EIGHTH EDITION

Dynamic Physical Education for Elementary School Children

VICTOR P. DAUER

Washington State University
Pullman, Washington

ROBERT P. PANGRAZI

Arizona State University
Tempe, Arizona

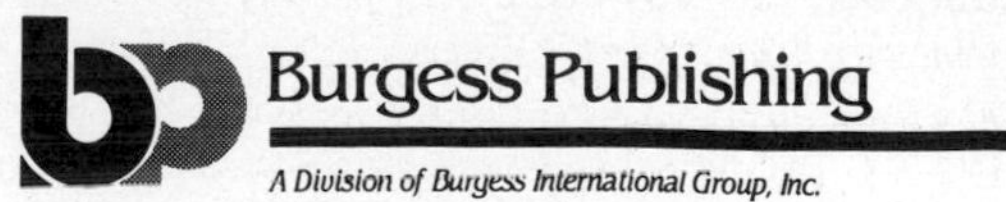

Development editor: Anne E. Heller
Assistant development editor: Charlene J. Brown
Copy editor: Betsey I. Rhame
Production coordinator: Melinda Berndt
Cover photographs: Robert P. Pangrazi

Printed in the United States of America

Library of Congress Cataloging in Publication Data

Dauer, Victor Paul, 1909–
Dynamic physical education for elementary school children.

Bibliography: p.
Includes index.
1. Physical education for children—United States.
2. Physical education for children—United States—Curricula. 3. Physical education for children—Study and teaching—United States. 4. Child development—United States. I. Pangrazi, Robert P. II. Title.
GV443.D32 1986 372.8′6′0973 85–29071
ISBN 0–8087–4444–5

Burgess Publishing
7110 Ohms Lane
Edina, MN 55435

J I H G F E D C B

To my wife, Alice, whose help, inspiration, and encouragement have been of inestimable value in the writing of this book and its revisions.

Victor P. Dauer

This book is dedicated with love and respect to my wife, Debbie, without whose aid, patience, and understanding my efforts would not have been possible.

Robert P. Pangrazi

Contents

Preface

The eighth edition of *Dynamic Physical Education for Elementary School Children* represents an exciting and major revision. The authors are deeply appreciative of the reception the text has received from professional personnel in teacher education. The text has enjoyed past success because of its focus on child development, general and specific physical education instructional procedures, and field-tested activity sequences. The wide variety of activities has always been a strength of *Dynamic Physical Education.*

Rather than rest on these laurels, we have continued to upgrade and update the materials. The field testing is an ongoing process. Before preparing the manuscript for the eighth edition, we asked selected physical education professionals specializing in teacher education to evaluate the seventh edition. Their critiques were analyzed, and pertinent recommendations were included in the eighth edition format. Individuals with acknowledged expertise and experience with children critiqued and rewrote several specific areas (rhythmics, gymnastics, and sports). Newer movements and practices also have been incorporated in the text. Among these are computer use and increased attention to fitness programs for kindergarten and primary-level children. Both of these emphases reflect the concerns expressed at recent national meetings of the American Alliance for Health, Physical Education, Recreation and Dance (AAHPERD).

In the eighth edition, we provide an answer to superintendents, principals, teachers, and parents concerning the *unique* contributions of a physical education program to the child's development and well-being. These unique contributions are (1) the development and maintenance of a personalized level of physical fitness, (2) the acquisition of movement competency, and (3) the understanding of movement and the mechanics of movement. To accomplish these goals, the physical education program must be largely instructional. This approach puts physical education on a par with the other instructional areas of the elementary school curriculum. A well-planned program goes far beyond mere recreation and entertainment.

The eighth edition text thus has a dual educational function: first, as a textbook for teacher training in physical education, and second, as a directive for implementing a sound physical education program in the public school. This edition represents a revision that will better meet both of these important needs. As with previous editions, the teacher trainee should retain the book as an important tool to be used often in future professional endeavors.

The textual organization has been revised to flow more logically to facilitate the professional preparation of the physical education instructor. The eighth edition begins with a review of the history and background of physical education. Chapter 2 gives aspiring teachers the background necessary to understand the effects of physical activity on children, the guidelines for planning safe activity participation, and the reasons why physical activity is important for the child's proper growth and development patterns. This chapter is based on current research being conducted by specialists in pediatric exercise and activity. It is the base on which the program is developed.

Chapter 3 offers the necessary principles and guidelines for effective teaching of motor skills. It is based on fundamental concepts from the fields of biomechanics and motor learning and development. Methodology for teaching motor skills and the mechanical principles and patterns of development in sport skills are covered.

Chapters 4 and 5 deal with curriculum development. The *whys* of curriculum and the steps necessary to develop a broad and varied curriculum based on the needs and characteristics of children are established. Teachers in training as well as practicing teachers need to understand how to fashion curriculum. Too often, teachers graduate having learned only bits and pieces of curriculum development but not how those pieces fit together to form a unified plan that covers the entire school year.

A major concern for both practicing teachers as well as those in training is class management. Chapter 6 deals with the skills involved in moving and managing children. Management skills are not inborn; they can be learned and mastered. Indeed, the current approach to teaching views the instruction process more as a science than an art. Allied to class management are teaching methodology and styles. Chapter 7 explores the range of teaching styles and the development of an environment that enhances learning.

Divergent and convergent movement are clearly distinguished in Chapters 8 and 9. In past editions, the methodology for stimulating divergent movement appeared in one part of the text, while the ideas and activity themes were found in another. We have changed this arrangement in the eighth edition. The themes and ideas now follow the methodology immediately, thus facilitating the teacher's transition from theory to practice. Convergent movement is defined, and new methodology for enhancing correct movement patterns is included.

In Chapter 10, we discuss human wellness. The chapter has been expanded to help teachers hold short yet relevant discussions in the physical education setting. Methodology to aid students in making meaningful decisions about their personal wellness is included so teachers can better understand the decision-making process. Chapters 11 and 12 on the special child and children with special needs also have been updated and expanded.

Since legal liability continues to be a major concern for physical education teachers, Chapter 13 has been completely rewritten to incorporate the current thinking on the subject. We delineate the situations that teachers should avoid, and we offer a checklist for analyzing possible situations that might give rise to a lawsuit.

In Chapter 14, we review procedures for student evaluation and microcomputer applications, which now contain the AAHPERD Health Related Physical Fitness Test. The methods and forms for the teacher's self-evaluation of the instructional process also are included. The microcomputer section discusses and gives examples of how personal computers can be used to enhance instruction and learning. Computer-assisted instruction, test reporting, and data gathering and analysis are among the topics covered. The actual forms and instructions for purchasing computer software also are provided.

In past editions, a major focus of the text has been on activity and units of instruction. The eighth edition retains this emphasis. The sport chapters in particular have been updated in light of current coaching and instructional methods.

Chapter 17 on rhythmic movement was revised by Jerry Poppen, supervisor of physical education for the Tacoma, Washington, public schools. He has an extensive and varied background in the rhythmics area, and has given the chapter a new, updated, exciting emphasis.

Chapter 21 on stunts and tumbling was evaluated and updated by John Spini, current coach of the women's gymnastic team at Arizona State University. He has taught gymnastics to young children for many years. The chapter reflects his broad experience and knowledge.

The soccer and volleyball chapters have been extensively revised. Ken Fox, a soccer coach from England, and Debbie Morgan were instrumental in updating the material. Both are currently finishing doctorates in physical education at Arizona State University.

We continue to perceive the need for a physical education program that is broad and varied as well as changing and dynamic. Through the various editions of the text, our constant attempt has been to develop a better physical education program that keeps pace with this rapidly changing profession. The eighth edition contains more than 150 new photographs and illustrations, thus maintaining the contemporary look of the text.

The fourth edition of *Lesson Plans for Dynamic Physical Education* was developed concurrently with the text. The new plans are enlarged and expanded to offer a different and unique set of lesson plans for grades K–2, 3–4, and 5–6. This organization allows for a greater range of activity and ensures the suitability of the plans to the development level and maturity of all youngsters.

A new, expanded edition of the *Instructional Resource Materials Package* accompanies the text and is available to adopters. Other available materials are a 16-mm color film illustrating the program, a video tape program with various lectures and ideas for using the text, and computer software programs for student and teacher evaluation. Our concern has been to offer a total package of materials that gives those instructors involved in professional preparation an integrated instructional approach.

In this latest revision, we are indebted to many people who have provided valuable suggestions and ideas. The teachers of the Mesa School District in Mesa, Arizona, and their supervisor, Gene Petersen, have contributed immeasurably by evaluating and augmenting the curriculum. Donald Hicks and Debbie Pangrazi have used the lesson plans and ideas for many years, and have provided valuable insights concerning content.

We thank the following reviewers for answering a survey questionnaire that helped give direction to our eighth edition revision: Rosalie Hedlund (Ottawa University, Ottawa, Kansas), Paul G. Schempp (Kent State University, Kent, Ohio), Laretha Leyman (State University of New York, Cortland), Patricia Keogh (Mankato State University, Mankato, Minnesota), Mark G. Fischman (Southern Illinois University at Carbondale), Scott Melville (Eastern Washington University, Cheney), Gary F. Hansen (University of Iowa, Iowa City), Stuart Daily (University of Wisconsin, Madison), Ken Renner (University of Central Florida, Orlando), Jody Wise (Fort Hays State University, Hays, Kansas), Jerry D. Poppen (Tacoma Public Schools, Tacoma, Washington), Elizabeth Griffin (San Diego State University, San Diego, California), Anne Simmons (University of Texas, Austin), John M. Pearson (Central Washington University, Ellensburg), and Brenda Bonheim (Liberty Baptist College, Lynchburg, Virginia).

Meaningful, successful textbooks are the result of cohesive teamwork between the publishing company and the authors. We are indebted to a professional group of people at Burgess Publishing. Special thanks go to Anne Heller for her sensitive and generous guidance. Betsey Rhame's insightful and comprehensive editing throughout this edition has been of immeasurable help in creating a clear, concise textbook.

We hope you find the eighth edition to be better than ever.

CHAPTER 1

Introduction to Physical Education

The overall goal of a general education and of physical education is to help individuals achieve optimum growth and development. This implies acceptance by the public as well as by school personnel that physical education is a full partner in the child's total educational program. The role of physical activity in developing a healthy life-style is well accepted, and people are beginning to understand the importance of a quality physical education program for youngsters.

The broad aim of education can be further defined as the development in children of the ability to achieve satisfaction as responsible, contributing citizens of society. Physical education, through a carefully planned and functionally sound program, can make significant contributions to this overall goal. To accomplish this goal, physical education should focus on and maximize the *unique* contributions it makes to the education of the individual, concentrating on educational outcomes that are not likely to be achieved through other subject areas in the total school curriculum.

The first of these unique outcomes is the promotion of physical development and the achievement of personal physical fitness goals. A second major goal is developing competency in a wide variety of physical skills, which allows students to function effectively in physical activities. A third outcome is establishing an understanding of movement and the pertinent principles governing motor skill performance. Should these goals not be accomplished in physical education classes, they will not be realized elsewhere in the curriculum.

In addition to these major contributions, a variety of goals are shared and complemented by other areas of the school program. The development of a satisfactory self-image, for example, can be accomplished in physical education, but is also enhanced in other areas of schoolwork. Other goals, such as safety skills, personal values, moral development, and cooperative and competitive attitudes are not unique to physical education. This does not reduce their importance, but should stress to the physical educator that physical fitness and skill development can only be accomplished through physical education programming. Without a systematic and organized physical education program, children will leave school not knowing how to maintain a satisfactory level of fitness, will not possess the adequate skills needed to perform a wide variety of adult recreational activities, and will not understand the meaning of movement.

When the three major child-centered goals, outcomes, or objectives are achieved, physical education becomes a full partner in the educational process. These basic objectives provide direction for developing a physical education instructional system that carefully monitors student accomplishment. Achieving these objectives also means meeting the needs of all children—those with physical handicaps, the retarded, the slow or delayed learners, children with motor problems, gifted children, disturbed individuals, children with impaired hearing or visual acuity, as well as those without handicaps, the so-called "normal" children. One can judge the quality of a program by how well it meets the needs of children who are less skilled and able—the unfit, the inept, and those with motor problems.

The instructor is the most important factor in the learning process. No matter what instructional method is used, a perceptive, analytical teacher is the key to a child's progress. A good teacher guides students to learn, to perceive themselves as learning, and to feel positive about themselves as learners. Students not only improve but also take note of their educational progress. The teacher is the most critical element in the educational process and is the creator of conditions for optimum learning.

The elementary school is the level at which students should explore, experiment, and come in contact with a wide range of physical education activity. The curriculum guide and the yearly schedule should feature a variety of activities so children can learn personal competencies and an appreciation of the many types of physical activity available. The critical selection of future activities for lifetime participation can proceed rationally when based on experience.

Developing a skill level that allows a child to compete with and be respected by peers has a strong impact on personal growth. A sense of belonging and peer acceptance are necessary attributes for a child's satisfactory self-concept. An unskilled child often avoids activity rather than risking the embarrassment of failure. The need for fitness and skill competency cannot be overemphasized. The world of the elementary school child is a physical one. Respect and esteem are generally given to those who accomplish physically and are physically fit.

Students should not only learn skills but must also acquire the knowledge related to skill performance. Not only is it important to give attention to correct technique, but the reasons for using the suggested techniques must also be stated. Students need to leave the program with a clear understanding of movement principles and how those principles apply to various skill performance areas. This understanding, coupled with skill performance, develops a foundation for self-analysis and improvement in later years.

In the affective domain, which deals with attitudes and values, social interchanges in the teaching environment—sharing, taking turns, fairness, and concern for others—should be in harmony with moral growth. The "hidden curriculum" merits attention. This is defined as the inherent qualities of the learning environment that affect attitudinal, moral, and emotional learning. The way the environment is structured, how the teacher presents information, and how youngsters are treated have a much greater impact on learning than the teacher's verbalization. The basic point is that teachers teach much by their actions, by their rules in the gym, and by how they respond to all students. Through the hidden curriculum, the instructor may model both desirable and undesirable behavior, which speaks loudly to students.

Physical education should be more than the experiencing of movement. It should be an essentially enjoyable experience for both teacher and students, and a well-developed program can contribute to the overall school atmosphere.

The physical education program should offer something for everyone. Programs that are sport-oriented only may meet the needs of those children who are skilled in the sport areas, but the less skilled children may have to persevere with minimal reinforcement for an entire school year. The *Dynamic Physical Education Program* can be described as a contemporary program with a wide range of activity presentations. It integrates and utilizes ideas from many areas, including sports, physical fitness, movement education, rhythms, and perceptual motor, individual, and dual activities. Such a physical education program is all-encompassing, and should present a balanced, comprehensive, child-centered curriculum for the development of all youngsters.

WHAT IS PHYSICAL EDUCATION?

Physical education is that phase of the general educational program that contributes, primarily through movement experiences, to the total growth and development of each child. Physical education is defined as education of and through movement, and must be conducted in a manner that merits this meaning. It should be an instructional program that gives adequate and proportional attention to all learning domains—psychomotor, cognitive, and affective.

Children acquire the ability to move effectively through a program centering on both versatility and quality of movement. Target goals for movement competency in children are best realized when the teacher has a clear understanding of growth and development principles, instructional strategies, and class management techniques. To understand children and to be able to manage them in a productive learning environment are necessary prerequisites for effective teaching.

Physical education should be concerned with human wellness. This necessitates cooperation with classroom teachers and an understanding of the overall school curriculum. The concept of human wellness is broader than the concept of good health, and relates to developing a total life-style that promotes well-being. This topic is discussed in detail in Chapter 10.

Teachers should focus on becoming educators of children, not simply activity organizers. The *how* should be coupled with the *why:* instructors need to adopt the practice of telling youngsters not only what to do but also the movement skill principles behind the actions. Viable alternatives should be presented to students. Guiding a physical education program that educates children is the domain of the professional, dedicated teacher. If physical education is to achieve acceptance as a full partner in the education process, it must be directed by well-trained, dedicated teachers who give high quality instruction.

EDUCATIONAL AND CULTURAL FORCES AFFECTING PHYSICAL EDUCATION

A better understanding of current programs in physical education can be gained by reviewing briefly the long history of physical education.

THE ANCIENT GREEKS AND SUBSEQUENT INFLUENCES

Among the ancients, the Greeks were the first to embrace the concept of physical activity to develop the whole human being. The goal of producing citizens with a high degree of physical prowess, who could defend the homeland, was basic to all ancient cultures. In their definition of sport participation, the Greeks also included other ideals, one of which was the grace and beauty of movement. The concept of the sportsperson as a moral individual was also considered important by them. Many of today's sports represent a heritage from the ancient Greeks and their great sport festivals, of which the Olympic Games are the best known. The modern Olympic oath is a tribute to the Greek ideals.

With the collapse of the Greek civilization, degeneration of the Olympic ideals soon set in, and rank professionalism took over sport competition. Under Roman rule, sport festivals became brutal spectacles, and the idealistic concepts of the Greeks were lost.

Little progress was made during the Dark and Middle Ages, and few practical programs appeared, although play and exercise began to be regarded as beneficial, primarily to enhance health.

PURITAN ETHICS AND THE EARLY AMERICAN SETTLERS

Early settlers in New England had little time to play, and students attended to the serious business of learning. To the Puritans, play was not just a waste of time; it was sinful. Virtue rested in hard work.

In subsequent decades, as frontier life became less demanding, hunting and fishing were no longer necessary for survival and became leisure activities. The British tradition of participation in archery, bowling, cricket, tennis, soccer, rugby, boxing, and track and field was important in the southern colonies. Still, the only physical activity in schools was the free play during recess.

THE GERMAN AND SWEDISH INFLUENCE BEFORE WORLD WAR I

During the 1800s, in both Germany and Sweden, physical education systems that centered on body development were established in the schools. Around the middle of the 19th century, German and Swedish immigrants to the United States introduced these concepts of physical education. The German system favored a gymnastic approach and required a good deal of equipment and special teachers. The Swedish system incorporated an exercise program in the activity presentations. The physical education program in many of the schools that adopted this system consisted of a series of exercises that children could perform in the classroom.

The need for equipment and gymnasiums posed problems for the schools that followed these systems, and many economy-minded citizens questioned the programs. A combination of games and calisthenics evolved and became the first scheduled physical education activity offered in some U.S. schools.

THE EMPHASIS ON GAMES AND SPORTS FROM WORLD WAR I TO THE 1950S

In training programs designed for soldiers during World War I, an emphasis on games and sports proved more effective than strict calisthenics. This shift to the use of games and sports for physical development spawned school programs with the same emphasis. Then, when two of John Dewey's cardinal aims of education stressed attention to physical activities, the development received impetus. These aims, the promotion of health and the worthy use of leisure time, became school curricular responsibilities. The school was also deemed responsible for molding social change, and a high value was placed on games and sports.

When about one third of the American men drafted in World War I were rejected as physically unfit for military service, the result was a new demand for physical education in the schools. State educational authorities legislated minimal weekly time requirements for physical activity in school programs. In many states, these laws established physical education as part of the school curriculum. The laws were, however, quantitative in nature, and little attention was given to program quality.

Programs stressing sports and games appeared in the secondary schools. The elementary programs became miniature models of these secondary programs, and could literally have been described by answering the question, "What games are we going to play today?" During the Depression years, equipment was difficult to secure, and teachers in the field were almost nonexistent. Physical education was relegated to a minor role, and in many cases was eliminated entirely.

During World War II, many new training programs for special groups appeared. Research proved the efficacy of physical fitness development, hospital reconditioning programs, and other innovative approaches. An improvement in the quality of physical education programs might have been expected after the war, but in fact little positive effect was evident in elementary school programs at that time.

THE RENEWAL OF INTEREST IN PHYSICAL FITNESS

Although physical fitness has always been considered an important goal in physical education, a renewed emphasis on fitness occurred in the 1950s, following the publication of comparative studies of fitness levels of U.S. and European children, which were based on the Kraus-Weber tests.[1] A study by Dr. Hans Kraus comparing strength and flexibility measurements of 4000 New York-area schoolchildren with a comparable sample of Central European children had far-reaching results. The press became concerned about the comparative weakness of U.S. children, and as a consequence of this concern, the present fitness movement was born.

One result of the uproar over physical fitness was the establishment of the President's Council on Physical Fitness and Sports, a potent force in promoting good physical fitness, not only among schoolchildren, but among citizens of all ages. Through its many publications, services, and promotions, the President's Council has had a major influence on school programs. In 1984, the President's Council sponsored the first National Youth Fitness Conference. The purpose of the conference was to renew emphasis on fitness and to call attention to the importance of physical fitness for youngsters.

The results of this new emphasis on fitness have been evident in elementary physical education programs. Existing programs were improved, and many programs were established where none existed. Administrators have become increasingly aware of the contributions that physical education can make to the growth and development of children.

MOVEMENT EDUCATION

Movement education introduced a fresh, new approach to providing learning experiences for children. Movement education originated in England and evolved for a number of reasons. It was a revolt against more formal programs, which included calisthenics and were command-oriented. This approach attempted to shift to the children the responsibility for their own progress. The methodology featured problem solving and an exploratory approach.

To some, movement education seemed to be the panacea for the ills of physical education. In some cases, adopting this approach led to the rejection of physical fitness-oriented activities, especially calisthenics, which were labeled as "training" and not education. Controversy arose regarding the application of movement principles to the teaching of specific skills, particularly athletic skills. There was some tendency to apply the methodology to the teaching of athletic skills without valid research evidence to support such practices.

Some instructors who stressed movement education believed that the child should first experience the movement pattern, manipulative object, or piece of apparatus without direction or instruction before any instructional sequences or challenges were introduced. Although little evidence shows that this principle results in significant educational progress, some advocates still defend the concept as the natural way of learning.

PERCEPTUAL-MOTOR PROGRAMS

All movement is essentially perceptual-motor movement, but the concern in perceptual-motor programs is corrective in nature and relates to remedying learning difficulties attributed to a breakdown in perceptual-motor development. Theorists hold that children progress through growth and developmental stages from head to foot (cephalocaudally) and from the center of the body outward (proximodistally) in an orderly fashion. When disruptions, lags, or omissions occur in this process, certain underlying perceptual-motor bases fail to develop fully, and this impairs the child's ability to function correctly.

Perceptual-motor programs grew out of concern for the slow learner, sometimes called the slow child or the delayed learner. Most children identified as such show motor coordination problems involving movement factors such as coordination, balance and postural control, image of the body and its parts, and relationships involving time and space. Perceptual-motor programs are a type of remediation for low-skilled children. The use of the term *perceptual-motor* to identify a separate program entity in physical education is diminishing.

Perceptual-motor elements are important additions to regular physical education programs. A variety of movement demands and challenges should be included in physical education classes, for instructional value lies both in limited perceptual-motor movements and in an exploratory, creative approach.

TITLE IX: EQUAL OPPORTUNITY FOR THE SEXES

Title IX of the Education Amendments, a federal ruling, has had a minor effect on elementary school physical education. Most programs in current use are coeducational. Title IX rules out any separation of the sexes and calls for all offerings to be coeducational. Organizing separate competitions for the sexes is permissible, provided that mixed participation in an activity can be determined to be hazardous, particularly for girls.

A second effect of Title IX relates to the elimination of sexism and sex-role typing. Human needs and opportunity must take precedence over the traditional sexual stereotypes of masculinity and femininity. Appreciation of the physical abilities of the opposite sex should be learned at an early age. Segregating children by sex in elementary school physical education programs is thus indefensible.

EQUAL RIGHTS FOR THE HANDICAPPED

Public Law 94–142 has given hope for a full education to the 3.5 to 4 million handicapped youngsters in the United

1. The Kraus-Weber tests, which served as an instrument in the study, are no longer regarded as a valid measurement of the physical fitness of elementary school children.

States. This federal law mandates that handicapped youngsters have the right to a free and public education, and that they be educated in the least restrictive educational environment possible. No longer can such children be assigned to segregated classes or schools unless a separate environment is determined *by due process* to be in the child's best interest.

The law has resulted in degrees of mainstreaming[2] (full or partial), with many handicapped children now participating in regular classes with nonhandicapped children. While the law is commendable and morally sound, it often necessitates changing the structure and educational procedures of the school as well as the viewpoints and attitudes of school personnel. Many teachers have neither the educational background, the experience, nor the inclination to handle handicapped children among their normal peers. The answer is not to ignore the problem but to provide teachers with the knowledge and attitudes that will allow them to function successfully with handicapped children. If they are to function in society when they become adults, handicapped children deserve and need the opportunity to participate with nonhandicapped youngsters.

In addition to the mainstreaming of handicapped students in normal classes, the law mandates the preparation of a specific program for each handicapped student, an individualized educational program (IEP). Establishing the child's due process committee, developing the IEP, and monitoring that program in the best interest of the student is a process of considerable challenge and magnitude. The process of developing an IEP can be used for nonhandicapped children as well and aids in making the educational process more personalized and individualized.

HUMAN WELLNESS AND HEALTHFUL LIVING

Today's educators are centering more attention on human wellness and healthful living. This focus is currently pushing physical educators to develop programs that teach more than fitness and skill activities. Wellness is a broader concept than being healthy. It is a dynamic state of well-being, which implies living fully and deriving the most from living.

Teaching for wellness involves teaching about concepts that will help students to develop a fitness plan for life. An understanding of valid principles of fitness development and a knowledge of the benefits of fitness will help students to maintain lifetime fitness. In addition, students should be taught what types of activities are useful for developing various fitness areas, and how to evaluate and prescribe activities for total body fitness.

Eating wisely, controlling weight, dealing with tension, understanding body (muscular) movement, getting sufficient rest and sleep, controlling posture, keeping in shape, and dealing with the forthcoming temptations of youth (use of alcohol, cigarettes, and drugs) are proper concerns of the physical educator.

The problem of weight control merits special attention in the elementary school. The obese child should be stimulated to become physically active. Unless life-style can be changed at an early age, obese children usually become obese adults.

More attention is now being devoted in the public schools to posture and posture problems, mostly in connection with physical fitness programs. Some states have instituted early screening to detect severe scoliosis (lateral curvature of the spine) and the recommendation of appropriate remedial treatment.

In experiencing movement patterns and skill-learning activities, the child learns to move and to understand the mechanical principles behind various movements. Within the instructional framework, basic kinesiological and mechanical principles must be related to movement patterns so that children can grasp the underlying basis of efficient movement.

Human wellness is an area in which physical education can have a lifelong impact on students. It is an area best handled when classroom teachers and physical education specialists work closely together. The common goal of wellness for all children should help physical education to become an integral part of the total curriculum.

NATIONAL CONCERN FOR QUALITY EDUCATION

The return to basics in elementary education has implications for physical education. The physical education program must be instructional in nature and of high quality if it is to be a part of the back-to-basics movement. In 1983, the National Commission on Excellence in Education presented a critical review of the total process of U.S. education in a report entitled *A Nation at Risk.*[3] In the report, physical education was not included as part of a basic education. Whether the omission was deliberate or happenstance is open to question. In the past, other deliberations and reports have included physical education as a part of basic instruction. Possibly the school experiences of commission members in the physical education area were largely an unorganized fun and games approach.

To conform to the concept of basic education, the fundamental target objectives that are expected to be accomplished in physical education at each grade level must be delineated. These child-centered outcomes must be measurable, and teachers and schools can then be held accountable

2. The term *mainstreaming,* used to describe the process of educating handicapped children in classes with nonhandicapped children, does not appear in the discussions and regulations of P.L. 94–142.

3. Gardner, David P. (Chair). 1983. A Nation at Risk: The Imperative for Educational Reform. A Report to the Nation and the Secretary of Education, U.S. Department of Education. The National Commission on Excellence in Education. *The Chronicle of Higher Education.* 26(10): 11–16.

for helping students reach a predetermined level of achievement.

A danger exists, however, in holding teachers accountable for student achievement levels. In self-defense, the teacher may turn to the use of memorization, drill, and rote learning, and may encourage practice mainly in those areas in which students will be tested. In physical education, this often means teaching only fitness activities so students will score well on the National Youth Fitness Test. This approach results in an inferior program that may satisfy the accountability concern of the instructor but does little to give students a well-rounded education.

A current trend is to extend education both downward and upward. With the appearance of preschool education and child-care centers, the downward aspects have become important to the elementary school physical educator. Head Start programs are another extension of the educational system.

ORGANIZATIONS, TRENDS, AND EVENTS AFFECTING PHYSICAL EDUCATION

The influences that tend to affect physical education have broadened in scope over the last two decades.

THE AMERICAN ALLIANCE FOR HEALTH, PHYSICAL EDUCATION, RECREATION, AND DANCE (AAHPERD)

The American Alliance for Health, Physical Education, Recreation and Dance,[4] through its section dealing with elementary school physical education, has had a marked influence nationally on elementary programs. AAHPERD delegates direction of elementary programs to the Council on Physical Education for Children (COPEC), a group of professionals with national area representation, supervised by Dr. Margie Hanson, staff AAHPERD consultant. COPEC has been active in producing publications and in scheduling conferences, workshops, and convention programs. Publications such as *Essentials of a Quality Elementary School Program* (1971) and *Guidelines for Children's Sports* (1979) provide national standards and shape program philosophy. Teacher education institutions are given direction with a publication outlining suggested teacher preparation guidelines.

AAHPERD, through other constituent committees, has published an informative handbook entitled *Personalized Learning in Physical Education* (1976) and has promoted several conferences and workshops on this topic.

4. This organization was formerly termed the American Association for Health, Physical Education and Recreation (AAHPER). In 1980, the name was changed to reflect a growing involvement in dance. In this text, the abbreviation AAHPERD will be used for all references to the organization, regardless of the actual organization name at the time.

The Second National (AAHPERD) Conference on Teacher Preparation for the Elementary School Specialist

This conference, sponsored by AAHPERD in October 1984, was particularly timely with respect to the current national concern about improving teacher performance in the public schools. Several significant teacher preparation measures were stressed, including the initial securing of a strong commitment from the teacher candidate. Candidates should be interested in children and in child progress. A strong teacher is one who has a strong commitment. Second, the conference emphasized the need for early field (preprofessional) experiences to provide a realistic background for professional courses. After participation in these experiences, candidates can decide whether they wish to continue in the teacher training program. The experience may involve observation and miniteaching but is not to take the place of later field experiences or cadet teaching. Concern was also expressed about improving the quality of all field experiences.

Other matters discussed included the basic background of teacher education professors. The conference consensus was that all professors should have had successful public or private school experiences teaching physical education to children. Valid documentation was mentioned as a necessary function of both teacher preparation and public school programs. The place of the liberal education in teacher preparation programs was also discussed, but no firm commitments were made. Accountability was given some attention. It was suggested that teacher preparation programs should suggest ways and means by which specialists can work effectively with principals, for the support of the principal is most important in the success of any school program.

THE AMERICAN MEDICAL ASSOCIATION (AMA)

Strong formal approval and support of physical education programs in the schools have come from the American Medical Association (AMA). The support originated with a statement adopted at the national convention of the AMA in 1960.

> Resolved, That the American Medical Association through its various divisions and departments and its constituent and component medical societies do everything feasible to encourage effective instruction in physical education for all students in our schools and colleges.

The 1960 resolution was reaffirmed in 1969, strongly supported by the AMA Committee on Exercise and Physical Fitness, a body that was not in existence at the time of the 1960 resolution. Today, the medical profession continues to support effective school programs and, in particular, good physical development.

THE NATIONAL EDUCATION ASSOCIATION (NEA) AND U.S. PUBLIC HEALTH SERVICE ENDORSEMENTS

Two significant groups have added their endorsement to physical education programs. The resolution adopted by the 1981 Representative Assembly of the National Education Association (NEA) reads, "The Association also believes that health and physical education programs should be developed and maintained commensurate with maturation levels of children."

The U.S. Public Health Service has launched an intensive effort to improve the health of Americans, citing the importance of physical fitness and exercise in preventive care. Although the emphasis on physical fitness and exercise is broad in scope, the schools have been singled out and charged to improve the quality of their physical education programs. The significance of this endorsement lies in the fact that, for the first time, the nation's principal health agency has officially recognized physical fitness and exercise as essential elements of preventive health care and as a critical component of physical education programs (President's Council on Physical Fitness and Sports 1981).

MOVEMENT EDUCATION AND PHYSICAL EDUCATION

Movement education, with its Laban-based methodology and movement factors, has had a strong impact on present-day physical education. These ideas were incorporated in elementary school programs, and the teachers called themselves *movement educators*. Movement education thus became a separate entity, and a dichotomy was created between physical educators and movement educators. The movement approach is a sound and valid approach to teaching divergent movement, and has broadened both the content and instructional strategies used in physical education programs. The problem arises when teachers limit themselves to movement education and accept Laban's concepts as the total program—rejecting past theory and the practice of physical education as "traditional."

Movement education originated in England in the 1930s, where it developed under the potent influence of Rudolph Laban's movement theory. Laban was not a physical educator. He constructed his theory with reference to drama, modern dance, and mime. Within these areas, he applied his theory to promote graceful, proficient, and efficient movement. He did not propose or recommend any specific movement system for school physical education programs.

The appropriateness of physical fitness in movement education became controversial. In Laban's books, the term *physical fitness* does not appear, and early movement education manuals published in England make no mention of fitness development. Movement educators deplored the rather formalized methodology used at that time to develop physical fitness. They perceived calisthenics and traditional gymnastics as training and of little educational value.

Laban's concepts and ideas were interpreted and adjusted for use in the public schools. The idea of movement themes was expanded beyond Laban's original scope, and new terminology was incorporated in the learning environment. Exploration, discovery, and student choice were inherent to the original Laban approach, and what became known as the *discovery* learning style of movement education began to find favor. Telling a child what to do and how to follow a movement pattern was seen as educational heresy. The focus was on keeping children active and happy. As one child put it: "Why do they always make me do what I feel like?"

A shift away from traditional school gymnastics, with the prescribed vaulting, balancing, and tumbling stunts, was reflected by the introduction of child-oriented apparatus designed for climbing, hanging, supporting, swinging, and traveling. This influenced an *educational gymnastics* approach, which used newly designed apparatus as well as some of the old, to incorporate Laban's movement factors and ideas of exploration and discovery.

Because apparatus availability was usually limited, classes were organized around station teaching. Three or more groups would be arranged at separate stations in an area, with each group working on a different movement problem. This approach was gradually carried over to other types of movement lessons, even when the availability of apparatus made it unnecessary.

An emphasis on *problem solving* became popular among movement educators. The term was used loosely to designate the accomplishment of open-ended tasks. True problem solving, in the narrow sense of the term, was attempted only occasionally. The theory holds that children may be stimulated to think, move, and react through discovery and problematic situations.

Today, the dichotomy between physical education and movement education is lessening. Physical education programs of the past may not have been as deficient as some movement educators claimed. Current physical education programs are designed to be as broad, challenging, and comprehensive as possible.

From the late 1970s to the present, a number of articles in the professional literature have deplored the separation of movement education and physical education, and have urged the elimination of movement education as a separate entity—even advocating abolishing the term. The most practical solution to the problem is to upgrade present-day physical education programs by applying all of the valuable new educational ideas that are relevant, including those of merit from movement education sources. This approach produces a contemporary and educationally sound program and is the focus of this text.

COGNITIVE LEARNING

Conceptual understanding (i.e., the application of abstract ideas drawn from experience) plays an important part in physical education. In the process of movement, the child learns to distinguish between near and far, strong and weak, light and heavy, and high and low. The child should also be given the opportunity to experiment with and thereby establish an understanding of such concepts as *curve, stretch, twist, turn, balance,* and *bounce.*

There is currently great emphasis on the need for cognitive development in the area of wellness. Choosing and practicing a healthy life-style is impossible if adequate knowledge is unavailable. Many important concepts dealing with the cognitive approach to wellness are found in Chapter 10.

AFFECTIVE LEARNING

Since the mid-1960s, many different approaches to values clarification and moral education have emerged. A large body of literature has been generated on the topic and many conflicting views have been expressed. In the 14th Annual Gallup Poll of the Public's Attitudes Toward Public Schools (1984), lack of discipline again heads the list of major problems confronting the public schools.

Values, feelings, beliefs, and judgments are receiving more attention in the schools and in physical education classes in particular. Awareness of the hidden curriculum and the part it plays in affective learning is an attendant facet of this emphasis. Firm guidelines for moral education have not been forthcoming, and school administrators are often hesitant to enter this domain. Such wellness issues as alcohol and drug abuse need to be dealt with in the elementary school years before students become regular users. In most cases, however, schools are reticent about confronting these issues for fear that some public element will disapprove vocally. Unfortunately, a small minority appears to have been able to keep this type of instruction from elementary school students.

Positive Self-Concept Development

This aspect of affective learning centers on the development of a positive self-concept as an important influence in shaping human behavior. A child's self-image is of vital importance in relationships with peers and teachers, and can affect individual learning progress. The ability to move with grace and confidence enhances a child's self-esteem. In contrast, the awkward, uncoordinated, or physically weak child is apt to be ridiculed for shortcomings and made to feel "different."

Physical educators can help children develop better self-concepts with a methodology that guarantees each child some measure of success during a lesson. Offering a wide variety of program activities and challenges tends to allow each child to find an area of interest in which success can be achieved.

YOUTH SPORT PROGRAMS

In the last decade, community youth sport programs have increased markedly, providing some early sport experiences for children. Many schools have also increased the variety of their sport offerings. This plethora of programs has made the teaching of physical education much more complex, for youngsters enter school with widely varying backgrounds. Some may have been taught by experts in private clubs or by amateurs in recreation programs, but others enter school with no previous sport experiences.

Most community programs rely on volunteer coaches whose only experience has been infrequent participation in a sport during childhood. Many of these volunteers have had little or no formal training in any of the related sport coaching areas. Not surprisingly, some youngsters leave sport programs with negative and unpleasant memories.

Concern about the quality of the coaching in these types of programs is justifiable. A number of associations are now providing informative literature, basic training, and certification programs for amateur coaches. Among these are the *National Youth Sports Coaches Association* and the *American Coaching Effectiveness Program.* Schools can encourage effective coaching programs by working with community groups to provide coaching clinics. A number of excellent coaching manuals are now available.

World of Sport Influences

The media, particularly television, project a kaleidoscopic panorama of sport activities and sport figures, which has a subtle and substantial effect on children. To emulate these popular figures becomes a goal of many youngsters, both boys and girls. Instructional programming in sport skills can capitalize on this influence by stressing the need for consistent and correct practice similar to that which high-level performers have followed for many years.

PROLIFERATION OF EQUIPMENT

A wealth of equipment and supplies for school programs has become available commercially. Wall-attached climbing frames, portable floor apparatus, climbing ropes on tracks, balance beam benches, parachutes, individual tug-of-war ropes, and various kinds of mats are items that should be considered. The many other pieces of equipment designed for tumbling, specialized movement patterns, and remedial work are not always necessary. Program needs must be examined carefully before these are purchased.

The supply of phonograph records seems endless, and the variety of physical education activities on records is extensive—active songs, creative stories and songs, folk dance, exercise programs, fundamental movement records, rope-jumping rhythms, various specialty dances, and aerobic dance. Most are long-play and 45 rpm, with 78 rpm records being phased out.

Some equipment can be constructed in the school rather than being bought ready-made. Suggestions for equipment that school personnel can make are in Chapter 34.

PROFESSIONAL PREPARATION

The preparation of professionals in elementary school physical education is trying to keep pace with the changes in philosophy and science in the field. Rather than train instructors to emphasize content and methodology, today's educational institutions are seeking to produce professionals who can teach children. To meet the needs of elementary school students, teachers must extend their expertise to interact with handicapped and retarded children, individuals with low-fitness levels, children with motor deficiencies, children from bilingual backgrounds, children from ghetto areas, and children from families of transient workers. When classroom teachers handle physical education without proper preparation, the children usually suffer from low-level physical experiences.

THE PHYSICAL FITNESS RESURGENCE

More attention and concern are being given to physical fitness training for kindergarten and primary school children. The AAHPERD Health Related Physical Fitness Test lists norms for children, beginning at the kindergarten level. Fitness development at the kindergarten and primary levels has been singled out for attention, with appropriate fitness programs being developed for the various primary grades. The AAHPERD Health Related Physical Fitness Test norms for the primary grades provide measures for evaluating fitness activities for those grades. The development of norms by the AAHPERD provides an important national stamp of approval for fitness training for young children.

AEROBIC EXERCISE PROGRAMS

Aerobic exercise programs have blossomed in many directions. *Aerobic activity* is defined as exercise for which the body is able to supply adequate oxygen for sustained performance over long periods of time. The conditioned participant can continue the activity for lengthy periods without reaching extreme breathlessness. Aerobic activity of sufficient intensity is excellent for developing cardiovascular fitness.

At the elementary school level, aerobic dance predominates among recognized aerobic forms of activity. It involves a series of exercise forms, dance steps, and modern dance prototypes. These dance programs have a variety of name designations such as Aerobic Dance, Aerobicize, Exercise Dance, and Jazzercise. Among the less organized aerobic forms are rope jumping, jogging, and bicycle riding. See Chapter 10 for guidelines for developing aerobic endurance.

COMMERCIALIZATION AND ACTIVITY CENTERS

Commercialization is rampant today in an effort to profit from the high level of interest in exercise, fitness, and related activities and remedial programs. Publications about exercise systems, diet, weight loss, muscular development, and stress reduction abound. Remediation is prescribed for weak abdominal muscles and faulty posture, and many correctional or developmental devices are also on the market along with the instructional literature.

Specialized centers that focus on various aspects of fitness, body development, weight loss, and recreation have become commonplace. Some are even nationally franchised. Today's schools have a responsibility to provide basic background information and experiences so students can form valid value judgments about the efficacy of such programs.

COMPUTER TECHNOLOGY

Computer technology has much to offer to elementary school physical education programming. Fitness evaluation and related standards can be incorporated in a system, and students can secure immediate feedback showing raw scores, percentile rank, and suggested activities for improving performance. Printouts for individualized programs can govern student contract methodology and ease the instructor's record-keeping burden. Computer software is becoming user friendly, which allows students to enter their evaluation results so the instructor does not have to record all class data.

Another important area of computer application is for special student programs and the writing of individualized educational programs (IEPs). The appropriate form can be called up on the computer screen, and the objectives and goals as well as accomplishments quickly typed in. The IEP can thus be brought up to date easily, relieving the tedious burden of manual recording and filling out a new form after each evaluation. Further discussion of computer applications can be found on pages 175–205.

ELEMENTARY SCHOOL PHYSICAL EDUCATION TODAY

Elementary school physical education has been influenced by many trends, organizations, and issues over a long period of time. Sound curricular programs cannot be developed unless we understand the historical impact of past events and the current concerns of a society. Educational programs are always affected by current events. For example, when the Soviet Union launched the satellite Sputnik, Americans became concerned about the quality of mathematics and science instruction in the public schools. In similar fashion, the Kraus-Weber test results caused U.S.

citizens to think that our youth were unfit compared with European children, and a renewed emphasis on fitness occurred.

Educational programs are generally responsive to the needs of society, and physical education has passed through periods of change due to historical and cultural events. The sum total of these various forces, trends, and issues results in a physical education program for children that is *well balanced and offers something for all children.* Fitness is an easily identified part of each lesson. Motor skill development is taught in a clear, concise manner, so youngsters learn proper movement patterns at an early age. Perceptual-motor activities are integrated in all lessons, so children learn such concepts as directionality, laterality, and spatial awareness. Wellness concepts are intertwined with other material and discussed regularly in order to enhance student understanding. Creativity and problem solving are centered around different teaching styles in an attempt to help students work out personal needs and challenges. Today, no single phase of physical education can be ignored at the expense of another. Physical education must be a systematic and progressive program that reaches out to children from all walks of life.

REFERENCES

AAHPERD. 1979. *Guidelines for children's sports.* Reston, Va.: AAHPERD.

AAHPERD. 1976. *Personalized learning in physical education.* Reston, Va.: AAHPERD.

President's Council on Physical Fitness and Sports. 1981. *Newsletter* (June). Washington, D.C.: President's Council on Physical Fitness and Sports.

CHAPTER 2

Children and Physical Activity

The purpose of this chapter is to identify important research and to apply it to the physical education setting. Physical activity is essential for the optimum growth and development of healthy children. Only regular strenuous activity will raise the child's level of fitness.

Many of the studies that are cited in this chapter can offer excellent justification for including physical education in the total school curriculum. For example, the strong concern about the correlation between heart disease and the lack of activity among children, the importance of developing skill competency in children so they have the tools to be active for a lifetime, and the relationship between activity and academic performance are all excellent points justifying the inclusion of a well-taught, well-organized physical education program.

PHYSICAL ACTIVITY AND HEART DISEASE

In a study (Glass 1973) conducted in the public schools of Iowa, more than 5000 children between the ages of 6 and 18 were examined over a two-year period. Of these children, 70% had symptoms of coronary heart disease, 7% had extremely high cholesterol levels, a large percentage had high blood pressure, and at least 12% were obese.

The life-styles of U.S. children need to be changed before their 8th birthday. Before this time, dietary and exercise patterns are relatively easy to change, but change becomes increasingly difficult as the child grows older. In examining the developmental history of arteriosclerosis in humans, Dr. Kenneth Rose (1973) notes that "the first signs appear around age 2 and the disease process is reversible until the age of 19."

According to Dr. John Kimball, a noted cardiologist at the University of Colorado, "Evidence is growing stronger that the earliest bodily changes leading to heart disease begin early in life" (Albinson and Andrews 1976). He also points out that more and more autopsy reports on children show blood vessels that have begun to clog with fatty deposits, which can eventually lead to heart attack.

Wilmore and McNamara (1974) examined 95 boys, age 8 to 12 years, in an effort to determine the extent to which coronary heart disease risk factors derived from an adult population were manifested in a group of young boys. They concluded that "coronary heart disease, once considered to be a geriatric problem, is now recognized as being largely of pediatric origin."

In a study by Gilliam et al. (1982), the intensity of voluntary activity patterns of 59 children were analyzed by recording heart rates. Results showed that children do not voluntarily engage in high-intensity activity and that prior to intervention, the training heart rate (160 beats per minute) was never reached. The authors concluded that daily activity patterns can be changed, and added an average of 35 minutes of high-intensity activity to the children's daily activities. Their contention is that coronary heart disease can be decreased through increased cardiovascular activity. They offered the following guidelines for better use of recess time for enhanced activity.

1. Set up an exercise trail on the school grounds. Encourage children to use it during recess, and record their accomplishments on a classroom chart.

2. Set up a large clock with a second hand on the playground and encourage children to check their pulse rate periodically to see if it is in the training zone.

3. Encourage all children to walk or run around the school playground before participating in recess.

Regardless of the approach used to increase activity, children seldom perform intense activity during free and leisure time. It is important that school administrators understand this point and realize that recess is not a substitute for physical education in any way, shape, or form.

AEROBIC METABOLISM

Maximal aerobic power is an individual's maximum ability to use oxygen in the body for metabolic purposes. The oxygen uptake of an individual, all other factors being equal, determines the quality of endurance-oriented performance. Adults interested in increasing endurance-based athletic performance therefore train extensively to increase aerobic power.

Maximal aerobic power is closely related to lean body mass, which explains the differences that occur between boys and girls. When maximum oxygen uptake is adjusted per kilogram of body weight, it shows little change for boys (no increase) and a continual decrease for girls (Bar-Or 1983). This decrease in females may be due to an increase in body fat and a decrease in lean body mass. When maximal oxygen uptake is not adjusted for body weight, it increases in similar amounts on a yearly basis for both boys and girls through age 12, even though boys have higher values as early as age 5.

The question arises as to whether training children will increase their aerobic performance. The research results differ. Some researchers have found an increase in aerobic power through training, while others report that training has no impact on the aerobic system. Particularly in children under 10 years of age, aerobic power appears to increase little with training, even though running performance improves. Bar-Or (1983) indicates that young children may either become more efficient mechanically or may improve in anaerobic metabolism. Another postulate is that young children are naturally active enough so that intergroup differences are negligible.

Even though children demonstrate a relatively high oxygen uptake, they do not perform up to this level because they are not economical in running or walking activities. An 8-year-old child running at 180 m per minute is operating at 90% of maximum aerobic power, while a 16-year-old running at the same rate is only at 75% of maximum. This explains why young children are less capable than adolescents and adults at competing over long distances, even though they can maintain a slow speed for long distances (Bar-Or 1983).

Children exercising at a certain work load perceive the activity to be easier than do adults working at a similar level. The Rating of Perceived Exertion was used and analyzed at different percentages of maximal heart rate (Bar-Or 1977). The question of why children perceive the exertion to be at a lesser level remains unanswered. However, many researchers are well aware of the rapid recovery rate of children after strenuous exercise, and exercise possibly does not demand as much of children as it does of adults. In any case, teachers should avoid judging work loads for children by their own perception of how strenuous the activity is. Second, teachers should use a child's rapid recovery rate to full advantage. Exercise bouts can be interspersed with restful stretching and nonlocomotor movements to maintain the amount of time devoted to exercise. Interval training can be particularly effective.

Finally, teachers should note that obesity takes a great toll on a child's aerobic power because of the greater metabolic cost of exercise. Obese children must perform at a higher percentage of their maximal oxygen uptake. Their maximal uptake values are unfortunately often lower than those of lean children. This gives them less reserve and makes them perceive higher exertion when performing a task. These reactions contribute to the well-known perception among teachers that "obese children don't like to run." What is needed is understanding by teachers that the obese child *is* working harder and that work loads must be adjusted accordingly.

GROWTH PATTERNS

Children go through a rapid period of growth from birth to age 5. From age 6 to the onset of adolescence, growth slows to a steady but increasing pattern. During adolescence, rapid growth occurs again until adulthood is reached. During the elementary school years, boys are generally taller and heavier. Girls reach the adolescent growth spurt first, and grow taller and heavier during the 6th and 7th grade years. Boys quickly catch up, however, and grow larger and stronger.

Young children have relatively short legs for their overall height. The trunk is longer in relation to the legs during early childhood. The ratio of leg length (standing height) to trunk length (sitting height) is similar for boys and girls through age 11. The head comprises one fourth of the child's total length at birth and about one sixth at age 6.

Steady growth during the elementary school years results in children becoming more aware of their body and moving the body comfortably. Since K–2 students have short legs, they are often "top heavy" when performing activities such as the Sit-up and V seat. They may fall more easily than adults, because their center of gravity is higher than it will be at maturity. The gradually lowering center of gravity gives children increased stability and balance, allowing them more opportunity to be successful at sport activities.

BODY PHYSIQUE

The child's physique can also affect the quality of motor performance. In general, children who possess a mesomorphic body type perform best in activities requiring strength, speed, and agility. The mesomorph is characterized as having a predominance of muscle and bone and is often labeled "muscled." These children usually perform well in most team sports, because these activities require strength, speed, and agility. On the other hand, the ectomorph is identified as extremely thin, with a minimum of muscle development, and is characterized as "skinny." These children usually perform poorly in activities requiring strength and power, but may do well in aerobic endurance activities such as jogging, cross-country running, and track and field. The third somatotype is the endomorph, who is soft and round, with an excess of digestive organs. These children are usually regarded as fat and often perform poorly in many areas, including aerobic and anaerobic skill-oriented activities. The obese child is generally at a disadvantage in all phases of the physical education program.

SKELETAL GROWTH

Activity affects skeletal growth. Vigorous activity can improve internal bone structure so that bones are much more resistant to pressure, tension, and, ultimately, to breakage. The bones also increase in diameter and mineralization in response to activity. Inactivity for prolonged periods causes demineralization and makes the bones more prone to fracture.

Vigorous activity appears to cause the bones to grow to a shape that is mechanically advantageous for muscle attachments (Rarick 1973). The skeletal system is not totally rigid and responds to stress by changing its posture. This mechanical advantage may allow the child to perform physical challenges at a higher level in later years when sport activities are more meaningful. This phenomenon probably explains why a small person can throw a baseball as fast as a larger person with longer levers. An increased mechanical advantage allows the smaller person (with shorter levers) to generate an increased force. This may be the benefit gained from throwing repetitively throughout the early childhood years.

MUSCULAR STRENGTH

In the elementary school years, muscular strength increases linearly with chronological age (Malina 1980). A similar yearly increase occurs until adolescence, at which time a rapid increase in strength occurs. Strength is related to body size and lean body mass. When differences in strength between the sexes are adjusted for height, there is no difference in lower body strength from age 7 through 17. When the same adjustment between the sexes is made for upper body strength, however, the boys have more upper extremity and trunk strength (Malina 1980). Boys and girls are thus competing on somewhat even terms in activities demanding leg strength, particularly if their size and mass are similar. On the other hand, in activities demanding arm or trunk strength, boys have a definite advantage, even if they are similar to the girls in height and mass. These considerations are important when pairing children for competition. Many problems occur when a student is paired with someone who is considerably taller and heavier and therefore stronger.

MUSCLE FIBER TYPE AND PERFORMANCE

The number of muscle fibers that an individual possesses is genetically determined. An increase in muscle size is accomplished by an increase in the size of each muscle fiber. The size of the muscles is determined first by the number of fibers, and secondarily by the size of the fibers. An individual is therefore somewhat muscularly limited by genetic restrictions.

Skeletal muscle tissue contains fibers that are fast contracting (fast twitch [FT]) and others that are slow contracting (slow twitch [ST]) (Saltin 1973). The percentage of fast versus slow contracting fibers varies from muscle to muscle and among individuals. The percentage of each type of muscle fiber is determined during the first weeks of postnatal life (Dubowitz 1970). Most individuals are believed to possess a 50–50 split, that is, half of the muscle fibers are FT and half are ST. A small percentage of people have a ratio of 60:40 (in either direction), and researchers have verified that some people possess an even more extreme ratio.

What is the significance of variation in the ratio of muscle fiber type? The ST fibers have a rich supply of blood and related energy mechanisms. This results in a slow contracting, fatigue-resistant muscle fiber that is well suited to endurance-type (aerobic) activities. In contrast, the FT fibers are capable of bursts of intense activity, but are subject to rapid fatigue. These fibers are well suited to activities demanding short-term speed and power (e.g., pull-ups, standing long jump, and shuttle run). The ST fibers would facilitate performance in the mile run or other endurance-oriented activity.

Surprisingly, children who do best in activities requiring FT fibers also apparently do best in distance running (Krahenbuhl and Pangrazi 1983). Muscle fiber metabolic specialization does not appear to occur until adolescence, making a strong argument for keeping all youngsters involved and interested in varied physical activity throughout the elementary years. A youngster who does poorly in elementary school may do quite well during and after adolescence when a high percentage of ST fibers will aid in the performance of aerobic activity. On the other hand, this same child may do poorly in a physical education program dominated by team sports that place a premium on quickness and strength. Designing a program that offers activities demanding a wide range of physical attributes (i.e., endurance, balance, flexibility) is thus essential.

STRENGTH AND MOTOR PERFORMANCE

Strength is an important factor in performing motor skills. A study by Rarick and Dobbins (1975) identified and ranked the factors that contribute to the motor performance of children. The factor identified as most important was strength or power or both in relation to body size. Youngsters who demonstrated high levels of strength in relation to their body size were more capable of performing motor skills than those with lower strength levels.

Obesity again has a negative impact. Deadweight (fat) was the fourth-ranked factor in the motor performance study and was weighted in a negative direction. The more obese a child was, the less proficient he was in performing motor skills. Deadweight is a negative factor because it reduces the child's strength in relation to body size. Obese children may be stronger than normal-weight children in absolute terms, but they are less strong when strength is adjusted for body weight. This lack of strength can cause obese children to perceive a strength-related task (e.g., Push-up or Sit-up) as much more difficult than the same task might seem to normal weight children. The need for varied work loads accompanied by teacher understanding and empathy is important for the obese child.

MATURITY

The concept of maturity is used often by teachers in physical education. Usually, elementary school children are identified as being early, late, or average maturers, with teachers examining the social maturity rather than the physical maturity of the child. Physical maturity, however, has a strong impact on the child's performance in physical education. The most commonly used method to identify maturity rate is to compare chronological age with skeletal age. Skeletal age gives a truer sense of the child's physical maturity and can be predicted by X-raying the wrist bones and comparing the development of the subject's bones with a set of standardized X rays (Gruelich and Pyle 1959). If a child's chronological age is ahead of her skeletal age, she is said to be a late (or slow) maturer. On the other hand, if the skeletal age is ahead of chronological age, the child is labeled an early (fast) maturer.

Early maturing children of both sexes are generally heavier and taller for their age than average or late maturing students. In fact, obese children (endomorphs) are often more mature for their age than normal-weight children. Early maturing children also have larger amounts of muscle and bone tissue due to their larger body size. However, the early maturer also carries a greater percentage of body weight as fat tissue (Malina 1980).

The motor performance of boys is related to skeletal maturity in that the more mature boy usually performs better on motor tasks (Clarke 1971). For girls, however, motor performance appears not to be related to physiological maturity. In fact, a study by Malina (1978) found that late maturation is commonly associated with exceptional motor performance.

MATURITY AND PHYSICAL EDUCATION

Physical education programs often place importance on learning at the same rate, even though this practice may be detrimental to the development of many students. Teachers sometimes expect all youngsters to do the same activity at the same time, regardless of skill level. Unfortunately, students are not maturing at the same rate and are therefore not at similar levels of readiness to learn.

Studies examining skeletal age (Gruelich and Pyle 1959, Krahenbuhl and Pangrazi 1983) consistently show that a five- to six-year variation in maturity exists in a typical classroom of youngsters. For example, a class of 3rd graders who are 8 years old chronologically would range in skeletal age from 5 to 11 years. Most teachers would not ask a 5-year-old kindergarten child to perform tasks that 11-year-olds are expected to accomplish. Teachers need to monitor and adjust program activities constantly to allow students to progress at a rate suitable to their level of maturity.

MATURITY AND SPORTS

Maturity also plays an important role in dictating which position a child will learn to play in a sport. Will he be a pitcher or right fielder, play in the line, or be quarterback? Often, these questions are answered for young children by adults, who may never allow a youngster an opportunity to realize her potential. In a study by Hale (1956), skeletally mature athletes were found to be playing in the skilled positions in the Little League World Series. Chronologically, the players were all 11 years old, with a skeletal age range similar to that described earlier. The most mature were pitchers and catchers, and the least mature played right field.

In this situation, the skeletally mature child is given more opportunities to throw at an early age (through pitching and catching) and becomes an even better thrower due to practice. The elementary school child who is immature plays right field, and seldom throws or catches. These children receive so much less throwing practice that it is improbable that they will ever become a pitcher or catcher.

PHYSICAL EDUCATION AND COMPETENCY

Physical education programs should allow students to practice all positions in various sport activities. In lead-up games and drills, all children should receive similar amounts of practice at all positions to develop broad competencies. If this does not occur, the gap between skilled and less skilled becomes greater, until the less skilled child eventually feels incompetent and drops out of sport activity on a permanent basis.

Appropriate instruction in physical education is necessary if children are to develop competency in various physical skills. During recess, children who practice skills without supervision receive feedback from peers based only on their actual performance level. Unfortunately, the practice of an incorrect technique does not make perfect; it does make the skill performance difficult to change at a later time.

Students base their physical activity choices on their competency level. If they feel competent at an activity, they may participate in that activity for the rest of their life, but if they feel incompetent, they will probably avoid the activity. Youngsters base 70% of their decisions (Hebron 1966) on their self-perceived level of competency formed by age 8. This reinforces the need for an instructionally oriented, broad, varied program, so children can find a variety of activities in which they can demonstrate competency.

A physical education program that contains a wide variety of activities is vital to the total development of children. While all children cannot be expected to like the same activities or even to possess similar abilities, limiting the number of activities offered will only limit the opportunities for all children to find success and develop competency.

INCOMPETENCY AND INACTIVITY

Students who feel incompetent in the physical skill area eventually drop out of physical education, and when they leave school have a negative opinion of an active life-style. Dropping out of physical education commonly occurs at the junior high school level, although the process often begins in the elementary school years.

Dropping out of activity because of elementary school performance is most unfortunate. Predicting who will be an outstanding athlete in junior or senior high school by observing elementary school performance is in fact quite difficult. In a study by Clarke (1968), athletes identified as outstanding in elementary school were seldom outstanding in junior high school, and predictions based on elementary school performance were correct only 25% of the time. Most people would believe that they had failed if they could pick horse races correctly only 25% of the time. Teachers, however, constantly label youngsters at an early age, even though their predictions are incorrect three out of four times.

PLACING CHILDREN IN ORGANIZED SPORTS AT A YOUNG AGE

No evidence supports the idea that starting a child at a young age ultimately allows the child to develop into an outstanding athlete. In fact, many excellent athletes, particularly in basketball, did not even play the sport until the high school years.

One reason why many parents and coaches push to have children start competing in a sport at an early age is that a better athlete appears to have been developed by the age of 8 or 9. The participating child may seem extremely gifted compared with the nonparticipant, because he has been practicing skills for four or five years. Naturally, this child looks advanced compared with a child who has not been in an organized program. In most cases, however, a child who is genetically more gifted quickly catches up to and surpasses an "early superstar" in one to three years. As Shephard (1984a) states, "Any advantage that is gained from very prolonged training probably lies in the area of skill perfection rather than in a fuller realization of physical potential."

There is some concern that children who have been in documented programs will burn out at an early age. A documented program is one in which extrinsic rewards are offered. Examples of such rewards are trophies, league standings that are published, ribbons, and excessive parental involvement. Some evidence shows that extrinsic motivation may ultimately decrease intrinsic motivation, particularly in children age 7 years and older. Thomas and Tennant (1978) found that younger children (age 5) perceived a reward as a bonus, thus adding to the joy of performing a throwing motor task. This effect decreased with age; by the age of 9 the reward was seen as a bribe, and intrinsic motivation appeared to be undermined. There is no substitute for allowing young children to participate in physical activity for the sheer enjoyment and excitement involved in moving and interacting with peers.

Why start children young? Many parents believe that children will never "catch up" if they do not begin as early as possible. As noted, this has not proved to be true, and physical educators need to share this message with parents. Another reason often given for starting children at a young age is tied to the commodity that only a child has—free time. Children supposedly have an abundance of free time that can be devoted to practice. Unfortunately, however, if the child shows promise, more practice becomes necessary "to ensure that all this talent is not lost." It is important to remind parents that life includes more than athletic development and that many youngsters have been maimed by an excessive sport emphasis at the expense of intellectual and social development.

OBESITY AND PHYSICAL ACTIVITY

Obesity restricts the motor performance of children. The study of childhood obesity has produced some disturbing findings. Many obese people appear to have a decreased tendency for muscular activity. As weight increases, the impulse for physical exertion further decreases. As children become more obese, they find themselves in a cycle that appears to be out of control. In most cases, physical activity may be the crucial factor in dealing with weight control (Chapter 12). In comparisons of the diets of obese and normal children, no substantial difference in caloric consumption was usually found. In fact, in some cases, obese children actually consumed less food than normal-weight children (Corbin and Fletcher 1968).

The lack of physical activity is common among obese children. In a study of 9th grade girls (Johnson et al. 1956), girls who were obese ate less but also exercised two-thirds less (in total time) than normal-weight girls. An examination of children in an elementary school in Massachusetts (Johnson et al. 1956) revealed that children gained more weight during the winter when they were less active. Movies taken of normal-weight and overweight children (Corbin and Fletcher 1968) demonstrated a great difference in activity level of the two groups, even though diets were quite similar.

Adults often make the statement, "Don't worry about excessive weight; it will come off when the child reaches adolescence." The opposite is usually true, however. Four out of 5 obese children grow into obese adults; however, 28 out of 29 obese teenagers become obese adults (Johnson et al. 1956). Children clearly do not *grow out* of obesity—they grow into it. Childhood obesity needs to be challenged at an early age, and this challenge must come from increased movement and activity.

OBESITY AND PERFORMANCE

As mentioned, obese children seldom perform physical activities on a level with leaner children (Bar-Or 1983). This is due to the greater metabolic cost of the obese child's exercise. Obese children require a higher oxygen uptake capacity to perform a given task. Unfortunately, their capacity is usually lower than that of normal-weight children, which means that they must operate at a higher percentage of their maximum capacity. This forces obese children to operate at a higher percentage of their aerobic capacity, so they have less reserve. The lack of reserve probably explains why these children perceive aerobic tasks as demanding and unenjoyable. Teachers should bear this in mind when they ask obese children to try to run as far and as fast as normal-weight children. The task *is* more demanding for the obese child.

Identifying whether obese children are less active due to genetic or environmental factors is difficult. In a study by Rose and Mayer (1968), 4- to 6-month-old babies were divided into groups based on their level of obesity. The most obese children had the fewest limb motions, expending only 20% of their total energy on physical activity. In contrast, the leanest babies expended 35% to 40% of their energy on physical activity.

Griffiths and Payne (1976) selected 4- and 5-year-old children for study based on their parents' level of obesity. At the time of the study, the children were of similar body composition. Children of obese parents were, however, less active and also ate less than the offspring of leaner parents. If the behavior continued, these children of obese parents would probably become obese due to lack of activity. The children's personal activity habits will have to change if they are to avoid obesity.

EXERCISING CHILDREN IN WARM CLIMATES

Teachers must be cautious when exercising youngsters in hot climates. The arrival of summer does not mean that exercise must stop, but certain measures should be used to avoid heat-related illness.

Children are not just little adults, and they do not adapt to extremes of temperature as effectively as adults for the following physiological reasons (Bar-Or 1983).

1. Children have a greater surface area/mass ratio than adults do. This allows a greater amount of heat to transfer between the environment and the body.

2. When walking or running, children produce more metabolic heat per unit mass than adults produce. Youngsters are not as efficient in executing movement patterns, so they generate more metabolic heat than adults performing a similar task.

3. Sweating capacity is not as great in children as in adults, resulting in a lowered ability to cool the body.

4. Ability to convey heat by blood from the body core to the skin is reduced in children due to a lower cardiac output at a given oxygen uptake.

These physiological differences clearly show that children are at a distinct disadvantage compared with adults when exercising in an environment in which the ambient air temperature is higher than the skin temperature.

Individuals do acclimatize to warmer climates. However, children appear to adjust to heat more slowly than adults (Bar-Or 1983). Often, children do not instinctively drink enough liquids to replenish fluids lost during exercise. The American Academy of Pediatrics Committee on Sports Medicine (1983) offers the following guidelines for exercising children in hot climates.

1. The intensity of activities that last 30 minutes or more should be reduced whenever relative humidity and air temperature are above critical levels (zone 3 in Figure 2.1). Information concerning relative humidity can be obtained from a nearby U.S. National Weather Service office or by use of a sling psychrometer (School Health Supplies, Box 409, 300 Lombard Rd., Addison, IL 60101; approximate cost $30) to compare dry-bulb and wet-bulb temperature levels.

2. At the beginning of a strenuous exercise program or after traveling to a warmer climate, the intensity and duration of exercise should be restrained initially and then increased gradually over a period of 10 to 14 days to accomplish acclimatization to the effects of heat.

3. Before prolonged physical activity, children should be fully hydrated. During the activity, periodic drinking (e.g., 150 ml of cold tap water every 30 minutes for a child weighing 40 kg) should be enforced.

4. Clothing should be lightweight and limited to one layer of absorbent material to facilitate evaporation of sweat and to expose as much skin as possible. Sweat-saturated garments should be replaced by dry ones. Rubberized sweat suits should never be used to produce weight loss.

The committee identifies children with the following conditions as being at a potentially high risk for heat stress: obesity, febrile (feverish) state, cystic fibrosis, gastrointestinal infection, diabetes insipidus, diabetes mellitus, chronic heart failure, caloric malnutrition, anorexia nervosa, sweating insufficiency syndrome, and mental deficiency.

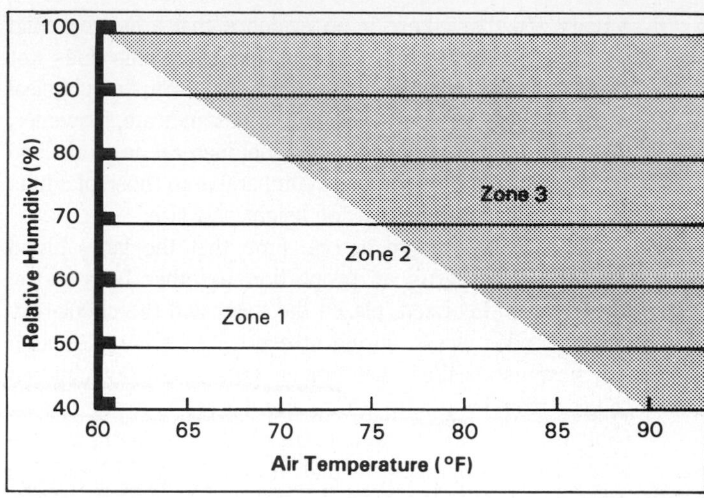

FIGURE 2.1. Weather guide for prevention of heat illness during prolonged strenuous exercise. (Adapted from THE PHYSIOLOGICAL BASIS OF PHYSICAL EDUCATION AND ATHLETICS, Third Edition, by Edward L. Fox and Donald K. Mathews. Copyright © 1981 by CBS College Publishing. Reprinted by permission of CBS College Publishing.)

DISTANCE RUNNING AND CHILDREN

The question of how much and how far children should be allowed to run often occurs, particularly in a competitive or training-for-competition setting. The answer is complex, since parents, teachers, or coaches seldom see the long-term effects. The American Academy of Pediatrics Executive Committee (1982) identifies some of the concerns:

> Lifetime involvement in a sport often depends on the type of early participation and gratification gained. Psychological problems can result from unrealistic goals for distance running by children. A child who participates in distance running primarily for parental gratification may tire of this after a time and quit, or the child may continue, chafing under the parental pressure. In either case, psychological damage may be done, and the child may be discouraged, either immediately or in the long run from participating in sports. A prepubertal child should be allowed to participate for the enjoyment of running without fear of parental or peer rejection or pressure. A child's sense of accomplishment, satisfaction, and appreciation by peers, parents, and coaches will foster involvement in running and other sports during childhood and in later life.

A strong position taken by the International Athletics Association Federation (IAAF) Medical Committee was recently reprinted (1983). In part, it states:

> The danger certainly exists that with over-intensive training, separation of the growth plates may occur in the pelvic region, the knee, or the ankle. While this could heal with rest, nevertheless definitive information is lacking whether in years to come harmful effects may result.
>
> In view of the above, it is the opinion of the committee that training and competition for long-distance track and roadrunning events should not be encouraged. Up to the age of 12, it is suggested that not more than 800 meters should be run in competition. An increase in this distance should be introduced gradually—with, for example, a maximum of 3000 meters in competition for 14 year olds.

MODERATION IN EXERCISE

As is usually the case, moderation is the best way to ensure that children grow up enjoying different types of physical activity. Moderate exercise, coupled with opportunities to participate in recreational activity, help to develop a lasting desire to move.

Educators are sometimes concerned that a child may be harmed physiologically by too much or too vigorous activity. To date, there is no evidence that a healthy child can be harmed through vigorous exercise. This does not mean that a child is capable of the same unadjusted physical work load as an adult. Evidence does indicate, however, that children can withstand a gradual increase in work load and are capable of work loads comparable to those of adults when the load is adjusted for height and size.

There was concern at one time that the large blood vessels do not grow in proportion to other body parts. This, it was theorized, placed the heart and the circulatory system under stress during strenuous exercise. Research has now established that fatigue causes *healthy* children to stop exercising long before any danger to health occurs (Shephard 1984a). In addition, the child's circulatory system is similar in proportion to that of an adult and is *not* at a disadvantage during exercise.

PHYSICAL EDUCATION AND INTELLECTUAL DEVELOPMENT

For years physical educators have attempted to demonstrate a relationship between physical education and a child's intellectual potential. Indeed, if intellectual development or academic achievement could be linked to physical performance, physical education would rank higher as an educational priority. However, according to Shephard (1984), "Strong proof is lacking." Shephard identifies the many limitations of such investigations, which include (1) studies of special populations such as the mentally handicapped or athletes, (2) "halo" effects, because teachers reward star performers with higher marks, (3) self-image gains by athletes due to teacher and peer praise, (4) short duration of training programs, (5) possible side effects from curtailment of academic instruction, and (6) use of retrospective data relating observed academic performance to measures of activity or physical ability.

In any case, physical educators can justify the inclusion of a physical education in the total school curriculum on the basis of two unique contributions—(1) motor skill development and (2) the understanding and maintenance of physical fitness. Since these contributions are unique to physical education and contribute to the physical well-being of youngsters, further convincing administrators and parents that intellectual development is enhanced by physical education should not be necessary. Few people will not support a physical education program if it aids, nurtures, and shows concern for the physical development of *all* children.

A study that has created much interest in this area is the Trois Rivieres regional experiment (Shephard 1984b). The study provides a well-conceived design for showing the contribution of added physical activity to the academic achievement of students throughout their primary school years. Gains in academic performance (in comparison with control students) were statistically significant in grades 2, 3, 5, and 6. The more active students received higher marks in French language, mathematics, English, and science, despite a 13% reduction in the time available for academic instruction.

Later evaluation of the study (Shephard 1984b) found that 6th grade students who participated in provincewide examinations continued to perform better. These results appear to counter the objection that more physical education will result in poorer academic performance due to less time spent in the classroom. Administrators need to consider this study, particularly today, when many schools have a back-to-basics emphasis. This emphasis usually means "back to the classroom," without physical activity or the arts. One wonders if this lack of concern for the body, our "home of the brain," is not detrimental to the children's total development. The ability to read becomes unimportant if one's health has degenerated. No priority in life is higher than physical well-being.

LONG-TERM EFFECT OF EXERCISE

Many experts believe that the physical activity undertaken in childhood has a lifetime impact. Saltin and Grimby (1968) conducted a research project to learn whether the benefits of childhood activity carried over to adult life. They compared the ability to adjust to effort of three groups of subjects age 50 to 59. One group was former athletes who had not participated in activity for over 20 years and who worked in sedentary jobs. A second group consisted of former athletes who kept up a regular training and exercise program during their adult years. The third group was individuals who were not athletes in youth and who were inactive as adults. Results showed that the nonathlete group was capable of the least effort (measured by maximal oxygen uptake). The group that was active during youth but took part in little activity during adulthood scored significantly higher than the nonathlete group. The athlete group that had maintained training scored a great deal higher than the other two groups. The essence of the study is that functional capacity as an adult appears to be partly a result of activity during the growing years.

In summary, accumulating evidence continues to show that the earliest years of a person's life are the most important in the development of future movement and activity patterns. A child who is active at an early age will probably be active as an adult.

REFERENCES

Albinson, J. G., and Andrews, G. M. 1976. *Child in sport and physical activity.* Baltimore: University Park Press.

American Academy of Pediatrics. 1982. Risks in long-distance running for children. *The Physician and Sportsmedicine* 10(8): 82–86.

American Academy of Pediatrics. 1982. Climatic heat stress and the exercising child. *The Physician and Sportsmedicine* 11(8): 155–159.

Bar-Or, O. 1983. *Pediatric sports medicine for the practitioner.* New York: Springer-Verlag.

Bar-Or, O. 1977. Age-related changes in exercise perception. In *Physical work and effort,* G. Borg, ed. New York: Pergamon Press.

Clarke, H. H. 1968. Characteristics of the young athlete: A longitudinal look. *Kinesiology Review* 3: 33–42.

Clarke, H. H. 1971. *Physical motor tests in the Medford boy's growth study.* Englewood Cliffs, N.J.: Prentice-Hall.

Corbin, C. B., and Fletcher, P. 1968. Diet and activity patterns of obese and non-obese elementary school children. *Research Quarterly* 39(4): 922.

Dubowitz, V. 1970. Differentiation of fiber types in skeletal muscle. In *Physiology and biochemistry of muscle as a food,* E. J. Briskey, R. G. Cassens, and B. B. Marsh, eds. vol 2. Madison, Wis.: University of Wisconsin Press.

Gilliam, T. B., et al. 1982. Exercise programs for children: A way to prevent heart disease? *The Physician and Sportsmedicine* 10(9): 96–108.

Glass, W. 1973. Coronary heart disease sessions prove vitally interesting. *California CAHPER Journal* (May/June): 7.

Griffiths, M., and Payne P. R. 1976. Energy expenditure in small children of obese and non-obese parents. *Nature* 260: 698–700.

Gruelich, W., and Pyle, S. 1959. *Radiographic atlas of skeletal development of the hand and wrist.* 2nd ed. Stanford, Calif.: Stanford University Press.

Hale, C. 1956. Physiological maturity of little league baseball players. *Research Quarterly* 27: 276–284.

Hebron, M. E. 1966. *Motivated learning.* London: Methuen & Co.

International Athletics Association Federation (IAAF). 1983. Not kid's stuff. *Sports Medicine Bulletin* 18(1): 11.

Johnson, M. L., Burke, B. S., and Mayer, J. 1956. The prevalence and incidence of obesity in a cross section of elementary and secondary school children. *American Journal of Clinical Nutrition* 4(3): 231.

Krahenbuhl, G. S., and Pangrazi, R. P. 1983. Characteristics associated with running performance in young boys. *Medicine and Science in Sports* 15(6): 486–490.

Malina, R. M. 1978. Physical growth and maturity characteristics of young athletes. In *Children and youth in sport; A contemporary anthology,* R. A. Magill, M. H. Ash, and F. L. Smoll, eds. Champaign, Ill.: Human Kinetics.

Malina, R. M. 1980. Growth, strength, and physical performance. In *Encyclopedia of physical education, fitness, and sports,* G. A. Stull and T. K. Cureton, eds. Salt Lake City: Brighton Publishing.

Rarick, L. G., ed. 1973. *Physical activity, human growth and activity.* New York: Academic Press.

Rarick, L. G., and Dobbins, D. A. 1975. Basic components in the motor performances of children six to nine years of age. *Medicine and Science in Sports* 7(2): 2.

Rose, H. E., and Mayer, J. 1968. Activity, calorie intake, fat storage and the energy balance of infants. *Pediatrics* 41: 18–29.

Rose, K. 1973. To keep people in health. *Journal of the American College Health Association* 22: 80.

Saltin, B. 1973. Metabolic fundamentals of exercise. *Medicine and Science of Sports* 5: 137–146.

Saltin, B., and Grimby, G. 1968. Physiological analysis of middle-aged and old former athletes, comparison with still active athletes of the same ages. *Circulation* 38(6): 1104.

Shephard, R. J. 1984a. Physical activity and child health. *Sports Medicine* 1: 205–233.

Shephard, R. J. 1984b. Physical activity and "wellness" of the child. In *Advances in pediatric sport sciences,* by R. A. Boileau. Champaign, Ill.: Human Kinetics Publishers.

Thomas, J. R., and Tennant, L. K. 1978. Effects of rewards on changes in children's motivation for an athletic task. In *Psychological perspectives in youth sports,* F. L. Smoll and R. E. Smith, eds. Washington: Hemisphere.

Wilmore, J. H., and McNamara, J. J. 1974. Prevalance of coronary heart disease risk factors in boys 8 to 12 years of age. *Journal of Pediatrics* 84(4): 4.

CHAPTER 3

The Basis of Movement Learning

A growing body of knowledge is available to guide teachers in developing a child's movement competency. That an understanding of the nature of movement learning contributes to more efficient teaching is rarely questioned. Movement becomes learning for children when it accomplishes something positive and helps them reach their educational potential. The process by which children learn movement skills is called *motor learning.* This can be self-learning, wherein the child through exploration and experimentation achieves some progress. However, the teacher takes youngsters beyond this stage by helping them consolidate positive gains, by adding new insights, and by coaching to higher levels of achievement.

If children are to enjoy movement, they need to achieve reasonable competency in executing movement patterns. Some educators believe that developing lifelong patterns of exercise depends critically on achieving a satisfactory competency level in physical activity during the elementary school years. Nash (1960) believed that the recreational skills learned before the age of 12 are the skills used in adult leisure.

To promote optimum learning that elicits the potential of each child, efficient teaching methods and methodology must be based on an understanding of motor learning. Teaching children to move efficiently and to achieve success and satisfaction in movement experiences is the key to establishing positive feelings toward activity. The teacher is therefore the key factor in guiding movement experiences so that learning occurs.

UNDERSTANDING MOTOR LEARNING

The learning process involved in mastering motor skills can be made more productive when teachers understand pertinent tenets from educational doctrine and motor learning research. The applications vary with the stage of learning, the activity presented, and the maturity of the children.

The development of motor skills is an individual matter, and wide variation occurs among children of similar chronological age. However, the sequence of skill development in youngsters is much the same and appears to progress in an orderly fashion. Experts on motor learning have identified three development patterns that typify the growth of children.

1. Development in general proceeds from head to foot (cephalocaudally), that is, coordination and management of body parts occur in the upper body before they are observed in the lower. The child can therefore throw before he can kick.
2. Development occurs from inside to outside (proximodistally). For example, the child can control her arm before she can control her hand. She can therefore reach for objects before she can grasp them.
3. Development proceeds from the general to the specific. Gross motor movements occur before fine motor coordination and refined movement patterns. As the child learns motor skills, nonproductive movement is gradually eliminated.

READINESS

One role of the teacher in teaching skills is to ascertain the time when children are capable and ready to learn, and then to design a learning environment that promotes the most effective development of the skills. The learning task must be within the capacity of the child.

A number of factors affect readiness, among them maturity level, previous practice, prerequisite skills, body management skills, and state of physical fitness. Interest in the activity plays a role in readiness levels, because people do things that interest them. In turn, if they do well at an activity, they become ready to learn more about the activity. People usually want to do well because of the social rewards that accompany success. Teachers should first offer worthwhile experiences that are based on students' existing interests, but they must then go further to establish new student interests and experiences.

Maturity level is defined as the gross physical and neural body management competencies necessary for the child to have a basis for success and to be challenged by the selected movement pattern. For example, a child must have the ability to track a moving object before she can become proficient in catching skills. If the child lacks the capability to perform a task, the activity should be modified in a progressive manner. For example, if a child cannot catch a small, rapidly moving object, asking her to play a game involving softball skills will have little value. Instead, she will benefit if the teacher brings out a large, brightly colored and slower moving object, such as a beach ball, for practice sessions.

Previous experience and prerequisite skills are usually the result of prior learning experiences. A child who began rope jumping in kindergarten and continued the experience would be ready for advanced activities that would frustrate a beginner of similar age. *Prerequisite skills* refers to the fundamental competencies needed for success in a later unit. As an example, dribbling, trapping, and kicking skills are necessary prerequisites for successful participation in the game of soccer.

Body management skills are a broad collection of skills needed for managing the body in a variety of environmental challenges. These skills include starting and stopping, avoiding collisions, dodging, changing direction, accelerating, and moving efficiently to meet challenges. Many of these skills originate in the lower grades.

Physical fitness levels have implications, too. Children who can resist fatigue and sustain the rigors of skill practice are more likely to achieve than those with an inadequate fitness level.

Most experts agree that each learner's optimum state of readiness is defined as the level at which the child learns most efficiently and with the least difficulty. Whenever possible, the teacher should identify that optimum state for each child. This state of readiness is often difficult to recognize because students mature at different rates. However, if attempts are not made to analyze each child's progress frequently and if the instruction is beyond the child's level of readiness, then frustration and withdrawal may occur.

In general, findings suggest that boys perform better at gross motor skills demanding strength and large-body movement, while girls perform better at motor skills requiring a higher degree of coordination, precision, flexibility, and balance. These tendencies may be sex differences or may be attributed to environment. Either way, they point out the need to offer youngsters an opportunity to participate in a variety of movement experiences to enhance readiness to learn. Often, specific skill activities are learned earlier when children have the advantage of enriched movement experiences during preschool years.

Generalizations about an individual or a group within an age range are of limited value, but can be a starting point for activity selection. Age-level characteristics provide information about average or typical development.

In the selection of learning activities for children, two decisions face the teacher. First, are the students ready for that type of activity? Second, at what level of difficulty in activity progression and challenge should instruction begin? In an activity unit, the authors recommend that the Start-and-Expand principle be adopted. The teacher begins at an entry level where all children can be successful, and then moves along the activity progression to a point at which difficulty in execution is encountered by the majority of the class. At this point, the teacher arranges the most effective learning situation for the development of the challenged skills. In most situations, children should be allowed to stay at a level that is within their learning capability.

MOTIVATION

Readiness implies that the child *can learn* and *is ready to learn.* When children are motivated, they *want to learn.* Capability and readiness have a physical and neural basis, while motivation is based on psychological drives. The learner must have some drive to act or little learning takes place. The teacher can have a marked effect on the child's motivational level.

The concept of "physical education" is often motivating to children, because they associate physical action with recess and play. This feeling must not be lost. Students' faces should light up when the classroom teacher announces that it is time to go to physical education class. This excitement can be augmented by introducing something new, something different, something challenging, or perhaps by trying a new teaching style.

In time, a shift in motivation from extrinsic to intrinsic factors should occur; emphasis should shift from teacher approval to personal satisfaction in task accomplishment. If the teacher expects students to be successful, students reflect this confidence in their ability and form realistic goals. On the other hand, if the teacher expects students to fail, they often live up to the negative expectation.

Learning why one is doing something is a strong motivator. Children learn more readily when they understand the *why* of activities. Students should be included as activity planners, since those who participate in the planning are more likely to support the activity.

The activity should be changed when fatigue, boredom, or lack of progress is evident among the children. Good teaching allows for rest or relaxation periods between practice sessions.

GOALS

Providing children with target goals toward which they strive is a means of motivation that merits separate discussion. Children are stimulated when they have a goal that is both challenging and attainable. The teacher should make sure that children understand the goals of the various activities. If these goals or performance objectives can be defined in a personal way by each child, the procedure gains significance and has unique value for the learner. Children need to feel that they have met a challenge and can say, "I did it."

A goal should be stated clearly so the learner knows when it has been reached. If the overall goal can be broken into subgoals, the instructional sequence is enhanced. Learning takes place effectively when the learner participates actively in selecting and setting goals and in planning ways to attain them. Often, the teacher can hold discussions to allow students to help in goal setting. Teaching aids such as movies, filmstrips, loop films, posters, and speakers also help both the teacher and students to determine desirable goals.

FEEDBACK AND REINFORCEMENT

Feedback and reinforcement are modifying factors in the learning process and in maintaining learning receptivity. Detrimental effects can occur when the feedback is unpleasant or negative. *Feedback* refers to the impressions, feelings, or concepts that a child derives from learning experiences. Feedback should provide information about the technical correctness of the movement and about the accuracy or adequacy of that response. *Reinforcement* implies a strengthening, a consolidation, and a shoring up of learning as a result of feedback.

Reinforcement is important in shaping learner behavior. Whatever is reinforced regularly becomes a part of the child's behavior pattern. The child is reinforced when he receives something pleasant (e.g., the teacher's attention, praise, and encouragement) or when something unpleasant is taken away (e.g., peer pressure or constant failure).

Children thrive on praise and encouragement; a positive approach is more meaningful than a negative one. When students lack confidence, praise and encouragement are even more important. Encouragement that indicates growth and improvement can help the child progress, and also helps her overcome fear of failure. Praise should be honest and give recognition when it is due.

Practice alone is not enough. The child must receive feedback that tells how movements can be improved. In the early stages of learning a new skill, the amount of close analysis should be minimal. As the child's ability increases, more specific feedback can be offered. If the movement pattern can be broken into progressive increments, the possibility for positive feedback is increased.

While general feedback ("nice going" or "good work") provides encouragement, it has little effect on specific factors in skill learning. Too much information, however, can confuse the learner. In analyzing a child's performance, the teacher should concentrate on one or two of the more salient points and leave other details for later, more advanced lessons.

Product feedback (without concern for the process of skill performance) can sometimes be erroneous. A child who manages to get the ball into a basket might believe that the process was correct because of the outcome, even though the technical points of the throw were performed incorrectly.

Another feedback method is for the teacher to discuss and stress to the class the critical points of a skill. The critique of student performance can then be based on a question such as "What are the important points we must remember to perform this skill efficiently?"

Finally, structured skill achievement tests can be used to measure student progress in the upper grades. The sport units lend themselves to skill testing, and self-testing gives students feedback about personal improvement without the stigma of comparison with classmates. Self-testing can also be relevant to the personal goals that a child has established.

TRANSFER OF MOVEMENT LEARNING

Simply defined, *transfer of learning* is the effect that the previous practice or acquisition of movement skills and concepts has on the student's ability to learn new skills. The theory of transfer has caused some controversy, and no absolute answers are available.

A child's learning efficiency depends in part on how fast she can adapt previously learned skills and transfer them to new skill acquisition. Transfer is not automatic, but occurs more readily *when the skill closely resembles previously learned patterns.* However, a learner may not cognitively recognize the similarity.

If teachers desire transfer of learning to occur, they must make a conscious effort to discuss and apply generalizations about skills and skill applications in similar situations. Transfer has a major limitation of which teachers must be aware: it is quite specific. For instance, learning to shoot a basketball will not make a student a better football passer. There seems to be more transfer from fundamental movement skills (e.g., walking, hopping, or jumping) to specific skills involving these components than there is between complex skills (e.g., shooting a basket and kicking a soccer ball).

In addition to transfer between similar tasks, theorists also hold that transfer is more probable if the original task is well learned. If, for example, the learner has a good understanding of the movement principles involved in the original task and has learned that task well, transfer of learning is more likely. Throughout the program, the relevance of pertinent movement principles should be stressed when they are applicable.

An interesting aspect of transfer is the schema theory

of motor learning (Schmidt 1976). According to this theory, a motor skill should be learned under a wide variety of conditions and should be practiced in as many varied situations as possible. Students thus perform the skill under a wide range of conditions. Schmidt's studies emphasize the importance of offering a broad and varied program of activity to elementary school youngsters.

PART METHOD VERSUS WHOLE METHOD OF TEACHING

Among teachers, there has long been much discussion about the teaching of movement skills by the part method and by the whole method. The *whole method* refers to the process of learning the entire skill or activity in one dose. The *part method* involves learning parts of the activity separately until all of the parts are learned, and then combining the parts to form a unified whole. The choice of the whole method or the part method depends on the complexity of the skill or activity to be learned. The teacher needs to decide whether the activity is simple enough to be taught as a whole or whether it should be broken into parts. Ideally, the skill should be practiced as a whole. If the child is failing to perform the skill as a whole, then it must be broken into subskills and each part practiced. Once the subskills are mastered, they can then be put together in proper sequence and practiced as a whole.

STRESS AND ANXIETY

Various emotional conditions may affect movement learning. Children feel challenged when confronted with a problem that they can solve successfully. They feel threatened when given a problem that they do not feel capable of handling, and this feeling usually interferes with the learning process. The teacher must anticipate and eliminate situations that might threaten students and cause excessive stress and anxiety.

The teacher should concentrate on praising progress and proper performance. Dwelling on criticism and identifying performances of poor quality encourage peer rejection. Enough equipment should be available so that each child is occupied in a movement task and has no time to ridicule less skilled children. Total student involvement helps reduce stress and anxiety.

Competition is usually disruptive when students are learning a complex skill. When competition is introduced in the early stages of skill learning, stress and anxiety are apt to cause more problems than when competition is introduced after the skill has been overlearned. Since most children in elementary school have not overlearned skills, teachers should avoid competition when learning a skill properly is the primary goal.

PROGRESSION

Logical progression is the heart of the learning process. *Progression* is defined as moving the learning process through ordered steps from the least challenging to the more challenging facets of an activity. For any child, the starting point in a lesson would be the challenge of a task that is one step above the student's present level. Individual differences do occur among children, however, and any one progression cannot satisfy everyone's requirements.

Motor skills can be ranked in a hierarchy from the simple to the complex. Complex skills are difficult, if not impossible, to attain when the fundamental skills have not been learned. The learning of fundamental motor skills requires considerable time and practice for refinement to take place. The fundamental skills must be overlearned so they can be performed automatically and without conscious effort. Eventually, this allows the child's thought processes to be directed toward learning new, complex movements or to thinking about strategy while performing sport activities.

Expansion *within an activity* may be the approach indicated. If the children are not capable of performing the activity at the lowest level, then the activity is not a suitable educational experience for the group.

Progression also involves the review of previously learned steps before proceeding to new material, and the concept further includes the development of prerequisite skills before experiencing a more complex activity. For example, a skill performed in place should precede the same skill performed while moving. A basketball dribble is simpler when done in place, and later can be expanded with the addition of locomotor movements. A further progression would be for the dribbler to retain control while being guarded.

LEARNING A NEW SKILL

Learning a new skill involves three separate but overlapping phases. The first is the introductory or cognitive phase, a relatively shorter period than the two following phases. The second phase is the practice phase and is the critical step in ensuring that children develop new skills correctly. The final phase involves consolidation, using the skill automatically in a setting that involves integrating a series of developed skills.

THE INTRODUCTORY PHASE

In the introductory phase, the student acquires an understanding of the task to be performed and forms a concept of what is to be done. The teacher must be able to verbalize the skill (i.e., discuss its component parts) so the children can follow the pattern of the task. Much of this is done in sequenced steps or in slow motion, depending on the type of challenge. Demonstration can emphasize the critical points of the skill. Loop films, videotaping, diagrams, and other visual aids help children to develop correct understanding. Students should have the opportunity to experiment with different, valid ways of performing a skill, rather than being confined to a single teacher-selected pattern.

In the early stages of learning, when emphasis is placed on exploration and experimentation with various skills, the approach should be a system of approximation and correction, rather than trial and error. Success can be determined when the approximation begins to resemble the desired movement pattern.

Reasonable form should be stressed. This ensures that youngsters will not have to relearn a skill later, because they learned an improper pattern. Proper patterns can be taught with individual differences taken into consideration.

The learner selects subroutines, serializes the needed movements, and is helped to discard those components that are incorrect or impede progress. At this point, little refinement occurs, but the basic form to be practiced is established and the learner begins to adopt a style.

Mime offers an important approach to establishing the basic techniques of a new motor skill. Students can be in mass formation and follow the directions of the leader. Without the implement (e.g., ball, bat, or other object), they can concentrate on the movement and can acquire a kinesthetic feeling for the skill. In this way, many can practice at one time, form can be emphasized, questions answered, and gross errors discovered at an early stage. The mime approach is most effective with the intermediate grades or with youngsters who already have some perception of the skill being taught.

THE PRACTICE PHASE

During the practice phase, the learner receives ongoing feedback, eliminates errors, and makes necessary adjustments. The task begins to be done with less conscious effort. Timing of the movement is refined during this phase, and execution is polished. Attention begins to shift from the process to the product. Emphasis must be placed on learning motor skills properly, and teachers should help young children to develop a reasonable competence level.

Children need repeated trials to learn a skill. Practice by itself, however, does not ensure that learning is occurring, unless the practice is purposeful. To be learned, motor patterns must be practiced correctly. During practice sessions, the teacher coaches and helps youngsters attain adequate levels of skill by analyzing and making corrections. The student expects an intelligent answer to the question "What am I doing wrong?" Coaching depends on powers of observation and development of keen recognition ability. Effective coaching techniques give students a feeling of confidence. The student should believe that, if she is having difficulty, the instructor will help her discover a different solution.

The following guidelines ensure maximum results from practice sessions.

1. *Groups.* Skills should be practiced in as small a group as possible given the students' skill levels and the equipment available. Each child should have a piece of equipment. In ball handling (i.e., throwing, catching, kicking, and other means of receipt and propulsion), maximum practice opportunity is achieved by partner organization, with one object being used by two children.

2. *Overlearning and retention.* The teacher must allow sufficient repetition to establish retention. This is the principle of overlearning. *Correct* form must be practiced until it becomes fixed. The more complex the skill and the higher the performance level, the more practice is needed to establish and maintain that level. Overlearning is achieved when a smooth, coordinated response or movement pattern is performed with little mental effort. How well a learned skill is retained depends on the degree of proficiency reached during practice and the degree of overlearning.

3. *Extended experiences.* In addition to sufficient repetition, multiple opportunities to experiment with various movement patterns are crucial to motor learning. Single experiences and one-time exposure have little effect. Children need an environment filled with a variety of sensual experiences. They crave almost continual activity and must be given the opportunity to repeat the same activity many times in recurring and varied ways. In what amounts to a vital drive toward development of new motor patterns, young children appear to have a natural desire to repeat, rework, and reiterate.

4. *Length of practice sessions.* Practice sessions that last a relatively shorter time and involve relatively fewer repetitions usually produce more efficient learning than longer sessions with more repetitions. Many educators believe that this is due to the young learner's mental fatigue in longer sessions. Other educators, however, believe that attention span is affected more by motivation than by learner age. Using varied approaches, challenges, and activities to develop the same skill helps maintain both teacher and student motivational levels. For example, the many different beanbag activities described later (pp. 295–297) offer novelty to maintain motivation yet still focus on throwing and catching skills.

5. *Distribution of practice sessions.* Practice sessions that occur over a longer time are usually more effective than many sessions crowded into a shorter time period. The combination of practice and review appears to be effective for youngsters. Activities can be taught in a short unit and practiced in review sessions spaced throughout the school year. In the initial stages of skill learning, it is particularly important that practice sessions be distributed in this way. In later stages, when success increases motivational levels, the individual practice sessions can be lengthened.

6. *Mental Practice.* Mental practice has the advantage of stimulating children to think about and review the activity that they are to perform. Some experience or familiarity with the motor task is requisite before the performer can derive value from mental practice. Mental practice should be used in combination with regular practice, not in place of it. Before performing the task, students can review mentally the critical factors and sequencing of the act. Thus mental practice has value in helping skill development.

7. *Observation.* Critical observation by the teacher is essential in the practice phase. Some observation system, which may involve recording, should be developed. The teacher centers first on the whole movement, then on the component parts. In particular, the teacher directs attention to the components that were stressed in the skill instructions. Observation should generate comments to help eliminate inefficient actions or errors. Comments should be predominantly positive in nature. Teachers should support comments by explanations as to why certain skill elements were selected.

THE CONSOLIDATION PHASE

The consolidation phase, also termed the automatic phase, is reached when the child performs easily, without stress, and with little, if any, conscious control. Few elementary school children reach this stage with specialized skills, although children may reach this level with some fundamental skills. The consolidation phase is not a strong consideration in elementary physical education. The continued practice of all skills under more challenging conditions should be the focus. Even overlearned skills need practice.

ENHANCING MOTOR LEARNING EXPERIENCES

A number of guidelines and considerations for effective motor learning have been presented in this chapter. Additional areas not covered previously are explored in this section.

1. The learning curve applies to learning physical skills. Increments of improvement are invariably larger in the early learning phases, and become smaller and smaller as the skill improves.

2. Motor learning is specific. To broaden the development of motor learning patterns, a variety of movement experiences should be offered. For example, to help a child acquire the generalized motor competency known as *locomotor movement* (e.g., walking, skipping, hopping, or leaping), experiences in many skills in a variety of situations should be planned. The child must learn not only the separate movements but must put them in combination and sequence (flow) through experimentation and exploration.

3. The "start them young" approach, sometimes promoted by misguided parents and occasionally by athletic coaches, is often the source of many problems for youngsters. This type of instruction is evident in some organized sport programs and attempts to teach sport skills at an increasingly early age. The available evidence does not show that teaching refined skills as early as possible produces a more proficient performer in the long run. Instead, proficiency seems to be a function of the child's interest in the activity, as well as related genetic and environmental factors. Emotional problems can occur when children are forced to engage in activities in which they have little interest or ability. A rich environment that offers many opportunities for children to explore and practice skills is the best training ground. Such an environment should be seen as a necessity and not as a luxury.

4. Laterality is an important concept to apply in skill development. If a child leads with his left foot while doing a follow step on the balance beam, the next experience should be performed with the right foot leading. In basketball, children should learn to dribble with either hand. For some skills, however, as in batting a softball, children may wish to retain one-sidedness.

5. Motor skills, particularly complex skills that involve sequencing, should be practiced in the same sequence and with about the same timing as in the natural act. Some skills can be slowed down, but to decrease the speed of performance to a point at which timing is lost adds a negative factor that would have to be corrected later. An example of a fundamental skill that can be slowed down effectively is skipping. The movement can be taught as a slow step-hop, with alternating feet. Conversely, if running is slowed down, it becomes an awkward movement with little meaning.

6. The addition of rhythm to a skill-learning situation does more than enhance the quality of movement; it adds breadth and motivation, because it capitalizes on the child's inherent love of rhythm. The rhythm must be appropriate to the movement pattern and tempo. Another aid to learning motor patterns is the selection of cue words. An example would be telling children to say the phrase "step, hop" as they learn how to skip.

7. The performance of overlearned skills is generally enhanced by competition, but competition diminishes the performance of new skills being learned. Suppose a relay is being used to enhance the performance of a skill. If the skill is simple (such as running or skipping) and is being performed by 4th graders, then competition will probably motivate the youngsters and cause them to give a better effort. On the other hand, if the skill is more complex (such as dribbling a soccer ball), the majority of 4th-grade students will probably be frustrated by competition and will do a poorer job. Since the majority of motor skills that youngsters learn in elementary school are *not* refined and overlearned, competition should be used with caution.

MECHANICAL PRINCIPLES INVOLVED IN SKILL PERFORMANCE

The effective performance of movement skills requires an understanding of mechanical principles. This section discusses concepts that teachers should understand and help youngsters to apply to skill performance. Intermediate-grade children should begin to analyze their performances (albeit in a somewhat rudimentary fashion) by applying some of these principles.

STABILITY

Stability reflects balance and equilibrium, which affect the performance of many sport skills. A stable base is necessary when one applies force to a projectile or absorbs force. Instability is useful in some activities, as when a rapid start is desired. (Instability is the basis of the sprinter's start.)

Children can be introduced to the following concepts.

1. The size of the base of support must be increased to achieve more stability. The base must be widened in the direction in which force is applied or from which force is absorbed.

2. The body's center of gravity must be closer to the base of support (i.e., lower) when stopping quickly or when applying or absorbing force (as in pulling). This lowering is accomplished by bending the knees and hips (Figure 3.1).

3. The center of gravity must be kept over the base of support (within the boundaries of the base) for stability and balance. When the center of gravity passes beyond the boundaries of the base, the person has lost his balance. In most activities, the head should be kept up and excessive body lean eliminated. Keeping the body weight centered over the base of support allows for a rapid start in any direction.

FORCE

Force is essentially a measure of the push or pull that one object or body applies to another. Force is necessary to move objects of various types and size. The larger the object to be moved, the greater the amount of force required to cause the movement. Generating large forces usually requires the involvement of large muscle groups and a greater number of muscles than does the generation of a smaller force.

Torque is the twisting or turning effect that a force produces when it acts eccentrically with respect to a body's axis of rotation. Torque is therefore a rotational movement. An understanding of torque facilitates the understanding of levers.

FIGURE 3.1. Pulling

Concepts that children can use include the following.

1. When resisting or applying force, the bones on either side of the major body joints should form a right angle to each other. This facilitates the development of high levels of torque by the muscles. A muscle is most effective at causing rotation when it pulls at a 90-degree angle.

2. The development of muscle tension is facilitated when the shortening phase is immediately preceded by a stretching phase. Many body movements use a stretch-shorten pattern naturally.

3. To generate greater force, body parts must be activated in a smooth, coordinated manner. For example, in throwing, the hips and trunk are rotated first and are followed in sequence by the upper arm, lower arm, hand, and fingers.

4. More force is generated when the number of muscles used is large. Muscles are capable of generating high levels of force when the contraction speed is low. For example, lifting a very heavy object rapidly is impossible.

5. Force should be absorbed over a large surface area and over as long a period of time as possible. An example of absorbing force over a large surface area is a softball player rolling after a dive through the air to catch a ball. The roll absorbs the force with the hands and the large surface area of the body. Absorbing force over a period of time implies moving, or giving, with the object. Examples are landing in a crash pad after a high jump or "giving" when catching a baseball pitch.

6. The follow-through in striking and throwing activities is necessary for the maximum application of force and the gradual reduction of momentum. An example is the continued swing of the baseball bat after striking the ball. Many errors in skill performance result from lack of follow-through (i.e., stopping the throwing arm after the ball has been released).

LEVERAGE AND MOTION

Body levers are necessary to amplify force into motion. Levers offer a mechanical advantage so that less effort is needed to accomplish tasks. Motion occurs after force has been applied or when force is absorbed.

A simple lever is basically a bar or some other rigid structure that can rotate about a fixed point when force is applied to overcome a resistance. Levers serve one of two functions: (1) Either they allow a resistance greater than the applied force to be overcome, or (2) they serve to increase the distance over which or the speed at which a resistance can be moved. In the human body, the individual segments act as levers as they rotate about the joints.

The following are characteristics of levers and the effects they have on movement.

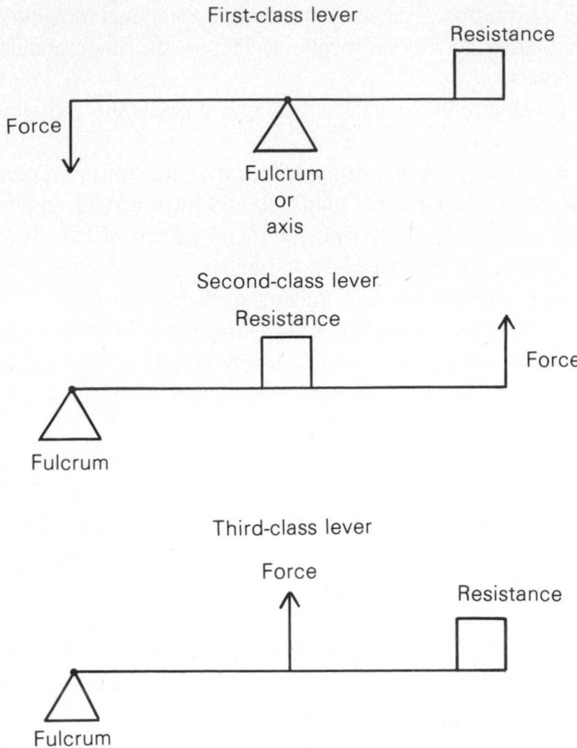

FIGURE 3.2. Types of levers

1. The three types of levers in the body are known as first-, second-, and third-class levers (Figure 3.2). Most of the body's levers are third-class levers, which have the point of force (produced by the muscles) between the fulcrum (joint) and the point of resistance (produced by the weight of the object to be moved).

2. Most of the levers in the body are used to gain a mechanical advantage for speed rather than to accomplish heavy tasks. Since the majority of levers are third class, students must learn to work within the body's structural and physical limits.

3. A longer force arm (distance from joint to point of force application) allows greater resistance to be overcome (Figure 3.3). This concept is useful if we are considering how to manipulate an external lever. For example, when we pry open a paint can, we apply force to the screwdriver away from the rim rather than near the paint can. This allows the screwdriver to act as a longer lever.

4. A longer resistance arm (distance from joint to point of resistance) allows greater speed to be generated (Figure 3.4). Rackets and bats are extensions of the arm, that is,

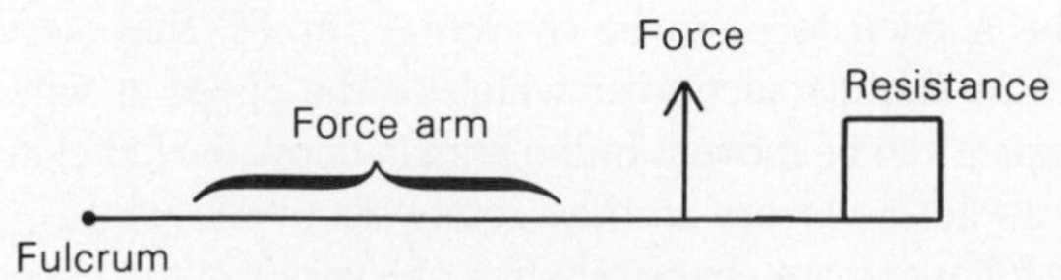

FIGURE 3.3. Longer force arm

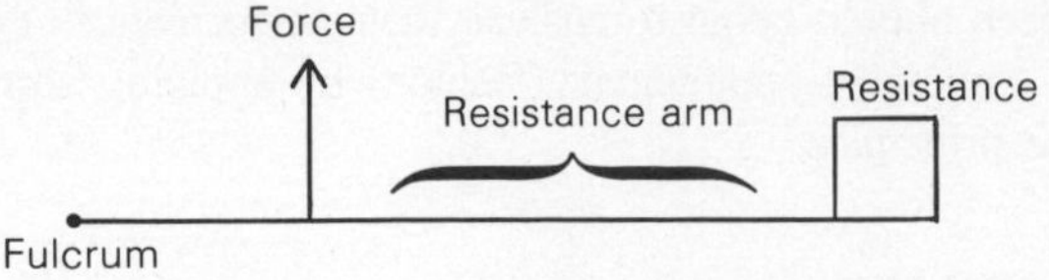

FIGURE 3.4. Longer resistance arm

they offer longer resistance arms for applying greater speed. The longer the racket or bat, therefore, the greater the speed generated. Unfortunately, however, longer levers are more difficult to rotate. This is why young baseball players are encouraged to choke up to make the bat easier to swing and control. Even though the lever is shortened, bat velocity (at point of contact with the ball) is probably not much reduced. The important result is that performance improves through more high-quality contacts.

MOTION AND DIRECTION

Since the majority of skills involved in physical activities are associated with propelling an object, students should understand the basic principles of motion and direction.

Children can be exposed to the following concepts.

1. The angle of release determines how far an object will travel. Theoretically, the optimum angle of release is 45 degrees. The human body has various limitations, however, which cause the optimum angle of projection to be well below 45 degrees. For example, the angle of projection for the shot put is 40 to 41 degrees; for the running long jump, it is 20 to 22 degrees.

2. A ball rebounds from the floor or from the racket at the same angle at which it is hit. However, various factors such as rotation applied to the ball, the type of ball, and the surface contacted by the ball can modify the rebound angle.

3. In most throwing situations, the propelled object should be released at a point tangent to the target. During throwing, for example, the arm travels in an arc, and the ball must be released when the hand is in line with the target.

APPLICATION OF MECHANICAL PRINCIPLES

As students are made aware of the existence of mechanical principles, they should start applying them in learning experiences. Some applications are discussed in this section.

STARTING AND STOPPING THE BODY

The following general principles can be applied to starting and stopping the body in any activity.

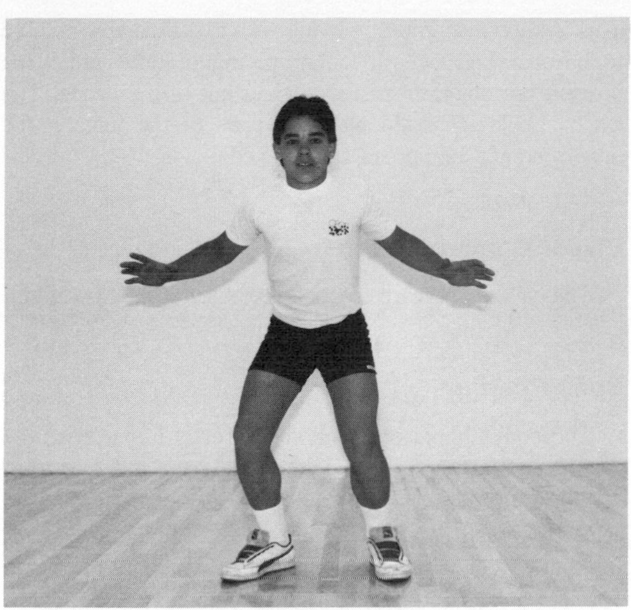

FIGURE 3.5. Ready position

Ready Position

In the ready position (Figure 3.5), the feet are spread to shoulder width. For some skills, one foot may be ahead of the other. The knees are bent slightly, the toes are pointed forward, and the weight is carried on the balls of the feet. In this position, the body can be moved equally well in any direction. The back should be reasonably straight, the head up, and the hands ready for action.

Fast Starts

When a fast start in a known direction is desired, the feet are usually spread and pointed in the direction of motion, and the body leans in the direction of the proposed movement (Figure 3.6). The center of gravity is moved forward and lowered somewhat by the body lean and by the increased bend at the knees. This causes a rapid shift of body weight in the direction of movement.

Absorbing Force

When the body is stopped quickly, force must be absorbed. The ankles, knees, and hips should bend to absorb force over as long a period of time as possible.

Falling

Falling is usually an undesirable movement or at least an unplanned activity. Since it occurs often in sports and in movement activities, however, it must be taught. The force of the fall should be absorbed over as large an area as possible. Rolling helps to spread the impact and can be accomplished by tucking the head and doing a Forward or Judo Roll (p. 394). The hands are placed on the ground, with wrists and elbows bent to absorb some of the force of landing.

PROPELLING OBJECTS

Throwing, striking, kicking, batting, and bowling all involve applying force to an object. The following principles govern these skills.

Visual Concentration

In object propulsion, the eyes focus on some point, fixed or moving, depending on the skill. The child should watch the ball in striking. In shooting a basket or in bowling, the child should fix the gaze on the target. In kicking, the child should keep the head down and watch the ball.

Pads of the Fingers

The pads of the fingers are the controlling element in many manipulative skills, particularly in ball skills. They increase touch control and have the ability to absorb force. Older children can learn to use the pads of the fingers for control and absorption.

Opposition

Opposition refers to the coordinated use of the arms and legs. In walking or running, leg movement is coordinated with arm movement on the opposite side of the body. In right-handed throwing, the forward step should be made with the left foot, that is, a step with the left foot means a forward swing with the right arm.

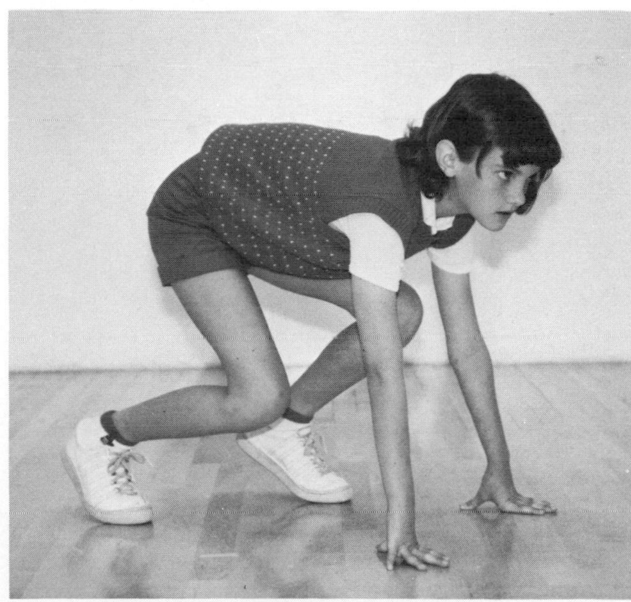

FIGURE 3.6. Alternate position for a fast start

Weight Transfer

The transfer of weight from the back to the front foot is a critical element in throwing, batting, striking, and bowling skills. Initially, the body weight is on the back foot, with the transfer occurring during execution of the skill.

Development of Torque

Development of torque involves total body coordination. In throwing or batting, the child should start with a forward motion of the hip and rotate the body, thus adding force to the thrown or batted ball.

Many skills require that the entire body be brought into play to perform the skill effectively. A child who throws primarily with the arm should be taught to bring the whole body into the action.

Follow-Through

Follow-through refers to a smooth projection of the already-initiated movement. The principle is vitally important in throwing, striking, batting, and kicking skills. In kicking, the instruction is to kick *through* the ball, not at it. In batting, the normal swing must be fully completed, not arrested after a hit.

CATCHING

Catching is an important skill in many activities and should be practiced with different objects, since each presents a different challenge.

Giving

The child should reach out for the object and then draw the object softly toward the body as the catch is made. This is known as *giving.* Giving with the arms allows force to be absorbed over a longer period of time and helps prevent the object from rebounding out of the hands. The catch should be made with the pads of the fingers; the fingers should be spread and relaxed.

Visual Concentration

The child must learn to track the object until it is caught.

Body Position

The body should be positioned directly in line with the incoming object, and the weight should be transferred from the front to the rear foot as the object is caught. This helps to spread the force of impact over time. The knees are bent as the catch is made to aid in absorbing the force. The feet are spread to increase body stability.

Protective Equipment

Baseball gloves are an example of protective equipment that should be used when the object to be caught is moving at a high rate of speed. The padding in the glove gives the catcher more time to absorb the impact of the ball.

REFERENCES

Nash, J. E. 1960. *Philosophy of recreation and leisure.* Dubuque, Iowa: Wm. C. Brown.

Schmidt, R. A. 1976. The schema as a solution to some persistent problems in motor learning theory. In G. E. Stelmach, ed. *Motor control: Issues and trends.* New York: Academic Press.

CHAPTER 4

Developing a Physical Education Curriculum: Theoretical Considerations

A curriculum is developed to give sequence and direction to the learning experiences of students. By necessity, decisions must be made concerning what experiences and activities should be included. Different approaches may be used to select and identify essential activities, but the selective criteria are based ultimately on the philosophical values of those involved in curriculum development.

This value base provides the philosophical foundation on which the program is developed. Expressed in this foundation is what the writers believe philosophically about children, schools, goals, the community, and learning through movement. These philosophical beliefs give weight to the relative importance of various program elements.

Closely allied to the value base is the conceptual framework, which is a set of concepts, beliefs, and basic convictions delineated to guide program development. Out of these grows the curriculum framework. The curriculum is formed through a clear understanding of the basic urges and developmental stages of children. The urges of children in relation to activity provide guidelines for program development. These strong drives, possessed by all people of all ages, govern activity participation.

The characteristics and interests of youngsters must also be understood before program objectives are developed. These differ from the basic urges in that they are age-specific. Whereas urges are found in all people regardless of age or maturity, characteristics and interests are allied closely to the child's developmental stage. Since children undergo considerable development and change from kindergarten through 6th grade, these characteristics and interests have strong educational implications for curricular planning.

At this point in the curriculum development, the writers formulate learning objectives based on the urges, characteristics, and interests of the learners. These objectives determine and direct the curriculum content. Indeed, curriculum content is really an organized list of learning opportunities designed to achieve expressed objectives for children. (Discussion of curriculum development is continued in Chapter 5, which explains how to select a balanced and comprehensive set of activities that meet the needs of all students.)

A PHILOSOPHICAL VALUE BASE

An initial step is the selection of an appropriate definition of physical education. *Physical education* is that portion of the child's overall education that is accomplished through movement. It is education about and involving movement. Simply experiencing movement is not an adequate physical education. The movement experiences must go beyond seeing how many times or in how many different ways a child can move. This process does have some value, particularly in the primary grades, but nevertheless represents low-level experiences. Physical education must be largely an instructional program if it is to acquire a full partnership in the child's overall education. Only quality programs based on developmental goals and with demonstrable, accountable outcomes achieve this respect.

Using the overriding general educational goal of U.S. schools—to develop an individual who can live effectively in a democracy—one then selects critical contributions that physical education can make to meet this goal. While physical education stresses essentially psychomotor goals, it can make a marked contribution to the cognitive and affective domains.

The physical education profession needs to reinforce

its position in education and to stress the unique contributions it makes to child development. These contributions can be made only by physical education as compared with other subject areas of the child's education. The three unique contributions of a quality physical education program are as follows.

1. *The development and maintenance of a personalized level of physical fitness.* For the instructor, this means more than pushing youngsters through demanding physical exercise. Teachers must give children the conceptual framework in which personal fitness is developed. This has extended implications for the concept of human wellness (i.e., teaching students how to maintain a vibrant and functional life-style throughout adulthood).

2. *The development and enhancement of movement competency.* Initially, this means developing broad areas of body management and general movement skills. As students mature, instructional progressions lead to increased skill in fundamental movements and later to specialized sport skills.

3. *An understanding of movement and movement principles.* This understanding includes Laban's concepts of movement and the understanding of both anatomical and mechanical principles that are necessary for critical performance.

A physical education program is of dubious value if it does not accomplish these three major goals, for these contributions are unique to the physical education area. Clearly, cognitive and affective outcomes, such as the development of reasoning powers and social skills, can be achieved also in academic settings. It is in physical education, however, that students learn how to diagnose, prescribe, and evaluate personal fitness qualities, how to develop lifetime sport skills, and how to analyze movement principles. They will leave school without these abilities if the physical education program is inadequate or nonexistent.

THE CONCEPTUAL FRAMEWORK UNDERLYING THE CURRICULUM

The conceptual framework consists of statements that characterize the curriculum. These concepts establish an umbrella for the activities and experiences included in the curriculum. The framework not only directs the activities but also reflects beliefs about education and the learner. The following are basic conceptual statements that should consistently guide the formulation of a child-centered, developmental curriculum.

1. *Physical education curriculum should be child-centered and developmentally oriented.* Activity selection must be based on the urges and characteristics of youngsters and geared to their developmental level. The child is the center of the curriculum, and experiences must be selected based on the needs of the child. At no time should an activity be selected because it is a favorite of the teacher, or avoided because the teacher lacks knowledge in an area. A professional looks beyond personal shortcomings—directly into the eyes of the learner.

2. *Each student is unique in terms of needs and learning capabilities.* All children have the right to reach their potential, and the curriculum must provide an opportunity for such achievement. Children should move at a pace that is challenging, educationally sound, and capable of enhancing their development. Individual differences must dictate the application of the curriculum, so that objectives, activities, and learning experiences meet the needs of individuals rather than the perceived needs of a single, unified group. Since students learn in different ways, alternate teaching methods and styles should be employed. Underlying all teaching approaches is the belief that students can and do learn independently, and that students must be given the opportunity to make personal decisions about what is important and relevant.

3. *Children should be seen as whole and complete beings.* This means extending the curriculum beyond the development of physical skills and personal fitness. In the cognitive area, associated learnings should accompany the development of physical fitness and skills. In developing physical fitness, for example, children should reach an understanding of why they are doing what they are doing. Skill development should feature not only the *how* but also the *why*. In the affective domain, achieving physical success plays a critical role in developing a positive self-concept. Children who achieve motor efficiency and are physically successful are usually better adjusted to school life than less capable, underdeveloped children. The hidden curriculum can have a strong effect on the development of desirable social qualities. The manner in which the learning environment and the instruction are structured has a powerful impact on student norms, values, and beliefs.

4. *Outcomes associated with student needs must be taught explicitly through physical education.* Activities must be directed and conducted in a manner that ensures that the objectives of physical education can be attained. The values of physical education are not gained automatically or by accident. Desired affective outcomes such as fair play, self-discipline, and peer cooperation do not result simply from participation in physical activities. Physical education must be mainly an instructional program, employing educationally sound teaching strategies.

5. *Movement is the basis of physical education.* Movement is essential if physical learning and accomplishment are to occur. Program quality can be evaluated in part by the degree of movement that *each* child experiences. Physical education implies activity. Children do not profit from standing in line, waiting for equipment to be arranged, listening to lengthy teacher explanations, or participating in an activity dominated by a few students.

6. *Learning must go beyond the immediate moment and offer each student the skills for a lifetime of use.* In today's society, the maintenance of physical fitness and wellness is of prime importance. The program must be vigorous and dynamic in nature to develop physiological fitness in students. Fitness, which serves as a foundation for the achievement of most motor skills, should be functional and presented in such a manner that varying work loads are allocated for each student. The emphasis should be on wellness and fitness for life.

Movement competency is the other important element in lifetime psychomotor development. Divergent movement activity—featuring exploration, choice, and attention to Laban's movement theory—develops the body management skills on which specialized motor skills can be based. Fundamental and specialized sport skills require correct and repetitive practice by children and are learned through convergent, or focused, movement activity. Movement concepts are important inclusions in developing these skills.

BASIC URGES OF CHILDREN

A basic urge is a desire to do or accomplish something. All children have these feelings, which may be hereditary or environmentally influenced. Basic urges are linked closely to societal influences and can be affected by teachers, parents, and peers. Usually, basic urges are similar among youngsters of all ages and are not affected by developmental maturity. These desires provide important direction for developing physical education curriculum and creating a program that is appropriate to the nature of the child.

THE URGE FOR MOVEMENT

Children have an insatiable appetite for moving, performing, and being active. They run for the sheer joy of running. For them, activity is the essence of living. The physical education program must satisfy this craving for movement.

THE URGE FOR SUCCESS AND APPROVAL

Children not only like to achieve; they also want their achievements to be recognized. They wilt under criticism and disapproval, whereas encouragement and friendly support promote maximum growth and development. Failure can lead to frustration, lack of interest, and inefficient learning. Successes should far outweigh failures, and students should achieve some measure of success during each class meeting.

THE URGE FOR PEER ACCEPTANCE AND SOCIAL COMPETENCY

Peer acceptance is a basic human need. Children want others to accept, respect, and like them. The school environment should offer ways to gain peer acceptance. Learning to cooperate with others, being a contributing team member, and sharing accomplishments with friends are important outcomes of the physical education program.

THE URGE TO COOPERATE AND COMPETE

Children enjoy working and playing with other children. They find satisfaction in being a necessary part of a group, and they experience sadness when others reject them. Cooperation should be taught prior to competitive experiences. Often, the joy of being part of a group far outweighs the gains from peer competition.

The urge to compete is evident in the child's desire to match physical skill and strength with peers. Children are willing to show this urge when they think they have a chance of winning. If the child has no opportunity to win, then the situation is not competitive and failure is preordained. Equated competition, in which each youngster has a chance to win, should be provided and monitored.

THE URGE FOR PHYSICAL FITNESS AND ATTRACTIVENESS

Every teacher should understand how eager boys and girls are to be physically fit and to possess a body that is agile and attractive. Teachers must recognize the humiliation suffered by a youngster who is weak, fat, crippled, or abnormal in any way. Programs should offer opportunity for self-improvement so youngsters can cope with subpar strength, obesity, lack of physical skill, and inadequate physical fitness. Teachers should monitor reward systems carefully so they acknowledge *every* child in the class.

THE URGE FOR ADVENTURE

The drive to participate in something different, adventuresome, or unusual impels children to participate in interesting new activities. Teachers should space inherently exciting activities throughout the curriculum. This tends to enhance the youngsters' level of anticipation and excitement.

THE URGE FOR CREATIVE SATISFACTION

Children like to try different ways of doing things, to experiment with different materials, and to explore what they can do creatively. Finding different ways to express themselves physically satisfies this urge for creative action.

THE URGE FOR RHYTHMIC EXPRESSION

All boys and girls enjoy rhythm. Rhythm implies movement, and children like to move. The program should offer a variety of rhythmic activities that all students can learn well enough to achieve satisfaction. Youngsters should also be shown the natural rhythm involved in all types of activity. Many effective and beautiful sport movements can be done rhythmically (e.g., shooting a lay-up, jumping a rope, and running hurdles).

THE URGE TO KNOW

Young people are naturally curious. They are interested not only in what they are doing but also in why they are doing it. Knowing *why* is a great motivator. It takes little time or effort to share with a class why an activity is performed and the contributions it makes to physical development.

CHARACTERISTICS AND INTERESTS—GUIDELINES FOR THE PROGRAM

The urges of children represent broad traits. Characteristics and interests represent more detailed facts that are age and maturity related. These are categorized according to the learning domains—psychomotor, cognitive, and affective (Table 4.1). Characteristics and interests provide critical guidelines for program development and offer insights as to the appropriate timing and sequencing of various activities. Bear in mind that these are general estimates and that youngsters vary a great deal both in physical and psychological maturity.

The authors recommend this approach, as opposed to the common practice of selecting activities based on teacher preference. Curriculums developed in the latter manner are often limited in scope and designed for the instructor rather than for the children.

OBJECTIVES OF PHYSICAL EDUCATION

Objectives must be selected according to their appropriateness based on the urges, characteristics, and interests of the children, and the potential of the physical education program to achieve the objectives. They must make a significant contribution to the overall goals of school and society—the development of a well-rounded individual capable of contributing to a democratic society. The objectives must also be able to bear critical examination with respect to the discussions presented earlier in this chapter. While in one sense objectives may seem idealistic, yet quality programs move children toward high-level achievement through

TABLE 4.1. CHARACTERISTICS AND INTERESTS OF CHILDREN

Kindergarten and First Grade

Characteristics and Interests	Program Guidelines
Psychomotor Domain	
Noisy, constantly active, egocentric, exhibitionistic. Imitative and imaginative. Want attention.	Include vigorous games and stunts, games with individual roles (hunting, dramatic activities, story plays), and a few team games or relays.
Large muscles more developed, game skills not developed.	Challenge with varied movement. Develop specialized skills of throwing, catching, and bouncing balls.
Naturally rhythmic.	Use music and rhythm with skills. Provide creative rhythms, folk dances, and singing movement songs.
May become suddenly tired but soon recovers.	Use activities of brief duration. Provide short rest periods or intersperse physically demanding activities with less vigorous ones.
Hand-eye coordination developing.	Give opportunity to handle different objects such as balls, beanbags, and hoops.
Perceptual abilities maturing.	Give practice in balance—unilateral, bilateral, and cross-lateral movements.
Pelvic tilt can be pronounced.	Give attention to posture problems. Provide abdominal strengthening activities.
Cognitive Domain	
Short attention span.	Change activity often. Give short explanations.
Interested in what the body can do. Curious.	Provide movement experiences. Pay attention to educational movement.
Want to know. Often ask *why* about movement.	Explain reasons for various activities and the basis of movement.
Express individual views and ideas.	Allow children time to be creative. Expect problems when children are lined up and asked to perform the same task.

TABLE 4.1/*continued*

Characteristics and Interests	Program Guidelines
Begin to understand the idea of teamwork.	Plan situations that require group cooperation. Discuss the importance of such.
Sense of humor expands.	Insert some humor in the teaching process.
Highly creative.	Allow students to try new and different ways of performing activities; sharing ideas with friends encourages creativity.
Affective Domain	
No sex differences in interests.	Set up same activities for boys and girls.
Sensitive and individualistic, self-concept very important. Accept defeat poorly.	Teach taking turns, sharing, and learning to win, lose, or be caught gracefully.
Like small-group activity.	Use entire class group sparingly. Break into smaller groups.
Sensitive to feelings of adults. Like to please teacher.	Give frequent praise and encouragement.
Can be reckless.	Stress safe approaches.
Enjoy rough-and-tumble activity.	Include rolling, dropping to the floor, and so on, in both introductory and program activities. Stress simple stunts and tumbling.
Seek personal attention.	Recognize individuals through both verbal and nonverbal means. See that all have a chance to be the center of attention.
Love to climb and explore play environments.	Provide play materials, games, and apparatus for strengthening large muscles (e.g., climbing towers, climbing ropes, jump ropes, miniature Challenge Courses, and turning bars).

Second and Third Grade

Characteristics and Interests	Program Guidelines
Psychomotor Domain	
Capable of rhythmic movement.	Continue creative rhythms, singing movement songs, and folk dancing.
Improved hand-eye and perceptual-motor coordination.	Give opportunity for manipulating hand apparatus. Provide movement experience and practice in perceptual-motor skills (right and left, unilateral, bilateral, and cross-lateral movements).
More interest in sports.	Begin introductory sports and related skills and simple lead-up activities.
Sport-related skill patterns mature in some cases.	Emphasize practice in these skill areas through simple ball games, stunts, and rhythmic patterns.
Developing interest in fitness.	Introduce some of the specialized fitness activities to 3rd grade.
Reaction time slow.	Avoid highly organized ball games that require and place a premium on quickness and accuracy.
Cognitive Domain	
Still active but attention span longer. More interest in group play.	Include active big-muscle program and more group activity. Begin team concept in activity and relays.
Curious to see what they can do. Love to be challenged and will try anything.	Offer challenges involving movement problems and more critical demands in stunts, tumbling, and apparatus work. Emphasize safety and good judgment.
Interest in group activities; ability to plan with others developing.	Offer group activities and simple dances that involve cooperation with a partner or a team.
Affective Domain	
Like physical contact and belligerent games.	Include dodgeball games and other active games, as well as rolling stunts.
Developing more interest in skills. Want to excel.	Organize practice in a variety of throwing, catching, and moving skills, as well as others.
Becoming more conscious socially.	Teach need to abide by rules and play fairly. Teach social customs and courtesy in rhythmic areas.
Like to perform well and to be admired for accomplishments.	Begin to stress quality. Provide opportunity to achieve.
Essentially honest and truthful.	Accept children's word. Give opportunity for trust in game and relay situations.
Do not lose willingly.	Provide opportunity for children to learn to accept defeat gracefully and to win with humility.
Sex difference still of little importance.	Avoid separation of sexes in any activity.

continued

TABLE 4.1/*continued*

Fourth, Fifth, and Sixth Grades

Characteristics and Interests	Program Guidelines
Psychomotor Domain	
Steady growth. Girls often grow more rapidly than boys.	Continue vigorous program to enhance physical development.
Muscular coordination and skills improving. Interested in learning detailed techniques.	Continue emphasis on teaching skills through drills, lead-up games, and free practice periods. Emphasize correct form.
Differences in physical capacity and skill development.	Offer flexible standards so all find success. In team activities, match teams evenly so individual skill levels are less apparent.
Posture problems may appear.	Include posture correction and special posture instruction; emphasize effect of body carriage on self-concept.
Sixth-grade girls may show signs of maturity. May not wish to participate in all activities.	Have consideration for their problems. Encourage participation on a limited basis, if necessary.
Sixth-grade boys are rougher and stronger.	Keep sexes together for skill development but separate for competition in certain rougher activities.
Cognitive Domain	
Want to know rules of games.	Include instruction on rules, regulations, and traditions.
Knowledgeable about and interested in sport and game strategy.	Emphasize strategy, as opposed to merely performing a skill without thought.
Question the relevance and importance of various activities.	Explain regularly the reasons for performing activities and learning various skills.
Desire information about the importance of physical fitness and health-related topics.	Include in lesson plans brief explanations of how various activities enhance growth and development.
Affective Domain	
Enjoy team and group activity. Competitive urge strong.	Include many team games, relays, and combatives.
Much interest in sports and sport-related activities.	Offer a variety of sports in season, with emphasis on lead-up games.
Little interest in the opposite sex. Some antagonism may arise.	Offer coeducational activities with emphasis on individual differences of all participants, regardless of sex.
Acceptance of self-responsibility. Strong increase in drive toward independence.	Provide leadership and followership opportunities on a regular basis. Involve students in evaluation procedures.
Intense desire to excel both in skill and physical capacity.	Stress physical fitness. Include fitness and skill surveys both to motivate and to check progress.
Sportsmanship a concern for both teachers and students.	Establish and enforce fair rules. With enforcement include an explanation of the need for rules and cooperation if games are to exist.
Peer group important. Want to be part of the gang.	Stress group cooperation in play and among teams. Rotate team positions as well as squad makeup.

goal accomplishment. A set of objectives provides children with target goals to be accomplished during their school career, and gives instructors a constant and clear direction.

PHYSICAL FITNESS

Objective: *The physical education program should provide all children with the opportunity to develop and maintain a level of physical fitness commensurate with individual needs.*

Since an appropriate level of fitness is essential to meet the needs of the individual and of the society, physical fitness should be one of the goals of education. Physical education can make an important contribution to fitness, one that cannot be accomplished in any other curriculum area.

A person who is physically fit possesses the strength and stamina to perform daily tasks without undue fatigue, and has enough energy left to enjoy leisure activity and to deal with emergencies. Strength, muscular endurance, flexibility, and cardiovascular endurance are qualities of fitness that should be developed through planned, progressive activity based on sound physiological principles. Fitness emphasis should also be given to posture and body composition.

The activities for children in kindergarten through 2nd grade are mostly informal challenges that emphasize movement and establish in the children the need for fitness activity on a regular basis. Beginning in grade 3, more fitness-oriented, specialized activities dominate the fitness development program. A portion of each class period should be allotted to fitness activities. Throughout the fitness emphasis, students should be taught the pertinent physiological, anatomical, and kinesiological principles governing personal fitness development.

Physical fitness instruction must be educational, so that each child is stimulated to take part in physical activity beyond the scope of the school program. A long-range goal is the maintenance of an appropriate level of fitness in later years. It is entirely possible that establishing the desire and the need in children to maintain fitness may be more important than the actual level of fitness established at a given time.

Fitness has other values, too. Peer status and relationships, particularly for boys, are improved for the child who is physically fit. The relationship between physical fitness and motor learning is strong, and the qualities of physical fitness—strength, endurance, and power, among others—are needed for optimum skill development.

MOVEMENT EXCELLENCE AND USEFUL PHYSICAL SKILLS

Objective: *The physical education program should help each child become competent in body management and in useful physical skills.*

To be graceful and skillful are sought-after goals. The hierarchy of skill development depends on competent body management, from which evolve fundamental skills as well as specialized skills. Figure 4.1 shows the relationship.

Competency in Body Management

Body management refers to the ability of the body as a whole to meet the challenges of the environment. Learning to manage the body involves greater control over gross movements and leads to increased skill.

The child controls the body in personal space, in general space in relation to others, in flight, and while suspended on apparatus. Children need to learn what the body can do and how to manage the body effectively in a variety of movement situations and challenges. This understanding incorporates Laban's concepts of space, time, force, and flow.

Good body management practices are related to the body's resistance to the force of gravity. Children should be able to manage their bodies efficiently with ease of movement and to accept good standards of posture and body mechanics as meaningful constituents of movement patterns.

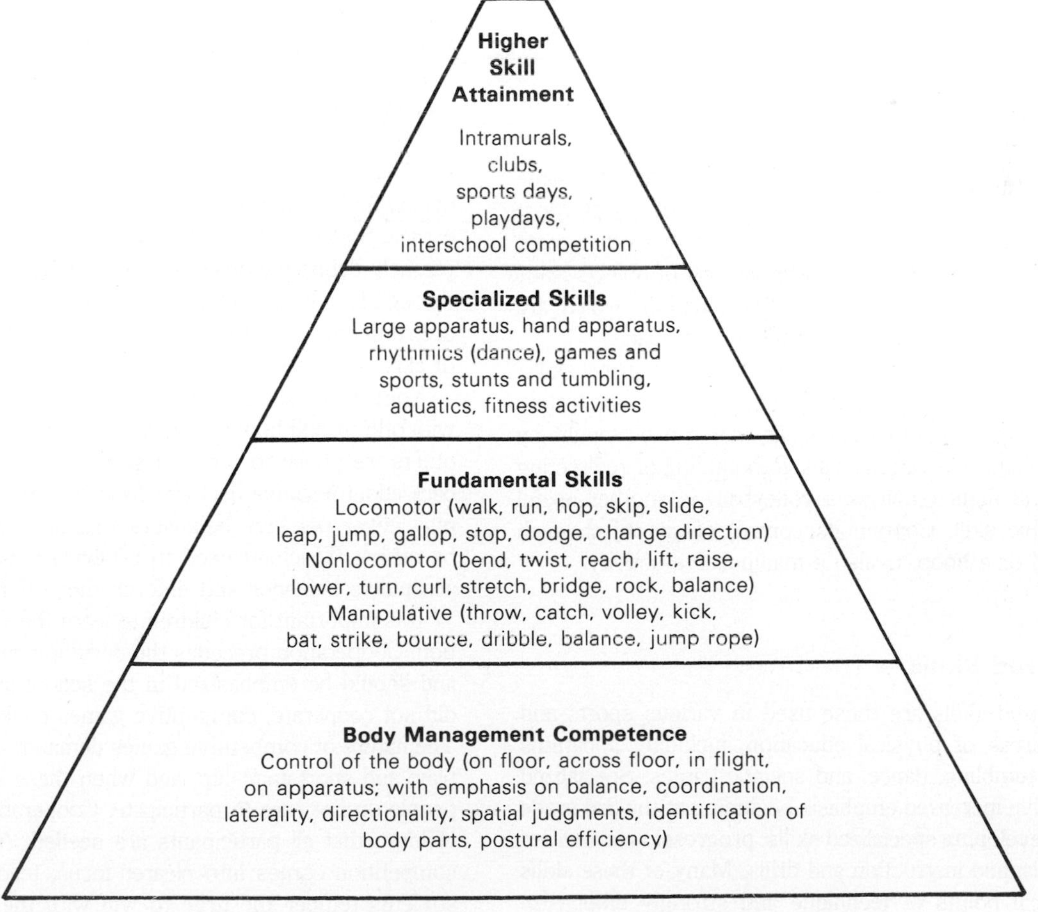

FIGURE 4.1. Continuum of program development based on skill development and attainment

Fundamental Skills

Fundamental skills are those utilitarian skills that children need for living and being. This group of skills is sometimes labeled *basic* or *functional.* The designation *fundamental skills* is preferrable, however, because these skills are normal, characteristic attributes necessary for every child to possess in order to function in the environment. Fundamental skills are given strong attention in the primary grades, and instruction continues at the intermediate level. For purposes of discussion, these skills may be divided into three categories.

Locomotor Skills

Locomotor skills are those used to move the body from one place to another or to project the body upward, as in jumping and hopping. They also include walking, running, skipping, leaping, sliding, and galloping.

Nonlocomotor Skills

Nonlocomotor skills are those performed in place, without appreciable spatial movement. These skills are not as well defined as locomotor skills. They include bending and stretching, pushing and pulling, raising and lowering, twisting and turning, shaking, bouncing, circling, and others.

Manipulative Skills

Manipulative skills are defined as those skills that come into play when the child handles some kind of object. Most of these skills involve the hands and feet, but other parts of the body can also be used. Manipulation of objects leads to better eye-hand and eye-foot coordination, which are particularly important for tracking items in space.

Manipulative skills are the basis of many game skills. Propulsion (throwing, batting, kicking) and receipt (catching) of objects are important skills that can be taught by using beanbags and various balls. Rebounding or redirecting an object in flight (such as a volleyball) is another useful manipulative skill. Continuous control of an object, such as a wand or a hoop, is also a manipulative activity.

Specialized Skills

Specialized skills are those used in various sports and in other areas of physical education, including apparatus activities, tumbling, dance, and specific games. Specialized skills receive increased emphasis beginning at the 3rd-grade level. In developing specialized skills, progression is attained through planned instruction and drills. Many of these skills have critical points of technique and strongly emphasize correct performance.

EXPERIENCING AND UNDERSTANDING MOVEMENT

Objective: *Each child should enjoy a broad experience in movement, leading to an understanding of that movement and the underlying principles involved.*

Through divergent movement activity, featuring a thematic presentation of educational movement, children should experience great diversity in their movement approaches. They should become familiar with and be able to apply the movement components of space, time, force, flow, and body factors. The emphasis on educational movement should continue through grade 3. In convergent movement, which emphasizes particular skills, the movement components have excellent application in stimulating breadth of experience in the teaching progressions.

Ancillary areas include the development of internal and external directionality, knowledge and location of body parts, and basic kinesiological understandings. The latter include the name, location, and function of selected muscles, joint movement actions, and the location and name of major bones. Further cognitive comprehensions involve mechanical principles and performance considerations important in executing skills.

SOCIAL DEVELOPMENT

Objective: *The physical education environment should be such that children can acquire desirable social standards and ethical concepts.*

Physical education classes should offer an environment of effective social living. Children need to internalize and understand the merits of participation, cooperation, and tolerance. Some terms, such as good citizenship and fair play, can help define the desired social atmosphere. The teacher, through listening, empathy, and gentle guidance, helps children differentiate between acceptable and unacceptable ways of expressing feelings.

Youngsters should become aware of how they interact with others, and how the quality of their behavior influences others' response to them. If students do not receive feedback about negative behavior from teachers and peers, they may never perceive behaviors that are strongly resented by others. Teachers need to establish reasonable limits of acceptable behavior and enforce those limits consistently.

It is important for children to learn the value of cooperation. Cooperation precedes the development of competition and should be emphasized in the school setting. If people did not cooperate, competitive games could not be played. The nature of competitive games demands cooperation, fair play, and sportsmanship, and when these are not present, people do not care to participate. Cooperative games teach children that all participants are needed. As the nature of competition comes into clearer focus, teachers must help students temper the urge to win with the realization that not all participants can be winners.

The hidden curriculum has been mentioned as having strong impact on social development. How the lesson is organized, the types of activities presented, how the teacher views students who do not win, and how handicapped children are treated give an implied message to students. The teacher's likes, dislikes, and personal conduct are important moral influences on children.

SAFETY SKILLS AND ATTITUDES

Objective: *Through physical education, children must acquire a knowledge of safety skills and habits, and develop an awareness of safety with respect to themselves and others.*

The school has both a legal and a moral obligation to provide a safe environment. Safety must be actively sought. The teacher should always conduct activity in a safe environment.

Instructional procedures in any activity must pay attention to safety factors, and good supervision is necessary to guide children in safe participation.

Water safety is an important facet of physical education. Although few elementary schools provide opportunities for aquatic instruction, students should be encouraged to seek swimming instruction on their own. Various community agencies should cooperate to provide a swimming and water safety program as one of the educational opportunities available to all children.

WHOLESOME RECREATION

Objective: *Through physical education, children should develop physical skills that allow them to participate in and derive enjoyment from wholesome recreational activities throughout their lifetime.*

The basic considerations of wholesome recreation are several. First, children must derive enjoyment from leisure-time activity so they will seek further participation. To this end, children should become proficient in a variety of motor skills and develop an adequate level of physical fitness. Most adults participate only in those activities in which they developed competency during childhood. Second, children need a rational basis for play. This can be established through activity orientations that can be carried over to other situations. Such activities should include a variety of games suitable for small groups and sport activities adapted to local situations. Third, children need to learn the social benefits of recreational activity.

The inclusion of fitness practice as a part of leisure activity is essential. Jogging and walking should be encouraged, since these are valuable both as personal and family activities.

The burden of providing broad orientation to skills, games, and fitness activities falls on the elementary school program. In high school, students have more and more choices and options for meeting activity requirements. Preparation in and orientation to many different activities during the elementary school years can provide a background for making the choices for a lifetime of recreational enjoyment.

POSITIVE SELF-CONCEPT

Objective: *Each child should develop a desirable self-concept through relevant physical education experiences.*

How children feel about their ability to cope with life is the *self-concept.* The self-concept is developed through the eyes of others. How teachers and parents respond to children communicates to youngsters that they are loved, capable, and contributing people. On the other hand, teachers and parents can also give children negative messages that they are incapable of learning and are unloved. Not only must the teacher understand the learner, each learner should also understand herself, for self-understanding is a powerful influence on human behavior.

The self-concept that a child develops is vital to the learning process. It can make learning possible, or it can hinder or block the ability to learn. If children believe that they belong, that they are loved and respected, and that their successes outweigh their failures, then they are well on the way to establishing a desirable self-concept. Teachers should focus on a student's strong points rather than on weaknesses. Students need also to learn how to accept positive feedback from peers, instead of discounting it. A plethora of activities should be presented to increase the children's chances of experiencing success.

Figure 4.2 shows how success and failure are related to self-concept development. The child approaches a task. If failure results, two undesirable directions are indicated. If success is the outcome, certain positive effects carry over to the self-concept.

The ability to move with grace, confidence, and ease helps a child regard himself in a favorable light. Achieving self-satisfying levels of skill competency and fitness can also make a child feel positive and assured. The child's concept of self is related, in part, to his physical skill competence. Positive achievement in physical education can be especially valuable to children who perform at a lower academic level but experience a measure of success in physical activities.

PERSONAL VALUES

Objective: *Through physical education, each child should acquire personal values that encourage living a full and productive life.*

A number of personal benefits can be derived from physical education programming. Through a task-oriented instructional approach, students work on improving their on-task times. Getting started, becoming involved, and trying to do one's best are commendable habits that should be reinforced. Enjoying activity participation and cooperating with others also contribute to positive mental health.

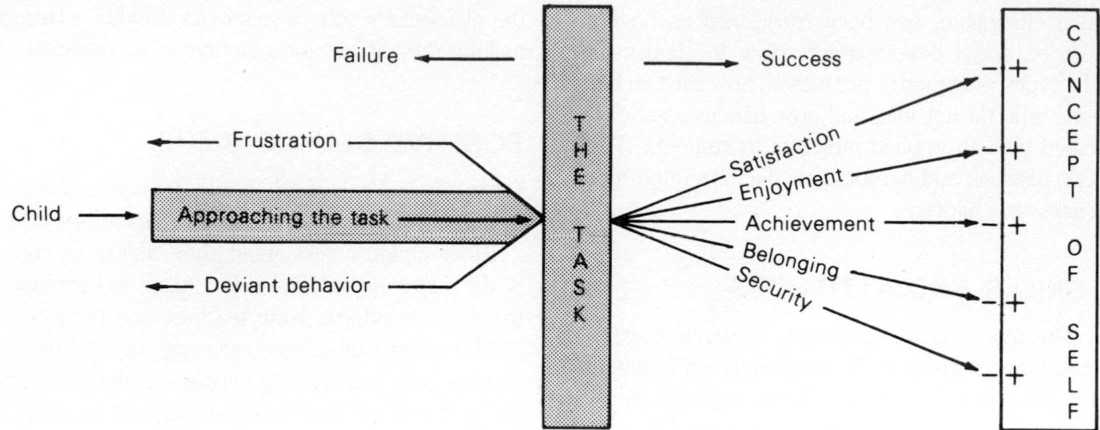

FIGURE 4.2. The child's self-concept

Programs should offer children opportunities to experience the creative satisfaction of problem solving. Throughout the year, ample opportunities for children to develop activity variations of their own should be integrated in the lessons. Children should also be encouraged to develop new patterns of movement and skill performance as they master the basics of different skills.

Active play should help children to find relief from tension. To have fun, take part freely, and express joy in physical activity are important to all youngsters. Children can learn to recognize tension, stress, and anxiety, and they can be taught different techniques for controlling and releasing internalized emotions.

Effective instructional technique challenges the child's cognitive processes. For example, a number of contrasting terms can be introduced or reinforced with appropriate movement challenges. Terms such as up-down, forward-backward, and heavy-light can be imbedded in movement directives. Serializing activities in a movement challenge affords practice in memory recall. An understanding and comprehension of important movement principles and fitness concepts are thus developed.

CHAPTER 5

Planning a Physical Education Program

The end result of curriculum planning and writing should be a product based on the desires, characteristics, and interests of children. It should reflect sound physical education philosophy and theory, support the objectives of the school system, and conform to the mores and culture of the community.

In building a physical education curriculum, a school or school system could take one of the following approaches:

1. Adopt a program model that is functioning in another locale, one that has been successful in terms of pupil achievement. The value base, conceptual framework, and program design are accepted in toto. Minor program changes are incorporated only to fit local school situations and preferences.
2. Adapt a model program. The selected program provides a starting point, from which the planners depart to make the program conform to local interests, preferences, and school philosophy. Two or more model programs might be melded into a cohesive unit.
3. Build a new model. The approach involves coordinating ideas from many sources to form a unified program. This is a difficult challenge, and the group performing the task must have enough breadth of experience and an extensive enough understanding of curriculum development to construct an educationally sound program. Physical education has long suffered from individual teachers "doing their own thing" and trying to develop a new curriculum based on inadequate experience.

The major purpose of planning is to formulate a written curriculum that gives direction and continuity to the program. The process must avoid three major errors common in curriculum construction: fragmentation, imbalance, and lack of continuity. The design should be definitive, presenting clearly the program focus for all grade levels, and the curriculum should be easily translated into action. Materials and lesson plans for implementing the program should be a part of the written curriculum.

THE ELEMENTARY SCHOOL PHYSICAL EDUCATION CURRICULUM COMMITTEE

Value judgments become a necessary part of the curricular process, for various instructional elements must be interpreted and assigned relative importance. Someone or some group must make these judgments. A school district physical education committee is an effective way to shape curriculum and share the responsibility for important decisions.

Input on formulating or revising the curriculum should come from all concerned sources. The physical education consultant or specialist should probably head the committee. Committee membership should be open to classroom teacher representatives from primary and intermediate levels, an administrator, parents (through the PTA), one or more community representatives (from community recreation or a service club, the Chamber of Commerce, or churches), and possibly selected elementary students.

The committee should meet regularly to review and upgrade the curriculum. A most important meeting occurs at the end of the school year, when modifications for the coming year are considered. A report on the year's program operation can also be presented at that meeting.

The committee's duties may extend beyond the physical

education program to include intramural and sport competition. In addition, the work of the committee should be coordinated with the program for the secondary school.

The primary mission of the committee is to establish and maintain a functional, practical, and educationally sound curriculum. A published curriculum must be in the hands of all elementary teachers and administrators, even those not directly involved in the program. This wide distribution is important so that the values gained in physical education—especially the ideas and practices relevant to human wellness—can be integrated with the values and practices taught in other fields.

A public relations plan, both inside and outside the school, should be devised by the committee to cover the new or updated curriculum. The committee should set yearly budget allocations and establish long-range plans for procuring equipment and improving facilities. An evaluation plan should be outlined to determine how well the program has achieved the stated goals, and to secure value judgments about the program from children, teachers, administrators, and parents.

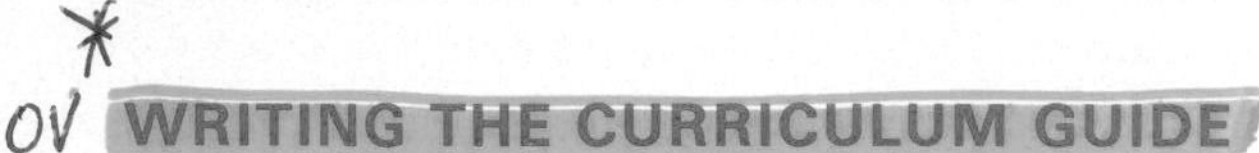

WRITING THE CURRICULUM GUIDE

The curriculum guide should be written in a systematic fashion. First, the curriculum philosophy must be established before the selection of activities and movement themes. The following steps should be followed in devising a meaningful, well-planned guide. (See Chapter 4 for an in-depth discussion of the first four steps.)

1. Articulate a philosophical program foundation that is based on what physical education can and should do for children. The philosophical statement focuses on the ultimate expectations that the program should accomplish.

2. Develop a conceptual framework that provides basic assumptions and guidelines for conducting the program. The conceptual framework includes statements that guide activity selection, detail how children learn and how activities should be presented, and explain the long-range learnings to be accomplished.

3. Examine and identify the urges, characteristics, and interests of children and the guidelines that these traits offer for curriculum development. This planning step assures a child-centered curriculum, which is based on knowledge of a child's development rather than on the preferences of teachers.

4. Adopt a set of objectives to be achieved by the students. These objectives are the guiding force in selecting activities for the curriculum. A clearly written set of objectives delineates what types of activity must be included to accomplish these goals.

After these four decisions have been made, the rest of the steps involve selecting activities and organizing them in a systematic presentation. Basically, a curriculum guide is a method of presenting activities that are based on the needs of children in a manner that represents proper learning progressions. This systematic presentation of activities must cover an entire school year. Each of the following steps in curriculum development is discussed in detail in the remaining chapters.

5. Select activities to be taught based on prior decisions about philosophy, conceptual framework, objectives, and characteristics and interests of children. No activities should be rejected if they meet the program objectives, unless they are judged detrimental to the health or development of children.

6. Organize appropriate instructional experiences to influence student learning. This involves writing instructional activity units that include sequential arrangement of activities and movement themes, necessary instructional procedures, and safety procedures.

7. Allocate the instructional activity units to specific grade levels. This step is the development of the vertical curriculum, and determines which activities will be taught from grade to grade. Horizontal curriculum planning differs from the vertical in that it involves sequencing activities *within* a grade level.

8. Outline a yearly plan. This involves sequencing the instructional activity units on a week by week basis. The outline is a necessary step to avoid running out of things to do, or not having enough time to teach everything. If selected activities are important, it is absolutely necessary that they be presented to children in a systematic fashion.

9. Develop the weekly lesson plan. This is a detailed plan that gives the instructor direction for instructional sequences. Failure to plan the week's activities can lead to a poorly presented instructional unit. Many times, if planning has not been done, a shortage of time or of instructional activities will occur.

10. Devise a systematic evaluation plan for the sole purpose of improving the curriculum. The curriculum guide is an instrument that gives direction to teaching. It presents a product that can be modified, improved, and evaluated. The guide provides for accountability when evaluation is planned. If the curriculum does not seem to accomplish designated program objectives, change will be necessary.

RESTRICTIVE FACTORS

When developing a curriculum guide for a school district, most people like to start with restrictive factors. Examples of restrictive factors are the amount and type of equipment, budget size, and cultural makeup of the community. Although this step needs to be examined carefully and implemented, it should not be undertaken before the ten steps already mentioned. The reason for this is that restrictive factors tend to circumvent and limit the curriculum scope and sequence. This can be a severe problem, because the curriculum guide should communicate to teachers, administrators, parents, and students what a well-conceived program is to be. It is a goal, a direction, and a destination for the future. If restrictive factors are considered too early in the planning process, the curriculum will be stunted and without direction for growth.

The following are examples of restrictive factors that limit the development of a broad and comprehensive curriculum. Although these factors may be limiting, they can also be handled in a creative fashion, which results in an effective curriculum. In summary, think big at the start and develop a comprehensive and ideal curriculum. Think restrictively second, modify the curriculum as necessary, and seek consistently to expand and develop the curriculum beyond these negative factors.

School Administrators

The support of school administrators has a significant impact on the curriculum. It is important for physical education teachers to interpret the program goals to administrators. Many administrators, like the general public, have misconceptions about physical education and its contribution to the overall education of students. Communication between the staff and the administration is a key factor if the curriculum is to be expanded and improved on a regular basis. In most cases, administrators will agree with and support the philosophy of the physical education faculty if they perceive that philosophy to be built on sound educational principles, which can be documented and evaluated.

The Community: People and Climate

The community needs to be considered when implementing a curriculum. Physical educators should become familiar with the types of people prevalent in the community. Occupations, religions, educational levels, cultural values, and physical activity habits are factors that can affect curriculum development. Parents have a strong influence on the activity interests and habits of their children.

The geographical location and the climate of the area are also important factors for consideration. The terrain of the mountains, deserts, or plains combined with the weather conditions particular to each area have an effect on people's activity interests. Extremely hot or cold climates influence markedly what activities can be arranged in the curriculum and at what time of the year they should be scheduled. Plans and alternatives for rainy climates and for extremely hot or frigid climates must be considered.

Facilities and Equipment

The available teaching facilities dictate in part the activities that can be offered. Facilities include the on-campus areas as well as off-campus areas in the neighboring community. Off-campus facilities may involve using a community swimming pool or park.

Equipment is important for presentation variety and for assuring the maximum practice time for students. It must be available in quality and quantity. In many cases, one piece of equipment per child is a necessity if students are to learn at an optimum rate. Equipment can be purchased with school funds or with special funds raised by students through demonstration programs. Some types of equipment can be constructed by school maintenance departments or as industrial arts projects. Yet another possibility is to have the students bring equipment, such as rackets and tennis balls, from home.

Laws and Requirements

Laws, regulations, and requirements at the national, state, and local level are factors that may restrict or direct a curriculum. Programs must be developed to conform to these laws. Examples of two national laws affecting physical education programs are Title IX of the Educational Amendments Act of 1972 and Public Law 94–142. The former enforces equal opportunities for both sexes, and the latter mandates equal access to educational services for handicapped students. The individual states have different laws that also affect physical education and that need to be considered.

Scheduling

The schedule or organizational pattern of the school has an impact on curriculum development. How many times per week the classes meet, the length of the class periods, and who teaches the classes are factors that must be considered. Many scheduling alternatives exist: daily, two or three times per week, and every other week. Periods can range from 20 to 45 minutes in length. The time frame involved has a strong effect on curriculum implementation. Whenever possible, schedules should be developed to enhance the educational program, and not for the convenience of principals or teachers.

Budget and Funding

The amount of funding allocated for purchasing new equipment and replacing old supplies has an impact on curriculum growth. This reinforces the need for a well-developed curriculum guide, because the guide states what equipment and apparatus are necessary to present a comprehensive program. It tells the administration what is needed and that the need is based on sound educational objectives. Equipment needs should be listed in order of priority so budget planners can make decisions about what is needed most and how much it will cost.

Physical educators must seek parity in funding with other school program areas. Students are not expected to learn to read and write without materials and supplies. In similar fashion, they cannot learn physical skills without the necessary equipment and supplies.

GUIDELINES FOR CURRICULUM PLANNING

1. A major thrust in formulating a curriculum is to outline what content should be taught and when. The document should be organized so a teacher of a particular grade level has little difficulty determining the program content.

2. Selected activities should be based on their potential to help students reach curriculum objectives. For example, selection should include regular activity of sufficient intensity to promote growth and physical fitness, as well as instructional sequences that lead to a broad range of movement competencies and skills. The elementary years are a time for experimentation, practice, and decision making about activities that are personally enjoyable. The more activities a youngster experiences, the greater the chance is that she will find a lifetime activity of high personal interest.

3. Program activities should be selected to promote the achievement of desirable behavioral changes, associated educational changes, and personal benefits. Behavioral changes in children are probably due more to instructional procedures and to the positive effects of participation than to activity selection. However, activities should be selected in such a way that the aforementioned changes and values *can* be achieved given appropriate instructional methods.

4. Today's programs are strongly concerned with associated cognitive and affective learning. Children should learn about their bodies through movement. When they receive perceptive guidance and coaching, they can choose the best way to perform skills and understand why they move as they do. The underlying principles and practices of physical fitness and wellness should be included in the cognitive domain.

5. The program should provide experiences that allow all children to succeed and to feel satisfaction. Much attention must be given to preventing failure. Enjoying participation while learning is a key to motivation. This enjoyment depends on achieving success, as measured by the child's efforts to meet challenges, rather than by the teacher's expectations. Special children should also be able to succeed.

6. Program content must rest on a foundation of efficient body management skills and fundamental movement skills geared to the developmental needs of the child. This implies an instruction-oriented program that leads to a goal of reasonable movement competency and concept acquisition. The Laban elements of time, space, force, and flow are incorporated in the entire program. At the primary level, this is accomplished through the medium of educational movement themes by using divergent movement. At the intermediate level, these concepts are applied at appropriate times in skill-learning situations. The activities should be organized in sequential fashion, beginning with easy experiences and proceeding to more difficult challenges.

7. Progression is the soul of learning, and the curriculum should reflect progression vertically (from grade to grade) and horizontally (within each grade and within each activity).

8. Additional opportunities should be offered in the form of intramurals, sport days, playdays, sport competition, and recreational play. Such programs give children who are especially interested and skilled an additional opportunity to perform, but these events should also be open to all who want to participate.

9. Certain activities are naturally seasonal and must be scheduled accordingly. Sports, in particular, are accepted more readily when they are offered during the time of year when high schools, colleges, and professionals are actively involved in the same sport.

10. School health instruction and physical education are separate but related areas and should be regarded as such in the elementary school curriculum. However, the practice of substituting health instruction for physical education during inclement weather may result in a dislike of health instruction. Health and physical education instruction can complement and reinforce each other, but the two should not share a designated time allotment.

11. Changes and trends in junior and senior high school physical education programs may affect significantly the makeup of the elementary school program. For example, at the present time, high school programs have limited requirements and emphasize a broad spectrum of elective activity offerings. The elementary school program needs to prepare students by supplying a background of activity, so students can gain the knowledge and experience needed to select specific sport activities later in their educational career.

12. Appropriate means of assessing student progress should be included. Determining fitness development is important, as well as monitoring skill development, cognitive learning, and attitude development toward physical activity.

13. The program must facilitate and encourage quality teaching. A properly designed program eases the burden of planning throughout the school year by sequencing activities in an educationally sound manner. It helps the teacher develop an approach that is translated easily into action.

PLANNING THE CURRICULUM

The end result of curriculum planning and writing should be a product based on the characteristics and interests of children and a product compatible with the objectives of the educational institution. Each of the following considerations is relevant when structuring and writing the curriculum.

DETERMINING AREAS OF PROGRAM EMPHASIS

Major areas of emphasis are determined based on program objectives. These areas can be allotted a percentage of program time based on the characteristics and interests of the students. This determination reveals to administrators, teachers, and parents the direction and emphasis of the program.

Table 5.1 shows program emphasis. The figures are subject to adjustment as needed. Each area must have its proportionate share of instructional time, and the percentage of time allotted to each program area should reflect the characteristics of youngsters in the respective grades.

The Physical Education Program for Kindergarten and Primary Children

Learner characteristics in the lower grades make it necessary to create an enjoyable as well as instructional learning environment. When children in this age group find joy and reward through physical activity, positive approach behaviors are developed that can last a lifetime.

A recent trend, long overdue, puts more emphasis on physical development, which is reflected in an increased apportionment of time for physical fitness activity. The development of norms for the lower grades for the AAHPERD Health Related Physical Fitness Test emphasizes this newer interest in physical development for younger children. Developmental fitness activities should be movement oriented, not just an extension downward of the activities designated for the intermediate level. Testing is now possible to ascertain individual progress, which is important for monitoring student growth and development.

Early activities for younger children are individual in nature and center on divergent movement and theme development. Children begin to learn about movement and move-

TABLE 5.1. **ELEMENTARY SCHOOL PHYSICAL EDUCATION PROGRAM EMPHASIS**

Activity	Suggested Yearly Percentage of Time for Each Grade			
Kindergarten-Primary Grades	**K**	**1**	**2**	**3**
Introductory (warm-up) activities	10	10	10	10
Fitness routines and activities	27	27	27	27
Educational movement	15	11	9	5
Fundamental skills	5	8	10	8
Rhythmic activities	17	16	16	13
Apparatus, stunts, tumbling	9	11	11	10
Sport skills and activities				10
Low-organized games	17	17	17	17
Swimming and water safety				*
Intermediate Grades		**4**	**5**	**6**
Introductory (warm-up) activities		10	10	10
Fitness routines and activities		27	27	27
Fundamental skills		5	5	2
Rhythmic activities		12	9	9
Apparatus, stunts, tumbling, combatives		12	12	12
Sport skills and related activities		17	20	23
Low-organized games and relays		17	17	17
Swimming and water safety		*	*	*

* Swimming and water safety is a recommended area of instruction for elementary school children. The emphasis on this area depends on the facilities and instruction available. If swimming is included in the school program, the percentage of time allotted to other activities is reduced proportionately.

ment principles. Through educational movement themes, they start to develop body identification and body management. Internal and external directionality should also be given attention. Refinement of fundamental skills occurs through convergent movement techniques, as the transition to specialized skills begins to occur by 3rd grade. Visual-tactile coordination is enhanced by using a variety of simple manipulative skills.

Throughout the primary-grade years, children should be allowed the opportunity to explore, experiment, and create activities without fear. While *not* stressing conformity, children need to absorb the how and also the why of activity patterns. Consideration for and cooperation with peers are important considerations, too, with less emphasis placed on group and team play. More group activities appear in the 2nd and 3rd grade curricula.

In addition to divergent and educational movement, simple rhythmics, appropriate stunts and tumbling activities, and low-organized games round out the program. A few sport skills are introduced in 3rd grade to provide a transition to sport programs at the intermediate level.

The Physical Education Program for Intermediate-Grade Children

A principal change in the program for the intermediate grades is a shift to more emphasis on specialized skills and sport activities. Football, track and field, volleyball, and hockey are added to the sport offerings in 3rd grade. More specialized sport skills are taught in the intermediate grades, as compared with the primary grades, with emphasis on quality of movement and correctness of patterns.

Emphasis is also placed on physical fitness and developmental activities. Organized and structured fitness routines are offered so students can begin to make decisions about personal approaches to maintaining fitness levels.

Less emphasis is placed on divergent movement experiences, and a larger percentage of instruction time is devoted to manipulative activity. Students move into the sport program after they learn the necessary skills and participate in lead-up games.

At this level, a measure of time is set aside for the rhythmic program and for the program area involving apparatus, stunts, and tumbling. Combatives assume importance for the intermediate grades as youngsters begin to enjoy the rigors of competition. If possible, swimming should be included at this level.

SWIMMING AND WATER SAFETY

Swimming and water safety have been mentioned as an important adjunct to the physical education program. The emphasis should be on "drownproofing," simple survival techniques, and basic swimming skills.

We do not attempt to cover instruction in these subjects. Experts have worked for many years to develop comprehensive approaches to swimming and water safety, and in-depth material is available from the American Red Cross.

The community is responsible for making swimming instruction available to *every* child, since full participation is the goal. The school may cooperate with or supplement outside programs, or a school-sponsored program may be necessary to reach every child. The crux of the matter is that some agency must get the job done, and if the school is involved in the program, a number of administrative decisions have to be made.

A primary consideration is who participates. Should all children be given the opportunity to have swimming instruction regardless of their ability? For some of the more skilled swimmers, program participation may be only a pleasant diversion from class work. If only nonswimmers or those with marginal skills take part, alternate activities and supervision must be provided for the students who remain at the school. Careful handling is indicated in such cases, so that those who are selected for the swimming program are not stigmatized as inept or having poor skills.

Since the swimming program usually involves busing and special fees, material support must be forthcoming from the administration. Sometimes parents are expected to pay children's fees, but this poses a problem for students whose parents cannot, or will not, assume the expense.

Cooperation with the municipal recreation department, the YMCA and the YWCA, nearby colleges, and similar agencies can solve the facility problem. In some cases, weather permitting, the program can use outdoor facilities during the month of May, a lax period before heavy summer use. The facility should have the capability of regulating the water temperature of the pool.

SELECTING APPROPRIATE ACTIVITIES

Activities should be selected that accomplish the program objectives, and selection of activities should be based on assessed contribution to the growth and development of students. This approach contrasts with selecting an activity because it is fun or because the teacher enjoys it. As many activities as possible should be gathered in the planning stage. The greater the number of activities considered, the more varied and imaginative the final program will be. If an activity can be performed safely by students and contributes to the physical education of the child, it should be integrated in the total curriculum.

ORGANIZING SELECTED ACTIVITIES INTO UNITS

After appropriate and varied activities have been selected, some organization scheme must be developed. A useful approach is to organize the ideas and activities into instructional activity units or sequences. The activities in these units should be organized along a continuum, from the easiest to the most difficult. As the units are taught and field-tested by children, the activity order may be changed. Organizing the activities in a progression (1) helps children meet with success rather than failure at the start of the unit, (2) ensures that safety and liability factors are met, since the activities are presented in proper sequence, and (3) aids teachers in finding a starting point for sound instruction. Instruction should begin with activities that *all* children can perform, and then move gradually to more challenging activities. This progression gives students a positive feeling about the unit and accomplishes skill review at the same time.

Another valuable technique is to develop a list of pertinent instructional procedures to remind teachers about various points of emphasis. These might include safety hints, notes on how to teach for quality, initial methods of equipment organization, ways to expand the activity for variety, and crucial factors to be emphasized for proper motor skill development.

ALLOCATING UNITS OF ACTIVITY TO GRADE LEVEL

Children's capability and readiness are major considerations in the placement of specific activities at various grade levels. Since a large number of activities is presented, some arbitrary decisions must be made about grade placement. Adjustments upward or downward with respect to age level can be made empirically after a period of class trial. Another factor also enters the picture. A specialist, if one is available, usually has more success in helping youngsters achieve criterion skill levels than someone who has had little or no training in the instructional area.

Table 5.2 can be used in program planning to ensure a broad program. Basically, it states that a particular unit should be part of a specific age-level program. The elements to be included, the approaches to be followed, and the instructional procedures to be used are discussed in later sections under separate activity presentations.

DEVELOPING A YEAR-LONG CURRICULUM PLAN

Many teachers have had experience with weekly activity units and have found the weekly approach superior to a daily schedule in which different activities are taught on different days. In a weekly unit, an activity is extended over an entire week. Combinations of activities and games can be used on the last day to keep the program varied and flexible.

The weekly plan has three major advantages. First, a teacher needs only one lesson plan for the week. The teacher's objective in the lesson is to move children along the path of learning at a comfortable rate. To some extent, what cannot be covered one day can wait until the next. Second, little orientation is needed after the first day. Safety factors, instructional techniques, and key points and concepts need only a brief review each day. Equipment needs are similar from day to day. Third, progression and learning sequences are evident; both the teacher and the children can see progress. The teacher can begin a unit with the activity basics and progress to a point at which instruction and skill practice are again indicated. This procedure provides needed review and adapts the activity to the group. The activity sequence for each day is built on the preceding lesson. If the teacher has difficulty or needs to investigate an approach, there is time between lessons to clear up questionable issues. Children also can be referred to resource material to study the activities for the next day or to clarify a point of difficulty from the past lesson.

An objection raised by some teachers is that a weekly unit program does not have enough variety and that children tend to tire of the same activities presented over a longer period. To remedy this, activities should be spaced so that the same type of activity is not practiced for more than two weeks in succession. If more time is needed for a specific unit, adding another week or two later in the year is the best strategy. The use of games and relays is another way to provide a change of pace when the motivational level of the class (and teacher) appears to be waning.

Some other combinations in weekly planning are in favor at present. One arrangement offers one type of activity on Monday, Wednesday, and Friday and another activity type on Tuesday and Thursday. Another approach is to reserve the games and relays for Friday of each week and to use the first four days for more sequential material. Both arrangements show elements of progression. The least desirable plan is to have a different program each day of

TABLE 5.2. SUGGESTED ALLOCATION OF ACTIVITIES TO GRADE LEVEL

Activity Area	Grade						
Educational Movement	K	1	2				
Fundamental Movement: Locomotor, Nonlocomotor	K	1	2				
Magic ropes	K	1	2				
Fundamental Skills: Manipulative	K	1	2	3	4	5	6
Beanbags	K	1	2	3	4		

continued

TABLE 5.2./*continued*

Activity Area	Grade						
Yarn or fleece balls	K	1	2				
Playground balls (8½ in.)	K	1	2	3	4		
Small balls (sponge, softball size)				3	4	5	6
Paddles and balls				3	4	5	6
Hoops	K	1	2	3	4	5	6
Jump ropes	K	1	2	3	4	5	6
Parachutes	K	1	2	3	4	5	6
Wands				3	4	5	6
Rhythmics (see Table 17.1, p. 245	K	1	2	3	4	5	6
Rope-jumping to music				3	4	5	6
Apparatus	K	1	2	3	4	5	6
Bounding boards	K	1	2				
Balance boards	K	1	2	3	4		
Balance beams	K	1	2	3	4	5	6
Benches	K	1	2	3	4	5	6
Climbing ropes	K	1	2	3	4	5	6
Climbing frames	K	1	2	3	4	5	6
Individual mats	K	1	2				
Jumping boxes	K	1	2				
Ladders and bars		1	2	3	4	5	6
Stunts and Tumbling	K	1	2	3	4	5	6
Pyramids				3	4	5	6
Combatives				3	4	5	6
Simple Games	K	1	2	3	4	5	6
Relays				3	4	5	6
Creative play	K	1	2				
Sport Skills and Activities				3	4	5	6
Basketball				3	4	5	6
Flag football					4	5	6
Indoor and outdoor hockey				3	4	5	6
Soccer				3	4	5	6
Softball (mostly skills)				3	4	5	6
Track and field				3	4	5	6
Volleyball						5	6

the week. This burdens the teacher with five different lesson plans.

Table 5.3 is an example of a year-long outline that illustrates the parallel listing of various lesson elements. The percentages given in Table 5.1 can be used to guide the development of the yearly plan to determine how many weeks of instruction should be devoted to a specific area. The total amount of instructional time required for fitness can be calculated by looking at the length of the daily period (in minutes), the number of times the classes meet (during the school year), and multiplying the total number of minutes by the percentage of time allotted.

As the curriculum becomes more organized, introductory activities, fitness development, and game activities, as well as the basic lesson focus for each week, can be incorporated in the yearly plan. A yearly plan similar to Table 5.3 ensures that youngsters learn many ways of warming up for activity and approximately 15 different methods of enhancing fitness. In addition, the children are exposed to 20 to 25 lesson-focus activities.

THE PHYSICAL EDUCATION LESSON

The physical education lesson for a particular class period should either grow out of a unit of instruction or be based on activity progressions. Each lesson should follow a written plan. Written lesson plans vary in form and length, depending on the activity and the background of the teacher. A

TABLE 5.3. **SUGGESTED YEARLY PLAN FOR GRADES THREE THROUGH FOUR**

Week	Introductory Activity	Fitness Development Activity	Lesson Focus Activity	Game Activity
1	Orientation and games			
2	Fundamental movements and stopping	Teacher-leader exercises	Beanbags	Crows and Cranes Potato Relays Battle Dodgeball
3	Move and Assume a Shape	Teacher-leader exercises	Throwing	Whistle Mixer Touchdown Chain Tag
4	Walk, Trot, and Sprint	Teacher-leader exercises	Soccer, lesson 1	Diagonal Soccer
5	Partner Over and Under	Teacher-leader exercises	Soccer, lesson 2	Mini-Soccer
6	Run, Stop, and Pivot	Circuit Training	Playground games	Running Dodgeball Steal the Treasure Addition Tag
7	European Rhythmic Running	Circuit Training	Long-rope jumping	Right Face, Left Face Cageball Target Throw
8	Magic Number challenges	Circuit Training	Playground balls	Bronco Dodgeball Whistle Ball One-Base Dodgeball
9	Stretching exercises	Pace running	Throwing, lesson 2	Recreational activity
10	Stretching exercises	Pace running	Jogging	Recreational activity
11	Locomotor and manipulative activity	Exercise to music	Rhythms, lesson 1: With equipment	Whistle Mixer Arches
12	Variety movements	Exercise to music	Hockey, lesson 1	Hockey Raceway Star Wars Hockey
13	New leader	Astronaut Drills	Hockey, lesson 2	Sideline Hockey Regulation Hockey
14	Group Over and Under	Astronaut Drills	Individual rope jumping	One-Base Dodgeball Right Face, Left Face
15	Low-organized games	Astronaut Drills	Stunts, tumbling, and combatives, lesson 1	Whistle Mixer Barker's Hoopla Over the Wall
16	Following activity	Astronaut Drills	Rhythms, lesson 2	Relays
17	Leapfrog	Grass Drills and partner resistance exercises	Benches	Cageball Kick-Over Squad Tag
18	Bridges by Three	Grass Drills and partner resistance exercises	Basketball, lesson 1	Captain Ball Captain Basketball
19	Jumping and hopping patterns	Challenge Course	Basketball, lesson 2	Sideline Basketball Around the Key

continued

TABLE 5.3 /*continued*

Week	Introductory Activity	Fitness Development Activity	Lesson Focus Activity	Game Activity
20	Milk Carton Fun	Challenge Course	Recreational activity	Recreational activity
21	Ball activities	Challenge Course	Balance beams	Couple Tag Alaska Baseball
22	Moving to music	Squad leader exercises	Stunts, tumbling, and combatives, lesson 2	Triangle Dodgeball Star Wars
23	European Rhythmic Running, with variations	Squad leader exercises	Wands	Jolly Ball Bombardment Circle Hook-on
24	Tortoise and Hare	Squad leader exercises	Rhythms, lesson 3	Jump the Shot Circle Team Dodgeball Club Guard
25	Bend, Stretch, and Shake	Continuity exercises	Throwing, lesson 3; individual and long rope jumping	Scatter Dodgeball Sunday
26	Move and Perform a Task on Signal	Continuity exercises	Hoops	Hand Hockey Loose Caboose
27	Tag games	Continuity exercises	Paddles and balls	Mini-Soccer
28	Combination movement patterns	Continuity exercises	Stunts, tumbling, and combatives, lesson 3	Pin Dodgeball Chain Tag
29	Marking	Exercises to music	Tug-of-War ropes, relays	Scooter Kickball Trees
30	European Rhythmic Running with equipment	Exercises to music	Rhythms, lesson 4	Arches Attention Relay Prone Relays
31	Creative routine	Walk, Trot, and Sprint	Track and field, lesson 1	Nonda's Car Lot Islands
32	Stretching exercises and light pace running		Track and field, lesson 2	Potato Shuttle Race
33	Stretching exercises and light pace running		Parachute activity	Relays
34	Four-Corners Movement	Walk, Trot, and Sprint	Frisbee	Frisbee Keep-Away Frisbee Golf
35	Long-rope routine	Parachute exercises	Softball, lesson 1	Throw It and Run Two-Pitch Softball Hit and Run
36	Squad leader movements	Parachute exercises	Softball, lesson 2	In a Pickle Batter Ball Tee Ball
Alternate Lessons				
A	Substitute	Substitute	Balance beams with manipulative equipment	Hand Hockey Nine Lives
B	Substitute	Substitute	Football, lesson 1	Five Passes Fourth Down
C	Substitute	Substitute	Football, lesson 2	Box Ball Flag Football
D	Substitute	Substitute	Softball, lesson 3	Slow-Pitch Softball Babe Ruth Ball Regular softball
E	Substitute	Substitute	Rhythms, lesson 5	Partner Stoop
F	Substitute	Substitute	Rhythms, lesson 6	Whistle March
G	Substitute	Substitute	Climbing ropes	Busy Bee Box Ball
H	Substitute	Substitute	Soccer, lesson 3	Mini-soccer

written plan ensures that thought has been given to the lesson before the children enter the activity area. It helps the teacher avoid spur-of-the-moment decisions that might affect the unity and progression of the material. The teacher can still modify the lesson, but the written plan keeps the central focus and purpose of the lesson intact.

Progression is more apt to occur in a lesson when the teacher uses the previous lesson plan as a guide. In future years, the teacher can refer back to the collection of weekly lesson plans for suggestions and improvements.

A lesson is divided into the following parts.

1. Introductory activity (3 minutes)
2. Fitness development activity (8 minutes)
3. Lesson focus (14 to 22 minutes)
   a. Review of previously presented materials
   b. New learning experiences
4. Closing activity (5 to 7 minutes)

The reason the time varies is due to variation in lesson length from school to school. The first set of numbers represents the time allotment for a 30-minute lesson, while the second set represents a 40-minute lesson. Certainly the numbers could be modified if a different length lesson were in effect. Each of the lesson parts is discussed in the following sections.

Introductory Activity

Children come to physical education class eager for movement, and the introductory activity is designed to satisfy this appetite, after which the lesson can proceed to the achievement of specific objectives. Introductory activity also serves as a warm-up that prepares the child's body for the activities to follow. While serving as an introductory activity, the movement patterns also have fitness implications, and should be related to and coordinated with fitness development activities, particularly for younger children in kindergarten through 2nd grade.

Generally, some type of gross, unstructured movement (usually based on locomotor movements) comprises the introductory activity. An enterprising teacher can employ many different activities and variations effectively as introductory activity. Examples are provided in Chapter 15.

Fitness Development Activity

The second part of the lesson devotes time to fitness development, which is defined as activities that have as major objectives the physical development of the body and the various qualities of physical fitness (i.e., strength, power, endurance, agility, flexibility, and speed).

The lesson plan should include stated doses so that a series of lessons shows an increase in work load. Physical fitness activities appropriate for inclusion in the physical education lesson are discussed in Chapter 16.

Lesson Focus

The lesson focus is the heart of the lesson. It presents the learning experiences dictated by the overall instructional plan. Before the new material is presented, the teacher should review and work with the activities of the preceding lesson until a satisfactory level of learning has been reached. In some instances, the entire lesson focus is taken up with such review.

After sufficient time is given to review, the new learning experiences are presented. These may be instruction in a particular skill, participation in a rhythmic activity, or progression in an area such as stunts and tumbling.

The length of time devoted to the lesson focus is determined in part by the time demands of the other three lesson areas. After introductory and fitness development activities, the remaining time (less the time allotment for the closing activity) can be given over to the lesson focus.

Closing Activity

The closing activity takes different forms. The lesson may be completed with a game that uses the skills being developed in the lesson, or the activity may be devoted simply to having fun by finishing up with any game or activity that children enjoy. In either case, the children should associate the day's experiences with a final feeling of pleasure.

The closing activity can also be an evaluation of the day's accomplishments—stressing and reinforcing important techniques and concepts. The teacher can entertain suggestions for future activities in other lessons.

At the close of the lesson, all equipment, apparatus, and supplies are returned to their proper storage place. The teacher should give definite assignments and emphasize student responsibility. Squads, under the direction of student leaders, can take care of storing equipment.

In some lessons, the closing activity may be minimal, or it may be deleted entirely. This might be the case when the game or other activity, which is the focus of the lesson, demands as much time as possible.

A SUGGESTED WRITTEN LESSON PLAN FORMAT

The lesson plan should contain all of the information necessary to provide a high-quality learning experience, including expected outcomes, progressions, means of organization, points to be emphasized, and reminders to the teacher. A well-structured lesson plan gives the teacher confidence and provides unity, completeness, and depth to the movement experiences in the lesson.

Although a lesson plan can cover a single day's lesson, it is more practical to write a plan that covers several days. During any one lesson, the instruction then proceeds as far as is educationally feasible and takes up again at that point during the next lesson. The same introductory activity, with some changes, and the same fitness development activities are repeated during the lesson series.

The teacher may deviate from the lesson plan when, for example, the learning potential can be enhanced by changes in sequence or by the addition of material, the relevance of which was not evident when the lesson was planned.

A lesson plan format can be developed to allow for the interchange of plans within a school district. If such a format is adopted, a supervisor can then issue lesson plans for the entire district.

The format presented here offers the teacher a workable and effective instrument for guiding the instructional process. The lesson plan contains the following components.

1. *General information.* Name of school, classroom or class involved, date, and activity are included.

2. *Arrangement of necessary supplies and equipment.* A list of materials, indicating the specific numbers of each item needed, is presented, along with a description of how the equipment should be arranged when the class enters.

3. *Lesson evaluation.* During and after the lesson, the teacher should note what material was covered and how successful it was. The teacher should make notes to herself on directions for future lessons. Some teachers may question the feasibility of writing out lesson plans—saying that it takes too much time and effort and that a written plan is unnecessary. A lesson plan, however, need be only precise enough to serve as an effective guide for the learning experiences. It does not need to be long; the length depends on the background of each instructor. Beginning teachers may want a more detailed plan than experienced instructors. A lesson plan should be seen as a functional tool. Some teachers may use only a word or a phrase to suggest an idea or a procedure, while others may want more detailed written directions.

4. *Description of the lesson plan.* The lesson is divided into four activity areas—introductory activity, fitness development activity, lesson focus, and closing or game activity. For each area, the plan should include a description of the content of the experiences, time allotted, organization of the activities, teaching hints, and expected student objectives (psychomotor, cognitive, and affective) and outcomes. The objectives may not be pure in a behavioral sense, but they should be statements that lend direction and continuity to the program. The outcomes should be formulated to be a constant reminder to the teacher, so teaching can be geared to reach these goals.

5. *Space for notes and references.* Finally, the plan should provide space for notes and references, so the teacher can write in evaluative comments and references to sources that offer more in-depth description.

Table 5.4 shows a sample plan for a lesson on long-rope jumping at the intermediate level.

EVALUATING AND MODIFYING THE CURRICULUM

Evaluation schedules and suggested techniques for modifying the curriculum should be built into the curricular structure. A number of sources can supply evaluative data—pupils, teachers, consultants, parents, and administrators. The type of data desired can vary. Achievement test scores can supply hard data to compare preassessments and postassessments with those of other programs. Subjective assessment might include likes and dislikes, value judgments, problem areas, and needed adjustments.

The evaluation schedule may select a limited area for assessment, or assessment can be broadened to cover the entire program. Collecting information is only the first step; the information must then be translated into action.

Modification of possible program deficiencies should be based on sound educational philosophy. If the program has weak spots, identifying the weaknesses and determining the causes are important steps to take.

A pilot or trial project can be instituted if the new curriculum represents a radical change. One school in the district might be chosen to develop a pilot program. Site selection should offer the program a strong opportunity to succeed, for success depends in large part on the educational climate of the school. In some cases, the experimental program might be implemented with only one class in a school. Enthusiastic, skilled direction is necessary for such projects. Much valuable information can be derived from the pilot process before an entire program is implemented throughout the school system.

Various interest groups may promote new approaches and ideas. These are welcome if the proposals are supported by valid evidence and if the new focus represents progress. Since change in itself is not progress, the bandwagon approach should be avoided.

Probably the most appropriate time to analyze evaluative data is during a curriculum committee meeting late in the school year. The committee can then consider modifications for the coming school year. Times may occur during the year, however, when problems arise that mandate immediate remedial measures.

Figure 5.1 is an example of an informal curriculum evaluation form that might be used regularly to evaluate the curriculum. Questions can be added to be more explicit about a specific curriculum.

TABLE 5.4 SAMPLE ELEMENTARY SCHOOL PHYSICAL EDUCATION LESSON PLAN (LONG-ROPE JUMPING, GRADES THREE THROUGH FOUR)

Movement Experience, Content	Organization and Teaching Hints	Expected Student Objectives and Outcomes
Introductory Activity (3 minutes): **European Rhythmic Running** Develop the ability to follow the leader, maintain proper spacing, and move to the rhythm of the tom-tom. Stop on a double beat of the tom-tom. Variation: Have leader move in different shapes and designs. Have class freeze and see if they can identify the shape or formation.	*Dynamic Physical Education,* pp. 207–208 Single-file formation with a leader. Start the class by moving feet, in place, to the beat of the tom-tom at a slow pace and gradually speed up. Add clapping hands. Add movement after the above is accomplished. The beat must be fast enough so that students move at a fast trot with knees up.	Psychomotor—The student will be able to move rhythmically with the beat of the tom-tom by the end of the week. Cognitive—The student will describe six sport and recreational activities in which the body moves rhythmically.
Fitness Development Activities (8 minutes): **Circuit Training** 1. Rope jumping 2. Push-ups 3. Agility Run 4. Arm Circles 5. Rowing 6. Crab Walk 7. Tortoise and Hare 8. Bend and stretch Begin with 20 seconds of activity, 10 seconds to change.	*Dynamic Physical Education,* pp. 232–235 Increase the amount of time at each station to 25 seconds and decrease the amount of rest between stations. The student must be able to perform the exercises well to ensure the effectiveness of Circuit Training. Emphasize quality of exercise rather than quantity.	Psychomotor—The student will be able to perform all exercises. Cognitive—The student will be able to state which circuit exercises develop the various areas of the body. Affective—Most fitness gains are made when the body is exercised past the point of initial fatigue. Discuss briefly the value of pushing oneself past the first signs of tiring.
Lesson Focus (14 to 22 minutes) **Long-Rope Jumping** 1. Run through turning rope, front door. 2. Run in front door, jump once, run out. 3. Run through turning rope, back door. 4. Run in back door, jump once, run out. 5. Try the following variations: a. Run in front door and out back door. b. Run in front door and out front door. c. Run in back door and out back door. d. Run in front or back door, jump a specified number of times, and run out. e. Run in front or back door, jump and do a quarter, half, and full turn in the air. f. Add individual rope.	*Dynamic Physical Education,* pp. 322–326 Groups of four to six children. Two children turn and the others jump. Make sure that all children get a chance to both turn and jump. For jumping front door, the rope is turned from its peak toward the jumper. For jumping back door, the rope is turned away from the jumper. Back door is much more difficult. Approach the rope at a 45-degree angle. Girls will probably be much more skilled in this activity. Turners maintain a constant rhythm with the rope. Children who have trouble jumping should face one of the turners and key their jumps to both the visual and audio cues (e.g., hand movement and sound of the rope hitting the floor).	Psychomotor—The student will be able to jump the rope a minimum of 15 times consecutively without a miss. Cognitive—In terms of physical exertion, 10 minutes of rope jumping is equal to 30 minutes of jogging. Affective—Rope jumping is neither a male nor a female activity. It is performed by boxers, football players, and dancers for fitness development. Cognitive—The student will learn to react to rope-jumping terms—front door, back door, Hot Pepper, High Water, and so on.

continued

TABLE 5.4./*continued*

Movement Experience, Content	Organization and Teaching Hints	Expected Student Objectives and Outcomes
g. Individual choice or with a partner. 6. Hot Pepper: *Gradually* increase the speed of the rope. Use the verse on p. 324. 7. High Water: *Gradually* raise the height of the rope while it is turning. 8. Have more than one child jump at a time. Students can enter in pairs or any other combination. Have jumpers change positions while jumping. 9. Have one of the turners jump the long rope. 10. Egg Beater: Two or more long ropes are turned simultaneously with four turners. 11. Double Dutch: Requires two long ropes turned alternately. Rope near jumper is turned front door and far rope back door. 12. Combination movements: Three or four ropes in sequence.	It might be helpful to review beanbags briefly as a change of pace (rest) activity. Try to eliminate excessive body movement while jumping (e.g., jumping too high). In Double Dutch, the jumper must jump twice as fast as each rope is turning to succeed. Students can be challenged to perform a different activity as they pass through each rope.	
Game (5 to 7 minutes) A game that does not contain too much activity is probably a good choice. The following are suggested: 1. Right Face, Left Face (p. 437) 2. Cageball Target Throw (pp. 439–440)	*Dynamic Physical Education,* pp. 415–445	

NOTE: Supplies and equipment needed—
One long jump rope (16 ft) for a group of four to six children
Seven individual jump ropes
Tom-tom

INFORMAL EVALUATION QUESTIONS

1. Are students incorporating physical activity in their life-style?
2. Are students participating in other school activities (e.g., intramurals, after-school sports) and such activities as Little League baseball?
3. Are students acquiring competence in physical skills?
4. Are students developing an understanding of personal fitness and wellness?
5. Are students reaching a desirable level of physical fitness through participation in the program?
6. Do students possess the requisite knowledge required to participate in a wide variety of sports, games, and exercises?
7. Have students acquired the social and emotional skills necessary for productive participation in school and society?
8. Does the curriculum leave students with a broad understanding of the wealth of physical activities available to them (balance)?
9. Does the curriculum allow students to leave school with a high level of competency in a few activities (depth)?
10. Does the curriculum follow a progressive sequence within the school year as well as between school years (horizontal and vertical curriculum)?

FIGURE 5.1. Sample informal curriculum evaluation form

CHAPTER 6

Effective Class Management

Effective class management skills are displayed by all successful teachers. The skills may vary among teachers in emphasis and focus, but collectively they characterize quality teaching. Effective teachers take guidance from these assumptions: that teaching is a profession, that students are in school to learn, and that the teacher's challenge is to promote learning. These assumptions imply a responsibility to a range of students, both those who accept instruction and those who do not. Teachers must maintain the faith that many students who have not yet found success will eventually do so. Instructing teachable children is relatively easy, but making appreciable gains among low-aptitude and indifferent students is the mark of an effective teacher.

THE TEACHER'S ROLE

The basic responsibility of the teacher is to direct learning toward target goals. Teachers should vary presentations and select instructional strategies appropriate to the capabilities of students and the nature of activity sequences. How teachers teach, not the characteristics of a particular teaching style, determines what students learn. No matter what the methodology or teaching strategy, a diagnostic-prescriptive approach is superimposed on all teaching processes. The teacher observes critically the pace of instruction and adjusts the instruction based on the students' reaction.

Effective class management and organizational skills create a relaxed environment that offers students a freedom of choice in harmony with class order and efficient teaching procedures. Management techniques include the mechanics of organizing a class, planning meaningful activities, and enhancing the personal growth of students. Effective teachers plan experiences to meet the needs of all students. Because skillful instructors have the ability to prevent problems before they occur, they spend less time dealing with deviant behavior. In short, teachers who fail to plan, plan to fail.

Teachers must be aware of the impact of their behavior on students. In many ways, teaching reflects the personality, outlook, ideals, and background of the teacher. A successful teacher provides high-quality learning experiences and communicates a zest for movement that is contagious. Teachers must also be aware of personal habits and attitudes that may affect youngsters negatively. Proper dress, a sound fitness level, and the willingness to participate with students reveal clearly how a teacher regards the profession and the subject.

A basic requisite for teachers is to model the behavior that they desire from students. This may mean moving quickly if they demand that students hustle. It may mean listening carefully to students or performing required fitness activities. Modeling desired behavior has a strong impact on students. The phrase "Your actions speak much louder than your words" has significant implications for teachers.

Successful teachers communicate to students a belief that the youngsters are capable, important, and self-sufficient. Stressing a positive self-concept and offering experiences to promote success are invaluable aids to learning. Students need to be reminded that the teacher enjoys seeing them achieve. They appreciate the teacher's concern and usually respond with increased efforts.

Effective teaching takes place without sarcasm, ridicule, or threats. Teachers must be aware of the limitations of their knowledge and admit when they do not have a ready answer to a question. A wise teacher tells the class that she will find the answer by the next class meeting. Humor heals many hurts. The teacher's ability to laugh with the children and at her own behavior is also an effective instrument for class rapport.

Teachers and students may become angry with one another in the class setting. In some cases, teachers communicate that they do not like the student who misbehaves, and this lowers the student's self-esteem. Teachers should tell students that the misbehavior is unacceptable and that it must stop. At the same time, however, the instructor should communicate to the student that he is an acceptable person who is still cared for and appreciated.

CLASS MANAGEMENT SKILLS

Class management skills are a prerequisite to instruction. Moving and organizing students requires the teacher's comprehension of various techniques and the students' effective acceptance of those techniques. Observers of the teaching process agree that if a class is unmanageable, it is unteachable.

Instructing students in management areas should not be viewed as a negative or punishing proposition. Most students and teachers enjoy a learning environment that is organized and efficient and allows a maximum amount of class time to be devoted to practicing an activity in a setting that encourages success and enjoyment. Teachers should remember that skills in management need to be practiced consistently throughout the school year.

Class management skills should be taught to students in a manner similar to physical skill teaching. All skills need to be learned through practice and repetition until they become second nature. If teachers view class management skills in this light, they will have more empathy for students who do not perform well. Just as students forget how to shoot a basketball correctly, so also they sometimes forget how to perform a management skill quickly. A simple statement to the effect that "It appears you forgot how to freeze quickly, let's practice," is much more positive than indicting a class for its carelessness and disinterest. One final thought—motor skills are practiced many times over without perfection ever being reached. Class management skills also must be practiced many times during the school year if students are to perform those skills effectively.

STARTING THE CLASS

A major goal of teachers is to have all students listening to directions given prior to activity. The instructions should be as specific and clear as possible. A teacher who talks longer than 30 seconds during any single instructional episode will begin to lose control of the class. For this reason, teachers should alternate instructional episodes with periods of activity. Too often, teachers sit students down and explain many different technical points of skill performance. In a series of points, most people remember only the first and last. This fact should help teachers understand the importance of giving students only one or two points on which to focus when performing a skill. This reduces the length of the instructional episode and also eliminates the students' frustration over trying to remember many points of technique.

Teachers should remember the admonition "How before What," which means explaining *how* an activity should be performed before telling *what* the specific activity is. An effective way to stimulate youngsters to listen is to signal the beginning and end of a practice session by using certain words. These signals could be "Begin!" or "Stop!" or the school nickname. Instructions might be "When I say Sun Devils [school nickname], I'd like you to. . . ." This method can lead to an enjoyable interchange between students and instructor, but should not be used to excess.

STOPPING THE CLASS

A consistent signal should be established for stopping the class. It does not matter what the signal is, as long as it means the same thing consistently. Often, having both an audio signal (such as a whistle blast) and a visual signal (raising the hand overhead) is effective, since some youngsters may not hear the audio signal if they are engrossed in activity. Regardless of the signal used to indicate a stop, it is usually best to select a different signal to start the class. If the children do not respond to the signal to stop, the procedure must be practiced. Asking the class to freeze on signal is a good practice method. As the children become more effective at stopping, their response should be reinforced. To evaluate class effectiveness in responding to the stop signal, the teacher can time the latency of the response to the signal (see Chapter 14). If a class takes longer than 5 seconds to freeze and get ready for the next command, stopping and listening probably should be practiced.

Teachers must strive for 100% cooperation when students are asked to stop. If some students stop and listen to directions and others do not, class morale soon degenerates. The teacher can easily scan the class to see if all students are stopped and ready to comprehend the next set of directions. If the teacher settles for less than full attention, students will fulfill those expectations.

ORGANIZING STUDENTS INTO GROUPS AND FORMATIONS

Instructors should know how to divide their classes into teachable groups. Often, simple games can be used to accomplish this in an enjoyable and rapid fashion. For example, the game called Back to Back (see pp. 420–421) can be used to teach children to find partners. The goal of the game is to get back to back with a partner as fast as possible. Other challenges can be to get foot to foot or shoulder to shoulder or to look into the eyes of a partner. Students without a partner are instructed to go to the center of the teaching area immediately and to find someone else without a partner. This gives students a secure feeling, as opposed to feeling unwanted while running around the area looking for a partner. Emphasis on rapid selection keeps children from looking for a favorite friend or telling someone that she is not wanted as a partner. If students insist on staying near a friend, the teacher tells the class to move throughout the area until they are adequately mixed and spread out.

Another effective game for arranging students in groups of a selected size is Whistle Mixer (see p. 435). When the whistle is blown a certain number of times, students form groups corresponding to the number of whistles and sit down to signify that they have the correct number in the group. Again, students who are left out go to the center of the area and find the needed number of members. Once this skill is mastered, students can move quickly into the proper size group depending on the number of whistle signals.

To divide the class into two equal groups, the teacher can have students get back to back with a partner. One partner sits down while the other remains standing. Those standing are asked to go to one area, and those sitting are then moved to the desired space. Getting into groups is a skill that needs to be learned and practiced on a regular basis.

Other suggestions for grouping by partners are to ask students to find a partner wearing the same color, with a birthday during the same month, with a phone number that has two similar numbers in it, and so forth. To arrange students in equal-size groups, the instructor can place an equal number of different colored beanbags or hoops on the floor. Students are asked to move throughout the area. On signal, they sit on a beanbag. All students with a red beanbag are in the same group, green beanbags make up another group, and so on.

An effective technique for moving a class into a single-file line is to have students run randomly throughout the area until a signal is given. On signal, while continuing to move, they fall in behind someone until a single line is formed. This exercise can be done while students are running, jogging, skipping, or walking. As long as students continue to move in behind the ones in front, the line will form automatically. The teacher or a student leader then leads the line into a desired formation or position.

Another method of moving a class into formation is to ask the students to get in various formations without talking. They can offer visual signals but cannot ask someone verbally to move. Two groups can be used to compete against one another to see which forms the desired formation fastest. Young students learn to visualize various shapes through this technique. Remember that a circle is the hardest of all formations for students to make and should be the last formation learned. Most circle games can be played in a square or rectangle that has rounded corners. If necessary, use cones to establish the corners of the shape.

USING SQUADS

Squad formation, when employed properly, can be an effective means of arranging youngsters. The following are guidelines for using squad formation to maximize teaching effectiveness.

1. Selection of squads or groups must never embarrass a child who might be chosen last. In no case should this be a "slave market" approach in which the leaders look over the group and visibly pick those whom they favor. The teacher can select the squads ahead of time for balance of ability level, or some students, chosen as captains, can pick squad members but the captains are then assigned to squads other than those they picked.

2. A designated location should be used for assembling students in squad formation. When the teacher wants students in squads, children move to the predesignated area, with squad leaders in front and the rest of the squad behind.

3. Squads are effective in providing opportunities for leadership and followership among peers. The teacher should make maximum use of squad leaders, so the youngsters regard being a leader as a privilege entailing certain responsibilities. Examples of leadership activities are gathering equipment for squads, moving squads to a specified location, leading squads through exercises or various introductory activities, and appointing squad members to certain positions in sport activities.

4. Squad leaders should be changed at least every three weeks, and the composition of squads should be altered every nine weeks. Each youngster must have an opportunity to lead.

5. In most cases, an even number of squads should be formed. This allows the class to be broken quickly into halves for games. Having a class of 30 students divided into six squads of only 5 members each means a small number of students per piece of apparatus in group activities.

6. A creative teacher makes the use of squads an exciting, worthwhile activity, not an approach that restricts movement and creativity. For example, cones can be numbered and placed in different locations around the activity area. When students enter the gym, they are instructed to find their squad number and assemble. The numbers might be written in a different language, or hidden in a mathematical equation or story problem. Another enjoyable experience is to spread out task cards in the area that specify how the squads are to arrange themselves. The first squad to follow instructions correctly can be awarded a point or some acknowledgment from the rest of the class. Examples of tasks for the squads might be arranging the members in a circle, sitting with hands on head, or arranging themselves in crab position in a straight line facing northwest. The task cards might specify what the children are to do for an introductory activity, or where they should go for the fitness development activity.

7. Allow youngsters to develop names for their squad. This helps them to feel part of a select group, and that feeling makes the activity more enjoyable for both teacher and students. Youngsters should be encouraged to develop pride in their squad.

LEARNING STUDENTS' NAMES

Effective class management is predicated on the teacher's learning the names of students. Praise, feedback, and correction go unheeded when the teacher addresses students as "Hey you!" Teachers should develop a system for learning names. One approach is to memorize three or four names per class period. The names are written on a note card, and those students are identified at the start of the period. At the end of the period, the teacher again identifies the students to see if she has learned their names. A sound practice is telling students that you are trying to learn their names. Once the first set of names has been memorized, a new set can be learned. At the start of class when the meeting occurs, those names learned previously can be reviewed and new students identified.

Another effective way to learn names is to take a Polaroid picture of each class and later identify students by keying names to the picture. The teacher identifies those students whom he knows and does not know before the start of the period. He then sets personal goals by calculating the percentage of students whose name he knows after each period.

PREPARING YOUNGSTERS FOR ACTIVITY

If children are to have the sense of security that comes from knowing what to do from the time they enter the instructional area until they leave the area when the lesson is finished, certain basic procedures must be practiced. A specified entry behavior minimizes management time and gets the children into activity as soon as possible.

If children must change shoes in the gymnasium, this should be accomplished as expediently as possible, since little lesson activity can occur until all have made the change. For younger children in classes taught by specialists, help from classroom teachers in putting on shoes and tying laces conserves learning time. Instruction and practice in tying laces is desirable.

Shoes may need to be marked for younger children, so the right and left shoe can be identified. (Position shoes so the inside edges are together, and then place corresponding marks on the shoes so the marks come together when the shoes are on the correct feet.) Having both gymnasium and street shoes marked with the child's name minimizes squabbling over ownership. A routine, orderly arrangement for street shoes should be established so the children can find their shoes quickly, without unnecessary scrambling, at the end of class.

Some efficient means should be devised for conveying to the specialist the names of children who are not to participate in the lesson. This decision is best made before children arrive at the lesson area. A note from the classroom teacher, listing the name and health problem of those who are to sit out or take part in modified activity, can be delivered to the specialist as children enter the room. The specialist should accept the information at face value. This avoids the time-consuming procedure of questioning students on the sidelines to determine what the problem is and what the solution should be.

Some teachers like to have children assemble for instruction immediately after the youngsters have changed their shoes. These teachers should understand that children are excited over the opportunity to be active and that sitting quietly and listening at this point is not a satisfying experience. Other teachers prefer to start with an introductory activity and then give any necessary instructions. A third plan is to teach the introductory and fitness activity before explanations about the lesson focus are given. Children can then sit and listen while they recover from the strenuous activity.

After the lesson is completed, exit procedures need to be enacted. Changing shoes and forming lines for the return to the classroom may be the only items that need structuring.

USING EQUIPMENT

The first and most important rule for the use of equipment such as balls, hoops, jump ropes, and the like is that every youngster must have a piece for personal use. When large equipment or apparatus is used, as many stations or groups as possible should be established. For a class of 25, six benches, mats, or jumping boxes should be available so students have only a short wait in line. One way to avoid standing and waiting a turn is to use return activities (see pp. 333–334). With this approach, students are asked to perform a task or tasks on their way to the end of the line.

Instructors must demonstrate the proper method of using equipment. Youngsters should be able to get a piece of equipment and work on it in an acceptable fashion. Equipment should always be placed in the same (home) position when the class is called to attention. For example, beanbags might be placed on the floor, balls placed between the feet, and jump ropes folded and placed behind the neck. Such routines avoid the problems of youngsters striking one another with the equipment, dropping it, or practicing activities when they should be listening. Positioning the equipment out of the student's hands is usually preferable.

Equipment should be distributed to students as rapidly as possible. When students wait for a piece of equipment, time is wasted. Often, teachers assign student leaders to get the equipment for a squad. This means that only the leaders are assigned a task, while others sit and wait. Probably the easiest and fastest method is to have the leaders place the equipment around the perimeter of the area. Youngsters then move on signal to a piece of equipment and begin practice immediately. The reverse procedure can be used for putting equipment away. This contrasts with the practice of placing the equipment in a bag and telling students to "run and get a ball." This approach usually results in youngsters being knocked down and bruised.

The child who first picks up a piece of equipment is entitled to retain possession of it. Others should respect this right and not attempt to grab the piece away from the individual. This principle also holds for space possession. The child who first steps inside a hoop, on a mat, or into any designated space is entitled to occupy that space.

DEVIANT BEHAVIOR

Some children display overt deviant behavior or have problems that get in the way of learning. Parents are becoming increasingly concerned about the permissive climate of the schools and the apparent lack of discipline. This concern puts pressure on the school administration, which in turn presses teachers to "make children mind."

UNDERSTANDING INDIVIDUALS

The labeling of children by peers and faculty members is a serious negative reinforcer for problem children. Teachers should try to see each child as a new person each day and to avoid statements such as "Are you doing that again?" or "Why can't you ever behave?" When possible, behavioral problems should be viewed as a lack in the child's education, rather than a personality defect.

Teachers sometimes misunderstand aggressiveness. Many children learn to be aggressive to get what they want. The aggressive child has not yet learned the self-discipline required to compete in an acceptable manner. Such a child may go to any extreme to finish first, or may compete so intensely that he becomes disliked. The teacher should offer the youngster guidance in tolerating himself and in treating others with compassion and care. Discussions to increase awareness of others' rights and feelings can be effective in easing this problem.

Shy, timid children may lack aggressiveness and may withdraw from participation. They may be afraid of failing and losing in activities. This type of child is more comfortable in situations that allow exploration and learning in relative privacy. The shy youngster becomes more outgoing through activities that offer individual participation at a comfortable pace and guarantee success.

Teachers must make a sincere effort to understand handicapped children and their special problems when faced with a mainstreaming situation. These children sometimes have deep and special psychological problems that require careful handling.

ESTABLISHING A POSITIVE TEACHING CLIMATE

Teachers' reactions to appropriate and inappropriate behavior are an effective procedure for increasing and decreasing specific behaviors. These reactions can be positive in the form of praise, or negative in the form of scolding. The available evidence shows that many teachers consistently use a high rate of negative reactions and a relatively low rate of positive reactions (Boehm 1974, Darst 1976, Hamilton 1974). Teachers need to focus positive reactions on appropriate student behaviors. This is an effective preventive disciplinary strategy that leads to a positive and productive environment.

Initially, teachers should emit positive reactions containing specific information at a high frequency. These reactions should occur immediately when students behave appropriately. Examples include:

1. Thanks for getting dressed and ready to participate so quickly.
2. Squad three has all good listeners.
3. John, way to follow directions.
4. Good hustle between stations. I like that a lot.
5. Sally and Sarah are working hard today.

Too often, teachers focus scolds on 1 or 2 students in the class while 29 or 30 other students receive little teacher attention for behaving appropriately. Teachers should avoid repeating too many general, positive statements like good job, good work, good hustle, way to go, good going, and nice work. Students can become satiated with such general statements and the statements then lose their effectiveness. It is also important to make sure that the intensity of the statement is commensurate with the student behavior. Students who are not behaving appropriately should not receive positive unqualified reactions from the teacher.

Scolds and other negative teacher reactions are sometimes necessary and useful in decreasing inappropriate behavior. It is important to deliver scolds infrequently but with a certain amount of severity. Teachers should attempt to remain unemotional and to focus on the student's inappropriate behavior. Students must understand that the scold is not focused on them as a person but on the undesirable behavior. The student must further understand what the appropriate behavior was in the given situation. The appropriate behavior is usually obvious, but students may need to be reminded of the rules.

Another useful teacher reaction is called *extinction.* This technique consists of ignoring certain behaviors that are not seriously disruptive to the learning environment. Many times, undesirable student behavior is maintained by the attention of the teacher and the peer group. For example, a student misbehaves, and the teacher publicly scolds the behavior. The student's friends laugh at the situation. This laughter reinforces the student, and the behavior will occur again. If the behavior is not seriously distracting, then ignoring the behavior coupled with a positive reaction for those students emitting an appropriate behavior may be effective. The teacher may also wish to explain to the class that they, too, should ignore the student's inappropriate behavior. In this way, the student loses the attention of both teacher and peers.

Teacher reactions play a powerful role in controlling student behavior and in establishing an effective, positive learning atmosphere. Careful plans should be made regarding the use of these reactions. Teachers can decide in advance on the specific student behaviors that will be praised, scolded, or ignored. Each teacher should develop a list of specific student behaviors and the accompanying teacher reaction. For example,

Praise	Scold	Ignore
Listening	Fighting	Talking out
Following directions	Pushing	Raising a hand
Hustling	Disrupting others	Snapping fingers
Being on time	Cursing	Showing off
Proper dress	Obscene gestures	Constantly asking questions

Various situations may require a different reaction. Teachers should strive, however, to be consistent in their reactions so students know what to expect and learn to behave accordingly.

DEALING WITH INAPPROPRIATE BEHAVIOR

Teachers need a consistent approach to dealing with undesirable behavior, an approach they feel comfortable implementing. The plan should be spelled out to students, so the youngsters know exactly what is acceptable and unacceptable behavior and understand what actions will be taken if they demonstrate the undesirable behavior. The desired behavior, as well as the consequences of undesired behavior, should be posted in the teaching area. Examples of desired behavior might be careful listening when the teacher is instructing, keeping one's hands off others, and performing promptly the activities presented by the teacher. In most cases, the list of desired behaviors should number between four and six items.

One possible set of consequences might be as follows:

First deviation: The student is warned quietly on a personal basis to avoid embarrassing him.

Second deviation: The student is told to go to a predesignated cooling-off spot. This might be a chair, an isolated area, or a refrigerator box. The student must stay there until she is ready to reenter the activity and demonstrate the desired behavior.

Third deviation: The student must go to the cooling-off box and stay for a predetermined time established prior to the infraction.

Fourth deviation: The student loses free-time privileges. This manifests itself through the student's serving time in detention. Detention is time that the student serves in a study hall atmosphere supervised by teachers on a rotating basis. Detention must be completed during the student's free time rather than the teacher's.

If these consequences do not work, the last alternative is to call the parents for a conference with the principal.

The teacher should try to avoid having negative feelings about the student and internalizing the student's misbehavior. In some cases, teachers become punitive in handling deviant behavior, and this destroys any chance for a worthwhile relationship. The way the misbehavior is dealt with should contribute to the development of a responsible, confident student who understands that all individuals who function effectively in society must adjust to certain limits. The teacher should try to forget about past bouts of deviant behavior and to approach the student anew in a positive fashion at the start of each class. If this is not done, the student soon becomes labeled, which makes behavioral change extremely difficult to accomplish and often causes the student to live up to the teacher's negative expectations.

BEHAVIOR GAMES

Behavior games are an effective strategy for changing student behaviors quickly in the areas of management, motivation, and discipline. If a teacher is having severe disruptive problems in any of these areas, a well-conceived behavior game may turn the situation around in a short period of time. These games can be packaged for a group of students to compete against each other or against an established criterion. The goal of the games is to use group contingencies to develop behaviors that enhance the learning environment and to eliminate behaviors that detract from the environment. Various forms of behavior games have been used successfully by physical educators (Darst and Whitehead 1975, McKenzie and Rushall 1973, Paese 1982).

Behavior games have been successful in solving these types of inappropriate behaviors: Nonattendance, tardiness, nondressing, cursing, talking out, low practice rates, and high rates of management time. The following is an example of a behavior game used successfully with 6th graders in an effort to improve management behaviors.

1. The class is divided into four squads. Each squad has a designated color for identification. Four boundary cones with appropriate colors are arranged to mark a starting area.

2. The rules of the game are as follows:

a. Each squad member has to be dressed and in the proper place at a designated starting time. Reward: 2 points.

b. Each squad member has to move from one activity to another activity within the specified time (10, 20, or 30 seconds) and begin the appropriate behavior. Reward: 1 point for each instance.

c. Each point earned is rewarded with one minute of free activity time on Friday. Free activity time includes basketball, Frisbee playing, rope jumping, flag football, or any other activity popular with students.

d. The squad with the most points for the week earns a bonus of 5 points.

3. The teacher explains the allotted time for each management episode (10, 20, or 30 seconds), and gives a "go" signal. At the end of the allowed time, the teacher signals "stop" and awards points for appropriate behavior.

4. Squads that are successful are praised by the teacher, and the points are recorded on a small card. The unsuccessful squads are not hassled or criticized, just reminded that they did not earn a point.

5. On Fridays, the appropriate squads are awarded the special free-time activities while the other squads continue with the regularly scheduled class activities.

6. The game is slowly phased out as students begin to manage themselves more quickly.

The results of this game were as follows:

1. The use of group contingencies and free-time activities reduced overall class management time.

2. The free-time activities were within the physical education curriculum objectives and served as a break from regular activities.

3. The free-time activities gave the teacher an opportunity to interact with students on a personal level.

4. The students enjoyed the competition and the feeling of success when they emitted appropriate behaviors.

5. The students enjoyed the free time with novelty activities.

6. The positive approach of the game seemed to improve the overall teaching-learning atmosphere. The students were more attentive and cooperative.

7. The teachers estimated that more time was available for instruction because of the reduction in management time.

Another important point in designing behavior games is that the games should be so structured that any student or squad is able to win the game. Each game need not generate a winner and loser. All participants should be able to win. Teachers must also be aware that one or two students may find it reinforcing to cause their team to lose the behavior game. They will try to break every game rule to make sure that their team loses consistently. In these cases, the teacher should have a special team discussion and possibly a vote to eliminate those students from the team and the game. These students could be sent to a time-out area or channeled into an alternative activity. They may even be asked to sit out an entire class. Again, caution is urged, because sitting out may be exactly what the student has in mind as a final goal.

Another effective behavior game can be used to help students persist at learning activities in a station-type approach. Often, teachers will set up four or five learning stations for activities such as basketball, volleyball, soccer, or football. Performance objectives or learning tasks are posted at each station for the students to practice. However, some of the students are not motivated and do not use their time productively until the teacher rotates to the station where they are working. The teacher then prods the group, hassles a few students, and may praise a few others. Overall, the environment is not productive, and the teacher gets tired of hassling unmotivated students. A possible solution to this situation is the following game:

1. Divide the class into four or five squads. Let the students pick a name for their squad.

2. Set up the learning stations with the activities to be practiced. An equal number of squads and learning stations is necessary.

3. Program a cassette tape with popular music. Short gaps of silence should be interspersed throughout the tape.

4. Tell students that if everyone in their squad is properly engaged in practicing the appropriate task, a point will be awarded to the squad at each gap in the music. If one or more persons are not engaged, then the point will not be awarded.

5. The points can be exchanged for minutes of free time for reinforcing motor activities such as Frisbee play or rope jumping. Fridays can be designated as reward day when the accumulated time is used.

6. The music can be changed regularly, and the interval between gaps should be changed and slowly increased until the gaps are eliminated. The music then serves as a discriminative cue for future practice time.

Many teachers have found that students enjoy exercising and practicing skills while listening to music. The music seems to enhance the motivational level and the productivity of the environment. Students might be allowed to bring their own music as a special reward for productive behavior. (Teachers should first make sure that the music is not offensive to others due to sexual, ethnic, or religious connotations.)

USING PUNISHMENT

Some types of misbehavior may require punishment. Deviant behavior such as deliberate disobedience, refusal to comply with a legitimate request, threats, and open and continued misbehavior demands action. Punishment should be meted out fairly, consistently, and as privately as possible so as not to embarrass the child. The punishment should be carried out immediately and should be designed to decrease the occurrence of misbehavior in the future. When punishing, the teacher must avoid being vindictive, holding grudges, or using harsh or inhumane gestures. If the punishment severely lowers the child's self-esteem, the deviant behavior may occur more frequently. Whenever a youngster's self-esteem is lowered, as when she is embarrassed in front of her peers, that student will attempt to rebuild it—often in unacceptable ways.

Punishing an entire class for the deviant behavior of a few youngsters is not only unfair but may trigger undesirable side effects. Students become hostile toward those who caused the loss of privileges, and this peer hostility lowers the level of positive social interaction. If the group as a whole is misbehaving, then punishing the entire group is perhaps appropriate.

Reciting rules and possible punishments and telling students what they should be doing have little lasting effect on behavior. Focus on positive behavior, and avoid either-or statements that issue an ultimatum to conform. If possible, offer students choices so they can choose to conform to acceptable alternatives. When deviant behavior manifests itself in a range of problems, establish priorities and proceed to correct one problem at a time.

EXPULSION: LEGAL CONSIDERATIONS

If serious problems occur, the physical education specialist should discuss the problems with the classroom teacher. Many times, the deviant behavior is part of a larger, more severe problem that is troubling the child. A cooperative approach may provide an effective solution. A group meeting involving parents, classroom teacher, principal, counselor, and physical education specialist may open avenues that encourage understanding and increase productive behavior.

Legal concerns involving the student's rights in disciplinary areas are an essential consideration. While minor infractions may be handled routinely, expulsion and other substantial punishments can be imposed on students only after due process. The issue of student rights is complicated, and most school systems have established guidelines and procedures for dealing with students who have been removed from the class or school setting. Youngsters should be removed from class only if they are disruptive to the point of interfering with the learning experiences of other children. Sending a child out of class is a last resort and means that both teacher and student have failed.

REFERENCES

Boehm, J. 1974. The effects of competency-based teaching programs on junior high school physical education student teachers and their pupils. Unpublished doctoral dissertation, The Ohio State University, Columbus, Ohio.

Darst, P. 1976. The effects of a competency-based intervention on student teaching and pupil behavior. *Research Quarterly* 47(3): 336–345.

Darst, P., and Whitehead, S. 1975. Developing a contingency management system for controlling student behavior. *Pennsylvania Journal for HPER* XLVI(3): 11–12.

Hamilton, K. 1974. The effects of a competency-based format on the behavior of student teachers and high school pupils. Unpublished doctoral dissertation, The Ohio State University, Columbus, Ohio.

McKenzie, T., and Rushall, B. 1973. Effects of various reinforcing contingencies on improving performance in a competitive swimming environment. Unpublished paper, Dalhousie University, Halifax, Nova Scotia, Canada.

Paese, P. 1982. Effects of interdependent group contingencies in a secondary physical education setting. *Journal of Teaching in Physical Education* (fall): 29–37.

CHAPTER 7

Teaching: Methodology and Styles

An understanding of three postulates should precede the study of teaching methods and styles. First, the teacher as an educator is the most important single factor in the educational process. A proficient instructor can select any appropriate teaching style and secure excellent educational returns from children.

A second postulate is that there is no one best way to teach. Naturally, one approach may be more appropriate depending on the desired outcomes of the educational experience. How an individual teaches should be determined by the target goals for children. The aim is high-quality teaching, rather than the application of a particular teaching style.

A third postulate is the importance of a diagnostic-prescriptive approach, in which the teacher monitors the class progress and adjusts the elements of the lesson. Critical observation skills are most important. The progress and responses of youngsters determine the succeeding elements of the lesson. While observation and analysis are important, it is more critical that the teacher provide feedback to the students and modify the tasks so that individual needs are met.

To ensure quality movement performance, the teacher should center on the following: (1) make sure that the child understands the instructions before performing, (2) stimulate the child to a high-level effort, and (3) see that each child completes the task as outlined, even if the response does not quite meet expectations. Directions should be clear and concise, and the teacher should offer appropriate feedback and reinforcement. These requisites are the characteristics of quality teaching, no matter what style is selected. The following section offers guidelines for effective communication with the learner.

COMMUNICATING WITH THE LEARNER

Communicating with the learner—indeed, with all learners—is critical for teachers, and communication skills can always be improved. Nonverbal communication is just as important as verbal communication.

If children are to get essential information, the teacher must encourage students to improve their listening skills, that is, the communication must get through each child's filter.

A major negative teacher communication practice—easy to identify but not so easy to eliminate—is the habit of talking too much. Beginning teachers often talk too long, until what they are saying passes the point of having any influence on the children. When youngsters have received the message, activity should begin. The aim is brevity.

A second, related aim is a balanced lesson with appropriate amounts of time devoted to management practices, initiation of activity, clarification of conceptual points, question-and-answer sessions, evaluation discussions, and activity participation. All are important, but time devoted to learning by doing should never be sacrificed for the sake of promoting an "academic" environment. Learning proceeds through physical education, not in spite of it.

A third communicative aim is clarity. An emphasis on following directions is part of the clarity of presentation. This does not mean that children are to take direction simply for its own sake but, rather, that they must learn to operate within the limits of the problem framework. Depending on the task at hand, these problems may be narrow, with some limitation, or broad, with considerable flexibility. Sequence-building is an excellent way to give practice in following directions. When a child does not respond to directions, the teacher needs to consider objectively whether the difficulty is in the communication or in the child's lack of ability to respond.

Before communication can take place, securing the children's undivided attention is necessary. Wait until they are reasonably quiet, then use a voice with enough volume to reach the group, but do not shout. Speak in terms consistent with the comprehension level and maturity of the children. Gradually add new words to their vocabulary, but avoid technical terms that they do not understand. In working with disadvantaged children, be sure that terms are appropriate and relevant to the group.

When phrasing the instructional points of a lesson, accent the positive. For example, tell children to "Land lightly," rather than saying "Don't land so hard." An easy way to emphasize the *why* of an activity is to say, "Do this because. . . ." If there are several different and acceptable ways to perform the movement patterns, be explicit. Show students the various ways, and discuss with them the reasons behind the technique differences. Children like to know the correct technique, even if it is beyond their sphere of accomplishment. Explain only enough, however, to get the activity under way successfully.

Limit the use of open-ended directives, and substitute those with precise goals. Instead of saying, "How many times can you . . . ?" or "See how many times you can . . . ," give children a definite target goal. Use directives like "See if you can . . . five times without missing," or "Show me five different ways you can. . . ." The teacher can ask the child to select a target goal. Using measurable and attainable goals is especially important when teaching slow learners or special education students.

Doing an activity in many different ways or doing it many times is a first step in the learning process, not an ultimate goal. Ask children to pick the best way and to practice that skill. Youngsters should be told to practice the skill until the habit feels right and then to move on to something else.

Certain teacher mannerisms may require attention and change. Avoid sermonizing at the least provocation. Excessive reliance on certain words and phrases—"okay," "all right," and the irritating "and uh"—are unappealing to children. Acquire instead a broad vocabulary of effective phrases for indicating approval and good effort.

If the classroom teacher has the responsibility for physical education instruction, he can make maximum use of the activity time by giving the more time-consuming explanations in the classroom before students go to the play area. Rules can be explained, procedures and responsibilities outlined, and formations illustrated on the blackboard.

When talking with a student, the teacher should make direct eye contact and assume a physical posture that tells the child nonverbally that she is paying attention. Facial and verbal cues reinforce this indication of interest. Remember that children want to understand and to be understood.

The judicious use of questioning can give direction, encourage new movements, discourage repetition of movements, and stress cognitive elements.

The teacher should respect students' opinions as long as he believes that they are sincere, and avoid humiliating a child who gives a wrong answer. Pass over inappropriate answers by directing attention to more appropriate responses.

Refrain from injecting personal opinion into the instructional question-answer process. At the end of the discussion, a summary of important points may be of value, however.

Do not be stunned, show surprise, or take offense if children comment negatively in response to a query asking for candid opinions about an activity or procedure. When opinions are honest, some are bound to be negative.

In dealing with young children, avoid answering individual questions until the entire explanation has been given. Questions can then be raised to clear up specific points. Youngsters should be seated if the discussion is to continue longer than 20 or 30 seconds.

DEVELOPING AN EFFECTIVE LEARNING ENVIRONMENT

General procedures applicable to many aspects of teaching physical education are presented in this section. Procedures for specific activity sequences are covered in the discussion of the specific activity.

Physical education is movement and learning through movement. All children, including physical underachievers, the handicapped, the overweight, and unskilled children, should be active in the learning situation. Teachers must make a conscious effort to avoid bias for certain students. Some teachers react unconsciously with distaste to overweight children or to those who are unkempt or dirty, which puts those children at an immediate disadvantage.

All children should be expected to work at or near their potential. Youngsters learn gradually that success is achieved through trying. If a teacher does not expect effort from students, the students will usually not make an effort.

In class, a happy medium should be found between quiet and boisterousness. Youngsters should be under control but able to express enthusiasm. Teachers soon learn to differentiate between noise related to purposeful activity and noise originating from disruptive behavior and lack of control.

Teachers need to recognize that the child's self-concept is learned and malleable. Achieving success and enjoying participation and the respect of peers are essential to forming a healthy ego. The fear of failure can be alleviated to some extent through achievable challenges, but children must also learn to tolerate some failure, to be willing to take risks, and to accept new obstacles to growth. The dignity of the child must be respected. For example, if a child does not understand how he is expected to move in an activity, the teacher should avoid using physical force to move him into position. A more humane approach is to explain the movement again and to show the child how the desired move is to be made.

Courtesy, fair play, and honesty are important social values that can be developed in the physical education setting through skillful lesson planning. Participation alone does not instill positive values in children. Team games and relays can help to develop group cooperation, fair play, and an attention to rules. Under adverse conditions, however, these games can also teach a child about cheating, winning at all costs, and disregarding rules. The instructional approach determines the result.

Movement experiences should offer ample time for experimentation and exploration, which means that children can practice an activity of choice. Background music helps when students are engaged in self-directed activities. If the music is quiet and relaxing, it tends to soothe and calm students.

DEMONSTRATIONS AND TEACHING

Demonstrations can illustrate variety or depth of movement, show something unique or different, point out items of technique or approach, illustrate different acceptable styles, and show progress.

The teacher or selected students can perform the demonstration. Care must be taken that the selected student can indeed accomplish the demonstration purpose. Rotating demonstration among many students is a sound practice. All children should have the chance to demonstrate at some time, but using the more skilled is difficult to avoid. Asking for volunteers tends to eliminate for these students the stigma of being the teacher's favorite.

The demonstration should be directed toward increasing the children's understanding of the movements presented by encouraging them to observe critically and to analyze what they have just seen. To this end, the demonstration should be followed by a period of practice.

DEMONSTRATION BY THE TEACHER

Be sure that all of the children can see and hear the performance. When explaining technique, the teacher should bring out the reasons behind the points. Teacher demonstration to establish proper technique can take a number of forms. He can show the proper starting position and then verbalize the instructions from that point on, or he can provide a more complete, point-by-point demonstration. The terminology should be clear, and the techniques demonstrated should be at the children's skill level.

The more critical the skill, the more demonstration is needed. For more flexible movement patterns, demonstrations may not be desirable, because they often lead to imitative behavior, which reduces creativity. In educational movement, the teaching goal is to develop movement variety and versatility. Demonstrations should therefore be used infrequently and not at the beginning of the lesson. Instead, children should be given the opportunity to develop individual approaches rather than imitating the style of another. A few basics presented early in the lesson, however, may give direction to the activity. Questions can be raised during the demonstration, but the teacher should not allow the question-and-answer period to take up too much time.

DEMONSTRATIONS BY INDIVIDUAL STUDENTS

The student demonstration is a most effective teaching technique, because it interjects children's own ideas into the lesson sequence. As students practice and move, the class can be stopped to let one child show what she has done. Teacher comments should be positive in nature, not derogatory. If the demonstration is unsatisfactory, the teacher can go on to another child without comment or reprimand, saying only, "Thank you, Janet. Let's see what Carl can do." Or the teacher might simply direct the children to continue practicing.

Selecting several children to demonstrate their achievement is usually preferable, so the other students can observe varied approaches. If partner or small-group work is undertaken, the same principle holds.

MULTIPLE DEMONSTRATIONS

The multiple demonstration is a valuable way to show what has been accomplished after a period of practice or at the end of a unit. One convenient way to organize this is to have squads demonstrate. The teacher can select one or more squads to perform, and then direct all children to return to activity. Other squads can have turns later. Another way to arrange such a demonstration is to have half of the class demonstrate while the other half watches.

TEACHERS WHO CANNOT DEMONSTRATE

Because of physical limitations, some teachers cannot demonstrate effectively. Few teachers who are not physical education specialists can do all physical activities well. Even the relatively skilled teacher at times needs to devise substitutions for an effective instructor demonstration.

Through reading, study, analysis of movement, and other devices, teachers should develop an understanding and a knowledge of the activities. Even if performing the activity is personally impossible, teachers must know how the activity should be done. Select skillful children to help demonstrate. Place more reliance on squad leaders and use the squad formation in skill drills. Be able to describe the skill, and use effective visual aids at appropriate points.

LEADERSHIP SKILLS

If children are to learn to lead as well as to follow, the program must provide social situations in which students have real leadership experiences. The very nature of the physical education program provides many jobs that can be distributed among students to give them opportunities to assume responsibility.

GUIDELINES FOR THE LEADERSHIP PROGRAM

The following guidelines are intended to help implement a leadership program.

1. Jobs assigned should be realistic and definite and should extend over a specified time period. Job descriptions should designate nonoverlapping areas of responsibility and should help orient children to the proper performance of duties.

2. The leadership program is not to be regarded as a time-saving device for the teacher. Furthermore, asking children to assume responsibilities without adequate guidance is unfair. The teacher must devote time and effort to the training of the leaders and must provide sufficient supervision.

3. If leadership practice is considered a developmental opportunity, then it follows that leadership is good for all children. Jobs should be rotated at specified times to give everyone some type of responsibility during the year.

4. Students should be held to a reasonable standard of job performance. They should be brought to the realization that being a leader requires planning, and they must set aside sufficient time to plan and discharge their duties.

5. Elementary school youngsters are not mature enough to be left in charge of a group for too long. Even a child with good leadership ability cannot cope with situations in depth.

6. Some consideration can be given to a leaders' club, which would include all of the leaders for a given period. Such a club can be organized within a class or on an all-school basis.

7. The use of leaders should improve the efficiency of the class. The most important element, however, is not leadership, but the quality of the physical education experience, which should not be allowed to suffer because too much emphasis is placed on leadership training.

8. Care must be taken to ensure that the leaders are not kept too busy to participate in the regular program. Assistant leaders, who assume head duties during the next leadership period, can be appointed. Continuity is preserved in this manner.

TYPES OF LEADERSHIP EXPERIENCES

The following kinds of experiences may prove valuable for children.

1. *Equipment manager.* A child designated as equipment manager can obtain, arrange, and return equipment for the day's activities.

2. *Area supervisor.* The duties of an area supervisor include marking fields, setting up boundaries, and seeing that the area is, in general, ready for activity. Indoors, this would entail duties like setting out mats or getting the public address system ready.

3. *Squad leaders.* Squad leaders can be responsible for simple tasks like keeping the squad in proper order for relays or stunt activities, or they can supervise skill teaching. Routine record keeping of individual performances and test scores can be part of their duties. (See also pp. 59–60.)

4. *Officials.* Officials need to have a thorough knowledge of the rules of the game. Enough officials can be assigned so that each official gets a chance to play in the activity and still hold the leadership position.

5. *Game leader, demonstrator, exercise leader.* Children can be assigned to choose and lead a game. If the activity or situation makes pupil demonstration desirable, the teacher can assign these duties to selected and properly directed students. Trained students can also lead these exercises.

6. *Monitors.* Special responsibilities can be assigned to monitors. Turning lights on and off, supervising the cleanup after class, and making safety inspections are duties that monitors can assume.

7. *Weekly equipment organizers.* A solution to the vexing problem of keeping the equipment in order is to have two to four students assigned to take responsibility for this task. Rearranging can be done late in the school day on Friday, or even after school. The equipment room is cleaned, materials are put away, and needed repairs are routed to the proper source. Each week then begins with an orderly equipment room.

TEACHING STYLES

Several teaching styles merit consideration. Figure 7.1 shows a continuum of teaching styles based on the degree of control exercised by the teacher. Competent teachers use more than one style and may even use a number of styles during a single lesson. The choice of teaching style depends on expected student outcomes, on the children's stage of progression, and on the activity. One reason for using different styles is to add novelty to the teaching situation, and so keep both learner and teacher motivated. Teachers should make a strong effort to experiment with different styles of teaching, and to persevere to make various styles effective. To some degree, each teacher's personality traits and aptitudes also determine which teaching styles are most suitable.

The nature of the activity should be considered in choosing the teaching style. For example, an individualized style

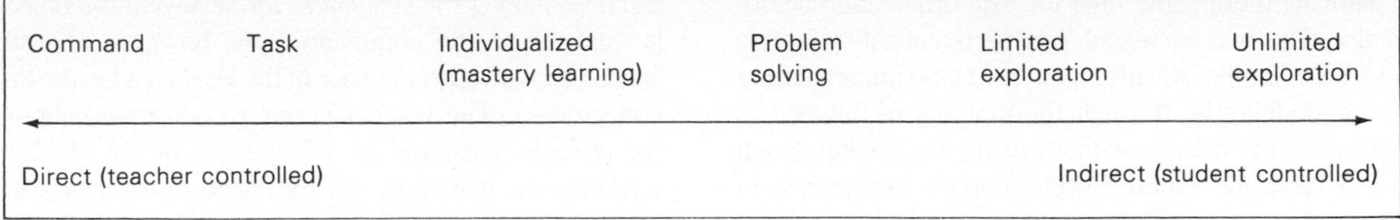

FIGURE 7.1. Continuum of teaching styles

of teaching is appropriate for a stunts and tumbling unit, whereas individual mat activities present an excellent opportunity for the unlimited exploration approach.

No matter which style is employed, the child needs to know the answers to three questions.

1. Where am I going? (What is it I am supposed to accomplish?)

2. How do I get there? (Is the teacher going to lead me, or do I have to attempt to find my own way?)

3. How will I know when I have arrived? (Do I evaluate myself, do I have a peer evaluate me, or is the teacher going to judge my performance?)

The answer to the first question is found in the goals or expected outcomes of the unit or lesson, which outline what the child is expected to accomplish. These goals can be expressed in terms of domains—psychomotor, cognitive, and affective. A point in favor of using this classification system is that many school districts have adopted the terminology and learning techniques implicit in this system. Most educators have an adequate background in these concepts, so we offer only a minimum explanation here.

The psychomotor domain deals with body competence, skill, and developmental outcomes, with the lesson objectives making specific reference to these areas. The pertinent cognitive elements are knowledge about the activity and other conceptual understandings. Cognitive elements go hand in hand with the development of psychomotor goals, and the teaching style selected should enhance this relationship. The affective domain, which is receiving increasing consideration from physical educators, deals with attitudes, feelings, and values. Many broad values, such as cooperation with others, fair play, and the like, can be furthered by an effective teaching style.

The answer to the second question—the *how*—involves the learning process, which outlines for the learner how to proceed in quest of the anticipated goals.

The third question concerns evaluation. Children are vitally interested in knowing whether they have achieved the anticipated goals. Evaluation comes first from the child, with respect to how she feels about what she has accomplished. More overt evaluation relies on established performance objectives, observations, tests, and achievement demonstrations that afford informal comparison with peers.

SELECTING THE APPROPRIATE TEACHING STYLE

Teachers should select a style most likely to enhance the child's learning experiences. As suggested by Figure 7.1, the teaching style should be chosen according to the degree of control the teacher plans to exert over lesson preparation, implementation, and evaluation. External factors are one consideration. If time is short, the command style may be best. On the other hand, if time permits experimentation with alternatives, the limited exploration style might also work well. An internal factor to be considered is the ability of the children to accept responsibility for their own learning. The teacher must analyze carefully the class's status in the psychomotor, cognitive, and affective domains, and then decide on the appropriate teaching style.

The teacher should also remember that good teaching techniques (being prepared, keeping all children active, and teaching with enthusiasm) are vital to successful teaching regardless of style. No single style is superior to another; each has its place and value for an effective teacher. One style may, however, be more appropriate than another in a given situation.

COMMAND STYLE

The command style is the most direct and teacher-controlled approach. The teacher prepares all facets of the lesson, is wholly responsible for instruction, and monitors the lesson progress by direct methods. Basically, the command style includes explanation, demonstration, and practice. The amount of time devoted to each is determined by the instructor. Evaluation is usually accomplished by the instructor, who has certain preset standards for student performance. Children are guided along almost identical paths toward similar goals.

When the command style is used, instructions should be brief and to the point, with as much action as possible following the instruction. Teachers sometimes make the mistake of talking in depth about a skill and including too many details in the introductory remarks, only to find that students usually forget all but the last few points. A demonstration that covers either part of the skill or the complete skill activity can shorten the time devoted to explanation.

When youngsters are introduced to new pieces of equipment, allowing them some time for experimentation before giving directions is often useful. Any pertinent safety factors should receive immediate attention. Dry runs (mime), during which the students go through the motions of the skill to get the feel of the activity without using implements (such as balls or bats) are helpful. During practice work, teachers should circulate among the students to help and coach.

Teachers use the command style more than they might imagine, because it is an efficient way to reach any teacher-selected goal. In situations in which discipline problems are a factor, the command style allows a tighter rein on class conduct. Teachers invariably use a command-dominated style with large classes. Another application of command style is in a situation in which a precise skill or a specific result is the goal. Such situations often arise during remediation of low fitness or motor deficiencies. With children who have lower levels of comprehension (e.g., the retarded), the command style is appropriate for accomplishing specific increments of progress. The directions are definite, and the children get needed practice in following directions.

Shortcomings of the command style are seen in the cognitive and affective areas of the learning process. Children have little chance to think or to make choices when they simply respond to command stimuli, and little consideration is given to what the children wish to do or accomplish.

When the command style is used, the perceptive teacher makes sure that it is personalized to the fullest extent possible. A good approach is to alternate or integrate other styles with the command style, so the directive is sometimes "Do it this way," and at other times "Do it your way."

TASK STYLE

When using the task style, the instructor is responsible for setting the lesson objectives, selecting the activities, and determining the sequences for achieving the objectives. In contrast to the command style, however, the student becomes involved in the pace of the lesson and in the instruction process. The teacher is not so concerned about how the class is organized or whether all of the children are working simultaneously on the same movement patterns. Instead, the teacher is more concerned with how the students are carrying out the defined task. Whereas success in the command style is judged by whether each child reaches the movement goal, in the task style the instructor accepts individual differences in accomplishment. This style may therefore motivate children who cannot achieve at the same level as the majority of the class.

Tasks can be presented verbally or printed on task cards. The student accomplishes the task at her own pace. She may find a partner to help or may even function as a member of a small group. The format might call for all students to give attention to the same problem or might allow them to work on different problems.

Task cards can be useful teaching devices. A number of different cards can be made to allow for progression. As a child finishes the task on one card, another card, describing the new task to complete, is issued to him. Cards for particular areas can be categorized according to the skill level required by the activity, from beginning (introductory) to intermediate to advanced. A sample task card for beginning skills in rope jumping is shown in Figure 7.2.

INDIVIDUALIZED STYLE

The individualized style is based on the concept of student-centered learning through an individualized curriculum. This style employs a variety of teaching strategies and allows the student to progress at an individual rate. Each student's needs are diagnosed, and a program is prescribed to address those needs. Clear objectives are stated in behav-

ROPE JUMPING—BEGINNING SKILLS

Needed: one jump rope

1. Check for proper size. The rope ends should come up to the armpits when the jumper is standing in the rope center.
2. Forward turning to the side: Hold the rope handles in one hand. Turn the rope forward to the side.
3. Jump and rebound! Without the rope, practice the jump and rebound until it is in good rhythm.
4. Combine jump and rebound with turning the rope to the side.
5. Slow-time jumping: With the hands holding the rope in normal rope-jumping position and with the rope started behind the back, try to perform regular rope jumping to slow-time rhythm.
6. Turn the rope 5 turns without a miss.
7. Turn the rope 10 turns without a miss.

FIGURE 7.2. Sample task card

ioral terms. The student is required to learn cognitive factors before moving to psychomotor tasks.

Certain materials and hardware are necessary to establish the proper learning environment for individualized instruction. Equipment is needed for loop films, transparencies, and audiotapes. Reference books, wall charts, and cards for recording student progress are also necessary. Useful equipment includes slide and overhead projectors, cassette tape recorders, screens, and chalkboards. A learning center that includes materials and equipment to direct the learning process can be established. Software for computers is available for use in learning centers (see Chapter 14). An example of a learning center is shown in Figure 7.3. Clearly, many other arrangements are also possible.

The individualized style of teaching basically follows five steps.

1. *Diagnosis.* Assessment is made to determine the student's present level of cognitive and psychomotor knowledge.

2. *Prescription.* Each student is given a learning package based on her present level of knowledge.

3. *Development.* The student works on tasks in the learning package until he is able to perform them successfully. Self-testing goals are offered, and the student decides after testing whether to proceed to the next step.

4. *Evaluation.* The student goes to the teacher for final evaluation. Both psychomotor and cognitive progress is evaluated at this point.

5. *Reinforcement.* If the student completes the tasks successfully, the teacher gives her positive reinforcement, records the data on the student's progress chart, and prescribes a new learning package based on the student's needs. If the student does not perform the task successfully, the teacher can offer possible alternatives for reaching the objective. The evaluation process gives the teacher an opportunity to counsel each student and to reinforce critical points.

Learning packages are at the core of the individualized style. The learning package is a student contract that provides the ingredients that the learner needs to accomplish various tasks and to put those tasks together in a meaningful sequence. The learning package consists of the following parts.

1. The content classification statement describes the task or concept to be learned. This could be a psychomotor task (such as the Cartwheel) or a cognitive task (such as learning about how to absorb force).

2. The purpose section explains what the package will do for the learner (e.g., "This contract provides you with activities that will enable you to perform the Cartwheel.").

3. The listed learning objectives tell the learner what he is to learn, under what conditions the learning will take place, and how he will perform when learning has occurred.

4. The diagnostic test (pretest) determines the student's knowledge and skill levels. The student is given a cognitive test as well as psychomotor tasks to perform for assessment.

5. The learning activities section offers different ways for the student to teach herself the skill, concept, or activity. In each contract, different choices should be available. The student can select any of the strategies to enhance learning. Some of the following strategies might be offered: the student can view and analyze loop films and transparencies, listen to audiotapes for instruction in cognitive tasks, read various books and manuals (referenced in advance by the instructor) describing the task, view videotapes offering

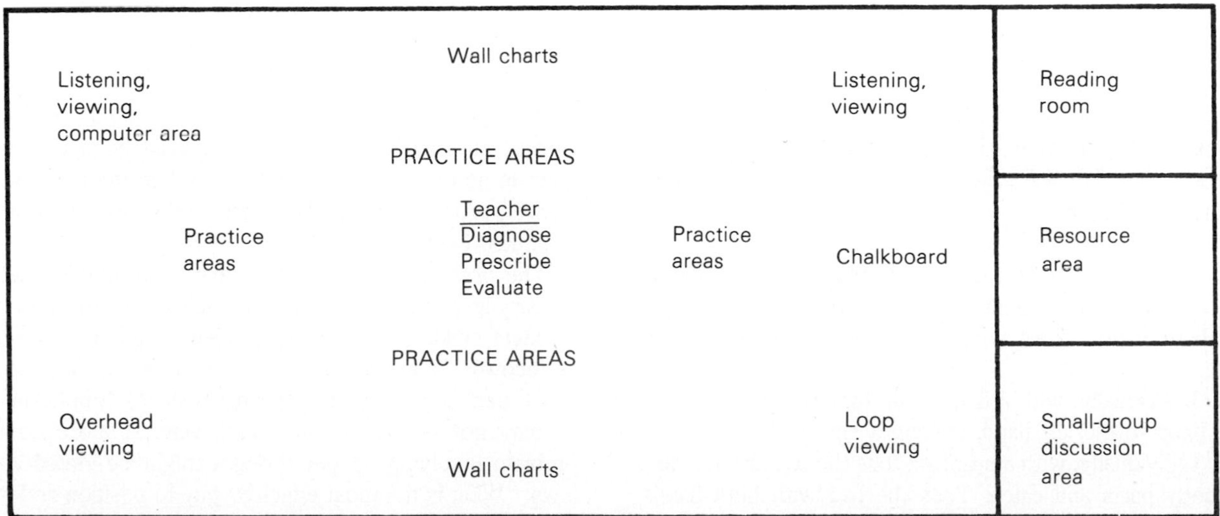

FIGURE 7.3. Organization of a learning center

demonstration and explanation of a skill to be performed, or study wall charts that break down the skill into its components. Students can also be directed to ask other students who have successfully completed the activity to help them practice.

6. The self-test is a phase that helps the student decide whether he is ready for the final test to be given by the teacher. The student can ask his peers to tell him whether he is ready for the final test.

7. The final test is an observable measure of the student's achievement. The psychomotor achievements are usually judged by the teacher, while the cognitive learnings are measured by a written exam.

In summary, the individualized style allows the student to control the rate of learning and to receive personalized feedback about progress. The teacher controls the material by designing the packages and by deciding the size of the learning increments. The student is encouraged to investigate different approaches to learning designated skills through written material, various audiovisual media, and contacts with peers. Experience in the learning process itself is a valuable acquisition that students can use later to learn new activities or skills.

Mastery Learning

Another approach to individualized instruction, which is becoming popular, is mastery learning. The approach places less emphasis on the cognitive domain and the need for extensive evaluation by peers and teachers. It is an instructional strategy in which the terminal target skill is broken into progressive subunits, each of which becomes in turn the focus of the learner. The key is the division of the final movement capability into progressive teachable units, each of which is to be mastered in order, thus providing an additive effect toward achieving the target competency. The approach is somewhat similar to contract teaching, but is more restricted in scope. The continuum of subunits must be mastered in turn before more complicated tasks are approached, and the number of subunits depends on the complexity of the skill.

For mastery learning, the skill of catching is offered as an illustration. For the sake of brevity, only four subunits are presented here.

1. Individually, with a fleece ball, toss with both hands and catch with both hands. Toss with the right and catch with both hands. Toss with the left and catch with both hands.

2. Individually, with a fleece ball, toss the ball from the right hand to the left hand, making a high arc.

3. Individually, with a beanbag, toss the bag around various body parts and catch. Toss the bag with both hands overhead and catch it behind the back with both hands.

4. Individually, with a beanbag and in an erect position, toss the bag high and catch as low as you can with both hands. Next, catch with the right and then the left hand as low as possible.

For each step, performance criteria need to be established. In step 1, to reach the mastery level, the child may be required to catch four out of five throws in each of the tasks. The final test would be to demonstrate capability in the terminal movement task.

Should the child fail the performance criterion for any step, practice is repeated and a second test session follows. This is the mastery element of the strategy. If the child fails the step test a number of times (say three or four), the step is abandoned, and the child moves to the next subunit.

Mastery learning as a strategy is useful in a number of ways. First, the child moves at an individualized pace and masters preliminaries needed for the target skill. The style is well suited to working with low-skilled and handicapped children. It also provides homework for children, enabling them to work during their spare time on areas needing improvement.

The process of the style can be outlined as follows:

1. The target skill or movement competency must be divided into sequenced, progressive units.

2. Prerequisite competency must be considered. Is the child ready?

3. Performance objectives for each of the successive learning units must be established.

4. Informal progress-testing can be carried on by the performer to determine readiness for more formal testing by the teacher or a peer.

5. When the child is ready, testing by the teacher determines pass or fail for a particular subunit. If the child passes, he moves to the next learning unit.

6. Should the child fail, he continues to practice, incorporating any alternatives or modification measures provided.

PROBLEM-SOLVING STYLE

The problem-solving style involves input, reflection, choice, and response. The problem must be structured so there is no one prescribed answer. When there is just one answer, problem solving becomes guided discovery, a type of limited exploration.

The problems selected will vary from simple ones for primary-level children to more complex ones for intermediate-level children. A simple problem might be expressed as follows: "What are the different ways you can bounce a ball and stay in your personal space?" Emphasis may or may not be placed on a *best* way. A more complex problem involving deeper thought might be stated as follows: "What is the most effective way to position and move your feet while guarding an opponent in basketball?" The solution could use an individual, partner, or group approach.

The following steps make up the problem-solving style.

1. *Presenting the problem.* The student is presented with a problem in the form of a question or statement that provokes thought and reflection. No demonstration or explanation of appropriate responses is given, because solutions should come from the child.

2. *Determining procedures.* The student must think about the procedures necessary for arriving at a solution. With younger children, the problems are simple and this phase is minimal. This step is important, however, because the assessment of how to proceed toward a solution has cognitive value. The child may need to define subproblems.

3. *Experimentation and exploration.* In experimentation, the student tries out different possible solutions, evaluates them, and makes a choice. In exploration, the goal is to seek breadth of activity. Self-direction is important, and the teacher acts in an advisory role—answering questions, helping, commenting, and encouraging, but not providing solutions. Sufficient time must be allotted for this phase.

4. *Observation, evaluation, and discussion.* Each child should have the opportunity to offer a solution and to observe what others have discovered. Various kinds of achievement demonstrations can be employed—by individuals, by small groups, by squads, or by part of the class. Discussion should center on justifying a particular solution.

5. *Refining and expanding.* After observing the solutions that others have selected and evaluating the reasoning behind the chosen solutions, each child should be given the opportunity to rework her movement patterns, incorporating ideas from others.

Children must understand that problems can be solved and that they can find the solutions. To do so, they must be equipped with techniques, so they can proceed under self-direction toward a sound solution.

One of the more difficult procedures in the problem-solving style is the designing of problems to which students do not already know the solution. On the surface, this sounds simple. If one student knows the answer, however, or secures the solution ahead of time, he may pass it on to the rest of the class, and the process of solving and exploring is lost. While the teacher should guide youngsters, the initiative for finding a solution lies with the students.

There are few limits to the areas that can be covered in the problem-solving approach. These include concepts, relationships, strategies, and proper use of skills for specific solutions.

LIMITED EXPLORATION STYLE

In limited exploration, the teacher is responsible for lesson preparation, subject matter selection, and the general direction of responses. The choice of specific responses is up to the student, since there is no set response for each limitation.

In most cases, exploration styles are best suited to teaching broad areas of movement and to developing multiple movement patterns for particular kinds of skills. When learning manipulative movements, for example, a child might show different ways to toss and catch a beanbag in place. The child can react within the limitation of catching while remaining in place. In another example, when children are working with partners to learn ball skills, they can show the different ways to bounce a ball back and forth between them. In this style, an example of fundamental movement teaching would be asking the child to show different ways to jump back and forth over a jump rope on the floor. The method can also be centered on the broader goal of exploring movement elements such as space, time, force, and flow. In this case, the limitation is only that movement elements be explored.

Guided Discovery

Another kind of limited exploration is guided discovery. A predetermined choice or result, of which the teacher is aware, is to be discovered by the students. Suppose, for example, that the teacher wants students to acquire the concept that in right-handed throwing the most efficient foot placement is a stride position with the left foot forward. Students are given different foot patterns for experimentation, with the goal of selecting the preferable pattern. They practice right-handed throwing with the following limitations: feet together, feet in a straddle position, feet in a stride position with the left foot forward, and feet in a stride position with the right foot forward. After practicing the four different foot positions, students choose which position seems best in terms of throwing potential.

Limited exploration is a useful approach for exploring and developing versatility in a particular kind of movement pattern. Progressions in manipulative activities are particularly adaptable to this teaching style. Limited exploration is a flexible style; at any time during a lesson, the style can be used to give children an opportunity to explore a particular situation.

UNLIMITED (FREE) EXPLORATION STYLE

In unlimited exploration, the only guidance from the teacher is selection of the instructional materials to be used and designation of the area to be explored. Two directives might be: "Today, for the first part of the period, you may select any piece of equipment and see what you can do with it." "Get a jump rope and try anything with it." No limits, except those dictated by safety, are imposed on the children. The teacher may need to forewarn or remind students how to use the equipment safely.

With exploration, the teacher avoids demonstrations and the praising of certain results too early, because these might lead to imitative and noncreative behavior. This does not mean, however, that the teacher is uninvolved. The teacher moves among the students—encouraging, clarifying, and answering questions on an individual basis. She should concentrate on motivating effort, since the student is responsible for being a self-directed learner. Teachers are wise to offer students the opportunity for self-direction in small doses, with the time being increased as the children become more disciplined.

Exploratory opportunities should be offered frequently, for this phase of learning takes advantage of the child's love of movement experimentation and allows the free exercise of natural curiosity. Self-discovery is a necessary and important part of learning, and students should have this concept reinforced by experiencing the joy of creativity.

DEVELOPING CREATIVITY

If a teacher expects children to be creative, she must introduce originality and personality into the teaching process. Some personalities are better suited to such emphasis and methods than others.

Through creativity, the child is stimulated to become a self-propelled learner, to develop habits of discovery and reflective thinking, and to increase retention of concepts. When children discover cognitive elements by themselves, the concepts are better retained and more easily retrieved for future use.

Another approach to encouraging creativity is for the teacher to set aside time at the beginning of a movement experience, before the child receives instruction, for the child to explore creatively. This usually involves a manipulatable object or piece of apparatus. For example, a child might be given a hoop and told, "Experiment with the different kinds of things you can do with it." Some educators believe strongly in this practice. They hold that direction stifles creativity and that the child should have the opportunity to try out, become familiar with, and explore the range of possibilities *before* more defined instruction occurs. Opposing this viewpoint are those who believe that only a low level of learning occurs without direction and that more productive and creative activity is possible when the teacher transmits simple basics before experimentation begins.

The teacher should provide creative opportunity during appropriate segments of the instructional sequence. This can take the form of asking children to add on to a movement progression just presented or to expand it in a new direction. Time for creativity should be designated in the lesson plan, and the lesson plan should be flexible enough to allow for creativity at teachable moments. A sound practice is allowing an opportunity for creativity after a few progressions have been established to give breadth to the movement patterns. Creativity is furthered by the judicious use of movement factors, particularly sequence building and continuity.

The creative process can be stimulated by a show-and-tell demonstration. After a period of exploration, emphasis should be on what types of movement patterns are possible when one creates. Children naturally observe others when they reach a block or are stymied in their thinking. Although concentration should be on developing one's own unique patterns, ideas from others can be a base on which to devise alternatives.

Creativity is an umbrella that can be superimposed on all activity. Care must be taken, however, to reject the premise that directed teaching is the antithesis of creativity and is disassociated from the creative process. For general movement patterns, choice can be injected early. For the more precise, specific skills, creativity can enter after the skills have been reasonably acquired. At that point, an exploratory approach leads to extension and better use of the practiced movement pattern.

PERSONALIZED LEARNING

Personalization means adjusting what is to be learned to the needs and characteristics of the learner. (See AAHPERD [1976] for a more detailed discussion of this concept.) Learners differ in many significant ways, and human variability must be a consideration in the teaching process. Children learn effectively at different rates and under different conditions. The task is to pace instruction at personalized rates and to offer a variety of instructional strategies using different conditions.

Several techniques help to personalize instruction. First, the teacher should physically or emotionally touch all children in the group. This means getting away from the traditional teaching position at the front of the class and moving among the children. The teacher should make it a point to reach every child during the presentation and to interact with each one both verbally and nonverbally. Such interaction is a strong motivating force. Recognizing and calling each child by name is fundamental to personalized instruction.

As a second technique, teacher comments should be perceptive and helpful. The teacher should focus on the specifics of what is good and what can be improved, rather than relying exclusively on general approvals such as "Good," "Fine," and so on.

A third means of personalizing instruction is to have enough equipment so each student can work at a task at his own pace. In addition, each child should have adequate opportunity to extend movement patterns. The start-and-expand technique (p. 360) provides personalization in the sense that every child achieves a measure of success. The slogan "There is always another way" applies: children have the opportunity to explore and find alternative solutions.

Personalization can also take the form of allowing options in the way responses are made to a challenge or in the way a skill is performed. Certainly inept or faulty movement responses should receive corrective attention, but it is equally important to give credit for a good individual effort and to call attention to achievement.

Finally, children should have opportunities to set their own goals. This obviates some of the justifiable criticism of the lockstep approach to fitness activities. In performing Curl-ups, for example, children can be allowed to set their own limits and to then strive toward the goal they themselves set.

TEACHING ENVIRONMENTS

How children are arranged or grouped for instruction is a decision that needs to be made early in the lesson-planning process. More than one arrangement can be used in a single lesson. The objectives and nature of the movement experiences, together with the space and equipment available, determine the type of grouping selected. There are three basic schemes, with numerous variations and subdivisions.

SINGLE-CHALLENGE FORMAT

In the single-challenge format, all children respond to the same challenge, whether as individuals, as partners, or as members of a group. This format allows the teacher to conduct the class according to a lesson plan that includes elements of guided progression. The single-challenge format is convenient for coaching and demonstrating, because all children are involved in similar activities.

Pacing is a problem with no easy solution, since the instruction must be personalized to meet each child's needs. Although individual children are recognized as having differences, yet the assumption is made that for all children at the same age a central core of activity is acceptable.

Many of the instructional procedures already discussed involve the single-challenge format, and for this reason, no further elaboration is made here.

MULTIPLE-GROUP (STATION) FORMAT

In the multiple-group (or station) format, the class is divided into two or more groups, each working on a different movement challenge. Some system of rotation is provided, and the children change from one activity to another.

Dividing a class into groups for station teaching is of value at times, particularly when supplies and apparatus are insufficient for an entire class to work on a single challenge. This arrangement can save time in providing apparatus experiences, because once the circuit is set, little change in apparatus is needed. The participants are changed, not the apparatus. Some system of rotation must be instituted, with changes either on signal or at will. Sometimes all stations are visited during a single class session, and in other cases, students make only a few station changes per session.

Class control and guidance sometimes become a problem with station format, since stopping the class to provide instruction and guidance is not practical. Two techniques can help. The first entails conducting the children, as a single group, around the circuit for a quick, preliminary orientation at each station. The second technique involves posting written guidelines at each station. The instructions should cover putting the station in order before moving on. These measures help make up for the fact that the teacher must divide her efforts over a number of stations. If a station has a safety hazard (e.g., rope climbing), the teacher may wish to devote more attention there.

The station format is well suited to theme development. Stations can be selected and materials provided to give students a thematic emphasis at each area. If creativity, exploration, and varied movement are primary goals, then station teaching is an effective format.

INDIVIDUAL-CHOICE FORMAT

In the individual-choice format, children select their movement experiences and rotate at will. They may get their equipment themselves or choose from pieces provided. This format should be used after children have established a basis for further exploration and creativity. They should be encouraged to practice on weak areas or to create beyond their present level. The period of individual choice should be one of creativity and development, not supervised free play.

Some teachers find the individual-choice format effective in the introductory activity section of the daily lesson. Occasionally, at the beginning of a class, the teacher can give the following directions: "For the first few minutes of our class period today, you may select and practice any movement pattern." The teacher can qualify this by enumerating the possibilities: "You may practice movements without equipment; you may select from the available balls, beanbags, wands, or hoops; or you may work on the climbing ropes, balance beams, or mats." A choice period can also be used to finish up a daily lesson or a unit of work. The choice can be limited to the activities and movements in the lesson or unit.

FORMATIONS FOR MOVEMENT AND SKILL INSTRUCTION

The teacher should devise an appropriate formation or arrangement to guide the children's learning experience in the intended activity. Different formations are needed for activities in place (nonlocomotor activities), activities in which children move (locomotor activities), and activities in which balls, beanbags, or other objects are thrown, kicked, caught, or otherwise received (manipulative activities). A number of formations have usefulness in more than one area.

MASS OR SCATTERED FORMATION

Children can be scattered throughout the area in random fashion so each student has his own personal space. This formation is useful for in-place activities and when individuals need to move in every direction. In locomotor movement, children should be courteous and avoid collisions. From the beginning, emphasis should be placed on not bumping into, colliding with, or interfering with other children. The scattered formation is basic to such activities as wands, hoops, individual rope jumping, and individual ball skills. Teachers must watch for children who go to the outskirts of the group and for close friends who gravitate to each other.

EXTENDED SQUAD FORMATION

Extended squad formation is a structured formation based on squad organization. In formal squad formation, members stand about 3 ft apart in a column. In extended formation, the squad column is maintained with more distance (10 to 15 ft) between members. Figure 7.4 shows a regular and an extended squad formation.

Regular Ⓛ XXXXXX

Extended Ⓛ X X X X X X

FIGURE 7.4. Regular and extended squad formation

PARTNER FORMATION

Partner formation is most important in throwing, catching, kicking, and receiving activities. One ball or object is needed for each pair. On the playground, where there is sufficient room, pairs can scatter. Indoors, keeping pairs aligned in somewhat parallel fashion minimizes problems with flying balls (Figure 7.5).

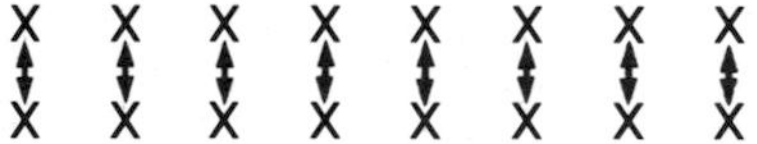

FIGURE 7.5. Partner formation

SMALL GROUPS (BY TWOS, THREES, OR FOURS)

The small-group formation is similar to the partner arrangement but includes a few more children. Children work together on either a fundamental movement problem or ball skills.

LANE OR FILE

Lane, or file, arrangement is the basic relay formation (Figure 7.6). It can be used for locomotor activity, with those in front moving as prescribed and then taking their place at the rear of the lane.

X X X X
X X X X
X X X X
X X X X
X X X X
X X X X

FIGURE 7.6. Lane, or file, formation

SQUAD FORMATION WITH LEADER

Squad formation with a leader (or lane-plus-one formation) is a useful relay formation, with possible minor application in skill practice. It has utility for throwing and catching skills. Each leader is positioned a short distance in front of the squad (Figure 7.7).

X X X X
X X X X
X X X X
X X X X
X X X X

Ⓛ Ⓛ Ⓛ Ⓛ

FIGURE 7.7. Squad formation with leader

SQUAD FORMATION RE-FORMING AT THE OTHER END OF THE SPACE

To re-form at the other end of the space from squad formation, the leading child in each squad begins his movement across the floor. When he is about halfway, the next child starts. The squad re-forms at the other end and gets ready for another movement (Figure 7.8).

Squad re-forms on this end

X X X X X
X X X X X
X X X X X
X X X X X
X X X X X
X X X X X

X X X X X
X X X X X
X X X X X
X X X X X
X X X X X
X X X X X

FIGURE 7.8. Squad formation re-forming at other end of space

LINE AND LEADER

Line-and-leader formation (Figure 7.9) is used often for throwing and catching skills. The leader passes back and forth to each line player in turn. It makes a nice revolving relay.

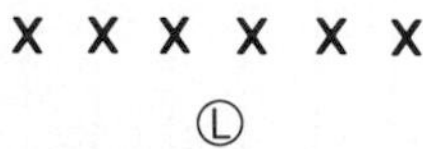

FIGURE 7.9. Line-and-leader formation

SEMICIRCLE AND LEADER

Semicircle-and-leader formation (Figure 7.10) is a variation of line and leader.

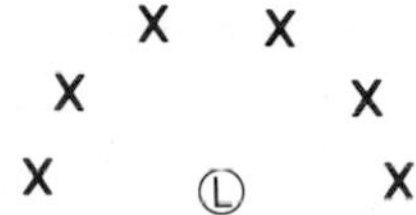

FIGURE 7.10. Semicircle-and-leader formation

CIRCLE

Circle formation (Figure 7.11) is useful for ball-handling skills such as passing, kicking, and volleying.

FIGURE 7.11. Circle formation

CIRCLE AND LEADER

Circle and leader is another ball-handling formation (Figure 7.12), which can serve as a basis for relays. The leader passes in turn to each member of the circle.

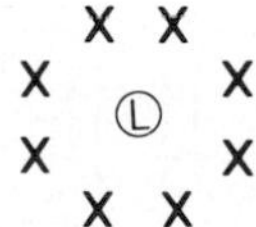

FIGURE 7.12. Circle-and-leader formation

DOUBLE LINE

Double-line formation is good for passing and kicking. Figure 7.13 shows a zigzag formation that is more efficient than positioning the corresponding players in each line opposite to each other. The ball is passed from one line to the next.

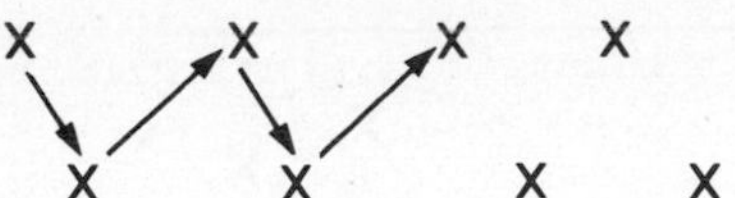

FIGURE 7.13. Double-line formation

REGULAR SHUTTLE FORMATION

In shuttle formation (Figure 7.14), the movement of the players is similar to that of a loom shuttle. The formation can be done with as few as three players, but more are generally used. It serves as the basis of passing and dribbling skills in hockey, soccer, and basketball, and of ball-carrying skills in football; it can also serve as a relay formation. Essentially, the player at the head of one line dribbles toward, or passes to, the player at the head of the other line. Each player keeps moving forward and takes a place at the end of the other half of the shuttle.

FIGURE 7.14. Regular shuttle formation

SHUTTLE TURN-BACK FORMATION

Shuttle turn-back formation (Figure 7.15) is used for passing, kicking, and volleying. The player at the head of one shuttle line passes to the player at the head of the other. After passing, each player goes to the back of her half of the shuttle.

FIGURE 7.15. Shuttle turn-back formation

SPECIAL FORMATIONS

The following special formations are useful for locomotor movements performed either around the room area or forward and backward. These formations are especially important in teaching fundamental locomotor skills.

AROUND THE AREA IN CIRCULAR FASHION

This formation has children moving about the area in a circular fashion (Figure 7.16). An objection to this arrangement is that it creates competition and generates conformity. Collisions, however, are not likely, and the teacher can observe the children more effectively.

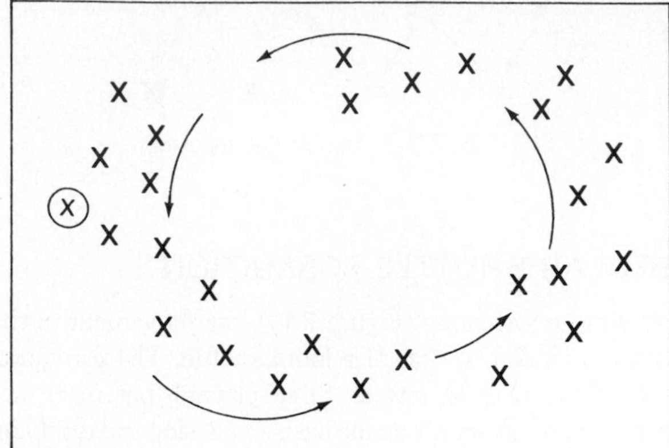

FIGURE 7.16. Moving around area in circular fashion

ON OPPOSITE SIDES, EXCHANGING POSITIONS

Children can also start on opposite sides of the gym and exchange positions (Figure 7.17). On signal, they cross to the opposite side of the area, passing through the opposite line without contact.

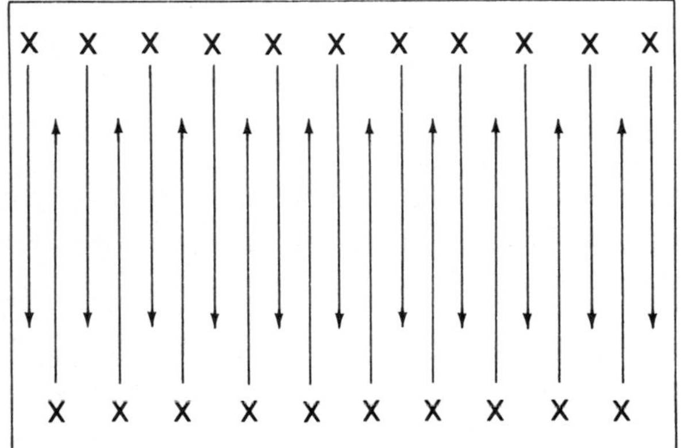

FIGURE 7.17. Exchanging positions on opposite sides

ON ADJACENT SIDES, CROSSING OVER

In another arrangement, children form in line on adjacent sides of the gym or area. The two lines of children then take turns crossing to the other side (Figure 7.18).

ON OPPOSITE SIDES, MOVING TO THE CENTER AND BACK

Another formation involves children starting on opposite sides and moving to the center and back. A line can be formed with ropes, wands, or cones to mark the center limit. Children move to the center of the area and then return to place (Figure 7.19).

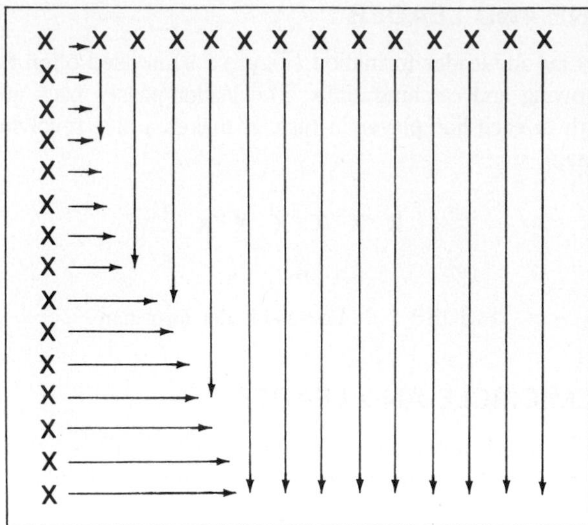

FIGURE 7.18. Crossing over on adjacent sides

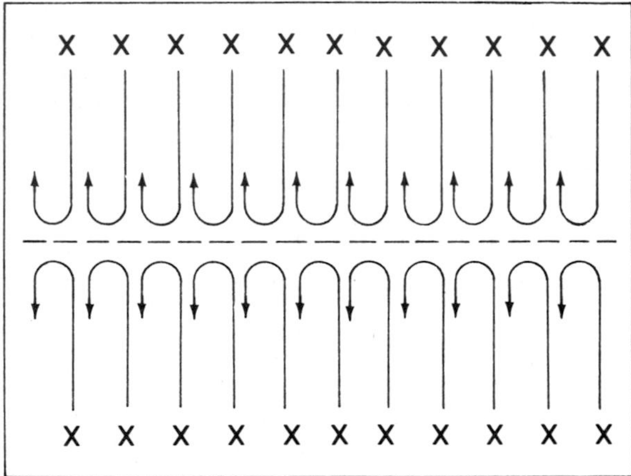

FIGURE 7.19. Moving to center and back on opposite sides

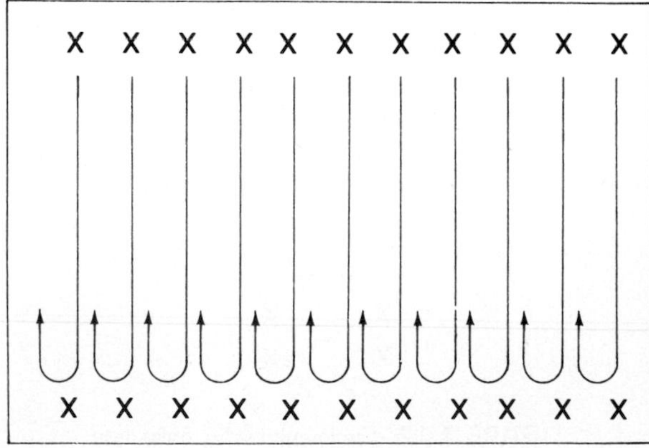

FIGURE 7.20. One line moving across and back on opposite sides

ON OPPOSITE SIDES, ONE LINE MOVING ACROSS AND BACK

In a variation of the previous movement, the two sides alternate turns. The line of children from one side crosses to a point near the other line, makes a turn, and then returns to place (Figure 7.20). After the one line has completed the movement, the other group takes a turn.

ON FOUR SIDES, EXCHANGING

The final formation has children starting on four sides and exchanging (Figure 7.21). The children on one pair of opposite sides exchange first, and then the others exchange. They alternate back and forth in this manner.

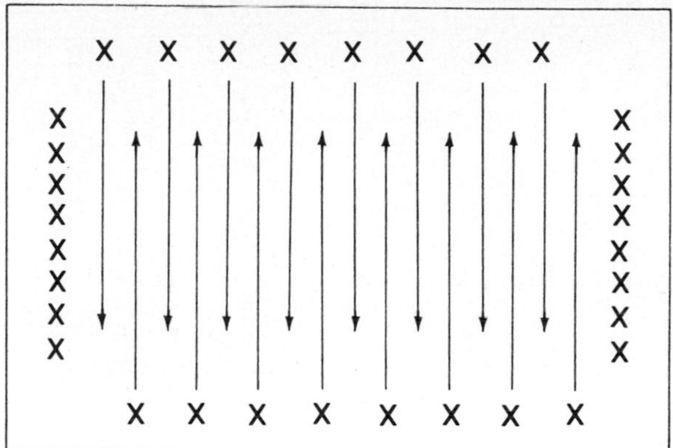

FIGURE 7.21. Exchanging on four sides

REFERENCE

AAHPERD. 1976. *Personalized learning in physical education.* Reston, Va.: AAHPERD.

CHAPTER 8

Divergent Movement: Developing Educational Movement Themes

The term *educational movement* is used to describe the educational approach to accomplishing divergent movement. It features a movement education approach using Laban's idea of themes. Educational movement is movement performed for its own sake, for increased awareness and understanding of the body as a vehicle for movement, and for the acquisition of a personal vocabulary of movement skills. It is the foundation of movement experiences and competencies. Gains for children, however, also come out of the teaching process by which movement goals are attained.

DEVELOPING GENERAL MOVEMENT PATTERNS

The following analysis of movement describes the overall movement patterns of the body in terms of four questions. When the four questions are answered, the parameters of the desired educational movement patterns can be established.

WHAT CAN THE BODY DO?

The possible movements of the body can be divided into two categories—locomotor and nonlocomotor movement. *Locomotor movements* transfer the weight from one body part to another in order to achieve linear movement. The ways that a child can move from here to there are innumerable and can provide many movement experiences. *Nonlocomotor movements* include the many ways that the body can be supported or balanced. One or more parts of the body can be anchored, while other body parts move with or against each other. Reaching, pulling, twisting, contracting, raising, and lowering are some of the nonlocomotor movements that a child can experience.

The development of body awareness depends on experience in specific locomotor and nonlocomotor movements and on experimentation with other body capabilities, such as assuming various shapes (e.g., curled, stretched, twisted, wide, and narrow). Knowing the names and locations of the separate parts of the body must come before any understanding of the functions and possibilities of movement can be achieved.

WITH WHAT AND WITH WHOM DOES THE CHILD MOVE?

Part of the child's movement experience is her relationship with the physical environment in which she moves (gymnasium, classroom, or playground), with the equipment she uses, and with the way she works (with other children or by herself).

The child must first learn to move with competence and to manage himself and a piece of equipment without interfering with other children. Only after the child has learned to handle himself reasonably well as an individual can he learn to work with another child. Finally, he develops a sensitivity to others and learns to work in a group, sharing experiences and judgments in a give and take situation that leads to greater social maturity.

WHERE CAN THE BODY MOVE?

Space has two aspects—general and personal. In general space, the child moves with consideration for others in executing locomotor movements. In personal space, the child is concerned only with her own movements. Some space factors are direction, level, pattern, size, and plane of movement.

HOW CAN THE BODY MOVE?

In addition to space factors, time, quality (or force), flow, and body factors are involved in movement. Time includes variation in speed (acceleration and deceleration) and rhythm. Qualities of movement include force of movement, expressive movement, and imitative movement. Flow can be either sustained (free) or interrupted (bound). Body factors describe the body and its parts in relation to the movement.

METHODOLOGY FOR TEACHING EDUCATIONAL MOVEMENT THEMES

In practice, educational movement is organized around themes, which can be categorized according to the general movement factors of space, time, force, flow, and the body. A theme of spatial movement might ask the child to explore different ways of moving in a specific direction or at a certain level. Time is featured in a theme asking the child to move at a fast or slow pace. A focus on flow is achieved by asking the child to link movements together in a particular way. Body factors can be related to the use of different parts of the body for support or movement.

Themes are seldom experienced in isolation. To some degree, the movement factors are characteristic of all movements. At times, however, one or more factors are given special attention and become the core of a lesson.

With younger children, the movement experiences are quite general, and identifying the different themes is not easy. During the primary years and later, the instruction can be guided toward more specific theme development.

The teacher must structure a learning environment in such a way that children learn to think for themselves and to accept a large part of the responsibility for their own learning. Through the process of acquiring movement competency, children should learn to follow directions, to listen, to think, and to solve movement problems in their own ways. The teacher should not dominate the lesson but should stimulate the children to use their own ideas in the movement experiences.

To the extent that the child expresses himself individually in movement, he can achieve a satisfactory measure of success for himself rather than simply fulfilling teacher-dominated or group standards. The child progresses according to innate abilities, stimulated by the teacher and the learning situation. No child need feel awkward or self-conscious because his performance does not measure up to predetermined standards. The fact that children differ in size, shape, maturity, and motor ability does not preclude success and satisfaction.

The emphasis in educational movement should be on activity and movement of a purposeful nature, with both quantity and quality of movement encouraged. Only in this way does movement become a sound educational experience. Too often, children undergo experiences without the necessary guidance and without the teacher's insistence that they perform the movement as well as possible. Care must be taken that doing movements in different ways does not deemphasize the value of performing well. We question the premise that the child's own choices about movement experiences are the overriding concern. The teacher's broader base of experience can be of great value to the child. A child should be encouraged to continue to experiment even after arriving at a solution that is satisfactory to her. There may be other effective ways, even a better way, to do something.

Some other values grow out of the process of selection. Children should be able not only to move with ease and efficiency but also to analyze critically their own movements and those of others. As a result, it is postulated that a safer learning environment will result, because children are neither forced nor urged to go beyond their capacities. They choose and perform individually when they have decided that they are ready.

EXPANDING MOVEMENT AND SECURING VARIETY OF RESPONSE

Space, time, qualities of movement, flow, and body factors are important ingredients in educational movement. Through their application in coaching and by suggestion, these elements are the means by which the teacher brings out the child's movement potential and develops the child's awareness of movement. Skill in the application of these factors is most essential if variety and depth of movement are to be attained. These elements can enhance the value of any teaching approach or style of teaching. Frequent reference is made to them throughout this book.

Space Factors

Space factors involve directions, level, relationship, pattern, size, plane of movement, and internal directionality. These can be varied as follows.

Direction—straight, zigzag, circular, curved, forward, backward, sideward, upward, and downward

Level—low, high, or in between

Relationship—above, below, near, far, ahead of, behind, over, under, through, in front of, to the side of, around, overhead, underneath

Pattern—squares, diamonds, triangles, circles, figure eights, and others

Size—large, small, or in between

Plane of movement—horizontal, vertical, or diagonal

Internal directionality—front and back, top and bottom, sides, and right-left discrimination

Time Factors

The time factor may be varied as follows.

Different speeds—slow, moderate, or fast
Acceleration or deceleration—increasing or decreasing the speed of movement
Rhythm—sudden, jerky, smooth, or even, and variation in rhythm

Force Factors (Qualities of Movement)

Three force factors or qualities of movement are important.

Force—light or heavy, strong or weak, sudden or sustained
Expressive movement—happy or sad, gay or restrained, angry or tranquil, rough or gentle
Imitative movement—imitating animals, personalities, machines, fictitious characters

Flow Factors

The flow factor establishes continuity of movement.

Interrupted flow (bound flow)—stopping at the end of a movement or part of a movement
Sustained flow (free flow)—linking together smoothly different movements or parts of a movement

Body Factors

A number of considerations in the use of the body can add variety to movement.

Shape—long or short, wide or narrow, straight or twisted, stretched or curled, symmetrical or asymmetrical
Weight bearing—different parts of the body supporting the weight or receiving the weight, different numbers of body parts involved in a movement or as body support
Execution—unilateral (one-sided), bilateral (both sides together), or cross-lateral (arm and leg on opposite sides)
Body-center orientation—leading with different parts of the body, moving away from or toward the center of the body
Body zones—front, back, right side, left side, upper body, lower body, center of gravity

WORKING ON APPARATUS

In addition to the factors just presented, variety in movement as the children work on large apparatus can be stimulated in the following ways.

1. Apparatus can be arranged in different sequences, combination, and numbers (Figure 8.1). Benches and balance beams, for example, can be placed on an incline, suspended higher than normal, or placed in combination with other equipment.

2. With apparatus work, a three-step process can be instituted. First, various ways to get on the apparatus are stipulated. Second, movements to do on the apparatus can be varied. For example, the teacher challenges the child to go over, under, around, or through the apparatus. The child can support her body in different fashions, using a variety of body factors. Finally, different means of dismounting, or getting off the apparatus, are specified.

3. Apparatus work can be combined with other activities. Combined activities might include one or more types of apparatus, as well as stations centering on manipulative activities or fitness challenges as part of a circuit. Such combinations are convenient when not enough pieces of apparatus are available to serve all children in single-activity organization.

EXTENDING MOVEMENT THROUGH CONTRASTING TERMS

Another means of increasing the child's understanding of movement possibilities is to employ terms that stress contrasts. The following list includes many common sets of contrasting terms that express either relationships between movements or descriptions of ways to move.

Above—below, beneath, under
Across—around, under
Around clockwise—around counterclockwise
Before—after
Between—alongside of
Big—little, small
Close—far
Crooked—straight
Curved—flat, straight
Diagonal—straight
Fast—slow
Forward—back, backward
Front—back, behind
Graceful—awkward
Heavy—light
High—low
In—out
In front of—behind, in back of
Inside—outside
Into—out of
Large—small
Near—far
On—off
On top of—under, underneath

FIGURE 8.1. Climbing frames combined with benches

Over—under, through
Right—left
Round—straight
Separate—together
Short—long, tall
Sideways—forward, backward
Smooth—rough
Sudden—sustained
Swift—slow
Tight—loose
Tiny—big, large
Top—bottom
To the right of—to the left of
Up—down
Upper—lower
Upside down—right side up
Upward—downward
Wide—narrow, thin
Zigzag—straight

Some of the terms may be grouped more logically in sets of three contrasts (e.g., forward—sideways—backward, up—down—in between, over—under—through). Word meanings also can be emphasized according to rank or degree (e.g., near—nearer—nearest, low—lower—lowest).

The use of contrasting terms is a fine basis for movement themes; children gain an understanding of the terms and learn to translate them into movement. Contrasting terms also provide a way for teachers to create variety. Instead of challenging a child to move fast, for example, the teacher guides him to contrast a fast movement with a slow movement.

PHRASING THE CHALLENGE OR THE QUESTION

Stimulating an effective movement response from children depends on the phrasing of the problem. Problems can be presented in the form of questions or statements that elicit and encourage variety, depth, and extent of movement.

Presenting a Problem

The following phrases illustrate challenging ways to present a problem.

1. Show me how a . . . moves. (Show me how an alligator moves.)

2. Have you seen a . . . ? (Have you seen a kangaroo jump?)

3. What ways can you . . . ? (What ways can you hop over the jump rope?)

4. How would you . . . ? How can you . . . ? (How would you dribble a ball, changing hands frequently?)

5. See how many different ways you can. . . . (See how many different ways you can hang from a ladder.)

6. What can you do with a . . . ? What kinds of things can you . . . ? (What can you do with a hoop?)

7. Can you portray a . . . ? (Can you portray an automobile with a flat tire?)

8. Discover different ways you can. . . . (Discover different ways you can volley a ball against a wall.)

9. Can you . . . ? (Can you keep one foot up while you bounce the ball?)

10. Who can . . . a . . . in such a way that . . . ? (Who can bounce a ball in such a way that it keeps time with the tom-tom?)

11. What does a . . . ? (What does a cat do when it is wet?)

12. Show . . . different ways to. . . . (Show four different ways to move across the floor.)

Securing Variety or Setting a Limitation

To stimulate alternatives or to impose a limitation, the following models are useful.

1. Try it again another way. Try to. . . . (Try to jump higher.)

2. See how far (many times, high, close, low). . . . (See how far you can reach with your arms.)

3. Find a way to . . . or find a new way to. . . . (Find a new way to jump over the bench.)

4. Apply . . . to. . . . (Apply a heavy movement to your run.)

5. How else can you . . . ? (How else can you roll your hoop?)

6. Make up a sequence. . . . (Make up a sequence of previous movements, changing smoothly from one movement to the other.)

7. Now try to combine a . . . with. . . . (Now try to combine a locomotor movement with your catching.)

8. Alternate . . . and. . . . (Alternate walking and hopping.)

9. Repeat the last movement, but add. . . . (Repeat the last movement, but add a body twist as you move.)

10. See if you can. . . . (See if you can do the movement with a partner.)

11. Trace (draw) a . . . with. . . . (Trace a circle with your hopping partner.)

12. Find another part of the body to. . . . Find other ways to. . . . (Find another part of the body to take the weight.)

13. Combine the . . . with. . . . (Combine the hopping with a body movement.)

14. In how many different positions can you . . . ? (In how many different positions can you carry your arms while walking the balance beam?)

15. How do you think the . . . would change if . . . ? (How do you think the balance exercise we are doing would change if our eyes were closed?)

16. On signal, . . . (On signal, speed up your movements.)

STIMULATING EFFORT

While stimulating variation does in a sense spur the children on to a better effort, it is also important for children to extend themselves within the movement itself. This is why the movement problem includes incentives, such as asking them to carry out tasks as far as possible or with abrupt or definite changes. Although competition among individuals is not an accepted concept in movement education, some challenges like "How far can you reach?" and "How far can you jump?" lend themselves to measurement. The number of floorboards covered or reached could be counted. The children can also use beanbags or other markers and place them as far away as they can possibly reach. The device of having children stretch or reach until they pull themselves from their base makes them extend their limits.

GIVING DEFINITIVE DIRECTIONS

Many of the previously presented directives for movement are open-ended statements calling for indefinite responses. Challenges asking for a specific number of responses should also be employed. The directive might use this form: "Find three different ways you can . . . ," or "Put together your sequence in two different ways." These challenges offer a definite objective, which prevents a student from becoming overly concerned about how many different ways are "enough." The element of success then becomes measurable. Specific directives are particularly useful when working with mentally retarded youngsters.

INSTRUCTIONAL SEQUENCES FOR IMPLEMENTING EDUCATIONAL MOVEMENT THEMES

This explorational approach, designed for teaching educational movement, also has value when the class is working with simple, fundamental convergent skills, such as introductory and low-level manipulative skills. The unique nature of educational movement dictates specialized instructional sequences so the movement objectives can be realized.

Five steps are suggested for development of educational movement outcomes, with the goals and progressions determining the sequence and depth of each step. The first two steps are reasonably fixed in the sequence, but the other three can be interchanged or one or more can be omitted, depending on lesson development. The instructional process can be keyed by the following directions: "Explore," "Discover and expand," "Analyze and select," and "Repeat and extend."

STEP ONE: SETTING AND DEFINING THE PROBLEM

The first step defines the problem for the student, setting the stage, focus, and limitations. The focus can be within broad or narrow limitations. It might elicit an exploratory response. The WHAT, WHERE, and HOW need definition.

What is the child to do? An action word must be supplied. In divergent movement, is the child to move a certain way, go over and under, explore alternatives, or experiment with some nonlocomotor movement? She may be directed to run, jump, or use some fundamental skill (convergent movement) in some particular way. With whom is the child to work—by herself, with a partner, or as a member of a group? Is there a choice involved? With what equipment or on what apparatus is the child to perform?

Where is the child to move? This is the spatial aspect. What space is to be used—personal or general? What directional factors are to be employed—path, level?

How is the child to move? What are the force factors (light—heavy, sudden—sustained)? What elements of time are involved (even—uneven, acceleration—deceleration)? What are the relationships (over—under—across, in front of—behind)? What body parts are involved for support? For locomotion?

In initiating divergent movement patterns, the challenge can be stated like this: "Let's see you move across the floor, changing direction as you wish, with a quick movement with one foot and a slow movement with the other."

As a basis for convergent movement, the teacher can say, "Show me how you can run in general space, changing directions and level at the same time, when I sound the drumbeat." If they are deemed appropriate, hints on technique can be added: "Remember to run lightly on your toes with a slight body lean and with your head up."

Contrasting terms can be a part of the original theme format, or they can be introduced in the second step.

STEP TWO: INCREASING VARIETY AND DEPTH OF MOVEMENT

The second step challenges the children's creativity and thinking processes. This step enhances their movements, provides depth to their experiences, increases variety of response, and encourages individual choice. Securing variety of response means that the teacher should insert challenges and suggestions that are based on factors for expanding movement discussed earlier in this chapter (pp. 82–83).

The teacher needs to develop effective techniques of observation and analysis to modify movement patterns through perceptive guidance. Coaching can be individual or group oriented.

In addition to using the factors for promoting variety, the teacher can encourage the children to expand their movement possibilities by asking them to find other ways to do the movement, since the original challenge may have been met by a single response. The teacher also can specify the number of responses desired.

STEP THREE: DEVELOPING QUALITY IN MOVEMENT

Although movement quality should be considered throughout the process, the third step gives special attention to quality. Too often, children are not encouraged to perform as well as they possibly can; their movement experiences often achieve only variety of movement and not quality.

Variety provides an important basis for the child's selection of a preferred movement pattern. Since there is no "right way" in divergent movement, the child must be guided to select the movement pattern that he deems the most efficient or the best and to consider such general characteristics as lightness, smoothness, efficient use and flow of different body parts, rhythm, and coordination. Attention must also be given to mechanical principles as they relate to the selected movement themes (see pp. 88–96). In teaching fundamental skills, add stress points to guide the child toward techniques appropriate to the skill involved.

All of the activities described in this text should be taught with an emphasis on performance quality. Children should be encouraged to choose freely and to practice freely, and to reach an understanding of their movement capabilities. They should not be made to conform to artificial standards.

STEP FOUR: BUILDING SEQUENCES AND COMBINING MOVEMENT PATTERNS

As a fourth step, the child can select certain movements that have been practiced and put them together in sequence, looking for good transition (flow) from one movement pattern to another. The child is challenged to imagine how she can put the movements together. In this step, either the child selects the movements and the number of movements to put in combination, or the teacher specifies some limitation on the number of combinations, the types of movement, or the order in which they are sequenced.

Achievement demonstrations are an excellent way to stimulate effort, since children love to show what they have put together. These demonstrations provide ideas and give the children a rough standard against which they can compare their own movement patterns.

The magic-number idea is also an excellent device for developing sequences. The directive might be: "Today our magic number is ten. Put together a sequence in which you link three different types of movement together so they total ten. (This could be three of one movement, four of another, and three of a third.) You choose your combination." Or the teacher can say, "The magic number is three. Put together three different types of movement, each of which is repeated three times."

STEP FIVE: CULMINATING ACTIVITY

Working with others is an important social goal, and partner and small-group work, used as a fifth step, can expand instructional opportunities. Here are some suggestions for working with a partner.

1. One child serves as an obstacle while his partner uses him in the development of a theme. The moving partner can go over, under, or around the stationary partner.

2. Partners observe and evaluate each other's movements. Observation should center on points that have been discussed, otherwise the critique might be of little value. The critique can serve as a learning device to enhance cognitive elements of both the observer and the performer.

3. Imitative movement is another possibility. One child performs a pattern and the other reproduces it, either by itself or as part of a sequence.

4. Children work together as partners to perform simultaneous parallel movements.

5. A child works cooperatively with a partner to form different shapes, designs, forms, letters, and figures, either in upright positions or on the floor.

6. Throwing and catching skills are greatly enhanced by partner work.

7. One partner supports wholly or partially the other's weight.

Group work should go beyond the accomplishments of individuals or partners. In educational movement, groups should be kept small (from three to six members), or too much time is devoted to getting the group organized and not enough time is spent on achieving movement goals.

Games and relays serve as vehicles for participation in newly experienced skills. Creative games are another excellent medium for the realistic extension of skill practice. An individual activity, a partner activity, or a small-group game can be created on the basis of skill development of the movement factor just experienced.

EXAMPLES OF EDUCATIONAL MOVEMENT THEMES

Lessons in educational movement stress development through selected themes. A movement theme focuses on a movement quality around which children build patterns and sequences. The purpose is to explore and experiment with the theme, gain a thorough understanding of the movement quality, and develop body awareness in the movement area. Development usually employs fundamental skills, which become concomitant movement goals related to the central movement theme.

Success is possible in educational movement as long as children move within the theme definition. They are allowed considerable latitude in movement patterns. Movement responses, however, must go beyond the challenge of "How many different ways can you . . . ?" A main goal for the teacher is to guide the child toward the best response that he is capable of producing. Quality must not be neglected in the interest of getting children to respond in different ways.

Theme development, as presented, uses few supplies and minimal equipment. Many themes can be developed by employing floor and wall-attached apparatus. Attention is given to this concept in the discussions of apparatus (Chapter 20), so this phase is not covered here.

Themes are identified by their contribution to general movement concepts of space, time, qualities of movement (force), flow, and body factors. Some themes draw from more than one area.

In most cases, formations for the children are not specified here. The teacher is referred to the section on teaching formations (pp. 76–79) for suggestions.

Care must be taken to express ideas and movement in correct terminology. When terminology is new or unfamiliar to the children, explanations should be given. The cognitive potential should be exploited whenever feasible. We have noted this in some of the movement descriptions, with particular attention to the explanation of prefixes.

Divergent movement themes are grouped under three classifications. Basic themes provide the foundation on which other themes are then developed. Early in movement development and concept acquisition, attention should be focused on establishing a knowledge of body parts and a good understanding of the concepts of personal and general space.

Themes for understanding the elements of movement are the second area of emphasis and constitute the bulk of the themes, which collectively cover Laban's movement elements and concepts. Some themes involve only a single movement principle or factor, while others involve two or more.

We have attempted to be specific in exploring the elements of movement, but in actuality, isolating a particular factor is difficult. For example, in exploring balance, movement possibilities are expanded through the application of body shape, level, and time factors. Since these three elements are often employed to broaden movement in other themes, they are given attention first, and are followed by the other elements in alphabetical order.

Some planners like to identify a main lesson theme and then to list a number of subthemes to be given attention. This is unnecessary and undesirable, because focus on the main theme is subordinated to the subthemes. By strongly emphasizing the theme under development, better application and achievement of the selected theme is realized.

Themes for expanded movement combinations are the third classification and cover three subcategories: (1) flow-sequencing and movement combinations, (2) cooperative partner activities, and (3) group activities. Flow-sequencing and movement combinations can be flexible in nature, which provides considerable student choice, or they can be specified by the teacher. Partner work and small-group activity, to a lesser degree, are possible with most themes. For example, partners can match each other's movements in the development of a theme. One partner matches the other in a particular balance position, traveling in general space or transferring weight. Some curriculum specialists like to include partner and group interactions in each daily lesson regime. A basic guideline, however, is that children should perform with a partner or as members of a group only those activities that could not be done individually.

BASIC THEMES

Body Awareness

Body awareness refers to knowing the name of the various body parts, to one's internal sense of the location of each part, and to the ability to control each part independently or in conjunction with others. The following body parts are to be learned.

1. Head—forehead, face, eyes, cheeks, eyebrows, nose, mouth, ears, jaw, chin, eyelashes, lips, hair

2. Upper body—neck, shoulders, chest, back, stomach, arms, forearms, elbows, wrists, hands, fingers, thumbs, palms

3. Lower body—waist, abdomen, hips, seat, thighs, knees, ankles, feet, arches, toes, heels, soles

Theme development can proceed as follows:

"We are going to see whether you can touch the body part I name. I will say, 'Touch your hips.' As soon as you do this, you reply to me, 'I am touching my hips.' "

Note: This approach is especially effective with kindergarten youngsters. It works particularly well when the teacher alternates from the head and upper body to the lower body so the children need to make gross motor changes.

"We are going to try some special ways of touching. Raise your right hand as high as you can—now down. Raise your left hand as high as you can—now down. Touch your left (or right) shoulder (elbow, knee, hip, ankle) with the right (or left) hand." (Try many combinations.)

"Now, point to a door (window, ceiling, basket) with an elbow (thumb, toe, knee, nose). Let's see if you can remember right and left. Point your left (or right) elbow to the window." (Try different combinations.)

"When I name a body part, let's see if you can make this the highest part of your body without moving from your place."

"Now, the next task is a little more difficult. Move in a straight line for a short distance and keep the body part named above all the other body parts. What body parts would be difficult to keep above all others?" (Possibilities are the eyes, both ears, both hips.)

"Touch the highest part of your body with your right hand. Touch the lowest part of your body with your left hand."

"Let's see if you can locate some of the bones in your body. When I name a bone, hold that bone, move and touch a wall, and return to your spot." (These challenges are dependent on bones that the children can identify. The same procedure can be used to identify selected muscles.)

"Now move around the room, traveling any way you wish." (The movement can also be limited.) "The signal to stop will be a word describing a body part. Can you stop and immediately put both hands on that part or parts?" (Or, "On *'Stop,'* hide the body part.") "You are to move around the room again. When I call out a body part, find a partner and place the body parts together."

"Toss your beanbag in the air. When I call out a body part, sit down quickly, and put the beanbag on that part, or on one of the parts named."

"This time, when I call out a body part, you are to move around the room as you wish, while holding with one hand a named body part. When I call out another name, change the type of movement and hold the part with the other hand as you move. Now I will call out two body parts. Have the parts touch each other." (This theme develops concepts of body awareness, space, and level.)

Exploring Personal Space

A graphic way to illustrate personal space is to have youngsters take an individual jump rope and double it. From a kneeling position, they swing it in a full arc along the floor. It should not touch another child or rope.

"Show us how big your space is. Keeping one foot in place, outline how much space you can occupy. Sit cross-legged and outline your space. Support your weight on different parts of your body and outline your space."

"Make yourself as wide (narrow, small, large, low, high) as possible. Try these from different positions—kneeling, balancing on the seat, and others. Show us what kinds of body positions you can assume while you stand on one foot. While you lie on your stomach. On your seat. Try the same with one foot and one hand touching the floor."

"Move from a lying position to a standing position without using your arms or hands. Return to lying."

"Can you stay in one place and move your whole self but not your feet? Sway back and forth with your feet together and then with your feet apart. Which is better?"

"In a supine position (on your back) move your arms and legs from one position slowly and then move them back quickly to where you started. Explore other positions."

"Keeping one part of your body in place, make as big a circle as you can with the rest of your body."

"Explore different positions while you keep one leg (foot) higher than the rest of your body. Work out a smooth sequence of three different positions."

"Pump yourself up like a balloon, getting bigger and bigger. Hold until I say, 'Bang!' "

"In your personal space, show me how a top spins. Keep your feet together in place. With your arms wide to the sides, twist and make your feet turn."

Note: Children should adjust their personal space so they do not intrude on the space of others. (This develops space and body factors.)

Moving in General Space

Goals in these movement experiences, in addition to developing movement competence, should also enhance (1) the ability to share space with other children, (2) the ability to move through space without bumping anyone, and (3) the ability to develop consideration for the safety of others.

"Run lightly in the area, changing direction without bumping or touching anyone until I call 'Stop.' Raise your hand if you were able to do this without bumping into anyone."

"Let's try running zigzag fashion in the area without touching anyone. This time, when I blow the whistle, change direction abruptly and change the type of movement."

"Run lightly in general space and pretend you are dodging someone. Can you run toward another runner and change direction to dodge?"

"Get a beanbag and drop it to mark your personal space. See how lightly, while under control, you can run throughout the area. When the signal is given, run to your spot, pick up your beanbag, put it on your head, and sit down (or give some other challenge). Try this skipping."

"We are going to practice orienteering (explain the term). Point to a spot on the wall, and see whether you can run directly to it in a straight line. You may have to stop and wait for others to pass so as not to bump into anyone, but you cannot change direction. Stay in a straight line. When you get to your spot, pick another spot, and repeat."

"What happens when general space is decreased? You had no problem running without touching anyone in the large space. Now let's divide the area in half with cones. Run lightly within this area so as not to touch or bump anyone. Now it's going to get more difficult. I'm going to divide the space in half once more, but first let's try walking in the new area. Now, run lightly." (Decrease the area as feasible.)

"Get a beanbag and mark your personal space. Run around the beanbag until you hear a 'Bang,' and then explode in a straight direction until I call 'Stop.' Return to your personal space."

"From your beanbag, take five (or more) jumps (hops, skips, gallops, slides) and stop. Turn to face home, and return with the same number of movements. Take the longest steps you can away from home, and then return home with tiny steps."

"Show me how well you can move with these combinations in general space: run—jump—roll, skip—spin—collapse. Now you devise a series of any three movements and practice them."

"Today our magic number is five. Can you move in any direction with five repetitions of a movement? Change direction and pick another movement to do five times. Continue."

"Blow yourself up like a soap bubble. Can you huff and puff? Think of yourself as a big bubble that is floating around. When I touch you, the bubble breaks, and you collapse to the ground. This time, blow up your bubble and float around. When you are ready, say, 'Pop,' so the bubble bursts."

"I am going to challenge you on right and left movements. Show me how you can change to the correct direction when I say either 'Right' or 'Left.' Now begin running lightly."

"This time, see whether you can run rapidly toward another child, stop, and bow to each other. Instead of bowing, shake hands, and say, 'How do you do!' "

"From your personal space, pick a spot on a wall. See whether you can run to the spot, touch it, and return without bumping anyone. This time, it's more difficult. Pick spots on two different walls, touch these in turn, and return."

THEMES FOR UNDERSTANDING ELEMENTS OF MOVEMENT

Body Shapes (Figure 8.2)

"Let's try making shapes and see whether we can name them. Make any shape you wish and hold it. What is the name of your shape, John? (Wide.) Try to make different kinds of wide shapes. Show me other shapes you can make. What is the name of your shape, Susie? (Crooked.) Show me different kinds of shapes that are crooked."

FIGURE 8.2. Forming different shapes

"Make yourself wide and then narrow. Now tall and then small. How about tall and wide, small and narrow, tall and narrow, and small and wide. Work out other combinations."

"Select three different kinds of shapes and move smoothly from one to another. This time I will clap my hands as a signal to change to a different shape."

"Select four different letters of the alphabet. On the floor, make your body shape successively like these letters. Try with numbers. Make up a movement sequence that spells a word of three letters. Show us a problem in addition or subtraction."

"Jump upward, making a shape in the air. Land, holding that shape. Begin with a shape, jump upward with a half turn, and land in another shape."

Note: Emphasize the kinds of shapes and reinforce the concept by having the children practice each kind of shape. This exercise can be divided into shapes formed while erect and shapes formed on the floor. (This theme develops body and flow factors.)

Levels

"Choose one way of traveling at a high level and another at a low level. Again, move at a high level and stop at a low level. Move at a low level and stop at a high level. Choose one way of traveling at a medium level and add this somewhere in your sequence—beginning, middle, or end."

"Select three different kinds of traveling movement with the arms at a high, medium, and low level. Link these movements together in a smooth sequence."

"Move on all fours with your body at a high level, a medium level, and then as low as possible. Try these movements with your face turned to the ceiling."

"Use a jump rope or a line or board in the floor as your path to follow. Begin at the far end. Show me a slow, low-level movement down and back. What other ways can you go down and back slowly and at a low level? Change to a fast, high-level movement. On what other levels can you move?"

"Combine a low, fast movement down with a high, slow movement on the way back. Explore other combinations. Make different movements by leading with different parts of your body."

Note: Each child has a path outlined by a rope, line, or board with a length of from 8 to 10 ft. This activity can also be organized by means of selected formations (pp. 75–79). The child soon realizes that if she exists in space, she must be at some level. The concept of level can be integrated in most movement challenges that emphasize other elements. (This theme develops space, time, and body factors.)

Time (Speed)

Speed involves the pace of action, which can be slow, fast, or any degree in between. Speed involves acceleration and deceleration, that is, the time factor can be either constant or employ acceleration or deceleration. Time also can be even or uneven.

"With your arms, do a selected movement slowly and then quickly. Move your feet slowly and then as rapidly as you can. Change your support base and repeat."

"In turn, stretch a part of your body slowly and then return it to place quickly, like a rubber band snapping. Stretch the entire body as wide as possible and snap it back to a narrow shape."

"Choose a way of traveling across the floor quickly and then do the same movement slowly. Do a fast movement in one direction and, on signal, change to a slow movement in another direction."

"Select a magic number between 10 and 20. Do that many slow movements and repeat with fast movements of the same count."

"Choose a partner. With your partner a little bit away from you, begin moving rapidly toward your partner and decelerate as you draw close. Move away by beginning slowly and accelerate until you return to where you started. Repeat. Select the kinds of movement you wish to use together."

"Staying in your own personal space, begin with some kind of movement and accelerate until you are moving as fast as you can. Reverse by beginning with a fast movement and then slow down until you are barely moving. Put together a sequence of two movements by beginning with one and accelerating, then changing to another movement and decelerating. Try doing two different body movements at the same time—one that accelerates and one that decelerates."

Note: Time concepts can be stressed by relating this movement to a car with its accelerator and brakes. Acceleration and deceleration can be combined with many types of movement and challenges. Explain the prefixes of the two words. (This theme develops time and flow factors.)

Balancing (Figure 8.3)

"Explore different ways you can balance on different surfaces of your body. Can you balance on three different parts of your body? On two? On one? Put together sequences of three or four balance positions by using different body parts or different numbers of body parts."

"Can you balance on a flat body surface? What is the smallest part of the body that you can balance on? Support the body on two dissimilar parts. On three dissimilar parts. Support the body on different combinations of body flats and body points."

FIGURE 8.3. Balancing on different body parts

"Use two parts of the body far away from each other to balance. Shift smoothly to another two parts."

"Balance on parts of the body forming a tripod (explain the term)."

"In a hands and knees position and later in a crab position, balance on the right arm and right leg, the left arm and left leg, the right arm and left leg, the left arm and right leg."

"Stand on your toes and balance, using different arm positions."

"Place a beanbag on the floor. How many different ways can you balance over it? Try with a hoop. How many different ways can you balance inside the hoop?"

"When I call out a body part or parts, you balance for 5 seconds on that part or part combinations." (Use knees, hands, heels, flats, points, and a variety of combinations.)

"Keep your feet together and sway in different directions without losing your balance. Can you balance on one foot with your eyes closed? Bend forward while balancing on one foot? Lift both sets of toes from the floor and balance on your heels? Now sit on the floor. Can you lift your feet and balance on your seat without hand support? Can you balance on your tummy without your feet or hands touching the floor?"

"In a standing position, thrust one leg out sideways and balance on the other foot."

Note: This theme could also be called SUPPORTING BODY WEIGHT. Balance positions should be maintained for 3 to 5 seconds before changing. The theme develops force and body factors.

Bridges (Figure 8.4)

"Show me a bridge made by using your hands and feet. What other kinds of bridges can you make? Can you make a bridge using only three body parts? Only two?"

"Show me a wide bridge. A narrow one. A short bridge. A long one. How about a high bridge? A low one? Can you make a bridge that opens when a boat goes through. Get a partner to be the boat and you be the bridge. If you are the boat, choose three ways of traveling under a bridge. Each time the boat goes under the bridge, the bridge should change to another means of support."

FIGURE 8.4. Making bridges

"Show me a bridge at a high level. At a low level. In between."

"Work up a sequence of bridge positions, going smoothly from one to the next." (This theme develops flow and body factors.)

Circles in the Body (Figure 8.5)

"Can you form full circles with your hands and arms at different joints—wrist, elbow, and shoulder? Now what circle can you make with your legs and feet? Try this lying on your back. Use other body joints to make circles."

"Travel in general space by skipping (running, hopping, sliding). Stop on signal and make moving, horizontal (vertical, inclined) circles with an arm. Repeat, but on signal lie down immediately on your back and make the specified circle with one foot."

"Show how a swimmer makes circles with the arms when doing the backstroke. Alternate arms and also move them together. Reverse the arm direction to make the crawl stroke. Make vertical circles with one and both arms across the body."

"Make a circle with one hand on the tummy and pat yourself on the top of the head with the other hand at the same time. Reverse hands."

"Select a partner. Match the arm circles the partner makes."

"Can you keep two different circles going at the same time? Make a circle turning one way, and another circle

FIGURE 8.5. Forming circles

turning the other way. Repeat, using twisting actions of the body parts making the circles."

Note: Carry this far enough to get children to explore most of their body and joint actions. This theme develops body factors.

Contrasting Movements

Contrasting movements have wide and frequent application in the development of other themes.

"Show me a fast movement. Now a slow one. Show me a smooth movement. Now a rough, jerky movement."

"Show me a wide shape. Now, an opposite one. A crooked shape. Now, its opposite. Show me a high-level movement and its contrast. Can you do a balanced movement? What is its opposite?" (Use light-heavy and other contrasts as well.)

"Pick two contrasting movements. When I clap my hands, do one, and change to the other when I clap again. What are the movements you did?"

Note: Stimulate children to think about and identify opposite movements. One approach is to name one quality and to see whether children can identify the opposite with a movement response. Another is to have children match their choices. Get further suggestions from the children. A list of terms and their opposites is found on p. 83. (This theme develops space, time, force, and flow factors.)

Flight

"Show me three different ways you can go through space. Try again, using different levels. Lead with different parts of your body."

"See how high you can go as you move through space. What helps you get height?"

"Practice various combinations for takeoff and landing. See if you can work out five different possibilities for taking off and landing, using one or both feet." (Possibilities are same to same [hop]; one foot to the opposite [leap]; one-foot takeoff, two-foot landing; two-foot takeoff, two-foot landing [jump]; two-foot takeoff, one-foot landing.)

"Run and jump or leap through the air with your legs bent. With your legs straight. With one leg bent and the other straight. Try it with your legs spread wide. With your whole body wide. With your whole body long and thin through the air."

"Project yourself upward beginning with the feet together and landing with the feet apart. Run, take off, and land in a forward stride position. Repeat, landing with the other foot forward."

"With a partner, find ways to jump over the partner as she changes shape."

"Using your arms to help you, run and project yourself as high as possible. Practice landing resiliently, with knees bent." (Explain *resiliently.*)

Note: Parallel lines 2 ft apart can represent a creek to be crossed. Other objects such as small cones, individual mats, and masking tape are useful. (This theme develops space, force, and body factors.)

Force

"Show me different kinds of sudden movements. Do a sudden movement and repeat it slowly. Put together a series of sudden movements. Put together a series of sustained movements. Mix sudden and sustained movements."

"Reach in different directions with a forceful movement. Crouch down as low as you can and explode upward. Try again, exploding forward. Move as if you were pushing something very heavy. Pretend you are punching a heavy punching bag."

"What kinds of movements can you do that are light movements? Can you make movements light and sustained? Light and sudden? Heavy and sustained? Heavy and sudden? Which is easier? Why?"

"Try making thunder (big noise with hands and feet) and then lightning (same movements without any noise), timing each with five slow counts."

"Can you combine heavy movements in a sequence of sudden and sustained movements? Can you make one part of your body move lightly and another part heavily?" (This theme develops force factors.)

Leading With Different Parts of the Body (Figure 8.6)

"As you move between your beanbags (lines, markers), explore ways that different parts of your body can lead movements. Add different means of locomotion. Work at different levels."

"Have a partner make a bridge and you go under, leading with different parts of the body. Can you find five different ways to go under with different body parts leading? Now try finding five ways to go over or around."

"What body parts are difficult to lead with?" (This theme develops body factors.)

FIGURE 8.6. Leading with a foot

Moving in Different Ways

"Discover different ways you can make progress along the floor without using your hands and feet. See whether you can walk with your seat. Let your heels help you."

"What ways can you move sideward or backward? What rolling movements can you make? Look carefully before you move, to make sure you have a clear space."

"Use large movements and travel through general space. Make your body into a straight line and move in straight lines, changing direction abruptly. With your body in a curved shape, move in a curved pathway."

"Each time you change direction, alternate a straight body and a straight path with a curved body shape and a curved path."

"Find ways of moving close to the floor with your legs stretched. Now move with your legs bent, keeping at a low level."

"As you travel forward, move up and down. As you travel backward, sway from side to side."

"Travel, keeping high in the air. Change direction and travel at a low level. Continue to alternate."

"Counting the four limbs (two arms, two legs), travel first on all four, then on three, next on an arm and a leg, and then on one leg. Now reverse the order."

"With your hands fixed on the floor, move your feet in different ways. Cover as much space as possible. With your feet fixed, move your hands around in different ways as far away from the body as you can. Move around general space the way a skater does. The way a person on a pogo stick does. Choose other ways. Change body direction as you move, but keep *facing* in the original direction." (This theme develops space and body factors.)

Moving Over, Under, Around, and Through Things

This theme is flexible and can use any available equipment as obstacles to go over, under, around, and through (Figure 8.7). It functions best in a rotating station system. Equipment can be already arranged, or the children can set it up themselves.

"Using the equipment, explore different ways you can go over, under, around, or through what you have set up. Lead with different parts of the body."

Note: Cones, wands, blocks, ropes, baseball bats, and chairs are examples of articles that can be used. This is an excellent partner or small-group activity. The theme develops space and body factors.

Moving With the Weight Supported on the Hands and Feet (Figure 8.8)

"Pick a spot away from your personal space and travel to and from that spot on your hands and feet. Try moving with your hands close to your feet. Far away from your feet. Show me bilateral, unilateral, and cross-lateral movements. Build up a sequence."

FIGURE 8.7. Moving over and under

"Experiment with different hand-foot positions. Begin with a narrow shape and with hands and feet as close together as possible. Extend your hands from head to toe until they are as far apart as possible. Extend the hands and feet as wide as possible and move. Now, try with the hands wide and the feet together. Reverse."

"Practice traveling so both hands and feet are off the ground at the same time. Go forward, backward, sideward."

"With your body straight and supported on the hands and feet (push-up position), turn the body over smoothly and face the ceiling. The body should remain straight throughout. Turn to the right and left. Recover to your original position."

"What kinds of animal movements can you imitate? Move with springing types of jumps. What shapes can you assume while you move?"

Note: The terms BILATERAL, UNILATERAL, and CROSS-LATERAL need explanation, including the significance of the prefixes. A selected movement formation is excellent for this activity. (This theme develops force, flow, and body factors.)

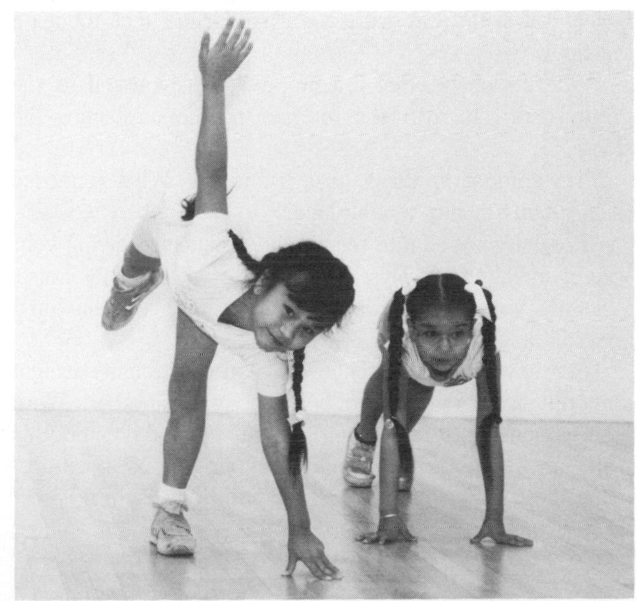

FIGURE 8.8. Taking the weight on the hands and feet

Planes of Movement

"Show me a variety of movements in a horizontal plane. In a vertical plane. In a diagonal plane. Put together combinations so you go in sequence from one type of movement to another."

"Here is a challenge. When I call out a plane of movement, respond with one that is correct. Ready?" (Specify the plane of movement.)

"Using a jump rope doubled in one hand, make circles in the different planes. Try the same with a hula hoop."

Note: This theme can be combined with circles in the body (p. 91).

Receiving and Transferring Weight

"Support the weight on two different body parts and then transfer the weight smoothly to another pair of parts. Add another pair of unlike parts if you can."

"Take a deep breath, let the air out, relax, and drop to the floor, transferring the weight from a standing position to a position on the floor. Can you reverse the process?"

"Show in walking how the weight transfers from the heel to the ball of the foot with a push-off from the toes. In a standing position, transfer the weight from the toes, to the outside of the foot, to the heel, and back to the toes. Reverse the order."

"Travel with a jump or a leap and then lower yourself gently to your back after landing. Repeat, only lower yourself smoothly to your seat."

"From a standing position, bend forward slowly and transfer the weight partially to both hands. Lift one foot into the air. Return it to the ground gently. Repeat with the other foot. Lift a hand and a foot at the same time and return them smoothly."

"Lower yourself in a controlled manner to take the weight on your tummy. Can you turn over and take the weight on your seat with your hands and feet touching the floor?"

"Select a shape. See if you can lower yourself to the ground and return to your original position, retaining the shape."

"Try some jump turns, quarter and half. What is needed to maintain stability as you land?"

"Project yourself into the air and practice receiving your weight in different ways. Try landing without any noise. What do you have to do? See how high you can jump and still land lightly."

"See how many different ways you can transfer weight smoothly from one part of your body to another. Work up a sequence of three or four movements and go smoothly from one to another, returning to your original position." (This theme develops force, flow, and body factors.)

Stretching and Curling

"In your own space, stretch out and curl. What different ways can you find to do this? Let's go slowly from a stretch to a curl and back to a stretch in a smooth, controlled movement. Curl your upper body and stretch your lower body. Now curl your lower body and stretch your upper body. Work out a smooth sequence between the two combinations."

"Show different curled and stretched positions on body points and on body flats. Go from a curled position on a flat surface to a stretched position supported on body points. Explore how many different ways you can support your body in a curled position." (This theme develops time, force, and body factors.)

Symmetrical and Asymmetrical Movements

"Show me different kinds of symmetrical movements. Now asymmetrical movements. Put together sequences of symmetrical and asymmetrical movements."

"Taking the weight on your hands, show symmetrical and asymmetrical movements of your legs."

"Run and jump high in the air, forming symmetrical shapes during flight."

Note: The terms need to be explained. The difference between these two types of movement can be used in many situations to provide another challenge. (This theme develops body factors.)

Taking the Weight on the Hands (Figure 8.9)

Establishing proper hand positioning for taking the weight on the hands (and later for the headstand) is important.

"Put your hands about shoulder width apart, with fingers spread and pointed forward. With knees bent, alternate lifting the feet silently into the air, one foot at a time. Pick a point ahead of your hands (2 ft or so), and watch it with your eyes. Keep from ducking your head between your arms."

"See whether you can take the weight on your hands for a brief time. How do you get your body into the air? What is the importance of the center of gravity? What different movements can you make with your feet while your weight is on your hands? See how long you can keep your feet off the ground. Repeat, trying to get your hips above your hands. Now add a twist at the waist to return your feet to the floor at a different spot."

"Try again, but shift the weight to one hand and land both feet at a different spot."

"Begin in a standing position and try to keep your feet over your head for as long as possible. Begin with the arms and hands stretched overhead, and repeat. Kick up one leg and then the other." (This theme develops force and body factors).

FIGURE 8.9. Taking the weight on the hands

Tension and Relaxation

"Make yourself as tense as possible. Now slowly relax. Take a deep breath and hold it tight. Expel the air and relax."

"Reach as high as possible with both hands, relax slowly, and drop to the floor. Tense one part of your body and relax another. Slowly shift the tension to the relaxed part, and vice versa."

"Run forward, stop suddenly in a tensed position, and then relax. Run in a tensed manner, change direction, and then run in a relaxed manner."

"Walk forward with tight, jerky movements. Change direction and walk with loose, floppy movements. Pretend you are a boxer by using short, tense movements. Now move your arms like a floppy rag doll."

THEMES FOR EXPANDED MOVEMENT COMBINATIONS

Flow Sequencing and Movement Combinations

Emphasis in sequencing should be on sustained flow. The sequences can be experienced individually or with partners.

The examples given here are in series of three or more challenges. If only two are pertinent to the situation, the teacher can select the first two movement patterns of a series. In introducing combinations, starting with just two movements and adding the third in time may be best.

Both locomotor and nonlocomotor movement can be put together in various combinations such as the following.

1. Run, leap, and roll.
2. Shake (all over), gallop, freeze.
3. Hop, collapse, and explode.
4. Whirl, skip, and sink slowly.
5. Creep, pounce, and curl.
6. Lift, grin, and roll.
7. Kneel, sway, and jump to the feet.
8. Run, stop to look, and explode.
9. Run on all fours, roll, and jump.
10. Do a Jumping Jack, slide, and jump-turn.
11. Hop, collapse, and creep.
12. Jump forward, shake, and whirl.
13. Rock on the heels, jump high, and sit down.
14. Sink slowly, roll, and jump-turn.
15. Click the heels right and left, do a jump half turn, and run backward.
16. Twist, skip, sit down, and smile.
17. Turn around three times, clap the hands twice behind the back, run, and balance on one foot.
18. Take fast, tiny steps in place; fall forward to the hands; and do a Log Roll right or left.
19. Take a deep breath, expel the air by saying "Ahhh," jump forward, spin, and sink.
20. Spin on your seat, roll forward, and take five jumps in the direction of the roll.
21. Make a high statue shape, on signal do a jump turn, skip, stretch, and melt.
22. Run, stretch, fall, and roll.
23. Roll in one direction, finish with a spring in the air, and then use a different roll to move in another direction.

Students should be challenged to put together combinations of their own choosing. The challenge can be open, or it can provide some limitation on the type of movement. In an example of the latter approach, the child might be directed to begin with some kind of rapid movement, followed by a balance position, and then to finish with a movement on all fours. (This theme develops flow, space, and body factors.)

Cooperative Partner Activities

Developing the ability to cooperate with others is an important educational goal. Problems should be realistic and give opportunity for discussion and decision making between partners. Depending on the activity, pairing children of reasonably equal achievement may be better. At other times, size, height, and weight can be pertinent factors.

Having children cooperate in solving problems has merit as a partner activity and is a good example of the kind of experience that a child cannot have alone.

1. One child is an obstacle, and the partner devises ways of going over, under, and around the positions the "obstacle" takes (Figure 8.10). Additional challenges are provided when one partner holds a piece of equipment such as a wand or hoop to govern movements.

2. One partner supports the weight of the other, either wholly or in part (Figure 8.11), or the two work together to form different kinds of figures or shapes. Bridges can be built.

3. One child does a movement and the other copies it or provides a contrasting movement.

4. One child moves and the other attempts to shadow her (do the same movements). This must be done slowly, with uninterrupted flow predominating.

5. One child moves and the other provides correction or critique.

6. Partners develop a parallel sequence with both moving together and in the same way.

7. Partners begin 15 to 20 yd apart and come together, using the same selected locomotor movement. They reverse direction and part, using another selected locomotor movement. Acceleration and deceleration have application here, as well as contrasting terms.

8. One child does a movement. The second child repeats the movement and adds another. The first child repeats both movements and adds a third, and so on. Some limit on the number of movements probably needs to be set.

9. Children form letters or figures with their bodies on the floor or in erect positions.

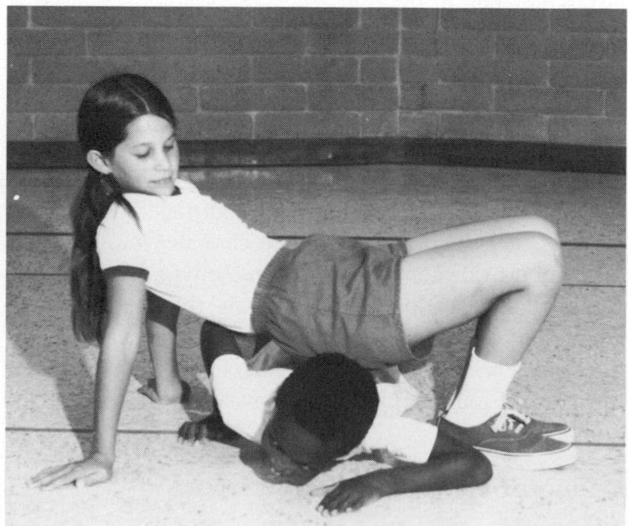

FIGURE 8.10. Going under a partner

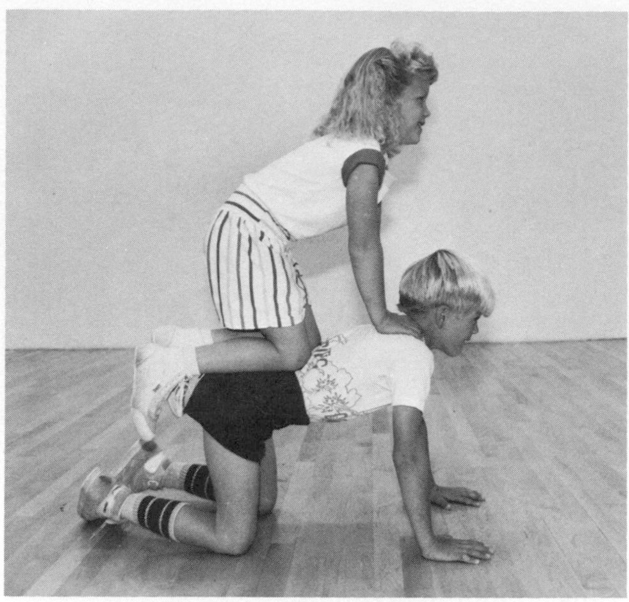

FIGURE 8.11. Supporting the partner's weight

Group Activities

Group work in movement activities is defined as a group of children working together on a movement task. Groups should be kept small so that each child makes a significant contribution. Much of the work can be confined to groups of three or four children, but groups up to squad size are practical. The task should be definite, so efforts are directed toward a common goal.

Most of the ways in which children can work with a partner are applicable, with modifications, to small-group work. Designing, inventing, or modifying a game makes an excellent group problem-solving activity. Coordinating group activity may be difficult, because groups work at different rates and may not be balanced with respect to the time required to complete a task. Some movement activities that are feasible for group work follow.

1. Children explore different ways to build a human tower.

2. Groups show different ways to support others wholly or in part.

3. Children practice copying activities. One child sets a movement pattern and the rest copy his actions.

4. Groups make a human merry-go-round.

5. Groups select and make a pyramid.

6. Children do parallel movements as a group.

7. Small groups (five is a good number) do over and under movements. Each child goes over and under the others in turn.

MOVEMENT CHALLENGES

A number of other ideas have value for stimulating children to purposeful movement.

FLOOR TARGETS

Lines can be used for jumping, hopping, and leaping activities. A jump rope laid lengthwise makes a fine floor target. Children begin at one end, go back and forth over the rope as they go down the line, and return down the rope back to place.

A hoop on the floor is an excellent stimulus to movement. Children do different movements in and out of and inside and around the hoop. A number of hoops in line provides excellent motivation.

A wand or a beanbag can be carried during various locomotor movements. On signal, the object is placed on the ground, and the child jumps back and forth across it.

FLOOR PATTERNS

Footprints can be painted or marked on the floor, and the children do movements guided by them. Lines, mazes, and different kinds of figures can be painted on blacktop to provide movement guides.

SPORTS

Various sport activities provide a basis for creative movements. Pretending to play hockey, football, or basketball is meaningful for both boys and girls.

INDIVIDUAL MATS

Individual mats are excellent for basic movements, both locomotor and nonlocomotor. The child does movements on, across, and around the mats (pp. 349–350).

FLASH CARDS

Flash cards can give direction to movements by depicting different patterns such as circles, triangles, and squares. A pair of numbers on a flash card gives direction to hopping patterns (see p. 102). The flash card might give a movement combination, such as run, leap, or roll.

MOVEMENT SUGGESTION BOX

An idea that is received enthusiastically by children is the movement suggestion box. This box, which should contain enough cards for the whole class, can be used in two ways. First, have movement challenges already written on the cards. Each child takes a card and responds to the challenge. This activity works well at the beginning of a lesson. The second method offers the children some movement choice. Cards covering three or more areas (e.g., mat activities, locomotor movements, nonlocomotor movements, and manipulative activities) can be in different box compartments. Children choose a card from the second area only after they finish the first task.

CHAPTER 9

Convergent Movement: Fundamental and Specialized Skills

When teaching convergent movement, the teacher guides instruction toward the acquisition of a particular skill, one that can be identified by name, such as walking, batting, bouncing, jumping, or pitching. (A convergent movement can usually be identified by the fact that its name ends in the suffix *ing.*) Convergent movement implies a limitation; the child must accomplish a specified target skill, even though the means to reach the goal may differ among individual learners.

The more precise the skill, the more critical the need is to establish proper technique. Correct technique should prevail over experimentation, even when the child is more comfortable with a known departure from accepted form. A child who throws right-handed and steps with the right foot as he throws should be induced to change to a left-footed (opposite side) step, since the right-footed (same side) step is an undesirable habit that needs to be changed. In most cases, changing an incorrectly learned motor pattern is much more difficult than teaching the correct pattern in the early years of development. As a general rule, the child should be made aware of the recommended techniques even if he chooses to retain the questionable pattern.

For convergent movement, a somewhat different instructional approach is indicated from that used for divergent movement. For a given skill, the range of acceptable techniques needs to be known and adhered to. In some cases, the range may be broad; in others, it may be quite limited. Perceptive guidance is essential in analyzing the child's performance. Progressions and pacing become important, and repetition aimed at establishing unconscious or automatic skill behavior is inherent in the lesson continuum.

Convergent movement embraces a broad spectrum of skills, from simple to complex. For simpler skills, exploration and creativity may be used, as in teaching divergent movement. Teaching the more complicated skills demands going *beyond* exploration and experimentation. The learning of these specialized skills requires a more direct approach based on researched techniques, valid progressions, and diligent practice. Practice needs to continue until the target skill becomes overlearned and automatic.

CONVERGENT MOVEMENT SKILLS

Understanding the various groups of skills that children need to learn is important. These skills set the foundation for adult activity and when learned correctly, performers move with confidence and style. All individual, dual, and team sport activities use fundamental and specialized skills of one type or another. If children feel incompetent in performing movement patterns, they will be hesitant to participate in various leisure activities throughout their life span. The following skills are grouped for ease of teaching and ease of comprehension by students. Although the skills are presented here individually, they are performed in an infinite number of combinations depending on the sport or activity.

FUNDAMENTAL SKILLS

Fundamental skills are those utilitarian skills that a child needs for living and being. This group of skills is sometimes labeled *basic* or *functional.* The designation *fundamental skills* is preferable to other labels, because the skills are normal, characteristic attributes necessary for the child to function in the environment. For purposes of discussion, the fundamental skills are divided into three categories.

Locomotor Skills

Locomotor skills are used to move the body from one place to another or to project the body upward, as in jumping and hopping. They include walking, running, skipping, leaping, sliding, and galloping. They form the foundation of gross motor coordination and involve large muscle movement.

Nonlocomotor Skills

Nonlocomotor skills are performed without appreciable movement from place to place. These skills are not as well defined as locomotor skills. They include bending and stretching, pushing and pulling, raising and lowering, twisting and turning, shaking, bouncing, and circling, among others.

Manipulative Skills

Manipulative skills come into play when the child handles some kind of object. Most of these skills involve the hands and feet, but other parts of the body can also be used. The manipulation of objects leads to better hand-eye and foot-eye coordination, which are particularly important for tracking items in space.

Manipulative skills are the basis of many game skills. Propulsion (throwing, batting, kicking) and receipt (catching) of objects are important skills that can be taught by using beanbags and various balls. Rebounding or redirecting an object in flight (such as a volleyball) is another useful manipulative skill. Continuous control of an object, such as a wand or hoop, is also a manipulative activity.

SPECIALIZED SKILLS

Specialized skills are those used in various sports and in other areas of physical education including apparatus activities, tumbling, dance, and specific games. In developing specialized skills, progression is attained through planned instruction and drills. Many of these skills have critical points of technique and strongly emphasize correct performance. Specialized skills are usually a combination of locomotor, nonlocomotor, and manipulative skills. In addition, they are situation-specific and involve a high level of refinement. Children in elementary school are usually introduced to these skills and allowed to practice them without excessive concern for a high level of performance.

FUNDAMENTAL LOCOMOTOR MOVEMENTS

In the descriptions that follow, fundamental locomotor movements are analyzed, and selected activities based on particular movements are presented. Suggested learning activities fall into two categories. The first category, suggested movement patterns, consists of movement-oriented sequences that do not require rhythm. The second category, rhythmic activities, consists of sequences that employ rhythmic background. Some of the activities in the first category could be set to rhythm. There is considerable overlap in the suggestions given for the respective locomotor movements. Most of the suggestions for walking patterns, for example, can be used for running.

When teaching fundamental locomotor movements, the same methodology used in teaching divergent movement (educational movement) can be employed with modifications made to restrict the variety of responses. The suggested movement patterns for each skill make provision for lesson plan construction. Instructors should understand the proper execution of the movement pattern and be able to describe the correct pattern, teach the factors that affect performance, and provide necessary coaching hints to improve performance.

Either a drum or appropriate recorded music is effective in reinforcing and expanding movement possibilities, particularly of the locomotor type. The character of the beat is critical if movements are to be achieved naturally and smoothly. Music designed for fundamental movement is especially valuable.

WALKING

In walking, the feet move alternately, with one foot always in contact with the ground or floor. This means that the stepping foot must be placed on the ground before the other foot is lifted. The weight of the body is transferred from the heel to the ball of the foot and then to the toes for push-off. The toes are pointed straight ahead, and the arms swing freely from the shoulders in opposition to the feet. The body is erect, and the eyes are focused straight ahead and slightly below eye level. The legs swing smoothly from the hips, with knees bent enough to clear the feet from the ground. Marching is a precise type of walk, accompanied by lifted knees and swinging arms.

Many different ways of walking should be experienced, but the underlying motive is to have the children move gracefully and efficiently in normal walking. Different walking patterns offer an excellent opportunity to stress posture.

Stress Points

1. The toes should be pointed reasonably straight ahead.

2. The arm movement should feel natural. The arms should not swing too far.

3. The head should be kept up and the eyes focused ahead.

4. The stride length should not be excessive. Unnecessary up-and-down motion is to be avoided.

Teaching Cues

1. Head up, eyes forward.
2. Point toes straight ahead.
3. Nice, easy, relaxed arm swing.
4. Walk quietly.
5. Hold tummy in, chest up.
6. Push off from the floor with the toes.

Directives for Suggested Movement Patterns

1. Walk in different directions, changing direction on signal.

2. While walking, bring the knees up and slap with the hands on each step.

3. Walk on the heels, toes, and sides of feet.

4. Gradually lower the body while walking (going downstairs) and raise yourself again slowly (going upstairs).

5. Walk with a smooth, gliding step.

6. Walk with a wide base on the tiptoes, rocking from side to side.

7. Clap the hands alternately in front and behind. Clap the hands under the thighs while walking.

8. Walk slowly, and then increase the speed gradually. Reverse the process.

9. Take long strides. Take tiny steps.

10. On signal, change levels.

11. Walk quickly and quietly. Walk heavily and slowly.

12. Change direction on signal, but keep facing the same way.

13. Walk gaily, angrily, happily. Show other moods.

14. Hold the arms in different positions. Make an arm movement each time you step.

15. Walk in different patterns—circle, square, triangle, figure eight.

16. Walk through heavy mud. On ice or a slick floor. Walk on a rainy day.

17. Walk like a soldier on parade, a giant, a dwarf, a robot.

18. Duck under trees or railings while walking.

19. Point your toes in different directions—in, forward, and out.

20. Walk with high knees. Stiff knees. One stiff knee. A sore ankle.

21. Walk to a spot, turn in place while stepping, and take off in another direction.

22. Practice changing steps while walking.

23. Walk with a military goose step.

24. Walk and change direction after taking the magic number of steps. (One child picks a magic number.)

Rhythmic Activities: With recorded music, the use of the phrase (eight counts) is critical. Children can walk one way during a phrase and then change to another type of walk during the next phrase.

1. Walk forward one phrase (eight counts) and change direction. Continue to change at the end of each phrase.

2. Use high steps during one phrase and low steps during the next.

3. Walk forward for one phrase and sideward during the next. The side step can be a draw step, or it can be of the grapevine type. To do a grapevine step to the left, lead with the left foot, stepping directly to the side. Cross the right foot *behind* the left, and then in front of the left on the next step with that foot. The pattern is a step left, cross right (behind), step left, cross right (in front), and so on.

4. Find a partner. Face each other and join hands. Pull your partner by walking backward as he resists somewhat (eight counts). Reverse roles. Now stand behind your partner and place the palms of your hands on partner's shoulders. Push your partner by walking forward as she resists (eight counts). Reverse roles.

5. Walk slowly, then gradually increase the tempo. Now begin fast and decrease. (Use a drum for this activity.)

6. Walk in various directions while clapping your hands alternately in front and behind. Try clapping the hands under a thigh at each step, or clap the hands above the head in time with the beat.

7. Walk forward four steps, and turn completely around in four steps. Repeat, but turn the other way the next time.

8. While walking, bring the knees up and slap with the hands on each step in time with the beat.

9. On any one phrase, take four fast steps (one count to each step) and two slow steps (two counts to each step).

10. Walk on the heels or toes or with a heavy tramp. Change every four or eight beats.

11. Walk with a smooth, gliding step, or walk silently to the beat.

12. Walk to the music, accenting the first beat of each measure. Now sway your body to the first beat of the measure. (Use a waltz with a strong beat.)

RUNNING

Running (Figure 9.1), in contrast to walking, is moving rapidly in such a manner that, for a brief moment, both

FIGURE 9.1. Running

feet are off the ground. Running varies from trotting (a slow run) to sprinting (a fast run for speed). The heels can take some weight in distance running and jogging. Running should be done with a slight body lean. The knees are bent and lifted, and the arms swing back and forth from the shoulders with a bend at the elbows. Additional pointers for sprinting are found in the track, field, and cross-country running unit (Chapter 32).

Running in these sequences should be done lightly on the balls of the feet. It should be a controlled run and not a dash for speed. Children can cover ground on the run, or they can run in place.

Stress Points

1. The balls of the feet should be used for sprinting.
2. The faster one desires to run, the higher the knees must be lifted. For fast running, the knees also must be bent more.
3. For distance running, less arm swing is used compared with sprinting for speed. Less body lean is used in distance running, with comfort being the key. The weight is absorbed on the heels and transferred to the toes.

Teaching Cues

1. Run on the balls of the feet.
2. Head up, eyes forward.
3. Bend your knees.
4. Relax your upper body.
5. Breathe naturally.
6. Swing the arms forward and backward, not sideways.

Directives for Suggested Movement Patterns

1. Run lightly throughout the area, changing direction as you wish. Avoid bumping anyone. Run zigzag throughout the area.
2. Run and stop on signal. Change direction on signal.
3. Run, turn around with running steps on signal, and continue in a new direction. Alternate turning direction.
4. Pick a spot away from you, run to it, and return without touching or bumping anyone.
5. Run low, gradually increasing the height. Reverse.
6. Run in patterns. Run between and around objects.
7. Run with high knee action. Slap the knees while running.
8. Run with different steps—tiny, long, light, heavy, crisscross, wide, and others.
9. Run with your arms in different positions—circling, overhead, stiff at your sides.
10. Run free, concentrating on good knee lift.
11. Run at different speeds.
12. Touch the ground at times with either hand while running.
13. Run backward, sideward.
14. Run with exaggerated arm movements. Run with a high bounce.
15. Run forward ten steps and backward five steps. Repeat in another direction. (Other tasks can be imposed after the ten steps.)
16. Run forward, then make a jump turn in the air to face in a new direction. Repeat. Be sure to use both right and left turns. Make a full reverse (180-degree) turn.
17. Run the Tortoise and Hare sequence (p. 209) and Ponies in the Stable (p. 209). These are interesting patterns.

Rhythmic Activities: Many of the suggested movements for walking are equally applicable to running patterns. Some additional suggestions for running include the following.

1. Walk during a phrase of music and then run for an equal length of time.
2. Run in different directions, changing direction on the sound of a heavy beat (or on a signal).
3. Lift the knees as high as possible while running, keeping time to the beat.
4. Do European Rhythmic Running (pp. 207–208) to supplement the running patterns described previously.

HOPPING

In hopping, the body is propelled up and down by one foot. The body lean, the other foot, and the arms serve to balance the movement. Children should change to the other foot after a short period. Hopping can be done in place or as a locomotor movement.

Stress Points

1. To increase the height of the hop, the arms must be swung rapidly upward.
2. Hopping should be performed on the ball of the foot.
3. Small hops should be used to start, with a gradual increase in height and distance of the hop.

Teaching Cues

1. Hop with good forward motion.
2. Stay on your toes.
3. Use your arms for balance.
4. Reach for the sky when you hop.
5. Land lightly.

Directives for Suggested Movement Patterns

1. Hop on one foot and then on the other, using numbered sequences such as 1–1, 2–2, 3–3, 4–4, 5–5, 2–1, 1–2, 3–2, 2–3, and so on. The first figure of a series indicates the number of hops on the right foot, and the second specifies the number of hops on the left foot. Combinations should be maintained for 10 to 20 seconds.
2. Hop, increasing height. Reverse.
3. See how much space you can cover in two, three, or four hops.
4. Hop on one foot and do a heel-and-toe pattern with the other. Now change to the other foot. See whether a consistent pattern can be set up.

5. Make a hopping sequence by combining hopping in place with hopping ahead.

6. Hop forward, backward, sideward.

7. Hop in different patterns on the floor.

8. Hop while holding the free foot in different hand positions.

9. Hold the free foot forward or sideward while hopping. Explore other positions.

10. Hop with the body in different positions—with a forward lean, a backward lean, a sideward balance.

11. Hop lightly. Heavily.

12. While hopping, touch the floor with the hands, first one and then both.

13. Hop back and forth over a line, moving down the line as you hop.

14. Trace out numbers or letters by hopping.

15. Turn around while hopping in place.

16. Hop forward and then backward according to a magic number (selected by a student). Repeat in another direction. Now add sideward hopping instead of going backward.

Rhythmic Activities: Combining rhythm with hopping patterns is more difficult than walking, running, or skipping to rhythm. The drumbeat is probably the best approach, although some recorded music designed especially for hopping also works well. Since hopping on one foot may fatigue students rapidly, the suggested patterns combine other locomotor movements with hopping.

1. Walk four steps, hop three times, rest one count.

2. Walk four steps, then hop four times as you turn in place. Repeat in a new direction.

3. Hop eight times on one foot (eight counts) and then eight times on the other.

4. Hop forward and backward over a line to the rhythm, changing feet each phrase (eight counts).

5. Combine skipping, sliding, or galloping with hopping.

6. Practice the step-hop to music. (The child takes a step followed by a hop on the same foot. This is a two-count movement.)

JUMPING

As a fundamental movement, jumping is taking off with both feet and landing on both feet (Figure 9.2). The arms help with an upswing, and the movement of the body combined with the force of the feet helps lift the weight. A jumper lands lightly on the balls of the feet with the knees bent. Jumping can be done in place or as a locomotor activity to cover ground.

Stress Points

1. The knees and ankles should be bent before takeoff to achieve more force from muscle extension.

2. The landing should be on the balls of the feet, with the knees bent to absorb the impact.

FIGURE 9.2. Jumping

3. The arms should swing forward and upward at takeoff to add momentum to the jump and to gain distance and height.

4. The legs must be bent after takeoff or the feet will touch the ground prematurely.

Teaching Cues

1. Swing your arms forward as fast as possible.
2. Bend your knees.
3. On your toes.
4. Land lightly with bent knees.
5. Jump up and try to touch the ceiling.

Directives for Suggested Movement Patterns

1. Jump up and down, trying for height. Try small and high jumps. Mix in patterns.

2. Choose a spot on the floor. Jump forward over the spot. Now backward and then sideward.

3. Jump with your body stiff and arms held at your sides. Jump like a pogo stick.

4. Practice jump turns in place—quarter, half, three-quarter, and full.

5. Increase and decrease your jumping speed. Increase and decrease the height of the jump.

6. Land with the feet apart and then together. Alternate with one foot forward and one backward.

7. Jump and land quietly. How is this done?

8. Jump, crossing and uncrossing the feet.

9. See how far you can go in two, three, and four consecutive jumps. Run lightly back to place.

10. Pretend you are a bouncing ball.

11. Clap the hands or slap the thighs while in the air. Try different arm positions.

12. Begin a jump with your hands contacting the floor.

13. Jump in various patterns on the floor.

14. Pretend you are a basketball center jumping at a

jump ball. Jump as high as you can. Jump from a crouched position.

Rhythmic Activities: Jumping is similar to hopping in the application of rhythm to the skill. Most of the patterns suggested for hopping to rhythm are suitable for jumping. Other suggestions follow.

1. Begin jumping slowly to the drumbeat and then accelerate. Begin jumping fast and decelerate to the beat.
2. Toss a ball upward and jump in time to the bounce. (The ball must be a lively one.)
3. Do varieties of the Jumping Jack. First, move your feet without any arm movement. Now add an arm lift to shoulder height, then lift the arm to a full overhead position. Work in body turns and different foot patterns.
4. Take a forward stride position. Change the feet back and forth to the rhythm.

Note: Jumping and hopping patterns to rhythm carry over to aerobic dancing.

SKIPPING

Skipping is a series of step-hops done with alternate feet. To teach a child to skip, have her take a step with one foot and a small hop on the same foot. The child then takes a step and a hop with the other foot. Skipping is done on the balls of the feet with the arms swinging to shoulder height in opposition to the feet.

An alternate way to teach skipping begins with the child holding a large ball (9 in. or more) in front of himself at waist height. The child steps with one foot and raises the other knee to touch the ball. This stimulates the hop. Repeat with the other foot and the opposite knee. Later, the child only pretends to hold a ball and continues the pattern. If children are having trouble skipping, slow down the step-hop sequence and call out "Step, hop" in rhythm.

Stress Points

1. Smoothness and rhythm are goals in skipping. Speed and distance are not.
2. The weight must be transferred from one foot to the other on the hop.
3. The arms swing in opposition to the legs.

Teaching Cues

1. Skip high.
2. Swing your arms.
3. Skip smoothly.
4. On your toes.

Directives for Suggested Movement Patterns: Many of the suggested movement patterns for walking and running can be applied to skipping, particularly those that refer to changing direction, stopping, making different floor patterns, and moving at different speeds and in different size increments. The following should be considered as well.

1. Skip with exaggerated arm action and lifted knees.
2. Skip backward.
3. Clap as you skip.
4. Skip with a side-to-side motion.
5. Skip twice on one side (double skip).
6. Skip as slowly as possible. Skip as fast as possible.

Rhythmic Activities: Almost all of the combinations suggested for walking and running are useful for skipping movements, and many combinations of skipping, walking, and running can be devised. The piece "Pop Goes the Weasel" is excellent music for skipping. On the "Pop," some movement challenge can be specified.

SLIDING

Sliding is done to the side. It is a one-count movement, with the leading foot stepping to the side and the other foot following quickly. Since the same foot always leads, the movement should be practiced in both directions. Sliding is done on the balls of the feet with the weight shifted from the leading foot to the trailing foot. Body bounce during the slide should be minimal.

Stress Points

1. Emphasize the sideways movement. Often, students move forward or backward, which is actually galloping.
2. Both directions should be used, so each leg has a chance to lead as well as to trail.
3. The slide is a smooth, graceful, and controlled movement.

Teaching Cues

1. Move sideways.
2. Do not bounce.
3. Slide your feet.

Directives for Suggested Movement Patterns

1. Lead in one direction with a definite number of slides, do a half turn in the air, and continue the slide leading with the other leg in the same direction. (A four-plus-four combination is excellent.)
2. Begin with short slides and increase length. Reverse.
3. Slide in a figure-eight pattern.
4. Change levels while sliding. Slide so the hands can touch the floor with each slide.
5. Slide quietly and smoothly.
6. Pretend to be a basketball defensive player and slide with good basketball position.
7. Slide with a partner.

Rhythmic Activities: With appropriate music, many of the above movement patterns can be set to rhythm. The use of the phrase (eight counts) to change direction or to insert another challenge is recommended.

GALLOPING

Galloping is similar to sliding, but progress is in a forward direction. One foot leads and the other is brought rapidly up to it. There is more upward motion of the body than in sliding. A helpful way to teach the gallop is to have children hold hands and slide in a circle, either to verbal cues or a drumbeat. Tell them to turn gradually to face the direction in which the circle is moving. This takes them naturally from a slide into a gallop. Next, have them drop hands, and permit free movement in general space.

Stress Points

1. The movement should be smooth and graceful.
2. Each foot should have a chance to lead.

Teaching Cues

1. Keep one foot in front of the other.
2. Now lead with the other foot.
3. Make high gallops.

Directives for Suggested Movement Patterns

1. Do a series of eight gallops with the same foot leading, then change to the other foot. Change after four gallops. Change after two gallops. (Later in the rhythmic program, the gallop is used to teach the polka, so it is important for children to learn to change the leading foot.)
2. Change the size of the gallops.
3. Gallop in a circle with a small group.
4. Pretend to hold reins and use a riding crop.
5. Gallop backward.

Rhythmic Activities: Since galloping is essentially a rhythmic movement, many of the patterns just described should be done to rhythm. Use of the phrase (eight counts) is important in helping the children to change the leading foot. Check previous sections on locomotor movements for other suggestions.

LEAPING

Leaping is an elongated step designed to cover distance or to go over a low obstacle. It is usually combined with running, since a series of leaps is difficult to maintain alone (Figure 9.3). The suggested movement patterns assume such combinations of running and leaping. Leaping should emphasize graceful flight through space.

Stress Points

1. Height and graceful flight are goals for which to strive.
2. Landing should be light and relaxed.

Teaching Cues

1. Push off and reach.
2. Up and over, land lightly.
3. Use your arms to help you gain height.

FIGURE 9.3. Leaping

Directives for Suggested Movement Patterns

1. Leap in different directions.
2. See how high you can leap.
3. Leap and land softly.
4. Vary your arm position when you leap. Clap your hands as you leap.
5. Leap with the same arm and leg forward. Try the other way.
6. Show a leap in slow motion.
7. Leap and turn backward.
8. Leap over objects or across a specified space.
9. Practice by playing Leap the Brook (p. 425).

Rhythmic Activities: Since the leap is essentially an explosive movement through space, it is difficult to apply rhythm to the movement. Children must gather themselves in preparation for the leap, which makes the movement nonrhythmic in nature.

FUNDAMENTAL NONLOCOMOTOR MOVEMENTS

Nonlocomotor movements include bending, twisting, turning (in place), moving toward and away from the center of the body, raising and lowering the parts of the body, and other body movements done in place. Nonlocomotor movements are not as easily divided between divergent and convergent movement as are locomotor and manipulative skills. Gross body movements to the limits of flexibility are important. Body control and a variety of movements that lead to effective body management are also important goals. Balance is another factor that should receive attention.

The nonlocomotor movements, with the exception of swinging, are not enhanced by rhythmic accompaniment. Many are controlled movements, done individually by the children. Music, however, makes swinging a delightful experience. Waltz music is best.

BENDING

Bending is movement at a joint. Emphasis should be on learning where the body bends, why it needs to bend,

FIGURE 9.4. Bending movements

and how many different bends are combined in various movements (Figure 9.4).

Stress Points

1. Bending as far as possible to increase flexibility and range of movement is a key goal.

2. The bending possibilities of many joints should be explored.

3. Time factors can be introduced in slow and rapid bending.

Teaching Cues

1. Bend as far as possible.

2. Bend one part while holding others steady.

Directives for Suggested Movement Experiences

1. Bend your body down and up.

2. Bend forward and backward, left and right, north and south.

3. Bend as many ways as possible.

4. Bend as many body parts as you can below your waist. Above your waist. Bend with your whole body.

5. Sit down and see whether you can bend differently from the ways you bent in a standing position.

6. Lie down and bend six body parts. Can you bend more than six? Now bend fewer.

7. Try to bend one body part quickly while you bend another part slowly.

8. Make a familiar shape by bending two body parts. Add two more parts.

9. Think of a toy that bends; see whether you can bend in a similar fashion.

10. Find a partner and bend with her. Have your partner make big bends while you make tiny bends.

11. Show me how you would bend to look funny. To look happy or sad. Bend slowly or quickly.

ROCKING AND SWAYING

Rocking occurs when the center of gravity is fluidly and gradually transferred from one body part to another. In rocking, the body is in a rounded position where it touches the floor. The term *swaying* implies a slower movement than rocking and is somewhat more controlled than rocking. In swaying, the base of support is unchanged.

Stress Points

1. Rocking is done best on a body surface that has been rounded. Arm movements and movements of other body parts can facilitate the rocking motion.

2. Rocking should be done smoothly and in a steady rhythm.

3. Rocking can be started with small movements and increased in extent, or vice versa.

4. Rocking and swaying should be done to the full range of movement.

5. Swaying maintains a stable base.

Teaching Cues

1. Rock smoothly.

2. Rock in different directions. At varying speeds.

3. Rock higher (farther).

4. Sway until you almost lose your balance.

Directives for Suggested Movement Experiences

1. Rock in as many different ways as you can (Figure 9.5).

2. Show me how you can rock slowly. Quickly. Smoothly.

3. Sit cross-legged with arms outstretched to the sides, palms facing the floor. Rock from side to side until the hands touch the floor.

4. Lie on your back and rock. Now point your arms and legs toward the ceiling as you rock.

5. Lie on your tummy with arms stretched overhead and rock. Hold your ankles and make giant rocks.

6. Try to rock in a standing position.

7. Rock and twist at the same time.

8. Lie on your back with knees up and rock from side to side.

FIGURE 9.5. Rocking variations

9. Show me two ways to have a partner rock you.

10. From a standing position, sway back and forth, right and left. Experiment with different foot positions. Sway slowly and rapidly. What effect does rapid swaying have?

11. Repeat swaying movements from a kneeling position.

12. Start with a small rocking motion and make it progressively bigger.

13. Choose three (or more) ways of rocking and see if you can change smoothly from one to the next.

SWINGING

Swinging involves an action of body parts that resembles a swinging rope or the moving pendulum of a clock. The teacher can put a weight on the end of a string about a yard long and demonstrate swinging motions. Note that most swinging movements are confined to the arms and legs.

Swinging is a rhythmic, smooth motion that is fun to do to waltz music. It is also effective to combine this movement with a step at the beginning of each measure of music. When experimenting with swinging movements, some children carry the swings to such an extreme that they make a full circle. With a musical background, swinging and circular movements can form sequences. Music is important, because it gives the children the feeling of the swing.

Stress Points

1. Swinging should be a smooth, rhythmic action.
2. The body parts involved in swinging should be relaxed and loose.
3. The extent of the swing movement should be the same on both sides of the swing.
4. Swinging movements should be as full as possible.

Teaching Cues

1. Loosen up; swing easy.
2. Swing fully; make a full movement.
3. Swing in rhythm.

Directives for Suggested Movement Experiences

1. Explore different ways to swing your arms and legs.
2. Work out swinging patterns with the arms. Combine them with a step pattern, forward and back.
3. Swing the arms back and forth, and go into full circles at times.
4. With a partner, work out different swinging movements (Figure 9.6). Add circles.
5. Work out swinging patterns and combinations. Form sequences with swinging and full-circle movements. (This activity is best done to waltz music with a slow or moderate tempo.)

TURNING

Turning is a movement involving rotation around the long axis of the body. The terms *turning* and *twisting* are sometimes used interchangeably to designate the movements of body parts. Actually, however, turning properly refers to movements of the body as a whole. In the movement experiences suggested here, action involves movement of the entire body. Movements of body parts are discussed under twisting.

FIGURE 9.6. Partner swinging

Stress Points

1. Maintaining balance and body control is important.
2. Turning should be tried in both directions, right and left.
3. Turns in standing position can be made by jumping, hopping, or shuffling with the feet.
4. Most turns are made in increments or multiples of quarter turns. Multiples should be practiced.
5. Turns should be practiced in body positions other than standing—seated, on the tummy or the back, and so forth.

Teaching Cues

1. Keep your balance.
2. In jump turns, land in a relaxed way with the knees relaxed.
3. Be precise in your movement, whether it is a quarter, half, or full turn.

Directives for Suggested Movement Experiences

1. In standing position, turn your body to the left and right, clockwise and counterclockwise.
2. Turn to face north, east, south, and west. (The teacher should post directions on the wall and might even introduce some in-between directions, northwest, for example.)
3. Stand on one foot and turn around slowly. Now turn around quickly. Now turn with a series of small hops. Try to keep good balance.

4. Show me how you can cross your legs with a turn and sit down. Can you get up again in one movement?

5. Every time you hear the signal, see whether you can turn around once, moving slowly. Can you turn two, three, or four times slowly on signal?

6. Lie on your tummy on the floor and turn your body slowly in an arc. Turn over so that you are on your back; turn back to your tummy again.

7. Find a friend and see how many different ways he can turn you and you can turn him.

8. Play Follow the Leader with your friend. You make a turn and she follows.

9. Begin with a short run, jump into the air, and turn to land facing in a new direction. Practice both right and left turns. Can you make a full reverse (180-degree) turn?

TWISTING

Twisting is the rotation of a selected body part around its own long axis (Figure 9.7). The joints of the following body parts can be used for twisting: spine, neck, shoulders, hips, ankles, and wrists. Twisting differs from turning in that twisting involves movement around the body part itself, while turning focuses on the space in which the entire body turns. Remember that the children are used to having some of these twisting movements called "turning."

Stress Points

1. Twisting should be extended as far as possible with good control.
2. The body parts on which the twist is based should be stabilized.
3. A twist in one direction should be countered by a reverse twist.
4. Some joints are better for twisting than others. (Explain why this is so.)

FIGURE 9.7. Twisting movements

Teaching Cues

1. Twist far (fully).
2. Twist the other way.
3. Hold the supporting parts firm.

Directives for Suggested Movement Experiences

1. Glue your feet to the floor. Can you twist your body to the left and to the right? Can you twist your body slowly? Quickly? Can you bend and twist at the same time? How far can you turn your hands back and forth?
2. Twist two or more parts of your body at the same time.
3. Twist one body part in one direction and another in the opposite direction.
4. Try twisting the lower half of your body without twisting the upper half.
5. See what parts you can twist while sitting on the floor.
6. Try to twist one body part around another part. Is it possible to twist together even more parts?
7. Balance on one foot and twist your body. Can you bend and twist at the same time?
8. Show me some different shapes that you can make by twisting your body.
9. Try to twist like a spring. Like a cord on a telephone.
10. Try to move and twist at the same time.
11. With the weight on your feet, twist as far as you can in one direction. Now take the weight on your hands and move your feet.

STRETCHING

Stretching is a movement that generally makes the body parts as long or as wide as possible. Stretching sometimes involves moving a joint through the range of movement. It is important for children to understand that stretching the muscles involves some minor discomfort and controlled movement. The muscle-stretching process is necessary for maintaining and increasing flexibility.

Stress Points

1. Stretching should be extended to the full range of movement.
2. Stretching exploration should involve many body parts.
3. Stretching should be done in many positions.
4. Stretching can be combined with opposite movements, such as curling.
5. Stretching is done slowly and smoothly.
6. Hold full stretching position for 10 seconds.

Teaching Cues

1. Stretch as far as possible. Make it hurt a little.
2. Find other ways to stretch the body part (joint).
3. Keep it smooth. Do not jerk.

Directives for Suggested Movement Experiences

1. Stretch as many body parts as you can.
2. Stretch your arms, legs, and feet in as many different directions as possible.
3. Try to stretch a body part quickly. Slowly. Smoothly.
4. Bend a body part and tell me which muscle or muscles are being stretched.
5. See how many ways you can stretch while sitting on the floor.
6. Lie on the floor and see whether you can stretch two, three, four, or five body parts at once.
7. Try to stretch one body part quickly while you stretch another part slowly.
8. From a kneeling position, see whether you can stretch to a mark on the floor without losing your balance.
9. Stretch your right arm while you curl your left arm.
10. Find a friend and show me how many ways you can help each other stretch.
11. Try to stretch and become as tall as a giraffe. (Name other animals.)
12. Stretch and make a wide bridge. Find a partner to go under, around, and over your bridge.
13. Bend at the waist and touch your toes with your fingers. See whether you can keep your legs straight while you are stretching to touch the toes.
14. Combine stretching with curling. With bending.
15. Stretch the muscles in your chest, back, tummy, ankles, wrists, and fingers.
16. Make a shape with your body. Now stretch the shape so it is larger.
17. As you move at a low level, curl and stretch your fingers.
18. Find a position in which you can stretch one side of the body.
19. Find a position in which you can stretch both legs far apart in the air. Now make the legs as narrow as possible.

PUSHING

Pushing is a controlled and forceful action performed against an object to move the body away from the object or to move the object in a desired direction by applying force to it (Figure 9.8).

Stress Points

1. A forward stride position should be used to broaden the base of support.
2. The body's center of gravity should be lowered.
3. The line of force is directed toward the object.
4. The back is kept in reasonable alignment, and the body forces gathered for a forceful push. Do not bend the waist.
5. The push should be controlled and steady.

FIGURE 9.8. Pushing

Teaching Cues

1. Broaden your foot base.
2. Use all your body forces.
3. Push steadily and evenly.
4. Lower yourself for a better push.

Directives for Suggested Movement Experiences

1. Stand near a wall and push it from an erect position, then push with the knees bent and one foot behind the other. In which position can you push with more force?
2. Push an imaginary object that is very light. Now imagine that you are pushing a heavy object.
3. Try to push a partner who is sitting on a jumping box, then try to push a partner who is sitting on a scooter. What changes must you make in your body position?
4. Push an object with your feet without using your arms or hands.
5. Sit down and push a heavy object with your feet. Can you put your back against the object and push it?
6. See how many different ways you can find to push the object.
7. Find a friend and try to push her over a line.
8. Sit back to back with your partner and see whether you can push him backward.
9. See if it is possible to lie on the floor and push.
10. Lie on the floor and push your body forward, backward, and sideward.
11. Lie on the floor and push yourself with one foot and one arm.
12. Put a beanbag on the floor and push it with your elbow, shoulder, nose, or other body part.
13. Move in crab position and push a beanbag.
14. Show me how you can push a ball to a friend.

PULLING

Pulling is a controlled and forceful action that moves an object closer to the body or the body closer to an object. If the body moves and an object is being pulled, then pulling causes the object to follow the body.

Stress Points

1. For forceful pulling, the base of support must be broadened and the body's center of gravity must be lowered.

2. The vertical axis of the body should provide a line of force away from the object.

3. Pulling should be a controlled movement with a minimum of jerking and tugging.

4. The hand grips must be comfortable if pulling is to be efficient. Gloves or other padding can help.

5. Pulling movements can be isolated in the body, with one part of the body pulling against the other.

Teaching Cues

1. Take a good grip.
2. Get your body in line with the pull. Lower yourself.
3. Widen your base of support.
4. Gather your body forces and pull steadily.

Directives for Suggested Movement Experiences

1. Reach for the ceiling and pull an imaginary object toward you quickly. Slowly and smoothly.

2. Use an individual tug-of-war rope and practice pulling against a partner. Do this with your hands and arms at different levels.

3. From a kneeling position, pull an object.

4. Try to pull with your feet while you sit on the floor.

5. Pretend to pull a heavy object while you are lying on the floor.

6. Clasp your hands together and pull as hard as you can.

7. Try pulling an object while you stand on one foot.

8. Hold hands with a partner, and pull slowly as hard as you can.

9. Have your partner sit down, and then see how slowly you can pull him.

10. With your partner sitting on the floor, see whether you can pull her to her feet.

11. Pull with different body parts.

12. Pull your partner by the feet as he sits on a rug square.

PULLING AND PUSHING

Combinations of pulling and pushing movements should be arranged in sequence. Musical phrases can signal changes from one movement to the other.

Balance-beam benches are excellent for practicing pulling and pushing techniques. Individual tug-of-war ropes provide effective pulling experiences.

The selected partner resistance exercises (pp. 230–231) are also good pulling and pushing experiences.

PATTERNS OF DEVELOPMENT IN SPECIALIZED SKILLS

Skills basic to a number of sports include catching, throwing, and kicking, among others. These are complex motor patterns, and stages of development have been identified, from initial stages through mature patterns of performance. An example of incorrect learning is often seen in throwing. Many youngsters never develop mature throwing patterns. Several factors contribute to this situation. Little emphasis is placed on correct form, and children are seldom encouraged to learn properly. If the skill-learning period does indeed occur in the early years, then teaching and encouraging the correct performance of specialized sport skills is necessary if proper development is to take place.

Most complex skills must be practiced at almost normal speed rather than in slow motion. Analysis of the following skills offers the teacher an idea of development sequence, which is more important to the learning process than the chronological age of the children. Suggested activity challenges for developing throwing, catching, and kicking skills are found in Chapter 18, Manipulative Activities.

THROWING

In throwing, an object is thrust into space and is accelerated through the movement of the arm and the total coordination of the body. Teachers should be aware that young children may need to go through two preliminary tossing stages before entering the stages of throwing.

The first toss is a two-handed underhand throw that involves little foot movement. A large ball, such as a beach ball, is best for teaching this type of throw, which begins with the ball held in front of the body at waist level. The child completes the toss by using only the arms, and sometimes has difficulty maintaining balance when encouraged to throw the ball for any distance.

The second toss is the one-handed underhand throw. In this toss, which resembles pitching a softball, the child begins to develop body torque and is able to shift the weight from the rear to the front foot. This toss requires a smaller object. Beanbags, fleece balls, and small sponge balls work well.

The following skill analysis deals with overhand throwing. The teacher should be concerned that children strive for proper form while throwing, rather than for distance or accuracy. A good rule to remember is that accuracy is a secondary goal if one is interested in developing patterns characterized by a full range of motion and speed. Throwing for accuracy can be introduced gradually as the pattern matures.

Stage One

Stage one of throwing generally can be observed between the ages of 2 and 3 years. This stage is basically restricted to arm movement from the rear toward the front of the body. The feet remain stationary and positioned at shoulder width, with little or no trunk rotation occurring (Figure 9.9). Most of the movement force originates from flexing the hip, moving the shoulder forward, and extending the elbow.

Stage Two

Stage two of throwing develops between the ages of 3½ years and 5 years. Some rotary motion is developed as the child attempts to increase the amount of force. This stage is characterized by a lateral fling of the arm, with rotation occurring in the trunk (Figure 9.10). Often, the child takes a step in the direction of the throw, although many children still keep their feet stationary. This throwing style sometimes looks like a discus throw rather than a baseball throw.

Stage Three

Typically, stage three is found among children age 5 to 6 years. The starting position is similar to that of stages one and two in that the body is facing the target area, the feet are parallel, and the child is erect. In this stage, however, the child steps toward the target with the foot on the same side of the body as the throwing arm. This allows for rotation of the body and shifting of the body weight forward as the step occurs. The arm action is nearer to the overhand style of throwing than is the fling of stage two, and there is also an increase in hip flexion. The throwing pattern of many students never matures beyond this stage.

Stage Four

Stage four is a mature form of throwing and allows the child to apply more force to the object being accelerated. The thrower uses the rule of opposition in this stage, taking a step in the direction of the throw with the leg opposite the throwing arm. This develops maximum body torque. The child addresses the target with the nonthrowing side of the body and strides toward the target to shift body weight. Beginning with the weight on the back leg, the movement sequence is as follows: (1) step toward the target, (2) rotate the upper body, and (3) throw with the arm (Figure 9.11.) The cue phrase used is "Step, turn, and throw." The elbow should lead the way in the arm movement, followed by forearm extension, and finally a snapping of the wrist. This pattern must be practiced many times to develop total body coordination. Through a combination of sound instruction and practice, the majority of youngsters should be able to develop a mature pattern of throwing by age 8 or 9 years.

CATCHING

Catching is a skill that involves using the hands to stop and control a moving object. Catching is more difficult for a child to learn than throwing, because he must be able to track the object with his eyes and to move his body into the path of the object at the same time. Another element that makes catching more difficult to master is fear of the object to be caught. When teaching the early stages of catching, instructors must be careful to use objects that

FIGURE 9.9. Throwing form, stage one

FIGURE 9.10. Throwing form, stage two

FIGURE 9.11. Throwing pattern, stage four

cannot hurt the receiver. Balloons, fleece balls, and beach balls move slowly, thus encouraging visual tracking, and they do not hurt the child if he is hit in the face.

Stage One

In stage one of catching, the child holds the arms in front of the body, with elbows extended and palms up, until the ball makes contact. She then bends the arms at the elbows (Figure 9.12). The catch is actually more of a trapping movement, since the arms press the ball against the chest. Children often turn their head away or close their eyes because of the fear response. They should be encouraged to watch the object rather than the person who is throwing the object.

Stage Two

In stage two, the child repeats much of the same behavior as in stage one. Rather than waiting for the ball to contact the arms, however, the child makes an anticipatory movement and cradles the ball somewhat.

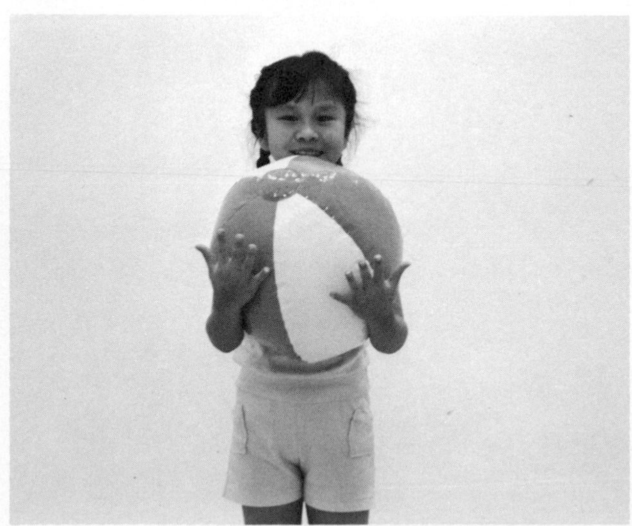

FIGURE 9.12. Catching form, stage one

FIGURE 9.13. Catching a large object, stage three

Stage Three

As the child's catching pattern matures, he prepares for the catch by lifting the arms and bending them slightly. The chest is used as a backstop for the ball. During this stage, the child attempts to make contact with the hands first and then to guide the object to the chest (Figure 9.13).

Stage Four

The fourth and final stage of catching, which should occur at approximately 9 years, is characterized by catching with the hands. The child can be encouraged to catch with the hands by decreasing the size of the ball to be caught. As the child continues to improve, she learns to give with the arms as she catches (see p. 30). The legs bend, and the feet are moved in anticipation of the catch.

KICKING

Kicking is a striking action executed with the feet. There are different types of kicking: punting (in which the ball is dropped from the hands and kicked before it touches the ground), and placekicking (kicking the ball in a stationary position on the ground) are two. A third type is soccer kicking, which is probably the most difficult of all kicking skills because the ball is moving before the kick is executed.

Stage One

In stage one, the body is stationary and the kicking foot is flexed as the child prepares for the kick. The kicking motion is carried out with a straight leg and with little or no flexing at the knee. Minimal movement of the arms and trunk occurs as the child concentrates on the ball.

Stage Two

In the second stage of kicking, the child lifts the kicking foot back by flexing at the knee. Usually, the child displays opposition of the limbs. When the kicking leg goes forward, her opposite arm moves forward. In stage two, the child's kicking leg moves farther forward as a follow-through motion than in stage one.

Stage Three

The child runs or walks toward the object to be kicked. There is an increase in the distance that the leg is moved, coupled with a movement of the upper body to counterbalance the leg movement.

Stage Four

The mature stage of kicking involves a preparatory extension of the hip to increase the range of motion. As the child runs to the ball and prepares to kick it, he takes a small leap to get the kicking foot in position. As the kicking foot is carried forward, the trunk leans backward, and the child takes a small step forward on the support foot to regain balance (Figure 9.14).

FIGURE 9.14. Kicking a soccer ball, stage four

CHAPTER 10

Human Wellness: Concepts for Better Living

If one were to ask a child what the concept of human wellness means, a typical answer might be to "feel good." The term means more, however, than just adequate health. It means attainment of a special type of life-style, and focuses on living life to the fullest.

Wellness programs, stressing personal wellness planning, are being established in major medical centers. Only recently, however, have the public schools given attention to the concept. For the child, wellness becomes a value issue and a search for understanding of how the body functions. Motivation is important, because most children have little cultural or educational background for learning the concepts of wellness. Many parents have had minimal exposure to wellness planning, and thus children need to be challenged to expand their involvement in enhancing their personal wellness life-style.

Human wellness is subject to individual interpretation by children as a result of their differing backgrounds and experiences. In the educational process, children become listeners and potential consumers. The goal of wellness education in the schools is to establish a fundamental basis for effective living. The approach at the elementary school level is threefold.

First, a sound physical education program contains knowledge that can contribute to the concepts of human wellness. A child needs to understand the human body and how it functions. This involves teaching rudimentary anatomy, simple physiology, and relevant movement principles. The information must be within a child's understanding and must be relevant to situations that a child faces.

The second step is to present selected concepts from various areas deemed important in establishing a broad coverage of wellness. Human wellness is not an entity in itself, but is composed of various interlocking areas that form a coordinated whole. What are the necessary concepts, for example, that should be stressed to achieve a better understanding of the physical fitness process? What nutrition basics does a child need to know?

The final step is to provide opportunity for application of the concepts through a variety of learning experiences. Without this step, the entire process is merely academic practice. The physical education learning environment should provide guidance to help children assimilate the substance of the wellness concepts.

WELLNESS IN THE PHYSICAL EDUCATION SETTING

Nowhere is it assumed that the achievement of wellness is the sole concern of physical education. Some aspects of wellness, such as development of a personalized level of physical fitness, are emphasized primarily in physical education. Other aspects can be developed cooperatively by planning with the classroom teachers.

A physical education teacher may justifiably raise the question: How can I develop physical fitness levels, teach skills, and accomplish all the topics listed under human wellness? Many of the topics may be included in the classroom health program, and added support from the physical education teacher is of immeasurable help.

There are many different approaches to the teaching of wellness in elementary school physical education classes. Physical activity is still the cornerstone of physical education, and we do not suggest the substitution of a knowledge-discussion program at the expense of activity. On the other hand, a strong case can be made that activity, without a knowledge base of *how* and *why,* is in the long run ineffective. If additional time cannot be found for teaching wellness activities, then discussions should be held to a 5-minute limit. Within the physical education setting, discussions longer than this usually give rise to inattention and disinterest.

Some districts have successfully designed programs that concentrate on wellness for a period of 2 to 4 weeks. This wellness instruction is spaced out during the school year. During those weeks, physical education classes per se are cancelled and moved to a classroom where the physical education specialist conducts the wellness sessions. This results in concentrated instruction in a setting (the classroom) that is conducive to cognitive and affective development. Many variations of this approach have been developed to accommodate the specific school parameters.

At best, the wellness approach becomes the pursuit of excellence, inspiring children to make the most of their physical and movement potential. At least, wellness instruction gives children a better understanding of the body and its possibilities, which can mean higher achievement.

INSTRUCTIONAL STRATEGIES FOR TEACHING WELLNESS

Physical education plays a large role in enhancing the fitness and skill levels of students so they have a background that allows them to develop an active life-style. Another program goal should also be to help young people make responsible decisions about wellness and its impact on their lives. People are faced with many decisions that can have either a positive or a negative impact on their level of wellness. The ability to make responsible decisions depends on a wide range of factors: understanding one's feelings and clarification of personal values, ability to cope with stress and personal problems, ability to make decisions, and impact of various factors on health.

DEVELOPING AWARENESS AND DECISION-MAKING SKILLS

The focus of wellness instruction should be to view the student as a total being. Stability is predicated on all parts fitting together in a smooth and consistent fashion. When a problem occurs, the balance of physiology, thinking, and function tends to be disrupted. Individuals then need to use their knowledge, coping ability, and decision-making skills to restore the equilibrium associated with personal stability. Teachers can try to help students understand their feelings, values, and attitudes, and the impact that these have on coping and decision making.

COPING SKILLS

Coping is the ability to deal with problems successfully. Learning to cope with life's problems is dependent on and interrelated with knowledge of self, decision-making skills, and the ability to relate to others. Specific skills dealing with coping include the following.

1. Admit a problem exists and face it. Coping with a problem is impossible when the problem is not recognized.

2. Define the problem and who owns it. Individuals must identify what needs to be coped with and to decide if the problem is theirs or belongs to others.

3. List alternative solutions to the problem. A basic step in decision making, problem solving, and coping is to identify what alternatives are open in a given situation.

4. Predict consequences for oneself and others. Once alternatives are identified, weighing the potential consequences of each, and then ranking them in order of preference is an important process.

5. Identify and consult sources of help. All possible sources of help available to assist in carrying out alternatives should be considered. In order to do this, students need to have some knowledge of the available resources or how to find resources.

6. Experiment with a solution and evaluate the results. If the decision did not produce satisfactory results, try another alternative. Evaluation of results also allows people to keep track of their ability to come up with satisfying solutions.

DECISION-MAKING SKILLS

Youngsters are faced with many life situations in which decisions must be made. Decision making is something that everyone does every day, often without thinking. Because it is a common act, it receives little attention until a person is faced with an important decision that has long-term consequences.

Although the schools attempt to help students learn how to make personally satisfying decisions, a major portion of teacher time is spent developing information for or supplying information to students. Although this teacher function is extremely important, it is only one part of the decision-making process. Teachers should ask themselves the question, "If you are going to provide information to others, what do you want them to do with that information?" Opportunities should be provided for students to put information to use.

Decision making is defined as a process in which a person selects from two or more possible choices. A decision cannot exist unless more than one course of action is available to consider. If a choice exists, the process of deciding may be used. Decision making enables the individual to reason through life situations, to solve problems, and, to some extent, to direct behavior.

There are no right answers for the decision made but, rather, the decision is judged by the student's effective use of a process that results in satisfying consequences. This criterion distinguishes decision making from problem solving. Problem solving usually identifies one best or right solution for everyone involved. When making decisions, students should consider each of the following steps.

1. *Gather information.* If meaningful choices are to be made, then gathering all available information is important. Information should be gathered from as many sources as possible. Students generally consider information valid if they see that it comes from many different sources and that it allows them to view both sides of an issue. Too often, teachers present students with information that supports only the instructor's point of view.

2. *Consider the available choices.* The next step is to consider all of the available choices. It does not make sense to consider alternatives that, in reality, have no possibility of being selected. Considering the choices is an important step if students are to realize that they have many different possibilities from which to choose and that what they choose will influence the direction of their life. In the school setting, many choices have been made for students, and they sometimes come to believe that others make all decisions for them and that they, in turn, bear no responsibility for their successes or failures.

3. *Analyze the consequences of choices.* When the various choices are delineated, students must consider the consequences that accompany each choice. If the consequences are ignored, the choice made may be unwise and detrimental to good health. Making wise decisions about wellness demands that students be aware of the consequences. This means understanding why some people choose to smoke or drink, even when they understand the negative consequences. The most important role of the teacher is to help students identify the positive and negative consequences without moralizing or telling the students how to think.

4. *Make a decision and implement it.* When all of the information has been gathered, students must make a decision and implement it in their life-style. These decisions are personal to each student and need not be revealed to others.

Skillful decision makers have greater control over their lives because they can reduce the amount of uncertainty in their choices and limit the degree to which chance or their peers determine their future. Two individuals may face a similar decision and make different choices, because each person is different and places differing values on outcomes. The individual makes each decision unique. Learning decision-making skills therefore increases the possibility that students can achieve their goals.

Decisions also have limits. Each decision is necessarily limited by what a person is capable of doing, by what a person is willing to do, and by the environment in which the decision is made. The environment in which decision-making skills are practiced is important to the development of these skills. A nonjudgmental atmosphere would seem most appropriate. Since the solutions differ for different people, the person making a decision should be free to select from any of the available choices, and should be willing to accept the probable consequences and results.

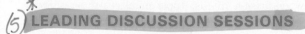

LEADING DISCUSSION SESSIONS

The success of discussions depends on how effectively the teacher is able to establish and maintain the integrity and structure of the lesson and the students' psychological freedom. Integrity and structure mean that all students are dealing with the same issue in a thoughtful and responsible way. Psychological freedom means that individual students participate to the degree they want to by (1) commenting when they choose to do so or refraining from comment when they so desire, (2) responding to directed questions or choosing to "pass" for the time being, (3) agreeing or disagreeing with what others in the group have said, or (4) deciding what data they need, if any, and reaching out to ask for that data. This demands certain teacher behavior to establish a meaningful environment. A brief description of the necessary teaching behaviors follows.

STRUCTURING

The purpose of structuring is to create a climate that is conducive to open communication by all parties. This is accomplished by outlining expectations and role relationships for both teacher and students. Structuring includes any of the following:

1. Establish the lesson climate at the beginning of the lesson by providing an explanation of what the students and teacher will be doing and how they will work together.

2. Maintain the established lesson structure by not allowing students to be pressured to respond and by seeing that no one's ideas are put down.

3. When necessary, add to or modify the lesson structure established at the beginning of the lesson. For example, this might involve changing to small group sessions rather than continuing a total class discussion.

FOCUS SETTING

The purpose of focus setting is to establish an explicit and common topic or issue for discussion. Since this teaching behavior is used in different circumstances, there are different ways it can be formulated:

1. The teacher may present a topic, usually in the form of a question, to the group for their discussion.

2. The teacher may use focus setting to restate the original question during the lesson or to shift to a new discussion topic because the students have indicated that they have finished discussing the original question.

3. The teacher may use focus setting to bring the discussion back to the original topic when a student unknowingly shifts to a new topic.

4. The teacher may use focus setting to label a discussion question presented by a student as a new topic and to allow discussion of that topic in place of a previous one.

CLARIFYING

The purpose of a clarifying teaching behavior is to invite a student to help the teacher better understand the substance or content of the student's comment. Whenever possible, the clarifying teaching behavior should give the student some indication of what the teacher does not understand. In addition, the teacher's remarks should be formulated in such a way that the burden of understanding is put on the teacher, rather than implying that the student is deficient because she cannot express herself effectively. Clarifying is used by teachers only when they do not understand. The teacher does not assume the responsibility of clarifying for other students.

ACKNOWLEDGING

An acknowledging teaching behavior informs a student who is talking to the teacher that the teacher understands what has been said and that the student's comments have made a contribution to the discussion. Unlike most teaching behaviors, this one can be implemented nonverbally as well as by verbal means.

How an acknowledging teaching behavior is worded and when it is used must be considered carefully. To use acknowledging only when the teacher understands and agrees, but to do something else when the teacher understands and disagrees, is to have seriously misunderstood the purpose and function of this teaching behavior. Acknowledging is intended to be a nonjudgmental way of saying "I understand."

TEACHER SILENCE

The purpose of teacher silence is to communicate to students through nonverbal means that it is their responsibility to initiate and carry on the discussion. Teacher silence is used only in response to student silence. It protects the students' rights and responsibility to make their own decisions about the topic being discussed. In one sense, this teaching behavior is a nonbehavior.

INSTRUCTIONAL AREAS REQUIRED FOR UNDERSTANDING HUMAN WELLNESS

The material in this section on wellness is couched in terms of the knowledges and understandings that elementary school students must develop. The areas presented are rudimentary and were chosen to illustrate clearly to future and practicing teachers what knowledge, concepts, and experiences children must become immersed in as a prelude to developing a value set that enhances personal wellness. Since most children with an abundance of good health have little concern about health, this unit should be the foundation for developing proper health attitudes later at the junior and senior high school level.

Students must understand two major categories of wellness concepts. The first is a basic knowledge of how the body functions, and how it can be maintained and finely tuned through proper care and activity. The second category consists of an awareness of the roadblocks that stand in the path of wellness. Some of these are stress, improper nutrition, obesity, anorexia, substance abuse, and personal safety problems.

We list first the basic knowledge in each area that can be imparted to children, followed by concepts that are deemed important. Learning activities are suggested for the purpose of applying the concepts in a situation that gives them meaning.

THE SKELETAL SYSTEM

The skeletal system (Figure 10.1.) is the framework of the body and consists of 208 separate bones. The bones act as a system of levers and are linked together by connections (joints) that allow movement. The bones are held together at the joints by ligaments and muscles. Ligaments are tough and incapable of stretching. They do not contract the way muscles do and are therefore subject to injury when the bones are moved beyond their natural range.

Joints that are freely movable are called *synovial joints.* Synovial fluid is secreted to lubricate the joint and reduce friction. A thin layer of cartilage also reduces friction at the ends of the bones. A disk, or meniscus, forms a pad between many of the weight-bearing joints for the purpose of absorbing shock. When a cartilage is damaged, joint dysfunction and pain can occur.

Muscular activity increases the weight-bearing stresses on bones. The bones respond to the added stress by increasing in mineral content and density, increasing in diameter, and reorganizing internal elements to cause an increase in bone strength. The bones serve as a mineral reserve for the body and can become deformed as a result of dietary deficiencies.

The bones and joints establish levers with muscles acting as the force. Three types of lever are identified and classified by the arrangement of the fulcrum, force, and resistance (see the illustration on p. 120).

The forearm is an example of a first-class lever when it is extended at the elbow joint (fulcrum) by the triceps muscle (Figure 10.2A). A second-class lever exists where the gastrocnemius raises the weight of the body to the

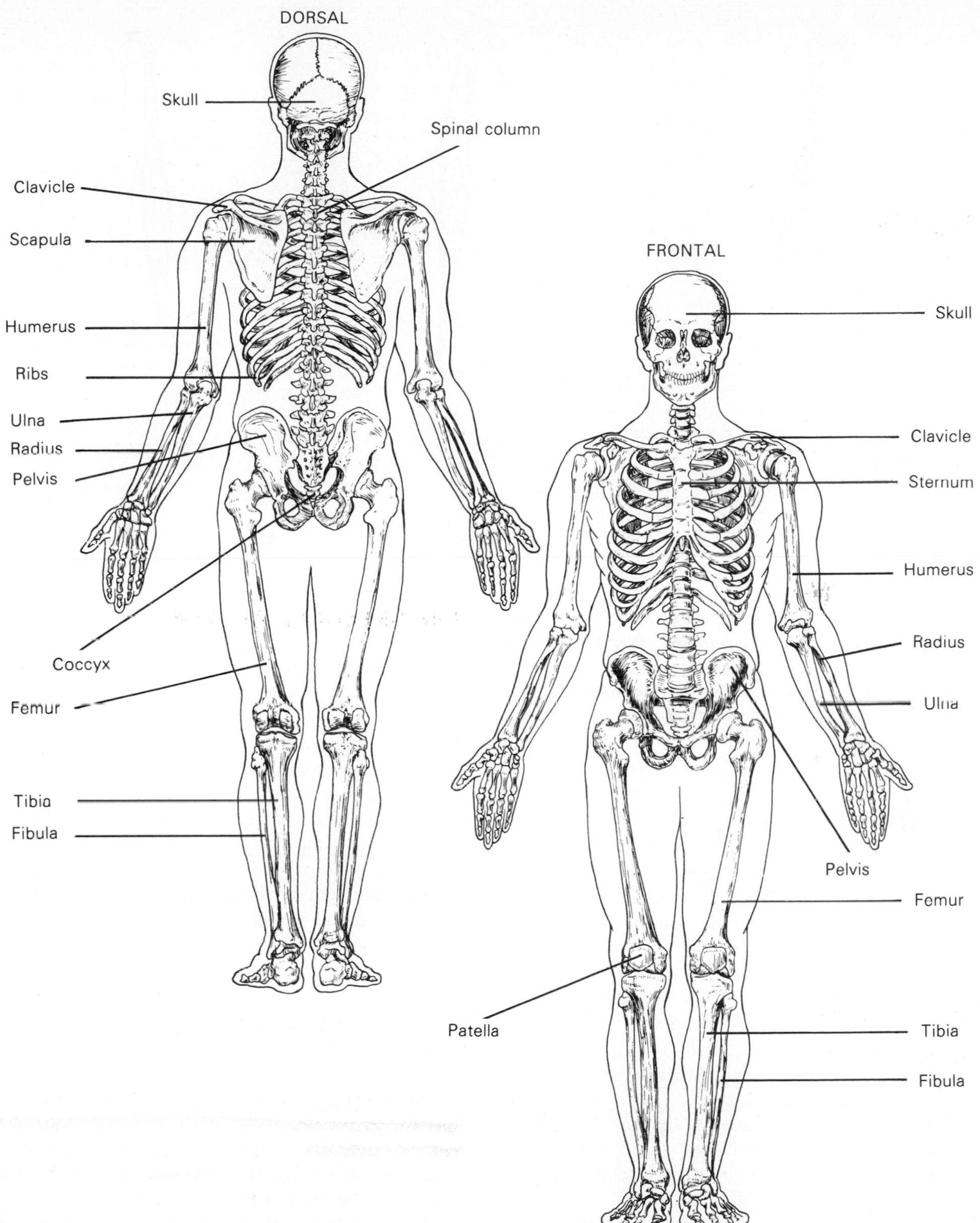

FIGURE 10.1. The skeletal system

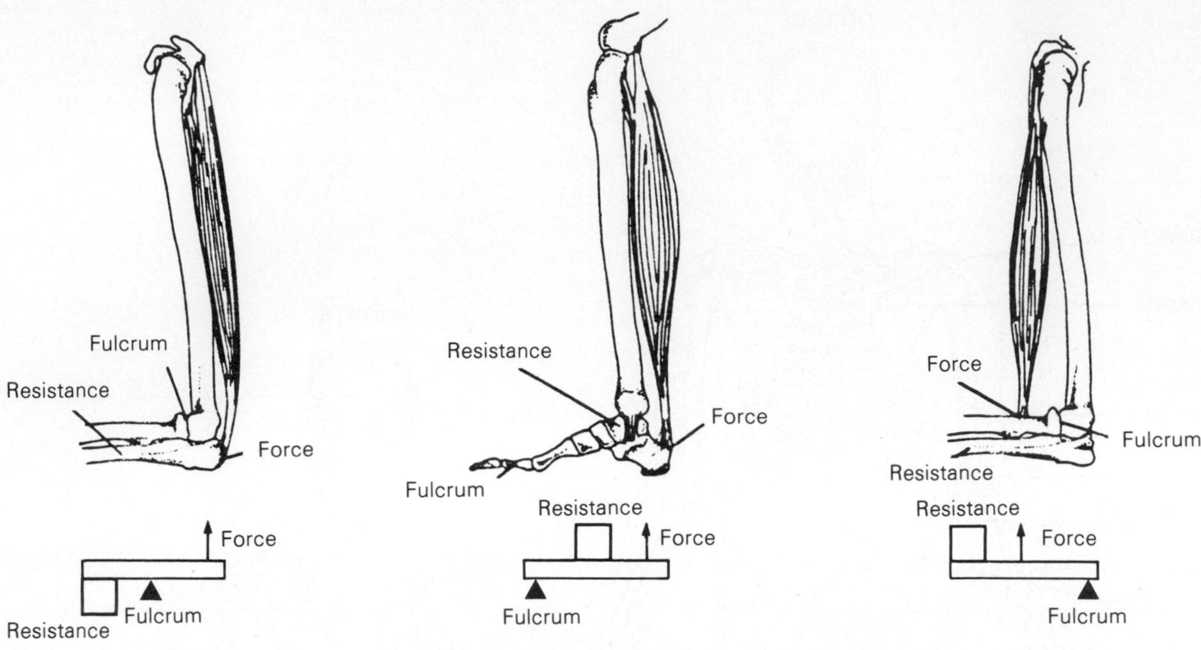

FIGURE 10.2. Types of levers in human joints

toes (Figure 10.2B). Examples of third-class lever actions are the movement of the biceps muscle to flex the forearm at the elbow joint (Figure 10.2C), the sideward movement of the upper arm at the shoulder joint by the deltoid muscle, and the flexion of the lower leg at the knee joint by the hamstring muscles.

Concepts

1. The skeletal system consists of 208 bones and determines the external appearance of the body.
2. Joints are places where two or more bones are fastened together to make a movable connection.
3. Bones are held together by ligaments and muscle tissue. The stronger the muscles surrounding the joint, the more resistant the joint is to injury.
4. Good posture results when the bones are in proper alignment. Alignment depends on the muscular system. When antigravity muscles are weak, greater stress is put on the joints, and poor posture results.
5. The bones and joints establish levers with muscles serving as the force.
6. The attachment of the muscle to the bone determines the mechanical advantage that can be gained at the joint. Generally, the farther from the joint the muscle attaches, the greater the force is that can be generated.
7. The body has three types of levers. These are classified by the arrangement of the fulcrum, force, and resistance.

Suggested Learning Experiences

1. Identify and locate major bones significant in body movement. The following are suggested.
   - **a.** Head—skull
   - **b.** Arm-shoulder girdle—radius, ulna, ribs, humerus, scapula (shoulder blade), clavicle (collarbone)
   - **c.** Chest—sternum (breastbone), ribs
   - **d.** Back-pelvis—spinal column, pelvis, coccyx
   - **e.** Thigh-leg—femur, tibia, fibula, patella (kneecap)
2. Identify the types of movement possible at selected joints. Study the neck, shoulder, elbow, wrist, spinal column, hip, knee, and ankle joints.
3. Catalogue the types of levers found in the body. Illustrate the fulcrum, force, and resistance points.
4. Obtain animal bones from a grocery store and analyze their various components. Cartilage, muscle attachments, ligaments, and bone structure can be studied in this way.
5. Obtain outdated X-ray films from physicians. These are excellent sources for identifying differences in various bones and joints.

THE MUSCULAR SYSTEM (FIGURE 10.3)

Muscles apply force to the bones to create movement. Muscles create movement always through contraction, never by pushing. When one set of muscles contracts, another set that pulls in the opposite direction must relax. This set is the antagonistic muscle group.

People are born with two distinct types of muscle fiber. These are often called fast-twitch and slow-twitch fibers. Slow-twitch fibers respond well to aerobic activities, whereas fast-twitch fibers are suited to anaerobic activities. This is one of the reasons why people perform differently in different physical activities. For example, those born with a high percentage of slow-twitch fibers would be suited to distance running but might do poorly in sprint races.

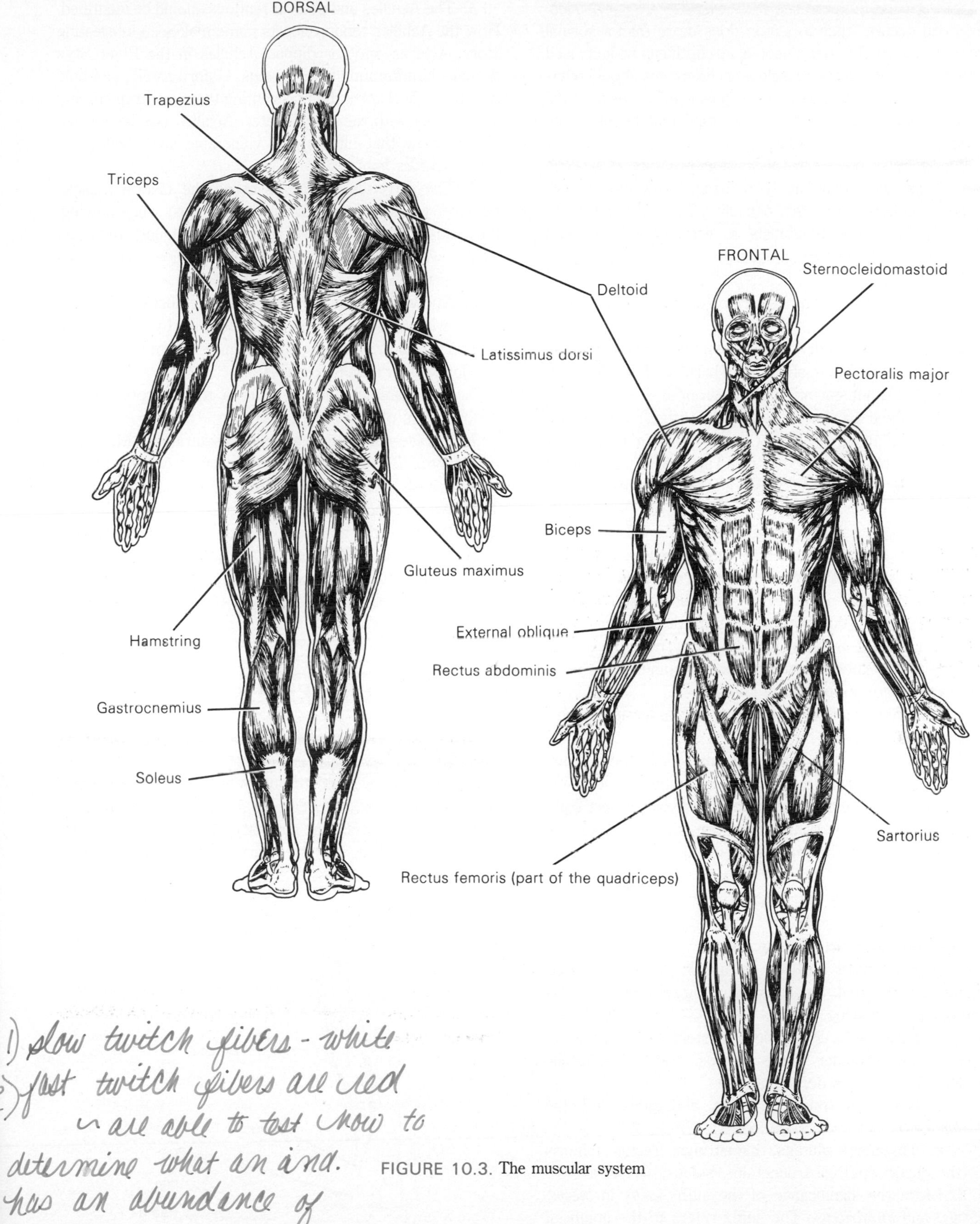

FIGURE 10.3. The muscular system

1) slow twitch fibers - white
2) fast twitch fibers are red
- are able to test how to determine what an ind. has an abundance of

Strength can be increased when muscles are overloaded. Overload occurs when a person does more than a normal amount of work. In young people, strength can be increased without a change in the muscle size. Exercises should overload as many muscle groups as possible to ensure total body development. Strength is an important factor in the development of motor skills.

Flexibility is the range of motion possible at a given joint. Exercises should apply resistance through the full range of motion to maintain flexibility. Extensor and flexor muscle groups are antagonists to each other, and both groups should be exercised equally.

Concepts

1. Muscles can pull and shorten (contract); they never push.

2. Flexors cause a decrease in joint angle, and extensors cause an increase. There should be a balance of development between these antagonistic muscle groups.

3. The fixed portion of a muscle (origin) usually has muscle fibers attached directly to the bone or may be attached by a tendon to the bone. The moving portion of the muscle forms a tendon, which attaches to a bone (insertion).

4. Overload with proper progression is necessary for muscle development. Muscles become strong in both boys and girls through exercise. After adolescence, boys' muscles will increase in size owing to the male hormone testosterone. Girls' muscles do not show the same degree of increase.

5. Muscles are important for proper posture. Good muscle tone makes good posture comfortable and puts a minimum amount of strain on the joints.

6. Different types of training are necessary for aerobic and anaerobic activity.

7. Muscles are composed of many small fibers. When these fibers contract, they do so according to the all-or-none principle, that is, if they contract, they contract completely. Differences in contraction strength of a muscle are a function of the percentage of muscle fibers recruited and asked to contract.

8. When muscles are fatigued, the muscle fibers will no longer contract.

Suggested Learning Experiences

1. Identify major muscles or muscle groups and their functions at the joint. Muscle groups suggested for elaboration are the following.

a. Head-neck—sternocleidomastoids

b. Arm-shoulder girdle—biceps, triceps, pectorals, deltoid, latissimus dorsi, trapezius

c. Body—abdominals (rectus abdominis and the obliques)

d. Thigh-leg—gluteus, hamstrings, rectus femoris (the quadriceps), gastrocnemius, soleus, sartorius

2. Learn the significance of the suffix *-ceps* in *biceps, triceps,* and *quadriceps.* The suffix refers to the points of origin (heads). The biceps has two points of origin (heads), the triceps has three, and the quadriceps has four.

3. The Achilles and patellar tendons should be identified. How the Achilles tendon got its name makes an interesting story. Achilles' mother dipped Achilles in the River Styx to make him immune from arrows. Unfortunately, she held him by the heel cord, thus preventing that area from coming into contact with the magic water. Achilles was later killed by an arrow that hit his one vulnerable spot, hence the name *Achilles tendon.*

4. The sartorius muscle is called the tailor's muscle, because, years ago, tailors sat cross-legged while sewing, thus causing the muscle to shorten. The tailors then had trouble with ordinary leg movements because of the shortened muscle.

5. Know approximately where each muscle originates and how it causes movement at the joint by attaching to a particular bone or bones. Recognize the muscles being developed by various exercises.

6. Study animal muscle under a microscope. Identify various parts of the muscle.

7. Involve students in a project featuring a "Muscle of the Month." The classroom teacher can cooperate by presenting basic facts about the muscle in classroom work. The physical education teacher can make drawings showing the anatomy of the muscle (origin, insertion, and location) (Figure 10.4) and post these in the gymnasium and classroom. Pay attention to spelling and pronunciation. Over a 2-year period, all of the suggested muscle groups can be studied.

THE CARDIORESPIRATORY SYSTEM

The cardiorespiratory system consists of the heart, lungs, arteries, capillaries, and veins. The heart is a muscular organ that pumps blood through the circulatory system—arteries, capillaries, and veins, in that order. The heart has its own blood vessels, the coronary arteries, which nourish it to keep it alive, for the heart draws no nourishment

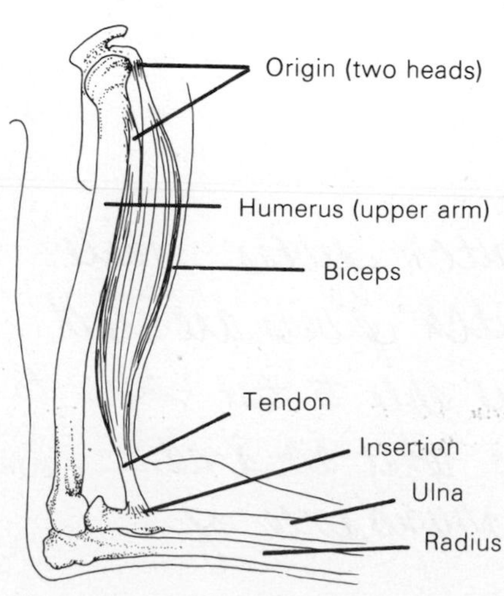

FIGURE 10.4. Anatomy of a muscle

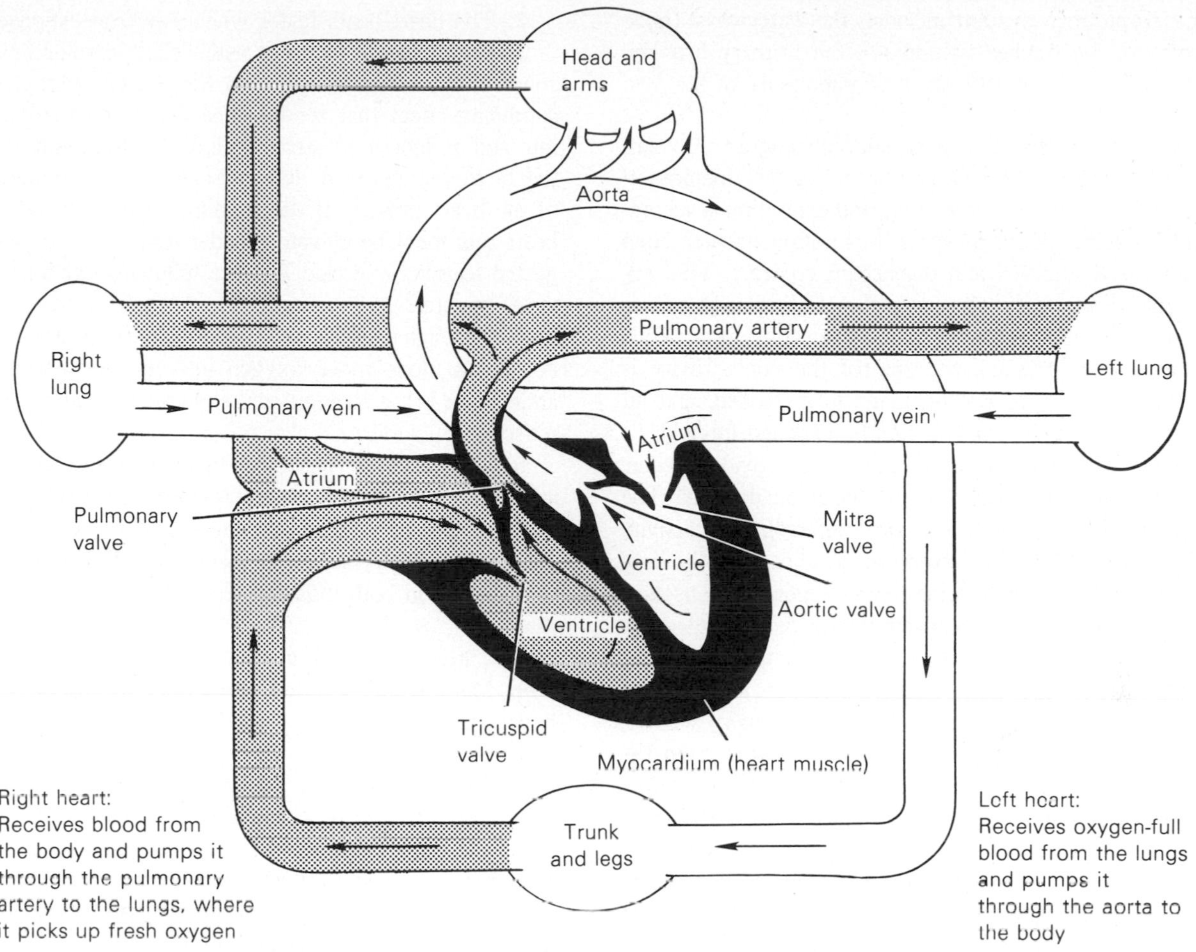

FIGURE 10.5. Structure of the heart (after the American Heart Association)

from the blood going through the chambers as it pumps. The blood supply to the heart is critical, and a decreased flow can damage the heart muscle. Decreased flow may result from a buildup of fatty deposits or from a blockage, either of which can be serious enough to be regarded as heart disease.

The heart has two chambers, the right and left ventricles (Figure 10.5). The left side of the heart pumps blood carrying nutrients and oxygen to the body through the arteries to the capillaries, where the nutrients and oxygen are exchanged for waste products and carbon dioxide. The waste-carrying blood is returned through the veins to the right side of the heart, from which the blood is routed through the lungs to discharge the carbon dioxide and pick up fresh oxygen. This oxygen-renewed blood returns to the left side of the heart to complete the circuit. Other waste products are discharged through the kidneys.

Each time the heart beats, it pumps both chambers. The beat is called the pulse, and its impact travels through the body. The pulse is measured in number of beats per minute. A pulse rate of 75 means that the heart is beating 75 times each minute. The output of the heart is determined by the pulse rate and by the stroke volume, the amount of blood discharged by each beat.

The pulse is measured by placing the two middle fingers of the right hand on the thumb side of the subject's wrist (Figure 10.6) while the subject is seated. Taking the pulse at the wrist is usually preferable to using the carotid artery (along the neck), because pressure on the carotid artery decreases blood flow to the brain. There is some debate on this point, however, and the carotid artery can be used by an adult taking a child's pulse. Pulse for baseline data should be taken two or three times to make sure it is accurate. The pulse is usually taken for 10 or 15 seconds and converted to a per minute rate by using the appropriate multiplier.

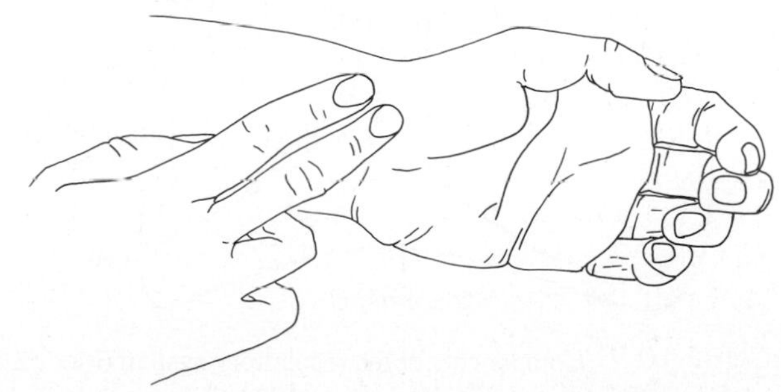

FIGURE 10.6. Taking the pulse at the wrist

The respiratory system includes the entryways (nose and mouth), the trachea (windpipe), the primary bronchi, and the lungs. Figure 10.7 shows components of the system.

Breathing consists of inhaling and exhaling air. Air contains 21% oxygen, which is necessary for life. Inspiration is assisted by muscular contraction, and expiration is accomplished by relaxing the muscles. Inspiration occurs when the intercostal muscles and diaphragm contract. This enlarges the chest cavity, and expansion of the lungs causes air to flow in as a result of reduced air pressure. When the muscles are relaxed, the size of the chest cavity is reduced, the pressure on the lungs is increased, and air flows from the lungs. Air can also be expelled forcibly.

The primary function of the lungs is to provide oxygen, carried by the bloodstream, to the cells on demand. The amount of oxygen needed will vary depending on activity level. When an individual exercises strenuously, the rate of respiration increases to bring more oxygen to the tissues. If the amount of oxygen carried to the cells is adequate to maintain the level of activity, the activity is termed *aerobic* (endurance) exercise. Examples are walking, jogging, and bicycling for distance. If, because of high-intensity activity, not enough oxygen can be brought to the cells, then the body continues to operate for a short time without oxygen. This results in an oxygen debt, which must be repaid later. In this case, the activity is termed *anaerobic* exercise.

After exercise, the respiratory rate gradually returns to normal. The recovery rate is faster if the oxygen debt built up during exercise was a small one. An individual has recovered from an oxygen debt when blood pressure, heart rate, and respiration rate have returned to preexercise levels.

Concepts

1. The heart is a muscular organ, and its development and maintenance are a function of the demands placed on it through exercise.

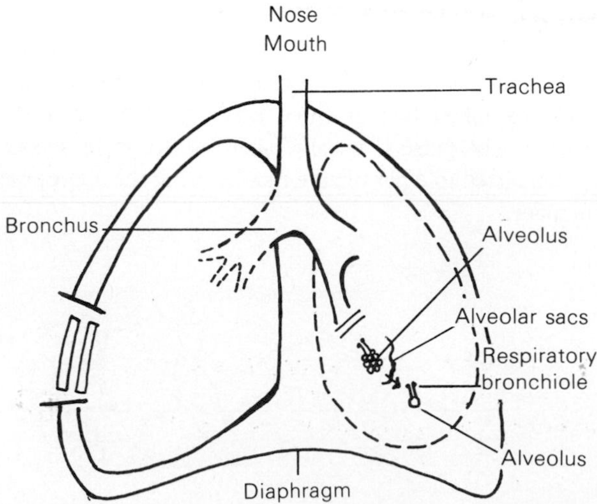

FIGURE 10.7. Components of the respiratory system (Modified from David K. Miller and T. Earl Allen. 1982. *Fitness: A lifetime commitment.* 2nd ed. Minneapolis: Burgess, p. 157.)

2. The heart beats faster when a person exercises.

3. An important factor in establishing cardiorespiratory conditioning is regular exercise. Regular exercise produces a training effect that results in a decreased resting heart rate and an increased stroke volume (the amount of blood the heart pumps each time it beats) due to hypertrophy of the heart muscle. If the training effect is to occur, the heart rate must be elevated to the training zone (see suggested learning exercise 7 in the following section) for 10 to 20 minutes.

4. Through exercise and training, the respiratory system is able to move more oxygen into the body because of an increase in the strength and endurance of the respiratory muscles.

5. The pulse rate varies depending on the level of fitness and other variables. Heart rate among girls usually averages 10 beats per minute more than among boys. As children grow older, their heart rate decreases. Fear, excitement, or a change in body position also affects the resting heart rate.

6. Cardiorespiratory conditioning is important for children. Many circulation and respiratory disorders in adults have a childhood origin.

7. Increased levels of cholesterol and other fats in the blood cause buildup of fatty deposits in the coronary arteries.

8. Some factors (e.g., heredity, sex, race, and age) that affect the cardiorespiratory system are impossible to control. Risk can be minimized, however, by controlling other factors such as smoking, body weight, diet, blood pressure level, and amount of regular exercise.

9. The immediate effects of exercise are to increase the rate of breathing and the volume of air brought into the lungs.

Suggested Learning Experiences

1. Emphasize the risk factors of cardiovascular disease. Use the acronym DANGER.

D—Don't smoke.
A—Avoid foods high in fat and cholesterol.
N—Now control high blood pressure and diabetes.
G—Get regular medical checkups.
E—Exercise each day.
R—Reduce if overweight.

2. Demonstrate and compare pulse rate in different body positions. Take the baseline pulse rate first (two or three times) with the subject in a sitting position. Take the pulse rate with the subject standing and lying down.

3. Using a single subject, show the relationship between exercise and heart action. Take the resting pulse and record it on the chalkboard. Have the subject run in place for 1 minute. Take pulse rate immediately for 10 seconds and record it. Continue taking the pulse at five 2-minute intervals to demonstrate recovery rate. (The pulse rate is approximately doubled after the stipulated exercise.) Discuss why pulse rate increases with exercise, and how the heart is strengthened through regular exercise.

4. Take the blood pressure immediately after exercise and again after resting for 3 minutes. Compare the difference.

5. To show how excess weight affects an individual, use two subjects of the same sex who are similar in build. Take the baseline pulse rate for each and record it. Give one subject 15 lb in added weight (use two 7½-lb weights), and have both subjects travel back and forth ten times across the width of the gym. Immediately take the pulse rates and record them. Compare the rates of the two subjects.

6. Compare pulse rate changes after different kinds of exercise—walking, running, rope jumping, and rope climbing. Standardize the exercise time factor at 1 or 2 minutes.

7. Calculate the heartbeat range that should be maintained to achieve the training effect and to ensure that the individual is not under- or overexercising. To do this, first determine the estimated maximum heart rate by taking 220 minus the student's age, then multiply the difference by 60% and by 80%. An example for a child of age 10 follows.

220 − 10 = 210
60% of 210 = 126
80% of 210 = 168

The heart rate range for this student to maintain while exercising is 126 to 168. The pulse rate should be checked during exercise to see whether the training effect is occurring. Charts showing exercising heart rate ranges should be placed on bulletin boards in the gymnasium so students can quickly translate the results.

8. Compare respiration rates before and after exercise.

9. Compare the volume of air moved before and after strenuous activity. Large plastic garbage bags can be used to collect expired air prior to exercise. After 2 minutes of exercise, expired air can be gathered in another bag. Compare the volume of air collected in the two bags.

EXERCISE AND THE MAINTENANCE OF PHYSICAL FITNESS

Physical fitness is defined as the ability to carry out daily tasks with vigor and alertness, without undue fatigue, and with ample energy to enjoy leisure pursuits and to meet unforeseen emergencies. Physical fitness can best be understood in terms of its components, each of which has a distinctive feature and contributes an essential element to the individual.

The most important measurable components of physical fitness are strength, power, and cardiorespiratory endurance. Agility and flexibility are only slightly less important. Speed, although a desirable attribute, is not sought directly in programs to develop physical fitness. Some tests for physical fitness include a measurement of speed as one test item, since measurements of speed may reflect indirectly other fitness components—strength, power, agility, and flexibility. Speed is, however, a valid goal of the overall physical education program.

Strength refers to the ability of a muscle or muscle group to exert force. To develop strength, the child's learning experiences should include a regular program of intense activity involving all large-muscle groups. Strength is necessary in skill performance. Without strength, a low standard of performance can be expected, because muscles give out before they can reach their potential.

Power implies using strength to apply force for effective movement. Power is based on strength and its application to movement. Maximum strength provides explosive movement for an all-out power effort.

Endurance refers to the ability of a muscle or muscle group to exert effort over a period of time. There are two major types of endurance. The first is *cardiorespiratory endurance* and refers to the ability to maintain total body activity for extended periods of time. People with adequate levels of cardiorespiratory fitness can postpone fatigue and continue performing muscular effort. Cardiorespiratory endurance is based on the movement of oxygen to the muscles at the cellular level so that a constant source of energy is available. *Muscular endurance* is the ability of the muscles to perform a desired activity without excessive fatigue. It is related to strength in that a stronger person is able to keep up muscular effort longer than a weaker person. Whereas cardiorespiratory endurance is related to general movement (i.e., walking or running), muscular endurance is related to specific activity (i.e., Push-ups, throwing, or jumping).

Agility refers to the ability to change direction swiftly, easily, and under good control. A particularly agile person is one who is hard to catch in a tag game. She can dodge and change direction well. Agility is necessary for individual safety. Many persons are alive and free from injury because they were agile enough to get out of the way of a moving object.

Flexibility is a person's range of movement at the joints. A particularly flexible individual can stretch farther, touch the toes more easily, and bend farther than others. Flexibility allows freedom of movement and the ready adjustment of the body to various movements.

Speed is the ability to move quickly. It is a necessary skill for many physical activities. Among fitness qualities, speed has high prestige, as illustrated by the fame of track stars and Olympic runners. Every child should be given the opportunity to strive for speed.

Two types of muscular contraction need to be defined. In *isotonic contraction,* the muscle shortens. There is obvious movement of some part of the body. In *isometric contraction,* the muscle maintains a fixed length. The contraction is held, and the involved body part does not move.

Concepts

1. Physical fitness is acquired only through muscular effort. Activity should be intense, regular, and varied enough to develop all components of physical fitness.

2. The maintenance of physical fitness must be ongoing; gains in fitness levels can be lost in a span of 6 to 8 weeks. Fitness is a lifelong pursuit.

3. Isotonic muscular contractions are the basis of muscular effort, with isometric contractions an important auxiliary.

4. To provide body symmetry, exercises for muscle development should involve similar work loads for extensor and flexor muscle groups. (Flexor muscles decrease the angle of a joint, and extensor muscles cause the return from flexion.)

5. To maintain fitness, a person must have a regular exercise program involving a relatively constant work load. To raise the level of fitness, the work load must be increased progressively.

6. Cardiorespiratory endurance is enhanced by moderate and continued activity, such as jogging, running, or swimming laps, over relatively long periods of time.

7. Exercise, to be beneficial, must be done properly. Certain exercises should be avoided (see p. 217).

8. Flexibility activities should feature static stretching. Muscles are stretched slowly and then held in the maximum position for 15 to 45 seconds. Ballistic stretching, which uses repetitive, forceful movements to stretch a muscle group, is not recommended.

9. Flexibility is specific to a given joint. Students should learn exercises that stretch all joints. General flexibility is the sum total of the flexibility of all joints. Measuring the range of motion at one or two selected joints can, however, give a general indication of overall flexibility.

10. Muscles must be strong enough not only to accomplish tasks but also to keep the joints in line for good posture.

Suggested Learning Experiences

1. Acquire a cardboard or wooden box about 10 in. high with a flat top. Sit on the floor with the legs together and flat on the floor so the soles are placed against the box side. Begin with arms placed behind the back and palms on the floor to support the body in an erect sitting position. Bring both arms forward slowly and bend the body forward, without bouncing, to touch the toes, the box, or beyond the edge of the box. Measure how many inches the student can reach beyond the edge of the box.

2. This experiment requires a large protractor (approximately 2 ft in diameter) and a goniometer, an instrument for measuring joint angles. A rough goniometer can be made from two pieces of wood or metal, each piece approximately 2 ft long, 2 in. wide, and ¼ in. thick. In each of the pieces, bore a hole about 1 in. from the end. Connect the two with a bolt and thumbscrew. Now open the goniometer so the two pieces form a straight line. In measuring the elbow joint, place the bolt at the center of the joint. Raise the forearm as far as possible and bring up one arm of the instrument to match the angle of the flexed movement. Tighten the thumbscrew to maintain the instrument angle. Rubber bands on the limbs can be used to hold the instrument in place. Measure the angle on the homemade protractor to quantify the individual's range of motion.

Physical fitness and fitness activities are further elaborated on in Chapter 16.

POSTURE

The maintenance of correct posture contributes to physical attractiveness and wellness. Posture refers to the habitual or assumed alignment and balance of the body segments while the body is standing, walking, sitting, or lying. In proper posture, all parts are in correct relationship to each other, and this balance is reflected in ease, gracefulness, poise, and efficiency of bearing. Posture is a reflection of the inner self. Appropriate posture radiates a positive self-image, while improper posture (e.g., slouching) reflects a poor mental image.

The association of posture with physical fitness is justified. The body must be in good enough physical condition to resist the constant pull of gravity and to maintain erect posture. The antigravity muscles, those that help support the body against the forces of gravity, must be exercised regularly to accomplish this with ease and without undue fatigue.

From a mechanical standpoint, the musculature involved in correct posture must be balanced to hold the bones and joints properly. Faulty alignment[1] can cause undue strain on supporting muscles and ligaments, which leads to early fatigue, muscle strain, and progressive displacement of postural support. In extreme cases, pain may result, and the position and function of vital organs, primarily those located in the abdomen, can be affected adversely.

The body adjusts to exterior forces applied to it. Unfortunately, this can result in poor posture. With elementary school children, incorrect posture may be simply a bad habit. As the child matures, however, poor posture becomes a growth characteristic. The muscles that activate the joints must, of necessity, adapt both in length and function to the faulty positions of the body segments.

WHAT IS CORRECT POSTURE?

Posture varies with the individual's age, sex, and body type. Very young children often toe out while standing and walking to provide a wider, more stable base. Standing position exhibits an exaggerated lumbar curve and rounded shoulders, which are normal at this developmental stage. By age 6 or 7, however, the lumbar curve is lessening and the prominent abdominal protrusion is beginning to disappear. At this stage, the feet and toes generally point ahead. Less rigid postural standards must be applied in

1. In the interest of keeping the discussion nontechnical, most technical terms describing various types of faulty alignment have not been used in this section.

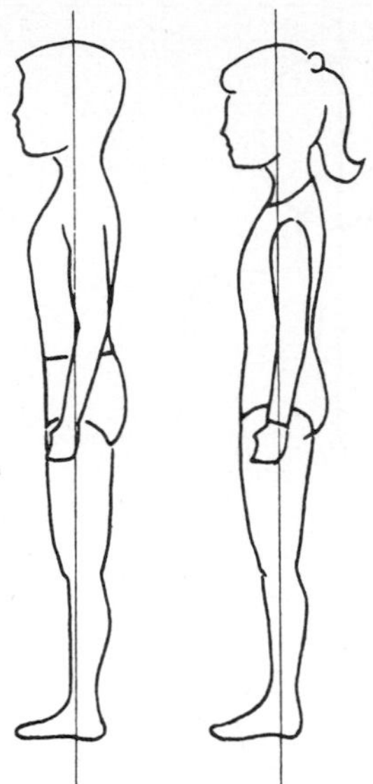
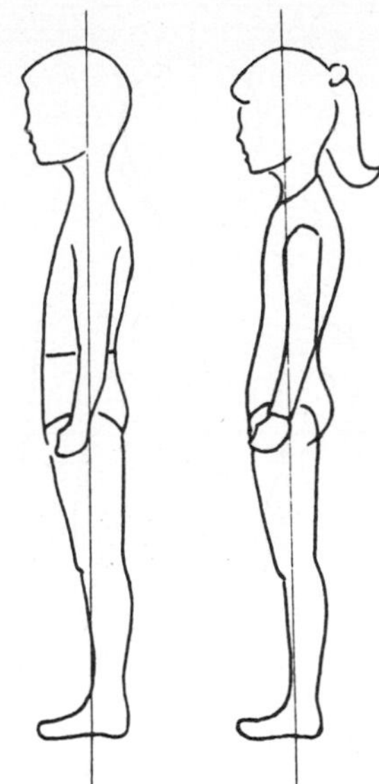
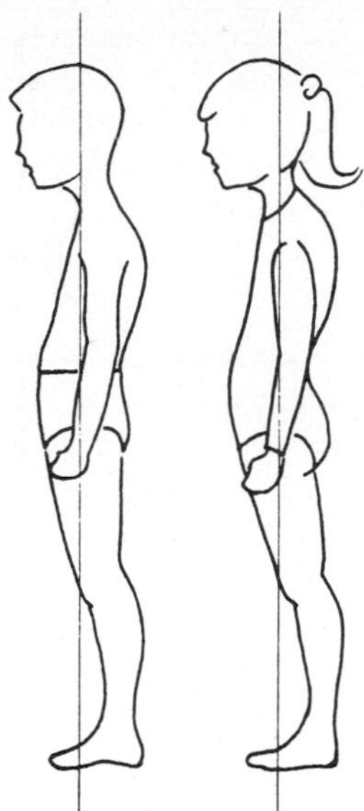

Correct Posture	Fair Posture	Poor Posture
Head up, chin in, head balanced above the shoulders with the tip of the ear directly above the point of the shoulders, eyes ahead Shoulders back and easy, chest up Lower abdomen in and flat Slight and normal curves in the upper and lower back Knees easy Weight balanced with toes pointed forward	Head forward slightly Chest lowered slightly Lower abdomen in but not flat Back curves increased slightly Knees back slightly Weight a little too far back on the heels	Head noticeably forward, eyes generally down Chest flat or depressed Shoulder blades show winged effect Abdomen relaxed and prominent Back curves exaggerated Knees forced back in back-kneed position Pelvis noticeably tilted down Weight improperly distributed

FIGURE 10.8. Characteristics of correct, fair, and poor posture

the lower grades. The educational process should assist the child in making the transition from the normal exaggerated curves of young children to proper adult posture in adolescence.

The entire body posture is based on proper positioning of the feet. When the feet are positioned correctly, then the rest of the body is more likely to line up properly. If weight is placed improperly on the heels with the knees in a locked position, then the pelvis is tilted forward (down), with a compensating increased lumbar curvature and rounded shoulders.

Toeing out during walking or standing is undesirable, because it can lead to progressive arch trouble and cause other problems such as less efficient walking and off-balance standing. Another undesirable adaptation occurs in the heel cord, which may curve outward where it joins the heel. Further change occurs as the bony structure of the foot slides toward the inside. This change culminates in a prominent inside malleolus. (The term *malleolus* refers to a bony protuberance.) The basic components of posture are illustrated in Figures 10.8 and 10.9.

LATERAL DEVIATIONS IN POSTURE

Consideration to this point has been mostly with the forward-backward plane of body movement, generally assessed from the side. The body also must be in balance in the lateral plane, as viewed from either front or back.

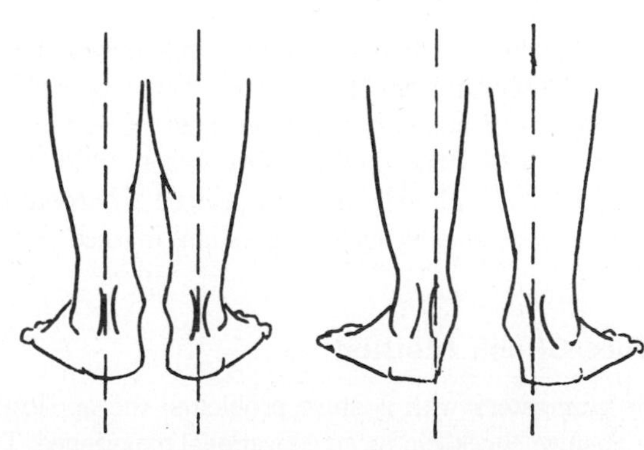

FIGURE 10.9. Normal and pronated heel cord

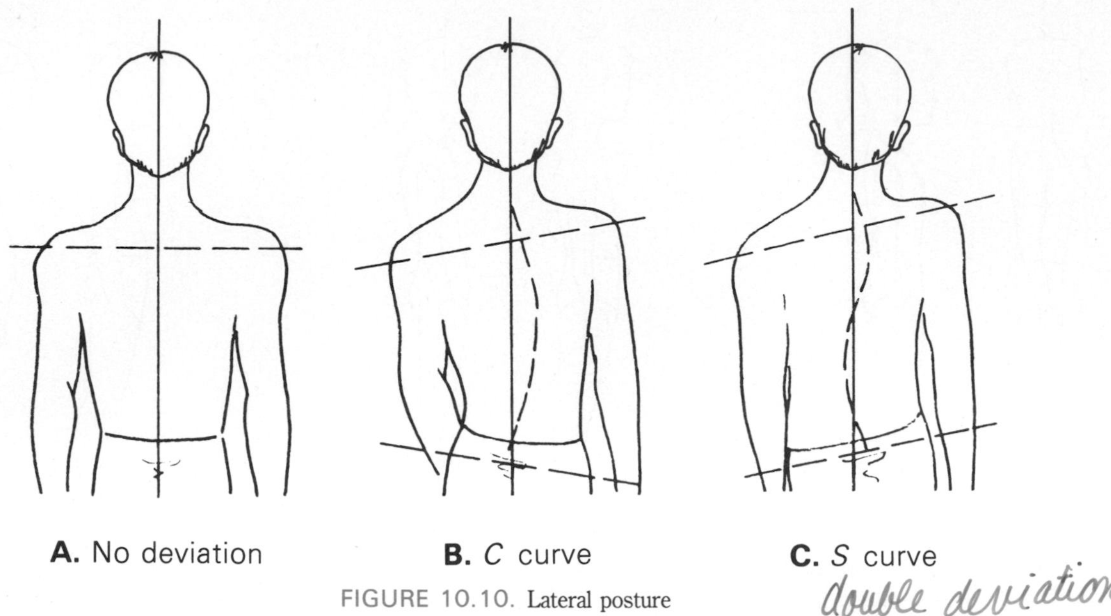

FIGURE 10.10. Lateral posture

The spinal column viewed from the back should show a straight, vertical line that divides the body into two symmetrical halves (Figure 10.10A).

A deviation occurs when this vertical line becomes either a single (*C*) curve (Figure 10.10B) or a multiple (*S*) curve (Figure 10.10C). Such deviations are coupled with one or more of the following body adjustments: (1) one shoulder higher than the other, (2) head tilts to one side, (3) hips not level, and (4) weight carried more on one leg than on the other. Marked deviations are noticeable, but moderate deviations are difficult to detect, especially when the body is clothed.

One way in which lateral curvature (scoliosis) can be detected is to have the child bend forward and touch the toes. A serious curvature is indicated when the ribs protrude on one side. Early attention to lateral curvature is important, because it generally gets worse instead of better with age. By the time the child reaches high school, the curvature is probably well established and difficult to remedy.

EVALUATING POSTURE

Since elementary school teachers are responsible for detecting and reporting any physical problems of children, some program of posture evaluation must be established. Evaluation can be done through observation, both formal and informal, and with measurement devices. Concentration should be on those individuals who exhibit marked posture deviations.

Posture Check Method

For youngsters with posture problems, the application of the posture check can be an educational experience. Two methods of recording are presented—an individual form (Figure 10.11) and a class form (Figure 10.12). The teacher may prefer the single sheet, which includes all of the class, but the individual form is easier for parents and administrators to interpret. The class form is more adaptable to class analysis and comparisons. Each item is rated 1, 2, or 3 on an ascending scale. By averaging the rating numbers, one obtains a mean rating for each child.

Some formal organization is needed for testing. Children can be examined a few at a time. A better evaluation is possible if they are in gym clothing or swimsuits, although this does require additional organization on the teacher's part.

Informal Observation

Any formal posture evaluation is an analysis of an assumed posture, which is not necessarily the posture used by the child in daily living. To offset this testing effect, posture checks can be made informally when young people are participating in classroom and physical education activities. How does each child walk, stand, or sit when not conscious of an observer? The teacher can make notes and supplement the formal posture check.

Ear-Shoulder Method

In normal posture, the lobe of the ear is directly above the point of the shoulder. Any departure from this relationship indicates a degree of back and shoulder roundness, and can be used as a measure of general posture deviation. When one body area is out of alignment, other body segments compensate proportionally. For example, if the head is forward, other parts of the body would protrude to counterbalance the poor alignment. If one measures the degree by which the head is forward, then one has an estimate of general posture. Measurement can be made with a wand or pointer and can be expressed in terms of the number

POSTURE CHECK REPORT

Name ______________ Grade ______ School ______________

Date ______________ Check made by ______________

SIDE VIEW

Head
Erect, chin in ______ Somewhat forward ______ Markedly forward ______

Upper Back
Shoulders back ______ Slightly rounded ______ Rounded ______

Lower Back
Slight natural curve ______ Moderately curved ______ Hollowed ______

Abdomen
Flat ______ Slightly protruded ______ Protruding ______

Knees
Relaxed ______ Slightly back ______ Hyperextended ______

Feet
Pointed ahead ______ Pointed out somewhat ______ Pointed out ______

FRONT AND BACK VIEW

Shoulders
Level ______ Slightly uneven ______ Considerably uneven ______

Hips
Level ______ Slightly uneven ______ Considerably uneven ______

Backs of Ankles and Feet
Heels and ankles straight ______ Turned out somewhat ______ Pronated ______

REMARKS

FIGURE 10.11. Individual posture check form

of inches the earlobe is positioned from the vertical line above the shoulder point. (In a deviated posture, the earlobe is usually forward, if anything.)

Videotaping and Self-Evaluation

An effective device to employ with children who have obvious posture problems is to videotape and play back pictures of the children standing, walking, and in other positions. In this way, they can observe themselves and make their own assessments using the posture check report. Roughly the same result can be accomplished with a Polaroid camera.

POSTURE AND THE INSTRUCTIONAL PROCESS

Posture is both a practice and a subject. The predominant emphasis should be on hints, corrections, reminders, and encouragement during all phases of the program. Even the simplest movements present postural challenges that give opportunities for incidental teaching. Strong postural impli-

CLASS POSTURE CHECK

Class ______________________ School ______________________

Date ____________ Teacher ______________________

CODE

Meets good postural standards 1

Slight but definite deviation 2

Marked deviation 3

NAME	Side View: Head and Neck	Side View: Neck	Side View: Upper Back	Side View: Lower Back	Side View: Abdomen	Side View: Knees	Side View: Feet	Front and Back View: Level of Shoulders	Front and Back View: Level of Hips	Front and Back View: Feet and Ankles	Remarks
1.											
2.											
3.											

FIGURE 10.12. Class posture check form

cations can be derived from exercises when the children understand the why of the movement.

Checking children for toeing out should be a part of every activity. The teacher should make sure that children understand the anatomical reasons for keeping the feet parallel.

Proper, well-fitting shoes are important for maintaining correct leg action during walking. Any shoe that distorts the normal shape and functioning of the foot should be avoided. Shoe heels that are worn down on the outside generally cause the foot to adjust incorrectly. The normal foot has an inside straight line from the heel up to and including the big toe. If worn long enough, any shoe that forces the big toe against the other toes can reshape the foot improperly. Tight, elastic socks also can force the big toe out of position.

At times, posture can be a subject of direct study. Values and advantages of good posture should be stressed. Emphasis is on helping children accept the responsibility for their own posture. Nagging and overzealousness on the part of the teacher or parents can have negative results.

The teacher should become skilled in providing the correct cues to help children achieve good posture. The following cues have value.

Feet—"Feet forward. Point feet straight ahead. Weight on entire foot."

Knees—"Knees easy. Knees straight but not stiff."

Lower back and abdomen—"Tuck your seat under. Flatten your tummy. Hips under. Flatten lower back."

Upper body—"Shoulders easy. Shoulder blades flat. Chest high. Raise chest."

Neck and head—"Stand tall. Chin in. Head high. Stretch tall. Chin easy. Eyes ahead."

Walking—"Walk tall. Feet forward. Eyes ahead. Arms relaxed."

Sitting—"Seat back. Sit erect. Rest against the back. Bend forward at the hips when working."

MUSCULAR DEVELOPMENT AND POSTURE

The overall physical education program should include vigorous physical activities that lead to general fitness and to strengthening of the muscle groups that hold the body in proper alignment. Strengthening the abdominal wall and the musculature of the upper back and neck helps maintain proper body alignment. Enough flexibility of the various body segments must be attained so that the child is able to move his body segments with ease and assume postural alignment. If weak musculature is the cause of poor posture, exercises and other activities to strengthen affected areas of the body should be prescribed. Development of muscle tone prevents fatigue, which results in body slump, from setting in so readily.

Many exercises (see pp. 221–228) can contribute to the maintenance of good posture. A group of special posture correction exercises is presented on pp. 228–230.

Referral

The perceptive teacher, observing children in study or play, can screen children who need attention because of poor posture. If the problem is beyond the scope of the classroom teacher, the child can be referred to the physical education specialist, nurse, principal, or an appropriate agency for help. After a corrective program has been set up, the teacher can help by encouraging the child to fulfill the prescribed remedial exercises.

If the problem is a serious lateral deviation, seeking outside help is desirable. Perhaps one leg is shorter than the other, or some other structural abnormality is present. The child must be made to realize that now is the time for correction. Later, correction will become more difficult, if not impossible.

Concepts

1. Most elementary school children are capable of assuming good posture.

2. A knowledge of the elements of good posture and a willingness to practice those elements are crucial to the maintenance of proper posture.

3. A satisfactory level of strength in the antigravity muscles is important to maintaining good posture.

4. Balanced muscular development and sufficient stamina are important in maintaining satisfactory posture.

5. Emotional outlook and self-image are factors that affect posture.

6. A well-poised body makes a person look more attractive, alert, and alive. Good posture can help one look and feel like a winner.

7. With poor posture, fatigue and muscular strain set in earlier, because the bones are out of line, which causes the muscles and ligaments to take on more work and strain than they should.

8. In sports, one can generally perform better if the body is in proper alignment.

9. Physical abnormalities can prevent a child from practicing good posture.

10. Good overall body flexibility helps in assuming good posture.

Suggested Learning Experiences

1. Practice proper posture so the body can adjust to proper alignment. Motivation is the most important element in establishing and maintaining good posture.

2. Develop an understanding and appreciation of proper posture through pictures, posters, demonstrations, and other media. Youngsters need to acquire consciously the desire for a well body.

3. Stress the values of good posture—feeling better, looking more attractive, being a winner, becoming a better performer, and being less tired.

4. Identify the antigravity muscles and single them out for development. When children are doing exercises, they can be taught to recognize and appreciate developmental possibilities.

5. All children must learn to recognize when their body is in good postural alignment. Establish the kinesthetic feeling by teaching children about proper foot and leg position, tucking the seat under, and lifting the rib cage by taking a deep breath. At the same time, tell them to stand tall, flatten the abdominal wall, and keep the head and shoulders in good position. They should then expel the air, and maintain the position without tenseness.

6. Use a wall or door to establish the feeling of correct alignment. Play "wallpaper" against the wall by making contact with the heels, calves, seat, elbows, shoulders, and back of the head. An alternate way to get into this position is to stand about 12 in. from a wall and assume a modified Skier's Sit (p. 395), with the thighs at about a 45-degree angle downward. In small increments, move the heels against the wall and, at the same time, slide the body upward until the legs are straight. The result is proper standing posture. Walk away from the wall without tenseness and return to the wall to check whether the proper position is held. A tom-tom can be used to provide rhythm for the walk.

POSITIVE SELF-CONCEPT

An individual's daily regimen should include a portion of time set aside for pleasurable play and satisfaction in physical activity. Physical participation can provide a good feeling, one that gives self-satisfaction, and can also aid in maintaining good mental health.

Physical activity can help develop an attractive body, thus allowing the child to make the most of genetic inheritance. One's self-image is boosted when one looks vibrant and sparkling. Neat and proper dress are beneficial, together with good grooming. The impression sent to others by the characteristics of good body development and proper carriage and proportion are unmistakable. For youngsters dissatisfied with their body contours, proper physical activity can be an important step toward correcting the problem and boosting self-image.

Concepts

1. Participating in physical activity makes one feel better.

2. Physical activity is a factor in making one more attractive.

3. The habit of regular participation in physical activity should be formed early in life.

4. To increase satisfaction with one's body, setting goals for desired changes and establishing a regimen to attain those goals is an effective approach.

Suggested Learning Experiences

1. Show pictures of athletes (both male and female) and discuss why they look exciting, attractive, and vibrantly alive.

2. Provide examples of television and movie personalities who maintain proper body proportions and attractiveness by specialized physical activity programs.

3. Discuss the many ways in which physical attractiveness is rewarded in our society, that is, through jobs, grades, acceptance, and so on.

4. Identify the features of physical appearance that are noticed by others (e.g., haircuts, new glasses, cleanliness, good posture, neat clothes). Our dress and grooming reflect our self-concept.

FACTORS RELATED TO WELLNESS

The following areas are important for students to understand. Wellness involves knowing what activities to avoid as well as what to do. In teaching about these activities, avoid preaching and indoctrination. Emphasis should be placed instead on showing students the pros and cons of various practices and the consequences of making certain decisions. The ultimate decision and responsibility rest with the student, not the teacher.

The major areas discussed in this section are nutrition and weight control; stress, tension, and relaxation; substance abuse; and personal safety. All are areas in which behavior can be modified to enhance the quality of life. Students' decisions in these areas may affect dramatically how they live and, sometimes, whether they will live.

NUTRITION AND WEIGHT CONTROL

Proper nutrition is necessary if one is to obtain an optimum level of physical performance from one's body. An area of emphasis in the physical education program should be balanced diet and weight control. Students must understand the reasons for maintaining a balanced diet and the impact of so-called junk foods on the body. All students are concerned about weight control and should understand how excessive caloric intake coupled with reduced exercise result in an accumulation of adipose tissue.

Students should learn about the elements of a balanced diet. The body needs fats, carbohydrates, proteins, minerals, and vitamins. A balanced diet draws from each of the four basic food groups: (1) milk and milk products, (2) meat, fish, and poultry with nuts and legumes as supplements, (3) fruits and vegetables, and (4) breads and cereals.

Moderation in the consumption of foods high in cholesterol and fat should be encouraged. Some cholesterol and fat are necessary for proper body function. When too much fat is ingested, however, cholesterol and triglyceride levels in the blood plasma increase. Many studies have shown a relationship between high cholesterol and triglyceride levels and coronary heart disease. (A blood test is needed to determine blood lipid levels.)

Children should be aware of which foods are high in fat and cholesterol. Some of the following are examples of foods high in cholesterol: eggs, cheese, cream, most beef and pork cuts, chocolate milk, shrimp, chocolate candy, cake and cookies, and ice cream.

Depending on the criteria used, anywhere from 30% to 50% of elementary school youngsters are overweight, meaning that their body weight is over the accepted limits for their age, sex, and body build. The large majority of cases of obesity occur as a consequence of inactivity or overeating or both. It is therefore important to learn about the caloric content of foods (as well as their nutritional value) in order to monitor the amount of calories ingested. Learning the amount of calories burned by different sports and individual activities is also important. For elementary school children, such levels of awareness may be difficult to achieve. However, students must gain the realization early that when caloric intake exceeds caloric expenditure, fat is stored. Experts agree that obese children do not in general consume more calories than children of normal weight. Rather, they exercise less.

Obesity is a roadblock to wellness. Life insurance companies judge overweight people as poor risks because of their shorter life expectancy. Excessive body fat makes the heart work much harder, increases the chance of having high blood pressure, and lowers the possibility of recovery from a heart attack. In youngsters, it has a detrimental effect on self-image. Students of normal weight find it much easier to perform the physical tasks that are the source of recognition from peers and adults. Overweight students are often punished more severely for misbehavior and may even receive lower grades for work similar to that of their normal-weight peers.

A systematic program for helping children to lose excess body fat can be found in Chapter 12. Body fat must be measured with skin calipers; a scale measures only total body weight. Youngsters involved in weight control programs often gain body weight as measured by a scale, even though they may actually have lost body fat. This weight gain is the replacement of fat mass by lean mass.

Concepts

1. The diet should be balanced and contain foods from each of the four basic groups. This ensures that the body is receiving essential nutrients.

2. Caloric expenditure (exercise) and intake (eating) must balance if weight is to be maintained. A weight-reduction program should include a reduction in caloric intake and an increase in daily exercise.

3. Activities vary in the energy they require. Individual needs must be considered in the selection of exercise activities.

4. Junk foods add little, if any, nutritional value to the diet and usually are high in calories.

5. Excessive weight makes it difficult to perform physical tasks. This results in less success and in less motivation to be active, thus increasing the tendency toward obesity.

6. Obesity increases the risk of heart disease and related health problems. It is a roadblock to human wellness and may decrease the longevity of the individual.

7. Scales are not an accurate indicator of a reduction in body fat. Skin calipers should be used to measure body fat.

Suggested Learning Experiences

1. Post a list of activities and their energy demands on the bulletin board. Discuss the selection of a strenuous activity as a daily exercise, especially for students who have a sedentary life-style.

2. Use skinfold calipers to measure body fat. The measurements can be compared with the amounts specified by the AAHPERD Health Related Physical Fitness Test Manual (1980) (see page 178).

3. Analyze the activity level of others in class. Record the exercise time and type of activities participated in daily for one week.

4. Maintain a food diary. Record all the food ingested daily and the amount of calories represented. Compare the amount of calories ingested with the amount of calories expended.

5. Discuss the ways in which society rewards physically fit individuals, and contrast this with the ways in which obese people are sometimes treated in our society and schools.

6. On the bulletin board, post a chart that compares the caloric content of junk foods with that of more acceptable foods.

A specific program for weight control is found on pages 156–158.

STRESS AND TENSION

Stress can be defined as a substantial imbalance between environmental demands and the individual's response capability. In situations that induce stress, the failure to meet the environmental demands usually has important consequences. For example, children can be pressured by parents' unrealistically high expectations, by their own desire to be accepted by peers, and by their desire to achieve to meet teacher expectations. Realistic, challenging, and attainable goals tend to eliminate many frustrating situations that could become stressful. Stress management is learning how to respond to situations that might cause tension. Both teacher and child must learn to recognize stressful symptoms before appropriate management techniques can be imposed.

We have much to say in this text about establishing an educationally sound learning environment. The emphasis in this discussion centers on what children should know about stress and what techniques they can learn to adopt to prevent stressful situations.

First, children need to recognize that individuals react differently to stressful situations. Some learn to handle stress in a productive fashion so that it actually increases their effectiveness. Some may not sense that a situation is stressful and so may remain calm through a crisis. How an individual perceives a situation usually determines whether it is stressful. Teachers can aid youngsters in achieving a productive and healthy outlook on life that will minimize stress.

A second area deals with the effects of stress on the body. Psychologically, stress can take the form of excitement, fear, or anger. Physical changes are also apparent when a person is under stress. The nervous system may respond to the stress through increased heart rate, increased blood pressure, increased respiration rate, increased muscle tension throughout the body, or decreased digestion (often accompanied by queasiness).

Unrelieved stress has detrimental effects on the body. It increases the risk of heart disease and can lead to insomnia and hypertension. Indigestion is common in stressed individuals, as is constipation. Backaches and general body aches often originate from stress. The inability to relieve stress through productive habits may lead to alcoholism, smoking, and drug abuse, usually among adults.

In the school setting, one antidote to stress is open communication between teacher and children. The teacher must be genuinely interested in helping children solve their problems and must give the impression to the children that she cares.

Teaching children to respect each other begins with the teacher showing genuine respect for students. Children need to recognize that how they act influences how other children act toward them. The key is for children to make the most of their abilities; to do their best and allow the consequences to occur as they may. Comparison with others should be avoided. A healthy perspective for competition is a target goal. Place the significance of winning or being the top performer in proper perspective, and concentrate on high personal effort and doing one's best. Children should be made aware of the need for classroom and gymnasium expectations, standards, deadlines, and behavior control, without which schools could not operate effectively. Standards and rules should be realistic and administered fairly and consistently.

Studies have shown that sports and moderate physical activity decrease tension. A side effect of involvement in organized sport activities is that the concentration required provides a diversion from stress and worry. Some experts believe that exercise applies stress to the body in a systematic fashion and thus prepares the body to deal with other stressful situations. One goal of teachers should be to provide students with productive and meaningful ways to relieve tension.

Coping skills should be taught to individuals who have characteristics or defects that tend to attract attention. Stress management is learning how, in this situation, to respond to uncomplimentary remarks and teasing. Behavior control should receive attention. A good adage to emphasize is that of stopping to think before you act.

RELAXATION

Motor learning promotes patterned movement and inhibits unnecessary muscles from interfering. This results in an ability to relax muscles not specifically required for task performance. Children should learn that relaxation is necessary to achieve top performance in demanding skills, particularly those involving accuracy. A basketball player takes a deep breath, expelling air, to relax before shooting a free throw. Reduction of tension results in conservation of energy and allows the task to be done efficiently and smoothly.

Sometimes, children need to think about whether to try to accomplish a skill at all costs. When performers try too hard at any activity, the result is usually an excess of effort and unnecessary motions. Tenseness produces inefficient motion and can be counterproductive.

Relaxation is a release of muscle tension that must be performed consciously. The first step in learning to relax is to recognize stress and tension. At times, children can be given short periods of complete relaxation, generally in a supine position on the floor.

Concepts

1. Stress affects all individuals to a certain degree. A certain amount of stress is necessary to stimulate performance.

2. The amount of stress that individuals experience depends on how they perceive the situation. Healthy perceptions are needed to cope effectively with stress.

3. When people have difficulty dealing with stress through productive means, they often attempt to relieve it through unhealthy and potentially dangerous means, such as alcohol, tobacco, and drug use, or inappropriate behaviors.

4. Stress causes changes in body functions. An awareness of these changes is necessary so students will know when they are under the influence of stress.

5. Stress may increase susceptibility to diseases and can cause psychosomatic illnesses.

6. Exercise is an excellent way to relieve stress and tension.

7. The body works more efficiently if all muscles unrelated to a given task are relaxed.

8. Relaxing antagonistic muscles is possible so that interference is minimized.

9. Relaxation is important in skills demanding concentration and accuracy.

10. Students need to learn to live up to their personal expectations, rather than to the expectations of others.

11. Deep breathing is a natural relaxant. Teach students to take several deep breaths if they feel tense.

Suggested Learning Experiences

1. Select a particular movement. Identify the muscles that are necessary for the movement and those that should be relaxed.

2. Hold an isometric contraction at the elbow joint. With the other hand, feel the contraction in the biceps and triceps. Do the same with other joints and muscles.

3. Tense all muscles and hold for a count of five; relax gently. Repeat as desired.

4. Try shooting a free throw while holding the breath. Inhale and exhale to relax, and then shoot the free throw. Discuss the difference.

5. Discuss overt changes in people when they are under stress. What is meant by "choking" in sports?

6. Discuss the role of perception in tension-building situations. How does it feel to be scared?

7. Discuss situations in physical education class that build stress, for example, failing in front of others, not being selected for a team, and being laughed at or yelled at for poor performance.

8. Identify physical activities that seem to relieve tension and stress. Discuss the relationship between involvement in activity and the reduction of stress.

9. Identify and discuss unproductive attempts to relieve stress, such as smoking, drinking, and taking drugs.

SUBSTANCE ABUSE

Substance abuse among elementary school youngsters is common. To make wise decisions in this area, children need to be aware of the impact these substances can have on their lives. Facts should be presented without moralizing or preaching. Making meaningful decisions is difficult for youngsters if most of the information they receive is from peers or moralizing adults.

Alcohol, tobacco, and drugs are deterrents to wellness and usually are detrimental to total health. These substances need to be discussed with youngsters, because children are in constant contact with them through parents, television, and friends. At regular and opportune intervals, the physical education teacher can supplement presentations made in the classroom.

Alcohol

Alcohol has both short-term and long-term effects. The short-term effects vary as a result of the depressant effect that alcohol has on the central nervous system. People become relaxed, aggressive, and active in differing degrees. Ultimately, lack of coordination and confusion occur if a great deal of alcohol is ingested.

Some long-term effects of excessive alcohol consumption may be liver damage, heart disease, and malnutrition. The greatest concern about long-term drinking is the possibility of becoming an alcoholic. The disease of alcoholism has the following components: (1) the loss of control of alcohol intake, (2) the presence of functional or structural damage (psychological and physical), and (3) the need to have alcohol to maintain an acceptable level of functioning.

Youngsters may drink for any of the following reasons: (1) curiosity, (2) a desire to celebrate with parents, (3) peer pressure, (4) to be like adults and appear more mature, (5) to rebel against the adult world, and (6) because their models or admired adults drink. Youngsters usually are ambivalent about alcohol: they know its detrimental effects, yet they see many of their friends and models using it. The problem is difficult, and understandings of moderate use and of abstinence are needed.

Tobacco

Tobacco use is common among youngsters. A long-term habit increases significantly the possibility of heart attack, stroke, and cancer. Chronic bronchitis and emphysema are diseases prevalent among smokers. A recent study revealed that the average life-span of long-term smokers is 7 years shorter than that of nonsmokers.

Children need to understand the impact of smoking on a healthy body. Teachers should discuss the reasons why people choose to smoke or not smoke. In the end, however, as with alcohol, youngsters must make a meaningful and personal choice. Youngsters who choose to smoke do so for reasons similar to those related to drinking.

Drug Abuse

The use of marijuana and hard-core drugs needs to be discussed. In athletics, discussion can center on the use by some athletes of pep pills, pain relievers, and steroids to improve performance.

The intent of this section is to create an awareness in teachers of the problem of substance abuse. We hope that teachers will use the excellent materials available to make presentations to students. Substance abuse is so contrary to the concept of physical wellness that physical educators must accept the challenge to increase awareness of the problem.

Concepts

1. The earlier one begins to smoke, the greater the risk to functional health.

2. Smoking is done for psychological reasons and makes no contribution to physical development.

3. People choose to smoke and drink for reasons of curiosity, status, and peer pressure.

4. Choosing a life-style different from the majority of one's friends takes courage.

5. When decisions about substance use are based on a lack of knowledge, they are often poor decisions. Wise and meaningful decisions can be made only after all alternatives and consequences are understood.

6. Substance abuse is often a misguided attempt to cope with problems and stress. Exercise and activity are more productive and healthy ways of coping.

7. The use of alcohol, tobacco, and drugs prevents people from enjoying certain activities.

8. It is much more important to make decisions based on personal need and direction than to be like everyone else. A positive feeling about oneself is more important than being "part of the crowd."

Suggested Learning Experiences

1. Identify some of the reasons why people choose or choose not to become involved in substance abuse.

2. Discuss the reasons why it is important to be your own person and to make meaningful personal decisions.

3. Develop a bulletin board listing the ways in which the tobacco and alcohol industries attempt to get people to use their products. Reserve a section for advertising (if any) that tries to convince people to abstain or to use moderation.

4. Youngsters often hear about the impairment in physical performance caused by smoking or drinking. Discuss athletes seen smoking or drinking on television and why they perform at high levels in spite of this abuse.

5. Youngsters want to be part of a group at any cost. Discuss how one admires those individuals who had the courage to be different. Examples might be da Vinci, Columbus, Helen Keller, Martin Luther King, or Louis Braille.

6. Discuss how individuals release tension in an attempt to feel good. Discuss productive releases of tension such as recreational pursuits, hobbies, and sports.

7. Develop displays identifying the various effects that alcohol, tobacco, and drugs have on the body. The effects can be discussed briefly at opportune times.

SAFETY AND FIRST AID

Safety and first aid have often been included in the physical education program because of the fact that a higher number of accidents occur in this setting than in any other part of the curriculum. Safety is an attitude and involves concern for one's welfare and health. An accident is an unplanned event or act that may result in injury or death. Oftentimes, accidents occur in situations that could have been prevented. The following are some of the most common causes of accidents: (1) lack of knowledge and understanding of risks, (2) lack of skill and competence to perform tasks safely, such as riding a bike or driving a car, (3) false sense of security, which leads people to think that accidents will happen only to others, (4) fatigue or illness, which affect physical and mental performance, (5) drugs and alcohol, and (6) strong emotional states such as anger, fear, or worry, which cause people to do things they might not do otherwise.

Traffic accidents are one area in which many deaths could be prevented. Wearing seat belts could reduce the number of deaths by half. Drinking alcohol while driving increases the risk of having an accident 20 times as compared with a nondrinking driver. Another factor that has reduced the number of traffic deaths is the 55 mph speed limit. Since students are going to be passengers in automobiles, an awareness of the possibility of serious injury should be a part of the wellness program.

Bicycles are another source of numerous accidents. Car

drivers have difficulty seeing bicycles, and the resulting accidents are frequently serious. Students need to learn bicycle safety. Often, the physical education setting is the only place where this is discussed. Instruction in bicycling for safety and fitness is usually well received by elementary school children.

Swimming-related accidents are the second leading cause of accidental death among young adults. More than 50% of all drownings occur when people unexpectedly find themselves in the water. Physical education programs should see that all students learn to swim and learn safety rules during their school career.

Physical education and sports are sources of injury in the school setting. Proper safety procedures and simple first aid techniques should be taught. Intermediate-grade students should know how to stop bleeding, treat shock, and administer mouth-to-mouth respiration, and cardiopulmonary resuscitation (CPR). Many physical education programs now include a required unit of instruction dealing with these topics. An estimated 100,000 to 200,000 lives could be saved if most bystanders knew CPR.

Basic Concepts

1. Accidents are unplanned events or acts that may result in injury. Most accidents could be avoided if people were adequately prepared and understood the necessary competencies and risks involved.

2. Wearing seat belts would decrease the number of deaths caused by automobile accidents.

3. Bicycles are often not seen by car drivers. Bicycling safety classes can lower the number of bicycle accidents.

4. Swimming-related accidents are the second leading cause of accidental death among young people. Drownproofing programs would decrease dramatically the number of deaths.

5. Basic first aid procedures to prevent further injury to victims are competencies that all students should possess.

Suggested Learning Experiences

1. Discuss the causes of different types of accidents and how many accidents could be avoided.

2. Identify the types of accidents that happen to different age-groups and why this is the case.

3. Identify the role of alcohol and drugs in the incidence of accidents. Why are these substances used in recreational settings?

4. Develop a bulletin board that demonstrates how to care for shock victims. Practice carrying out the steps in a mock procedure.

5. Have an Accident Day and let students stage different types of accidents that require treatment such as stoppage of bleeding, artificial respiration, or CPR.

6. Outline the steps to follow in case of a home fire. Discuss how many fires could be prevented.

7. Conduct a bicycle safety fair. Have students design bulletin boards and displays that explain and emphasize bicycle safety.

REFERENCE

AAHPERD. 1980. *Health related physical fitness test manual.* Reston, Va.: AAHPERD.

CHAPTER 11

The Special Child: Guidelines for Program Development

"My teachers have really been great. They can't seem to do enough for me. . . . People are handicapped in many ways, but the ones who don't try to understand the problems of others are really the handicapped." The foregoing statement was made by a visually impaired student.[1]

When the Education for All Handicapped Children Act (Public Law 94-142) was passed in 1975, those teaching physical education were perhaps unprepared for the impact of the law on their programs. The law brought new requirements in physical education teaching and mandated duties for teachers who said that they had little or no time to meet these new responsibilities. These teachers now have handicapped children participating in their programs, and special attention must be paid to whether the program meets certain target goals.

The law mandates equal access for the handicapped to educational services equivalent to those available to the nonhandicapped. The emphasis is on *equal opportunity for all,* including the handicapped, to achieve an education that meets their personal needs.

By due process, the handicapped child must be placed in an educational setting deemed to be in his best interests. This may involve placement in regular classes with nonhandicapped peers, which is termed *mainstreaming.*[2] The education of each handicapped child, according to the law, is to be guided by an individualized educational program (IEP), which is formulated by the child's established guidance committee. Since this procedure represents a radical change in school structure, the understanding and acceptance of the spirit of the law has been only marginal. Some school districts have reacted with global assignments in mainstreaming to meet the terms of the law. Because of the abrupt change in school operation, teacher's attitudes in some cases were bound to be negative. Many teachers have little expertise in handling handicapped children, and some of these instructors resent the additional burdens imposed on an already full teaching load.

To ensure the successful integration of the handicapped into the regular school program, the strong advocacy and commitment of school administration officials is essential. Two viewpoints of compliance occur. The first is compliance with the letter of the law. The second, which is more valid and more difficult, is compliance with the spirit of the law. Compliance with the law should not involve tasks to be gotten out of the way but, rather, should involve a way of thinking and a means of helping handicapped children to reach their potential. The law, with its ramifications and purposes, needs to be understood by all. The functioning staff is then more likely to implement the process according to the spirit of the law.

In-service education is needed to focus on meeting problems as they occur. The intent of mainstreaming is to meet the needs of the handicapped without modifying or detracting from the instruction of other students—not a simple task. Long-range goals to be realized for the handicapped are achieving their full educational potential, finding a place in society, acquiring independence in school and in domestic activity, being able to travel in the community with assurance, participating in community leisure activities, and developing a vocation.

1. National Education Association. 1978. *Education for all handicapped children: Consensus, conflict, and challenge.* Washington, D.C.: NEA, p. 33.

2. The term "mainstreaming" does not appear in P.L. 94-142. It is an education term coined to denote placement of handicapped children in classes with nonhandicapped peers.

Implementing P.L. 94-142 is further complicated by the wide variety of ailments among the handicapped, particularly those with retardation. Because these children have lived with failure, many have low fitness levels, are poorly skilled, and exhibit behavioral problems. Social and emotional growth is critical, coupled with the development of a satisfactory self-concept. A physical education program based on the student's needs must offer experiences to help offset these deficiencies.

No easy solution comes to mind. Not enough valid research has been done to provide guidelines for conducting these programs. Amendments to the law now direct attention to providing background, understanding, and expertise in undergraduate teacher education programs, so that teachers are better trained to help handicapped students.

THE SPECIAL CHILD AND PHYSICAL EDUCATION

Special children are identified by the law as those having any of the following problems to such a degree that the condition interferes with their learning: mental retardation, visual impairment, partial hearing or deafness, speech impairment, orthopedic impairment, learning disability, serious emotional disturbance, and neurological impairment (epilepsy, palsy, or other nervous disability). Unfortunately, some children may have more than one of these handicaps, which seriously complicates educational planning.

P.L. 94-142 specifies that each handicapped child must receive the special attention necessary to meet his educational needs. The law further specifies that each handicapped child is to be educated in the least restrictive environment possible. This means that the schools must provide a range of services, from placement in regular classes with nonhandicapped peers (mainstreaming) to more restrictive environments.

Determination of placement is in the hands of the child's guidance committee, which might consist of the principal, the classroom teacher, the physical education specialist, a special education consultant, the school nurse, and the parents. A feature of the law involves the parents' right to protest what they may deem to be an inappropriate placement of their child. This, in extreme cases, has led to civil court battles. Some type of school supervisory body, to which appeals could be made, would be a more reasonable approach. The child's committee is also responsible for seeing that the IEP is implemented.

Prudent placement in a least restricted educational setting means that the setting must be as normal as possible (normalization), while ensuring that the child can fit in and achieve success in that placement. The placement may be mainstreaming but is not confined to this approach. Several categories of placement can be defined relevant to physical education classes.

1. *Full mainstreaming.* Handicapped students function as full-time members of a regular classroom group. Within the limitations of their handicap, they participate in physical education with nonhandicapped peers.

2. *Mainstreaming for physical education only.* Handicapped children are not members of the regular classroom groups but participate in physical education with that group.

3. *Partial mainstreaming.* Students take part in selected physical education experiences but do not attend on a full-time basis because they can meet with success in only some of the offerings. Their developmental needs are usually met in special classes.

4. *Special developmental classes.* Handicapped students are in segregated special education classes.

5. *Reverse mainstreaming.* Nonhandicapped children are brought into a special physical education class to promote intergroup peer relationships.

Segregation can be maintained only if it is in the best interests of the child. The thrust of segregated programs should be to establish a level of skill and social proficiency that will enable the special child to be transferred eventually to a less restricted learning environment.

The emphasis on placement in the least restrictive environment in which the child, as an individual, can profit most is the cornerstone of the educational process. Handicapped children, working on their own, often have been denied opportunities to interact with peers and to become a part of the social and academic classroom network. However, the process represents more than just moving the child from a self-contained special education class to a more normal situation. Due process requires an appropriate determination, and the program must be tailored to the child.

INDIVIDUALIZED EDUCATIONAL PROGRAMS

P.L. 94-142 requires that an individualized educational program (IEP) be developed for each handicapped child receiving special education and related service. The IEP must be written by a special education representative, the child's parents, the teachers who have direct responsibility for implementing the IEP, and, if possible, the child herself. The child is involved relative to degree of maturity and ability to comprehend. This program identifies the child's unique qualities and determines educationally relevant strengths and weaknesses. A plan is then devised based on the diagnosed strengths and weaknesses.

Assessment is a vital part of collecting baseline information about the handicapped student's physical and motor abilities. In evaluating these, attention must be given to knowledge and understanding of movement and to values and attitudes toward physical activity. When valid instruments are available, rigorous measurement should occur. Medical examinations should be part of the assessment process when a medical problem is apparent. On the basis of the entire assessment, the degree to which the youngster can participate in the regular program is then established, and the needed support services identified. Generally speaking, if a child scores below the 30th percentile on test items with valid norms, this area of deficiency should receive special attention. Scores below the 50th percentile indicate an area of concern and possible focus.

Schools should seek out handicapped children and provide service, since some parents may not readily identify a child as handicapped. Permission must be secured from parents to assess such children to determine whether they can be categorized as special students. The distinction between normal and marginally handicapped children is not clearly defined.

One trait that should be included in assessment procedures is that of self-confidence. Self-confidence can have a marked impact on the child's success in the mainstreaming assignment. *Self-confidence* in this context refers to the strength of the child's belief in himself to execute successfully the behaviors necessary to achieve a required outcome or to meet the environmental challenges. This attribute is important to skill performance. Assessment of self-confidence can be made by subjective means or by formal assessment procedures. The child's feelings and anxiety about the mainstreaming placement are of great importance.

Developing and sequencing objectives for the student is the first step in formulating the IEP. Short-range and long-range goals should be delineated, and data collection procedures and testing schedules established to monitor the child's progress. Materials and strategies to be used in implementing the IEP should also be established. Finally, methods of evaluation to be used are determined in order to monitor the student's progress and the effectiveness of the program. (Computer assistance is helpful in relieving laborious hand recording.) Movement to a less restrictive environment should be based on achievement of specified competencies that are necessary in the new environment.

Continued and periodic follow-up of the child is necessary. Effective communication between special and regular teachers is essential, because the child's progress needs careful monitoring. At the completion of the designated time period or school year, a written progress report should be filed along with recommendations for action during the coming year. Here, again, the computer can be of valuable assistance.

A program for the summer months is often an excellent prescription to ensure that improvement is maintained. Records should be complete so that information about the youngster's problem and the effects of long-term treatment are always available.

MAINSTREAMING SPECIAL STUDENTS INTO PHYSICAL EDUCATION CLASSES

Although mainstreaming is especially applicable to physical education, few valid guidelines are available to provide direction. Misconceptions and confusion about mainstreaming can result in the placement of disabled students in physical education classes that are not in line with their needs. Financial considerations and other pressures often cause handicapped children to be placed in situations for reasons other than educational need.

The concern is no longer whether to mainstream, but how to mainstream effectively. The physical educator is faced with increasing numbers of handicapped children with diverse impairments. Many instructors are not qualified to handle this situation. Changing how teachers teach is difficult, but in this situation the same effect must be accomplished both in terms of attitude and instructional expertise. The learning strategies that the instructor is familiar with and has been using successfully may not be appropriate for the handicapped. Attitudinal change is also crucial. The teacher must not only accept the child as a full-fledged participant but also must assume the responsibilities that go along with special education.

An early consideration in planning the IEP is whether the child is ready for mainstreaming. Many handicapped children have severe developmental lags, which become insurmountable factors working against their successful integration in normal classes. Prior physical education intervention in special classes is a viable solution. The IEP needs to spell out what competencies are to be achieved and to what degree before the child is mainstreamed into the regular class. The child must be physically able to accomplish a portion of the program without much, if any, assistance and another portion with assistance. For some students, placement might be limited to certain activities in which success can be achieved.

When a child is deemed ready for placement, consultation between the physical education teacher and the special education supervisor is of prime importance. The thrust should center on what the child can do rather than what she cannot do. Any approach that treats the handicapped as cripples dehumanizes them. Full information is due the physical education teacher *before* the child appears. This procedure should also be implemented when the child moves from one mainstreaming situation to another.

The support services and the assistance of the special education department should not be withdrawn when the child is mainstreamed. A team approach is vital. If conditions indicate special help, it should be provided.

Both the regular and handicapped students must have opportunities to make appropriate progress. The educational needs of the handicapped must be met without jeopardizing the progress of other students. This does not rule out some activity modifications so the handicapped can be included. Some adapted equipment may also be necessary. Wholesale restructuring of the program could, however, be counterproductive.

The teacher is advised to help all students understand the problems related to being handicapped. A goal should be to have students understand, accept, and live comfortably with persons who have handicaps. They should recognize that the handicapped are functional and worthwhile individuals who have innate abilities and can make significant contributions to society. The concept of understanding and appreciating the handicapped is one that merits positive development and should not be left to chance. An approach that has achieved some success in helping nonhandicapped children understand and accept handicapped children in a normalized setting concentrates on three aspects.

1. Recognize the similarities among all people—their hopes, rights, aspirations, and goals.

2. Try to understand human differences and center on the concept that all people have handicaps. For some, the handicaps are of such nature and severity that they interfere with normal living.

3. Explore ways to deal with those who differ and stress the acceptance of all children as worthwhile individuals. The handicapped deserve consideration of their handicaps, based on empathetic understanding. Overhelp should be avoided.

For the handicapped, educators must identify early the area of greatest need. Children should routinely develop acceptable work behaviors between and among fellow students and for the teacher. The special child should not be permitted to use a handicap as a crutch or as an excuse for substandard work. The child should also not be allowed to manipulate people into helping with tasks he is capable of doing. Coping skills need to be developed, because the handicapped do encounter teasing, ignorance, and rejection at varying times.

Now that the mainstreamed child, the regular students, and the teacher have undergone preliminary preparation, consideration can be given to integrating the disabled into the learning environment. Mainstreaming should allow the child to make commendable educational progress, to achieve especially in those areas outlined in the IEP, to learn to accept limitations, to observe and model appropriate behavior, to become more socially accepted by others, and in general to become a part of the real world. Some guidelines for successful integration of the handicapped into physical education follow.

1. In addition to participation in the regular program of activities, meeting the target goals as specified in the IEP is important. This can involve resources beyond the physical education class, including special work and homework.

2. Build ego strength; stress abilities. Eliminate established practices that unwittingly contribute to embarrassment and failure.

3. Foster peer acceptance, which begins when the teacher accepts the child as a functioning, participating member of the class.

4. Concentrate on the child's physical education needs and not on the disability. Give strong attention to fundamental skills and physical fitness qualities.

5. Provide continual monitoring and assess periodically the child's target goals. Anecdotal and periodic record keeping are implicit in this guideline.

6. Be constantly aware of the child's feelings and anxiety concerning her progress and integration. Provide positive feedback as a basic practice.

7. Tailor the regular program to meet the unique capacities, physical needs, and social needs of the handicapped.

8. Provide individual assistance and keep the handicapped active. Peer or paraprofessional help may be needed. On-task time is important.

9. Consult regularly with the special education consultant.

10. Give consideration to more individualization within the program so the handicapped can fit in more easily. The individualized approach for the handicapped must be based on the target goals of the IEP.

11. Strong consideration must be given to the use of computer programs for recording data and generating meaningful reports.

12. Alter and modify game rules and activities. Encourage the entire class to suggest possibilities that allow handicapped children to participate and compete in a meaningful manner. Another section develops this topic in detail.

HEALTH AND SAFETY PRECAUTIONS IN TESTING AND ACTIVITY

Assessment procedures provide data on which to base the child's program. However, the assessment process must be implemented cautiously because some disabled students who are not physically fit may show signs of discomfort or physiological distress as a result of effort to pass or produce high-level scores. Instructors should be aware of symptoms and conditions that indicate a need to modify the intensity of activity.

The intensity of the testing or exercise should be decreased or terminated when any of the following symptoms appears:[3] Extended periods of breathlessness, signs of unusual fatigue, muscle twitching or shakiness, headaches, unusual pain, severe pounding of the heart, nausea or vomiting. In addition, a number of conditions may require medical consultation before testing procedures can be instituted.

MODIFYING PARTICIPATION

Special education children need additional consideration at times when participating in group activities, particularly when the activity is competitive. Much depends on the

3. Based on a publication by the Maryland State Department of Education. 1983. *Teacher's helper—physical fitness for handicapped students.* Baltimore: Maryland State Department of Education, p. 8.

physical condition of the child and the type of impairment. Children like to win in a competitive situation, and resentment can be created if a team loss is attributed to the presence of a handicapped child. Equalization is the key. Rules can be changed for everyone so the handicapped child has a chance to contribute to group success. On the other hand, children need to recognize that everyone, including the handicapped and the inept, has a right to play. Some suggestions for modification follow.

1. Determine the most desirable involvement for the handicapped by analyzing participants' roles in game and sport activities. Determine the role or position that will make the special child's experience as natural or normal as possible.

2. Adapt rules to prevent failure for the handicapped. For example, for a batter with limited mobility in a softball-type game, require that the ball be thrown to second base and then to first for the out. In relay races in which mobility is again a factor, let the handicapped child lead off, with enough of a start to minimize the mobility factor. Involve students in the adaptation process.

3. Modify participation time to reduce fatigue, particularly for a child with braces. Substitute freely.

4. Provide matching or substitution. Match another child on borrowed crutches with a child on braces. Two players can be combined to play one position. A student in a desk chair with wheels can be matched against a wheelchair child. Permit substitute courtesy runners.

5. Be careful in situations that might devalue the child socially. In arranging teams, do so by chance or by teacher choice. Never use the degrading method of having captains choose from a group of waiting children. Elimination games should be changed so that points are scored instead of players being eliminated. The procedure of scoring a number of points against a player can also be modified. For example, in dodgeball games, charge only one score against a handicapped child with limited mobility.

6. Equalize teams so that no one team is overbalanced with handicapped children. Sometimes the handicapped child can be placed on a team with better players.

7. Modify the equipment and facilities. For example, nets can be lowered or paths shortened. The special child might use a larger bat or a batting tee.

8. If vision is a problem, change the size of the targets or change the striking implements. Brightly colored objects aid the visually impaired child, and balls can be thrown more slowly to the child to facilitate batting. Some teachers have had success in placing small bells inside some balls so that youngsters can track the ball by sound.

9. Students with hearing problems can learn hand signals, and teachers can develop the habit of offering both verbal and visual signals when teaching special students.

10. Youngsters can substitute skills for each other. For example, a child may be able to strike an object but may lack the mobility to run. Another student can run for her.

11. Offer many individual and dual activities. Handicapped youngsters often need to build confidence in their skill before they want to participate with others. Individual activities give children a greater amount of practice time without the pressure of failing in front of peers.

The aim of these techniques is to make the handicapped less visible so they are not set apart from their more able classmates. Using the handicapped as umpires or scorekeepers should be a last resort. Overprotectiveness benefits no one and prevents the special student from experiencing challenge and personal accomplishment. The tendency to underestimate the abilities of the handicapped must be avoided.

TEACHER BEHAVIOR AND THE MAINSTREAMING PROCESS

The success or failure of the mainstreaming process rests largely on the interaction between the teacher and the disabled child. There is no foolproof, teacher-proof system. Certainly the role of the physical education instructor, whether he be a specialist or a classroom teacher, has been greatly changed by P.L. 94-142.

Purposes and derived goals are perhaps more important to the handicapped child than to so-called normal peers. Proper levels of organic fitness and skill are vital for healthful living for the handicapped. Such levels enable them to compete with peers.

All teachers have to accept responsibility for meeting the needs of children, including those with handicapping conditions that permit some degree of mainstreaming. Teachers need to be able to judge when referral for special assistance or additional services is in order. Physical education specialists must be able to do the following: (1) analyze and diagnose motor behavior of the handicapped, (2) provide appropriate experiences for remediation of motor conditions needing attention, and (3) register data as needed on the child's personal record. Classroom teachers who have a minimal background in physical education will need help from a consultant or specialist to accomplish these goals.

Record keeping needs to be emphasized. A short period, perhaps the 5 minutes between classes, could be set aside to accomplish the task promptly. The abhorrent practice by some administrators of running one class on top of the other without any time between classes hardly gives the physical education teacher time for record keeping.

To work successfully with the handicapped, teachers must know the characteristics of the specific handicap and how it affects learning. The teacher should also know how to assess the motor and fitness needs of the child, and how to structure remediation to meet the demonstrated needs. These evaluations are further complicated by the need to gather information relevant to integrating the handicapped child into the regular program.

Referrals should be kept to a minimum. Teachers should have at least two alternate strategies in reserve in case the original method fails. Referral to the special education teacher then becomes a last resort.

Explanations and directions should be couched in terms that all students, including the retarded, can understand. Be sure that the handicapped students understand what is to be accomplished before the learning experiences begin, especially when working with the hearing-impaired. Concentrate on finding something special in which the handicapped children can excel. Try to find some activity through which they can achieve peer regard. In particular, these youngsters should be expected to work to their full capacity. Do not accept a performance that is inferior in terms of the child's abilities.

Avoid placing special children in situations in which success is not likely. Conversely, give them opportunities that make the best use of their talents. Stress the special objectives of the handicapped. Concentrate on steps along the way to meet these objectives. Obvious increments of improvement toward terminal objectives are excellent motivators for both children and teachers. Let youngsters know that you as a teacher are vitally interested in their progress.

Apply multisensory approaches in teaching the handicapped. Visual and auditory modes of learning may not reach slow learners. Manipulate the child through a given movement to communicate the correct "feel." Touch or rub the involved part of the body to provide tactile stimulation. Emphasis should be on helping these children perform the skill, not doing it for them.

The presence of special children in the physical education class requires the teacher to become more effective, which ultimately results in an improved program for all. Ideally, all children in the class, not only the handicapped, would have IEPs so the teacher could monitor the individual progress of all students.

Teachers should seek sources of information to aid them in dealing effectively with handicapped children. Books about the handicapped and suggested guidelines for dealing with special children are available. Information covering specific disabilities is also available. Short-term workshops can be organized featuring knowledgeable individuals with successful programs who can help solve specific problems. Larger school systems may organize in-service education for physical education teachers.

UTILIZING MICROCOMPUTER SERVICES

Microcomputers are becoming increasingly available in schools all over the country. The computer is a time-saving device that can take over the record-keeping chores required by the provisions of P.L. 94-142. Printouts of present and past status reports can be made available on demand. The computer also can provide comparisons with established norms, especially in physical fitness areas, and it can record progress toward the target goals set by the IEP. The advantage of the microcomputer is that it minimizes the time necessary for recording student progress. In addition, computerized graphic compilations facilitate quick comprehension of progress reports.

Another significant computer service is related to informational printouts. The due process regulations of P.L. 94-142 might be one such topic. Information concerning specific disabilities could be made readily available. Guidelines for formulating the IEP are yet another printout possibility. Long- and short-term objectives can be retrieved from a growing data bank.

Relevant information can be made available to students concerning their progress. This serves as excellent motivation and stimulates a systematic approach to the attainment of spotlighted achievements. The same information can also be the basis for reports to parents and other adults who are interested in the child. These reports serve as motivating factors to enhance parental cooperation.

PARENTAL SUPPORT

Having parents on the IEP committee establishes a line of communication between home and school and involves parents in the corrective process. Some kind of home training or homework may be recommended, particularly with younger children. If home training is indicated, two factors are important. First, parents must be committed in terms of time and effort. Their work need not be burdensome but must be done regularly in accordance with the sequenced learning patterns. Second, the school must supply printed and sequenced learning activities for a systematic approach to the homework. Materials should be understandable so that what is to be accomplished is not in doubt. Parents should see obvious progress in their child as assignments unfold.

Older handicapped children may also accept some responsibility for home training, relegating the parent to the role of an interested spectator who provides encouragement. Even if homework is not in the picture, parental interest and support are positive factors. The parents can help their youngster realize what skills have been learned and what progress has been made.

POSTURE FOR THE HANDICAPPED

The normalization process has directed attention to posture as a factor in peer acceptance. Since many handicapped children have low physical fitness levels, posture problems often occur in this group. One aim of mainstreaming is to make the special child less visible, hence the need to help handicapped children achieve acceptable posture. Values received from an attractive appearance include better acceptance by peers and more employment opportunities later. It is crucial to correct an idiosyncratic gait or an appearance that exudes the impression of deviance. These are often problems for mentally retarded children.

Early identification of a problem and inclusion of a posture correction program are important. The physical educator is often best qualified to initiate and supervise this program. Informal screening should include several tasks—walking, sitting, and stair climbing. Height, weight, and body type affect posture. Obesity may need to be considered in amelioration. Once identification is made, a more detailed analysis of the subject's posture can follow (see p. 129 for a posture check form). The degree of postural abnormality governs whether referral is indicated. Videotaping can provide baseline data from which to monitor corrections. Achieving an acceptable posture is both a short-term (progress) and long-term (achievement) goal to be included in the child's IEP.

Exercise and physical conditioning procedures can be selected to help develop antigravity musculature and to provide flexibility training. These must be combined with comprehensive movement training so the child learns to move as skillfully and gracefully as possible. Muscular relaxation techniques may help. A well-rounded physical education program is important and should be reinforced by corrective exercises.

Referral for severe conditions or for postural conditions that are difficult to correct should involve the support services of a physician or an orthopedic specialist. Braces may be needed, particularly for lateral curvature (scoliosis).

The psychosocial aspects of posture should be considered, with attention focused on the establishment of a good self-concept and effective social relations. Behavior management can focus on the motivation for better postural habits in standing, walking, sitting, lifting, and general movement. Proper posture should become a habit. Postural correction for the handicapped is a complex process that must be included as an integral part of the IEP.

SPECIFIC TYPES OF HANDICAPS

To assist a child with a handicap, an understanding of the handicap and what it means to the child is essential. Basic information is provided here, and additional materials can be secured from special education consultants. National associations offer information about various handicaps and suggest ways of helping special children.

MENTAL RETARDATION

The capacity of the mentally retarded child is deficient and does not allow the child to be served by the standard program. Deficient mental functioning is a question of degree, usually measured in terms of intelligence quotient (IQ). Mildly retarded children (with IQs ranging roughly from 50 to 75 or 80) are most often mainstreamed in both physical education and the regular classroom. Children with IQs below 50 usually cannot function in a regular classroom environment; they need special classes. These children are generally not mainstreamed and so are excluded from the following discussion.

Academically, mildly retarded children (also termed *educable mentally retarded*) are slower to understand directions, to follow directions, to complete tasks, and to make progress. Conceptually, they have difficulty pulling facts together and drawing conclusions. Their motivation to stay on task is generally lower. Academic success may have eluded them. These realities must be considered in the physical education setting. Improvement in these areas is a goal to be achieved.

Do retarded children differ physically from other students? In a study comparing 71 educable mentally retarded boys with 71 normal boys, age 6 to 10 years, the following was noted.

> Differences between the retarded and the normal in respect to opportunities to be physically active tend to be substantial. Similarly, the motivation to be physically active may be less in the retarded, a reflection of their general motor ineptness. The relatively large proportion of subcutaneous tissue in the retarded is more than suggestive of a physically inactive life resulting in a corresponding low level of motor performance (Dobbin, Garron, and Rarick 1981: 7).

In another study (Ulrich 1983), a comparison was made of the developmental levels of 117 handicapped and 96 educable mentally retarded children with respect to criterion-referenced testing of 12 fundamental motor skills and 4 physical fitness skills. The investigation supports the findings of the previous study in that the educable mentally retarded students lagged 3.5 years behind normal children in motor skill development, as based on the researcher's selected criterion reference point. The investigator attributes this lag to a lack of opportunity for movement experiences at an early age. The handicapped children were from special education classes, not from a mainstreaming situation.

Studies of mildly retarded students support the assumption that they can learn, but do so at a slower rate and not to the depth of normal mentally functioning children. To help the mildly retarded develop their capacities so they can become participating members of society, the learning process should concentrate on fundamental skills and fitness qualities. Unless this base is established, the retarded child faces considerable difficulty later in learning specialized skills. Minimizing skill and fitness lags can help ease the child into mainstream living.

The fitness approach involves motivation, acquisition of developmental techniques, and application of these to a personalized fitness program. The retarded child reacts well to goal setting, provided the goals are challenging yet attainable.

The pace of learning depends on the degree of retardation. Before a retarded child can learn, he needs to know what is expected and how it is to be accomplished. Common sense must govern the determination of progress increments. These should be challenging but within the performer's grasp. Often, past experiences have made retarded children the victims of a failure syndrome. The satisfaction of accomplishment must supplant this poor self-image.

EPILEPSY

Epilepsy is a dysfunction of the electrical impulses that the brain emits. It is not an organic disease. It can happen at any period of life but generally shows up during early childhood. Many children, with proper care and medication, overcome this condition and live normal lives.

Epilepsy is a hidden handicap. A child with epilepsy looks, acts, and is like other children except for unpredictable seizures. Unfortunately, epilepsy carries an unwarranted social stigma. A child with epilepsy meets with a lack of acceptance, even when adequate explanations are made to those sharing the child's environment. A major seizure can be frightening to others. Revulsion is another possible reaction of observers.

Gaining control of seizures is often a long procedure, involving experimentation with appropriate anticonvulsive medication in proper doses. Fortunately, most epilepsy can be controlled or minimized with proper medication. One factor in control is to be sure that the child is taking the medication as prescribed.

Sometimes a child can recognize signs of seizure onset. If this occurs in a physical education class, the child should have the privilege of moving to the sideline without permission. A seizure may, however, occur without warning. The instructor should know the signs of a seizure and react accordingly. The teacher may be the first (even before the child) to recognize that a seizure is imminent.

Three kinds of seizure are identified. A petit mal seizure involves a brief period (a few seconds) of blackout. No one is aware of the problem, including the child. Sometimes it is labeled inattention and thus is difficult to identify. A psychomotor epileptic seizure is longer lasting (perhaps a few minutes) and is characterized by involuntary movements and twitching. The child acts like a sleepwalker and cannot be stopped or helped. The affected youngster does not respond when addressed and is unaware of the seizure. A grand mal seizure is a total seizure with complete neurological involvement. The child may become unconscious and lose control of the bladder or bowels, resulting in loss of urine, stool, or both. Rigidity and tremors can appear. The seizure must run its course.

Two points are important. First, throughout any seizure or incident, the teacher must preserve a matter-of-fact attitude and try not to exhibit pity. Second, the teacher must educate the other children to understand and empathize with the problem. Stress what the condition is and, later, what it is not. Explain that the behavior during a seizure is a response to an unusual output of electrical discharges from the brain. Everyone needs these discharges to function in normal living, but the person with epilepsy is subject to an unusual amount of the discharges, which results in unusual activity. The condition involves a natural phenomenon that gets out of control.

Children need to understand that the seizure must run its course. When the seizure is over, everyone can resume normal activity, including the involved child, although the child may be disoriented and uncoordinated for a brief period of time. Offer the child the option of resting or returning to activity. Proper emotional climate of the class is established when the teacher maintains an accepting and relaxed attitude.

Information about epilepsy should be a part of the standard health curriculum in the school, rather than a reaction to an epileptic seizure or to the presence of a student who may have seizures. Epilepsy can be discussed as a topic relevant to understanding the central nervous system. Certain risks are involved if the lessons have as their focus the problems of a particular child, because this may heighten the child's feelings of exclusion and place disproportionate attention on what might have been a relatively inconsequential aspect of her life. (This caution does not rule out helpful information being given to peers when a seizure has taken place.)

In the event of a grand mal seizure, some routine procedures should be followed. Have available a blanket, a pillow, and towels to clean up any mess that might occur. Make the child comfortable if there is time. Do not try to restrain her. Put nothing in the mouth. Support the child's head on the pillow, turning it to one side to allow the saliva to drain. Remove from the area any hard or sharp objects that might cause harm. Secure help from a doctor or nurse if the seizure continues more than 3 or 4 minutes or if seizures occur three or more times during a school day. Always notify the school nurse and the parents that a seizure had occurred. Assure the class that the seizure will pass and that the involved child will not be harmed or affected.

Recommendations regarding special modes of conduct and guidelines governing participation in school activities must come from the child's physician, since most epileptic children are under medical supervision. The instructor should stay within these guidelines while avoiding being overprotective.

Today's approach is to bring epilepsy into the open. A concerted effort should be made to educate today's children so that traditional attitudes toward the condition can be altered. Perhaps tomorrow's adults will then possess a better understanding. The child with epilepsy is a normal, functioning individual except at the time of a seizure. Epilepsy is not a form of mental illness, and most persons with epilepsy are not mentally retarded. Program adaptations are not indicated except as specified by the child's physician.

VISUAL IMPAIRMENT

Mainstreaming for the visually impaired must be handled carefully and with common sense. The visually impaired designation includes those who are partially sighted as well as those who are legally blind. One has only to move about in a dark room to realize the mobility problems faced by a visually impaired child. This disability poses movement problems and puts limits on participation in certain types of physical activity. Total mainstreaming may not be a viable solution. There is a need to bring the child in contact with other children, however, and to focus on the child's unique qualities and strengths.

Visually impaired children have to develop confidence in their ability to move freely and surely within the limits of the handicap. Since limited mobility often leads to reduced activity, this inclination can be countered with a specialized physical fitness and movement program in which the lack of sight does not prove insurmountable. The child can take part in group fitness activities with assistance as needed. Exercises should pose few problems. Rope jumping is an excellent activity. Individual movement activities, stunts and tumbling, rhythms and dances (particularly partner dances), and selected apparatus activities can be appropriate. Low balance beams, bench activities, climbing apparatus, and climbing ropes may be within the child's capacity. Manipulative activities, involving tactile senses, are not always appropriate. If the child has some vision, however, brightly colored balls against a contrasting background in good light can permit controlled throwing, tracking, and catching. Through the selection of activities, the sense of balance should be challenged regularly to contribute to sureness of movement. Since vision is limited, other balance controls also need to be developed.

The visually impaired child ordinarily cannot take visual cues from other children or the teacher, so explanations must be precise and clear. For some situations, an assigned peer can monitor activity, helping as needed or requested. In running situations, the helper can hold hands with the visually impaired child. Another way to aid the child is with physical guidance until the feel of a movement pattern is established. This should be a last choice, however, occurring only after the child has had a chance to interpret the verbal instructions and still cannot meet the challenge. Touching a part of the child's body to establish correct sequencing in a movement pattern also can be of help.

Empathy for and acceptance of the visually impaired child are most important. The task of monitoring movement and helping this child should be considered a privilege to be rotated among class members. If participation in the selected class activity is contraindicated, the monitor can help provide an alternate activity.

AUDITORY IMPAIRMENT

Auditorally impaired children are those who are deaf or who must wear hearing aids. In physical education classes, these children are capable of performing most, if not all, activities that nonhandicapped children can perform. Since most instruction is verbal, a deaf child is isolated and often frustrated in a mainstreaming situation unless other means of communication are established. Accomplishing this while keeping the class functioning normally constitutes a problem of considerable magnitude.

Some advocates for the deaf contend that implementing P.L. 94–142 with its emphasis on mainstreaming is not appropriate for deaf children and thwarts their development. Teaching the deaf is a challenging and specialized process, requiring different communication techniques. Many deaf children have poor or unintelligible speech and inevitably develop a language gap with the hearing world. Sign language, lip reading, and speech training are all important facets of communicative ability for the deaf.

Certainly hearing-impaired children can perform physically and at the same level as children with normal hearing when given the opportunity. One successful approach to teaching both the hearing impaired and normal youngsters is to use contract or task card techniques. Written instructions can be read loudly by the teacher or monitor. Pairing children with severe hearing loss with other children can be a frustrating experience for both, but meaningful possibilities also exist. Such a pairing necessitates lip reading, the use of verbal cues, or strong amplification on a hearing aid. Visual cues, featuring a "do as I do" approach, can stimulate certain types of activity.

The deaf child should be near the teacher to increase the opportunities to read lips and receive facial cues. Keep the class physically active. Avoid long delays for explanations or question-and-answer periods. This becomes a blank time for the hearing impaired, and leads to frustration and aggressive action. For rhythmics, some devices can be of benefit. Keep record player speakers on the floor to provide vibration. Use a metronome or blinking light. For controlling movement patterns, hand signals should be developed for starting, stopping, moving to an area, assembling near the teacher, sitting down, and so on.

Static and dynamic balance problems are prevalent among hearing-impaired children. Focus on activities that challenge balance and insist on proper procedures. Have the child maintain the position or movement for 10 to 15 seconds and recover to the original position, all in good balance.

Integrating deaf children in the regular physical education class setting is a process that must be handled with common sense. The experience should be satisfying to the deaf child or it is a failure. No easy solution exists.

ORTHOPEDIC HANDICAPS

Orthopedic handicaps in children encompass a wide range of physical ailments, some of which may involve external support items such as splints, braces, crutches, and wheelchairs. A few postpolio cases may be encountered.

Generalizing procedures for such a wide range of physical abnormalities is difficult. Children with orthopedic handicaps usually function on an academic level with other children and are regular members of a classroom. As such, they appear with the class for physical education.

Instructional focus must be on what the child can do and on the physical needs that are to be met. Mobility is a problem for most, and modification is needed if the class activity demands running or agility. Individualized programs are made to order for this group, because the achievement goals can be set within the child's capacity to perform. Individual and dual sports offer a carry-over to leisure participation. Try to develop proficiency in lead-up skills for badminton, deck tennis, archery, and other such sport activities in which the child may be interested. Swimming and water sports should be encouraged, and children in wheelchairs should be encouraged to acquire basketball and volleyball skills as preparation for possible participation in organized wheelchair games in later life.

For wheelchair children, certain measures are implicit. Special work is needed to develop general musculature to improve conditions for coping with the handicap and to prevent muscle atrophy. In particular, wheelchair children need strong arm and shoulder musculature to transfer in and out of the wheelchair without assistance. Flexibility training to prevent and relieve permanent muscle shortening (contracture) should be instituted. Cardiorespiratory training is needed to maintain or improve aerobic capacity, since immobility in the chair decreases activity. From these experiences, the wheelchair child should derive a personal, functioning program of activity that she can carry over into daily living.

Time devoted to special health care after class must be considered for children with braces or in wheelchairs. Children with braces should inspect skin contact areas to look for irritation. If the child has perspired, a washcloth and towel will help him freshen up and remove irritants. Wheelchair children can transfer to a canvas lawn chair and allow the wheelchair to dry out. Sitting in the canvas chair also allows air to circulate more freely around the child's body. (A folding lawn chair should be kept available.) Schedules can be adjusted so time for this care is available. Scheduling the class during the last period before lunch or recess or at the end of the day allows this time.

Children with temporary conditions (fractures, sprains, strains) are handled on an individual basis, according to physician recommendations. Remedial work may be indicated.

OTHER HANDICAPPING CONDITIONS

A range of other handicapping conditions may be encountered. These include cardiac problems, cerebral palsy, asthma, emotional disturbances, and diabetes.

Children with cardiac problems are generally under the guidance of a physician. Limitations and restrictions should be followed to the letter. The child should, however, be encouraged to work to the limits of the prescription.

An asthmatic child has restricted breathing capacity. The condition carries a warning against activities that can cause breathing distress. The child should be the judge of her physical capacity and when rest is indicated.

Cerebral palsy, like epilepsy, has strong negative social implications. Peer education and guidance are necessary. The signs of cerebral palsy are quite visible and, in severe cases, result in odd, uncoordinated movements and a characteristic gait. Medical supervision indicates the limits of the child's activities. Children with cerebral palsy are usually of normal intelligence; their chief problem is control of movement. An important goal is ensuring that they can achieve competency in performing simple movements. The excitability threshold is critical and must not be exceeded. Many need support services for special training in both neural and movement control.

Disturbed children represent an enigma for mainstreaming. They have been removed from the regular classroom situation because they may cause a disruption and because they need psychological services. Physical education seems to be one area in which they can find success. Each case is different, however, and generalization is difficult.

Occasionally, a diabetic child may be found in a physical education class. Diabetes is an inability to metabolize carbohydrates that results from the body's failure to supply insulin. Insulin is taken either orally or by injection to control serious cases. If the child is overweight, a program of weight reduction and exercise prescription are partial solutions. Diabetics are usually under medical supervision. Knowing that a diabetic child is in a physical education class is important, because the child must be monitored to detect the possibility of hypoglycemia (abnormally low blood sugar level). The condition can be accompanied by trembling, weakness, hunger, incoherence, and even by coma or convulsions. The solution is to raise the blood sugar level immediately through oral consumption of simple sugar (e.g., skim milk, orange juice) or some other easily converted carbohydrate. The diabetic usually carries carbohydrates, but a supply should be available to the instructor. Immediate action is needed because low blood sugar level can be dangerous, even leading to loss of life. The diabetic probably has enough control to participate in almost any activity. This is evidenced by the number of diabetic professional athletes, who meet the demands of high activity without difficulty.

NATIONALLY VALIDATED HELP PROGRAMS

For several years, nationally validated programs of proven practices in special education have been available for adoption. Portions of many of these programs are in or related to physical education. These programs are funded and endorsed by the U.S. Office of Education. Some deal with screening, assessment, and curriculum for young children with special needs. Others feature management practices associated with special children. A number deal with early recognition and intervention so the child can be fitted more successfully into the mainstreaming situation. Information pertaining to these programs can be secured from state departments of education or from the U.S. Office of Education.

REFERENCES

Dobbin, D. A., Garron, R., and Rarick, G. L. 1981. The motor performance of educable mentally retarded and intellectually normal boys after covariate control for differences in body size. *Research Quarterly* 52(1): 6–7.

Ulrich, D. A. 1983. A comparison of the qualitative motor performance of normal, educable, and trainable mentally retarded students. In *Adapted physical activity,* Eason, R. L., Smith, T. L., and Caron, F., eds. Champaign, Ill.: Human Kinetics Publishers.

CHAPTER 12

Programs for Children With Special Needs

The current emphasis on equal education for all has focused attention on children with special needs. Physical education can offer solutions to relevant problems through activity-oriented programs. Instruction has long been aimed at training the physically adept, with little concern or empathy shown for the less gifted. The programs presented in this chapter are for underachievers in physical fitness, children with weight problems, and children with motor deficiencies.

UNDERACHIEVERS IN PHYSICAL FITNESS

Underachievers in physical fitness, often called low-fitness children, can be helped through prescriptive programs of physical activity tailored to their needs. The program for underachievers also can be used as the activity program for obese children. To a lesser degree, the program for underachievers can be applied to handicapped children who have deficiencies in fitness that need special attention. Often, these children have experienced little success and have been held in low regard by classmates. Working with such children can be a rewarding experience, because the results, in many cases, are phenomenal, and the physical well-being and the personalities of such children are as a consequence dramatically changed.

The program for the underachiever usually is scheduled for the intermediate grades but can include the lower grades. Children need to accept responsibility for their program and progress. An underachiever should be in the program only if she wishes to help herself. Primary-level children usually do not have the maturity or motivation to accept this personal responsibility.

When the AAHPERD Health Related Physical Fitness Test[1] (p. 178) is used for screening purposes, an individual is rated as an underachiever if one or more of the results on the test items are below the 25th percentile.

Another means of selection instituted by a school system in the Northwest might be considered. Within a school, teachers, principal, and specialist make a list of the names of children who are judged to need attention. From this list, those children thought to have the greatest need are selected. The children are interviewed and screened, and if they are eligible, are included in the program. The advantage of this method of selection is that the entire school population does not need to be tested in order to identify the underachievers. Teachers usually know through observation which children need help.

The approach to helping underachievers must be systematic. Four documents are suggested.

1. *Letter to parents.* The letter provides an explanation to the parents and contains a return portion on which parents consent to the child's participation in the program. The letter should also deal with the physical examination procedure.

2. *Program description.* A description of the program should accompany the letter to parents. This description spells out all of the necessary program details, including time schedule and means in which the problem will be handled. Some explanation of fitness concepts probably should be included. The description should be complete

1. Full details on this test can be found in the *Health Related Physical Fitness Test Manual,* AAHPERD (1980).

enough to enable parents to make a rational decision about the child's participation. A formalized brochure or compilation can impress parents that the approach is systematic, well-planned, and educationally sound.

3. *Letter to the physician.* The letter to the family physician should be in the form of a physical examination notice specifying the informational items needed. In particular, the letter should request notification of any conditions that need remediation and any findings that might affect the remedial program. The physician should recommend one of three choices—unrestricted participation, participation with stated restrictions, or no participation.

4. *Form for students.* Each student is given a form that describes the basics of physical fitness, outlines his personal program, and provides space for him to check off his activities (Figure 12.1).

In general, if possible, a sound procedure is to have each child in the program examined by a physician. The school should absorb the cost of the examination for those

FIGURE 12.1. Student's form to assess fitness

STUDENT'S FORM

School District Individual Fitness Program
Step Up to Better Fitness

Name ______________________________ Date ____________

School ______________________ Grade ____________ Circle: Boy Girl

This is your program to help you become more physically fit. Please read it carefully, because it can help a great deal, depending on how well you follow directions and work to improve.

What Is Physical Fitness?

Good physical fitness for you means that your body has enough strength, endurance, power, and flexibility to help you do well the things you like so you can get more fun and enjoyment out of living.

What Can Good Physical Fitness Do for You?

Being physically fit does not have the same value for everyone, but most people agree that physical fitness can help you in these ways:

1. You get more fun out of what you are doing, because you can do things better without becoming easily tired. You can play longer, jump farther, and do other kinds of activities better.
2. You will enjoy your schoolwork more and play better, because you are able to do the same things other boys and girls in your class can do and keep up with them.
3. You are helping yourself toward a better and fuller life. Becoming physically fit can make you look better and can help you grow up to become the kind of person you want to be.
4. If you are interested in playing sports, becoming physically fit is most important.

How Can You Help Yourself to Better Fitness?

First, you must be willing to follow the work program outlined for you and to try your best.

Second, you must think of how you can help yourself toward better fitness by improving your eating, sleeping, and other daily living habits. Are you eating the right kinds of food and enough of them? Are you eating a variety of foods, including fruit, vegetables, and milk? Are you in bed and asleep by at least 9:30 if you are in the primary grades, or by 10:00 if you are in grades 4, 5, or 6? Do you play outdoors and are you active generally, or do you just sit and watch TV?

To become physically fit, you have to do more activities and keep at them longer than you did before. Here is what you should do to improve your fitness. Strive to increase gradually the amount of activity you do (as appropriate to the different recommended activities by increasing distance, number of repetitions, or length of activity time, or by selecting a more challenging activity). Remember that the activities you select must be done regularly and correctly to get maximum benefit. In the scoring table, mark down the number of days each week that you did the activity.

FIGURE 12.1./*continued*

	Weeks											
A. General Activity (two items) Do at least two of the following:	1	2	3	4	5	6	7	8	9	10	11	12
1. Jogging—3 or 4 times per week												
2. Rope jumping—daily												
3. Interval running—3 or 4 times per week												
4. Running in place—daily												
B. Increasing Arm Strength (three items) 1. Do either:												
Chins—daily												
Flexed-Arm Hang—daily												
2. Do Push-ups—daily												
3. Do one of the following:												
Crab Walks—daily												
Rope climbing—daily												
Selected isometrics using a wand—daily												
C. Strengthening Abdominal (Tummy) Muscles (one item) Do one of the following daily:												
1. Partial Curl-ups												
2. Full Curl-ups												
3. Curl-ups for time (time limit, 30–60 seconds)												
D. Body Twisting and Stretching Exercises (two items) Do two of the following:												
1. Sitting Toe Toucher												
2. Windmill												
3. Trunk Twister												
4. Body Circles (both directions)												
5. Side Flex												

E. Leisure Activities

Take part in one or more of the following three to four times per week in your leisure time:

______ Bicycling	______ Skiing	______ Bowling	______ Roller-skating
______ Ice-skating	______ Soccer	______ Hiking	______ YMCA or YWCA activities
______ Swimming	______ Basketball	______ Baseball	______ Scouting fitness activities

continued

FIGURE 12.1/*continued*

DESCRIPTION OF ACTIVITIES

A. General Activities

1. Jogging: Set the distance and make it without stopping. Keep as fast a pace as possible, but slow down if needed. Maintain a steady pace.
2. Rope jumping: Use fast turning. Use the basic two-foot jump or alternate feet. Set a bout of 50 or 100 turns. Decide on the number of bouts, or set a time limit and jump for that long.
3. Interval running: Set a course of either 50 or 100 yards with two markers. Run down to the marker as fast as possible. Turn and walk back to original place. Repeat for one unit. Decide on the number of units before you begin.
4. Running in place: Count only the left foot. Fifty counts per bout. Increase the number of bouts gradually.

B. Arm Strength

1. Chins (Pull-ups) or a Flexed-Arm Hang: Set three trials for either. If no Pull-ups can be done, use the Flexed-Arm Hang.
2. Push-ups: Use the letdown first, then push up. Let down slowly. Keep the body straight.
3. Crab Walk: Do back and forth (round trips) between lines 5 yards apart. Touch one line with a foot and the other line with a hand. Try to keep the seat up.
4. Rope climbing: Go up and down several times.
5. Isometrics: Use a broom handle or a similar stick. Do sets of three or four isometrics, using different arm positions.

C. Abdominal Exercises

1. Partial Curl-ups: Lie on the back, feet flat on the floor and knees bent. The hands are laid flat, palms down, on top of the thighs with arms stretched. Slide the hands forward, leading first with the chin, until the head, shoulders, and upper body are off the floor. Hold for ten counts and release.
2. Full Curl-ups: Lie on the back with feet flat and knees bent. The fingers are clasped behind the head. Touch the inside of the opposite knee with the elbow, alternating sides. Hook the toes under something.
3. Curl-ups for Time: Time yourself doing Full Curl-ups.

D. Body Activities

1. Sitting Toe Toucher: Sit on the floor with the body erect, hands braced to the side and back, feet forward and reasonably together. Bring the arms overhead toward the ceiling, then bend forward slowly, bringing the hands as far forward toward the toes as possible. Forcibly continue stretching for 10 seconds. Recover.
2. Windmill (four-count exercise): Stand, feet apart and arms out to the side, palms down. Twist down and touch one hand to the opposite foot. Recover. Repeat to the other side. Set the number of exercises.
3. Trunk Twister (four-count exercise): Stand, feet apart, fingers clasped behind the head, elbows out. Bend forward, twist one elbow down, twist the other down, recover. Set the number of exercises.
4. Body Circles (eight-count exercise): Stand in the same starting position as for number 3, except bend the body forward at the waist. Circle one way on four counts, then circle the other way on four counts. This is one complete set. Decide on the number of sets.
5. Side Flex (two-count exercise): Lie on the side with lower arm extended along the floor in an overhead position. The upper arm is at the side. The head rests on the lower arm, and the legs are extended, one on top of the other. Lift the upper arm and upper leg as high as possible. Lower. This is one repetition. Do so many on the right side, and so many on the left.

E. Leisure Activities

Count these only if you spend at least 30 minutes doing the activity. You may select different activities to meet the three to four per week count.

children whose parents have financial problems. A less acceptable alternative is to have parents certify that to their knowledge and according to previous physical examinations, the child has no disabilities that would prevent participation in the program.

The school district should explain to the local medical association or to individual doctors, by letter, the nature of the program and the need for their cooperation. In this way, special arrangements and fees for the examinations might be established, and the physicians would be alerted to the purpose of the program when the children came in for their examination.

After the children are selected for the program and parental and medical approvals are secured, each child undergoes a short orientation period. At this time, the candidate is given the Student's Form as the basis for her effort.

Goals, including subgoals, are set by the supervisor and the child. Some retesting may be needed. Reinforcing the child's commitment is important. The orientation should provide the child with a full explanation of the program and the procedures that he is to follow. The program should operate for a specified period of time, say 10 to 12 weeks. The basic program concept is to have the child improve his own fitness, rather than forcing improvement.

An alternate means of stimulating the student is the contract approach. The student signs a Physical Fitness Contract (see Figure 12.2) that stipulates specifically the fitness assignment. The activities appear in the same format as on the Student's Form.

The program for underachievers is in addition to, not in place of, the regular physical education program. The supervisor meets weekly with the child, either individually

PHYSICAL FITNESS CONTRACT

Name ______________________________ Date ______________

School ______________________ Grade ______________ Circle: Boy Girl

I agree to do the following activity program to the best of my ability for ________weeks.

GENERAL ACTIVITY

1. Rope Jumping. 50 turns, 4 bouts.
2. Running in place. 50 counts on left foot, 4 bouts.

ARM STRENGTH

1. Chins. 3 chins, 3 bouts. Increase number.
2. Push-ups. 5 first week, increase each week.
3. Crab walks. 6 trips. Increase number.

ABDOMINAL STRENGTH

1. Full Curl-ups. 10 curl-ups. Increase number.

BODY TWISTING AND STRETCHING

1. Toe Toucher. 4 stretches. Increase time and number.
2. Body Circles. 6 sets. Increase number of sets.

LEISURE ACTIVITIES

1. Roller Skating
2. Bicycling
3. Soccer

I agree to participate at least 4 times per week total in these activities.

Signed ______________________

FIGURE 12.2. Physical fitness contract

or in a very small group, assesses progress, and sets the work load for the coming week. The child is encouraged to work during free time both at school and at home. Encouragement should be positive, and it is quite critical that progress be evident to both the child and the parents. The parents' part is one of encouragement and understanding rather than pressuring or forcing the child.

Friendly encouragement by the physical education instructor (if different from the supervisor) and by the classroom teacher is of help. These individuals can also provide follow-up after the program is completed to help the child maintain a proper state of fitness.

A posttest should be administered to evaluate the effectiveness of the program. In addition, the classroom teacher should solicit the reactions of the physical education teacher, the parents, and the child. Parents can allude to observed changes in personality, attitude, or participation on the part of the child.

CHILDREN WITH WEIGHT PROBLEMS

Obesity is a common problem in the United States, and the solution is neither simple nor immediate. It is a difficult and sensitive issue. Each case is different, and the approach must fit the subject.

Obesity can be defined in terms of percentages. Roughly speaking, a child who is between 10% and 20% over the weight designated appropriate for her age and height would be classified as overweight. A child who is 20% or more over the ideal is classified as obese. (These percentages vary from one source to another.) The advantage of a percentage definition is that it is meaningful to parents. Skinfold measurement with calipers is a more scientific means of identifying obese individuals. Skinfolds can be converted to a percent body fat reading to make the measurement meaningful to parents and children. For research purposes, converting the readings to a percentage is not desirable, but for a student-oriented program, the procedure is acceptable. Basically, the simplest test is the appearance of the child: if he looks obese, he is!

In any solution, the basic factors involved in obesity must be considered. These factors include genetics, emotional stability, hormonal functions, and intake-activity relationships. The overwhelming odds are that a fat child will stay fat. About 85% of obese children must fight weight gain for the rest of their lives (Eden 1975). The assumption that obese children normally grow out of the condition is a fallacy. Some parents rationalize the problem, maintaining that their child "still has some baby fat but will grow out of it later." Unless active measures are taken, the chances of solving the child's problem are small.

Heredity and environment are difficult to separate as causes for obesity, yet weight gain runs in families. If one parent is obese, about half of his children will probably be obese adults. This ratio jumps to 80% when both parents are obese (Eden 1975).

One theory supports the importance of finding an early solution for obesity. According to this theory, during childhood the obese child develops more fat cells than a child of normal weight, and the number of fat cells is carried over to adolescence and adulthood. An individual who has more fat cells is more prone to becoming overweight than a person who has fewer. The obvious implication is that weight-control measures should occur early, before the fat cells increase in number. During adult life, the number of fat cells is thought not to increase, but rather to enlarge in size.

Obese children often experience physical activities in ways different from children of normal weight. Success in physical activity is difficult for obese children to attain. When compared with their peers, heavy children are often physically inept. They may be the object of ridicule or the butt of jokes. Their peers sometimes call them names, such as Fatso, Tubby, and Lard Bucket. Children can be hurt deeply and driven even farther from active living, a direction opposite from the one they so desperately need to follow.

Not only does obesity impede the development of motor skills and limit the child's success in physical activities, it also contributes to heart disease, because obese people are generally more inactive than their peers.

The most common factor in obesity is an imbalance between caloric intake and energy expenditure. Many obese children fail to involve themselves in enough physical activity to burn up the calories they ingest. Excess calories are then stored in fat cells, and the child is pushed farther into obesity.

A practical method for determining obesity uses calipers to measure skinfolds (Figure 12.3). Calipers are relatively inexpensive, and the measurement can be done quickly. The skinfold of the triceps muscle is representative of the whole body. To measure the triceps skinfold, the skin on the back of the child's upper arm is pinched with thumb and forefinger. The calipers are then applied to the skinfold, indicating a reading in millimeters. Three readings should be taken and the results averaged. Table 12.1 can be consulted to see whether the child should be rated as obese. To compare how much body fat a child has with others of the same age and sex, consult the AAHPERD Health Related Physical Fitness Test percentile scores listed on page 178.

Another method is less scientific but offers a reasonable estimate. It is called the pinch test (Figure 12.4). Several skinfold pinches are made with the thumb and forefinger on such areas as the back of the upper arm, the side of the lower chest, the abdomen, and the back just below the shoulder blades. If a skinfold of more than 1 in. can be picked up, the child is considered obese. A skinfold between 0.5 and 1 in. is in the acceptable range. Some children are so obviously obese that measurement is hardly needed.

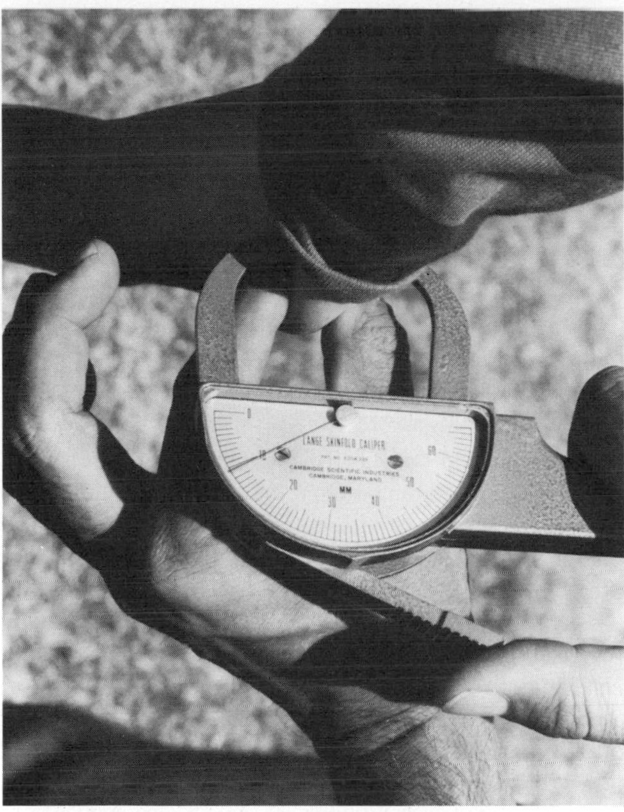

FIGURE 12.3. Measuring skinfold with calipers

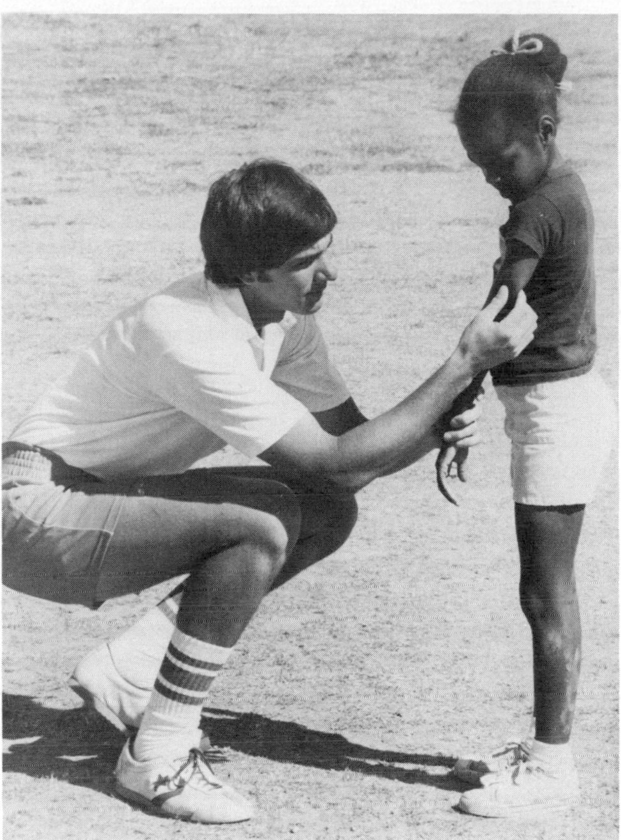

FIGURE 12.4. The pinch test

The solution to an obesity problem involves attention to both diet and activity. Unfortunately, this means that the child must alter her life-style, which requires adjustment not only in school life but also in home life. Without a genuine commitment from the child and without the cooperation of the child's parents, a remedial program can have little chance of success. For some children, commitment to the program is a relatively easy step, because they resent being fat and have wanted to do something about their obesity but have not known quite what to do. A protracted time commitment is important, because the remedial program must turn into a program for living or the child will revert to old habits. Getting parents to cooperate can be more difficult, especially if they themselves are obese. The parents may give lip service to cooperation but may in reality do nothing to change the home life-style that contributes to the child's obesity.

TABLE 12.1. **MINIMUM THICKNESS OF TRICEPS SKINFOLD INDICATING OBESITY**

Age	**Thickness (in Millimeters)**	
	Boys	Girls
5	12	14
6	12	15
7	13	16
8	14	17
9	15	18
10	16	20
11	17	21
12	18	22
13	18	23

SOURCE: C. C. Seltzer and J. Mayer. 1965. A simple criterion of obesity. *Postgraduate Medicine* 38(2): A101.

Counseling is an important part of the program for fighting obesity and should include both conferences with the child and support through printed instructions. The program of activity for the underachiever in physical fitness (see pp. 149–154) is also excellent for the obese child. Getting the child to follow the activity prescription is vital. This is where the physical educator's emphasis should lie.

Dealing with diet is extremely complex and involves changing the eating habits not only of the obese child but of parents and siblings, too. This is complicated by the fact that, in some cases, the obese child's diet is not substantially different from that of normal-weight classmates. It is also difficult for a child to change the food received at home, so diet control must be relegated to a minor role in the weight-control program. If the child can be influenced to eat moderately at mealtime and to avoid snacking between meals, much has been accomplished, and the child's diet at school can be monitored.

TREATING OBESITY: DEVELOPING A SUCCESS PROFILE

Any weight-control project should include the whole school and involve the classroom teacher, because it is necessary to use some class time for conferences with the children in the program. Probably the intermediate level is the most feasible time to deal directly with weight problems, since children at this level become more sensitive to their appearance and their relationships with peers. At the primary level, children usually have little motivation to deal with the problem.

The following is a step-by-step approach to developing a success profile for obese children in the elementary school setting. It is written in outline form and attempts to offer a systematic approach to dealing with youngsters who have this serious handicap. In many programs, youngsters are selected for treatment because someone feels uneasy about their physical predicament. More meaningful is a selection based on the youngsters' ability to deal successfully with the problem. This approach assumes that certain individuals are better suited to treatment than others. Not treating a child may be the better solution if the treatment outcome is likely to be failure, because failure only reinforces the child's belief that there is little hope, even when teachers want to help. The following approach picks children who show a success profile after initial testing.

INITIAL SCREENING OF POTENTIAL CANDIDATES

1. Explain the program to classroom teachers and emphasize the need for their support.

2. Ask classroom teachers to identify potential candidates.

3. Discuss with the classroom teacher the possibility of success for each candidate.

4. Hold a discussion with each of the students to explain the nature of the problem, the possibility of treatment, and whether the student would like to participate.

5. Select students to be tested based on the comments of the classroom teachers, the student's comments, and the opinion of the physical education specialist.

EVALUATION AND SELECTION OF STUDENTS

This is the critical step in developing a successful program. Students must be selected who are capable of implementing the program objectives. An approach that has worked well is to develop a success profile that is a compilation of selected data on each potential candidate. The following are areas that can be included.

1. *AAHPERD Health Related Physical Fitness Test* data, which includes the following.

a. Skinfolds: Children can be selected for inclusion in the program if they fall between the 15th and 40th percentile on the *AAHPERD Health Related Physical Fitness Test* norms. In most cases, youngsters outside this range are usually not obese or are too obese for treatment in a physical education setting. Severe cases may require medical attention and counseling beyond the scope of the physical education specialist.

b. Sit and reach for flexibility.

c. Sit-ups to evaluate abdominal strength.

d. Mile run-walk to evaluate cardiovascular endurance. Teachers should emphasize the ***walk*** aspect, because many of these children are not in condition to try running a mile.

2. Height and weight: This data is collected only for the purpose of communicating with parents about where their child ranks in relation to others (percentile ranking). Standard height and weight charts can be used and are available from Ross Laboratories, Columbus, OH 43216.

3. *Children's Attitude Toward Physical Activity* (CATPA) evaluation: This scale gives an indication of the child's feeling about participation in physical activity.

4. *My Physical Self-Concept* evaluation: This instrument offers results that reflect how children feel about themselves physically.

5. Assessment of the Fitness Council: This council consists of the classroom teacher, principal, school nurse, and counselor.

6. Assessment of the elementary school physical education specialist.

All of these factors are weighed in a relative fashion with the exception of the skinfold measurement. If the student does not fit into the percentile range discussed previously, then she should not be selected because the possibility of failure is too great. All other factors are weighed, and those children are selected who have the most positive self-concept, the most positive attitude toward physical activity, the highest fitness level, and the most positive assessment by the fitness council and the specialist. The success profile form (Figure 12.5) can be used to analyze the data.

PARENTAL INVOLVEMENT

1. Meet with parents of selected students for a conference to explain the program. Topics covered in the meeting should be objectives of the program, operation and organization of the program, data gathered on the success profile, parent responsibilities, and need for follow-up conferences.

2. Give parents a handout explaining the program and the related responsibilities of the parents and child. This will allow them to discuss the program at home.

3. Parents should leave the meeting with a clear understanding that the program is terminated if either the child or parent fails to perform his or her duties.

Name ____________________

Pre ________ Post ____________

SUCCESS PROFILE

1. Height and weight
   a. Height __________ inches
   b. Height __________ percentile
   c. Weight __________ pounds
   d. Weight __________ percentile
2. Skinfold measurements
   a. Triceps __________ mm
   b. Subscapular __________ mm
   c. Percent body fat __________
3. Physical fitness attitude inventory (CATPA)
   a. Score __________ (336 possible)
4. My Physical Self-concept evaluation (Osgood's Semantic Differential Technique)
   a. Score __________ (70 possible)
5. Physical fitness test evaluation
   a. Sit-ups __________
   b. Sit and Reach __________
   c. One-mile Run-Walk __________
6. Parent support __________
7. Classroom teacher support __________
8. Student interest __________
9. PE teacher interest __________

FIGURE 12.5. Success profile form for analyzing data relevant to weight control program participation

4. Give parents a "permission for my child to participate" form and ask them to return it within a stipulated time. This allows the parent and child to discuss whether they really want to participate.

IMPLEMENTATION OF THE PROGRAM

After the students have been selected, a conference with each student must be arranged. Conferences should be conducted on a weekly basis and should not be held during the student's free time, if possible.

1. The conference should last 10 to 20 minutes.
2. A student notebook should be developed, which is the property of the student. He should be able to personalize it and make it something he values. Included in the notebook are the forms that define the student's work load and contain notes and information about exercise, nutrition, and weight control. Included also should be a form for communicating with parents about the child's progress. A parental checkoff sheet stating that the youngster completed the weekly fitness assignment is necessary.

Assigning Fitness Activity

The following guidelines should be used when developing activity for obese children.

1. Assigned activity should be aerobic in nature to increase the caloric expenditure.

2. Exercise prescription should be based on the individual's tolerance for exercise. Start at a level that ensures success.

3. Record assigned activity in order to increase gradually the amount of activity and to ensure overload. Computer recording should be considered.

4. If possible, find aerobic activities that the child enjoys. The assignment should not be in lieu of activity already performed. Offer two or three choices for variety.

5. Assignments should be made in terms of minutes per day. Start with 10 minutes and increase 2 minutes per week, until a maximum of 30 to 40 minutes of exercise a day is reached.

6. Suggested activities are walking, skateboarding, roller-skating or ice-skating, bike riding, motocrossbiking, hiking, unorganized sport activities, orienteering, jogging, swimming, and rope jumping.

Follow-up Activities

1. Every third week, parents should receive some type of communication that discusses the youngster's progress. This might be a note, phone call, computer printout, or personal visit.

2. The physical education teacher should visit regularly with the classroom teacher and explain how the youngster is progressing, what treatment is being used, and those areas to be reinforced in the classroom.

The program emphasizes treating systematically those children who have the characteristics to succeed. If students are selected properly, the program success rate can be very high.

CHILDREN WITH MOTOR DEFICIENCIES

Specialized programs for children with motor deficiencies should be an integral part of the school's overall approach to ameliorating deficiencies, which usually includes other special programs such as speech and reading programs, psychological services, and behavioral management. Programs for the motor deficient are not a substitute for physical education but are an addition to regular participation in physical education classes.

In addition to the programs for special education children discussed previously (see pp. 138–143), two types of programs can be identified for remedying motor deficiency. The first program category concerns children with academic problems, labeled *specific learning disabilities* (SLDs). Children with these problems were formerly targets of *perceptual-motor training,* a term that has lost its usefulness.[2] The second type of program concerns children who exhibit motor deficiencies to a degree that does not allow them to participate successfully in movement activities with peers.

2. A cogent article by Reid (1981) expresses well the position we take with respect to perceptual-motor programs.

SPECIAL LEARNING DISABILITIES AND MOTOR DEFICIENCIES

A specific learning disability is sometimes called a specific language disability. The two terms are interchangeable, and both are referred to as SLDs. A child with SLD has academic performance problems despite an average or above-average IQ. He often exhibits problems such as slow, laborious reading; bizarre and inconsistent spelling; reversing of letters and numbers; clumsy, awkward, and sloppy handwriting; difficulty processing what he hears; hyperactivity and inattentiveness; apparent laziness or behavioral problems; or a discouraged attitude because success is not achieved often.

The learning-disabled often suffer from motor deficiencies and exhibit movement and perceptual problems. This brings physical education into play. Formerly, these learning deficiencies and motor problems were postulated to be the result of a lack of sequential development in the perceptual-motor realm. Proponents of this theory believed that if a corrective program of selected movement activities and motor proficiency development (perceptual-motor programs) could be instituted, then motor proficiency and academic performance would improve. Unfortunately, research has shown collectively that perceptual-motor programs are usually ineffective in remediating learning difficulties. All movement activities are perceptual-motor in nature. To designate certain activities as "perceptual-motor activities" is confusing and inappropriate. Nevertheless, for two decades educators have used the term to mean activities that enhance balance, laterality, agility, spatial awareness and control, hand-eye coordination, rhythm, and body awareness and image.

Although perceptual-motor programs per se are no longer considered effective, the qualities said to be enhanced by them should be given strong attention in a balanced physical education program. Even though research indicates that perceptual-motor programs fail to ameliorate academic learning difficulties, all children with motor deficiencies, including the learning-disabled, need a special corrective program to help with motor difficulties.

In such a program, attention should center on breaking the failure syndrome that these children often experience in the school environment. Many children with disabilities accept failure as the natural course because, no matter how hard they try, the effort does not seem to be enough. Program goals must be twofold—to give children a taste of success and to improve their motor proficiency so they can participate successfully with peers and earn peer regard. Children should achieve success in a noncompetitive environment with activities that are a challenge but within their range of achievement. The SLD child can find satisfaction in movement experiences to compensate some for lack of academic success. These successful experiences become in turn the means for development of a proper body image and self-concept. Other values realized from the remedial program include the following.

1. The child develops listening habits and learns to follow directions.

2. The child learns to reproduce as specified, including putting tasks together in specified sequence.

3. The child learns to stay on task.

4. The child develops pride in achievement, which can stimulate more interest in school and thus stimulate an increased overall effort in classroom work.

5. The child is singled out for special attention and is expected to do well; therefore she does well. Studies show that children do as well as teachers expect them to do.

CLUMSINESS OR INEPTNESS

An observant teacher can screen for further study those children who exhibit clumsiness and ineptitude in accomplishing movement tasks. The child may be able to walk or run reasonably well but may have trouble in skipping, sliding, or galloping. Simple throwing and catching tasks may meet with little success when target skills are deficient. If a child's sense of spatial relationships is deficient, he may collide with objects and classmates more frequently than is normal. This child should be assessed with a motor proficiency test.

MOTOR PROFICIENCY TESTS

Assessment of motor ability is the first step in a remedial program. The number of motor ability tests available is amazing, with a conservative estimate showing more than 250 tests (Wade 1981). Most of these are achievement, as opposed to process-oriented, tests. Achievement tests measure how fast, how far, how many times, or what target score. Process-oriented test items give attention to qualitative changes characterizing movement patterns and relate the movement to a valid developmental sequence norm.

Achievement tests are more easily administered than process-oriented tests, although the latter are considered more valid in terms of motor development. It is much simpler to measure for 10 seconds the balance of a child standing on the preferred leg than to identify what stage the child's throwing pattern assumes in comparison to a scale within the child's age bracket.

An example of one useful test, the *Bruininks-Oseretsky Test of Motor Proficiency,*[3] bears examination. The battery of eight subtests covers gross motor ability, upper limb coordination, and fine motor ability as follows. Four gross motor subtests measure (1) running speed and agility, (2) balance, (3) bilateral coordination, and (4) strength. Upper limb coordination is tested by bouncing and catching balls and by moving and touching body parts. Three fine motor subtests measure (1) response speed, (2) visual-motor control, and (3) upper limb speed and dexterity. The complete battery contains 46 test items distributed among the eight subtests. A short form emphasizes the same eight subtests but consists of only 14 items. The short form takes approximately 20 minutes to administer. The applicable age range is from 4 years, 6 months, to 14 years, 5 months. Standard scores and percentile ranks are available.

A plus for the Bruininks test is that the importance of strength in performing gross motor skills is recognized. Before a child can acquire skill proficiency, she must have a necessary reservoir of strength to practice and accomplish the skill. Many of the items in the fine motor section are not physical education items. These involve pencil accuracy tests, sorting and collecting items, and accomplishing small tasks with accuracy. This portion of the test may be more valuable to a classroom teacher than to a physical educator.

The selection of a proper test as an assessment tool is difficult. First, one must determine the nature of the motor ineptitude and then select motor tasks or developmental sequences that give a clue to the degree of ineptitude. Both of these decisions involve subjective judgments, meaning that test results will always differ because human judgment cannot be stabilized.

3. Test copies and examiner's manual for administering the tests are available from Bruininks-Oseretsky Test of Motor Proficiency, American Guidance Service, Inc., Circle Pines, MN 55014.

REMEDIAL MEASURES FOR THE MOTOR DEFICIENT

An important goal of any remedial program is to provide training to help the deficient child better understand her body and become more proficient and effective in executing movement patterns. The critical issue is effective assessment. Without this, the remedial program has little basis. Assessment should identify deficiencies in achievement and in movement patterns. The remedial clinician should be interested in item results (product) and movement patterns (process) through which the overall test results were attained. The approach to remediation is threefold: (1) give attention to physical fitness qualities, (2) provide broad training in physical education activities, and (3) ameliorate specific deficiencies revealed through assessment procedures.

Physical Fitness

Motor-deficient children tend to be less active than their more skilled peers and usually rank lower in physical fitness qualities. If a child is inactive enough to be classified as an underachiever in physical fitness, the suggestions to help underachievers (pp. 149–154) are appropriate. Otherwise, attention should center on the specific fitness qualities that need development. Basic to the program is developing an understanding of the body—how it functions and how to keep it in proper condition.

Broad Training in Physical Education Experiences

The foundation for the training portion of the program should be fundamental locomotor and manipulative skills taught in a structured, progressive manner. Individual activities done to rhythm, such as rope jumping to music, European Rhythmic Running, rhythmic ball bouncing and dribbling, and selected dance numbers, can supplement and have value. Tumbling, stunts, and apparatus activities offer additional possibilities. These activities should combine sound instructional patterns with emphasis on enjoyment. Teachers should recognize that children enjoy activities in which they find success. The thrust is therefore to get the children to participate successfully in regular, everyday physical education experiences.

Another approach to consider is supplemental instruction (if needed) for current activities in the regular physical education program. This may raise the child's level of skill so that he can compete on an equal basis with peers in the regular physical education class.

Ameliorating Specific Deficiencies

The importance of the assessment process is evident. Specific deficiencies are listed for remediation, with suggestions for appropriate action. If there are many deficiencies, the examiner should establish priority and select critical remediations for early action. The successful correction of one or two items is preferable to a blanket approach to remediation, which may fail.

The method of attack should be a structured, diagnostic teaching approach that follows sound motor-learning principles. Repetition and practice, with an on-task approach for the child, should be stressed. When the student has accomplished the target skill level, proficiency can be tested.

PERCEPTUAL-MOTOR ACTIVITIES

Even though the term *perceptual-motor training* has lost critical meaning, some activity approaches in these programs still have value. For example, laterality, which is defined as the ability to control and move corresponding parts of the body independent of or in conjunction with each other, is a major focus in regular physical education programs and has been singled out for special attention in perceptual-motor programs. In this instance, as in others, the distinction between regular physical education and perceptual-motor activities is difficult to perceive.

To enhance laterality, a variety of movement patterns and combinations that include unilateral, bilateral, cross-lateral, and independent movements should be offered. Independent movements entail separate movements of a dissimilar nature of two or more limbs. The object is to offer a broad range of experiences so the child can learn to move with ease and assurance in executing various movements. Angels in the Snow (Figure 12.6) and crawling and creeping patterns are examples of movement sequences that can be employed to enhance laterality. These movements are used infrequently in regular physical education classes because of their corrective nature.

FIGURE 12.6. Angels in the Snow

The movement pattern Angels in the Snow received the name from a traditional snow activity in which children lie in the snow on their backs and move their arms in an arc from a position overhead along the ground to their sides, thus outlining angel wings. In the exercise, children lie on the back, with legs together and arms at the sides. On command, designated limbs move, the arms moving along the floor to a position above the head, and the legs moving apart. Commands can single out one limb or two, or a full bilateral action in which both arms and both legs move. The commands are given as follows: "Right arm, left leg—out, (pause) back." The words "out" and "back" are alternated so the movement pattern is repeated from six to ten times.

The following movements generally comprise the patterns.

1. Bilateral—both arms, both legs, both arms and both legs

2. Unilateral—right (or left) arm, right (or left) leg, right arm and right leg together, left arm and left leg together

3. Cross-lateral—right arm and left leg, left arm and right leg

Angels in the Snow was originally designated as an individual exercise in which the leader pointed to an arm or a leg and said, "Move that arm (or leg)." This, however, proved unsuitable for group work.

Crawling can follow the same basic patterns.

1. Unilateral—crawling forward on hands and knees, using the arm and leg on the same side together

2. Bilateral—moving forward, reaching out with both hands, and then bringing the feet up to the hands (Bunny Jump)

3. Cross-lateral—crawling forward, moving the right arm and left leg at the same time, and vice versa

Unilateral and cross-lateral creeping also can be employed. (Creeping differs from crawling in that the child assumes a prone position in creeping, while she is on hands and knees in crawling. The terms often are used interchangeably, however.) Variations on crawling and creeping patterns are as follows.

1. Move forward, backward, sideward; make quarter turns right and left.

2. Turn the head first toward the leading hand and then opposite to it, coordinating with each step.

ADMINISTRATION OF THE CORRECTIVE PROGRAM

For any corrective program, classes should be small. Assignment to corrective proficiency classes usually is included as part of the physical educator's normal teaching load. A special period during the day can be set aside for the class, or the class can meet before school, during the lunch hour, or after school.

Parental cooperation is most helpful. The program is more effective if the child does additional work outside of class to improve motor proficiency. A brochure outlining the goals and suggested activities enables parents to help the child with homework. Record keeping is a requirement; each child should have a separate folder.

REFERENCES

AAHPERD. 1980. *Health related physical fitness test manual.* Reston, Va.: AAHPERD.

Eden, A. 1975. How to fat-proof your child. *Reader's Digest* 107(December): 150–152.

Reid, G. 1981. Perceptual-motor training: Has the term lost its utility? *JOPERD* 52(6): 38–39.

Wade, M. G. 1981. A plea for process-oriented tests. *Motor Development Academy Newsletter* (winter): 1–4.

CHAPTER 13

Legal Liability and Proper Care of Students

The nature of physical education is such that it is a high-risk activity. Teachers entering the profession must assume that there will be more opportunity for accidents in their area than in an academic setting. More than 50% of all accidents in the school setting occur in physical education. Facilities and equipment such as baseball bats, hockey sticks, gymnastic equipment, and playground equipment can be sources of injury. Activities in the curriculum offer ample opportunity for accidents and personal injury. Football, wrestling, softball, gymnastics, and track and field have higher accident rates than other activities. These statistics are not presented to alarm teachers but to increase awareness of the situation. The teacher's responsibility lies in creating a safe environment for students—one in which risk and the opportunity for injury are minimized.

All students have a right to freedom from injury caused by others or due to participation in a program. Courts have ruled that teachers owe their students a duty of care to protect them from harm. Teachers must offer a standard of care that any reasonable and prudent professional with similar training would apply under the given circumstances. A teacher is required to exercise the teaching skill, discretion, and knowledge that members of the profession in good standing normally possess in similar situations. Lawsuits usually occur when citizens believe that this standard of care was not exercised.

Liability is a responsibility to perform a duty to a particular group. It is an obligation to perform in a particular way that is required by law and enforced by court action. Teachers are bound by contract to carry out their duties in a reasonable and prudent manner. Liability is always a legal matter. It must be proved in a court of law that negligence occurred before one can be held liable.

TORT LIABILITY

Tort liability is a lawsuit for breach of duty. It is concerned with the teacher-student relationship and is a legal wrong that results in direct or indirect injury to another individual or to property. The following is a legal definition of a tort as stated in *Black's Law Dictionary* (1968):

> A private or civil wrong or injury, other than breach of contract, for which the court will provide a remedy in the form of an action for damages. Three elements of every tort action are: existence of legal duty from defendant to plaintiff, breach of duty, and damage as proximate result.

In tort liability, the court can give a monetary reward for damages that occurred. The court can also give a monetary reward for punitive damages if a breach of duty can be established. Usually, the court rewards the offended individual for damages that occurred due to the negligence of the instructor or other responsible individual. Punitive damages are much less common.

NEGLIGENCE AND LIABILITY

Liability is usually concerned with a breach of duty through negligence. Lawyers must examine the situation that gave rise to the injury to establish if liability can be determined. Four major points must be established to determine if a teacher was negligent.

Duty

The first point to examine is that of duty owed to the participants. Did the school or teacher owe students a duty of care that implies conforming to certain standards of conduct? When examining duty or breach of duty, the court always looks at reasonable care that a member of the profession in good standing would provide. In other words, to determine a reasonable standard, the court uses the conduct of other teachers as a standard for comparison.

Breach of Duty

The teacher must commit a breach of duty by failing to conform to the required duty. After it is established that a duty was required, it must be proved that the teacher did not perform that duty. Two situations are possible: (1) the teacher did something that was not supposed to be done (e.g., put boxing gloves on students to solve their differences), or (2) the teacher did not do something that should have been done (e.g., failed to teach an activity by using proper progressions).

Injury

An injury must occur if liability is to be established. If no injury or harm occurs, there is no liability. Further, it must be proved that the injured party is entitled to compensatory damages for financial loss or physical discomfort.

Proximate Cause

The failure of the teacher to conform to the required standard must be the proximate cause of the resulting injury. It must be proved that the injury was caused by the teacher's breach of duty. It is not enough to prove simply that a breach of duty occurred. It must simultaneously be shown that the injury was a direct result of the teacher's failure to provide a reasonable standard of care.

FORESEEABILITY

A key to the issue of negligence is foreseeability. The courts expect that a trained professional is able to foresee potentially harmful situations. Was it possible for the teacher to predict and anticipate the danger of the harmful act or situation and to take appropriate measures to prevent it from occurring? If the injured party can prove that the teacher should have foreseen the danger involved in an activity or situation (even in part), the teacher will be found negligent for failing to act in a reasonable and prudent manner.

This points out the need to examine all activities, equipment, and facilities for possible hazards and sources of accident. As an example, a common game in the school setting is bombardment or dodge ball. During the game, a student is hit in the eye by a ball and loses her vision. Was this a foreseeable accident that could have been prevented? Were the balls being used capable of inflicting severe injury? Were students aware of rules that might have prevented this injury? Were the abilities of the students somewhat equal, or were some capable of throwing with such velocity that injury was predictable? These types of questions would likely be considered in court in an attempt to prove that the teacher should have been able to predict the overly dangerous situation.

TYPES OF NEGLIGENCE

Negligence is defined by the court as conduct that falls below a standard of care that is established to protect others from unreasonable risk of harm. Several different types of negligence can be categorized.

Malfeasance

Malfeasance occurs when the teacher does something improper by committing an act that is unlawful and wrongful, with no legal basis. This type of negligence is illustrated by the following incident. A male student misbehaved on numerous occasions. In desperation, the teacher gave the student a choice of punishment—a severe spanking in front of the class or running many laps around the field. The student chose the former and suffered physical and emotional damage. Even though the teacher gave the student a choice whereby he could have avoided the paddling, the teacher is still liable for any harm caused.

Misfeasance

Misfeasance occurs when the teacher follows the proper procedures, but does not perform according to the required standard of conduct. Misfeasance is based on an action that is performed improperly so it does not meet a required standard. It is usually the subpar performance of an act that might have been lawfully done. An example would be the teacher's offering to spot a student during a tumbling routine and then not doing the spotting properly. If the student is injured due to a faulty spot, the teacher can be held liable.

Nonfeasance

Nonfeasance is based on lack of action in carrying out a duty. This is usually an act of omission; the teacher knew the proper procedures, but failed to follow them. Teachers can be negligent if they act or fail to act. Understanding and carrying out proper procedures and duties in a manner befitting members of the profession are essential. In contrast to the misfeasance example, nonfeasance would involve a teacher's knowing that it is necessary to spot certain gymnastic routines, but failing to do so. It should be added here that the courts have expected teachers to behave with more skill and insight than parents (Strickland et al. 1976). Teachers are expected to behave with greater competency than responsible parents because they have been educated to meet a high standard of professional training.

Contributory Negligence

The situation is different when the injured student is partially or wholly at fault. Each student is expected to exercise sensible care and to follow directions or regulations to protect himself from injury. This responsibility is always directly related to the maturity, ability, and experience of the child. For example, most states have laws specifying that a child under 7 years of age is incapable of contributory negligence (Baley and Matthews 1984). Improper behavior by the injured party as cause of the accident is contributory negligence, because the injured party *contributed* to the resulting harm. To illustrate contributory negligence, assume that the teacher has explained thoroughly the safety rules to be followed while hitting softballs. As students begin to practice, one of them runs through a restricted area that is well marked and is hit by a bat. Depending on the age and maturity of the child, the possibility is strong that the student will be held liable for his actions.

Comparative or Shared Negligence

Under the doctrine of comparative negligence, the injured party can recover only if she is found to be less negligent than the defendant (the teacher). Where statutes apply, the amount of recovery is generally reduced in proportion to the injured party's participation in the circumstances leading to the injury.

COMMON DEFENSES AGAINST NEGLIGENCE

It should be clear at this point that negligence must be proved in a court of law. Undoubtedly, teachers are often negligent in carrying out their duties, yet the injured party does not take the case to court. If the teacher is sued, some of the following stands may be taken in an attempt to show that the teacher's action was not the primary cause of the accident.

Contributory Negligence

As described, this defense attempts to convince the court that the injured party acted in a manner that was abnormal. In other words, the injured individual did not act in a manner that was typical of students of similar age and maturity. The defense would attempt to demonstrate that the activity or equipment in question had been used for years with no record of accident. A case would be made based on the manner of presentation—how students were taught to act in a safe manner—and that the injured student acted outside the parameters of safe conduct. A key point in this defense is whether the activity was suitable for the age and maturity level of the participants.

Act of God

The defense in this situation is to put the cause of injury on forces beyond the control of the teacher or the school. The case is made that it was impossible to predict that an unsafe condition would occur, but through an act of God, the injury occurred. Typical acts would be a gust of wind that blew over a volleyball standard, a cloudburst of rain that made a surface slick, or a flash of lightning that struck someone on the playing field. The act of God defense can be used only in those cases in which injury would still have occurred had reasonable and prudent action been taken.

Proximate Cause

This defense attempts to prove that the accident was not caused by the negligence of the teacher. There must be a close relationship between the breach of duty by the teacher and the injury. This is a common defense in cases dealing with proper supervision. The student is participating in an activity supervised by the teacher. When the teacher leaves the playing area to get a cup of coffee, the student is injured. The defense tries to show that the accident would have occurred regardless of whether the teacher was there or not.

Assumption of Risk

Clearly, physical education is a high-risk activity when compared with most other curriculum areas. The participant assumes the risk of an activity when she chooses to be part of that activity. The assumption of risk defense is seldom used by physical education teachers because students are not often allowed to choose to participate or not participate. An elective program that allows students to choose desired units of instruction might find this a better defense than a totally required program. Athletic and sport club participation is by choice, and players do assume a greater risk in activities such as football or gymnastics.

AREAS OF RESPONSIBILITY

Teachers need to be keenly aware of those areas in which they may be found negligent in fulfilling their responsibilities. These areas most often lead to lawsuits when teachers fail to conduct themselves in a reasonable, prudent, and careful manner.

SUPERVISION

Teachers have a responsibility to supervise students in all school settings and are accountable for this duty. The two types of supervision are *general* and *specific.* General supervision refers to always being physically present in the gymnasium or on the field. It also means that the teacher will be immediately available to any student who needs assistance or aid. A common general supervision situation occurs when a student is injured. The teacher sometimes judges that he must take the student to the nurse and therefore leaves the rest of the class unattended. If an accident occurs while the class is unattended, the teacher may be found negligent. Either another student must attend the injured party, or another teacher must be secured to attend the class.

When conducting general supervision duties, the teacher must be able to see all participants. Teachers should have a plan of rotation (written, if necessary) that allows contact with all students. Discipline in the supervised area is a necessity. If the court proves that the injury occurred due to lack of student control, the teacher may be held liable. Specific supervision requires that the instructor be with a certain group of students. An example might be the need to spot students who are performing difficult gymnastic activities. If certain pieces of apparatus require special care and proper use, the teacher should have rules and regulations posted near the apparatus.

The following guidelines help ensure that proper supervision occurs:

1. All school activities must be supervised, regardless of the situation. The teacher may have to answer a phone call, go to the bathroom, secure more equipment, or discipline a student privately. Before doing any of these, another qualified supervisor must be secured. A class should never be split and sent to different areas if both areas cannot be supervised simultaneously.

2. Be aware of any possible dangers in the area. If the playing field has sprinkler heads that could cause injury, they should be marked with cones. If glass or other debris is on the field, the area should be marked off and avoided. The supervisor is responsible for being aware of these situations and keeping students from them. The teacher must always inspect the activity area for possible hazards.

3. Have safety rules posted in the area. Students should be made aware of the posted rules, and they should receive related instruction and guidance in interpreting the rules. When rules are modified, they should be rewritten in proper form. There is no substitute for documentation when defending one's policies and approaches.

4. Arrange and teach the class so that all students are always in view. This means supervising from the perimeter of the area. A teacher who is at the center of the student group with her back to many students will find it impossible to supervise a class safely and effectively.

5. Do not leave equipment and apparatus unsupervised at any time if it is accessible to other students in the area. An example would be equipment that is left on the playing field between classes. If other students in the area have easy access to the equipment, they may use it in an unsafe manner, and the teacher can be found liable if an injury occurs.

6. Do not agree to supervise activities in which you are unqualified to anticipate possible hazards. If this situation arises, a written memo should be sent to the department head or principal stating your lack of insight and qualification. Keep a copy for your files.

7. The number of supervisors should be determined by the type of activity, the size of the area, and the number and age of the students.

INSTRUCTION

The major area of concern involving instruction is whether the student received adequate instruction before or during activity participation. Adequate instruction means (1) teaching how to perform the activity correctly and how to use equipment and apparatus properly and (2) teaching necessary safety precautions. If instructions are given, they must be correct, understandable, and include proper technique, or the instructor can be held liable. The risk involved in an activity must be communicated to the learner.

The age and maturity level of the students play an important role in the selection of activities. Younger students require more care, instructions that are easy to comprehend, and clear restrictions in the name of safety. Students have a lack of appropriate fear in some activities, and the teacher must be aware of this in discussing safety factors. A very young child may have little concern about performing a high-risk activity if an instructor is nearby. This places much responsibility on the instructor to give adequate instruction and supervision.

Careful planning is a necessity. Written curriculum guides and lesson plans should offer a well-prepared approach that can withstand scrutiny and examination by other teachers and administrators. Lesson plans should be developed that include proper sequence and progression of skill. Teachers are on defensible grounds if they can show that the progression of activities was based on presentations made by experts and was followed carefully during the teaching act. District and state guidelines enforcing instructional sequences and restricted activities should be checked closely.

Proper instruction demands that students not be forced to participate. If a youngster is required to perform an activity against her will, the teacher may be open to a lawsuit. In a lawsuit dealing with stunts and tumbling (Appenzeller 1970), the court held the teacher liable when a student claimed that she was not given adequate instruction in how to perform a stunt called "roll over two." The teacher was held liable because the student claimed that she was forced to try the stunt before adequate instruction was offered. Gymnastics and tumbling are areas in which lawsuits are prevalent due to a lack of adequate instruction. Posting the proper sequence of skills and lead-up activities may be useful to ensure that they have been presented properly. Teachers need to tread the line carefully between helpful encouragement and forcing students to try new activities.

Since for many teachers the use of punishment is a part of the instructional process, the consequences of its use should be examined carefully before implementation. Physical punishment that brings about permanent or long-lasting damage is certainly indefensible. The punishment used must be in line with the physical maturity and health of the student involved. A teacher's practice of having students perform laps when they have misbehaved might go unchallenged for years. However, what if an asthmatic student or a student with congenital heart disease is asked to run and has an attack? What if the student is running unsupervised and is injured from a fall or suffers heat exhaustion? In these examples, defending the punitive practice would be difficult. We also believe that it is difficult to defend making students perform physical activity for misbehavior under any circumstance. In any case, if a child is injured while performing a physical punishment, the teacher is usually liable and is held responsible for the injury.

The primary point to remember about instruction is that the teacher has a duty to protect students from unreasonable physical or mental harm and a duty to avoid any acts or omissions that might produce such harm. The teacher is educated, experienced, and skilled in the area and must be able to predict situations that might be harmful.

The following points can help the teacher in planning for meaningful and safe instruction:

1. Sequence all activities in a unit of instruction and develop a written lesson plan. Most problems occur when snap judgments are made under the pressure and strain of the teaching situation.

2. Eliminate high-risk activities. If in doubt, discuss the activities with other experienced teachers and administrators.

3. Never force students to perform an activity. The activities used in the curriculum must be within the developmental limits of the students. Since the range of maturity and development within a class is usually wide, some activities may be beyond the ability level of various students.

4. If students' grades are based on the number of activities in which they try to participate, then some students may feel forced to try all activities. Teachers should make it clear to students that the choice to participate belongs to them. When they are afraid of getting hurt, they can elect not to perform an activity.

5. Include in the written lesson plan the necessary safety equipment. The lesson plan should detail how equipment is to be arranged, the placement of mats, and where the instructor will carry out supervision.

6. Activities included in the curriculum should be based on the contribution that they make to the growth and development of students. It makes little sense in a court of law to say that the activity was included "for the fun of it" or "because the students liked it." The activities included should be based on the constructs of the curriculum and the consensus of experts.

7. If a student states that he is injured or brings a note from parents stating that he is not to participate in physical activity, the teacher must honor the communication. These excuses are almost always given at the start of the period when the teacher is busy with many other duties (e.g., getting equipment ready, taking roll, and opening lockers). It is impossible to make a thoughtful judgment at this time. The school nurse is qualified to make these judgments when they relate to health and should be used in that capacity. If the excuses continue over a long period of time, the teacher or nurse should have a conference with the parents to rectify the situation.

8. Make sure that the activities included in the instructional process are in line with the available equipment and facilities. An example is the amount of space available. If a soccer lead-up activity is brought indoors because of inclement weather, it may no longer be a safe and appropriate activity.

9. If spotting is required for the safe completion of activities, it must always be done by the instructor or by trained students. Teaching students how to spot is as important as teaching them physical skills. Safe conduct must be learned.

10. Have a written emergency care plan posted in the gymnasium. This plan should be approved by health care professionals and should be followed to the letter when an injury occurs.

EQUIPMENT AND FACILITIES

The equipment and facilities used in the physical education program must allow safe participation in activity. The choice of apparatus and equipment should be based on the growth and developmental levels of the students. For example, allowing elementary school children to use a horizontal ladder that was designed for high school students may result in a fall that causes injury. Hazards found on playing fields need to be repaired and eliminated. The legal concept of an "attractive nuisance" should be understood. This implies that some piece of equipment or apparatus, usually left unsupervised, was so attractive to children that they could not be expected to avoid it. When an injury occurs, even though students may have been using the apparatus incorrectly, the teachers and the school are often held liable because the attractive nuisance should have been removed from the area when unsupervised.

Teachers should develop a written checklist of equipment and apparatus for the purpose of recording regularly scheduled safety inspections. The date of inspection is noted to show that inspection occurs at regular intervals. If corrective action is needed, the principal or an appropriate administrator should be notified *in writing.* Telling them verbally is not enough, because this approach affords little protection to the teacher. If a potentially dangerous situation exists, rules or warnings should be posted so students are made aware of the risk before participating.

Proper installation of equipment is critical. Climbing equipment and other equipment that must be anchored should be installed by a reputable firm that guarantees its work. When examining an apparatus, inspecting the installation at the same time is important. Maintenance of facilities is also important. Grass should be kept short and the grounds inspected for debris. Holes in the ground should be filled and loose gravel removed. A proper finish that prevents excessive slipping should be used on indoor floors. Shower rooms should have a roughened floor finish applied to prevent falls when the floors are wet.

The facilities should be used in a safe manner. Often, the side and end lines of playing fields for sports such as football, soccer, and field hockey are placed too close to walls, curbings, or fences. The boundaries should be moved in to allow adequate room for deceleration, even though the size of the playing area may be reduced. In the gymnasium, students should not be asked to run to a line that is close to a wall. Another common hazard is baskets positioned too close to the playing area. The poles that support the baskets must be padded.

The proper use of equipment and apparatus is important. Regardless of the state of equipment repair, if it is misused, it may result in an injury. Students must receive instruction in the proper use of equipment and apparatus before it is issued to them and used. All safety instruction should be included in the written lesson plan to ensure that all points are covered.

ATHLETIC PARTICIPATION

When students are involved in extracurricular activity, teachers (coaches) are still responsible for the safe conduct of activities. A common error that gives rise to lawsuits is the mismatching of students on the basis of size and ability. Just because the competitors are the same sex and choose to participate does not absolve the instructor of liability if an injury occurs. The question the court examines is whether an effort was made to match students according to height, weight, and ability. The courts are less understanding about mismatching in the physical education setting than in an athletic contest, but mismatching is a factor that should be considered in any situation.

Participants in extracurricular activities should be required to sign a responsibility waiver form. The form should explain the risks involved in voluntary participation and discuss briefly the types of injuries that have occurred in the past during practice and competition. Supervisors should remember that waiver slips do not waive the rights of participants, and that teachers and coaches can still be found liable if injuries occur. The waiver form does communicate clearly, however, the risks involved and may be a strong "assumption of risk" defense.

Participants should be required to have a medical examination before participating. Records of the examination should be kept in the files and should be identified prominently in cases of physical restriction or limitation. Students should not be allowed to participate unless they purchase medical insurance, and evidence of coverage should be kept in the folders of athletic participants.

Preseason conditioning should be undertaken in a systematic and progressive fashion. Starting the season with a mile run for time makes little sense if students have not been preconditioned. Coaches should be aware of guidelines dealing with heat and humidity. For example, in Arizona, guidelines are to avoid strenuous activity when the temperature exceeds 85 degrees and the humidity exceeds 40% (Stone 1977). When these conditions are exceeded, running is curtailed to 10 minutes and active games to 30 minutes. Drinking water should be available and given to students on demand.

Whenever students are transported, teachers are responsible for their safety both en route and during the activity. Licensed drivers and school-approved vehicles should always be used. Travel plans should include official approval from the appropriate school administrator. One special note: if the driver receives expenses for the trip, the possibility of his being held liable for injury increases dramatically. Many insurance policies also do not cover drivers who receive compensation for transporting students. If a teacher is transporting students and receiving reimbursement, a special insurance rider that provides liability coverage for this situation should be purchased.

SAFETY

The major thrust of safety should be to prevent situations that cause accidents. It is estimated that over 70% of injuries that occur in sport and other related activities could be prevented through proper safety procedures. On the other hand, some accidents will occur despite precautions, and proper emergency procedures should therefore be established to cope with any situation. A comprehensive study of injuries received in sports and related activities was conducted by the Consumer Product Safety Commission (1975). This study involved a network of computers in 119 hospital emergency rooms that channeled injury data to a central point. The sports and activities that produced the most injuries were, in order, football, touch football, baseball, basketball, gymnastics, and skiing. The facility that produced the most disabling injuries was the swimming pool.

Learning to recognize potential high-risk situations is probably the most important factor in preventing accidents. Teachers must possess a clear understanding of the hazards and potential dangers of an activity before they can establish controls. Instructors cannot assume that participants are aware of the dangers and risks involved in various activities. They must be told of the dangers and risks before participation.

GUIDELINES FOR SAFETY

1. In-service sessions in safety should be administered by experienced and knowledgeable teachers. Department heads may be responsible for the training, or outside experts can be employed to undertake the responsibility. Giving in-district credit to participating teachers is a strong indication of the district's desire to nurture the use of proper safety techniques.

2. Medical records should be reviewed at the start of the school year. Students who are atypical or handicapped should be noted and identified within each class listing. Identifying these individuals before the first instructional day is important. If necessary, the teacher or school nurse can call the doctor of a handicapped or activity-restricted student to inquire about the situation and discuss any special needs.

3. At the beginning of the school year, a safety orientation should be conducted with students. This should include discussions of potentially dangerous situations, class conduct, and rules for proper use of equipment and apparatus. Teachers should urge students to report any condition that might cause an accident.

4. Safety rules for specific units of instruction should be discussed at the onset of each unit. Rules should be posted and brought to the attention of students regularly. Posters and bulletin boards can promote safety in an enjoyable and stimulating manner.

5. If students are to act as instructional aides, they should be trained. Aides must understand the techniques of spotting, for example, and must receive proper instruction if they are to be a part of the educational process.

6. If equipment is faulty, it should be removed completely from the area until it is repaired. Along the same lines, equipment should not be modified or used for something other than its original intended purpose.

7. An inventory of equipment and apparatus should include a safety checklist. At the end of the school year, equipment in need of repair should be sent to proper agents. If the cost of repair is greater than 40% of the replacement cost, discarding the equipment or apparatus is advisable.

8. Equipment should be purchased on the basis of quality and safety as well as potential use. Many lawsuits occur because of unsafe equipment and apparatus. The liability for such equipment may rest with the manufacturer, but this has to be proved, which means that the teacher must state, in writing, the exact specifications of the desired equipment. The process of bidding for a lower priced item may result in the purchase of less safe equipment. If the teacher has specified the proper equipment, however, the possibility of being held liable for injury is reduced.

9. Whenever an injury occurs, it should be recorded and a report placed in the student's file. An injury report should also be filed by type of injury, for example, ankle sprains or broken arms. The report should list the activity and the conditions to facilitate analysis at regular intervals. The analysis may show that injuries are occurring regularly during a specific activity or on a certain piece of equipment. This process can give direction for creating a safer environment or for defending the safety record of a sport, activity, or piece of equipment.

THE SAFETY COMMITTEE

A safety committee can meet at regular intervals to establish safety policies, to rule on requests for allowing high-risk activities, and to analyze serious injuries that have occurred in the school district. This committee should develop safety rules that apply districtwide to all teachers. It may determine that certain activities involve too high a risk for the return in student benefit. Acceptable criteria for sport equipment and apparatus may be established by the committee.

The safety committee should include one or more high level administrators, physical education teachers, health officers (nurse), parents, and students. A point to remember is that school administrators are usually indicted also when lawsuits do occur, because they are held responsible for program content and curriculum. Their representation on the safety committee is therefore important. In addition, students on the committee may be aware of possible hazards, and parents may voice concerns often overlooked by teachers.

Safety should be publicized throughout the school on a regular basis, and a mechanism should exist that allows students, parents, and teachers to voice concerns about unsafe conditions.

ASSESSING THE HEALTH STATUS OF STUDENTS

Periodic health examinations do not uncover every health problem related to participation in physical activity. Some conditions may appear only after exercise. In other instances, the condition may develop after an examination and may have an important bearing on the health status of the student.

The task of screening children who respond poorly to exercise is not difficult, because it involves identifying certain observable conditions that are indications of an abnormality. The Committee on Exercise and Fitness of the American Medical Association lists these observable signs that may accompany or follow exercise and be indications for referral to a physician. In any case, if the teacher identifies some of these symptoms, the school nurse should be notified and asked to examine the student. Teachers, regardless of their experience and expertise, should never try to make medical diagnoses or decisions.

1. *Excessive breathlessness.* Some breathlessness is normal with exercise, but if it persists long after exercise, it is cause for medical referral.

2. *Pale or clammy skin.* Pale or clammy skin or cold sweating following or during exercise is not a normal reaction to physical activity within the usual temperature range of the gymnasium or playing field.

3. *Unusual fatigue.* Excessive fatigue, as evidenced by unusual lack of endurance or early failure to maintain moderate activity, suggests the need for medical referral. Attributing such reactions to lack of effort is unwise until possible organic causes have been ruled out.

4. *Persistent shakiness.* Unusual weakness or shakiness that continues for more than 10 minutes following vigorous exercise is cause for concern.

5. *Muscle twitching or tetany.* Muscular contractions such as twitching or tetany, whether localized or generalized, sometimes occur as an unusual reaction to exercise.

In addition, such medical symptoms as headache, dizziness, fainting, broken sleep at night, digestive upset, pain not associated with injury, undue pounding of the heart or irregular heartbeat, disorientation, or personality change are contraindications of normal functioning. The committee cautions that an occasional episode need not alarm the instructor, but recurring or persisting patterns of any of these symptoms, particularly when related to activity, indicates the need for medical review.

THE EMERGENCY CARE PLAN

Establishing procedures for emergency care and notification of parents in case of injury is of utmost importance in providing a high standard of care for students. In order to plan properly for emergency care, all physical education teachers should have first aid training. First aid is the immediate and temporary care given in an emergency before the physician arrives. Its purpose is to save life, prevent aggravation of injuries, and alleviate severe suffering. If there is evidence of life-threatening bleeding or if the victim is unconscious or has stopped breathing, the teacher must administer first aid. When already injured persons may be further injured if they are not moved, then moving them is permissible. As a general rule, however, an injured party should not be moved unless absolutely necessary. If there is any indication of back or neck injury, the head must be immobilized and should not be moved without the use of a spine board. Remember the purpose of first aid—to save life. The emergency care plan should consist of the following steps:

1. Administration of first aid to the injured student is the number one priority. Treat only life-threatening injuries. If a school nurse is available, she should be called immediately to the scene of the accident. Emergency care procedures should indicate whether the student can be moved and in what fashion. It is critical that the individual applying first aid avoid aggravating the injury.

2. Unless the injury is so severe that the student must be taken directly to the hospital emergency care unit, the parents should be notified. Each student's file should list home and emergency telephone numbers where parents can be reached. If possible, the school should have an arrangement with local emergency facilities so a paramedic unit can be called immediately to the scene of a serious accident.

3. In most cases, the student should be released to a parent or a designated representative. Policies for transportation of injured students should be established and documented.

4. A student accident report should be completed promptly while the details of the accident are clear. Figure 13.1 is an example of an accident report form that covers the necessary details. The teacher and principal should both retain copies and send additional copies to the administrative office.

PERSONAL PROTECTION: MINIMIZING THE EFFECTS OF A LAWSUIT

In spite of proper care, injuries do occur, and lawsuits may be initiated. Two courses of action are necessary to counteract the effects of a suit.

Liability Insurance

Teachers may be protected by school district liability insurance. Usually, however, teachers must purchase a policy. Most policies provide for legal services to contest a suit and will pay indemnity up to the limits of the policy ($300,000 liability coverage is most common). Most policies give the insurance company the right to settle out of court. If this occurs, some may infer that the teacher was guilty, even though the circumstances indicate otherwise. Insurance companies usually settle out of court to avoid spending a lot on legal fees to try to win the case in court.

Record Keeping

The second necessary course of action is to keep complete records of accidents. Many lawsuits occur months or even years after the accident, when memory of the situa-

STUDENT ACCIDENT REPORT
_______________ SCHOOL

In all cases, this form should be filed through the school nurse and signed by the principal of the school. The original will be forwarded to the superintendent's office, where it will be initialed and sent to the head nurse. The second copy will be retained by the principal or the school nurse. The third copy should be given to the physical education teacher if accident is related.

Name of injured _______________ Address _______________

Phone _______________ Grade _______________ Home room _______________ Age_______________

Parents of injured _______________

Place of accident _______________ Date of accident _______________

Hour _______________ A.M. P.M. Date reported _______________ By whom _______________

Parent contact attempted at _______________ A.M. P.M. Parent contacted at _______________ A.M. P.M.

DESCRIBE ACCIDENT, GIVING SPECIFIC LOCATION AND CONDITION OF PREMISES _______________

____

NATURE OF INJURY _______________
(Describe in detail)

CARE GIVEN OR ACTION TAKEN BY NURSE OR OTHERS _______________

____

REASON INJURED PERSON WAS ON PREMISES _______________
(Activity at time—i.e., lunch, physical education, etc.)

STAFF MEMBER RESPONSIBLE FOR STUDENT SUPERVISION AT TIME OF ACCIDENT _______________

____

IS STUDENT COVERED BY SCHOOL-SPONSORED ACCIDENT INSURANCE? _____ Yes _____ No

MEDICAL CARE RECOMMENDED _____ Yes _____ No

WHERE TAKEN AFTER ACCIDENT _______________
(Specify home, physician, or hospital, giving name and address)

BY WHOM _______________ AT WHAT TIME _______________ A.M. P.M.

FOLLOW-UP BY NURSE TO BE SENT TO CENTRAL HEALTH OFFICE

REMEDIATIVE MEASURES TAKEN _______________
(Attach individual remarks if necessary)

School _______________ Principal _______________

Date _______________ Nurse _______________

On the back of this sheet, list all persons familiar with the circumstances of the accident, giving name, address, telephone number, age, and location with respect to the accident.

FIGURE 13.1. Sample accident report form

tion is fuzzy. Accident reports should be filled out immediately after an injury. The teacher should take care to provide no evidence, oral or written, that others could use in a court of law. Do not attempt to make a diagnosis or to specify the supposed cause of the accident in the report.

If newspaper reporters probe for details, the teacher should avoid describing the accident beyond the basic facts. When discussing the accident with administrators, only the facts recorded on the accident report should be discussed. Remember that school records can be subpoenaed in court proceedings. The point here is not to dissemble, but to be cautious and avoid self-incrimination.

A SAFETY AND LIABILITY CHECKLIST

The following checklist can be used to monitor the physical education environment. Any situations that deviate from safe and legally sound practices should be rectified immediately.

Supervision and Instruction

1. Are teachers adequately trained in all of the activities that they are teaching?

2. Do all teachers have evidence of a necessary level of first aid training?

3. When supervising, do personnel have access to a written plan of areas to be observed and responsibilities to be carried out?

4. Have students been warned of potential dangers and risks, and advised of rules and the reasons for rules?

5. Are safety rules posted near areas of increased risk?

6. Are lesson plans written? Do they include provisions for proper instruction, sequence of activities, and safety? Are all activities taught listed in the district curriculum guide?

7. When a new activity is introduced, are safety precautions and instructions for correct skill performance always communicated to the class?

8. Are the activities taught in the program based on sound curriculum principles? Could the activities and units of instruction be defended on the basis of their educational contributions?

9. Do the methods of instruction recognize individual differences among students, and are the necessary steps taken to meet the needs of all students, regardless of sex, ability, or disability?

10. Are substitute teachers given clear and comprehensive lesson plans so they can maintain the scope and sequence of instruction?

11. Is the student evaluation plan based on actual performance and objective data rather than on favoritism or arbitrary and capricious standards?

12. Is appropriate dress required for students? This does not imply uniforms, only dress that ensures the safety of the student.

13. When necessary for safety, are students grouped according to ability level, size, or age?

14. Is the class left unsupervised for teacher visits to the office, lounge, or bathroom? Is one teacher ever asked to supervise two or more classes at the same time?

15. If students are used as teacher aides or to spot others, are they given proper instruction and training?

Equipment and Facilities

1. Is all equipment inspected on a regular basis, and are the inspection results recorded on a form and sent to the proper administrators?

2. Are "attractive nuisances" eliminated from the gymnasium and playing field?

3. Are specific safety rules posted on facilities and near equipment?

4. Are the following inspected periodically?

a. Playing field for presence of glass, rocks, and metal objects

b. Fasteners holding equipment such as climbing ropes, horizontal bars, or baskets

c. Goals for games, such as football, soccer, and field hockey, to be sure that they are fastened securely

d. Padded areas such as goal supports

5. Are mats placed under apparatus from which a fall is possible?

6. Are playing fields arranged so participants will not run into each other or be hit by a ball from another game?

7. Is a log maintained recording the regular occurrence of an inspection, the equipment in need of repair, and when repairs were made?

8. Are landing pits filled and maintained properly?

Emergency Care

1. Is there a written procedure for emergency care?

2. Is a person properly trained in first aid available immediately following an accident?

3. Are emergency telephone numbers readily accessible?

4. Are telephone numbers of parents available?

5. Is an up-to-date first aid kit available? Is ice immediately available?

6. Are health folders maintained that list restrictions, allergies, and health problems of students?

7. Are health folders reviewed by instructors on a regular basis?

8. Are students participating in extracurricular activities required to have insurance? Is the policy number recorded?

9. Is there a plan for treating injuries that involves the local paramedics?

10. Are accident reports filed promptly and analyzed on a regular basis?

REFERENCES

Appenzeller, H. 1970. *From the gym to the jury.* Charlottesville, Va.: The Michie Company.

Baley, J. A., and Matthews, D. L. 1984. *Law and liability in athletics, physical education, and recreation.* Boston: Allyn and Bacon.

Black's law dictionary. 4th ed. 1968. St. Paul: West Publishing Co.

Stone, W. J. 1977. Running and running tests for Arizona school children. *Arizona JOHPERD* 21: 15–17.

Strickland, R., Phillip, J. F., and Phillips, W. R. 1976. *Avoiding teacher malpractice.* New York: Hawthorn Books.

U.S. Consumer Product Safety Commission. 1975. *Hazard analysis of injuries relating to playground equipment.* Washington, D.C.: U.S. Government Printing Office.

CHAPTER 14

Evaluation and Microcomputer Applications

Educators have been accused of spending millions of dollars on innovations but very little money to see if those innovations are worthwhile. The heart of evaluation is to determine whether the learning environment is accomplishing progress toward learning objectives established for children. Evaluation should concern itself with pupil progress, teacher performance, and program effectiveness.

Student evaluation can be formal or informal and can focus on individual or group progress. Teacher evaluation can be used to improve the instructional process or to secure data for measuring teacher effectiveness. Program evaluation examines critically the total program or selected program areas. What is effective needs to be retained and enhanced, and what is deficient needs to be corrected.

EVALUATION OF STUDENTS

Two types of evaluation pertain to students, namely, process evaluation and product evaluation. Process evaluation relates to the performance of general movement patterns with the correct technique. The form used to execute the movement is the point of focus, rather than the outcome of the skill performed.

Product evaluation focuses on performance outcomes in terms of measurable increments of what the child can do. For example, if product evaluation were applied to fundamental ball skills, the concern would be with how far the ball was thrown, while process evaluation would focus on the quality of the throwing pattern.

It is sometimes helpful to think of product versus process in terms of how teachers view the instructional environment. A product-oriented teacher does not show as much concern for how the students feel about learning, or about the technique and form used when performing skills. In a game of basketball, the primary area of product concern would be the outcome of the game—winning or losing. The process-oriented teacher, on the other hand, is more concerned that students develop proper patterns of skill performance and positive attitudes toward the activity. The outcome of the game would be secondary to the learning experience. The epitome of product orientation is an athletic situation in which the coach might say, "I don't care if you like it or not, as long as we win." In all likelihood, most teachers find themselves somewhere between the two viewpoints and place varying amounts of emphasis on process and product.

Three problems confront the evaluator. The first is to devise a system of recording that is efficient, valid, and not excessively time consuming. The second concerns the number of times a trait needs to be observed or measured before it can be considered reliable. A third problem pertains to the amount of in-class and out-of-class time needed for effective evaluation. Take the case of the physical education specialist who handles 600 or more students each day. How does the specialist evaluate this number of students adequately and record the items properly? In some cases, microcomputers can be helpful in expediting data analysis (see pp. 201–203).

PROCESS EVALUATION

Some motor learning specialists hold that the first concern in the psychomotor domain is process evaluation: Can the child perform the general motor pattern using the correct technique? Later, concern can be directed toward the product of the pattern.

Two means of process evaluation seem to dominate. In the first, stages of motor skill development are identified. The lowest stage would be one in which the child begins roughly to learn the pattern. The final stage is a mature pattern in which the child has accomplished the skill technique to a degree of appropriate usefulness for her age level. In between would be a number of intermediate steps linking the initial to the mature pattern.

To employ this type of process evaluation, the teacher needs to have accurate knowledge of the different stages so the child's pattern can be categorized through observation techniques. Videotaping is useful for viewing the skill performance a number of times and in slow motion. As an example, normative data might show that a 4th-grade child should be in stage three of development. If this age child tests at the first stage of development, a developmental deficiency is indicated.

A second means of process evaluation involves a checklist format. The movement criteria governing proper technique for the pattern are listed, and the child's performance is checked against these points. Limiting coverage to two or three of the more critical points of technique is usually best. Ratings for each point can be on a 3-point scale, namely, no conformance, partial conformance, and complete conformance. These could be numbered 0, 1, and 2, respectively, providing a point scale for comparisons. The record sheet can be organized so that the achievement levels are listed, and the evaluator circles the appropriate number.

PRODUCT EVALUATION

Product evaluation is concerned with how far, how accurate, how many times, how much, and how fast. It does not deal with the technique used to perform the skill. The point of concern is the performance outcome. Both subjective and objective means of assessment are employed. Three approaches are useful for identifying entry-level behavior and monitoring progress in areas of skill performance and behavioral patterns.

CHECKLISTS

Checklists have long been used as a system of reporting progress to parents. A regular class list with skills added across the top of the sheet is one means of recording class progress. It can alert the teacher to youngsters who are in need of special help. If grading is based on the number of activities that students can master, the checklist can deliver this information. Checklists are usually most effective when skills are listed in the sequence in which they should be learned. In this way, the teacher can gear the teaching process to diagnosed needs. To avoid disrupting the learning process, the teacher records student progress informally while students are practicing. Figure 14.1 is a sample checklist for rope jumping.

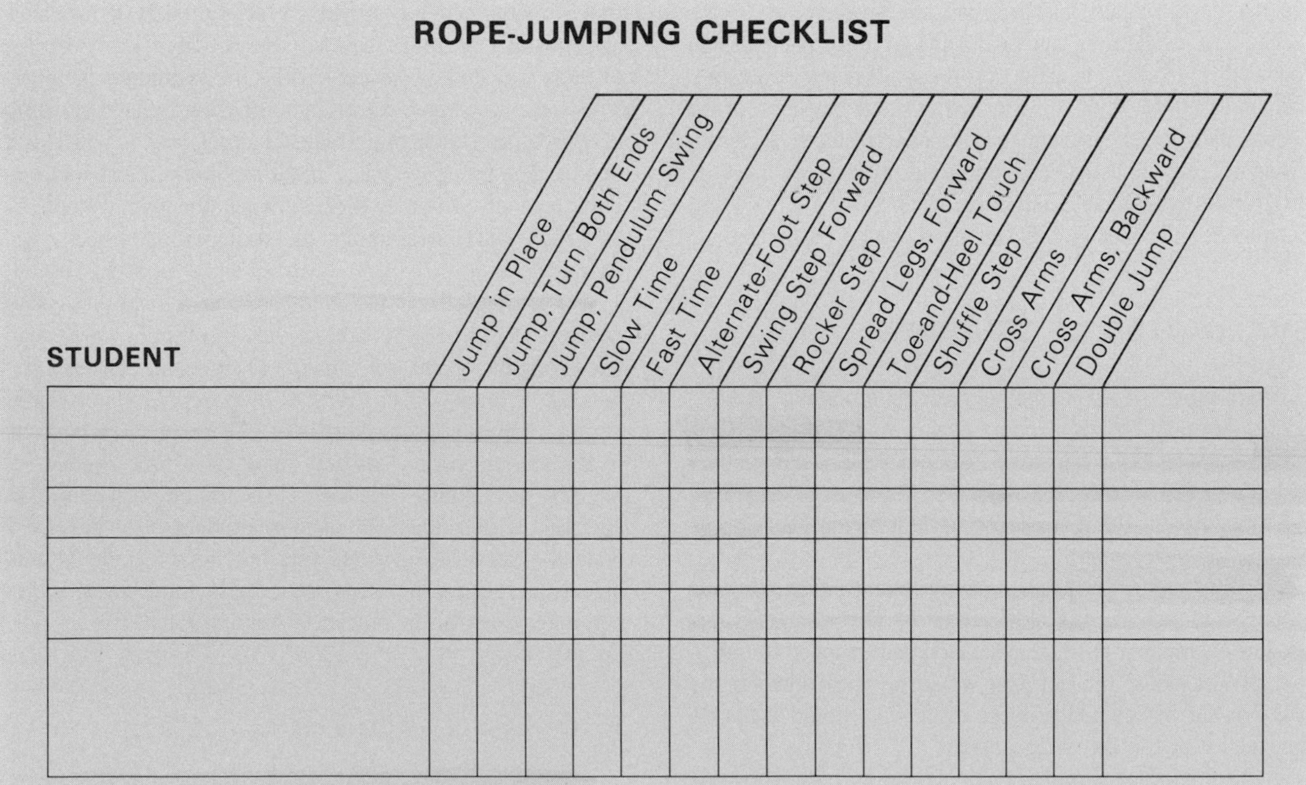

ROPE-JUMPING CHECKLIST

STUDENT	Jump in Place	Jump, Turn Both Ends	Jump, Pendulum Swing	Slow Time	Fast Time	Alternate-Foot Step	Swing Step Forward	Rocker Step	Spread Legs, Forward	Toe-and-Heel Touch	Shuffle Step	Cross Arms	Cross Arms, Backward	Double Jump

FIGURE 14.1. Sample skill checklist

ANECDOTAL RECORD SHEETS

A record sheet that contains student names and has room for comments about student behavior can also be used to assess student progress. A record of student progress can be reinforcing to both student and teacher. Often, neither is able to see much progress over a long period. With anecdotal records, teachers can inform students of their initial skill level as compared with present performance.

A tape recorder is an excellent tool for recording anecdotal information. The recorder can be used during observation, and anecdotes can be written down at a later time. This process helps the teacher learn the names and behavior patterns of students and leads to an increased empathy for participants. Observations can be recorded at the start of the unit and compared with observations made at a later date as instruction proceeds. A sample record sheet is illustrated in Figure 14.2.

Student Self-Evaluation

Students in the intermediate grades are capable of self-evaluation. They can be given lists of performance objectives and told to make judgments about their achievements. If more objectivity is desired, students can evaluate each other, or groups of two or three students can evaluate one another. Self-evaluation reduces the amount of teacher time required and gives the teacher more time for instruction. The ability to evaluate oneself and the desire to be evaluated are important outcomes of any effective program.

STANDARDIZED TESTS

Standardized tests are useful for evaluating measurable outcomes. The tests have been administered to large samples of youngsters, and the results are available for comparative purposes. Most of the tests require that exact testing procedures and protocol be followed. The disadvantages of standardized tests are their inflexibility and the need for specialized equipment.

Throughout the school year, testing should be done at least twice. Testing at the beginning of the school year can identify low-fitness children and emphasize those directions the program should take. Testing at the end of the school year can provide information about program and student accomplishments.

Testing is a problem for the unassisted teacher. It is difficult for children to supervise each other and secure reliable measurements. A plan in which the school enlists the help of the community school organization is advised. Interested parents make excellent testers. A team of parents can be established on a schoolwide or districtwide basis, depending on the situation. Those school districts that have such a plan in operation report enthusiastic support for testing and for the entire physical education program.

Testers must undergo orientation and training. A trial run with one class or with a small group helps iron out most difficulties. The testing program should be organized efficiently. Each tester is given detailed instructions for each station. If enough parents are available, having two testers at each station is helpful. One carries a clipboard and does the recording while the other does the testing.

Two systems of recording information can be used. One is to have class lists at each station. The other is for each child to have an individual record card, which she carries from station to station. The first method is speedier, but care must be taken to match the correct name with the performance. The class lists have to be transferred to individual cards after the testing is over. Some school districts record data on computer opscan cards. This provides a

Class Ms. Massoney **ANECDOTAL RECORD SHEET** Date 2/14/83

Bob: Is making progress on the backward jump. Sent a jump rope home with him for practice.

Gene: Seems to be discouraged about rope jumping. Called parents to see if there is a problem outside of school.

Linda: Discussed the need for helping others. She is going to be a cross-aged tutor for next two weeks, as her performance in batting is excellent.

FIGURE 14.2. Sample anecdotal record sheet

ready means of data analysis and eliminates laborious hand tabulation of results.

The test results, or at least an interpreted summary, should become part of the child's permanent health record and should be included in the periodic progress report to parents. The school report card should contain a section devoted to the physical fitness of the student. Test results for each class and for the school as a whole should be interpreted in light of national norms and in comparison with local achievement. Testing is meaningless unless the evaluators have a concern for raising the children's performance levels and upgrading the physical education program.

AAHPERD HEALTH RELATED PHYSICAL FITNESS TEST

The AAHPERD Health Related Physical Fitness Test is a four-item test used to diagnose the functional health of students. The items evaluate cardiorespiratory function, body composition, and abdominal and low back-hamstring function. For an in-depth discussion of the test, the AAHPERD *Health Related Physical Fitness Test Manual* (1980) should be consulted. The following is a description of the test items followed by the norms for each.

Sum of Skinfold Fat

Purpose: The purpose of the test is to evaluate the level of fatness or body composition.

Equipment: Skinfold calipers are necessary. The inexpensive plastic calipers are suitable substitutes.

Test Description: Two skinfold fat sites (triceps and subscapular) are measured easily and correlate well with total body fat. The triceps skinfold is measured over the triceps muscle of the right arm halfway between the elbow and the acromion process of the scapula with the skinfold parallel to the longitudinal axis of the upper arm. The subscapular site (right side of the body) is ½ in. below the angle of the scapula and in line with the natural cleavage lines of the skin.

The recommended testing procedure is:

1. Firmly grasp the skinfold between the thumb and forefinger and lift up.

2. Place the contact surfaces of the caliper ½ in. above or below the finger.

3. Slowly release the grip on the calipers, which enables them to exert their full tension on the skinfold.

4. Read skinfold to nearest 0.5 mm after needle stops (1 to 2 seconds after releasing grip on caliper).

Interpretation: The higher the percentile score, the less fat the child is (Tables 14.1 and 14.2). The criterion for a desired degree of fatness for children is above the 50th percentile.

Modified Sit-up

Purpose: The purpose of the Sit-up[1] is to evaluate abdominal muscular strength and endurance.

Equipment: Mats can be used to create a comfortable surface, and a stopwatch is necessary to time the test.

Test Description: The student lies on his back with knees flexed and feet flat on floor, with the heels between 12 and 18 in. from the buttocks. The arms are crossed on the chest with the hands on opposite shoulders. The feet are held by a partner to keep them in touch with the testing surface. The student curls to the sitting position. Arm con-

1. We prefer the term "Curl-up" for this movement, but we use the term "Sit-up" here since this is AAHPERD terminology.

TABLE 14.1. PERCENTILE NORMS: AGES 6–18* FOR SUM OF TRICEPS PLUS SUBSCAPULAR SKINFOLDS (MM) FOR BOYS†

	Age											
Percentile	6	7	8	9	10	11	12	13	14	15	16	17
95	8	9	9	9	9	9	9	9	9	9	9	9
75	11	11	11	11	12	12	11	12	11	12	12	12
50	12	12	13	14	14	16	15	15	14	14	14	15
25	14	15	17	18	19	22	21	22	20	20	20	21
5	20	24	28	34	33	38	44	46	37	40	37	38

SOURCE: Reprinted by permission of the American Alliance for Health, Physical Education, Recreation and Dance, 1900 Association Drive, Reston, VA 22091.

* The norms for age 17 may be used for age 18.

† Based on data from F. E. Johnston, D. V. Hamill, and S. Lemeshow. (1) *Skinfold thickness of children 6–11 years* (Series II, No. 120, 1972), and (2) *Skinfold thickness of youths 12–17 years* (Series II, No. 132, 1974). U.S. National Center for Health Statistics, U.S. Department of HEW, Washington, D.C.

TABLE 14.2. **PERCENTILE NORMS: AGES 6–18* FOR SUM OF TRICEPS PLUS SUBSCAPULAR SKINFOLDS (MM) FOR GIRLS†**

	Age											
Percentile	6	7	8	9	10	11	12	13	14	15	16	17
95	9	10	10	10	10	11	11	12	13	14	14	15
75	12	12	13	14	14	15	15	16	18	20	20	20
50	14	15	16	17	18	19	19	20	24	25	25	27
25	17	19	21	24	25	25	27	30	32	34	34	36
5	26	28	36	40	41	42	48	51	52	56	57	58

SOURCE: Reprinted by permission of the American Alliance for Health, Physical Education, Recreation and Dance, 1900 Association Drive, Reston, VA 22091.

* The norms for age 17 may be used for age 18.

† Based on data from F. E. Johnston, D. V. Hamill, and S. Lemeshow. (1) *Skinfold thickness of children 6–11 years* (Series II, No. 120, 1972), and (2) *Skinfold thickness of youth 12–17 years* (Series II, No. 132, 1974). U.S. National Center for Health Statistics, U.S. Department of HEW, Washington, D.C.

tact with the chest must be maintained. The chin should remain tucked on the chest. The Sit-up is completed when the elbows touch the thighs. To complete the movement, the student returns to the down position in which the mid-back makes contact with the testing surface.

The number of correctly executed Sit-ups performed in 60 seconds is the score. Rest is allowed between Sit-ups, and the student should be aware of this before starting. The goal is to perform as many Sit-ups as possible.

Interpreting Test Results: Weak abdominal muscles are a contributing factor in the development of low back pain. Students who score below the 50th percentile (Tables 14.3 and 14.4) on this test are encouraged to improve abdominal

TABLE 14.3. **PERCENTILE NORMS: AGES 5–18 FOR SIT-UPS FOR BOYS**

	Age												
Percentile	5	6	7	8	9	10	11	12	13	14	15	16	17+
95	30	36	42	48	47	50	51	56	58	59	59	61	62
75	23	26	33	37	38	40	42	46	48	49	49	51	52
50	18	20	26	30	32	34	37	39	41	42	44	45	46
25	11	15	19	25	25	27	30	31	35	36	38	38	38
5	2	6	10	15	15	15	17	19	25	27	28	28	25

SOURCE: Reprinted by permission of the American Alliance for Health, Physical Education, Recreation and Dance, 1900 Association Drive, Reston, VA 22091.

TABLE 14.4. **PERCENTILE NORMS: AGES 5–18 FOR SIT-UPS FOR GIRLS**

	Age												
Percentile	5	6	7	8	9	10	11	12	13	14	15	16	17+
95	28	35	40	44	44	47	50	52	51	51	56	54	54
75	24	28	31	35	35	39	40	41	41	42	43	42	44
50	19	22	25	29	29	32	34	36	35	35	37	33	37
25	12	14	20	22	23	25	28	30	29	30	30	29	31
5	2	6	10	12	14	15	19	19	18	20	20	20	19

SOURCE: Reprinted by permission of the American Alliance for Health, Physical Education, Recreation and Dance, 1900 Association Drive, Reston, VA 22091.

strength and endurance as well as back, hip, and posterior thigh flexibility.

Sit and Reach

Purpose: The purpose of the sit-and-reach test is to evaluate the flexibility of the low back and posterior thighs.

Equipment: The test apparatus consists of a sit-and-reach box that can be constructed or purchased. Detailed instructions for constructing the box are illustrated in the AAHPERD *Health Related Physical Fitness Test Manual* (1980).

Test Description: Students remove their shoes and sit down at the test apparatus with knees fully extended and the feet shoulder width apart. The feet should be flat against the end board of the box. The arms are extended forward with one hand placed on top of the other to perform the test. The student reaches directly forward, palms down, along the measuring scale four times and holds the position of maximum reach on the fourth trial. The position of maximum reach must be held for 1 second.

Interpreting Test Results: A score above the 50th percentile on this test is considered a normal level of flexibility (Tables 14.5 and 14.6). Scores below the 50th percentile represent poor extensibility in at least one of the following areas: posterior thigh, low back, or posterior hip. Poor flexibility in these areas is a contributing factor in the development of musculoskeletal problems.

Distance Runs

Purpose: The purpose of the distance runs is to measure maximal functional capacity and cardiorespiratory endurance.

Equipment: Either of the two distance run tests can be administered on a 440-yd or 400-m track or on any other flat, measured area. A stopwatch is needed for timing the runs.

Test Description: Norms are available for each of the two distance runs. They are the 1-mile run for time and the 9-minute run for distance. The decision as to which of the two tests to administer should be based on facilities, equipment, time limitations, administrative considerations, and personal preference of the teacher.

1. *One-mile run.* Students are instructed to run 1 mi in the fastest time possible. As they cross the finish line, elapsed time should be called to the runners (or their part-

TABLE 14.5. PERCENTILE NORMS: AGES 5–18 FOR SIT AND REACH (CM) FOR BOYS

	Age												
Percentile	5	6	7	8	9	10	11	12	13	14	15	16	17+
95	32	34	33	34	34	33	34	35	36	39	41	42	45
75	29	29	28	29	29	28	29	29	30	33	34	36	40
50	25	26	25	25	25	25	25	26	26	28	30	30	34
25	22	22	22	22	22	20	21	21	20	23	24	25	28
5	17	16	16	16	16	12	12	13	12	15	13	11	15

SOURCE: Reprinted by permission of the American Alliance for Health, Physical Education, Recreation and Dance, 1900 Association Drive, Reston, VA 22091.

TABLE 14.6. PERCENTILE NORMS: AGES 5–18 FOR SIT AND REACH (CM) FOR GIRLS

	Age												
Percentile	5	6	7	8	9	10	11	12	13	14	15	16	17+
95	34	34	34	36	35	35	37	40	43	44	46	46	44
75	30	30	31	31	31	31	32	34	36	38	41	39	40
50	27	27	27	28	28	28	29	30	31	33	36	34	35
25	23	23	24	23	23	24	24	25	24	28	31	30	31
5	18	18	16	17	17	16	16	15	17	18	19	14	22

SOURCE: Reprinted by permission of the American Alliance for Health, Physical Education, Recreation and Dance, 1900 Association Drive, Reston, VA 22091.

ners). Walking is permitted, but the objective is to cover the distance in the shortest possible time.

2. *Nine-minute run.* Students are instructed to run as far as possible in 9 minutes. The students continue to run until a whistle is blown when 9 minutes have elapsed. They then stand in place until their distance has been recorded. The distance that each student runs is recorded to the nearest 10 yd or 10 m. Walking is permitted, but the objective is to cover as much distance as possible during the 9 minutes.

Interpretation: Students can be compared with persons of the same age and sex based either on the norms in Tables 14.7 and 14.8 or on locally developed norms. Note that the time or the distance reflects not only cardiorespiratory fitness but also may reflect in part the child's inherited characteristics, running skill, relative leanness, and motivation to do well.

WELLNESS PROFILE

A wellness profile can be developed to identify and assess factors that, if left untreated, could result in later health problems. Typically, schools gather the majority of this data at one time or another but fail to collate it and make it available to teachers and parents. The wellness profile should be included in the student's permanent record. Results should be sent home to parents so that they are aware of their youngster's health status. The wellness profile is not intended to diagnose disease but to offer basic measurements of health status. If measurements give cause for concern, parents can make the decision to visit the family physician.

The letter to parents in Figure 14.3 illustrates the type of data that can be collected. Desirable ranges can be offered with a brief explanation for each area. A health assessment team that includes school nurses, physical education instructors, and clerical aides can assess a classroom of students in approximately 20 minutes, with the exception of the 1-mile run. Other data that can be included in the wellness profile are results of visual screening, auditory screening, posture checks, and immunization and medical examination records.

EVALUATING THE INSTRUCTIONAL PROCESS

The instructional process has often been evaluated by use of methods such as intuition, checklists, rating scales, and observation. Over the years, these methods have proved

TABLE 14.7. PERCENTILE NORMS: AGES 5–18 FOR THE ONE-MILE RUN (MINUTES AND SECONDS) FOR BOYS

	Age												
Percentile	5	6	7	8	9	10	11	12	13	14	15	16	17+
95	9:02	9:06	8:06	7:58	7:17	6:56	6:50	6:27	6:11	5:51	6:01	5:48	6:01
75	11:32	10:55	9:37	9:14	8:36	8:10	8:00	7:24	6:52	6:36	6:35	6:28	6:36
50	13:46	12:29	11:25	11:00	9:56	9:19	9:06	8:20	7:27	7:10	7:14	7:11	7:25
25	16:05	15:10	14:02	13:29	12:00	11:05	11:31	10:00	8:35	8:02	8:04	8:07	8:26
5	18:25	17:38	17:17	16:19	15:44	14:28	15:25	13:41	10:23	10:32	10:37	10:40	10:56

SOURCE: Reprinted by permission of the American Alliance for Health, Physical Education, Recreation and Dance, 1900 Association Drive, Reston, VA 22091.

TABLE 14.8. PERCENTILE NORMS: AGES 5–18 FOR THE ONE-MILE RUN (MINUTES AND SECONDS) FOR GIRLS

	Age												
Percentile	5	6	7	8	9	10	11	12	13	14	15	16	17+
95	9:45	9:18	8:48	8:45	8:24	7:59	7:46	7:26	7:10	7:18	7:39	7:07	7:26
75	13:09	11:24	10:55	10:35	9:58	9:30	9:12	8:36	8:18	8:13	8:42	9:00	9:03
50	15:08	13:48	12:30	12:00	11:12	11:06	10:27	9:47	9:27	9:35	10:05	10:45	9:47
25	17:59	15:27	14:30	14:16	13:18	12:54	12:10	11:35	10:56	11:43	12:21	13:00	11:28
5	19:00	18:50	17:44	16:58	16:42	17:00	16:56	14:46	14:55	16:59	16:22	15:30	15:24

SOURCE: Reprinted by permission of the American Alliance for Health, Physical Education, Recreation and Dance, 1900 Association Drive, Reston, VA 22091.

FIGURE 14.3. Example of a wellness profile (Much of this material has been adapted with permission from a program developed by Dr. Thomas Crow, Clovis Public Schools, Clovis, CA 93612.)

WELLNESS PROFILE

To the parent/guardian of ______________________:

Your child's health status was recently examined as part of the Health Evaluation Program in the ____________School District. Listed below are your child's results and the corresponding percentile score in his/her age group. An explanation of the items included in this screening is given below.

HEALTH COMPONENT	**SCORE**	**PERCENTILE SCORE**
Sit-and-reach test	______ centimeters	__________
Sit-ups (1 minute)	______ repetitions	__________
Aerobic field test		
1-mile run/walk	______ minutes:seconds	__________
9-minute run/walk	______ distance covered	__________
Skinfold	______ % body fat	__________
Height	______ inches	__________
Weight	______ pounds	__________
Blood pressure		
Systolic	______ mm/Hg	Normal range ____ to ____
Diastolic	______ mm/Hg	Normal range ____ to ____
Dental/oral inspection	______________________________	
Hearing (audiometer)	______ Acceptable	____ Needs Attention

The program is not meant to diagnose disease but to indicate basic measurements of health. If you are concerned or are advised by school authorities to seek medical attention for your child, please take this form to your doctor or clinic. Please feel free to contact the school nurse if you have any questions.

Sincerely,

____

EXPLANATION OF WELLNESS PROFILE ITEMS

Sit-and-reach test:	The sit-and-reach test measures flexibility of the lower back and hamstring (back of the thigh) muscle group. A lack of flexibility in this area often contributes to low back pain.
Sit-ups:	Sit-ups measure the strength of the abdominal muscle group. Strength in this area is important for proper posture and to prevent low back pain.
Aerobic field test:	The aerobic field test consists of running and walking one mile in the fastest time possible. This test is the best single indicator of cardiorespiratory endurance, which is important in preventing heart disease.
Skinfold:	This measurement relates to the amount of fat a person carries. People who have too much fat are more likely to develop problems such as diabetes (excessive sugar in the blood) and high blood pressure.

FIGURE 14.3/*continued*

Height and weight:	These are general measurements of a child's growth. It is important that growth be observed regularly to ensure that the body is developing normally.
Blood pressure:	Blood pressure is recorded using two values. The top number (systolic) represents the pressure in the arteries when the heart is pumping blood. The bottom number (diastolic) represents the pressure in the arteries when the heart is at rest. High blood pressure increases the risk of heart disease.
Dental and oral inspection:	An inspection of the gums and teeth is conducted to document any noticeable inflammation, sores, cavities, and other abnormalities.
Hearing check:	A hearing test is given to check the acuity of the ears at different frequencies. If "needs attention" is checked, a physician should be consulted.

INTERPRETING THE RESULTS

Results are in two categories. The first is the raw score showing the actual performance of your child. The second score is the percentile score and allows comparison of your child's performance with that of other children of similar age. For example, if your child scored in the 60th percentile, it means that he/she scored higher than 60% of the students tested. It also means that 40% of students evaluated scored higher than your child. By examining the listed percentile scores, you can get a general indication of your child's health status.

to be relatively ineffective in assessing the quality of instruction. The use of intuition relies on the expertise of a supervisor who observes the instructor and then recommends changes, thus reinforcing specific practices. The improvement based on such recommendations is difficult to identify, because little or no quantification is offered.

Checklists and rating scales are used often and give the appearance of objective, quantified evaluation (Figures 14.4, 14.5, 14.6). Unfortunately, the ratings are often quite unreliable and become more so when the number of choice points increases. The scales and checklists are open to a broad spread of interpretation depending on the experience and capacity of the rater. Most of the evaluation done by the use of checklists and rating scales is subject to the impressions and opinions of the evaluator rather than being based on objective data.

The inherent weakness of checklists necessitates the need for developing a systematic method of observing teachers that quantifies the teaching processes. In its purest form, the data gathered is reliable and can be used for research studies. In this section, we describe teacher observation methods that are systematic in nature and feasible for self-evaluation. The methods advocated emphasize the use of systematic observation for self-improvement. If readers choose to conduct research projects, the Siedentop text *Developing Teaching Skills in Physical Education* (1983) should be consulted as a primary resource. Another relevant text for developing research techniques is *Systematic Observation Instrumentation for Physical Education* by Darst et al. (1983). The techniques described in the following section have been simplified to facilitate implementation by classroom and physical education teachers in the typical school setting.

METHODS FOR SYSTEMATICALLY OBSERVING INSTRUCTION

Information based on the systematic observation of instruction can be gathered in a variety of ways. The first step in the process is to define the area to be evaluated. The second step is to then delineate a precise definition of the behavior that occurs within the defined area. Definitions should be written and followed consistently if the data is to be meaningful. The methods require little more than pencil, paper, tape recorder, and stopwatch. A videotape recorder can add another dimension, but is not a necessity.

EVENT RECORDING

In simplest terms, this involves recording the number of times a predefined event occurs during a specified time period. Event recording identifies the frequency with which a certain behavior occurs. The quantity of events is recorded, not the quality of events. For example, a teacher might want to know the number of times that she interacted with individual students or the number of times a positive statement was made. The defined event could be the number of practice attempts that students receive after a skill has

FIGURE 14.4. Example of a teacher evaluation checklist

LESSON OBSERVATION-INSTRUCTOR ASSESSMENT

RATING SCALE

3 Competent, good, high level
2 Moderate, satisfactory
1 Needs improvement
X Not observed or not applicable

Date ____________
Instructor ____________
Evaluator ____________
Grade Level ____________
Activities ____________

PERSONAL QUALITIES — **COMMENTS**

____ 1. Appearance: neatness, appropriate dress
____ 2. Poise, confidence, self-control
____ 3. Enthusiasm, energy
____ 4. Voice: clarity, force, effectiveness

TEACHING SKILLS AND CLASSROOM MANAGEMENT — **COMMENTS**

____ 1. Facilities and equipment prepared
____ 2. Supplies: efficient handling
____ 3. Effective behavior level and control
____ 4. Safety precautions: taught, observed
____ 5. Effective use of time: verbal and movement
____ 6. Efficient movement of students, use of space

COMMUNICATION SKILLS—RAPPORT WITH STUDENTS — **COMMENTS**

____ 1. Conveys ideas clearly and effectively
____ 2. Maintains student interest and enthusiasm
____ 3. Uses student ideas and suggestions
____ 4. Sensitive to student needs
____ 5. Interacts with students
____ 6. Provides positive reinforcement, encourages

THE LESSON — **COMMENTS**

____ 1. Shows good planning, preparation
____ 2. Teaching methods appropriate to content
____ 3. Adapts, adjusts to students' abilities
____ 4. Appropriate progressions
____ 5. Provides for maximum participation
____ 6. Accomplishes objectives

FIGURE 14.4/*continued*

_____ 7. Allows for exploration, creativity

_____ 8. Provides for critique, evaluation

GENERAL COMMENTS

What were the strong points or commendable aspects of the lesson presentation? What suggestions are made for improving or strengthening the quality of the presentation?

EVALUATION FORM

Activity ______________________________ Date __________

Student Teacher ______________________________ Elementary _______ Secondary ________

College Supervisor ______________________ Cooperating Teacher ____________________

This evaluation of student teaching serves as a tangible basis for discussion among the cooperating teacher, the college supervisor, and the student. The following symbols will be used: Plus (+) indicates a positive feature of the student teacher's work; minus (–) indicates a need for improvement.

TEACHING COMPETENCIES

☐ Appearance
☐ Use of language
☐ Voice
☐ Enthusiasm
☐ Poise
☐ Creativity

☐ Planning and organization
☐ Execution of lesson-teaching technique
☐ Knowledge of subject
☐ Demonstration of skills
☐ Appropriate progression
☐ Provisions for individual differences
☐ Class management-control
☐ Adaptability, foresight
☐ Appropriate choice of activity

COMMENTS:

FIGURE 14.5. Example of a student teacher rating scale

Student Teacher ______________ Activity ______________ Grade ______________

	5	4	3	2	1	Comments
1. Use of language						
2. Quality of voice						
3. Personal appearance						
4. Class management						
5. Presentation and teaching techniques						
6. Professional poise						
7. Enthusiasm, interest						
8. Adaptability, foresight						
9. Adequate activity						
10. Knowledge of subject						
11. Appropriate use of student help						
12. Demonstration (if any)						
13. Progression (if applicable)						
14. General organization						

General evaluation
- 5–Superior
- 4–Above average
- 3–Average
- 2–Below average
- 1–Poor

Evaluating Teacher

____

Date ______________________________

FIGURE 14.6. Example of a student teacher rating scale

been introduced, or the number of times the teacher asks the class to stop and come to attention. Usually, event recording results are divided by the number of minutes in the evaluation session to give a rate per minute. This allows some comparison of lessons that involve different content or teaching styles.

To minimize the amount of time needed for observation and data analysis, a sampling technique can be used. For example, if the lesson is 30 minutes long, four bouts of recording, each lasting 2 minutes and spread throughout the lesson, would reduce the burden of recording and still give representative results. Any observable teacher behavior, student behavior, or behavior between teacher and student can be recorded when the behavior has been defined clearly.

DURATION RECORDING

Whereas event recording offers insight into the frequency of certain behaviors, duration recording reveals the length of the behavior in terms of minutes and seconds. Time is the measure used in this type of recording. As with event recording, the duration recording does not have to involve an entire lesson. Using representative sampling techniques, generalizations about the entire session can be made based on three or four bouts of observation lasting 3 minutes each.

The data are usually converted to percentages so comparisons can be made from lesson to lesson. This is done by dividing the length of the total observation into the amount of time accumulated involving a specific behavior. For example, if 20 minutes of observation took place and if the student was observed to be in activity for 10 of the 20 minutes, then the percentage of time spent in activity would be 50%. This is expressed as, "50% of the total time was spent in activity." This approach is best used when one desires to identify the duration of certain behaviors, such as practice, managerial, or instructional behaviors.

INTERVAL RECORDING

Interval recording is most often used to record individual behavior patterns. In interval recording, the intervals should be 6 to 12 seconds in length, with one interval for observing and the other for recording. For example, if one were using 6-second intervals during a 1-minute session, five intervals would be for observing and five for recording the results. According to Siedentop (1983), having at least 90 data points (observe-record equals 1 point) is necessary to establish the validity of the technique. Using 6-second intervals, it would be possible to generate 100 data points in 20 minutes.

The data generated from this technique are usually converted to a percentage of the data points in which the behavior occurred. If, for example, the behavior occurred in 40 of 100 data points, the figure would be 40%. The percentage could then be compared from lesson to lesson. A simple way to keep track of intervals is to wear a headset from a recorder that "beeps" every 6 seconds (see p. 203 for a discussion of using a computer to time and enter data). The observer can alternate observing and recording with each signal. This technique is reliable, particularly when intervals are short, and can be used to analyze academic learning time and other types of observable behavior.

PLACHECK SAMPLING

Placheck (*Pl*anned *a*ctivity *check*) recording is similar to interval recording in that behavior is observed at different intervals. However, this technique is used to observe group behavior. At regular intervals during a lesson, the observer scans the group for 10 seconds. The scan takes place from the left to right side of the instructional area, and the observer might take note, for example, of which students were not on task. Only one observation per student is used. The observer does not go back and change the decision, even if the student changes behavior during the 10-second interval.

This technique is usually used to identify student effort, productive activity, and participation. Recording the smaller number of students exhibiting a behavior is easier. For example, if the teacher is interested in identifying the percentage of students involved in the assigned activity, it might be easier to record the number of students *not* participating. The intervals should last for 10 seconds and be randomly spaced throughout the lesson. There should be eight to ten observation intervals. Again, signals to observe can be recorded on a tape recorder at random intervals to cue the observer. This technique yields valuable information concerning the behavior of a group.

SYSTEMATIC OBSERVATION FOR SELF-IMPROVEMENT

Each teacher has different strengths, weaknesses, and concerns for improvement. The approach used for systematic observation for self-improvement may vary greatly from teacher to teacher. The teacher needs to decide which variables she wants to evaluate and then needs to determine the best possible way to record and monitor the data.

Starting simple and evaluating one area is usually preferable, since recording more than one variable at a time may frustrate and confuse. After the teacher decides which behavior needs to be changed, a plan for meaningfully evaluating the behavior area is developed. This means identifying the behavior that affects the desired educational outcome and deciding which method of observation will be most effective. At that point, a coding form is developed to facilitate recording of the data.

Coding sheets should be specific to each situation and suited to the teacher. Areas on the sheet should provide for recording of the teacher's name, the date, the focus and content of the lesson, the grade level and competency of the students, the duration of the lesson, and a short description of the evaluation procedure. The sheets should be consistent for each type of behavior so the instructor can compare progress throughout the year.

Deciding what behavior to record depends on the instructor's situation. For example, can the data be gathered by students who are not participating? Can another teacher gather the data easily? Can the data be gathered from an audiotape or is a videotape necessary? Is the instructor willing to let others gather the information, or does he believe that keeping the data confidential is important? These and other considerations determine what areas the teacher is able to evaluate. In most cases, the teacher is least threatened by self-evaluation techniques and is more willing to change when change is not required by outside authorities. The routine daily teaching behavior is least changed when outside observers are not present, so self-evaluation techniques are more likely to reveal the actual patterns exhibited in day-to-day teaching.

Many areas that can be evaulated are suggested later in this section with appropriate coding forms. These are, however, only examples that can be modified easily to meet the specific needs of the instructor. The important point is that teachers should make self-evaluation an ongoing, integral part of the teaching process. They should think continually about ways to improve. Teachers seldom stay the same; they either improve or their performance tapers off.

IMPROVING THE QUALITY OF INSTRUCTION

Quality instruction results when an effective teacher implements a well-planned lesson. Many successful teachers have learned how to do this over a period of years through the inefficient method of trial and error. Unfortunately, sheer experience does not guarantee that one will grow into an outstanding teacher. Witness the fact that there are many experienced yet mediocre teachers. The key to improving teaching ability is experience coupled with meaningful feedback about the teacher's performance.

Often, teachers find it difficult, if next to impossible, to find someone capable of offering evaluative feedback. Principals and curriculum supervisors may be too busy to evaluate teaching regularly, or they may not possess the skills necessary for the systematic observation of teaching behavior. This only accentuates the importance of finding ways to self-evaluate one's teaching as the primary avenue for improvement. Without regular and measurable means of evaluation, improving the quality of teaching becomes next to impossible. Teachers have long been told to talk less, move more, praise more, learn more names, and increase student practice time—all without documented methods of measurement. This section shows the many phases of teaching behavior that are observable and therefore measurable. These data can be gathered by the teacher, by teaching peers, or by selected students.

Our emphasis in evaluation is on the do-it-yourself approach. Feedback that is gained in the privacy of one's office is easier to digest and less threatening. Teachers may set personal goals and chart their performance privately. When teachers choose to evaluate their own teaching procedures, they are usually willing to change. This attitude is in contrast to the resistance that teachers feel when principals and supervisors choose to evaluate and dictate change. Instructors often doubt the validity of the latter process and reject change.

INSTRUCTIONAL TIME

The teaching process is not educational if teachers do not instruct. The "throw out the ball" approach is nothing more than leisure activity in a school setting. Instructors should be aware of the amount of instruction that they offer students. Finding a meaningful balance between instruction and practice is also important. An observer can tally the number of instructional episodes and the length of each episode. At a later time, the average length of an instructional episode can be evaluated, as well as the percentage of the lesson that was used for instruction. Generally, episodes should be short and frequent, with an attempt made to limit each episode to 30 seconds or less.

How to Do It

1. Design a form for duration recording.

2. Have a colleague or a nonparticipating student turn on the stopwatch every time the instructor begins an instructional episode, or record the lesson using an audiotape recorder and time the instructional episodes at the end of the day. Be sure to establish consistency in identifying the difference between instructional and management episodes.

3. Total the amount of time spent on instruction.

4. Convert the amount of time to a percentage of the total lesson time by dividing the total lesson time into the time spent on instruction. The average length of an instruction episode can be determined by dividing the amount of instructional time by the number of instructional episodes. Figure 14.7 is an example of a form that might be used.

CLASS MANAGEMENT TIME

Effective teachers are efficient managers of students. Management time is usually that time when no instruction or practice is taking place. Management occurs when students are moved into various formations, when equipment is gathered or put away, and when directions are given relative to these areas. Figure 14.8 is an example of a form that can be used to evaluate the amount of management time. This form involves duration recording using a stopwatch.

The amount of time being used for class management and the length and number of episodes are meaningful data for a teacher to have. The number of episodes and the length of each can be recorded by an observer. These data are useful for analyzing how much lesson time is devoted to management. The instructor may be alerted to an inefficient organizational scheme, or she may realize that students are not responding quickly to explanations and requests.

How to Do It

1. Design a form that gathers the desired data (Figure 14.8).

2. Record the lesson with an audiotape recorder. Then time the episodes of management and note each episode in a box on the form.

3. Total the amount of management time and divide it by the length of the period to compute the percentage of management time in the lesson.

4. Total the number of episodes and divide this number into the amount of time devoted to management to find the average length of a management episode.

INSTRUCTIONAL ANALYSIS

Teacher ________ Observer ________

Class ________ Grade ________ Date and Time ________

Lesson Focus ________ Comments ________

Starting Time ________ End Time ________ Length of Lesson ________

PRACTICE

INSTRUCTION

MANAGEMENT

Total time: Pract ________ Inst ________ Mgmt ________ Dead ________

Percent of lesson for: Pract ________ Inst ________ Mgmt ________ Dead ________

No. of episodes: Pract ________ Inst ________ Mgmt ________ Dead ________

Average length of episodes: Pract ________ Inst ________ Mgmt ________ Dead ________

FIGURE 14.7. Sample form for instructional analysis duration recording

PRACTICE TIME (TIME ON TASK) AND DEAD TIME

For students to learn physical skills, they must be involved in meaningful physical activity. Physical education programs have a finite amount of scheduled time per week. Practice time or time on task has also been identified by some as ALT-PE (Metzler 1979). This is an acronym for Academic Learning Time-Physical Education. It is student time spent practicing skills in a setting in which students can experience accomplishment. Instructors need to gather data about the amount of time that students are involved in productive, on-task activity. In one well-regarded school district, the authors found that the average amount of activity time per 50-minute period was only 9 to 12 minutes. Certainly one could question whether much learning was taking place in this program.

To evaluate practice time, duration recording is the most effective method. A student or fellow teacher can observe a lesson and time those periods when students are involved in practicing skills. Figure 14.9 is an example of the results of a duration recording for practice time. The goal should

MANAGEMENT TIME

Teacher ______________________ Observer ______________________

Class ______________ Grade __________ Date and Time ______________

Lesson Focus ______________________ Comments ______________________

Starting Time __________ End Time __________ Length of Lesson ______________

Total management time __________

Percent of class time devoted to management __________

Number of episodes ________ Average length of episodes __________

FIGURE 14.8. Sample form for evaluation of management time

be to increase the amount of time devoted to skill practice. For example, a teacher might choose to increase the amount of practice time by using more equipment, by using only those drills that demand a minimum of standing in line, or by streamlining the amount of verbal instruction given.

Another type of time that can be measured while evaluating practice time is *dead time.* Dead time occurs when students are off task or are doing something unrelated to practice, management, or instruction. Examples might be standing in line waiting for a turn, doing nothing because instructions were not understood, or playing a game (such as softball) and literally doing nothing other than waiting to field a ball.

How to Do It

1. Design a form for collecting the data (Figure 14.10).

2. Have a nonparticipating student or colleague identify a representative student who will be used for the evaluation. This student is observed to see when she is involved in practice. This is a critical step. The student chosen should be neither exceptional nor below par; her behavior should give a realistic picture of practice time. When the identified student is not involved in on-task practice, management,

Teacher: Debbie Massoney
School: Whittier Elementary

Parts of the lesson	Practicing	Inactive, off task, listening
Introductory activity	1.5 min	0.5 min
Fitness development	6.5 min	1.5 min
Lesson focus	10.0 min	4.0 min
Game	5.0 min	1.0 min
Total	23.0 min	7.0 min

FIGURE 14.9. Results of a duration recording for practice time

PRACTICE TIME

Teacher ______________________ Observer ______________________

Class ______________ Grade __________ Date and Time ______________

Lesson Focus ______________________ Comments ______________________

Starting Time __________ End Time __________ Length of Lesson ______________

Total practice time __________

Percent of class time devoted to practice __________

Number of episodes __________ Average length of episodes __________

FIGURE 14.10. Sample form for collecting data on practice time

or instructional activity, the episode is recorded as dead time. An easy way to calculate dead time is to subtract the combined amounts of time used for practice, management, and instruction from the total length of the lesson.

3. Turn on the stopwatch when the students are involved in practice activity. Record the interval of practice.

4. Total the amount of time devoted to student practice (in minutes) and divide it by the length of the lesson. This computes the percentage of practice time in a lesson. Total the amount of dead time and divide it by the length of the lesson to compute the percentage of dead time.

RESPONSE LATENCY

How quickly do students respond when commands or signals are given? This is the essence of identifying response latency. Response latency may occur either when instructions are given to begin practicing an activity or to stop an activity. An observer records the amount of time that elapses from the moment when a command is given to start or stop activity and the moment when the students actually begin or stop. The amount of elapsed time is the response latency and is wasted time. An accompanying criterion needs to be set for the percentage of students who are expected to be on task. It is not unreasonable to expect 100% of the students to respond to the command. If less than 100% of the class is expected to respond, a gradual loss of class control may occur.

The average amount of response latency can be calculated so the instructor can set a goal for improving this student behavior. A certain amount of response latency is to be expected. Few groups of students stop or start immediately. However, most instructors have a strong feeling about the amount of latency that they are willing to tolerate. After more than a 5-second response latency, teachers usually become uneasy and expect the class to stop or start.

How to Do It

1. Develop a form on which to gather the data (Figure 14.11).

2. Have a nonparticipating student or colleague time the response latency that occurs when the class is asked to stop (start). The clock should run from the time the command to *Stop* is given until the next command is given or until the class is involved in productive behavior. Remember that starting and stopping response latency are two separate behaviors that must be recorded separately.

3. Identify the number of response latency episodes and divide this number into the total amount of time devoted to response latency to calculate the average episode length.

STUDENT PERFORMANCE

Some classes will have a greater percentage of students performing at optimum level than others. This may mean

RESPONSE LATENCY

Teacher ______________________ Observer ______________________

Class ______________ Grade ________ Date and Time ______________

Lesson Focus ______________ Comments ______________________

Starting Time ________ End Time ________ Length of Lesson ______________

STARTING RESPONSE LATENCY

STOPPING RESPONSE LATENCY

Total amount of starting response latency ________

Percent of class time devoted to response latency ________

Number of episodes ________ Average length of episodes ________

Total amount of stopping response latency ________

Percent of class time devoted to response latency ________

Number of episodes ________ Average length of episodes ________

FIGURE 14.11. Sample form for evaluating response latency

that a class is poorly motivated, does not understand instructions, or is out of control. In any case, instructors should evaluate the percentage of students who are performing in a desired manner. This can be accomplished by means of the placheck (Planned Activity Check) observation technique (Siedentop 1983). The placheck can be used to identify a range of behavior. The instructor determines the area of evaluation. Examples of areas that might be evaluated are student performance of the stipulated activity, productive behavior, effort, and interest in the activity. Once the results are determined, teachers can begin to increase the percentage of students involved in the desired observable behavior.

How to Do It

1. Design a form for recording the desired data. Figure 14.12 is an example of a form that can be used for placheck observation. In this case, the same form can be used to identify three different types of student performance.

2. Place eight to ten "beeps" at random intervals on a tape recording to signal when a placheck should be conducted.

3. Scan the area in a specified and consistent direction from left to right each time the tape-recorded signal is heard. The class is scanned for 7 to 10 seconds while the observer records the number of students who are engaged in the desired behavior.

STUDENT PERFORMANCE

Teacher ______________________ Observer ______________________

Class ______________ Grade ________ Date and Time ____________

Lesson Focus ______________ Comments ______________________

Starting Time ________ End Time ________ Length of Lesson ____________

ACTIVE/INACTIVE

ON TASK/OFF TASK

EFFORT/NONEFFORT

Number of plachecks ________

Total number of students ________

Number of students not on desired behavior ____________

Percentage of students not on desired behavior ____________

FIGURE 14.12. Sample form for placheck observation

4. Convert the data to a percentage by dividing the total number of students into the number of unproductive students and then multiplying the result by 100. Eight to ten plachecks spaced throughout a class period yield valid information about class conduct.

INSTRUCTIONAL FEEDBACK

The type of feedback that teachers offer to students strongly affects the instructional presentation. Instructors can analyze their interaction patterns with students and set meaningful goals for improvement. Oftentimes, students and teachers assume that teaching is an art and that one is born with the necessary qualities. If one accepts this assumption, then to work on developing useful patterns of communication is unnecessary. In fact, nothing could be further from the truth. Developing successful communication skills is a process that all teachers must accept. Few teachers enter the profession with the ability to communicate with warmth and clarity. The process of change creates discomfort and concern but ultimately pays dividends. The following areas can be evaluated to get feedback for implementing useful change.

Praise and Criticism

When students are involved in activity, teachers give a great deal of feedback dealing with student performance. This feedback can be positive and constructive or negative and critical in nature. It is easy to ask a student or peer to record the occurrence of praise and criticism. The recordings can then be tallied and evaluated at the end of the day. The number of instances is calculated and the ratio of positive to negative comments. With this information, the instructor can begin to set goals for increasing the number of comments per minute and modifying the ratio of positive to negative comments. It is not unusual for a teacher to average one to two comments per minute with a positive to negative ratio of four to one.

INSTRUCTIONAL FEEDBACK

Teacher ______________________ Observer ______________________

Class ______________________ Grade ____________ Date and Time ______________

Lesson Focus ______________________ Comments ______________________

Starting Time ____________ End Time ____________ Length of Lesson ______________

Interactions unrelated to skill performance	+								
	−								
General instructional feedback	+								
	−								
Specific positive instructional feedback									
Corrective instructional feedback									
First names									
Nonverbal feedback	+								
	−								

Ratio + to −/nonskill related ____________

Ratio + to −/skill related ____________

FIGURE 14.13. Sample form for tallying teaching behaviors

General Versus Specific

Feedback to students can be specific or general in nature. To illustrate, "good job," "way to go," and "cut that out" are general in nature. General feedback can be positive or negative; it does not specify the behavior being reinforced. In contrast, specific feedback identifies the student by name and reinforces an actual behavior; it also might be accompanied by a valuing statement. An example would be "Michelle, that's the way to keep your head tucked! I really like that forward roll!"

To evaluate in this area, the number of general and specific feedback instances is tallied. Since feedback can be positive or negative in nature, this distinction can also be made as part of the tallying process. The use of first names is important in personalizing the feedback and directing it to the right individual. The number of times that first names are used could be totaled. The number of valuing statements can also be evaluated. All of these categories should be divided by the length of the lesson (in minutes) to render a rate per minute. Figure 14.13 is an example of a form that can be used to tally behaviors described in this section.

Positive feedback should be specific whenever possible so students are aware of what they performed well. An instructor might say, "Your goal kick was exactly where it should have been!" This type of feedback creates a positive feeling in a class and thus is important. Sometimes, however, teachers overuse general positive feedback to such a point that it becomes an habitual form of communication (e.g., "good job," "nice serve," "way to go"). Such nonspecific feedback does not identify the desirable behavior and may soon be ignored by students. An undesirable behavior may also be reinforced when feedback is general.

Corrective Instructional Feedback

Effective teachers are usually excellent at coaching students to higher levels of performance. This involves giving performers meaningful corrective feedback. Corrective feedback should focus on improving the performance of the participant. Teachers should ignore poor performances if students are already aware of them.

Corrective instructional feedback should be specific when possible so performers know what it is that they must correct. An example of corrective instructional feedback would be, "You struck the soccer ball much too high. Try to strike it a little below center." This type of feedback tells the student what was incorrect about the skill attempt and how to perform the skill correctly.

Nonverbal Feedback

Much feedback about performance can be given nonverbally. Certainly this is meaningful to students and may be equal to or more effective than verbal forms of communication. Examples of nonverbal feedback that could occur after a desired performance are a pat on the back, a wink, a smile, a nod of the head, the thumbs-up sign, or clapping the hands. Nonverbal feedback can also be negative—a frown, shaking the head in disapproval, walking away from a student, or laughing at a poor performance.

It is possible to tally the number of positive and negative nonverbal behaviors exhibited by a teacher. A student or another instructor can do the tallying. Students are often better at evaluating the instructor in this domain because they are keenly aware of what each of the instructor's mannerisms means.

How to Do It

1. Design a form to collect the data.

2. Have a student evaluate the lesson, or audiotape a lesson for playback and evaluation at a later time (videotape if evaluating nonverbal behavior).

3. Record the desired data to be analyzed. It is usually best to take one category at a time when beginning. For example, analyze the use of first names during the first playback, and then play the tape again to evaluate corrective feedback.

4. Convert the data to a form that can be generalized from lesson to lesson (e.g., rate per minute, rate per lesson, or ratio of positive to negative interaction).

STUDENT CONTACT AND TEACHER MOVEMENT

When instructors are involved in the teaching process, they are in constant contact with students. Contact means that they are moving and offering personalized feedback to youngsters. The number of times an instructor becomes personally involved with a student can be counted. This type of feedback differs from total class interaction and demands that the instructor have keen insight into each student and his particular concerns.

Allied to this area is that of teacher movement. Instructors often develop a particular area in the gymnasium from which they feel comfortable teaching. Before instruction can begin, they move back to this area. This causes students to drift to different areas depending on how they feel about the activity or the instructor. Students who like the instructor will move closer to her, whereas students who dislike the teacher or are uneasy about the activity may move as far away as possible. This results in a cycle in which effective performers are always near the instructor, and students who may be somewhat deviant are always farther away and difficult to observe.

These patterns can be avoided if the instructor moves throughout the teaching area. Teacher movement can be evaluated by dividing the area into quadrants and tallying the number of times the instructor moves from one section to another. The amount of time spent in each quadrant can also be tallied. A teacher goal should be to spend approximately the same amount of time in each area. When students cannot predict where the teacher will be next, they have a greater tendency to remain on task.

It is more accurate to record the amount of time a teacher stays in a quadrant. The length of time can be recorded on the form in relationship to where the teacher stands. At the end of the lesson, the amount of time spent in each quadrant by the teacher can be analyzed.

Another useful technique is to code the type of teacher behavior that occurs at each teacher movement into a new quadrant. For example, an "M" might signal management activity, an "I" instructional activity, and an "A" activity time. This would reveal not only the amount of time the instructor spent in each area but where the teacher moved to conduct different types of activity.

How to Do It

1. Develop a coding form such as that shown in Figure 14.14.

2. Ask a nonparticipating student or colleague to record the desired data on teacher movement. Another alternative is to videotape the lesson and evaluate it at a later time.

3. Evaluate the data by calculating the number of moves per lesson, and the number of moves during instruction, management, and practice.

EVALUATION OF THE PHYSICAL EDUCATION PROGRAM

The elementary school physical education program should be evaluated regularly to ensure that it is being developed in the direction of the stated program goals. Evaluation instruments can be written that are in line with the program philosophy and are designed specifically for individual districts. Figure 14.15 is an instrument that can serve as an example to be adapted, depending on district needs and goals.

This self-evaluation instrument can be used to expose serious program deficiencies and operational difficulties. The results, including program strengths and weaknesses, can be shared with administrators or used by teachers to evaluate a program that they have developed. The instrument can also be used to compare programs or to identify effective programs.

In the instrument, evaluative statements are written as a set of standards that, when met, ensure an effective program. Four areas are listed for evaluation: (1) philosophy of the program, (2) instructional procedures, (3) curricular offerings, and (4) facilities, equipment, and supplies. The entire instrument can be used, or any of the four areas can be evaluated individually. Evaluators should read each

TEACHER MOVEMENT

Teacher ______________________ Observer ______________________

Class ______________ Grade ______________ Date and Time ______________

Lesson Focus ______________________ Comments ______________________

Starting Time ______________ End Time ______________ Length of Lesson ______________

Total number of moves ______________

Number of moves (I) ______________ (M) ______________ (A) ______________

FIGURE 14.14. Form for evaluating teacher movement-student contact

statement and determine the extent to which there is compliance with the accepted standard. The appropriate scale score is then circled. Comments can be made at the end of each section. Each statement should be rated and assigned points on the following basis: a rating of 3 represents complete compliance (the program meets the standard fully, without deficiencies), 2 represents adequate compliance with room for improvement, 1 represents minimal compliance (im-

FIGURE 14.15. Sample form for evaluating the physical education program

COMPREHENSIVE PROGRAM EVALUATION

PROGRAM PHILOSOPHY

1.	Physical education is regarded by the administration as an integral part of the total curriculum and is dedicated to the same curricular goal, the fullest possible development of each pupil for living in a democracy.	0	1	2	3
2.	The curriculum guide states the program philosophy that is used for direction.	0	1	2	3
3.	A written and up-to-date sequential curriculum is available and used by all instructors.	0	1	2	3
4.	The course of study includes units of activity appropriate for the grade levels.	0	1	2	3
5.	Lesson plans are developed from the course of study and are used as the basis for instruction.	0	1	2	3
6.	The physical education program is a developmental program in which youngsters learn through movement sequences that are planned and arranged in sequential fashion.	0	1	2	3
7.	A meaningful progression of activities is evident from grade to grade and within each grade.	0	1	2	3
8.	Students are classified in physical education classes according to grade level or developmental level.	0	1	2	3
9.	Students are scheduled in the physical education program on a regular basis. Music, field trips, and extracurricular activities are not accepted as substitutes for physical education.	0	1	2	3
10.	Children are taught the "why" of physical activity in relation to appropriate psychological and physiological principles.	0	1	2	3
11.	Youngsters are given physical examinations before entering school (kindergarten) and at the 4th-grade level. The results of the exam are used to determine the extent of participation in physical education.	0	1	2	3
12.	Students are excused from physical education on a long-term basis only when they can submit a physician's statement indicating medical concern and the duration of the excuse.	0	1	2	3
13.	Appropriate arrangements are made for students with medical, religious, or temporary health excuses.	0	1	2	3
14.	A nurse or teachers with suitable first aid training are available in case of accident.	0	1	2	3
15.	Grading procedures are consistent with those used in other subject areas.	0	1	2	3
16.	The budget specified for equipment and supplies for physical education is adequate.	0	1	2	3
17.	Physical education demonstration programs are offered regularly for purposes of public relations and general information.	0	1	2	3
18.	The services of an elementary physical education specialist or consultant are available.	0	1	2	3
19.	Classroom teachers use effectively the services of the physical education specialist or consultant to supplement and improve physical education instruction.	0	1	2	3
20.	When physical education is supplemented by an activity of the classroom teacher, the specialist or consultant provides adequate aid.	0	1	2	3
21.	Physical education specialists have a personal, written plan for professional growth and development. This plan might include graduate work, workshops, conferences, conventions, and independent study.	0	1	2	3
22.	In-service sessions are organized for improvement of instruction in physical education based on demonstrated need.	0	1	2	3

continued

FIGURE 14.15/*continued*

		0	1	2	3
23.	Physical education instruction is evaluated regularly by an appropriate supervisor. This information is used to provide immediate feedback for the purpose of improving instruction.	0	1	2	3
24.	A broad intramural program is present with a variety of activities to suit the needs of boys and girls.	0	1	2	3
25.	Any extramural activities are an outgrowth of the instructional program and are limited to the intermediate grades.	0	1	2	3

Comments:

INSTRUCTIONAL PROCEDURES

1.	Instructors use sound class management techniques during instruction.	0	1	2	3
2.	Students are allowed to participate in program planning, activity selection, and evaluation.	0	1	2	3
3.	Teachers are familiar with different styles of teaching and use them when the need arises.	0	1	2	3
4.	Leadership opportunities such as demonstrating, officiating, planning, and leading peers are offered to students.	0	1	2	3
5.	Instructors are strong models for students. They possess an appropriate level of fitness and dress properly for physical activity.	0	1	2	3
6.	The minimum amount per class of time allotted for physical education activity is 30 minutes.	0	1	2	3
7.	Each class receives physical education instruction a minimum of three times per week, excluding recess and supervised play.	0	1	2	3
8.	Class sizes are similar to those allotted to classroom teachers, with a maximum of 35 students.	0	1	2	3
9.	Program activities are coeducational in nature.	0	1	2	3
10.	Disciplinary measures in physical education instruction do not include expulsion from class or punishment using physical activity.	0	1	2	3
11.	Youngsters wear appropriate clothing and shoes to physical education so that attire does not restrict activity.	0	1	2	3
12.	Systematic testing is used at regular intervals to evaluate the effectiveness of the program.	0	1	2	3
13.	There is a special program for low-fitness students.	0	1	2	3
14.	There is a special program for obese students.	0	1	2	3
15.	Grading plans (when required) are based on established criteria and indicate the extent to which each student has achieved course objectives.	0	1	2	3
16.	There is an annual review and evaluation of the curriculum for purposes of revision and adjustment.	0	1	2	3
17.	Procedures for dealing with accidents, including administration of first aid, reporting, and follow-up, are in written form.	0	1	2	3
18.	Teachers have knowledge of liability concerns in physical education. Instruction and programming reflect this knowledge through prudent practices.	0	1	2	3
19.	Facilities, equipment, curriculum, and teaching methods are analyzed regularly to reduce the possibility of accidents.	0	1	2	3
20.	Facilities, equipment, and curriculum areas that might be liabilities are reported in writing to appropriate administrators.	0	1	2	3
21.	Bulletin boards, charts, pictures, and other visual materials are posted and used in the instructional process.	0	1	2	3
22.	Teaching aids such as films, slides, and models are used to enrich and supplement instruction.	0	1	2	3
23.	A learning center containing reading materials appropriate to the reading and interest level of youngsters is available for physical education.	0	1	2	3

FIGURE 14.15/*continued*

Comments:

CURRICULAR OFFERINGS

1. The physical education program provides learning experiences to help each child attain the following:				
a. A personalized level of physical fitness and body conditioning	0	1	2	3
b. Suitable skills in a variety of educational movement patterns on the ground and on appropriate apparatus	0	1	2	3
c. Manipulative skills leading to the development of specialized skills	0	1	2	3
d. Specialized skills related to games, rhythms, tumbling, stunts, and sport activities	0	1	2	3
e. Knowledge of rules, techniques, and strategy related to specialized skills	0	1	2	3
f. Desirable social standards and ethical behavior	0	1	2	3
g. Proper safety practices for self and others	0	1	2	3
h. Competence in activities that can be used during leisure time	0	1	2	3
i. Knowledge and understanding of concepts leading to human wellness	0	1	2	3
2. Activities are organized and adjusted to suit the maturity and skill levels of youngsters.	0	1	2	3
3. All children are considered important and the program is adjusted to suit the maturity and skill levels of youngsters.	0	1	2	3
4. The program offers something for all children: boys and girls, skilled and unskilled, physically fit and low-fitness youngsters, and special education students.	0	1	2	3
5. Each lesson has a portion of time (7 to 10 minutes) devoted to physical fitness activities.	0	1	2	3
6. The physical education program emphasizes and allocates enough time at the appropriate grade level for each of the following areas.				
a. Educational movement patterns	0	1	2	3
b. Fundamental skills including locomotor, nonlocomotor, manipulative, and specialized skills	0	1	2	3
c. Rhythmic activities	0	1	2	3
d. Stunts, tumbling, and combatives	0	1	2	3
e. Games and relays	0	1	2	3
f. Sports and lead-up activities	0	1	2	3
7. The program in the primary grades emphasizes educational movement.	0	1	2	3
8. An up-to-date professional library is available for the physical education specialist and faculty.	0	1	2	3
9. There is an aquatic program in either the public schools or in the community recreation program (or another agency) so that all children have the opportunity to learn to swim.	0	1	2	3
10. Both indoor and outdoor teaching stations are assigned for physical education instruction.	0	1	2	3
11. The yearly curriculum is planned and written so that a wide variety of activities is offered.	0	1	2	3
12. Units of instruction last no longer than 3 weeks and include skill instruction.	0	1	2	3

Comments:

continued

FIGURE 14.15/*continued*

FACILITIES, EQUIPMENT, AND SUPPLIES

1. Facilities include teaching stations that allow all students a minimum of three classes per week.	0	1	2	3
2. Maximum use of facilities for physical education instruction is apparent.	0	1	2	3
3. Outdoor facilities meet the basic acreage standard of 5 acres plus 1 acre for each additional 100 students.	0	1	2	3
4. Outdoor facilities include the following.				
a. Areas where different age groups can play without interference from each other	0	1	2	3
b. Areas for court games	0	1	2	3
c. Cement or asphalt spaces marked with a variety of game patterns	0	1	2	3
d. Backstops and goals for softball, soccer, and basketball	0	1	2	3
e. Suitable fencing for safety and control	0	1	2	3
f. Outdoor playground equipment including climbing apparatus, turning bars, and tetherball areas	0	1	2	3
5. The outdoor area is free from rocks, sprinkler heads, and other hazards that might cause injury.	0	1	2	3
6. Indoor facilities meet the following standards.				
a. Clean, sanitary, and free from hazards	0	1	2	3
b. Well lighted, well ventilated, heated, cooled, and treated for proper acoustics	0	1	2	3
c. Surfaced with a nonslip finish and include painted game area lines	0	1	2	3
7. There is periodic inspection of all facilities and equipment, both indoor and outdoor, and a written report is sent to the appropriate administrators.	0	1	2	3
8. Storage facilities are adequate for supplies and portable equipment.	0	1	2	3
9. Adequate provision is made for off-season storage of equipment, apparatus, and supplies.	0	1	2	3
10. An office is provided for the physical education instructor; it includes a shower, and is located near the instruction area.	0	1	2	3
11. Basic supplies are sufficient in the following areas.*				
a. Manipulative equipment (one piece for each child): fleece balls, small balls, beanbags, wands, hoops, and jump ropes	0	1	2	3
b. Sport and game balls: softballs, footballs, volleyballs, basketballs, soccer balls, tetherballs, and cageballs in sufficient numbers	0	1	2	3
c. Sport and game supplies: cones, pinnies, track-and-field standards, jumping pits	0	1	2	3
d. Testing equipment: measuring tapes, stopwatches, calipers to measure skinfold thickness, and specialized apparatus	0	1	2	3
12. Sufficient materials are available for a varied rhythmic program: variable-speed record player, records, drums, tambourines, and percussion instruments	0	1	2	3
13. Capital-outlay items for the indoor facility include the following.				
a. Minimum of six tumbling mats (4 by 8 ft or larger)	0	1	2	3
b. Individual mats (32)	0	1	2	3
c. Sufficient climbing apparatus so that at least one half of the class can be active at one time. Apparatus should include wall bars, chinning bars, horizontal bars, climbing ropes on tracks, and ladders.	0	1	2	3
d. Balance beam benches (at least 6)	0	1	2	3
e. Jumping boxes (at least 8)	0	1	2	3
f. Basketball goals, volleyball nets, hockey goals	0	1	2	3

Comments:

* For a comprehensive list of equipment needed, see pp. 581–582.

provement is necessary to reach functional compliance), 0 represents no compliance (the deficiency is serious and a detriment to an effective program).

MICROCOMPUTER APPLICATIONS

The use of computers to aid in teaching and evaluating students is an important consideration. Computers are most effective when they are programmed to execute menial and repetitive tasks. They are often used in the evaluation process because evaluative results are quantifiable and can be translated into a meaningful report by using a computer program.

No field is changing more rapidly than the field of computers and related software. This section should be read with the understanding that it is impossible to keep up-to-date on the new software by reading textbooks. In many cases, by the time a text is published that explains how to use certain software, the software has already become obsolete. This section is a statement of the computer applications that are currently available. Rapid changes may cause this discussion to become quickly outdated.

The following discussion reflects the many computer applications in a physical education setting. Certainly using a microcomputer is not a substitute for evaluation or instruction, but should be seen as an additional instructional tool. A first step in understanding computer applications is to understand clearly what a computer can and cannot do. All too often, a computer is purchased and sits idle, gathering dust, because its capabilities were misunderstood.

REPORTING FITNESS TEST RESULTS

Several software programs are currently available from AAHPERD for evaluating the fitness levels of students. All of the programs require that youngsters be tested and that the test results be entered into the computer. This is usually the point at which the process slows down. How are the results to be entered into the computer? Should each student enter his own data? Can the students learn how to enter the data and in what order it is to be entered? Are students capable of entering the data quickly and accurately, or will the teacher have to enter the data for 900 children? Would this be possible, or would it take more time than doing the compilations by hand? If a report is desired, will there be a time delay in waiting for the printer to finish printing the report? These questions are not intended to discourage the use of the computer, but only to raise critical points for consideration.

The payoff for using the computer is that the final printed report is usually personalized, easy to interpret, and meaningful to parents. Figure 14.16 is a screen from the *Health Fitness Profile for Children* program (Hastad and Plowman 1984) and illustrates how the AAHPERD fitness test results can be shown graphically by a computer. The program automatically compares raw scores with national norms and offers a printed exercise prescription.

Another advantage of using the computer is that the data can be stored on disk. When the same students are tested at a later date, the scores can be compared to see if improvement has occurred. It is also possible to generate quickly the means for all test items so group performances can be compared. Reports can be generated for parents or for students or for both.

DEVELOPING FITNESS NORMS

Teachers and school districts want to know how their students perform relative to other students. The AAHPERD Youth Fitness Test (1976) and the AAHPERD Health Related Physical Fitness Test (1980) are examples of tests that offer normative data based on large samples of students. These tests make it easy to compare the students in a local school district with a national sample.

WELLNESS REPORTS

Communicating with parents about the health status of their child is becoming increasingly important. One way to enhance public relations is not only to share the results of testing with parents but also to tell them *what* the results mean in terms of their child's health status.

The Pangrazi-Dauer *Wellness Profile* software program asks students to enter their data into the computer. The areas evaluated can be found on the Wellness Profile described earlier in this chapter. Once all of the data is typed in, a printout is generated that states the student's performance, the significance of each area analyzed, and a recommended minimum level. Parents are advised to consult their family physician if the child's scores are below the recommended minimums. This program is available from Burgess Publishing, 7110 Ohms Lane, Edina, MN 55435.

NUTRITIONAL ANALYSIS

Many programs are currently available for nutritional analysis. These programs are highly structured and demand that users analyze their diet carefully. In most cases, programs of this nature are probably most useful for individual students who are overweight or malnourished.

The programs ask for personal information such as age, weight, height, sex, and amount of physical activity. These data are then used to calculate the individual's caloric, fiber, protein, and lipid needs. The next step is to record the types and amounts of foods eaten daily. A report is then generated that lists calories ingested and expended, the nutrient value for all foods, and the sum total of all nutrients ingested. These data enable an instructor to see if the youngster has met the recommended dietary allowances (RDA)

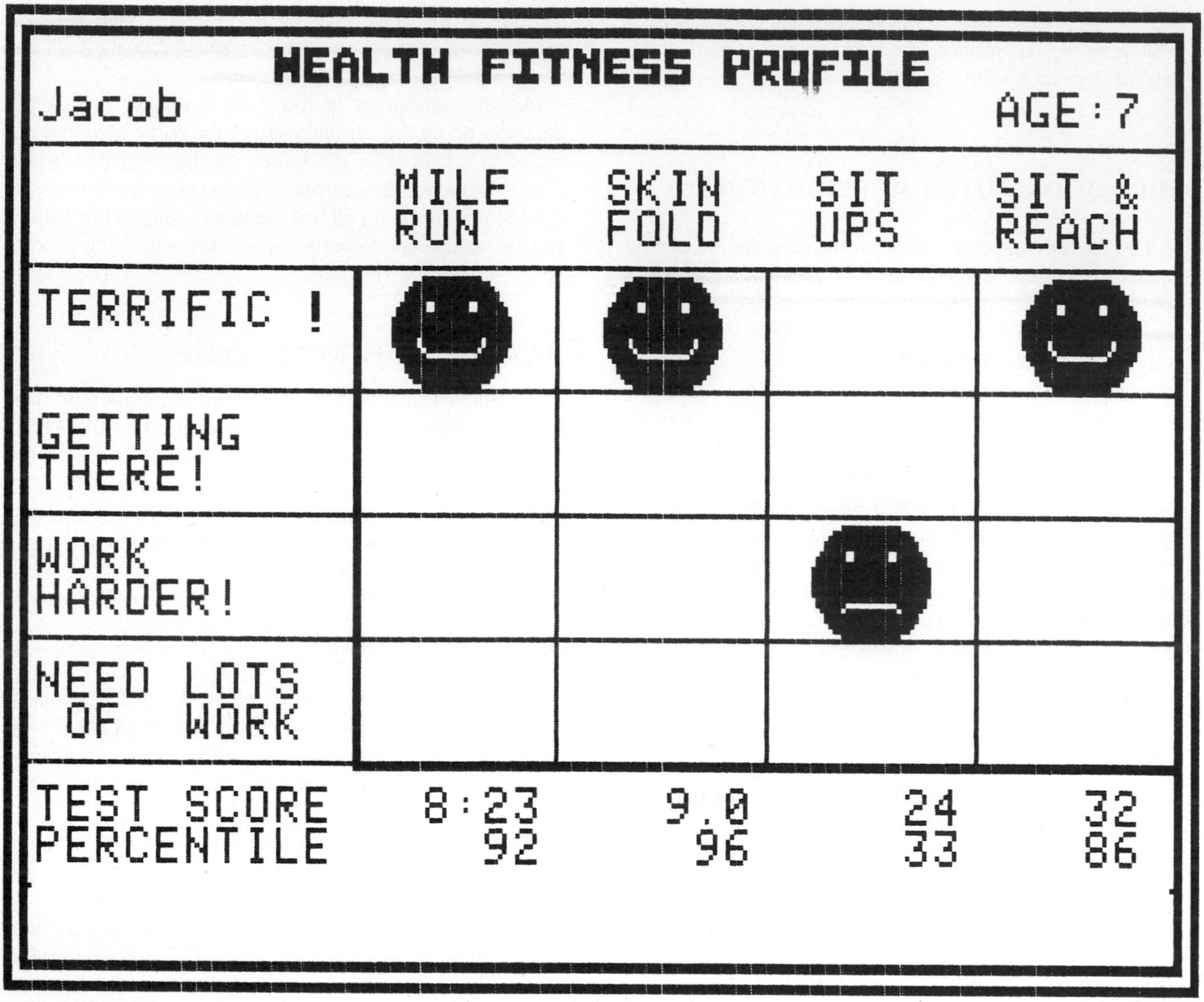

HEALTH FITNESS PROFILE

Jacob AGE: 7

	MILE RUN	SKIN FOLD	SIT UPS	SIT & REACH
TERRIFIC !	☺	☺		☺
GETTING THERE!				
WORK HARDER!			☹	
NEED LOTS OF WORK				
TEST SCORE	8:23	9.0	24	32
PERCENTILE	92	96	33	86

FIGURE 14.16. Health Fitness Profile for Children (Reprinted from D. Hastad and S. Plowman, 1984, *Health Fitness Profile for Children*)

required and whether the amount of calories ingested was excessive.

Another interesting computer application found in some nutritional programs is in the area of caloric expenditure. The software predicts the amount of calories expended in performing a specific exercise for a specified amount of time. The program tells the user that to burn off a certain number of calories eaten, she will need to perform a given activity for a certain length of time.

RAPID RECORDING OF FIELD-BASED DATA

A problem that becomes quickly apparent to any teacher doing testing in the field is the recording of the results. The Department of Physical Education at Arizona State University has developed a system that includes immediate transmission of test results onto a computer disk. The system involves the use of potentiometers to measure movement. Software has been written that translates this movement into numerical data.

Figure 14.17 shows skin calipers, a sit-and-reach box, and a hand dynamometer, all of which are connected directly to a computer. Using this method, the teacher can measure a child and the data is entered immediately and automatically into the computer. The data is stored on disk and can be analyzed at a later time. This approach offers a tremendous reduction in the time required for gathering and recording data. The obvious need is for a computer placed at the point of testing.

Card Reader

Another useful piece of hardware is a card reader. This device allows scores to be marked on a card and fed into

FIGURE 14.17. Testing children using the on-line data collection system

the reader. Customized cards (Figure 14.18) to meet a wide variety of needs can be printed so that a considerable range of data can be read. The card reader is connected directly to the computer, so data can be placed directly on disk for later analysis. This piece of hardware is of value when large amounts of data are being gathered on a regular basis.

PRESCRIBING ACTIVITIES

Teachers often have difficulty finding activities that will help remedy student shortcomings. An example of a computer program applicable to this area is the *Prescriptive Activities* program developed by Pangrazi, Cicciarella, and Dauer (1983). Initially, the program asks the teacher to identify the student's area of weakness. Areas listed are cardiovascular fitness, obesity, flexibility, coordination, and strength in the upper body, lower body, or trunk region. After an area has been identified, the program lists activities to help remediate the area that is deficient. The activities listed are from this text and offer the teacher a wide variety from which to choose. The program is particularly useful for classroom teachers or specialists who are working with individualized programs. It is available from Burgess Publishing.

WORD PROCESSING AND DATABASE PACKAGES

A large number of reports can be generated using database and word processing packages. A major use of database software is for entering and storing data, sorting data, and generating a report that makes the data easy to read and analyze for results. For example, with database software the operator can create a form on the monitor that tells what data to enter and how to enter it. Following the form instructions, a teacher or student can enter test scores and store the data on disk. The data can then be sorted (e.g., by best performance, alphabetically by last name, or by date of birth). Any variable entered can be used as the primary sort variable. A printout is then generated and used for instructor analysis or to report student performance.

Word processing software that contains a data merging feature is now available for generating reports. The advantage of a word processor lies in the easy modification of a report to meet changing needs. The merging factor takes the file of data generated using the database and places the data in the report in proper sequence.

ANALYSIS OF TEACHING BEHAVIOR

Software that allows for an analysis of teaching behavior is becoming available. An example of this type of software is the *ALT-PE Micro Computer Data Collection System* developed by Metzler (1984). If the reader is not cognizant of the technique for measuring Academic Learning Time in Physical Education (ALT-PE), a description can be found in the text by Darst et al. (1983). Basically, the ALT-PE program analyzes the amount of time engaged in physical education content activity at an easy level of difficulty and gives a description of student time involvement in physical education.

The process of recording and analyzing the data by hand is difficult and time consuming. The software program is excellent in that it offers a mode for entering the data directly into the computer and then gives a printout as soon as analysis of the lesson is finished. The ALT-PE software measures the length of an observation interval and causes the computer to beep a signal that it is time to enter data at regular intervals. When all data have been gathered, the program runs a data analysis and generates a printout. The software can be purchased from METZSOFT, 328 Loudon Road, Blacksburg, VA 24060.

GRADING

Software packages are available for generating grade reports. (An excellent package can be purchased from Sensible Software, 6619 Perham Drive, West Bloomfield, MN 48033.) The package allows for class sizes of up to 40 students, and the instructor can weight tests differently. The program can generate printouts that show cumulative percentages for all students, for the results of a particular student, or for the class as a whole, and a report containing students' final percentages and letter grade. The program is simple to operate and can facilitate the grading process. Scores for other factors such as attendance and effort can be weighted and entered into the report.

CREATING TESTS

Software programs are also available for writing multiple-choice tests. After a battery of test items has been developed, the software selects randomly a desired number of questions for the test. The program will also change the

FIGURE 14.18. Samples of optical scan cards

order of the choices offered for each question. This allows the instructor to generate a variety of exams that contain different test questions with different choice orders. An example of this type of software is *Test Writer,* which is available from Burgess Publishing, 7110 Ohms Lane, Edina, MN 55435.

Another novel piece of software is *Crossword Magic,* which is available from L & S Computerware, 1589 Fraser Drive, Sunnyvale, CA 94087. This software develops crossword puzzles from answers and clues given by the teacher. The instructor can then use the crossword puzzle as a test or an instructional tool. A variety of puzzles can be developed to focus on such areas of instruction as movement principles, game rules, and techniques of skill performance.

COMPUTER-ASSISTED INSTRUCTION

Computer-assisted instruction can be used with elementary school youngsters in cognitive areas requiring drill and practice. The advantage of this approach is that it offers the student immediate feedback on a correct or incorrect answer. Some type of reinforcement along with feedback can be built into the instructional software.

Areas that can be developed effectively for computer-assisted instruction are quizzes related to various sport strategies, safety rules and regulations, components of and guidelines for developing fitness, and various aspects of school procedure such as grading and discipline. The cognitive information can be built into crossword puzzles, word searches, fill in the blanks, and true and false questions. When the correct answer is supplied by the student, a reinforcing response is flashed on the screen (e.g., "Exactly right! You must be brilliant."). On the other hand, if an incorrect answer is supplied, the response might be, "Sorry, that is incorrect. Go back and read page 2 of your handout to identify the correct answer."

The application of computer-assisted instruction is individual. It allows students to proceed at a rate that is meaningful to them. Conceivably, students might be released for a short interval from physical education activity to learn to use the computer. Once students can use the computer, the teacher's group instruction duties might be reduced and teachers could then work on an individualized basis with students.

An excellent source of software for computer-assisted instruction is CompTech Systems Design, P.O. Box 516, Hastings, MN 55033. We have used software that covers the following topics: cardiorespiratory fitness, the heart and exercise, youth fitness test, sports terminology for aquatics, individual dual sports, volleyball, basketball, comprehensive programs for bowling and biking, and more. Many of the programs contain graphics that make the instruction clear and easy to comprehend.

REFERENCES

AAHPERD. 1980. *Health related physical fitness test manual.* Reston, VA.: AAHPERD.

AAHPERD. 1984. *Technical manual: Health related physical fitness.* Reston, Va.: AAHPERD.

AAHPERD. 1976. *Youth fitness test manual.* Reston, VA.: AAHPERD.

Darst, P. W., Mancini, V. H., and Zakrajsek, D. B. 1983. *Systematic observation instrumentation for physical education.* West Point, NY: Leisure Press.

Hastad, D. N., and Plowman, S. A. 1984. Health fitness profile for children ages 6–12. (Computer software developed at Northern Illinois University, DeKalb, Ill.)

Metzler, M. W. 1984. *ALT-PE Micro computer data collection system.* Blacksburg, Va.: METZSOFT.

Pangrazi, R. P., Cicciarella, C. E., and Dauer, V. P. 1983. *Fitness and wellness through dynamic physical education.* Minneapolis: Burgess Publishing.

Siedentop, D. 1983. *Developing teaching skills in physical education,* Palo Alto, Calif.: Mayfield Publishing Co.

CHAPTER 15

Introductory Activities

Introductory activities are the first item of attention in the recommended lesson plan (pp. 49–51). They can take many forms, and teachers are urged to create and develop activities of their own. The chief characteristic of introductory activities is their vigorous nature. Gross movements (generally locomotor activities) are employed. Introductory activities should challenge every student with movement and should allow considerable freedom of movement. They should not be rigidly structured.

Introductory activities are used in the first 2 or 3 minutes of the lesson for the following reasons.

1. To warm children up physiologically and prepare them for the strenuous fitness activity to follow.

2. To prepare children psychologically to move. Children often enter the physical education area unready to move. A few minutes are needed to develop the proper frame of mind.

3. To review management skills quickly with a class. Since introductory activities require little instruction, teachers can work on getting the attention of the class and preparing the children to stop quickly on signal.

4. To ensure that children are immediately active upon entering the gym. This dissipates excess energy and establishes the proper tone (purposive, under control) for the class.

Since the introductory activities constitute the first activity youngsters receive when entering the gymnasium, they should begin the activities with moderate intensity and gradually increase to full speed. Introductory activities involve gross motor movement that can be done at a slow pace in the initial stages of warming up. For example, if using Rhythmic Running as an introductory activity, children could begin by walking. As they warm up, the movement could be increased to a run. Another example involving Group Over and Under would be to have the children moderately move over, around, and under other students. After both sets of students have had a chance to warm up, the activity can be done at full speed. This accomplishes the goal of physiologically preparing the body for the physical fitness section of the lesson.

EUROPEAN RHYTHMIC RUNNING

Some type of Rhythmic Running is done in many European countries to open the daily lesson. The European style is light, rhythmic running to the accompaniment of some type of percussion, usually a drum or tom-tom. Skilled runners do not need accompaniment but merely keep time with a leader.

Much of the running follows a circular path, but it can follow other patterns. To introduce a group of children to Rhythmic Running, have them stand in circular formation and clap to the beat of the drum. Next, as they clap, have them shuffle their feet in place, keeping time. Following this, have them run in place, omitting the clapping. Finally, have them run in a prescribed path. That the running be light, bouncy, and rhythmic is essential, and it must keep time with the beat. A successful running pattern calls for each child to stay behind the person in front, to maintain proper spacing, and to lift the knees in a light, prancing step.

A number of movement ideas can be combined with the rhythmic running pattern.

1. On signal (a whistle or a double beat on the drum), runners freeze in place. They resume running when the regular beat begins again.

2. On signal, runners make a full turn in four running steps, lifting the knees high while turning.

3. Children clap hands every fourth beat as they run. Instead of clapping, runners sound a brisk "Hey!" on the fourth beat, raising one arm with a fist at the same time.

4. Children run in squad formation, following the path set by the squad leader.

5. On signal, children run in general space, exercising care not to bump into each other. They return to a circular running formation on the next signal.

6. Students alternate between running with high knee action and regular running.

7. Runners change to a light, soundless run and back to a heavier run. The tone of the drum can control the quality of the movement.

8. Students use Rhythmic Running while handling a parachute.

9. On the command "Center," children run four steps toward the center, turn around (four steps), and run outward four steps to resume the original circular running pattern.

10. On signal, runners go backward, changing the direction of the circle.

11. Students carry a beanbag or a ball. Every fourth step, they toss the bag up and catch it while running.

12. A leader moves the class through various formations. A task that is enjoyable and challenging is crossing lines of children while they alternate one child from one line in front of one youngster from another line.

13. The class moves into various shapes on signal. Possible shapes might be a square, rectangle, triangle, or pentagon. The Rhythmic Running must be continued while the youngsters move into position.

14. When a signal is given, each class member changes position with another student and then resumes the activity. An example might be to change position with the student opposite in the circle.

15. Since the movement is rhythmic, students can practice certain skills, such as a full turn. The turn can be done to a four-count rhythm and should be more deliberate than a quick turning movement that lacks definition.

16. When the tom-tom stops, children scatter and run in random fashion. When the beat resumes, they return to circular formation and proper rhythm.

GROSS MOVEMENTS AND CHANGES

Most movements of the gross movement type stress locomotor activities, but some include manipulative and nonlocomotor activities. The movements should involve the body as a whole and provide abrupt change from one movement pattern to another. A routine can begin with running and then change to another movement pattern that is either specified by the teacher or left up to the children. Signals for change can be supplied with a voice command, whistle, drumbeat, or handclap. Children love to be challenged by having to change with the signal. Each part of a routine should be continued long enough for good body challenge and involvement but not so long that it becomes wearisome.

Running provides much of the basis for gross movement activities, but other activities of a vigorous nature can be employed. The suggested activities are classified roughly according to type and whether they are individual or partner or group oriented.

INDIVIDUAL RUNNING AND CHANGING MOVEMENTS

Free Running

Students run in any direction, changing direction at will.

Running and Changing Direction

Children run in any direction, changing direction on signal. As a progression, specify the type of angle (e.g., right, obtuse, 45-degree, 180-degree). Alternate right and left turns.

Running and Changing Level

Children run high on their toes and change to a lower level on signal. Require runners to sometimes touch the floor when at the lower level.

Running and Changing the Type of Locomotion

On signal, runners change from running to free choice or to a specified type of locomotion (e.g., walking, jumping, hopping, skipping, sliding, or galloping).

Running and Stopping

Students run in various directions and, on signal, freeze. Stress stopping techniques and an immobilized position.

Running and Spiking

Children run and, on signal, stop, then jump as high as possible and pretend to spike a volleyball. The jump can be repeated one or more times before the run resumes. A variation is using a basketball jump. Youngsters can pair up informally and jump against one another.

Run and Assume a Shape

Pupils run and, on signal, assume a statue pose. Allow choice or specify a limitation.

Tortoise and Hare

When the teacher calls out "Tortoise," the children run slowly in general space. On the command "Hare," they change to a rapid, circular run. During the latter, stress good knee lift.

Ponies in the Stable

Each child has a stable, his spot or place on the floor. This can be marked with a beanbag or a hoop. On the initial signal, children gallop lightly (like ponies) in general space. The next signal tells them to trot lightly to their stable and to continue trotting lightly in place.

Adding Fitness Challenges

Running (or other locomotor movements) can be combined with fitness activities. During the signaled stop, exercises such as Push-ups and Curl-ups can be done.

Move and Perform a Task on Signal

Youngsters move and perform a task on signal. Tasks can be individual or partner activities. Examples are Seat Circles (p. 374), Balances (p. 371), Wring the Dishrag (p. 368), Partner Hopping (p. 381), Twister (p. 382), and Chinese Get-up (p. 382).

Run, Stop, and Pivot

Students run, stop, and then pivot. This is an excellent activity for game skill development. Youngsters enjoy it especially when they are told to imagine that they are basketball or football players.

Triple *S* Routine

The triple *S*'s are speed, style, and stop. Children are in scatter formation throughout the area. On the command "Speed," they run in general space rapidly while avoiding contact with others. On "Style," all run in style (easy, light, loose running) in a large, circular, counterclockwise path. On the command "Stop," all freeze quickly under control. Repeat as necessary.

Agility Run

Pick two lines or markers 5 to 10 yd apart. Students run (or use other locomotor movements) back and forth between the lines for a specified time (10, 15, or 20 seconds). Students can add a personal challenge by seeing how many times they can move back and forth within the given time limit.

OTHER INDIVIDUAL MOVEMENT COMBINATIONS

Upright Movement to All Fours

Youngsters begin with a movement in upright position and change to one on all fours.

Secret Movement

The teacher has written a number of movements on cards and selects one. Direction is given by saying, "I want you to show me the secret movement." The children select a movement and continue that movement without change until they are signaled to stop, whereupon the teacher identifies those who performed the movement on the card. The movement is then demonstrated by those who chanced upon it, and all perform it together. If no one comes up with the movement pattern on the card, repeat the activity by asking the children to change their responses.

Airplanes

Children pretend to be airplanes. When told to take off, they zoom with arms out, swooping, turning, and gliding. When they are commanded to land, they drop to the floor in prone position, simulating a plane at rest. To start their engines and take off, they can perform a series of push-ups and move up and down while simulating engine noise.

Combination Movement

Directives for combination movement can establish specified movements or allow some choice. The limitation might be to run, skip, and roll, or to jump, twist, and shake. Another approach is to set a number for the sequence and let the children select the activities. Say, "Put three different kinds of movement together in a smooth pattern." (See page 95 for other suggestions.)

Countdown

The teacher begins a countdown for blast-off: "Ten, nine, eight, seven, six, five, four, three, two, one—blast-off!" The children are scattered, and each makes an abrupt, jerky movement on each count. On the word "Blast-off," they run in different directions until the stop signal is given.

Magic Number Challenges

A challenge can be issued like this: "Ten, ten, and ten." Children then put together three movements, doing ten repetitions of each. Or the teacher could say, "Today we are going to play our version of Twenty-one." Twenty-one becomes the magic number that is to be fulfilled with three movements, each of which is done seven times.

Crossing the River

A river can be set up as the space between two parallel lines about 40 ft apart, or it can be the crosswise area in a gymnasium. Each time the children cross the river, they employ a different type of locomotor movement. Children should be encouraged not to repeat a movement. Play is continuous over a minute or so.

Four Corners

A square or a rectangle is laid out, with a marker at each corner. As the child turns each corner, she changes to a different locomotor movement. Sometimes a rectangular formation with both short and long sides is desirable. More demanding movements can be specified for the short sides. Indoors, it may be advisable to set up two courses, each in a half of the gymnasium.

Jumping and Hopping Patterns

Each child has a home spot. The teacher provides jumping and hopping sequences to take children away from and back to their spot. The teacher could say, "Move with three jumps, two hops, and a half turn. Return to place the same way." The teacher should have on hand a number of sequences. Action can extend beyond simply jumping and hopping.

Leading With Body Parts

Students move throughout the area with some body part leading. Try using various body parts such as elbow, fingers, head, shoulder, knees, and toes. Try the same exercise with different body parts trailing. Try moving and leading with two different body parts. Try with three. Try also with combinations of body parts trailing the body. Children can jog with some body part leading or trailing. On signal, tell them to make a new body part lead or trail the body.

Move, Rock, and Roll

Each youngster procures an individual mat and places it on the floor. Students are challenged to move around, over, and on the mats. When a signal is given, children move to a mat and try different ways of rocking and rolling. Rocking on different parts of the body can be specified, and different body rolls can be suggested. As another challenge, tell the children to do a rock or a roll or both on a mat, get up and run to another mat, and repeat the sequence. Older children enjoy seeing how many mats they can move to within a certain amount of time.

INDIVIDUAL RHYTHMIC MOVEMENTS

Musical Relaxation

Musical relaxation can be conducted with a drum or appropriate recorded music. Children run in time to the rhythm. When the rhythm stops, each reclines on the back, closes the eyes, and remains relaxed until the music begins again.

Moving to Rhythm

The possibilities with rhythm are many. Rhythm can guide locomotor movements, with changes in tempo being part of the activity. The intensity of the sound can be translated into light or heavy movements.

Moving to Music

Pieces such as the Bleking song (p. 268) and "Pop Goes the Weasel" (p. 265) can provide a basis for creative movement. These are two-part pieces, so a nonlocomotor movement can be done to the first part and a locomotor movement to the second.

Folk Dance Movement

Use a record or tape recording to stimulate different types of rhythmic movement such as polka, schottische, and two-step. Youngsters can move around the room practicing the steps dictated by the music.

INDIVIDUAL MOVEMENTS WITH MANIPULATION

Individual Rope Jumping

Each child runs with rope in hand. On the signal to change, the child stops and begins to jump rope.

Hoop Activities

Each child runs holding a hoop. When the signal is given to stop, the child either does hula-hooping or lays the hoop on the floor and uses it for hopping and jumping patterns.

Wand Activities

Movements similar to those done with jump ropes and hoops can be performed with wands. After they run and stop, the children do wand stunts.

Milk Carton Fun

Each child has a milk carton stuffed with crumpled newspapers and secured with cellophane tape. The children kick the cartons in different directions for 1 minute.

Ball Activities

Youngsters dribble balls as in basketball or (outside) as in soccer. When a change is signaled, they stop, balance on one leg, and pass the ball under the other leg, around the back, and overhead, keeping both control and balance. Other challenges can be supplied that involve both movement with the ball and manipulative actions performed in place.

Beanbag Touch and Go

Beanbags are spread throughout the area. On signal, youngsters move and touch as many different beanbags as possible with their hands. Different body parts can be specified for children to use for touching. Different colors of beanbags can be selected, and the command might be "Touch as many blue beanbags as possible with your elbow."

Children can also move to and around a beanbag. The type of movement can be varied. For example, they might skip around the yellow beanbags with the left side leading. Change the movement as well as the direction and leading side of the body. Another enjoyable activity for youngsters is to trace out a shape (e.g., triangle, circle, square) as they move from beanbag to beanbag.

Disappearing Hoops

Each child gets a hoop and places it somewhere on the floor. Offer challenges such as "Move through five blue hoops, jump over four yellow hoops, and skip around six green hoops." On signal, the children move to find a hoop and balance inside it. As youngsters are moving, take away two or three hoops. At the signal, some students will not find a hoop. Those left out then offer the class the next movement challenge. Different challenges and stunts inside the hoops can be specified.

PARTNER AND GROUP ACTIVITIES

Marking

The children can do what the British call *marking.* Each child has a partner who is somewhat equal in ability. One partner runs, dodges, and tries to lose the other, who must stay within 3 ft of the runner. On signal, both stop. The chaser must be able to touch her partner to say that she has marked him. Partners then change roles.

Following Activity

One partner leads and performs various kinds of movements. The other partner must move in the same fashion. This idea can be extended to squad organization.

Group Over and Under

Half of the children are scattered. Each is in a curled position, face down. The other children leap or jump over the curled children. On signal, reverse the groups quickly. Instead of being curled, the children form arches or bridges, and the moving children go under these. A further extension is to have the children on the floor alternate between curled and bridge positions. If a moving child goes over the curled position, the floor child changes immediately to a bridge. The moving children react accordingly.

Bridges by Threes

Three children in a group can set up an interesting movement sequence using bridges. Two of the children make bridges, and the third child goes under both bridges and sets up her own bridge. Each child in turn goes under the bridges of the other two. Different kinds of bridges can be specified, and the bridges can be arranged so that a change in direction is made. An over-and-under sequence also provides interest. The child vaults or jumps over the first bridge then goes under the next bridge before setting up her own bridge.

Shooting Star

Students gather around the teacher in the center of the area. Like a shooting star, they explode and run rapidly from the teacher as far as possible before the whistle blows. Students then return to the teacher by using desired or designated locomotor movements. The activity is best done outside.

New Leader

Squads or small groups run around the area, following a leader. When the change is signaled, the last person goes to the head of the line to lead. Groups of three are ideal for this activity.

Manipulative Activities

Each child has a beanbag. The children move around the area, tossing the bags upward and catching them as they move. On signal, they drop the bags to the floor and jump, hop, or leap over as many bags as possible. On the next signal, they pick up any convenient bag and resume tossing to themselves. Having one fewer beanbag than children adds to the fun. Hoops can also be used in this manner. Children begin by using hoops in rope-jumping style or for hula-hooping. On signal, the hoops are placed on the floor, and the children jump in and out of as many hoops as they can. Next, they pick up a nearby hoop and resume the original movement pattern. The activity can be done with jump ropes, too.

Body Part Identification

Enough beanbags for the whole class are scattered on the floor. The children either run between or jump over the beanbags. When a body part is called out, the children place that body part on the nearest beanbag.

Leapfrog

Two, three, or four children can make up this sequence. The children form a straight or curved column, with all except the last child in line taking the leapfrog position. The last child leaps over the other children in turn, and after going over all, gets down so the others can go over him. Lines should curve around to avoid running into other jumpers.

Drill Sergeant

Another movement is performed as a squad activity. A drill sergeant gives these kinds of commands for the movement sequence to be performed: "Walk, jump twice, and roll." "Run, jump-turn, and freeze (pose)." "Shake, jump-turn, and roll." "Seal Walk, Forward Roll, and jump." The squad leader should be told about the activity ahead of time so she can prepare some patterns, or she should be given cards with suggested patterns written on them. To add a realistic flavor, the sergeant can call the squad members to attention, give them the directions, and then call, "Move!" Younger children, especially, love to play soldiers.

CREATIVE AND EXPLORATORY OPPORTUNITIES

Another approach of interest to children is providing creative and exploratory opportunities at the beginning of a lesson. Some examples follow.

1. Put out enough equipment of one type (hoops, balls, wands, or beanbags) so all children have a piece of equipment with which to explore. This can be open exploration, or the movement can follow the trend of a prior lesson, thus supplying extension to the progression.
2. Have available a number of manipulative items. The children select any item they wish and decide whether to play alone, with a partner, or as a member of a small group.
3. Make available a range of apparatus, such as climbing ropes, climbing apparatus, mats, boxes, balance beams, balance boards, and similar items. Manipulative items can be a part of the package, too. The children choose the area in which they want to participate.

TAMBOURINE-DIRECTED ACTIVITIES

The tambourine can signal changes of movement, because it can produce two different kinds of sound—the tinny noise made by vigorous shaking and the percussive sound made by striking the instrument. Movement changes are signaled by changing from one sound to the other.

Shaking Sound

1. The children remain in one spot but shake all over. These should be gross movements.
2. The children shake and gradually drop to the floor.
3. The children scurry in every direction.
4. The children run lightly with tiny steps.

Drum Sound

1. Students make jerky movements to the percussive beat.
2. They jump in place or through space.
3. Youngsters do locomotor movements in keeping with the beat.
4. Responding to three beats, the children collapse on the first beat, roll on the second, and form a shape on the third.

Combinations

To form a combination of movements, select one from each category (shaking or percussive). When the shaking sound is made, the children perform that movement. When the sound is changed to the drum sound, the children react accordingly.

GAMES AND MISCELLANEOUS ACTIVITIES

Selected games are quite suitable for introductory activities, provided that they keep all children active, are simple, and require little teaching. Usually, a familiar game is used so that little organizational time is needed. Some appropriate games are listed.

Addition Tag (p. 431)
Back to Back (p. 420)
Circle Hook-on (p. 436)
Couple Tag (p. 427)
Loose Caboose (p. 433)
One, Two, Button My Shoe (p. 421)
Squad Tag (p. 434)
Touchdown (p. 438)
Whistle Mixer (p. 435)

Some running patterns also can be established. Children can run laps. A Challenge Course or a cross-country type of circuit can be set up.

CHAPTER 16

Incorporating Physical Fitness Into the Program

All children have the right to become strong, quick, agile, and flexible. It is the responsibility of the school to provide opportunities for them to achieve the goal of developing and maintaining a level of physical fitness that allows them to live fully and achieve well.

Should this development be a by product, a concomitant goal, of general program activities, or should it be achieved directly? We take the position that both approaches should be employed to help all children develop and maintain a level of physical fitness commensurate with their needs. The key lies in motivating the child to take responsibility for personal fitness. How much the school can accomplish toward this end depends on the values placed on physical development in the curriculum. Physical fitness rarely occurs by chance. It usually is the result of an individual's knowing what to do to stay in top condition and then transforming this knowledge into regular activity.

THE BROAD PROGRAM OF PHYSICAL FITNESS

There is much more to acquiring physical fitness than just providing physical fitness routines in the program. The components of a broad program are as follows:

1. *Get students to assume responsibility for their personal fitness development.* This includes helping students set personal goals that have meaning. It implies an extension of fitness development beyond recess and free time in school, as well as application to the home and community environment.

2. *Provide an understanding of how fitness is developed.* This implies an explanation of the value of the procedures followed in class sessions so children understand the purpose of all fitness developmental tasks.

3. *Develop cognition of the importance of fitness for wellness.* Students should understand how to perform fitness activities and why these activities should be performed. They need to know the values derived from maintaining a minimal fitness level.

4. *Provide basic explanations of rudimentary anatomy and kinesiology.* Children should learn the names and locations of major bones and muscle groups, including how they function in relation to selected joint action. Knowledges should relate to fitness actions appropriate to the maturity level of students.

5. *Provide a sound fitness development program that is part of each session.* This is the culmination—the show-me-how procedures that embody the first four program points.

Teachers should examine how the physical education program and accompanying instruction communicate the importance of fitness to children. Most children understand the importance of brushing one's teeth to preserve them. In comparison, few children understand clearly the importance of exercise to personal health. Too often, the area deleted from physical education instruction is physical fitness. This communicates to children that fitness is the least important aspect of physical education. In fact, the values shared with children should develop the comprehension that physical fitness is the foundation of skill performance, personal health, and wellness.

COMPONENTS OF PHYSICAL FITNESS

Many components of physical fitness have been identified: strength, power, cardiorespiratory endurance, agility, flexibility, and speed. This discussion is concerned primarily with those components that are health related. They are flexibility, muscular strength and endurance, body composition, and cardiovascular endurance. These components can be measured by the AAHPERD Health Related Fitness Test (1980) and are important in maintaining wellness.

FLEXIBILITY

Flexibility is the range of movement through which a joint or sequence of joints can move. Inactive individuals tend to lose flexibility, whereas frequent movement tends to retain the range of movement. Through stretching activities, the length of muscles, tendons, and ligaments is increased. The ligaments and tendons tend to retain their elasticity through constant use.

Flexibility is important to fitness; a lack of flexibility can create problems for individuals. People who are flexible are less subject to injury in sport, usually possess sound posture, and may have less low back pain. Many physical activities demand a wide range of motion to generate maximum force.

Two types of stretching activity have been used to develop flexibility. Ballistic stretching (strong bouncing movements) was the most commonly used until recently, but has come under scrutiny since it may initiate the stretch reflex. This reflex is an involuntary response to a stimulus (stretch) and causes the muscle to contract. The reflex may cause muscle soreness and strain and may not develop an increased range of motion.

Static, controlled stretching, without bounce, is effective because it does not induce the stretch reflex. It involves gradually increasing the stretch to the point of discomfort, backing off slightly to where the position can be held comfortably, and maintaining the stretch for an extended time. Static stretching is safer and less prone to cause injury. This method of stretching can be used to reduce muscle soreness or to prepare for strenuous activity. The length of time to hold the stretch can be started at 5 to 10 seconds and increased gradually up to 30 to 45 seconds.

MUSCULAR STRENGTH AND ENDURANCE

Strength is the ability of muscles to exert force; it is an important fitness component for learning motor skills. Most activities that students are involved in do not build strength in the areas where it is most needed—the arm-shoulder girdle and the abdominal region.

Muscular endurance is the ability to exert force over an extended period of time. Endurance postpones the onset of fatigue so that activity can be performed for lengthy periods. Most sport activities require that muscular skills, such as throwing, kicking, and striking, be performed many times without fatigue.

When muscular strength is a desired training outcome, it is necessary to lift or move maximum work loads with minimal repetitions. Strength development is accompanied by muscle hypertrophy, an increase in the number of muscle fibers recruited, and an increase in oxygen use capacity.

To develop muscular endurance, a low-resistance, high-repetition work load is suggested. For most athletes, a balance of the two is probably most useful. Usually, muscular strength and endurance workouts should be conducted three days per week.

BODY COMPOSITION

Body composition is now regarded as an integral part of health-related fitness. Body composition is the proportion of body fat to lean body mass. After the thickness of selected skinfolds has been measured, the percentage of body fat is calculated by using formulas.

Attaining physical fitness is difficult when an individual is obese. An understanding of caloric intake and expenditure (see Chapter 10) is important to weight control. It is possible to eat enough to gain weight regardless of the amount of exercise performed. Since the wellness status of individuals is dependent on body composition, students must learn about the concepts and consequences in this area.

CARDIOVASCULAR ENDURANCE

This element plays an important role in living a healthy life-style and may be the most important element of fitness. Cardiovascular endurance is the ability of the heart, the blood vessels, and the respiratory system to deliver oxygen efficiently over an extended period of time.

To develop cardiovascular endurance, activity must be aerobic in nature. Activities that are continuous and rhythmic in nature require that a continuous supply of oxygen be delivered to the muscle cells. During aerobic exercise, oxygen that the body uses in a given period of time is called the maximum oxygen uptake and is the best indicator of cardiovascular endurance. Activities that stimulate development in this area are paced walking, jogging, biking, rope jumping, aerobic dance, swimming, and continuous movement sports such as basketball or soccer.

In contrast to aerobic activity is anaerobic exercise, an activity that is so intense that the body cannot supply oxygen at the cellular level. The body can therefore continue the activity for a short time only. Examples of anaerobic activity are sprinting, running up stairs, or an all out effort in any sport.

DEVELOPING PHYSICAL FITNESS

The following points deal with enhancing the level of fitness in students. Students should leave a physical education program keenly aware of these basic principles and able to apply them to a personal fitness program.

OVERLOAD

To increase the present level of physical fitness, the body must be overloaded beyond what is normally done. To ensure that systematic overloading occurs, students should be able to prescribe their own work loads using the acronym FIT as a guide. The letters FIT stand for Frequency, Intensity, and Time. The variables are interrelated, and changing one may require a change in another.

Frequency determines the number of exercise sessions an individual will do per week. Three workouts per week is the frequency minimum if benefits are to accrue. In many physical education programs, youngsters meet perhaps once or twice a week. Given that frequency, some teachers believe that there is little reason to teach physical fitness activities. This is a critical error in judgment, because eliminating physical fitness suggests to children that it is unimportant. Another error in this line of reasoning is the assumption that children cannot be taught cognitive understandings of physical fitness even if fitness activities are presented only once a week.

Time is the length of each exercise bout. For developing cardiovascular endurance, the minimum amount of aerobic exercise should be 5 to 8 minutes. The intensity of the exercise has an impact on the length of time devoted to the fitness session. In most situations, monitoring the duration of the activity is more feasible than monitoring the intensity. An example would be a running activity in which the teacher is torn between monitoring the amount of time required to move versus timing the speed (intensity) at which the activity should be performed.

To monitor *intensity* in aerobic activity, the heart rate should be calculated. Proper intensity requires that the heart rate reach the training state, which is 60% to 80% of the maximum heart rate. Time and intensity can also be monitored in strength development. Most strength activities are of high intensity, therefore requiring an increase in duration through an increased number of sets or repetitions.

Progression is important to maintaining motivation and reducing the chance of injury. Progression of work loads should be increased gradually by increasing both the intensity and duration of the exercise. Physical fitness activities should be structured to progress gradually. Teachers can be overenthusiastic about developing fitness in a short amount of time. They need to remember that maintaining fitness is an ongoing process that must be performed for a lifetime. The important point is to maintain the desire to exercise. A reasonable progression throughout the school year helps to ensure that this occurs.

TRAINING HEART RATE

The heart rate can be used to determine exercise intensity. It gives an indication of whether the work load should be increased or decreased. To monitor heart rate, palpate at the wrist or carotid artery. When the pulse is palpated at the wrist, it should be done near the joint, on the thumb side, using the index and middle fingers. To locate the pulse at the carotid artery, find the Adam's apple and slide the index and middle fingers to either side. Apply only slight pressure to allow blood flow to continue while taking the pulse.

To count the heart rate, begin within 5 seconds after stopping exercise. The count should be taken for 10 seconds and then multiplied by 6 to give the heart rate per minute. To enhance the level of cardiovascular endurance, the heart rate must be elevated to the training state. Using the following formula, the heartbeat range that should be maintained during exercise can be calculated.

1. Determine the estimated maximum heart rate by taking 220 minus the person's age.
2. Multiply the difference by 60% and 85%.

The two results provide the heart rate range per minute that should be maintained while exercising. For example, if a child is age 10, subtract 10 from 220, which equals 210. Now multiply 210 by 60% and 85%. The result means that a heart rate between 126 and 178 beats per minute should be maintained during exercise to reach the training state.

Once the training heart rate has been determined, the exercise routine can be undertaken. At the conclusion of the workout, monitor the heart rate. If it is above the beats per minute allowed by the formula, reduce the intensity. On the other hand, if the heart rate is low, increase the intensity of aerobic exercise.

ISOTONICS, ISOMETRICS, AND ISOKINETICS

The majority of exercises used for routines involve isotonic contractions. These are contractions of a muscle through its full range of motion. Walking, jogging, calisthenics, and bicycling are examples of activities that involve isotonic contractions.

Isometric contractions occur without muscle movement. Here, the contraction is made against an immovable object, and the muscles do not shorten as they do in isotonic contraction. Isometric contractions are somewhat controversial as a means to develop strength, although isometrics do appear to be effective. To receive results, contractions should be an all-out effort held for 8 to 12 seconds. A shortcoming of isometrics is that they build strength only at the angle of contraction. For this reason, they should be implemented at a range of joint angles in an attempt to develop strength throughout the complete range of motion.

Isokinetic contractions are a type of isotonic contraction that requires the use of special machines. Isokinetic contractions are maximum contractions throughout the complete range of motion. Isokinetic devices control the work load mechanically, so the resistance and rate of movement are maintained regardless of the mechanical advantage that occurs as the contraction is near completion. For strength development, isokinetic exercises appear to be more effective than either isotonic or isometric exercises (Miller and Allen 1982). However, the requirement of special equipment probably makes this type of exercise impractical for most school settings.

SPECIFICITY OF EXERCISE

Physical conditioning should match the demands that a sport or activity makes on the individual. *Specificity* implies that all skills and activities are unique and require training that is geared specifically to each. The implication of specificity is that exercising a certain part or component of the body develops only that part. This emphasizes the importance of a balanced approach to fitness. For example, if one chooses only to jog for fitness, the cardiovascular system will be developed. Flexibility, however, will decrease in the lower back and hamstrings, and abdominal strength will decrease. Muscular power, as revealed by the vertical jump, will decrease also. Balancing the approach to fitness by including flexibility, strength development, and cardiovascular endurance activity in the exercise regimen is thus desirable.

INSTRUCTIONAL PROCEDURES FOR FITNESS ACTIVITIES

1. Students should move into an appropriate formation quickly. Methods for accomplishing this include scattering so that each student has sufficient personal space, going to prearranged places (sport names or numbers painted on the floor help), and using extended squad formation (the squad stays in line but extends spacing between members from front to back, as shown on p. 76).

2. When introducing a new exercise, show children briefly how it is to be done. Give the purpose of the exercise and its value, including the muscle groups involved. Take children through the exercise by parts (count by count) until it is mastered, and then speed up to normal tempo. Remind children about key performance points and proper form.

3. Work load depends on the number of repetitions and other factors. In setting repetitions, the instructor can be guided by ranges specified in the exercise section that follows. Begin with the lower figure and add one or two repetitions or sets each week.

4. The development potential of certain exercises can be enhanced by incorporating positions that are held, as in isometric exercises. A position can be held for a period of time (8 to 12 seconds) with a nearly maximal contraction.

5. For some exercises, the instructor can allow students to set personal limits informally. This works well with Curl-ups, Push-ups, and similar exercises in which the limits can be based on individual capacity. For example, children might be requested to do one (or two) repetitions for each year of their age.

6. Instructors should develop some rhythmic means of starting exercises, such as "Ready—begin." For halting, the voice is lowered and the tempo slowed during the last series of counts, which now becomes "One, two, and halt." The words "and halt" are substituted for the last two counts of the final series.

7. Each exercise has a particular rhythm or tempo that is most effective. Some experimentation is necessary to determine the appropriate rhythm. Children enjoy exercises performed in an even, rhythmic manner.

8. A counting system should be employed to keep track of the number of repetitions. Series counting can include the repetitions "One-two-three-one, one-two-three-two, one-two-three-three, one-two-three-four."

9. Response cadence counting by the students adds a motivational factor and gives students a role in the exercise routine. The leader names or describes the exercise, specifies the number of repetitions, and puts the group in starting position. The following dialogue then takes place.

Leader: Ready—exercise.

Group: Ready—exercise. One-two-three-four, one-two-three-two (and so on, in unison).

If eight repetitions are desired, the group stops itself with the following:

Group: Eight-two-and-halt.

The cadence should be clipped, sharp, and moderate in intensity. Shouting should be avoided.

10. Good postural alignment should be maintained. In exercises in which the arms are held in front, to the sides of the body, or overhead, the abdominal wall needs to be tensed and flattened for proper positioning of the pelvis. In most activities, the feet should be pointed reasonably forward, the chest should be up, and the head and shoulders in good postural position.

11. Exercises, in themselves, are not sufficient to develop cardiovascular endurance. Additional activity in the form of running, rope jumping, or some other vigorous work load is needed to round out fitness development.

12. Fitness instruction should be included in the daily physical education lesson plan with a specific time allotted to activities devoted exclusively to fitness development. It is possible to develop an appropriate level of fitness through a daily program of 8 to 12 minutes of activity when the activity is well planned for maximum involvement.

AVOIDING HARMFUL PRACTICES AND EXERCISES

The following points contraindicate certain exercise practices and should be considered when offering fitness instruction.

1. When developing abdominal strength, the Sit-up with the knees bent should be used instead of the straight-legged Sit-up. When the legs are bent at the knee, the abdominal muscles are isolated from the psoas muscle group. This concentrates development on the abdominals rather than on the lower back area and avoids development of an excessive lower back curve. Sit-ups should be performed with a smooth curling movement with the chin tucked. This avoids the bouncing and jerking motion often observed.

2. When stretching exercises are performed, the pressure applied should be smooth and constant. Students should stretch to the point of discomfort, then back off slightly and hold that position. Bouncing to further the range of motion should be avoided. Stretching exercises should be done under control in a slow and sustained manner.

3. If forward flexion is done from a sitting position in an effort to touch the toes, the bend should be from the hips, not the waist.

4. Straight leg raises from a supine position should be avoided because they may strain the lower back. The problem can be somewhat alleviated by placing the hands under the small of the back.

5. Deep knee bends (full squats) should be avoided. They may cause damage to the knee joints. (Note that deep knee bends as an exercise have little developmental value.) Much more beneficial is flexing the knee joint to 90 degrees.

6. In stretching exercises from a standing position, the knees should not be hyperextended. The knee joint should be relaxed rather than locked. In all stretching activities, participants should be allowed to judge their range of motion. Expecting all students to be able to touch their toes is an unrealistic goal, particularly in early stages of development.

7. Caution must be used in placing stress on the neck. Examples of activities in which caution should be used are the Inverted Bicycle, Wrestler's Bridge, and the Sit-up with the hands behind the head. Most of these activities can be avoided or work loads carefully adjusted to the capacity of the student.

FITNESS ACTIVITIES FOR KINDERGARTEN THROUGH GRADE TWO

Fitness activities for young children should have the potential for developing components of physical fitness and exercising the various body areas. The entire lesson for any one day should provide activity to meet recommended physical demands. In particular, introductory activity and fitness development activity, the first two parts of the lesson, should combine to provide broad coverage by including activities for each of these five areas: (1) trunk, (2) abdomen, (3) arm-shoulder girdle, (4) legs and cardiorespiratory system, and (5) flexibility.

Many selected movement patterns contribute to more than one body area. Some contribute to all five. A fitness activity is generally counted as developing the area that is its main focus. The five exercise areas can be developed by combining the introductory-development phase of the lesson.

Inventiveness, imagination, and perceptiveness in using movement suggestions from children are the keys to providing adequate experiences. Each child works individually without competition from others. It is important that all children be stimulated to strenuous effort.

The following are examples of how a teacher might stimulate children to develop abdominal and shoulder girdle strength. To present activity based on the Partial Curl-up (p. 225), the instructor, after getting the children into the starting position, might challenge them in this manner: "Work your fingers up to the top of your knees, raising your head and shoulders. Can you see your toes? Do this several times."

A way to develop movement sequences with the Push-up (pp. 222–223) is to begin with a controlled descent to the floor from the top position. "Let's pretend we are going to have a flat tire. When I say 'Bang,' lower yourself slowly to the floor as if you were a tire going flat. What kind of noise does air make when it is escaping from a tire?" Children can pretend to have a blowout (fast action) or a slow leak (very slow action). "Can you push yourself back up, keeping your body pretty straight? If you have trouble, try doing it first on your knees." Other ways of working informally with the push-up position are presented on p. 219.

TRUNK DEVELOPMENT

Movements that include bending, stretching, swaying, twisting, reaching, and forming shapes are important inclusions. No particular continuity exists, except that a specified approach should move from simple to more complex. A logical approach is to select one or more movements and to use them as the theme for the day. Vary the position the child is to take—standing, lying, kneeling, or sitting. From the selected position, stimulate the child to varied movements based on the theme for the day. Examples of different trunk movements follow.

Bending

"Bend in different ways."

"Bend as many parts of the body as you can."

"Make different shapes by bending two, three, and four parts of the body."

"Bend the arms and knees in different ways and on different levels."

"Try different ways of bending the fingers and wrist of one hand with the other. Use some resistance. (Explain *resistance.*) Add body bends."

Stretching

"Keeping one foot in place, stretch your arms in different directions, stepping as you move with the free foot. Stretch at different levels."

"Lying on the floor, stretch one leg different ways in space. Stretch one leg in one direction and the other in another direction."

"Stretch as slowly as you wish and then snap back to original position."

"Stretch with different arm-leg combinations in several directions."

"See how much space on the floor you can cover by stretching. Show us how big your space is."

"Combine bending and stretching movements."

Swaying and Twisting

"Sway your body back and forth in different directions. Change the position of your arms."

"Sway your body, bending over."

"Sway your head from side to side."

"Select a part of the body and twist it as far as you can in one direction and then in the opposite direction."

"Twist your body at different levels."

"Twist two or more parts of your body at the same time."

"Twist one part of your body while untwisting another."

"Twist your head to see as far back as you can."

"Twist like a spring. Like a screwdriver."

"Stand on one foot and twist your body. Untwist."

"From a seated position, make different shapes by twisting."

Forming Shapes

Children like to form different shapes with their bodies, and this interest should be used to aid in trunk development. Shapes can be formed in almost any position—standing, sitting, lying, or while balancing on parts of the body or moving. Shapes can be curled or stretched, narrow or wide, big or little, symmetrical or asymmetrical, twisted or straight.

ABDOMINAL DEVELOPMENT

The best position for exercising the abdominal muscles is supine on the floor or on a mat. Challenges should lift the upper and lower portions of the body from the floor, either singly or together. The following are possible directives.

"Sit up and touch both sets of toes with your hands."

"Sit up and touch your right toe with your left hand. Do it the other way."

"Bring up your toes to touch behind your head."

"With hands to the side, bring your feet up straight and then touch them with the right hand. With the left hand."

"Lift your knees up slowly, an inch at a time."

"Pick your heels up about 6 inches off the floor and swing them back and forth. Cross them and twist them."

"Lift your head from the floor and look at your toes. Wink your right eye and wiggle your left foot. Reverse."

Selected abdominal exercises (pp. 224–226) can be modified to provide suitable challenges. The approach should be informal, using directives like "Can you . . . ?" or "Show me how you can. . . ."

ARM-SHOULDER GIRDLE DEVELOPMENT

Movement experiences contributing to arm-shoulder girdle development can be divided roughly into two groups. The first group includes activities in which the hands and arms support the body weight either wholly or in part. The second group includes activities in which the arms are free but are stimulated to move in many different ways.

ARM-SUPPORT ACTIVITIES

The teacher should make use frequently of the activities listed for the stunts and tumbling program (pp. 363–375). In addition, selected movement challenges that stress the arms and shoulder girdle are of value.

Animal Walks and Selected Stunts

Alligator Crawl (p. 364)
Puppy Dog Run (p. 364)
Cat Walk (p. 364)
Rabbit Jump (p. 368)
Lame Dog Walk (p. 369)
Seal Crawl (p. 375)
Crab Walk (pp. 369–370)
Turn-Over (p. 372)
Frog Jump (p. 376)
Measuring Worm (p. 376)
Frog Handstand (p. 378)
Turtle (p. 383)
Wheelbarrow (p. 389)

Movement Challenges—Various Body Positions

"Practice taking the weight completely on your hands."

"In crab position, keep your feet in place and make your body go in a big circle. Do the same from push-up position."

"In crab position, let's see you go forward, backward, and to the side. Turn around, move very slowly, and so on."

Successively from standing, supine, and hands-knees positions: "Swing one limb (arm or leg) at a time, in different directions and at different levels."

"Combine two limb movements (arm-arm, leg-leg, or arm-leg combinations) in the same direction and in opposite directions. Vary the levels."

"Swing the arms or legs back and forth and go into giant circles. In supine position, make giant circles with the feet."

In a bent-over position, "Swing the arms as if swimming. Try a backstroke or a breaststroke. What does a sidestroke look like?"

"Make the arms go like a windmill. Turn the arms in different directions. Accelerate and decelerate."

"How else can you circle your arms?"

"Pretend a swarm of bees is around your head. Brush them off and keep them away."

Movement Challenges Based on the Push-up Position

Each child assumes the push-up position (Figure 16.1), which provides a base of operation. The challenges require a movement and then a return to the original push-up position.

"Lift one foot high. Now the other foot."

"Bounce both feet up and down. Move the feet out from each other while bouncing."

"Inch the feet up to the hands and go back again. Inch the feet up to the hands and then inch the hands out to return to the push-up position."

FIGURE 16.1. Push-up position

"Reach up with one hand and touch the other shoulder behind the back."

"Lift both hands from the floor. Try clapping the hands."

"Bounce from the floor with both hands and feet off the floor at the same time."

"Turn over so the back is to the floor. Now complete the turn to push-up position."

"Lower the body an inch at a time until the chest touches the floor. Return."

There is value in maintaining the push-up position for a length of time. The various tasks both interest and challenge youngsters. The informal and individual approach stimulates the children to good effort.

The crab position can be used in a similar fashion. Many of the same directives listed for the push-up position can be used with modification for the crab position. The side-leaning rest position is another that can be employed.

LEG AND CARDIORESPIRATORY DEVELOPMENT

Leg and cardiorespiratory development activities can include a wide range of movement challenges, either in general space or in place. The introductory phase of the lesson often incorporates some type of running activity. Most of the activities in this section work best when activities from the previous three sections are integrated with them to develop a total body fitness routine. In other words, combine activities from the trunk, abdominal, and arm-shoulder girdle sections with the leg and cardiorespiratory activities.

Running Patterns

Running in different directions
Running in place
Ponies in the Stable (p. 209)
Tortoise and Hare (p. 209)
European Rhythmic Running (pp. 207–208)
Running and stopping
Running and changing direction on signal

Jumping and Hopping Patterns

Jumping in different directions back and forth over a spot
Jumping or hopping in, out, over, and around hoops, individual mats, or jump ropes laid on the floor
Jumping or hopping back and forth over lines, or hopping down the lines

Rope Jumping

Individual rope jumping—allow choice.

Combinations

Many combinations of locomotor movements can be suggested, such as run, leap, and roll, or run, jump-turn, and shake. Other combinations can be devised. (See p. 95 for others.)

Miniature Challenge Courses

A miniature Challenge Course (Figure 16.2) can be set up indoors or outdoors. The distance between the start and finish lines depends on the type of activity. To begin, a distance of about 30 ft is suggested, but this can be adjusted. Cones can mark the course boundaries. The course should be wide enough for two children at a time to move down it.

Each child performs the stipulated locomotor movement from the start to the finish line, then turns and jogs back to the start. The movement is continuous. Directions should be given in advance so that no delay occurs. The number of children on each course should be limited to normal squad size or fewer. The following movements can be stipulated.

All types of locomotor movements—running, jumping, hopping, sliding, and so on

Movements on the floor—crawling, Bear Walk, Seal Crawl, and the like

Movements over and under obstacles or through tires or hoops

A Challenge Course could have the following elements, in this order: (1) crawling under two cone sets, (2) rolling down an inclined mat, (3) log-rolling up an inclined mat, (4) moving up and down a three-step structure, and on the final climb, jumping and rolling, (5) crawling through a barrel or one or more tires, (6) walking a balance beam, and (7) pulling the body down a bench in prone position.

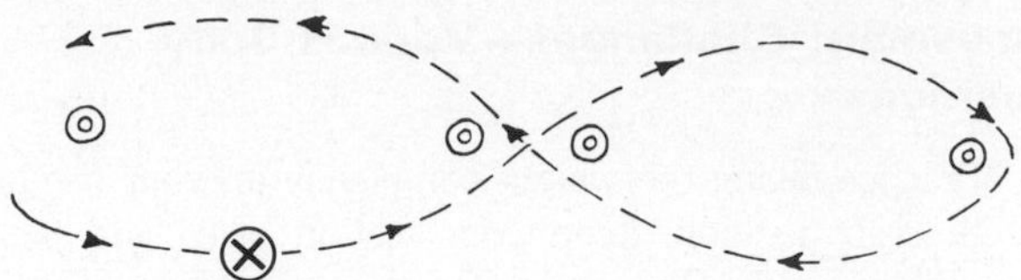

FIGURE 16.3. Figure-eight hopping circuit

Circular Movements

Each child selects a spot on which the hands are maintained. Directives to children in this position can be as follows.

"Keeping the body straight, walk the feet in a full circle back to place. Change direction. Try with the back to the floor."

"Keep the feet in place and walk the hands in a full circle. Vary as in the previous movement."

Figure-Eight Movements

Four cones or beanbags are placed as shown in Figure 16.3 for a figure-eight hopping circuit. Children change feet at the end of each full circuit. Skipping, jumping, galloping, and sliding can be used in place of hopping.

Four-Corners Movement Formation

A rectangle is formed by four cones. The student moves around the rectangle. Each time the child goes around a corner, he changes the movement pattern. On long sides, rapid movement such as running, skipping, or sliding should be designated. Moving along short sides, the student can hop, jump, or do animal walks. Vary clockwise and counterclockwise directions.

Using the four-corners ideas as a basis, other combinations can be devised. For example, the pattern in Figure 16.4 requires running along one of the long sides and sliding along the other. One of the short sides has mats and requires three Forward Rolls, while the other short side requires an animal walk on all fours.

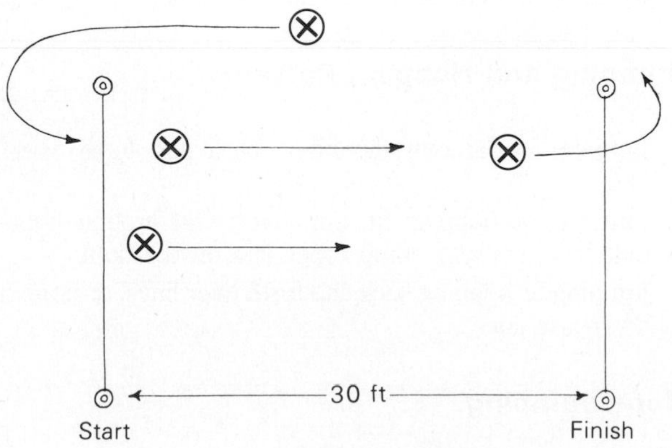

FIGURE 16.2. Miniature Challenge Course

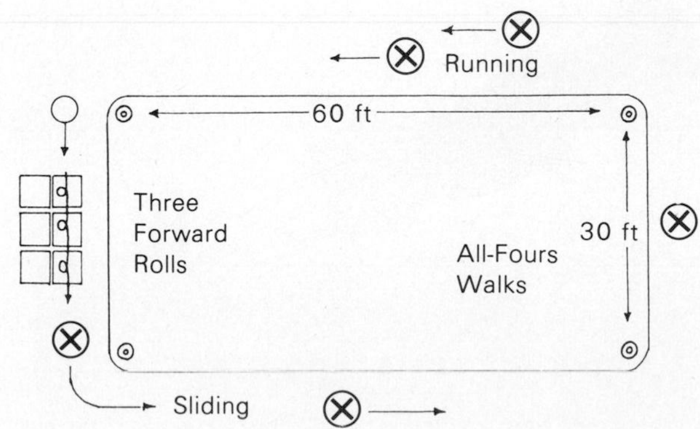

FIGURE 16.4. Four-corners movement formation

Measurements can vary according to the ages of the children and the movement tasks involved. Outdoors, four rectangles can be laid out. Indoors, at least two should be established. Too much crowding and interference occur when only one rectangle is used for the average-size class.

Fitness Using Routines and Equipment

Parachute activities (pp. 306–309) provide many physical challenges for various body areas. Astronaut Drills (p. 236) can be modified to good effect for younger children. Circuit Training (pp. 232–235) can also be adapted to fit the needs of grades kindergarten through 2. Stations can include some fun-oriented or manipulative activities on an informal basis in addition to exercise routines. Bounding boards (p. 352) are highly recommended as a station activity. Other activities of value are going over and under hurdles, activities with jumping boxes, manipulative activities with beanbags or balls, hula-hoop or wand stunts, individual mat activities, climbing ropes, and activities with tires in stands. Hoops laid in floor patterns (p. 314) provide excellent movement challenges. Bicycle or automobile tires can serve the same purpose. Floor apparatus makes excellent circuit stations.

FITNESS ACTIVITIES FOR GRADES THREE THROUGH SIX

In contrast to the program for the lower grades, the emphasis on fitness in grades 3 through 6 shifts to more structured drills and routines, with less stress on exploratory movement. Figure 16.5 shows a sample program for grades 3 through 6 that includes various fitness routines scheduled over a 36-week period. Some adaptation to school schedules may be necessary.

FITNESS DEVELOPMENT ACTIVITY

WEEK	ACTIVITY
1–4	Exercises
5–8	Circuit Training
9–10	Astronaut Drills
11–12	Continuity exercises
13–16	Exercises to music
17–18	Grass Drills and partner resistance
19–22	Squad leader exercises
23–26	Circuit Training
27–28	Challenge Courses
29–30	Jogging
31–32	Selected movement sequences
33–34	Aerobic dancing
35–36	Parachute exercises and activities

FIGURE 16.5. Sample fitness development program, grades 3–6

A program of fitness for the year should lead off with teacher-leader exercises, since these are the basic exercises for many of the other drills. It is helpful if the exercises have catchy or descriptive names. Once children associate the exercise with a characteristic name, little time is wasted in getting the activity under way.

EXERCISES FOR DEVELOPING FITNESS ROUTINES

Selected exercises fall into the following categories: (1) flexibility, (2) arm-shoulder girdle, (3) abdominal, (4) leg and agility, and (5) trunk twisting and bending. In any one class session, the exercises should number from 6 to 10. Included in each lesson should be 2 exercises from the arm-shoulder girdle group and at least 1 from each of the other categories. Specific exercises should be changed at times, with a minimum of 12 exercises being included in the year's experiences.

Several approaches ensure variety in exercise selection. One system is to select a basic group of exercises. Assume that 12 exercises are selected. These could be divided into two sets of 6 each, with the selection meeting the standards of category coverage previously discussed. Some teachers like to alternate sets day by day. Others prefer to have one set in effect for a week or two before changing.

As a time-saver, teachers can make up sets of exercises on cards, using a different colored card for each of the categories. In this manner, the teacher can be assured of full developmental coverage by having students select a card from each color group, with the stipulation of two from the arm-shoulder girdle group.

Recommended exercises are presented under each of the five categories. Stress points, modifications, variations, and teaching suggestions are presented when appropriate. Teachers can supplement the listed exercises with some of their choice, provided the exercises are fundamentally sound.

FLEXIBILITY EXERCISES

Many exercises contribute to the development of flexibility. Those included in this section, however, have flexibility as their main goal. The exercises presented here can be done in unison or informally at each student's own pace and capacity.

Bend and Stretch

Starting Position: Stand erect, with hands on hips, and feet shoulder width apart and pointing forward.

Cadence: Slow

Movement: Bend down gradually, taking three counts to touch the floor. Recover on the fourth count. Knees can be flexed somewhat if needed.

Beginning Dosage: Eight repetitions

Variation: *Cross-Foot Toe Touch*—Same as Bend and Stretch, except cross one foot in front of the other. Do half of the repetitions in this position and then reverse the feet.

Sitting Stretch

Starting Position: Sit on the floor with legs extended forward and feet about 1 yd apart. The hands are clasped behind the neck, with elbows pointed forward and kept close together (Figure 16.6).

Cadence: Slow or at will

Movement: Gradually bend forward, taking three counts to bend fully. Recover to sitting position on the fourth count.

Beginning Dosage: Eight repetitions

Stress Point: Bend from the hips. Knees may be relaxed if necessary.

Variation: Instead of bending straight forward, bend first toward the left knee, then forward, and then toward the right knee. Reverse the direction during the next sequence.

Partner Rowing

Starting Position: Partners sit facing each other, holding hands with palms touching and fingers locked. The legs are spread and extended to touch soles of partner's feet.

Cadence: Slow or at will

FIGURE 16.6. Sitting stretch position

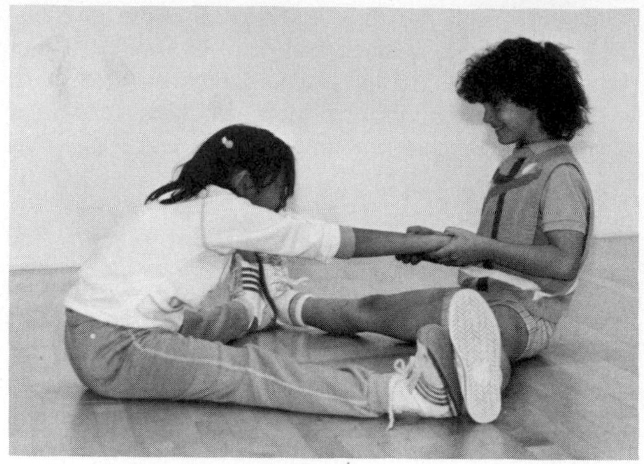

FIGURE 16.7. Partner Rowing

Movement: One partner bends forward, with the help of the other pulling backward, to try to bring the chest as close to the floor as possible (Figure 16.7). Reverse direction. Pairs should work individually.

Beginning Dosage: Eight sets, forward and back

Variation: *Steam Engine*—With both partners in the sitting position, alternate pulling hands back and forth like a pair of steam-engine pistons. Do eight sets, right and left combined twists.

ARM-SHOULDER GIRDLE EXERCISES

Arm-shoulder girdle exercises for this age-group include both arm-support and free-arm types.

Push-ups

Starting Position: Assume the push-up position (p. 219), with the body straight from head to heels.

Cadence: Moderate or at will

Movement: Keeping the body straight, bend the elbows and touch the chest to the ground, then straighten the elbows, raising the body in a straight line.

Beginning Dosage: Five repetitions

Stress Points: The movement should be in the arms. The head is up, with the eyes looking ahead. The chest should touch the floor lightly, without receiving the weight of the body. The body remains in a straight line throughout, without sagging or humping.

Modification: If children are unable to perform the activity as described, have them start with knees or hips in contact with the floor.

Variation: After gaining some competence in doing Push-ups, try the following four-count sequence: (1) halfway down, (2) all the way down, (3) halfway up, and (4) up to starting position. Another interesting variation is to put an 8½-in. playground ball under the chest, which is then lowered to touch the ball. Smaller balls add more challenge.

Teaching Suggestion: Controlled movement is a goal; speed is not desirable. Most Push-ups should be done at will, allowing each child to achieve individually.

Reclining Pull-Ups

Starting Position: One pupil lies in supine position. Partner is astride, with feet alongside the reclining partner's chest. Partners grasp hands with interlocking fingers, with other suitable grip, or with an interlocked wrist grip.

Cadence: Moderate to slow

Movement: Pupil on floor pulls up with arms until the chest touches partner's thighs. The body remains straight, with weight resting on the heels (Figure 16.8). Return to position.

Beginning Dosage: Four to five repetitions

Stress Points: Supporting student should keep the center of gravity well over the feet by maintaining a lifted chest and proper head position. The lower student should maintain a straight body during the Pull-up and move only the arms.

Variations

1. Raise as directed (count 1), hold the high position isometrically (counts 2 and 3), return to position (count 4).

2. Set a target number. On the last repetition, hold the raised (high) position for eight counts.

FIGURE 16.8. Reclining Pull-ups

FIGURE 16.9. Arm Circles

Arm Circles

Starting Position: Stand erect, with feet apart and arms straight out to the side (Figure 16.9).

Cadence: Moderate

Movement: Do eight forward 12-in. circles with palms up, moving arms simultaneously. Then do eight backward 12-in. circles with palms down, moving arms simultaneously. The number of circles executed before changing can be varied.

Beginning Dosage: Three sets of forward and backward circles

Stress Point: Correct posture should be maintained, with the abdominal wall flat and the head and shoulders held back.

Crab Kick

Starting Position: Crab position, with the body supported on the hands and feet and the back parallel to the floor. The knees are bent at right angles. On all crab positions, keep the seat up and avoid body sag.

Cadence: Moderate

Movement: Kick the right leg up and down (counts 1 and 2) (Figure 16.10). Repeat with the left leg (counts 3 and 4).

Beginning Dosage: Twelve repetitions with each leg

Crab Alternate-Leg Extension

Starting Position: Assume crab position.

Cadence: Fast

FIGURE 16.10. Crab Kick

FIGURE 16.11. Flying Angel

Movement: On count 1, extend the right leg forward so it rests on the heel. On count 2, extend the left leg forward and bring the right leg back. Continue alternating.

Beginning Dosage: Ten sets, right and left combined

Crab Full-Leg Extension

Starting Position: Assume crab position.

Cadence: Moderate

Movement: On count 1, extend both legs forward so that the weight rests on the heels. On count 2, bring both feet back to crab position.

Beginning Dosage: Twelve extensions

Crab Walk

Starting Position: Assume crab position.

Cadence: None

Movement: Move forward, backward, sideward, and turn in a small circle right and left.

Beginning Dosage: Fifteen seconds of movement

Flying Angel

Starting Position: Stand erect, with feet together and arms at sides.

Cadence: None—no counting after initial signal

Movement: In a smooth, slow, continuous motion, raise the arms forward with elbows extended and then upward, at the same time rising up on the toes and lifting the chest, with eyes following the hands (Figure 16.11). Lower the arms sideward in a flying motion and return to starting position.

Beginning Dosage: Six repetitions

Stress Points: The abdominal wall must be kept flat throughout to minimize lower back curvature. The head should be back and well up. The exercise should be done slowly and smoothly, under control.

Variation: Move the arms forward as if doing a breaststroke. The arms are then raised slowly, with hands in front of the chest and elbows out, to full overhead extension. Otherwise, the movement is the same as the Flying Angel.

Other Exercises

In addition to the preceding exercises, the following from the posture exercise section should be considered.

Hook Lying (p. 228)
Swan (p. 228)
Tailor (pp. 228–229)

ABDOMINAL EXERCISES

For most exercises stressing abdominal development, the child starts from supine position on the floor or on a mat. To involve the abdominal muscles from this position, the child can lift the legs, the upper body, or both at the same time. If the upper body is lifted, the movement should begin with a roll-up, moving the head first so the chin makes contact or near contact with the chest, thus flattening and stabilizing the lower back curve. The bent-knee position places greater demand on the abdominal muscles. Two excellent exercises for abdominal development that do not use the supine position are the Leg Extension and the Mad Cat.

The isometric principle can be applied to most abdominal exercises, that is, the position should be held without movement for about 8 seconds.

Having three levels of Curl-ups allows better adaptation to individual differences. At times, the instructor may specify that the group do curl-up exercises and may allow individual students to choose the one they desire.

The Toe Toucher strengthens the muscles of the abdomen, thighs, and hips. It also stretches the hamstring muscles, and this further aids in the development of suppleness and flexibility. The massaging effect on the abdominal viscera is also beneficial.

Partial Curl-up

Starting Position: Lie on the back, with feet flat and knees bent, and with hands flat down on top of thighs.

Cadence: Moderate or at will

Movement: Leading with the chin, slide the hands forward until the fingers touch the kneecaps, then lift the head, shoulders, and upper body from the floor (Figure 16.12). Hold for eight counts and return to position.

Beginning Dosage: Eight to ten repetitions. The verbal count can be given as "Up (lift), two, three, four, five, six, seven, down." Another method is to give only the "up" command. Students count to themselves and return to position individually.

Sit-up (AAHPERD Health Related Physical Fitness Test Position)

Starting Position: Lie on the back with feet flat and knees bent. Insteps should be held by a helper. The arms are crossed on the chest with hands on opposite shoulders.

Cadence: Moderate or at will

Movement: Move up (Figure 16.13) and then back down in a two-count pattern. This Sit-up can also be done as an eight-count exercise, moving up on one count, holding for six counts, and moving down on the last count.

Beginning Dosage: Five repetitions

Stress Points: Roll up, with the chin first. Move the chest as close to the knees as possible.

FIGURE 16.12. Partial Curl-up

FIGURE 16.13. Modified timed sit-up position

Variations

1. Start with the arms along the floor overhead.

2. *Sit-up for Time.* Set a specified time; 30 seconds is reasonable. Attempt to do as many Sit-ups as possible during that time. A partner can count the repetitions. The body must make a full upward movement and a full return to the floor.

Curl-up With Twist

Starting Position: Lie on the back with feet flat and knees bent. The insteps should be held by a helper. Fingers are clasped behind the head.

Cadence: Moderate or at will

Movement: Sit up and touch the right knee with the left elbow. Repeat, alternating elbows (Figure 16.14).

Beginning Dosage: Five repetitions

Variations

1. Touch the outside of the knee with the elbow.

2. Touch both knees in succession. The sequence is up, touch left, touch right, and down.

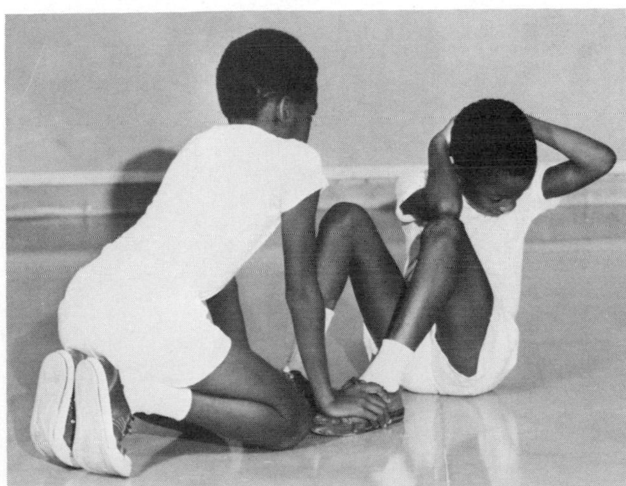

FIGURE 16.14. Curl-up With Twist

Rowing

Starting Position: Lie on the back with arms extended overhead along the floor.

Cadence: Slow—can be irregular

Movement: Curl up in one continuous movement, bringing the knees to the chest and extending the arms beyond the knees, parallel to the floor. Hold for a moment, squeezing hard. Return to position.

Beginning Dosage: Five to seven repetitions

Variation: On three successive up movements, bring the knees to the right, to the center, and to the left.

Leg Extension

Starting Position: Sit on the floor with legs extended and hands on hips.

Cadence: Moderate

Movement: With a quick, vigorous action, raise the knees and bring both heels as close to the seat as possible (Figure 16.15). The movement is a drag with the toes touching lightly. Return to position.

Beginning Dosage: Eight repetitions

Variation: Alternate bringing the knees to the right and left of the head.

Toe Toucher

Starting Position: Lie flat on the back, with feet about 2 ft apart and arms extended overhead.

Cadence: Slow, irregular

Movement: Roll up, thrust the arms forward, and touch the toes, keeping the knees straight. Roll back to original position. Raise the legs, swinging them overhead; keeping the knees straight, touch the toes to the ground behind the head. Slowly lower the legs to starting position.

Beginning Dosage: Three to four repetitions

FIGURE 16.15. Leg Extension

Other Exercises

Another useful exercise of this type is the Mad Cat, found with the posture exercises on p. 229.

LEG AND AGILITY EXERCISES

Leg and agility exercises should feature rhythmic, graceful motion with emphasis on control.

Running in Place

Starting Position: Stand with arms bent at the elbows.

Cadence: Slow, fast, and then slow

Movement: Run in place. Begin slowly, counting only the left foot. Speed up somewhat, raising the knees to hip height. Then run at full speed, raising the knees hard. Finally, slow down. The run should be on the toes.

Beginning Dosage: Twenty seconds

Variations

1. *Tortoise and Hare.* Jog slowly in place. On the command "Hare," double the speed. On the command "Tortoise," slow the tempo to original slow jogging pace.
2. March in place, lifting the knees high and swinging the arms up. Turn right and left on command while marching. Turn completely around to the right and then to the left while marching.
3. *Fast Stepping.* Step in place for 10 seconds as rapidly as possible. Rest for 10 seconds and repeat five or more times.

Jumping Jack

Starting Position: Stand at attention.

Cadence: Moderate

Movement: On count 1, jump to a straddle position with arms overhead. On count 2, recover to starting position.

Beginning Dosage: Ten repetitions

Variations

1. Begin with the feet in a stride position (forward and back). Change feet with the overhead movement.
2. Instead of bringing the feet together when the arms come down, cross the feet each time, alternating the cross.
3. On the completion of each set of eight counts, do a quarter turn right. (After four sets, the child is facing in the original direction.) Do the same to the left.
4. *Modified Jumping Jack.* On count 1, jump to a straddle position with arms out to the sides, parallel to the floor, and palms down. On count 2, return to position.

Treadmill

Starting Position: Assume push-up position, except that one leg is brought forward so the knee is under the chest (Figure 16.16).

FIGURE 16.16. Treadmill

Cadence: Moderate

Movement: Reverse the position of the feet, bringing the extended leg forward. Change back again so the original foot is forward. Continue rhythmically alternating feet.

Beginning Dosage: Ten steps with the right foot counting only the right foot

Stress Points: The head should be kept up. A full exchange of the legs should be made, with the forward knee coming well under the chest each time.

TRUNK-TWISTING AND BENDING EXERCISES

Many exercises involve twisting or bending; a few involve both. The twisting or bending should be done throughout the full range of movement. Movements should be large and vigorous.

The Trunk Twister reaches and strengthens all muscles of the trunk. It has excellent postural benefits, and results in increased flexibility in the lower back region.

Trunk Twister

Starting Position: Stand with feet shoulder width apart and pointed forward. The hands are clasped behind the head, the elbows are held backward, and the chin is in.

Cadence: Slow

Movement: Bend downward, keeping the knees straight. Recover slightly. Bend downward again and simultaneously rotate the trunk to the left and then to the right (Figure 16.17). Return to original position, pulling the head back, with chin in.

Beginning Dosage: Eight sets

Bear Hug

Starting Position: Stand with feet comfortably spread and hands on hips.

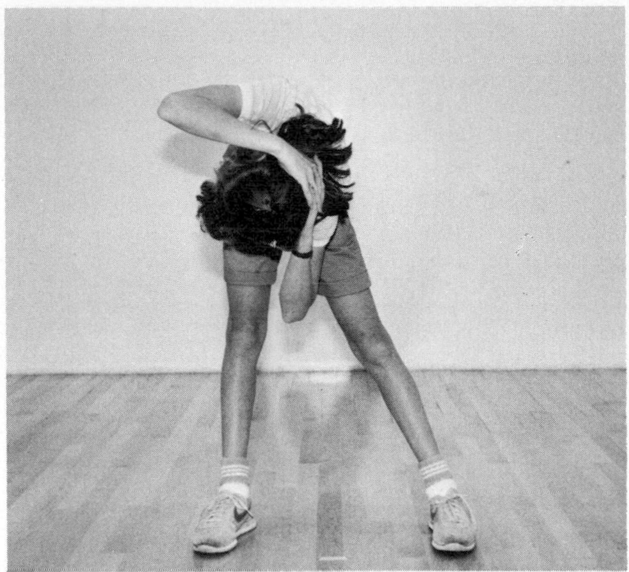

FIGURE 16.17. Trunk Twister

Cadence: Slow

Movement: Take a long step diagonally right, keeping the left foot anchored in place. Tackle the right leg around the thigh by encircling the thigh with both arms. Squeeze and stretch (Figure 16.18). Return to position. Tackle the left leg. Return to position.

Beginning Dosage: Eight sets, right and left legs combined

Stress Point: The value in flexibility comes from slow, controlled stretching.

Side Flex

Starting Position: Lie on one side with lower arm extended overhead. The head rests on the lower arm. The legs are extended fully, one on top of the other.

FIGURE 16.18. Bear Hug

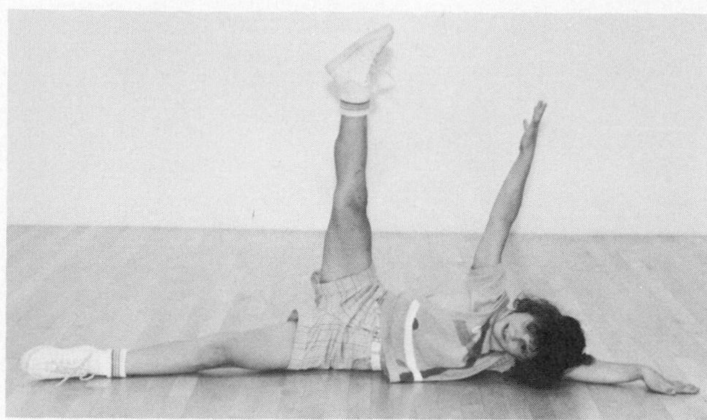

FIGURE 16.19. Side Flex

Cadence: Moderate

Movement: Raise the upper arm and leg diagonally (Figure 16.19). Repeat for several counts and change to the other side.

Beginning Dosage: Eight repetitions on each side

Variation: *Side Flex, Supported*—Similar to the regular Side Flex but more demanding. A side-leaning rest position is maintained throughout (Figure 16.20).

Body Circles

Starting Position: Stand with feet shoulder width apart, hands on hips, and body bent forward.

Cadence: Moderate

Movement: Make a complete circle with the upper body. A specified number of circles should be made to the right and the same number to the left.

Beginning Dosage: Five circles each way

Variations

1. Circle in one direction until told to stop, then reverse direction.

FIGURE 16.20. Side Flex, Supported

2. Change to a position in which the hands are clasped behind the neck and the elbows are kept wide. Otherwise, the exercise is the same. (This is more demanding than the regular Body Circles.)

Windmill

Starting Position: Stand with feet shoulder width apart and arms extended sideward with palms down.

Cadence: Moderate

Movement: Bend and twist at the trunk, bringing the right hand down to the left toe. Recover to starting position. Bend and twist again, but bring the left hand to the right toe. Recover to starting position.

Beginning Dosage: Twelve sets, right and left combined

Stress Point: The arms and legs should be kept straight throughout.

SPECIALIZED POSTURE CORRECTION EXERCISES

Exercises to correct posture problems should be done slowly and under control. Positions can be held, as in isometric exercise, thus helping to strengthen the designated muscle groups and to develop the feel of correct posture.

HEAD, SHOULDER, AND UPPER BACK DEVELOPMENT

Hook Lying

Starting Position: Lie on the back with feet flat on the floor, knees bent, arms out in wing position, and palms up.

Movement: Press the elbows and head against the floor, keeping the chin in. Hold for six to eight counts.

Beginning Dosage: Six to eight repetitions

Swan

Starting Position: Lie prone (facedown), the arms extended sideward with palms down.

Movement: Raise the upper back, head, and arms in an exaggerated swan dive position (Figure 16.21). The chin is kept in, and the movement is limited to the upper back. Hold for eight counts.

Beginning Dosage: Four repetitions

Tailor

Starting Position: Sit tailor fashion (cross-legged) with trunk erect, fingers locked on the back of the head, and elbows out (Figure 16.22).

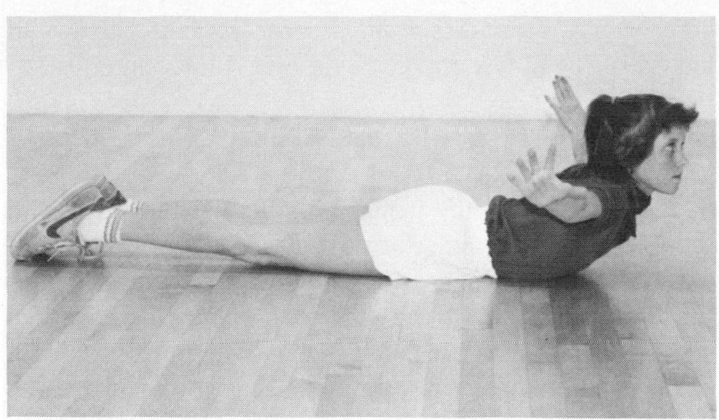

FIGURE 16.21. Swan

Movement: Force the head and elbows back slowly against pressure. Be sure that the erect body position does not change. Keep the abdominal wall flat.

Beginning Dosage: Ten repetitions

Wall Sit

Starting Position: Sit as in the Tailor but against a wall. The forearms rest naturally on the thighs.

Movement: Flatten the upper back and shoulders against the wall and put the chin down and in. Flatten the lower back, bringing it close to the wall by tensing the lower abdominal muscles and lifting up on the pelvis. Holding this fixed position, perform the following movements slowly and smoothly. First, raise the arms forward (pause) and overhead (pause); return. Then raise the arms forward (pause) and sideward to touch the wall; return. Finally, raise the arms sideward to horizontal (pause) and then diagonally upward; return. The palms are upward during the entire movement.

Beginning Dosage: Fifteen seconds

FIGURE 16.22. Tailor

ABDOMINAL MUSCLE DEVELOPMENT

Mad Cat

Starting Position: Get down on the hands and knees, with the back sagging somewhat.

Movement: Arch the back, rounding it as much as possible with a forcible contraction of the abdominal muscles (Figure 16.23). Hold for eight counts and return to position.

Beginning Dosage: Six repetitions

Pelvis Tilter

Starting Position: Lie on the back with feet flat on the floor, knees bent, arms out in wing position, and palms up.

Movement: Flatten the lower back, bringing it closer to the floor by tensing the lower abdominals and lifting up on the pelvis. Hold for eight counts. Tense slowly and release slowly.

Beginning Dosage: Five to seven repetitions

FOOT DEVELOPMENT

Floor Scratching (Sand Scraping)

Starting Position: Sit on a chair or stand with bare feet flat on the floor.

Movement: Using the toes, scratch the floor by bringing the toes toward you forcibly on the floor.

Beginning Dosage: Ten repetitions

Floor Creeping

Starting Position: Sit or stand with bare feet flat on the floor.

FIGURE 16.23. Mad Cat

Movement: Using the toes, pull the foot forward with the heels sliding. Change to the other foot.

Beginning Dosage: Ten repetitions of each foot

Marble Transfer

Starting Position: Sit on a chair or a bench. Have ready a marble (or a wadded piece of paper).

Movement: Pick up the marble with the right foot and bring it up to the left hand. Transfer the marble to the right hand and bring the left foot up to put the marble back on the ground.

Beginning Dosage: Eight repetitions

Knot Tying With Feet

Starting Position: Stand

Movement: Lay a jump rope on the floor. Tie a knot in the rope, using one foot only. Repeat with the other foot.

Beginning Dosage: Five repetitions, right and left

Foot Carry

Starting Position: Stand. Have a narrow piece of felt or a rope tied in a loop about 1 ft in diameter.

Movement: Grasp the loop with the toes of one foot and hop a short distance. Repeat, changing the loop to the other foot.

Beginning Dosage: Ten repetitions on each foot

PARTNER RESISTANCE EXERCISES

Partner resistance exercises are useful for building strength, but they produce little increase in cardiorespiratory endurance. Consequently, they should be regarded as an addition to the overall fitness program and not as a substitute for any other phase of the program. Partner resistance exercises are especially valuable when used in conjunction with activities that demand considerable endurance, such as Grass Drills, jogging, or Astronaut Drills.

Partner resistance exercises can strengthen specific muscle groups, and so have value in correcting posture and in helping the physically underdeveloped child. The exercises are simple and enjoyable; children can do them as homework. Children should be made aware of the muscle group developed by each exercise.

Partners should be somewhat matched in size and strength so they can challenge each other. The exercises are performed through the full range of motion at each joint and take 8 to 12 seconds to complete. The partner providing the resistance says, "Ready," and begins the slow count. Positions are then reversed.

In addition to the partner resistance exercises presented here, similar resistance exercises can be performed with individual tug-of-war ropes, as described in Chapter 18.

Arm Curl-up

Exerciser keeps the upper arms against the sides with the forearms and palms forward. Partner puts her fists in exerciser's palms (Figure 16.24). Exerciser attempts to curl the forearms upward to the shoulders. To develop the opposite set of muscles, partners reverse hand positions. Push down in the opposite direction, starting at shoulder level.

Forearm Flex

Exerciser extends the arms and places the hands, palms down, on partner's shoulders. Exerciser attempts to push partner into the floor. Partner may slowly lower himself to allow the exerciser movement through the range of motion. Try with the palms upward.

Fist Pull-Apart

Exerciser places the fists together in front of the body at shoulder level. Exerciser attempts to pull the hands apart while partner forces them together with pressure on the elbows. As a variation, with fists apart, the exerciser tries to push them together. Partner applies pressure by grasping the wrists and holding exerciser's fists apart.

Butterfly

Exerciser starts with arms straight and at the sides. Partner, from the back, attempts to hold the arms down while exerciser lifts with straight arms to the sides. Try

FIGURE 16.24. Arm Curl-up

with arms above the head (partner holding) to move them down to the sides.

Camelback

Exerciser is on all fours with head up. Partner sits lightly or pushes on exerciser's back, while exerciser attempts to hump the back like a camel.

Back Builder

Exerciser spreads the legs and bends forward at the waist with head up. Partner faces exerciser, and places clasped hands behind exerciser's neck. Exerciser attempts to stand upright while partner pulls downward (Figure 16.25).

Swan Diver

Exerciser lies in prone position with arms out to the sides and tries to arch the back, while partner applies pressure to the lower and upper back area.

Scissors

Exerciser lies on one side, while partner straddles exerciser and holds the upper leg down. Exerciser attempts to raise the top leg. Reverse sides and lift the other leg.

Bear Trap

Starting from a supine position on the floor, spread the legs and then attempt to move them together. Resistance is provided by partner who tries to keep the legs apart.

FIGURE 16.25. Back Builder

FIGURE 16.26. Knee Bender

Knee Bender

Exerciser lies in prone position with legs straight and arms pointing ahead on the floor. Partner places the hands on the back of exerciser's ankle. Exerciser attempts to flex the knee while partner applies pressure (Figure 16.26). Reverse legs. Try in the opposite direction, starting with the knee joint at a 90-degree angle.

Push-up With Resistance

Exerciser is in push-up position with arms bent, so the body is about halfway up from the floor. Partner straddles or stands alongside exerciser's head and puts pressure on the top of the shoulders by pushing down (Figure 16.27). The amount of pressure takes judgment by the partner. Too much causes the exerciser to collapse.

FIGURE 16.27. Push-up With Resistance

DEVELOPING PHYSICAL FITNESS ROUTINES

When planning fitness routines, the instructor should establish variety in activities and include a number of different approaches. This tends to minimize the inherent weaknesses of any single routine.

STUDENT LEADER EXERCISES

At times, selected students should lead either single exercises or an entire routine. Careful instruction is needed, and students should realize that prior practice is essential for them to lead their peers effectively in a stimulating exercise session. Probably the greatest difficulty is in maintaining a steady, even, and appropriate cadence. Starting and stopping the exercise are also sources of difficulty. The student leader should be given directions concerning the number of repetitions and should use a counting system that keeps track of progress. The teacher should ask for volunteers or make assignments, so students can practice ahead of time. No child should be forced to lead, because this can result in failure for both the child and the class.

A unique formation that requires four student leaders can be arranged in the following manner. A student leader stands on each of the four sides of the formation (Figure 16.28). The sequence of leaders is generally clockwise, but it could be otherwise. The first leader, after finishing an exercise, gives the command, "Right face!" The children are now facing the second leader, who repeats the process. Two more exercises and direction changes bring the children back to the original leader. This formation can be adjusted to employ two leaders positioned on opposite sides of the formation. The command after the exercise led by the first leader would be "About face!"

SQUAD LEADER EXERCISES

Squad organization is valuable for providing students with opportunities to lead exercises. Each leader takes her squad to a designated area and puts the squad through exercises. The procedure works best as a planned activity with prior announcement to the squad leader. Giving the squad leader a card specifying the sequence of exercises and the number of repetitions is helpful. The squad leader can assign various members of the squad to lead exercises.

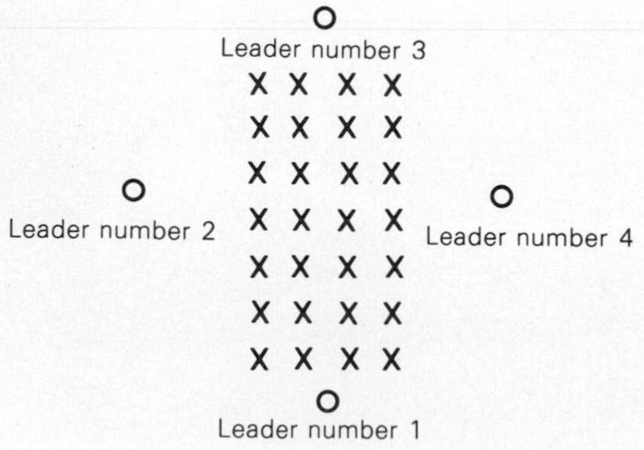

FIGURE 16.28. Four-leader formation

COMBINED EXERCISE ROUTINES

An interesting fitness activity can be fashioned by combining exercises in the following manner. Make it a rule that, after an exercise is given (in the normal way), the children immediately do a prescribed floor exercise, such as a Push-up or Curl-up. The teacher direction could be "We are going to do a series of exercises. Just as soon as you finish an exercise, you will immediately do five Push-ups without waiting for any direction from me." This system works better when the directed exercises are performed from a standing position, so either the Push-ups or the Curl-ups require a definite position change. After the children have completed the floor exercise, they stand immediately and await the next directed exercise from the teacher. Other combinations can be put together. For example, exercises can be alternated with running, jumping, or hopping in place.

EXERCISES TO MUSIC

Exercises to music add another dimension to developmental experiences. Many commercial record sets with exercise programs are available, but a most effective approach is to rely on the tape recorder. The teacher then has control over the selection, sequence, and number of repetitions, and the routine can be adapted to the particular needs and characteristics of the group. The usual starting and halting procedures are easily incorporated in taped sequences.

Appropriate music for taping can be found in basic movement record sets—polkas, waltzes, marches, jazz music, and other selections. Using a skilled pianist as an accompanist is also possible, a practice that is in vogue in some European countries.

A group of students can be assigned to make up an exercise routine to music and to put it on tape. This gives them some input into the program.

CIRCUIT TRAINING

In Circuit Training, each of several stations has a designated fitness task. The student moves from station to station, generally in a prescribed order, completing the designated fitness task at each station.

The exercise tasks constituting the circuit should contribute to the development of all parts of the body. In addition, activities should contribute to the various components of physical fitness (strength, power, endurance, agility, and flexibility).

Instructional Procedures

1. Each station provides an exercise task that the child can learn and perform without the aid of another child. As the child moves from one station to the next, the exercises that directly follow each other should make demands on different parts of the body. In this way, the performance at any one station does not cause local fatigue that could affect the ability to perform the next task.

2. Before the children begin the course, giving them sufficient instruction in the activities is important so they can perform correctly at each station. Youngsters should be taught how to count the number of repetitions when a system of counting is employed.

3. The class can be so distributed that some children are starting the circuit at each station. This method keeps the demands on equipment low. For example, if there are 30 children for a circuit of six stations, then 5 children start at each spot.

4. A tape recorder can be used effectively to give directions for the circuit. Music, whistle signals, and even verbal directions can be prerecorded. The tape provides a rigid time control and gives a measure of consistency to the circuit. Using tapes also frees the teacher for supervisory duties.

Timing and Dosage

In general, a fixed time limit at each station seems to be the best plan for Circuit Training at the elementary school level. Each child attempts to complete as many repetitions as possible during the time allotted at a station. The work load can be increased by increasing the amount of time at each station. A suggested progressive timetable is as follows.

Time Period	*Seconds at Each Station*
Introduction (first day)	15
First two weeks	20
Second two weeks	25
After four weeks	30

A 10-second interval should be established to allow children to move from one station to the next. Later, this can be lowered to 5 seconds. Students may start at any station, as designated, but they must follow the established station order.

A second method of timing is to sound only one signal for the change to the next station. According to this plan, the child ceases activity at one station, moves to the next, and *immediately* begins the task at that station without waiting for another signal.

Another means of increasing the activity demands of the circuit is to change the individual activities to more strenuous ones. For example, a station could specify Knee or Bench Push-ups and later change to regular Push-ups, a more demanding exercise. Another method of adding effort is to have each child run a lap around the circuit area between station changes.

The amount of activity can also be increased by dividing the class in halves. One half is on the circuit and the other is running lightly around the area. On signal to change, the runners go to the circuit, and the circuit players change to runners. Make a rule that runners change direction (clockwise and counterclockwise) on successive runs. Try to limit the number of stations to six.

One method of operating the circuit employs variable doses at each of the stations, depending on the child's abilities. The repetitions at each station are established by the following formula. Red represents a modest challenge; all children can do these. White represents a moderate challenge. Blue represents a considerable challenge. Under this system, the number of Push-ups might be 10 on the red circuit, 15 on the white, and 20 on the blue. Each child is assigned to complete the red, white, or blue circuit depending on his capacity and fitness level. Some experimentation will be needed to set repetition progressions at each of the stations.

Since children progress at an individual rate from station to station, the problem of sufficient equipment and space at each station is an important consideration. Placing signs at each station to designate the number of repetitions for each color is useful.

Indoor Circuits

The manner in which an indoor circuit is organized can vary. Equipment is a consideration, and we recommend that exercise tasks be selected from those requiring a minimum of equipment.

The number of stations can vary but probably should be no fewer than six and no more than nine. (Figures 16.29 and 16.30 show a six- and a nine-station course, respectively.) Signs at the different stations can include the name of the activity and any necessary cautions or stress points for execution. When children move between lines as limits (as in the Agility Run), traffic cones or beanbags can be used to mark the designated boundaries.

Suggested Activities

A circuit should always include activities for exercising the arm-shoulder girdle and for strengthening the abdominal wall. A variety of activities are suggested and classified in the following section. One activity can be selected from each classification.

General Body Activities

Rope jumping: Use single-time speed only.
Jumping Jack (p. 226)
Running in Place: Lift the knees.

Six-station course

1 Running in place	2 Curl-ups	3 Arm Circles
6 Crab Walk	5 Trunk Twister	4 Agility Run

Supplies and equipment: Mats for Curl-ups (to hook toes)
Time needed: 4 minutes—based on 30-second activity limit, 10 seconds to move between stations

FIGURE 16.29. Sample six-station circuit training course

Arm-Shoulder Girdle Exercises

Crab Walk (p. 224): Two parallel lines are drawn 6 to 8 ft apart. Start with hands on one line and feet pointing toward the other. Move back and forth between the lines in crab position, touching one line with the heels and the other with the hands.

Crab Kick (p. 223): Start in crab position and alternate with the right and the left foot kicking toward the ceiling.

Leg Exercises

Step-ups: One bench is needed for every three children at this station. Begin in front of the bench, stepping up on the bench with the left foot and then up with the right foot. Now step down in rhythm, left and then right. The next class period, begin with the right foot to secure comparable development. Be sure that the legs are fully extended and that the body is erect when on top of the bench.

Treadmill (pp. 226–227)

Straddle Bench Jumps: Straddle a bench and alternate jumping to the top of the bench and back to the floor. Since the degree of effort depends on the height of the bench, benches of various heights should be considered. These can be constructed in the form of small, elongated boxes 4 ft long and 10 in. wide with height ranging from 8 to 10 in. A 4-ft-long box accommodates two children at a time.

Agility Runs—Legs and Endurance

Agility Run—Touch With the Toes: Two lines are established 15 ft apart. Move between the two lines as rapidly as possible, touching one line with the right foot and the other with the left.

Agility Run—Touch With the Hand: Same as above, except touch the lines with alternate hands instead of with the feet.

Arm Circles—Arms and Shoulders

Standing Arm Circles (p. 223).

Lying Arm Circles: Lie prone, with arms out to the sides. Alternate forward and backward arm circling, chang-

Nine-station course

1 Rope jumping	2 Push-ups	3 Agility Run	4 Arm Circles
8 Windmill	7 Treadmill	6 Crab Walk	5 Rowing
9 Hula-Hooping (or any relaxing "fun" activity)			

Supplies and equipment: Jumping ropes, mats for knee Push-ups (if used), hoops (if used)
Time needed: 6 minutes—based on 30-second activity limit, 10 seconds to move between stations

FIGURE 16.30. Sample nine-station circuit training course

ing after five circles in each direction. The head and shoulders are lifted from the ground during the exercise.

Curl-ups (p. 225): Anchor the feet. Use a mat and hook the feet under the edge to provide the support that ordinarily is supplied by another person.

Alternate Toe Touching: Begin on the back with arms extended overhead. Alternate by touching the right toe with the left hand and vice versa. Bring the foot and the arm up at the same time and return to the flat position each time.

Flexibility and Back Exercises

Bend and Stretch (pp. 221–222)
Windmill (p. 228)
Trunk Twister (p. 227)

Potpourri

Other exercises, stunts, and movements can be used, some in combination. In leg exercises, for example, the task can be designated as 25 running steps in place and then 5 Pogo Stick jumps (p. 373) in place, with the whole task repeated. If the gymnasium is equipped with chinning bars, horizontal ladders, and climbing ropes, circuits can make use of these. Some activities—basketball dribbling, traveling over and under obstacles, tumbling stunts, and manipulative activities—can be included as station tasks to liven things up. Hula-hoop activities are attractive, and gym scooters add a different dimension to many routine movements.

Outdoor Circuits

An outdoor circuit around a 220-yd track or around a comparable area can combine running and station tasks. Fewer stations are needed than in indoor circuits because exercising of the legs is accomplished by the running.

Tasks are performed either for a specified time period or on a work load basis. Work load for each task can be established by counting the number of repetitions or sets that a child can do in a minute and then using half of that figure as the dosage.

When a time change is signaled or when the work load is accomplished, each participant runs one lap around the area counterclockwise past the station where she just performed and on to the next station. This is repeated until each station has been completed. Stations should be located inside the track so there is no interference with the runners. Laps are run briskly at good speed.

This type of circuit can be used with a jogging trail also, and is sometimes called a *parcourse.* At specified points, different tasks can be performed along the course.

CONTINUITY DRILLS

Continuity drills originated in Europe. Continuity exercises, done snappily and with vigor, are enjoyable experiences for youngsters.

Children are in extended squad formation or scattered. Each has a jump rope. They alternate between rope jumping and exercises. A specified time period governs the length of the rope-jumping episode, which should be done in fast time (single jumps). At the signal to stop rope jumping, children drop the ropes and immediately take position for the selected exercise. The exercises demand a down-body position and are in a two-count cadence. When children are positioned for the exercise, the leader says, "Ready!" All children do one repetition of the exercise, counting out loud the two-count cadence. For each repetition, they wait until the leader initiates the repetition with a "Ready," and each child then responds with the action and the cadence count "One, two."

The sequence of rope jumping and selected exercises can follow this pattern.

First signal: Begin rope jumping.

Second signal: Drop ropes and take push-up position. On each command of "Ready," do one Push-up to a two-count cadence. Repeat as needed.

Third signal: Resume rope jumping.

Fourth signal: Drop ropes and go to a supine position with arms overhead along the floor, preparatory to doing the Rowing exercise (p. 226). On the command "Ready," perform the exercise to the two-count cadence. Repeat as needed.

Fifth signal: Resume rope jumping.

Sixth signal: Drop ropes and take a crab position, preparatory to doing a Crab Full-Leg Extension (p. 224). On the signal "Ready," thrust both feet forward to an extended leg position with the weight momentarily on the heels, and then draw the legs back to the crab position in a fast two-count cadence. Repeat.

Seventh signal: Resume rope jumping.

Eighth signal: Go into a side-lying position on the left side for the Side Flex (pp. 227–228). On the "Ready," perform a Side Flex in a two-count cadence. After performing one repetition, roll immediately over to the other side. On the next command, perform a Side Flex on that side and then roll back to original position.

Ninth signal: Finish, or do one more session of rope jumping.

The number of repetitions should depend on the age and physical condition of the group. Some experimentation may be necessary to determine the length of the rope-jumping periods. As in Circuit Training, a tape recorder can signal changes of movement and supply appropriate music for rope jumping.

GRASS DRILLS

A grass drill, as an adaptation of a football drill, requires the performer to alternate from a standing position to a down position on the grass. The activities are strenuous and are performed in quick succession at top speed. Progress is gained by increasing the length of the work period. Alertness, quick reaction, and agility are needed in the drills. The drills are executed in place, so almost any formation is appropriate as long as there is sufficient space between performers.

Basic Grass Drills involve moving rapidly from one of three basic positions to another on the commands "Go," "Front," and "Back."

1. "Go" signals running in place at top speed on the toes, with knees raised high, arms pumping, and body bent forward slightly at the waist.

2. "Front" signals dropping to the ground in prone position, with hands underneath the body, ready to push off and change position. The head should point toward the center of the circle or toward the front of the room. The feet are extended back and kept together.

3. "Back" signals lying flat on the back, with arms alongside the body and palms down. The head-to-leg direction is opposite to that of the front position.

Basic Grass Drills can be operated in two ways. The choice occurs after the "Go" signal, which starts children running in place.

1. *Continuous motion.* In this method, when the command "Front" or "Back" is given, the child goes immediately to the appropriate position and comes back to the running position without a second command.

2. *Interrupted motion.* In this method, instead of coming automatically back to the running position, the child stays in the front or back position until a change is called.

A number of variations can be built on the basic Grass Drill by adding different positions to front and back, as for the Push-up, Crab, V-up (p. 394), Side-Leaning Rest, Reverse Push-up, Turtle (p. 383), and Seat Balance (full turn, right and left). Instead of running on "Go," Fast Stepping can be substituted. Isometrics can be done while running.

ASTRONAUT DRILLS

In Astronaut Drills, children are spaced about 6 ft apart and are told to walk in a circular pattern or along the gymnasium perimeter. A succession of locomotor movement directives is then given, interspersed with commands to walk; or the circle can be stopped, and the children can perform certain movements in place. They then resume walking. The following movements and tasks can be incorporated in the routine. The teacher can be creative.

1. Various locomotor movements, such as hopping, jumping, running, sliding, skipping, giant steps, and walking high on the toes.

2. Movement on all fours—forward, backward, or sideward—with respect to the direction of walking. Repeat backward and forward using the Crab Walk.

3. Stunt movements, such as the Seal Walk, Gorilla Walk, and Bunny Jump.

4. Upper torso movements and exercises that can be done while walking, such as Arm Circles, bending right and left, and body twists.

5. Various exercises in place, always including an abdominal development activity.

Astronaut Drills can be adapted successfully to any level, kindergarten through 6th grade. Careful selection of movements is the key. While the emphasis is on physical development, educational implications must not be overlooked. Correct and coach form as the situation dictates. Children who lag can be moved toward the inner part of the circle; allow more active children to pass them on the outside.

The children's enjoyment comes from being challenged by a variety of movements. The teacher should note the possibilities on a card or even have a full plan similar to the one following.

1. Walk.

2. On all fours, move.

3. Walk again.

4. High on the toes, walk. Reach the arms high while walking on the toes.

5. Feet first, Crab-Walk.

6. Walk. Arms out to the side, circle forward and backward. (Chest up, tummy flat.)

7. Stop, face center. Do some kind of push-up activity.

8. Walk. Reach out with the hands and slap the thighs with the hands while walking.

9. Stop, face center. Do as many Curl-ups as you can in 10 seconds.

10. Hop. Change to the other foot.

11. Stop, face center. Rock on the tummy.

12. Jump, pogo-stick style (with stiff knees).

13. Run, with knees high.

14. Walk, with giant steps.

15. Stop, face center. Do Windmills for 10 seconds.

16. Trot, run.

CHALLENGE COURSES

The Challenge Course is becoming increasingly popular as a tool for fitness development in the elementary schools. Challenge Courses can be divided roughly into two types—the outdoor (generally permanent) and the indoor (portable).

The courses can be run against a time standard or done for the exercise value. A course should be designed to exercise all parts of the body through a variety of activities. By including running, vaulting, agility tasks, climbing, hanging, crawling, and other activities, the teacher can ensure good fitness demands. Equipment such as mats, parallel bars, horizontal ladders, high-jump standards, benches, and vaulting boxes can be used to make effective Challenge Courses. A variety of courses can be designed, depending on the length of the course and the tasks included. Indoors, space is an important factor. Some schools fortunate enough to have a suitable wooded area on the school grounds have established permanent courses.

A sample indoor course, including a climbing rope, is illustrated in Figure 16.31. The total equipment list for this course is as follows.

Three benches (16 to 18 in. high)
Four tumbling mats (4 by 8 ft)
Four hoops or tires
One pair of high-jump standards with crossbar
One climbing rope
One 36-in. vaulting box or wooden horse
Five chairs

LEG AND AGILITY ROUTINES

Several movement routines can provide challenges for the legs and increase agility. The routines are probably best suited to the outdoors, but they can be adapted to the gymnasium.

Walk, Trot, and Sprint

Four cones can outline a square or rectangular area 30 to 40 yd on a side. (Indoors, the circumference of the gymnasium is used.) Children are scattered around the perimeter, all facing in the same direction. The signals are given with a whistle. On the first whistle, children begin to walk. On the next whistle, they change to a trot. On the third whistle, they run as rapidly as they can. Finally, on the fourth whistle, they walk again. The cycle is repeated as many times as the capacity of the children indicates. Faster-moving youngsters should pass on the outside of the area.

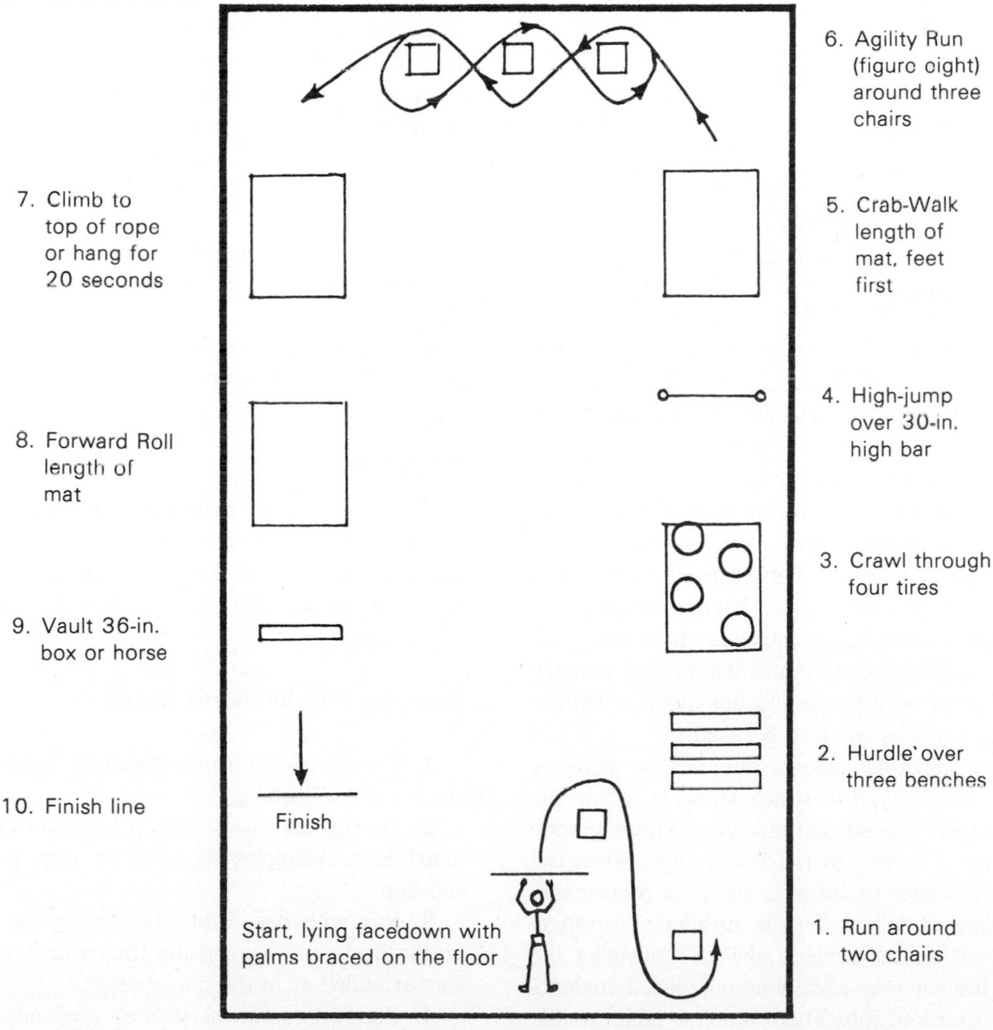

FIGURE 16.31. Indoor Challenge Course

Timed Activities

Children can be stimulated to good effort if they know that they are being timed and are competing against other children. Timing can be done for 30, 45, or 60 seconds or for some other interval. The following should be considered as timed activities.

1. *Rope jumping for time.* The object is to turn the rope as fast as possible during the time limit. The number of successful jumps is counted.

2. *Agility run between lines.* Two lines are selected at any convenient distance between 10 and 20 ft, so all children are challenged with the same distance. The child runs between the lines, touching each one alternately with a hand. The number of circuits is counted.

Additional Routines

European Rhythmic Running (pp. 207–208) is excellent, or children can run laps. Rope jumping can be used with or without musical accompaniment. The basketball group defensive drill (p. 488) should be used at times. Marking (p. 211) should also be considered.

MOVEMENT EXPERIENCES

Movement experiences, previously described in the program for younger children (Chapter 8), can be adapted effectively for older youngsters, These activities are a welcome change of pace from other routines.

AEROBIC DANCING

Aerobic dancing is one of the most popular fitness activities for people of all ages. It develops cardiorespiratory fitness as well as strength and flexibility. Bright and snappy music increases effort, duration, and intensity, while reducing the boredom associated with some fitness tasks.

Aerobic dancing is a mixture of Rhythmic Running, various fundamental movements, dance steps, swinging movements, and stretching challenges. Dances are choreographed for particular pieces of music, which have a definite, pronounced beat and a swinging, stimulating character. Rock and roll, disco, ballroom dance, folk dance, and country swing music all serve well for developing routines. (Music for rope-jumping routines can also be used.)

Aerobic dance generally follows one of two patterns. The first is the leader type in which students follow the actions of the leader. The second involves a choreography based on a piece of music. In the leader type, when the music begins, the leader performs a series of movements and the other dancers follow. This is an informal arrangement that depends on the leader's skill in motivating the followers. The teacher may lead, although skilled students can also do an excellent job. There are few limits to the range of activities a leader can present. Those activities involving a position on the floor do often present sight-line problems. The leader may integrate manipulative equipment (i.e., balls, jump ropes, hoops, wands) with the movement activities.

The second method is the scheduled routine. For elementary school children, routines should be kept uncomplicated. When the music has run through a repetition or phrase, the movement patterns can change. Children can design routines to the music of their choice. For most routines, music should have a tempo of 120 to 140 beats per minute.

Instructional Procedures

1. Use movement increments that are organized by units of 4, 8, or 16 counts. When phrases in the music are repeated, it is often desirable to repeat the previous dance step.

2. Vary the movements. Places where the activity slows down and eases should be alternated with strenuous movements.

3. Dance steps should be relatively simple. Students are working on increasing their fitness levels rather than on becoming competent dancers. Stress continuous movement (moving with the flow) rather than perfection of routines. Running and bouncing steps that children can follow easily are effective and motivating.

4. Routines motivate more children when they do not appear to be a dance. Being able to finish the routine should be a challenge. Both boys and girls should feel comfortable with the activity.

5. Establish cue words to aid youngsters in following routines. Examples are "Bounce," "Step," "Reach," and "Jump."

6. Energetic and positive teachers have a significant impact on class enthusiasm.

Basic Steps

The following are basic steps and movements that can be used to develop a wide variety of routines. The majority are performed to four counts, although this can be varied, depending on the skill of the participants and the goals of the teacher.

Running and Walking Steps

1. Do directional runs—forward, backward, diagonal, sideways, and turning.

2. Do rhythmic runs, with a specific movement on the fourth beat. Examples are knee lift, clap, jump, jump-turn, and hop.

3. Run with flair. Run while lifting the knees, kicking up the heels, or slapping the thighs or heels, or run with legs extended as in the goose step.

4. Run with arms in various positions—on the hips, in the air above the head, and straight down.

Movements on the Floor

1. *Sit-ups.* Modify these in various ways, for example, by using four counts: up to knees (count 1), touch the floor (count 2), back to knees (count 3), and return to the floor (count 4). V-ups can be held for two counts and rested for two counts.

2. *Side Leg Raises.* Do these with a straight leg while lying on the side of the body.

3. *Alternate Leg Raises.* While on the back, raise one leg to meet the opposite hand. Repeat, using the opposite leg or both legs.

4. *Rhythmic Push-ups.* Do these in two- or four-count movements. A four count would be as follows: halfway down (count 1), nose touched to the floor (count 2), halfway up (count 3), and arms fully extended (count 4).

5. *Crab Kicks and Treadmills.* Do these to four counts.

Upright Rhythmic Movements

1. *Lunge variations.* Perform a lunge, stepping forward on the right foot while bending at the knee, and extending the arms forward and diagonally upward (counts 1 and 2). Return to starting position by bringing the right foot back and pulling the arms into a jogging position (counts 3 and 4). The lunge can be varied by changing the direction of the move and the depth and speed of the lunge.

2. *Side Bends.* Begin with the feet apart. Reach overhead while bending to the side. This movement is usually done to four beats: bend (count 1), hold (counts 2 and 3), and return (count 4).

3. *Reaches.* Reach upward alternately with the right and left arms. Reaches can be done sideways also and are usually two-count movements. Fast alternating one-count movements can be done, too.

4. *Arm and Shoulder Circles.* Make Arm Circles with either one or both arms. Vary the size and speed of the circles. Shoulder shrugs can be done in a similar fashion.

Jumping Jack Variations

1. Jump with arms alternately extended upward and then pulled in toward the chest.

2. Do Side Jumping Jacks with regular arm action while the feet jump from side to side or forward and backward together.

3. Do variations with the feet—forward stride alternating, forward and side stride alternating, kicks or knee lifts added, feet crossed, or heel-toe movements (turning on every fourth or eighth count).

Bounce Steps

1. *Bounce and clap.* This is similar to a slow-time jump-rope step. Clap on every other bounce.

2. *Bounce, turn, and clap.* Turn a quarter or half turn with each jump.

3. *Three bounces and clap.* Bounce three times and bounce and clap on the fourth beat. Turns can be performed.

4. *Bounce and rock side-to-side.* Transfer the weight from side to side, or forward and backward. Add clapping or arm swinging.

5. *Bounce with body twist.* Hold the arms at shoulder level and twist the lower body back and forth on each bounce.

6. *Bounce with floor patterns.* Bounce and make different floor patterns such as a box, diagonal, or triangle.

7. *Bounce with kick variations.* Perform different kicks such as knee lift, kick, knee lift and kick; double kicks; knee lift and slap knees; and kick and clap under knees. Combine the kicks with two- or four-count turns.

Activities With Manipulative Equipment

1. Use a jump rope. Perform basic steps such as forward and backward, and slow and fast time. Jump on one foot, cross the arms, and while jogging, swing the rope from side to side with the handles in one hand.

2. Use beanbags. Toss and catch while performing various locomotor movements. Use different tosses for a challenge.

3. Use a hula hoop. Rhythmically swing the hoop around different body parts. Perform different locomotor movements around and over hoops.

4. Try movements with balls. Bounce, toss, and dribble, and add locomotor movements while performing tasks.

Sample Routine

1. March in place, circling the arms in large circles (16 counts).

2. Take side-lunge position, hold, and circle the right arm (8 counts). Reverse, circling with the left arm (8 counts).

3. Bounce forward twice, slapping the thighs. Bounce backward twice, thrusting the arms in the air. Repeat four times (16 counts).

4. Bounce and do a clap turn. Turn a quarter turn on every second bounce. Repeat four times clockwise (8 counts) and four times counterclockwise (8 counts).

5. Repeat numbers 3 and 4 above.

6. Do a grapevine step to the right with a clap and hop on the fourth beat. Repeat to the left. Repeat the sequence four times (32 counts).

7. Do a Jumping Jack variation, extending the arms up and out. Repeat four times (32 counts).

8. Bounce and twist (16 counts), with arms in thrust position.

9. Do eight Side Jumping Jacks in a two-count movement (16 counts).

10. Bounce, bounce, bounce, and clap in a four-count movement. Repeat four times (16 counts). Turn right and left on each bounce (i.e., right, front, left, front).

11. Do Goose Step Running forward, with a clap on the fourth beat (16 counts). Move backward in the same way. Repeat.

12. Repeat bounce and twist routine (16 counts). Arms are in thrust position.

13. Do Rhythmic Running with a clap on every fourth beat (16 counts).

JUMP UP AND APPLAUD FOR THE PERFORMANCE!

JOGGING

Jogging, a good fitness activity for any age, can lead to regular activity habits and to a personal jogging program. *Jogging* is defined as easy, relaxed running at a pace that a person can maintain for long distances without undue fatigue or strain. It is the first level of locomotion above walking.

The school should provide instruction in jogging techniques and in planning a personal progressive jogging program. Instruction can be offered during physical education time, but the activity itself should be done primarily during recess, at the noon hour, after school, or during other free times.

Jogging is unique in that it takes no special equipment, can be done almost anywhere, is an individual activity, consumes relatively little time, and is not geared to any particular time of day. For most people, it is an exercise in personal discipline, which can enhance the self-image and raise the confidence level.

Types of Jogging Programs

Three types of jogging programs can be considered. The first is the jog-walk-jog method, which is generally employed in introductory jogging programs. One way to apply this system is to have the child cover a selected distance by a combination of jogging and walking. The child jogs until she feels the need to walk, and walks until she feels like jogging again. Progression is realized by having the child gradually eliminate as much of the walking as possible while maintaining the selected distance.

Another way to use the jog-walk-jog method is to divide the selected distance into specified increments of jogging and walking. For example, the jogger, to cover a quarter mile, could jog 110 yd, walk 55 yd, jog 110 yd, walk 55 yd, and jog the remaining 110 yd.

A second method is to jog for the entire set distance; the jogger increases or decreases the pace in response to the body's reaction to the exercise. Better endurance is needed for this procedure than for the jog-walk-jog method.

A third method maintains the pace but builds in progressions by gradually increasing the distance. Combinations of the three methods are also possible.

Instructional Procedures

1. Authorities generally recommend that jogging be done on alternate days, to allow for recovery from the effects of the day's workout. Some joggers, however, like to run every day, alternating between heavy and light workouts.

2. The teacher should not be concerned about foot action, since the child selects naturally the means that is most comfortable. Arm movement should be easy and natural, with elbows bent. The head and upper body should be held up and back. The eyes look ahead. The general body position in jogging should be erect but relaxed. Jogging on the toes should be avoided.

3. Beginning distances for elementary school children should offer challenge, but not to the point of causing distress or undue fatigue. A suggested beginning distance is 440 yd, with the stipulation that the child adjust this distance to his individual requirements. Children should increase the distance gradually until they are running a mile or more.

4. Jogging should not be a competitive, timed activity. Each child jogs at her own pace. Racing belongs in the track program. A good technique for encouraging youngsters to run at a comfortable pace is to have them select a partner of equal ability with whom to jog. If they cannot visit with each other while jogging, they are probably running too fast. The teacher should not give excessive praise to the first youngsters to finish their jogging, because this encourages the children to race rather than jog, and the students without speed would seldom receive praise under such a system. Another reason to avoid speed is that racing keeps youngsters from learning to pace themselves. For developing endurance, it is more important to run for a longer time at a slower speed than to run at top speed for a shorter distance.

Random Running

In schools in which physical education classes meet only two or three days a week, classroom teachers can use the Random Running Program (RRP) to help children develop an effective conditioning program. In this program, the classroom teacher sends youngsters outside to run randomly in any direction at their own speed. The only teacher responsibility is to clock the children for the specified time and to encourage the youngsters to keep running. The timetable in Figure 16.32 offers a good starting point for the intermediate grades. For primary-age children, the time element should be halved.

For indoor jogging, the teacher can determine how many laps of the gymnasium equal one quarter mile. A system to equalize the effect of direction is to jog counterclockwise on odd-numbered days and clockwise on even-numbered days. Jogging, however, is better as an outdoor activity.

Jogging is a relatively safe physical education activity.

Week	Time (in Minutes)
1	3
2	3.5
3	4
4	5
5	5.5
6	6
7	6.5
8	7
9	7.5
10	8
11	9
12	10

FIGURE 16.32. Running timetable

The chance of injury or physiological damage occurring is minimal, because the child's inborn "governor" stops him before any damage can occur. Nevertheless, two cautions must be observed. First, children with certain types of handicaps, such as cardiac abnormalities, asthma, and diabetes, should jog within stipulated medical limitations. Second, progression in jogging programs should be *slow*. The development of endurance for jogging is the result of a deep, systemic capacity, which changes slowly in response to the body's demands.

Motivational Techniques

A number of devices can be used to stimulate jogging. The teacher can keep record sheets of the total distance jogged by each individual. Each student reports jogging progress to the teacher. The individual mileage sheet could have a total of 100 miles recorded in quarter-mile increments. Certificates of commendation might be given for totals of 50 or 100 miles of jogging.

Another motivator is the cross-country contest, during which one class may challenge others to jog a set distance between their hometown and another city. The first class to run the total mileage is the winner. A United States map on which the children record their class progress helps to keep the contest alive. Each runner contributes his distance to the class total.

The song "California Here I Come" can provide the basis for a jogging song, with children making up verses. Student artwork and posters illustrating catchy phrases such as "Jog a bit and keep fit," "Get the beat—use your feet," and "Jogging is tops" can stimulate interest in the activity. The use of manipulative equipment during jogging is sometimes a good technique for keeping youngsters moving. Examples include playing catch with a football or Frisbee while running, kicking a soccer ball while running, or running with a jump rope.

TESTING FOR PHYSICAL FITNESS

A testing program is essential to the fitness program. Testing should uncover low-fitness students, measure the status of the rest of the students, determine areas needing improvement, create motivation for the students, and provide material for public relations. Certainly much of the effectiveness of the physical education program can be measured with respect to how well it meets the challenge of fitness. At a minimum, testing should take place at the beginning and end of the school year. Another test could be administered in the middle of the year to check progress at the halfway point. The progress of low-fitness children could be checked more often. Tests and testing procedures for physical fitness can be found in Chapter 14.

After the underachiever in physical fitness has been identified, a remedial program should be instituted. These programs, together with measures to help overweight children, are described in Chapter 12.

THE EXTENDED FITNESS PROGRAM

The school physical education program cannot provide all of the necessary physical activity for proper development. However, it must provide a good beginning and the motivation to improve fitness. The school can extend program experiences into other areas.

The school playground should provide suitable play space and be equipped with appropriate apparatus, so it can function as a laboratory for the learning experiences of the physical education program. Climbing structures, monkey rings, horizontal ladders, and exercise bars are examples of the kinds of playground equipment that have good fitness development potential.

A Challenge Course can be a part of the school's outdoor opportunities. Challenge Courses can be set up compactly or arranged on an extended layout. Many schools have also laid out jogging courses on the school grounds.

An intramural program that grows out of the experiences of the physical education activities should be operated for both boys and girls. Saturday morning recreational programs also can extend the opportunities. A sound interschool competitive program is a further extension, mostly for the benefit of the more skilled. Special clubs, such as sport groups, tumbling clubs, and dance clubs, provide outlets for specific interests.

Municipal recreation programs, particularly during the summer vacation months, can take up some of the slack when schools are not in session. Recreational groups can also cooperate with the school in operating the school facilities during Christmas and spring vacation.

MOTIVATING CHILDREN TO MAINTAIN PHYSICAL FITNESS

The physical education program can provide strong motivation, which is important if the child is to be stimulated to good effort in achieving and maintaining fitness. Some considerations for motivation follow.

1. The school can adopt the award system promoted nationally by the President's Council on Physical Fitness and Sports, which recognizes commendable levels of physical fitness as measured by the AAHPERD Youth Fitness Test (1976) of the council. However, the school system may wish to base its award system on the more meaningful AAHPERD Health Related Physical Fitness Test (1980). Awards such as iron-on patches and certificates are available for high achievers. See Chapter 14 for more information on the AAHPERD test.

2. A second type of award is for commendable progress. This type of award serves to reward low achievers in physical development who are working hard to achieve satisfactory levels. The system also enables the school to recognize significant achievement that is nevertheless short of the higher standards set for awards like those of the President's Council.

3. The bulletin boards in the gymnasium and in the classrooms can be used to publicize items of interest about fitness. The material should be kept up-to-date.

4. Although it is misguided to believe that everyone can achieve above the average, the publication of school norms and records gives students a goal.

5. The use of visual aids should be exploited. A number of good films dealing with fitness are available. Write to the President's Council on Physical Fitness and Sports, Washington, D.C. 20201.

6. An excellent motivation for fitness is for each child to understand the values of physical fitness and the physiology of its development and maintenance.

7. An understanding of the muscle groups and of bone functions adds interest to the fitness process.

8. Cooperation at home is essential. Children are more likely to be fit when their parents are concerned about fitness.

9. Physical education exhibitions and school demonstrations for parents can feature the topic of fitness.

10. The child's current level of fitness should be an item on the periodic school report to parents.

11. Some caution is urged in the use of contests between classes or between schools based on fitness statistics. This can place undue pressure on low-fitness children and lead to undesirable peer relationships.

REFERENCES

AAHPERD. 1980. Lifetime health related physical fitness test manual. Reston, Va.: AAHPERD.

AAHPERD. 1976. Youth fitness test manual. Reston, Va.: AAHPERD.

Miller, D. K., and Allen, T. K. 1982. *Fitness: A lifetime commitment.* Ed. 2. Minneapolis: Burgess Publishing.

CHAPTER 17

Rhythmic Movement

Rhythm is the basis of music and dance. Rhythm in dance is simply expressive movement made with or without music. All body movements tend to be rhythmic—the beating of the heart, swinging a tennis racquet, wielding a hammer, or throwing a ball. Most movements that take place in physical education class contain elements of rhythm. This chapter deals with dance forms, movements performed in time to musical accompaniment, or movements based on a specific theme as in creative rhythm activities.

The movement potential of children can be stimulated with music and other rhythmic forms, adding much to the physical education program. Rhythm can arouse in the child a higher intensity of movement, longer participation and interest, and increased enjoyment. All children derive pleasure from moving to rhythm.

Movement to rhythm should begin early in the child's school career and continue throughout. Rhythmic activities are particularly appropriate for younger children. A sizable portion of the kindergarten through 2nd grade program should be devoted to such activities. One of the problems in incorporating rhythmic activities in the program is the vast amount of material available, which requires judicious selection to present a broad, progressive program. Another problem is that many teachers are hesitant about the subject area. If teachers prepare properly, they will be more comfortable with rhythms and will find that these activities are a favorite of children.

Early experiences should center on functional and creative movement forms. The program must go beyond being a collection of movement songs and folk dances, and it must be more than the teacher playing records for the children. Effective planning is necessary to gear the program to meet children's rhythmic needs.

To develop the child's rhythmic potential, a focus on considered listening, as opposed to random hearing, is important. The characteristics of the rhythmic background must be perceived by the child if they are to be translated into relevant movement. Understanding and perception of the structure and meaning of rhythm evolve gradually as the child moves to meter, accents, intensity, mood, and phrases. The ability to start and stop as the rhythm dictates is a prerequisite for efficient rhythmic movement. Children must move in time and under control if the movement is to be classified as rhythmic.

Some social values can be stressed through boy-girl relationships in the elementary grades, although many of the rhythmic activities currently labeled as boy-girl partner dances can also be conducted without regard to sex typing. Nevertheless, social graces and common courtesy are important goals in the rhythmic program and should be taught in a sensitive manner. In the intermediate grades, there should be opportunity for individual dances, particularly of the modern type.

Fundamental skills (pp. 99–110) are inherently rhythmic in execution, and the addition of rhythm can enhance development of these skills. An important component of children's dance is, therefore, fundamental rhythms. Instruction should begin with and capitalize on locomotor skills that the children already possess—walking, running, hopping, and jumping.

When performing rhythmic activities, children should move with good posture, keeping aimless and excessive movements of body parts to a minimum. Opportunity is present for both incidental and direct instruction in moving gracefully.

Rhythmic activities also provide a vehicle for expressive

movement. These activities offer opportunity for broad participation and personal satisfaction for all, since children personalize their responses within the framework of the idea. The youngsters should have a chance to create unique rhythmic responses within action songs and dances.

The vigorous nature of many rhythmic activities fulfills the criterion of developmental movement, particularly in gross motor activities for primary-level children. Rope skipping to music (pp. 330–331) and aerobic dance (pp. 238–240) are emphasized in the intermediate program. Exercise to music is another interesting fitness activity that uses rhythm.

SOURCES OF RHYTHMIC ACCOMPANIMENT

Essential to any rhythmic program is rhythm that draws from the children the desired motor patterns and expressive movement. If children are to move to a rhythm, it must be stimulating, appropriate for the expected responses, and appealing to the learners.

DANCE DRUM AND TOM-TOM

Skillful use of a drum or tom-tom adds much to rhythmic experiences. The teacher can interject drumbeats into many movement patterns. A major use of the drumbeat is to guide the movement from one pattern to another by signaling tiny increments of change with light beats that control the flow.

Some practice is necessary to learn how to beat a drum efficiently. The motion in striking is essentially a wrist action, not an arm movement. If the instructor has problems keeping time, she can cue on a competent performer to find the correct rhythm. Instead of a drum, some teachers have success with a small, resonant, wooden tube struck with a hard striker. It provides a definite, piercing beat. Two bamboo sticks, each about 12 in. long, are also a reasonable substitute for a drum.

RECORD PLAYER

Probably the most common source of accompaniment is the record player. The record player can be started and stopped efficiently and makes locating the beginning of each piece easy. An appropriate record player for physical education meets the following criteria:

1. Provides enough volume to be heard throughout the gymnasium

2. Possess variable speeds: 33, 45, and 78 RPM

3. Has a speed control, enabling the record to be played either faster or slower than originally recorded without distortion, a major help when teaching a dance.

On gymnasium floors, protection against needle bounce is needed. Some kind of permanent installation for both the record player and the storage of records should be considered, particularly in new construction or renovation. Overhead speakers provide better sound. At the very least, a record player should be assigned to the gymnasium. The rhythmic program is hindered markedly if the teacher has to check out a record player from the library whenever one is needed.

Each school and teacher should build a collection of records. Good record sets created especially for physical education movement patterns and dance are available from a number of sources. Physical education records should be stored in the physical education facility, rather than in the school library. Storage should be so arranged that each record has its assigned place and is readily available. Keeping extra copies of the more frequently used records in reserve is an excellent practice, especially in centralized equipment distribution centers for larger school systems. Student operators of the record player need proper instruction so record damage is minimized.

PIANO

The piano provides excellent accompaniment when the player has a suitable skill level. It has one drawback: the teacher who plays and must read music is not able to observe the children, let alone help the children with their movement patterns.

TAPE RECORDER

The tape recorder offers possibilities for rhythmic accompaniment not found in other sources. It provides a way for children to create and record their own accompaniment. Voice directions can be superimposed over music; this is useful for establishing an exercise sequence. Tape recorders are especially valuable in providing background for creative rhythms for which changes of music are desirable.

When using a tape recorder for square dancing or folk dancing, select a recorder that has a counter. The tape should be labeled as to where each song can be found, otherwise valuable class time is wasted looking for the starting point for each piece on the tape. The one drawback is that the tape recorder cannot vary tempo.

OTHER SOURCES OF RHYTHM

Some other sources of rhythmic accompaniment merit consideration. In action songs, the children can learn the music and the words and so provide their own accompaniment.

The tambourine can play a useful role in the rhythmic program, and rhythm bands can give direction. Primary-level classrooms usually have instruments available for the rhythm band. Guitar music provides good background rhythm and still allows the teacher, if he is the guitarist, to observe the activity of students.

CHARACTERISTICS OF RHYTHMIC BACKGROUND

Music has essential characteristics that children should recognize, understand, and appreciate. These characteristics are also present to varying degrees in other purely percussive accompaniment.

Tempo is the speed of the music. It can be constant or show a gradual increase (acceleration) or decrease (deceleration).

Beat is the underlying rhythm of the music. Some musicians refer to the beat as the pulse of the music. The beat can be even or uneven. Music with a pronounced beat is easier to follow.

Meter refers to the manner in which the beats are put together to form a measure of music. Common meters used in rhythmics are 2/4, 3/4, 4/4, and 6/8.

Certain notes or beats in a rhythmic pattern receive more force than others, and this defines *accent.* Usually, accent is applied to the first beat of a measure and generally is expressed by a more forceful movement in a sequence of movements.

The *intensity* of music can be loud, soft, light, or heavy. *Mood* is related to intensity but carries the concept deeper into human feelings. Music can interpret many moods—happiness, sadness, gaiety, fear, stateliness, and so on.

A *phrase* is a natural grouping of measures. In most cases, a phrase consists of eight underlying beats. Phrases of music are put together into rhythmic *patterns.* Children should learn to recognize when the pattern repeats or changes.

THE RHYTHMIC MOVEMENT PROGRAM

ACTIVITIES

Rhythmic activities should be scheduled in the same manner as other phases of the program and not regarded as fillers, rainy-day programs, or recreational outlets. The rhythmic program should be balanced and include activities from each of the categories of rhythmic movement. Table 17.1 shows recommended types of rhythmic activities for each grade level.

SKILL PROGRESSIONS

Another factor in program construction is the progression of basic and specific dance steps. Dances employing the following skills and steps appear in each of the respective grade-level programs.

TABLE 17.1. **TYPES OF RHYTHMIC ACTIVITY**

	Grade Level						
Activity	K	1	2	3	4	5	6
Fundamental rhythms	X	X	X	X	S	S	S
Creative rhythms	X	X	X	X			
Singing movement songs	X	X	X				
Folk dances	S	S	X	X	X	X	X
Mixers				S	X	X	X
Aerobic dancing				S	X	X	X
Square dancing						S	X
Rope jumping to music			S	S	X	X	X
Musical games			S	S	S	S	S
Rhythmic gymnastics					S	S	S

NOTE: X means that the activity is an integral part of the program. S means that the activity is given only minor emphasis.

Kindergarten—fundamental locomotor movements. (Skipping and sliding are taught and practiced, but students are not expected to master them.)

First grade—fundamental locomotor movements.

Second grade—fundamental locomotor movements, usually consisting of combinations of two or more skills; the Bleking step.

Third grade—fundamental locomotor movements, more combinations of locomotor skills, the step-hop, and the grand right and left.

Fourth grade—advanced combinations of locomotor skills, marching, basic Tinikling steps, and introductory square dancing steps.

Fifth grade—the grapevine step, schottische, polka, intermediate Tinikling steps, and square dancing.

Sixth grade—the two-step, advanced Tinikling step, square dancing, and an understanding of all steps introduced at earlier grade levels.

INSTRUCTIONAL PROCEDURES

1. Establishing the correct tempo is important in most rhythmic activities—fundamental and creative rhythms, folk dance, and so on. The tempo should take into account the stage of learning. During beginning instruction, the tempo should probably be slowed somewhat, but not to such an extent that it distorts the movement pattern. The tempo can then be increased gradually to the normal speed. If a teacher has trouble determining the correct tempo, she should focus on a child with good rhythmic movement and pace the beat to that child's movements.

2. When the class is practicing patterns without music prior to performing with recorded music, students should practice without music until they can perform the pattern at the tempo of the record. Learning a movement pattern at one tempo and then trying to perform at another adds an unnecessary challenge.

3. Teachers should have definite starting and stopping signals for dancers, such as "Ready and begin," or "Ready—now," and "Stop." The signal for dancers to begin should be given on the musical phrase just before the start of a full pattern. On a phrase of eight beats, starting signals can be given on the fifth and seventh beats of the phrase.

4. During the initial presentation of a rhythm, children should be familiarized with what is to follow. The teacher should analyze the music for the children, stating its mood, tempo, accents, phrases, and meter.

5. Active listening, as differentiated from simple hearing, is vital. When children listen for phrasing, they become aware of the changes in and effects of the music. Sometimes active listening can be done early in the rhythmic activity. Especially when teaching folk dance, it is important.

6. To gain a sense of rhythm, children can follow the beat with hand or foot sounds. The hands can be clapped together or slapped lightly on parts of the body. The toes can be tapped against the floor, the heels pounded lightly on the floor, the soles or the sides of the feet brought together, or the whole foot can be stamped. Partners can help emphasize the beat. One partner claps the first four beats of a phrase and the other claps the second four beats.

7. Spoken cues can help children gain mastery of rhythmic patterns, but cueing techniques need practice. Spoken cues should be rhythmically correct, particularly when given before the introduction of music. Cues can vary in type. Some involve simple counting—"One, two, three, four." Others involve rhythm—"Slow, slow, fast-fast-fast." Another type uses descriptive words—"Step, step, step, hop," as in the schottische. The cue for the next movement can be given when the prior movement is drawing to a close—"One, two, three, and turn"—or the word "turn" can be spoken alone at the appropriate time. As skills progress, cues should be shortened and finally eliminated.

8. In the lower grades, teachers need not be concerned about strict mechanics. Children should be held to standards appropriate to their age. Individual help can be given as needed, but the teacher should not hold the class to the pace of a slow learner. Tips for graceful carriage, good form, and efficient movement should be included in the instruction.

9. The teacher is freed to give more instructional attention to the class when a child or another adult handles the record player. There should be definite signals for starting and stopping the music. Volunteers from the intermediate grades can help with primary-level rhythm classes.

10. When working with a class in circle formation, the teacher should observe from outside the circle. When the teacher is located inside the circle, a portion of the class is always out of view.

11. The parachute provides interesting variations to many rhythmic activities. When its addition to the dances presented in this chapter is practical, the fact is noted.

FUNDAMENTAL RHYTHMS

Fundamental rhythms should be an outgrowth of the movement activities with which the children are already familiar, such as walking (stepping), running, jumping, and hopping. To these acquired skills, rhythm is added. Fundamental rhythms are emphasized in the primary grades and are extended to the intermediate level on a smaller scale.

The general purpose of a fundamental rhythms program is to provide a variety of fundamental movement experiences, so the child can learn to move effectively and efficiently and develop a sense of rhythm. While the creative aspect of fundamental rhythms is important, even more important is first establishing a vocabulary of movement competencies for each child.

The skills in a fundamental rhythm program are important as the background for creative dance and also as the basis for the more precise dance skills of folk, social, and square dance, which follow later in school programs. (Fundamental skills were described, together with teaching hints and stress points, in Chapter 9.)

LOCOMOTOR MOVEMENTS

Even types of locomotor movement are walking, running, hopping, leaping, jumping, draw steps, and such variations as marching, trotting, stamping, and twirling. Uneven types are skipping, galloping, and sliding.

NONLOCOMOTOR MOVEMENTS

Simple nonlocomotor movements are bending, swaying, twisting, swinging, raising, lowering, circling, and rotating various parts of the body.

Mimetics are striking, lifting, throwing, pushing, pulling, hammering, and other common tasks.

MANIPULATIVE MOVEMENTS

Manipulative movements involve object handling such as ball skills. Other objects such as hoops, wands, and even chairs can be used.

INSTRUCTIONAL PROCEDURES

1. Success depends on the teacher's initiating and guiding simple patterns. Of prime importance is the class atmosphere, which should be one of enjoyment. Furthermore, the accompaniment must be suitable for the movements to be experienced.

2. The element of creativity should not be stifled in a program of fundamental rhythms. The instruction can be directed toward a specific movement (like walking), and a reasonable range of acceptable performance, which permits individual creativity, can be established.

3. Teachers who feel awkward or insecure about developing rhythmic programs with a strong creative approach will find the fundamental rhythms a good starting point. Combining rhythmic movement with those movements that students enjoy can be the beginning of a refreshing and stimulating experience for both teacher and child.

4. The approach to fundamental rhythms should be a mixture of direct and indirect teaching. Many of the movements do have standard or preferred techniques. For example, there is a correct way to walk, and children should recognize and learn such fundamentals. Within the framework of good technique, however, a variety of movement experiences can be elicited.

IDEAS FOR USING FUNDAMENTAL RHYTHMIC MOVEMENTS

Presented in the following paragraphs are ideas that provide a basis for breadth and variety of movement in the fundamental rhythmic movements program. Children love change and the challenge of reacting to change. They can be encouraged to change the movement pattern or some aspect of it (direction, level, body leads, and so on) at the end of a musical phrase. Music provides the cues for change, and the children must plan ahead for the upcoming change.

Changes can be signaled by variations in the drumbeat. A heavy, accented beat, for example, can signal a change in direction or type of movement. Stops and starts, changes to different rhythms, and other innovations are within the scope of this process. The intensity of the drumbeat can call for light or heavy movements or for different levels of movement—high, middle, or low. As an example of how to do this, picture a class of children walking heavily in general space to a heavy, even beat. The teacher sounds one extra-heavy beat, whereupon students change direction abruptly, now moving very lightly on the toes to a light, even beat. This sequence finishes with another heavy beat, which causes the children again to change direction abruptly and to change their movement as indicated by the next sequence of beats. The opportunities for intriguing movement combinations are many.

The use of different parts of the body, singly and in various combinations, is important in establishing movement variety. Different positions of the arms and legs can vary the ways of moving. The child can perform high on the toes, with toes in or out; on the heels, with stiff knees; kicking high in front or to the rear, with knees brought up high; in a crouched position; and in many other positions.

The arms can swing at the sides or be held stiff, be held out in front, or held overhead. The arms can move in circles or in different patterns. The body can bend forward, backward, or sideward, and it can twist and turn. By combining different arm, leg, and body positions, the children can assume many interesting position variations. Changes in body level and patterns of movement for outlining circles, squares, triangles, and other shapes also add interest. Ideas and suggestions for using fundamental skills with rhythm are found in Chapter 9.

CREATIVE RHYTHMS

Creativity should be part of all dance and rhythmic activities, with the scope of the activity determining the degree of freedom. Creative rhythms, however, provide a special program area in which creativity is the goal and functional movement is secondary. The emphasis is on the process and not the movement outcomes.

Creativity manifests itself in the opportunity for each child to respond expressively within the scope of the movement idea, which can range from total freedom to stated limits. The child's judgment should be respected, and the teacher should look for original interpretations. Stimulation should be positive in nature, guiding the movement patterns by suggestions, questions, encouragement, and challenges that help children to structure their ideas and add variety. Careful guidance is necessary to fan the spark of self-direction, since freedom in itself does not automatically develop creativity.

INSTRUCTIONAL PROCEDURES

1. Appropriate music or rhythmic background is important; otherwise, movement can become stilted. An atmosphere of creative freedom must be established. The class should be comfortable, relaxed, and free from artificial restraints.

2. In analyzing the setting, the teacher should ask himself, what is the basic idea? What expressive movements can be expected? What are the guidelines or boundaries of movement? What space are the children to use?

3. Listening is an important element, because children must get the mood or sense of the rhythmic background. Some questions that can be posed to the children are "What does the music make us think of?" and "What does the music tell us to do?" If the movement or interpretation is preselected, little time need be wasted in getting under way. Provide enough music so the children can grasp the impact. Have them clap the beat if necessary, and then move into action.

4. Use action-directing statements such as, "Let's pretend we are . . . ," "Let's try being like . . . ," "Try to feel like a . . . ," and "Make believe you are. . . ."

5. In some lessons, the initial focus may be on the selection of appropriate rhythmic background. This is the case when children formulate a creative rhythm of the dramatic type and then seek suitable music for their dance.

6. Children must be given time to develop and try out their ideas and to come up with solutions. This is an open-ended process that has a variety of solutions. Coaching and guidance are important aspects at this stage. Application of time, space, force, flow, and body factors is essential. Teachers should move with the children and encourage large, free movement of all body parts. Use the entire area and fill in the empty places in general space. Allow plenty of time for exploration.

7. As children mature and come to understand their role in creative rhythm lessons, they should be asked to put together a pattern that has aesthetic value. Repeat sequences three or four times so the children can consolidate their movement patterns.

8. Demonstration must be handled carefully with respect for each child and her created movement patterns. Demonstration can be given by individuals, groups, or by the entire class, but *not* by the teacher.

SUGGESTIONS FOR CREATIVE RHYTHMS

The following approaches offer suggestions for development of creative ideas.

Understanding and Relating to Rhythm

Teachers can bring in the idea of meter (2/4, 3/4, 4/4, and 6/8 times) and have children move in time to the meter. Other movements can illustrate even and uneven time, accents, phrasing, and other elements of rhythmic structure.

Fundamental Motor Rhythms

Creativity can be developed through various locomotor movements. The use of the drum is recommended. A skillful teacher can vary the tempo, signal movement changes, and provide a variety of interesting activities. The teacher pounds out a beat for the children to move to according to the rhythm provided. Some variety can be added by the following devices.

1. On a single loud beat, each student changes direction abruptly, turns around, or jumps or leaps in the air.

2. A quick, heavy, double beat signals children to stop in place without any further movement or to fall to the floor.

3. Various changes in beat and accent pattern can be given, with children instructed to follow the pattern with movement.

Records designed for fundamental movements are excellent teaching aids. The records should have sections featuring separate skills and sections to guide movement combinations. These can be used for both instruction and creative activities. As an example, children who are seated in a circle tap out a rhythm with lummi sticks. After the rhythm is sufficiently established, half of the class moves in general space to the rhythm, which is continued by those who remain seated.

Another instructional option is using a tape recorder. The tape should contain 10 to 12 rhythmic units. Each unit features 15 to 20 seconds of an appropriate rhythm (piano or recorded music) to which a fundamental movement can be performed. At the end of each unit, a bell is rung or a gong struck. The children move to the rhythm, and at the sound of the bell or gong, they freeze in a pose of their choosing. When the next rhythm begins, the sequence is repeated.

Expressive Movement

Children can express moods and feelings and show reactions to colors and sounds by improvising dances or movements that demonstrate different aspects of force or gestures that depict different feelings. A piece of music is played and is followed by a discussion of its qualities and how it makes the children feel. Children may interpret the music differently. Moods can be described as happy, gay, sad, brave, fearful, cheerful, angry, solemn, silly, stately, sleepy, funny, cautious, bold, or nonchalant.

Identification

There are endless subject sources for identification and interpretation. Each child can take on the identity of a familiar character, creature, or object. The following ideas should be useful.

1. Animals—elephants, ducks, seals, chickens, dogs, rabbits, lions, and others

2. People—soldiers, fire fighters, sailors, nurses, various kinds of workers, forest rangers, teachers, cowboys and cowgirls, and so on

3. Play objects—seesaws, swings, rowboats, balls, various toys, and many other common articles with which children play

4. Make-believe creatures—giants, dwarfs, gnomes, witches, trolls, dragons, pixies, and fairies

5. Machines—trains, planes, jets, rockets, automobiles, bicycles, motorcycles, tractors, elevators, and the like

6. Circus characters—clowns, various trained animals, trapeze artists, tightrope performers, jugglers, acrobats, and bands

7. Natural phenomena—fluttering leaves, grain, flowers, rain, snow, clouds, wind, tornadoes, hurricanes, volcanoes, and others

8. *Star Wars* characters—Darth Vader, Starships, C-3PO, R2-D2, Chewbacca, Luke Skywalker, Landspeeder machines, and the Force

Dramatization

Dramatization and rhythm are useful vehicles for group activity. Suitable background music or rhythmic accompaniment is a necessary ingredient. Excellent recordings are available, from short numbers lasting a minute or two to more elaborate productions like those found in the *Dance-a-Story* series (RCA Victor).

Here are some useful ideas for dramatic rhythms.

1. Building a house, garage, or other building project.
2. Making a snowman, throwing snowballs, going skiing.
3. Flying a kite, going hunting or fishing, going camping.
4. Acting out stories about astronauts, cowboys and cowgirls, fire fighters, explorers.
5. Interpreting familiar stories, such as "Sleeping Beauty," "The Three Bears," or "Little Red Riding Hood."
6. Doing household tasks such as chopping wood, picking fruit, mowing the lawn, cleaning the yard, washing dishes, and vacuuming.
7. Celebrating holidays like Halloween, the Fourth of July, Thanksgiving, or Christmas, or dramatizing the seasons.
8. Playing sports such as football, basketball, baseball, track and field, swimming, tennis, and golf.
9. Divide the class in groups of three or four, and assign each group a sport other than one of the major sports. Have them develop a series of movements dramatizing that sport to the class. Have the remaining groups guess which sport is being presented. Slow-motion movements add to this activity.
10. Plan a trip through a haunted house. A record by Hap Palmer ("Movin'," KIMBO EA 546) has an excellent sequence about being in a haunted house.
11. Have the children make a motor. One student starts by getting into a position of choice in the middle of the floor and by putting one body part in motion. The motion should be a steady, rhythmic movement. The remaining students, one at a time, attach on to the first person, and each person puts one body part in motion. As each person hooks on to the motor, his level should be lowered. After all are attached, a machine with many moving parts is the result.
12. Act out the children's favorite parts in popular movies. Having the children perform to the original sound track brings realism to the performance.
13. Select a favorite poem ("Old Mother Hubbard," "Pat-a-Cake," "The Giant") and design a sequence of activities to fit the meaning of the poem. Stories have excellent appeal.

An example that shows how an idea can be exploited for a lesson on creative rhythm is called "The Wind and the Leaves." One or more children are chosen to be the wind, and the remaining children are the leaves. Two kinds of rhythm are needed; a tambourine can be used. The first rhythm should be high, fast, and shrill, indicating the blowing of the wind. The intensity and tempo should illustrate the speed and force of the wind. The second rhythm should be slow, measured, and light, to represent the leaves fluttering in the still air and finally coming to rest at various positions on the ground. During the first rhythm, children representing the wind act out a heavy gust. While this is going on, the leaves show what it is like to be blown about. During the second rhythm, the wind is still and the leaves flutter to the ground. Other characterizations can be added. For example, street sweepers can come along and sweep up the leaves.

Another lesson strategy is to divide the class in groups and to give each group the task of acting out an idea with percussive accompaniment. Each group puts on a performance for the others. At completion, the other groups guess what the interpretation was. In this game, the interpretations should not be too long.

A tape recorder can be of value in creating dramatic rhythms. Bits of music and other accompaniment can be put together as desired. This procedure allows a story or idea to be structured against its own individually designed rhythmic background.

Creating Dances

A wide range of creative endeavor is possible in making up dances. Efforts can vary from construction of simple routines to formulation of a complete dance to a new or familiar piece of music. Students need to analyze the characteristics of the piece, determine the kinds of movement best suited to the musical elements, and design an appropriate movement routine or dance. This works best with small groups.

CREATIVE RHYTHMS IN THE INTERMEDIATE GRADES

Although children in the intermediate grades generally have outgrown activities such as imitating animals and objects, other creative activities are appropriate and desirable. Creative rhythms involving fundamental skills can be valuable learning experiences for intermediate-grade children. The movements should be vigorous and challenging to gain acceptance by the more skilled. Ball bouncing and dribbling routines done to music have strong appeal.

Some caution should be exercised in the use of creative activities of a dramatic and expressive nature in the upper grades. At a time when children are looking forward to becoming more adult, activities of this type may seem to them like turning back the clock.

MOVEMENT SONGS

Movement songs include action songs and singing games. The latter term is losing favor, because few of the songs can really be labeled "games." In these rhythmic activities, children usually sing the verses, and the verses tell the children how to move. Considerable latitude in movement is usually the case, because the children follow and interpret the action picture of the words. A movement song can be an interpretation of an old story or fable, a celebration, or some kind of task.

INTRODUCING A SONG

The following steps provide a logical sequence for presentation of a movement song.

1. *Background.* Tell something about the song by discussing its nature and meaning.

2. *Analyzing the music.* Have the children listen critically to the music. They can clap to the beat.

3. *Learning the verses.* Write the verses on a blackboard or poster board to speed learning and save time. Learning one verse at a time and putting each verse into action after learning the words is in general the better learning procedure. Sometimes the music teacher and the physical education teacher can cooperate. The children can learn the music and the verses during the music period, and can add the action during the activity period.

4. *Adding the action.* Arrange the children in formation quickly and proceed with the action. Encourage creative interpretation as determined by the framework of the movement song. Begin with the largest workable activity part that the children can handle at one time. After this part is learned, add other increments.

5. *Including variations.* Be alert to possible variations that may be suggested by the children.

INSTRUCTIONAL PROCEDURES

1. Make sure that the background source of music is loud enough for all children to hear as they sing. Otherwise, the singing will soon be out of time with the background music. After the children learn the verses and can sing reasonably well, the music source may not be needed.

2. Where a key figure is the center of attention, several children should assume the part so attention is shared and more children are involved.

3. Allow children to alter the last line of a song occasionally to provide a surprise ending. A different last line can be composed, and the children can match their actions to it.

FOLK DANCE AND OTHER DANCE ACTIVITIES

A folk dance is defined as a traditional dance of a given people. In this concept, a definite pattern or dance routine is usually specified and followed. Folk dance is one phase of a child's education that can assist in bringing about international understanding. A country's way of life and many other habits are often reflected in its folk music. From these dances, children gain an understanding of why people from certain countries act and live as they do, even though modern times may have changed the life-style from that of days gone by. Since folk dances depict the character of a people, these dances were never intended to be changed. However, to promote the joy of folk dance among elementary-level children, some slight modifications, which do not change greatly the inherent nature of the dance, may be instituted. Substituting a double handhold for a closed position, or a basic handhold for a varsovienne position, are examples of acceptable changes.

Other values of folk dancing include the coordination and skill development that can take place. From folk dancing, children gain a background for future social dancing. They develop the ability to move to rhythm, and to coordinate hands and arms with feet and legs.

Folk dances for the kindergarten and primary level normally consist of simple fundamental locomotor movements, either singly or in combination. Dances such as the two-step, polka, and schottische, with more specialized steps, are found at the intermediate level. The first consideration for teaching folk dance is whether children know the basic step. If instruction is indicated, this can be handled in one of two ways. The first way is to teach the step separately, before teaching the dance. The second is to teach the dance in its normal sequence, giving specific instruction at the time when the step appears. The first method is usually more efficient, because the children can concentrate on one element, the step.

INTRODUCING A DANCE STEP

The ability level of the group and the degree of difficulty of the dance step influence the manner in which instruction proceeds. Several approaches may be necessary to ensure that everyone has acquired sufficient skill. The following considerations are important.

Analysis of the Step

Explain and discuss the characteristics of the rhythm and of the accents and foot pattern in relation to the rhythm.

1. Have children listen to the music.

2. Have them clap their hands or tap their feet to the rhythm. Emphasize the accents with a heavier clap or tap.

3. Use the blackboard to illustrate the relationship of the step to the music.

4. Demonstrate the step.

Selection of Formation

Select the formation most suitable for teaching, keeping it as informal as possible. Scattered formation is the simplest of the arrangements. Single-circle formation involves no partners, while double-circle formation is with partners.

Position of the Dancers

In general, each child practices first individually and later with a partner. When starting with a partner, children can assume the side-by-side position first, and then the closed position later, if that position is the goal. Another approach to reaching the closed dance position is to have partners face each other but stay at arm's length, with hands joined.

Method of Presentation

The sequence of presentation can be repeated as dancers move from individual formation to working with partners.

1. Use a walk-through, talk-through approach without music and at a reduced tempo.

2. Increase the practice speed, still without music.

3. Practice with music. The tempo can be slowed to approximate the practice speed.

4. Apply the step to a simple sequence.

The relationship of cues to the accompaniment is important. The tempo of cues should be increased gradually to approximate the tempo of the music. Music should be at a slow and comfortable tempo for learning, and the tempo can then be increased gradually.

INTRODUCING NEW DANCES

Much of the procedure for teaching a new step is applicable with some modification to teaching an entire dance. The following instructional sequence is presented with the assumption that the basic dance step has been learned and that the class is now ready to proceed with the dance itself.

1. With the children sitting informally or in formation for the dance, tell them about the dance and its characteristics.

2. Have the children listen to and analyze the music for accents, phrases, or changes.

3. As a general rule, if the dance is short, use the whole teaching approach. If it is a longer dance with several different parts, use the part-whole method. Teach the largest learning part possible.

4. A technique of value is to have the children learn half of a two-part dance or a third of a three-part dance and then to put that part to music. When the music comes to the part the children do not know, have them listen while waiting for a repetition of the portion that they have learned. Listening to the music during the unknown part of the piece gives children a chance to observe the tempo changes and to fix the relationship of the parts to the whole.

When walking the students through the dance without music, practice at a slowed tempo until the pattern is learned. Before putting the learned sequence to music, make sure that the students can perform the pattern at the speed of the music.

5. Teach the remaining portions of the dance and then put them together, beginning at a slowed tempo and gradually increasing to the normal tempo.

6. Add refinements such as partner changes (if the dance is a mixer), points of technique, and other details.

GENERAL INSTRUCTIONAL PROCEDURES FOR DANCES

1. The instructor should know the dance, have the instructional sequences determined in advance, and have the music set at the right tempo.

2. Get the group into formation as quickly as possible, since children can grasp the dance better when they are in formation.

3. Arrange for partners quickly and efficiently. Change partners frequently. Boys or girls can move forward or backward one place. Extras should be rotated into partner dances. A good way to change is to have the dancers stand in place at the completion of the dance and leave that place only when replaced by an extra. Another way to include extras is to have the extra person replace one of the dancers every time the dance repeats itself.

4. Watch for fatigue, particularly when the dance patterns are quite demanding, for fatigue destroys enjoyment of the dance. If necessary, shorten the number of repetitions.

5. Let the group know beforehand the number of repetitions the dance will go through. Either announce this before the dance begins or arrange a signal for the last repetition. Cue with a phrase such as "Once more" or "Last time," or use a hand signal. Some folk dances repeat patterns several times. Be alert for boredom; call a halt before the pattern is run into the ground.

6. Make frequent use of mixers, because they provide opportunity for sociability, add interest, and give everyone an equal opportunity to meet others. At times, a class can invite another class to join in a dance party, usually to do dances they both have learned. Some mixers are simple and upbeat, providing a welcome change from folk dancing, especially if the class has just finished learning a serious, difficult dance.

7. Stress the enjoyment and pride that come from knowing a dance well and executing it properly.

ARRANGING FOR PARTNERS

Arranging for partners can be a source of deep hurt or embarrassment for some children. To be acceptable, a method of arranging for partners must avoid the situation in which children are looked over and overlooked. Some suggestions follow.

1. Dancing boy-girl fashion in the traditional mode is not always necessary. When starting a dance program with a class that has never danced before or with students who are uncomfortable with each other, or if the class has a major imbalance of boys and girls, allow the students to dance with a partner of their choice. If this places boys with boys and girls with girls, allow that arrangement.

Try putting colored pinnies on half of the children. Instead of giving directions for the girl's part, call it out as "The people in red on the outside of the circle do. . . ." Be careful not to label one group as playing the role of boys or girls. Change partners frequently, and sooner or later the members of both sexes will dance with members of the opposite sex.

2. In a follow-the-leader approach, the teacher puts on some brisk marching music and begins walking among the students who are scattered in general space. As the teacher passes a student, she taps the student on the shoulder, and he gets in line behind the teacher. Subsequent students go to the end of the line when tagged by the teacher until all students are chosen. This allows the teacher to arrange students as the teacher wishes—boy, girl, or just to separate children who do not work well together.

3. Have children walk down the center of the room by twos. The boys are on the right side and the girls are on the left, both facing toward the same end of the room. All march forward to the end of the room, turn toward each other, and march down the center into circle formation.

4. Boys join hands in a circle formation, and each girl steps behind a boy. Reverse the procedure, and have the girls make the circle, or have the half of the class wearing red pinnies form the circle.

5. Boys stand in a circle facing counterclockwise, while girls form a circle around them facing clockwise. Both circles move in the direction in which they are facing and stop on signal. The boy takes the girl nearest him as his partner.

6. Two squads can be assigned to establish partners. The boys in one squad are paired off with the girls in the other. The squad leaders can supervise this process.

7. For square dances, take the first four couples from any of the previous formations to form a set. Continue until all sets are formed.

FORMATIONS FOR MOVEMENT SONGS AND FOLK DANCES

The formations illustrated in Figure 17.1 cover almost all action songs and dances. The teacher should be able to verbalize the formations, and the children should be able to take their places in formations without confusion. The formations are classified as single-circle, double-circle, and other formations.

DANCE POSITIONS

In most dance positions, the boy holds his hand or hands palms up and the girl joins the grip with a palms-down position. The following dance positions or partner positions are common to many dances.

Partners Facing Position

In partners facing position, as the name suggests, the partners are facing. The boy extends his hands forward with palms up and elbows slightly bent. The girl places her hands in the boy's hands.

Side-by-Side Position (Figure 17.2)

In side-by-side position, the boy always has his partner to the right. The boy offers his right hand, held above the waist, palm up. The girl places her left hand in his raised hand.

Closed Position

Closed position is the social dance position. Partners stand facing each other, shoulders parallel, and toes pointed forward. The boy holds the girl's right hand in his left hand out to the side, at about shoulder level, with elbows bent. The boy places his right hand on the girl's back, just below her left shoulder blade. The girl's left arm rests on the boy's upper arm, and her left hand is on the boy's right shoulder.

Open Position

To get to open position from closed position, the boy turns to his left and the girl to her right, with their arms remaining in about the same position. Both face in the same direction and are side by side.

Skaters' Position (Figure 17.3)

Skaters' position is the crossed-arm position in which the dancers stand side by side, facing the same direction, with the right hand held by partner's right and the left by partner's left.

Varsovienne Position

Boy and girl stand side by side and face the same direction. The girl is slightly in front and to the right of the boy. The boy holds the girl's left hand in his left hand in front and at about shoulder height. She brings her right hand directly back over her right shoulder, and the boy reaches behind her at shoulder height and grasps that hand with his right.

THE FOLK DANCE PROGRESSIONS

A folk dance progression should be followed in every school. By so doing, several benefits are derived. Special dances are reserved for each grade level. It is appropriate

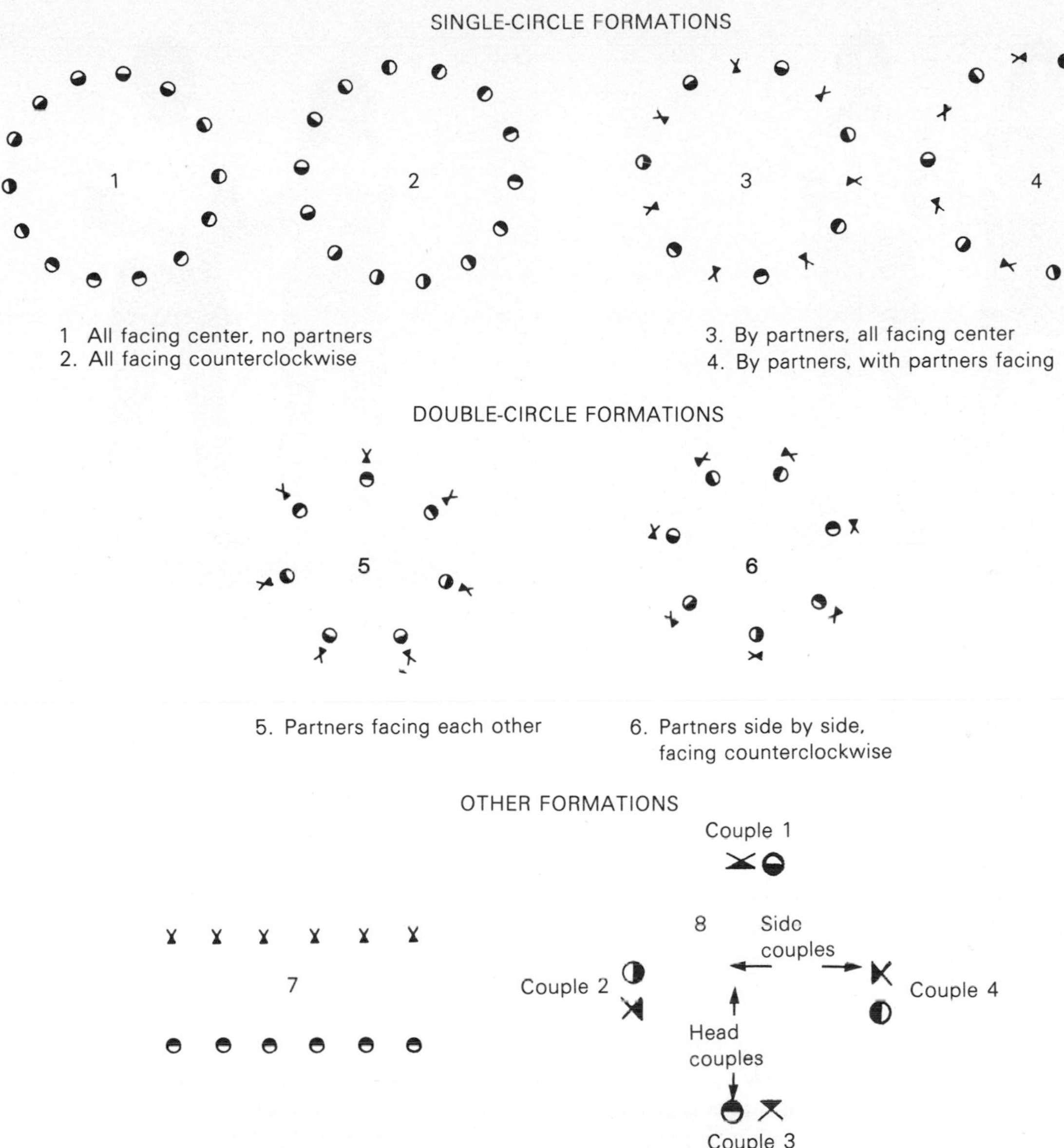

FIGURE 17.1. Dance formations

and often desirable for the teacher to review and use dances assigned to a prior grade level. However, a teacher should not teach folk dances assigned to grade levels ahead. Adherence to this practice reserves some special dances for each grade level and ensures that students have new dance experiences each year.

The folk dances included in the progressions that follow are of appropriate challenge level for the grade level to which they are assigned. This has been determined through field experience.

Regarding level of difficulty, teachers must keep in mind that if a group of students is lacking in rhythmic background, then the dances assigned to them in the progression may be too difficult. A 6th-grade class, for example, lacking in dance skills may need to begin with easier 4th-grade level dances. However, never insult a class by starting the children on material below their maturity level.

The sequence of dances given here for the various grade levels may be the appropriate order in which to present them to students. Arranging folk dances in order of difficulty for any grade level presents some problems, but following the listed order of the dances is a logical way to present them to a class. The teacher can skip dances but still follow the general order.

DANCES FOR KINDERGARTEN CHILDREN

The dances in the kindergarten section consist of action songs and some basic folk dances. Some of the dances

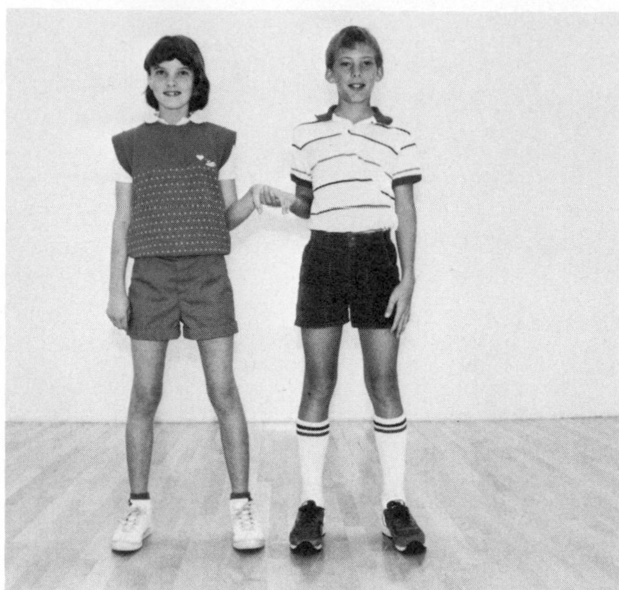

FIGURE 17.2. Side-by-side position

FIGURE 17.3. Skaters' position

are individual; others require partners. The dances demand only simple locomotor steps. The rhythms emphasizing body part identification should be performed accurately.

Dances	*Skills*
Looby Loo	Running step or skipping, body identification
Let Your Feet Go Tap, Tap, Tap	Skipping
Pease Porridge Hot	Running, turning in a circle
How D'Ye Do My Partner	Walking or skipping with a partner, bowing, curtsy
Hokey Pokey	Body identification and nonlocomotor movements
Movin' Madness	Keeping time, creativity
Popcorn Man	Skipping and jumping
Danish Dance of Greeting	Light running step, bowing
Chimes of Dunkirk (Var. 1)	Turning with a partner in a small circle, changing partners

Looby Loo (English)

Records: Hoctor HLP-4026; Folkraft 1184; Russell 702; Columbia 10008D; Lloyd Shaw LS, E-4

Skill: Skipping

Formation: Single circle, facing center, hands joined

Chorus

Here we dance looby loo
Here we dance looby light
Here we dance looby loo
All on a Saturday night.

Verses

1 I put my right hand in,
I take my right hand out,
I give my right hand a shake, shake, shake,
And turn myself about.
2 I put my left hand in, . . .
3 I put my right foot in, . . .
4 I put my left foot in, . . .
5 I put my head way in, . . .
6 I put my whole self in, . . .

Directions: The chorus is repeated before each verse. During the chorus, all children skip around the circle to the right. On the verse part of the dance, the children stand still, face the center, and follow the directions of the words. On the words "and turn myself about," they make a complete turn in place and get ready to skip around the circle again. The movements should be definite and vigorous. On the last verse, they jump forward and then backward, shake vigorously, and then turn about.

The dance can be made more fun and more vigorous by changing the tasks in the song. Try these tasks: Right side or hip, left side or hip, big belly, backside.

Let Your Feet Go Tap, Tap, Tap (German)

Records: Folkraft 1184; Lloyd Shaw E-7, E-20

Skill: Skipping

Formation: Double circle, partners facing

Directions

Verse	Action
Let your feet go tap, tap, tap,	Tap the foot three times.
Let your hands go clap, clap, clap,	Clap the hands three times.
Let your finger beckon me,	Beckon and bow to partner.
Come, dear partner, dance with me.	Join inside hands and face counterclockwise.
Chorus	
Tra, la, la, la, la, la, la, and so on.	All sing and skip counterclockwise.

This dance can be done to the tune of "Merrily We Roll Along," with a little adjustment for line 2. If children are having difficulty with skipping, substitute a walking or running step.

Pease Porridge Hot (English)

Records: Folkraft 1190, Lloyd Shaw E-8

Skills: Running, turning in a circle

Formation: Double circle, partners facing

Verse

Pease porridge hot,
Pease porridge cold,
Pease porridge in a pot,
Nine days old!
Some like it hot,
Some like it cold,
Some like it in a pot,
Nine days old!

Directions: The dance is in two parts. The first is a pat-a-cake rhythm done while the children sing the verse. During the second part, partners dance in a circular movement.

Part I

Line 1: Clap the hands to the thighs, clap the hands together, clap the hands to partner's hands.

Line 2: Repeat the action of line 1.

Line 3: Clap the hands to the thighs, clap the hands together, clap the right hand against partner's right, clap one's own hands together.

Line 4: Clap the left hand to partner's left, clap one's own hands together, clap both hands against partner's hands.

Lines 5–8: Repeat lines 1–4.

Part II: Join both hands with partner and run around in a small circle, turning counterclockwise for the first four lines and ending with the word "old!" Reverse direction and run clockwise for the remainder of the verse. Move one step to the left for a new partner. An elbow-swing could be used.

Variation

Part I: Children are seated on the floor, facing their partner, with hands braced in back for support. The movements are done with the feet instead of the hands. Instead of clapping the hands to the thighs, knock both heels against the floor. In the partner interaction, the feet do the work of the hands.

Part II: Have each child spin on her seat in one direction during the first eight measures and then spin the other way during the next eight. Each child must keep her knees up and her heels near her seat while spinning to avoid contact with her partner, or have the children crawl around until they are ready to select another partner for the next sequence of the song.

How D'Ye Do, My Partner (Swedish)

Records: Folkraft 1190; Hoctor HLP-4026; Lloyd Shaw E-3

Skills: Bowing, curtsying, skipping

Formation: Double circle, partners facing, boys on inside

Verse

How d'ye do, my partner?
How d'ye do today?
Will you dance in the circle?
I will show you the way.

Directions

Measures	Action
1–2	Boys bow to their partner.
3–4	Girls curtsy.
5–6	Boy offers his right hand to the girl, who takes it with her right hand. Both turn to face counterclockwise.
7–8	Couples join left hands and are then in skaters' position. They get ready to skip when the music changes.
9–16	Partners skip counterclockwise in the circle, slowing down on measure 15. On measure 16, the girls stop and the boys move ahead to secure a new partner.

Hokey Pokey (American)

Records: Capitol 2427; McGregor 6995; Old Timer 8086, 8163; Folkraft 6026; Lloyd Shaw E-25, 4B-6056

Skills: Turning, shaking, and other nonlocomotor movements

Formation: Single circle, facing center

Verse

Line 1: You put your right foot in,
Line 2: You put your right foot out,
Line 3: You put your right foot in
Line 4: And you shake it all about;
Line 5: You do the hokey pokey
Line 6: And you turn yourself around.
Line 7: That's what it's all about.

Directions: During the first four lines, the children act out the words. During lines 5 and 6, they hold their hands overhead with palms forward and do a kind of hula while turning around in place. During line 7, they stand in place and clap their hands three times.

The basic verse is repeated by substituting, successively, the left foot, right arm, left arm, right elbow, left elbow, head, right hip, left hip, whole self, and backside. The final verse finishes off with the following:

You do the hokey pokey,
You do the hokey pokey,
You do the hokey pokey.
That's what it's all about.

On each of the first two lines, the children raise their arms overhead and perform a bowing motion with the arms and upper body. On line 3, all kneel and bow forward to touch the hands to the floor. During line 4, they slap the floor six times, alternating their hands in time to the words.

Teaching Suggestions: Encourage the youngsters to make large and vigorous motions during the hokey pokey portions and during the turn around. This adds to the fun.

The records all feature singing calls, but the action sequence of the different records varies. The children should sing lightly as they follow the directions given on the record.

Movin' Madness (American)

Records: Folkraft 1188; Lloyd Shaw E-9, E-20; Pioneer 3016

Skills: Keeping time with the music

Formation: Scattered

Directions: The music is in two parts.

Part I: The tempo is slow, slow, fast-fast-fast. The children do any series of movements of their choice to fit this pattern, repeated four times. The movements should be large, gross motor movements.

Part II: During the second part (chorus) of the music, the children do any locomotor movement in keeping with the tempo. The step-hop, a light run, or a jig would probably fit the tempo of Part II best.

Teaching Suggestions: Have the youngsters clap the rhythm. They should pay particular attention to the tempo in Part I. The music is bleking, a dance presented later in the 3rd grade program. The music for "I See You" is also suitable, but note that the movements in Part I are repeated twice instead of four times. The Part II music is suitable for skipping, sliding, or galloping.

The Popcorn Man (American)

Record: Folkraft 1180 ("The Muffin Man")

Skills: Jumping, skipping

Formation: Single circle, facing center, hands at sides. One child, the Popcorn Man, stands in front of another child of the opposite sex.

Verses

1. Oh, have you seen the Popcorn Man,
The Popcorn Man, the Popcorn Man?
Oh, have you seen the Popcorn Man,
Who lives on ____ Street?
2. Oh, yes, we've seen the Popcorn Man,
The Popcorn Man, the Popcorn Man.
Oh yes, we've seen the Popcorn Man,
Who lives on ____ Street.

Directions

Verse 1: The children stand still and clap their hands lightly, with the exception of the Popcorn Man and his partner. These two join hands and jump lightly in place while keeping time to the music. On the first beat of each measure, a normal jump is taken, followed by a bounce in place (rebound) on the second beat.

Verse 2: The Popcorn Man and his partner then skip around the inside of the circle individually and, near the end of the verse, each stands in front of a child, thus choosing a new partner.

Verse 1 is then repeated, with two sets of partners doing the jumping. During the repetition of verse 2, four children skip around the inside of the circle and choose partners. This procedure continues until all children have been chosen.

The children choose the name of a street to put in the verses.

Dance of Greeting (Danish)

Records: Hoctor HLP-4026; Folkraft 1187; Merit Audiovisual-Folk Dance Fundamentals

Skills: Running or sliding, bowing, curtsying

Formation: Single circle, all face center. Each boy stands to the left of his partner.

Directions

Measures	Action
1	All clap, clap, and bow to partner (girl curtsies).
2	Repeat but turn the back to the partner and bow to the neighbor.
3	Stamp right, stamp left.
4	Turn around in four running steps.
5–8	Repeat the action of measures 1–4.
9–12	All join hands and run to the left for four measures (16 counts).
13–16	Repeat the action of measures 9–12, taking light running steps in the opposite direction.

Variation: Instead of a running step, use a light slide.

Chimes of Dunkirk, Var. 1 (French-Belgian)

Records: Lloyd Shaw E-7, E-21; Hoctor HLP-4026; Folkraft 11

Skills: Turning in a small circle with a partner, changing partners

Formation: Double circle, partners facing

Directions

Measures	Action
1–2	Stamp three times in place, right-left-right.
3–4	Clap the hands three times above the head (chimes in the steeple).
5–8	Turn with partner. The boy places both hands on his partner's hips; the girl places both hands on her partner's shoulders. Taking four steps, they turn around in place. On the next four counts, the girl (on the outside) moves one person to her left with four steps. Repeat the sequence from the beginning.

Teaching Suggestion: An alternative to the turn described is to do an elbow-turn by linking right elbows.

DANCES FOR FIRST-GRADE CHILDREN

The 1st-grade folk dance program is made up of movement songs and folk dances that are introductory in nature and involve simple formations and uncomplicated changes. The movements are primarily basic locomotor skills and hand gestures or clapping sequences. There are dances both with and without partners. First graders can become excellent dancers, remembering quite a long pattern of movements. They normally show gracious courtesy to their partners, making this an exciting grade level to teach.

Dances	Skills
Did You Ever See a Lassie	Walking at 3/4 time, creativity
Jump Jim Jo	Jumping, running, draw step
Children's Polka	Step-draw
Chimes of Dunkirk (Var. 2)	Turning with a partner, skipping
Seven Jumps	Step-hop, balance, control
Ach Ja	Walking, sliding
Eins Zwei Drei	Walking, heel-toe step, sliding
Shoemaker's Dance	Skipping, heel and toe

Did You Ever See a Lassie (Scottish)

Records: Folkraft 1183; Lloyd Shaw E-4

Skill: Walking at 3/4 time

Formation: Single circle, facing halfway left, with hands joined; one child in the center

Verse

Did you ever see a lassie (laddie), a lassie, a lassie?
Did you ever see a lassie do this way and that?
Do this way and that way, and this way and that way?
Did you ever see a lassie do this way and that?

Directions

Measures	Action
1–8	All walk to the left in a circle with hands joined. (Since this is fast waltz time, the dancers should take one step to each measure.) The child in the center gets ready to demonstrate some type of movement.
9–16	All stop and copy the movement suggested by the child in the center.

As the verse starts over, the center child selects another to do some action in the center and changes places with her.

Jump Jim Jo (American)

Records: Folkraft 1180; Lloyd Shaw E-10; Merit Audiovisual-Folk Dance Fundamentals

Skills: Jumping, running, draw step

Formation: Double circle, partners facing, both hands joined

Directions

Measures	Verse
1–2	Jump, jump, oh jump Jim Jo
3–4	Take a little whirl, and around you'll go,
5–6	Slide, slide, and point your toe,
7–8	You're a jolly little fellow when you jump Jim Jo.

Measures	Action
1–2	Do two jumps sideward, progressing counterclockwise, followed by three quick jumps in place. Jump (counts 1 and), jump (2 and), jump (1), jump (and), jump (2), pause (and).
3–4	Release hands and turn once around in place with four jumps (two jumps per measure). Finish facing partner and rejoin hands.
5	Take two sliding steps sideward, progressing counterclockwise. Slide sideward (count 1), together (and), repeat (2 and).
6	Partners face counterclockwise with inside hands joined and tap three times with the toe of the outside foot.
7–8	Take four running steps forward, then face partner, join both hands, and end with three jumps in place.

Children's Polka (German)

Records: Folkraft 1187; Hoctor HLP-4026; Lloyd Shaw E-7

Formation: Single circle of couples, partners facing

Directions

Measures	Action
1–2	Take two step-draw steps toward the center of the circle, ending with three steps in place.
3–4	Take two step-draw steps away from the center, ending with three steps in place.
5–8	Repeat the pattern of measures 1–4.
9	Slap own knees once with both hands; clap own hands once.
10	Clap both hands with partner three times.
11–12	Repeat the pattern of measures 9–10.
13	Hop, placing one heel forward, and shake the forefinger at partner three times.
14	Repeat the "scolding" pattern with the other foot and hand.
15–16	Turn once around in place with four running steps and stamp three times in place.

Chimes of Dunkirk, Var. 2 (French-Belgian)

Records: Folkraft 1188; Lloyd Shaw E-7, E-21; Merit Audiovisual Folk Dances for Beginners

Formation: Single circle of couples, partners facing

Directions

Measures	Action
1–2	Stamp three times in place.
3–4	Clap own hands three times.
5–8	Do a two-hand swing with partner. Join both hands with partner and turn once clockwise with eight running or skipping steps.

	Chorus Action
1–8	Circle left, singing, "Tra, la, la, la, la, . . ." All join hands and circle left with 16 running or skipping steps, ending with a bow.

Variations: The dance can also be used as a mixer by the girl's advancing one partner to her left.

Instead of a two-hand swing with partner, use the shoulder-waist position. The boy places his hand on his partner's waist, and the girl places her hands on her partner's shoulders.

To facilitate forming the circle for the chorus, make a four-step turn instead of an eight-step turn on measures 5–8. This gives the children four counts to get ready for the circle formation and four counts to make the circle.

Seven Jumps (Danish)

Records: Methodist M-108; Victor 45-6172, 21617

Skills: Step-hop, balance, control

Formation: Single circle, hands joined

Directions: There are seven jumps to the dance. Each jump is preceded by the following action.

Measures	Action
1–8	The circle moves to the right with seven step-hops, one to each measure. On the eighth measure, all jump high in the air and reverse direction.
9–16	Circle to the left with seven step-hops. Stop on measure 16 and face the center.
17	All drop hands, place their hands on hips, and lift the right knee upward with the toes pointed downward.
18	All stamp the right foot to the ground on the signal note, then join hands on the next note.
1–18	Repeat measures 1–18, but do not join hands.
19	Lift the left knee, stamp, and join hands.
1–19	Repeat measures 1–19, but do not join hands.
20	Put the right toe backward and kneel on the right knee. Stand and join hands.
1–20	Repeat measues 1–20; do not join hands.
21	Kneel on the left knee. Stand and join hands.
1–21	Repeat measures 1–21; do not join hands.
22	Put the right elbow to the floor with the cheek on the fist. Stand and join hands.
1–22	Repeat measures 1–22; do not join hands.
23	Put the left elbow to the floor with the cheek on the fist. Stand and join hands.

Measures	Action
1–23	Repeat measures 1–23; do not join hands.
24	Put the forehead on the floor. Stand and join hands.
1–16	Repeat measues 1–16.

Teaching Suggestion: This dance was performed originally in Denmark by men as a control-elimination dance. Those who made unnecessary movements or mistakes were eliminated. Emphasize control.

Variation: An excellent variation is to do the dance with a parachute. The dancers hold the parachute taut with one hand during the step-hops. The chute is kept taut with both hands for all jumps except the last, during which the forehead touches the chute on the floor.

Ach Ja (German)

Records: Evans, Child Rhythms VII; Lloyd Shaw E-2

Skills: Walking, sliding

Formation: Double circle, partners facing counterclockwise, boys on the inside, inside hands joined

Verse

When my father and my mother take the children to the fair,
Ach Ja! Ach Ja!
Oh, they haven't any money, but it's little that they care,
Ach Ja! Ach Ja!
Tra la la, tra la la, tra la la la la la la
Tra la la, tra la la, tra la la la la la la
Ach Ja! Ach Ja!

Directions: Explain that "Ach Ja" means "Oh yes."

Measures	Action
1–2	Partners walk eight steps in the line of direction.
3	Partners drop hands and bow to each other.
4	Each boy then bows to the girl on his left, who returns the bow.
5–8	Measures 1–4 are repeated.
9–10	Partners face each other, join hands, and take four slides in the line of direction (counterclockwise).
11–12	Four slides are taken clockwise.
13	Partners bow to each other.
14	The boy bows to the girl on his left, who returns the bow. To start the next dance, the boy moves quickly toward this girl, who is his next partner.

Eins Zwei Drei

Records: Hoctor HLP-4026; Folkraft 1522

Formation: Single circle of couples (the girl on her partner's right) facing the center and numbered alternately couple 1, 2, 1, 2

Directions: Explain that "Eins, Zwei, Drei" means "one, two, three," in German.

Measures	Figure 1 Action
1–2	Couples 1 take three steps toward the center of the circle as they clap their hands by brushing them vertically like cymbals, (count 1–3), pause (count 4).
3–4	Couples 1 repeat measures 1–2, walking backward to place.
5–8	Couples 1 face, join both hands, and take four slides toward the center of the circle and four slides back to place. The boy starts with his left foot, the girl with her right.
9–16	Couples 2 repeat measures 1–8.
	Figure 2 Action
17	The boy turns and touches his right heel sideward as he shakes his right index finger at partner. The girl does the same with her left heel and left index finger.
18	Repeat measure 17 with the corner, reversing footwork and hands.
19–20	Repeat measures 17–18.
21–24	All join hands and circle left with eight slides.
25–32	Repeat measures 17–24, reversing the direction of the slides.

Shoemaker's Dance (Danish)

Records: Hoctor HLP-4026; Folkraft 1187; Merit Audiovisual Folk Dances for Beginners; Lloyd Shaw E-5, E-20

Formation: Double circle, partners facing, with the boy's back to the center of the circle.

Figure 1 Verse

Wind, wind, wind the bobbin,	Wind, wind, wind the bobbin,
Wind, wind, wind the bobbin,	Wind, wind, wind the bobbin,
Pull, pull	Pull, pull
Clap, clap, clap.	Tap, tap, tap.

Measures	Figure 1 Action
1	With arms bent and at shoulder height, and with hands clenched to form fists, circle one fist over the other in front of the chest (winding thread).
2	Reverse the circular motion and wind the thread in the opposite direction.
3	Pull the elbows back vigorously twice (pulling and tightening the thread).

Measures	Figure 1 Action
4	Clap own hands three times.
5–7	Repeat the pattern of measures 1–3.
8	Tap own fists together three times (driving the pegs).

Figure 2 Verse

Heel and toe and away we go,
Heel and toe and away we go,
See my new shoes neatly done,
Away we go to have some fun.

Figure 2 Action

9–16	Partners face counterclockwise, inside hands joined. Skip counterclockwise, ending with a bow.

Variation of Figure 2

9	Place the heel of the outside foot forward (counts 1 and), and point the toe of the outside foot in back (2 and).
10	Take three running steps forward, starting with the outside foot and pausing on the last count.
11–12	Repeat the pattern of measures 9–10, starting with the inside foot.
13–16	Repeat the pattern of measures 9–12, entire "heel and toe and run, run, run" pattern dance, four times singing:

DANCES FOR SECOND-GRADE CHILDREN

The 2nd-grade program includes many activities similar to those in the 1st grade program, but more emphasis is placed on partner-style dances and on changes of partner. The dance patterns tend to become more definite, and more folk dances are included. The movements are still primarily of the simple locomotor type, with additional and varied emphasis on more complicated movement patterns.

Dance	Skills
Jolly Is the Miller	Walking (marching), skipping
Carrousel	Draw step, sliding
Turn the Glasses Over	Walking, wring the dishrag
Jingle Bells (Var. 1)	Sliding, elbow swing, skipping
Bombay Bounce	Hesitation step, side step
Bleking	Bleking step, step-hop
Nixie Polka	Bleking step, running or shuffle step
Bingo	Walking, grand right and left

Jolly Is the Miller (American)

Records: Old Timer 8089; Folkraft 1192; American Play Party 1185; Lloyd Shaw E-10.

Skill: Marching

Formation: Double circle, partners facing counterclockwise, boys on the inside, with inside hands joined. A Miller is in the center of the circle.

Directions

Verse	Action
Jolly is the Miller who lives by the mill; The wheel goes round with a right good will One hand on the hopper and the other on the sack; The right steps forward and the left steps back.	All sing. The children march counterclockwise, with inside hands joined. During the second line when "the wheel goes round," the dancers turn their outside arm in a circle to form a wheel. The children change partners at the words "right steps forward and the left steps back." The Miller then has a chance to get a partner. The child left without a partner becomes the next Miller.

Variation: In this version, extra boys (Millers) are inside the circle, or extra girls are outside the circle. This version involves calls. The action of the first three lines is the same; all sing the first three lines.

Call	Action
The boys (or girls) keep going and the girls (or boys) turn back.	Drop hands, and one line reverses (boys or girls). Extra children now join the line.
The girls (or boys) go back, all around the ring.	Continue walking in opposite directions.
Right by each handsome (or sweet young) thing.	Continue walking in opposite directions.
Keep on going and you'll sure be glad	Continue walking in opposite directions.
When I tell you, boys (or girls) to grab, grab, grab.	Boys and girls now pair off and march counterclockwise around the ring. Extra boys go to the center, or extra girls go to the outside.

Call	Action
Now take your partner and you all promenade. Promenade the ring with that pretty little thing.	Using skaters' (promenade) position, walk around the circle until the music changes. Shift to inside hands joined and get ready to repeat.

Carrousel (Swedish)

Records: Folkraft 1183; Lloyd Shaw E-13; Merit Audiovisual-Folk Dance Fundamentals

Skills: Side steps, sliding

Formation: Double circle, facing inward. The inner circle, representing a merry-go-round, joins hands. The outer players, representing the riders, place their hands on the hips of the partner in front.

Verse

Little children, sweet and gay,
Carrousel is running; it will run to evening.
Little ones a nickel, big ones a dime.
Hurry up, get a mate, or you'll surely be too late.

Chorus

Ha, ha, ha, happy are we,
Anderson and Peterson and Henderson and me,
Ha, ha, ha, happy are we,
Anderson and Peterson and Henderson and me.

Directions: During the verse, the children take slow draw steps (step, close) to the left. This is done by taking a step to the side with the left foot (count 1) and closing with the right (count 2) to get the merry-go-round slowly underway. Four slow stamps replace the draw steps with the words "Hurry *up*, get a *mate*, or you'll *surely* be too *late*." A stamp is made on each of the italicized words. The circle then comes to a halt.

During the chorus, the tempo is increased, and the movement is changed to a slide. Be sure to have the children take short, light slides, or the circle gets out of control.

All sing during the dance.

Variation: This dance can be done with a parachute. Try first with single children (no riders) and then with riders.

Turn the Glasses Over (American-English)

Record: Folkraft 1181

Formation: A circle of couples face counterclockwise, the girl on partner's right. Extra boys or girls are in the center. Couples are in skaters' position, hands crossed in front, right hands joined over left.

Directions

Measures	Verse	Action
1–4	I've been to Harlem, I've been to Dover,	The couples walk counterclockwise, singing. At the words "turn the glasses over," they raise their arms, keeping the hands joined, and turn under the raised arms, making one complete outward "dishrag" turn. The children must anticipate the turn and be prepared to start in time to complete the movement by the end of the phrase.
5–8	I've traveled this wide world all over,	
9–12	Over, over, three times over,	
13–16	Drink all the lemonade, and turn the glasses over.	
	Chorus	
1–4	Sailing east, sailing west,	The girls or all children in the outer circle continue walking counterclockwise, while the boys or those in the inner circle turn and walk clockwise. An extra player or players joins one of the circles and continues with the group. At the words "girl in the ocean," the boys take the nearest girl for a new partner. Those children left without a partner go to the center.
5–8	Sailing over the ocean,	
9–12	You better watch out when the boat begins to rock	
13–16	Or you'll lose your girl in the ocean.	

Jingle Bells, Var. 1 (Dutch)

Record: Folkraft 1080

Skill: Swing, skipping

Formation: Double circle, partners facing, with both hands joined

Measures	Action
1–2	Partners take eight slides counterclockwise in the circle.
3–4	Partners turn so they are standing back-to-back, and take eight more slides in the line of direction. This move is best made by dropping the front hands and swinging the back hands forward until the dancers are standing back-to-back. They rejoin the hands that are now in back. Make this move with no loss of rhythm.
5–6	Repeat the action of measures 1–2. To get back to the face-to-face position, let go of the back hands and swing the front hands backward, allowing the bodies to pivot and face again.
7–8	Repeat measures 3–4.
	Chorus Action
1	Clap own hands three times.
2	Clap both hands with partner three times.
3	Clap own hands four times.
4	Clap both hands with partner once.
5–8	Right elbow-swing with partner. Partners hook right elbows and swing clockwise with eight skips.
9–12	Repeat the clapping sequence of measures 1–4.
13–16	Left elbow-swing with partner for eight skips, finishing in the original starting position, ready to repeat the entire dance with the same partner; or do a left elbow-swing with partner for four skips, which is once around, then all boys or children in the inner circle skip forward to the girl ahead and repeat the entire dance from the beginning with a new partner.

Bombay Bounce

Record: Any good rock, jive, or jazz record with a moderately fast beat

Skills: Hesitation step, side step

Formation: Scattered, all facing forward

Part I (16 counts): Do eight side hesitation steps in place. Take a short step to the left, and touch the right foot to the left. Return with the right foot, and touch with the left. Clap on each second beat (2, 4, 6, 8), coordinating with the touch. The cue is left, touch (clap); right, touch (clap); and so forth.

Part II (16 counts): Take two side steps to the left, then two to the right. Clap on counts 4 and 8. The cue is left, close; left, close (clap); right, close; right, close (clap). Repeat the pattern.

Part III (16 counts): Take four side steps left and four side steps right. Clap only on count 8. Cue is left, close (four times); right, close (four times).

Part IV (16 counts): Take four steps forward and four steps backward, four steps backward and four steps forward. Clap on counts 4 and 8. The cue is forward, 2, 3, 4 (clap); backward, 2, 3, 4 (clap); backward, 2, 3, 4 (clap); forward 2, 3, 4 (clap).

Teaching Suggestion: Have the youngsters bring a favorite record from home. They like the "mature" feeling of dancing to up-beat music. Variations are possible (i.e., in Part IV, instead of four steps, use three steps and a kick (swing).

Bleking (Swedish)

Records: Folkraft 1188; Lloyd Shaw E-9, E-20; Merit Audiovisual-Folk Dances for Everyone

Skills: Bleking step, step-hop

Formation: Single circle, partners facing, both hands joined. Boys face counterclockwise and girls clockwise.

Directions

Part I—The Bleking Step: Cue by calling "Slow-slow, fast-fast-fast."

Measure	Action
1	Hop on the left foot and extend the right heel forward with the right leg straight. At the same time, thrust the right hand forward. Hop on the right foot, reversing the arm action and extending the left foot to rest on the heel.
2	Repeat the action with three quick changes—left, right, left.
3–4	Beginning on the right foot, repeat the movements of measures 1 and 2.
5–8	Repeat measures 1–4.

Part II —The Windmills: Partners extend their joined hands sideways at shoulder height.

Measure	Action
9–16	Partners turn in place with a repeated step-hop. At the same time, the arms move up and down like a windmill. The turning is done clockwise, with the boy starting on his right foot and the girl on her left. At the completion of the step-hops (16), the partners should be in their original places ready for Part I again.

Variations

1. Change from original positions to a double circle, partners facing, the boys with back to the center. Part I is as described. For Part II, all face counterclockwise, and partners join inside hands. Partners do the basic schottische of "step, step, step, hop" throughout Part II (p. 277).

2. Another excellent variation is to do the dance with partners scattered in general space. Part I is as described. For Part II, the children leave their partners and step-hop in various directions around the dancing area. When the music is about to change back to Part I, each performer finds a partner wherever she can, and the dance is repeated.

3. Bleking is excellent music for creative dance, with the stipulation that the children maintain individually the bleking rhythm of "slow-slow, fast-fast-fast" during Part I and do any kind of movement in place that they wish. During Part II, they may do any locomotor or other movement that they choose.

Nixie Polka (Swedish)

Record: Folkraft 6185; Merit Audiovisual-Folk Dance Fundamentals

Skills: Bleking step

Formation: Single circle, all facing center, with one or more children scattered inside the circle

Measures	Action 1
1–4	With hands joined, all spring lightly onto the left foot and extend the right foot forward, heel to ground, toe up. Next, spring lightly onto the right foot and extend the left foot forward. Repeat this action until four slow bleking steps are completed.
5–8	All clap hands once and shout "Hey!" The center child then runs around the inside of the circle, looking for a partner. She selects one. They join both hands and run lightly in place until the music is finished. This refrain is repeated, so the children have time to get back to the center of the circle.
	Action 2
1–4	The center dancer and her partner, with both hands joined, repeat the action of measures 1–4. All dancers in the circle also repeat the action of measures 1–4.
5–8	On the first count, all clap hands, shouting "Hey!" The center dancer then about-faces and places both hands on the shoulders of her partner, who now becomes the new leader. In this position, both shuffle around the inside of the circle, looking for a third person to dance with. The music is repeated again to allow ample time to return to the center.
	Action 3
1–4	The action of measures 1–4 is repeated, with the new dancer facing the circle and the two others facing him.
5–8	On the first count, all clap hands, shouting "Hey!" The two people in the center then about-face. All three now face the center to form a line of three dancers with a new leader who looks for a fourth dancer. The music is repeated.

The entire dance is thus repeated, accumulating dancers with each repetition. There should be one center dancer for each dozen dancers in the circle.

Bingo (American)

Records: Folkraft 1189; Lloyd Shaw E-13, E-20; Merit Audiovisual-Folk Dances From Near and Far

Skills: Walking, right-and-left grand

Formation: Double circle, partners side-by-side and facing counterclockwise, boys on the inside and inside hands joined

Note: Bingo is a favorite of young people. The singing must be brisk and loud. The dance is in three parts.

Directions

Part I: Partners walk counterclockwise around the circle, singing the following refrain.

A big white dog sat on the back porch and Bingo was his name.
A big white dog sat on the back porch and Bingo was his name.

Part II: All join hands to form a single circle, the girl on her partner's right. They sing (spelling out) with these actions.

Song	Action
B-I-N-G-O,	All take four steps into the center.
B-I-N-G-O,	All take four steps backward.
B-I-N-G-O,	All take four steps forward again.
And Bingo was his name.	Take four steps backward, drop hands, and face partner.

Part III: Shake right hands with the partner, calling out *B* on the first heavy note. All walk forward, passing their partner, to meet the oncoming person with a left handshake, calling out *I* on the next chord. Continue to the third person with a right handshake, sounding out the *N.* Pass on to the fourth person, giving a left handshake and a *G.* Instead of a handshake with the fifth person, face each other, raise the arms high above the head, shake all over, and sound out a long, drawn-out *O.* The fifth person becomes the new partner, and the dance is repeated.

Variations

1. A real desperado by the name of Ringo actually had quite a reputation as a gunman, and his name can be used in the dance. The wording of the verses is then changed as follows.

There was a fast gunman in the West and Ringo was his name!
There was a fast gunman in the West and Ringo was his name!
R-I-N-G-O, (Repeat three times.)
And Ringo was his name.

2. The dance can be adapted to the use of a parachute. At the end of Part II (the end of the line "And Bingo was his name") the boys face the chute and hold it with both hands, lifting it to shoulder level. The girls drop their hands from the parachute and get ready to move clockwise. On each of the letters B-I-N-G-O, they move inside the first boy, outside the next, and so on, for five changes. They then take a new place as indicated and get ready to repeat the dance. The next sequence can have the girls remaining in place, holding the chute, while the boys move counterclockwise.

DANCES FOR THIRD-GRADE CHILDREN

In the 3rd grade, the emphasis is definitely on folk dance. Locomotor skills are still the basis of the movement patterns, but in most of the dances, the patterns are more difficult than in the 2nd grade. At this level, each dance always has at least two parts, and may have three or more. Since the movement patterns are longer, the part-whole teaching method is used more often with this age-group. The dances for the 3rd grade are vigorous and fast-moving, which makes them exciting for youngsters to perform.

Dance	Skills
Bridge of Avignon	Skipping, mimicking
Pop Goes the Weasel	Walking, skipping, turning under
Teddy Bear Mixer	Walking, pausing, changing partners
Csebogar	Skipping, sliding, draw step, elbow swing
Gustaf's Skoal	Walking (stately), skipping, turning
Polly Wolly Doodle	Slide, turns, elbow swing
Patty Cake (Heel and Toe) Polka	Heel and toe step, sliding, elbow swing
Oh, Susanna	Walking, grand right and left, skipping
La Raspa	Bleking step, running, elbow swing

Bridge of Avignon (French)

Records: Folkraft 1191; Lloyd Shaw E-3; Merit Audiovisual-Folk Dance Fundamentals

Skills: Skipping and mimicking

Formation: Circle of couples facing counterclockwise, inside hands joined

Measures	Chorus
1–2	On the Bridge of Avignon,
3–4	They are dancing, they are dancing
5–6	On the Bridge of Avignon
7–8	They are dancing in a ring.
	Verse 1
1–2	Gentlemen all do this way,
3–4	Then they all do this way.
	Verse 2
1–2	Ladies all do this way,
3–4	Then they all do this way.
	Verse 3
1–2	Soldiers all do this way,
3–4	Then they all do this way.
	Verse 4
1–2	Angels all do this way,
3–4	Then they all do this way.
	Verse 5
1–2	Street boys all do this way,
3–4	Then they all do this way.

Directions

Measures	Chorus Action
1–8	All skip counterclockwise, facing forward and singing.
	Verse 1 Action
1–2	Partners face each other, and with great mimicry make an elaborate bow.
3–4	All move one place right to a new partner and repeat the bow.
	Verse 2 Action
1–2	Partners face and curtsy, the boys holding their trousers out—pretending to be girls. Again, this is done with much exaggeration.
3–4	All move one place right to meet a new partner and repeat curtsy.
	Verse 3 Action
1–2	Salute each other.
3–4	Move to a new partner.
	Verse 4 Action
1–2	Angels either pray or fly.
3–4	Move to a new partner.

Measures	Chorus Action
	Verse 5 Action
1–2	Stick the thumbs in the ears and wiggle the fingers while sticking out the tongue.
3–4	Move to a new partner.

There is one additional repeat of music for teachers to improvise their own action. (Have the children locate Avignon, France, on a map.)

Pop Goes the Weasel (American)

Records: Folkraft 1329; Folk Dancer 1329; Lloyd Shaw E-7, E-21, E-26 (reduced tempo); Merit Audiovisual-Folk Dances From Near and Far.

Skills: Walking, skipping, turning under

Formation: A circle of "sets of four," couple facing couple with girl on partner's right. Couples facing clockwise are no. 1 couples; couples facing counterclockwise are no. 2 couples.

Directions

Measures	Action
1–4	Join hands in a circle of four and circle left, once around, with eight skipping or sliding steps.
5–6	Take two steps forward, raising the joined hands, and two steps backward, lowering the hands.
7–8	"Ones" pop the "Twos" under (i.e., couples no. 1 raise their joined hands to form an arch and pass the no. 2 couples under). All walk ahead to meet a new couple.

Repeat as desired.

Variations

1. Dancers are in sets of three, all facing counterclockwise. Each forms a triangle with one child in front and the other two with joined hands forming the base. The front dancer reaches back and holds the outside hands of the other two dancers. The groups of three are in a large

Measures	Action
1–2	Sets of three skip forward four times (counterclockwise).
3–4	Sets of three skip backward four times (clockwise).
5–6	Sets of three skip forward four times (counterclockwise).
7–8	On "Pop goes the weasel," the two back dancers raise their joined hands, and the front dancer backs up underneath to the next set. This set, in the meantime, has "popped" its front dancer back to the set behind it.

2. "Pop Goes the Weasel" is excellent for stimulating creative movement. The music actually consists of a verse and a chorus part. During the verse part, the children can slide, gallop, or skip until the "Pop" line, at which time they make a half or full turn in the air. During the chorus, they can do jerky nonlocomotor movements. Other options include ball routines, in which the children dribble in time to the music during the verse and pass the ball around various parts of the body during the chorus. Another variation involves ropes. The children carry a jump rope while skipping, sliding, or galloping. During the chorus, they jump in time to the music, and on the word "Pop," they try to do a double jump.

Teddy Bear Mixer (American)

Records: Any version of Teddy Bear's Picnic; Glow Worm Folkraft 1158; Lloyd Shaw E-11

Skills: Walking, pausing, partner change

Formation: Double circle of couples facing counterclockwise, girl on right side of partner, inside hands joined. Walking step is used throughout.

Directions

Measures	Action
1	Walk, 2, 3, pause: Starting with the boy's left foot (girl's right), walk three steps in the line of direction and pause.
2	Back, 2, 3, pause: Starting with the boy's right foot (girl's left), walk backwards three steps in the reverse line of direction and pause.
3	Separate, 2, 3, pause: Starting on the left foot, the boys move three steps toward the center of the circle and pause. Starting on the right foot, the girls move away from the center of the circle three steps and pause. At the completion of the third step, a handclap may be used during the pause.
4	Together, 2, 3, pause: Starting on the boy's right foot (girl's left), both move toward each other, rejoining inside hands.
5	Walk, 2, 3, pause: Repeat no. 1.
6	Back, 2, 3, pause: Repeat no. 2.
7	Separate, 2, 3, pause: Repeat no. 3.
8	Diagonally, 2, 3, pause: Starting with the boy's right foot (girl's left), both move together diagonally, with the boy moving forward to the girl ahead to acquire a new partner for the next repetition.

Csebogar (Hungarian)

Records: Folkraft 1196; Lloyd Shaw E-15; Merit Audiovisual-Folk Dances for Beginners

Skills: Skipping, sliding, draw step, elbow swing

Formation: Single circle, partners facing center, hands joined with girls on the right

Directions
Part I

Measures	Action
1–4	Take seven slides to the left.
5–8	Take seven slides to the right.
9–12	Take four skips to the center and four backward to place.
13–16	Hook right elbows with partner and turn around twice in place, skipping.

Part II: Partners face each other in a single circle with hands joined.

Measures	Action
17–20	Holding both of partner's hands, take four draw steps (step, close) toward the center of the circle.
21–24	Take four draw steps back to place.
25–26	Go toward the center of the circle with two draw steps.
27–28	Take two draw steps back to place.
29–32	Hook elbows and repeat the elbow-swing, finishing with a shout and facing the center of the circle in the original formation.

Variation: Instead of elbow-swing, partners can use the Hungarian turn. Partners stand side-by-side and put the right arm around the partner's waist. The left arm is held out to the side, with the elbow bent, the hand pointing up, and the palm facing the dancer.

Gustaf's Skoal (Swedish)

Records: Hoctor HLP-4027; Lloyd Shaw E-11, E-22; Merit Audiovisual-Folk Dances for Everyone

Skills: Walking (stately), skipping, turning

Formation: The formation is similar to a square dance set of four couples, each facing center. The boy is to the left of his partner. Couples join inside hands; the outside hand is on the hip. Two of the couples facing each other are designated the head couples. The other two couples, also facing each other, are the side couples.

Directions: The dance is in two parts. During Part I, the music is slow and stately. The dancers perform with great dignity. The music for Part II is light and represents fun.

Part I

Measures	Action
1–2	The head couples, inside hands joined, walk forward three steps and bow to the opposite couple.
3–4	The head couples take three steps backward to place and bow to each other. (The side couples hold their places during this action.)
5–8	The side couples perform the same movements, while the head couples hold their places.

The dancers then repeat the entire figure.

Part II

Measures	Action
9–12	The side couples raise their joined hands to form an arch. The head couples skip to the center, where they meet the opposite partners. Each, after dropping his partner's hand, takes the inside hand of the facing dancer and skips under the nearest arch. After going under the arch, they drop hands and head back home to their original partner.
13–16	All clap hands smartly on the first note of measure 13 while skipping. They skip toward their partner, join both hands, and skip once around in place.

The action of measures 13–16 is repeated. The head couples form the arches, and the side couples repeat the pattern just finished by the head couples.

Variation: During the first action sequence of Part I (in which the dancers take three steps and bow), a shout of "Skoal" and raising the right fist high above the head as a salute can be substituted for the bow. The word *skoal* is a toast. (Note that the dancers' hands are not joined.)

Polly Wolly Doodle (American)

Record: Merit Audiovisual-Folk Dance Fundamentals

Skills: Sliding, turning, walking

Formation: Double circle of dancers, partners facing with both hands joined, the boy with his back to the center of the circle

Measures	Music A
1–4	Oh, I went down south for to see my Sal,
5–8	Sing polly wolly doodle all the day.
9–12	My Sally am a spunky gal
13–16	Sing polly wolly doodle all the day.
	Verse 2
1–4	Oh, my Sal she am a maiden fair,
5–8	Sing polly wolly doodle all the day,
9–12	With laughing eyes and curly hair,
13–16	Sing polly wolly doodle all the day.
	Music B
1–4	Fare thee well, fare thee well,
5–8	Fare thee well, my fairy fay,
9–12	For going to Louisiana for to see my Susyanna,
13–16	Sing polly wolly doodle all the day.

Directions

Measures	Action (Music A)
1–4	All slide four steps—boys to left, girls to right, counterclockwise.

Measures	Action (Music A)
5–8	Drop hands and all turn solo circle, boys to left, girls to right, with five stamps in this rhythm: 1—2—1, 2, 3. (Stamp on the word "polly," stamp on the other foot on the word "doodle," and take three quick stamps on the word "day.")
9–16	Repeat measures 5–8, but in the opposite direction, boys moving to right and girls to left.
	Action (Music B)
1–4	Both bow to each other, boys with hands on hips, girls holding skirts.
5–8	With four walking steps (or skipping steps), both move backward, away from each other.
9–12	Both move diagonally forward to own left to meet a new partner.
13–16	With the new partner, elbow swing in place using a skipping step.

Repeat the dance from the beginning with the new partner.

Patty Cake (Heel and Toe) Polka (International)

Records: Folkraft 1260; MacGregor 5003-B; Lloyd Shaw E-12, 228

Skills: Heel and toe polka step, sliding, elbow-swing, skipping

Formation: Double circle, partners facing, the boy in the inner circle with his back to the center. Both hands are joined with partner. The boy's left and the girl's right foot are free.

Directions

Measures	Part I Action
1–2	Heel-toe twice with the boy's left and the girl's right foot.
3–4	Take four slides sideward to the boy's left, progressing counterclockwise. Do not transfer the weight on the last count. Finish with the boy's right and the girl's left foot free.
5–8	Repeat the pattern of measures 1–4, starting with the boy's right and the girl's left foot, progressing clockwise. Finish with the partners separated and facing.
	Part II Action
9	Clap right hands with partner three times.
10	Clap left hands with partner three times.
11	Clap both hands with partner three times.
12	Slap own knees three times.
13–14	Right elbow-swing with partner. Partners hook right elbows and swing once around with four walking steps, finishing with the boy's back to center.
15–16	Progress left to a new partner with four walking steps.

Repeat the entire dance with the new partner.

Oh, Susanna (American)

Records: Merit Audiovisual-Folk Dances From Near and Far; Folkraft 6178, 1186; Lloyd Shaw E-14, E-23

Skills: Grand right and left, skaters' position

Formation: Single circle, all facing center, girl on the boy's right

Directions

Measures	Part I Action
1–4	The girls walk forward four steps and back four, as the boys clap hands.
5–8	Reverse, with the boys walking forward and back, and the girls clapping time.
	Part II Action
1–8	Partners face each other, and all do a grand right and left by grasping the partner's right hand, then passing to the next person with a left-hand hold. Continue until reaching the seventh person, who becomes the new partner.
	Chorus
1–16	All join hands in skaters' position with the new partner and walk counterclockwise around the circle for two full choruses singing: "Oh Susanna, oh don't you cry for me, For I come from Alabama with my banjo on my knee."

Repeat the dance from the beginning, each time with a new partner. For variety in the chorus, skip instead of walk, or walk during the first chorus and swing one's partner in place during the second chorus.

Variation

Formation: Partners stand in a single circle, all facing center with the girl on the boy's right, hands joined

Directions

Measures	Action
1–8	Take eight sliding steps to the right, then eight sliding steps to the left.
9–12	Take four steps to the center, and four steps back to place.
13–16	Release hands. The girls walk four steps toward the center of the circle and four steps back. The boys stand in place and clap hands.
17–20	The boys go to the center while the girls clap hands.
21–24	Do-si-do with partner.
25–28	Do-si-do with the corner.
29–32	Everyone promenades around the circle, or the boy promenades with the corner lady.

La Raspa (Mexican)

Records: Imperial 1084; Folkraft 1119, 1457; Merit Audio-visual-Folk Dances From Near and Far; Lloyd Shaw E-8

Skills: Bleking step, running, elbow-turn

Formation: Couples scattered around the room

Directions: *La raspa* means "the rasp" or "the file," and the dance movements are supposed to represent a rasp or file in action. The dance is in two parts. Directions are the same for both partners.

Part I: To begin, the partners face each other, the girl pretending to hold her skirt and the boy with his hands behind his back. The step is similar to the bleking step (p. 262).

Measures	Part I Action
1–4	Beginning right, take one bleking step.
5–8	Turn slightly counterclockwise away from partner (right shoulder to right shoulder) and, beginning left, take one bleking step.
9–12	Repeat action of measures 1–4, facing opposite direction (left shoulder to left shoulder).
13–16	Repeat action of measures 1–4, facing partner.

Part II: Partners hook right elbows; left elbows are bent and left hands are pointed toward the ceiling.

Measures	Part II Action
1–4	Do a right elbow-swing, using eight running or skipping steps. Release and clap the hands on the eighth count.
5–8	Do a left elbow-swing, using eight running or skipping steps. Release and clap the hands on the eighth count.
9–16	Repeat the actions of measures 1–8.

Variation 1: Face partner (all should be in a single-circle formation for this version) and do a grand right and left around the circle. Repeat Part I with a new partner.

Variation 2: All face center or face a partner and do the bleking or *raspa* step. On each pause, clap own hands twice.

MIXERS (INTERMEDIATE GRADES)

A mixer is an activity in which all dancers regularly exchange partners. Almost any dance can involve a partner exchange and could therefore be classified as a mixer. Many of the dances listed in the primary section suggest a partner exchange at the end of each basic dance pattern. We include a special section on mixers so the teacher can set aside some quick and easy dances to be used at several grade levels to serve the following purposes:

1. Provide fun through dance.

2. Create a less formal atmosphere than many dances allow.

3. Provide quick and easy accomplishment, thus reinforcing success through dance.

4. Help break the ice for older children who are less experienced with rhythmic activities and who are sometimes hesitant to work with members of the opposite sex. Mixers can pave the way for more difficult dances to come.

When teaching dance in the elementary physical education program, having children change partners often is a wise practice. The folk dances suggested for the upper grades contain partner exchanges. The dances included in this "Mixers" section can be used at several different grade levels and in most cases have more frequent partner exchanges than the other dances listed for the upper grades.

Dance	Grade Level
The Bird Dance	3–6
Irish Washerwoman	3–6
E-Z Mixer	3–6
Wild Turkey Mixer	3–6
Jiffy Mixer	3–6
Tennessee Wig Walk	4–6
Inside-Out Mixer	4–6
Jugglehead Mixer	5–6

The Bird Dance (Chicken Dance)

Record: Avia Disk AD-831-A

Skills: Skipping or walking, elbow-swing or star

Formation: Circle or scatter formation, partners facing

Directions

Measures	Part I Action
1	Four snaps—thumb and fingers, hands up
2	Four flaps—arms up and down, elbows bent
3	Four wiggles—hips, knees bent low
4	Four claps

Measures	Part II Action
1	With a partner, do either a right-hand star with 16 skips or 16 walking steps, or do an elbow-swing.
2	Repeat with the left hand. On the last four counts of the last swing, everyone changes partners. If dancing in a circle formation, the girls advance forward counterclockwise to the next boy partner. If dancing in a scattered formation, everyone scrambles to find a new partner.

Irish Washerwoman

Records: Folkraft 1155; Merit Audiovisual-Folk Dances From Near and Far; Lloyd Shaw E-11

Skills: Walking, swinging, promenade

Formation: Single circle, couples facing center, girl to the right of her partner, hands joined

Directions: Dancers follow the call.

Call	Action
All join hands and go to the middle.	Beginning left, take four steps to the center.
And with your big foot keep time to the fiddle.	Stamp four times in place.
And when you get back, remember my call.	Take four steps backward to place.
Swing your corner lady and promenade all.	Swing the corner lady and promenade in the line of direction.

Dancers keep promenading until they hear the call again to repeat the pattern.

E-Z Mixer

Record: Grenn 15008

Skills: Walking and elbow-swing, or swing in closed position

Formation: Circle formation with couples in promenade position, inside hands joined, facing counterclockwise

Directions

Measures	Action
1–2	With the girl on the boy's right, walk forward four steps (walk, 2, 3, 4); back out to face center in a single circle (out, 2, 3, 4).
3–4	The girls walk to the center (walk, 2, 3, 4), and back out of the center (out, 2, 3, 4).
5–6	The boys take four steps to the center, turning one half left face on the fourth step (walk, 2, 3, turn left face). They take four steps toward the corner (out, 2, 3, 4).
7–8	The boys swing the corner girl twice around, opening up to face counterclockwise, back in starting position, to begin the dance again.

Any piece of music with a moderate 4/4 rhythm is appropriate for this basic mixer.

Wild Turkey Mixer

Record: Euclid, OH 44117

Skills: Walking, elbow-swing

Formation: Trios (three people, either sex) abreast facing counterclockwise around the circle

Directions

Measures	Action
1–8	The trios promenade 16 steps around the circle. (As a line of three, with the right and left person holding the near hand of the center person, all walk 16 steps forward.)
9–12	The center person (Wild Turkey) turns the right-hand person once around with the right elbow.
13–16	The Wild Turkey turns the left-hand person with the left elbow, and then moves forward to repeat the dance with the two new people in front of him.

The same dance can be adapted to other pieces of music. With a faster tempo, the elbow-swings are done with a skip instead of a walk.

Jiffy Mixer

Records: Windsor 4684; Kimbo KEA-1146

Skills: Heel-and-toe step, chug step

Formation: Double circle, partners facing with both hands joined. The boy's back is to the center of the circle. The elbows should be bent slightly.

Directions: The Windsor record has an introduction. Directions are for boys; the girls' actions are opposite.

Measures	Action (Introduction)
1–4	Wait, wait, balance apart (push away on the left foot and touch the right). Balance together (forward on the right and touch the left).

The Dance

Measures	Action
1–4	Heel, toe; heel, toe; side, close; side, touch. (Strike the left heel diagonally out and return to touch the toe near the right foot. Repeat. Do a side step left with a touch, moving in the line of direction.)
5–8	Heel, toe; heel, toe; side, close; side, touch. (Repeat in the reverse line of direction, beginning with the right foot.)
9–12	Chug, clap. Repeat three more times. (Release hands and take four chug steps backward, clapping on the up beat.)
13–16	Walk to the right, 2, 3, 4. (Starting with the left foot, take four slow, swaggering steps diagonally to the right, progressing to a new partner.)

The chug step is done by dragging both feet backward. The body is bent slightly forward.

Teaching Suggestions

1. The dance can be introduced by having all join hands in a single circle, facing inward. There are no partners and no progressions to new partners.

2. The dancers can be in the butterfly position for the first eight measures of the dance. (The butterfly position is taken by partners holding hands with the arms outstretched to the sides.)

Tennessee Wig Walk (American)

Records: Decca 28846; Kimbo KEA-1146

Skills: Sidestep, boogie woogie step

Formation: Double circle, partners facing. Partners do not hold hands.

Directions: Actions are for the boys. The girls reverse the directions.

Measures	Action
1	Step left, close right, step left, touch right to left, and clap.
2	Step right, close left, step right, touch left to right, and clap.
3–4	Repeat the actions of measures 1 and 2.
5–6	Do a boogie woogie step in the line of direction. Pivot on the heels, move both toes left, pivot on the toes, and move both the heels left. Repeat three times.
7	Both boys and girls do two side steps left (left, close right, step left, close) to position themselves in front of a new partner.
8	Slap the thighs, clap the hands together, and clap the partner's hands.

Repeat the dance with a new partner.

Inside-Out Mixer

Record: Any record with a pronounced beat—jive, rock, or jazz—suitable for walking at a moderate speed

Skills: Walking, reverse circle

Formation: Three children standing side-by-side, facing counterclockwise, with inside hands joined

Directions

Measures	Action
1–4	Take eight walking steps forward.
5–8	Form a small circle and circle left in eight steps back to place.
9–12	The center person walks forward under the raised arms opposite, pulling the other two under to reverse the circle (back-to-back).
13–16	The trio circles left in eight steps, returning to place. When almost back to place, drop hands. The center person walks forward counterclockwise, and the other two walk clockwise (the way they are facing) to the nearest trio for a change of partners.

Note that the first circle left moves clockwise, and the second counterclockwise. A pinney can be worn by the center person for identification.

Jugglehead Mixer (American)

Records: Columbia 52007 ("Little Brown Jug"); Old Timer 8051

Skills: Two-step, elbow-turn (forearm grasp)

Formation: Couples facing counterclockwise, the boy on the inside, with right and left hands joined in the crossed-arm (skaters') position

Directions: The action described is for the boy. Directions are opposite for the girl.

Measures	Call	Action
1–4	Two-step left and two-step right, walk-2-3-4.	Do a two-step left and a two-step right and take four walking steps forward.
5–8		Repeat measures 1–4.
9–10	Turn your partner with the right.	The boy takes the girl's right hand with his right and walks around that girl to face the girl behind him.
11–12	Now your corner with your left.	The boy turns the girl behind him with his left hand.
13–14	Turn your partner all the way around.	The boy turns his own partner with the right hand, going all the way around.

Measures	Call	Action
15–16	And pick up the forward lady.	The boy steps up one place to the girl ahead of him, who becomes his new partner.

Teaching Suggestion: When the boy turns the girl, he should slide his hand along the girl's wrist and use a forearm grasp for the turns.

DANCES FOR FOURTH-GRADE CHILDREN

Dances for 4th graders still consist primarily of the basic locomotor skills, but these are now performed in more complex combinations and intricate formations. The dances are all lively and vigorous. (Directions for the Tinikling Dance and the Lummi Sticks are printed in the section titled "Specialty Dances.")

At the 4th grade level, the teacher should be concerned mainly with teaching the basics of each of these activities. We assume that the 5th and 6th grade programs will offer continued practice. At the end of the 6th-grade year, students should be able to perform these dances with quality and flair.

Dance	Skills
Grand March	Marching
Green Sleeves	Walking, right- and left-hand stars
Ve David	Walking, pivot, buzz-step turn
Jingle Bells (Var. 2)	Skipping, skaters' position, sliding, elbow swing
Virginia Reel	Walking or skipping, arm turn, do-si-dos, sashay (sliding), reel the set
Crested Hen	Step-hops, turning under
Troika	Running step, turning under
Tinikling (pp. 282–285)	
Lummi Sticks (pp. 289–290)	

Grand March (American)

Record: Any good march or square dance record

Skills: Controlled walking, grand march figures

Formation: The girls are on the left side of the room, facing the end, and the boys are on the right side, facing the same end. This is the foot of the hall. The teacher or caller stands at the other end of the room, the head of the hall. An alternate formation is to put half of the class on each side of the room and to designate each half with different colored pinnies.

Directions

Call	Action
1. Down the center by twos.	**1.** The lines march forward to the foot of the hall, turn the corner, meet at the center of the foot of the hall, and march in couples toward the caller (Figure 17.4), with inside hands joined. The girls' line should be on the proper side so that, when the couples come down the center, the boy is on the girl's left. Odd couples are numbered 1, 3, 5, and so forth. Even couples are numbered 2, 4, 6, and so on.
2. Twos left and right.	**2.** The odd couples go left and the even couples go right around the room and meet at the foot of the hall.
3. Down the center by fours.	**3.** The couples walk down the center, four abreast.
4. Separate by twos.	**4.** When they approach the caller, odd couples go left and even couples right. They meet again at the foot of the hall.
5. Form arches.	**5.** Instead of coming down the center, odd couples form arches and even couples tunnel under. Each continues around the sides of the hall to meet at the head.
6. Other couples arch.	**6.** Even couples arch, and odd couples tunnel under. Each continues around the sides of the room to the foot.
7. Over and under.	**7.** The first odd couple arches over the first even couple, then ducks under the second even couple's arch. Each couple goes over the first couple and under the next. Continue around to the head of the hall.

Call	Action
8. Pass right through.	**8.** As the lines come toward each other, they mesh and pass through each other in the following fashion: All drop handholds. Each girl walks between the boy and girl of the opposite couple and continues walking to the foot of the hall.
9. Down the center by fours.	**9.** Go down the center four abreast.
10. Fours left and right.	**10.** The first four go left around the room, and the second four go right. The fours meet at the foot of the hall.
11. Down the center by eights.	**11.** Go eight abreast down the center.
12. Grapevine.	**12.** All persons in each line join hands and keep them joined. The leader takes either end of the first line and starts around the room with the line trailing. The other lines hook on to form one long line.
13. Wind it up.	**13.** The leader winds up the group in a spiral formation, like a clock spring. He makes the circles smaller and smaller until he is in the center.
14. Reverse (unwind).	**14.** The leader turns and faces in the opposite direction and walks between the lines of winding dancers. He unwinds the line and leads it around the room.
15. Everybody swing.	**15.** After the line is unwound, everybody does a square dance swing.

Teaching Suggestions: The leaders (couples 1 and 2) should maintain an even, steady pace and not hurry, or the march becomes a race.

When one set of couples forms arches (as in movements 5 and 6) for the other set of couples to tunnel under, the arches should be made with the inside arms, and the couples should continue marching while they form the arches.

Green Sleeves (English)

Records: Folkraft 6175; Lloyd Shaw E-11; Merit Audiovisual-Folk Dances for Beginners

Skills: Walking, star formation, over and under

Formation: Circle, facing counterclockwise, boys on the inside, inside hands joined. The couples are numbered 1 and 2. Two couples form a set.

Directions

Measures	Call	Action
1–8	Walk	Walk forward 16 steps.
9–12	Right-hand star	Each member of couple 1 turns individually to face the couple behind. All join right hands and circle clockwise (star) for eight steps.
13–16	Left-hand star	Reverse and form a left-hand star. Circle counterclockwise. This should bring couple 1 back to place, facing in the original direction (counterclockwise).
17–20	Over and under	Couple 2 arches, and couple 1 backs under four steps while couple 2 moves forward four steps. Couple 1 then arches, and couple 2 backs under (four steps for each).
21–24	Over and under	Repeat the action of measures 17–20.

Ve David (Israeli)

Records: Folkraft 1432; Hoctor HLP-4028

Skills: Walking, pivoting, buzz-step turn

Formation: Circle of couples facing counterclockwise, girl on partner's right. Inside hands joined, right foot free.

Directions

Measures	Figure I Action
1–2	All walk forward and form a ring. Take four walking steps forward, starting with the right foot and progressing counterclockwise, then

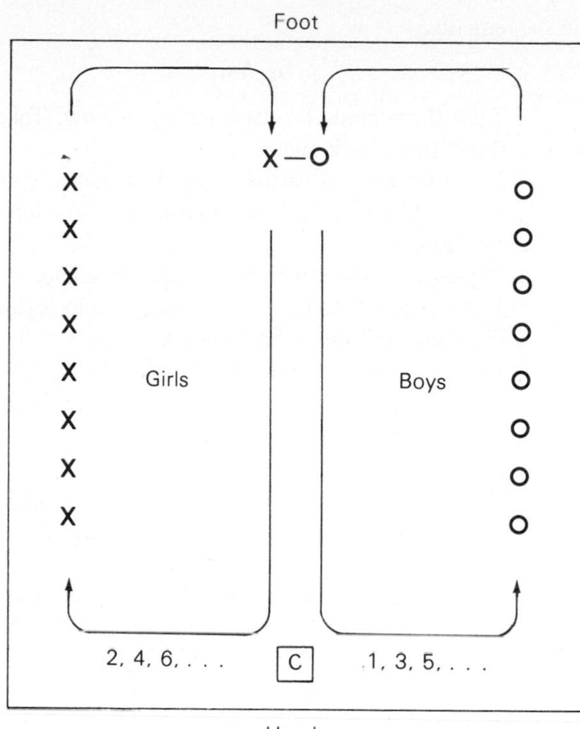

FIGURE 17.4. Formation and action for grand march

Measures	Figure I Action
	back out taking four walking steps to form a single circle, facing center, with all hands joined.
3–4	All forward and back. Four steps forward to center and four steps backward, starting with the right foot.

Measures	Figure II Action
1–2	Girls forward and back; boys clap. The girls, starting with the right foot, walk four steps forward to the center and four steps backward to place while the boys clap.

Measures	Figure III Action
1–2	Boys forward, circle to the right and progress to a new partner; all clap. The boys, clapping hands, walk four steps forward to the center, starting with the right foot. They turn right about on the last "and" count and walk forward four steps, passing their original partner and progressing ahead to the next girl.
3–4	Swing the new partner. The boy and his new partner swing clockwise with right shoulders adjacent, right arms around each other across in front, and left arms raised—pivoting with right foot for an eight count "buzz-step" swing.

Repeat the entire dance.

Jingle Bells, Var. 2 (Dutch)

Record: Folkraft 1080

Skills: Skipping, skaters' position, sliding, elbow-swing

Formation: Circle of couples facing counterclockwise, girl on partner's right. Skaters' position, hands crossed in front, right hands joined over left, right foot free.

Directions

Measures	Music A Action
1–2	Take four skips forward and four skips backward, starting with the right foot free.
3–4	Repeat the pattern of measures 1–2.
5	Do four slides to the right, away from the center of the circle.
6	Now do four slides left, toward the center.
7–8	Execute eight skips, making one turn counterclockwise, with the boy pivoting backward and the girl moving forward. Finish in a double circle, partners facing, with the boy's back to the center.

Measures	Music B Action
1	Clap own hands three times.
2	Clap both hands with partner three times.
3	Clap own hands four times.
4	Clap both hands with partner once.
5–8	Right elbow-swing with partner. Partners hook right elbows and swing clockwise for eight skips.
9–12	Repeat clapping pattern of measures 1–4.
13–16	Left elbow-swing with partner using eight skips and finishing in the original starting position to repeat the entire dance with the same partner; or left elbow-swing with partner once around, then all of the boys or children in the inner circle skip forward to the girl ahead and repeat the entire dance with a new partner.

Virginia Reel (American)

Records: Folkraft 1141, 1249; Melody House 74; Lloyd Shaw E-12, E-23; Hoctor HLP-4027

Skills: Skipping (forward and back), arm turn, do-si-dos, sliding (sashay), reeling

Formation: Six couples in a longways set of two lines facing, the boys in one line and the girls in the other. The boy on the left of his line and the girl across from him are the head couple.

Directions: During the first part of the dance, all perform the same movements.

Measures	Call	Action
1–4	All go forward and back.	Take three steps forward, curtsy or bow. Take three steps back and close.
5–8	Right hands around.	Move forward to partner, join right hands, turn once in place, and return to position. Use a forearm grasp.
9–12	Left hands around.	Repeat the action with a left forearm grasp.
13–16	Both hands around.	Partners join both hands, turn once in a clockwise direction, and move backward to place.
17–20	Do-si-do your partner.	Partners pass each other, right shoulder to right shoulder and then back-to-back, and move backward to place.
21–24	All go forward and back.	Repeat the action of measures 1–4.
25–32	Head couple sashay.	The head couple, with hands joined, takes eight slides down to the foot of the set and eight slides back to place.
33–64	Head couple reel.	The head couple begins the reel with linked right elbows and turns one-and-one-half times. The boy is then facing the next girl, and his partner is facing the next boy. Each member in the head couple then links left elbow with the person facing and turns once in place. The head couple meets again in the center and turns once with a right elbow-swing. The next dancers down the line are turned with a left elbow-swing, and then the head couple returns to the center for another right elbow-turn. The head couple thus progresses down the line, turning each dancer in order. After the head couple has turned the last dancers, they meet with a right elbow-swing but turn only halfway around and sashay back to the head of the set.
65–96	Everybody march.	All couples face toward the head of the set, with the head couple in front. The head girl turns to her right and the head boy to his left, and each goes behind the line, followed by the other dancers. When the head couple reaches the foot of the set, they join hands and make an arch, under which all other couples pass. The head couple is then at the foot of the set, and the dance is repeated with a new head couple.

The dance is repeated until each couple has had a chance to be the head couple.

Variation: Versions of this dance vary. Some allow time in the beginning for a do-si-do after the both hands around (measures 13–16), and some do not. The teacher should check all phrasing before presenting the dance to the class.

Technically, the dance is written for eight couples in each set. For the head couple to reel all couples in the set, they must not miss one beat of the music, or they will be behind the phrasing for the reel section. When introducing the dance to a class for the first time, having only six couples in each set is helpful. If a couple then gets a beat behind the music for the reeling section, they still can stay in time to the music, and with a little luck, finish before the "casting off" section begins.

Crested Hen (Danish)

Records: Folkraft 1154, 1194; Hoctor HLP-4027; Merit Audiovisual-Folk Dances for Beginners

Skills: Step-hop, turning under

Formation: Sets of three, which can be two girls and a boy, two boys and a girl, or three of the same sex. One child is designated the center child.

Directions

Part I

Measures	Action
1–8	Dancers in each set form a circle. Starting with a stamp with the left foot, each set circles to the left, using step-hops.

The figure is repeated. Dancers reverse direction, beginning again with a stamp with the left foot and following with step-hops. The change of direction should be vigorous and definite, with the left foot crossing over the right.

Part II: During this part, the dancers use the step-hop continuously while making the pattern figures. The outside dancers release their hands to break the circle and stand on either side of the center person, forming a line of three with the center dancer while retaining joined hands with her.

Measures	Action
9–10	The dancer on the right moves forward in an arc to the left and dances under the arch formed by the other two.
11–12	After the right dancer has gone through, the two forming the arch turn under (dishrag), to form once again a line of three.
13–16	The dancer on the left then repeats the pattern, moving forward in an arc under the arch formed by the other two, who turn under to unravel the line.

As soon as Part II is completed, dancers again join hands in a small circle. The entire dance is repeated. Another of the three can be designated the center dancer.

Troika (Russian)

Records: Folkraft 1170; Hoctor HLP-4027; Lloyd Shaw WT-10010

Skills: Running step, turning under

Formation: Trios face counterclockwise. The center dancer and two partners may be one boy with two girls, one girl with two boys, or all boys or all girls. Start with hands joined in a line of three. The body weight is on the left foot; the right foot is free.

Directions

Measures	Part I Action
1	Take four running steps diagonally forward right, starting with the right foot.
2	Take four running steps diagonally forward left, starting with the right foot.
3–4	Take eight running steps in a forward direction, starting with the right foot.
5–6	The center dancer and her left-hand partner raise joined hands to form an arch and run in place. Meanwhile, the right-hand partner moves counterclockwise around the center dancer with eight running steps, goes under the arch, and back to place. The center dancer unwinds by turning under the arch.
7–8	Repeat the pattern of measures 5–6, with the left-hand partner running under the arch formed by the center dancer and her right-hand partner.
	Part II Action
9–11	The trio joins hands and circles left with 12 running steps.
12	Three stamps in place (counts 1–3), pause (count 4).
13–15	The trio circles right with 12 running steps, opening out at the end to re-form in lines of three facing counterclockwise.
16	The center dancer releases each partner's hand and runs under the opposite arch of joined hands to advance to a new pair ahead. Right- and left-hand partners run in place while waiting for a new center dancer to join them in a new trio.

DANCES FOR FIFTH-GRADE CHILDREN

At the 5th-grade level, children should be adept dancers, especially if they have had folk dancing at earlier grade levels. If the students do not have a well-developed dance background, the teacher may be wise to spend time on the program recommended for the 4th grade.

The dances for the 5th grade include dance patterns that must be performed with skill and finesse. At this level, patterns become longer, requiring more concentration and memorization. The schottische and polka step make their first appearance in these dances.

Fifth-Grade Dances	Skills
Tennessee Wig Walk	Grapevine step, brush step
D'Hammerschmiedsgselln	Clapping routine, step-hops
Alley Cat	Grapevine step, touch step, knee lifts
Alunelul	Step behind step, grapevine step, stomping
Hora	Stepping sideward, step-swing
Horse and Buggy Schottische	Schottische step
Jessie Polka	Step and touch, polka step
Klumpakojis	Walking, stars, polka step
Tinikling (pp. 282–285)	
Lummi Sticks (pp. 289–290)	

Tennessee Wig Walk (American)

Records: Folkraft M60051; Kimbo KEA-1146

Skills: Grapevine step, brush step

Formation: Double circle, boys facing counterclockwise, girls facing clockwise, side-by-side with right hands joined and raised to shoulder height.

Directions

Measures	Part I Action
1–2	Touch left toe on the floor to the inside (toward partner) once, then to the outside (away from partner) once.
3–4	Step the left foot behind the right so the legs are crossed; step the right foot one step to the right; then close the left foot to the right.
5–6	Touch the right toe on the floor to the inside (toward partner) once, then to the outside (away from partner) once.
7–8	Step the right foot behind the left so the legs are crossed; step the left foot one step to the left; then close the right foot to the left.
	Part II Action
9–12	Starting with the left foot (right hands still joined at shoulder level height), take three steps and a brush step with the right foot, in a circle, to change places with partner (left-right-left-brush). Continuing on around, complete the circle with another left-right-left-brush.
13–16	Back in the original starting position, drop partner's hand, and progress forward (boy counterclockwise, girl clockwise) with a left-right-left-brush. Bypass the first oncoming partner and with one more left-right-left-brush, take the second partner in line as the new partner.

Repeat from the beginning.

D'Hammerschmiedsgselln (Bavarian)

Records: Folkraft 1485; Lloyd Shaw E-18, E-19

Skills: Clapping routine, step-hops

Formation: Circle of four: either two couples with girl on partner's right, or four boys

Directions: Translated, the title of the dance means "The Journey Blacksmith."

Measures	Chorus Action
1–16	First opposites (boys 1 and 3, or the two girls) do a clapping pattern beginning on the first count of measure 1, while the others (boys 2 and 4, or the two boys) do a clapping pattern beginning on first count of measure 2. The pattern is performed as follows: With both hands, slap own thighs (count 1), own chest (count 2), and clap own hands together (count 3). Opposites clap right hands (count 4), left hands (count 5), and both hands (count 6).
	Figure I
17–24	Join hands and circle left with step-hops.
25–32	Circle right in the same manner.
	Figure II—Star
1–16	Repeat the chorus action.
17–24	Right-hand star with step-hops.
25–32	Left-hand star in the same manner.
	Figure III—Big Circle
1–16	Repeat the chorus action.
17–24	Circles of four open to form one large circle, and circle left with step-hops.
25–32	Reverse direction, continuing with step-hops.

Variation: As a mixer, try the following sequence.

Measures	Action
1–16	Use the chorus clapping pattern described.
17–24	As in Figure I or II, circle left, or do a right-hand star with step-hops (or simple walking steps).
25–32	Do eight step-hops with the corner in general space or in any comfortable position, progressing anywhere.

Repeat the entire sequence with a new foursome.

Alley Cat (American)

Records: ATCO 45-6226; Columbia CL-2500; Atlantic 13113

Skills: Grapevine step, touch step, knee lifts

Formation: None, although all should face the same direction during instruction

Directions

Measures	Action
1–2	Do a grapevine left and kick: step sideward left, step right behind left, step left again, and kick. Repeat to the right.
3–4	Touch the left toe backward, bring the left foot to the right, touch the left toe again backward, bring the left foot to the right, taking the weight. Repeat, beginning with the right toe.
5–6	Raise the left knee up in front of the right knee and repeat. Raise the right knee up twice, similarly.
7–8	Raise the left knee and then the right knee. Clap the hands once and make a jump quarter turn to the left.

When the routine is repeated three times, the dancer should be facing in the original direction.

Teaching Suggestion: The actions should be done with appropriate body motions. Devise other dance routines.

Alunelul (Romanian)

Records: Hoctor HLP-4027; Folkraft 1549; Lloyd Shaw WT-10005; Folk Dancer MH-1120

Skills: Step behind step, grapevine step, stomping

Formation: Single circle, hands on shoulders on both sides, arms straight

Directions: The Romanians are famous for rugged dances. This dance is called "Little Hazelnut." The stomping action represents the breaking of the hazelnuts. The title is pronounced "ah-loo-NAY-loo."

Measures	Part I Action
1–2	(5 steps + 2 stomps) sidestep right, step left behind right, sidestep right, step left behind right, sidestep right, stomp twice.
3–4	Beginning with the left foot, repeat the action but with reverse footwork.
5–8	Repeat the action of measures 1–4.
	Part II Action
1–2	(3 steps + 1 stomp) sidestep right, left behind right, sidestep right, stomp. Sidestep left, right behind left, sidestep left, stomp.
3–4	Repeat the action of measures 1–2.
	Part III Action
5–6	In place, step right, stomp left; step left, stomp right; step right, stomp left, stomp left.
7–8	Beginning left, repeat action of measures 5–6.

Teaching Suggestion: The stomps should be made close to the supporting foot. In teaching the dance, scatter the dancers in general space so they can move individually.

Hora (Israeli)

Records: Folkraft 1110; Merit Audiovisual-Folk Dances From Near and Far; Lloyd Shaw FK-1118

Skills: Stepping sideward, step-swing

Formation: Single circle, facing center, hands joined. The circle can be partial.

Note: The Hora is regarded as the national dance of Israel. It is a simple dance, which expresses joy. The traditional Hora is done in circle formation, with the arms extended sideward and the hands on the neighbors' shoulder. It is best to introduce the dance with hands joined in a circle. The dance can progress counterclockwise or clockwise. The clockwise version is presented here.

There is an Old and a New Hora, as done in Israel. The New Hora is more energetic, with the dancers springing high in the air and whirling around with shouts of ecstasy. The Hora can be done to many tunes, but the melody of "Hava Nagila" is the favorite.

Directions—Old Hora: Step left on the left foot. Cross the right foot in back of the left, with the weight on the right. Step left on the left foot and hop on it, swinging the right foot forward. Step-hop on the right foot and swing the left foot forward.

The same step is repeated over and over. The circle may move to the right also, in which case the same step is used, but the dancers begin with the right foot.

Directions—New Hora: Face a little to the left and run two steps: left, right. Jump on both feet positioned close together. Hop on the left foot, swinging the right foot forward. Take three quick steps in place: right, left, right. Continue in the same manner, moving always to the left.

If the circle moves to the right, do the same steps, but start on the right foot.

The Hora often begins with the dancers swaying in place from left to right as the music builds. Gradually the dance increases in pace and intensity. Shouts accompany the dance as the participants call to each other across the circle. The words *Hava Nagila* mean "Come, let us be gay!"

TEACHING THE SCHOTTISCHE STEP

The schottische is actually a light run, but when students are learning, it should be practiced as a walking step. (This is also true in polka instruction.) Lively music will quicken the step later. The cue is "Step, step, step, hop; step, step, step, hop; step-hop, step-hop, step-hop, step-hop." A full pattern of the schottische, then, is three steps and a hop, repeated once, and followed by four step-hops. The boy starts on the left foot and his partner on the right. The step can be learned first in a single circle, and can be practiced later by couples in a double circle. An effective way to introduce the schottische is with the "Horse and Buggy Schottische."

Horse and Buggy Schottische (American)

Records: Folkraft 1166; Lloyd Shaw E-14

Skill: Schottische step

Formation: Couples in sets of four in a double circle, facing counterclockwise. Couples join inside hands and give outside hands to the other couple (Figure 17.5).

Directions

Part I: All run forward: step, step, step, hop; step, step, step, hop.

Part II: During the four step-hops, one of three movement patterns can be done.

1. The lead couple drops inside hands and step-hops around the outside of the back couple, who move forward

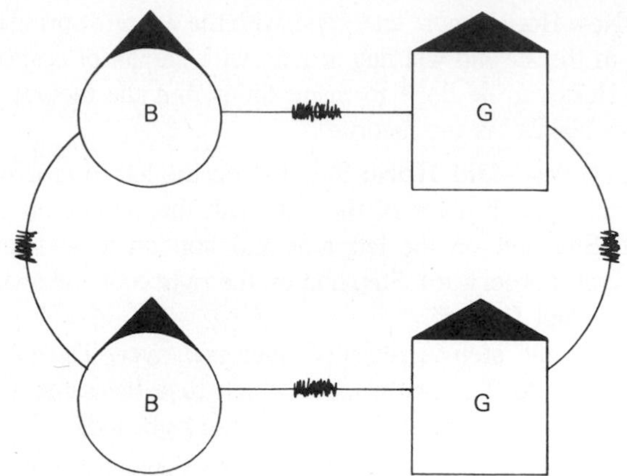

FIGURE 17.5. Schottische formation

during the step-hops. The lead couple then joins hands behind the other couple, and the positions are reversed.

2. The lead couple continues to hold hands and moves backward under the uprasied hands of the back couple, who untwist by turning away from each other.

3. Alternate 1 and 2.

Variation: During Part I, the grapevine step provides a nice challenge. Step left diagonally, right behind left, left and hop; step right diagonally, left behind right, right and hop. Part II action is the same.

TEACHING THE TWO-STEP

Children can be taught the forward two-step by simply moving forward on the cue "Step, close, step," starting on the left foot and alternating thereafter. The close-step is made by bringing the toe of the closing foot to a point even with the instep of the other foot. All steps are almost slides, a kind of shuffle step.

The two-step described above is nothing more than a slow gallop, alternating the lead foot. One way to help students learn the step-close-step pattern is to put them in a single circle and have them gallop forward. They should all start on the left foot and move forward eight slow gallops. Stop the class and have them put their right foot forward and repeat the gallops. Continue this pattern, and have the students make the change from galloping with their left foot forward to galloping with their right foot forward without stopping. When they make this transition, they should bring the right foot forward in a walking step—the weight being on the left foot. Reverse the procedure when moving the left foot forward. The movement should be very smooth. When the students master this pattern, repeat the sequence, but do four gallops with each foot forward. After this pattern is mastered, repeat the pattern with two gallops on each foot. When students can do this, they are performing the forward two-step.

Next, arrange the children by couples in a circle formation, boys on the inside, all facing counterclockwise. Repeat the instruction, with both partners beginning on the left foot. Practice the two-step with a partner, with the boy beginning on his left foot and the girl starting on her right. In the next progression, the children move face-to-face and back-to-back.

TEACHING THE POLKA STEP

The polka and the two-step are much alike. They both have a step-close-step pattern. The two-step is simply step-close-step, but the polka is step-close-step-hop. Technically, the polka is best described as hop-step-close-step (or hop-step-together-step). However, the first description is probably more helpful when working with beginning students.

The polka step can be broken down into four movements: (1) step forward left, (2) close the right foot to the left, bringing the toe up and even with the left instep, (3) step forward left, and (4) hop on the left foot. The series begins with the weight on the right foot.

Several methods can be used to teach the polka:

1. *Step-by-step rhythm approach.* Analyzing the dance slowly, have the class walk through the steps together in even rhythm. The cue is "Step, close, step, hop." Accelerate the tempo to normal polka time and add the music.

2. *Gallop approach.* A method preferred by many elementary instructors is the gallop approach. (Review the previous section on teaching the two-step, which uses the gallop.) The approach is the same, but add the polka hop and speed up the tempo. When moving the right foot forward, a hop must be taken on the left foot. When moving the left foot forward, the hop is on the right foot.

3. *Two-step approach.* Beginning with the left foot, two-step with the music, moving forward in the line of direction in a single circle. Accelerate the tempo gradually to a fast two-step and take smaller steps. Without stopping, change to a polka rhythm by following each two-step with a hop. Use a polka record for the two-step, but slow it down considerably to start.

4. *Partner approach.* After the polka step has been learned individually by one of the three methods, the step should be practiced with partners in a double-circle formation, boys on the inside and all facing counterclockwise, with inside hands joined. The boys begin with the left foot and the girls with the right.

Jessie Polka

Record: Folkraft 1093, 1071

Skills: Step and touch, two-step or polka

Formation: Circle, couples facing counterclockwise with inside arms around each other's waist

Directions

Measures	Part I Action
1	Heel step: Beginning left, touch the heel in front, then step left in place.

Measures	Part I Action
2	Touch the right toe behind, then touch the right toe in place, or swing it forward, keeping the weight on the left foot.
3	Touch the right heel in front, then step right in place.
4	Touch the left heel to the left side, sweep the left foot across in front of the right. Keep the weight on the right.
	Part II Action
5–8	Take four two-steps or polka steps forward in the line of direction.

Variation: The dance may be done as a mixer by having the girl turn out to the right on the last two two-steps and come back to the boy behind her. The boys continue to move forward on the last two two-steps, to make it easier to meet the girl coming toward them.

Klumpakojis (Swedish)

Records: Folkraft 1419; Merit Audiovisual-Folk Dances for Beginners

Skills: Walking, stars, polka step

Formation: Couples in a circle, side-by-side, all facing counterclockwise, with the girl to the boy's right

Directions

Measures	Part I Action
1–4	With inside hands joined, free hand on hip, all walk briskly around the circle for eight steps counterclockwise.
5–8	Turn individually to the left, reverse direction, change hands, and walk eight steps clockwise.
	Part II Action
9–12	Face partner and join right hands (making certain the right elbow is bent). The left hand is on the hip. With partner, walk around clockwise for eight walking steps. Change hands and repeat the eight steps, reversing direction.
	Part III Action
13–16	Listen to the musical phrase, then stamp three times on the last two counts. Listen to the phrase again, then clap own hands three times.
17–20	Now shake the right finger at partner, 1, 2, 3. Shake the left finger, 1, 2, 3.

Measures	Part III Action
21–24	Turn solo to the left, clapping partner's right hand once during the turn. Use two walking steps to make the turn, and finish facing partner.
25–32	Repeat the action of measures 16–24.
	Part IV Action
33–40	With inside hands joined, do 16 polka steps (or two-steps) forward, moving counterclockwise. (Later, as the dance is learned, change to the skaters' position.) On polka steps 15 and 16, the boy moves forward to take a new partner while handing the original partner to the boy in back. New couple joins inside hands.

DANCES FOR SIXTH-GRADE CHILDREN

As the culmination of the elementary dance program, the dances for 6th-grade children should display rhythmic skills performed with a relatively high degree of competence. The dance progression for the 6th grade ranges from a dance that is performed in a circle but introduces square-dance moves, to dances that put the two-step and polka step to use, and even to dances featuring the charleston and schottische. Students at this level also should become proficient at a variety of tinikling dance steps.

To accomplish these recommended activities, students need a strong rhythmic background. If they are not well prepared, the 4th and 5th grade activities should be reviewed. Allow time to diagnose and to become familiar with the students' skill level.

Dance	Skills
Oh Johnny	Shuffle step, swing, allemande left, do-si-do, promenade
Ten Pretty Girls	Walking, grapevine
Teton Mountain Stomp	Walking, banjo position, sidecar position, two-step
Kalvelis	Polka, swing
Doudlebska Polka	Polka, walking
Cotton-Eyed Joe	Two-step
Korobushka	Schottische
Tinikling (pp. 282–285)	
Square Dance (pp. 285–288)	

Oh Johnny (American)

Records: Folkraft 1037; Bowmar B-2056LP; Mack 2042

Skills: Shuffle step, swing, allemande left, do-si-do, promenade

Formation: Single circle of couples facing in, girl on right side of partner. Dancers use a shuffle step.

Directions

Call	Action
You all join hands and you circle in the ring.	All join hands and circle counterclockwise for eight steps.
Stop where you are, give your partner a swing.	All stop; the boys swing with their partner.
Swing that little girl behind you.	The boys turn to their left and swing the corner girl.
Now swing your own if she hasn't flown.	The boys swing with their partner again.
And allemande left with the corner girl.	The boys turn to their left and do an allemande left with their corner.
And you do-si-do with your own.	The boys turn to their right and do a do-si-do with their partner.
Then you all promenade with the sweet corner maid singing, "Oh Johnny, Oh Johnny, Oh!"	The boys promenade counterclockwise with the corner girl, who becomes the new partner for the next repetition.

Ten Pretty Girls (American)

Records: Folkraft 1036; Merit Audiovisual-Folk Dances for Beginners

Skills: Walking, grapevine

Formation: Circle of groups of any number, with arms linked or hands joined, all facing counterclockwise

Directions

Measures	Action
1–2	Front, side, back, step, step: Starting with the weight on the right foot, touch the left foot in front, swing the left foot to the left and touch, swing the left foot behind the right foot and put the weight on the left foot, step to the right, close the left foot to the right.
3–4	Front, side, back, step, step: Repeat, starting with the weight on the left foot and moving to the right.
5–6	Walk, 2, 3, 4: Take four walking or strutting steps forward, starting on the left foot.
7–8	Swing, swing, stamp, stamp, stamp: Swing the left foot forward with a kicking motion; swing the left foot backward with a kicking motion; stamp left, right, left, in place.

Repeat the entire dance 11 times, starting each time with the alternate foot.

The dance can be used as a mixer when performed in a circle by groups of three. On measures 7–8, have the middle person move forward to the next group during the three stamps.

Teton Mountain Stomp (American)

Records: Folkraft 1482; Classroom Materials Company, Album 8, Just for Dancing

Skills: Walking, banjo position, sidecar position, two-step

Formation: Single circle of partners in closed dance position, boys facing counterclockwise, girls facing clockwise

Directions

Measures	Action
1–4	Side, close; side, stomp; side, close; side, stomp: Step to the left toward the center of the circle on the left foot, close right foot to the left, step again to the left on the left foot, stomp right foot beside the left but leave the weight on the left foot. Repeat this action, but start on the right foot and move away from the center.
5–8	Side, stomp; side, stomp; walk, 2, 3, 4: Step to the left toward the center on the left foot; stomp the right foot beside the left. Step to the right away from the center on the right foot, and stomp the left foot beside the right. In "banjo" position (modified closed position with right hips adjacent), the boy takes four walking steps forward (left-right-left-right), while the girl takes four steps backward, starting on her right foot (right-left-right-left).
9–12	Change and walk: 3, 4, change, and progress, 3, 4. Partners change to sidecar position (modified closed position with left hips adjacent) by each making a one half turn to the right in place, the boy remaining on the inside and the girl on the outside. The boy walks backward (left-right-left-right), while the girl walks four steps forward (left-right-left-right). Partners change back to banjo position with right hips adjacent by each making a left-face one half turn; then they immediately release from each other. The boy walks forward four steps (left-right-left-right) to meet the second girl approaching him, while the girl walks forward four steps (right-left-right-left) to meet the second boy approaching her.
13–16	Two-step, two-step, two-step, two-step: New partners join inside hands and do four two-steps forward, beginning with the boy's right foot and the girl's left.

Variation: If the dancers are skillful enough, use the following action for measures 13–16. New partners take the closed dance position and do four turning two-steps, starting on the boy's left (girl's right) and make one complete right-face turn while progressing in the line of direction.

Kalvelis (Little Blacksmith) (Lithuanian)

Record: Folkraft 1418

Skills: Polka step, swing

Formation: Circle of couples facing center, the girl on partner's right, all hands joined in a single circle with the right foot free

Directions

Measures	Figure I Action
1–8	Circle right with seven polka steps, ending with three stomps.
9–16	Circle left with seven polka steps, ending with three stomps.
	Chorus
1–2	Clap own hands four times, alternating, left hand onto own right, then right hand onto own left.
3–4	Right elbow-swing with four skips.
5–6	Repeat the clapping pattern of measures 1–2.
7–8	Left elbow-swing with four skips.
9–16	Repeat the pattern of measures 1–8.
	Figure II Action
1–8	The girls dance three polka steps forward toward the center, ending with three stamps. They then turn to face their partner and return to place with three polka steps forward, ending with three stamps, facing center again.
9–16	The boys repeat the pattern of measures 1–8, but dance more vigorously, stamping on the first beat of each measure.
	Chorus
1–16	As described.
	Figure III Action
1–16	Grand right and left around the circle with polka steps, meeting a new partner on the last measure.
	Chorus
1–16	As described, but with a new partner.

Doudlebska Polka

Records: Folkraft 1413; Lloyd Shaw E-16, E-19

Skills: Polka step, walking

Formation: Either one large circle or several smaller circles scattered around the floor. The following description is for one large circle.

Directions

Measures	Part I Action
1–8	Partners assume the ballroom position and do a regular polka around the circle, one couple following another. They should do a heavy two-step polka. Beginners can use a varsovienne position instead of the ballroom position.
	Part II Action
9–16	The boy puts his right arm around the girl's waist as they stand side-by-side, while the girl puts her left hand on the boy's right shoulder. The boy puts his left hand on the shoulder of the boy in front. This closes the circle. The boys move sideward to the center to catch up with the boy ahead. In this position, all march forward counterclockwise and sing loudly, La, La, La, and so forth. This takes 32 walking steps.
	Part III Action
17–24	The boys face the center, and the girls drop behind their partner. The girls turn to face the other way, clockwise, and polka around the circle (around the boys) with their hands on hips. At the same time, the boys, who face center, clap a rhythm as follows: clap hands twice, then extend both hands, palms outward, toward the neighbor on each side, and clap hands once with the neighbor. Repeat this pattern over and over. For variation, the boys may slap a thigh occasionally, or duck down, or cross their arms when clapping the neighbor's hand.

At the end of part III, the boys turn around, take whatever girl is behind them, and resume the dance from the beginning. If some children are without a partner, they move to the center and thus find a partner.

Extra boys or girls can enter the dance during the clapping part for boys, and the girls can join the ring to polka around the outside. Those left without a partner wait for the next turn. When the group is large, several circles can be made, and it is perfectly proper for unpartnered girls to steal into another circle. The polka in this case is done anywhere around the room. During the march, make circles of any number of people.

Cotton-Eyed Joe

Records: Folkraft 1255; Merit Audiovisual-Holiday Folk Dances

Skills: Two-step

Formation: Couples facing, arranged in a circle, boy's back to center

Directions

Part Ia Action

Take the ballroom position. Starting with the boy's left (girl's right) foot, do a heel-and-toe (touch heel to side, then touch same toe beside the other foot). Next, do a two-step, starting on the boy's left (girl's right) foot and moving counterclockwise. A two-hand hold may be substituted for the ballroom position.

Repeat the sequence by doing a heel-and-toe and a two-step in the other direction (clockwise), starting on the boy's right foot (girl's left).

Part Ib Action

Drop hands and turn away from each other (boy to the left, girl to the right) with four two-steps.

Part IIa Action

Face partner, but do not hold hands. Both move sideward to the right, taking seven tiny side steps. Repeat in the other direction.

Part IIb Action

Assume the ballroom position and do four two-steps, turning around the circle.

Variation

Part Ib Action

In the turning solo, instead of two-steps, do a lively jig or polka. Girls can swish their skirts, while the boys use their arms "cake-walk" style. Dancers may also toss their hands overhead while shaking them, then drop their hands behind the back, alternating an up and down hand movement with each step.

Korobushka (Russian)

Records: Folkraft 1170; Hoctor HLP-4028; Lloyd Shaw WT-10005

Formation: Double circle, boy's back to the center, with partners facing and both hands joined. The boy's left and the girl's right foot are free.

Directions

Measures	Part I Action
1–2	Take one schottische step away from the center (the boy moving forward, the girl backward) starting with the boy's left and the girl's right foot.
3–4	Repeat the pattern of measures 1–2, reversing direction and footwork.
5–6	Repeat the pattern of measures 1–2, ending on the last count with a jump on both feet in place.
7	Hop on the left foot, touching the right toe across in front of the left foot (count 1). Hop on the left foot, touching the right toe diagonally forward to the right (count 2).
8	Jump on both feet in place, clicking the heels together (count 1), pause, and release the hands (count 2).
	Part II Action
9–10	Facing partner and beginning with the right foot, take one schottische step right, moving away from partner.
11–12	Facing and beginning with the left foot, take one schottische step left, returning to partner.
13–14	Joining right hands with partner, balance forward and back: step forward on the right foot (count 1), pause (count 2), rock back on the left foot in place (count 3), pause (count 4).
15–16	Take four walking steps forward, starting with the right foot, and change places with partner.
17–24	Repeat the pattern of measures 9–16, returning to place.

Variation: To use the dance as a mixer, during measures 19–20, move left to the person just before partner and continue with this new partner.

Tinikling (Philippine Islands)

Records: RCA Victor LPM-1619; Mico TM-006; Children's Book and Music Center PE-637, PE-613 (includes three sets of poles), PE-707; Kimbo KEA-8095, KEA-9015; Hoctor, Bamboo Hop

Skills: Tinikling steps

Formation: Sets of fours scattered around the room. Each set has two strikers and two dancers (Figure 17.6).

Note: The dance represents a rice bird as it steps, with its long legs, from one rice paddy to another. The dance is popular in many countries in Southeast Asia, where different versions have arisen.

Directions: Two 8-ft bamboo poles and two crossbars on which the poles rest are needed for the dance. A striker kneels at each end of the poles; both strikers hold the end of a pole in each hand. The music is in waltz meter, 3/4 time, with an accent on the first beat. The strikers slide and strike the poles together on count 1. On the other two beats of the waltz measure, the poles are opened about 15 in. apart, lifted an inch or so, and tapped twice on the crossbars in time to counts 2 and 3. The rhythm "close, tap, tap" is continued throughout the dance, each sequence constituting a measure.

Basically, the dance requires that a step be done *outside* the poles on the close (count 1) and that two steps be done *inside* the poles (counts 2 and 3) when the poles

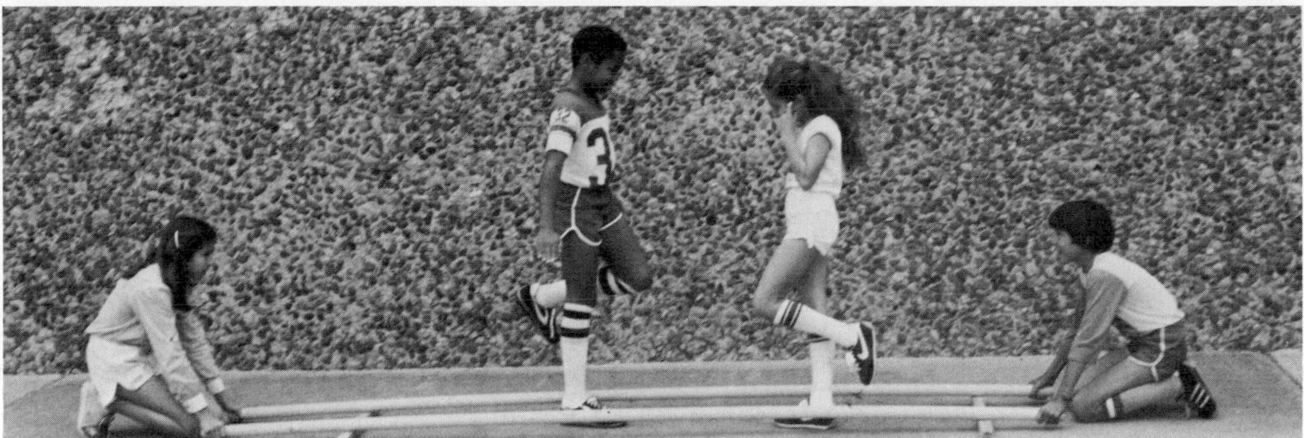

FIGURE 17.6. A tinikling set

are tapped on the crossbars. Many step combinations have been devised.

The basic tinikling step should be practiced until it is mastered. The step is done singly, although two dancers are performing. Each dancer takes a position at an opposite end and on the opposite side so her right side is to the bamboo poles.

Count 1: Step slightly forward with the left foot.

Count 2: Step with the right foot between the poles.

Count 3: Step with the left foot between the poles.

Count 4: Step with the right outside to dancer's own right.

Count 5: Step with the left between the poles.

Count 6: Step with the right between the poles.

Count 7: Step with the left outside to the original position.

The initial step (count 1) is used only to get the dance underway. The last step (count 7) to original position is actually the beginning of a new series (7, 8, 9—10, 11, 12).

Some tinikling dances and records guide the dancers with a different type of rhythm (tap, tap, close), necessitating adjustment of the steps and patterns in these descriptions.

Tinikling steps also can be adjusted to 4/4 rhythm, (close, close, tap, tap), which requires the poles to be closed on two counts and open on the other two. The basic foot pattern is two steps outside the poles and two inside. For the sake of conformity, we present all routines in the original 3/4 time (close, tap, tap). If other rhythms are used, adjust accordingly.

The dancer can go from side to side, or she can return to the side from which she entered. The dance can be done singly, with the two dancers moving in opposite directions from side to side, or the dancers can enter from and leave toward the same side. Dancers can do the same step patterns or do different movements. They can dance as partners, moving side-by-side with inside hands joined, or facing each other with both hands joined.

Teaching Suggestion: Steps should be practiced first with stationary poles or with lines drawn on the floor. Wands or jump ropes can be used as stationary objects over which to practice. Because the dance is popular and lots of fun, a number of sets of equipment should be available so many children can be active.

To gain a sense of the movement pattern for 3/4 time, slap both thighs with the hands on the "close," and clap the hands twice for movements inside the poles. For 4/4 time, slap the right thigh with the right hand, then the left thigh with the left hand, followed by two claps. This routine should be done to music, with the poles closing and opening as indicated. Getting the feel of the rhythm is important.

Other Tinikling Steps and Routines

Crossover Step: The crossover step is similar to the basic tinikling step, except that the dancer begins with the right foot (forward step) and steps inside the poles with the left foot, using a cross-foot step. Each time the dancer steps in or out, he has to use a cross-step.

Rocker Step: For the rocker step, the dancer faces the poles and begins with either foot. As she steps in and out (forward and backward), she makes a rocking motion with her body.

Circling Poles: For circling the poles, the dancer positions himself as in the basic tinikling step (Figure 17.7) and executes the following movements.

Measure 1

Count 1: Step slightly forward with the left foot.

Count 2: Step with the right foot between the poles.

Count 3: Step with the left foot between the poles.

Measure 2

Count 1: Step with the right foot outside the poles to the right.

Counts 2 and 3: With light running steps, make a half circle to a position for the return movement.

Measures 3 and 4: The dancer returns to his original

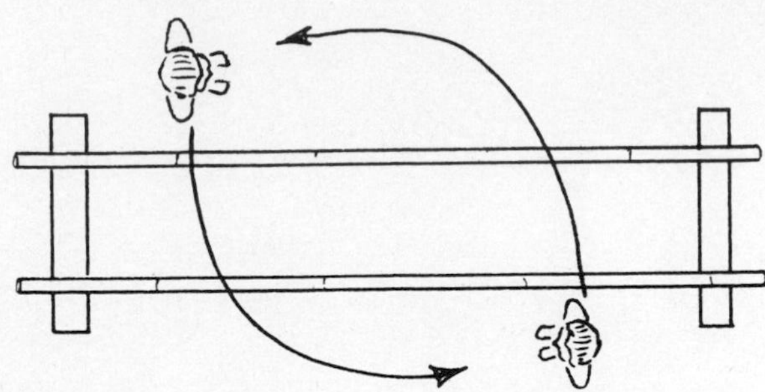

FIGURE 17.7. Circling poles for tinikling

position using the same movements as in measures 1 and 2.

Fast Tinikling Trot: The fast tinikling trot is similar to circling the poles, except that the step goes twice as fast and thus requires only two sets of three counts. Instead of having the side of the body to the poles, as in the basic tinikling step, the dancers face the poles. The following steps are taken.

Measure 1

Count 1: Shift the weight to the left foot and raise the right foot.

Count 2: Step with the right foot between the poles.

Count 3: Step with the left foot outside the poles and begin turning to the left.

Measure 2

Count 1: Step with the right foot outside the poles, completing the left turn to face the poles again.

Count 2: Step with the left foot inside the poles.

Count 3: Step outside with the right foot.

The next step is done with the left foot to begin a new cycle. The movement is a light trot with quick turns. Note that the step outside the poles on count 3 in each measure is made with the poles apart.

Side Jump: The dancer begins the side jump with her side toward the poles. She can execute the jump from either side.

Measure 1

Count 1: Jump lightly in place.

Counts 2 and 3: Jump twice between the poles.

Measure 2

Count 1: Jump lightly in place (other side).

Counts 2 and 3: Jump twice between the poles.

The feet should be kept close together to fit between the poles. The dancer can exit to the same side from which he entered, or he can alternate sides. Another way to enter and exit is by facing the poles and jumping forward and backward rather than sideward. When jumping sideward, one foot can be kept ahead of the other in a stride position. This position can be reversed on the second jump inside the poles.

Cross-Step: To do the cross-step, the dancer begins with the basic tinikling position, and uses the following sequence.

Measure 1

Count 1: Cross-step across both poles with the left foot, hopping on the right side.

Counts 2 and 3: Hop twice on the right foot between the poles.

Measure 2

Count 1: Hop on the left foot outside the poles to the left.

Counts 2 and 3: Hop twice again on the right foot between the poles.

Straddle Step: The dancer does a straddle jump outside the poles on count 1 and executes two movements inside the poles on counts 2 and 3. Let the dancers explore the different combinations. Jump turns are possible.

Line of Poles: Three or more sets of poles are about 6 ft apart. The object is to dance down the sets, make a circling movement (as in Circling Poles), and return down the line in the opposite direction (Figure 17.8). The dancer keeps his right side toward the poles throughout.

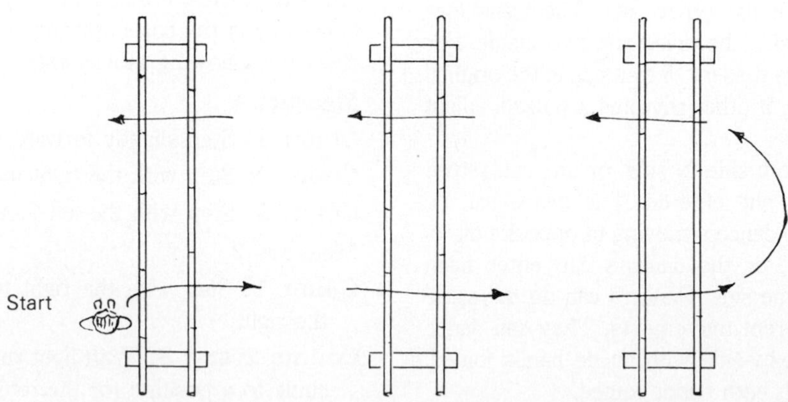

FIGURE 17.8. Movement through line of poles for tinikling

During measure 1 (three counts), the dancer does a basic tinikling step, finishing on the right side of the first set of poles. During measure 2 (three counts), he uses three light running steps to position himself for the tinikling step at the next set of poles. When he gets to the end, he circles with three steps to get in position for the return journey.

Square Formation: Four sets of poles can be placed in a square formation for an interesting dance sequence (Figure 17.9). Four dancers are positioned as shown. The movements are as follows: During measure 1, each dancer does a tinikling step, crossing to the outside of the square. On measure 2, the dancers circle to position for a return tinikling step. During measure 3, the dancers do a tinikling step, returning to the inside of the square. On measure 4, they rotate counterclockwise to the next set of poles with three running steps.

Teaching Suggestions: The basic tinikling step must be mastered if the children are to enjoy the activity. Tell them to look ahead (*not* at the poles), so they learn by thinking and doing and not by gauging the pole distances visually.

Four Pole Set: This arrangement features two longer crossbars, on which two sets of poles rest, leaving a small space between the poles when the sets are open. Four clappers control the poles. Two dancers begin by each straddling a set of poles on opposite ends, so the dancers face each other. Changes in foot pattern should be made every 16 measures, which for most records is a full pattern of music. The following steps and routines are suggested.

1. Straddle, jump, jump, exiting on measure 16 to the left.

2. Do the basic tinikling step, exiting on the left foot.

3. Do the basic tinikling step, first on one's own set of poles and then on the other set of poles. As the dancer comes out of the first set of poles with the right foot, she makes a half turn to do the tinikling step through the other poles. On the return, she makes another half turn in the middle to face and return to her original position. Repeat the sequence twice.

4. Do the same routine as in no. 3, but move diagonally, passing the oncoming dancer with right shoulder to right shoulder, in effect, changing places. (Do not use half turns.) Turn around in six steps and return to position. Repeat.

5. Jump to a straddle position with one foot in each of the pole openings. On "close," jump to the space between the sets. On measure 16, the dancer jumps out to the left on both feet.

6. Two-footed step: Jump twice with both feet inside the first set of poles, to the space between, twice inside the second set, and out. Return. Repeat twice.

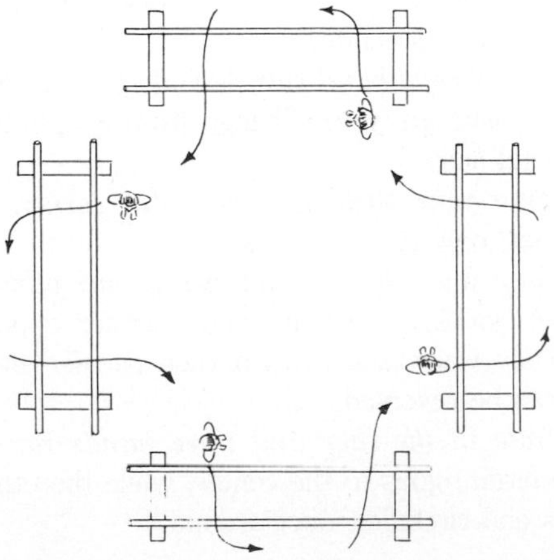

FIGURE 17.9. Square formation for tinikling

INTRODUCTORY SQUARE DANCE

Introductory square dance should be just that—introductory. In no case should the goal be finished, accomplished square dancing. The emphasis should be on enjoyment and learning the basics within the maturity capabilities of elementary school children. This can involve, however, considerable skill and polish.

The teacher's first problem arises because square dancing is such a broad and colorful activity with numerous figures, patterns, and dances. The large quantity of materials (introductory, intermediate, and advanced) poses a selection problem given the limited amount of program time that can be allocated to the activity. A further complication is the fact that the same figures have different names and are performed in different ways in different parts of the country.

A second concern relates to calling square dances and square dance figures. Square dance fun begins with an effective caller, and calling takes practice. In a few instances, youngsters can develop into satisfactory callers.

One solution is to select from the numerous square dance records with calls that are on the market. Records that have the music and calls on one side and the music only on the other side are useful. Directions are usually supplied with the records.

Singing calls should be used. For these, the calls can be done by one individual, by a group, or by the entire class. Singing calls are fun to dance to, because youngsters know what is coming next.

A third concern is the appropriate grade level for square dance teaching. Some sources hold that square dance instruction should begin modestly in the 4th grade, with the impetus increasing in the 5th and 6th grades. This does not rule out the use of square dance-related figures in folk dances taught earlier.

Square dance as a specialized dance activity requires the application of appropriate methodology. Some teaching suggestions follow.

1. In early figure practice or patter calls, pairing off by sex is not important. Let boys dance with boys and girls with girls if necessary. Avoid labeling one position for boys and one for girls, because any boys who play the girl's position may be subject to ridicule. In a couple, one partner becomes the left partner and the other the right. The goal is, however, to have boys dance with girls, and vice versa.

2. The shuffle step should be used, rather than the skipping or running step that beginners usually tend to use. The shuffle step makes a smoother and more graceful dance, has better carryover to other dancing, and conserves energy. It is a quick walk, almost a half glide, in time to the music and is done by reaching out with the toes in a gliding motion. The body should be in good posture position and should not bounce up and down on each step.

3. Teach the children to listen to the call. Equally important is that they know what the call means. They should have fun, but they must be quiet enough to hear the call.

4. It is important to follow the caller's directions and not to move too soon. The children should be ready for the call and then move at the proper time.

5. Generally, the caller explains the figures, has the children walk through the patterns, and then calls the figures.

6. The teacher should remember that there are many different ways to do different turns, swings, hand positions, and so on, and as many opinions on how these should be done. Settle on good principles and stick with them.

7. When a set becomes confused, each couple should return to their home position and try to pick up from that point. Otherwise, the choice is to wait until the dance is over or a new sequence has started.

8. Change partners at different times during the dancing. Have each boy move one place to his right and take a new partner, or have all of the girls (or boys) keep their positions and have their partners change to another set.

The Movement Approach to Square Dance

Many square dance terms can be taught using a movement approach. The students are scattered in general space. A piece of country western music with a strong beat is played. Anytime that students hear the call, they perform the same task with the person nearest to them.

Two calls are basic. "Hit the lonesome trail" directs students to promenade individually in general space in diverse directions. This call can be inserted at any time to move the students in new directions. The other basic call is "Stop where you are and keep time to the music." Students stop and beat time to the music with light claps. Other calls can be selected from the following list.

1. *Right (or left) elbow-swing.* With a forearm grasp, turn your partner once around and return to place.

2. *Honor your partner, honor your corner.* Bow to one person, then bow to another.

3. *Do-si-do your partner, do-si-do your corner.* Pass around one person, right shoulder to right shoulder, and back to place. Repeat with another person.

4. *Allemande left with the old left hand.* Using a forearm grasp, turn your partner around counterclockwise.

5. *All around your left-hand corner. Seesaw your pretty little taw.*[1] Pass around one student, left shoulder to left shoulder. Move to another student and pass around, right shoulder to right shoulder. Return to place.

6. *Star to the right.* Grasp right hands about shoulder height, with elbows somewhat bent. Circle (star) once around. The left-hand star reverses the maneuver.

7. *Two-hand swing.* Partners grasp both hands, lean away from each other, and circle clockwise once around.

8. *Go forward and back.* Move forward with three steps and a touch toward another person, who is moving similarly toward you. Move back to place with three steps and a touch.

9. *Grin at your partner; wave to your corner.* As described.

10. *Double elbow-turn.* Lock right elbows and turn two steps. Turn one half turn in two steps to lock left elbows. Turn in the opposite direction for four steps.

Note that there are no boy or girl roles. The two-handed swing is to be used instead of the regular buzz-step swing.

The next teaching strategy is to divide the class into groups of four. Use a call such as "Circle up, four hands round." Groups of four circle clockwise. There usually will be extras. If there are three extras, one person can pretend to have a partner. Rotate the extras in and out.

Circle fours until all groups are formed. With the call "Break and swing," the fours separate into pairs within the foursome. Position the pairs so they face each other. Use the terms "left partner" and "right partner" instead of boy and girl. If convenient, when there are mixed pairs put the girl on the right. Some attention can be directed to getting back to home place.

The following figures can be practiced in fours.

1. *Circle to the left (or right).* Join hands and circle once around as indicated.

2. *Form a right- (or left-) hand star.* Hold right hands at about shoulder height and turn clockwise. A left-hand star reverses the direction.

3. *Form a right-hand star, how do you do, back with the left and how are you?* Change from a right-hand star to a left-hand star.

4. *Honor your partner, honor your corner.* Bow to your partner; bow to your corner.

5. *Swing your opposite and swing your partner.* The left partner walks toward the right partner opposite and swings. They walk back to their own partner and swing. The call can be reversed.

6. *Birdie in the cage and three hands round.* One child (the birdie) goes to the center, while the other three join hands and circle left once around.

1. "Taw" refers to partner.

7. *The birdie hops out and the crow hops in.* The birdie joins the circle and another child goes in the center.

8. *Pass right through and pass right back.* Reach with the right hand to touch the opposite's right hand and exchange places. The left partner gives his left hand to his partner, puts his arm around the partner, and turns one half turn in place. The action is repeated to get couples back to home place.

9. *Go into the middle and come back out; go into the middle and give a little shout.* This is done from a circle-right or circle-left formation. The dancers face center and come together. Repeat again, but with a light shout.

10. *Round and round in a single file; round and round in frontier style.* From a circle-left or circle-right formation, the dancers drop hands and move in a single file.

11. *Dive for the oyster—dig for the clam.* Usually after circling left once around, one couple goes partially under the raised joined hands of the other couple. The other couple repeats the same maneuver. Stepping should be: in, 2, 3, touch; out, 2, 3, touch.

12. *Square on through.* Join right hands with the opposite (the one you are facing), and pull on through. Face partner and join left hands to pull on through again. To bring the couples back to home place, repeat with the opposite and partner.

13. *When you get home, everybody swing.* This is a convenience call to break a circling maneuver and get couples back to home position.

The caller can use the "Hit the lonesome trail" call at any time to break up the makeup of the fours, and then reorganize later with different combinations of students.

The formation using two couples can be accomplished in the traditional manner of boy-girl partners. This would necessitate placing the couples, rather than using the happenstance type of organization described previously.

Square Dance Formation

Each couple is numbered around the set in a counterclockwise direction. It is important that the couples know their position. The couple with their backs to the music is generally couple 1, or the head couple. The couple to the right of them is number 2, and so on. While *the* head couple is number 1, the term *head couples* includes both couples 1 and 3. In some dances, couples 2 and 4 are the *side couples.*

With respect to any one boy (gent), the following terms are used.

Partner—the girl at his side
Corner or corner lady—the girl on the boy's left
Right-hand lady—the girl in the couple to the boy's right
Opposite or opposite lady—the girl directly across the set

Other terms that are used include these.

Home—the couple's original or starting position
Active or leading couple—the couple leading or visiting the other couples for different figures

Once the square dance formation has been introduced, the figures and patter calls discussed previously should be practiced in the full formation of four couples. Although there is some repetition of material already presented in the movement approach section, the following figures merit discussion with the square dance formation as the background.

American Square Dance Figures

Some common square dance figures are the following.

1. *Honor your partner.* Partners bow to each other.

2. *Honor your corner.* The boy bows to his corner, who returns the bow.

3. *Elbow-swing.* The boy turns his partner with a right-hand swing, using a forearm grasp.

4. *Allemande left.* The boy faces his corner, grasps the corner with a left-forearm grip, walks around the corner, and returns to his partner. The next figure is generally a right-and-left grand.

5. *Right-and-left grand.* All face their partner, touch right hands, walk past the partner, and touch left hands with the next person in the ring, and so on down the line. This causes boys to go in one direction (counterclockwise) around the circle and girls to go in the other direction, alternately touching right and left hands until partners meet again. The girl reverses direction by turning under the uplifted joined right hands, and the couple promenades home.

6. *Promenade.* The couple walks side-by-side, right hand joined to right hand and left to left in a crossed-arm (skaters') position. They walk around the square once and return to home position.

7. *Swing your partner (or corner).* The boy and girl stand side-by-side with right hip against right hip. The dancers are almost in social dance position, except that the boy's right arm is more around to the girl's side than back at the shoulder blade. The dancers walk around each other with a slight lean away from each other until they reach their starting position.

8. *Right-and-left through (and back).* Two couples pass through each other, girls to the inside, touching right hands passing through. After passing through, the boy takes the girl's left hand in his left, puts his right hand around her waist, and turns her in place so the couples are again facing each other. On "Right and left back," the figure is repeated, and the couples return to place.

9. *Ladies chain.* From a position with two couples facing each other, the girls cross over to the opposite boy, touching right hands as they pass each other. When they reach the opposite boy, they join left hands with him. At the same time, each boy places his right arm around the girl's waist and turns her once around to face the other couple. On "Chain right back," the girls cross back to their partner in a similar figure.

10. *Do-si-do your partner* (*or corner*). Partners walk around each other, passing right shoulder to right shoulder, and return to place.

11. *All around your left-hand lady, seesaw your pretty little taw.* The boy does a do-si-do with his corner and then passes around his partner, left shoulder to left shoulder.

12. *Do-pass-so.* Partners join left hands and walk around each other. They release, and with right hands joined, walk around their corner. The boy then returns to his partner, they take left hand in left hand, and he turns her in place with his right arm around her waist. The turning movement is similar to the figure used in right-and-left through and ladies chain.

13. *Circle right* (*or left*). All eight dancers join hands and circle. The caller can add "Into the center with a great big yell." The circle usually is broken up with a swing at home place.

Selecting Square Dances and Records

In past years, the types of square dances suggested for elementary students were traditional square dances using a patter call. Today, square dancing is a popular form of adult recreation. Two reasons for the resurgence of square dancing as an adult activity are the singing call and the use of modern music.

Instead of recommending a series of square dances for each grade level, we suggest that teachers choose instructional records that present a progression of calls. Many sources offer such instructional records or square dances with calls. Securing an instructional square dance book to supplement the information in this presentation also will be helpful.

Sources for square dance records and books are:

Bob Ruff Records
8459 Edmaru Avenue
Whittier, CA 90605

Stocks a wide variety of square dance and folk dance records.

Children's Music and Book Center
2500 Santa Monica Boulevard
Santa Monica, CA 90404

Stocks Melody House records.

Dance Record Distributors/Folkraft Records
12 Fenwick Street
Newark, NJ 07114

Educational Activities, Inc.
P.O. Box 392
Freeport, NY 11520

Educational Record Sales
157 Chambers Street
New York, NY 10007

Distributor for the products quoted in dance descriptions:

Merit Audiovisual Records—a series of seven LPs
Folk Dances for Fun and Fitness Series
Folk Dances From Round the World Series
Several instructional square dance records

Hoctor Products for Education
159 Franklin Turnpike
Waldwich, NJ 07463

Kimbo
P.O. Box 477
Long Branch, NJ 07740

Stocks records of all types.

Lloyd Shaw Foundation, Sales Division
12225 Saddle Strap Row
Hudson, FL 33567

Stocks records of all types.

FAD DANCING

Fad dances that take a high degree of skill to perform should be used in the total rhythms program to provide motivation and fun. As this chapter is being written, break dancing is the major fad dance in America. One way to work break dancing into a lesson is to capitalize on the students' knowledge and skill. Use the squad leader or "follow me" approach.

Students appreciate the teacher's showing interest in dance areas that are also of major interest to them. Other fad dances that have been adapted recently for inclusion in physical education lessons are country western line dances and the line hustles of the disco era. Often, local social dance instructors are willing to visit a school and teach the fundamentals of current fad dances.

CULMINATING EVENTS FOR THE RHYTHMS UNIT

Country Western Day

After all grade levels have reached a specified performance level in square dancing, a country western day can be sponsored by the school. Teachers and students should be encouraged to wear country western style clothing all day, and then during the last hour of the school day, the student body can have a square dance. It is important to include activities that everyone, from kindergarten students to 6th graders, can do together. The movement approach presented previously can help achieve this goal.

May Festival

In the spring when the rhythm program is drawing to a close, it is exciting to feature in a May festival all of the dances learned. To have this activity include everyone, each class or grade level should make a dance presentation. The announcer should describe the history and background of each dance,[2] and the festival should end with the entire school performing the Maypole Dance.

LUMMI STICKS

Activities that use lummi sticks are appropriate for grades 3 through 6. Lummi sticks are smaller versions of wands; they are 12 to 15 in. long. Some believe that lummi sticks were a part of the culture of the Lummi Indians in northwest Washington. Others give credit to South Pacific cultures for the origin of the sticks. The actual origin remains obscure.

The chant (Figure 17.10) sets the basis for the movements and should be learned first, so it becomes automatic. Most lummi stick activities are done by partners, although some can be done individually. Each child sits cross-legged, facing her partner at a distance of 18 to 20 in. Children adjust this distance as the activities demand. The sticks are held in the thumb and fingers (not the fist) at about the bottom third of the stick.

Routines are based on sets of six movements; each movement is completed in one count. Many different routines are possible. The basic ones only are presented here. The following one-count movements are used to make up routines.

Vertical tap: Tap both sticks upright on the floor.

Partner tap: Tap partner's stick (right stick to right stick, or left to left).

End tap: Tilt the sticks forward or sideward and tap the ends on the floor.

Cross-tap: Cross hands and tap the upper ends to the floor.

Side tap: Tap the upper ends to the side.

Flip: Toss the stick in air, giving it a half turn, and catch other end.

Tap together: Hold the sticks parallel and tap them together.

Toss right (or left): Toss the right-hand stick to partner's right hand, at the same time receiving partner's right-hand stick.

Pass: Lay the stick on the floor and pick up partner's stick.

Toss right and left: Toss quickly right to right and left to left, all in the time of one count.

A number of routines, incorporating the movements described, are presented here in sequence of difficulty. Each routine is to be done four times to complete the 24 beats of the chant.

1. Vertical tap, tap together, partner tap right, vertical tap, tap together, partner tap left.
2. Vertical tap, tap together, pass right stick, vertical tap, tap together, pass left stick.
3. Vertical tap, tap together, toss right stick, vertical tap, tap together, toss left stick.
4. Repeat nos. 1, 2, and 3, but substitute an end tap and flip for the vertical tap and tap together. Perform the stated third movement (e.g., end tap, flip, partner tap right, end tap, flip, partner tap left).
5. Vertical tap, tap together, toss right and left quickly, end tap, flip, toss right and left quickly.
6. Cross-tap, cross-flip, vertical tap (uncross arms), cross-tap, cross-flip, vertical tap (uncross arms).
7. Right flip side—left flip in front, vertical tap in place, partner tap right. Left flip side—right flip in front, vertical tap in place, partner tap left.
8. End tap in front, flip, vertical tap, tap together, toss right, toss left.
9. Vertical tap, tap together, right stick to partner's left hand, toss own left stick to own right hand. Repeat. This is the circle throw.
10. Same as in no. 9, but reverse the circle.

2. Consult specialty dance books for a description of the various dances.

FIGURE 17.10. The Lummi Stick Chant

Lummi stick activities are another example of movement patterns that can be the basis for creativity. Let the children design their own sequences.

The activity can be done by four children with a change in the timing. One set of partners begins at the start, and the other two start on the third beat. All sing together. In this way, the sticks are flying alternately.

Some excellent records are available for Lummi stick activities and merit consideration. They are: Educational Activities AR-104; Children's Book and Music Center PE-868, PE-163, PE-195; Hoctor-Lummi Sticks; Kimbo 2000, 2014, 2015.

GAMES USING RHYTHMIC BACKGROUNDS

A number of interesting games use music as a part of the game. Most are simple in principle and are based on the idea of movement changes when the music changes or stops. Some are similar to the old game of Musical Chairs.

KINDERGARTEN THROUGH GRADE TWO

Circle Stoop

Children are in a single circle, facing counterclockwise. A march or similar music, or a tom-tom beat, can be used. The children march in good posture until the music stops. As soon as a child no longer hears the music or the tom-tom beat, he stoops and touches both hands to the ground without losing his balance. The last child to touch both hands to the ground and those children who lost balance pay a penalty by going into the mush pot (the center of the circle) and waiting out the next round of the game. The children must march in good posture, and anyone stooping, even partially, before the music stops should be penalized. The duration of the music should be varied, and the children should not be able to observe the stopping process if a record player is used.

Variations

1. Using suitable music, have the children employ different locomotor movements, such as skipping, hopping, or galloping.

2. Vary the stopping position. Instead of stooping, use positions like the Push-up, Crab, or Lame Dog, or balancing on one foot or touching with one hand and one foot. Such variations add to the interest and fun.

Freeze

The children are scattered about the room. When the music starts, they move throughout the area—guided by the music. They walk, run, jump, or use other locomotor movements, depending on the selected music or beat. When the music is stopped, they freeze and do not move. Any child caught moving after the cessation of the rhythm pays a penalty.

A tom-tom or a piano is a fine accompaniment for this game, because the rhythmic beat can be varied easily and the rhythm can be stopped at any time.

Variations

1. Specify the level at which the children must freeze.

2. Have the children fall to the ground or balance or go into a different position, such as the Push-up, Crab, Lame Dog, or some other defined position.

Take Me Out to the Ball Game

This activity involves a rhythmic pantomime of the game of baseball. As an introduction, the group sings the verse. When they sing "One, two, three," they hold the right arm out to the side, as an umpire does, indicating the three strikes by holding up the three fingers in succession. On the words "You're out," they point the thumb of the right hand vigorously over their right shoulder.

Formation: Singly or in small groups facing front, or in single circle formation facing center with one person as the leader in the center

Verse

Take me out to the ball game.
Take me out to the crowd.
Buy me some peanuts and crackerjack,
I don't care if I never get back.
And it's root, root, root for the home team
If they don't win it's a shame.
For it's one, two, three strikes you're out,
At the old ball game.

Pitcher: (Underhand) All stand facing forward, feet together, on an imaginary pitcher's mound. Hold the ball in the right hand, and swing the right arm back slowly for an underhand pitch. Pitch the ball, taking one step forward with the left foot, and at the same time, swing the right arm forward. Bring the right foot forward to join the left. Return to the original position, completing the action during the first four measures. Repeat this pantomime seven times.

Batter: All stand with the left side turned toward the front, each holding an imaginary bat in front of her. Pound on home plate twice, swing the bat upward over the right shoulder and strike at the ball, completing the action during the first four measures. Repeat seven times.

Catcher: All stand facing forward, crouching, knees bent. Catch the ball, straighten the knees, and throw ball overhand, stepping forward on the left foot. Return to the original position, completing the action during the first four measures. Repeat seven times.

Shortstop: All stand facing forward, legs apart, and knees bent. Slap the thighs once, slap the mitt once, stop a grounder, then rise and throw the ball overhand, stepping forward on the left foot. Return to the original position, completing the action during the first four measures. Repeat seven times.

Statues

In this musical game, which is similar to Freeze, all children become statues when the music stops and hold for a count of five. If a child moves during the count, she must stay out of the game during the next sequence and help the teacher judge whether any of the statues moves. The type of statue can be specified (e.g., funny, pretty, ugly, or balancing statues).

Right Angle

A tom-tom can be used to provide the rhythm for this activity. Some of the basic rhythm records also have suitable music. The children change direction at right angles on each heavy beat or change of music. The object of the game is to make the right-angle change on signal and not to bump into other players.

GRADES THREE THROUGH SIX

Arches

The game is similar to London Bridge. An arch is placed in the playing area. (To form an arch, two players stand facing one another with hands joined and arms raised.) When the music starts, the other players move in a circle, passing under the arch. Suddenly, the music stops, and the arch is brought down by dropping the hands. All players caught in an arch immediately pair off to form other arches, keeping in a general circle formation. If a caught player does not have a partner, he waits in the center of the circle until one is available. The last players caught (or left) form arches for the next game.

The arches should be warned not to bring down their hands and arms too forcefully, so the children passing under are not pummeled. Children wearing glasses also need consideration. Glasses should be removed, or the children with glasses can be part of an arch at the start.

Variation: Different types of music can be used, and the children can move according to the pattern of the music.

Whistle March

A record with a brisk march is needed. The children are scattered around the room, individually walking in various directions and keeping time to the music. A whistle is blown a number of times. At this signal, lines are formed of that precise number of children, no more and no fewer. To form the lines, the children stand side-by-side with locked elbows. As soon as a line of the proper number is formed, it begins to march to the music counterclockwise around the room. Any children left over go to the center of the room and remain there until the next signal. On the next whistle signal (a single blast), the lines break up, and all walk individually around the room in various directions.

When forming a new line, make a rule that children may not form the same combinations as in the previous line.

Partner Stoop

The game follows the same basic principle of stooping as in Circle Stoop, but it is played with partners. The group forms a double circle, with partners facing counterclockwise, which means that one partner is on the inside and one is on the outside. When the music begins, all march in the line of direction. After a short period of marching, a signal (whistle) is sounded, and the inside circle reverses direction and marches the other way—clockwise. The partners are thus separated. When the music stops, the outer circle stands still, and the partners making up the inner circle *walk* to rejoin their respective outer circle partners. As soon as a child reaches her partner, they join inside hands and stoop without losing balance. The last couple to stoop and those who have lost balance go to the center of the circle and wait out the next round.

Insist that players walk when joining their partner. This avoids the problem of stampeding and colliding with others.

Variation: The game can be played with groups of three, instead of partners. The game begins with the groups of three holding hands and marching abreast, counterclockwise, in triple-circle formation. On the signal, the outside player of the three continues marching in the same direction. The middle player of the three stops and stands still. The inside player reverses direction and marches clockwise. When the music stops, the groups of three attempt to reunite at the spot where the middle player stopped. The last three to join hands and stoop are put in the center for the next round.

Squad Leader Dance

Each squad forms a spaced column. The child in front is the leader. When the music starts, the leader does movements in time to the rhythm, leading the squad around the room, with all squad members performing as the leader does. When the music is stopped, all pause and the leader goes to the rear of the squad. The child now in front becomes the new squad leader, and the activity is repeated. Change leaders until all have had a turn.

Follow Me

The game has its basis in the phrasing of the music. The children are in circle formation, facing in, with a leader in the center. The leader performs a series of movements of his choice, either locomotor or nonlocomotor, for the duration of one phrase of music (eight beats). The children imitate his movements during the next musical phrase. The leader takes over for another set of movements, and the children imitate during the next phrase. After a few changes, the leader picks another child to take his place.

Variations

1. Have the children follow the leader's movements as she performs. This means changing movement as the leader changes and performing as the leader does, with everyone keeping the rhythm. A change is made as soon as the leader falters or loses her patterns or ideas.

2. The game can be played with partners. One partner performs during one phrase, and the other partner imitates his movements during the next phrase. The teacher can decide which couple is making the most vivid and imaginative movements and is doing the best job of following the partner's movements.

CHAPTER 18

Manipulative Activities

A manipulative activity is one in which a child handles some kind of play object, usually with the hands but possibly with the feet or other body parts. As fundamental skills, manipulative activities invite application of educational movement methodology, adding an important dimension to movement experiences. Manipulative activities develop both hand-eye and foot-eye coordination as well as dexterity.

Activities with balloons, hoops, wands, beanbags, balls of various types, tug-of-war ropes, and parachutes round out a basic program. Deck tennis rings, rubber horseshoes, lummi sticks, Frisbees, and scoops enrich the offerings.

Activities with jump ropes are important in the program, because they offer multiple possibilities—manipulative activity, rhythmic activity, and fundamental movement. Because of the complexity and interrelatedness of the activities, a separate chapter (Chapter 19) is devoted to activities with jump ropes.

Balloons, beanbags, and yarn balls provide the first throwing and catching activities for younger children. A soft object reduces the fear that younger children have of catching an object. After the introductory skills are mastered, other types of balls and more demanding skills can be brought in. Since early competency in handling objects provides a basis for later, more specialized skills, the basic principles of skill performance (pp. 26–30) have strong application, particularly as related to throwing and catching skills.

The start-and-expand approach is sound for teaching manipulative activities. Start the children at a low level of challenge so all can achieve success, and then expand the skills and experiences from that base. In progression, most activities begin with the individual approach and move later to partner activity. Partners should be of comparable ability.

PROGRESSION AND MOVEMENT THEMES

The activities in the manipulative area are presented in progression, in the form of either movement themes or movement tasks and challenges. The reliance on movement themes as opposed to simply listing a series of activities in progression permits the teacher to have greater flexibility. For example, the first movement theme in beanbag activities is entitled "Tossing to self in place." Suggestions for the development of this theme follow. Teachers can take either of two approaches. They can develop one or two themes in depth, exhausting all of the possibilities, or they can select a few activities from a number of themes, moving from one to the other with more dispatch. In the latter case, when the lesson is repeated the following day, the teacher can use the same themes but pose different challenges.

CREATIVE OPPORTUNITIES IN MANIPULATIVE ACTIVITIES

Opportunity for creative expression should be offered on a planned basis when the possibilities of a series of challenges have been exhausted or before the start of another movement theme. The lesson plan should include reference to creative opportunity in the progressions.

REINFORCING SKILLS WITH CREATIVE GAMES

Skills can be reinforced and enhanced through creative games. Children can be given a brief outline of a game situation on which they can structure a game applying the skills just learned. Specification of the game situation can range from open choice to creativity within guidelines. In either case, the focus is on using the skills just learned. As an example, the teacher might tell youngsters to create a game embodying a certain skill in which they are to select the needed equipment, outline the game space and specify number of participants, and set the rules, including scoring. More specifically, the teacher might outline certain conditions, such as use of two hoops and two Indian clubs, space limitations of two lines 20 to 30 ft apart, and competing sides of two against two. Within those parameters, students would then create a game.

Creative games can be oriented toward individuals, partners, or small groups. Groups should be kept small, or individual input becomes minimal. Different kinds of equipment can be specified (e.g., mats, wands, goals, and benches). After a period of time, different games can be demonstrated. While the creative process certainly has excellent value, the focus on the skill to be practiced must not be lost.

ACTIVITIES WITH BALLOONS

Balloons provide interesting movement experiences and emphasize hand-eye coordination. Success can be achieved with balloons when students may not be ready for ball skills. Keeping a balloon afloat is within the capability of young children and special education students. The activity can be expanded to challenge 1st- and 2nd-grade children as well.

Balloons are inexpensive and readily available. Extras are needed, since there is always breakage. The balloons should be of good quality and spherical in shape. At times, however, oddly shaped balloons can provide a change of pace. Balloons should be inflated only moderately, because high inflation increases the chance of breakage. Sometimes, a penny or a small washer can be put inside a balloon to give it an odd flight pattern.

INSTRUCTIONAL PROCEDURES

1. After blowing up each balloon, twist the neck and fix it with a twist tie of the type used to close plastic bags. This permits the balloon to be deflated easily and reused. Tying a knot in the neck makes deflating difficult.
2. Blowing up balloons for a class is quite a chore. Teach children to do this (some may require help). As soon as a child has successfully blown up a balloon, she can practice keeping it in the air.
3. Stress fingertip control and tactile contact.
4. Tell children to play only with their own balloon.

RECOMMENDED ACTIVITIES

1. Begin with free exploration, having children play *under control* with their balloon. The objective is to have the children gain a sense of the balloon's flight.
2. Introduce specific hand, finger, and arm contacts. Include using alternate hands; contacting at different levels (low, high, in between); jumping and making high contact; using different hand contacts (palm, back, side, and different fist positions); using different finger combinations (two fingers, index finger, thumb only, others); and using arms, elbows, and shoulders.
3. Expand the activity to use other body parts. Establish contact sequences with three or four body parts. Use various levels and body shapes.
4. Bat from various body positions—kneeling, sitting, lying (Figure 18.1).
5. Use an object to control the balloon (e.g., a lummi stick, a ball, a stocking paddle).
6. Restrict movement. Keep one foot in place. Keep one or both feet within a hoop or on a mat or carpet square.
7. Work with a partner by alternating turns, batting the balloon back and forth, employing follow-the-leader patterns, and so on.
8. Introduce some aspects of volleyball technique, including the overhand pass, the underhand pass, and the dig pass. Begin with a volleyball serve. Make this informal and on a "let's pretend" basis. Check the volleyball unit (pp. 561–571) for technique suggestions.
9. Propel a balloon upward. Pick up a hoop from the floor, pass it around the balloon, replace the hoop on the floor, and keep the balloon from touching the ground.
10. Have four to six children seated on the floor in a small circle. Each circle gets two balloons to be kept in the air. Children's seats are "glued" to the floor. Once a

FIGURE 18.1. Batting balloons from different body postions

balloon hits the floor, it is out of play. Play for a specified time (30 to 60 seconds).

11. If balloons can be spared, tie one to each child's ankle with a lead of 1 or 2 ft. Children try to burst each other's balloons. As soon as a child has had his balloon burst, he is eliminated. This can be a squad contest.

ACTIVITIES WITH BEANBAGS

Activities with beanbags provide valuable learning experiences for elementary school children at all levels. All parts of the body can be brought into play. For tossing and catching, though, the beanbag encourages manipulation with the hands; playground balls lead to arm and body catching.

Beanbag activities can be used in the intermediate-grade program, provided the activities are selected carefully to challenge students. The more challenging partner activities—juggling, different and unique methods of propulsion, and the split-vision drill (p. 297)—are examples of suitable activities.

INSTRUCTIONAL PROCEDURES

1. Make sure beanbags are at least 6 in. square. This size balances well and can be controlled on various parts of the body, thus offering greater challenge to intermediate-level children.

2. Throwing and catching skills involve many intricate elements. Emphasize the principles of opposition, eye focus, weight transfer, and follow-through. It is important for children to track the object being caught and to focus on the target when throwing.

3. Stress laterality and directionality when teaching throwing and catching skills. This means that children should be taught to throw, catch, and balance beanbags with both the left and right side of their body. They should learn to catch and throw at different levels.

4. Children should throw at chest height to a partner, unless a different type of throw is specified. Teach all types of return—low, medium, high, left, and right.

5. In early practice, stress a soft receipt of the beanbag by giving with the hands, arms, and legs. *Giving* involves the hands going out toward the incoming beanbag, and bringing it in for a soft landing.

6. In partner work, keep distances between partners reasonable, especially in introductory phases. Fifteen feet or so seems to be a reasonable starting distance.

7. In partner work, emphasize skillful and varied throwing, catching, and handling of the beanbag. Throwing too hard or out of range, to cause the partner to miss, should be avoided.

Most activities are classified as individual or partner activities. A few activities are for groups of three or more.

INDIVIDUAL ACTIVITIES

Tossing to Self in Place

1. Toss with both hands, with right hand only, and with left hand only. Catch the same way. Catch with the back of the hands.

2. Toss the beanbag progressively higher. Reverse.

3. Hold the beanbag in one hand and make large arm circles (imitating a windmill). Release the bag so it flies upward, and then catch it.

4. Toss from side to side, right to left (reverse), front to back (reverse), and around various body parts in different combinations.

5. Toss upward and catch with hands behind the back. Toss upward from behind the body and catch in front. Toss upward and catch on the back, on the knees, on the toes, and on other body parts.

6. Hold the bag at arm's length in front of the body, with palms up. Withdraw hands quickly from under the bag, and catch it from on top in a palms-down stroke before it falls to the floor.

7. Toss upward and catch as high as possible. As low as possible. Work out a sequence of high, low, and in between.

8. Toss upward and catch with the body off the floor. Try tossing as well as catching with the body off the ground.

9. Toss in various fashions while seated and while lying.

10. Toss two beanbags upward and catch a bag in each hand.

Adding Stunts in Place

1. Toss overhead to the rear, turn around, and catch. Toss, do a full turn, and catch.

2. Toss, clap the hands, and catch. Clap the hands more than once. Clap the hands around different body parts.

3. Toss, do pretend activities (e.g., comb hair, wash face, brush teeth, shine shoes), and catch.

4. Toss, touch different body parts with both hands, and catch. Touch two different body parts, calling out the name of the parts. Touch two body parts, clap the hands, and catch.

5. Toss, kneel on one knee, and catch. Try this going to a sitting or lying position. Reverse the position order, coming from a lying or sitting position to a standing position to catch.

6. Toss, touch the floor, and catch. Explore with other challenges. Use heel clicks or balance positions.

7. Bend forward, reach between the legs, and toss the bag onto the back or shoulders.

8. Reach one hand over the shoulder, drop the beanbag, and catch it with the other hand behind the back. Reverse the hands. Drop the beanbag from one hand behind the back and catch it with the other hand between the legs.

Put the beanbag on the head, lean back, and catch it with both hands behind the back. Catch it with one hand.

Locomotor Movements

1. Toss to self, moving to another spot to catch. Toss forward, run, and catch. Move from side to side. Toss overhead to the rear, run back, and catch.

2. Add various stunts and challenges described previously. Vary with different locomotor movements.

Balancing the Beanbag on Various Body Parts

1. Balance the beanbag on the head. Move around, keeping the beanbag in place. Sit down, lie down, turn around, and so on.

2. Balance the beanbag on other parts of the body and move around. Balance on top of the instep, between the knees, on the shoulders, on the elbows, under the chin. Use more than one beanbag.

Propelling With Various Body Parts

1. Toss to self from various parts of the body—the elbow, the instep, the knees, the shoulders, between the feet, between the heels.

2. Sit and toss the bag from the feet to the hands. Practice tossing in a supine position. From a supine position, pick up the bag between the toes and place it behind the head, using a full curl position. Go back and pick it up, returning it to place.

Juggling

1. Begin with two bags and juggle them in the air. (See pp. 301–302 for instructions on juggling.)

2. Juggle three.

Other Activities

1. From a wide straddle position, push the beanbag between the legs as far back as possible. Jump in place with a half turn and repeat.

2. Take the same position as above. Push the bag back as far as possible between the legs, bending the knees. Without moving the legs, turn to the right and pick up the bag. Repeat to the left.

3. Stand with feet apart and hold the beanbag with both hands. Reach as high as possible (with both hands), bend backward, and drop the bag. Reach between the legs, and pick up the bag.

4. On all fours, put the bag in the small of the back. Wiggle and force the bag off the back without moving the hands or knees from place.

5. In crab position, place the beanbag on the stomach, and try to shake it off. Put it on the back and do a Mule Kick (pp. 376–377).

6. Push the beanbag across the floor with different body parts, such as the nose, shoulder, or knee.

7. Each student drops a beanbag on the floor. See how many different ways students can move over, around, and between the beanbags. As an example, jump three bags, crab-walk around two others, and cartwheel over one more.

8. Spread the legs about shoulder width. Bend over and throw the beanbag between the legs and onto the back. Next, throw the beanbag all the way over the head, and catch it.

PARTNER ACTIVITIES

Tossing Back and Forth

1. Begin with various kinds of two-handed throws—underhand, overhead, side, and over the shoulder. Change to one-handed tossing and throwing.

2. Throw at different levels, at different targets, right and left.

3. Throw under the leg, around the body. Center as in football. Try imitating the shot put and the discus throw. Try the softball (full arc) throw.

4. Have partners sit cross-legged about 10 ft apart. Throw and catch in various styles.

5. Use follow activities, in which one partner leads with a throw and the other follows with the same kind of throw.

6. Jump, turn in the air, and pass to partner.

7. Toss to partner from unexpected positions and from around and under different body parts.

8. Stand back-to-back and pass the bag around both partners from hand to hand as quickly as possible. Also try moving the bag around and through various body parts.

9. Toss in various directions to make partner move and catch.

10. Run around partner in a circle, tossing the bag back and forth.

11. Propel two beanbags back and forth. Each partner has a bag, and the bags go in opposite directions at the same time. Try having one partner toss both bags at once in the same direction, using various types of throws. Try to keep three bags going at once.

Propelling Back and Forth With Different Body Parts

1. Toss the bag to partner with foot or toe, from on top of the feet and from between the feet, with elbow, shoulder, head, and any other body part. Use a sitting position.

2. With back to partner, take a bunny-jump position. With the bag held between the feet, kick the bag back to partner. Try kicking with both feet from a standing position.

3. Partners lie supine on the floor with heads pointing toward each other, about 6 in. apart. One partner has a beanbag between the feet and deposits it in back of her head. The other partner picks up the bag with his feet (which are over his head) and places it on the floor by his feet after returning to a lying position. With both partners in backward curl position, try to transfer the bag directly from one partner to the other with the feet.

GROUP ACTIVITIES AND GAMES

Split-Vision Drill

A split-vision drill from basketball can be adapted to beanbags. An active player faces two partners about 15 ft away. They are standing side by side, a short distance apart.

Two beanbags, one in the hands of the active player and the other with one of the partners, are needed for the drill. The active player tosses her bag to the open partner and *at the same time* receives the bag from the other partner. The two bags move back and forth between the active player and the other two, alternately (Figure 18.2). After a period of time, change positions.

Target Games

Wastebaskets, hoops, circles drawn on the floor, and other objects can be used as targets for beanbag tossing. Target boards with holes cut out are available from commercial sources. Holes can be triangles, circles, squares, and rectangles, thus stressing form concepts.

Beanbag Quoits

The game is played in the same way as horseshoes. A court is drawn with two spots on the floor about 20 ft apart. Spots can be made with masking tape and should be 1 in. in diameter. Each competitor has two bags, a different color for each player. Tosses are made from behind one spot to the other spot. The object is to get one or both bags closer to the mark than the opponents do. If a bag completely blocks out the spot, as viewed from directly overhead, the player scores 3 points. Otherwise, the bag nearest the spot scores 1 point. Games are 11, 15, or 21 points. In each round, the player winning the previous point tosses first.

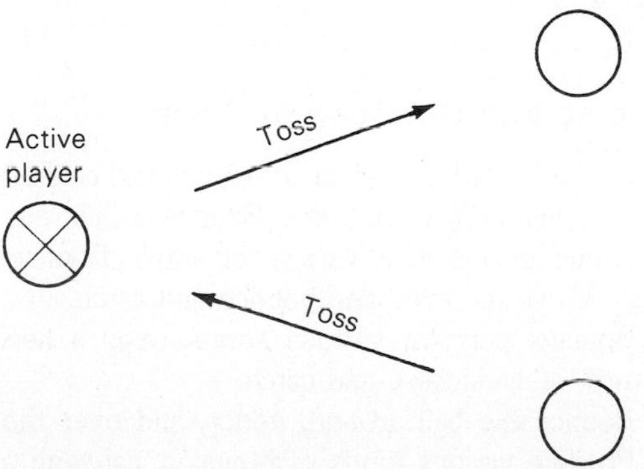

FIGURE 18.2. Split-vision drill for beanbags

Other Games

Children love to play One Step (p. 431). Teacher Ball (p. 423) is also readily adaptable to beanbags.

FUNDAMENTAL BALL SKILLS

Included in this section are the fundamental ball skills in which the child handles balls without the aid of other equipment such as a bat or paddle. Ball skills are mostly of two types: (1) hand-eye skills, including throwing, catching, bouncing, dribbling (as in basketball), batting (as in volleyball), and rolling (as in bowling), and (2) foot-eye skills, including kicking, trapping, and dribbling (as in soccer).

TYPES OF BALLS

For younger children, sponge rubber, yarn, and fleece balls are all excellent for introductory throwing and catching, because they help overcome the fear factor. (See Chapter 34 for instructions on how to make balls from yarn.) The innovative teacher can probably come up with other suitable objects, such as crumpled-up newspaper balls wrapped with cellophane tape, papier-mâché balls, stitched rolls of socks, and stuffed balloons.

The whiffle ball, a hollow plastic ball with holes cut in the surface, is also useful. Scoops, either commercial or home constructed, provide an extension of whiffle ball activities.

Another type of ball that has value is a soft softball, a much softer version of the regular softball. It is suitable for catching and throwing but does not hold up well if batted.

The inflated rubber playground ball (8½-in. size) should be the ball used for most of the children's ball-handling experiences. Balls should be inflated moderately so they bounce well, but not overinflated, which makes them difficult to catch. Overinflation can also distort the ball's spherical shape.

Some attention should be given to the color of the balls. In a study comparing blue, yellow, and white balls against a black background and a white background, "blue and yellow balls produced significantly higher catching scores than did a white ball" (Morris 1976). However, no data were provided for the common playground balls of red color.

TYPES OF ORGANIZATION

Instruction in the lower grades should begin with individual work and progress to partner and group activities. After the children have acquired some skill, a lesson can include both individual and partner activities.

In propelling the ball back and forth between partners, the children can progress from rolling the ball, to throwing with one bounce, to throwing on the fly. Be sure that a disparity in skill level between partners does not cause a problem for either. A skilled child can help a less skilled child, but the more skilled individual may resent being restricted.

Group work should be confined to small groups (of three to six), so each child can be active, and should include activities not possible in individual or partner activity.

Distance between partners should be short at first and should be lengthened gradually. The concept of targets is introduced by directing the children to throw the ball to specified points. Later, a change from a stationary target to a moving target maintains progression. Relays are useful for reinforcing learning, but the skills should be learned reasonably well before application in a relay.

INSTRUCTIONAL PROCEDURES

1. The principles of skill performance (pp. 26–30) have strong application to ball handling skills—particularly visual concentration, follow-through, arm-leg opposition, weight transfer, and total body coordination—and should be incorporated in the instructional sequences and be part of the coaching process. Balls should be handled with the pads of the fingers and should not be palmed.

2. In catching, soft receipt of the ball is achieved by giving with the hands and arms. The hands should reach out somewhat to receive the ball and then cushion the impact by bringing the ball in toward the body in a relaxed way.

3. To catch a throw above the waist, the hands should be positioned so the thumbs are together. To receive a throw below the waist, the little fingers should be kept toward each other and the thumbs kept out.

4. In throwing to a partner, unless otherwise specified, the throw should reach the partner at about chest height. At times, different target points should be specified—high, low, right, left, at the knee, and so on.

5. A lesson should begin with basic skills within the reach of all and progress to more challenging activities.

6. Laterality is an important consideration. Right and left members of the body should be given practice in turn.

7. Split-vision should be incorporated in bouncing and dribbling. Children should learn to look forward, rather than at the ball, when bouncing and dribbling. A split-vision drill (p. 297) is of value for throwing.

8. Tactile senses can be enhanced by having the children dribble or bounce the ball with the eyes closed.

9. Rhythmic accompaniment, particularly for bouncing and dribbling activities, adds another dimension to ball skills.

10. Enough balls should be available so each child has one.

11. The problem of uncontrolled balls can be solved by telling children to ignore stray balls since someone is sure to be coming after them.

Activities with balls are presented with the 8½-in. rubber playground ball in mind. Some modification is needed if the balls used are smaller or are of the type that does not bounce, as is the case with yarn, fleece, or sponge rubber balls.

INDIVIDUAL ACTIVITIES

Each child has a ball and practices alone. In the first group of individual activities, the child remains in the same spot. Next, he rebounds against a wall. (The wall should be reasonably free of projections and irregular surfaces so the ball can return directly to the student.) In the third group of activities, the child performs alone while on the move.

Controlled Rolling and Handling in Place

1. In a wide straddle position (other possible positions are seated with legs crossed or outstretched and push-up position), place the ball on the floor, and roll it with constant finger guidance between and around the legs.

2. Roll the ball in a figure-eight path in and out of the legs.

3. Reach as far to the left as possible with the ball and roll it in front of you to the other side. Catch it as far to the right of the body as possible.

4. Turn in place and roll the ball around with one hand in a large circle.

5. Roll the ball around while lying on top of it. Roll the ball around the floor while on all fours, guiding it with the nose and forehead.

6. With the back moderately bent, release the ball behind the head, let it roll down the back, and catch it with both hands.

7. Make different kinds of bridges over the ball while using the ball as partial support for the bridge.

8. Starting with one arm above the head, roll the ball down that arm, behind the back, down the other arm, and then catch it.

Bouncing and Catching in Place

1. Beginning with two hands, bounce and catch the ball. Bounce a given number of times. Bounce at different levels. Bounce one-handed in a variety of ways. Bounce under the legs. Close the eyes and bounce and catch.

2. Bounce, perform various stunts (e.g., a heel click, body turn, or handclap), and catch.

3. Bounce the ball around, under, and over the body.

4. Practice various kinds of bounces, catching all with the eyes closed.

5. Bounce the ball with various body parts, such as the head, elbow, or knee.

6. Bounce the ball, using consecutive body parts (for example, the elbow and then the knee), and catch.

Tossing and Catching in Place

1. Toss and catch, increasing height gradually. Toss from side to side. Toss underneath the legs, around the body, and from behind. Add challenges while tossing and catching. Clap the hands one or more times, make body turns (quarter, half, or full), touch the floor, click the heels, sit down, lie down, and so on.

2. To enhance body part identification, toss and perform some of the following challenges: touch the back with both hands, touch the back with both hands by reaching over both shoulders, touch both elbows, touch both knees with crossed hands, touch both heels with a heel slap, and touch the toes. Be sure to catch the ball after completing each challenge. The teacher or a leader can quickly call out the body part, and the class must respond with a toss, touch, and catch.

3. Toss upward and catch the descending ball as high as possible; as low as possible. Work out other levels and create combinations. Catch with crossed arms.

4. From a seated position, toss the ball to self from various directions. Lie down and do the same. Toss with the feet.

5. Practice catching by looking away after the ball is tossed upward. Experiment with different ways of catching with the eyes closed.

Batting to Self in Place

1. Bat the ball as in volleyball by using the fist, an open hand, or the side of the hand.

2. Bat and let the ball bounce. Catch in different fashions.

3. Rebound the ball upward, using different parts of the body. Let it bounce. Practice serving to self.

4. Bat and rebound the ball so it does not touch the ground. Change position while doing this.

5. Bat the ball, perform a stunt, and bat again.

Foot Skills in Place

1. Put the toe on top of the ball. Roll the ball in different directions, keeping the other foot in place but retaining control.

2. Use a two-foot pickup, front and back. This is done by putting the ball between the feet and hoisting it to the hands.

3. From a seated position with legs extended, toss the ball with the feet to the hands.

4. Try doing a full curl with the ball between the feet, retaining control until the ball is again placed on the floor. Try bringing the ball between the feet to a point directly over the body. With the arms outstretched for support, lower the feet with the ball to the right and left.

5. In a supine position, hold the ball on the floor above the head. Do a Curl-up, bring the ball forward, touch the toes with it, and return to supine position.

6. Drop the ball, and immediately trap it against the floor with one foot. Try to bounce the ball with one foot.

Dribbling Skills in Place

1. Dribble the ball first with both hands and then with the right and the left. (Emphasize that the dribble is a push with good wrist action. Children should not bat the ball downward.) Use various number combinations with the right and left hands. Dribble under the legs in turn and back around the body. Kneel and dribble. Go from standing to lying, maintaining a dribble. Return to standing position. Dribble the ball at different levels and at various tempos.

2. Dribble without looking at the ball. Dribble and change hands without stopping the dribble. Dribble with the eyes closed. Dribble the way the Harlem Globetrotters do.

Throwing Against a Wall (Catching on the First Bounce)

1. Throw the ball against the wall, and catch the return after one bounce. Practice various kinds of throws—two-handed, one-handed, overhead, side, baseball, chest pass.

2. Throw at a target mounted on the wall.

Throwing Against a Wall (Catching on the Fly)

Repeat the throws used in the previous activity, but catch the return on the fly. It may be necessary to move closer and to have the ball contact the wall higher.

Batting Against a Wall (Handball Skills)

1. Drop the ball, and bat it after it bounces. Keep the ball going as in handball.

2. Serve the ball against the wall as in volleyball. Experiment with different ways to serve.

Kicking Against a Wall and Trapping (Foot-Eye Skills)

1. Practice different ways to control kicking against the wall and stopping (trapping) the ball on the return. Try using the foot to keep returning the ball against the wall on the bounce.

2. Put some targets on the wall and kick the ball at a target. See how many points are scored after ten kicks.

Rolling on the Move

1. Roll the ball, run alongside it, and guide it with the hands in different directions.

2. Roll the ball forward, then run and catch up with it.

Tossing and Catching on the Move

1. Toss the ball upward and forward. Run forward and catch it after one bounce. Toss the ball upward in various directions (forward, sideward, backward), run under it, turn, and catch it on the fly.

2. Add various stunts and challenges such as touching the floor, clicking the heels, or turning around.

Batting on the Move

With first the right and then the left hand, bat the ball upward in different directions, and catch it on the first bounce or on the fly.

Practicing Foot Skills on the Move

Dribble the ball (soccer style) forward and in other directions. Dribble around an imaginary point. Make various patterns while dribbling, such as a circle, square, triangle, or figure eight.

Dribbling on the Move

1. Dribble (basketball style) forward using one hand, and dribble back to place with the other. Change direction on a signal. Dribble in various directions, describing different pathways. Dribble in and around cones, milk cartons, or chairs.

2. Place a hoop on the floor. Dribble inside the hoop until a signal is sounded, then dribble to another hoop and continue the dribble inside that hoop. Avoid dribbling on the hoop itself.

Practicing Locomotor Movements While Holding the Ball

1. Hold the ball between the legs and perform various locomotor movements.

2. Try holding the ball in various positions with different body parts.

PARTNER ACTIVITIES

Rolling in Place

Roll the ball back and forth to partner. Begin with two-handed rolls and proceed to one-handed rolls. When partner rolls the ball, pick it up with the toe and snap it up into the hands.

Throwing and Catching in Place

1. Toss the ball to partner with one bounce, using various kinds of tosses. Practice various kinds of throws and passes to partner.

2. Throw to specific levels and points—high, low, right, left, at the knee, and so on. Try various throws—from under the leg, around the body, backward tosses, and centering as in football.

3. Throw and catch over a volleyball net.

4. Work in a threesome, with one person holding a hoop between the two partners playing catch. Throw the ball through the hoop held at various levels. Try throwing through a moving hoop.

Batting in Place (Volleyball Skills)

1. Toss the ball upward to self and bat it two-handed to partner, who catches and returns it in the same manner. Serve as in volleyball to partner. Partner makes a return serve. Toss the ball to partner, who makes a volleyball return. Keep distances short and keep the ball under control. Try to keep the ball going back and forth as in volleyball.

2. Bat the ball back and forth on one bounce. Bat it back and forth over a line, wand, jump rope, or bench.

Kicking in Place

1. Practice different ways of controlled kicking between partners and different ways of stopping the ball (trapping).

2. Practice a controlled punt, preceding the kick with a step on the nonkicking foot. Place the ball between the feet and propel it forward or backward to partner.

3. Practice foot pickups. One partner rolls the ball, and the other hoists it to self with extended toe.

Throwing From Various Positions in Place

Practice different throws from a kneeling, sitting, or lying position. (Allow the children to be creative in selecting positions.)

Two-Ball Activities in Place

Using two balls, pass back and forth, with balls going in opposite directions.

Follow Activities in Place

Throw or propel the ball in any manner desired. Partner returns the ball in the same fashion.

Throwing and Catching Against a Wall

Alternate throwing and catching against a wall. Alternate returning the ball after a bounce, as in handball.

Throwing on the Move

1. One child remains in place and tosses to the other child, who is moving. The moving child can trace different patterns, such as back and forth between two spots or in a circle around the stationary child. (Spatial judgments must be good to anticipate where the moving child should be to receive the ball. Moderate distances should be maintained between children.)

2. Practice different kinds of throws and passes as both children move in different patterns. (Considerable space is needed for this type of work.) Practice foot skills of dribbling and passing.

3. Partners hold the ball between their bodies without using the hands or arms. Experiment with different ways to move together.

4. Carrying a ball, run in different directions while partner follows. On signal, toss the ball upward so the child following can catch it. Now change places and repeat the activity.

JUGGLING

Professional juggling is done with specialized objects such as balls, rings, clubs, and wands. For juggling at the elementary school level, small, tight beanbags, sponge balls, or fleece balls (Figure 18.3) are most often used. An excellent medium for teaching beginners is sheer, lightweight scarves that are 18 to 24 in. square. These move slowly, so children can visually track them. As youngsters find success with scarves, they can progress to beanbags and finally to balls.

FIGURE 18.3. Juggling with fleece balls

Two balls can be juggled with one hand, and three balls can be juggled with two hands. Juggling can be done in a crisscross fashion, which is called *cascading,* or it can be done in a circular fashion, called *showering.* Cascading is considered the easier of the two styles and should be the first one attempted.

Much practice is necessary to learn to juggle, and there will be a lot of misses during the acquisition of this skill. The object is to eliminate the misses gradually until the student acquires the art of keeping the balls in the air.

INSTRUCTIONAL PROCEDURES

1. Juggling requires accurate, consistent tossing, and this should be the first emphasis. The toss should be from 2 to 2.5 ft upward and somewhat inward, since the ball is tossed from one hand to the other.

2. The fingers, not the palms, should be used in tossing and catching. Stress relaxed wrist action.

3. The student should look upward to watch the balls at the peak of their flight, rather than watching the hands.

4. The balls should be caught about waist height and released a little above this level.

5. Two balls must be carried in the starting hand, and the art of releasing only one must be mastered.

6. Progression should be working successively with one ball, then two balls, and finally three balls (Figure 18.4).

RECOMMENDED PROGRESSION FOR CASCADING

1. Using one ball and one hand only, toss the ball upward (2 to 2.5 ft), and catch it with the same hand. Begin with the dominant hand, and later practice with the other. Toss quickly, with wrist action. Then handle the ball alternately with right and left hands, tossing from one hand to the other.

2. Now, with one ball in each hand, alternate tossing a ball upward and catching it in the *same* hand so that one ball is always in the air. Begin again with a ball in each hand. Toss on an inward path to the other hand. To keep the balls from colliding, toss under the incoming ball. After some expertise has been acquired, alternate the two

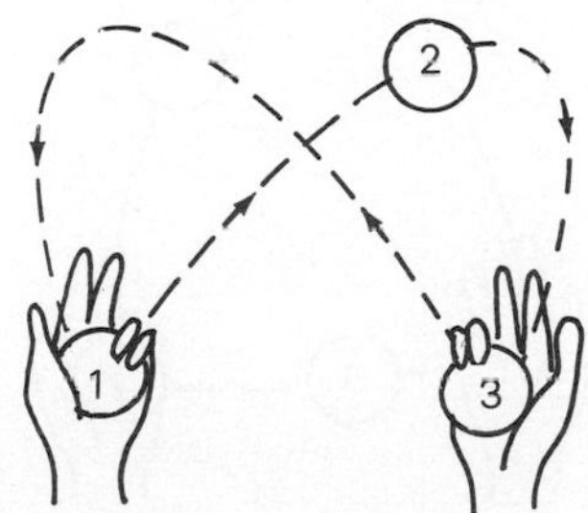

FIGURE 18.4. Cascading with three balls and two hands

kinds of tosses by doing a set number (four to six) of each before shifting to the other.

3. Hold two balls in the starting hand and one in the other. Toss one of the balls in the starting hand, toss the ball from the other hand, and then toss the third ball. This is juggling.

RECOMMENDED PROGRESSION FOR SHOWERING

1. The showering motion is usually counterclockwise. Hold one ball in each hand. Begin by tossing with the right hand on an inward path and then immediately toss the other ball from the left directly across the body to the right hand. Continue this until the action is smooth.

2. Now, hold two balls in the right hand and one in the left. Toss the first ball from the right hand on an inward path and immediately toss the second on the same path. At about the same time, toss the ball from the left hand directly across the body to the right hand (Figure 18.5).

3. A few children may be able to change from cascading to showering and vice versa. This is a skill of considerable challenge.

ACTIVITIES WITH SCOOPS AND BALLS

Scoops made out of bleach bottles or similar containers (see Chapter 34) can add another dimension to throwing and catching skills (Figure 18.6). Scoops should follow playground ball activity, since a smaller ball is used, such as a tennis ball or a 2¼-in. sponge rubber or fleece ball. The following activities are recommended.

INDIVIDUAL ACTIVITIES

1. Put the ball on the floor, and pick it up with the scoop. Toss the ball upward, and catch it with the scoop. Throw the ball against a wall, and catch it in the scoop. Put the ball in the scoop, throw it in the air, and catch it. Throw the ball against a wall with the scoop, and catch it with the scoop.

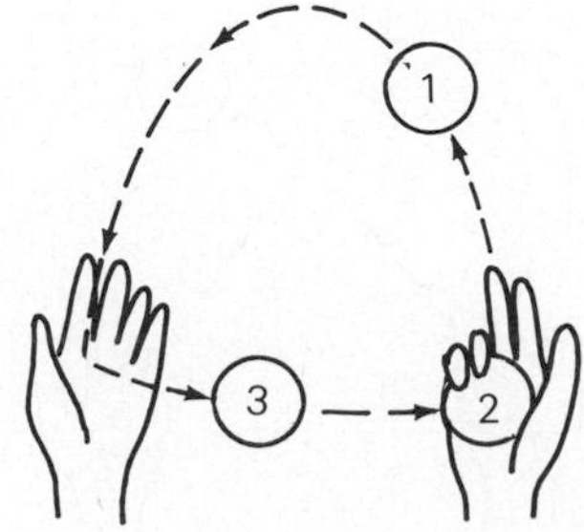

FIGURE 18.5. Showering with three balls and two hands

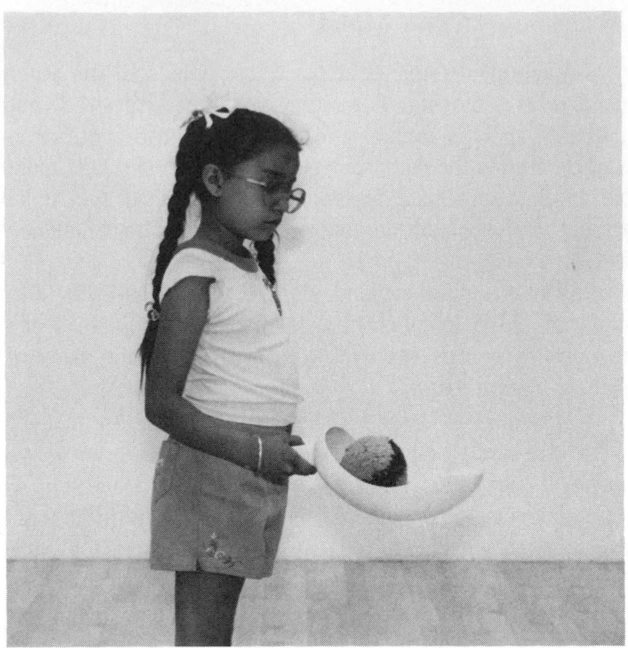

FIGURE 18.6. Catching a fleece ball with a scoop

2. Throw the ball, switch the scoop to the opposite hand, and catch. Toss the ball upward from the scoop, perform a stunt, such as a heel click or a body turn, and catch the ball in the scoop.

3. Toss the ball upward, and catch it as low as possible; as high as possible. Toss it a little higher each time, and catch it in the scoop. Tell students to toss the ball so they have to stretch to catch it. (Most activity should begin with a toss from the free hand and later employ a toss from the scoop.)

PARTNER ACTIVITIES

1. One partner rolls the ball on the floor, and the other catches it in the scoop. Partners throw the ball back and forth and catch it in the scoop. Play One Step (p. 431) while playing catch to add some challenge to the activity.

2. One partner tosses the ball from the scoop, and the other partner catches. Throw the ball from the scoop at different levels, and catch it at different levels. Throw and catch from various positions, such as sitting, back to back, prone, and kneeling.

3. Work with more than one partner, with more than one ball, and with a scoop in each hand. (Follow or matching activities are also excellent for scoops.)

GAMES AND RELAYS

Many games and relays can be played using scoops. Many school districts are now playing lacrosse with the scoops and a whiffle ball. Set up a lesson in which the children devise games for themselves that use the scoop and a ball.

BOWLING ACTIVITIES

Children in kindergarten and the two lower grades should practice informal rolling. In about the 3rd grade, the emphasis should change from informal rolling to bowling skills, and this emphasis should continue through the 6th grade.

Bowling skills begin with a two-handed roll and progress to one-handed rolls using both the right and left hand. Various targets can be used, including Indian clubs, milk cartons, small cones, blocks, and even humans.

The regular (8½-in.) rubber playground ball is excellent for teaching bowling skills. Volleyballs and soccer balls also can be used. Stress moderate speed in the motion of the ball. The ball should roll off the tips of the fingers with good follow-through action.

The four-step approach is the accepted form for tenpin bowling, and its basis can be set in class work. The teacher is referred to bowling manuals for more details, but here is the technique, in brief form, for a right-handed bowler.

Starting position: Stand with the feet together and the ball held comfortably in both hands in front of the body.

Step one: Step forward with the right foot, pushing the ball forward with both hands and a little to the right.

Step two: Step with the left foot, allowing the ball to swing down alongside the leg on its way into the backswing.

Step three: Step with the right foot. The ball reaches the height of the backswing with this step.

Step four: Step with the left foot, and bowl the ball forward.

As cues, the teacher can call out the following sequence for the four steps: "Out," "Down," "Back," and "Roll."

Bowling activities are organized mostly as partner or group work. When targets are being used, having two children on the target end is desirable. One child resets the target, while the other recovers the ball. The following are partner activities unless otherwise noted. A fine game for rounding off the activities is Bowling One Step (p. 431).

1. Employ a wide straddle stance, and begin with two-handed rolls from between the legs.

2. Roll the ball with first the right and then the left hand. The receiver can employ the foot pickup, done by hoisting the ball to the hands with the extended toe.

3. Practice putting different kinds of spin (English) on the ball. (For a right-handed bowler, a curve to the left is called a ***hook ball,*** and a curve to the right is a ***backup ball.***)

4. Get into groups of three (Figure 18.7), and employ human straddle targets. Using a stick 2 ft long, make marks on the floor for the target child who is in the middle, between the two bowlers. She stands so the inside edges of her shoes are on the marks, thus standardizing the target spread. (Targets must keep their legs straight and motionless during the bowling. Otherwise, they can make or avoid contact with the ball and upset the scoring system.) Start from a moderate distance (15 to 20 ft) at first, and adjust as proficiency increases. Scoring can be 2 points for a ball that goes through the legs without touching and 1 point for a ball that goes through but touches the leg.

5. Use Indian clubs, milk cartons, or even regular bowling pins as targets. Begin with one and progress to two or three. (Plastic bowling pins are available. Other targets might be a wastebasket lying on its side—the ball is rolled into it—or a 3-lb coffee can for a smaller ball.)

ACTIVITIES WITH PADDLES AND BALLS

The present popularity of racket sports makes it imperative that the schools give attention to racket skills. For primary-level children, the nylon-stocking paddle (see Chapter 34 for its construction) can be used to introduce the racket sports. Much of this early activity is devoted to

FIGURE 18.7. Bowling through human straddle target

informal, exploratory play. Different types of objects can be batted—table tennis balls, newspaper balls, shuttlecocks, and tennis balls.

For children in the 3rd through 6th grade, plastic or wooden paddles (see Chapter 34) and appropriate balls are used, with instruction laying a basis for future play in racket ball, table tennis, squash, and regular tennis.

The activities, particularly paddle tennis, take considerable space. If played outdoors, balls roll hither and thither. The emphasis must be on controlled stroking.

INSTRUCTIONAL PROCEDURES FOR NYLON-STOCKING PADDLES

1. Most of the stroking should be volleys, although when the balls do bounce, some ground strokes can be done.

2. There must be good individual control before proceeding to partner work. Remember that rallies for young children tend to be quite brief.

3. Teach something about grip, but let the children experiment with the kinds of activities they wish to do.

RECOMMENDED ACTIVITIES

1. Toss the ball, and hit it upward. Try to hit it a second time. Hit it forward, chase it, and hit it back. Explore different ways of stroking.

2. Hit it against a wall, retrieve it, and continue. Try different strokes.

3. Work with a partner. One can toss the ball to the other, who then hits it back.

4. Use a spherical balloon. Keep it up individually, or propel it back and forth between partners.

INSTRUCTIONAL PROCEDURES FOR WOODEN OR PLASTIC PADDLES

1. All paddles should have leather wrist thongs. The hand goes through the leather loop before grasping the paddle. No play should be permitted without this safety precaution.

2. Proper grip must be emphasized, and seeing that children maintain this is a constant battle. The easiest method to teach the proper grip is to have the student hold the paddle perpendicular to the floor and shake hands with it (Figure 18.8). Young people tend to revert to the inefficient hammer grip, so named because it is similar to the grip used on a hammer.

3. Accuracy and control should be the primary goals. The children should not be concerned with force or distance.

4. The wrist should be held reasonably stiff, and the arm action should be a stroking motion.

5. Early activities can be attempted with both the right and left hand, but the dominant hand should be developed in critical skills.

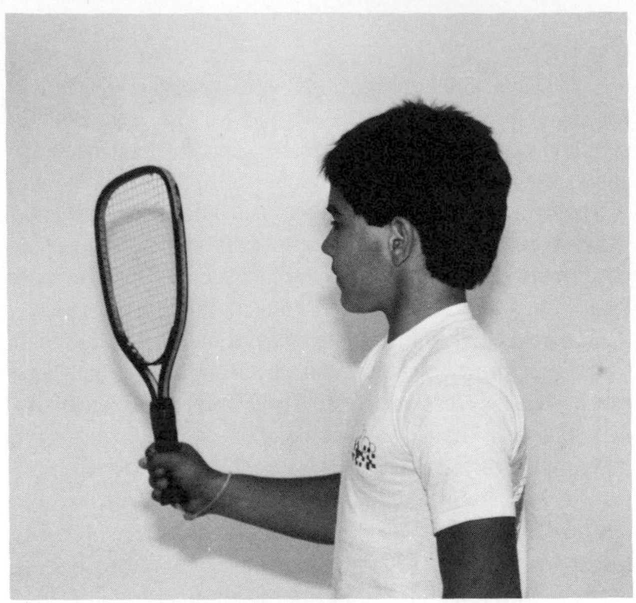

FIGURE 18.8. The handshake grip

6. During a lesson, related information about racket sports may be quite relevant.

7. Practice in racket work should move from individual to partner work as quickly as is feasible, because partner work is basic to racket sports.

8. For the forehand stroke, the body is turned sideways so that, for a right-handed player, the left side points in the direction of the hit.

9. For the backhand stroke, the thumb is placed against the handle of the racket for added support and force, and the body is turned sideways so that the shoulder on the side of the racket hand points in the direction of the stroke.

10. During either type of stroke, a step is made with the foot that is forward with respect to the direction of the stroke.

11. A volley is made with a sort of punch stroke. The hitter faces in the direction of the hit, and the racket is pushed forward rather than being stroked. To practice volleys, students need a firm surface from which the ball can rebound.

INDIVIDUAL ACTIVITIES

1. Place a ball on the paddle and attempt to keep it from falling off. As skill increases, attempt to roll the ball around the edges of the paddle.

2. Using the paddle, rebound the ball upward. Bounce it on the paddle without letting it touch the floor. Bounce it off the paddle upward, and catch it with the other hand. Increase the height of the bounce.

3. Dribble the ball with the paddle, first while stationary and then while moving. Change the paddle from hand to hand while the ball is bouncing off the floor.

4. Alternate bouncing the ball in the air and on the floor.

5. Bounce the ball off the paddle upward and catch it with the paddle. This requires giving with the paddle to create a soft home for the ball.

6. Put the ball on the floor and scoop it up with the paddle. Start dribbling on the ball without touching it with the hands. Put a reverse spin on the ball, and scoop it up into the air.

7. Bounce the ball off the paddle into the air and turn the paddle to the other side as you bounce the ball.

8. Bat the ball into the air and perform the following stunts while the ball is in the air: touch the floor, do a heel click (single and double), clap the hands, turn completely around. Do various combinations of these activities.

PARTNER ACTIVITIES

Beginning partner activity should involve feeding (controlled throwing) by one partner and the designated stroke return by the other. In this way, the child can concentrate on the stroke without worrying about the competitive aspects of the activity.

1. Return partner's feed with a forehand stroke. Return backhand. Switch roles.

2. Stroke back and forth with partner, first forehand and then backhand.

3. Play back and forth over a net. The "net" can be a jump rope lying on the floor crosswise to the field of play, a wand supported on blocks or cones, or a bench. (See Chapter 34 for a diagram of a home-constructed net.)

4. Volley partner's feed. Volley back and forth with partner. (In the volley, the ball does not touch the floor.)

5. Play doubles. Partners on each side alternate turns returning the ball.

6. Volley using a whiffle ball. (A whiffle ball moves slowly and allows the children time to position their feet properly.) Play with a partner. Allow the ball to bounce before returning it. Perform stunts while the ball is in the air.

7. Dribble the ball with your paddle and try to pull a flag from an opponent's pocket without losing control of the ball.

8. While moving with a partner, keep the ball in the air by alternating bounces.

ACTIVITIES WITH FRISBEES (FLYING DISKS)

Frisbee activities are popular with children of all ages, but younger children may need considerable guidance to develop skills.

THROWING THE DISK

Backhand Throw

The backhand grip (Figure 18.9) is used most often. The thumb is on top of the disk, the index finger along the rim, and the other fingers underneath. To throw the Frisbee with the right hand, the child stands in a sideways position with the right foot toward the target. She steps toward the target and throws the Frisbee in a sideways motion across the body, snapping the wrist and trying to keep the disk flat on release.

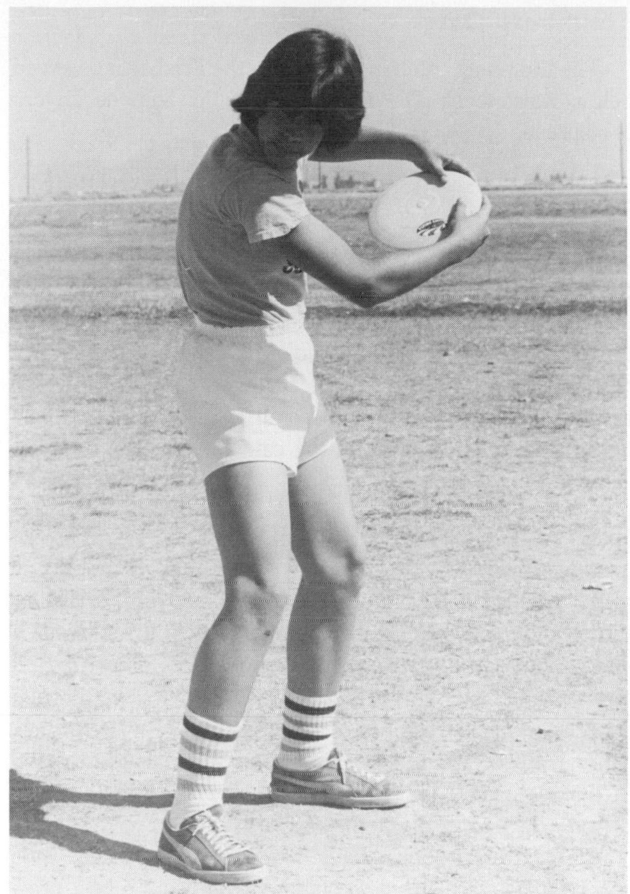

FIGURE 18.9. Gripping the Frisbee for a backhand throw

Underhand Throw

The underhand throw uses the same grip as in the backhand throw, but the child faces the target and holds the disk at the side of the body. He steps forward with the leg opposite the throwing arm as he brings the Frisbee forward. When the throwing arm is out in the front of the body, he releases the Frisbee. The trick to this throw is learning to release the disk so it is parallel to the ground.

CATCHING THE DISK

Thumb-Down Catch

The thumb-down catch is used for catching when the disk is received at waist level or above. The thumb is pointing toward the ground. The Frisbee should be tracked from the thrower's hand. This clues the catcher about any tilt on the disk that may cause it to curve.

Thumb-Up Catch

The thumb-up catch is used when the Frisbee is received below waist level. The thumb points up, and the fingers are spread.

Trick Catches

The disk can be caught in different positions. The two most popular trick-catch positions are behind the back and between the legs. In the behind-the-back catch, the thumb-up technique is used, and the disk is caught with the arm that is farthest away from the thrower. For the between-the-legs catch, the thumb-up catch is also used, and one leg can be lifted to facilitate the catch.

INSTRUCTIONAL PROCEDURES

1. When the disk is thrown, it should be parallel to the ground at release. If it is tilted, a curved throw results.

2. Good throwing principles should be followed. Students should step toward the target and follow through on release of the disk.

3. If space is limited, the Frisbees should be thrown in the same direction. Students can line up on either side of the area and throw across to each other.

4. Each child should have a disk so that practice time can be maximized. However, most activities are best practiced by pairs of students using one disk.

5. Youngsters can develop both sides of the body by learning to throw and catch the disk with either hand. The teacher should design the activities so youngsters get both right-hand and left-hand practice.

6. In the early stages, emphasis should be on proper technique.

7. Since a Frisbee is somewhat different from the other implements that children usually throw, devote some time to teaching form and style in throwing and catching. Avoid drills that reward speed in throwing and catching.

RECOMMENDED ACTIVITIES

1. Throw the Frisbee at different levels to a partner.

2. Catch the Frisbee, using various catching styles and hand positions.

3. Throw a curve by tilting the disk. Try curving it to the left, the right, and upward. Throw a slow curve and then a fast slider.

4. Throw a bounce pass to partner. Throw a low, fast bounce. Throw a high, slow bounce.

5. As the catcher, do various stunts after the disk has left partner's hand. Examples are a full turn, heel click, handclap, or touching the ground.

6. Throw the disk with the nondominant hand. Try to throw for accuracy first, and then strive for distance.

7. Make the disk respond like a boomerang. Throw into the wind at a steep angle and see whether it comes back to you.

8. Throw the Frisbee into the air, run, and catch it. Try to increase the throwing distance and still make the catch before the disk touches ground.

9. Have partner hold a hoop as a target. See how many times you can throw the Frisbee through the hoop. Play a game of One Step in which you move back a step each time you throw the disk through the hoop. When you make two misses in a row, partner gets a chance to try.

10. Place a series of hoops on the ground. Different colored hoops can signify different point values. Have a contest with partner to see who can earn more points in five throws.

11. Play catch while both partners are moving. Try to throw the disk in front of partner so she does not have to break stride to catch it.

12. Throw for distance. Try to throw farther than partner by using a series of four throws.

13. Throw for both distance and accuracy. Using a series of four or more throws, try to reach a goal that is a specified distance away. Many different objects can be used as goals, such as basket standards, fence posts, and trees. (This could be the start of playing Frisbee Golf, which is becoming a popular recreational sport.)

14. Set a time limit of 30 seconds. Within this time, see how many successful throws and catches can be made. A certain distance apart must be set for all pairs, and missed catches do not count as throws.

15. Working in groups of three, try to keep the disk away from the person in the middle. The children can establish their own rules as to when someone else must move to the middle.

16. In groups of three, with one person in the middle, try to throw the Frisbee through the middle person's legs. A point is scored each time the disk is thrown through the legs without touching. The legs must be spread about shoulder width.

PARACHUTE PLAY

Parachute play can be enjoyed by all children from 1st through 6th grade. Activities must be selected carefully for younger children, since some of the skills presented would be difficult for them. One parachute is generally sufficient for the normal-size class of 30 children.

Parachutes come in different sizes, but those with diameters ranging from 24 to 28 ft are suitable for a regular class. Parachutes 10 to 12 ft in diameter are available for smaller groups.

Each parachute has an opening near the top to allow trapped air to escape and to keep the parachute properly shaped. Most parachutes are constructed of nylon. A parachute should stretch tight when it is pulled on by children spaced around it. One that does not do so has limited usefulness.

VALUES OF PARACHUTE PLAY

Parachutes provide a new and interesting means of accomplishing physical fitness goals—good development of strength, agility, coordination, and endurance. Strength development is focused especially on the arms, hands, and shoulder girdle. At times, however, strength demands are made on the entire body.

A wide variety of movement possibilities, some of which are rhythmic, can be employed in parachute play. Locomotor skills can be practiced while manipulating the parachute. Rhythmic beats of the tom-tom or appropriate music can guide locomotor movements. Parachute play provides many excellent cooperative group learning experiences.

GRIPS

The grips used in handling the parachute are comparable to those employed in hanging activities on an apparatus. Grips can be with one or two hands, overhand (palms facing away), underhand (palms facing toward), or mixed (one hand underhand and the other overhand). The grips should be varied.

INSTRUCTIONAL PROCEDURES

1. Certain terms peculiar to parachute activity must be explained carefully. Terms such as *inflate, deflate, float, dome,* and *mushroom* need to be clarified when they are introduced.

2. For preliminary explanations, the parachute can be stretched out on the ground in its circular pattern, with the children seated just far enough away so they cannot touch the parachute during instructions. When the children hold the parachute during later explanations, they should retain their hold lightly, letting the center of the parachute drop to the ground. Children must be taught to exercise control and not to manipulate the parachute while explanations are in progress.

3. The teacher explains the activity, demonstrating as needed. If there are no questions, the activity is initiated with a command such as "Ready—begin!"

4. Squads can be used to form the parachute circle, with each squad occupying a quarter of the chute's circumference. Squads are useful for competitive units in game activity.

5. The teacher must watch for fatigue, particularly with younger children.

Activities are presented according to type, with variations and suggestions for supplementary activities included. Unless otherwise specified, activities begin and halt on signal. Pupils' suggestions can broaden the scope of activity.

EXERCISE ACTIVITIES

Exercises should be done vigorously and with enough repetitions to challenge the children. In addition to the exercises presented, others can be adapted to parachute play.

Toe Toucher

Sit with feet extended under the parachute and hold the chute taut with a two-hand grip, drawing it up to the chin. Bend forward, and touch the grip to the toes. Return parachute to stretched position.

Curl-Up

Extend the body under the parachute in curl-up position, so the chute comes up to the chin when held taut. Do Curl-ups, returning each time to the stretched chute position.

Dorsal Lift

Lie prone, with head toward the parachute and feet pointed back, away from it. Grip the chute and slide toward the feet until there is some tension on it. Raise the chute off the ground with a vigorous lift of the arms, until head and chest rise off the ground. Return.

V-Sit

Lie supine, with head toward the chute. Do V-ups by raising the upper and lower parts of the body simultaneously into a V-shaped position. The knees should be kept straight.

Backward Pull

Face the parachute and pull back, away from its center. Pulls can be made from a sitting, kneeling, or standing position.

Other Pulls

With arm flexed, do Side Pulls with either arm. Other variations of pulling can be devised.

Hip Walk and Scooter

Begin with the parachute taut. Move forward with the Scooter (p. 380) and Hip Walk (p. 381). Move back to place with the same movement until the chute is taut again.

Elevator

Begin with the chute taut and at ground level. On the command "Elevator up," lift the chute overhead while keeping it stretched tight. On the command "Elevator down," lower the chute to starting position. Lowering and raising can be done quickly or in increments. Levels can also bring in body part identification, with children holding the chute even with their head, nose, chin, shoulders, chest, waist, thighs, knees, ankles, and toes.

Running in Place

Run in place while holding the chute at different levels. Grass Drills (p. 236) can be performed while holding on to the chute.

Isometrics

Hold the chute taut at shoulder level and try to stretch it for 10 seconds. Many other isometric exercises can be performed with the parachute to develop all body parts.

DOME ACTIVITIES

To make a dome, children begin with the parachute on the floor, holding with two hands and kneeling on one knee. To trap air under the chute, children stand up quickly, thrusting their arms above the head (Figure 18.10), and then return to starting position (Figure 18.11). Some or all of the children can change to the inside of the chute on the down movement. Domes also can be made while moving in a circle.

Students Under the Chute

Tasks for under the chute can be specified, such as turning a certain number of turns with a jump rope, throwing and catching a beanbag, or bouncing a ball a number of times. The needed objects should be under the chute before the dome is made.

Number Exchange

Children are numbered from one to four. The teacher calls a number as the dome is made, and those with the number called must change position to be under the dome before the chute comes down. Locomotor movements can be varied.

FIGURE 18.10. Making a dome

FIGURE 18.11. The dome

MUSHROOM ACTIVITIES

To form a mushroom, students begin with the chute on the ground, kneeling on one knee and holding with two hands. They stand up quickly, thrusting the arms overhead. Keeping the arms overhead, each walks forward three or four steps toward the center. The arms are held overhead until the chute is deflated.

Mushroom Release

All children release at the peak of inflation and either run out from under the chute or move to the center and sit down, with the chute descending on top of them.

Mushroom Run

Children make a mushroom. As soon as they move into the center, they release holds and run once around the inside of the chute, counterclockwise, back to place.

ACTIVITIES WITH SMALL MANIPULATIVE OBJECTS

Ball Circle

Place a basketball or a cageball on the raised chute. Make the ball roll around the chute in a large circle, controlling it by raising or lowering the chute. Try the same with two balls. A beach ball is also excellent.

Popcorn

Place a number of beanbags (from six to ten) on the chute. Shake the chute to make them rise like corn popping (Figure 18.12).

FIGURE 18.12. Popping popcorn

Team Ball

Divide the class in half, each team defending half of the chute. Using from two to six balls of any variety, try to bounce the balls off the opponents' side, scoring 1 point for each ball.

Poison Snake

Divide into teams. Place from six to ten jump ropes on the chute. Shake the chute and try to make the ropes hit players on the other side. For each rope that touches one team member, that team has a point scored against it. The team with the lower score is the winner.

Circular Dribble

Each child has a ball suitable for dribbling. The object is to run in circular fashion counterclockwise, holding on to the chute with the left hand and dribbling with the right hand, retaining control of the ball. As an equalizer for left-handers, try the dribbling clockwise.

The dribble should be started first, and then, on signal, children start to run. If a child loses his ball, he must recover it and try to hook on at his original place.

Hole in One

Use four or more plastic whiffle balls the size of golf balls. The balls should be of two different colors. The class is divided into two teams on opposite sides of the chute. The object is to shake the other team's balls into the hole in the center of the chute.

OTHER ACTIVITIES

Merry-Go-Round Movements

Merry-go-round movements, in which children rotate the chute while keeping the center hole over the same spot, offer many opportunities for locomotor movements, either free or to the beat of a tom-tom. European Rhythmic Running is particularly appropriate. Also appropriate are fundamental movements, such as walking, running, hopping, skipping, galloping, sliding, draw steps, and grapevine steps. The parachute can be held at different levels. Holds can be one- or two-handed.

Shaking the Rug and Making Waves

Shaking the Rug involves rapid movements of the parachute, either light or heavy. Making Waves involves large movements to send billows of cloth up and down. Waves can be small, medium, or high. Different types of waves can be made by having children alternate their up and down motions, or by having the class work in small groups around the chute. These small groups take turns showing what they can do. For a more demanding activity, children can perform locomotor movements while they shake the rug.

Chute Crawl

Half of the class, either standing or kneeling, stretches the chute at waist level parallel to the ground. The remaining children crawl under the chute to the opposite side from their starting position.

Kite Run

The class holds the chute on one side with one hand. The leader points in the direction they are to run while holding the chute aloft like a kite.

Running Number Game

The children around the chute count off by fours; then they run lightly, holding the chute in one hand. The teacher calls out one of the numbers. Children with that number immediately release their grip on the chute and run forward to the next vacated place. They must put on a burst of speed to move ahead.

Routines to Music

Like other routines, parachute activities can be adapted to music. A sequence should be based on eight counts, with the routine composed of an appropriate number of sequences.

Tug-of-War

For team Tug-of-War, divide the class in halves. On signal, teams pull against each other and try to reach a line located behind them. Another approach that is often more enjoyable for primary-age children is an individual tug, in which all children pull in any direction they desire.

Action Songs and Dances

A number of action songs, games, and dances can be performed while children hold on to a parachute. The following are suggested: Carrousel (p. 261), Bingo (p. 263), and Seven Jumps (p. 258).

ACTIVITIES WITH WANDS

Wands have been used in physical education programs for many years, but only recently have a wide variety of interesting and challenging activities been developed. Wands can be made from ¾-in. maple dowels or from a variety of broom and mop handles. If two lengths are chosen, make them 36 in. and 42 in. If only one size is to be used, a length of 1 m is recommended. Wands are more interesting when they are painted with imaginative designs, a chore that can be a class project.

Wands are noisy when they hit the floor. Putting rubber crutch tips on each end of a wand alleviates most of the noise and makes it easier to pick up. The tips should be put on with mucilage.

The year's supply of wands should include five or six extras beyond the number of children. There will be some breakage.

Wands serve the physical education program in four ways: (1) challenge activities, (2) stunts, (3) exercises, and (4) combative activities. Challenge activities, stunts, and exercises are presented here, and combatives are presented in Chapter 22. The recommended level for the introduction of wand stunts is the 3rd grade, but the challenge activities can be introduced earlier.

INSTRUCTIONAL PROCEDURES

1. Since wands are noisy when dropped, the children should hold their wands with both hands or put them on the floor during instruction.

2. Many wand activities require great flexibility, which means that not all children are able to do them. Girls usually perform flexibility stunts better than boys.

3. An adequate amount of space is needed for each individual, because wand stunts demand room.

4. Wands are not to be used as fencing foils. Put a stop to any such nonsense at once.

CHALLENGE ACTIVITIES WITH WANDS

Challenge activities offer a relatively unstructured approach and allow for problem solving. The following are only a few of the many possible challenges. The children can develop other ideas.

1. Can you reach down and pick up your wand without bending your knees?

2. Try to balance your wand on different body parts. Watch the top of the wand to get cues on how to retain the balance.

3. Can you hold your stick against the wall and move over and under it?

4. Let's see whether you can hold the stick at both ends and move through the gap.

5. Can you spin the wand and keep it going like a windmill?

6. Let's see how many different ways you can move over and around your wand when it is on the floor.

7. Put one end of the wand on the floor and hold the other end. How many times can you run around your wand without getting dizzy?

8. Place one end of the wand against a wall. Holding the other end and keeping the wand against the wall, duck underneath. Place the wand lower and lower on the wall and go under.

9. Place the wand between your feet and hop around as though you are on a pogo stick.

10. Throw your wand in the air and catch it.

11. Hold the wand vertically near the middle. Can you release your grip and catch the wand before it falls to the floor?

12. Have a partner hold a wand horizontally above the floor. Jump, leap, and hop over the wand. Gradually raise the height of the wand.

13. Put your wand on the floor and try making different kinds of bridges over it.

14. Place the wand on the floor. Curl alongside it, just touching it. Curl at one end of the wand.

15. Balance the wand vertically on the floor. Release the wand and try to complete different stunts—clapping the hands, doing a heel click, touching different body parts—before the wand falls to the floor.

16. Put the wand on the floor and see how many ways you can push it, using different body parts.

INDIVIDUAL WAND STUNTS

Wand Catch

Stand a wand on one end and hold it in place with the fingers on the tip. Loop the foot quickly over the stick, letting go of the wand briefly but catching it with the fingers before it falls. Do this right and left for a complete set. Try to catch the wand with just the index finger.

Thread the Needle (V-Seat)

Maintaining a V-seat position, with the wand held in front of the body with both hands, bend the knees between the arms and pass the wand over them and return, *without touching* the wand to the legs. Try with the ankles crossed.

Thread the Needle (Standing)

Holding the wand in both hands, step through the space, one leg at a time, and return without touching. Step through again, but this time bring the wand up behind the back, over the head, and down in front. Reverse. Try from side to side with the stick held front and back.

Grapevine

Holding the wand near the ends, step with the right foot *around* the right arm and over the wand inward, toward the body (Figure 18.13). Pass the wand backward over the head and right shoulder (Figure 18.14), and continue sliding the wand down the body until you are standing erect with the wand between the legs. Reverse the process back to original position. Try with the left foot leading.

FIGURE 18.13. Beginning the Grapevine

FIGURE 18.14. Grapevine, second stage (head ducks under, and wand is passed down the back)

Back Scratcher

Hold the wand with an underhand grip (palms up), arms crossed in front of the body (Figure 18.15). Bend the elbows so the wand can go over and behind the head. Attempt to pass the wand down the length of the body from the back of the shoulders to the heels. Do not release the grip on the wand. The wand is worked down behind the back while the arms stay in front of the body.

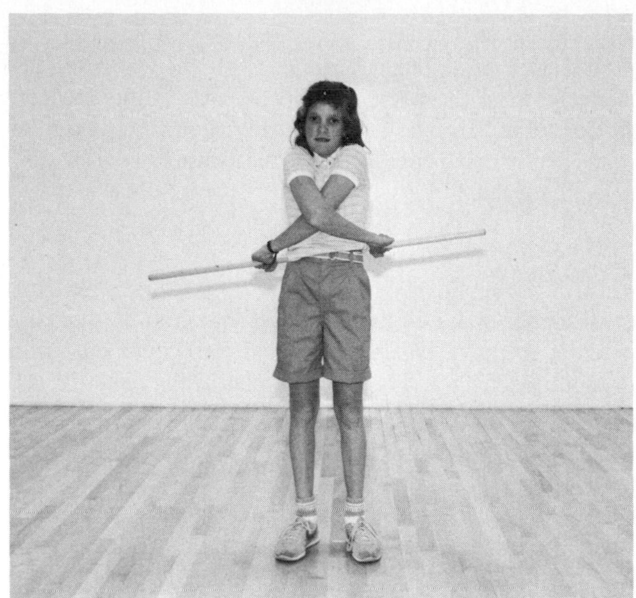

FIGURE 18.15. Back Scratcher (wand has been passed overhead and is now being forced down the back)

Wand Whirl

Stand the wand upright in front of the body. Turn around quickly and grasp the wand before it falls. Do the movement both right and left. Try making two full turns and still catching the wand before it falls.

Twist Under

Grasp the upright wand with the right hand. Twist around under the right arm without letting go of the wand, taking it off the floor, or touching the knee to the floor. Repeat, using the left arm.

Jump Wand

Holding the wand in front with the fingertips of both hands, jump over it. Jumping back is not recommended, because the wand can hit the heels and cause an awkward fall. (A rope or a towel can be substituted for the wand if children are having difficulty.)

Balancing the Wand

Balance the wand vertically with one hand. Experiment with different hand and finger positions. Walk forward, backward, and sideward. Sit down, lie down, and move into other positions while keeping the wand balanced. Keep the eyes on the top of the wand. Balance the wand horizontally on the hands, arms, feet, and thighs. Balance it across the back of the neck. In crab position, balance it across the tummy.

The Sprinter

Get into a sprinter's position, with the wand on the floor, between the feet, and perpendicular to the direction of the sprint. Change the feet rapidly, alternating over the wand. Try moving both feet together forward and backward over the wand.

Crab Leap

Place the wand on the floor. Get into crab position and attempt to move the feet back and forth over the wand without touching it. Try this with alternating feet.

Long Reach

Stand with legs extended and feet spread about 12 in. apart. Hold a wand in the left hand, and use it like a third limb. With a piece of chalk in the right hand, reach forward as far as possible and make a mark. Use the wand as a support and see whether the mark can be bettered.

Merry-Go-Wand

Place the wand vertically on the floor about 2 ft in front of the body. Bend over, and place the forehead on the upper end of the wand. Using a crossover step, go all the way around the wand without letting it fall to the floor. The hands must be kept on the small of the back.

Wand Bridge

On a mat, start in a straddle stance with legs straight. Hold a wand near one end, with the other end above the head and pointed toward the ceiling. Bend backward, place the wand on the mat behind you, and walk the hands down the wand. Return to standing position.

Wand Twirl

Children in the class who have baton-twirling experience can show the class some points of technique.

PARTNER WAND STUNTS

Partner Catch

Partners face each other a short distance (5 ft) apart, each holding a wand in the right hand. On signal, each throws the wand to the partner with the right hand and catches the incoming wand with the left. Distances can be increased somewhat.

Partner Change

Partners face each other a short distance (5 ft) apart. Each has a wand standing upright, held on top by the right hand. On signal, each runs to the other's wand and tries to catch it before it falls. This can also be done in the same way as the Wand Whirl, with each whirling to the other's wand. Try with a small group of five or six. On signal, all move to the next wand.

Turn the Dishrag

Partners face each other and grasp a wand. When ready, they perform a dishrag turn (p. 368).

Jump the Wand

One partner moves the wand back and forth along the floor, while the other partner jumps over it. To add challenge, partners should change the tempo of movement and raise the level of the wand.

Wand Reaction

One partner holds the wand horizontally. The other partner places one hand directly above the wand, palm down. When the wand is dropped, the person with her hand over the wand tries to catch it before it strikes the floor.

Cooperative Movements

Holding a wand between them, partners stand toe-to-toe and circle either way with light foot movements. Together, partners squat down and stand up. Sit down and come up. Kneel and hold the wand overhead as they face each other. Bend sideways and touch the wand to the floor.

ISOMETRIC EXERCISES WITH WANDS

The isometric exercises with wands presented here are mainly grip exercises. A variety of grips should be employed. With the wand horizontal, use either the overhand or underhand grip. With the wand in vertical position, grip with the thumbs pointed up, down, or toward each other. Repeat each exercise with a different grip. Exercises can also be repeated with the wand in different positions—in front of the body (either horizontal or vertical), overhead, or behind the back. Hold each exercise for 8 to 12 seconds.

Pull the Wand Apart

Place the hands 6 in. apart near the center of the wand. With a tight grip to prevent slippage and with arms extended, pull the hands apart. Change grip and position.

Push the Wand Together

Hold the wand as previously, except push the hands together.

Wand Twist

Hold the wand with both hands about 6 in. apart. Twist the hands in opposite directions.

Bicycle

Holding the wand horizontally throughout and using an overhand grip, extend the wand outward and downward. Bring it upward near the body, completing a circular movement. On the downward movement, push the wand together, and on the upward movement, pull the wand apart.

Arm Spreader

Hold the wand overhead with hands spread wide. Attempt to compress the stick. Reverse force, and attempt to pull the stick apart.

Dead Lift

Partially squat and place the wand under the thighs. Place the hands between the legs and try to lift. Try also with hands on the outside of the legs.

Abdominal Tightener

From a standing position, place the wand behind the buttocks. With hands on the ends of the wand, pull forward and resist with the abdominal muscles.

STRETCHING EXERCISES WITH WANDS

Wands are useful for stretching, bending, and twisting movements.

Side Bender

Grip the wand and extend the arms overhead with feet apart. Bend sideways as far as possible, maintaining straight arms and legs. Recover, and bend to the other side.

Body Twist

Place the wand behind the neck, with arms draped over the wand from behind. Rotate the upper body first to the right as far as possible and then to the left. The feet and hips should remain in position. The twist is at the waist.

Body Twist to Knee

Assume body twist position. Bend the trunk forward and twist so that the right end of the wand touches the left knee (Figure 18.16). Recover, and touch the left end to the right knee.

FIGURE 18.16. Body Twist to Knee

Shoulder Stretcher

Grip the wand at the ends in a regular grip. Extend the arms overhead and rotate the wand, arms, and shoulders backward until the stick touches the back of the legs. The arms should be kept straight. Those who find the stretch too easy should move their hands closer to the center of the wand.

Toe Touch

Grip the wand with the hands about shoulder width apart. Bend forward, reaching down as far as possible without bending the knees. The movement should be slow and controlled. Try the same activity from a sitting position.

Over the Toes

Sit down, flex the knees, place the wand over the toes, and rest it against the middle of the arch. Grip the stick with the fingers at the outside edge of the feet. Slowly extend the legs forward, pushing against the stick and trying for a full extension of the legs.

ACTIVITIES WITH HOOPS

Most hoops manufactured in the United States are plastic, but Europeans sometimes use wooden ones. The plastic variety is less durable but more versatile. Extra hoops are needed, because some breakage will occur. The standard hoop is 42 in. in diameter, but it is desirable to have smaller hoops (about 36 in.) for younger children. Hoops with lead shot inside are of no advantage.

INSTRUCTIONAL PROCEDURES

1. Hoops produce noisy activity. The teacher may find it helpful to have the children lay their hoops on the floor when they are to listen.

2. Hoops can be a creative medium for children. Allow them free time to explore their own ideas.

3. Give the children an adequate amount of space in which to perform, for hoops require much movement.

4. In activities that require children to jump through hoops, instruct the holder to grasp the hoop lightly, so as not to cause an awkward fall if a performer hits it.

5. Hoops can serve as a "home" for various activities. For instance, the children might leave their hoops to gallop in all directions and then return quickly to the hoop on command.

6. Hoops are good targets. A hoop can be made to stand by placing an individual mat over its base (p. 349).

7. When teaching the reverse spin with hoops, have the students throw the hoop up, in place, rather than forward along the floor. After they learn the upward throw, they can progress to the forward throw for distance.

RECOMMENDED ACTIVITIES

Hoops as Floor Targets

Each child has a hoop, which is placed on the floor. A number of movement challenges can give direction to the activity.

1. Show what different patterns you can make by jumping or hopping in and out of the hoop.

2. Do a Bunny Jump and a Frog Jump into the center and out the other side.

3. Show what ways you can cross from one side of the hoop to the other by taking the weight on your hands inside the hoop.

4. What kinds of animal walks can you do around your hoop?

5. On all fours, show the kinds of movements you can do, with your feet inside the hoop and your hands outside. With your hands inside the hoop and your feet outside. With one foot and one hand inside, and one foot and one hand outside.

6. (Set a time limit of 15 to 30 seconds.) See how many times you can jump in and out of your hoop during this time. Now try hopping.

7. Balance on and walk around the hoop. Try to keep your feet from touching the floor.

8. Curl your body inside the hoop. Bridge over your hoop. Stretch across your hoop. See how many different ways you can move around the hoop.

9. Pick up your hoop and see how many different machines you can invent. Let your hoop be the steering wheel of a car. What could it be on a train or boat?

10. Jump in and out of the hoop, using the alphabet. Jump in on the vowels and out on the consonants. Use odd and even numbers in the same way. Vary the locomotor movements.

11. Get into the hoop by using two different body parts. Move out by using three parts. Vary the number of body parts used.

12. Get organized in squads or comparable groups, and divide the hoops. Arrange the hoops in various formations, and try different locomotor movements, animal walks, and other ways of maneuvering through the maze (Figure 18.17). (After the children have gained some experience, this can become a follow-the-leader activity.)

Hoop Handling

1. Spin the hoop like a top. See how long you can make it spin. Spin it again, and see how many times you can run around it before it falls to the floor.

2. Hula-hoop using various body parts such as the waist, legs, arms, and fingers. While hula-hooping on the arms, try to change the hoop from one arm to the other. Lie on the back with one or both legs pointed toward the ceiling and explore different ways the legs can twirl the hula hoop. Hula-hoop with two or more hoops.

3. Jump or hop through a hoop held by a partner. Further challenge can be added by varying the height and angle of the hoop.

4. Roll the hoop and run alongside it. Change direction when a command is given.

5. Hula-hoop on one arm. Throw the hoop in the air, and catch it on the other arm.

6. Hold the hoop and swing it like a pendulum. Jump and hop in and out of the hoop.

7. Use the hoop like a jump rope. Jump forward, backward, and sideward. Do a crossover with the hands.

8. Roll the hoop with a reverse spin to make it return to you. The key to the reverse spin is to pull down (toward

FIGURE 18.17. Hopping through hoop formations

the floor) on the hoop as it is released. Roll the hoop with a reverse spin, and jump over it and catch it as it returns. Roll the hoop with a reverse spin, and as it returns, hoist it with the foot and catch it. Roll the hoop with a reverse spin, kick it up with the toe, and go through the hoop. Roll the hoop with a reverse spin, run around it, and catch it. Roll the hoop with a reverse spin, pick it up, and begin hooping on the arm—all in one motion.

9. Play catch with a partner. Play catch with two or more hoops.

10. Hula-hoop and attempt to change hoops with a partner.

11. Have one partner roll the hoop with a reverse spin, and the other attempts to crawl through the hoop. (This is done most easily just after the hoop reverses direction and begins to return to the spinner. Some children can go in and out of the hoop twice.)

12. Tell partners to spin the hoops like tops and see who can keep theirs spinning longer.

GAMES WITH HOOPS

Musical Hoops

Hoops, one fewer than the number of children, are placed on the floor. Players are given a locomotor movement to do. On signal, they cease the movement, find a hoop, and sit cross-legged in the center of it. Music can be used, with the children moving to the music and seeking a hoop when the music stops.

Around the Hoop

The class is divided into groups of three, with children in each group numbered 1, 2, and 3. Each threesome sits back-to-back inside a hoop. Their heels may need to be outside the hoop. The leader calls out a direction (right or left) and names one of the numbers. The child with that number immediately gets up, runs in the stipulated direction around the hoop, then runs back to place and sits down. The winner is the first group sitting in good position after the child returns to place.

Hula Hoop Circle

Four to six children hold hands in a circle, facing in, with a hoop dangling on one pair of joined hands. They move the hoop around the circle and back to the starting point. This requires all bodies to go through the hoop. Hands can help the hoop move, but grips cannot be released.

RHYTHMIC GYMNASTICS

Rhythmic gymnastics became popular during the 1970s and was followed by acceptance as an official sport competition in the 1984 Olympic Games. The activities are broad in scope and merit far more explanation than can be presented in this context.

Essentially, activities in rhythmic gymnastics are routines done to music by a performer using different pieces of manipulative equipment. The routine can be either individual, partner, or team competition. The most common pieces of equipment used are balls, jump ropes, hoops, ribbons, and clubs. Wands, flags, and scarves are sometimes included, but not in national or international competition. The latter will not be discussed in this presentation, nor will partner or team competition.

Many movement qualities, such as balance, poise, grace, flow of body movement, coordination, rhythm, and kinesthetic sense, grow out of serious participation in rhythmic gymnastics. Fitness qualities of agility, flexibility, and proper posture are also developed. Furthermore, skill in handling the various pieces of manipulative equipment is enhanced, because these skills must be mastered before they can be organized into a routine set to music.

Participants, after initial practice in skill development, should work with music. The music should be light, lively, and enjoyable to the gymnast. Most record companies dealing in music for physical education stock specialized records for gymnastic movement, with different selections specified for various pieces of equipment. Most records contain directions for suggested routines. There is no substitute, however, for teacher ingenuity in helping children expand their movements.

ORGANIZING THE PROGRAM

The activities presented here focus on balls, jump ropes, hoops, and streamers, all of which ordinarily are covered in the elementary program. The club is one of the most difficult of the hand apparatus to use and is therefore not an item for instruction in elementary school programs.

The goal of rhythmic gymnastics is continuous body movement with the selected piece of equipment. Composition goals are originality, variety of movement, use of the performing area, and smoothness of transition. Harmony of movement with the music and execution factors are also important. The length of a competitive routine is 1 minute to 1 minute and 30 seconds, but performing time should be shortened for youngsters. The primary goal is the personal satisfaction that students receive from participating in the program. Offering students an introduction to these activities is more important than the competitive aspect.

Probably the most practical way to include rhythmic gymnastics in the curriculum is a dual approach. The basic skills are taught to all children in physical education classes, then through the intramural program or through a sport club, students can choose on an elective basis to participate in competition. Instructors often lack background in these activities. This problem may be solved by bringing in dance instructors from private clubs to introduce the activities.

DEVELOPING ROUTINES

Routines for the elementary level should be uncomplicated and based on learned skills. Aesthetics, although important as skill develops, should be of secondary emphasis. Ballet and modern dance movements, along with dance steps, are normal conclusions in high-level competition.

In developing routines to music, children need to remember that most music is based on units of 8 or 16 counts. An effective way to form a routine is to devise ribbon movements to consume 12 counts and to do the Elevator (p. 366) as a 4-count filler, ending each series with the hands in front of the waist. For example:

Forward circles on the right side (6 counts)
Forward circles on the left side (6 counts)
Elevator (coming down) (4 counts)

In this fashion, the routine can consist of a number of 16-count units, each of which is concluded with the Elevator (4 counts).

For any one piece of apparatus, certain skill areas can be specified. It is then up to the participant to include these at some point in the routine.

Figure 18.18 is an example of a simple routine using balls. The numbers refer to the floor area in the figure where each activity should be performed.

1. Bounce the ball in place.
2. Bounce the ball while moving forward slowly.
3. Run forward while making swing tosses from side-to-side.
4. Bounce the ball and make a full turn.
5. Run in a figure-eight pattern.
6. Toss the ball up and catch it with one hand.
7. Finish with a toss and catch behind the back.

RHYTHMIC GYMNASTIC BALL SKILLS

The ball should be of sufficient size so it cannot be grasped by the hand, but must rest in the hand and be controlled by balance. For elementary school children, use either a 6-in. or 8-in. ball. Balls should be moderately inflated.

In handling the ball, the fingers should be closed and slightly bent, with the ball resting in the palm. In throwing, the ball can roll from the fingertips. After catching, the ball returns immediately to the palm.

The following ball skill areas are considerations:

1. *Throwing and catching movements.* Emphasize tossing in a variety of ways to self and catching. The skills can be done in place or in combination with locomotor movements or dance steps.

2. *Bouncing movements.* These include single bounces and dribbling as in basketball, either in place or moving.

3. *Rolling movements.* The variety of rolling movements is interesting. Rolling the ball and following it on the floor represents one stunt area. Rolling the ball on various parts of the body is another.

4. *Swinging movements (also circular movements).* Swinging movements are more difficult than they first appear. The ball must be retained in the palm while the movements are performed.

5. *Balancing movements.* These are the spirals, curls, and other balances that are inherent to rhythmic gymnastics.

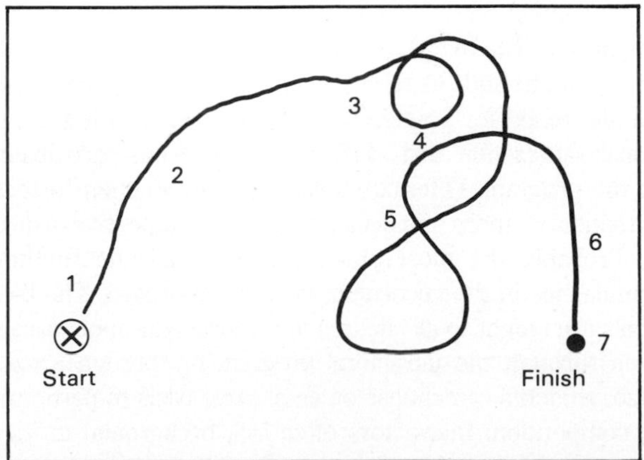

FIGURE 18.18. Floor pattern for routine using balls

RHYTHMIC GYMNASTIC ROPE ROUTINES

As with ball routines, jump-rope routines can be categorized in a number of areas. Most important is that the participant be able to do the basic jumps with consumate skill. Ropes can be used full length, folded in half, or folded in fourths. Knotting the end of the rope makes it easier to handle. Proper length is determined by standing on the center of the rope with one foot and extending the rope ends to the outstretched hands at shoulder level. Handles are not appropriate. Most rope jumping is done with the hands far apart. The rope should not touch the floor, but should pass slightly above it. The jumping techniques used for rhythmic gymnastics obviously differ from those taught in the physical education class. The following are examples of movements that can be performed using jump ropes.

1. *Jumping movements.* A number of basic steps are used, with the rope turning forward or backward. Techniques include moving to simple locomotor steps or dance steps such as the schottische or polka. Single, double, and even triple turns are also used.

2. *Swinging movements.* A variety of swinging movements are done in frontal, vertical, or horizontal planes with single, doubled, or quadrupled ropes. Ropes may be held in one hand or in both hands.

3. *Balance movements.* Balance movements add variety and permit the performer to catch his breath. These involve held body positions, with the rope underneath the foot or hooked around a foot.

4. *Wrapping movements.* The rope can be wrapped around the body or around various body parts. Most wrap-around stunts are done with the long single rope, but the folded rope can be used.

5. *Tossing and catching movements.* Tossing and catching movements present considerable difficulty. Many follow swinging movements. Tossing and catching can be done with one hand or with both hands.

RHYTHMIC GYMNASTIC HOOP MOVEMENTS

The basic hoop stunts and challenges (pp. 313–315) should first be mastered. The same hoop used in physical education classes is suitable for these routines. The hoop may be held, tossed, or caught in one or both hands and with a variety of different grips. Hoops may turn forward or backward. Some suggested rhythmic movements with hoops follow.

1. *Swinging movements.* The swinging movement should be very large. Good alignment between body and hoop is important. Hoops can be swung in a frontal, sagittal, or horizontal plane. The movements can be done in place or involve locomotion.

2. *Turning movements.* This movement entails turning the hoop, usually with both hands but sometimes with one. The hoop also can be spun on the ground.

3. *Circling movements.* These are the movements most characteristic of hoop activities. Hoops can be twirled by the hand, wrist, arm, leg, or body (hula hooping). Changes are made from one hand or wrist to the other.

4. *Tossing and catching movements.* The hoop can be tossed high in the air with one or both hands. The catch should be one-handed, between the thumb and index finger. Most tosses grow out of swinging or circling movements.

5. *Rolling movements.* The hoop can be rolled on the floor, either forward or reverse (return) rolling, or can be rolled on the body in diverse ways. If rolled along the floor, various jumps are executed over the rolling hoop. The hoop can be rolled along one arm to the other, on the front or back of the body.

6. *Jumping movements.* The hoop, turned forward or backward, can be used in a manner similar to a jump rope.

RHYTHMIC GYMNASTIC RIBBON MOVEMENTS

Ribbon movements are spectacular and make effective demonstrations. Official ribbon length is around 20 ft, but for practical purposes, shorter lengths are used at the elementary school level.

Ribbons can be made easily in a variety of colors. A rhythmic flow of movement is desired, featuring circular, oval, spiral, and wavelike shapes. A light flowing movement is the goal, with total body involvement. The dowel or stick, to which the ribbon is attached, should be an extension of the hand and arm. Laterality is also a consideration. The following are some basic ribbon movements.

1. *Swinging movements.* The entire body should coordinate with these large swinging motions.

2. *Circling movements.* Large circles should involve the whole arm; smaller circles involve the wrist. Circles are made in different planes—frontal, sagittal, and horizontal.

3. *Figure-eight movements.* Figure eights are also made in the three planes. The two halves of the figure eight should be the same size and on the same plane level. The figure can be made with long arm movements or with movements of the lower arm or wrist.

4. *Serpentine movements.* Serpentines can be made in the air or on the floor. These are done with continuous up and down hand movements, using primarily wrist action.

5. *Spiral movements.* The circles in the spiral can be of the same size or of an increasing or decreasing progression. Spirals can be made from left to right or the reverse.

6. *Throwing and catching movements.* These skills are usually combined with swinging, circling, or figure-eight movements. The ribbon is tossed with one hand and is caught with the same hand or with the other hand. Throwing and catching is a difficult maneuver.

ACTIVITIES WITH INDIVIDUAL TUG-OF-WAR ROPES

An individual tug-of-war rope is a rope about 5 ft long with a loop on each end. (See Chapter 34 for instructions on making individual tug-of-war ropes.)

Tug-of-war ropes help in the development of strength, because contestants must use maximum or near-maximum strength in the contests. These strength demands may continue over a short period of time. Since considerable effort is demanded in some cases, force concepts are concomitant learnings. An in-depth discussion of instructional procedures and formations for conducting combative activities is found in Chapter 22.

INSTRUCTIONAL PROCEDURES

1. Contests should be between opponents of comparable ability. Each child should have a chance to win sometimes.

2. Plan a system of rotation so children meet different opponents.

3. Caution students not to let go of the rope. If the grip is slipping, they should inform the other student, renew the grip, and start over.

4. Individual ropes are excellent for partner resistance activities. A few of these activities should be practiced each time the children use the ropes.

5. Make clear the starting routine so each contestant understands. Make definite rules about what constitutes a win and how long a contest must endure to be called a tie.

6. A line on the floor perpendicular to the direction of the rope makes a satisfactory goal for determining a win. One child pulls the other forward until he is over the line. If the distance seems too short, two parallel lines can be drawn 8 to 10 ft apart, with the object now being to pull the opponent out of the area between the lines. Another criterion for a win could be for children to pick up objects placed behind them.

PARTNER ACTIVITIES

Children should try the following ways of pulling. The tug-of-war rope offers good possibilities in movement exploration. Let students try to devise ways other than those mentioned by which they can pull against each other.

1. Pull with the right hand only, the left hand only, both hands.

2. Grasp with the right hand, with the body supported on three points (the left hand and the feet). Change hands.

3. Pull with backs toward each other, with the rope between the legs, holding with one hand only.

4. Opponents get down on all fours, with feet toward each other. Hook the loops around one foot of each opponent. For each contestant, the force is provided by both hands and the foot that remains on the floor.

5. Opponents get into crab position, and pull the rope by hooking a foot through the loop (Figure 18.19).

6. Opponents face each other and stand on one foot only. Each contestant tries to pull the other off balance without losing her own balance. If the raised foot touches the floor, the other person is declared the winner.

7. Contestants stand with opposite sides toward each other. They hold a tug-of-war rope with opposite hands and move apart until the rope is taut. The goal is to make the other person move his feet by pulling and giving on the rope. The legs must be kept straight, and only the arms can be used in the contest.

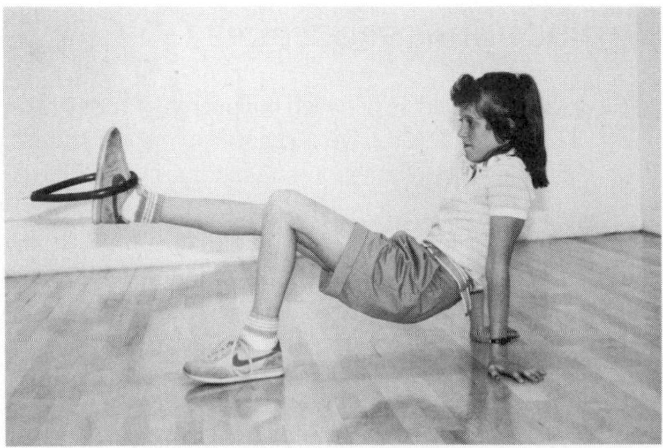

FIGURE 18.19. Pulling in crab position

8. Students stand 10 ft away from the rope, which is on the floor. On signal, they run to the rope, pick it up, and have a tug-of-war. Contestants can start from different positions, such as Push-up, Sit-up, or Crab.

9. Instead of opponents pulling each other across a line, each one tries to pull the other toward a peg or Indian club placed behind her so that she can pick up the object.

10. Two individual ropes are tied together at the center so four loops are available for pulling. Four Indian clubs form a square, and four children compete to see who can pick up his club first.

11. Two children pull against two others. The rope loops should be made big enough so that both can secure handholds on each end. They can use right hands only or left hands only.

12. For a Japanese Tug-of-War, two children take hold of a rope, each with both hands on a loop. The children are positioned close enough together so there is some slack in the rope. A third child grasps the rope to make a 6-in. bend at the center, and the contestants then pull the rope taut so there is no slack (Figure 18.20). On the signal "Go," the third child drops the loop, and the opponents try to pull each other off balance. To move a foot is to lose.

13. Group contests are possible. (See p. 588 for a diagram of rope arrangements suitable for groups.)

PARTNER RESISTANCE ACTIVITIES

The children should follow good exercise principles, exerting sufficient force (near maximum), maintaining resistance through the full range of motion for 8 to 10 seconds, and stabilizing the base so the selected part of the body can be exercised.

As in other activities, grip can be varied. The upper grip (palms away from performer) and the lower grip (palms toward performer) are usually used. Occasionally, a mixed grip, with one hand in upper position and one hand in lower position, can be used.

The force is a controlled pull, not a tug. The partner should not be compelled to move out of position. Much of the exercise centers on the hands and arms, but other parts of the body come into play as braces. Partners work together, both in the same position. (The exercises also

FIGURE 18.20. Japanese Tug-of-War

can be done by one person, with the other end of the rope attached firmly to some part of the building.) One or more basic activities are suggested for each position, and the teacher and the children can devise others. Laterality must be kept in mind so the right and left sides of the body receive equal treatment.

Partners Standing With Sides Toward Each Other

1. Use a lower grip. Do a flexed-arm pull, with elbows at right angles.

2. Use an upper grip. Extend the arm from the side at a 45-degree angle. Pull toward the side.

3. Use a lower grip. Extend the arm completely overhead. Pull overhead.

4. Loop the rope around one ankle. Stand with feet apart. Pull with the closer foot.

Partners Standing, Facing Each Other

1. Use a lower grip. Do a flexed-arm pull, with one and then both hands.

2. Use an upper grip. Extend the arms at the side or down. Pull toward the rear.

3. Use an upper grip. Pull both hands straight toward chest.

4. Use an upper grip. Extend the arms above head. Pull backward.

Partners Sitting, Facing Each Other

1. Repeat the activities described for standing position (Figure 18.21).

2. Hook the rope with both feet. Pull.

Partners Prone, Facing Each Other

1. Use an upper grip. Pull directly toward the chest.

2. Use a lower grip. Do a flexed-arm pull.

Partners Prone, Feet Toward Each Other

1. Hook the rope around one ankle. With knee joint at a right angle, pull.

2. Try with both feet together.

PULLING RESISTANCE ACTIVITIES

Using mostly the standing positions, work out resistance exercises like the following: One child pulls and makes progress with eight steps. The other child then pulls her back for eight counts. The addition of music makes this an interesting activity. The child being pulled must provide enough resistance to make the puller work reasonably hard.

FIGURE 18.21. Partner resistance activity in sitting position

GAME WITH TUG-OF-WAR ROPES

Hawaiian Tug-of-War

The playing area for Hawaiian Tug-of-War is the gymnasium or playground. Two parallel lines are drawn about 20 ft apart. The game is between two people, but as many pairs as are in a class can play. An individual tug-of-war rope is needed for each pair.

An individual tug-of-war rope is laid on the floor at right angles to, and midway between, the two parallel lines. The two children position themselves so that each is standing about 1 ft from one of the loops of the rope. They are in position to pick up the rope and pull against each other on signal.

The object of the game is to pull the other child so as to be able to touch the line behind. The magic word is "Hula." This is the signal to pick up the rope and begin to pull. Children must not reach down and pick up the rope until "Hula" is called. The teacher can use other commands, such as "Go" and "Begin," to deceive the children.

MANIPULATIVE ACTIVITIES WITH FOOTSIES

The program of manipulative activities can be expanded with any number of objects that may have limited or local popularity. Footsies are one such object. (Directions for constructing a footsie can be found in Chapter 34.) Some activities involving footsies are these.

1. Turn the footsie with the right foot and then with the left foot, clockwise and counterclockwise.

2. Travel forward, backward, and sideward while twirling the footsie.

3. Turn around in place in the same direction as the footsie. Now turn the opposite way.

4. Bounce a ball while twirling. Toss the ball and catch it. Play catch with a partner.

FOOTBAG ACTIVITIES

A footbag is an official object used in footbag skills and games. The construction varies with the manufacturer, although most footbags are constructed of leather and are stitched internally for durability. Normal size is about 2 in. in diameter, and the weight is a little over 1 oz. The object of the activities is to keep the bag in the air by means of foot contact.

The kicking motion used for footbag activities is new to most participants because of the lift, which is performed by lifting the foot upward, not away from the body. The lifting motion enables the footbag flight to be directed upward for controlled consecutive kicks and passes. The ball is soft and flexible, with no bounce. It must be designed specifically as a footbag.

Several points contribute to successful footbag work. The basic athletic stance (ready position) is used with the feet at approximately shoulder width and pointed straight ahead. Knees are bent slightly, with the weight lowered.

There should be equal use of both feet for lifting and kicking. The rule of the support (nonkicking) foot merits attention in maintaining balance and keeping the body in a crouched position. Eye focus on the footbag is essential. Kicking speed should be slow; most beginners tend to kick too quickly. The kicking speed should be about that of the descending footbag. *Slow* and *low* are the key words in kicking.

The arms and upper body are used for balance and control. For the outside and back kicks, an outstretched arm, opposite to the kicking foot and in line with it, aids in maintaining balance. The near arm is carried behind the body so as not to restrict the player's vision. For inside kicks, the arms are relaxed and in balanced position.

To begin, start with a hand toss to self or with a courtesy toss from another player. A restriction is made that touching the footbag with any part of the body above the waist is a foul and interrupts any sequence of kicks.

Footbag skills should begin at the intermediate-grade level. Three basic kicks are recommended.

1. *Inside kick.* This kick is used when the footbag falls low and directly in front of both shoulders. Use the inside of the foot for contact by turning the instep and the ankle upward to create a flat striking surface. Curling the toes under aids in creating a flat striking surface. Contact with the footbag is made at about knee level.

2. *Outside kick.* This kick is used when the footbag falls outside of either shoulder. The outside of the foot is used by turning the ankle and knee in to create a flat striking surface. With the kicking foot now parallel to the playing surface, use a smooth lifting motion, striking the footbag at approximately knee level. Pointing the toes up aids in creating a flat surface.

3. *Back kick.* This kick is somewhat similar to the outside kick and serves when the footbag goes directly overhead or is approaching the upper body directly. The hips and body must rotate parallel to the flight direction to enable the footbag to pass while still maintaining constant eye contact. Lean forward in the direction of the footbag's flight and allow it to pass by before executing the kick.

Play can take different forms.

1. *Individual play.* An individual attempts to see how many consecutive times she can keep the footbag in play. One point is scored for each kick.

2. *Partner play.* Partners alternate kicking the footbag. Score 1 point for each alternate successful kick.

3. *Group Play.* A circle of four or five individuals is the basic formation. Rules governing consecutive kicks are (a) all members of the circle must have kicked the footbag for a consecutive run to count, and (b) return kicks are prohibited, that is, a kicker may not receive a return kick from the person to whom he kicked the footbag.

Footbag play is an enjoyable activity, but the skills are not easily learned. Persistence and patience are needed. There will be many misses before students slowly gain control. Many physical education suppliers carry footbags, but if sources are needed and information is desired, write to: World Footbag Association, 1317 Washington Avenue, Suite 7, Golden, CO 80401.

REFERENCE

Morris, G. S. 1976. Effects ball and background color have upon the catching performance of elementary school children. *Research Quarterly* 47: 409–15.

CHAPTER **19**

Activities With Jump Ropes

Rope jumping is an excellent activity for conditioning all parts of the body. It increases coordination, rhythm, and timing, while offering a wide range of challenges. It is a useful activity to teach children, because it can carry over to later life and be an exercise activity that adults perform in the privacy of their homes. It is an especially good activity for obese children, because it increases their exercise level and leads to a more active life-style.

Rope jumping can be taught during any part of the school year and can be used as a fitness or lesson focus activity. It is a creative medium, for there is no limit to the number of routines and steps that can be developed and mastered. When used in programs for parent and teacher groups, this activity stimulates excellent audience response.

As a point of interest, some educators refer to rope jumping as *rope skipping.* The term *rope jumping* should be used instead, because jumping is the predominant skill in this activity.

Rope jumping is a learned skill, so it is difficult to allocate the various activities to grade levels. Rope-jumping activities in this chapter have been grouped in three categories: (1) movements guided by rope patterns, (2) long-rope jumping, and (3) individual rope jumping.

MOVEMENTS GUIDED BY ROPE PATTERNS

Ropes can be placed on the floor in various fashions to serve as stimuli for different locomotor and nonlocomotor movements. The activities should stress creative responses within the limits of the challenge. The educational movement factors of space, time, force, and flow can be interwoven in the activity. The key is teacher ingenuity in providing direction for the movement patterns. The child can move as an individual, with a partner, or as a member of a small group.

Generally, a rope is placed in a straight line or in a circle. Geometric figures can be formed, however, and numbers or letters of the alphabet featured. The discussions are organized around these patterns.

ROPE FORMING A STRAIGHT LINE

When the rope is placed in a straight line, one approach is for the child to begin at one end and to perform activities as he moves down the line. Much of the movement can be based on hopping or jumping. The child then returns, back up the line, to the starting point. Movement suggestions follow.

1. Hop back and forth across the rope, moving down the line. Return, using the other foot.

2. Jump lightly back and forth down the line. Return.

3 Hop slowly, under control, down the line. Hop rapidly back.

4. Jump so the rope is between the feet each time, alternately crossing and uncrossing the feet.

5. Move on all fours, leading with different body parts.

6. Do Crouch Jumps back and forth across the rope. Vary with three points and then two points of contact.

7. Jump as high as possible going down the line and as low as possible coming back.

8. Hop with a narrow shape down and a different shape back.

9. Walk the rope like a tightrope.

10. Begin with a bridge and move the bridge down the line. Return with a different bridge.

11. Lie across the rope, holding one end. Roll down the line, causing the rope to roll around the body. Unroll the rope back to position.

12. Do a movement with the rhythm slow-slow, fast-fast-fast, going down the line, and repeat coming back.

13. "Pull" yourself down the line, and "push" yourself back.

For the following movements, the child is positioned close to the center of the line and simply moves back and forth across it without materially changing her relative position.

1. Hop back and forth across the line. Jump back and forth.

2. Go over with a high movement. Come back with a low one.

3. Do a Bunny Jump across and back. A Frog Jump. A Crouch Jump.

4. Lead with different parts of the body back and forth. Propel with different parts.

5. Get into a moderately crouched position over the rope. Jump the feet back and forth over the rope.

6. Take a Sprinter's Position with the rope between the feet. Alternate the feet back and forth over the rope.

7. Jump back and forth lightly on the tiptoes.

8. Go back and forth, employing different shapes.

9. With toes touching the rope, drop the body forward across the rope, taking the weight on both hands. Walk the hands forward, out to the limit.

10. Pretend the rope is a river. Show different kinds of bridges that you can make over the river.

ROPE FORMING A CIRCLE

With the rope in a circle, children can do movements around the outside clockwise and counterclockwise—walking, skipping, hopping, sliding (facing toward and away from the circle), jumping, running, and galloping. The following activities can be done with hoops also.

1. Hop in and out of the circle, moving around. Jump.

2. Jump directly in and then across. Jump backward.

3. Jump in, collapse, and jump out, without touching the rope.

4. Begin in the center of the circle. Jump forward, backward, and sideward, each time returning to the center.

5. Place the feet in the circle and walk the hands all around the outside of the circle. Place the hands inside and the feet outside. Face the floor, the ceiling, and to the side.

6. Inside the circle, make a small shape. Make a large shape so you are touching all sides of the circle.

7. Do a Tightrope Walk clockwise and counterclockwise.

8. Jump and click the heels, landing inside the circle. Repeat, going out.

9. Do jump turns inside the circle without touching the rope—quarter turns, half turns, and full turns.

10. Jump in with a Bunny Jump. Jump out. Try with a Frog Jump.

11. Take the weight on the hands inside the circle so the feet land on the other side. Try a Cartwheel.

ROPE FORMING VARIOUS FIGURES

Have the rope form different figures, such as geometric shapes, letters, and numbers. In addition to the following challenges, many of the previous ones can be applied here, too.

1. With the rope and your body, form a triangle, a square, a rectangle, a diamond shape, and a figure eight.

2. With the rope and your body, form a two-letter word. Form other words.

3. Get a second rope and make your own patterns for hopping and jumping.

4. Toss the rope in the air and let it fall to the floor. Try to shape your body into the same figure that the rope made on the floor.

PARTNER ACTIVITY

Partner activity with ropes is excellent. Partners can work with one or two ropes, and can do matching, following, or contrasting movements. Add-on is an interesting game: one partner does an activity and the other *adds on* an activity to form a sequence.

GROUP ACTIVITY

Group activity with jump ropes also has good possibilities. Each child brings her rope to the group. Patterns for hopping, jumping, and other locomotor movements can be arranged with the ropes. An achievement demonstration after a period of practice allows each group to show the patterns that they have arranged and the movements that can be done in the patterns. A further extension is to leave the patterns where they are and to rotate the groups to different locations.

LONG-ROPE JUMPING

Five or six children is an appropriate group size for practicing long-rope skills. Two members of the group turn the rope while the others practice jumping. Students need to be taught how to turn the rope properly, and time should be allotted for this. All children should have equal opportunity to turn the rope. The teacher can signal when changes should occur.

Long jump ropes must be heavy enough to carry the rhythm and should be 9 to 16 ft in length. The exact length depends on the age and skill of the children; the longer the rope, the more difficult it is to turn. One end of the rope can be fastened with a snap to an eye bolt fixed on a post or to the side of a building. This eases the task of turning and allows more children to be actively jumping.

Children should understand the terms used to describe entry into the long jump rope. *Front door* means entering from the side where the rope is turning forward and toward the jumper after it reaches its peak. *Back door* means entering from the side where the rope is turning backward and away from the jumper. To enter front door, the jumper follows the rope in and jumps when it completes the turn. To enter back door, the jumper waits until the rope reaches its peak and moves in as the rope moves downward. Learning to enter at an angle is usually easier, but any path that is comfortable is acceptable.

Chants are suggested for many of the jumping sequences. Rope-jumping chants represent a cultural heritage. In many cases, children have their own favorites. Traditionally, many chants used girls' names, because rope jumping was considered a feminine activity. Today, however, this has changed, and both sexes participate in rope-jumping activities with equal vigor and success. Several of the chants included have been modified to reflect this change.

INTRODUCTORY SKILLS

Some introductory skills and routines follow.

1. Holders hold the rope in a stationary position 6 in. above the ground. Jumpers jump over, back and forth. Raise the rope a little each time. Be sure to hold the rope loosely in the hands. This is called Building a House.

2. Ocean Wave is another stationary jumping activity. Turners make waves in the rope by moving the arms up and down. Jumpers try to time it so they jump over a low part of the wave.

3. Holders stoop down and wiggle the rope back and forth on the floor. Jumpers try to jump over the rope and not touch it as it moves. This activity is called Snake in the Grass.

4. Holders swing the rope in a pendulum fashion. Jumpers jump the rope as it passes under them. This establishes basic jumping patterns.

5. The jumper stands in the center between the turners, who carefully turn the rope in a complete arc over the jumper's head. As the rope completes the turn, the jumper jumps over it and exits immediately in the direction in which the rope is turned.

6. Children run through the turning rope (front door) without jumping, following the rope through.

7. While the rope is being turned, the jumper runs in (front door), jumps once, and runs out immediately.

8. Children can play school and go through the following sequence, trying to pass to the 6th grade. To pass kindergarten, run through the turning rope. To pass 1st grade, run in, take one jump, and run out. For 2nd through 6th grade, increase the number of jumps by one for each grade. When the jumper misses, she becomes a turner.

9. When they have difficulty with the rhythm, children can practice off to one side without actually jumping over the rope. A drumbeat can reinforce the rhythm with alternating heavy (jump) and light (rebound) beats.

10. Children have fun turning the rope under a bouncing ball, which must be lively. Turners stand ready, and a third child tosses a ball upward so it will remain in one spot while bouncing. Turners adjust the speed of the turning as the bounces become smaller and more rapid. A count can be kept of the number of successful turns before the ball ceases bouncing.

11. When children can jump a number of times consecutively, they are ready for a simple chant like the following.

Susie had a baby.
She called it Tiny Tim.
She put him in the bathtub,
To see if he could swim.
He drank up all the water.
He ate up all the soap.
He tried to eat the towel,
But it wouldn't go down his throat.
Susie called the doctor.
Susie called the nurse.
Susie called the lady,
With the alligator purse. [Exit]

INTERMEDIATE SKILLS, ROUTINES, AND CHANTS

Intermediate routines require the jumper to be able to go in front door, jump, and exit front door, and to do the same sequence back door. Enough practice in the simple jumping skills and exits should be held so that confidence is fortified; students then can turn to more intricate routines. Entries and exits should be varied in the following routines.

1. Jumpers run in, jump a specified number of times, and exit.

2. Children can add chants that dictate the number of jumps, which are followed by an exit. Here are some examples.

Tick tock, tick tock,
What's the time by the clock?
It's one, two, [up to midnight].

I like coffee, I like tea,
How many girls (boys) are wild about me?
One, two, three, [up to a certain number].

Hippity hop to the barber shop,
How many times before I stop?
One, two, three, [and so on].

Bulldog, poodle, bow wow wow,
How many doggies have we now?
One, two, three, [and so on].

Lady, lady (laddie, laddie) at the gate,
Eating cherries from a plate.
How many cherries did she (he) eat?
One, two, three, [and so on].

3. Children can label their first jump "kindergarten" and exit at any "grade." To graduate from high school, the exit would be at the 12th grade. Each grade should be sounded crisply in succession.

4. Kangaroo (or White Horse) gets its name from the jump required for back-door entry, in which the jumper resembles a kangaroo or a leaping horse. The jumper calls out "Kangaroo," takes the entry jump through the back door, and exits. Next time, he calls out "Kangaroo one!" and adds a jump. Successive jumps are called and added until a designated number is reached.

5. Children can vary the two-footed jump by using right and left hops and heel-and-toe steps. Another challenge is to turn the rope over a line parallel to it and have the jumper jump back and forth over the line. The jumper can vary foot position—feet together, feet apart, stride forward and back.

6. Jumpers can vary the pattern with turns. Make four quarter turns until facing the original direction. Reverse the direction of the turns.

7. Youngsters can add stunts as directed by selected chants.

Teddy Bear, Teddy Bear, turn around.
Teddy Bear, Teddy Bear, touch the ground.
Teddy Bear, Teddy Bear, show your shoe.
Teddy Bear, Teddy Bear, you better skidoo.

Teddy Bear, Teddy Bear, say your prayers.
Teddy Bear, Teddy Bear, go upstairs.
Teddy Bear, Teddy Bear, turn out the light.
Teddy Bear, Teddy Bear, say good night.

Mama, mama (daddy, daddy), I am sick.
Get the doctor quick, quick, quick.
Mama, mama, turn around.
Mama, mama, touch the ground.
Mama, mama, are you through?
Mama, mama, spell your name.

8. In Hot Pepper, turners turn the rope faster and faster, while the jumper tries to keep up with the increased speed. The following chants are good for Hot Pepper.

Mabel, Mabel, set the table.
Bring the plates if you are able.
Don't forget the salt and
Red hot pepper!

(On the words "Red hot pepper," the rope is turned as fast as possible until the jumper misses.)

Pease porridge hot, pease porridge cold,
Pease porridge in a pot, nine days old.
Some like it hot, hot, hot!

Ice cream, ginger ale, soda water, pop.
You get ready 'cause we're gonna turn hot!

9. In Calling In, the first player enters the rope and calls in a second player by name. Both jump three times holding hands, and then the first runs out. The second player then calls in a third player by name. Both jump three times holding hands, and the second player exits. Players should be in an informal line, since the fun comes from not knowing when one is to enter.

10. Children can enter and exit according to the call in the following chants.

In the shade and under a tree,
I'd like ____ to come in with me.
He's (she's) too fat and I'm too stout.
He stays in and I'm getting out.

Calling in and calling out,
I call ____ in and I'm getting out.

House for rent,
Inquire within.
When I move out,
Let ____ move in.

11. In High Water, the rope is turned so that it becomes gradually higher and higher off the ground.

At the beach, at the sea,
The waves come almost to the knee.
Higher, higher, [and so forth].

12. In Stopping the Rope, the jumper (a) stops and lets the rope hit her, (b) stops the rope by straddling it, (c) stops with the legs crossed and the rope between the feet, or (d) stops the rope by stamping on it. The following chants work well, with accompanying actions as indicated.

Mister, Mister, kiss my sister.
(Mother, Mother, kiss my brother.)
If you don't, you stop like this!

Junior, Junior, climb the tree.
Junior, Junior, slap your knee.
Junior, Junior, throw a kiss.
Junior, Junior, time to miss.

13. Two, three, or four children can jump at a time. After some skill has been achieved, children in combination can run in, jump a specified number of times, and run out, keeping hands joined all the time.

14. Two, three, or four children can start as a small moving circle. They run in and jump in a circle, keeping the circle moving in one direction. They run out as a circle.

15. The jumper takes in a ball or other object. Bounce the ball while jumping. Try balancing a beanbag on a body part while jumping.

16. A partner stands ready with a ball and tosses it back and forth to the jumper while he jumps.

17. For Chase the Rabbit, four or five jumpers are in single file with a leader, the Rabbit, at the head. The Rabbit jumps in any manner she wishes, and all of the others must match her movements. If anyone misses, he must go to the end of the line. If the Rabbit misses or stops the rope, she goes to the end of the line, and the next child becomes the new Rabbit. Set a limit on how long a Rabbit can stay at the head of the line.

18. In On Four Cylinders, the challenge is to do activities in a series of fours—four of one kind of jump, four of another, and so on. The number of series can be specified, and the child has a choice of what he wishes to include. (Tell the children that their "engines are running on four cylinders.")

19. In Begging, a jumper runs in and works his way up the rope toward one of the turners. As he jumps, he says, "Father, Father, give me a dollar." The turner replies, "Go see your mother." The jumper works his way toward the other turner and says, "Mother, Mother, give me a dollar." The turner replies, "Go to your father." This continues until a miss occurs or until one of the turners says in reply, "Get out" or "Get lost," at which time the jumper exits.

20. In Setting the Table, a jumper enters and starts jumping. A partner stands ready with at least four beanbags. While the following verse is recited, the partner tosses in the beanbags one at a time, and the jumper catches and places them in a row on the side (with the upward swing of the rope) and then exits.

Mable, Mable, set the table
  [toss in one bag],
Bring the plates if you are able
  [toss in another bag],
Don't forget the bread and butter
  [toss in the other two bags].

21. Partners can go in and perform a number of stunts, such as Wring the Dishrag (p. 368), Partner Hopping (pp. 381–382), or Bouncing Ball (p. 367). Examine the partner stunts for other selections.

22. Children can enter and begin with a hop (one foot), then make a jump (two feet), add a hand touch next (three feet), and then jump with both hands and feet (four feet). Selected movements on hands and feet, such as Rabbit Jumps or Push-ups, can be executed.

23. In Blind Man, single or multiple jumpers enter and begin jumping to this chant.

Peanuts, popcorn, soda pop,
How many jumps before you stop?
Close your eyes and you will see
How many jumps that this will be!

The eyes remain closed during the jumping, which continues to a target number or a miss.

24. One or both holders can go inside and jump, turning with their outside hands. First attempts should begin with a pendulum swing and proceed to a full turn.

25. Children can make up chants, beginning from scratch or filling in blank spaces in a rough format such as the following. (The material to be inserted is in parentheses.)

(Suzy, Suzy) dressed in (yellow)
Went upstairs to (kiss a fellow).
How many (kisses) did she (get)?
One, two, [and so on].

(Joe, Joe) dressed in (white)
Went upstairs to (say good night).
How many (steps) did he (take)?
One, two, [and so on].

JUMPING TWO ROPES

Turning two ropes simultaneously requires practice, and time must be allotted for this. Handling two ropes is quite fatiguing, so turners should be rotated frequently. The following routines are interesting.

1. In Double Dutch, two ropes are turned alternately. The rope near the jumper is turned front door, while the rope away from the jumper is turned back door.

2. In Double Irish, two ropes are turned the reverse of their directions in Double Dutch.

3. In Egg Beater, two large ropes are turned at right angles simultaneously by four turners (Figure 19.1). Try three or four ropes simultaneously.

4. In Fence Jumping, two ropes are held motionless about 2 ft apart, parallel to each other and about 12 in. above the ground. The players jump or hop in and out of

FIGURE 19.1. The Egg Beater

the ropes in various combinations. The children can devise many different methods.

5. The jumper uses an individual rope while jumping under the long rope. The jumper must jump fast time with the individual rope. Both ropes should be turned the same way at first. Later, the long rope can be turned in the opposite direction. Partners can jump together.

FORMATION JUMPING

For formation jumping, four to six long ropes with turners can be placed in various patterns, with tasks specified for each rope. Ropes can be turned in the same direction, or the turning directions can be mixed. Several formations are illustrated in Figure 19.2.

INDIVIDUAL ROPE JUMPING

In individual rope jumping, the emphasis should be on establishing the basic turning skills and letting the children create their own routines and progress on their own. Individual rope jumping is particularly valuable as part of the conditioning process for certain sports. It lends itself to prescribed doses based on number of turns, length of participation, speed of the turning rope, and various steps.

Since rope jumping is of a rhythmic nature, the addition of music is a natural progression. Music adds much to the activity and enables the jumper to create and organize routines to be performed to the musical pieces. The most effective approach is probably a combination of experiences with and without music.

The best ropes are made of plastic links and have turning handles. Sash cord and hardweave synthetic ropes are satisfactory also.

The length of the rope will be different for different children. It should be long enough so the ends reach to the child's armpits (Figure 19.3) or slightly higher when the child stands on its center. Preschool children generally use 6-ft ropes, and the primary-level group needs mostly 7-ft ropes, with a few 6-ft and 8-ft lengths. Grades 3–6 need a mixture of 7-ft and 8-ft ropes. A 9-ft rope serves well for most instructors.

Weight is a factor in choosing ropes, too. They must be heavy enough to maintain the momentum of turning. The center of the rope can be weighted with some cord to give it added momentum for sideways skipping.

Posture is an important consideration in rope jumping. The body should be in good alignment, with the head up and the eyes looking straight ahead. The jump is made with the body in an erect position. A slight straightening of the knees provides the lift for the jump, which should be of minimal height (about 1 in.). The wrists supply the force to turn the rope, with the elbows kept close to the body. A pumping action and lifting of the arms is unnecessary. The landing should be made on the balls of the feet, with the knees bent slightly to cushion the shock. Usually, the feet, ankles, and legs are kept together, except when a specific step calls for a different position.

Most steps can be done in any of three different rhythms—slow time, fast time, or double time. In slow-time rhythm, the performer jumps over the rope, rebounds, and then executes the second step (or repeats the original step) on the second jump. The ***rebound*** is simply a hop in place as the rope passes over the head. Better jumpers bend the knees only slightly, without actually leaving the floor on rebound. The object of the rebound is to carry the rhythm between steps. The rope is rotating slowly, passing under the feet on every other beat, and the feet also move slowly, since there is rebound between each jump.

In fast-time rhythm, the rope rotates in time with the music, one turn per beat (120 to 180 turns per minute, depending on the tune's tempo), and the performer executes a step only when the rope is passing under the feet.

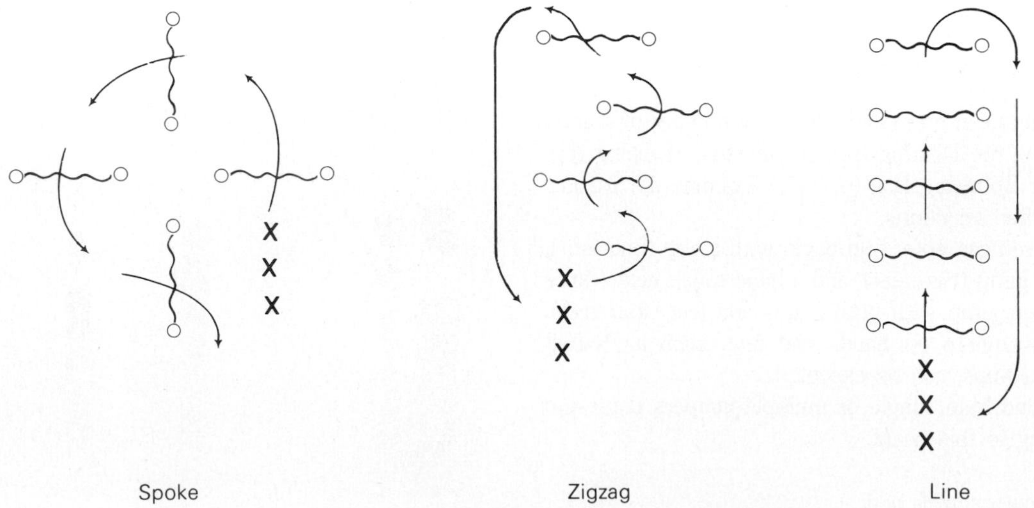

FIGURE 19.2. Formations for jumping rope

FIGURE 19.3. Correct jump-rope length

In double-time rhythm, the rope is turned at the same speed as for slow time, but rather than taking the rebound, the performer executes another step while the rope is passing over the head. Double time is the most difficult rhythm to master. When the feet are speeded up, there is a tendency to speed up the rope turning also, and this is wrong.

INSTRUCTIONAL PROCEDURES

1. Enough ropes should be available for each child to have one appropriate for her size. Ropes can be color-coded for length.

2. When the ropes do not have handles, the ends should be wrapped in tape or dipped in wax to prevent fraying.

3. Ropes should be hung or individually bundled for storage; otherwise, tangles can occur.

4. Starting positions, with the rope behind the feet for forward turning and in front of the feet for backward turning, should be explained.

5. The instruction can begin with slow-time rhythm and the basic two-footed jump.

6. Before the children start the actual jumping, there are two important instructional procedures to follow. First, students should jump without the rope to the correct rhythm. For slow time, this would be a jump and then a rebound step. The children can pretend that they are turning the rope. Second, the children take both ends of the rope in one hand and turn the rope without jumping. The rope is turned in a forward arc to one side of the body. The two steps can then be combined, so the children are simulating jumping while the rope is turned at the side. The next procedure is regular jumping.

7. Music can be added as soon as the jumpers have gotten through the first stages of jumping. Music provides a challenge for continued jumping.

8. In the primary-level group, some children cannot jump, but by the 3rd grade, all children who have had some experience should be able to jump. Children who cannot jump may be helped by the pendulum swing of the long rope, or the teacher or an older student can jump with the child inside an individual rope. Cues such as "Jump" or "Ready—jump" should be used, too.

9. To collect ropes at the completion of a rope-jumping activity, have squad leaders or two or three other children act as monitors. They put both arms out to the front or to the side at shoulder level. The other children then drape the ropes over their arms (Figure 19.4). The monitors return the ropes to the correct storage area.

COMBINATION POSSIBILITIES

Numerous combinations of steps and rope tricks are possible in rope jumping. Some ideas are the following.

1. Changes in the speed of the turn—slow time, fast time, and double time—can be made. Children should be able to shift from one speed to another, particularly when the music changes.

2. Developing expertise in various foot patterns and steps is important. Children should practice changing from one foot pattern to another.

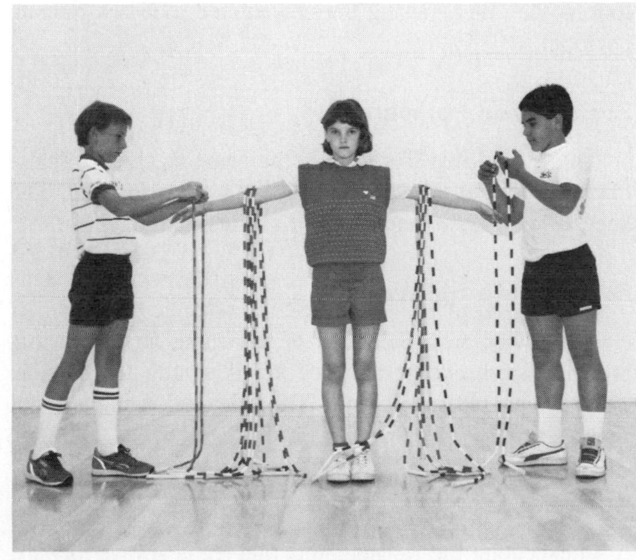

FIGURE 19.4. Collecting the ropes

3. The crossed-hands position should be tried both forward and backward.

4. Moving from a forward to a backward turn and returning should be practiced.

5. Double turns, during which the rope passes under the feet twice before the jumper lands, are possible. A few children may be able to do a triple turn.

6. Children should try to move forward, backward, and sideward, employing a variety of steps.

7. Backward jumping is quite difficult, but it can be accomplished and explored. Most steps can be done backward or modified for the backward turn.

8. Speedy turns can be practiced. Have children see how fast they can turn the rope for 15 or 30 seconds.

9. Many interesting routines can be done with partners. These are discussed later (p. 330).

BASIC STEPS

Most of the basic steps presented here can be done in all three different rhythms—slow time, fast time, and double time. After the youngsters have mastered the first six steps in slow time, the teacher may wish to introduce fast and double time. The Alternate-Foot Basic Step and Spread Legs Forward and Backward are two steps that seem to work well for introducing double-time jumping.

Two-Foot Basic Step

In the Two-Foot Basic Step, the jumper jumps over the rope with feet together as it passes under the feet, then she takes a preparatory rebound while the rope is over the head.

Alternate-Foot Basic Step

In the Alternate-Foot Basic Step, as the rope passes under the feet, the weight is shifted alternately from one foot to the other, raising the unweighted foot in a running position.

Swing-Step Forward

The Swing-Step Forward is the same as the Alternate-Foot Basic Step, except the free leg swings forward. The knee is kept loose, and the foot swings naturally.

Swing-Step Sideward

The Swing-Step Sideward is the same as the Swing-Step Forward, except the free leg is swung to the side. The knee should be kept stiff. The sideward swing is about 12 in.

Rocker Step

In executing the Rocker Step, one leg is always forward in a walking-stride position. As the rope passes under the feet, the weight is shifted from the back foot to the forward foot. The rebound is taken on the forward foot while the rope is above the head. On the next turn of the rope, the weight is shifted from the forward foot to the back foot, repeating the rebound on the back foot.

Spread Legs Forward and Backward

For Spread Legs Forward and Backward, the jumper starts in a stride position (as in the Rocker) with weight equally distributed on both feet. As the rope passes under the feet, the jumper jumps into the air and reverses the position of the feet.

Cross Legs Sideward

In Cross Legs Sideward, as the rope passes under the feet, the jumper spreads the legs in a straddle position (sideward) to take the rebound. As the rope passes under the feet on the next turn, the jumper jumps into the air and crosses the feet with the right foot forward. He then repeats with the left foot forward and continues this alternation.

Toe-Touch Forward

To do the Toe-Touch Forward, the jumper swings the right foot forward as the rope passes under the feet and touches the right toe on the next count. She then alternates, landing on the right foot and touching the left toe forward.

Toe-Touch Backward

The Toe-Touch Backward is similar to the Swing-Step Sideward, except that the toe of the free foot touches to the back at the end of the swing.

Shuffle Step

The Shuffle Step involves pushing off with the right foot and sidestepping to the left as the rope passes under the feet. The jumper lands with the weight on the left foot and touches the right toe beside the left heel. The step is repeated in the opposite direction.

Skier

The Skier is a double-foot jump similar to a technique used by skiers. A chalked or painted line is needed. The jumper stands on both feet to one side of the line. Jumping is done sideways back and forth over the line. Children should try it forward and backward.

Heel-Toe

In the Heel-Toe, as the rope passes under the feet, the jumper jumps with the weight landing on the right foot while touching the left heel forward. On the next turn of the rope, he jumps, lands on the same foot, and touches the left toe beside the right heel. This pattern is repeated with the opposite foot bearing the weight.

Heel Click

The jumper does two or three Swing-Steps Sideward, in slow time, in preparation for the Heel Click. When the right foot swings sideward, instead of a hop or rebound when the rope is above the head, the jumper raises the left foot to click the heel of the right foot. This is repeated on the left side.

Step-Tap

In the Step-Tap, as the rope passes under the feet, the jumper pushes off with the right foot and lands on the left. While the rope is turning above the head, she brushes the sole of the right foot forward and then backward. As the rope passes under the feet for the second turn, she pushes off with the left foot, lands on the right, and repeats.

Schottische Step

The Schottische Step can be done to double-time rhythm, or it can be done with a varied rhythm. The pattern is step, step, step, hop (repeat), followed by four step-hops. In varied rhythm, three quick turns in fast time are made for the first three steps and then double-time rhythm prevails. The step should be practiced first in place and then in general space. Schottische music should be introduced.

Bleking Step

The Bleking Step has the pattern slow-slow, fast-fast-fast. The rope should turn to conform to this pattern. The step begins with a hop on the left foot with the right heel forward, followed by a hop on the right with the left heel forward. This action is repeated with three quick changes—right, left, right. The whole pattern is then repeated, beginning with a hop on the right foot with the left heel extended. If done to the music for the Bleking dance (pp. 262–263), four Bleking steps of slow-slow, fast-fast-fast are done. The second part of the music (the chorus) allows the children to organize a routine of their own. They must listen for changes in the music.

CROSSING ARMS

Once the basic steps are mastered, crossing the arms while turning the rope provides an interesting variation. Crossing the arms during forward turning is easier than crossing behind the back during backward turning. During crossing, the hands exchange places. This means that, for forward crossing, the elbows are close to each other. This is not possible during backward crossing. Crossing and uncrossing can be done at predetermined points after a stipulated number of turns. Crossing can be accomplished during any of the routines.

DOUBLE TURNING

The double turn of the rope is also interesting. The jumper does a few basic steps in preparation for the double turn. As the rope approaches the feet, he gives an extremely hard flip of the rope from the wrists, jumps from 6 to 8 in. in height, and allows the rope to pass under the feet twice before landing. The jumper must bend forward at the waist somewhat, which increases the speed of the turn. A substantial challenge for advanced rope jumpers is to see how many consecutive double-turn jumps they can do.

SHIFTING FROM FORWARD TO BACKWARD JUMPING

To switch from forward to backward jumping without stopping the rope, any of the following techniques can be used.

1. As the rope starts downward in forward jumping, rather than allowing it to pass under the feet, the performer swings both arms to the left (or right) and makes a half turn of her body in that direction (i.e., facing the rope). On the next downward swing, she spreads the arms and starts turning in the opposite direction. This method also works for shifting from backward to forward jumping.

2. When the rope is directly above the head, the performer extends both arms, causing the rope to hesitate momentarily. At the same time, he makes a half turn in either direction and continues skipping with the rope turning in the opposite direction.

3. From a crossed-arm position, as the rope is going above the performer's head, she may uncross the arms and turn simultaneously. This starts the rope turning and the performer jumping in the opposite direction.

SIDEWAYS SKIPPING

In sideways skipping, the rope is turned laterally with one hand held high and the other extended downward. The rope is swung around the body sideways. To accomplish this, the jumper starts with the right hand held high overhead and the left hand extended down the center of the body. He swings the rope to the left, at the same time raising the left leg sideways. Usually the speed is slow time, with the rebound taken on each leg in turn. Later, better jumpers may progress to fast-time speed. The rope passes under the left leg, and the jumper then is straddling the rope as it moves around his body behind him. He takes the weight on the left foot, raising the right foot sideways. A rebound step on the left as the rope moves to the front brings the jumper back to the original position.

INDIVIDUAL ROPE JUMPING WITH PARTNERS

Many interesting combinations are possible when one child turns the individual rope and one or more children jump with him. For those routines in which the directions call for a child to run into a jumping pattern, it may be more effective to begin with the child already in position, before proceeding to the run-in stage.

1. The first child turns the rope and the other stands in front, ready to run in.

a. Run in and face partner, and both jump. (The child not turning can place her hands on the other's waist or shoulders.)

b. Run in and turn back to partner, and both jump.

c. Decide which steps are to be done; then run in and match steps.

d. Repeat with the rope turning backward.

e. Run in with a ball, and bounce it during the jumping.

2. Partners stand side by side, clasp inside hands, and turn the rope with outside hands.

a. Face the same direction, and turn the rope.

b. Face opposite directions, clasp left hands, and turn the rope.

c. Face opposite directions, clasp right hands, and turn the rope.

d. Repeat routines with inside knees raised.

e. Repeat routines with elbows locked. Try other arm positions.

3. The first child turns the rope while the second is in back of him, ready to run in. She runs in and grasps partner's waist or shoulders, and they jump together (engine and caboose).

4. The children stand back to back, holding a single rope in their right hand.

a. Turn in one direction—forward for one and backward for the other.

b. Reverse direction.

c. Change to left hands, and repeat.

5. Three children jump. One turns the rope forward; one runs in, in front; and one runs in behind. All three jump. Try with the rope turning backward.

6. Two jumpers, each with a rope, face each other and turn both ropes together, forward for one and backward for the other, jumping over both ropes at once. Turn the ropes alternately, jumping each rope in turn.

7. The partner turning jumps in a usual individual rope pattern. The other is positioned to the side. The turning partner hands over one end of the rope, and the other maintains the turning rhythm and then hands the rope back.

a. Try from the other side.

b. Turn the rope backward.

8. Using a single rope held in the right hand, partners face each other and turn the rope in slow time. With the rope overhead, one partner makes a turn to the left (turning in) and jumps inside the rope. He exits by turning either way. See if both can turn inside.

MOVEMENT SEQUENCES TO MUSIC

The opportunities for creative activity in movement sequences performed to music are unlimited. Good music is essential; it must have a definite beat and a bouncy quality. Pieces with a two-part format, usually labeled the verse and the chorus, are excellent. The change from the verse to the chorus signals changes in rope-jumping pattern.

Many of the records listed in Chapter 17 can be used quite successfully for rope jumping to music. Schottisches, marches, and polkas provide good background. Jazz music and rock-and-roll pieces also serve well. In addition, special records for rope jumping are available from commercial sources. Some that have proved successful include those listed below.

1. Music listed for the rhythmic program (Chapter 17) includes these records.

The Popcorn Man (p. 256)
Looby Loo (p. 254)
Bleking (pp. 262–263)
Pop Goes the Weasel (p. 265)
Schottische (pp. 277–278)
Polka (pp. 278–279)

2. Among the special rope-jumping records, Ball Bouncing and Rope Skipping (Album 12, Durlacher PR280) is especially good. Teachers will discover many other records and albums that work well as the children progress and become more familiar with the various rope-skipping activities and techniques.

3. Rock-and-roll, disco, and modern jazz records are good for intermediate children who like to structure routines to modern music. Many youngsters have favorites that they can bring from home.

DEVISING SEQUENCES TO MUSIC

Devising jumping sequences is a good opportunity for the children to create their own routines to selected records. Simple changes from slow time to fast time can introduce this activity. Later, different steps can be incorporated, crossing and uncrossing arms can be included, and then the turning direction can be varied. Partner rope-jumping stunts can also be adapted to music. Suggestions for incorporating different steps in the sequences follow.

1. "Pop Goes the Weasel" has a definite verse and chorus change. The children can switch from slow-time jumping to fast-time jumping on the chorus.

2. Bleking offers an interesting change in rope speed. The rhythm is slow-slow, fast-fast-fast (four times). The rope should be turned in keeping with the beat. Later, the bleking step can be added.

3. With the Schottische, children can do the schottische step in place twice, and for the chorus, they can do four moving step-hops in different directions.

4. To "Little Brown Jug," a four-part routine can be done to four rounds of the music.

First verse—Two-Foot Basic Step (slow time)
Chorus—Two-Foot Basic Step (fast time)
Second verse—Alternate-Foot Basic Step (slow time)
Chorus—Alternate-Foot Basic Step (fast time)
Third verse—Swing-Step Forward (slow time)
Chorus—Swing-Step Forward (fast time)
Fourth verse—Swing-Step Sideward (slow time)
Chorus—Swing-Step Sideward (fast time)

ASSESSMENT OF INDIVIDUAL ROPE JUMPING

Individual rope-jumping stunts, because of their specificity and individuality, can be adapted easily to learning packages and contract teaching. Skill assessment can be based on the accomplishment of a stated maneuver in so many turns of the rope. The assessment can be organized progressively, or it can be grouped by beginning, intermediate, and advanced tests. An example of a beginning test follows. All test items are done first in slow time and then in fast time.

1. Two-Foot Basic Step—10 turns
2. Alternate-Foot Basic Step—10 turns
3. Turning rope backward—10 turns
4. Alternate crossing arms—10 turns
5. Running forward—20 turns

Intermediate and advanced tests can be organized similarly.

CHAPTER 20

Apparatus Activities

Children have an innate desire for the physical expression that apparatus allows them. Part of the fundamental makeup of children is to want to run, jump, throw, swing, and climb. Apparatus plays a large role in the child's overall physical development.

Exercising on overhead and climbing apparatus benefits the arm and shoulder girdle. The child learns to manage his body free of ground support. The flexibility and stretching effects from apparatus activities have value in the maintenance of posture.

Equipment placed on the floor provides important extensions of educational movements. Individual response should be stressed. Further variety in apparatus activities can be achieved by the addition of hand apparatus such as beanbags, balls, wands, hoops, blocks, and other items. Individual or partner manipulative activities performed on apparatus add yet another dimension to movement possibilities.

Combinations of different pieces of apparatus often offer more challenges to children than single pieces. For example, jumping boxes used with balance beams and individual mats allow a wider variety of activity than boxes used alone.

Attention to form depends on the type of activity. Emphasis should be on giving the activity a good try and on doing the movements as well as one can. The teacher should think in terms of minimal and maximal performance standards, taking individual differences into consideration. The start-and-expand technique (see p. 360) is useful for this kind of approach.

Many apparatus activities involve a three-part sequence: (1) mounting, or getting on, the apparatus, (2) doing a skill or meeting a challenge, and (3) dismounting. Some attention should be given to the dismount. It should be a controlled movement, with a landing in bent-knee position with the weight balanced over the balls of the feet. The child should land under control and hold the position momentarily. Many challenges, such as shapes through the air, turns, and stunts following the landing, can be structured into dismounts.

Teachers must establish traffic rules stipulating when the next child starts her turn. Return routes to the starting point can be established, too. Children should be instructed in spotting techniques in addition to activity performance.

At some point in all apparatus activity sequences, generally at the end, the teacher provides an opportunity for creativity by telling the children to come up with something different from what was presented in the sequences.

RETURN ACTIVITIES

The use of return activities increases the movement potential of apparatus. *Return activity* has the child perform some kind of movement task on her way back to her place in line. This technique avoids the children's having to stand in line after they have finished their task on the apparatus. To increase the challenge of the return activity, a marker can be placed some distance in front of the apparatus. Before their apparatus routine, students must perform the return activity on the way to the marker, after the apparatus routine, on their way from the marker, and to the end of the line.

The return activity is usually a change from the instructional emphasis. The teacher's concentration is centered on the lesson activities, so the return movements should demand little supervision. Choice and exploration characterize return activities.

Return activity in combination with bench activity might

have the child performing on the bench, accomplishing the dismount, and doing a Forward Roll on the way back to place. Three children are active: one is performing, another is dismounting, and the third is rolling (Figure 20.1).

HANDLING EQUIPMENT

Children should be instructed in the proper setup and storage of apparatus and mats. Guidelines can be established with the following points in mind. Usually children should handle apparatus only with a teacher's guidance.

1. The order of assembly is first to bring out large pieces and position and assemble them. Next, smaller pieces are attached and small parts positioned. Lastly, mats are positioned for safety in dismounting, and any necessary hand apparatus is set out.

2. To remove apparatus, the procedure is reversed. All pieces should be returned to the proper storage area.

3. Materials should be carried, not dragged, across the floor. For particular pieces that need cooperation among the children, designate the number of children and the means of carrying. Safety considerations are important.

4. Traffic patterns should be established when needed. If large materials have to go through a doorway into a storage room, one piece at a time can be brought in, with the first group of children exiting before the next piece is brought in by another group of children.

5. If the entire class is not needed for removal of the apparatus, appoint a squad or a small group to handle the tasks. Meanwhile, send the other children on their way.

ACTIVITIES WITH CLIMBING ROPES

Climbing ropes offer high-level developmental possibilities for the upper trunk and arms as well as good training

FIGURE 20.1. Return activity

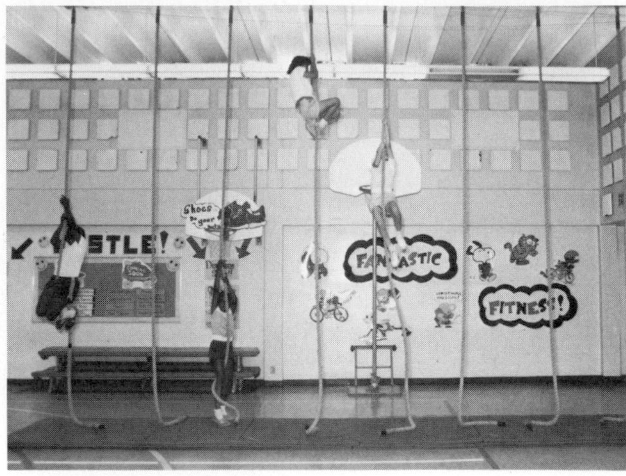

FIGURE 20.2. Rope climbing on an eight-rope set

in coordination of different body parts (Figure 20.2). Adequate grip and arm strength are prerequisites for climbing. Becoming accustomed to the rope and gaining confidence are important early goals. Many children need to overcome a natural fear of height.

INSTRUCTIONAL PROCEDURES

1. Mats should be placed under all ropes.

2. The hand-over-hand method should be used for climbing and the hand-over-hand method for descending.

3. Caution the children not to slide; sliding can cause rope burns on the hands and legs.

4. If a climber becomes tired, he should stop and rest. Proper rest stops should be taught as part of the climbing procedure.

5. Children also should be taught to leave enough margin for a safe descent. No child should go higher than her strength allows.

6. Spotters should be used initially for activities in which the body is inverted.

7. Rosin in powdered form and magnesium chalk aid in gripping. It is particularly important that they be used when the rope becomes slippery.

8. Children swinging on the ropes should be instructed to make sure that other children are out of the way.

9. Marks to limit the climb can be put on the rope with adhesive tape. A height of 8 to 10 ft above the floor is reasonable until a child demonstrates proficiency.

10. If the ceiling is higher than 15 or 16 ft, a wooden stop (circle) positioned on the rope to limit climbing beyond that height is suggested.

PRELIMINARY ACTIVITIES

Progression is important in rope climbing, and the fundamental skill progressions should be followed.

Supported Pull-Ups

In supported pull-up activities, a part of the body remains in contact with the floor. The Pull-up is hand-over-hand and the return is hand-over-hand.

1. Kneel directly under the rope. Pull up to the tiptoes and return to kneeling position.
2. Start in a sitting position under the rope. Pull up; the legs are supported on the heels. Return to sitting position.
3. Start in a standing position. Grasp the rope, rock back on the heels, and lower the body to the floor. Keep a straight body. Return to standing position.

Hangs

In a hang, the body is pulled up in one motion and held up for a length of time (5, 10, or 20 seconds). Progression is important.

1. From a seated position, reach up as high as possible and pull the body from the floor, except for the heels. Hold.
2. Same as the previous stunt, but pull the body completely free of the floor. Hold.
3. From a standing position, jump up, grasp the rope, and hang. This should be a Bent-Arm Hang with the hands about even with the mouth. Hold.
4. Repeat the previous stunt, but add leg movements—one or both knees up, bicycling movement, Half Lever (one or both legs up, parallel to the floor), Full Lever (feet up to the face).

Pull-ups

In the Pull-up, the body is raised and lowered repeatedly. The initial challenge should be to accomplish one Pull-up in the defined position. The number of repetitions should be increased with care. All of the activities described for hangs are adaptable to Pull-ups. The chin should touch the hands on each Pull-up.

Inverted Hang

For the Inverted Hang, both hands reach up high. The rope is kept to one side. The performer jumps to a bent-arm position, and at the same time, brings the knees up to the nose to invert the body, which is now in a curled position. In a continuation of the motion, the feet are brought up higher than the hands, and the legs are locked around the rope. The body should now be straight and upside down. In the learning phase, teachers should spot.

Swinging and Jumping

For swinging and jumping, a bench, box, or stool can serve as a takeoff point. To take off, the child reaches high and jumps to a bent-arm position. Landing should be with bent knees.

1. Swing and jump. Add half turns and full turns.
2. Swing and return to the perch. Add single- and double-knee bends.
3. Jump for distance, over a high-jump bar, or through a hoop.
4. Swing and pick up an Indian club, and return to the perch.
5. Carry objects (e.g., beanbags, balls, deck tennis rings). A partner, standing to the side away from the takeoff bench, can put articles to be carried back on the takeoff perch by placing each article between her knees or feet.
6. Not using a takeoff device, run toward a swinging rope, grasp it, and gain momentum for swinging.

CLIMBING THE ROPE

Scissors Grip

For the Scissors Grip, approach the rope and reach as high as possible, standing with the right leg forward of the left. Raise the back leg, bend at the knee, and place the rope *inside* of the knee and *outside* of the foot. Cross the forward leg over the back leg, and straighten the legs with the toes pointed down (Figure 20.3). This should give a secure hold. The teacher can check the position.

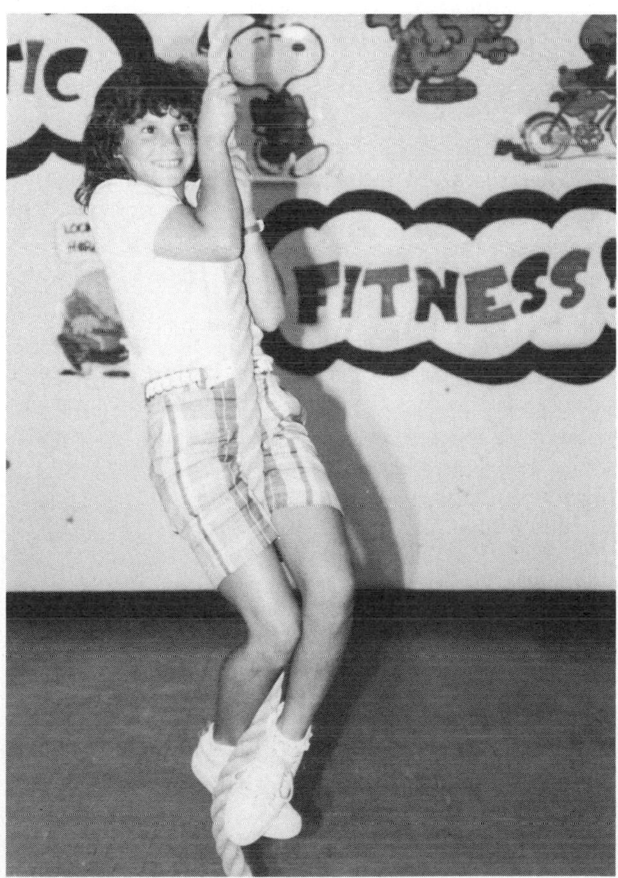

FIGURE 20.3. The Scissors Grip

To climb using the Scissors Grip, raise the knees up close to the chest, the rope sliding between them, while supporting the body with the hand grip. Lock the rope between the legs and climb up, using the hand-over-hand method and stretching as high as the hands can reach. Bring the knees up to the chest, and repeat the process until you have climbed halfway. Later, strive for a higher climb.

Leg-Around Rest

To do the Leg-Around Rest, wrap the left leg completely around the rope, keeping the rope between the thighs. The bottom of the rope then crosses over the instep of the left foot *from the outside.* The right foot stands on the rope as it crosses over the instep, providing pressure to prevent slippage. To provide additional pressure, release the hands and wrap the arms around the rope, leaning away from the rope at the same time.

To climb using the Leg-Around Rest, proceed as in climbing with the Scissors Grip, but loosen the grip each time and re-form higher up on the rope.

DESCENDING THE ROPE

There are four methods to descend the rope. The only differences are in the use of the leg locks, since the hand-over-hand is used for all descents.

Scissors Grip

From an extended scissors grip position, lock the legs and lower the body with the hands until the knees are against the chest. Hold with the hands, and lower the legs to a new position.

Leg-Around Rest

From the leg-around rest position, lower the body until the knees are against the chest. Lift the top foot, and let the feet slide to a lower position (Figure 20.4). Secure with the top foot and repeat.

Instep Squeeze

Squeeze the rope between the insteps by keeping the heels together. Lower the body while the rope slides against the instep.

Stirrup Descent

Have the rope on the outside of the right foot and carry it over the instep of the left. Pressure from the left foot holds the position. To get into position, let the rope trail along the right leg, reach under, and hook it with the left instep. When the pressure from the left leg is reduced, the rope slides smoothly while the descent is made with the hands.

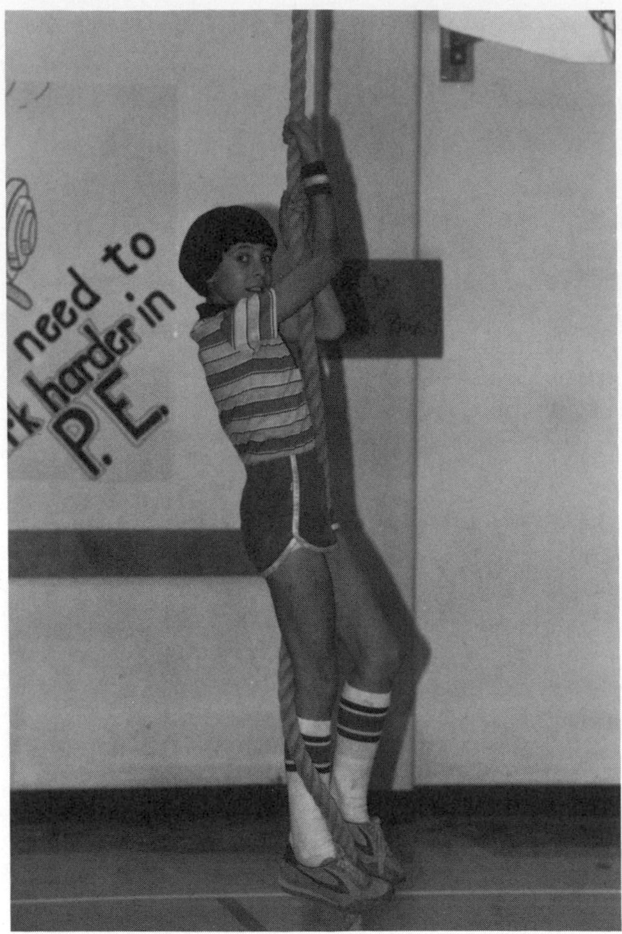

FIGURE 20.4. The Leg-Around Rest

OTHER CLIMBING ACTIVITIES

Climbing for Time

To climb for time, a stopwatch and a definite mark on the rope are needed. The height of the mark depends on the children's skill and capacity. Each child should have three trials (not in succession, however), with the best time recorded. Children should start from a standing position with hands reaching as high as desired. The descent should not be included in the timing, because too much emphasis on speed in descent may incite the children to drop or may promote rope burns.

Climbing Without Using the Feet

The strenuous activity of climbing without using the feet should be attempted only by the more skilled. During early sessions, the mark should not be set too high. Climbers start from a sitting position. The activity can be timed.

Organizing a Tarzan Club

The teacher can put a marker at the top limit of the rope. Each child who climbs to and touches the marker becomes a member of the Tarzan Club. A Super-Tarzan Club can be formed for those who can climb to the marker without using their feet. The climber must start from a sitting position on the floor.

STUNTS USING TWO ROPES

Two ropes hanging close together are needed for the following activities.

Straight-Arm Hang

To do the Straight-Arm Hang, jump up, grasp one rope with each hand, and hang with the arms straight.

Bent-Arm Hang

Perform as for the Straight-Arm Hang, but bend the arms at the elbows.

Arm Hangs With Different Leg Positions

1. Do single- and double-knee lifts.
2. Do a Half Lever: Bring the legs up parallel to floor and point the toes.
3. Do a Full Lever: Bring the feet up to the face and keep the knees straight.
4. Do a Bicycle: Pedal as on a bicycle.

Pull-ups

The Pull-up is the same as on a single rope, except that each hand grasps a rope.

Inverted Hangs

1. Hang with the feet wrapped around the ropes.
2. Hang with the feet against the inside of the ropes.
3. Hang with the toes pointed and the feet not touching the ropes (Figure 20.5).

Skin the Cat

From a bent-arm position, kick the feet overhead and continue the roll until the feet touch the mat. Return to the starting position. A more difficult stunt is to start from a higher position, so the feet do not touch the mat. Reverse to original position.

Climbing

1. Climb up one rope, transfer to another, and descend.
2. Climb halfway up one rope, cross over to another rope, and continue to climb to the top.

FIGURE 20.5. Spotting an inverted hang on two ropes (holding the performer's hands ensures confidence and safety)

3. Climb both ropes together without using the legs. This is difficult and requires the climber to slide one hand at a time up the ropes without completely releasing the grip.
4. Climb as on a single rope, with hands on one rope and feet on the other rope.

ACTIVITY SEQUENCES

Rope-climbing activities are conducive to forming sequences through which the child can progress. The following sequence represents the kind of progressive challenges that can be met.

1. Jump and hang (10 seconds).
2. Pull up and hold (10 seconds).
3. Scissors climb to blue mark (10 ft).
4. Scissors climb to top (15 ft).
5. Demonstrate Leg-Around Rest (10 ft).
6. Do an Inverted Hang, with body straight (5 seconds).

The teacher can structure three achievement levels from the activities included in this chapter. Perhaps each level could be given a characteristic name and organized as a task card or a contract project.

ACTIVITIES WITH HORIZONTAL LADDERS AND CLIMBING FRAMES

Horizontal ladders and climbing frames (Figure 20.6) are manufactured in a variety of models. The most usable ladder is one that can be stored against the wall out of the way. If the ladder can be inclined, the movement possibilities are extended.

The climbing frame pictured offers youngsters an exciting climbing environment.[1] It is stored against the wall and can be moved into position by students. The frame can be purchased in two or three sections and offers great flexibility for climbing activities. Climbing ropes, horizontal ladders, balance beams, and rope-climbing ladders can be attached to the frame. The climbing frames can be combined with climbing ropes for instructional purposes, with half of the class on each type of apparatus.

Horizontal ladders and climbing frames provide a good lead-up activity for rope climbing, because their rigidity makes them easier to climb. Grip strength and arm-shoulder girdle development are enhanced by the suspension of body weight. This development can help improve posture.

INSTRUCTIONAL PROCEDURES

1. The opposed-thumb grip, in which the thumb goes around the bar, is important. In most activities, the back of the hands should face the child. (This is the upper grip.) The grip should be varied occasionally, making use of the lower grip (palms toward the face) and the mixed grip (one hand facing one way and one the other).

2. Whenever the child is doing an Inverted Hang, spotters should be present.

3. Speed is not the goal of climbing activity. In fact, the longer the child hangs from the ladder, the more beneficial the activity is. There is value in simply hanging.

4. In activities involving movement across the ladder, all children should travel in the same direction.

5. Mats must be placed under the climbing apparatus when it is in use.

6. Children should be instructed in the dismount. They should land in a bent-leg position, on the balls of the feet.

7. Children should not be forced to climb the wall-attached climbing frames. Many children have a natural fear of height and need much reassurance before they will climb. If necessary, climb the frame with the child until confidence grows.

1. This frame is manufactured in Canada by Laurentian Gymnastic Industries and can be purchased in the United States from Robert Widen Company, P.O. Drawer 2075, Prescott, AZ 86301.

FIGURE 20.6. Climbing frame

ACTIVITIES WITH HORIZONTAL LADDERS

Hangs

Hangs should be performed with the opposed-thumb grip and usually with straight arms. Encourage children to hang in a bent-arm position, however, to involve more muscles in the upper arm. The following variations of the hang are suggested.

1. Keep the legs straight and point the toes toward the ground.

2. Lift the knees as high as possible toward the chest.

3. Lift the knees and pedal the bicycle.

4. Bring the legs up parallel to the ground, with the knees straight and the toes pointed.

5. Touch one or both toes to a rung or to the side of the ladder.

6. Bring the feet up and over one rung and hook the toes under a second rung. Release the hand grip, and hang in an inverted position.

7. Stand on a box if necessary to get in position for a Flexed-Arm Hang. Hang as long as possible with the chin even with the hands.

8. Swing the body back and forth.

9. Swing back and forth and jump as far as possible. Vary with turns.

10. Hang from the ladder, first with one hand and then with the other.

Traveling Activities

Throughout the suggested traveling activities, have the children use different body shapes.

1. Travel the length of the ladder, using the rungs. Start by traveling one rung at a time, and then skip one or more rungs to add challenge.

2. Travel the length of the ladder, using both side rails. Now use one rail only to travel the ladder.

3. Hang with both hands on the side rails. Progress the length of the ladder by jumping both hands forward at once.

4. Hang with both hands on the same rung. Progress by jumping both hands forward simultaneously.

5. Travel underneath the ladder in monkey fashion, with both hands and feet on the rungs. Try with the feet on the side rails.

6. Travel the length of the ladder carrying a beanbag, a ball, or any similar object.

7. Travel the length of the ladder sideways and backward.

8. Travel the length of the ladder, doing a half turn each time a move is made to a new rung.

9. Get a partner. Each child starts at one end of the ladder, and they pass each other along the way.

ACTIVITIES WITH WALL-ATTACHED OR FLOOR-SUPPORTED CLIMBING FRAMES

Wall-attached climbing frames are excellent pieces of equipment because of the movement possibilities they offer and the ease of getting them into action. Floor-supported apparatus are available in considerable variety and combinations, but more time and effort are involved in their assembly and disassembly.

The use of different parts of the body for supporting, moving, and leading should be explored. Different shapes can be part of the experiences. As the body moves upward, across, and downward, different parts of the body can lead. The body can hang free or be supported in different fashions. A key is to provide different challenges and to encourage imaginative and clever responses.

Getting on the Frame

If other apparatus (such as a bench) is attached to the frame, the entry onto the bench can be defined. Without a bench, the entry could be a climb or a jump to hanging position or could be by means of an attached climbing rope. Certain body parts can be specified to leave the floor last.

"Can you get on so your hands are the last to leave the floor?"

"See whether you can get on so your seat is the last to touch the floor."

"Explore getting on with your body lying on the floor sideways (or prone or supine)."

Partner activity also can be employed (e.g., "Work out different ways your partner can help you get on the frame.").

Performing on the Frame

The activities on the frame vary according to the type of frame used. In general, what the child is to do while climbing upward can be defined. Challenges can be set for moving at one level on the frame. The teacher can also specify positions to be assumed, hangs to be held, and balances to be made. Other static activities can be specified. If multiple frames with bars, ladders, or poles between them are present, the movement from one section to another can be defined. Listing all of the possible challenges here is not feasible. The possible challenges are limited only by the versatility of the teacher. A few examples should suffice.

"Try moving up the ladder so your hands move first in any change of position and are followed by your feet. Descend so your feet move first. Next time, reverse the procedure."

"Go halfway up the frame on one side, then go in and out the openings as you move at the same level across the frame. Continue upward, and move back across the frame as you wish. Move downward to the halfway mark, repeating the in-and-out movements but leading with a different body part. Descend as you wish."

"Climb until you can cross to the next section. Do so by using the hands only. Descend."

"Climb upward, and as you go up, hang for a few seconds with your feet free before you go to the next rung. Descend by using your hands only."

Follow-the-leader activities are excellent, as are magic number activities. If the magic number is five, for example, the child does five different kinds of movement in total, or five on the upward path and five on the descent.

Dismounting From the Frame

Dismounting can be varied to include jumping down, dropping from a hanging position, touching the ground first with a specified part of the body, or adding stunts after the dismount.

"Can you dismount so your hands touch first?"

"See whether you can dismount with a jump that includes a half turn."

"When you drop to the mat, finish with a forward or backward roll."

"In your jump dismount, show us different shapes."

ACTIVITIES WITH CARGO NETS

Cargo nets provide experiences similar to those with climbing frames, but the stability of the fixed apparatus is missing. The same general approaches can be applied to cargo nets as to climbing frames. The teacher should point out that the movements of one child affect those of the others.

Nets can be dropped like window shades from the ceiling, or they can be suspended from four corners to provide different kinds of experiences. Those dropped from the ceiling can be anchored also to the floor to give some stability. Cargo nets are available with some wall-attached frames. The storage of nets presents problems, for they are heavy and cumbersome.

ACTIVITIES ON THE EXERCISE BAR (LOW HORIZONTAL BAR)

Horizontal bars should be installed on the playground in a series of at least three at different heights. Indoor bars can be freestanding and have adjustable heights. Care must be taken that they are properly secured.

The primary program should be limited to hangs, travels, and simple stunts. To perform many of the more complicated stunts on the bar, sufficient arm strength is necessary to pull the body up and over the bar. Some of the youngsters in the 3rd grade will begin to have this capacity, but the emphasis in the primary grades should be on the more limited program.

In the intermediate program, attention should turn to gymnastic stunts. The advanced skills are, however, difficult, and the teacher should not be discouraged by the children's apparent lack of progress.

INSTRUCTIONAL PROCEDURES

1. Only one child should be on a bar at one time.
2. The bar should not be used when it is wet.
3. The basic grip is the opposed-thumb grip, facing away.

ACTIVITY SEQUENCES

Hangs

To hang from the bar, point the feet, one or both knees up, in a Half or Full Lever (p. 335). Bring the toes up to touch the bar inside the hands. Outside the hands. Use different body shapes.

Swings

Swing back and forth, release the grip, and propel the body forward. Land in a standing position.

Moving Along the Bar

Begin at one side and move hand against hand to the other end of the bar. Move with crossed hands. Travel with different body shapes.

Sloth Travel

Face the end of the bar, standing underneath. Grasp the bar with both hands, and hook the legs over the bar at the knees like a sloth. In this position, move along the bar to the other end. Return by reversing the movement.

Arm and Leg Hang

Grasp the bar with an upper grip. Bring one of the legs up between the arms, and hook the knee over the bar.

Double-Leg Hang

Perform as in the previous stunt, but bring both legs between the hands and hook the knees over the bar. Release the hands, and hang in the inverted position. If the hands touch or are near the ground, a dismount can be made by releasing the legs and dropping to a crouched position on the ground.

Skin the Cat

Bring both knees up between the arms as in the previous stunt, but continue the direction of the knees until the body is turned over backward. Release the grip and drop to the ground.

Skin the Cat Return

Perform as in the preceding stunt, but do not release the hands. Bring the legs back through the hands to original position.

Front Support

Grasp the bar with an upper grip, and jump to a straight-arm support on the bar. Jump down.

Front Support Push-off

Mount the bar in the same way as for a Front Support. In returning to the ground, push off straight with the arms and jump as far back as possible.

Tummy Balance

Jump to the bar as in the preceding stunt. Position the body so you can balance on the tummy with hands released.

Sitting Balance

Jump to the bar as for a Front Support. Work the legs across the bar, so a sitting balance can be maintained. If you lose your balance backward, grasp the bar quickly and bend the knees.

Tumble Over

Jump to a front-support position. Change the grip to a lower grip. Bend forward and roll over to a standing position under the bar.

Single-Knee Swing

Using the upper grip, swing one leg forward to hang by the knee. Using the free leg to gain momentum, swing back and forth.

Side Arc

Sit on the bar with one leg on each side, both hands gripping the bar in front of the body. Lock the legs, and fall sideways. Try to make a complete circle back to position. Good momentum is needed.

Single-Leg Rise

Using the position of the Single-Knee Swing, on the backswing and upswing, rise to the top of the bar. The down leg must be kept straight. Swing forward (down) first, and on the backswing, push down hard with straight arms. A spotter can assist by pushing down on the straight leg with one hand and lifting on the back with the other.

Knee Circles

Sit on top of the bar, with one leg over and one under the bar. Lock the feet. With the hands in an upper grip, shift the weight backward so the body describes a circle under the bar and returns to place. Try this with a forward circle, with hands in a lower grip. Note that considerable initial momentum must be developed for the circle to be completed.

ACTIVITIES ON THE BALANCE BEAM

Balance beam activities contribute to control in both static and dynamic balance situations (Figure 20.7). The balance beam side of a balance beam bench is ideal for such activities, with its 2-in.-wide and 12-ft-long beam. Balance beams come in many other sizes, however, and can be constructed from common lumber materials (see Chapter 34). Some teachers prefer a wider beam for kindergarten and 1st-grade children, and in particular, for special education children. The students should graduate to the narrower beam as soon as the activities on the wider beam no longer seem to challenge them.

FIGURE 20.7. Walking on a balance beam bench

Some other ideas for balance equipment are also interesting. A pole with ends shaped to fit the supports can be substituted for the flat balance beam. The pole is more challenging. Another idea is constructing a beam that begins with a 2-in. width and narrows to a 1-in. width at the other end. Beams of varying widths (from 1 to 4 in.) can be used also. The children progress from the wider to the narrower beams. A variety of widths is preferable for handicapped children.

INSTRUCTIONAL PROCEDURES

1. Children should move with controlled, deliberate movements. Speed is not a goal. The teacher should advise performers to recover their balance before taking another step or making another movement.

2. In keeping with the principle of control, children should step slowly on the beam, pause momentarily in good balance at the end of the activity, and dismount with a small, controlled jump from the end of the beam when the routine is completed.

3. Mats can be placed at the end of the bench to cushion the dismount and to allow for rolls and stunts after the dismount.

4. Visual fixation is important. Children should look straight ahead rather than down at the feet. Eye targets can be marked on or attached to walls to assist in visual fixation. This fixation allows balance controls other than vision to function more effectively. From time to time, movements can be done with the eyes closed, entirely eliminating visual control of balance.

5. Children should be told to step off the beam when they lose their balance, rather than teetering and falling off awkwardly. Allow the performer to step back on the beam and to continue the routine.

6. Success in a balance beam activity can be based on two levels. The lower level allows the performer to step off the beam once during the routine. The higher level demands that the student remain on the beam throughout. For both levels, the children should pause *in good balance* at the end of the beam before dismounting.

7. Both laterality and directionality are important. Right and left feet should be given reasonably equal treatment. For example, if a performer does steps leading with the right foot, the next effort should be made leading with the left foot. Directions right and left should be given equal weight. A child naturally uses the dominant side and direction, but must be encouraged to perform with both sides.

8. The child next in line should begin when the performer ahead is about three quarters of the distance across the beam.

9. Return activities (see pp. 333–334) are a consideration for enhancing the breadth of activity.

10. A child or the teacher can assist the performer. The assistant holds his hand palm up, ready to help the performer if and when help is needed.

ACTIVITY SEQUENCES

Activities for the balance beam are presented as a progression of movement themes. The teacher can develop fully all of the activities and possibilities within a theme before proceeding to the next theme, or she can take a few activities from each theme and cover more territory.

Activities on Parallel Beams

Activities on two parallel beams are presented first as lead-up practice for the single-beam tasks. The beams should be placed about 10 to 30 in. apart. The parallel-beam activities can be done alone or with a partner when more security is desired.

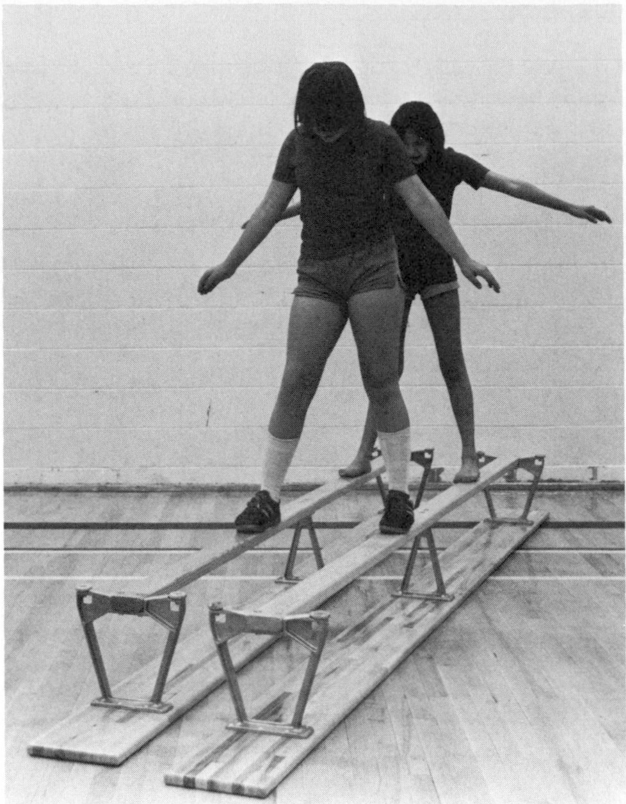

FIGURE 20.8. Walking on parallel beams

1. With a partner, join inside hands and walk forward, backward, and sideward. Walk sideward, using a grapevine step. Hold a beanbag in the free hand.

2. Without a partner, perform various animal walks, such as the Crab Walk, Bear Walk, Measuring Worm, and Elephant Walk.

3. With one foot on each beam, walk forward, backward, and sideward (Figure 20.8).

4. Step to the opposite beam with each step taken.

5. Progress the length of the beams with hands on one beam and feet on the other.

6. Progress to the middle of the beams and perform various turns and stunts, such as picking up a beanbag, moving through a hoop, and stepping over a wand.

Movements Across the Full Length of a Single Beam

1. Perform various locomotor tasks, such as walking, follow steps, heel-and-toe steps, side steps, tiptoe steps, the grapevine step (step behind, step across), and so on.

2. Follow different directions—forward, backward, sideward.

3. Use different arm and hand positions—on the hips, on the head, behind the back, out to the sides, pointing to the ceiling, folded across the chest.

4. Move across the beam—assuming different shapes.

5. Balance an object (beanbag or eraser) on various body parts—on the head, on the back of the hands, on the shoulders. Try balancing two or three objects at once.

Half-and-Half Movements

Half-and-Half Movements repeat the movements, arm positions, and balancing stunts described previously, except that the performer goes halfway across the beam using a selected movement and then changes to another type of movement on the second half of the beam.

Challenge Tasks or Stunts

For challenge tasks, the performer moves halfway across the beam with a selected movement, performs a particular challenge or stunt at the center, and finishes his movements on the second half of the beam. Examples of challenges or stunts that can be performed at the center of the beam are these.

1. Balances—Forward Balance (p. 371), Backward Balance (p. 372), Stork Stand (p. 366), Seat Balance (p. 386).

2. Stunts—Knee Dip (p. 379), Back Finger Touch (p. 387).

3. Challenges—Make a full turn, pick up a beanbag at the center, pick up some paper at the center with the teeth, do a Push-up.

More Difficult Movements Across the Beam

1. Hop the length of the beam—forward, sideward, and backward.

2. Do the Cat Walk (p. 364), Rabbit Jump (pp. 268–269), Lame Dog Walk (p. 269), Seal Crawl (pp. 375–376), or Crab Walk (pp. 269–270).

3. Do various locomotor movements with the eyes closed.

4. Walk to the center of the beam and do a Side-Leaning Rest. Try on the other side as well.

5. Walk to the center and do a complete body turn on one foot only.

Activities With Wands and Hoops

1. Carry a wand or hoop. Step over the wand or through the hoop in various fashions.

2. Step over or go under wands or hoops held by partner.

3. Twirl a hula hoop on the arms or around the body while moving across the beam.

4. Balance a wand on various body parts while moving across the beam.

5. Balance a wand in one hand and twirl a hoop on the other hand and proceed across the beam.

Manipulative Activities With Self

1. Using one or two beanbags, toss to self in various fashions—over the head, around the body, under the legs.

2. Using a ball, toss to self. Circle the ball around the body, under the legs.

3. Bounce a ball on the floor. On the beam. Dribble on the floor.

4. Roll a ball along the beam.

Manipulative Activities With a Partner

With a partner standing beyond the far end of the beam, toss and throw a beanbag or ball back and forth. Have partner toss for a volleyball return. Bat the ball (as in a volleyball serve) to partner.

Stunts With a Partner

1. Do a regular and a reverse Wheelbarrow (p. 389) with the supporting performer keeping the feet on the floor.

2. Partners start on opposite ends of the beam and move toward each other with the same kind of movement, do a balance pose together in the center, and return to their respective end of the beam.

3. Partners start on opposite ends of the beam and attempt to pass each other without losing their balance and without touching the floor. Find different ways to pass.

ACTIVITIES ON BENCHES

The balance beam bench is effective in developing strength and balance. Bench activities are challenging to children and offer a variety of movement possibilities.

INSTRUCTIONAL PROCEDURES

1. All activities on the benches should be broken down into three distinct parts—the approach to and mounting of the bench, the actual activity on the bench, and the dismount from the bench.

2. Mats should be placed at the ends of the benches to facilitate the dismount and various rolls and stunts executed after the dismount.

3. Benches can be positioned horizontally or inclined. They can also be combined with other equipment for variation and greater challenge.

4. Four to five children is the maximum number that should be assigned to one bench.

5. The child next in turn should begin when the performer ahead is about three quarters of the way across the bench.

6. Return activities (pp. 333–334) add to the activity potential.

7. Speed is not a goal in bench activities. Movements should be done deliberately and carefully, with attention given to body control and body management.

8. Attention also should be paid to laterality and directionality. For example, if a child hops on the right foot, the next effort should be made on the left foot. In jump turns, both right and left movements should be used.

ACTIVITY SEQUENCES

Animal Walks

Perform various animal walks on the bench, such as the Seal Crawl (pp. 375–376), Cat Walk (p. 264), Lame Dog Walk (p. 269), and Rabbit Jump (pp. 268–269).

Locomotor Movements

Perform various locomotor movements along the length of the bench, such as stepping on and off the side of the bench, jumping on and off the side of the bench, hopping on and off the side of the bench, skipping on the bench, and galloping on the bench.

Pulls

Pull the body along the bench, using different combinations of body parts. Use the arms only, the legs only, the right leg and the left arm, or the left leg and the right arm. Pull along the bench, using the following positions.

1. Prone position (headfirst and feetfirst) (Figure 20.9)
2. Supine position (headfirst and feetfirst) (Figure 20.10)
3. Side position (headfirst and feetfirst)

Various leg positions (such as legs up in a half-lever position, knees bent, and so on) should be used in performing pulls and pushes. Those body parts not being used to pull can be used to carry a piece of manipulative equipment, such as a beanbag, ball, or wand. Employ different body shapes. Try the Submarine (one foot in the air like a periscope).

Pushes

Push the body along the bench, using different parts of the body as discussed for pulls. Push the body, using the following positions.

1. Prone position (headfirst and feetfirst)
2. Supine position (headfirst and feetfirst)
3. Side position (headfirst and feetfirst)

Movements Along the Side of the Bench

Proceed alongside the bench in the following positions with the hands on the bench and the feet on the floor as far from the bench as possible.

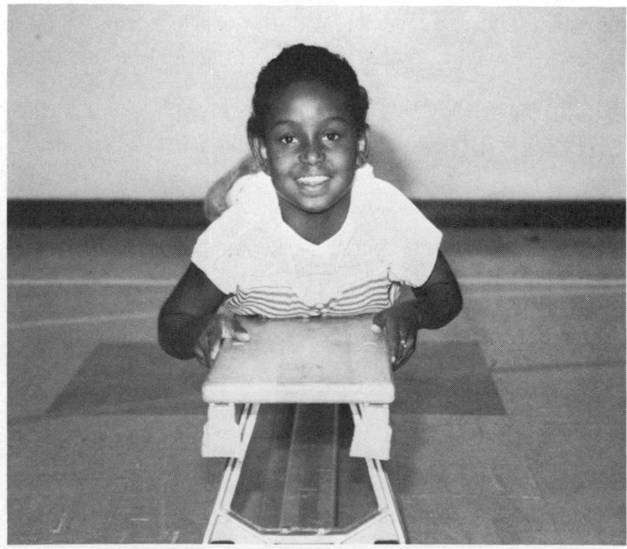

FIGURE 20.9. Prone movements, headfirst

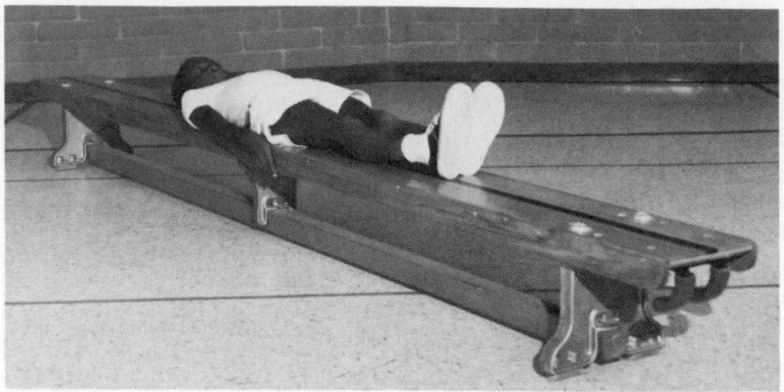

FIGURE 20.10. Supine movements, feetfirst

1. Prone position
2. Supine position
3. Turn-over (proceed along the bench, changing from prone to supine positions)

Repeat these positions with the feet on the bench and the hands on the floor as far from the bench as possible.

Scooter Movements

Sit on the bench and proceed along it without using the hands in the following ways.

1. Do a Scooter. Proceed with the feet leading the body. Try to pull the body along with the feet.
2. Do a Reverse Scooter. Proceed as for the Scooter but with the legs trailing and pushing the body along the bench.
3. Do a Seat Walk. Proceed forward by walking on the buttocks. Use the legs as little as possible.

Crouch Jumps

Place both hands on the bench and jump back and forth over it. Progress the length of the bench by moving the hands forward a few inches after each jump.

1. Do a regular Crouch Jump (Figure 20.11). Use both hands and both feet. Jump as high as possible.
2. Do a Straddle Jump. Straddle the bench with the legs, take the weight on the hands, and jump with the legs as high as possible.
3. Use one hand and two feet. Do a Crouch Jump, but eliminate the use of one hand.
4. Use one hand and one foot. Perform the Crouch Jump, using only one hand and one foot.
5. Stand to one side, facing the bench, with both hands on it. With stiff arms, try to send the seat as high as possible into the air. Add the Mule Kick (p. 376) before coming down.

FIGURE 20.11. Crouch jumping

Basic Tumbling Stunts

Basic tumbling stunts can be incorporated in bench activities—the Back Roller (p. 365), Backward Curl (p. 370), Forward Roll (p. 370) (Figure 20.12), Backward Roll (p. 377), and Cartwheel (p. 379).

Dismounts

All bench activities in which the child moves from one end of the bench to the other should end with a dismount. The following dismounts are suggested. Many other stunts can be used.

1. Single jump (forward or backward) (Figure 20.13).
2. Jump with turns (half turn, three-quarter turn, or full turn).
3. Jackknife—Jump, kick the legs up, and touch the toes with the fingertips. Keep the feet together.
4. Jackknife Split—Same as the Jackknife, but spread the legs as far as possible.

FIGURE 20.12. Doing a Forward Roll on the bench

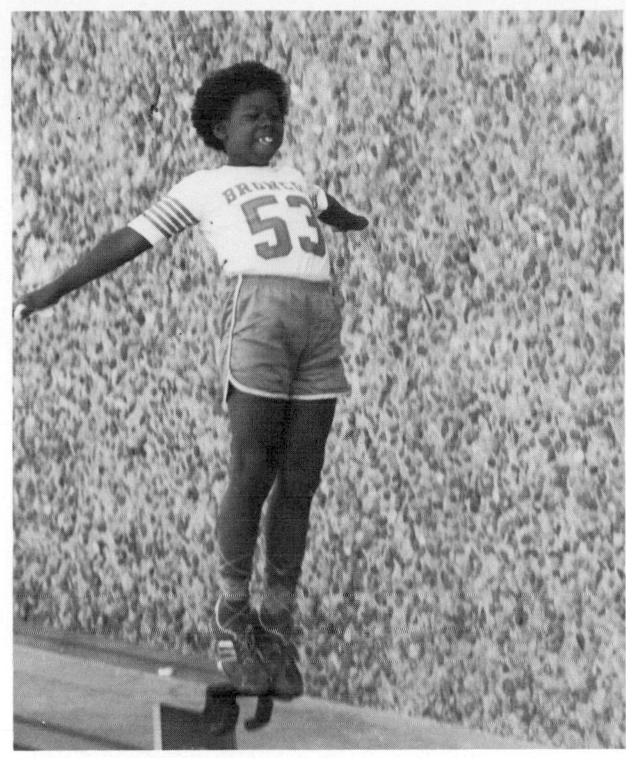

FIGURE 20.13. Dismounting from a bench

5. Jump to a Forward Roll.
6. Backward jump to a Backward Roll.
7. Side jump to a Side Roll (p. 364).
8. Judo Roll.
9. Jump with combinations of the above stunts.

ADDITIONAL EXPERIENCES ON BENCHES

1. The range of activities can be extended with the addition of balls, beanbags, hoops, and wands. Wands and hoops can be used as obstacles to go over, under, around, or through. Basic balance and manipulative skills can be incorporated in the activity with balls and beanbags.

2. Two can perform at one time, each child near one end of the bench, doing different balance positions on the bench.

3. Children love to go over and under a row of benches arranged in a kind of obstacle course. Some of the benches can be supported by jumping boxes, making them excellent for vaulting activities.

4. A bench can be supported by two jumping boxes and used as a vaulting box. Each bench is long enough to accommodate three children. They can jump off it, Mule Kick on it, and vault over it.

5. Four benches can be placed in a large rectangle (Figure 20.14), with a squad standing at attention on top of each bench. On signal, each squad gets off its bench, runs

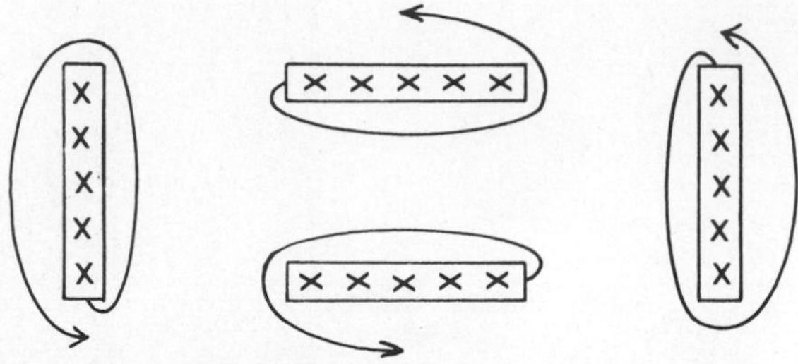

FIGURE 20.14. Rectangular bench activities

around the outside of the other three benches, and then runs back to its own bench. The first squad back and at attention on the bench is the winner.

6. Benches can be placed in a square formation, with children moving around the square and doing a different movement on each bench.

7. One end of the bench can be placed on a jumping box or on another bench. Children receive jumping practice by running up the incline and striving for jump height at the end of the bench.

8. Benches are appropriate for some partner activities. Partners can start on each end and pass through or around each other, reversing original positions. Wheelbarrow Walks are also suitable.

9. Another enjoyable activity is arranging the benches in a course as illustrated in Figure 20.15. A student is chosen to lead the squad or class through the Challenge Course. A different activity must be performed at each bench.

ACTIVITIES WITH JUMPING BOXES

Jumping boxes can be constructed or purchased. They provide opportunities for children to jump from a height and propel the body through space. Activities with jumping boxes are generally confined to the primary grades.

Boxes can be of varying heights. For kindergarten and 1st grade, heights of 8 in. and 16 in. are suggested. For the 2nd and 3rd grade, heights of 12 in. and 24 in. are more challenging. Boxes can be built with 18-by-18-in. sides for the two taller heights and 16-by-16-in. sides for the two lower heights. This enables the smaller boxes to be stored inside the larger ones. The box top should be padded and covered with durable leather or plastic. A rubber floor pad can be placed under the box to protect the floor and to prevent sliding. Plans for constructing boxes are in Chapter 34.

Many of the suggested activities can be done from a step platform. Heavy wooden chairs (never folding chairs) with backs removed can be used as higher platforms.

INSTRUCTIONAL PROCEDURES

1. Attention should be given to landing in proper form. Lightness, bent-knee action, balance, and body control should be stressed.

2. Mats should be used to cushion the landing.

3. The exploratory and creative approach is important; there are few standard stunts in jumping box activities.

4. No more than four or five children should be assigned to each series of boxes.

5. Additional challenges can be incorporated by the use of hoops, wands, balls, and the like. Rolling stunts after the dismount extend the movement possibilities.

6. Return activities work well with boxes.

7. Children should strive for height and learn to relax as they go through space.

ACTIVITY SEQUENCES

The activities that follow can be augmented easily. Let the children help expand the activity.

Various Approaches to the Boxes

The approach to the boxes can be varied by performing movements such as these.

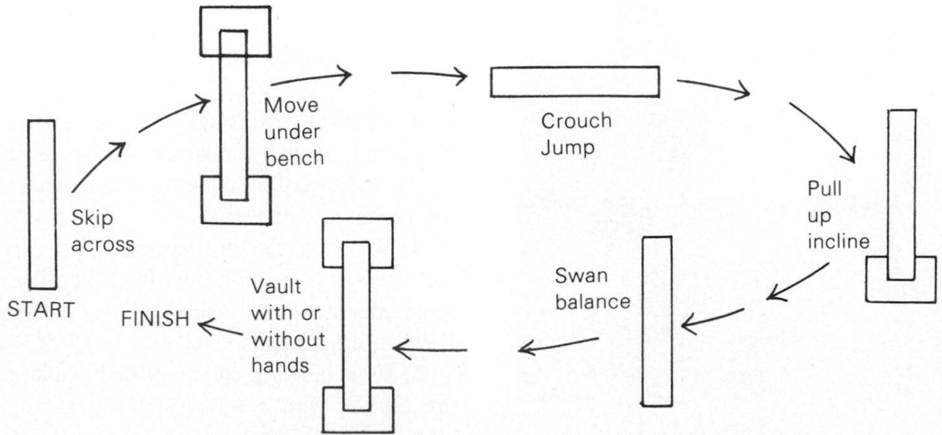

FIGURE 20.15. Challenge Course using benches

1. Fundamental locomotor movements—run, gallop, skip, and hop
2. Animal walks—Bear Walk, Crab Walk, and so on
3. Moving over and under various obstacles—jumping over a bench, moving through a hoop held upright by a mat, doing a Backward Roll on the mat
4. Rope jumping to the box—students try to continue jumping while mounting and dismounting the box

Mounting the Box

Many different combinations can be used to get onto the box.

1. Practice stepping onto the box (mounting) by taking the full weight on the stepping foot and holding it for a few seconds. This develops a sense of balance and tends to stabilize the support foot.
2. Mount the box, using locomotor movements such as a step, jump, leap, or hop. Perform various turns—quarter, half, three-quarter, and full—while jumping onto the box.
3. Use a Crouch Jump to get onto the box.
4. Back up to the box and mount it without looking at it.
5. Mount the box while a partner tosses you a beanbag.
6. Make various targets on top of the box with a piece of chalk, and try to land on the spot when mounting.

Dismounting the Box

The following dismounts can be used to develop body control.

1. Jump off with a quarter turn, half turn, or full turn.
2. Jump off with different body shapes—stretching, curling up in a ball, jackknifing.
3. Jump over a wand or through a hoop.
4. Jump off, and do a Forward Roll or a Backward Roll.
5. Change the above dismounts by substituting a hop or a leap in place of the jump.
6. Increase the height and distance of the dismount.
7. Dismount in various directions, such as forward (Figure 20.16), backward, sideward, northward, and southward.
8. Jump off, using a jackknife or wide straddle dismount.
9. Perform a balance stunt on the box and then dismount.

After the class has learned the basic movements used with jumping boxes, continuous squad motion can be incorporated. The squad captain is responsible for leading her group through different approaches, mounts, and dismounts. The same activity cannot be used twice in succession.

FIGURE 20.16. Jump dismounting from a 16-in. box

Addition of Equipment

Various pieces of equipment enhance box activities. Some suggestions follow.

1. Throw beanbags up while dismounting, or try to keep one on your head while mounting or dismounting the box.
2. Try to dribble a playground ball while performing the box routine.
3. Jump through a stationary hoop, held by a partner, while dismounting (Figure 20.17), or use the hoop as a jump rope and see how many times you can jump through it while dismounting.
4. Jump over or go under a wand.

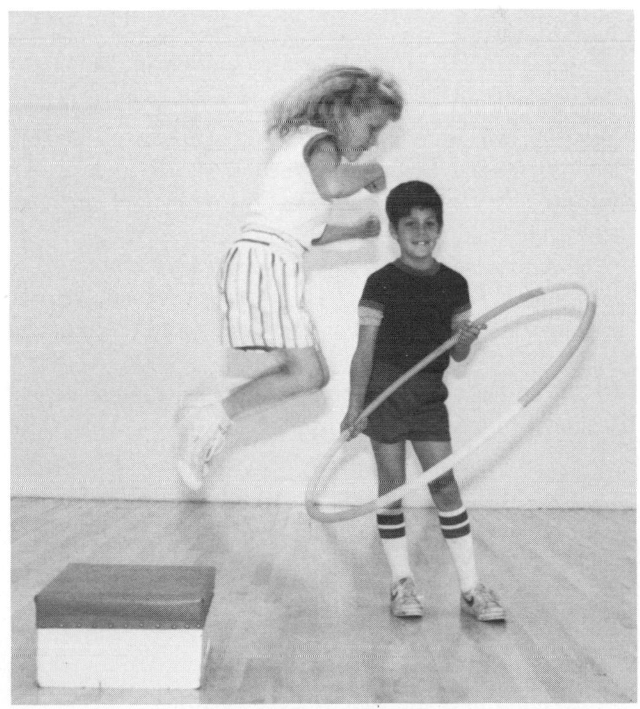

FIGURE 20.17. Jumping through the hoop

Box Combinations

Boxes can be arranged in a straight line and in other patterns. Children do a different movement over each box as though running a Challenge Course.

ACTIVITIES WITH MAGIC ROPES

Magic ropes come from Germany. Each rope is similar to a long rubber band. Magic ropes can be made by knitting wide rubber bands together, or they can be constructed from ordinary ¾-in. elastic tape available in most clothing stores. Children place their hands through loops on each end and grasp the rope. Ropes should be long enough to stretch to between 30 and 40 ft (see Chapter 34).

A major advantage of the magic rope is its flexibility; children have no fear of hitting it or tripping on it while performing. Ropes should be stretched tight, with little slack.

INSTRUCTIONAL PROCEDURES

1. Two or more children are rope holders while the others are jumping. The teacher should develop some type of rotation plan, so all children participate as holders.

2. Many variations can be achieved with the magic ropes by changing the height or by raising and lowering opposite ends of the ropes.

3. The jumping activities are strenuous and should be alternated with activities that involve crawling under the ropes.

4. The class should concentrate on *not* touching the rope. The magic rope can help develop body perception in space if the rope is regarded as an obstacle to be avoided.

5. Better use can be made of the rope with an oblique approach, which involves starting at one end of the rope and progressing to the other end by using jumping and hopping activities. In comparison, the straight-on approach allows the child to jump the rope only once.

6. A total of 8 to 12 ropes is needed for a class, 2 for each squad. Squads are excellent groups for this activity, because the leader can control the rotation of the rope holders.

7. The child next in turn begins when the child ahead is almost to the end of the rope.

ACTIVITY SEQUENCES

Activities With Single Ropes

Start the ropes at a 6-in. height and raise them progressively to add challenge.

1. Jump over the rope (Figure 20.18).

2. Hop over the rope.

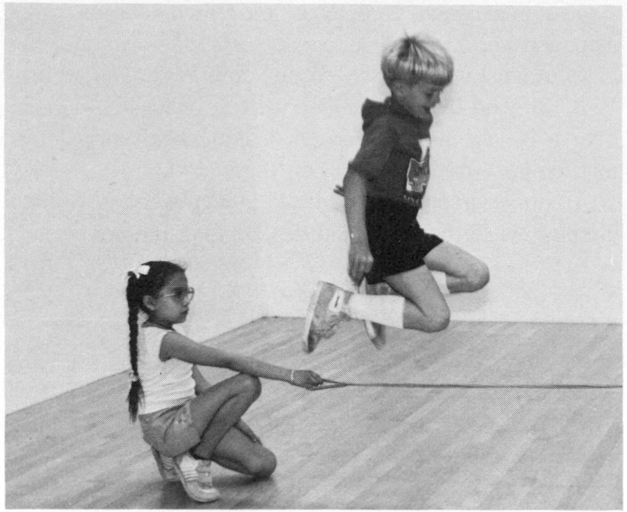

FIGURE 20.18. Jumping over a single magic rope

3. Jump and perform various body turns while jumping.

4. Make different body shapes and change body size while jumping.

5. Crawl or slide under the rope.

6. Crouch-jump over the rope.

7. Hold the rope overhead, and have others jump up and touch it with their foreheads.

8. Gradually lower the rope, and do the limbo under it without touching the floor with the hands.

9. Jump over the rope backward without looking at it.

10. Perform a Scissors Jump over the rope.

Activities With Double Ropes

Vary the height and spread of the ropes.

1. Do these activities with the ropes parallel to each other.

- **a.** Jump in one side and out the other.
- **b.** Hop in one side and out the other (Figure 20.19).

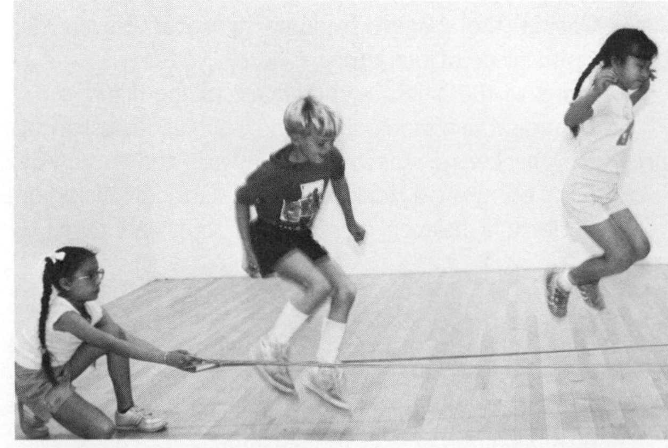

FIGURE 20.19. Hopping in and out of two magic ropes

c. Crouch-jump in and out.

d. Perform various animal walks in and out of the ropes.

e. Do a long jump over both of the ropes.

f. Perform a stunt while jumping in between the two ropes. Possible stunts are the Heel Click, body turn, handclap, and Straddle Jump.

g. Jump or leap over one rope and land on the other rope.

2. With the ropes crossed at right angles to each other, do these activities.

a. Perform various movements from one area to the next.

b. Jump into one area and crawl out of that area into another.

3. With one rope above the other to effect a barbed-wire fence, do these activities. Vary the height and distance apart of the ropes. This adds much excitement to the activity because the children are challenged not to touch the ropes.

a. Step through the ropes without touching.

b. Crouch-jump through.

Miscellaneous Activities With Magic Ropes

These miscellaneous activities are useful, too. The class should be given time to create their own ideas with the ropes and other pieces of equipment.

1. Perform the various activities with a beanbag balanced on the head. Perform while bouncing a ball.

2. Use four or more ropes to create various floor patterns.

3. Use a follow-the-leader plan to add variety to the activity.

4. Create a Challenge Course with many ropes for a relay.

ACTIVITIES WITH INDIVIDUAL MATS

Individual mats have an English origin and are the basis for many exploratory and creative movements. Essentially, the mat serves as a base of operation or as an obstacle to go over or around.

Mats vary in size, with the most popular being 20 by 40 in. and 24 by 48 in. Standard thickness is 0.75 in., but this also varies. The mat should have a rubber backing to prevent slipping. Rubber-backed indoor-outdoor carpeting of good quality makes excellent mats.

INSTRUCTIONAL PROCEDURES

1. Educational movement techniques are very important in mat work.

2. Body management and basic skills of locomotor and nonlocomotor movement should be emphasized.

3. Mats should be far enough apart to allow free movement around them.

4. Each child should have a mat.

ACTIVITY SEQUENCES

Rigid adherence to the sequence presented below is not necessary. The activities are quite flexible and require only fundamental skills.

Command Movements

In command movements, children change movement on command. The commands used are the following:

"Stretch": Stretch your body out in all directions as wide as possible.

"Curl": Curl into a tight little ball (Figure 20.20).

"Balance": Form some kind of balanced position.

"Bridge": Make a bridge over the mat.

"Reach": Keeping one toe on the mat, reach out as far as possible across the floor in a chosen direction.

"Rock": Rock on any part of the body.

"Roll": Do some kind of roll on the mat.

"Twist": Make a shape with a part of the body twisted.

"Prone": Lie prone on the mat.

"Melt": Sink down slowly into a little puddle of water on the mat.

"Shake": Shake all over, or shake whatever parts of the body are designated.

"Fall": Fall to the mat.

"Collapse": The movement is similar to a fall but follows nicely after a bridge.

Sequencing can be established in several ways. The children can emphasize flow factors by moving at will from one movement to another, or changes can be made on a verbal signal or on the beat of a drum. The magic number concept can be used too.

Another means of exploration is selecting one of the movement challenges—say, "Stretch"—and changing from one type of stretch position to another. If "Balance" is selected, the movement sequence can begin with a balance

FIGURE 20.20. Curl activities on individual mats

on six body parts; then the number can be reduced by one on each signal until the child is balancing on one body part. Different kinds of shapes can be explored.

Movements On and Off the Mat

Children do different locomotor movements on and off the mat in different directions. Turns and shapes can be added. Levels are another good challenge.

1. Take the weight on the hands as you go across the mat.

2. Lead with different body parts as you go on and off the mat. Move on and off the mat with a specified number of body parts (one, two, three, four, five) used for landing.

3. Jump backward, forward, sideward. Make up a rhythmic sequence. Move around the area, jumping from mat to mat.

Movements Over the Mat

Movements over the mat are similar to the preceding movements, but the child goes completely over the mat each time.

Movements Around the Mat

Locomotor movements around the mat are done both clockwise and counterclockwise.

1. Do movements around the mat, keeping the hands on the mat. Now do movements around, keeping the feet on the mat.

2. Change to one foot and one hand on the mat. Vary with the crab position.

3. Work out combinations of stunt movements and locomotor activities, going around the mats. Reverse direction often.

4. Move throughout the area, running between the mats, and on signal jump over a specified number of mats.

Activities Using Mats As a Base

1. Stretch and reach in different directions to show how big the space is.

2. Do combination movements away from and back to the mat. For example, do two jumps and two hops or six steps and two jumps.

3. Use the magic-number concept.

4. See how many letters you can make. Find a partner, put your mats together, and make your bodies into different letters and numbers.

Mat Games

Each child is seated on a mat. On signal, each rises and jumps over as many different mats as possible. On the next signal, each child takes a seat on the nearest mat. The last child to be seated can pay a penalty. The game can also be played by eliminating one or two mats so one or two children are left without a home base. The teacher can stand on a mat or turn over mats to put them out of the game. To control roughness, the rule should be that the first child to touch a mat gets to sit on it.

A variation of this game is to have each child touch at least ten mats and then sit cross-legged on his own mat, or a child can be required to alternate touching a mat and jumping over the next mat until a total of ten is reached. "See how many mats you can cartwheel or jump over in 10 seconds." Change the challenge and try again.

Developmental Challenges

1. Experiment with Curl-ups (partial or full). (This can be done informally and on a challenge basis.)

2. From a sitting position on the mat, pick up the short sides of the mat and raise the feet and upper body off the floor. Try variations of the V-up (p. 394).

Manipulative Activities

Keeping one foot on the mat, maintain control of a balloon in the air, either with a hand, a nylon-stocking paddle, or a lummi stick. Try the same activity with a stocking paddle and a paper ball. The number of touches, or strokes, can be counted. Try with both feet on the mat.

ACTIVITIES WITH CARPET SQUARES

Most mat activities can be adapted to carpet samples (usually 12- or 16-in. squares) purchased at a carpet store. Most kinds of carpet slide readily on the floor, so other activities are possible too. One child can pull another by using either a wand or a jump rope, with the rider seated or kneeling on the square. Another activity is to use the squares as though crossing the river on ice cakes. One child can do this and shift squares herself, or a partner can shift the squares.

ACTIVITIES ON BALANCE BOARDS

Balance boards are small devices on which the child stands and tries to keep his balance (Figure 20.21). Generally, they have either a circular or square platform about 15 in. wide and a rounded bottom to provide the balance challenge. A rubber pad should be used to protect the floor surface.

FIGURE 20.21. Balancing on a balance board

Activities with balance boards are somewhat limited, consisting of maintaining balance with a variety of challenges. The balance boards are quite useful when a variety of apparatus is put out and children are allowed to explore on the various pieces.

INSTRUCTIONAL PROCEDURES

1. Consider beginning with a single-axis board. This makes simpler demands and is good for handicapped children and those having difficulty balancing on a board with a rounded bottom.

2. Another board of value has a 4-in.-square bottom that provides a flat surface for better stability. The bottom square can be reduced in size for more challenge (see Chapter 34).

3. Provide a variety of boards.

ACTIVITY SEQUENCES

1. Secure a balanced position on the board. Change the position of the arms—folded on the chest, at the sides, outstretched to the sides or forward, or placed on the head, shoulders, hips, or knees.

2. Secure balance, and gradually lower the body to touch the board.

3. Change from a two-foot to a one-foot balance. Change from one foot to the other. Turn completely around on the board. Move the feet together and then move them apart. Stand on the tiptoes. Close the eyes and balance.

4. Tilt forward until the front edge of the board touches the floor, and return to the starting position. Try tilting backward, right, and left.

5. Mount and dismount from various sides of the board. Hop or jump off the board in different directions.

6. Bounce and catch a ball with two hands while maintaining balance.

7. Toss a ball in the air and catch it with both hands.

8. Try bouncing and tossing with one hand.

9. Dribble a ball, and keep track of the number of successful bounces made without losing balance.

10. Twirl a hoop on various body parts while maintaining balance.

11. Jump-rope on the board.

12. Do various activities with the eyes closed.

13. Balance on various body parts, such as the knees, tummy, and seat.

14. Touch different body parts as specified while balancing. Touch opposites (touch the right shoulder with the left hand, the left ear with the right hand, and so on).

15. Pick up a beanbag from the board.

16. Balance on the board with a partner.

17. Start from a standing position on the board and move to a kneeling position. Reverse and move to standing position.

18. Toss and catch beanbags, balls, or hoops with a partner. Twirl a hoop and change it from performer's arm to partner's without stopping or losing balance.

ACTIVITIES ON BONGO BOARDS

The bongo board is a single-axis balance board with a movable cylinder that allows the board to be shifted back and forth over the cylinder. Edges are fixed completely around the board underneath to prevent the cylinder from moving out from under the board. Commercial varieties generally feature a track in the center to keep the roller in line. This is a feature worth duplicating in boards constructed at home or school (see Chapter 34).

INSTRUCTIONAL PROCEDURES

1. The single-axis balance board can be regarded as a lead-up to bongo board activity.

2. Bongo board activity functions best as a station activity.

3. Children should not underestimate bongo board challenges; there is some danger from falling.

ACTIVITY SEQUENCES

All of the suggested activities except no. 2 can be accomplished on a single-axis balance board (with a fixed cylinder).

1. To mount, place the board on the roller so that one end is on the floor. Step on this end first, and then place the other foot on the high end. Bring the lower end off the floor, and shift the board along the roller until the roller is in the center. Hold and balance. (This is the basic position.)

2. Shift the board back and forth on the roller with an easy motion, beginning with a small shift and increasing somewhat, under control.

3. Take the basic position. Turn on the balls of the feet and face one end. (This is the turned position.) Face back to the basic position. Turn the other way.

4. Assume the basic position. Slowly bring the feet together, and then spread them again.

5. Begin with the basic position. Move to the turned position. Gradually move the feet until they are positioned together over the roller. Return to original position.

6. From the basic stance, jump lightly and land. Increase the height of the jumps.

7. Toss and receive beanbags and balls from a partner while in the basic stance. Do the same while in the turned position.

8. Maintaining the basic position, stoop and touch the board. Try picking up a beanbag from the board.

9. Handle hoops or juggle beanbags or balls while in balance.

10. Touch body parts as specified. Touch opposites (touch the left knee with the right hand and so on).

ACTIVITIES ON BOUNDING BOARDS

Bounding boards provide a unique type of movement similar to bouncing on a trampoline. They can be constructed easily from a piece of ¾-in. plywood, sized 2 by 6 ft. The board is supported on pieces of 4-by-4-in. lumber, which are padded on the underside with carpet to protect the floor. The plywood must be a quality product with few knots. Marine plywood, though expensive, is the best (see Chapter 34).

INSTRUCTIONAL PROCEDURES

1. Two children can work with one board. After performing, one child moves forward to leave the board and return to place. Return activity can be used.

2. Emphasis should be on lightness, height, and relaxation during the bounding.

3. Bounding, for the most part, should be done in the center of the board.

4. The activity is for younger children only. Older children can damage or break the boards.

5. The board supports should be cushioned or rubber matting placed on the floor to prevent damage to the floor surface.

ACTIVITY SEQUENCES

1. Bound in the center with both feet. With one foot.

2. Bound in the center, using turns and different arm positions. Add handclaps.

3. Move across the board, using jumping and hopping. Return. Add turns and handclaps.

4. Bound with numbered foot combinations, alternating two, three, or four hops on one foot and then changing to the other. These are called twosies, threesies, and foursies.

5. To the previous skills, add forward and backward leg extensions and leg changes sideward.

6. Use different numbers of hops when alternating, such as hopping once on the right foot and twice on the left. Use other combinations, such as 2–3, 2–4, and so on.

7. Add rope jumping at slow time and fast time. Use hoops.

8. Hold a specified body part while bounding.

ACTIVITIES WITH GYM SCOOTERS

Gym scooters make excellent devices for developmental activity when used properly. The minimum number is one scooter for two children, unless the scooters are used for relays only. In that case, four or six scooters will suffice for an average size class.

Two rules are important in the use of scooters. First, children are not to stand on scooters as they would on skateboards. Second, scooters, with or without passengers, are not to be used as missiles.

Children can work individually or in pairs. A child working alone can do many different combinations by varying the method of propulsion and the method of supporting the body. Children can propel the scooter with their feet, their hands, or both. The body position can be kneeling, sitting, prone, supine, or even sideways. The body weight can be wholly or partially supported on the scooter. The variation of space factors, particularly direction, adds interest.

When children work in pairs, one child rides and the other pushes or pulls. The rider's weight may be wholly supported by the scooter or partially supported by the scooter and partially supported by the partner.

Educational movement methodology is applicable to scooter work, but care should be exercised so the scooter activities are developmental and not just a fun session. Scooters are excellent for relays, and many games can be adapted for their use.

ACTIVITIES WITH TIRES

Activities with tires are challenging to children and easy on the school budget. The tires should be washed, and they can be painted to make them more appealing. Make the painting a school project in conjunction with the classroom teacher or art specialist.

INSTRUCTIONAL PROCEDURES

1. Tire size is not important, and tires of different sizes can be used.
2. Tires are generally used outside, because considerable space is needed.
3. Tire stands are necessary for activities with the tires set upright (see Chapter 34 for construction).
4. Creativity should be emphasized in working with tires.
5. Some system for getting the tires and returning them to the storage area is necessary.

ACTIVITY SEQUENCES

Activities With Tires Placed on the Ground

1. Jump in and out of the tire, forward and backward, and side to side.
2. Stand in the tire, and jump out as far as possible.
3. Take a push-up position with hands on the tire and feet outstretched. Walk the feet in a large clockwise circle and then in a counterclockwise circle. Reverse and put the feet on the tire and walk the hands.
4. Run, hop, skip, gallop, and slide around the tire clockwise and counterclockwise. Add different animal movements.
5. Run and jump into the center of the tire without touching it. Sink down and exit like a frog.
6. Use the Bunny Jump, the Frog Hop, and the Pogo Jump to move into the center and out.
7. Balance on one foot inside the tire, close the eyes, hold for a few seconds, and hop out with the eyes closed.
8. Do a Straddle Jump in and out of the tire.
9. Gradually increase and decrease the height of the jumps inside the tire.
10. Make a bridge, with the hands inside the tire and the feet outside. Move the bridge around the tire. Explore with different kinds of bridges, some with the feet inside the tire and the hands out. Can you make a bridge completely across the tire? Try inverting the bridge.
11. Show the different kinds of balances and locomotion you can do by standing or moving on the sides of the tire.
12. Stack two tires, and leap, jump, or otherwise move in and out. Add a third tire if you think you can make it.

Activities With Tires Placed in Patterns and Combinations

Tires can be placed in various combinations, either touching one another or spaced a bit apart, depending on the movement challenges. They can be placed in a straight line or in different curved patterns.

1. Run, jump, hop, and use various animal walks through the patterns.
2. Jump through the patterns with one foot on the tire sides.
3. Experiment with straddle-jumping patterns so that one foot is outside and one inside the tires. Try some crisscross jumping.
4. Jump through the tires without touching the sides. Increase the height of the jump slightly each time you move down the line of tires.
5. Run through on the sides. Form figure eights and do circular movements on the sides while walking or running lightly.
6. Stack two tires to add challenge to the patterns.

Handling the Tires

Handling the tires can be either an in-place activity or a rolling activity. Partner activities should be part of the experiences.

1. Spin the tire, and see what you can do while moving around the tire as it spins.
2. Roll the tire. Try to get in front of it and stop it. Try getting in front of it and jumping over it as it rolls. Roll it at a target.
3. Experiment with different ways to lift and hold the tire in the air. Can you get it overhead?
4. With a partner, roll the tire back and forth. Roll so your partner can jump the tire. Set a target in between you and your partner and see which of you can hit the target.
5. Work out a few contests with your partner. Try a tug-of-war with a tire. Devise other contests, either pulling or pushing.
6. Let your partner roll a tire in a path crossing your path, and see whether you can hit his tire with your tire.

Other Activities With Tires

1. Play Beanbag Horseshoes with the tires as targets. Score 1 point for each beanbag that lands inside the tire, or 2 points for landing a bag inside the tire and 1 point for landing a bag on the tire side.
2. Use the tire in a rolling relay or as an obstacle to jump in or to run around, through, or on.
3. With tires mounted on stands, explore different ways to go through, over, or around.

ACTIVITIES ON STILTS

Stilts are made in different fashions and heights. Generally, the step provides about a 4-in. support. The step should be 6 to 12 in. high for beginners. Greater heights of 18, 24, and 30 in. challenge the more skilled, but mounting the higher stilts is a problem. A jumping box, a sturdy chair, or a ladder may be necessary for mounting. The stilts should reach a foot or two above the shoulders when the student is on them.

Stilts made from tin cans have some value for younger children, but the balancing challenge is not as meaningful as with regular stilts. Activities on tin-can stilts can follow the described patterns in most cases.

INSTRUCTIONAL PROCEDURES

1. Stilts are regarded mostly as outdoor equipment. If used indoors, they should have rubber pads at the bottom to minimize slippage.

2. The exploratory approach should predominate, because the children need to move at their own pace in these activities.

3. First, master mounting and initial stepping. Mounting can be done from the ground or from a raised surface.

ACTIVITY SEQUENCES

1. Move in different directions—forward, backward, and sideward. Try moving while keeping one stilt always forward or backward.

2. Try pattern-walking for a challenge. Use tires or other obstacles to create various patterns.

3. Walk the stilts apart in small increments. Bring them back together again.

4. Try to balance momentarily on one stilt and pivot on one stilt.

5. Jump in place with the stilts. Try to move while jumping. Try hopping (this is a bit more difficult).

6. Using a low (8-in.) jumping box, step up on the box and down again. (The top of the box should have a nonslip surface. A stair platform of two or three steps can be negotiated by the more skilled, if there is provision against slippage. Spotters should be available.)

MISCELLANEOUS APPARATUS ACTIVITIES

Solid chairs (not the folding type) can provide the base for jumping and climbing patterns. The backs can be removed to make stools.

Unicycles are unique and attractive instruments for movement. These are not mastered easily, but they intrigue children. Expense is a factor. The high school shop could make them as a project.

Skateboards are a fact of life, and perhaps some attention to technique and safety can be included in the physical education program. This could be an after-school activity.

Roller-skating has been found to be an excellent activity for both handicapped and normal children. Fitting skates, however, is quite time consuming.

We question the use of the regular trampoline for elementary school physical education classes. With only one child bouncing at a time, the other children stand inactive. The hazards posed by trampolines have caused some administrators to take a hard look at their inclusion in the school program on any level. Justifying the inclusion of the trampoline in the elementary school program is difficult because of the space it takes up when not in use and the difficulty of moving or storing the apparatus. Most trampolines in elementary school programs were inherited from high school programs, for the expense of purchase can hardly ever be justified. Perhaps the logical use of the trampoline is with a special interest group in a gymnastics program under qualified supervision.

CHAPTER 21

Stunts and Tumbling

Gymnastic activities are an important part of every child's overall experience in physical education and can make a significant contribution to the goals of physical education. Through the stunts and tumbling program, such personal characteristics as dedication and perseverance can be furthered, for stunts are seldom mastered quickly. Since much of the work is individual, the child faces a challenge and has the opportunity to develop resourcefulness, self-confidence, and courage. When a challenging stunt is mastered, satisfaction, pride of achievement, and a sense of accomplishment contribute to improved self-esteem.

Social interplay is provided by the various partner and group stunts requiring cooperative effort. The social attributes of tolerance, helpfulness, courtesy, and appreciation for the ability of others grow out of the lessons when the methodology is educationally sound. Further group consciousness develops from the child's increased concern for her own safety and that of others. Children learn to use proper spotting techniques and to help others execute stunts.

Important physical values can emerge from an instructionally sound gymnastics program. Body management opportunities are presented, and coordination, flexibility, and agility are enhanced. The opportunity to practice control of balance is present in many activities. Visual control of balance can be eliminated occasionally by having children close their eyes, thus making demands on other balance controls.

The raw physical demands of holding positions and executing stunts contribute to the development of strength and power in diverse parts of the body. Many stunts demand support, wholly or in part, by the arms, thus providing needed development of the often weak musculature of the arm-shoulder girdle. Gymnastics activities also contribute to overall physical fitness.

In addition, stunts and tumbling activities offer a wonderful opportunity for children to acquire fundamental concepts such as right and left, near and far, wide and narrow, up and down, and forward and backward.

PROGRESSION AND GRADE-LEVEL PLACEMENT

Progression is the soul of learning experiences in the stunts and tumbling program. In this text, activities are allocated in progression from grade to grade. It is essential that the order of these activities be reasonably maintained. Adherence to grade-level placement is secondary to this principle. If children come with little or no experience in these activities, the teacher should start them on activities specified for a lower grade.

Another key point to the organization of the activities is their division into six basic groups: (1) animal movements, (2) tumbling and inverted balances, (3) balance stunts, (4) individual stunts, (5) partner and group stunts, and (6) partner support activities. This arrangement allows the teacher to pick activities from each group for a well-balanced lesson. Too often, teachers concentrate on tumbling activities, and children become bored and tired. Selecting stunts from all of the groups forestalls boredom and allows more students to meet with success.

The heart of a gymnastic program is the standard tumbling activities, such as rolls, stands, springs, and related stunts commonly accepted as basic to such a program. In performing the following activities, emphasis should be placed on exposure and overcoming fear. Perfect technique is less important than developing positive approach behaviors. The suggested progression of the *basic* activities is presented in the following list. Descriptions of these activities and more are found in the programs at the indicated grade levels.

Kindergarten and First Grade

Rolling Log
Side Roll
Forward Roll (Tuck Position)
Back Roller

Second Grade

Forward Roll (Straddle Position)
Backward Curl
Backward Roll (Handclasp Position)
Climb-up
Three-Point Tip-up
Mountain Climber—Handstand Lead-up Activity
Switcheroo—Handstand Lead-up Activity

Third Grade

Forward Roll (Pike Position)
Backward Roll (Inclined)
Backward Roll (Regular)
Frog Handstand (Tip-up)
Half Teeter Totter—Handstand Lead-up Activity
Cartwheel

Fourth Grade

Forward Roll to a Walkout
Forward Roll Combinations
Backward Roll Combinations
Headstand Practice and Variations
Teeter Totter—Handstand Lead-up Activity
Handstand

Fifth Grade

Forward and Backward Roll Combinations
Back Extension
Headstand Variations
Wall Arch
Handstand Against a Wall
Freestanding Handstand
Cartwheel and Round-off
Judo Roll

Sixth Grade

Forward and Backward Roll Combinations
Developing Gymnastic Routines
Straddle Press to Headstand
Headspring
Walking on the Hands
Walk-Over

The kindergarten and primary-level program relies on simple stunts with a gradual introduction to tumbling stunts classified as lead-ups or preliminaries to more advanced stunts. Stunts requiring exceptional body control, critical balancing, or substantial strength should be left for higher grades.

The intermediate-level program is built on activities and progressions from the primary-level program. Emphasis is placed on standard gymnastic activities, with the accompanying need for learning spotting techniques. While most stunts at the primary level can be performed with a certain degree of choice, for the intermediate-level stunts more conformance to correct technique is desirable. In general, the intermediate-level activities place higher demands on strength, control, form, agility, balance, and flexibility.

Most activities at the primary level can be done—at least in some fashion—by most students, but certain activities at the intermediate level may be too challenging for some students. The teacher should arrange lessons for the upper grades that include stunts that everyone can do, stunts that are moderately challenging, and stunts that are quite challenging.

PRESENTING ACTIVITIES

WARM-UP AND FLEXIBILITY ACTIVITY

Normal introductory activity and fitness development activity usually supply sufficient warm-up for the stunts and tumbling lesson. If additional stretching seems warranted, take a wide straddle position with the feet about 3 ft apart and the toes pointed ahead. With arms out to the sides, bend, twist, and generally stretch in all directions. Next, touch the floor with the hands to the front, sides, and back, with little bending of the knees.

Extra flexibility is required in the wrists, ankles, and neck. The following activities, which focus on these areas, can be used prior to participating in the gymnastic activities.

Wrists

1. Extend one arm forward. With the other hand, push the extended hand down, thus stretching the top of the wrist and forearm muscles. Hold the position for eight counts. Next, pull the hand backward and hold for eight counts to stretch the wrist flexor muscles.

2. Clasp the fingers of both hands in front of the chest. Make circles with both hands and stretch the wrists.

Ankles and Quadriceps

1. Kneel and sit on both feet. Smoothly and gently lean backward over the feet, using the arms to support the body.

2. In a sitting position, cross one leg over the other. Use the hands to help rotate each foot through its full range of motion. Reverse legs and repeat.

Neck

1. In a sitting position, slowly circle the head in both directions through the full range of motion.

2. In the same position, hold the chin against the chest for eight counts. Repeat with the head looking backward as far as possible. Look to each side and hold for eight counts.

Lower Back and Shoulders

Begin in a supine position. Place the hands back over the head on the mat so the fingers point toward the toes. Bridge up by extending the arms and legs. While in the bridge position, slowly rock back and forth.

EFFECTIVE CLASS MANAGEMENT

One of the justifiable criticisms of stunts and tumbling lessons is that children must wait in line for turns on the mat. Having to take turns is not in itself undesirable, but waiting must be controlled so that everyone is reasonably active. Sometimes, however, having the students watch what others are doing is desirable. How the children are arranged depends on the activities selected and whether mats are required. The following list will help establish priorities.

1. Whenever possible, all children should be active and performing. When mats are not required for the activities, there is little problem. Individual mats can be used for many of the simple balances and rolling stunts, particularly at the kindergarten and 1st-grade level. When larger mats are required, teachers must be more ingenious. Ideally, each group of three students should have a mat. When return activities are used in conjunction with groups as small as three, there is little standing around. Small groups also work well when spotting and other types of cooperation are needed.

2. When the number of mats is limited, children can perform across the mats sideways. On a 6-ft-long mat, two children can tumble sideways. An 8-ft-long mat can be used by three performers at the same time. With this arrangement, the focus is on single rolls, but an occasional series of rolls lengthwise on the mat is not ruled out. The ends of the mats can be used for various stands, as long as the children do not fall toward each other.

3. If children are to do a lot of tumbling lengthwise down the mats, there should be at least six mats per class. When eight mats are available, the squad formation can be used, with each squad having access to two mats.

4. Station teaching should be considered, especially when equipment is limited. Careful planning is necessary to ensure that the experience stresses progress and diligence. All stations can involve tumbling and inverted balance experiences, or only a few tumbling and inverted balance stations can be included with the other stations featuring less demanding activities. The arrangement might include Forward and Backward Rolls at the first station, Headstands at the second, Cartwheels at the third, and partner stunts at the fourth. Wall charts listing the activities in progression provide excellent guidance. A chart illustrated with stick figures can be made as a class project.

5. The contract or task card approach is particularly effective for tumbling and stunts.

FORMATIONS FOR TEACHING

Some formations that organize the class for gymnastic activities follow.

1. *Squad line formation.* Mats are placed in a line, with the squads lined up behind the mats. Each child takes a turn and goes to the end of the squad line, with the others moving up. An alternate method is for each child to perform and then return to a seated position.

2. *Squad file formation.* A file formation can be arranged. The teacher stands in front, and the children perform toward him. As soon as a child has completed her turn, she goes to the end of the line. A weakness of this formation is that, at times, some children may be hidden from the teacher by other children, which poses problems of control.

3. *Semicircular formation.* The squad file formation can be changed readily to a semicircular arrangement. This formation directs attention toward the teacher, who stands in the center. Groups are separated more than in squad file formation.

4. *Hollow rectangle.* The squads perform on the sides of a hollow rectangle. The advantage of this formation is that children can watch each other. If the teacher is in the center, however, some portion of the class will be blocked.

5. *U-shaped formation.* The mats are placed in the shape of a U. This formation allows good control for the teacher, and children are able to see what their classmates are doing.

6. *Double-row formation.* In this formation, three groups form a row on one side and three on the other. The teacher is never far from any one group, and the children can also observe each other.

7. *Demonstration mat.* One mat is placed in a central position and is used exclusively for demonstrations. Little movement is necessary for the children to be able to see the demonstrations.

RETURN ACTIVITIES

Return activities (discussed on pp. 333–334) work best when children perform lengthwise down the mat. Each child turns in a designated direction (right or left) at the end of the mat and uses that pathway to do the return task. A popular return activity makes use of a magic number. Instructions for the return are given in this way. "Today, our magic number for return activity is five." Children can solve the magic number problem by doing, for example, three jumps and two hops or four Push-ups and one Frog Jump.

REVIEW

Review of the learning experiences from the previous lesson or lessons is important to maintain continuity. Difficulties from previous lessons should be discussed and solved. More activity variety can then be developed, and performance quality can be given consideration.

DESCRIPTION AND DEMONSTRATION OF NEW GYMNASTIC ACTIVITIES

In presenting an activity, teachers find the following sequence helpful.

1. *Significance of the name.* Most stunts have a characteristic name, and this should be given attention by the teacher. If the stunt is of an imitative type, the animal or character represented should be described and discussed.

2. *Description of the activity.* Stunts can be approached in terms of three parts—starting position, execution, and finishing position. Most stunts have a defined starting position. To perform properly, the child should understand what position to assume as the first step. Next, key movements for proper execution of the activity should be stressed. Such factors as how far to travel, how long to balance, and how many times a movement should be done must be clarified. In some gymnastic activities, a definite finishing position or action is part of the stunt. In balancing stunts, it is important that the child return to a standing (or some other) position without losing balance and without moving the feet.

3. *Demonstration of the activity.* Three levels of demonstration are recognized: (a) minimal demonstration in the form of the starting position, (b) slow, step-by-step demonstration of the entire stunt, with an explanation of what is involved, and (c) execution of the stunt as the students would normally do it. The teacher should keep in mind that children need to analyze and solve problems. Too much demonstration defeats this goal. Explanation and demonstration should cover only one or two points. Try not to demonstrate too far in advance, but rather, show only those points necessary to get the activity underway. Add further details and refinements as the instruction progresses. Demonstrations have a place later in the instruction sequence also. These later demonstrations can use students to show the successful execution of activities that others are having difficulty performing. Demonstrations at the end of a unit can show what has been achieved. Each squad or group can demonstrate its achievements in turn.

OPPORTUNITIES FOR PRACTICE AND IMPROVEMENT

The character of each stunt determines the amount of practice needed and the number of times the stunt should be performed. Teachers should analyze a stunt thoroughly enough so they can verbalize the small points necessary for proper performance.

A reasonable standard of performance should be maintained. The teacher must answer the child's basic question, "Did I do it?" The instruction should make clear to the child what is involved in satisfactory performance so the child knows whether her execution is within the bounds of correct performance.

Many stunts require a position to be held for a short time. At first, the child should merely do the stunt. Later, the position can be held for 3 seconds and then 5 seconds.

Practice and repetition are essential in establishing effective movement patterns. Often, a teacher leaves an activity too soon for progress to have occurred. The following system is suggested. When explanations and demonstrations are completed and the children begin practice, each child in rotation should go through the stunt at least twice. When each child in the group has had the desired turns at an activity, the group remains in formation, waiting for the next instruction. If this system is to function properly, groups must be about the same size and must move at about the same speed. A teacher can ascertain at a glance whether the class is ready for the next instruction.

An alternate method is to allow the class to practice the activity a desired number of times. On the command or whistle to "freeze," the class stops whatever they are doing without returning to formation. Directions are then given for the next activity, and the class resumes practicing. This method decreases the amount of management time spent waiting for each squad to finish and return to formation.

VARIETY OF RESPONSE

Variety of movement can be secured in two general ways. The first way is to make use of the suggestions for variations incorporated in the stunt descriptions. The second is to use educational movement principles. The activity potential of any one stunt can be extended by the use of time, space, force, flow, and body factors and by creative expression. One or more of these factors can be varied to stimulate variety of movement and to provide exploratory activity.

The concepts of directionality and laterality should be

established so the children use both the right and left side without waiting to be told. If a balancing stunt is done on one foot, then the next time it should be tried on the other. If a roll is made to the right, a comparable roll should be made to the left. A teacher may wish to develop the stunt thoroughly on one side before making the change to the other side, but ultimately, the change should be made.

WAVE (OR RIPPLE) EFFECT

An interesting movement and sequence pattern can be injected into the instruction with the use of the wave (or ripple) effect. This should be used only after the students have achieved reasonable competency in the movements.

A squad is a group of suitable size to carry out the wave effect. The children form a line alongside a series of mats laid lengthwise. The wave effect can go in either direction, but generally moves from the performers' right to their left. The child on the right begins a stunt, followed quickly in turn by each successive child. The stunt movement appears to move along the line like a wave. The timing must be precise, with each child moving in succession.

The wave effect is an excellent culmination of a unit or lesson series. It is also effective in demonstrations performed for parent-teacher groups and other groups.

SAFETY CONSIDERATIONS

Safety is a foremost consideration in the gymnastic program. The inherent hazards of an activity and how to avoid them must be included in the instructional procedures. Spotting techniques are particularly necessary in the intermediate-level program. Only a few kindergarten and primary-level stunts require spotting.

SPOTTING

The purpose of spotting is twofold. First and most important is the performer's safety and the prevention of injury. Of secondary importance is the guiding of the performer through the stunt to help him develop a proper body awareness.

When spotting for safety, the goals are to assist the performer, to help support the body weight, and to prevent a hazardous fall. The first two tasks can be anticipated and included in the instruction, because the stunt determines what assistance should be given and how the spotter should aid in receiving the weight. Saving the performer from a fall is more difficult, because such intervention cannot be fully anticipated.

In assisting, the spotter should take a firm hold on the performer. In positioning herself, the spotter must consider the direction of the stunt. She may need to move with the performer as he executes the stunt. The spotter must be careful, however, not to provide so much help that her aid becomes a hindrance; she should avoid wrestling the performer into position.

The spotter's receiving the full weight of a performer occurs infrequently in the elementary school program. This happens in activities in which the child travels through the air in performing some kind of jumping or vaulting stunt. Assistance is given to help cushion the return to the floor. For cautious children, this type of help enables them to do the stunt and to get the feel of it. Later, as they become more sure of themselves, the help can be eliminated.

Each stunt should be analyzed with safety in mind, and a trained spotter should be assigned routinely. It is important for spotters to know both the stunt and the spotting techniques. Sufficient time must be allotted to teach correct spotting techniques.

Children should ask others to spot when they are learning a new stunt, and they, in turn, should be willing to assist others in spotting as needed.

OTHER SAFETY CONSIDERATIONS

Emphasis should be placed on how to fall. Children should be taught to roll out of a stunt when they lose their balance. When doing Headstands and Handstands, they should try to return to the floor in the direction from which they started. The return is facilitated by bending at the waist and the knees.

Pockets should be emptied, and lockets, glasses, watches, and other articles of this nature removed. A special depository for these articles should be provided, or they can be left in the classroom.

Teachers must guard against fatigue and strain in young children. The children should be encouraged but not forced to try stunts. Care should be taken not to use peer pressure to stimulate participation.

ADDITIONAL METHODOLOGY CONSIDERATIONS

INSTRUCTIONAL PROCEDURES

1. Although mats are not necessary for some stunts, it is wise to include stunts requiring mats in every lesson. Children like to perform on mats, and rolling stunts using mats are vital to the gymnastic program.

2. Many partner stunts work well only when partners are about the same size. If the stunt requires partner support, the support child should be strong enough to hold the weight of the other.

3. No two children are alike. Respect individual differences, and allow for different levels of success.

4. Relating new activities to those learned previously is important. An effective approach is to review the lead-up stunt for an activity.

5. Horseplay and ridicule have no place in a stunts and tumbling program. Children should have fun, but not at the expense of the performance of less-talented classmates.

6. Proper gym shoes are a help, but children can tumble in bare feet (not socks) if necessary.

7. When a stunt calls for a position to be held for a number of counts, use a standard counting system (e.g., "One thousand one, one thousand two. . . ." or "Monkey one, monkey two. . . .").

8. At times, the teacher can have children work in pairs, with one child performing and the second providing a critique.

9. In using small hand apparatus (wands, hoops, and the like) with stunts, having one item for each child is best. If this is not possible, a minimum of two pieces is needed for each group, so the child next in line does not have to wait for the return of the required object. One person, generally the leader of the group, should be designated to secure and return hand apparatus.

10. Shifting of mats should not be necessary during the course of instruction. In arranging a gymnastic routine for a day's lesson, the mat stunts should be grouped. The tumbling mats should be bordered with velcro so that, once fastened, they stay fastened together.

11. Soft background music can occasionally contribute to a pleasant atmosphere, but it should be low enough in volume so as not to interfere with the instruction.

12. The beat of a drum or tom-tom can direct controlled movements. Children should change position in small increments as guided by the beat. In Lowering the Boom (p. 372), for example, children can lower themselves a little each time the drum sounds.

START-AND-EXPAND TECHNIQUE

The start-and-expand technique should be applied to stunts when feasible. Consider someone teaching a simple Heel Click (p. 367). The instructor begins by saying, "Let's see all of you jump high in the air and click your heels together before you come down." (This is the start.) "Now, to do the stunt properly, you should jump into the air, click your heels, and land with your feet apart with a nice bent-knee action to absorb the shock." (This is the expansion.) Further expansion could be adding a quarter or half turn before landing, clapping the hands overhead while clicking the heels, or clicking the heels twice before landing. In general, the start is made simple, so all children can experience some measure of success. The instruction then expands to other elements of the stunt, with variations and movement factors added and refined as indicated.

SOCIAL FACTORS

Proper attire is essential. On days when stunts are scheduled, girls can change to slacks or shorts. The best solution, however, is to have all children change to gym uniforms.

Children should have fun with their friends during these activities, but they should not be allowed to laugh at an inept child. A social goal that should be stressed is cooperation—with a partner, in a small group, with the entire class, and with the teacher. Showing consideration in taking turns is important.

Children should be taught to have respect for equipment and to care for it. Mats should be lifted clear of the ground, not dragged, when being moved.

BASIC MECHANICAL PRINCIPLES

Certain mechanical principles should be established as the foundation of an effective gymnastic program. If children can build on these basic principles, instruction is facilitated. (Consult Chapter 3 if more in-depth coverage is desired.)

1. Momentum needs to be developed and applied, particularly for rolls. Tucking, starting from a higher point, and preliminary raising of the arms are examples of ways to increase momentum.

2. The center of weight must be positioned over the center of support in balance stunts, particularly in the inverted stands.

3. In certain stunts, such as the Headspring, the hips should be projected upward and forward to raise the center of gravity for better execution.

4. In stunts in which the body is wholly or partially supported by the hands, proper positioning of the hands is essential for effective performance. The hands should be approximately shoulder width apart, and the fingers should be spread and pointed forward.

STUNT CHECK-OFF SYSTEM

Some teachers like to establish a check-off system to keep track of student progress. Two systems are suggested. The first simply checks those stunts that the student has completed. The second differentiates between a stunt done well and one meeting the minimum requirements. In the latter system, the teacher can make a diagonal line (/) for a stunt meeting minimum requirements and a cross over that line, an X, for a stunt well done. A list of stunts with the children's names, by squad, can be posted on the bulletin board or kept on squad cards for convenient access during the lesson.

Some cautions need to be observed. The list should not result in peer pressure. Also, the student's sense of achievement may be distorted if the main interest is in getting stunts marked off on the list.

BASIC GYMNASTIC POSITIONS

Students should be able to recognize and demonstrate those basic positions that are unique to gymnastics. Empha-

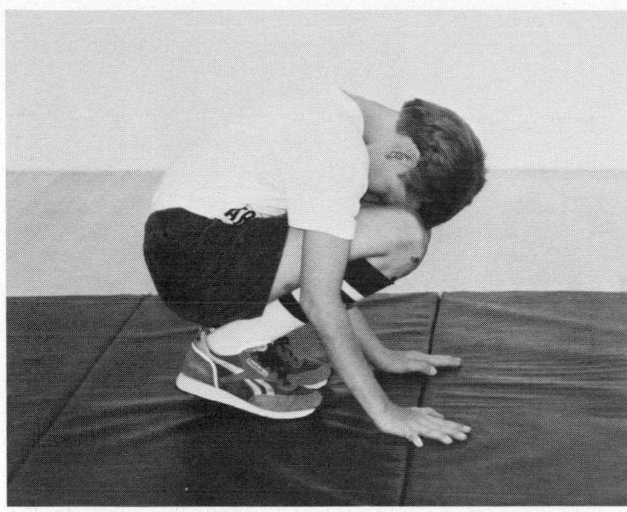

FIGURE 21.1. Tuck position

sis at the elementary level should be placed on a clear understanding of how the positions are performed, rather than on pure technique.

Tuck Position

The tuck position is performed with the legs bent and the chin tucked to the chest. Students can be cued to "curl up like a ball." There are three different tuck positions, and students should know all of them: the Sitting Tuck (Figure 21.1), the Standing Tuck, and the Lying Tuck.

Pike Position

The pike position is performed by bending forward at the hips and keeping the legs straight. The three basic pike positions are the Sitting Pike (Figure 21.2), the Standing Pike, and the Lying Pike.

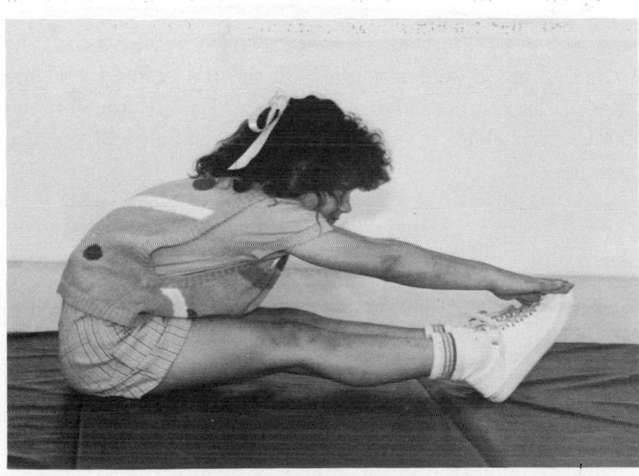

FIGURE 21.2. Pike position

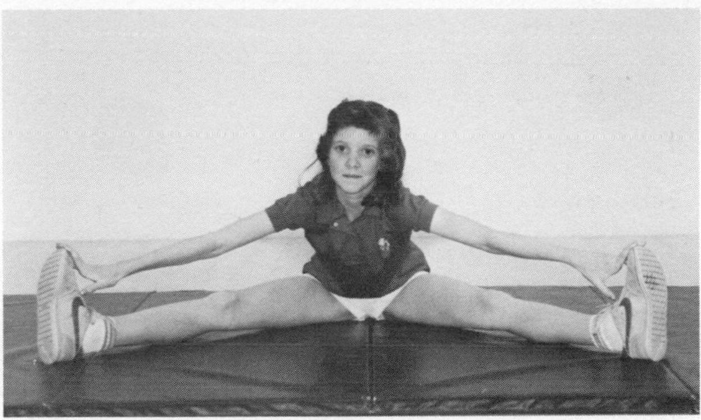

FIGURE 21.3. Straddle position

Straddle Position

The straddle position is accomplished by bending forward at the hips and spreading the legs apart to the sides as far as possible. The legs should be kept straight. Variations of the straddle position are the Sitting Piked Straddle (Figure 21.3), the Standing Piked Straddle, and the Lying Piked Straddle.

Front Support Position

This position is similar to the push-up position. The body is straight with the head up (Figure 21.4).

Back Support Position

The back support position is an inverted push-up position. The body is kept as straight as possible (Figure 21.5).

GYMNASTIC DANCE POSITIONS

Attitude

An attitude is a position in which the body weight is supported on one leg while the other leg is lifted and bent

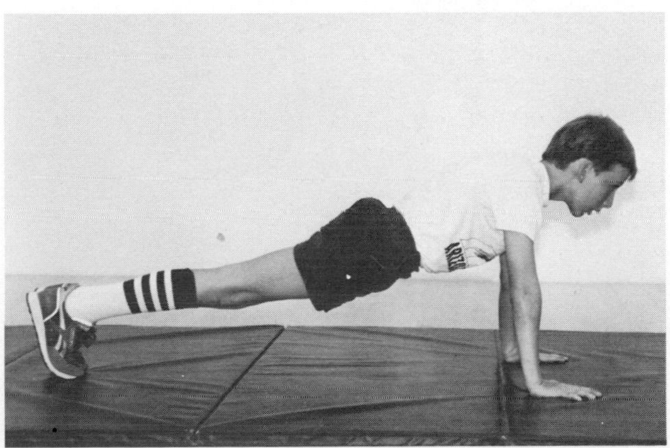

FIGURE 21.4. Front support position

FIGURE 21.5. Back support position

at the knee. The arm on the side of the lifted leg is usually bent over the head, and the other arm is extended at the side (Figure 21.6).

Lunge Position

In lunge position, the nonsupporting rear leg is straight while the forward, supporting leg is bent at the hip and knee. Most of the weight is placed on the forward leg. The arms are extended, and the head is up with the eyes forward (Figure 21.7).

Plié

A Plié is the bending of the knees. Both knees are bent, the arms are extended at right angles to the sides, and the seat is tucked to maintain a flat abdominal wall. The Plié teaches children how to absorb the force of the landing. There are different plié positions, but the basic purpose of the Plié in gymnastic instruction is to teach landing with grace and control.

FIGURE 21.6. Attitude

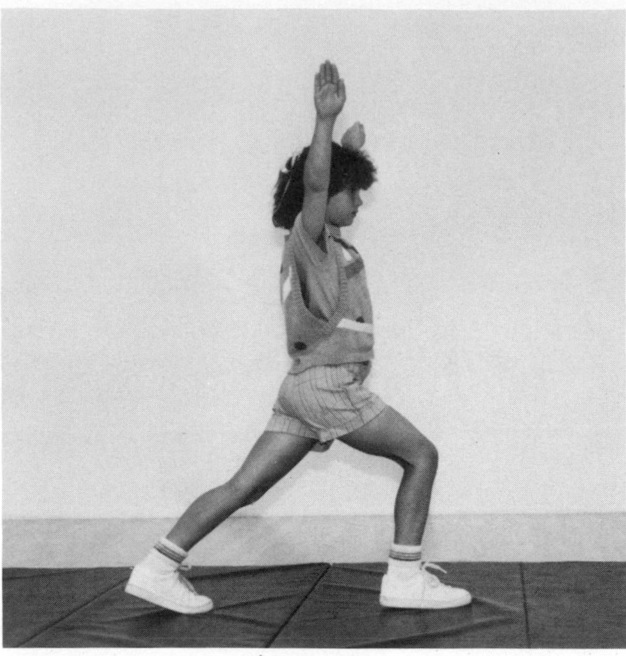

FIGURE 21.7. Lunge position

Relevé

The Relevé is an extension movement from the plié position. The movement goes from the plié (knees bent) position to the extended position. Extension should be complete through all of the joints, stretching upward from the balls of the feet.

Arabesque

In the arabesque position, the weight is supported on one leg while the other leg is extended to the rear. The extended leg is kept straight with the toe pointed, and the chest is kept erect (Figure 21.8). The Back Extension and the Cartwheel are often brought to completion with an Arabesque.

Jumps

Three jump variations are used commonly in gymnastic dance. They are the Tuck Jump, the Pike Jump, and the Straddle Jump. These jumps are simply a jump with the prescribed position added. The arms are raised in a lifting motion to increase the height of the jump and to enhance balance. The impact of the landing is absorbed at the ankles and knee joints.

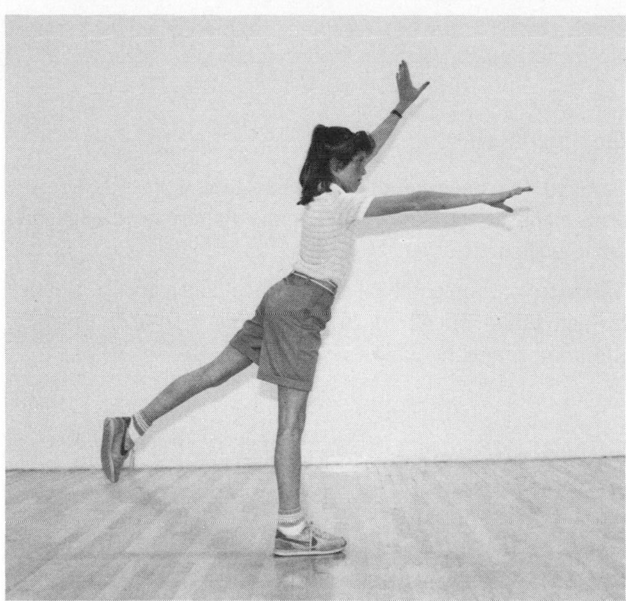

FIGURE 21.8. Arabesque

Chassé

The Chassé is a slide. This basic locomotor movement involves one leg chasing the other out of position. It is done close to the floor with a light spring in the step.

KINDERGARTEN AND FIRST-GRADE PROGRAM

The kindergarten and 1st-grade program consists primarily of imitative walks and movements, plus selected balance stunts and rolls. The Forward Roll is practiced, but its refinement is left to later grades. The Back Roller is practiced as a prelude to the Backward Roll.

The teacher should be concerned with the creative aspects of the activities as well as with performance standards. Children at this level tend to do stunts in different ways because of their different interpretations of what is required.

Directional concepts and a basic understanding of common movement terminology should have a prominent place in the instruction. The *why* of activity should be explained to the children.

Animal Movements

Alligator Crawl
Kangaroo Jump
Puppy Dog Run
  Cat Walk
  Monkey Run
Bear Walk
Gorilla Walk

Tumbling and Inverted Balances

Rolling Log
Side Roll
Forward Roll
Back Roller

Balance Stunts

One-Leg Balance
Double-Knee Balance
Head Touch
Head Balance
One-Legged Balance Stands
  Kimbo Stand
  Knee-Lift Stand
  Stork Stand

Individual Stunts

Directional Walk
Line Walking
Fluttering Leaf
Elevator
Cross-Legged Stand
Walking in Place
Jump Turns
Rubber Band
  Pumping Up the Balloon
Rising Sun
Heel Click

Partner and Group Stunts

Bouncing Ball
Seesaw
Wring the Dishrag

ANIMAL MOVEMENTS

Alligator Crawl

Lie facedown on the floor with elbows bent. Move along the floor in alligator fashion, keeping the hands close to the body and the feet pointed out (Figure 21.9). First, use unilateral movements, that is, right arm and leg moving together, then change to cross-lateral movements.

Kangaroo Jump

Carry the arms close to the chest with the palms facing forward. Place a beanbag or ball between the knees. Move in different directions by taking small jumps without dropping the object.

Puppy Dog Run

Place the hands on the floor, bending the arms and legs slightly. Walk and run like a happy puppy. Look straight ahead. Keeping the head up, in good position, strengthens

FIGURE 21.9. Alligator Crawl

the neck muscles (Figure 21.10). Go sideward, backward, and so on. Turn around in place.

Variations

1. *Cat Walk.* Use the same position to imitate a cat. Walk softly. Stretch at times like a cat. Be smooth and deliberate.

2. *Monkey Run.* Turn the hands and feet so the fingers and toes point in (toward each other).

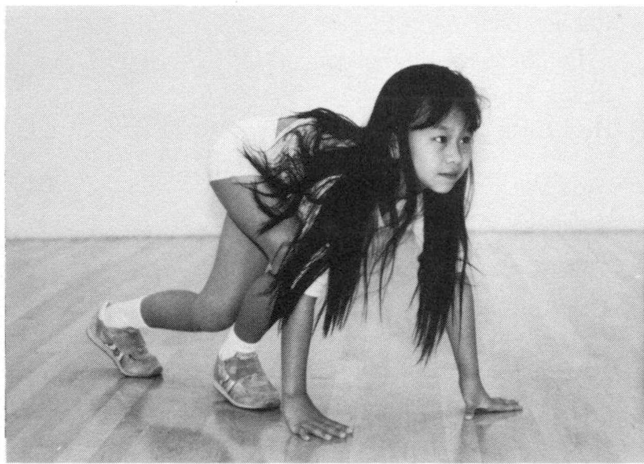

FIGURE 21.10. Puppy Dog Run

Bear Walk

Bend forward and touch the ground with both hands. Travel forward slowly by moving the hand and foot *on the same side* together (i.e., first the right hand and foot and then the left hand and foot) (Figure 21.11). Make deliberate movements.

FIGURE 21.11. Bear Walk

Variation: Lift the free foot and arm high while the support is on the other side.

Gorilla Walk

Bend the knees and carry the trunk forward. Let the arms hang at the sides. Touch the fingers to the ground while walking.

Variation: Stop and beat on the chest like a gorilla. Bounce up and down on all fours with hands and feet touching the floor simultaneously.

TUMBLING AND INVERTED BALANCES

Rolling Log

Lie on the back with arms stretched overhead (Figure 21.12). Roll sideways the length of the mat. The next time, roll with the hands pointed toward the other side of the mat. To roll in a straight line, keep the feet slightly apart.

Variation: Alternately curl and stretch while rolling.

Side Roll

Start on the hands and knees, with one side toward the direction of the roll. Drop the shoulder, tuck both the elbow and the knee under, and roll over completely, returning to the hands-and-knees position. Momentum is needed to return to the original position. Practice rolling back and forth from one hand-and-knee position to another.

Forward Roll

Stand facing forward, with the feet apart. Squat and place the hands on the mat, shoulder width apart, with elbows against the insides of the thighs. Tuck the chin to the chest and make a rounded back. A push-off with the hands and feet provides the force for the roll (Figure 21.13). Carry the weight on the hands, with the elbows bearing the weight of the thighs. If the elbows are kept against the thighs and the weight is assumed there, the force of the roll is transferred easily to the rounded back. Try to roll forward

FIGURE 21.12. Rolling Log

FIGURE 21.13. Forward Roll

to the feet. Later, try with the knees together and no weight on the elbows.

The spotter should kneel alongside the child and place one hand on the back of the child's head and the other under the thigh for a push, finishing with an upward lift on the back of the neck (Figure 21.14).

FIGURE 21.14. Spotting the Forward Roll (One hand is on the back of the head and one is under the thigh.)

Back Roller

Begin in a crouched position with knees together and hands resting lightly on the floor. Roll backward, securing momentum by bringing the knees to the chest and clasping them with the arms (Figure 21.15). Roll back and forth rhythmically. On the backward movement, go well back on the neck and head. Try to roll forward to original position.

FIGURE 21.15. Back Roller

If you have difficulty rolling back to original position, cross the legs and roll to a crossed-leg standing position. (This stunt is a lead-up to the Backward Roll.)

BALANCE STUNTS

One-Leg Balance

Lift one leg from the floor. Later, bring the knee up. The arms should be free at first and then assume specified positions—folded across the chest, on the hips, on the head, or behind the back.

Double-Knee Balance

Kneel on both knees, with the feet pointed to the rear. Lift the feet from the ground and balance on the knees. Vary the position of the arms. Experiment with different arm positions.

Head Touch

On a mat, kneel on both knees, with feet pointed backward and arms outstretched backward for balance. Lean forward slowly and touch the forehead to the mat. Recover to position (Figure 21.16). Vary the arm position.

Head Balance

Place a beanbag, block, or book on the head (Figure 21.17). Walk, stoop, turn around, sit down, get up, and so on. The object should be balanced so the upper body is in good posture. Keep the hands out to the sides for balance. Later, vary the position of the arms—folded across the chest or placed behind the back or down the sides. Link together a series of movements.

One-Legged Balance Stands

Each of the following stands should be done with different arm positions, starting with the arms out to the sides and then folded across the chest. Have the children devise other arm positions.

Each stunt can be held first for 3 seconds and then for 5 seconds. Later, the eyes can be closed during the count. The child should recover to original position without loss of balance or excessive movement. Stunts should be repeated, using the other leg.

FIGURE 21.16. Head Touch

FIGURE 21.17. Head Balance

1. *Kimbo Stand.* With left foot kept flat on the ground, cross the right leg over the left to a position in which the right foot is pointed partially down and the toe is touching the ground.

2. *Knee-Lift Balance.* From a standing position, lift one knee up so the thigh is parallel to the ground and the toe is pointed down. Hold. Return to starting position.

3. *Stork Stand.* From a standing position, shift all of the weight to one foot. Place the other foot so the sole is against the inside of the knee and thigh of the standing leg (Figure 21.18). Hold. Recover to standing position.

INDIVIDUAL STUNTS

Directional Walk

For a left movement, begin in standing position. Do all of the following simultaneously: take a step to the left, raise the left arm and point left, turn the head to the left, and state crisply "Left." Close with the right foot back to standing position. Take several steps left and then reverse.

FIGURE 21.18. Stork Stand

The Directional Walk is designed to aid in establishing right-left concepts. Definite and forceful simultaneous movements of the arm, head (turn), and leg (step) coupled with a crisp enunciation of the direction are the ingredients of this stunt.

Line Walking

Use a line on the floor, a chalked line, or a board. Walk forward and backward on the line as follows. First, take regular steps. Next, try follow steps, the front foot moving forward and the back foot moving up. The same foot always leads. Then do heel-and-toe steps, bringing the back toe up against the front heel on each step. Finally, hop along the line on one foot. Change to the other foot. The eyes should be focused ahead.

Fluttering Leaf

Keeping the feet in place and the body relaxed, flutter to the ground slowly, just as a leaf would do in autumn. Swing the arms back and forth loosely to accentuate the fluttering.

Elevator

With the arms out level at the sides, pretend to be an elevator going down. Lower the body a little at a time by bending the knees, but keep the upper body erect and the eyes forward. Return to position. Add a body twist to the downward movement. (A drum can be used.)

Cross-Legged Stand

Sit with the legs crossed and the body bent partially forward. Respond appropriately to these six commands.

"Touch the right foot with the right hand."
"Touch the left foot with the right hand."
"Touch the right foot with the left hand."
"Touch the left foot with the left hand."
"Touch both feet with the hands."
"Touch the feet with crossed hands."

The commands should be given in varied sequences. The child must interpret that his right foot is on the left side and vice versa. If this seems too difficult, have the children start with the feet in normal position (uncrossed).

Variation: Do the stunt with a partner, one child giving the commands and the other responding as directed.

Walking in Place

Pretend to walk vigorously by using the same movements as in walking but without making any progress. This is done by sliding the feet back and forth. Exaggerated arm movement should be made. (Children can gain or lose a little ground. Two children can walk alongside each other, with first one and then the other going ahead.)

Jump Turns

Do jump turns (use quarter turns and half turns) right and left, as directed. The arms should be kept outstretched to the sides. Land lightly without a second movement.

Jump turns reinforce directional concepts. Number concepts can also be developed with jump turns. The teacher calls out the number as a preparatory command and then says, "Move." Number signals are: "One" for a left quarter turn, "Two" for a right quarter turn, "Three" for a left half turn, and "Four" for a right half turn. Give the children a moment after the number is called and before the "Move" command.

Rubber Band

Get down in a squat position with the hands and arms clasped around the knees. On the command "Stretch, stretch, stretch," stretch as tall and as wide as possible. On the command "Snap," snap back to original position.

Variation: *Pumping Up the Balloon*—One child, the pumper, is in front of the other children, who are the balloons. The pumper pretends to use a bicycle pump to inflate the balloons. The balloons get larger and larger until the pumper shouts, "Bang," whereupon the balloons collapse to the floor. The pumper should give a "shoosh" sound every time a pumping motion is made.

Rising Sun

Lie on the back. Using the arms for balance only, rise to a standing position.

Variation: Fold the arms over the chest. Experiment with different positions of the feet. The feet can be crossed, spread wide, both to one side, and so on.

Heel Click

Stand with the feet slightly apart, jump up, and click the heels, coming down with the feet apart (Figure 21.19). Try with a quarter turn right and left.

Variations

1. Clap the hands overhead as the heels are clicked.

2. Join hands with one or more children. Count, "One, two, THREE," jumping on the third count.

3. Begin with a cross-step to the side, then click the heels. Try both right and left.

FIGURE 21.19. Heel Click

4. Try to click the heels twice before landing. Land with the feet apart.

PARTNER AND GROUP STUNTS

Bouncing Ball

Toss a *lively* utility ball into the air and watch how it bounces lower and lower until it finally comes to rest on the floor. From a bent-knee position with the upper body erect, imitate a ball by beginning with a high bounce and gradually lowering the height of the jump to simulate a ball coming to rest. Children should push off from the floor with the hands to gain additional height and should absorb part of the body weight with their hands as well. Toss a real ball into the air and move with the ball.

Variations: Try this with a partner, one partner serving as the bouncer and the other as the ball (Figure 21.20). Reverse positions. Try having one partner dribble the ball in various positions.

FIGURE 21.20. Bouncing Ball

Seesaw

Face and join hands with a partner. Move the seesaw up and down, one child stooping while the other rises. Recite the words to this version of "Seesaw, Margery Daw."

Seesaw, Margery Daw,
Maw and Paw, like a saw,
Seesaw, Margery Daw.

Variation: Jump upward at the end of the rise each time.

Wring the Dishrag

Face and join hands with a partner. Raise one pair of arms (right for one and left for the other) and turn under, continuing a full turn until back to original position (Figure 21.21). Take care not to bump heads. Reverse.

Variation: Try the stunt at a lower level, using a crouched position.

SECOND-GRADE PROGRAM

The 2nd-grade program should start with a review of the kindergarten and 1st-grade stunts. The Forward Roll from the straddle position should be practiced. The Backward Curl and the handclasped version of the Backward Roll are significant inclusions at this grade level. Additional stunts expand the opportunities for practicing balance.

Children of this age-group are amenable to coaching, compared with those of the previous level, and some attention can be given to performance factors.

Animal and Character Movements

Rabbit Jump
Elephant Walk
Siamese Twin Walk
Tightrope Walk
Lame Dog Walk
Crab Walk

FIGURE 21.21. Wring the Dishrag

Tumbling and Inverted Balances

Forward Roll (straddle position)
Backward Curl
Backward Roll (handclasp position)
Climb-up
Three-Point Tip-up
Mountain Climber (handstand lead-up activity)
Switcheroo (handstand lead-up activity)

Balance Stunts

Balance Touch
Single-Leg Balances
- Forward Balance
- Backward Balance
- Side Balance

Hand-and-Knee Balance
Single-Knee Balance

Individual Stunts

Lowering the Boom
Turn-Over
Thread the Needle
Heel Slap
Pogo Stick
Top
Turk Stand
Push-up
Crazy Walk
Seat Circle

Partner and Group Stunts

Partner Toe Toucher
Double Top
Roly Poly

ANIMAL AND CHARACTER MOVEMENTS

Rabbit Jump

Crouch with knees apart and hands placed on the floor. Move forward by reaching out with both hands and then bringing both feet up to the hands. The eyes look ahead.

The teacher should emphasize that this is a jump rather than a hop because both feet move at once. Note that the jump is a bilateral movement.

Variations

1. Try with knees together and arms on the outside. Try alternating with knees together and apart on successive jumps. Go over a low hurdle or through a hoop.

2. Experiment with taking considerable weight on the

hands before the feet move forward. To do this, raise the seat higher in the air when the hands move forward.

Elephant Walk

Bend well forward, clasping the hands together to form a trunk. The end of the trunk should swing close to the ground. Walk in a slow, deliberate, dignified manner, keeping the legs straight and swinging the trunk from side to side (Figure 21.22). Stop and throw water over the back with the trunk. Recite the following verse while walking, and move the trunk appropriately.

The elephant's walk is steady and slow,
His trunk like a pendulum swings to and fro.
But when there are children with peanuts around
He swings it up and he swings it down.

Variation: With a partner, decide who will be the mahout (the elephant keeper) and who will be the elephant. The mahout walks to the side and a little in front of the elephant, with one hand touching the elephant's shoulder. Lead the elephant around during the first two lines of the poem, and then during the last two lines release the touch, walk to a spot in front of the elephant, and toss the elephant a peanut when the trunk is swept up. Return to the elephant's side and repeat the action.

Siamese Twin Walk

Stand back to back with a partner. Lock elbows (Figure 21.23). Walk forward, backward, and sideward in unison.

Tightrope Walk

Select a line, board, or chalked line on the floor as the high wire. Pretend to be on the high wire, and do various tasks with exaggerated loss and control of balance. Add tasks such as jumping rope, juggling balls, and riding a bicycle. Pretend to hold a parasol or a balancing pole while performing.

Children should give good play to the imagination. The teacher can set the stage by discussing what a circus performer on the high wire might do.

FIGURE 21.22. Elephant Walk

FIGURE 21.23. Siamese Twin Walk

Lame Dog Walk

Walk on both hands and one foot. Hold the other foot in the air as if injured. Walk a distance and change feet. The eyes should look forward. Move backward also and in other combinations. Try to move with an injured front leg.

Crab Walk

Squat down and reach back, putting both hands on the floor without sitting down. With head, neck, and body level, walk forward, backward, and sideward (Figure 21.24).

Children have a tendency to lower the hips. The teacher should emphasize that the body is kept in a straight line.

Variations

1. As each step is taken with one hand, slap the chest or seat with the other.

2. Move the hand and foot on the same side simultaneously.

3. Try balancing on one leg and the opposite hand for 5 seconds.

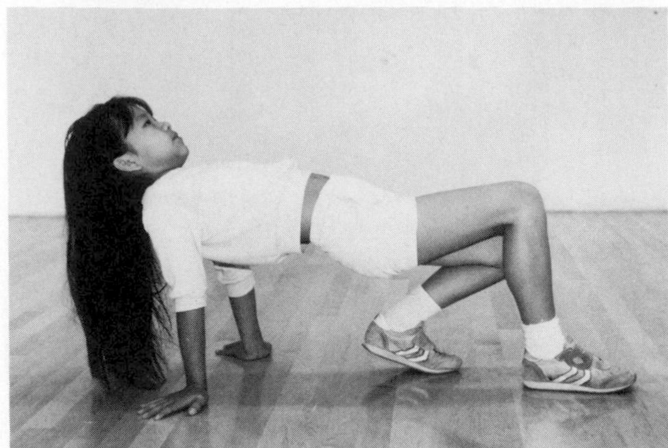

FIGURE 21.24. Crab Walk

TUMBLING AND INVERTED BALANCES

Forward Roll (Straddle Position)

Start with the legs spread in the straddle position. Bend forward at the hips, tuck the head, place the hands on the mat, and roll forward. A strong push with the hands at the end of the roll is necessary to return to the standing position.

Forward Roll Practice

Review the Forward Roll (tucked), with spotting and assistance as necessary. Work on coming out of the roll to the feet. Grasping the knees at the end of the roll is of help.

Variations

1. Roll to the feet with ankles crossed.
2. Try to roll with knees together.

Backward Curl

Approach this stunt in three stages. For the first stage, begin in a sitting position, with the knees drawn up to the chest and the chin tucked down. The arms are placed out to the sides as the shoulders make contact with the mat. Roll backward until the weight is on the shoulders (Figure 21.25). The feet and legs come back over the head so the toes touch the mat. Roll back to starting position.

Now, for stage two, perform the same action as before, but place the hands alongside the head on the mat while rolling back. The fingers are pointed in the direction of the roll, with palms down on the mat. (A good cue is "Point your thumbs toward your ears and keep your elbows reasonably close to your body.")

Finally, for stage three, perform the same action as in stage two, but start in a crouched position on the feet, as in a deep-knee bend, with the back toward the direction of the roll. Momentum is secured by sitting down quickly and bringing the knees to the chest.

FIGURE 21.25. Backward Curl

This, like the Back Roller, is a lead-up to the Backward Roll. The hand pressure is important. Teach the children to push hard against the floor to take the pressure off the back of the neck.

Variations

1. Touch the knees behind the head instead of the toes.
2. Keep a beanbag between the feet and deposit it behind the head, returning to position. Next, curl back and pick up the beanbag, returning it to original position.
3. Sit with legs crossed and hands grasping the feet. Roll backward, touching the floor overhead with the feet. Return to position. (This is a more difficult Backward Curl, which only a few children may be able to do.)

Backward Roll (Handclasp Position)

Clasp the fingers behind the neck, with elbows held out to the sides (Figure 21.26). From a crouched position, sit down rapidly, bringing the knees to the chest for a tuck to secure momentum. Roll completely over backward, taking much of the weight on the forearms (Figure 21.27). In this method, the neck is protected.

Teachers can have early success in teaching the backward roll by beginning with this approach. Children should be reminded to keep their elbows back and out to the sides to ensure maximum support and minimal neck pressure.

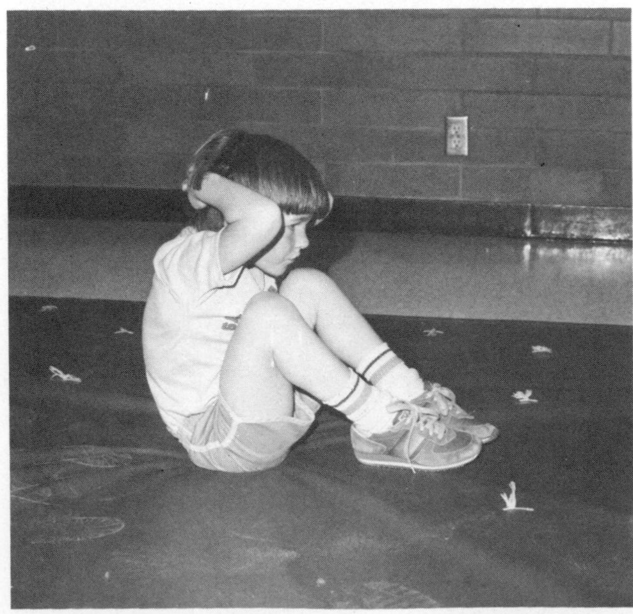

FIGURE 21.26. Handclasp Position

FIGURE 21.27. Backward Roll

Climb-up

Begin on a mat in a kneeling position, with hands placed about shoulder width apart and the fingers spread and pointed forward. Place the head forward of the hands, so the head and hands form a triangle on the mat. Walk the body weight forward so most of it rests on the hands and head. Climb the knees to the top of the elbows. (This stunt is a lead-up to the Headstand.)

In the Climb-up as well as in the Three-Point Tip-up, overweight or weak children may need spotting. This is done by placing one hand on the child's shoulder and the other on the back of the thigh.

Variation: Raise the knees off the elbows.

Three-Point Tip-up

Squat down on the mat, placing the hands flat, with fingers pointing forward. The elbows should be inside and pressed against the inner part of the lower thighs. Lean forward, slowly transferring the body weight to the bent elbows and hands until the forehead touches the mat (Figure 21.28). Return to starting position.

The Three-Point Tip-up ends in the same general position as the Climb-up, but with the elbows on the inside of the thighs. Some children may have better success by turning the fingers in slightly, thus causing the elbows to point outward more and offering better support at the thigh contact point. This stunt is a lead-up to the Headstand and the Handstand done at later levels.

Variation: Tuck the head and do a Forward Roll as an alternate finishing act.

Mountain Climber

This activity is similar to the exercise known as the Treadmill. The weight is taken on the hands with one foot forward and one foot extended back, similar to a sprinter's start. When ready, the performer switches foot position with both feet moving simultaneously. This activity is a lead-up to the Handstand and teaches children to support the body weight briefly with the arms.

FIGURE 21.28. Three-Point Tip-up

Switcheroo

This Handstand lead-up activity begins in the front lunge position with the arms overhead. In one continuous movement, bend forward at the hips, place the hands on the mat, and invert the legs over the head. Scissor the legs in the air, and then reverse the position of the feet on the mat. Repeat in a smooth and continuous motion.

BALANCE STUNTS

Balance Touch

Place an object (eraser, block, or beanbag) a yard away from a line. Balancing on one foot, reach out with the other foot, touch the object (no weight should be placed on it) (Figure 21.29), and recover to the starting position. Reach sideward, backward.

Variation: Try placing the object at various distances. On a gymnasium floor, count the number of boards to establish the distance for the touch.

Single-Leg Balances

1. *Forward Balance.* Extend one leg backward until it is parallel to the floor. Keeping the eyes forward and the arms out to the sides, bend forward, balancing on the other leg (Figure 21.30). Hold for 5 seconds without moving. Reverse legs. (This is also called a Forward Scale.)

FIGURE 21.29. Balance Touch

FIGURE 21.30. Forward Balance

2. *Backward Balance.* With knee straight, extend one leg forward, with toes pointed. Keep the arms out to the sides for balance. Lean back as far as possible. The bend should be far enough back so the eyes are looking at the ceiling.

3. *Side Balance.* Stand on the left foot with enough side bend to the left so the right (top) side of the body is parallel to the floor. Put the right arm alongside the head and in line with the rest of the body. Reverse, using the right leg for support. (Support may be needed momentarily to get into position.)

Hand-and-Knee Balance

Get down on all fours, taking the weight on the hands, knees, and feet, with toes pointed backward. Lift one hand and the opposite knee (Figure 21.31). Keep the free foot and hand from touching during the hold. Reverse hand and knee positions.

FIGURE 21.31. Hand-and-Knee Balance

Single-Knee Balance

Perform the same action as in the previous stunt, but balance on one knee (and leg), with both arms outstretched to the sides (Figure 21.32). Use the other knee.

INDIVIDUAL STUNTS

Lowering the Boom

Start in push-up (front-leaning rest) position. Lower the body slowly to the floor. The movement should be controlled so the body remains rigid.

Variations

1. Pause halfway down.
2. Go down in stages, inch by inch. (Be sure that the children understand the concept of an inch as a measure of distance.)
3. Go down slowly to the accompaniment of noise simulating air escaping from a punctured tire. Try representing a blowout, initiated by an appropriate noise.
4. Go down in stages by alternating lowering movements of the right and left arm.
5. Vary the stunt with different hand-base positions, such as fingers pointed in, thumbs touching, and others.

Turn-Over

From a front-leaning rest position, turn over so the back is to the floor. The body should not touch the floor. Continue the turn until the original position is reassumed. Reverse the direction. Turn back and forth several times. The body should be kept as rigid as possible throughout the turn.

Thread the Needle

Touch the fingertips together in front of the body. Step through with one foot at a time while keeping the tips in contact (Figure 21.33). Step back to original position. Next, lock the fingers in front of the body, and repeat the stunt. Finally, step through the clasped hands without touching the hands.

FIGURE 21.32. Single-Knee Balance

FIGURE 21.33. Thread the Needle

Heel Slap

From an erect position with hands at the sides, jump upward and slap both heels with the hands (Figure 21.34).

Variation: Use a one-two-three rhythm with small preliminary jumps on the first and second counts. Make a quarter or half turn in the air. During a jump, slap the heels twice before landing.

Pogo Stick

Pretend to be on a pogo stick by keeping a stiff body and jumping on the toes. Hold the hands in front as if grasping the stick (Figure 21.35). Progress in various directions. (The teacher should stress upward propelling action by the ankles and toes, with the body kept stiff, particularly at the knee joints.)

FIGURE 21.34. Heel Slap

FIGURE 21.35. Pogo Stick

Top

From a standing position with arms at the sides, try jumping and turning to face the opposite direction, turning three quarters of the way around, or making a full turn to face the original direction. Land in good balance with hands near the sides. No movement of the feet should occur after landing. Turn both right and left. (Number concepts can be stressed in having the children do half turns, three-quarter turns, and full turns.)

Variation: Fold the arms across the chest.

Turk Stand

Stand with feet apart and arms folded in front. Pivot on the balls of *both* feet, and face the opposite direction. The legs are now crossed. Sit down in this position. Reverse the process. Get up without using the hands for aid, and uncross the legs with a pivot to face in the original direction. Little change should occur in foot position (Figure 21.36).

FIGURE 21.36. Turk Stand

Push-up

From a front-leaning rest position, lower the body and push up, back to original position. Be sure that the only movement is in the arms, with the body kept rigid. (Since the Push-up is used in many exercises and testing programs, it is important for the children to learn proper execution early.)

Variation: Stop halfway down and halfway up. Go up and down by inches.

Crazy Walk

Progress forward in an erect position by bringing one foot behind *and around* the other to gain a little ground each time (Figure 21.37). (The teacher can set a specified distance and see which children cover the distance in the fewest steps.)

Variation: Reverse the movements and go backward. This means bringing the foot in front and around to gain distance in back.

Seat Circle

Sit on the floor, with knees bent and hands braced behind. Lift the feet off the floor and push with the hands, so the body spins in a circle with the seat as a pivot (Figure 21.38). Spin right and left.

Variation: Place a beanbag between the knees or on the toes and spin without dropping it.

FIGURE 21.37. Crazy Walk

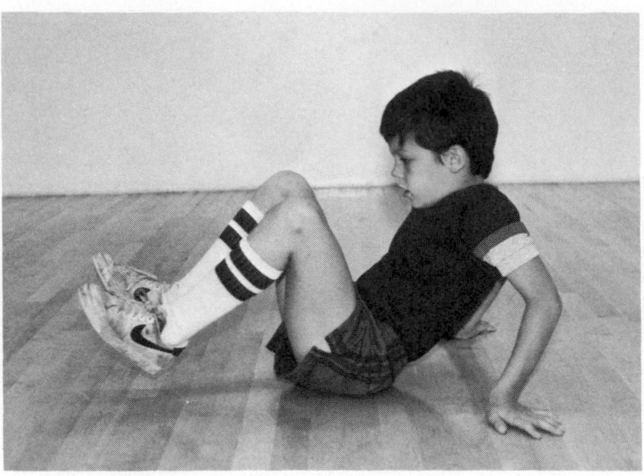

FIGURE 21.38. Seat Circle

PARTNER AND GROUP STUNTS

Partner Toe Toucher

Partners lie on their backs with heads near each other and feet in opposite directions. Join arms with partner using a hand-wrist grip, and bring the legs up so the toes touch partner's toes. Keep high on the shoulders and touch the feet high (Figure 21.39). Strive to attain the high shoulder position, since this is the point of most difficulty. (Partners should be of about the same height.)

Variation: One partner carries a beanbag, a ball, or some other article between the feet. She transfers the object to her partner, who lowers it to the floor.

Double Top

Face partner and join hands. Experiment to see which type of grip works best. With straight arms, lean away from each other and at the same time move the toes close to partner's (Figure 21.40). Spin around slowly in either direction, taking tiny steps. Increase speed.

FIGURE 21.39. Partner Toe Toucher

FIGURE 21.40. Double Top

Variations

1. Use a stooped position.
2. Instead of holding hands, hold a wand and increase the body lean backward. Try the stunt standing right side to right side.

Roly Poly

Review the Rolling Log. Four or five children lie facedown on the floor, side by side. The last child does a Rolling Log over the others and then takes a place at the end. Continue until all have rolled twice.

THIRD-GRADE PROGRAM

In the 3rd grade, more emphasis can be placed on form and quality of performance than at previous levels. More partner and group stunts are included in the program. The Headstand and Cartwheel are important additions to the tumbling area. Stunts such as the Frog Handstand, Mule Kick, and Half Teeter-Totter give children experience in taking the weight totally on the hands.

Animal Movements

Cricket Walk
Seal Crawl
  Reverse Seal Crawl
  Elbow Crawl
Frog Jump
Measuring Worm
Walrus Walk
Mule Kick

Tumbling and Inverted Balances

Forward Roll to a Walkout
Backward Roll (inclined)
Backward Roll (regular)
Headstand
Frog Handstand (Tip-up)
Half Teeter-Totter (handstand lead-up)
Cartwheel

Balance Stunts

One-Leg Balance Reverse
Tummy Balance
Knee Dip

Individual Stunts

Reach-Under
Stiff Person Bend
Coffee Grinder
Curl-up
Scooter
Hip Walk
Long Bridge
Heelstand
Wicket Walk

Partner and Group Stunts

Partner Hopping
Partner Twister
Partner Pull-up
Chinese Get-up
Rowboat

ANIMAL MOVEMENTS

Cricket Walk

Squat. Spread the knees. Put the arms between the knees, and grasp the outside of the ankles with the hands. Walk forward or backward. Chirp like a cricket. Turn around right and left. See what happens when both feet are moved at once!

Seal Crawl

Start in the front-leaning rest position, the weight supported on straightened arms and toes. Keeping the body straight, walk forward, using the hands for propelling force and dragging the feet (Figure 21.41). Keep the body straight and the head up.

Variations

1. Crawl forward a short distance and then roll over on the back, clapping the hands like a seal, with appropriate seal barks.
2. Crawl with the fingers pointed in different directions, out and in.
3. *Reverse Seal Crawl.* Turn over and attempt the crawl dragging the heels.
4. *Elbow Crawl.* Assume the original position but with weight on the elbows. Crawl forward on the elbows (Figure 21.42).

FIGURE 21.41. Seal Crawl

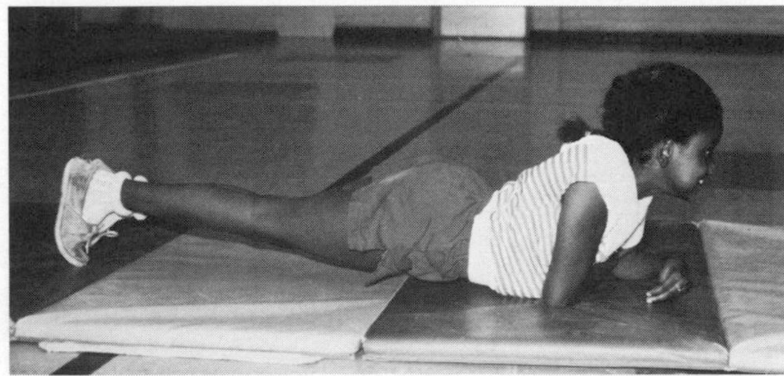

FIGURE 21.42. Elbow Crawl

5. Use the crossed-arm position for a more challenging stunt.

Frog Jump

From a squatting position, with hands on the floor slightly in front of the feet, jump forward a short distance, landing on the hands and feet simultaneously (Figure 21.43). Note the difference between this stunt and the Rabbit Jump. Emphasis eventually should be on both height and distance. The hands and arms absorb part of the landing impact to prevent excessive strain on the knees.

Measuring Worm

From a front-leaning rest position, keeping the knees stiff, inch the feet up as close as possible to the hands.

FIGURE 21.43. Frog Jump

FIGURE 21.44. Measuriing Worm

Regain position by inching forward with the hands. Keep the knees straight, with the necessary bending occurring at the hips (Figure 21.44).

Walrus Walk

Begin in a front-leaning rest position, with fingers pointed outward. Make progress by moving both hands forward at the same time (Figure 21.45). Try to clap the hands with each step. (Before doing this stunt, review the similar Seal Crawl and its variations.)

Variation: Move sideways so the upper part of the body describes an arc while the feet hold position.

FIGURE 21.45. Walrus Walk

Mule Kick

Stoop down and place the hands on the floor in front of the feet. The arms are the front legs of the mule. Kick out with the legs while the weight is supported momentarily on the arms (Figure 21.46). Taking the weight on the hands is important. The stunt can be learned in two stages. First, practice taking the weight momentarily on the hands. Next, add the kick.

FIGURE 21.46. Mule Kick

Variation: Make two kicks before the feet return to the ground.

TUMBLING AND INVERTED BALANCES

Forward Roll to a Walkout

Perform the forward roll as described previously, except walk out to a standing position. The key to the Walkout is to develop enough momentum to allow a return to the feet. The leg that first absorbs the weight is bent while the other leg is kept straight.

Backward Roll (Inclined)

If possible, the Handclasp Backward Roll should be practiced on an inclined mat. The gentle incline allows the youngster to learn to develop momentum in a nonthreatening manner. An inclined mat can be made by leaving one mat folded and laying a crash pad or another mat over it.

Backward Roll (Regular)

In the same squat position as for the Forward Roll, but with the back to the direction of the roll, push off quickly with the hands, sit down, and start rolling over on the back. The knees should be brought to the chest, so the body is tucked and momentum is increased. Quickly bring the hands up over the shoulders, with palms up and fingers pointed backward. Continue rolling backward with knees close to the chest. The hands touch the mat at about the same time as the head. It is vitally important at this point to push hard with the hands to release pressure on the neck. Continue to roll over the top of the head and to push off the mat until the roll is completed (Figure 21.47).

Proper hand position can be emphasized by telling the children to point their thumbs toward their ears and to spread their fingers for better push-off control.

In spotting, care must be taken never to push a child from the hip, thus forcing the roll. This puts undue pressure on the back of the neck. The proper way to aid the child who has difficulty with the stunt is as follows: The spotter stands in a straddle position, with the near foot alongside the spot where the performer's hands and head will make contact with the mat (Figure 21.48). The other foot is one stride in the direction of the roll. The critical point is for the spotter to lift the hips just as the head and hands of the performer make contact with the mat. This is accomplished by taking the back hand and reaching across to the far hip of the performer, getting under the near hip with the near hand. The lift is applied on the front of the hips just below the beltline. The object is to relieve the pressure on the neck.

FIGURE 21.47. Regular Backward Roll

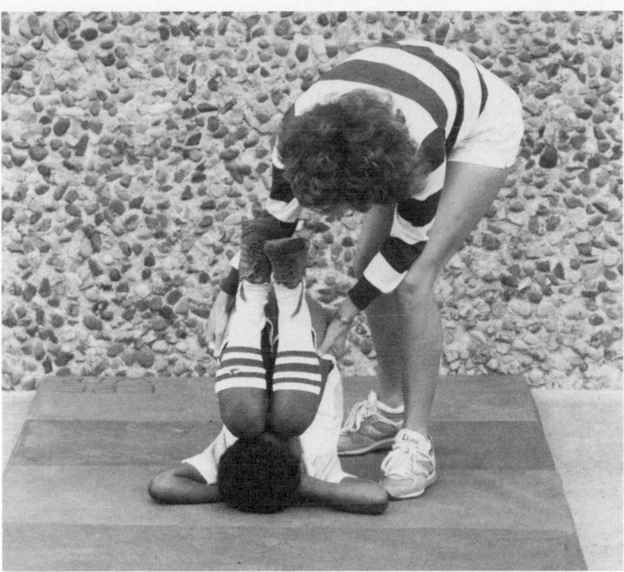

FIGURE 21.48. Spotting the Backward Roll (The lift is at the hips of the roller. The performer should be lifted, not forced, over.)

Rather than spotting the youngster who is having trouble doing the Backward Roll, it may be wise to return to the Handclasp Backward Roll and to practice on an inclined mat.

Headstand

Two approaches are suggested for the Headstand. The first is to relate the Headstand to the Climb-up, and the second is to go directly into a Headstand, using a kick-up to achieve the inverted position. With either method, maintaining the triangle position of the hands and the head is essential.

In the final inverted position, the feet should be together, with legs straight and toes pointed. The weight is evenly distributed among the three points—the two hands and the forward part of the head. The body should be aligned as straight as possible.

The safest way to come down from the inverted position is to return to the mat in the direction that was used in going up. Recovery is helped by bending at both the waist and the knees. The child should be instructed, in the case of overbalancing, to tuck the head under and go into a Forward Roll. Both methods of recovery from the inverted position should be included in the instructional sequences early in the presentation.

FIGURE 21.49. Headstand based on the Climb-up

Headstand Based on the Climb-up

Take the inverted position of the Climb-up (p. 371) and move the feet slowly upward to the headstand position (Figure 21.49), steadied by a spotter only as needed.

The spotter is stationed directly in front of the performer and steadies her as needed. The spotter can first apply support to the hips and then transfer to the ankles as the climb-up position is lengthened into a Headstand. If the spotter cannot control the performer, he must be alert to moving out of the way when the performer goes into a Forward Roll to come out of the inverted position.

Headstand Based on the Kick-up

Keeping the weight on the forward part of the head and maintaining the triangle base, walk the feet forward until the hips are high over the body, somewhat similar to the climb-up position. Keep one foot on the mat, with the knee of that leg bent, and the other leg extended somewhat backward. Kick the back leg up to the inverted position, following quickly with a push by the other leg, thus bringing the two legs together in the inverted position (Figure 21.50). The timing is a quick one-two movement.

When learning, children should work in units of three. One child attempts the stunt with a spotter on each side. Positions are rotated. Each spotter kneels, placing the near hand under the shoulder of the performer. The performer then walks the weight above the head and kicks up to

FIGURE 21.50. Headstand based on the Kick-up

FIGURE 21.51. Spotting the Headstand

position. The spotter on each side supports by grasping a leg (Figure 21.51).

The teacher should emphasize the importance of the triangle formed by the hands and the head and the importance of having the weight centered on the forward part of the head. Most problems that occur during performance of the Headstand come from an incorrect head-hand relationship. The correct positioning has the head placed the length of the performer's forearm from the knees and the hands placed at the knees. A useful technique to aid children in finding the proper triangle is to mark the three spots on the mat with chalk (more lasting spots can be made with paint).

It is not desirable to let children stay too long in the inverted position or to hold contests to see who can remain in the Headstand longest. Most of the responsibility for getting into the inverted position should rest with the performer. Spotters may help some, but they should avoid wrestling the performer up. The goal of the kick-up method is to establish a pattern that can be used in other inverted stunts.

Frog Handstand (Tip-up)

Squat down on the mat, placing the hands flat, with fingers pointing forward and elbows inside and pressed against the inner part of the knees. Lean forward, using the leverage of the elbows against the knees, and balance on the hands (Figure 21.52). Hold for 5 seconds. Return to position. The head does not touch the mat at any time. The hands may be turned in slightly if this makes better contact between the elbows and the insides of the thighs. (This stunt follows from the Three-Point Tip-up.)

Half Teeter-Totter

This is continued lead-up activity for the Handstand. Begin in the Lunge Position and shift the weight to the

FIGURE 21.52. Frog Handstand

hands. Kick the legs up in the air to a 135-degree angle, then return to the feet. This activity is similar to the Switcheroo, except the feet are kicked higher without switching foot position.

Cartwheel

Start with the body in an erect position, arms outspread and legs shoulder width apart. Bend the body to the right and place the right hand on the floor. Follow this, in sequence, by the left hand, the left foot, and the right foot (Figure 21.53). Perform with a steady rhythm. Each body part should touch the floor at evenly spaced intervals. The body should be straight and extended when in the inverted position. The entire body must be in the same plane throughout the stunt, and the feet must pass directly overhead.

Children who have difficulty with the Cartwheel should be instructed to concentrate on taking the weight of the body on the hands in succession. They need to get the feel of the weight support and later can concentrate on getting the body into proper position. After the class has had some practice in doing Cartwheels, a running approach with a skip can be added before takeoff.

In spotting, the spotter stands behind the performer and moves with her. To assist, the spotter assumes a crossed-arm position and grasps the performer at the waist. The spotter's arms uncross as the performer wheels.

FIGURE 21.53. Cartwheel

FIGURE 21.54. One-Leg Balance Reverse

BALANCE STUNTS

One-Leg Balance Reverse

Assume a forward balance position (p. 371). In a quick movement, to give momentum, swing the free leg down and change to the same forward balance position facing in the *opposite* direction (a 180-degree turn) (Figure 21.54). No unnecessary movement of the supporting foot should be made after the turn is completed. The swinging foot should not touch the floor.

Tummy Balance

Lie prone on the floor with arms outstretched forward or to the sides and palms down. Raise the arms, head, chest, and legs from the floor and balance on the tummy (Figure 21.55). The knees should be kept straight.

Knee Dip

Grasp the right instep behind the back with the left hand while balancing on the left foot. Using the other arm for balance, lower and touch the floor with the bent knee. Regain balance (Figure 21.56). Try with the other leg.

During the learning stages, the teacher can place a book under the knee being lowered, thus making the stunt easier. If the student has difficulty, another child can support from

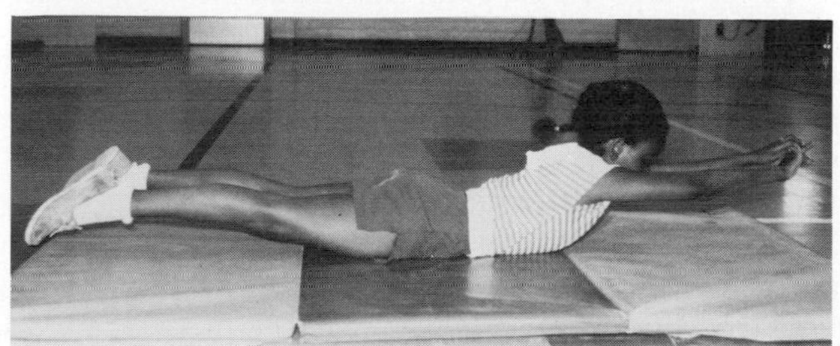

FIGURE 21.55. Tummy Balance

FIGURE 21.56. Knee Dip

behind. This activity should be done on a tumbling mat to protect the knee.

Variation: Hold the right foot with the right hand, and vice versa.

FIGURE 21.57. Stiff Person Bend

INDIVIDUAL STUNTS

Reach-Under

Take a position with the feet pointed ahead (spaced about 2 ft apart) and toes against a line or a floor board. Place a beanbag two boards in front of, and midway between, the feet. Without changing the position of the feet, reach one hand behind and between the legs to pick up the beanbag. Now pick up with the other hand. Repeat, moving the beanbag a board farther away each time.

Variation: Allow the heels to lift off the floor. Use the other hand.

Stiff Person Bend

Place the feet about shoulder width apart and pointed forward. Place a beanbag 6 in. behind the left heel. Grasp the right toe with the right hand, thumb on top. Without bending the knees, reach the left hand outside the left leg and pick up the beanbag without releasing the hold on the right toe. Gradually increase the distance of the reach. Reverse sides (Figure 21.57).

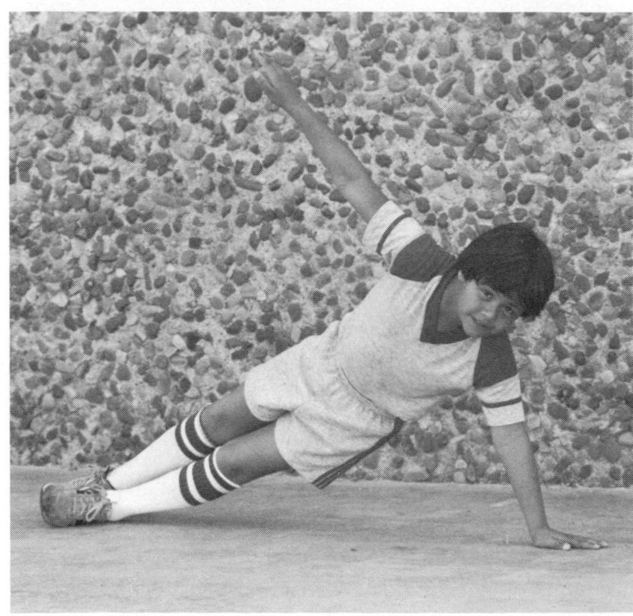

FIGURE 21.58. Coffee Grinder

Coffee Grinder

Put one hand on the floor, and extend the body to the floor on that side in a side-leaning rest position. Walk around the hand, making a complete circle and keeping the body straight (Figure 21.58). The stunt should be done slowly, with controlled movements. The body should remain straight throughout the circle movement.

Curl-up

Two children work together, with one child holding the other's feet. The performer lies on the back with knees up, forming an angle of 90 degrees at the knee joint. The feet are flat (soles down) on the floor. The hands, with fingers interlaced, are behind the lower part of the head. Curl up, alternately touching the right and left elbow to the opposite knee. One touch is made on each Curl-up.

Students should be encouraged to find different ways to perform the Curl-up to make it more challenging. The teacher should make sure that the child returns the head completely to the floor each time.

Scooter

Sit on the floor with legs extended, arms folded in front of the chest, and chin held high. To scoot, pull the seat

FIGURE 21.59. Scooter

toward the heels, using heel pressure and lifting the seat slightly (Figure 21.59). Extend the legs forward again and repeat the process. (This is an excellent activity for abdominal development.)

Hip Walk

Sit in the same position as for the Scooter, but with arms in thrust position and hands making a partial fist. Progress forward by alternate leg-seat movements. The arm-leg coordination is unilateral.

Long Bridge

Begin in a crouched position with hands on the floor and knees between the arms. Push the hands forward a little at a time until an extended push-up position is reached (Figure 21.60). Return to original position. (The teacher should challenge children to extend as far forward as they can and still retain the support.)

FIGURE 21.60. Long Bridge

Variations

1. Begin with a forward movement and then change to a sideward movement, establishing as wide a spread as possible.
2. Work from a crossed-hands position.

Heelstand

Begin in a full squat position with the arms dangling at the sides. Jump upward to full leg extension with the weight on both heels and fling the arms out diagonally. Hold momentarily, then return to position (Figure 21.61). Several movements can be done rhythmically in succession.

Wicket Walk

Bend over and touch the floor with the weight *evenly* distributed on the hands and feet, thus forming a wicket. Walk the wicket forward, backward, and sideward. Keep the arms and legs as nearly vertical as possible (Figure 21.62). Be sure the knees are reasonably straight, for the stunt loses much of its flexibility value if the knees are bent too much. A common error in the execution of this stunt is to keep the hands positioned too far forward of the feet. (The stunt gets its name from the child's position, which resembles a wicket in a croquet game.)

FIGURE 21.61. Heelstand

PARTNER AND GROUP STUNTS

Partner Hopping

Partners coordinate hopping movements for short distances and in different directions and turns. Three combinations are suggested.

1. Stand facing each other. Extend the right leg forward to be grasped at the ankle by partner's left hand. Hold right hands and hop on the left leg (Figure 21.63).
2. Stand back to back. Lift the leg backward, bending

FIGURE 21.62. Wicket Walk

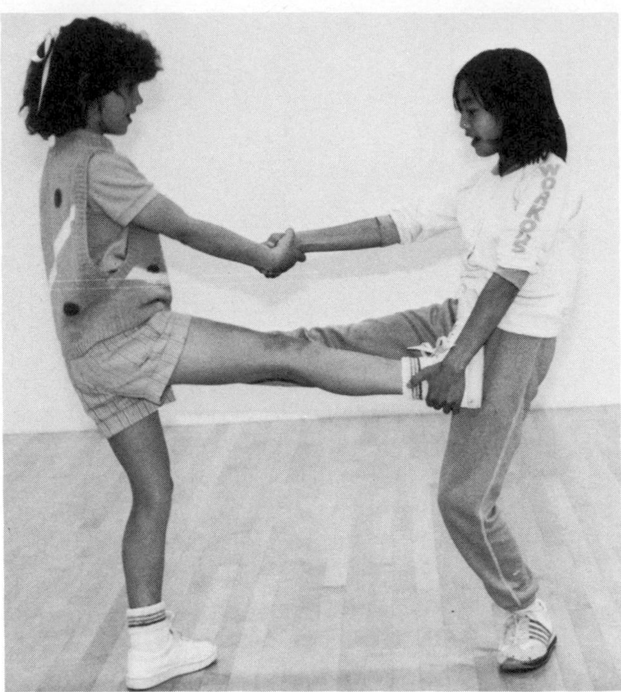

FIGURE 21.63. Partner Hopping

the knee, and have partner grasp the ankle. Hop as before.

3. Stand side by side with inside arms around each other's waist. Lift the inside foot from the floor, and make progress by hopping on the outside foot.

If either partner begins to fall, the other should release the leg immediately. Reverse foot positions.

Partner Twister

Partners face and grasp right hands as if shaking hands. One partner swings the left leg over the head of the other and turns around, taking a straddle position over his partner's arm (Figure 21.64). The other swings his right leg over the first, who has bent over, and the partners are now back to back. First partner continues with the right leg and faces in the original direction. Second partner swings his left leg over the partner's back to return to the original face-to-face position. Partners need to duck to avoid being kicked by each other's feet as the legs are swung over.

Variation: The stunt can be introduced by grasping a wand instead of holding hands.

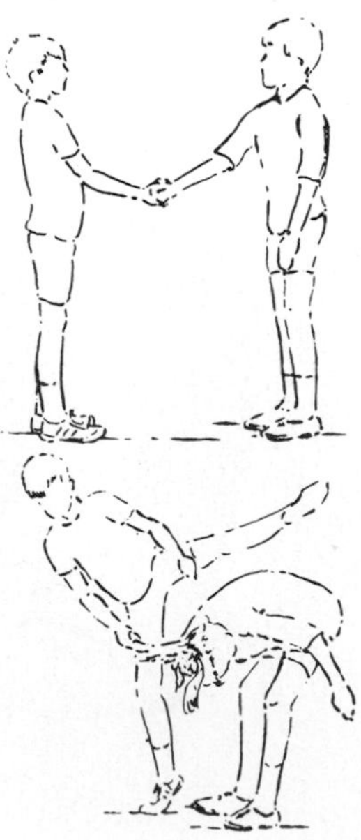

FIGURE 21.64. Partner Twister

Partner Pull-up

Partners sit facing each other in a bent-knee position, with heels on the floor and toes touching. Pulling cooperatively, they come to a standing position (Figure 21.65).

Variation: Try with feet flat on the floor.

FIGURE 21.65. Partner Pull-up

Chinese Get-up

Partners sit back to back and lock arms. From this position, they try to stand by pushing against each other's backs (Figure 21.66). Sit down again. If the feet are sliding, do the stunt on a mat.

Variations

1. Try with three or four children.

2. Try from a halfway-down position, and move like a spider.

Rowboat

Partners sit on the floor or on a mat, facing each other with legs apart and feet touching. Both grasp a wand with

FIGURE 21.66. Chinese Get-up

both hands. Pretend to row a boat. Seek a wide range of movement in the forward-backward rowing motion. (The stunt can be done without a wand by having the children grasp hands.)

FOURTH-GRADE PROGRAM

The 4th-grade program continues the emphasis on the Forward Roll and the Backward Roll with variations and combinations. The Teeter-Totter and Handstand are presented as students begin to become proficient in inverted balancing. Partner support stunts are introduced. Flops or falls are another addition. At this level, teachers should place more emphasis on form and dressing up the stunt.

Animal Movements

Double-Lame Dog
Turtle
Walrus Slap
  Reverse Walrus Walk

Tumbling and Inverted Balances

Forward Roll (pike position)
Forward Roll Combinations
Backward Roll Combinations
Headstand Practice and Variations
Teeter-Totter
Handstand

Balance Stunts

Leg Dip
Balance Jump
Seat Balance
Face-to-Knee Touch
Finger Touch

Individual Stunts

Knee Jump to Standing
Individual Drops
  Knee Drop
  Forward Drop
  Dead Body Fall
Stoop and Stretch
Tanglefoot
Egg Roll
Toe Touch Nose
Toe Tug Walk

Partner and Group Stunts

Leapfrog
Wheelbarrow
Wheelbarrow Lifting
Camel Lift and Walk
Dump the Wheelbarrow
Dromedary Walk
Centipede
Double Wheelbarrow

Partner Support Stunts

Double Bear
Table
Statue
Lighthouse
Hip-Shoulder Stand

ANIMAL MOVEMENTS

Double-Lame Dog

Support the body on one hand and one leg (Figure 21.67). Move forward in this position, maintaining balance. The distance should be short (5 to 10 ft), since this stunt is strenuous. Different leg-arm combinations should be employed such as cross-lateral movements (right arm with left leg and left arm with right leg).

Variation: Keep the free arm on the hip.

Turtle

Hold the body in a wide push-up position with the feet apart and the hands widely spread (Figure 21.68). From this position, move in various directions, keeping the plane of the body always about the same distance from the floor. Movements of the hands and feet should occur in small increments only.

Walrus Slap

From the front-leaning rest position, push the body up in the air quickly by force of the arms, clap the hands together, and recover to position. Before doing this stunt, review the Seal Crawl (pp. 375–376) and the Walrus Walk (p. 376).

FIGURE 21.67. Double-Lame Dog

FIGURE 21.68. Turtle

Variations

1. Try clapping the hands more than once.
2. Move forward while clapping the hands.
3. *Reverse Walrus Walk.* Turn over, and do a Walrus Walk while facing the ceiling. Clapping the hands is quite difficult in this position and should be attempted only by the more skilled. Work on a mat.

TUMBLING AND INVERTED BALANCES

Forward Roll (Pike Position)

Begin the piked Forward Roll in a standing pike position. Keep the legs straight and bend forward at the hips. Place the hands on the mat, bend the elbows, and lower the head to the mat. Keep the legs straight until nearing the end of the roll. Bend at the knees to facilitate returning to the feet.

Forward Roll Combinations

Review the Forward Roll, with increased emphasis on proper form. Combinations such as the following can be introduced.

1. Do a Forward Roll preceded by a short run.
2. Do two Forward Rolls in succession.
3. Do a Leapfrog (p. 389) plus a Forward Roll.
4. Do a Forward Roll to a vertical jump in the air, and repeat.
5. Do a Rabbit Jump plus a Forward Roll.
6. Hold the toes while doing a Forward Roll.

Backward Roll Combinations

Review the Backward Roll. Continue emphasis on the Push-off with the hands. Combinations to be taught are these.

1. Do a Backward Roll to a standing position. A strong push by the hands is necessary to provide enough momentum to land on the feet.
2. Do two Backward Rolls in succession.
3. Do a Crab Walk into a Backward Roll.
4. Add a jump in the air at the completion of a Backward Roll.

Headstand Practice and Variations

Continue work on the Headstand. Try the following variations. (Spot as needed.)

Variations

1. Clap the hands and recover. The weight must be shifted momentarily to the head for the clap. (Some children will be able to clap the hands twice before recovery.)
2. Use different leg positions—legs split sideward, legs split forward and backward (Figure 21.69), and knees bent.
3. Holding a utility ball or a beanbag between the legs, go into the Headstand, retaining control of the ball.

Teeter-Totter

The Teeter-Totter is the final lead-up activity for the Handstand. It is performed in a manner similar to the Half Teeter-Totter, except that the feet are held together for a moment in the handstand position before returning to the standing position.

Handstand

Start in the lunge position. Do a Teeter-Totter to the inverted position. The body, which is extended in a line from the shoulders through the feet, should be kept straight with the head down. It is helpful to teach the correct position first in a standing position with the arms overhead and the ears between the arms.

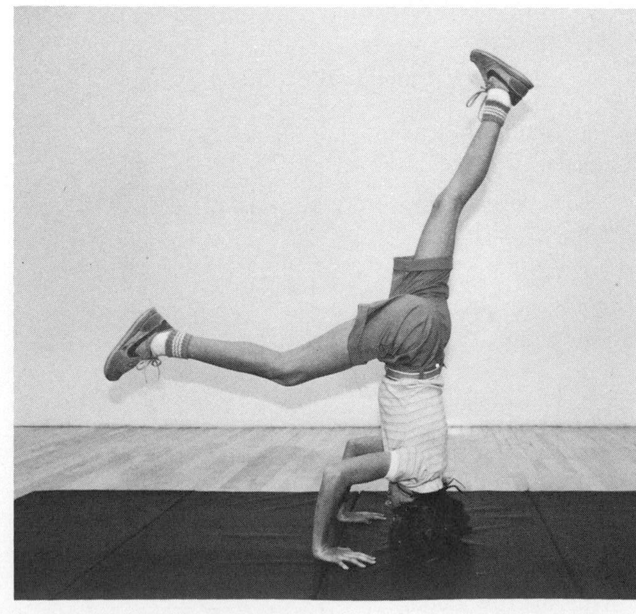

FIGURE 21.69. Headstand variation

The Handstand can be done with double or single spotting. In double spotting, the spotters are stationed on both sides of the performer. Each spotter should have a firm grip with one hand beneath the performer's shoulder. The other hand can assist the lift by upward pressure on the thigh (Figure 21.70). The performer walks the hips forward until they are over the hands and then kicks up with one foot, pushing off with the other and raising that leg to join the first in the inverted position (Figure 21.71). The rhythm is a one-two count.

In single spotting, the spotter takes a stride position, with the forward knee bent somewhat (Figure 21.72). The performer's weight is transferred over the hands, and the body goes into the handstand position with a one-two kick-up. The spotter catches the legs and holds the performer in an inverted position (Figure 21.73).

BALANCE STUNTS

Leg Dip

Extend both hands and one leg forward, balancing on the other leg. Lower the body to sit on the heel and return without losing the balance or touching the floor with any part of the body. Try with the other foot. (Another child can assist from the back by applying upward pressure to the elbows.)

Balance Jump

With hands and arms out to the sides and body parallel to the ground, extend one leg back and balance the weight

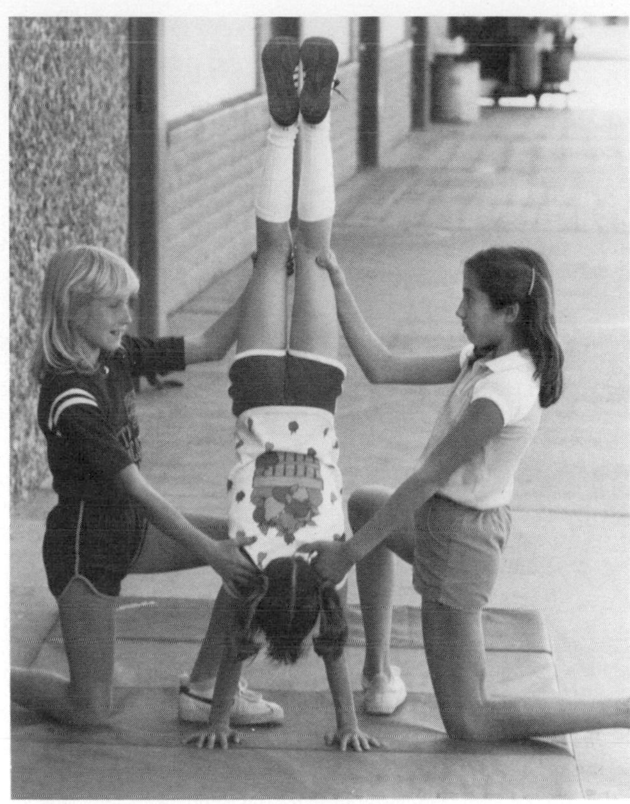

FIGURE 21.71. Double Spotting for the Handstand, second stage

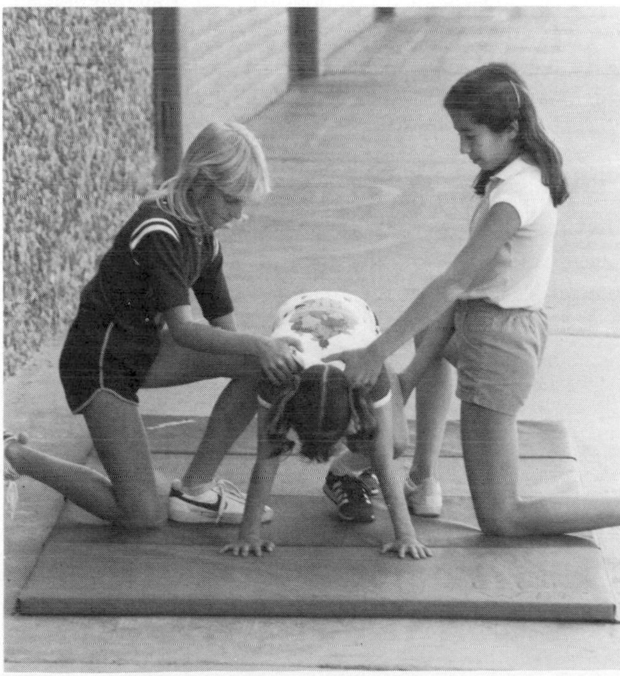

FIGURE 21.70. Double Spotting for the Handstand, first stage (Note the hand support under the shoulders.)

FIGURE 21.72. Single spotting for the Handstand, first stage (The performer's shoulder is against the spotter's leg.)

FIGURE 21.73. Single spotting for the Handstand, second stage (Note knee pressure against performer's shoulder.)

on the other leg (Figure 21.74). Quickly change balance to the other foot, maintaining the initial position but with the feet exchanged (Figure 21.75). Keep the body parallel to the ground during the change of legs. Try with arms outstretched forward. Working in pairs might be helpful. One student critiques the other's performance to make sure that the arms and body are straight and parallel to the floor.

Seat Balance

Sit on the floor, holding the ankles in front, with elbows inside the knees. The feet are flat on the floor, and the

FIGURE 21.74. Balance Jump, starting position

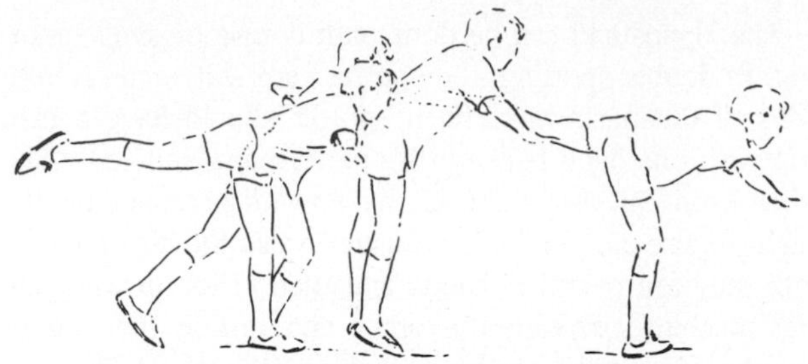

FIGURE 21.75. Balance Jump

knees are bent at approximately a right angle. Raise the legs (toes pointed) so the knees are straight (Figure 21.76), and balance on the seat for 5 seconds.

FIGURE 21.76. Seat Balance

Face-to-Knee Touch

Begin in a standing position with feet together. Placing the hands on the hips, balance on one foot, with the other leg extended backward. Bend the trunk forward, and touch the knee of the supporting leg with the forehead (Figure 21.77). Recover to original position.

Teachers can have the children begin by keeping the arms away from the sides for balance and then stipulate the hands-on-hips position later. In the learning stages, assistance can be given from behind by supporting the leg extended backward, or the child can place one hand against a wall.

FIGURE 21.77. Face-to-Knee Touch

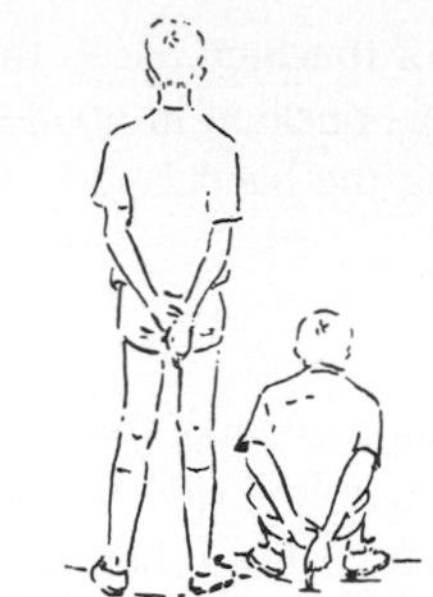

FIGURE 21.78. Finger Touch

FIGURE 21.79. Knee Jump to Standing

Finger Touch

Put the right hand behind the back with the index finger straight and pointed down. Grasp the right wrist with the left hand. From an erect position with the feet about 6 in. apart, squat down and touch the floor with the index finger (Figure 21.78). Regain the erect position without losing balance. Reverse hands. (In the learning stages, the teacher can use a book or the corner of a mat to decrease the distance and make the touch easier.)

INDIVIDUAL STUNTS

Knee Jump to Standing

Kneel, with seat touching the heels and toes pointing backward (shoelaces against the floor). Jump to a standing position with a vigorous upward swing of the arms (Figure 21.79).

It is easier to jump from a smooth floor than from a mat, because the toes slide more readily on the floor. If a child has difficulty, allow him to come to a standing position with the feet well spread.

Variation: Jump to a standing position, doing a quarter turn in the air in one quick motion. Try a half turn.

Individual Drops

Drops, or falls, can challenge children to achieve good body control. Mats should be used. The impact of a forward fall is absorbed by the hands and arms. During the fall, the body should maintain a straight-line position. Make sure that little change in body angles occurs, particularly at the knees and waist.

Knee Drop

Kneel on a mat, with the body upright. Raise the feet up, off the floor, and fall forward, breaking the fall with the hands and arms (Figure 21.80).

Forward Drop

From a forward balance position (p. 371) on one leg with the other leg extended backward and the arms extended forward and up, lean forward slowly, bringing the arms toward the floor. Continue to drop forward slowly until overbalanced, then let the hands and arms break the fall (Figure 21.81). The head is up, and the extended leg is raised high, with knee joints kept reasonably straight. Repeat, changing position of the legs.

Dead Body Fall

Fall forward from an erect position to a down push-up position (Figure 21.82). A slight bend at the waist is permissible, but the knees should be kept straight, and there should be no forward movement of the feet.

Stoop and Stretch

Hold a beanbag with *both* hands. Stand with heels against a line and feet about shoulder width apart. Keeping the knees straight, reach between the legs with the beanbag and *place* it as far back as possible. Reach back and pick it up with both hands.

Variations

1. Bend at the knees, using more of a squatting position during the reach.

FIGURE 21.80. Knee Drop

FIGURE 21.81. Forward Drop

FIGURE 21.82. Dead Body Fall

2. Use a piece of chalk instead of a beanbag. Reach back and make a mark on the floor. Try writing a number or drawing a small circle or some other figure.

Tanglefoot

Stand with heels together and toes pointed out. Bend the trunk forward and extend both arms down between the knees and around behind the ankles. Bring the hands around the outside of the ankles from behind and touch the fingers to each other (Figure 21.83). Hold for a 5-second count.

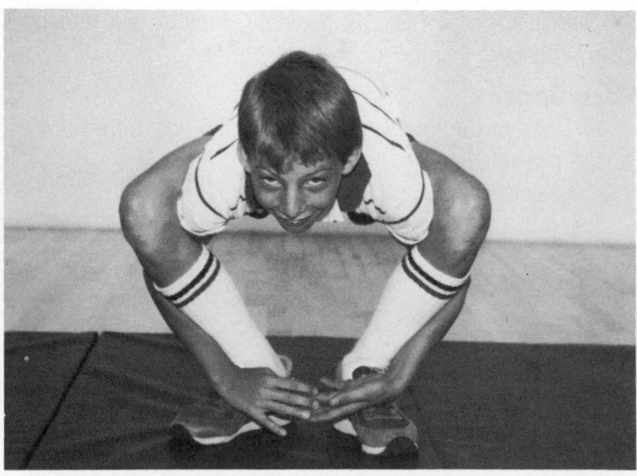

FIGURE 21.83. Tanglefoot

Variation: Instead of touching, clasp the fingers in front of the ankles. Hold this position in good balance for 5 seconds without releasing the handclasp.

Egg Roll

In a sitting position, assume the same clasped-hands position as for Tanglefoot. Roll sideways over one shoulder, then to the back, then to the other shoulder, and finally back up to the sitting position (Figure 21.84). The movements are repeated in turn to make a full circle back to place. The secret is a vigorous sideward movement to secure initial momentum. If mats are used, two should be placed side by side to cover the extent of the roll. (Some children can do this stunt better from a crossed-ankle position.)

FIGURE 21.84. Egg Roll

Toe Touch Nose

From a sitting position on the floor, touch the toe of either foot to the nose with the help of both hands. Do first one foot and then the other.

More flexible youngsters will be able to place the foot on top of the head or even behind the neck. Although this is a flexibility exercise, caution should be used; the leg can be forced too far.

Variation: Perform from a standing position. Touch the toe to the nose, and return the foot to original position without losing balance. Try the standing version with eyes closed.

Toe Tug Walk

Bend over and grasp the toes with thumbs on top (Figure 21.85). Keep the knees bent slightly and the eyes forward. Walk forward without losing the grip on the toes. Walk backward and sideward to provide more challenge. Walk in various geometric patterns, such as a circle, triangle, or square. (This stunt can be introduced in an easier version by having the children grasp the ankles, thumbs on the insides, and perform the desired movements.)

FIGURE 21.85. Toe Tug Walk

Variation: Try doing the walk with the right hand grasping the left foot, and vice versa.

PARTNER AND GROUP STUNTS

Leapfrog

One student forms a *back*. A leaper takes a running start, lays her hands flat on the back at the shoulders, and vaults over the low student. Backs are formed at various heights (Figure 21.86). To form a low back, crouch down on the knees, curling into a tight ball with the head tucked well down. To form a medium back, reach down the outside of the legs from a standing position and grasp the ankles. The feet should be reasonably spread and the knees straight. The position must be stable in order to absorb the shock of the leaper. To form a high back, stand stiff-legged, bend over, and brace arms against the knees. The feet should be spread, the head down, and the body braced to absorb the vault.

Leapfrog is a traditional physical education activity, but the movement is actually a jump-and-vault pattern. The take-off must be made with both feet. At the height of the jump, the chest and head must be held erect to avoid a forward fall. The teacher should emphasize a forceful jump to achieve height, coordinated with light hand pressure to vault over the back. Landing should be done lightly and under good control, with a bent-knee action.

FIGURE 21.86. High, medium, and low leapfrog positions

Variations

1. Work in pairs. Alternate leaping and forming the back while progressing around the room.

2. Have more than one back for a series of jumps.

3. Using the medium back, vault from the side rather than from the front. The vaulter's legs must be well spread, and the back must keep the head well tucked down.

4. Following the Leapfrog, do a Forward Roll on a mat.

Wheelbarrow

One partner gets down on the hands with feet extended to the rear and legs apart. The other partner (the pusher) grasps partner's legs about halfway between the ankles and the knees. The wheelbarrow walks forward on the hands, supported by the pusher (Figure 21.87). Movements should be under good control.

Children have a tendency to grasp the legs too near the feet. The pusher must not push too fast. The wheelbarrow should have the head up and look forward. Fingers should be pointed forward and well spread, with the pads of the fingers supporting much of the weight. The pusher should carry the legs low and keep the arms extended.

Wheelbarrow Lifting

Partners assume the wheelbarrow position. The pusher lifts partner's legs as high as possible without changing the hand position. The pusher should be able to lift the

FIGURE 21.87. Wheelbarrow

legs enough so the lower child's body is at an angle of about 45 degrees to the floor.

Variation: The pusher brings the legs up to the level described, changes the handgrip to a pushing one, and continues to raise the lower child toward a handstand position. The lower child keeps the arms and body straight.

Camel Lift and Walk

In the wheelbarrow position, the wheelbarrow raises her seat as high as possible, forming a camel. The camel can lower herself or walk in the raised position.

Dump the Wheelbarrow

Get into wheelbarrow position. Walk the wheelbarrow over to a mat. The lower child ducks the head (chin to waist), raises the seat (bending at the waist), and exits from the stunt with a Forward Roll. The pusher gives a little push and a lift of the feet to help supply momentum.

Dromedary Walk

One child (the support) gets down on the hands and knees. The other child sits on her, facing the rear, and fixes the legs around the support's chest. The top child leans forward, so she can grasp the back of the support's ankles. Her arms are reasonably extended (Figure 21.88). The support takes the weight off the knees and walks forward with the top child's help.

Centipede

One child, the stronger and larger individual, gets down on the hands and knees. The other child faces the same direction and places the hands about 2 ft in front of the support's. He then places his legs and body on top of the support. The knees should be spread apart and the heels locked together. The centipede walks with the top child using hands only and the supporting child using both hands and feet. The support should gather the legs well under while walking and not be on the knees.

FIGURE 21.88. Dromedary Walk

FIGURE 21.89. Centipede

Variation: More than two can do this stunt (Figure 21.89). After getting into position, the players should keep step by calling "Right" and "Left" out loud.

Double Wheelbarrow

Two children assume the same position as for the Centipede, except that the under child has the legs extended to the rear and the feet apart. A third child stands between the legs of the under child, reaches down, and picks up the legs of the lower child (Figure 21.90). The Double Wheelbarrow moves forward with right and left arms moving together.

An easy way to get into position for this activity is to form the front of the wheelbarrow first and then to pick up the legs of the second child. This stunt usually is done by three children but can be done by more.

PARTNER SUPPORT STUNTS

Several considerations are important in the conducting of partner support stunts at this level. The lower child

FIGURE 21.90. Double Wheelbarrow

(the support) should keep the body as level as possible. This means widening the hand base so the shoulders are more nearly level with the hips. The support performer must be strong enough to handle the support chores. Spotters are needed, particularly when the top position involves a final erect or inverted pose. The top child should avoid stepping on the small of the lower child's back. In the Lighthouse and the Hip-Shoulder Stand, the top performer can remove the shoes, making the standing position more comfortable for the support. When holding the final pose, the top child should fix the gaze forward and relax as much as possible while maintaining the position.

Double Bear

The bottom child gets down on the hands and knees. The top child assumes the same position directly above the support, with hands on the shoulders and knees on the hips of the support (Figure 21.91). Touch up the final position by holding heads up and backs straight.

Table

The bottom performer assumes a crab position. The top performer straddles this base, facing the rear, and positions the hands on the base's shoulders, fingers pointing toward the ground. She then places her feet on top of base's knees, forming one crab position on top of another (Figure 21.92). As a final touch, the heads are positioned so the eyes look up toward the ceiling, and the seats are lifted so the backs are straight.

Statue

The first child gets down in crab position. The second child straddles either foot, facing the child in crab position. With the help of a third person, he mounts each knee of the base child so the statue is standing erect (Figure 21.93). Hold the position for a few seconds. Partners should be facing each other. The top child should not mount with back toward the base child. (Spotters are important and must not be eliminated until the stunt is mastered.)

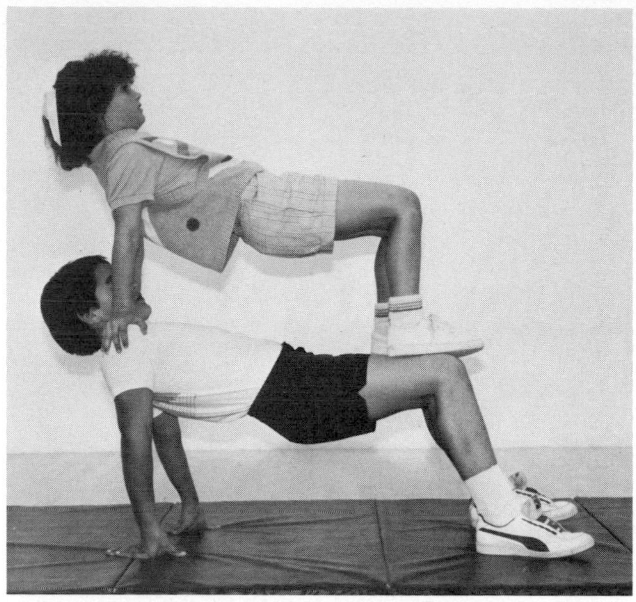

FIGURE 21.92. Table

Lighthouse

The support gets down on the hands and knees. The top child completes the figure by standing on the support's shoulders and facing in the same direction. The lighthouse stands erect with hands out to the sides (Figure 21.94).

FIGURE 21.91. Double Bear

FIGURE 21.93. Statue

FIGURE 21.94. Lighthouse

Variation: The support turns around in a small circle, while the partner keeps the standing balance.

Hip-Shoulder Stand

The support is on the hands and knees, with hands positioned out somewhat so the back is level. The top child faces to the side and steps up, first with one foot on support's hips and then with the other on the shoulders (Figure 21.95).

A spotter should stand on the opposite side and aid in the mounting. Care must be taken to avoid stepping on the small of the support's back.

FIGURE 21.95. Hip-Shoulder Stand

FIFTH-GRADE PROGRAM

The teacher should review stunts from the 4th grade. Repetition is valuable, because many 5th-grade activities are based on the simpler stunts performed in the 4th grade.

The children at this stage should be quite skillful in both the Forward and the Backward Roll. Routines involving these rolls can be expanded. The Judo Roll, Cartwheel with Round-Off, and Eskimo Roll continue the mat-type activities. Improvement in the Headstand is expected. Except for review, animal movements are not appropriate at this level.

Tumbling and Inverted Balances

Forward and Backward Roll Combinations
Back Extension
Headstand Variations
Wall Arch
Handstand Against a Wall
Freestanding Handstand
Cartwheel and Round-Off
Judo Roll

Balance Stunts

Fish Hawk Dive
High Dive
V-up
Push-up Variations
Flip-Flop

Individual Stunts

Wall Walk-up
Skier's Sit
Curl-up Practice
Rocking Horse
Heel Click (Side)
Walk-Through
Jump-Through
Circular Rope Jump

Partner and Group Stunts

Double Scooter
Eskimo Roll (Double Roll)
Tandem Bicycle
Circle High Jump
Stick Carries
Two-Way Wheelbarrow

Partner Support Stunts

Back Layout
Front Sit
Flying Dutchman

FIGURE 21.96. Alternating Forward and Backward Rolls

TUMBLING AND INVERTED BALANCES

Forward and Backward Roll Combinations

Combinations from the 4th grade should be reviewed. The following routines can be added.

1. Begin with a Forward Roll, coming to a standing position with feet crossed. Pivot the body to uncross the feet and to bring the back in the line of direction for a Backward Roll (Figure 21.96).

2. Hold the toes, heels, ankles, or a wand while rolling. Use different arm positions, such as out to the sides or folded across the chest. Use a wide straddle position for both the Forward Roll and the Backward Roll.

Back Extension

Carry the Backward Roll to the point where the feet are above and over the head. Push off vigorously with the hands, shoot the feet into the air, and land on the feet.

Headstand Variations

Review the various aspects of the Headstand, using the single-spotter technique as needed. Vary with different leg positions. Add the two-foot recovery. After the stand has been held, recover by bending at the waist and knees, pushing off with the hands, and landing on the feet back in the original position.

Wall Arch

Take a position with the shoulders against a wall and the feet about 2 ft out from the wall. Place the hands against the wall, employing the position used in the Backward Roll. Without moving the feet, work the hands downward to give the body an arch shape (Figure 21.97). Recover to position.

If the activity is too difficult, students can move their feet or make other adjustments. It may be necessary to spot and to lower the performer gradually to the arched position.

FIGURE 21.97. Wall Arch

Handstand Against a Wall

Using a wall as support, do a Handstand. The arms must be kept straight, with the head between the arms (Figure 21.98). Some performers like to bend the knees so the soles of the feet are against the wall.

FIGURE 21.98. Handstand Against a Wall

A critical point in the Handstand Against a Wall is to position the hands the correct distance from the wall. It is better to be too close than too far. Being too far can cause the performer to collapse before the feet gain the support of the wall. A mat should be used in the preliminary stages.

Freestanding Handstand

Perform a Handstand without support. Students must learn to turn the body when a fall is imminent, so they land on the feet. (Spotters can be used to prevent an awkward fall.) Move the hands to help control the balance.

Cartwheel and Round-off

Practice the Cartwheel, adding a light run with a skip for a takeoff. To change to a Round-off, place the hands somewhat closer together during the early Cartwheel action. Bring the feet together and make a quarter turn to land on both feet, with the body facing the starting point. The Round-off can be followed by a Backward Roll.

Judo Roll

For a left Judo Roll, stand facing the mat with the feet well apart and the left arm extended at shoulder height. Bring the arm down, and throw the left shoulder toward the mat in a rolling motion, with the roll made on the shoulder and the upper part of the back (Figure 21.99). Reverse for a right Judo Roll. Both right and left Judo Rolls should be practiced. Later, a short run and a double-foot takeoff should precede the roll.

The Judo Roll is a basic safety device to prevent injury from tripping and falling. Rolling and taking the fall lessen the chances of injury. The Judo Roll is essentially a Forward Roll with the head turned to one side. The point of impact is the back of one shoulder and the finish is a return to the standing position.

Variations

1. Roll to the feet and to a ready position.

2. Place a beanbag about 3 ft in front of yourself and go beyond the bag to start the roll.

FIGURE 21.99. Judo Roll

BALANCE STUNTS

Fish Hawk Dive

Place a folded paper on the floor, with the edge up. Kneel on one leg, with the other leg extended behind and the arms out for balance. Lean forward, pick up the paper with the teeth, and return to position without losing balance. Begin the stunt using an 8½-by-11-in. piece of paper folded lengthwise. It may be necessary to have someone hold the paper. If the stunt is done successfully, fold the paper a second time so a lower target is presented.

High Dive

Fold a piece of paper as for the Fish Hawk Dive. Using the arms for balance and standing on one foot only, try to pick up the paper with the teeth. If this seems too difficult, shorten the distance to the paper by elevating it on a box or a book.

V-up

Lie on the back, with arms overhead and extended. Keeping the knees straight and the feet pointed, bring the legs and the upper body up at the same time to form a V shape. The entire weight is balanced on the seat (Figure 21.100). Hold the position for 5 seconds.

This exercise, like the Curl-up, is excellent for development of the abdominal muscles. It is quite similar to the Seat Balance, except for the starting position.

Variation: Place the hands on the floor in back for support. (This makes an easier stunt for those having trouble.)

Push-up Variations

Begin the development of push-up variations by reviewing proper push-up techniques. The only movement is in

FIGURE 21.100. V-up

the arms. The body should come close to, but not touch, the floor. Explore the following variations.

Monkey Push-up

Point the fingers toward each other. Next, bring the hands close enough for the fingertips to touch.

Circle-O Push-up

Form a circle with each thumb and forefinger.

Fingertip Push-up

Get up high on the fingertips.

Different Finger Combinations

Do a Push-up using four, three, or two fingers only.

Extended Push-up

Extend the position of the hands progressively forward or to the sides.

Crossed Push-up

Cross the arms. Cross the legs. Cross both.

One-Legged Push-up

Lift one leg from the floor.

One-Handed Push-up

Use only one hand, with the other outstretched or on the hip.

Exploratory Approach

See what other types of Push-ups or combinations can be created.

Flip-Flop

From a push-up position, propel the body upward with the hands and feet, doing a Turn-Over (Figure 21.101). Flip back. The stunt should be done on a mat. (Review the Turn-Over from the 2nd grade activity section before having students try this stunt.)

FIGURE 21.101. Flip-Flop

INDIVIDUAL STUNTS

Wall Walk-up

From a push-up position with feet against a wall, walk up the wall backward to a handstand position (Figure 21.102). Walk down again.

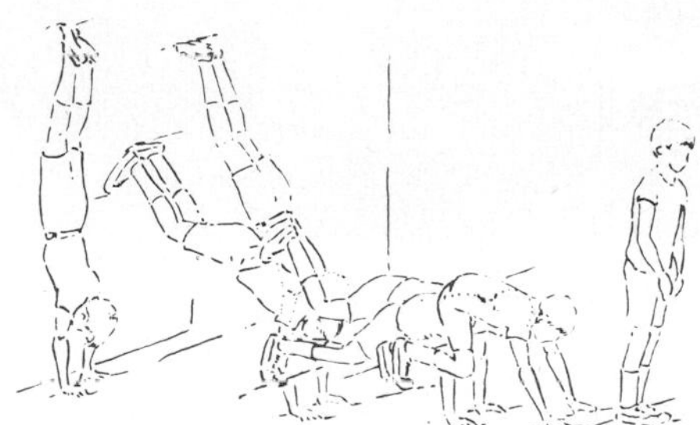

FIGURE 21.102. Wall Walk-up

Skier's Sit

Assume a sitting position against a wall with the thighs parallel to the floor and the knee joints at right angles. (The position is the same as if sitting in a chair, but of course, there is no chair.) The arms are held in front of the chest. The feet should be flat on the floor and the lower legs straight up and down (Figure 21.103). Try to sit for 30 seconds, 45 seconds, and 1 minute.

The Skier's Sit is an isometric type of activity and is excellent for developing the knee extensor muscles. It is done by skiers to develop the muscles used in skiing.

Variation: Support the body with crossed legs. A more difficult stunt is to support the body on one leg, with the other leg extended forward.

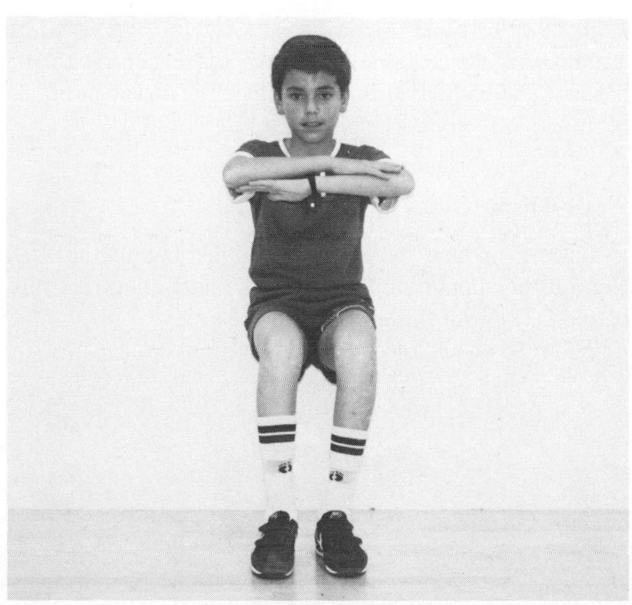

FIGURE 21.103. Skier's Sit

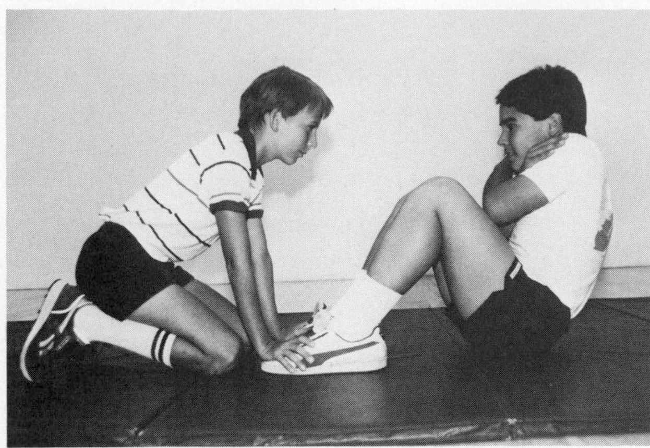

FIGURE 21.104. Curl-up position

Curl-up Practice

Lie on the back with the feet apart and flat on the floor. Bend the knees at approximately a right angle. With the arms folded in front of the chest, curl up so the folded arms touch the knees each time (Figure 21.104). An alternate version is to place the hands, with fingers interlaced, behind the lower head. The left elbow touches the right knee on the first Curl-up, and the right elbow touches the left knee on the next.

Start with 10 to 15 Curl-ups and gradually increase the number during the year. Done properly and regularly, this exercise helps to maintain good posture. A partner can hold the feet down and count the repetitions.

Rocking Horse

Lie facedown on a mat with arms extended overhead, palms down. With back arched, rock back and forth (Figure 21.105). (Some children may need to have someone start them rocking.)

Variation: Reach back and grasp the insteps with the hands. (The body arch is more difficult to maintain in this position.) Also try rocking from a side position.

Heel Click (Side)

Balance on one foot, with the other out to the side. Hop on the supporting foot, click the heels, and return to balance. Try with the other foot.

The child should recover to the one-foot balance position without excessive foot movement. The teacher should insist on good balance.

FIGURE 21.105. Rocking Horse

FIGURE 21.106. Walk-Through

Variations

1. Take a short step with the right foot leading. Follow with a cross-step with the left and then a hop on the left foot. During the hop, click the heels together. To hop on the right foot, reverse these directions.
2. Jump as high as possible before clicking the heels.
3. Combine right and left clicks.

Walk-Through

From a front-leaning rest position, walk the feet through the hands, using tiny steps, until the body is fully extended with the back to the floor (Figure 21.106). Reverse the body to original position. The hands stay in contact with the floor throughout.

Jump-Through

Starting in a front-leaning rest position, jump the feet through the arms in one motion. Reverse with another jump, and return to original position. The hands must push off sharply from the floor, so the body is high enough off the floor to allow the legs to jump under. (The child may find it easier to swing a little to the side with one leg, going under the lifted hand, as indicated in Figure 21.107.)

Circular Rope Jump

Crouch down in a three-quarter knee bend, holding a folded jump rope in one hand. Swing the rope under the feet in a circular fashion, jumping it each time (Figure 21.108). Reverse the direction of the rope. Work from both right and left sides with either a counterclockwise or clockwise turn of the rope.

Variations

1. Perform the rope jump with a partner.
2. Jump using different foot patterns (e.g., one foot or alternate feet) and using slow and fast time.

FIGURE 21.107. Jump-Through

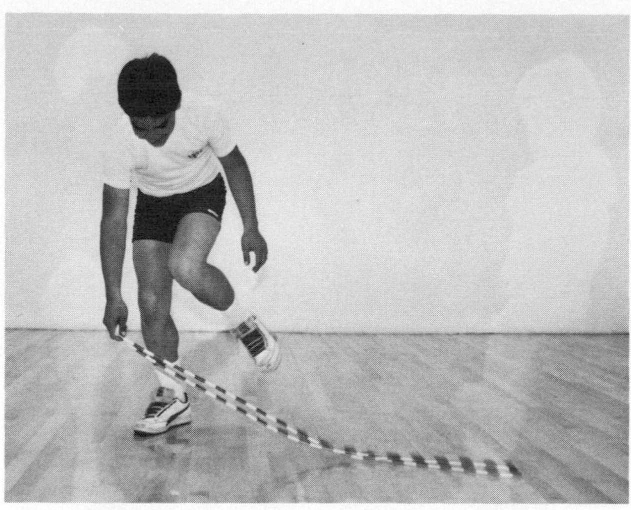

FIGURE 21.108. Circular Rope Jump

3. Establish standards for declaring a class champion in different areas. Some categories could be maximum number of turns in 30 seconds, most unique routine, and most jumps without a miss.

PARTNER AND GROUP STUNTS

Double Scooter

Two children about the same size face each other, sitting on each other's feet (Figure 21.109). With arms joined, scoot forward or backward with cooperative movements. When one child moves his seat, the other child should help by lifting with her feet. Progress is made by alternately flexing and extending the knees and hips. (Review the Scooter, pp. 380–381, before doing this stunt.)

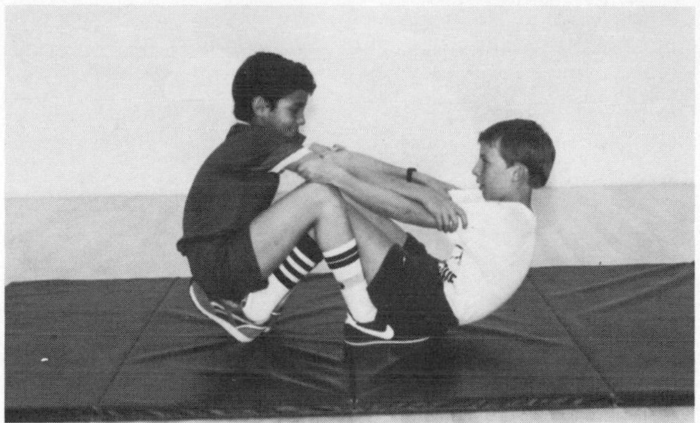

FIGURE 21.109. Double Scooter

Eskimo Roll (Double Roll)

One child lies on a mat with his feet in the direction of the roll. The other takes a position with feet on either side of the first child's head. The first child reaches back and grasps the other's ankles with thumbs on the inside and then raises his own feet, so that the other child can similarly grasp his ankles. The second child propels her hunched body forward, while the first sits up and takes the position originally held by the other (Figure 21.110). Positions then are reversed, and the roll continues.

Be sure that the top child hunches well and ducks the head to cushion the roll on the back of the neck and shoulders. Also, when the top child propels herself forward, bent arms should momentarily take the weight. It is important that the underneath child keep his knees bent.

Tandem Bicycle

One child forms a bicycle position, with back against a wall and knees bent, as if sitting. The feet should be placed under the body. The second child backs up and sits down lightly on the first child's knees. Other children may be added in the same fashion, their hands around the waist of the player immediately in front for support (Figure 21.111). Forward progress is made by moving the feet on the same side together.

Circle High Jump

Stand in circles of three, each circle having children of somewhat equal height. Join hands. One child tries to jump over the opposite pair of joined hands (Figure 21.112). To be completely successful, each circle must have each child jump forward in turn over the opposite pair of joined hands. (Jumping backward is not recommended.) To reach good height, an upward lift is necessary. Try two small preliminary jumps before exploding into the jump over the joined hands.

FIGURE 21.110. Eskimo Roll

FIGURE 21.111. Tandem Bicycle

FIGURE 21.112. Circle High Jump

Variation: Precede the jump with a short run by the group. A signal can be sounded so all know when the jump is to occur during the run.

Stick Carries

Children of similar weight stand in groups of three, each group having a sturdy broom handle about 4 ft long. Using movement exploration techniques, two of the children carry the third with the broom handle (Figure 21.113). The child who is carried may be partially or wholly supported by the handle. Exchange positions. (It is better to use special sticks for this purpose, because ordinary wands may break.)

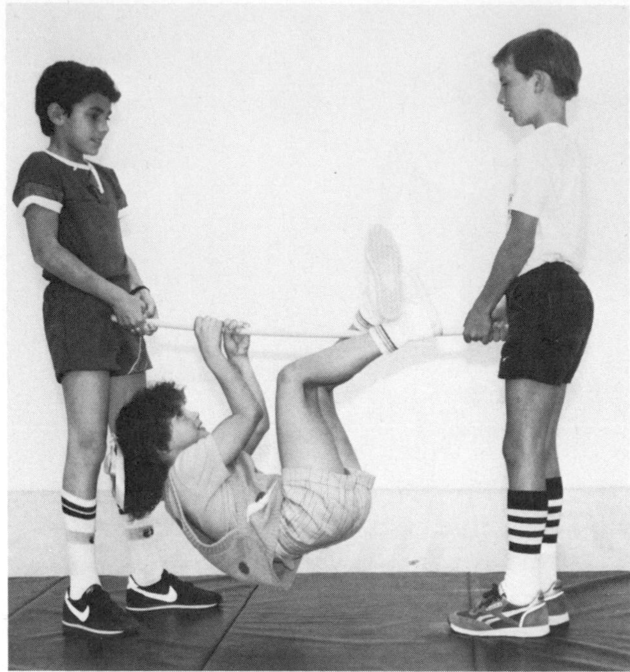

FIGURE 21.113. Stick Carry

Two-Way Wheelbarrow

One child holds two wheelbarrows, but with one in front and one behind. The child secures the front wheelbarrow first in a normal wheelbarrow position. The back wheelbarrow assumes position by placing the ankles over the already established hand position of the holder (Figure 21.114). (Review the various wheelbarrow activities from the 4th grade progression before doing this stunt.)

PARTNER SUPPORT STUNTS

Back Layout

The under, or support, partner lies on the back, with arms outstretched and palms down for support. The legs are raised, and the feet are positioned as if pushing up

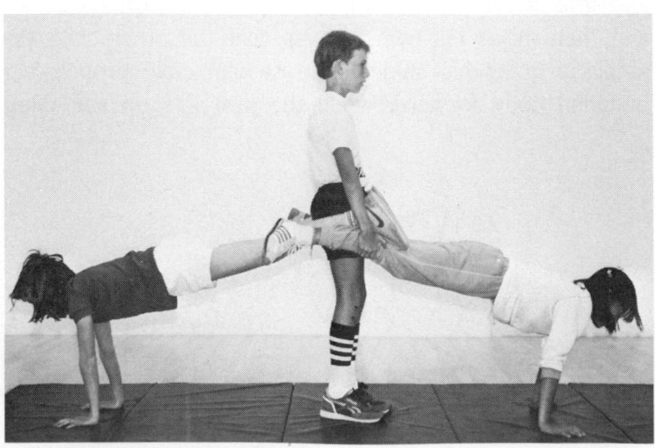

FIGURE 21.114. Two-Way Wheelbarrow

FIGURE 21.115. Back Layout

the ceiling. The support bends the knees, and the partner lies back, resting the small of the back on support's soles. The top partner balances in a layout position with arms out to the sides for balance and body in a slight curve. The bottom partner reaches up and gives support to the top child's arms to provide stability (Figure 21.115). (A spotter can help position the top partner.)

Front Sit

The support gets down in the same position as for the Back Layout. The top partner straddles the support, so the support and the top partner are looking at each other. The top partner backs up to sit on support's feet. As the support raises the top partner in a seated position, the top partner extends the legs forward, so the support can reach up and grasp them to stabilize the seated position (Figure 21.116). (Spotting should be done from behind.)

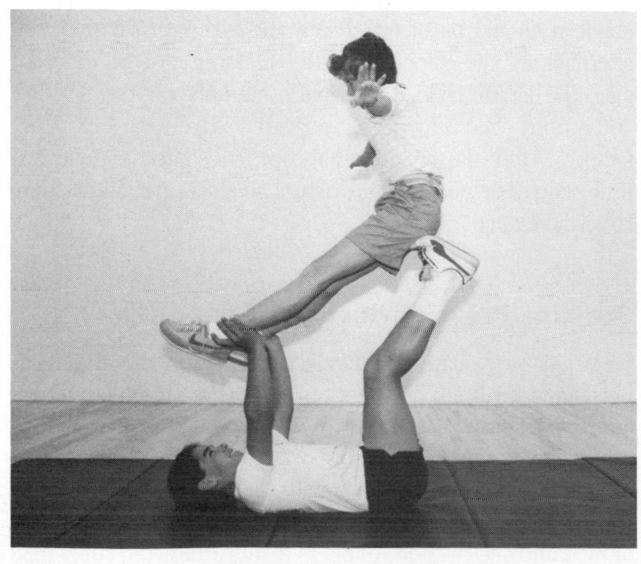

FIGURE 21.116. Front Sit

FIGURE 21.117. Flying Dutchman

Flying Dutchman

The support takes a position as for the Back Layout. The top child takes a position facing the support, grasping support's hands and at the same time bending over support's feet. The support then raises the top partner from the floor by extending the knees. The top child arches the back and can then release the grip and put the arms out level to the sides in a flying position (Figure 21.117). A little experimentation determines the best place for the foot support. (Spotting should be available for getting into position and for safety.)

SIXTH-GRADE PROGRAM

In the 6th grade program, practice continues on the basic rolls, with attention centered on variations and combinations. The stunts from the 5th grade should be reviewed. The 6th-grade program adds a number of stunts that children find quite challenging. Such stunts as the Headspring, Front Seat Support, Elbow Balance, Straddle Press to Headstand, and Walk-Over provide sufficient breadth for even the most skilled. It is difficult for all the children to accomplish the entire list of stunts.

Particular attention should be paid to the gymnastic-type stunts. While there is still opportunity at this level for exploration and individual expression, more emphasis is placed on execution, conformity, and form.

Tumbling and Inverted Balances

Forward and backward roll combinations
Developing gymnastic routines
Straddle Press to Headstand
Handstand variations
Headspring

Walking on the Hands
Walk-Over

Balance Stunts

Long Reach
Toe Jump
Handstand Stunts
Front Seat Support
Elbow Balance

Individual Stunts

Bouncer
Pretzel
Jackknife
Heel-and-Toe Spring
Single-Leg Circle (Pinwheel)

Partner and Group Stunts

Partner Rising Sun
Triple Roll
Quintuplet Roll
Dead Person Lift
Injured Person Carry
Merry-Go-Round

Partner Support Stunts

Knee-and-Shoulder Balance
Press
All-Fours Support
Angel
Side Stand

TUMBLING AND INVERTED BALANCES

Forward and Backward Roll Combinations

Put together different combinations of Forward Rolls and Backward Rolls. The emphasis should be on choice, exploration, and self-discovery. Variations can involve different approaches, execution acts, and finishes. Try the following variations of the Forward Roll.

1. Hold the toes, heels, ankles, or a wand and roll.
2. As above, but cross the hands.
3. Roll with hands on the knees or with a ball between the knees.
4. Roll with arms at the sides, folded across the chest, or on the back of the thighs.
5. Press forward from a front-leaning rest position and go into the roll.

Try the following suggestions with the Backward Roll.

1. Begin with a Stiff-Legged Sitdown, and go into the roll.
2. Push off into a Back Extension (p. 393), landing on the feet.
3. Roll to a finish on one foot only.
4. Roll with hands clasped behind the neck.
5. Roll with a ball between the knees.
6. Walk backward using a Crab Walk and then roll.

In addition to these, combine Forward Rolls with Backward Rolls in various ways.

Developing Gymnastic Routines

The teacher can put together in sequence various stunts and other movements. The problems might be structured like these.

1. Specify the number and kind of stunts and movements to be done and the sequence to be followed. For example, tell the child to do a balance stunt, a locomotor movement, and a rolling stunt.
2. Arrange the mats in some prescribed order so they become the key to the movement problems. Two or three might be placed in succession, three or four in a U shape, or four in a hollow-square formation. There should be some space between mats, depending on the conditions stated in the problem. The problem could be presented like this. "On the first mat, do a Forward Roll variation and then a movement to the next mat on all fours. On the second mat, do some kind of balance stunt, and then proceed to the next mat with a jumping or hopping movement. On the third mat, you have a choice of activity." The problem can also be stated in more general terms, and the children can do a different stunt or variation on each mat and a different movement between mats.
3. Have partners work out a series of stunts. The paired children should be of equal size and strength, so they can alternate as the support. If the children are of different size, the larger child can provide support for the smaller, and a third child may act as a spotter to take care of safety factors. After the children have practiced for a period of time, each partnership can demonstrate the routines they have developed.

Straddle Press to Headstand

Begin by placing the hands and head in the triangular headstand position. The feet are in a wide straddle position and the hips are up. Raise the hips slowly by pressing to a point over the base of support. Slowly raise the legs to a straddle position, and finish with the legs brought together in regular headstand position. All movement is done as a slow, controlled action. (This is a more difficult stunt than the regular Headstand.)

Handstand Variations

Practice the regular Handstand, as done in the 5th grade. The first two stages of the Handstand, done with double spotting and then single spotting with knee support (pp. 385–386), should be reviewed. Progression can then follow this order.

1. Single spotting, without knee support
2. Handstand Against a Wall
3. Freestanding Handstand
4. Walking on the Hands
5. Stunts against a wall

For single spotting without knee support, the performer and the spotter face each other 4 or 5 ft apart. The performer lifts both arms and the left leg upward as a preliminary move, with the weight shifted to the right leg. The lifted arms and forward leg come down forcefully to the ground, with the weight shifted in succession to the left leg and then to the arms. The right leg is kicked backward and upward for initial momentum, and is followed quickly by the left leg. The downward thrust of the arms, coupled with the upward thrust of the legs, inverts the body to the handstand position. The placement of the hands should be about 2 ft in front of the spotter, who reaches forward and catches the performer between the knees and the ankles (Figure 21.118).

Headspring

With forehead and hands on the mat and knees bent, lean forward until almost overbalanced. As the weight begins

FIGURE 21.118. Single spotting for the Handstand

FIGURE 21.119. Headspring

to overbalance, raise the feet sharply and snap forward, pushing with the hands. As the feet begin to touch the ground, snap the body to a bent-knee position (Figure 21.119). Keep control of balance and rise to a standing position.

Two spotters should be used, one on each side of the performer. Each spotter places one hand under the performer's back and the other hand under a shoulder. The spotters should give the performer a lift under the shoulders to help him snap to the standing position.

Some instructors like to introduce this stunt going over a rolled-up mat, which provides more height for the turn. A slight run may be needed to get the proper momentum.

Walking on the Hands

Walk on the hands in a forward direction, bending the knees slightly, if desired, for balance. (Walking can be done first with a spotter supporting, but this support should be minimal.)

Variation: Walk on the hands, using a partner. The performer does a Handstand, and the partner catches her feet. The performer then walks the hands forward until they are on the partner's feet. The two walk cooperatively.

Walk-Over

Do preliminary movements as if for the Handstand. Let the legs continue beyond the handstand position and contact the floor with a one-two rhythm. The body must be well arched as the leading foot touches the floor. Push off with the hands and walk out. (A spotter can support under the small of the back.)

BALANCE STUNTS

Long Reach

Place a beanbag about 3 ft in front of a line. Keeping the toes behind the line, lean forward on one hand and reach out with the other hand to touch the beanbag (Figure 21.120). Recover in one clean, quick movement to the original position, lifting the supporting hand off the floor. Increase the distance of the bag from the line.

FIGURE 21.120. Long Reach

Toe Jump

Hold the left toe with the right hand (Figure 21.121). Jump the right foot through without losing the grip on the toe. Try with the other foot. (The teacher should not be discouraged if only a few can do this stunt, for it is quite difficult.)

Handstand Stunts

Try these challenging activities from the handstand position against a wall.

1. Turn the body in a complete circle, maintaining foot contact with the wall throughout.

2. Shift the support to one hand and hold for a moment.

3. Do an Inverted Push-up, lowering the body by bending the elbows and then returning to handstand position by straightening the elbows.

Front Seat Support

Sit on the floor, with the legs together and forward. Place the hands flat on the floor, somewhat between the

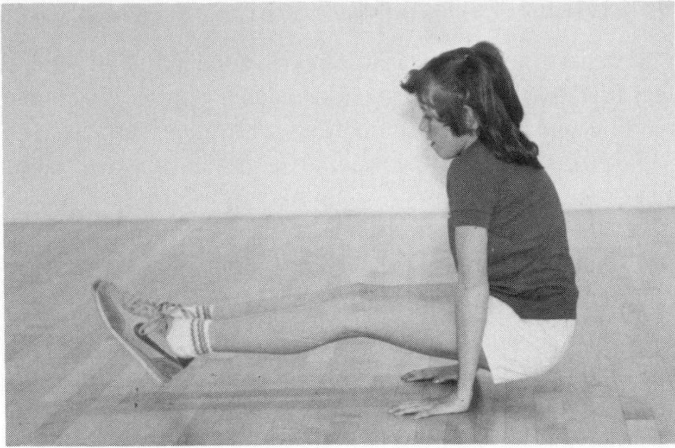

FIGURE 21.122. Front Seat Support

hips and the knees, with fingers pointed forward. Push down so the hips come off the floor, with the weight supported on the hands and heels. Next, lift the heels and support the entire weight of the body on the hands for 3 to 5 seconds (Figure 21.122). (Someone can help the performer get into position by giving slight support under the heels.)

Elbow Balance

Balance the body facedown horizontally on two hands, with elbows supporting the body in the hip area. To get into position, support the arched body with the toes and forehead. Work the forearms underneath the body for support, with fingers spread and pointed to the back. Try to support the body completely on the hands for 3 seconds, with elbows providing the leverage under the body (Figure 21.123). (Slight support under the toes can be provided.)

The Elbow Balance presents a considerable challenge. The teacher should take time to discuss the location of the center of gravity. The elbow support point should divide the upper and lower body mass.

FIGURE 21.121. Toe Jump

FIGURE 21.123. Elbow Balance

INDIVIDUAL STUNTS

Bouncer

Start in a push-up position. Bounce up and down with the hands and feet leaving the ground at the same time. Try clapping while doing this. Move in various directions. Turn around.

Pretzel

Touch the back of the head with the toes by raising the head and trunk and bringing the feet to the back of the head. Try first to bring the toes close enough to the head so the head-to-toe distance can be measured by another child with a handspan (the distance between the thumb and little finger when spread) (Figure 21.124). If this distance is met, then try touching one or both feet to the back of the head. (Girls are usually better at this stunt because they have more flexibility.)

Jackknife

Stand erect with hands out level to the front and a little to the side. Jump up and bring the feet up quickly to touch the hands. Vary by starting with a short run. Be sure the feet come up to the hands, rather than the hands moving down to the feet (Figure 21.125). Do several Jackknives in succession. The takeoff must be with both feet, and good height must be achieved.

Heel-and-Toe Spring

Place the heels against a line. Jump backward over the line while bent over and grasping the toes. (Lean forward slightly to allow for impetus and then jump backward over the line.) Try jumping forward to original position.

To be successful, the child should retain the grasp on the toes. The teacher can introduce the stunt by first having the children grasp their ankles when making the jumps. This is less difficult.

FIGURE 21.124. Pretzel

FIGURE 21.125. Jackknife

Single-Leg Circle (Pinwheel)

Assume a squatting position, with both hands on the floor, left knee between the arms, and right leg extended to the side. Swing the right leg forward and under the lifted right arm, under the left leg and arm, and back to starting position (Figure 21.126). Several circles should be made in succession. Reverse position, and try with the left leg.

FIGURE 21.126. Single-Leg Circle

PARTNER AND GROUP STUNTS

Partner Rising Sun

Partners lie facedown on the floor, with heads together and feet in opposite directions. They hold a volleyball or a basketball (or a ball of similar size) between their heads (Figure 21.127). Working together, they stand up and return

FIGURE 21.127. Partner Rising Sun

FIGURE 21.128. Triple Roll

to position while retaining control of the ball. Do not touch the ball with the hands.

A slightly deflated ball works best. Some caution is necessary to prevent bumping heads if the ball is suddenly squeezed out.

Triple Roll

Three children get down on their hands and knees on a mat, with heads all in the same direction to one of the sides. The performers are about 4 ft apart. Each is numbered, 1, 2, or 3, with the number 1 child in the center. Number 2 is on the right and number 3 is on the left. Number 1 starts rolling toward and under number 2, who projects himself upward and over the player beneath him. Number 2 is then in the center and rolls toward number 3, who projects himself upward and over number 2. Number 3, in the center, rolls toward and under number 1, who, after clearing number 3, is back in the center. Each performer in the center thus rolls toward and under the outside performer (Figure 21.128). (Review the Side Roll, p. 364, before doing this stunt.)

The children should be taught that, as soon as they roll to the outside, they must get ready to go over the oncoming child from the center. There is no time for delay. The upward projection of the body to allow the rolling child to go under is important.

Quintuplet Roll

Five children can make up a roll series. They are numbered 1 through 5, as shown in Figure 21.129. Numbers 3 and 5 begin by going over numbers 2 and 4, respectively, who roll under. Number 1 goes over number 3 as soon as she appears. Each then continues to go alternately over and under.

FIGURE 21.129. Quintuplet Roll

FIGURE 21.130. Dead Person Lift

Dead Person Lift

One child lies on the back, with body stiff and arms at the sides. Two helpers stand, one on each side of the "dead" person, with hands at the back of the neck and fingers touching. Working together, they lift the child, who remains rigid, to a standing position (Figure 21.130). From this position, the child is released and falls forward in a Dead Body Fall.

Injured Person Carry

The "injured" child lies on the back. Six children, three on each side, kneel down to do the carry. The lifters work their hands, palms upward, under the person to form a human stretcher, then they lift her up (Figure 21.131). (The "injured" child must maintain a stiff position.) They walk a short distance and set the person down carefully.

Merry-Go-Round

From 8 to 12 children are needed. Half of the children form a circle with joined hands, using a wrist grip. The remaining children drape themselves (each over a pair of joined hands) to become riders. The riders stretch out their bodies, faces up, toward the center of the circle, with the weight on the heels. Each rider then leans back on a pair

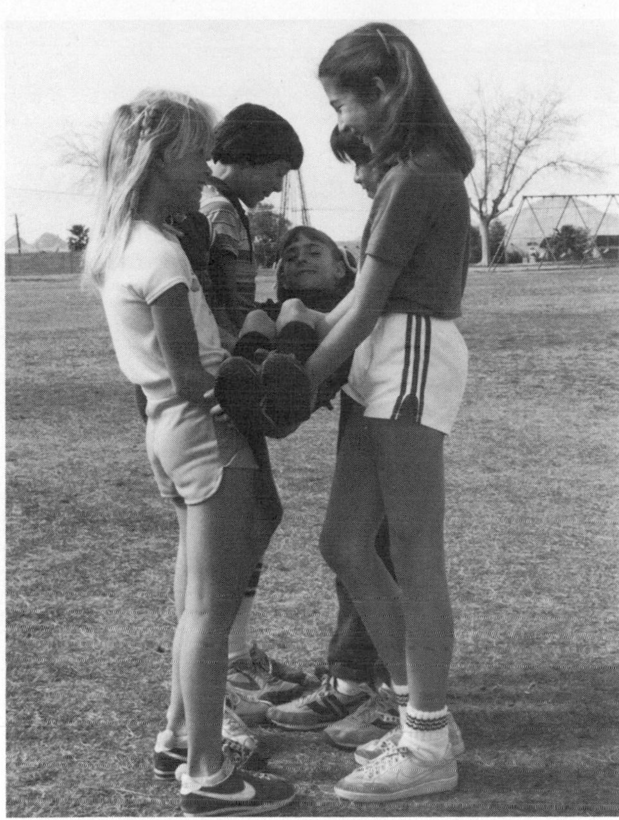

FIGURE 21.131. Injured Person Carry

of joined hands and connects hands, *behind* the circle of standing children, with the riders on either side. There are two sets of joined hands—the first circle, or merry-go-round, and the riders (Figure 21.132). The movement of the Merry-Go-Round is counterclockwise. The circle children, who provide the support, use sidesteps. The riders keep pace, taking small steps with their heels.

FIGURE 21.132. Merry-Go-Round

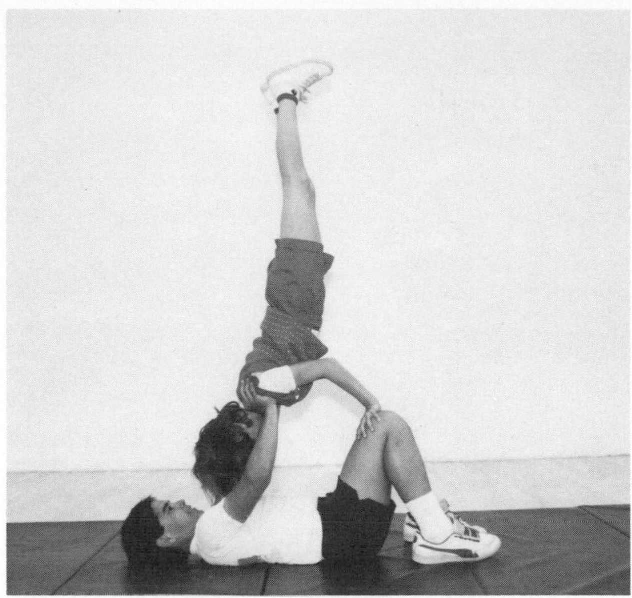

FIGURE 21.133. Knee-and-Shoulder Balance

PARTNER SUPPORT STUNTS

The basic instructions for partner support stunts (pp. 390–391) should be reviewed.

Knee-and-Shoulder Balance

The support partner is on the back, knees well up and feet flat on the floor. He puts the hands out, ready to support the shoulders of the top child. The top child takes a position in front of the support's knees, placing the hands on them. The top performer leans forward so that his shoulders are supported by the hands of the bottom partner, and he kicks up (Figure 21.133).

Spotters are needed on both sides of the pair. If the top child begins to fall, the support partner should maintain the support under the shoulders so the top child will land on the feet. Key points for the top partner are to keep the arms straight and the head up, and to look directly into the support partner's eyes.

Press

The bottom partner lies on the back, with knees bent and feet flat on the floor. The top partner takes a straddle position over the bottom partner, facing the support's feet. Performers then join hands with each other. The top partner sits on the joined hands, supported by the bottom partner, and rests the legs across the bottom partner's knees (Figure 21.134). Both performers should keep the elbows quite straight. Hold for a specified time.

All-Fours Support

The bottom performer lies on the back, with legs apart and knees up. The hands are positioned close to the shoul-

FIGURE 21.134. Press

ders, with palms up. The top performer stands on the partner's palms and leans forward, placing his hands on the support performer's knees. The support raises the top performer by lifting with the arms. The top performer is then in an all-fours position, with feet supported by the bottom performer's extended arms and hands supported by the bottom performer's knees (Figure 21.135).

Angel

The top performer stands in front of the support partner. Both face the same direction. The support squats down, placing the head between the legs of the top performer. Support rises, so the top partner is sitting on support's shoulders. The top performer then proceeds to take a position on support's knees. Support must lean well back for balance, removing the head from between the top performer's legs. The top performer stands erect on support's knees, with arms held level, out to the side. The bottom performer takes hold of the top's thighs and leans back

FIGURE 21.135. All-Fours Support

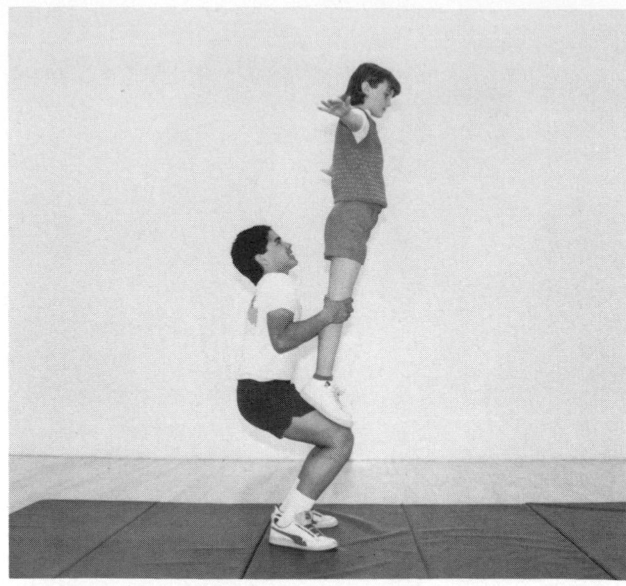

FIGURE 21.136. Angel

to place the pose in balance (Figure 21.136). Hold for 5 seconds. (Children need to experiment to determine the best way to achieve the final position.)

Side Stand

The support partner gets down on the hands and knees to form a rigid base. The top performer stands to the side, bends over the support's back, and hooks the hands, palms up, well underneath the support's chest and waist. He leans across, steadying with the hands, and kicks up to an inverted stand (Figure 21.137). (Spotters are needed on the far side.)

Variation: The top performer, instead of hooking hands underneath, grasps the bottom performer's arm and leg.

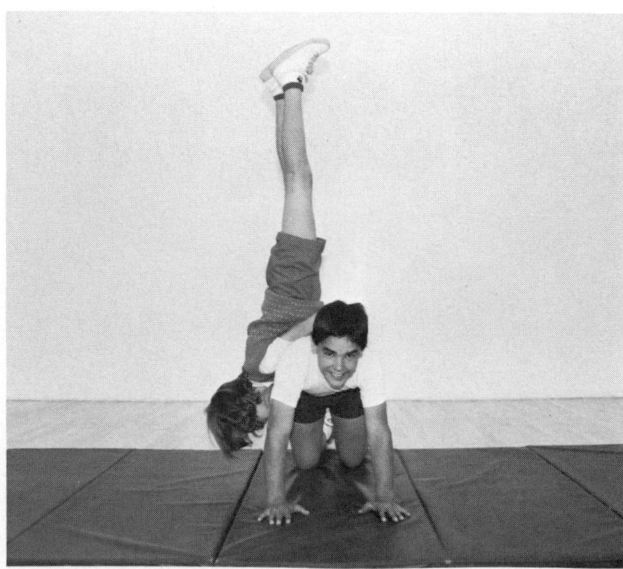

FIGURE 21.137. Side Stand

PYRAMIDS

Making pyramids is a pleasurable activity for children and uses many of the skills learned in the stunts and tumbling program. The emphasis in this section is on smaller pyramid groups. Larger pyramids can be formed by three of the smaller groups. Pyramids provide an opportunity for movement exploration and creativity, since a variety of figures can be made. While the examples presented (Figure 21.138A–F) are composed of three performers, four

FIGURE 21.138. Pyramid formations

and five performers can be combined in similar formations.

Children should stand at attention along a line on the floor or along the edge of the mats. On the first signal, all base performers get into position and top performers move to place. On the second signal, all top performers mount and get into position. On the third signal, top performers place their hands out to the sides or up for the finishing touch. This signal shows the pyramid in all its glory. On the fourth signal, the pyramid is disassembled, and children move to the line and stand at attention.

Children should not do pyramids unless the appropriate balance skills have been mastered. Stunts using only one performer or pairs should be practiced as preliminaries to pyramid building.

The problem-solving approach can be used to encourage the children to devise different pyramids. They can begin in groups of three and progress to larger groups. Smaller groups provide more opportunity for contributions by individual members. Some types of pyramids made by groups of three are shown in Figure 21.138A–F.

CHAPTER 22

Combative Activities

Combatives offer students an opportunity to match their strength and wits against others. The foundation for such activities as wrestling, boxing, judo, and fencing lies deep in the social structure. Combatives should begin in the 4th grade and continue through the remaining school years. Most of the emphasis is on individual competition, but some group activity is included.

Keeping a proper perspective is important when using combative activities. The goal is to give students an opportunity to test themselves. There is little to be gained by trying to determine a class champion or by placing youngsters in situations in which they continually lose. In most cases, the teacher is wise to try a specific combative a few times and then to move on to another activity.

Combatives can be used effectively in conjunction with stunts and tumbling. Often, tumbling activities are not physically demanding, and combatives can provide a change of pace and renewed excitement. On the other hand, a day's lesson dealing wholly with combatives may be too exhausting for children.

Activities with individual tug-of-war ropes (Chapter 18) should be included as part of the combative experiences at each level. The teacher can combine them with the combative activities suggested in this chapter.

INSTRUCTIONAL PROCEDURES

1. Instructions for the contest should be as explicit as necessary. The starting position should be defined so that both contestants begin from an equal and neutral position. What constitutes a win must be defined, and so must the number of trials permitted.

2. When contestants of unequal ability are matched, contests become uninteresting and injuries may result. The matching of contestants should be done in such a way that all children can win at least part of the time.

3. Fair play should be stressed. Children should be encouraged to find strategies and maneuvers to gain success, but always within the framework of the rules.

4. Safety factors are a greater necessity in group contests than in individual combat. Good supervision and a quick whistle are needed. Children should freeze when the whistle is blown. In tug-of-war contests, no one should let go suddenly, thus sending other children sprawling backward.

5. Contests can be started simultaneously on a signal by the teacher, or the approach can be more flexible—allowing children to start contests on their own.

6. Laterality is important. Contests should be done with the right side (arm or leg), the left side, and both sides.

7. Body position can be varied. Children can stand, crouch, sit, or lie for the same contest.

8. Work out a system of rotation, so each contestant has more than one opponent.

9. When a stick is required for the contest, a strong broomstick is a better implement than a wand. Only very sturdy wands should be used.

FORMATIONS FOR COMBATIVE ACTIVITIES

Because of their nature, combative activities require special formations. Except in the pair arrangement, some type of rotational plan should be used that ensures a variety of partners of equal ability.

PAIRS

In the pair formation, each child is paired with another of comparable ability. Starting or stopping the contests can be by instructor signal or at the will of the contestants. This formation keeps everyone active and is more informal than others.

GROUPS OF THREE

Children can also be divided into groups of three. In any group, two players compete against each other and the third child acts as the referee. Opponents are changed and the other child referees. One more change completes a round.

WINNER-LOSER ELIMINATIONS BY GROUPS OF FOUR

Four evenly matched contestants can be grouped. In each activity, they are matched by pairs, with the winners of one contest competing for first place and the losers competing for third. To save time, in the next combative activity each individual competes against the partner with whom he just finished competing.

SUGGESTED ACTIVITIES

FOURTH GRADE

Hand Wrestle

Starting Position: Contestants place right foot against right foot and grasp right hands in a handshake grip. The left foot is planted firmly to the rear for support.

Action: Try to force the other, by hand and arm pressure, to move either foot. Any movement by either foot means a loss.

Variations

1. Stand left foot against left foot and contest with left hands.

2. Stand balanced on the right foot and clasp right hands. A player loses if the right foot is moved or if the back foot touches the ground. Try with the left foot and left hand. The foot off the ground can be held with the free hand.

Finger Fencing

Starting Position: Contestants stand on the right foot and hold the left foot with the left hand.

Action: Hook index fingers of the right hands, and try to push the opponent off balance. Change feet and hands. Any movement of the supporting foot means a loss.

Touch Knees

Starting Position: Contestants stand on both feet and face each other.

Action: Touch one of the opponent's knees without letting the opponent touch yours. Five touches determine the victor.

Variations

1. Grasp left hands, and try to touch the knees with the right hand. The first one to touch wins that bout.

2. Either with hands free or with left hands grasped, try to step lightly on the other's toes.

Grab the Flag

Starting Position: Opponents are on their knees, facing each other on a tumbling mat. Each has a flag tucked in the belt near the middle of the back.

Action: Remain on the knees at all times. Try to grab the flag from the other.

Variation: Try this as a group contest in which contestants pull flags until a champion is established.

Rooster Fight

Starting Position: Players stoop down and clasp hands behind the knees.

Action: Try to upset the other player or cause the handhold to be released.

Variations

1. Squat down and hold the heels with the hands. A player loses when she is upset or when her hands come loose from her heels.

2. Try this as a group contest. Children stand around the edges of an area large enough to contain the group. On signal, they come forward and compete team against team or as individuals. A child that is pushed out of the area is eliminated. The last one left is the winner.

Palm Push

Starting Position: Contestants face each other, standing 12 in. apart. They place the palms of their hands together and must keep them together throughout the contest.

Action: Try to push the opponent off balance.

Variation: Use a wand instead of pushing the palms together.

Bulldozer

Starting Position: Opponents are on their hands and feet (not knees), facing each other, with right shoulders touching.

Action: Try to push (not bump) each other backward. Pushing across the mat or across a restraining line determines the winner. Change shoulders and repeat.

FIFTH GRADE

Breakdown

Starting Position: Opponents are in a front-leaning rest (push-up) position, facing each other.

Action: Using one hand, try to break down the other's position by pushing or dislodging his support while still maintaining your own position.

Variation: Try the contest with each contestant in wheelbarrow position with the legs held by a partner.

Elbow Wrestle

Starting Position: Contestants lie on the floor or sit at a table and face each other. Their right hands are clasped, with right elbows bent and resting on the surface, and right forearms pressed against each other.

Action: Force the other's arm down while keeping the elbows together. Raising the elbow from the original position is a loss.

Variation: Change to a position using the left arm.

Indian Wrestle (Leg Wrestle)

Starting Position: Opponents lie on their backs on the floor or on a mat, with heads in opposite directions, trunks close, and near arms locked at the elbow.

Action: Three counts are given. On each of the first two counts, lift the leg nearer to the opponent to a vertical position. On the third count, hook legs with the opponent near the foot. Try to roll the opponent over backward.

Variation: Use the right and left legs in turn.

Catch-and-Pull Tug-of-War

Starting Position: Two teams face each other across a line.

Action: Try to catch hold of and pull any opponent across the line. When a player is pulled across the line, he waits in back of the opposing team until time is called. The team capturing the most players wins.

Teaching Suggestion: Pulling by catching hold of clothing or hair is not permitted. The penalty is disqualification. Players may cross the line to pull if they are securely held by a teammate or by a chain of players.

Variation: Have those pulled across the line join the other team. This keeps all children in the game.

Stick Twist

Starting Position: Contestants face each other with their feet approximately 12 in. apart. They hold a wand above their heads with both hands, the arms completely extended.

Action: On signal, try to bring the wand down slowly without changing the grip. The object is to maintain the original grip and not to let the wand twist in the hands. The wand does not have to be forced down, but rather, should be moved down by mutual agreement. It can be moved completely down only if one player allows it to slip in her hands.

Toe Touch

Starting Position: Contestants face each other. Each places both hands on the opponent's shoulders.

Action: On signal, try to step lightly on the opponent's toes without letting him step on your toes. Keep score by counting the number of touches made.

Variation: Try this contest with groups of four or more opponents.

Crab Contest

Starting Position: Both contestants are in crab position with seats held high.

Action: On signal, try, by jostling and pushing, to force the other's seat to touch the mat.

Variation: Place a beanbag on the tummy. Try to knock the opponent's beanbag to the floor.

SIXTH GRADE

Most combatives for 4th- and 5th-grade students are beneficial and enjoyable at the 6th-grade level as well. A review adds to the variety of the 6th-grade program.

Shoulder Shove

Starting Position: Each contestant raises the left leg, holding the ankle with the right hand and holding the right elbow with the left hand.

Action: Try to bump the other person off balance with the left shoulder so that one of her hands releases its position.

Teaching Suggestion: The teacher or a referee should call a loss when the left hand releases the right elbow, because this is difficult for the opponent to see. Dropping the hold on the ankle is definite and visible.

Variations

1. Stand on one foot and fold the arms. Try to knock the other player off balance, so the uplifted foot touches the ground.

2. Using a 6- or 8-ft circle, try to force the opponent out of the circle.

3. Use a kangaroo theme. Carry a volleyball between the legs at the knees. Try to maintain control of the ball while shoving the opponent with the shoulder.

Wand Wrestle

Starting Position: Players face each other, grasping a wand between them. The grips must be fair, with each child having an outside hand.

Action: By twisting and applying pressure on the wand, try to get the opponent to relinquish his grip.

Variations

1. *Basketball Wrestle.* Use a basketball instead of a wand. Each should have the same grasp advantage at the start.

2. Squat down while maintaining a grip on the wand. Attempt to take away the wand or to upset the opponent.

Chinese Pull-up

Starting Position: Two students sit on the floor and face each other, with knees straight and soles of the feet against the opponent's. Each bends forward, and they grasp a wand between them.

Action: Pull the other player forward to cause him to release the grip. Only straight pulling is allowed.

Teaching Suggestion: To provide a straight pull, one player should have both hands on the inside and the other both hands on the outside, rather than having alternate grip positions.

Wand Lift

Starting Position: Two contestants stand facing each other and hold a 3-ft-long stick or wand between them. Each holds one end of the stick with the right hand, using an underhand grip. Each places the left hand, in an overhand grip, next to and touching the opponent's right-hand grip. The elbows are bent at approximately a right angle.

Action: Press down with the left hand and lift with the right to bring the stick up to a vertical position. The body can be braced for action, but body motion should be minimal. This contest is meant to be a test of pure strength.

Variation: Try with a left-hand lift.

Sitting Elbow Wrestle

Starting Position: Contestants sit on a mat, back-to-back, with elbows locked. The legs are spread wide.

Action: Pull to the left in an attempt to tip the opponent.

Variations

1. Reverse direction.

2. Position the legs so the knees are bent and the soles of the feet are flat on the mat.

Power Pull

Starting Position: One contestant stands with fingers touching in front of and close to her chest. The other person stands facing the opponent and grasps her wrists.

Action: On signal, the contestant holding the wrists attempts to pull the opponent's fingers apart. A straight pull (no jerking) is the action.

Rope Tug-of-War

Starting Position: Two equal teams face each other on opposite ends of a rope. A piece of tape marks the center of the rope. Two parallel lines are drawn about 10 ft apart. At the start, the center marker on the rope is midway between the lines.

Action: Try to pull the center marker over your team's near line.

Teaching Suggestion: The rope should be long enough to accommodate the children without crowding. It should be at least ¾ in. in diameter. Children should never wrap the rope around the hands, arms, or body in any manner.

Variation: Use different positions for pulling—with the rope overhead (teams have their backs toward each other), with one hand on the ground, or from a seated position (with feet braced on the floor).

Four-Team Tug-of-War

Starting Position: Four teams line up as shown in Figure 22.1. A special rope is needed, the size and extent of which

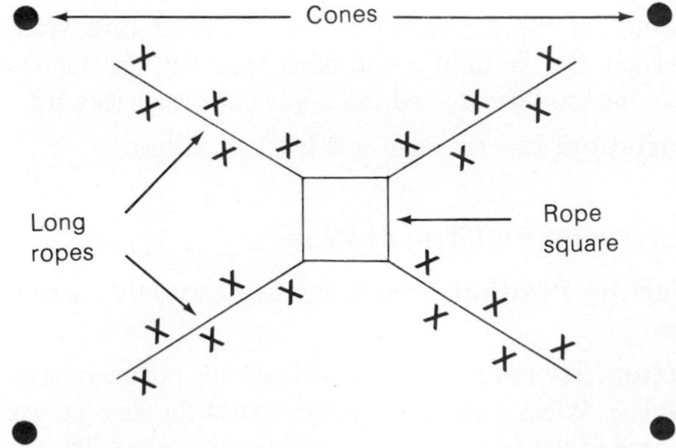

FIGURE 22.1. Formation for Four-Team Tug-of-War

depend on the number of children. A cone, an Indian club, or a beanbag is placed an equal distance behind each team.

Action: Pull, on signal, in the direction of your team's cone. A team wins when the player on the end of the rope can knock over the cone, or pick up the club or beanbag, without losing contact with the rope.

Teaching Suggestion: An automobile tire can be substituted for the center rope square. Simply tie four tug-of-war ropes to the tire.

Variation: Try this as a three-team contest, with the center figure a rope triangle.

CHAPTER 23

Games

As an integral part of the physical education program, games need to be scrutinized carefully and evaluated in terms of what they offer children. Games that involve only a few children, games that allow some children to dominate, and games that offer little in the way of skill development are being eliminated from the repertoire of traditional activities.

Children can create and modify games to meet their needs. Through these experiences, intermediate-level children learn about game components and how to change different components in a meaningful way.

Teachers should view games as a valuable contribution to the child's total development. Through games, children can experience success and accomplishment. In addition, some of the social objectives accomplished through a game encounter are the development of social skills, acceptance of rule parameters, and a better understanding of oneself in a competitive and cooperative situation.

Games are a laboratory where children can apply newly learned skills in a meaningful way. Many games help to develop the large-muscle groups and enhance the child's ability to run, dodge, start, and stop under control while sharing space with others. Cognitive development is also enhanced as children learn to understand and follow rules. By applying strategy in games, children learn the importance of alertness and the mental aspect of participation.

EVALUATING GAMES

Teachers learn to evaluate games by looking at various facets—the skills required, the number of participants, the complexity, length, and progression. As teachers become adept at game evaluation, they can use this skill to select new games and to modify games previously learned to ensure that the activities are suited to the maturity and skill level of the children.

The game should first be evaluated in terms of the skills that are required to participate successfully. If children have not yet learned and overlearned a skill, they will almost certainly not be able to learn and apply that skill in a game setting. For example, children may be able to throw with proper form, but they may not be able to throw accurately in a game setting. They may be able to hit a stationary object but not a moving target.

Children must learn to cooperate with teammates and to compete against peers. The larger the number of teammates and competitors, the more difficult the game becomes. Cooperating with teammates is just as difficult as competing in a meaningful fashion. Teachers should use a progression of games, moving from partner activities to small-group games to team games. Many games are actually more effective when played in small groups, because the participants get to handle objects more often and to be leaders more often.

The number of rules and the degree of strategy applicable in a game are important considerations. Primary-level children typically have difficulty playing a game that has many rules and probably will not enjoy such an activity. If extensive strategy is required, students must have overlearned the physical skills so they can apply their concentration to the mental aspect of the game. Complex games require team members to play specific roles, and some of these roles (e.g., goalkeeper or line positions) may not appeal to many youngsters. In contrast, many popular games are spontaneous in nature and demand little concentration.

Children should receive positive feedback from the game experience. Many games must be played for a long period of time before the outcome is determined. The younger the children, the less willing they are to wait for the outcome; feedback must be immediate. Children become bored and tire of playing long games. Fatigue is also a factor in the interest level of children, and the teacher must watch carefully for signs of it.

Games require a combination of skills. A game in which children must sequence many skills may result in failure or frustration for many. Lead-up games are developed for the express purpose of limiting the number of skills needed for successful participation. The instructor should look at the number of skills required and build a progression of games that gradually increases the use of skill combinations.

CREATING OR MODIFYING GAMES

Games can be modified and new variations created by the teacher or the students or by both together. For example, a teacher may observe that a specific game is not meeting the desired objectives. She decides to modify or change the game to facilitate skill development. In another situation, the teacher may stop the class and ask them to help make the game better and more meaningful. Alternatives can be implemented and the newly created activity tested to see whether it is indeed more effective. With intermediate-level students, the teacher can offer some parameters for developing a game and then allow the children to work as a group to implement the activity. Ground rules can be established to facilitate group dynamics. The teacher can suggest voting on a rule change or can specify a maximum number of changes allowed per period.

If students and teachers are to make meaningful modifications, they must understand how to analyze a game. The most recognized elements that structure games are desired outcomes, skills, equipment, rules or restrictions, number of players, and scheme of organization. Morris (1980) has provided an extensive approach to game analysis. Readers are referred to this text if they are interested in game modification.

Instructors should remember that youngsters need to learn how and what to modify and that they need to practice the process. Some suggestions to start youngsters thinking are the following.

1. Change the distance to be run by decreasing or increasing it. For example, in Star Wars go around once instead of twice.

2. Change the means of locomotion. Use hopping, walking, skipping, or galloping instead of running.

3. Play the game with one or more partners. The partners can move and act as if they were a single child.

4. Change the method of tagging in simple tag games. Call out "Reverse" to signal that the chaser is to become the tagger and vice versa.

5. Make goals or restricted areas larger or smaller. In Over the Wall (Chinese Wall), the restraining area should be made larger or smaller or its shape can be changed.

6. Vary the boundaries of the game. They can be made larger or smaller, as dictated by the number of players.

7. Change the formation in which the game is played. For example, Circle Kickball could be played in a square or triangular shape.

8. Change the requirements necessary for scoring. In Hand Hockey, students might be required to make four passes before a shot is taken.

9. Increase the number of players, taggers, or runners. The amount of equipment used can also be increased. For example, in Nine Lives, the more fleece balls used, the more practice the youngsters get in throwing at a moving target.

10. Change the rules or penalties of the game. For example, players might be allowed a maximum of three dribbles or might be allowed to hold the ball for no more than 3 seconds.

Many of the games in this chapter have been modified by students and teachers. These variations are presented with the description of each game.

COOPERATION AND COMPETITION

Most games require cooperation and competition. Cooperation involves two or more children working together to achieve a common goal. Competition is characterized by opponents working against each other as each tries to reach a goal or reward. An in-depth look at competition is offered in Chapter 26. The teacher should strive always to emphasize cooperation rather than competition and to develop a spirit of working together, a concern for teammates, and an appreciation of the collective skills of the group.

Achieving a balance between offense and defense in games is important. In tag and capture games, there should be an opportunity to remain safe as well as a strong challenge to be at risk and elude capture. Teachers should evaluate the game components continually and modify them in the interest of retaining an enjoyable environment. Teams should be somewhat equal so all participants have an opportunity to find success. There is no motivation when there is no opportunity to win. Emphasizing cooperation reinforces for children the need to play with all classmates regardless of ability level. Teachers should rotate students regularly so children have the chance to play with all of their classmates and to play on equal teams. Rotation plans should include handicapped youngsters.

SAFETY

Safety is a primary consideration in game situations. The play area should be checked for dangerous objects and hazards. Tables, chairs, equipment, and apparatus can become dangerous when a high-speed game is underway. Children should learn to move in a controlled fashion and to use the entire playing area to avoid collisions. They must be taught to stop playing immediately when a signal is given. This is an important prerequisite for later sports experiences.

Dodgeball games require special consideration because participants may sustain injury if not supervised properly. The value of dodgeball games is in the throwing practice. Students have few opportunities to practice throwing with velocity, which is necessary to develop mature throwing form.

The many foam-rubber balls on the market make excellent projectiles for dodgeball activities. They do not sting or cause injury. Fleece balls are also excellent for games in which balls are thrown at a close distance. (Playground balls should not be used.) Rules should be established that penalize for striking others above the waist. Restraining lines can be drawn to keep students an adequate distance apart and to allow them enough reaction time to dodge the oncoming ball.

Another excellent idea for modifying dodgeball games for safety is to throw at objects other than students. For example, Cageball Target Throw and Pin Dodgeball offer different targets, yet still provide throwing practice.

In games that involve a goal line, a wall should never be used as the goal. Rather, lines should be drawn 10 ft from the wall to allow for deceleration. Cones also can be used to mark the deceleration zone.

INSTRUCTIONAL PROCEDURES

1. The instructor must study the game before attempting to teach it. Safety hazards should be identified, difficult concepts anticipated, and the game adapted to the class and the situation. Physical preparations should be completed prior to teaching. Boundaries should be established and equipment made ready for distribution.

2. When presenting a new game to a class, the teacher should put the youngsters in the formation that they are going to use. They can then sit and be comfortable while listening to instructions. Directions should be as brief as possible, and the children should try the game quickly. A useful rule of thumb is to offer minimal instruction to get the game underway and then gradually to implement the more subtle rules. Try the game first, and then answer any questions that the students may have. This ensures that they have some perception of the game and how it is to proceed.

3. Having a trial period during the first stages of learning a game is important. This avoids the possibility of the children's feeling resentful about losing a point or being caught because they did not understand the activity.

4. Social learning should be enhanced through game experiences. Allow the children to call infractions or penalties on each other and on themselves. Youngsters must learn to accept calls made by officials as an integral part of any game situation. When disagreements occur, the teacher should adopt the role of arbitrator, rather than taking one side or the other. Children thus learn negotiation skills and eventually should resolve many differences among themselves rather than having the teacher decide each issue.

5. In the early phases of a game, instruction should continue. The teacher can look for opportunities to stop the game briefly and offer instruction or correction. Coaching hints for improving performance are also a part of the game environment.

6. Games are enjoyable when they are novel. Often, it is effective to stop the game at the height of interest. Children will then look forward to playing it the next time. In addition, a wide variety of games should be offered to stimulate interest.

7. The instructor must make sure that all children have a chance to participate in those games that require taking turns. A good policy for games in which numbers are called is to write the numbers down on a card. Caution must be used in games that eliminate children. If children must be eliminated, it should be for one or two turns only, and they should then be allowed back in the game. Another solution is to have play continue until a few youngsters are eliminated. Then the rest of the players can be declared winners.

8. The teacher should have a rotation plan that allows all children to play an equal amount of time. The object is to avoid the situation in which winners stay on the court and losers sit out, receiving much less practice than the better players.

9. If identifying teams is difficult, use pinnies, crepe paper armbands, colored shoulder loops, or flag football belts.

SELECTION OF GAMES

The majority of games in this chapter were selected because of their activity potential for all children. All games should be analyzed to identify the skills that children must practice before playing. Drills and skill practice become more meaningful when children comprehend that the skill is to be used in an enjoyable game situation.

Games for kindergarten through 2nd grade do not require a high degree of specialized sport skill. Most use basic locomotor skills and offer an environment in which children can practice and participate successfully. These games can be modified easily to allow all children to have enjoyable experiences.

Specialized sport skills are necessary for success in many

games for 3rd- through 6th-grade children. Ball-handling skills are challenged through the medium of game activity. Movement skills, with emphasis on agility, become important for success. Teachers should offer opportunities for children to practice these skills outside of competitive situations.

Games for intermediate-grade children fall into two categories: sport-related games and those games not specifically related to a sport. This chapter presents games in the latter category. Lead-up games relating to the various sports are presented in those chapters dealing with each sport. Chapter 17 also offers games that emphasize various rhythm components. Finally, Chapter 24 offers many relays that can provide enjoyable game experiences.

In the programs that follow, specific games are suggested for each grade level. In contrast to games for the lower grades, the activities for the intermediate level are more difficult to allocate to a specific grade. In many cases, the allocations involve arbitrary decisions. Some allocation system of games to grade level is important, however, to ensure that children have new experiences for each school year.

The intermediate program should make use of any appropriate games from the lower grades. Modifications of rules and boundaries allow these games to be used on many levels, even in junior and senior high school programs. The intermediate-level games presented here should be supplemented by the lead-up games presented in the chapters on the various sports.

GAMES FOR KINDERGARTEN CHILDREN

The game program for the kindergarten level features mostly individual games and creative play. Little emphasis is placed on team play or on games that have a scoring system. The games are simple, easily taught, and not demanding of skills. Beanbags are used in some of the activities, but ball games are not particularly appropriate for this level. Dramatic elements are present in many of the games, while others help establish number concepts and symbol recognition. Games based on stories or poems are popular with kindergarten children. Some of the games suggested for the 1st grade may also be appropriate.

Suggested Games

Colors
Fire Fighter
Jack Frost and Jane Thaw
Marching Ponies
Mother, May I?
Popcorn
The Scarecrow and the Crows
Statues
Tommy Tucker's Land

Colors

Playing Area: Playground, gymnasium, classroom

Players: Entire class

Supplies: Colored paper (construction paper) cut in circles, squares, or triangles for markers

Skills: Color or other perceptual concepts, running

Five or six different colored markers should be used, with a number of children having the same color. The children are seated in a circle with a marker in front of each child.

The teacher calls out a color, and everyone having that color runs counterclockwise around the circle and back to place. The first one seated upright and motionless is declared the winner. Different kinds of locomotor movement can be specified, such as skipping, galloping, walking, and so on. After a period of play, the children leave the markers on the floor and move one place to the left.

Variation: Shapes (e.g., circles, triangles, squares, rectangles, stars, and diamonds) can be used instead of colors, as can numbers or other articles or categories, such as animals, birds, or fish. This game has value in teaching identification and recognition.

Fire Fighter

Playing Area: Playground, gymnasium, classroom

Players: Entire class

Supplies: None

Skill: Running

A fire chief runs around the outside of a circle of children and taps a number of them on the back, saying, "Fire fighter," each time. After making the round of the circle, the chief goes to the center. When she says, "Fire," the fire fighters run counterclockwise around the circle and back to place. The one who returns first and is able to stand in place motionless is declared the winner and the new chief.

The chief can use other words to fool the children, but they run only on the word "Fire." This merely provides some fun, since there is no penalty for a false start. The circle children can sound the siren as the fire fighters run.

Jack Frost and Jane Thaw

Playing Area: Playground, gymnasium, classroom

Players: Entire class

Supplies: A white streamer for Jack Frost, a streamer of another color for Jane Thaw

Skills: Running, dodging, holding position

The children are scattered and move to avoid being frozen (tagged) by Jack Frost, who carries a white streamer in one hand. Frozen children must remain immobile until touched (thawed) by Jane Thaw, identified by a streamer of a different color. Freezing occurs instantly, but thawing is a more gradual process. Two Jack Frosts can help keep the action moving.

Marching Ponies

Playing Area: Playground, gymnasium, classroom

Players: Entire class

Supplies: None

Skills: Marching, running

One child, the ringmaster, crouches in the center of a circle of ponies formed by the other children. Two goal lines on opposite sides of the circle are established as safe areas. The ponies march around the circle in step, counting as they do so. At a predetermined number (whispered to the ringmaster by the teacher), the ringmaster jumps up and attempts to tag the others before they can reach the safety lines. Anyone tagged joins the ringmaster in the center and helps catch the other children the next time. The game should be reorganized after six to eight children have been caught. Those left in the circle are declared the winners.

Variation: Other characterizations, such as lumbering elephants, jumping kangaroos, and the like, can be tried. A child who suggests a unique movement could be allowed to be the ringmaster.

Mother, May I?

Playing Area: Playground, gymnasium

Players: Eight to ten

Supplies: None

Skills: Fundamental locomotor movements

Starting and finishing lines are established about 40 ft apart. In a gymnasium, the game can proceed sideways across the floor. One child is it and stands between the two lines. The rest of the children stand on the starting line. The object of the game is to reach the finish line first. The child who is it tells one of the players how many steps can be taken and what kind. The player must ask, "Mother, may I?" and await the answer before moving. (If a boy is in the center, the call is "Daddy, may I?") If a player fails to ask the question before moving, she goes back to the starting line. Even when the question is asked, the one who is it may say no. The steps should be varied to provide different kinds of movement. Baby steps, scissors steps, giant steps, hopping steps, bunny steps (jumps), and others are appropriate. The first to reach the finish line is it for the next game.

Popcorn

Playing Area: Playground, gymnasium, classroom

Players: Entire class

Supplies: None

Skills: Curling, stretching, jumping

The teacher should give a short preliminary explanation of how popcorn pops in response to the heat applied. Half of the children are designated as popcorn; they crouch down in the center of the circle formed by the rest of the children. The circle children, also crouching, represent the heat. One of them is designated the leader, and his actions serve as a guide to the other children. The circle children gradually rise to a standing position, extend their arms overhead, and shake them vigorously to indicate the intensifying heat. In the meantime, the popcorn in the center starts to pop. This should begin at a slow pace and increase in speed and height as the heat is applied. In the final stages, the children are popping up rapidly. After a time, the groups change places and the action is repeated.

The Scarecrow and the Crows

Playing Area: Playground, gymnasium, classroom

Players: Entire class

Supplies: None

Skills: Dodging, running

The children form a large circle representing the garden, which one child, designated the scarecrow, guards. From six to eight crows scatter on the outside of the circle, and the scarecrow assumes a characteristic pose inside the circle. The circle children raise their joined hands and let the crows run through, into the garden, where they pretend to eat. The scarecrow tries to tag the crows. The circle children help the crows by raising their joined hands and allowing them to leave the circle, but they try to hinder the scarecrow. If the scarecrow runs out of the circle, all of the crows run immediately into the garden and start to nibble at the vegetables, while the circle children hinder the scarecrow's reentry.

When the scarecrow has caught one or two crows, a new group of children is selected. If, after a reasonable period of time, the scarecrow has failed to catch any crows, a change should be made.

Statues

Playing Area: Playground, gymnasium

Players: Entire class

Supplies: None

Skills: Body management, applying force, balance

Children are scattered in pairs around the area. One partner is the swinger and the other the statue. The teacher voices a directive, such as "Pretty," "Funny," "Happy," "Angry," or "Ugly." The swinger takes the statue by one or both hands, swings it around in a small circle two or three times (the teacher should specify), and releases it. The statue then takes a pose in keeping with the directive, and the swinger sits down on the floor.

The teacher or a committee of children can determine which children are the best statues. The statue must hold the position without moving or be disqualified. After the winners are announced, the partners reverse positions. Children should be cautioned that the purpose of the swinging is to position the statues and that it must be controlled.

Variation: In the original game, the swinging is done until the directive is called. The swinger then immediately releases the statue, who takes the pose as called. This gives little time for the statue to react. Better and more creative statues are possible if the directive is given earlier.

Tommy Tucker's Land

Playing Area: Playground, gymnasium, classroom

Players: Eight to ten

Supplies: About ten beanbags for each game

Skills: Dodging, running

One child, Tommy Tucker (or Tammi Tucker, if a girl), stands in the center of a 15-ft square, within which the beanbags are scattered. Tommy is guarding his land and the treasure. The other children chant,

> I'm on Tommy Tucker's land,
> Picking up gold and silver.

The children attempt to pick up as much of the treasure as they can while avoiding being tagged by Tommy. Any child who is tagged must return the treasure and retire from the game. The game is over when only one child is left or when all of the beanbags have been successfully filched. The teacher may wish to call a halt to the game earlier if a stalemate is reached. In this case, the child with the most treasure becomes the new Tommy.

Variation: This game can be played with a restraining line instead of a square, but there must be boundaries that limit movement.

GAMES FOR FIRST-GRADE CHILDREN

The games for the 1st grade fall into two categories—(1) running and tag games and (2) ball games. Few team activities are included, because children at this level are quite individualistic and team play is beyond their capacities. The ball games require only the simple skills of throwing and catching. In addition to the games presented here, the kindergarten games should be reviewed.

Suggested Games

- Animal Tag
- Back to Back
- Blind Duck
- Midnight
  - Lame Wolf
- Old Man (Old Woman)
- One, Two, Button My Shoe
- Squirrel in the Trees
- Tag Games (Simple)
  - Locomotor Tag
  - Frozen Tag
- Where's My Partner?
- Ball Passing
- Stop Ball
- Teacher Ball (Leader Ball)

Animal Tag

Playing Area: Playground, gymnasium

Players: Entire class

Supplies: None

Skills: Imagery, running, dodging

Two parallel lines are drawn about 40 ft apart. The children are divided into two groups, each of which takes a position on one of the lines. The children in one group get together with their leader and decide what animal they wish to imitate. Having selected the animal, they move over to within 5 ft or so of the other line. There, they imitate the animal, and the other group tries to guess the animal correctly. If the guess is correct, they chase the first group back to its line, trying to tag as many as possible. Those caught must go over to the other team.

The second group then selects an animal, and the roles are reversed. If the guessing team cannot guess the animal, however, the performing team gets another try. To avoid confusion, the children must raise their hands to take turns at naming the animal. Otherwise, many false chases will occur. If the children have trouble guessing, then the leader of the performing team can give the initial of the animal.

Back to Back

Playing Area: Playground, gymnasium, classroom

Players: Entire class

Supplies: None

Skills: Fundamental locomotor movements

The number of children must be uneven. (If not, the teacher can play.) On signal, each child stands back to back with another child. One child will be without a partner. This child claps the hands for the next signal, and all children change partners, with the extra player from the previous game seeking a partner.

Variation: Considerably more activity can be achieved by putting in an extra command. After the children are in partner formation back to back, the teacher says, "Everybody run (skip, hop, jump, slide)!" Other commands, such as "Walk like an elephant," can also be given. The children move around in the prescribed manner. When the signal is sounded, they immediately find a new partner and stand back to back.

Blind Duck

Playing Area: Gymnasium, classroom

Players: 10 to 15

Supplies: A wand, broomstick, cane, or yardstick

Skills: Fundamental locomotor movements

One child, designated the duck (Daisy if a girl, Donald if a boy), stands blindfolded in the center of a circle and holds a wand or similar article. She taps on the floor and tells the children to hop (or perform some other locomotor movement). The children in the circle act accordingly, all moving in the same direction. Daisy then taps the wand twice on the floor, which signals all children to stop. Daisy moves forward with her wand, still blindfolded, to find a child in the circle. She asks, "Who are you?" The child responds, "Quack, quack." Daisy tries to identify this person. If the guess is correct, the identified child becomes the new duck. If the guess is wrong, Daisy must take another turn. After two unsuccessful turns, another child is chosen to be the duck.

Midnight

Playing Area: Playground

Players: 6 to 15

Supplies: None

Skills: Running, dodging

A safety line is established about 40 ft from a den in which one player, the fox, is standing. The others stand behind the safety line and move forward slowly, asking, "Please, Mr. Fox, what time is it?" The fox answers in various fashions, such as "Bedtime," "Pretty late," "Three-thirty." The fox continues to draw the players toward him. At some point, he answers the question by saying "Midnight," and then chases the others back to the safety line. Any player who is caught joins the fox in the den and helps to catch others. No player in the den may leave, however, until the fox calls out "Midnight."

Variation: *Lame Wolf*—The wolf is lame and advances in a series of three running steps and a hop. Other children taunt "Lame Wolf, can't catch me!" or "Lame Wolf, tame wolf, can't catch me!" The wolf may give chase at any time. Children who are caught join the wolf and must also move as if lame.

Old Man (Old Woman)

Playing Area: Playground, gymnasium, classroom

Players: Entire class

Supplies: None

Skills: Fundamental locomotor movements

A line is established through the middle of the area. Half of the children are on one side and half are on the other. There must be an odd person, the teacher or another child. The teacher gives a signal for the children to move as directed on their side of the line. They can be told to run, hop, skip, or whatever. At another signal, the children run to the dividing line, and each reaches across to join hands with a child from the opposite group. The one left out is the old man (if a boy) or the old woman (if a girl). Children may reach over but may not cross the line. The odd person should alternate sides, so the old man or woman can be on the other side at times.

Variation: The game also can be done with music or a drumbeat, with the players rushing to the center line to find partners when the rhythm stops.

One, Two, Button My Shoe

Playing Area: Playground, gymnasium

Players: Entire class

Supplies: None

Skill: Running

Two parallel lines are drawn about 50 ft apart. One child is the leader and stands to one side. The rest of the children are behind one of the lines. The leader says, "Ready." The following dialogue takes place between the leader and the children.

Children: One, two.

Leader: Button my shoe.

Children: Three, four.

Leader: Close the door.

Children: Five, six.

Leader: Pick up sticks.

Children: Seven, eight.

Leader: Run, or you'll be *late!*

As the children carry on the conversation with the leader, they toe the line, ready to run. When the leader says the word "late," the children run to the other line and return. The first child across the original line is the winner and becomes the new leader. The leader can give the last response ("Run, or you'll be late!") in any timing she wishes—pausing or dragging out the words. No child is to leave before the word "late" is uttered.

Squirrel in the Trees

Playing Area: Playground, gymnasium

Players: 16 to 30

Supplies: None

Skills: Fundamental locomotor movements

A number of trees are formed by two players facing each other and holding hands or putting hands on each other's shoulders. A squirrel is in the center of each tree, and one or two extra squirrels are outside. A signal to change is given. All squirrels move out of their tree to another tree, and the extra players try to find a free tree. Only one squirrel is allowed in a tree.

Teaching Suggestion: As a system of rotation, when each squirrel moves into a tree, he can change places with one of the players forming the tree. The rotation is important, because it ensures that all children are eventually active.

Tag Games (Simple)

Playing Area: Playground with established boundaries, or gymnasium

Players: Any number

Supplies: None

Skills: Fundamental locomotor movements, dodging

Tag is played in many ways. Children are scattered about the area. One child is it and chases others, trying to tag one of them. When a tag is made, she says, "You're it." The new it chases other children.

Variations

1. Touching a specified type of object (e.g., wood, iron) or the floor or an object of a specified color can make a runner safe.

2. Children can be safe by doing a particular action or by striking a certain pose.

a. *Stoop Tag.* Players touch both hands to the ground.

b. *Stork Tag.* Players stand on one foot (the other cannot touch).

c. *Turtle Tag.* Players get on their backs, feet pointed toward the ceiling.

d. *Hindoo Tag.* Players make an obeisance with forehead to the ground.

e. *Nose-and-Toe Tag.* Players touch the nose to the toe.

f. *Back-to-Back Tag.* Players stand back to back with any other child.

g. *Skunk Tag.* Players reach an arm under one knee and hold on to the nose.

3. *Locomotor Tag.* The child who is it specifies how the others should move—skipping, hopping, jumping. The tagger must use the same kind of movement.

4. *Frozen Tag.* Two children are it. The rest are scattered over the area. When caught, they are "frozen" and must keep both feet in place. Any free player can tag a frozen player and thus release her. The goal of the tagger is to freeze all players. Frozen players can be required to hop in place until released.

Where's My Partner?

Playing Area: Playground, gymnasium, classroom

Players: Entire class

Supplies: None

Skills: Fundamental locomotor movements

Children are in a double circle by couples, with partners facing. The inside circle has one more player than the outside. When the signal is given, the circles skip (or walk, run, hop, or gallop) to the right. This means that they are skipping in opposite directions. On the command "Halt," the circles face each other to find partners. The player left without a partner is in the mush-pot (the center area of the circle). When play starts again, this child enters either circle. The circles should be reversed after a time.

Variation: The game can also be played with music or a drumbeat. When the music stops, the players seek partners.

Ball Passing

Playing Area: Playground, gymnasium, classroom

Players: Entire class

Supplies: Five or six different kinds of balls for each circle

Skill: Object handling

The class is divided into two or more circles, with no more than 15 children in any one circle. Each circle consists of two or more squads, but squad members need not stand together.

The teacher starts a ball around the circle; it is passed from player to player in the same direction. The teacher introduces more balls until five or six are moving around the circle at the same time and in the same direction. If a child drops a ball, he must retrieve it, and a point is scored against his squad. After a period of time, a whistle is blown, and the points against each squad are totaled. The squad with the lowest score wins. Beanbags, large blocks, or softballs can be substituted for balls.

Stop Ball

Playing Area: Playground, gymnasium

Players: About half the class

Supplies: A ball

Skills: Tossing, catching

One child, with hands over the eyes, stands in the center of a circle of children. A ball is tossed clockwise or counterclockwise from child to child around the circle. Failing to catch the ball or making a bad toss incurs a penalty. The child must take one long step back and stay out of the game for one or two turns.

At a time of her own selection, the center player calls, "Stop." The player caught with the ball steps back and stays out for two turns. The center player should be allowed three or four turns and then be changed.

Teacher Ball (Leader Ball)

Playing Area: Playground, gymnasium

Players: Five to eight

Supplies: A volleyball or rubber playground ball

Skills: Throwing, catching

One child is the teacher or leader and stands about 10 ft in front of the others, who are lined up facing him. The object of the game is to move up to the teacher's spot by not making any bad throws and by not missing any catches. The teacher throws to each child in turn, beginning with the child on the left, who must catch and return the ball (Figure 23.1). Any child making a throwing or catching error goes to the end of the line, on the teacher's right. Those in the line move up, filling the vacated space.

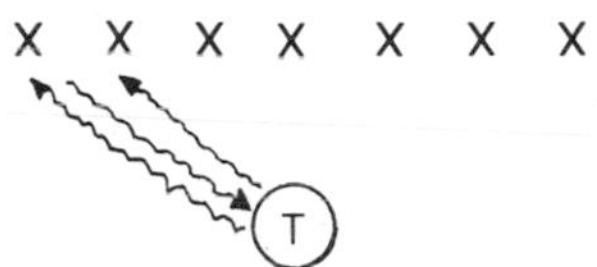

FIGURE 23.1. Formation for Teacher Ball

If the teacher makes a mistake, he must go to the end of the line, and the child at the head of the line becomes the new teacher. The teacher scores a point by remaining in position for three rounds (three throws to each child). After scoring a point, the teacher takes a position at the end of the line, and another child becomes the teacher.

Teaching Suggestion: This game should be used only after children have a minimal competency in throwing and catching skills. It can be a part of the skill-teaching program.

Variation: The teacher can suggest specific methods of throwing and catching, such as "Catch with the right hand only," or "Catch with one hand and don't let the ball touch your body."

GAMES FOR SECOND-GRADE CHILDREN

The games program for the 2nd grade is quite similar to that for 1st grade. The 2nd-grade teacher should make use also of all games presented in the 1st grade. The simple ball games of the 1st grade have particularly good value.

Suggested Games

Cat and Mice
Change Sides
Charlie Over the Water
Flowers and Wind
Forest Ranger
Hill Dill
Hot Potatoes
Leap the Brook
March Attack
May I Chase You?
Mousetrap
Red Light
Bottle Bat Ball
Circle Straddle Ball
Roll Dodgeball

Cat and Mice

Playing Area: Playground, gymnasium, classroom

Players: 10 to 30

Supplies: None

Skills: Running, dodging

The children form a large circle. One child is the cat and four others are the mice. The cat and mice cannot leave the circle. On signal, the cat chases the mice inside the circle. As they are caught, the mice join the circle. The last mouse caught becomes the cat for the next round.

Teaching Suggestions: The teacher should start at one point in the circle and go around the circle selecting mice so that each child gets a chance to be in the center.

Sometimes, one child has difficulty catching the last mouse or any of the mice. If this is the case, the children forming the circle can take a step toward the center, thus constricting the running area. The teacher should cut off any prolonged chase sequence.

Change Sides

Playing Area: Playground, gymnasium

Players: Entire class

Supplies: None

Skill: Body management

Two parallel lines are established 30 ft apart. Half of the children are on each line. On signal, all cross to the other line, face the center, and stand at attention. The first group to do this correctly wins a point. Children must be cautioned to use care when passing through the opposite group. They should be spaced well along each line; this allows room for them to move through each group. The locomotor movements should be varied. The teacher may say, "Ready—walk!" Skipping, hopping, long steps, sliding, and other forms of locomotion can be specified. The position to be assumed at the finish can be varied also.

Teaching Suggestion: Because success depends on getting across first, the teacher should watch for shortcutting of the rules and talk this problem over with the children.

Variation: The competition can be by squads, with two squads on each line.

Charlie Over the Water

Playing Area: Playground, gymnasium

Players: 8 to 12

Supplies: A volleyball or playground ball

Skills: Skipping, running, stopping, bowling

The children are in circle formation with hands joined. One child, Charlie (or Sally, if a girl), is in the center of the circle, holding a ball. The children skip around the circle to the following chant.

Charlie over the water,
Charlie over the sea,
Charlie caught a bluebird,
But he can't catch *me!*

On the word "me," Charlie tosses the ball in the air and the children drop hands and scatter. When Charlie catches it, he shouts, "Stop!" All of the children stop immediately and must not move their feet. Charlie rolls the ball in an attempt to hit one of the children. If he hits a child, that child becomes the new Charlie. If he misses, he must remain Charlie, and the game is repeated. If he misses twice, however, he picks another child for the center.

Flowers and Wind

Playing Area: Playground, gymnasium

Players: 10 to 30

Supplies: None

Skill: Running

Two parallel lines long enough to accommodate the children are drawn about 30 ft apart. The children are divided into two groups. One is the wind and the other the flowers. Each of the teams takes a position on one of the lines and faces the other team. The flowers select secretly the name of a common flower. When ready, they walk over to the other line and stand about 3 ft away from the wind. The players on the wind team begin to call out flower names—trying to guess the chosen flower. When the flower has been guessed, the flowers run to their goal line, chased by the players of the other team. Any player caught must join the other side. The roles are reversed and the game is repeated. If one side has trouble guessing, a clue can be given to the color or size of the flower or the first letter of its name.

Forest Ranger

Playing Area: Playground, gymnasium, classroom

Players: Entire class

Supplies: None

Skill: Running

Half of the children form a circle and face the center. These are the trees. The other half of the children are forest rangers and stand behind the trees. An extra child, the forest lookout, is in the center. The forest lookout starts the game by calling, "Fire in the forest. *Run, run, run!*" Immediately, the forest rangers run around the outside of the circle to the right. After a few moments, the lookout steps *in front* of one of the trees. This is the signal for each of the rangers to step in front of a tree. One player is left out, and she becomes the new forest lookout. The trees become rangers, and the rangers become trees. Each time the game is played, the circle must be moved out somewhat, because the formation narrows when the rangers step in front of the trees.

Hill Dill

Playing Area: Playground

Players: 10 to 50

Supplies: None

Skills: Running, dodging

Two parallel lines are established 50 ft apart. One player is chosen to be it and stands in the center between the lines. The other children stand on one of the parallel lines. The center player calls,

Hill Dill! Come over the hill,
Or else I'll catch you standing still!

The children run across the open space to the other line, while the one in the center tries to tag them. Anyone caught helps the tagger in the center. The first child caught is it for the next game. Once the children cross over to the other line, they must await the next call.

Hot Potatoes

Playing Area: Gymnasium, playground, classroom

Players: Entire class

Supplies: Six balls or beanbags for each group

Skill: Object handling

Children are seated close enough together in small circles (8 to 12 per circle) so that objects can be handed from one to another around the circle. Balls or beanbags or both are passed around the circle, a few items being introduced at a time. The point of the game is to pass the balls or beanbags rapidly so as not to get stuck with more than one object at a time. If this happens, the game is stopped and the player with more than one object moves back and waits. After three are out of the circle, the game starts over. The teacher should begin the game with two or three objects and gradually add objects until someone has more than one at a time.

Variation: The passing direction can be reversed on signal.

Leap the Brook

Playing Area: Gymnasium (or any area with a flat surface)

Players: Entire class

Supplies: None

Skills: Leaping, jumping, hopping, turning

A brook is marked off on the floor for a distance of about 30 ft. For the first 10 ft, it is 3 ft wide; for the next 10 ft, it is 4 ft wide; for the last 10 ft, it is 5 ft wide. The children form a single file and jump over the narrowest part of the brook. They should be encouraged to do this several times, using different styles of jumping and leaping. After they have satisfactorily negotiated the narrow part, they move to the next width, and so on (Figure 23.2).

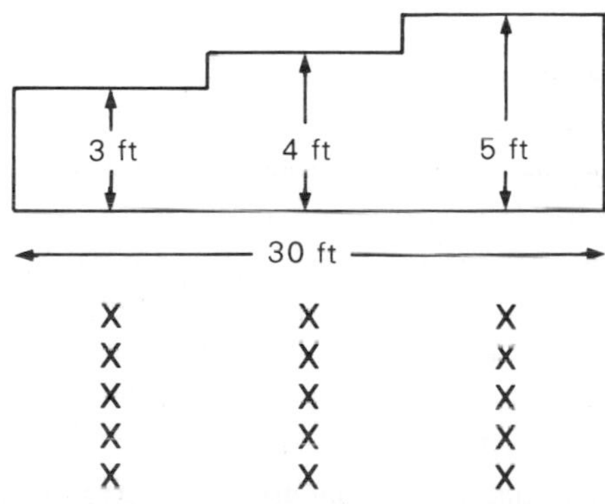

FIGURE 23.2. Formation for Leap the Brook

Teaching Suggestion: The teacher should stress landing lightly on the balls of the feet in a bent-knee position. Good form should be stressed throughout the game. The selection of the distances is arbitrary, and the distances can be changed if they seem unsuitable for any particular group of children.

Variation: Children can use different means of crossing the brook—leaping, jumping, hopping. They also can vary the kinds of turns to be made—right or left, or quarter, half, three-quarter, or full. They should use different body shapes, different arm positions, and so on.

March Attack

Playing Area: Playground, gymnasium

Players: 25 to 40

Supplies: None

Skills: Marching, running

Two parallel lines are drawn about 60 ft apart. The children are divided into two teams. One team takes a position on one of the lines, with their backs to the area. These are the chasers. The other team is on the other line, facing the area. This is the marching team. The marching team moves forward on signal, marching in good order, toward the chasers. When they get reasonably close, a whistle or some other signal is given, and the marchers turn and run back to their line, chased by the other team. Any marcher caught before reaching the line changes to the chase team. The game is repeated, with the roles exchanged.

May I Chase You?

Playing Area: Playground

Players: 10 to 30

Supplies: None

Skills: Running, dodging

The class stands behind a line long enough to accommodate all. The runner stands about 5 ft in front of the line. One child in the line asks, "May I chase you?" The runner replies, "Yes, if you are wearing ____," naming a color, an article of clothing, or a combination of the two. All who qualify immediately chase the runner until she is tagged. The tagger becomes the new runner. The children can think of other ways to identify those who may run.

Mousetrap

Playing Area: Playground, gymnasium, classroom

Players: 20 to 40

Supplies: None

Skills: Skipping, running, dodging

Half of the children form a circle with hands joined and face the center. This is the trap. The other children are on the outside of the circle. These are the mice. Three signals are given for the game. These can be word cues or other signals. On the first signal, the mice skip around, outside the circle, playing happily. On the second signal, the trap is opened (the circle players raise their joined hands to form arches). The mice run in and out of the trap. On the third signal, the trap snaps shut (the arms come down). All mice caught inside join the circle.

The game is repeated until all or most of the mice are caught. The players then exchange places, and the game begins anew. A child should not run in and out of the trap through adjacent openings.

Variation: This game is excellent with a parachute. The chute drops down and traps the mice.

Red Light

Playing Area: An area 60 to 100 ft across

Players: Entire class

Supplies: None

Skills: Fundamental locomotor movements, stopping

A goal line is established at one end of the area. The object of the game is to move across the area successfully without getting caught. One player is the leader and stands on the goal line. The leader turns away from the players, claps the hands five times, and turns around on the fifth clap. In the meantime, the players move toward the goal line, timing their movements to end on the fifth clap. If the leader catches any movement by any person, that person is required to return to the starting line and begin anew. After the leader turns away, he can turn back immediately to catch any movement. Once he begins clapping, however, five claps must be completed before he turns around. The first child to reach the goal line successfully without being caught in an illegal movement is the winner and becomes the leader for the next game.

Variations

1. An excellent variation of the game is to have the leader face the oncoming players. He calls out "Green Light" for them to move and "Red Light" for them to stop. When the leader calls other colors, the players should not move.

2. Different types of locomotion can be explored. The leader names the type of movement (e.g., hop, crawl, skip) before turning his back to the group.

3. The leader can specify how those caught must go back to place—walk, hop, skip, slide, crawl.

Teaching Suggestion: In the original game of Red Light, the leader counts rapidly, "One, two, three, four, five, six, seven, eight, nine, ten—red light," instead of clapping five times. This has proved impractical in most gymnasiums, however, because the children moving forward cannot hear the counting. Clapping, which provides both a visual and an auditory signal, is preferable.

Bottle Bat Ball

Playing Area: Playground

Players: Three or four

Supplies: A plastic bottle bat, whiffle ball, batting tee (optional), home plate, base marker

Skills: Batting, retrieving balls

A home plate is needed, and a batting tee can be used. Foul lines should be marked wide enough so as not to be restrictive.

The batter gets three pitches (or swings) to hit a fair ball, or she is out. The pitches are easy (as in slow-pitch softball), so the batter has a good chance to hit the ball. The batter hits the ball and runs around the base marker and back to home. If the ball is returned to the pitcher's mound before the batter reaches home, she is out. (A marker should designate the pitcher's mound.) Otherwise, the batter has a home run and bats again. One fielder other than the pitcher is needed, but another can be used. The running distance to first base is critical. It can remain fixed or can be made progressively (one step) longer, until it reaches such a point that the fielders are heavily favored.

Teaching Suggestions: The game should make use of a plastic bottle bat and fun (whiffle) ball. A rotation system should be established when an out is made.

Variation: A batting tee can be used.

Circle Straddle Ball

Playing Area: Playground, gymnasium, classroom

Players: 10 to 15

Supplies: Two volleyballs or rubber playground balls

Skills: Ball rolling, catching

Children are in circle formation, facing in. Each stands in a wide straddle stance with the side of the foot against the neighbor's. The hands are on the knees. Two balls are used. The object of the game is to roll one of the balls between the legs of another player before he can get his hands down to stop the ball. Each time a ball goes between the legs of an individual, a point is scored. The players having the fewest points scored against them are the winners.

Teaching Suggestion: The teacher should be sure that the children catch and roll the ball, rather than batting it. Children must keep their hands on their knees until a ball is rolled at them. After some practice, the following variation can be played.

Variation: One child is in the center with a ball and is it. The other children are in the same formation as before. One ball is used. The center player tries to roll the ball through the legs of any child. She should mask her intent, using feints and changes of direction. Any child allowing the ball to go through his legs becomes it.

Roll Dodgeball

Playing Area: Playground, gymnasium

Players: 20 to 30

Supplies: Many volleyballs or rubber playground balls

Skills: Ball rolling, dodging

Half of the children form a circle, and the other half are in the center. Balls are given to the circle players. The circle players roll the balls at the feet and shoes of the center players—trying to hit them. The center players move around to dodge the balls. A center player who is hit leaves the center and joins the circle.

After a period of time or when all of the children have been hit, the teams trade places. If a specified time limit is used, the team having the fewer players hit wins, or the team that puts out all of the opponents in the shorter time wins.

Teaching Suggestion: The instructor can have the children practice rolling a ball first. Balls that stop in the center are dead and must be taken back to the circle before being put into play again. The preferable procedure is to have the player who recovers a ball roll it to a teammate, rather than return to place with the ball.

GAMES FOR THIRD-GRADE CHILDREN

Compared with the programs of the first two grades, the 3rd-grade games program undergoes a definite change. The chase and tag games become more complex and demand more maneuvering. Introductory lead-up games make an appearance. The interests of the children turn to games that have a sport slant, and kicking, throwing, catching, batting, and other sport skills are beginning to mature. Games from the 2nd-grade program should be reviewed, however.

Suggested Games

- Busy Bee
- Couple Tag
  - Triplet Tag
- Crows and Cranes
  - Blue, Black, and Baloney
- Fly Trap
- Follow Me
- Galloping Lizzie
- Jump the Shot
- Nonda's Car Lot
- Steal the Treasure
  - Bear and Keeper
- Balance Dodgeball
  - Footsie Dodgeball
- Bat Ball
  - Shotgun Ball
- Bounce Ball
- Circle Team Dodgeball
- Club Guard
- Competitive Circle Contests
  - Individual Dodgeball
  - Circle Club Guard
  - Touch Ball
- One Step
  - Bowling One Step

Busy Bee

Playing Area: Playground, gymnasium, classroom

Players: Entire class

Supplies: None

Skills: Fundamental locomotor movements

Half of the children form a large circle, facing in, and are designated the stationary players. The other children seek partners from this group, and stand in front of the stationary players. An extra child in the center is the busy bee. The bee calls out directions such as "Back to back," "Face to face," "Shake hands," "Kneel on one knee (or both)," and "Hop on one foot." The other children follow these directions.

The center child then calls out, "Busy bee." Stationary players stand still, and their partners seek other partners while the center player also tries to get a partner. The child without a partner becomes the new busy bee.

Teaching Suggestions: Children should be instructed to think about the different movements that they might have the class do if they become the busy bee. In changing partners, children must select a partner other than the stationary player next to them. After a period of time, the active and stationary players are rotated. Different methods of locomotion should also be used when the children change partners.

Variations

1. All children who have not repeated any partner during a specified number of exchanges (say, ten) and who have not been caught as the busy bee are declared winners.
2. Instead of standing back to back, children lock elbows and sit down as in the Chinese Get-up (p. 382). After they sit down and are declared safe, they can get up, and the game proceeds as described.

Couple Tag

Playing Area: Playground, gymnasium

Players: Entire class

Supplies: None

Skills: Running, dodging

Two goal lines are established about 50 ft apart. Children run in pairs, with inside hands joined. All pairs, except one, line up on one of the goal lines. The pair in the center is it. They call "Come," and the children, keeping hands joined, run to the other goal line. The pair in the center, also retaining joined hands, tries to tag any other pair. As soon as a couple is caught, they help the center couple. The game continues until all are caught. The last couple caught is it for the next game.

Variation: *Triplet Tag*—The game can be played with sets of threes. Tagging is done with any pair of joined hands. If a triplet breaks joined hands, it is considered caught.

Crows and Cranes

Playing Area: Playground, gymnasium

Players: Entire class

Supplies: None

Skills: Running, dodging

Two goal lines are drawn about 50 ft apart. Children are divided into two groups—the crows and the cranes. The groups face each other at the center of the area, about 5 ft apart. The leader calls out either "Crows" or "Cranes," using a cr-r-r-r-r-r sound at the start of either word to mask the result. If "Crows" is the call, the crows chase the cranes to the goal line. If "Cranes" is the call, then the cranes chase. Any child caught goes over to the other side. The team that has the most players when the game ends is the winner.

Variations

1. Instead of facing each other, the children stand back to back, about a foot apart, in the center.

2. The game can be played with the two sides designated as red and blue. A piece of plywood painted red on one side and blue on the other can be thrown into the air between the teams, instead of having someone give calls. If red comes up, the red team chases, and vice versa.

3. *Blue, Black, and Baloney.* On the command "Blue" or "Black," the game proceeds as described. On the command "Baloney," no one is to move. The caller should draw out the bl-l-l-l sound before ending with one of the three commands.

4. Another variation of the game is to have a leader tell a story using as many words beginning with *cr-* as possible. Words that can be incorporated in a story might be *crazy, crunch, crust, crown, crude, crowd, crouch, cross, croak, critter.* Each time one of these words is spoken, the beginning of the word is lengthened with a drawn out cr-r-r-r sound. No one may move on any of the words except *crows* or *cranes.*

Fly Trap

Playing Area: Playground, gymnasium

Players: Entire class

Supplies: None

Skills: Fundamental locomotor movements

Half of the class is scattered around the playing area, sitting on the floor in cross-legged fashion. These children form the trap. The other children are the flies, and they buzz around the seated children. When a whistle is blown, the flies must freeze where they are. If any of the trappers can touch a fly, that fly sits down at that spot and becomes a trapper. The trappers must keep their seats glued to the floor.

The game continues until all of the flies are caught. Some realism is given to the game if the flies make buzzing sounds and move their arms as wings.

Teaching Suggestions: Some experience with the game enables the teacher to determine how far apart to place the seated children. After all (or most) of the flies have been caught, the groups trade places. The method of locomotion should be changed occasionally also.

Follow Me

Playing Area: Playground, gymnasium

Players: 8 to 30

Supplies: A marker for each child (Squares of cardboard or plywood can be used; individual mats or beanbags work well.)

Skills: All locomotor movements, stopping

Children are arranged in a rough circle, each standing or sitting with one foot on a marker. An extra player is the guide. He moves around the circle, pointing at different players and asking them to follow. Each player chosen falls in behind the guide. The guide then takes the group on a tour, and the members of the group perform just as the guide does. The guide may hop, skip, do stunts, or execute other movements, and the children following must do likewise. At the signal "Home," all run for places with a marker. One child is left without a marker. This child chooses another guide.

Teaching Suggestions: Making the last child the new leader is not a good idea, because this causes some children to lag and try to be last. Another way to overcome the tendency to lag is to make the first one back the guide. The teacher can also use a special marker; the first one to this marker becomes the new leader. A penalty can be imposed on the one who does not find a marker.

Galloping Lizzie

Playing Area: Playground

Players: 10 to 15

Supplies: A beanbag or fleece ball

Skills: Throwing, dodging, running

One player is it and has a beanbag or fleece ball. The other players are scattered around the playground. The player with the beanbag or fleece ball runs after the others and attempts to hit another player below the shoulders with the object. The person hit becomes it, and the game continues. The tagger must throw the bag or ball, not merely touch another person with it.

Variation: A pair of children is it, with one of the players handling the beanbag or ball. A specific kind of toss can be called for (e.g., overhand, underhand, left-handed).

Jump the Shot

Playing Area: Playground, gymnasium

Players: 10 to 20

Supplies: A jump-the-shot rope

Skill: Rope jumping

The players stand in circle formation. One player with a long rope stands in the center. A soft object is tied to the free end of the rope to give it some weight. An old, deflated ball makes a good weight. The center player turns the rope under the feet of the circle players, who must jump over it. Anyone who touches the rope with the feet is eliminated and must stand back from the circle.

Variation: The circle should be re-formed after three or four children have been eliminated. The center player should be cautioned to keep the rope along the ground. The rope speed can be varied. A good way to turn the rope is to sit cross-legged and turn it over the head.

Nonda's Car Lot

Playing Area: Playground, gymnasium

Players: 20 to 35

Supplies: None

Skills: Running, dodging

One player is it and stands in the center of the area between two lines established about 50 ft apart. The class selects four brands of cars (e.g., Honda, Datsun, Volkswagen, Ford). Each student then selects a car from the four but does not tell anyone what it is.

The tagger calls out a car name. All students who selected that name attempt to run to the other line without getting tagged. The tagger calls out the cars until all students have run. When a child (car) gets tagged, she must sit down at the spot of the tag. She cannot move but may tag other students who run too near her. When the one who is it calls out "Car lot," all of the cars must go. The game is played until all students (cars) have been tagged.

Steal the Treasure

Playing Area: Playground, gymnasium, classroom

Players: 8 to 12

Supplies: An Indian club

Skill: Dodging

A playing area 20 ft square is outlined, with a small circle in the center. An Indian club placed in the circle is the treasure. A guard is set to protect the treasure. Players then enter the square and try to steal the treasure without getting caught. The guard tries to tag them. Anyone tagged must retire and wait for the next game. The player who gets the treasure is the next guard.

Teaching Suggestion: If getting the treasure seems too easy, the child can be required to carry the treasure to the boundary of the square without being tagged.

Variation: *Bear and Keeper*—Instead of a treasure, a bear (seated cross-legged on the ground) is protected by a keeper. Anyone who touches the bear without being tagged becomes the new keeper, with the old keeper becoming the bear.

Balance Dodgeball

Playing Area: Playground, gymnasium

Players: Entire class

Supplies: An 8-in. foam rubber ball for each child who is it

Skills: Throwing, dodging

Children are scattered over the area. Two or more children have a ball each and are it. Children are safe from being hit when they are balanced on one foot. This means that one foot must be off the ground and the other foot, which is supporting the weight, must not be moved. Hits must be made below the shoulders. Anyone legally hit becomes it.

Teaching Suggestion: To avoid having the tagger stand by a child—waiting for him to lose his balance or touch a foot to the ground—the tagger can be required to count rapidly to ten, at which time the tagger must leave and seek another child.

Variation: *Footsie Dodgeball*—To be safe from being hit, the child must have both feet off the ground (e.g., as when jumping or sitting with feet raised).

Bat Ball

Playing Area: A field approximately 70 by 70 ft

Players: 16 to 30

Supplies: A volleyball (or similar ball)

Skills: Batting, running, catching, throwing

A serving line is drawn across one end of the field, and a 3-by-3-ft base is established about 50 ft from the serving line. Children are divided into two teams. One team is scattered over the playing area. The other team is behind the serving line, with one player at bat. The batter puts the ball in play by batting it with a hand into the playing area. To be counted as a fair ball, the ball must land in the playing area or be touched by a member of the fielding team. As soon as the ball is hit, the batter runs to the base and back across the serving line. In the meantime, the fielding team fields the ball and attempts to hit the runner below the shoulders with it.

Fielders may not run with the ball. It must be passed from fielder to fielder until thrown at the batter. A pass may not be returned to the fielder from whom it was received. Violation of any of these rules constitutes a foul.

A run is scored each time the batter hits a fair ball, touches the base, and gets back to the serving line without being hit. A run is also scored if the fielding team commits a foul.

The batter is out when the ball is caught on the fly.

Two consecutive foul balls also put the batter out. The batter is out when hit by a thrown ball in the field of play. Sides change when three outs are made.

Variation: *Shotgun Ball*—The entire batting team runs each time there is a fair ball. The defensive team tries to hit as many of the runners as possible. Instead of touching the base, the runners round it from either direction and return to the serving line. Each safe runner scores a run. More outs (six to ten) should be allowed before the teams change sides.

Bounce Ball

Playing Area: Rectangular court 40 by 60 ft

Players: 16 to 30

Supplies: Volleyballs or rubber playground balls of about the same size

Skills: Throwing, ball rolling

The court is divided into halves (30 by 40 ft each). The children form two teams. Each team occupies one half of the court and is given a number of volleyballs. One or two players from each team should be assigned to retrieve balls behind their own end lines. The object of the game is to bounce or roll the ball over the opponents' end line. A ball thrown across the line on a fly does not count.

Two scorers are needed, one at each end line. Players can move wherever they wish in their own area but cannot cross the center line. After the starting signal, the balls are thrown back and forth at will.

Variation: A row of benches is placed across the center line. Throws must go over the benches and bounce in the other team's area to score.

Circle Team Dodgeball

Playing Area: Playground, gymnasium

Players: 20 to 40

Supplies: A number of 8-in. foam rubber balls

Skills: Throwing, dodging

Children are divided into two teams, one of which forms a large circle. The other team is grouped together inside the circle. Balls are given to the circle players. When the starting signal is given, the circle players try to hit the center players. Any center player hit below the shoulders is eliminated and leaves the circle. The teams trade places, and the scores are compared to determine the winner.

Scoring can be done in any of several ways.

1. Count the number of center players remaining after 60 seconds of throwing.

2. Time by seconds how long it takes to eliminate all of the center players.

3. Count the center players remaining after a specified number of throws.

4. Give the circle players a point for each successful hit. The center players who are hit are not eliminated.

Teaching Suggestion: If some children tend to hog the action, a rule that no player may throw more than three times in any one action can be used to distribute the throws among the children.

Club Guard

Playing Area: Gymnasium, smooth surface outdoors

Players: Eight to ten

Supplies: An Indian club, a volleyball

Skill: Throwing

A circle about 15 ft in diameter is drawn. Inside the circle at the center, an 18-in. circle is drawn. The Indian club is put in the center of the small circle. One child guards the club. The other children stand outside the large circle, which is the restraining line for them.

The circle players throw the ball at the club and try to knock it down. The guard tries to block the throws with the legs and body. She must, however, stay out of the small inner circle. The outer circle players pass the ball around rapidly so that one of the players can get an opening to throw, since the guard needs to maneuver to protect the club. Whoever knocks down the club becomes the new guard. If the guard steps in the inner circle, she loses the place to whoever has the ball at that time.

Teaching Suggestion: A small circle cut from plywood (or a hula hoop or similar object) makes a definite inner circle so that determining whether the guard steps inside is easier. The outer circle should also be definite.

Variation: More than one club can be in the center.

Competitive Circle Contests

Playing Area: Playground, gymnasium

Players: 20 to 30

Supplies: Volleyballs or 8-in. foam rubber balls, two Indian clubs

Skills: Throwing, catching

Two teams arranged in independent circles compete against each other. The circles should be of the same size; lines can be drawn on the floor to ensure this. The players of each team are numbered consecutively, so each player in one circle corresponds to a player in the other circle. The numbered players, in sequence, go to the center of the opponents' circle to compete for their team in any of the following activities.

1. *Individual Dodgeball.* The circle players throw at the center player from the other team. The circle that hits the center player first wins a point. Use 8-in. foam rubber balls only.

2. *Circle Club Guard.* The center player guards an Indian club. The circle that knocks down the club first wins a point. The ball should be rolled at the club.

3. *Touch Ball.* The circle players pass the ball from one to another while the center player tries to touch it. The center player who touches the ball first wins a point for the respective team. In case neither player is able to touch the ball in a reasonable period of time, the action should be cut off without awarding a point.

After all players have competed, the team with the most points wins. For Individual Dodgeball and Circle Club Guard, there must be three passes to different people before the ball can be thrown at the center. Establishing circle lines may be necessary to regulate throwing distance.

One Step

Playing Area: Playground

Players: Any number of pairs, depending on the space available

Supplies: A ball or beanbag

Skills: Throwing, catching

Two children stand facing each other about 3 ft apart. One has a ball or a beanbag. The object of the game is to throw or toss the ball in the stipulated manner, so the partner can catch it *without moving his feet* on or from the ground. When the throw is completed successfully, the thrower takes one step backward and waits for the throw from her partner. Children can try to increase their distance to an established line, or the two children who move the greatest distance apart can be declared the winners. Variables to provide interest and challenge are type of throw, type of catch, and kind of step. Throwing can be underhand, overhand, two-handed, under one leg, around the back, and so on. Catching can be two-handed, left-handed, right-handed, to the side, and so on. The step can be a giant step, a tiny step, a hop, a jump, or some similar movement.

When either child misses, moves the feet, or fails to follow directions, the partners move forward and start over. A double line of children facing each other makes a satisfactory formation.

Variation: *Bowling One Step*—In groups of squad size or smaller, each of the players in turn gets a chance to roll the ball at an Indian club or bowling pin. A minimal distance (5 to 10 ft) is established, so most bowlers can hit the pin on the first try. The player takes a step backward each time the pin is knocked down, and keeps rolling until he misses. The winner is the child who has moved the farthest from the pin. Instead of backward steps, stipulated distances (5, 10, 15, and 20 ft) can be used.

GAMES FOR FOURTH-GRADE CHILDREN

At the 4th-grade level, a number of new games are suggested. The 3rd-grade games also should be reviewed.

Suggested Games

Addition Tag
Alaska Baseball
Box Ball
Cageball Kick-Over
Hand Hockey
  Scooter Hockey
Jump-the-Shot variations
Loose Caboose
Nine Lives
Running Dodgeball
Squad Tag
Trades
Trees
Whistle Mixer

Addition Tag

Playing Area: Playground

Players: Entire class

Supplies: None

Skills: Running, dodging

Two couples are it, and each stands with inside hands joined. These are the taggers. The other children run individually. The couples move around the playground, trying to tag with the free hands. The first person tagged joins the couple, making a trio. The three then chase until they catch a fourth. Once a fourth person is caught, the four divide and form two couples, adding another set of taggers to the game. This continues until all of the children are tagged.

Teaching Suggestions: Some limitation of area should be established to enable the couples to catch the runners; otherwise, the game moves slowly and is fatiguing. The game moves faster if started with two couples. A tag is legal only when the couple or group of three keeps their hands joined. The game can be used as an introductory activity, since all of the children are active.

Alaska Baseball

Playing Area: Playground

Players: Entire class

Supplies: A volleyball or soccer ball

Skills: Kicking, batting, running, ball handling

The players are organized in two teams, one of which is at bat while the other is in the field. A straight line

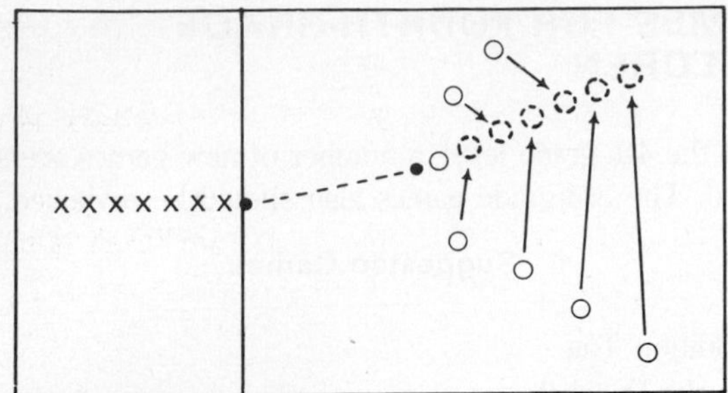

FIGURE 23.3. Formation for Alaska Baseball

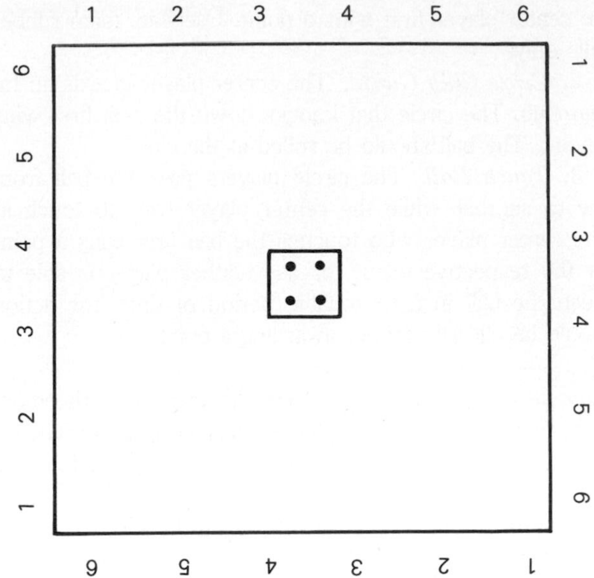

FIGURE 23.4. Formation for Box Ball

provides the only out-of-bounds line, and the team at bat is behind this line at about the middle. The other team is scattered around the fair territory (Figure 23.3).

One player propels the ball, either batting a volleyball or kicking a stationary soccer ball. His teammates are in a close file behind him. As soon as the batter sends the ball into the playing area, he starts to run around his own team. Each time the runner passes the head of the file, the team gives a loud count.

There are no outs. The first fielder to get the ball stands still and starts to pass the ball back overhead to the nearest teammate, who moves directly behind to receive it. The remainder of the team in the field must run to the ball and form a file behind it. The ball is passed back overhead, with each player handling the ball. When the last field player in line has a firm grip on it, she shouts, "Stop." At this signal, a count is made of the number of times the batter ran around his own team. To score more sharply, half rounds should be counted.

Five batters or half of the team should bat; then the teams should change places. This is better than allowing an entire team to bat before changing to the field, because players in the field tire from many consecutive runs.

Variation: Regular bases can be set up, and the batter can run the bases. Scoring can be in terms of a home run made or not, or the batter can continue around the bases, getting a point for each base.

Box Ball

Playing Area: Playground, gymnasium

Players: Entire class

Supplies: A sturdy box, 2 ft square and about 12 in. deep; four volleyballs (or similar balls)

Skills: Running, ball handling

The class is divided into four even teams, with six to ten players per team. Each team occupies one side of a hollow square at an equal distance from the center. Players face inward and number off consecutively from right to left (Figure 23.4).

A box containing four balls is put in the center. The instructor calls a number, and the player from each team who has that number runs forward to the box, takes a ball, and runs to the head of his line, taking the place of player number 1. In the meantime, the players in the line have moved to the left just enough to fill in the space left by the runner. On reaching the head of the line, the runner passes the ball to the next person and so on down the line to the end child. The last child runs forward and returns the ball to the box. The first team to return the ball to the box scores a point.

The runner must not pass the ball down the line until he is in place at the head of the line. The ball must be caught and passed by each child. Failure to conform to these rules results in team disqualification. Runners stay at the head of the line, retaining their original number. Keeping the lines in consecutive number sequence is not important.

Cageball Kick-Over

Playing Area: Playground (grassy area), gymnasium

Players: 14 to 20

Supplies: A cageball, 18-in., 24-in., or 30-in. size

Skill: Kicking

Players are divided into two teams and sit facing each other, with legs outstretched and soles of the feet about 3 ft apart. While maintaining the sitting position, each player supports her weight on the hands, which are placed slightly to the rear.

The teacher rolls the cageball between the two teams. The object of the game is to kick the ball over the other team, thereby scoring a point. After a point is scored, the teacher rolls the ball into play again. A good system of rotation is to have the player on the left side of the line take a place on the right side after a point is scored, thus moving all of the players one position to the left. When the ball is kicked out at either end, no score results, and the ball is put into play again by the teacher.

Variation: The children can be allowed to use their hands to stop the ball from going over them.

Hand Hockey

Playing Area: Playing field about 100 by 100 ft

Players: 24 to 30

Supplies: A soccer ball or volleyball

Skills: Striking, volleying

The players are on two teams. Half of the players on each team are guards and are stationed on the goal line as defenders. The other half are active players and are scattered throughout the playing area in front of their goal line (Figure 23.5).

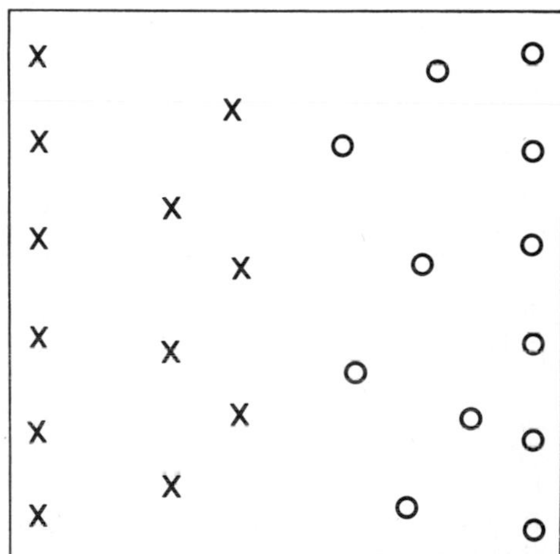

FIGURE 23.5. Formation for Hand Hockey

The object of the game is to bat or push the ball with either hand so it crosses the goal line that the other team is defending. Players may move the ball as in hockey but may not throw, hoist, or kick it. The defensive goal line players are limited to one step into the playing field when playing the ball.

The ball is put into play by being rolled into the center of the field. After a goal has been scored or after a specified period, guards become active players, and vice versa. An out-of-bounds ball goes to the opposite team and is put into play by being rolled from the sidelines into the playing area. If the ball becomes entrapped among players, play is stopped, and the ball is put into play again by a roll from the referee.

Players must play the ball and not resort to rough tactics. A player who is called for unnecessary roughness or for illegally handling the ball must go to the sidelines (as in hockey) and remain in the penalty area until the players change positions. Players should scatter and attempt to pass to each other rather than bunch around the ball.

Variation: *Scooter Hockey*—The active center players from each team are on gym scooters. The position that each child takes on the gym scooter can be specified or can be a free choice. Possible positions are kneeling, sitting, or balancing on the tummy. A hard surface is needed. This game version is usually played indoors on a basketball court.

Jump-the-Shot Variations

Playing Area: Playground, gymnasium, classroom

Players: 10 to 30

Supplies: A jump-the-shot rope

Skill: Rope jumping

Before the following variations are played, the Jump-the-Shot game described for the 3rd grade should be reviewed.

1. Squads line up in spoke formation (Figure 23.6). Each member does a specified number of jumps (from three to five) and then exits. The next squad member in line must come in immediately without missing a turn of the rope. A player scores a point for the squad when he comes in *on time,* jumps the prescribed number of turns, and exits successfully. The squad with the most points wins.

2. Couples line up in the same formation. They join inside hands and stand side by side when jumping.

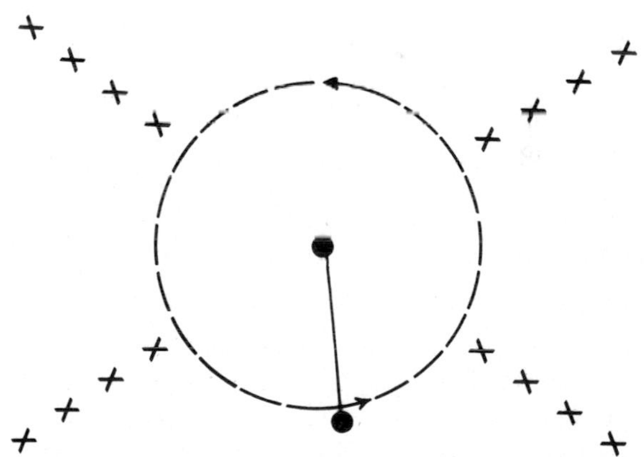

FIGURE 23.6. Spoke formation for Jump-the-Shot

Loose Caboose

Playing Area: Playground, gymnasium

Players: 12 to 30

Supplies: None

Skills: Running, dodging

One child is designated as the loose caboose and tries to hook on to a train. Trains are formed by three or four children standing in column formation with each child placing the hands on the waist of the child immediately in front.

The trains, by twisting and turning, endeavor to keep the caboose from hooking on to the back. Should the caboose manage to hook on, the front child in the train becomes the new caboose. Each train should attempt to keep together. If the number of children is 20 or more, there should be two cabooses.

Nine Lives

Playing Area: Gymnasium, classroom, any hard-surfaced area

Players: Entire class

Supplies: Fleece balls

Skills: Throwing, dodging

Any number of fleece balls can be used, the more the better. At a signal, players get a ball and hit as many people as possible. When a player counts that she has been hit nine times, she leaves the game and stands against a wall until a new game is started. A player may run anywhere with a ball or to get a ball, but he may possess only one ball at a time. Players must not be hit in the head. This puts the thrower out.

Teaching Suggestion: Children often cheat about the number of times they have been hit. A few words about fair play may be necessary, but a high degree of activity is the important game element.

Variations

1. For a ball caught on the fly, a designated number of hits may be taken away.

2. Either left- or right-hand throwing can be specified.

Running Dodgeball

Playing Area: Playground, gymnasium

Players: 20 to 30

Supplies: A number of 8-in. foam rubber balls

Skills: Running, throwing, dodging

Two parallel lines drawn about 40 ft apart form a gauntlet. The gauntlet is about 60 ft in length. The players are divided into two teams. One team does the throwing and the other runs the gauntlet. The throwing team's players are divided, with half on one side of the gauntlet and half on the other. The other players line up at one end of the gauntlet and try to run through without getting hit. They can run separately or all together (Figure 23.7).

The throwing team may recover the balls lying in the running area but must return to the sides before throwing. After a count is made of the successful runners, the teams trade places, and the game is repeated.

Variations

1. Instead of running once down the gauntlet, the players run down and immediately start back. They score a point only when they make the round trip without being hit.

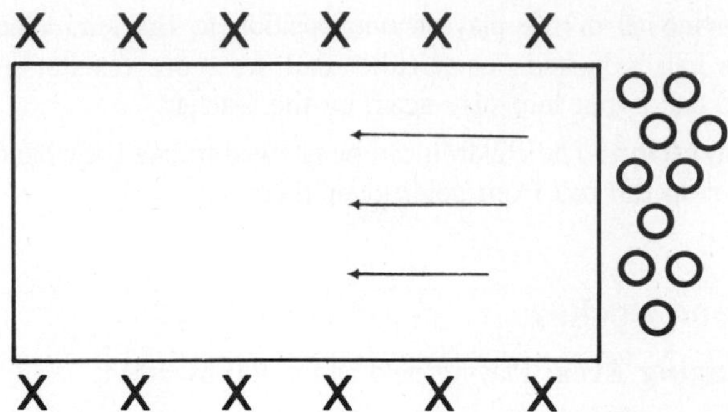

FIGURE 23.7. Formation for Running Dodgeball

2. An excellent variation can be played by rolling instead of throwing the balls. This causes the runners to jump high to avoid being hit.

Squad Tag

Playing Area: Playground, gymnasium

Players: Entire class

Supplies: Pinnies or markers for one squad, stopwatch

Skills: Running, dodging

An entire squad acts as taggers. The object is to see which squad can tag the remaining class members in the shorter time. The tagging squad should be marked. They stand in a football huddle formation in the center of the area. Their heads are down, and their hands are joined in the huddle. The remainder of the class is scattered as they wish throughout the area. On signal, the tagging squad scatters and tags the other class members. When a class member is tagged, she stops in place and remains there. Time is recorded when the last person is tagged. Each squad gets a turn at tagging.

Teaching Suggestion: Children should be cautioned to watch for collisions, because there is much chasing and dodging in different directions. Definite boundaries are needed.

Trades

Playing Area: Playground, gymnasium, classroom

Players: Entire class

Supplies: None

Skills: Imagery, running, dodging

The class is divided into two teams of equal number, each of which has a goal line. One team, the chasers, remains behind its goal line. The other team, the runners, approaches from its goal line, marching to the following dialogue.

Runners: Here we come.

Chasers: Where from?

Runners: New Orleans.

Chasers: What's your trade?

Runners: Lemonade.

Chasers: Show us some.

Runners move up close to the other team's goal line and proceed to act out an occupation or a specific task that they have chosen previously. The opponents try to guess what the pantomime represents. On a correct guess, the running team must run back to its goal line chased by the others. Any runner tagged must join the chasers. The game is repeated with roles reversed. The team ending with the greater number of players is the winner.

Teaching Suggestion: If a team has trouble guessing the pantomime, the other team should provide hints. Teams also should be encouraged to have a number of activities selected so little time is consumed in choosing the next activity to be pantomimed.

Trees

Playing Area: Playground, gymnasium

Players: Entire class

Supplies: None

Skills: Running, dodging

Two parallel lines are drawn 60 ft apart. All players, except the one who is it, are on one side of the area. On the signal "Trees," the players run to the other side of the court. The tagger tries to tag as many as possible. Any player tagged becomes a tree, stopping where tagged and keeping both feet in place. He cannot move the feet but can tag any runners who come close enough. The child who is it continues to chase the players as they cross on signal until all but one are caught. This player becomes it for the next game.

To speed up the action, two or more taggers may be chosen. Children cross from side to side only on the signal "Trees."

Whistle Mixer

Playing Area: Playground, gymnasium, classroom

Players: Entire class

Supplies: A whistle

Skills: All basic locomotor movements

Children are scattered throughout the area. To begin, they walk around in any direction they wish. The teacher blows a whistle a number of times in succession with short, sharp blasts. The children then form small circles with the number in the circles equal to the number of whistle blasts. If there are four blasts, the children form circles of four—no more, no less. Any children left out are eliminated. If a circle is formed with more than the specified number, the entire circle is eliminated.

After the circles are formed and the eliminated children have moved to the sidelines, the teacher calls, "Walk," and the game continues. In walking, the children should move in different directions.

Variation: A fine version of this game is done with the aid of a tom-tom. Different beats indicate different locomotor movements—skipping, galloping, slow walking, normal walking, running. The whistle is still used to set the number for each circle.

GAMES FOR FIFTH-GRADE CHILDREN

In addition to the new games presented here, the 4th-grade games should be reviewed.

Suggested Games

- Battle Dodgeball
- Bombardment
- Bronco Dodgeball
- Circle Hook-on
- Jolly Ball
- Right Face, Left Face (Maze Tag)
  - Streets and Alleys
- Scooter Kickball
- Star Wars
- Sunday
- Touchdown
- Whistle Ball

Battle Dodgeball

Playing Area: Playground, gymnasium

Players: 16 to 30

Supplies: Two 8-in. foam rubber balls

Skills: Throwing, dodging

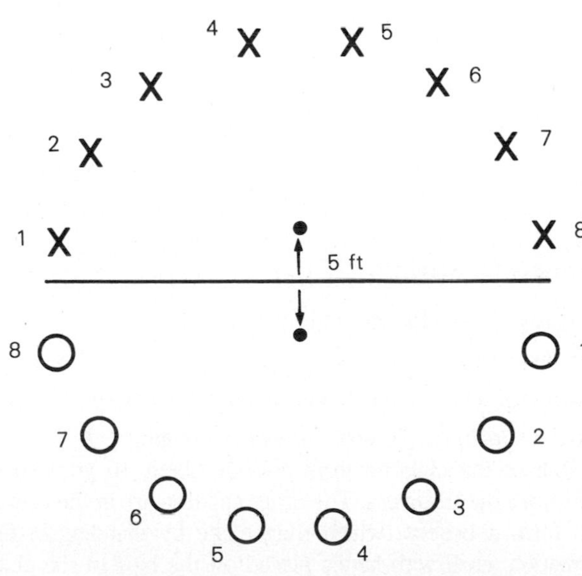

FIGURE 23.8. Formation for Battle Dodgeball

Two teams form one circle, each occupying half. Players on each team are numbered consecutively. For any one number, there is a player on each team. Two foam rubber balls are placed about 5 ft apart in the center of the circle, one on each side of a center line that separates the teams (Figure 23.8).

The teacher calls out a number. The two players with that number run forward; each picks up a ball and tries to hit the other with it. Players on the perimeter of the circle may retrieve balls and pass them to their teammates in the center, but each competing player must stay in her half of the circle. The winning player scores a point for her team. Play can continue to a certain number of points or until each player has had a turn in the center.

Variation: Two numbers and four balls can be used, so that two compete against two. The game can continue until one or both are hit.

Bombardment

Playing Area: Gymnasium

Players: 20 to 30

Supplies: 12 Indian clubs for each team, four to six rubber playground balls

Skill: Throwing

A line is drawn across the center of the floor from wall to wall. This divides the floor into two courts, each of which is occupied by one team. Another line is drawn 25 ft from the center line in each court. This is the club line. Each team spaces its Indian clubs along this line. Each team has at least two balls.

The object of the game is to knock over the other team's clubs, not to throw at the opponents. Players throw the balls back and forth but the players cannot cross the center line. Whenever a club is knocked over by a ball or accidentally by a player, that club is removed. The team with the most clubs standing at the end of the game is declared the winner. Out-of-bounds balls can be recovered but must be thrown from inside the court.

Variations: Clubs can be reset instead of removed. Two scorers, one for each club line, are needed. Rolling the balls is an excellent modification.

Bronco Dodgeball

Playing Area: Playground, gymnasium

Players: 15 to 20

Supplies: Two or more 8-in. foam rubber balls

Skills: Catching, passing, throwing, dodging

Half of the children form a circle about 10 yd across. These are the throwers. The other children are in the center and form a bronco, which they make by standing in file formation, each with hands placed on the hips of the child immediately in front. The object of the game is to hit the rear member of the bronco with the ball. This is the only child who may be hit legally. The bronco moves around, protected by the child at the head of the file, who may not use his hands.

As soon as the child at the rear of the bronco is hit, that player leaves the circle and the next child on the end becomes the target. If the bronco breaks during the maneuvering, all of the children to the rear of the break are eliminated. The circle and bronco players should be exchanged.

Teaching Suggestion: Five or six children are as many as can maneuver conveniently as a bronco, but two broncos can occupy the center. The instructor should stress quick passing and throwing.

Circle Hook-on

Playing Area: Playground, gymnasium, classroom

Players: Four

Supplies: None

Skills: Dodging, body management

One child plays against three others, who form a small circle with joined hands. The object of the game is for the lone child to tag a designated child in the circle. The other two children in the circle, by dodging and maneuvering, attempt to keep the tagger away from the third member of the circle. The circle players may maneuver and circle in any direction but must not release hand grips. The tagger, in attempting to touch the protected circle player, must go around the outside of the circle. She is not permitted to go underneath or through the joined hands of the circle players.

Teaching Suggestion: The teacher should watch for roughness by the two in the circle protecting the third. Children should be of about equal physical ability. If, after a time, the chaser is not successful, the players should rotate.

Variations

1. A piece of cloth, a handkerchief, or a flag is tucked in the belt in back of the child. The fourth child, the tagger, tries to pull the flag from the belt.

2. Instead of tagging, the chaser tries to hook on to the child being protected.

Jolly Ball

Playing Area: Playground, gymnasium

Players: 20 to 30

Supplies: A cageball 24 in. or larger (or a pushball 36 to 48 in.)

Skill: Kicking

Four teams are organized, each of which forms one side of a hollow square (Figure 23.9). The children sit down, facing in, with hands braced behind them (crab position). The members of each team are numbered consecutively.

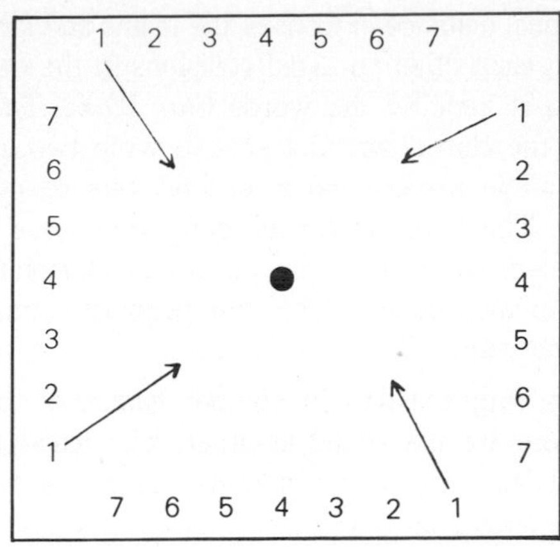

FIGURE 23.9. Formation for Jolly Ball

Each child waits until his number is called. Four active players (one from each team) move in crab position and try to kick the cageball over any one of the three opposing teams. The sideline players can also kick the ball. Ordinarily, the hands are not used, but this could be allowed in the learning stages of the game.

A point is scored against a team that allows the ball to go over its line. A ball that goes out at the corner between teams is dead and must be replayed. When a point is scored, the active children retire to their teams, and another number is called. The team with the fewest points wins the game. This game is quite strenuous for the active players, so they should be rotated after a reasonable length of time when there is no score.

Variation: Two children from each team can be active at once.

Right Face, Left Face (Maze Tag)

Playing Area: Playground, gymnasium

Players: 25 to 35

Supplies: None

Skills: Running, dodging

Children stand in rows that are aligned both from front to rear and from side to side. A runner and a chaser are chosen. The children all face the same way and join hands with the players on each side. The chaser tries to tag the runner who runs between the rows with the restriction that he cannot break through or under the arms. The teacher can help the runner by calling "Right face" or "Left face" at the proper time. On command, the children drop hands, face the new direction, and grasp hands with those who are then on each side, thus making new passages available. When the runner is caught or when the children become tired, a new runner and chaser are chosen.

Variations

1. Directions (north, south, east, west) can be used instead of the facing commands.

2. *Streets and Alleys.* The teacher calls, "Streets," and the children face in one direction. The call "Alleys" causes them to face at right angles.

3. The command "Air raid" can be given, and the children drop to their knees and make themselves into small balls, tucking their heads and seats down.

4. Having one runner and two chasers speeds up the action.

Scooter Kickball

Playing Area: Gymnasium, basketball court

Players: 20 to 30

Supplies: A cageball, gym scooters for active players

Skill: Striking with various body parts

Each team is divided into active players (on scooters) and goal defenders. The active players are seated on the scooters, and the goal defenders are seated on the goal line, with feet extended. The object of the game is to kick the cageball over the goal line defended by the opposite team. The players are positioned as shown in Figure 23.10.

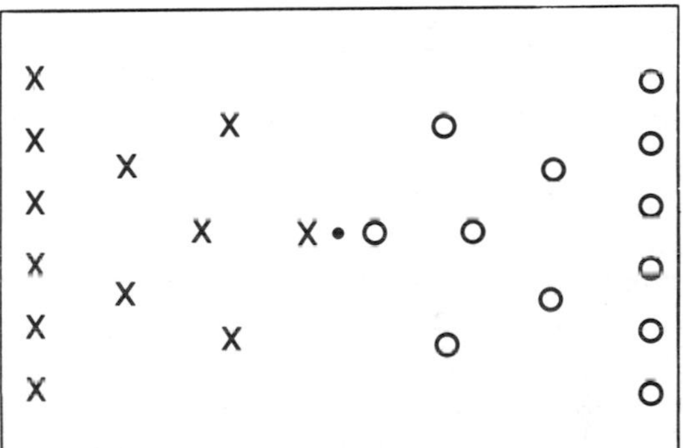

FIGURE 23.10. Formation for Scooter Kickball

The game starts with a face-off of two opposing players on scooters at the center of the court. The face-off is also used after a goal is scored. The active players on scooters propel the ball mainly with their feet. Touching the ball with the hands is a foul and results in a free kick by the opposition at the spot of the foul. A player also may use the head and body to stop and propel the ball.

The players defending the goal are seated on the goal line. They may not use their hands either, but use of the feet, body, and head is permitted. (If scoring seems too easy, then the defenders can be allowed to use their hands.) Defenders should be restricted to the seated position at the goal line; they are not permitted to enter the field of play to propel or stop the ball.

Teaching Suggestions: If the sidelines are close to the walls of the gymnasium, out-of-bounds balls need not be called because the ball can rebound from the wall. The number of scooters determines the number of active players.

The game works well if half of the players from each team are in the center on scooters and the other half are goal defenders. After a goal or after a stipulated time period, active players and goal defenders exchange places.

Some consideration should be made for glasses, otherwise they might be broken. Any active player who falls off a scooter should be required to seat herself again on the scooter before becoming eligible to propel the ball.

Variation: If there are enough scooters for everyone, the game can be played with rules similar to soccer. A more restricted goal (perhaps half of the end line) can be marked with standards. A goalie defends this area. All other players are active and can move to any spot on the floor. The floor space should be large enough to allow some freedom of play. Putting too many active players in a relatively small space causes jamming.

Star Wars

Playing Area: Playground, gymnasium, classroom

Players: Entire class

Supplies: Four Indian clubs

Skill: Running

A hollow square, about 10 yd on each side, is formed by four teams, each of which occupies one side, facing in. The teams should be even in number, and the members of each team should count off consecutively from right to left (Figure 23.11). This means that one person on each team has the same number as one child on each of the other three teams. The children are seated cross-legged.

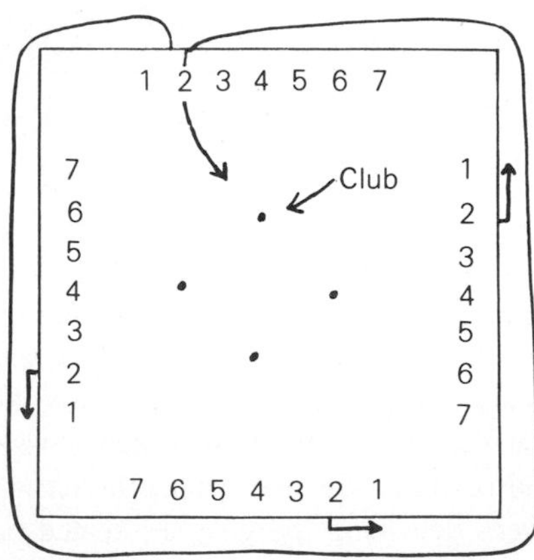

FIGURE 23.11. Star Wars formation

A number is called by the teacher. The four children with the number run to the right, all the way around the square, and through their *own* vacated space toward the center of the square. Near the center, in front of each team, stands an Indian club. The first child to put the Indian club down on the floor is the winner. The clubs should be at an equal distance in front of the teams and far enough away from each other to avoid collisions in the center.

Scoring is kept by the words *Star Wars.* The player who puts the club down first gets to write two letters of the name. The player who is second gets to put down one letter. The lettering can be done in a space in front of each team, where the name would be reasonably protected from the runners. The first team to complete the name is the winner.

Teaching Suggestion: In number games of this type, the numbers are not called in order. The teacher should keep a tally to make sure that every number is called.

Variation: Instead of being seated, each child can take a prone position, as if ready to do a Push-up. The teacher gives a preliminary command, such as "Ready," and each child comes up to a push-up position. The teacher then calls the number. The children with other numbers return to the prone position. Each child does a Push-up every time a number is called.

Sunday

Playing Area: Playground, gymnasium

Players: Entire class

Supplies: None

Skills: Running, dodging

Two parallel lines are drawn about 50 ft apart. One player is it and stands in the center of the area between the two lines. All of the other children are on one of the two lines. The object is to cross to the other line without being tagged and without making a false start.

Each line player stands with her front foot on the line. The line players must run across the line immediately when the tagger calls, "Sunday." Anyone who does not run immediately is considered caught. The tagger can call other days of the week to confuse the runners. No player may make a start if another day of the week is called. The tagger must be careful to pronounce "Monday" in such a way that it cannot be confused with "Sunday." If confusion does occur, "Monday" can be eliminated from the signals for the false start.

Teaching Suggestion: "Making a start" must be defined clearly. To begin, it can be defined as a player moving either foot. Later, when the children get better at the game, a forward movement of the body can constitute a start.

Touchdown

Playing Area: Playground, gymnasium

Players: 20 to 30

Supplies: A small object that can be concealed in the hand

Skills: Running, dodging

Two parallel lines about 60 ft apart are needed. Two teams face each other, each standing on one of the parallel lines. One team goes into a huddle, and the members decide which player is to carry an object to the opponents' goal line. The team moves out of the huddle and takes a position like a football team. On the charge signal "Hike," the players run toward the opponents' goal line, each player holding the hands closed as if carrying the object. On the charge signal, the opponents also run forward and tag the players. On being tagged, a player must stop immediately and open both hands to show whether or not he has the object.

If the player carrying the object reaches the goal line without being tagged, she calls, "Touchdown" and scores 6 points. The scoring team retains possession of the object and gets another try. If the player carrying the object is tagged in the center area, the object is given to the other team. They go into a huddle and try to run it across the field to score.

Whistle Ball

Playing Area: Playground, gymnasium, classroom

Players: Entire class

Supplies: A ball for each group of six to eight players

Skills: Passing, catching

Eight or fewer children stand in circle formation. A ball is passed rapidly back and forth among them in any order. The object is to be the player who stays in the game the longest. A child sits down in place if he makes any of the following errors.

1. He has the ball when the whistle blows. (The teacher should set a predetermined time period, at the end of which a whistle is blown. The time period can be varied from 5 to 20 seconds.)

2. He makes a bad throw or fails to catch a good throw.

3. He returns the ball directly to the person from whom it was received.

Teaching Suggestion: One way to control the time periods is to appoint a child as timer and to give her a list of the time periods, a whistle, and a stopwatch. The timer should be cautioned not to give any advance indication of when the stop signal will be blown. An automatic timer enhances the game. When the game gets down to two or three players, declare them the winners and begin anew.

GAMES FOR SIXTH-GRADE CHILDREN

Children in the 6th grade are becoming sophisticated, and much of their games experience should come from the sports program. Good use should be made of any of the games for the other grades. The 5th-grade games, in particular, should be reviewed.

Suggested Games

Barker's Hoopla
Cageball Target Throw
Chain Tag
  Catch of Fish
More Jump-the-Shot Variations
One-Base Dodgeball
Over the Wall (Chinese Wall)
Pin Dodgeball
Squad Dodgeball
Octopus
Whammy Team Handball
Galactic Empire and Rebels

Barker's Hoopla

Playing Area: Playground, gymnasium

Players: 20 to 30

Supplies: Hoops, beanbags

Skills: Running, dodgeball

Four hoops are arranged in the corners of the playing area. Any distance between hoops can be used, but 25 to 30 ft is a challenging distance. Five to six beanbags are placed in each hoop. The class is divided into four equal teams, one behind each hoop. This is their home base. The object of the game is to steal beanbags from other hoops and return them to the hoop that is home base for each respective team.

The following rules are in effect.

1. A player can take only one beanbag at a time. That beanbag must be taken to the player's home base before she can return for another one.

2. Beanbags cannot be thrown or tossed to the home base, but must be carried over the vertical plane of the hoop before being released.

3. No player can protect the home base or its beanbags with any defensive maneuver.

4. Beanbags may be taken from any hoop.

5. When the stop signal is given, every player must freeze immediately and release any beanbags in possession. Any follow-through of activities to get a final score is penalized.

The team with the most beanbags in the home-base hoop is declared the winner.

Cageball Target Throw

Playing Area: Gymnasium space about the size of a small basketball court

Players: 10 to 30

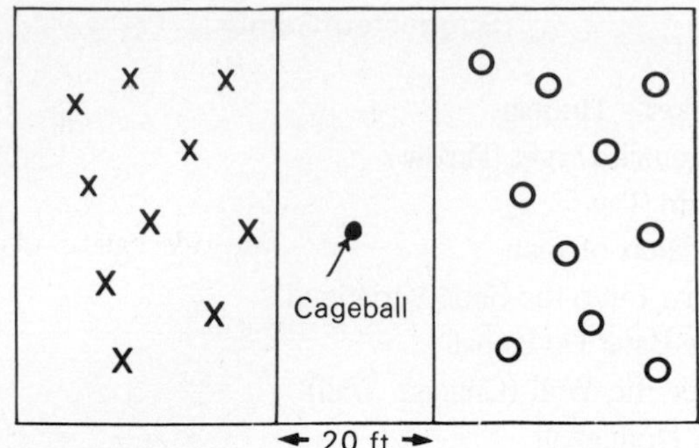

FIGURE 23.12. Formation for Cageball Target Throw

Supplies: A cageball (18 to 30 in.), 12 to 15 balls of various sizes

Skill: Throwing

An area about 20 ft wide is marked across the center of the playing area, with a cageball in the center (Figure 23.12). The object of the game is to throw the smaller balls against the cageball, thus forcing it across the line in front of the other team. Players may come up to the line to throw, but they may not throw while inside the cageball area. A player may enter the area, however, to recover a ball. No one is to touch the cageball at any time, nor may the cageball be pushed by a ball in the hands of a player.

Teaching Suggestion: If the cageball seems to roll too easily, it should be deflated slightly. The throwing balls can be of almost any size—soccer balls, volleyballs, playground balls, or whatever.

Variation: Two rovers, one from each team, can occupy the center area to retrieve balls. These players cannot block throws or prevent a ball from hitting the target. They are there for the sole purpose of retrieving balls for their team.

Chain Tag

Playing Area: Playground

Players: 20 to 40

Supplies: None

Skills: Running, dodging

Two parallel lines are established about 50 ft apart. The center is occupied by three players who form a chain with joined hands. The players with free hands on either end of the chain do the tagging. All other players line up on one of the parallel lines.

The players in the center call, "Come," and the children cross from one line to the other. The chain tries to tag the runners. Anyone caught joins the chain. When the chain becomes too long, it should be divided into several smaller chains.

Variation: *Catch of Fish*—The chain catches the children by surrounding them like a fishing net. The runners cannot run under or through the links of the net.

More Jump-the-Shot Variations

Playing Area: Playground, gymnasium, classroom

Players: 10 to 16

Supplies: A jump-the-shot rope

Skill: Rope jumping

Before the following variations are tried, the jump-the-shot routines and variations listed for the 4th-grade program should be reviewed.

1. Two or more squads are in file formation facing the rope turner. Each player runs clockwise (against the turn of the rope), jumping the rope as often as necessary to return to the squad (Figure 23.13).

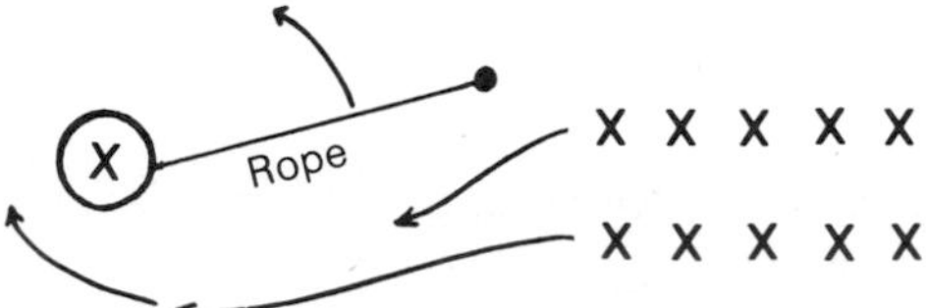

FIGURE 23.13. Jump-the-Shot variation

2. Each player runs counterclockwise and tries to run around the circle before the rope can catch up with him. If this happens, he must jump to allow the rope to go under him. The best time for a player to start his run is just after the rope has passed.

3. Players can try some of the stunts in which the hands and feet are on the ground—to see whether they can have the rope pass under them. The Rabbit Jump, push-up position, Lame Dog, and others are possibilities.

One-Base Dodgeball

Playing Area: Playground, gymnasium

Players: 16 to 30

Supplies: A base (or standard), a volleyball

Skills: Running, dodging, throwing

A home line is drawn at one end of the playing space. A base or standard is placed about 50 ft in front of the home line. Two teams are formed. One team is scattered around the fielding area, the boundaries of which are determined by the number of children. The other team is lined up in single file behind the home line (Figure 23.14).

The object of the game is for the fielding team to hit the runners *below* the shoulders with the ball. Two runners at a time try to round the base and head back for the home line without being hit. The game is continuous, meaning that as soon as a running team player is hit or crosses the home line, another player starts immediately.

The fielding team may not run with the ball but must pass it from player to player, trying to hit one of the runners.

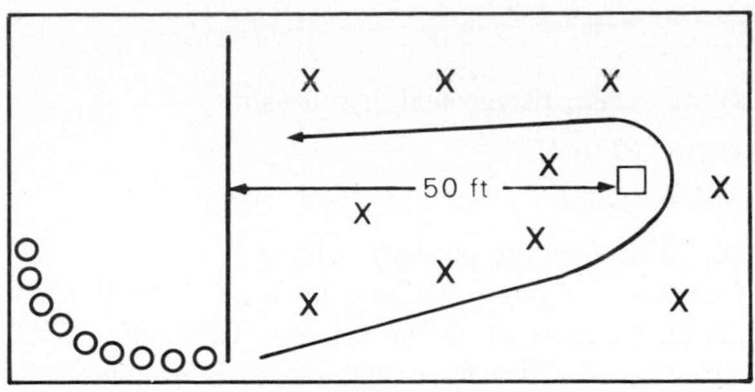

FIGURE 23.14. Formation for One-Base Dodgeball

The running team scores a point for each player who runs successfully around the base and back to the home line.

At the start of the game, the running team has two players ready at the right side of the home line. The others on the team are in line, waiting for a turn. The teacher throws the ball anywhere in the field, and the first two runners start toward the base. They must run around the base from the right side. After all of the players have run, the teams exchange places. The team scoring the most points wins.

Teaching Suggestions: To hit a runner, players on the fielding team should make short passes to a person close to the runner. They must be alert, because two children at a time are running. The next player on the running team must watch carefully, so she can start the instant one of the two preceding runners is back safely behind the line or has been hit.

Over the Wall (Chinese Wall)

Playing Area: Playground

Players: Entire class

Supplies: None

Skills: Running, dodging

Two parallel goal lines are drawn about 60 ft apart. Two additional parallel lines about 3 ft apart are laid out parallel to the goal lines in the middle of the game area. This is the wall (Figure 23.15). Side limits have to be established.

One player is it and stands on, or behind, the wall. All of the other players are behind one of the goal lines. The tagger calls, "Over the wall." All of the players must then run across the wall to the other goal line. The child who is it tries to tag any player he can. Anyone caught helps catch the others. Players also are considered caught when they step on the wall. They must clear it with a leap or a jump and cannot step on it anywhere, including on the lines. After crossing over to the other side safely, players must wait for the next call. The game can be made more difficult by increasing the width of the wall. The taggers can step on or run through the wall at will.

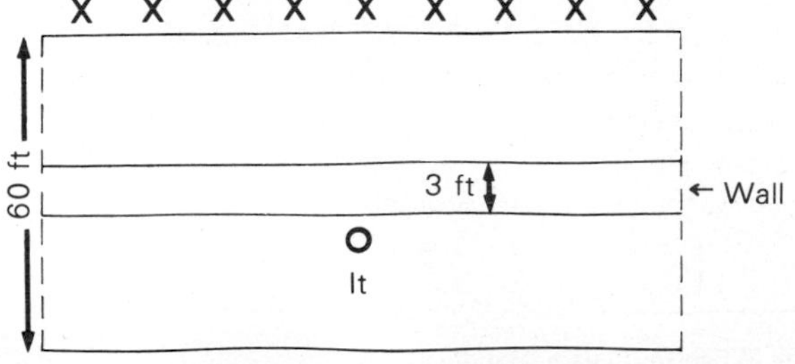

FIGURE 23.15. Formation for Over the Wall

Pin Dodgeball

Playing Area: Gymnasium

Players: Entire class

Supplies: Many playground balls, twelve Indian clubs

Skills: Throwing, dodging, catching

Two teams of equal number play the game. Each team is given many playground balls and six Indian clubs (Figure 23.16). A court 30 by 60 ft or larger with a center line is needed. The size of the court depends on the number of children in the game. The object of the game is to eliminate all of the players on the opposing team or to knock down all of their Indian clubs. The balls are used for *rolling* at the opposing team members or to knock down their clubs. Each team stays in its half of the court.

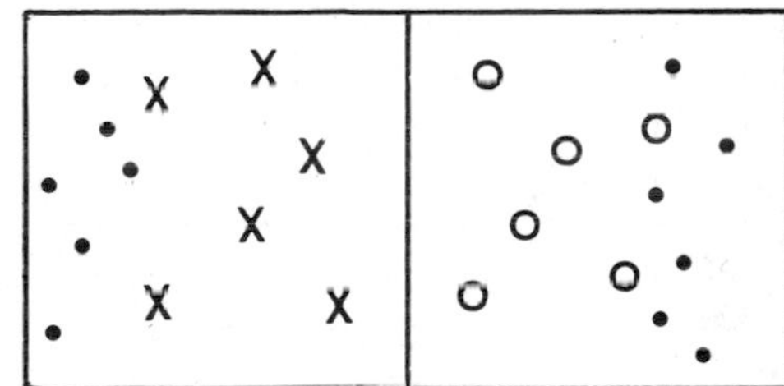

FIGURE 23.16. Formation for Pin Dodgeball

A player is eliminated if any of the following occurs.

1. She is hit by any ball at any time, regardless of the situation.

2. She steps over the center line to roll or retrieve a ball. (Any opposing team member hit as a result of such a roll is not eliminated.)

3. She attempts to block a rolling ball with a ball in her hands and the ball touches her in any manner.

A foul is called when a player holds a ball longer than 10 seconds without rolling at the opposing team. Play stops and the ball is given to the opposing team.

The Indian clubs are put anywhere in the team's area. Players may guard the clubs but must not touch them. When a club is down, even though knocked unintentionally by a member of the defending team, it is removed immediately from the game. The game is over when all players from one team have been eliminated or when all clubs on one side have been knocked down.

Teaching Suggestion: Players who are eliminated should move immediately to the sidelines and sit down. A referee should be positioned at one side of the court near the center line.

Squad Dodgeball

Playing Area: Basketball floor or other area with definite boundaries

Players: Entire class

Supplies: Two deflated volleyballs

Skills: Throwing, dodging

Each squad has a turn at being throwers. The other squad occupies a basketball court or a similar well-defined area. The object of the game is to eliminate the children inside the court. The game starts with two balls placed in the center jump circle and the throwing squad lining up on one end line. On signal, the throwing squad runs forward, picks up the balls, and begins to eliminate dodgers by hitting them below the shoulders with a ball.

Members of the throwing squad may not move when in possession of the ball. This means that the throwers must pass the ball rapidly from one squad member to another to put the ball in strategic position for a hit. With two balls in play, the action moves quickly. Dodgers who are hit should leave the playing area immediately. Dodgers who step on or outside a boundary line are eliminated and must leave the playing area immediately. The time required to eliminate all of the other players is recorded, and the squad with the lower elapsed time is the winner.

Octopus

Playing Area: Playground, gymnasium

Players: 10 to 15

Supplies: None

Skills: Maneuvering, problem solving

Octopus is a game that gets its name from the many hands joined together in the activity. The children stand shoulder to shoulder in a tight circle. Everyone thrusts the hands forward and reaches through the group of hands to grasp the hands across the circle. Players must make sure that they do not hold both hands of the same player. Players also may not hold the hand of an adjacent player. The object is to untangle the mess created by the joined hands by going under, over, or through fellow players. No one is permitted to release a hand grip during the unravelling.

What is the end result? Perhaps one large circle or two smaller connected circles. In a normal-size class, two groups may compete against each other to see which can untangle first. If, after a period of time, the knotted hands do not seem to unravel, call a halt and start over.

Whammy Team Handball

Playing Area: Handball courts superimposed on a basketball court (Figure 23.17)

Players: Two teams with eight per team—four forwards, three guards, and one goalie.

Supplies: An official handball (a soccer ball or volleyball may be substituted); two goals, one on each end; stopwatch

Skills: Passing, guarding, shooting (as in handball)

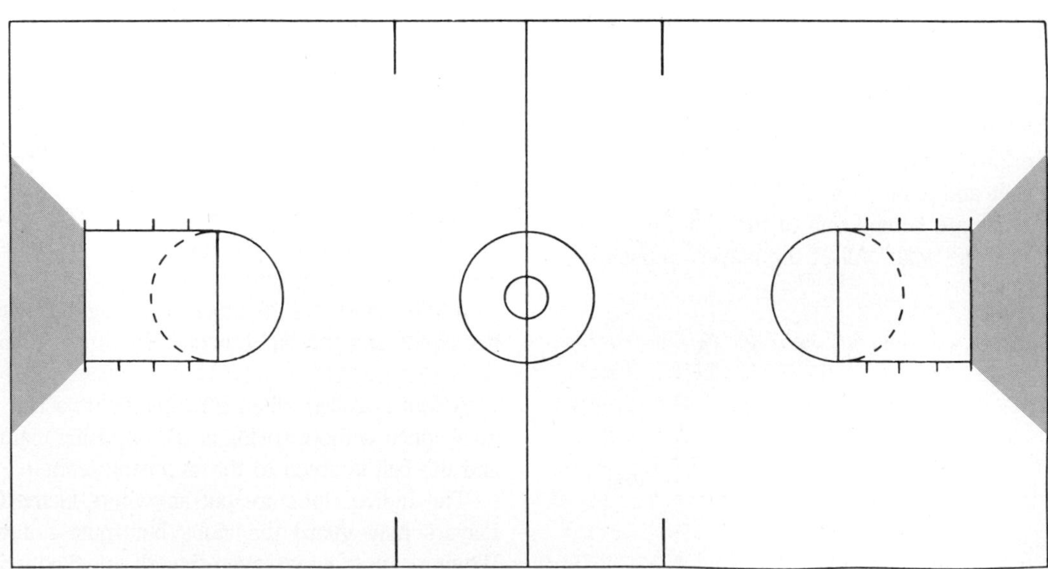

FIGURE 23.17. Handball court markings for Whammy Team Handball

The goal area is formed by a line drawn with tape or chalk across the free-throw lane. The line should be drawn halfway between the circle and the end out-of-bounds line. From where this line joins the lane lines, it is extended on each side to the end out-of-bounds line at an angle of about 45 degrees.

Two volleyball or high-jump standards can be used to form each goal. A crossbar or jump rope can be used for the top of the goal, which is preferably 6 ft above the floor. Stiff, folding tumbling mats also can be used, but should be placed on chairs. The goal width is determined by the basketball foul lines. Hockey goals can be used, but are a bit small.

The object of the game is to score by throwing the ball past the goalie into the goal. The ball must be thrown into the goal from the playing area. This must be accomplished within a 30-second period after the ball crosses the center line, or the defending team gets the ball out of bounds at the center line.

Four forwards compete against three defensive players and the goalie. Defensive players must stay in their backcourt, and likewise, offensive players must remain in their forecourt.

A player has 3 seconds to pass or shoot the ball, otherwise it goes to the other team at the closest sideline. The referee supervises this time limit.

No personal contact of any kind is permitted, nor may a player bat the ball out of another's hand. All tie balls go to the defensive team out of bounds. A player with the ball may not travel. The rules for traveling are the same as for basketball. A player receiving the ball is allowed the normal basketball one-two step count.

All balls that cross into the goal area belong to the goalie. No one may go into the goal area to recover a ball. Offensive players are permitted a single dribble just before shooting. At no other time may they dribble.

An offensive player may "crash" into the goal area after releasing the ball in an attempt to score, provided that her last step before releasing the ball was in the playing area. She must return immediately to the playing area without playing the ball and without interfering with the goalie in any manner.

After a goal is scored, the goalie takes the ball out of bounds and passes it to a teammate. The goalie may leave the goal area to help teammates work the ball into the forecourt for offensive play.

Six-minute quarters are suggested, with the offense and defense of each team trading roles each quarter.

Fouls are called for personal contact and unnecessary roughness. The foul shooter takes a position at the basketball free-throw line and throws at the goal with only the goalie defending. He is permitted the single dribble. Successful foul shots count the same as regular goals. For other violations, the ball is awarded to the offended team out of bounds. A timer is needed to call the 30-second limit.

Note: Since team handball is an official Olympic sport, children should become familiar with the activity. The teacher must be patient, because the strategies of the game are not common knowledge among children or teachers.

Galactic Empire and Rebels

Playing Area: Indoors—basketball court; outdoors—a square, 100 ft on a side. A prison is marked off on each end (Figure 23.18).

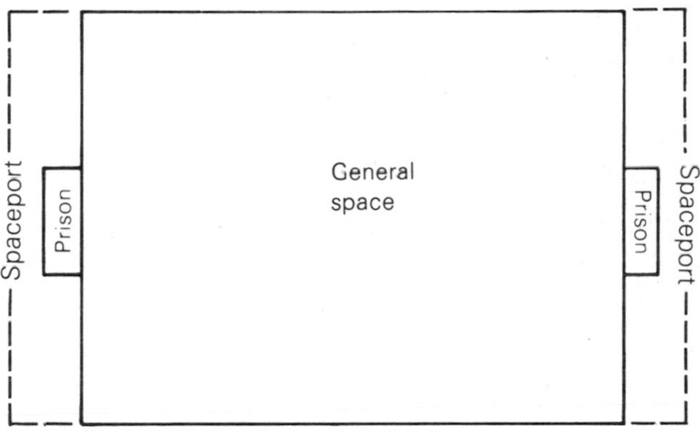

FIGURE 23.18. Galactic Empire court markings

Players: Two teams, 8 to 15 on a team

Supplies: None

Skills: Chasing, fleeing, dodging

Each team's spaceport is behind the end line, where the single space fighters are stationed, waiting to issue against the enemy. To begin, one or more space fighters from either team move from their spaceport to entice enemy fliers for possible capture. A flyer leaving the spaceport may capture only opposing flyers who *previously* have left their respective spaceport. This is the basic rule of the game. A flyer may go back to his spaceport and be eligible immediately to issue again to capture an opponent who was already in general space. The technique of the game is to entice enemy flyers close to the spaceport so fellow flyers can issue and capture (tag) an opposing flyer.

As an illustration of how the game proceeds: Rebel flyer no. 1 moves into general space to entice Empire flyer no. 1 so he can be captured. Rebel flyer no. 1 turns back and heads for her spaceport, chased by Empire flyer no. 1. Rebel flyer no. 2 now leaves her spaceport and tags Empire flyer no. 1 before the Empire flyer can tag Rebel flyer no. 1. The Empire flyer is now a prisoner.

A player captured by an opposing flyer is taken to the tagger's prison—both captor and captive are given free passage to the prison. In prison, the captives form a chain gang, holding hands and extending the prisoners' line toward their own spaceport. The last captive is always at the end of the prisoners' line with one foot in the prison. Captives can be released if a teammate can get to them without being tagged. The released prisoner (only the end one) is escorted back to her own spaceport and both players are given free passage.

The game becomes one of capturing opposing flyers and securing the release of captured teammates. Flyers stepping over the sideline automatically become prisoners. One or two players in the spaceport should be assigned to guard the prison.

Set a time limit of 10 minutes for the contest, and declare the team with the most prisoners the winner.

MISCELLANEOUS PLAYGROUND GAMES

The following games are useful only for small groups, but children do enjoy playing them on the playground.

Suggested Games

Four Square
  Chain Spelling
Two Square
Tetherball

Four Square (Grades Three Through Six)

Playing Area: Any hard surface

Players: Four (Others wait in line for a turn.)

Supplies: A playground ball or volleyball

Skill: Batting a ball

Lines are drawn as shown in Figure 23.19. The squares should be numbered 1, 2, 3, and 4. A service line is drawn diagonally across the far corner of square 1. The player in this square always serves and must stay behind the line when serving.

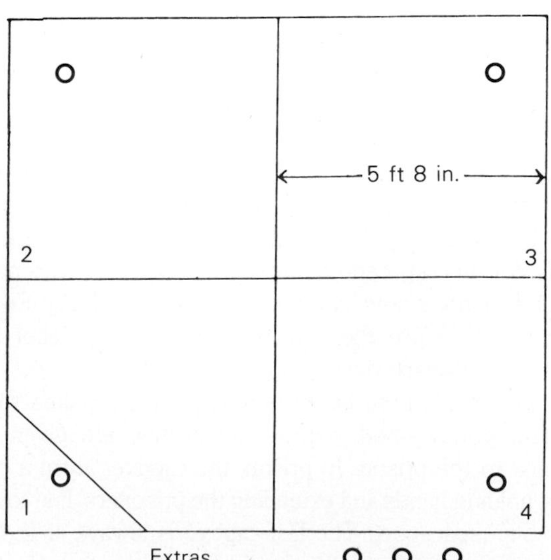

FIGURE 23.19. Formation for Four Square

The ball is served by dropping and serving it underhanded from the bounce. If the serve hits a line, the server is out. The server can hit the ball after it has bounced once in his square. The receiver directs it to any other square with an underhand hit. Play continues until one player fails to return the ball or commits a fault. Any of the following constitutes a fault.

1. Hitting the ball sidearm or overhand
2. Landing a ball on a line between the squares (A ball landing on an outer boundary is considered good.)
3. Stepping into another square to play the ball
4. Catching or carrying a return volley
5. Allowing the ball to touch any part of the body except the hands

When a player misses or commits a fault, she goes to the end of the waiting line and all players move up. The player at the head of the waiting line moves into square 4.

Variations

1. A 2-ft circle can be drawn at the center of the area. Hitting the ball into the circle constitutes a fault.

2. The game can be changed by varying the method of propelling the ball. The server sets the method. The ball can be hit with a partially closed fist, the back of the hand, or the elbow. A foot or knee also can be used to return the ball. The server calls "Fisties," "Elbows," "Footsies," or "Kneesies" to set the pattern.

3. *Chain spelling.* The server names a word, and each player returning the ball must add the next letter in the sequence.

Two Square (Grades Three Through Six)

Playing Area: Any hard surface

Players: Two (Others wait in line for a turn.)

Supplies: A playground ball or volleyball

Skill: Batting a ball

The basic rules and lines are the same as for Four Square, except that only two squares are used. If there are players waiting for a turn, the active player who misses or fouls can be eliminated as in Four Square. If only two players wish to play, score can be kept. The ball must be served from behind the baseline.

Tetherball (Grades Two Through Six)

Playing Area: Any hard surface

Players: Two to four, but generally two

Supplies: A tetherball assembly (pole, rope, and ball)

Skill: Batting a ball

The first server is picked by lot. One player stands on each side of the pole. The server puts the ball in play by tossing it in the air and hitting in the direction he chooses. The opponent must not strike thc ball on the first swing around the pole. On its second swing around the pole, she hits the ball back in the opposite direction. As the ball is hit back and forth, each player tries to hit it so the rope winds completely around the pole in the direction in which he is hitting the ball. The game is won by the player who succeeds in doing this or whose opponent forfeits the game by making a foul. A foul is any of the following.

1. Hitting the ball with any part of the body other than the hands or forearms
2. Catching or holding the ball during play
3. Touching the pole
4. Hitting the rope with the forearms or hands
5. Throwing the ball
6. Winding the ball around the pole below the 5-ft mark

After the opening game, the winner of the preceding game serves. Winning four games wins the set.

REFERENCE

Morris, G. S. D. 1980. *How to change the games children play.* Ed. 2. Minneapolis: Burgess Publishing.

CHAPTER 24

Relays

Relays add enjoyment, interest, and competition to some phases of physical education. When conducted properly, they can help develop fitness, movement skills, and social objectives. Children learn to cooperate with others in the interest of winning, to conform to rules and directions, and to use skills in situations of stress and competition. If the relays are not conducted in a sound way, however, the child may learn to win by cheating.

Relays should not be overused in the program. Instructors sometimes turn too readily to relays to solve motivation problems, because relays often interest the children. Few skills, however, are learned in a relay, because the emphasis is on winning rather than on learning. Another inherent problem with relays is that the majority of children are inactive—standing in line waiting for their turn. For these reasons, relays should be used sparingly and only at opportune times.

Relays should feature skills that children have already overlearned. It is an unreal expectation to think that children will learn skills in a competitive relay situation. A point to remember when using relays is that, when a skill is overlearned, a competitive situation will increase the level of performance. When a skill has not been overlearned, however, competition will lower the level of performance. In the latter case, children forget to perform the skill correctly in their haste to win. Overemphasis on winning compounds this problem.

A few instructional supplies such as blocks, pie plates, and standing pegs are needed for relays. These can be kept in special containers. Otherwise, items required for relay races are taken from the regular physical education supplies.

TYPES OF RELAYS

Three types of relays can be identified.

1. *Regular relays.* In regular relays, each player completes the chore when he has his turn and then retires from the action.

2. *Revolving relays.* In revolving relays, each player participates both when she has her turn and also as part of the relay task. Arch Ball and Corner Fly are ball-handling relays in which each player handles the ball on each turn.

3. *Modified relays.* Modified relays are number-calling relays. These are not true relays in the sense that one player completes a chore and tags off the next player. They have their place in the program, however, by providing an opportunity for alertness and quick reaction when the child's number is called.

INSTRUCTIONAL PROCEDURES

1. Four to six players on a team is usually a good number. Too many on a team drags out the race, and children lose interest.

2. If teams have uneven numbers, some players on the smaller teams should run twice, or a rotational system should be set up in which players take turns waiting out. All children on teams with fewer members must also take turns; otherwise, the more skilled runners may always run twice, which is undesirable.

3. Each team should have a captain to arrange the order, be responsible for the application of the rules, and help keep the action under control. After the race, captains can be asked about their team's conformity to the rules.

4. It is helpful, particularly in revolving relays, to identify the last runner or finishing player with an armband, pinny, or colored shirt. This keeps the teacher informed of the progress of the race.

5. Infractions of the rules should be penalized. Relays are a social learning experience. The children are in a situation in which they must conform to rules or be assessed a penalty. A team can be disqualified, points can be deducted, or other penalties imposed. All teams and players should be penalized on an equal basis.

6. The finishing order must be determined properly. In giving instructions, the teacher should be definite about the start, the turning point, and the finishing act. In some races, crossing the line can be the finishing act. In others, some act or held position may be specified.

7. A marker should be used as a turning point to eliminate arguments. Cones, Indian clubs, jump standards, and beanbags make effective markers. With cones and Indian clubs, knocking over the marker is a disqualification unless the runner resets it before proceeding.

8. Encouraging teams to win is fundamental. Too much emphasis on winning, however, makes the skilled resent being on a team with those of lesser ability. The idea of winning at any cost must be discussed.

9. Distances need to be modified when movements such as the Puppy Dog Run, the Crab Walk, and others with heavy physical demands are used.

10. Relays should be demonstrated so each team understands the procedures. A simple demonstration by one individual may suffice, or the entire team can practice the routine. If a new relay does not seem to have been started properly, stop the activity and review the instructions. A well-received practice is to try the relay first before embarking on a serious competitive run.

11. For modified relays, the teacher should make up a card with a list of numbers to ensure that all numbers are called.

12. Traffic rules should be clear. In most cases, the way to the right governs. When the runner goes around the turning point, she does it from the right (counterclockwise), returning past the finish line on the right side. Some procedures to ensure a fair tagging off of the next runner should be instituted. Runners should not leave the restraining line before being tagged. Exchanging a baton or a beanbag can help ensure fair play.

13. To avoid putting too much stigma on the less-skilled players, these members should be placed in the middle of the team. Discretion can be used when moving players to avoid the stigma of being labeled a poor performer. If these students occupy a starting or finishing position, other students can observe easily their lack of skill.

TEACHING THE RELAY CONCEPT

At the 2nd-grade level, experience in handling beanbags and yarn balls in relay sequences may be of value in teaching the concept of taking turns. Children can be grouped in a line (side-by-side) formation and can pass the articles to the end of the line. In a circle formation, they can pass around a beanbag. The object of these activities is to pass well and not to drop the article. Attention can be given to which group finishes first. Learning to participate in this kind of activity and to cooperate with others is basic to the relay concept.

Another way to develop the relay concept is to place the squads or teams in a file formation and to proceed as follows.

1. The first child (the head of the file) on each team is instructed to move toward and around a given turning point a short distance away and to return to place. The first child to complete this action successfully wins a point for the team.

2. The head child is then told to go to the rear of the line, and the next child has a turn.

3. The next step is for the child to move directly, without delay, to the rear of the line after completing a turn. The procedure of going around the designated side of the turning point and returning down the correct aisle for safety purposes can be introduced.

4. A beanbag can be exchanged between runners. Children are instructed not to run until they have the beanbag.

SELECTED RELAYS FOR GRADES THREE THROUGH SIX

Most of the relays presented here can be done successfully by children in grades 3 through 6, depending on their previous experience and skill level. No attempt has been made to classify the relays by grade level. The relay movements are arranged roughly according to increasing difficulty.

BEANBAG RELAYS

Beanbag relays make a good starting point for younger children, because beanbags can be handled more easily than balls.

Beanbag Pass Relay

Players are in a line, standing side by side. The player on the right starts the beanbag, which is passed from one player to the next down the line. When it gets to the end of the line, the relay is over. The teacher should be sure that each player handles the bag. Children should rotate positions in line.

In the next stage, a revolving relay can be developed in which each member of the team rotates from the right of the squad to the left. When each child has had an opportunity to be the lead member of the group, the relay is finished. This relay can be varied with an underleg pass. The child passes the beanbag underneath one leg to the next player.

Circle Beanbag Pass Relay

Players stand in a circle, facing out, but close enough so the beanbag can be handed from player to player. One circuit begins and ends with the same player. The underleg pass can be used in this formation also.

Carry-and-Fetch Relay

Players are in closed squad formation, with a hoop or circle positioned up to 30 ft in front of each team. The first runner on each team has a beanbag. On the command "Go," this player carries the beanbag forward and puts it inside the hoop; then she returns and tags off the next runner. The second runner goes forward, picks up the beanbag, and hands it off to the third runner. One runner carries the beanbag forward and the next runner fetches it back. Different locomotor movements can be specified.

Beanbag Circle Change Relay

Players are in lane formation. Two hoops or circles are about 15 and 30 ft in front of each team. A beanbag is in the far hoop (Figure 24.1). The first runner runs forward, picks up the beanbag, and moves it to the inner hoop. The next player picks it up and takes it back to the other hoop. The beanbag must rest inside the hoop.

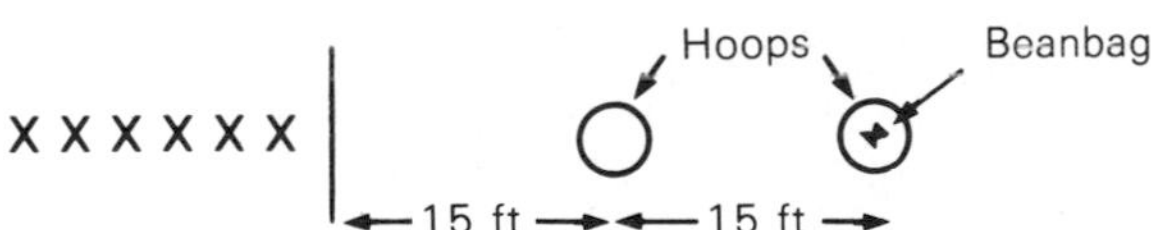

FIGURE 24.1. Formation for Beanbag Circle Change Relay

The Farmer and the Crow Relay

Runners are in lane formation. A line is drawn about 20 ft in front of the teams. The first runner of each team is the farmer, the second runner the crow, and so on. The farmer has five beanbags. On the signal "Go," the farmer hops forward and drops the five beanbags in a reasonably spaced fashion, with the last beanbag placed beyond the drawn line. The farmer then runs back and tags the next player, the crow. The crow runs to the farthest beanbag, begins hopping, and as he hops picks up the beanbags. The crow hands the five beanbags to the third runner, another farmer, who puts the objects out again.

Whenever a player has a beanbag, he hops; when he has no beanbags, he runs. The last beanbag should be placed beyond the far line, because this determines how far each player has to move. The relay can be done with only hopping allowed.

LANE RELAYS WITHOUT EQUIPMENT

In lane relays, each runner runs in turn. The race is over when the last runner finishes. Lane relays are usually regular relays. Different types of movements can be used to challenge the runners.

1. Locomotor movements—walking, running, skipping, hopping, galloping, sliding, jumping

2. Stunt and animal movements—Puppy Dog Run (pp. 363–364), Seal Crawl (p. 375), Bear Walk (p. 364), Rabbit Jump (pp. 368–369), Frog Jump (p. 376), Crab Walk (p. 369)

3. Restricted movements—heel-and-toe walk, sore toe walk (hold the left foot with the right hand), walking on the heels, Crazy Walk (p. 374), Toe Tug Walk (pp. 388–389)

Partner relays are also challenging and fun.

1. Children run (walk, skip, gallop, hop) with partners (inside hands joined) just as a single runner would.

2. Children face each other with hands joined (as partners), slide one way to a turning point, and slide back to the starting point—leading with the other side.

3. *Wheelbarrow Relay.* One person walks on her hands while the partner holds her by the *lower legs,* wheeling her down to a mark. Positions are switched for the return. Distances should not be too long.

LANE RELAYS WITH EQUIPMENT

The use of equipment can be added to basic lane relays.

1. *All Up, All Down Relay.* Three Indian clubs are set in a small circle about 20 ft in front of each team. The first player runs forward and sets the clubs up one at a time, using only one hand. The clubs must stand. The next player puts them down again, and so on.

2. A short line (24 in.) is drawn about 20 ft in front of each team. An Indian club stands on one side of the line. Each player must run forward and stand the Indian club on the other side of the line, using one hand only.

3. Two adjacent circles are drawn about 20 ft in front of each team. Three Indian clubs stand in one of the circles. A player runs forward and moves the clubs, one at a time, standing each club in the other circle. The next player moves the clubs back, one at a time, to the original circle, and so forth.

4. *Roll-and-Set Relay.* Each team has a mat and an Indian club. The mat is placed lengthwise in front of the team (40 to 60 ft away), and the club is between the team and the mat. The first player runs toward the mat, picking up the club. Carrying the club in one hand, he does a Forward Roll, sets the club beyond the far edge of the mat, and runs back and tags off the next player. This player runs to the club, picks it up, does a Forward Roll on the way back, and sets the club in the original spot. The players alternate in this fashion until all have run. The club must stand each time, or the player must return and make it stand.

Three-Spot Relay

Three parallel lines are drawn in front of the teams to provide three spots for each team (Figure 24.2). Each player is given three tasks to perform, one at each spot. She then runs back and tags off the next player, who repeats the performance. Suggestions for the tasks are these.

1. Lie prone.
2. Lie supine.
3. Do an obeisance (i.e., touch the forehead to the floor).
4. Do a nose-and-toe (i.e., touch the toe to the nose from a sitting position).
5. Do a specified number of hops, jumps, Push-ups, or Curl-ups.
6. Perform a designated stunt, such as the Coffee Grinder or Knee Dip.
7. Jump rope for a specified number of turns.

The runner must perform according to the directions at each spot, completing the performance before moving to the next spot. Other task ideas can be used. The winning team selects the requirements for the next race.

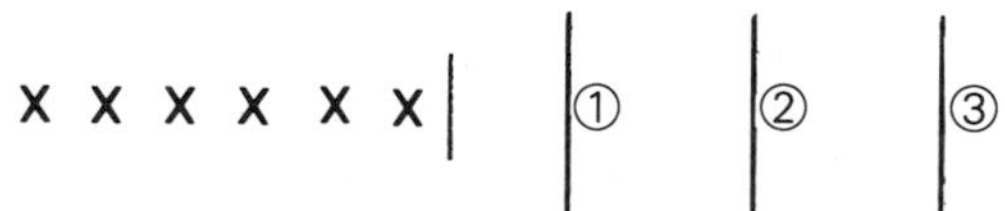

FIGURE 24.2. Formation for Three-Spot Relay

Gym Scooter Relays

Each team has a gym scooter. Scooters lend themselves to a variety of movements, both with individuals and with partners. Scooters should not, however, be used as skateboards. Some suggestions for individual movements are these.

1. Sit on the scooter and propel with the hands or feet.
2. Kneel and propel with the hands.
3. Lie facedown and move in alligator or swimming fashion.

Partner activity can feature any of several approaches. Partners can operate as a single unit, doing the task and passing the scooter to the next pair, or one partner can push or pull the other to the turning point, where they exchange roles and return to the starting line. A third approach is for the pusher to become the rider on the next turn. Some partner actions are these.

1. Rider kneels, and partner pushes or pulls.
2. Rider sits in a Seat Balance, and partner pushes or pulls on the rider's feet.
3. Rider does a Tummy Balance, and partner pushes on the feet.

A wheelbarrow race also can be done with the down person supporting the hands on the scooter.

Potato Relay

A small box about a foot square is placed 5 ft in front of each lane. Four 12-in. circles are drawn at 5-ft intervals beyond the box (Figure 24.3). This makes the last circle 25 ft from the starting point. Four blocks or beanbags are needed for each team.

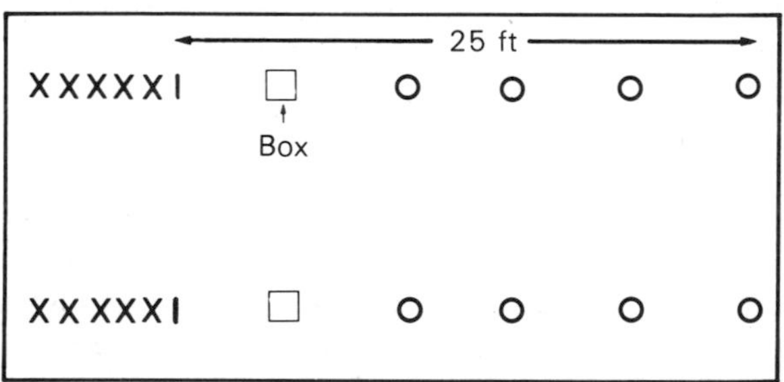

FIGURE 24.3. Formation for Potato Relay

To start, the blocks are placed in the box in front of each team. The first runner goes to the box, takes a single block, and puts it in one of the circles. She repeats this performance until there is a block in each circle; then she tags off the second runner. This runner brings the blocks back to the box, one at a time, and tags off the third runner, who returns the blocks to the circles, and so on.

Using a box to receive the blocks makes a definite target. When the blocks are taken to the circles, some rules must be made regarding placement. The blocks should be considered placed only when they are inside or touching a line. Blocks outside need to be replaced before the runner can continue. Paper plates or pie plates can be used instead of circles drawn on the floor.

Variation: The race can also be done with Indian clubs. Instead of being placed in a box, they are in a large circle at the start.

Sack Race

Sack races have long been a popular picnic event and hold strong attraction for children. Each team has a sack, and the runners must progress with their feet inside the sack. Either lane or shuttle formation can be employed. In lane formation, the sacked runner goes around a marker, returns to the team, and gives the sack to the next participant. Another way to run the race is to have the runner move while in the sack to a marker, get out of the sack, and run back to the head of the line. In shuttle formation, the first runner moves in the sack across the area and gives the sack to the next runner.

Sturdy grain sacks made of burlap hold up well. Large plastic bags can be used, but they are more breakable, especially on rough surfaces.

LANE RELAYS WITH BALLS

A number of interesting lane relays (some regular and some revolving) feature ball-handling skills. The balls should be handled crisply and cleanly. A mishandled ball must reenter the race at the point of error.

Bounce Ball Relay

A circle is drawn 10 to 15 ft in front of each team. The first player runs to the circle, bounces the ball once, runs back to the team, and *gives* the ball to the second player, who repeats the routine. Each player has a turn, and the team whose last child carries the ball over the finish line first wins. To vary the relay, players can bounce the ball more than once.

Kangaroo Relay

The first player in each lane holds a ball between the knees. She jumps forward, retaining control of the ball, rounds the turning point, jumps back to the head of the file, and hands the ball to the next player. If a player loses the ball from between the knees, she must stop and replace it. Slightly deflated balls are easier to retain.

Basketball or Soccer Ball Dribbling Relays

See Chapters 27 and 30 for some suggested basketball and soccer ball dribbling relays.

Bowling Relay

The player at the head of each team has a ball. A line is drawn 15 to 20 ft in front of each team. The first player runs to the line, turns, and rolls the ball back to the second player. The second player must wait behind the starting line to catch the ball and then repeats the pattern. The race is over when the last player has received the ball and carried it over the forward line.

Crossover Relay

The Crossover Relay is similar to the Bowling Relay, except that the ball is thrown instead of rolled.

OBSTACLE RELAYS

Obstacle relays involve some kind of task that the runners must do.

Over-and-Under Relay

A magic rope is stretched about 18 in. above the floor to serve as the turning point. Each runner jumps over the rope and starts back immediately by going under the rope.

Figure-Eight Relay

Three or four cones are spaced evenly in front of each team. Players weave in and out in figure-eight fashion.

Bench Relays

Several interesting races can be run using benches. A balance beam bench or an ordinary bench stands in front of each of two teams in lane formation. The following races are suggested.

1. Run forward, jump over the bench, jump back again, return, and tag off.

2. Run to the bench, pass a beanbag underneath it, run around the bench, pick up the beanbag, and return to the team. Give the beanbag to the next player.

3. Place a beanbag about 3 ft in front of the bench. The first player runs forward, picks up the beanbag, and jumps over the bench as she carries the bag. She then drops the bag on the far side of the bench, jumps back over the bench, returns to the line, and tags off. The next runner jumps over the bench, picks up the bag, jumps back over the bench with it, and places it on the floor near original position. The pattern is alternately carrying the bag over and bringing it back to the near side.

Eskimo Relay

Teams are in lane formation, with each team having two squares of cardboard about 2 by 2 ft. The cardboards represent cakes of ice, and the task is to use the cardboards as stepping stones. Players race two at a time. One player is the stepper, and one handles the cardboards. The stepper may not touch the floor. The handler can handle the cardboards to the turning point and then exchange places with the stepper. An alternative is to have the handler convey the stepper back to the starting point, give the cardboards to the next player at the head of the line, and then become the new stepper.

Variation: The race can also be run in shuttle formation. Since the partners go both ways during the race, the stepper and the cardboard handler exchange places halfway.

Jack Rabbit Relay (Jump Stick Relay)

Each runner carries a broomstick or wand, 1 m in length. A turning point is established about 30 ft in front of each lane. The race starts with the first player in line running forward around the turning point and back to the head of the line (Figure 24.4). In the meantime, the next player takes a short step to the right and gets ready to help with the stick. The runner with the stick returns on the left side and shifts the stick to the left hand. The second player reaches out with the right hand and takes the other end of the stick. The two then pass the stick under the others in the line, who must jump up to let it go through. When the stick has passed under all players, the original player releases the grip and remains at the end of the line. The second runner runs around the turning point and returns, and the next player in line helps with the stick, becoming the next runner when the stick has gone under all of the jumpers. Each player repeats until all have run.

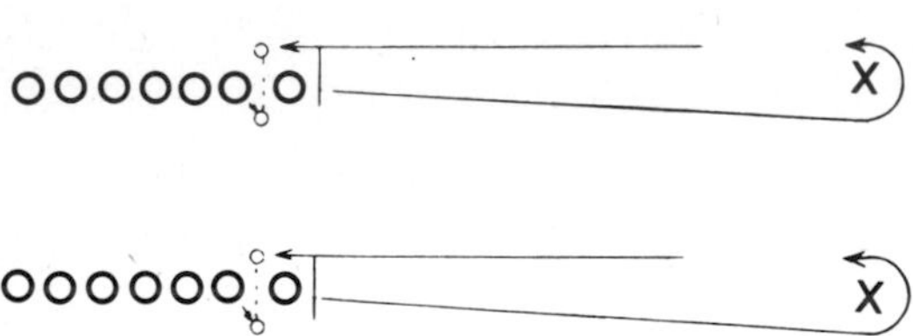

FIGURE 24.4. Formation for Jack Rabbit Relay

To end the race properly takes a little doing. The simplest way is to call the race complete when the last runner crosses the line with the wand. Another way is to have the last runner, helped by the original first runner who by now has rotated to the front of the line, carry the wand under the team. The last runner releases the wand, and the first runner returns the wand to the head of the line.

Teaching Suggestion: If children are unfamiliar with the relay, practice is needed. When they carry the stick back, under the jumpers, they should hold it close to the ground.

Hula Hoop Relay

Each team consists of a file of five or six children who join hands. The leader, in front, holds a hoop in the free hand. The object is to pass the hoop down the line so that all bodies go through it, until the last person holds the hoop. The last person takes the hoop to the head of the line, and the process is repeated until the original leader is again at the head. The children may manipulate the hoop with their hands as long as they keep their hands joined. They should lock little fingers if necessary. All team members must pass through the hoop, including the last person.

The hoop can be moved around a circle of children with hands joined. The hoop starts on a pair of joined hands. When it has gone around the circle, over all of the bodies, and returned to the same spot, the race is over.

REVOLVING TEAM BALL RELAYS

Arch Ball Relay

Each team is in lane formation. Each player, using both hands, passes a ball overhead to the next person, and so on to the back player. The last player, on receiving the ball, runs to the head of the column, and the activity is repeated. The race is over when the original front player comes back to his spot at the head of the line. Each player must clearly handle the ball.

Right and Left Relay

The action is the same as for Arch Ball, except that the ball is handed to the person behind with a side turn. The first turn is to the right, and the next person turns to the left.

Straddle Ball Relay

Players are in lane formation. Each player takes a wide straddle stance, forming an alley with the legs. The ball is rolled down the alley to the back person, who runs to the front with it and repeats the activity. Players may handle the ball to help it down the alley, but it is not required that each person do so.

Over and Under Relay

Players take a straddle position in lane formation. The first player hands the ball overhead with both hands to the player behind, who in turn hands the ball between his legs to the next player. The ball goes over and under down the line.

Pass and Squat Relay

One player (number 1) with a ball stands behind a line 10 ft in front of his teammates, who are in lane formation (Figure 24.5).

Number 1 passes the ball to number 2, who returns the ball to number 1. As soon as he has returned the ball to number 1, number 2 squats down so the throw can be made to number 3, and so on, down the file. When the last person in line receives the ball, she does not return

⑥⑤④③② |←10 ft→| ①

FIGURE 24.5. Formation for Pass and Squat Relay

it but carries it forward, straddling the members of her team, including number 1, who has taken a place at the head of the file. The player carrying the ball forward then acts as the passer. The race is over when the original number 1 player receives the ball in the back position and straddles the players to return to his original position.

Some care must be taken that the front player in the file is behind the team line as the passing starts. After the straddling, repositioning the file is necessary. Each player should form a compact ball during the straddling activity. This is an interesting relay, but some practice is needed for it to function properly.

CIRCLE PASS RELAYS

Circle Pass Relays involve ball handling in a circular formation.

Simple Circle Relay

Each team forms a separate circle of the same size. At first, the circle should be small enough so that players can hand the ball to each other. The leader of each group starts the ball around the circle by handing it to the player on her right. As soon as the ball gets back to the leader, the entire team sits down. The first team to be seated in good formation wins.

Later, the circle can be enlarged so the ball must be passed from player to player. More than one circuit of the circle can be specified. The leader can hold the ball aloft to signal completion.

Circle-and-Leader Relay

A circle 15 to 20 ft in diameter is formed. One player is in the center with a ball. The ball is passed in succession to each of the players. The race is over when the ball is returned to the center player by the last circle player. Different passes can be specified.

Corner Fly (Spry) Relay

The players are in a line or semicircle facing the leader (Figure 24.6), who has a ball. The ball is passed to and received from each player, beginning with the player on the left. When the last player receives the ball, he calls out, "Corner fly," and takes the position of the leader. The leader takes a position in the line to the left. In the meantime, all players adjust positions to fill the spot vacated by the new leader. The relay continues, with each player becoming the leader in turn. When the original leader returns to the spot in front of the team, the relay is over.

A marker can be placed behind the leader so the last player in line, when she receives the ball, runs around the marker to the leader's spot. This gives a little more time for the team to shift places and get ready for the new leader.

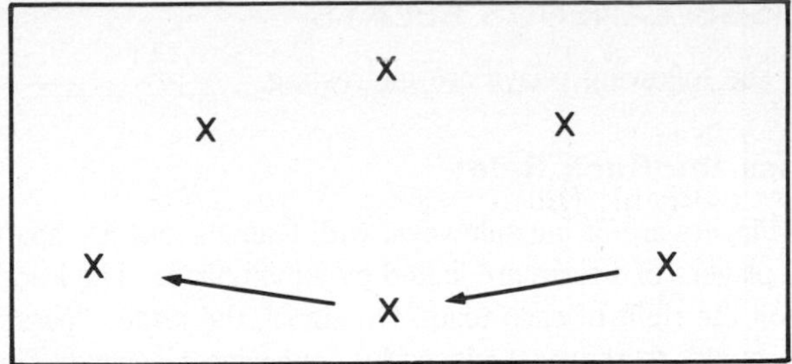

FIGURE 24.6. Formation for Corner Fly Relay

If a team is one person short of the number of players on the other teams, two consecutive passes could be made by the leader to the first person. Alternately, the initial leader might take two turns (first and last), which means another person comes forward after the second turn to provide the finish.

Tadpole Relay

One team forms a circle, facing in, and has a ball. Another team is in lane formation about 10 ft behind the circle (Figure 24.7). The object of the game is to see how many times the ball can be passed completely around the circle while the other team completes a relay. Each player from the team in lane formation runs in turn around the outside of the circle and tags off the next runner until all have run. In the meantime, the ball is being passed around the circle on the inside. Each time the ball makes a complete circuit, the circle players count the number loudly. After the relay is completed and the count established, the teams trade places and the relay is repeated. The team making the higher number of circuits by passing is the winner. The relay gets its name from the shape of the formation, which resembles a tadpole.

Variation: Different types of passes and different methods of locomotion provide variation.

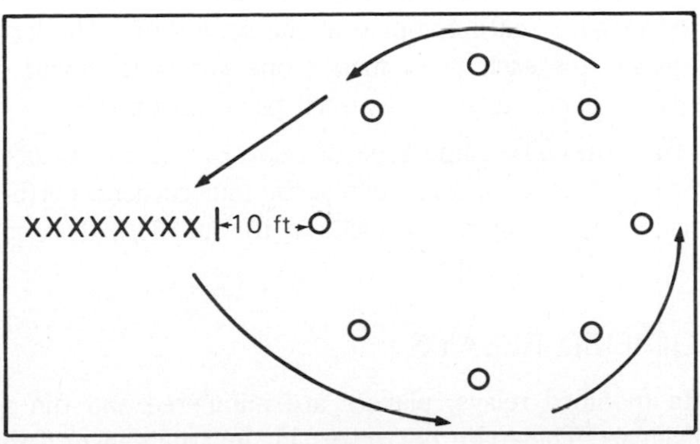

FIGURE 24.7. Formation for Tadpole Relay

MISCELLANEOUS RELAYS

The following relays are interesting.

Pass the Buck Relay

Players are facing sideways, with teams about 5 ft apart. All players of a team are linked by joined hands. The leader is on the right of each team. On signal, the leader "passes the buck" to the next player by squeezing his hand. This player in turn passes the squeeze to the next, and so on down the line. The end player, when she receives the buck, runs across the front of the team and becomes the new leader. She starts the squeeze, and it is passed down the line. Each player in turn comes to the front of the line, with the original leader finally returning to the head position.

Rescue Relay

Lane formation is used, with the first runner behind a line about 30 ft in front of the team (Figure 24.8). The first runner runs back to the team, takes the first player in line by the hand, and "rescues" him by leading him back to the 30-ft line. The player who has just been rescued then runs back to the team and gets the next player, and so on, until the last player has been conducted to the line.

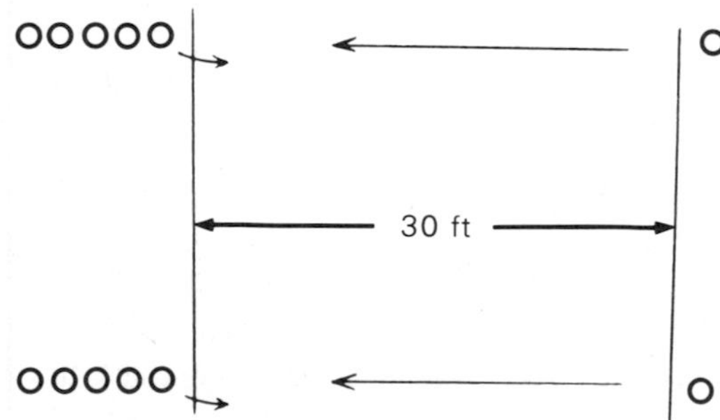

FIGURE 24.8. Formation for Rescue Relay

Around-the-Bases Relay

Four bases are laid out as in a baseball diamond. Two teams, lined up at opposite bases on the inside of the diamond (Figure 24.9), compete at the same time. The lead-off player for each team makes one complete circuit of the bases and is followed by each player in turn.

Variations: The same type of relay can be run indoors by using chairs or Indian clubs at the four corners. Further variations can require the children to run more than one lap or circuit on a turn.

MODIFIED RELAYS

In modified relays, players are numbered and run as individuals. These are not relays in the true sense of the term.

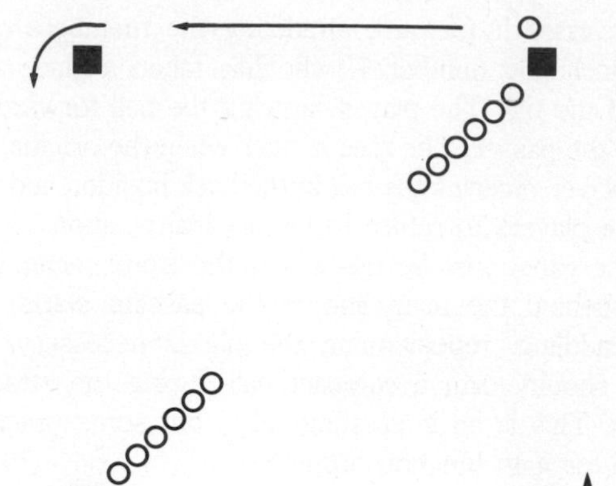

FIGURE 24.9. Formation for Around-the-Bases Relay

Attention Relay

The players on each team are facing forward in lane formation with team members about arm's distance apart. The distance between the teams should be about 10 ft. Two turning points are established for each team—one 10 ft in front of the team and the other 10 ft behind (Figure 24.10). Players are numbered consecutively from front to rear. The teacher calls, "Attention." All come to the attention position. The teacher calls out a number. (The route of player no. 2 is shown in Figure 24.10.) The player on each team holding that number steps to the right, runs around the front and the back markers, and returns to place. The rest of the team runs in place. The first team to have all members at attention, including the returned runner, wins a point.

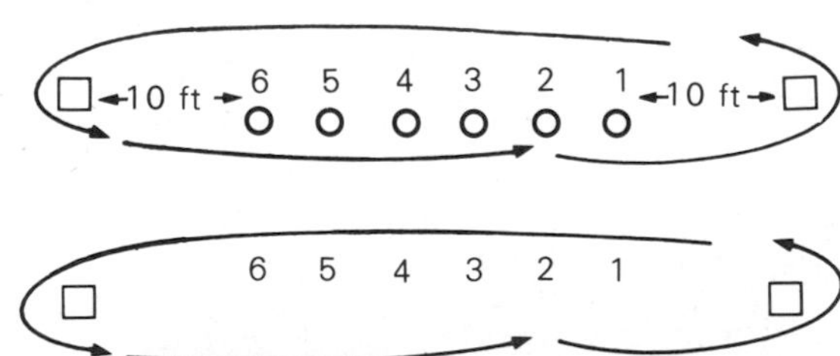

FIGURE 24.10. Formation for Attention Relay

The numbers should not be called in consecutive order, but all numbers should be called. There must be enough distance between teams so runners do not collide.

Variations

1. Different means of locomotion can be used.

2. The teams can be organized by pairs, and two can run at one time, holding inside hands.

3. *Under the Arch.* The leader calls two consecutive numbers, say, numbers 3 and 4. Immediately, numbers 3 and 4 on each team face each other and form an arch by raising both hands. The players in front of the arch (numbers

1 and 2) run forward around the front marker, around the back marker, and then back to place, passing under the arch. The players behind the arch run under the arch first, around the front marker, around the back marker, and back to place. When all have returned to place, the arch players drop hands and resume position. The first team to be at attention is the winner. The running is always forward at the start. Each player follows the person ahead, keeping in numbered order. Each goes around the front marker, around the back marker, and back to place after passing under the arch.

4. Each team stands on a bench. With the teams standing at attention, a number is called, and that team member jumps down from the bench, runs completely around it, and runs back to his place on top of the bench.

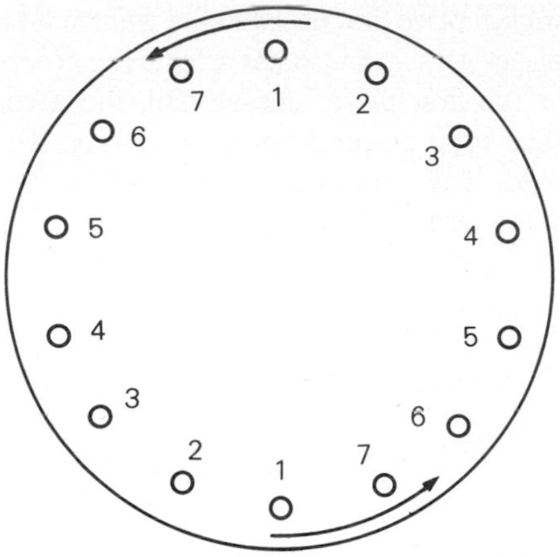

FIGURE 24.11. Formation for Circular Attention Relay

Circular Attention Relay

Two teams form a circle, with players facing counterclockwise and each team occupying half of the circle. The players of each team are numbered consecutively (Figure 24.11). The teacher calls the group to attention and then calls a number. The children with that number (one on each team) immediately run counterclockwise around the circle and back to place, and stand at attention. The first to get back to place scores a point for the team. All numbers should be called.

Variation: A variation is Circle Leapfrog. All players crouch on their knees, facing counterclockwise, with the forehead supported in cupped hands on the floor. When a number is called, the runner straddles or leapfrogs all of the children around the circle, returns to place, and resumes the original position. Scoring is the same as in Circular Attention.

Supine Relay

Players lie supine on the floor, in a circle, with their heads toward the center of the circle and hands joined. The members of each team are numbered consecutively. When a number is called, the player with that number runs around or over the players on her team (Figure 24.12), and then returns to her place, assuming the supine position with hands rejoined. The first player back scores a point for the team. The game can continue to a definite score or until all numbers are called.

Variations: The following are fun for the children.

1. *Human Hurdle.* Each team forms a small circle and sits with backs to the center. The action is the same as for the Supine Relay.

2. *Cyclone.* This is a team race, with the team getting

FIGURE 24.12. Supine Relay

back to original place first declared the winner. At the signal, the first player gets up and starts around the group. Immediately after the first player passes him, the second player follows. The third player follows as soon as the first two have passed. The remaining players follow in the same manner. When the first player gets back to place, she takes her original seated position. Each player in turn goes around until she is back to her original place. The last player cannot move until all of the other players have gone by. When he gets back to place, the race is over.

CHAPTER 25

Conducting Physical Education in the Classroom

At times it is desirable to supplement the regular program by conducting physical education in the classroom. When the weather is good, little need exists, because more than one class can use playground facilities. Adverse weather, however, creates facility problems when indoor (gymnasium) space is inadequate for a daily program or is nonexistent. The choice is then between conducting physical education in the classroom, with its inherent limitations, or having the children forgo their activity experiences for the day.

Providing an *instructional* physical education program in the classroom setting involves the careful selection and teaching of appropriate activities in a challenging environment. Children should make progress toward physical fitness and skill development through the classroom presentations. Merely entertaining the students with a variety of classroom games is much less demanding but is not instructional. Games can be part of the offerings but should not be the only emphasis.

SITUATIONS REQUIRING PHYSICAL EDUCATION IN THE CLASSROOM

Several situations confront the teacher with respect to classroom-based physical education.

THE SPLIT GYMNASIUM-CLASSROOM PROGRAM

Where facilities are available but inadequate for a daily program, classes held in regular physical education facilities have to be supplemented with classroom physical education. In a school where 20 classrooms share a gymnasium, a particular classroom may be scheduled only twice a week for regular physical education. The classes in the gymnasium are supplemented by lessons held in the classroom to meet the statutory time requirements.

Because the schedule usually is set at the beginning of the school year, a curriculum for a combination classroom-gymnasium physical education experience can be prepared. Planning must cover both the regular and the classroom programs. The more rugged activities and skill instruction are covered in the regular program. To the classroom are allocated those activities suitable for limited space. When weather permits outdoor scheduling, the classroom program is passed over.

CLASSROOM PHYSICAL EDUCATION

When no suitable gymnasium facilities are present, physical education that cannot be conducted on the playground must be scheduled in the classroom. Planning for this situation should include two programs—one for the playground and one for the classroom. The classroom program should be in sequential lessons, which follow consecutively as indoor program days occur. The arrangement should give special attention to fitness development.

THE OCCASIONAL CLASSROOM PHYSICAL EDUCATION LESSON

Sometimes emergency situations require that the physical education lesson be taught in the classroom because the usual facility is not available. This is the most difficult situation for which to plan. Program emphasis usually has to be shifted, because the active program of the gymnasium or playground is not suitable for classroom conditions. Since this situation is occasional and unexpected, the lesson can revolve mostly around fun and games. Activity should not be omitted altogether, or the children will be disappointed about losing their gymnasium time.

THE RELAXATION PERIOD

The relaxation period is designed to provide a break in the day's routine. It is a kind of safety valve that allows children to release tension. Because it is a supplement to the regular physical education experiences, the relaxation period should provide activities different from those in the regular program. The relaxation period is usually short, not more than 10 minutes or so. Relaxation activities and games make up the bulk of the experiences. Finger plays are excellent relaxation activities for younger children.

GUIDELINES FOR CLASSROOM AND LIMITED-SPACE ACTIVITIES

The following considerations are relevant in some degree to one or more of the situations described previously.

THE NOISE PROBLEM

Children must recognize that activity is a privilege and that their cooperation is essential. They need to keep exuberance under control so their activity does not interfere with other classes. (This can be a significant problem if one classroom is directly above another.) If possible, an entire section of the school should have physical education periods at the same time. When all classes in the same part of the building are playing simultaneously, they will not disturb each other.

EQUIPMENT AND SUPPLIES

If there is to be an appreciable amount of classroom physical education, a set of equipment and supplies separate from that used in the regular physical education program is needed. Having a supply cart that contains the items most used is an efficient system. The cart can be rolled directly into the classroom and saves sending monitors to a central point to carry items back to the classroom. Equipment carts that contain portable balance beams, light folding mats, balance boards, individual mats, and other equipment are also time-savers.

Each classroom should have a special collection of games, targets, manipulative objects, and other items for indoor play. Many of the items can be constructed by the children. Only supplies that will not damage the classroom should be used. Small sacks stuffed with excelsior, fleece balls, beanbags, yarn balls, rolled-up socks sewn together, balloons, and other articles of this nature can be used with little danger.

PREPARING THE FACILITIES

When classroom desks and chairs are movable, a variety of activities are possible. Furniture can be pushed together to permit circle activities and rhythmic activities. Chairs and desks can be pushed to one side to form an open space. If mats, balance beams, or benches are to be used, several wider aisles can be made by pushing adjacent rows together. Rotating station groups offers excellent possibilities.

Instruction should be given in how to prepare desks for moving. All personal items must be put away, desk tops cleared, and books and other objects stacked underneath in such a way that they will not fall out when the desks are moved. Projecting items that might cause tripping should be placed in safe positions. Windows should be opened and the room temperature lowered.

If desks and chairs are fixed, then space is more limited. Established aisles should be used, and as much space as possible cleared. Halls have a low priority for use. The noise permeates the entire building, and activity interferes with the passage of students.

CONDUCTING ACTIVITIES

The teacher must plan judiciously to extract as much activity as possible from the experiences. As many children as possible should engage in activity at one time. Taking turns may sometimes be necessary, but standing around and waiting should be minimized.

Safety is a concern. Inactive children should keep their feet well under their desks to avoid tripping players who are using the aisles.

Multiple-group organization (station teaching) can be used to increase the amount of activity per child. A specific space is designated for each station area, and the progressions to be followed are clearly defined. Organizing five or six stations prevents having too many children at any one. Children spend a specified period at each station and rotate on signal. One of the stations can be a fitness corner (see the "Fitness Development" section). The stations also could be used for fitness circuit training.

Cleanliness can be a problem and may limit or eliminate activities in which children are on the floor. Individual mats or carpet squares can be a partial solution. Sweeping or vacuuming takes time and is disruptive.

PROGRAM SUGGESTIONS (9)

Classroom physical education should try to achieve the same activity balance as the regular physical education program. Categories to be considered include fitness development, isometric conditioning exercises, rhythmics, manipulative activities, stunts and tumbling, apparatus activities, movement experiences, finger plays, and games and relays. Possibilities in each of these categories are discussed.

FITNESS DEVELOPMENT

Fitness activities can be adapted to classroom work. Many exercises are quite appropriate, including selected isometric exercises. Group exercises are occasionally useful but should not be overworked. Aerobic dance is particularly well suited to classroom exercise.

Circuit Training (see Chapter 16) is quite appropriate. The circuit could consist entirely of fitness activities or could combine fitness activities and other movement tasks.

A fitness corner permanently installed in the classroom is an excellent idea. This usually consists of a support beam mounted high on a wall or on the ceiling from which a variety of equipment—rings, hoops, trapezes, climbing poles and ladders, and climbing ropes—is hung. Several types are available from commercial sources. The equipment should be compact yet able to accommodate six or more children. Rubber bands made from inner tubes cut in two widths (1½ and 2 in.) are useful for resistance exercises. A chart describing the kinds of resistance exercises can be posted. Some means of storage must be devised, or the articles will be scattered around the classroom.

ISOMETRIC CONDITIONING EXERCISES FOR CLASSROOM USE

Isometric exercises are characterized by having virtually no movement of the body part but a high degree of muscular tension. The muscles undergo a holding contraction of eight slow counts. To prevent movement, the pulling, pushing, or twisting action is usually braced against some external force. This can be a desk, chair, wall, door frame, the floor, or a special isometric apparatus. Alternatively, one set of muscles can be worked against another, either individually or with a partner.

In the regular classroom, where narrow confines and furniture limit activity, isometrics have special value because they involve no movement. Many exercises can be done by children seated at their desks, with the desks used as braces.

Maximum or near-maximum tension of the muscle group must be reached and held for approximately 8 seconds. Repetition of an exercise at any one session is not needed, because maximum development is gained from one contraction at an exercise session. Contractions should be performed at different joint angles to ensure strength development throughout the full range of movement.

Isometric exercises are presented in five categories: (1) abdominals, (2) arms, chest, and shoulders, (3) back, (4) legs, and (5) neck. In each case, the arms provide the stabilizing force for the specified development, so in a sense, all of the exercises benefit the arms and shoulders.

Abdominals

1. Sit straight against a backrest. Hold the edges of the chair with the hands. Pull the stomach in hard against the backrest.

2. Sit with hands (palms down, fingers extended) on the lower portion of the top of the thighs. Press down with the hands and up with the legs. (This exercise can also be done by placing the hands on the knees and lifting the straightened legs.)

3. Stand about 4 ft behind a chair. Bend forward at the waist until the hands can be put on the back of the chair (the elbows are straight). With a strong downward pull from the abdominal wall and the arms, pull down against the chair.

Arms, Chest, and Shoulders

1. Stand or sit. Clasp the fingers together in front of the chest with forearms held parallel to the floor (elbows out). Pull against the fingers to force the elbows out. Be sure to keep the chest up, the shoulders back, and the head erect.

2. Stand or sit. Using a grip with the palms together and the fingers interlocked (knuckles upward), push the palms together. Be sure the elbows are up and out.

3. Sit. Drop the hands, straight down, to the sides. Curl the fingers under the seat. Pull up with the shoulders, keeping the body erect.

4. Sit. Rest the thumb and near part of the hands on top of the chair seat. Push to raise the seat completely off the chair. Hold.

5. Stand or sit. With the left palm up and the right palm down, clasp the hands in front of the body, chest high. Press down with the right hand, resisting with the left. Reverse.

6. Sit. Grasp two books (with a total thickness of about an inch) in an opposed thumb grip. Squeeze hard with both hands.

7. Sit or stand. Put both hands on top of the head. Slide the hands toward the elbows so that each grasps an elbow. Raise the arms high and attempt to pull them apart while resisting with the hands on the elbows.

Back

1. Sit, bent forward and grasping the toes. Pull upward with the back while holding the toes.

2. Sit. Slide the hands forward to grasp the knees. From a slightly forward bend, pull back against the knee pressure. This exercise can also be done by placing the hands under the thighs near the knees.

3. Sit. Grasp the right hand under the chair. Apply pressure by leaning to the left. Reverse direction.

Legs

1. Sit with legs outstretched, the right ankle over the left. Press down with the right leg. Reverse position. Bend the knees and repeat right and left.

2. Sit, leaning forward. Cup the right hand around the outside of the left knee and vice versa. Force the knees outward against the inward pressure of the hands.

3. Sit, leaning forward. Place the cupped right hand against the inside of the left knee and vice versa. Force the knees together against the outward arm pressure.

Neck

1. Stand or sit. Clasp the hands behind the back of the head. Keeping the elbows well out, force the head back against the pressure of the hands.

2. Sit or stand. Place both hands flat against the forehead. Move the head forward against the pressure.

3. Sit or stand. Place the heel of the right hand against the head above the ear. Force the head to the right against the arm pressure. Repeat on the left side.

Isometric exercises using wands can be adapted for the classroom (see pp. 312–313). Instead of using a 1-m wand, consider the lummi stick or a 12-in. section of broom handle.

RHYTHMICS

Rhythmics are easily adapted to classroom activity, particularly when circle space can be arranged by moving the furniture to the center of the room. Rhythmic activities done in place are ideal, because children can be scattered in the available space. Selections featuring identification of body parts and individual movement are excellent for younger children. Lummi stick rhythms should be considered. If enough pathways in and around the furnishings can be arranged, fundamental movements guided by a drum or recorded music provide controlled activity. Chapter 17, on rhythmic activities, contains additional ideas.

MANIPULATIVE ACTIVITIES

Selected manipulative activities can be used in the classroom. The major restriction is that many of the throwing, catching, kicking, rebounding, and batting activities do not suit the classroom situation.

Prevention of facility damage is an overriding factor. Manipulative articles that cannot damage the facilities—balloons, yarn balls, paper balls, beanbags, and 8-in. foam rubber balls—are preferable. Target games in which the article is tossed or rolled at a target are recommended.

Balloons, particularly for younger children, provide excellent challenges. A group of five or six children can be assigned two balloons. They try to keep the balloons aloft for a stipulated time period, while remaining glued to their chairs or the floor. A balloon that touches the floor is out of play.

Individual activities in which a child handles an object are implemented easily. Children can balance beanbags on various body parts or toss and handle beanbags individually in a controlled situation. Juggling with scarves or small juggling balls is within the scope of classroom activities.

Depending on room size, a small (12- to 16-ft) parachute might be used. Wands for isometric exercises and ropes placed on the floor can stimulate a wide range of activity.

STUNTS AND TUMBLING

If there is room for six mats, a full-fledged tumbling program is feasible. With room for only one or two mats, tumbling is best used as a station teaching circuit. Individual stunt activities that demand little movement, especially in-place balance stunts, are examples of suitable activity.

APPARATUS ACTIVITIES

The apparatus available in the fitness corner can be used in an apparatus program. The difficulty of moving apparatus to the classroom, setting it up, and returning it is a serious limitation. Low, portable balance beams have value, because these can be set up in aisles. A workable idea is to have apparatus set up at one or two stations. Balance boards, bounding boards, bongo boards, jumping boxes, and magic ropes are possible apparatus items for the stations.

MOVEMENT EXPERIENCES

Movement experiences in which children remain in personal space, either seated or standing, can take a number of directions. For younger children, reinforcing the concept of laterality is excellent activity. Commands that stimulate laterality are as follows.

"Point to the right, to the left, in front of you, behind you."

"Can you point your thumbs up, down, toward each other, away from each other? In the same direction to the right, to the left?"

"Put your arms out wide, forward, up high, down low."

"Turn your toes in, out. To the right, left."

"See if you can bend down, bend backward, to the right, to the left."

Identifying different body parts by touching provides similar experiences. Children can be asked to touch various body parts with the right hand, the left hand, and with both hands. Mirroring the movements of the teacher aids in visual recognition. The teacher makes various movements with the arms, and children mirror the movements. Later, they can try to copy the movements instead of mirroring them.

Hopping patterns (1-1, 2-2, 1-2, 2-1) can be specified,

with the first number representing the number of hops on the right foot and the second referring to hops on the left foot.

The Haida War Canoe Paddle is an interesting activity. (The Haidas were warlike Indians who lived along the coast of British Columbia and traveled great distances in large canoes.) Each child uses a ruler as a paddle. The child at the head of the row is the bow paddler. All keep time with the bow paddler on the same side of the row. When the bow paddler shifts to the other side, all paddlers follow suit.

Other ideas like the following can generate creative activity. Children can pretend to reel in a fish, catch fireflies, pound a hammer, pump up a tire, and so on. Poems also can elicit movement, particularly poems with specific movement commands. Two examples are provided. The first one starts with the children seated.

Two Little Hands

Two little hands go clap, clap, clap.
Two little feet go tap, tap, tap.
Two little knuckles go rap, rap, rap.
A quick jump from the chair,
Two little arms high in the air,
Two little fists grasp the hair.
Two little feet go jump, jump, jump.
Two little fists go thump, thump, thump.
Two little arms go pump, pump, pump.
One little body turns round and round,
One makes a face just like a clown,
One little body sits quietly down.

Exercise Time

I put my hands up high,
I put them way down low.
I put them way out wide,
And turn them up just so.
I jump with two feet fast,
I jump with two feet slow.
I turn round and round like a top,
Then I hold my head just so.
I move my hands like wings,
And then I try to swim.
I quickly sit way down
And look around with a grin.

FINGER PLAYS

Finger plays have a long and rich heritage representing many cultures. They have appeared in innumerable forms. They offer fine relaxation and digital movements and are appropriate as classroom movement experiences because they can be done while the children are seated at their desks. Finger plays are used mostly as activity for primary children. Several examples are included. The children can recite the lines in unison.

The Church

Words	Suggested Actions
Here is the church,	Fold the hands as in prayer in front of the chest.
Here is the steeple.	Raise both forefingers up high.
Open the doors	Reverse the hands so that the palms are up and the fingers spread.
And see all the people.	Wiggle the fingers.

Fingers

Words	Suggested Actions
Thumbkin, pointer man, middle man tall,	Extend the fingers of the left hand on top of the desk.
Ring man, wee man, great men all.	Beginning with the thumb, lift each finger with the right hand and let it fall heavily.

The Rain

Words	Suggested Actions
Pitter, patter, pitter, patter,	Do light finger drumming on the desk.
Hear the raindrops say.	
But, if a sunbeam should peep out,	Touch the fingers overhead, making a sun.
They'd make a rainbow gay.	Separate the arms with a wide sweep, showing the rainbow.
Rumble, rumble, rumble, rumble,	Double the fists up, and roll the knuckles on the desk.
Hear the thunder say.	Hold the arms overhead, fingers touching.
But soon the clouds will all be gone,	Bring the hands down to the desk and run the fingertips rapidly back and forth.
And we'll go out to play.	

Open and Close

Words	Suggested Actions
Open, close them; open, close them.	Hold the arms out, diagonally upward, and open and close the fingers.
Give a little slap.	Slap the thighs.
Open, close them; open, close them.	As before.
Lay them in your lap!	As directed.

GAMES AND RELAYS

The games and relays in this section are those that have particular relevance to classroom use. Except for target games, the equipment needs are minimal.

TARGET GAMES

Basketball Bounce

Formation: Individual or by teams

Players: Two to six for each basket

Supplies: A basketball, volleyball, or other rubber ball and a wastepaper basket

Each player in turn stands behind a line that is 5 to 10 ft from a wastepaper basket. Five chances are allowed to bounce the ball on the floor and into the basket. Five points are scored for each successful basket.

Beanbag Pitch

Formation: File, by rows

Players: Two to six for each target

Supplies: Beanbags and a small box for each team

A target box is placed at the head of each row. A pitch line is drawn 10 to 15 ft in front of the target. From behind the line, each player takes a specified number of pitches at the box. Scores are recorded for each player, and the team with the highest score wins. Many other targets are possible. The children can design them.

Bowling

Formation: File, by rows

Players: Two to six for each target

Supplies: A bowling pin or pins and balls for rolling

Many bowling games are possible in the classroom, with the aisles used as the alleys. Various kinds of balls can be rolled. The target can be a single pin or a group of pins, and competition can be between individuals in a row or between rows. Children can design their own bowling games.

Chair Quoits

Formation: File

Players: Two to six for each target

Supplies: A chair for each group and five deck tennis rings or rope rings

A line is established about 10 ft from a chair turned over so the legs point toward the thrower. Each player throws the five rings. A ringer on the back legs scores 10 points, and one on the front legs scores 5 points. Score should be kept for several rounds.

Variation: Fruit jar rings can be used with the chair or with other targets. Special peg targets can be constructed (see p. 592).

Tic-Tac-Toe

Formation: None

Players: Two to four for each target

Supplies: A tic-tac-toe target board, six beanbags or yarn balls of one color and six of another

The tic-tac-toe target is constructed from 1-by-4-in. boards standing on end to make a throwing target a little less than 4 in. deep, with each of nine squares separated by a 1-in. wide border. The spaces themselves are 1 ft square. The target is mounted on a 4-by-4-ft piece of sturdy plywood. A prop should be placed behind the board so it is tilted at about a 45-degree angle (Figure 25.1).

The object of the game is to get three squares covered in a line in any direction. Only one beanbag is permitted in a square. If a second beanbag lands inside a square, it is removed. The game can be played one against one or partners against partners. Alternate sides toss at the target.

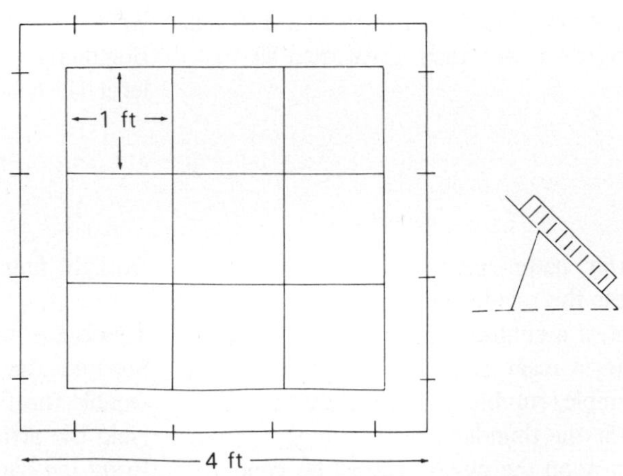

FIGURE 25.1. Tic-tac-toe target

The teacher might consider presenting the general outline of the game and letting the children make up their own rules and scoring system.

GAMES WITH LIMITED MOVEMENT

Animals Move

Formation: Standing in the aisles between desks or scattered

Players: Entire class

Supplies: None

The player who is it stands at the front of the room and calls out the name of a mammal, bird, fish, or reptile and a movement. For instance, the leader might call out, "Horses fly. Birds crawl. Salmon swim." When the leader states a correct relationship, the class must move accordingly. In the latter case, they would make a swimming movement. When an incorrect relationship is given, the children should not move. Those who move at the wrong time can sit down and wait until a new leader is selected. Games should be kept short, so all children have a chance to lead and no one has to sit out too long.

Teaching Suggestion: As the children become skilled at the game, the teacher should stress quality movement. The children can be encouraged to improve their hopping, flying, or jumping.

Bicycle Race

Formation: Rows

Players: Half the class

Supplies: Desks

The children stand in the aisle between two rows of desks. Alternate rows perform at a time. Each child places one hand on her own desk and one on the desk next to her. On the signal "Go," the child, supported by her hands, imitates a bicycling motion with her legs. The child who rides the longest without touching the floor with the feet is the winner for the row. Winners can compete later for bicycle riding champion of the room.

Do This, Do That

Formation: Scattered

Players: Entire class

Supplies: None

One child is the leader and performs various movements, accompanied by commands of "Do this" or "Do that." All players execute the movements accompanied by "Do this." If the directions are "Do that," no one is to move. Those who move at the wrong time are eliminated and sit down in place. The game continues until some of the children have been eliminated. The game is then re-formed with another leader, who is selected from the children who were not caught.

Abbacadaba

Formation: Seated

Players: Entire class

Supplies: None

One child is the leader and walks among the seated children. The leader suddenly points to a child and says, "Abbacadaba." This child must immediately put both hands to her ears. The child directly behind must put both hands on top of his head. The children on either side must cover the ear next to Abbacadaba with the near hand and the nose with the other hand. Play with duds as penalties. Three duds mean an out.

The game can be made harder by adding more intricate movement tasks. For instance, the children on either side can hold the near ear with the opposite hand and the nose with the other hand.

Variation: *Billy Goat*—The leader points to a child and says, "Billy Goat." The child answers, "Ba-a-a-ah." The children on each side of the billy goat put their hands alongside the head to simulate horns.

Imitation

Formation: Scattered

Players: Entire class

Supplies: Record player and records

A leader stands in front of the class and performs for a musical phrase (eight counts) with any kind of movement he wishes. For the next eight counts, the children imitate the same movements in the same sequence. The leader sets another round of movements, and the children again imitate. After a time, the leader selects another child to be the new leader.

O'Grady Says

Formation: Scattered

Players: Entire class

Supplies: None

A leader stands in front and calls out various military commands, such as "Right face," "Left face," "About face," "Attention," and "At ease." The players are to follow *only* when the command is preceded by the words "O'Grady says." Anyone moving at the wrong time is eliminated and must sit down. Additional commands involving other movements can be used. To be effective, the commands must be given rapidly.

Put Hands

Formation: Scattered, either standing or seated

Players: Entire class

Supplies: None

One child is the leader and stands in front of the class. The leader gives certain directions verbally and then tries to confuse the class by doing something else. He might say, "Put your hands on top of your head" and put his own hands on top of his shoulders. Those who follow his actions instead of his words have a point scored against them. Possible directions are the following.

"Put your hands on your shoulders (toes, knees, head, chest)."

"Reach out to the side (to the front, to the back, up high)."

"Put your right (left) hand on your shoulder (behind your back)."

After a short time, the leader should be changed.

Variation: Other movements can be introduced, such as "Right hand point west," "Left hand forward, right hand to the sky," and "Head right, jump left."

Shuffle Foot

Formation: Scattered, by pairs

Players: Two

Supplies: None

One person is the "same," the other is the "different." The two children stand facing each other about 3 ft apart. They clap three times, and on the third clap each puts a foot forward. If the feet are the same (right, right; left, left), the student designated the same wins. If the feet are different, the other child wins. The game goes on to a set number of points.

Simon Says

Formation: Scattered, standing or seated

Players: Entire class

Supplies: None

One player is selected to be Simon and stands in front of the class. Simon gives a variety of commands, such as "Stand up," "Clap your hands," "Turn around," and others. She may or may not precede a command with the words "Simon says." No one is to move unless the command is preceded by these words. Those who move at the wrong time are eliminated and must sit out the game. The leader gives commands rapidly, changing to different movements. Simon tries to confuse the class by doing all of the movements.

Snap

Formation: Seated in a circle

Players: 10 to 15

Supplies: None

The game involves a three-count rhythm. The children must practice the rhythm well before the game can be successful. On count 1, the children slap their knees; on count 2, they clap their hands; and on count 3, they snap their fingers.

Each child in the circle has a number. The leader calls a number on the third count. The player whose number was called then calls another number when he snaps the fingers. The object of the game is to maintain a precise rhythm, calling the numbers back and forth across the circle.

The following are errors.

1. Breaking the rhythm
2. Not calling another number after yours has been called
3. Calling when your number has not been called
4. Calling the number of a player who has been eliminated

Players are eliminated after they have made three errors.

Sticky Hands

Formation: Small circle

Players: 6 to 12

Supplies: None

Children stand close together in a circle. They extend their hands, which are sticky like glue. Once a child grasps a hand, she cannot let go. The children reach into the mass of hands and across the circle to find two hands (belonging to different people), which they grasp. The grips must not be released. By stepping over and around, twisting under and through, the group tries to unscramble itself.

Where, Oh Where?

Formation: Seated at desks or in a circle on the floor

Players: Entire class

Supplies: A spool or other small object that can be hidden in a closed hand

One child is chosen to be it and turns his back to the group while hiding his eyes. The object is passed among the children, from hand to hand, until a signal is given. The person who is it turns around and attempts to guess who has the object. He gets three guesses. All of the children, including the one who has the object, do various movements and stunts to confuse the guesser. The object must be held in the hand, however. If the guess is correct, the child with the object becomes the new guesser. If the guess is incorrect, the one who is it tries again. If a child misses on three turns in a row, he should choose another child to be it.

If the number of children in the class is large, two children can be it, thus doubling the chance of a correct guess.

Who's Leading?

Formation: Circle, either sitting at desks or on the floor

Players: Entire class

Supplies: None

One child is it and steps away from the circle and covers the eyes. The teacher points to a child in the circle, who becomes the leader. The leader starts any motion he chooses with the hands, the feet, or any body part. All of the children follow his movements. The child who is it uncovers her eyes and watches the group, as they change from one motion to another, to try to determine who is leading. Players should cover up for the leader, who also tries to confuse the guesser by looking at other players. The child who is it gets three guesses. If not successful, she chooses another child to be it. If she does guess correctly, she gets another turn, but a limit of three turns should be imposed.

Teaching Suggestion: The game seems to work best when the guesser is positioned in the center of the circle, because she cannot then observe all of the children at once. The children can also be standing, but this gets tiring.

GAMES WITH LOCOMOTOR MOVEMENT

Alphabet Mix

Formation: Circle, standing

Players: Entire class

Supplies: Flash cards (optional)

One player is chosen to be the leader. All players are given a letter of the alphabet. The leader calls out two letters, and the circle players having those letters must change places. At the same time, the leader tries to get to one of their places before they can complete the exchange. The player left without a place becomes the next leader.

Variation: The teacher can make a set of flash cards with letters on them, and the children change places when their letter is flashed. Each player can also be assigned a word and two words can then be flashed to enhance word-recognition skills. More than two letters or two words also may be called.

Around the Row

Formation: Rows

Players: As many as are in a row

Supplies: None

The game is played by rows, with an extra player for each row. On the command "March," children walk around the row. On signal, they stop marching and attempt to get a seat. One player is left out. The game continues to the next row, using the player left out as the extra. Walking only (no running) is permitted. Roughness should not be tolerated.

Balloon Football

Formation: Two lines facing each other 4 to 6 ft apart

Players: Entire class

Supplies: Balloon or light beach ball

The class is divided into two teams. Players sit in their chairs and keep one hand on the back of the chair throughout the game. The balloon or beach ball is tossed between the two teams. Both teams try to bat it over the heads of their opponents so the ball touches the floor behind the opposing team. Each touchdown scores a point. A student should be placed behind each team to serve as scorekeeper and ball retriever. The balloon should be put into play at different places along the two lines to prevent action from being concentrated among a few players.

Balloon Volleyball

Formation: Standing, sitting on the floor, or seated at desks

Players: Entire class

Supplies: Two balloons and available extras in case of breakage

Children are positioned on both sides of a rope stretched just above their reach. They try to bat a balloon back and forth across the rope. The balloon can be batted as often as necessary. Two balloons used at once provide good action. A system of rotation should be set up, so all players have a chance to occupy a position near the rope. Scoring is accomplished when one side fails to control a balloon and allows it to touch the floor or a wall.

Variation: A small marble or button placed *inside* the balloon causes it to take an erratic path, which adds interest to the game.

Blind Man's Bluff

Formation: Small circle

Players: Eight to ten

Supplies: A blindfold for each circle

One child is blindfolded and stands in the center of a small circle of children. Another child is chosen to be inside the circle also, and the blind man tries to catch her. As the quarry dodges, the blind man calls, "Where are you?" The others must respond immediately by making a sound like a baby chick, "Cheep, cheep!"

When the blind man has caught the other player, he tries to identify the player by feeling the face, arms, and clothes. Identification does not affect the outcome of the game but simply adds to the fun. Two other children are chosen to replace the first two players.

Teaching Suggestion: Circles should be kept small, otherwise catching is difficult and protracted. The blindfold must be effective, for the game is spoiled if the child can see under it. The game is usually confined to kindergarten through 2nd grade.

Variation: The circle children can make a buzzing sound (z-z-z-z-z-z), which becomes louder as the blind man nears the quarry.

Classroom Mousetrap

Formation: Circle

Players: Entire class

Supplies: None

Several pairs of children form arches around the circle. The arches remain up until the teacher says "Snap"; then they are brought down. The other children (the mice) scurry through the arches and try to avoid being caught. Anyone caught forms additional arches.

Colors

Formation: Scattered, standing or seated

Players: Entire class

Supplies: A set of flash cards of different colors

The teacher flashes a color card. All children touch five different objects of that color and return to position. There is no scoring, just activity.

Variation: Shapes can be the focus. The teacher holds up a shape (triangle, circle, square), and the children seek five articles of that same shape to touch.

Floor Ping-Pong

Formation: None

Players: Two to four

Supplies: A table tennis ball and a paddle for each player

A regular table tennis court is marked off on the floor. Play proceeds as in regular table tennis. Games should be short (10 points), so many children can be accommodated. A makeshift net can be set up with blocks and a wand.

Hide the Beanbag

Formation: Scattered

Players: 15 to 20

Supplies: A small beanbag

One child, the searcher, stands to the side with eyes covered. The other children sit cross-legged. One child is given the beanbag and must hide it by sitting on it.

The searcher moves among the children—trying to locate the beanbag. The children clap softly as the searcher moves about; they clap louder when he nears the child with the beanbag. The searcher tries to identify the one with the beanbag. If the guess is correct, another child is selected to be the searcher. If the identification fails, the searcher tries again (up to three guesses), and then another child becomes the searcher.

Teaching Suggestion: The teacher should choose the child to hide the beanbag. This is an opportunity to involve shy or less popular children in the game.

Hunter, Gun, Rabbit

Formation: Two lines facing each other

Players: Entire class

Supplies: None

The children are divided into two teams, which line up facing each other. They can sit or stand. Each team has a captain. The teams decide privately on one of the following three imitations.

1. Hunter—bring the hands up to the eyes and pretend to be looking through binoculars.
2. Gun—bring the hands and arms up to a shooting position and pretend to shoot.
3. Rabbit—put the hands in back of the head with fingers pointed up, and move the fingers back and forth like moving rabbit ears.

A signal is given, and each team pantomimes its choice. In scoring, the following priorities hold.

1. If one side is the hunter and the other the gun, the hunter wins because the hunter shoots the gun.
2. If one team selects the gun and the other imitates a rabbit, the gun wins because the gun can overcome the rabbit.
3. If one side is the rabbit and the other the hunter, the rabbit wins because it can outrun the hunter.
4. If both teams have the same selection, no point is scored.

The first team to score 10 points wins.

Teaching Suggestion: The teacher should keep the game moving. One way to do this is to have the child on the right of each line go down the line and whisper the choice to the team members. The child then positions herself on the left, and a new child is at the right of each line, ready to select the next imitation.

Lost Children

Formation: Scattered

Players: Entire class

Supplies: None

Desks are left in their usual position. One child is chosen to be the police officer and leaves the room. The other children walk around the room. The teacher or leader calls the police officer back and says, "The children are lost. Will you please take them safely home?" The officer then takes each child to his own seat. The players stay where they are until the officer seats them. Success for the police officer is determined by the number of children she can seat correctly. The officer is not permitted to look in the desks or in books for clues to correct seating.

Orienteering

Formation: Standing

Players: Entire class

Supplies: Chart of a compass face (optional)

Students stand to the right of their desks. Either the teacher or a chosen student stands facing the class. This person calls out various directions—north, southwest, and so on. The rest of the class must quickly face in the proper direction. When students turn in the wrong direction, they can either sit down or have a point scored against them.

Variations

1. To introduce children to a compass and to simple orienteering skills, a chart with the face and directional needle of a compass can be used. The leader turns away from the class, places the needle in a certain direction, and then shows the compass to the class. The class responds by turning toward the proper direction.

2. Regular orienteering can be done on a modified basis by setting up a course with the path to be followed described in terms of numbers of steps in a given compass direction. Inside some buildings, however, compasses are not accurate.

Ten, Ten, Double Ten

Formation: None

Players: Entire class

Supplies: A small object

All of the children except one leave the classroom. The child left in the room places the object in a spot that is visible but not too easily found. The children return to the room. As soon as a child sees the object, he pretends to search for another moment, so he does not give away the position. He then calls out, "Ten, 10, double 10, 45, 15, buckskin 6," and sits down. The other children continue to search. The child who found the object first gets to place it for the next game. The children who find it last, or any who do not find it at all, must remain in their seats for the next turn.

Who Am I?

Formation: Small circle or scattered

Players: 8 to 16

Supplies: None

The children recite this verse in unison:

> This morning as I walked down the street
> Whom do you think I chanced to meet?

One child is the demonstrator and proceeds to pantomime an action (e.g., fire fighter, police officer, banker, baseball player, and so forth). The children try to guess what the action represents. If a guesser is successful, he becomes the new demonstrator. If no one guesses, the present demonstrator gets another turn, after which another child takes over.

Zoo

Formation: Seated

Players: Entire class

Supplies: None

Children are in their regular seats. Seven children are chosen to stand in front of the class, and one of them is selected as the leader. The leader directs each of the other six children to choose a favorite animal and then places them in a line, saying the animal name as she does so.

On signal, the six children, performing in the order in which they were just announced by the leader, imitate the animal that they have chosen (10 to 15 seconds should be allowed for this). On a second signal, the rest of the children stand, wave their arms, and jump or hop in place (turning around if they wish). They then sit down, close their eyes, cover them with their hands, and put their head down on the desk.

The leader then arranges the six animals in a different order. When this has been done, the seated children raise their heads. Another signal is given, and the animals perform once again for a short period. Once this has been accomplished, any seated child can volunteer to place the six children in their original positions, naming the animal in each case. If the child succeeds in placing the animals in their original standing position and in calling them by their chosen animal name, he becomes an animal in the zoo and chooses a name for himself. The child then takes his place among the animals, and the game continues until 12 children (or some other designated number) are in the zoo. Other categories such as flowers, Mother Goose characters, play characters, and so on can be used.

RELAYS

Relays should be included occasionally in the classroom program. Most of the appropriate relays involve object handling or a task. Few classrooms have sufficient space for a variety of relays. Some relays can use the regular seating arrangement, but others may require special formations. Relays using the blackboard for spelling, word formation, and arithmetic can be of value, but not as scheduled physical education activities.

Flag Chase

Formation: Hollow square, seated in chairs

Players: Entire class

Supplies: Four flags (or beanbags), chairs for all competitors, and a marker centered 3 ft in front of each team

The class is divided into four even teams, facing center and seated on the sides of the square, with a marker in front of each team. The player on the left end of her team has a flag. On signal, this player runs to the marker, goes around it from the right (counterclockwise), and then runs to the seat on the right of the team. In the meantime, all players have moved one place to the left, vacating the right seat. The runner sits in the vacant chair, and the flag is passed down the line to the left. The player now in the left-most seat becomes the new runner and runs the same course as the previous runner. The race ends when the flag has been returned to the lead-off runner in the original position in the left seat.

Variations: An under-the-leg pass can be used, with the stipulation that the flag must go under all legs during transit. The run around the marker can be omitted, with the runner going directly from the left to the right seat.

Overhead Relay

Formation: File, by rows

Players: Entire class

Supplies: A beanbag, eraser, or similar object for each team

Each row forms a team. The first person in each row has in front of her the object that is to be passed to the desk behind. At the signal to pass, this child claps the hands, picks up the object, and passes it overhead to the child behind. The next child places the object on his desk, claps the hands, and then passes the object overhead. When the last child in the row receives the object, he runs forward to the head of the row, using the aisle to the right. *After* he has passed by, each child, using the *same* aisle, moves back one seat. The child who has come to the front then sits down in the first seat, places the object on the desk, claps the hands, and passes the object overhead. This continues until the children are back in their original seats and the object is on the front desk. The first row finished wins.

OTHER GAMES AND RELAYS

The games and relays in Chapters 23 and 24 should be examined for possible inclusion.

CHAPTER **26**

Implementing the Sports Program

Sport activities are so much a part of the American scene that little justification is needed for their inclusion in the elementary school program. The sports program has long been a major part of the elementary curriculum. Although for years attention was focused on boys, today's sports program provides challenges for all—boys and girls, the skilled and the unskilled, the handicapped and the nonhandicapped.

Few elementary school administrators would tolerate heavy emphasis on the development of those few boys who promise to become high school varsity players. The need for a rational, educationally sound approach is apparent. The program must meet the needs and interests of elementary school children and must be geared to their development. Inherent in sport activities are the many physical, educational, personal, and social values that schools should exploit in the best interests of children.

Sports selected for inclusion in the program are basketball, touch football, hockey, soccer, softball, track and field, and volleyball. These activities are modified for the elementary school curriculum. The broad goal of the sports program is to create interest in and provide background for immediate and future participation. Instructional sequences should be organized so that children develop a reasonable level of skill, have the opportunity to compete in lead-up and modified sports, and acquire necessary cognitive elements.

A balanced sports program has a three-pronged approach. Class instruction provides opportunities for all to learn the basics of a sport. Intramurals grow out of this base and provide additional instruction, practice, and opportunities for competition. Finally, a controlled interschool (extramural) competitive program provides additional experiences for the more skilled and interested children.

ORGANIZING THE SPORTS PROGRAM

This section discusses organizational and instructional elements common to the sports selected for the program. Specifics concerning each sport are found in the separate sport chapters (Chapters 27 through 33).

SAFETY

Good physical conditioning is an important prerequisite to competitive play. Fatigue must be controlled and attention given to matters of physical and mental stress. Safety instruction is essential, since each sport has particular hazards.

FACILITIES AND EQUIPMENT

Proper equipment and supplies are a primary consideration. Preparation of facilities, particularly outdoors, must be anticipated. Fields should be laid out and lined. Additional information about the requirements for specific sports can be found in the respective sport chapter.

An adequate quantity of equipment should be available so that standing and waiting for turns occurs seldom. In many cases, official balls are not needed, and substitutes can be used.

ORGANIZING TEAMS FOR EQUAL COMPETITION

The squad, with a designated leader, is an effective unit for instructional purposes, particularly for rotating (or station) instruction. Small-group organization within squads allows maximum activity. Most introductory phases of instruction should make use of groups of four or fewer children.

Homogeneous and heterogeneous groups have both advantages and disadvantages. Having skilled and unskilled players together when the activity demands a great deal of progression and ability is often a disadvantage. In a relay involving basket shooting, for example, a team might never win because of the poor performance of one player. Such a problem is solved by letting good players play on a team together and compete against another team of good shooters. This arrangement makes the competition more meaningful. The other side of the coin is that, in many situations, playing with athletes who are more skilled improves the performance and success of less skilled players. Heterogeneous grouping might increase the opportunities for youngsters to help each other reach team or group goals. One guideline is to avoid keeping the same teams for too long a time. Frequent rotation of team members gives students the opportunity to play with all peers and at the same time counteracts the problem of frequent losing because of the deficiencies of one or two students.

Choosing teams can be done in any of the following ways.

1. Names can be drawn out of a hat, or the children can pick colored tags out of a hat. Youngsters with tags of the same color are on the same team.

2. Leaders are elected by the students, who, in turn, go to a captain of their choice. (The number of members on a team does, however, have to be limited.)

3. Four to six leaders can be selected by the teacher or elected by their classmates. They choose teams in a private session outside of the classroom.

4. Depending on ability levels, the class can be arranged by height or weight and separated into teams. This is particularly useful in activities in which heavier and stronger children have an advantage.

LEAD-UP GAMES

Lead-up games emphasize only one or two skills and serve as a laboratory for the sport they precede. Each lead-up game should be analyzed for the skills involved. When a lead-up game is included in a unit, it becomes the focal game for the unit. More than one lead-up game can be the unit focus.

The following points should be kept in mind when lead-up games are used.

1. Lead-up games should not replace drills. Drills are used when students have not learned specific skills, whereas lead-up games are used to practice skills that have been learned.

2. Drills usually maximize the amount of practice time that each student receives in a given period. Lead-up games are for putting skills to use in a competitive situation. The amount of time that each student practices a skill will vary, depending on skill level and aggressiveness. Skills are best learned when the pressure of competition is absent.

3. Lead-up games should involve as many youngsters as possible at one time and should use as much equipment as possible. The more times a youngster participates, the more opportunity he has to develop a positive attitude toward the sport involved.

SKILLS PRACTICE THROUGH CREATIVE GAMES

Creative games made up by the children are an excellent supplement to the practice of sport skills, and the result is usually a realistic game at the children's own level. Creative games are not regarded as substitutes for lead-up games, but they do offer a quick and convenient practice situation.

The creative game may be one that children design without restriction, or it can include limiting factors specified by the teacher. The emphasis is on extended development of skills. Games can be organized on an individual, partner, or team basis, as specified by the teacher or students.

Creative games supply an important opportunity for observation. The teacher can determine the direction that skills practice should take. The instructor may find, for example, that skill development is already sufficient for game activities, or that further practice or attention should be focused on certain details.

MODIFYING ACTIVITIES

Most sport activities need modification to enable elementary children to derive enjoyment and achieve success. Changing selected elements increases the probability of successful participation. The most important consideration in modifying a sport is allowing the children to use and learn proper movement patterns. For example, many children learn to throw a basketball at a 10-ft-high basket, rather than learning to shoot properly. A modification would be to lower the basket and reduce the size and weight of the ball, so the children could learn proper form. Otherwise, patterns learned and practiced for a period of 2 or 3 years are difficult, if not impossible, to alter. The following ideas may make activity more effective.

1. Decrease the number of players on a side, particularly in soccer and football games.

2. Shorten the field or court.

3. Shorten the playing time.

4. Lower nets and baskets.

5. Make scoring easier by increasing the size of goals, removing goalies, or substituting a different kind of scoring.

6. Change to more appropriate equipment, such as softer softballs, a beach ball in place of a volleyball, or junior-size footballs and basketballs.

7. Use zones to guarantee more position play.

8. Change rules to increase successful play. For instance, move up the serving distance or allow an assist on the serve in volleyball.

OFFICIATING

When children are to officiate, some instructional time must be devoted to teaching them how. Rules should be clarified and posted, and simple officiating techniques covered. Impartial enforcement teaches respect for rules.

Some self-officiating is desirable, particularly in out-of-bounds decisions. A child can clarify an out-of-bounds decision by saying, "I touched it last."

INSTRUCTIONAL PROCEDURES

1. The principles of motor learning (Chapter 3) have a direct bearing on the acquisition of sport skills and should be incorporated in instruction and coaching during practice. The *how* and *why* of an activity are inseparable in sport instruction. If a child is asked to perform a skill in a certain manner, she should know why.

2. Each player should practice all skills, and the pattern of practice should reflect this. Rotation during lead-up games ensures that each child receives experience at all positions and that play is not dominated by a few skilled individuals.

3. Instruction should include critical points of the skill. Noting similarities to other skills establishes basic concepts and aids transfer. Individual coaching during practice is a vital part of instruction. Students should be encouraged to concentrate on correct execution, and the instructor should circulate among students to see that this occurs.

4. Students should be encouraged to participate, to evaluate, and to make adjustments to movement patterns during skill practice. They must be given many opportunities to try various aspects of the skill and to make individual decisions. Small groups permit experimentation without undue peer or performance pressure.

5. Relays that function as skill drills should be used with caution, because students in their haste to win often revert to sloppy performance.

6. Critique sessions can be valuable. Part of the group (half of the class or one squad) can demonstrate what has been achieved, and the rest of the class can provide the critique, with the emphasis on positive feedback. Critiques between partners should be considered.

7. A skilled performer can be introduced to motivate students, provide technical help, and answer questions. Another motivational device is to arrange a trip to a ball game. Special arrangements can be made for groups, with help provided for those children who cannot afford tickets.

8. Most sports have an interesting origin and history, and the school library should contain materials about sports. A presentation by a student of the background of a sport also stimulates interest.

YOUTH SPORTS PHILOSOPHY

Youth sports give rise to the many problems of dealing with competitive situations. The precedent set by professional, college, and even high school sports programs often fosters a philosophy of winning at all costs at the elementary school level. A coaching manual entitled *Youth Sports Guide for Coaches and Parents* (Thomas 1977) contains a "Bill of Rights for Young Athletes" (Figure 26.1) and offers insight into the many facets of a youth sports program.

BILL OF RIGHTS FOR YOUNG ATHLETES

1. Right of opportunity to participate in sports regardless of ability level.
2. Right to participate at a level that is commensurate with each child's developmental level.
3. Right to have qualified adult leadership.
4. Right to participate in safe and healthy environments.
5. Right of each child to share in the leadership and decision making of their sport participation.
6. Right to play as a child and not as an adult.
7. Right to proper preparation for participation in the sport.
8. Right to an equal opportunity to strive for success.
9. Right to be treated with dignity by all involved.
10. Right to have fun through sport.

FIGURE 26.1. Bill of Rights for Young Athletes (Thomas 1977, p. 44)

The following points are useful for examining competitive situations.

1. Competitive situations can be rewarding for those students capable of winning regularly. Highly skilled children usually enjoy competition, because they have a chance of finding success. The teacher should be guided by the feelings of *low-achieving* youngsters in evaluating the effect of competition on the children.

2. When children compete, the teacher should emphasize enjoyment of the activity by everyone. In unfortunate cases, children receive the teacher's attention and approval only when they win. This places a heavy premium on winning.

3. There is some evidence (Greene and Lepper 1975) to show that extrinsic rewards, such as ribbons or trophies, actually decrease a child's motivation to participate in an activity. When the extrinsic motivation is removed, the child may no longer want to participate simply for fun. In some cases, this response may generalize to all physical activity. Emphasis should be placed on the joy of participation rather than on the importance of receiving a reward. If rewards are given, however, they should be based on achievement, rather than on mere participation.

4. All children should have a chance to succeed. This might be accomplished by careful grouping, by pairing children with others of similar ability, and by making comparisons based on improvement and effort rather than on sheer ability. For example, competitive situations might be varied by matching individuals against others of somewhat equal ability, thus keeping the goals of competition within the student's level of achievement. Another useful form of competition is autocompetition, in which the students compete against themselves and try to improve on their past performances.

5. The practice of starting children as young as possible in a sport pursuit so they supposedly will develop into better athletes is questionable. No evidence supports the contention that starting youngsters at an early age accomplishes this goal. The youngster who has started early may reach a psychological or physical peak at a younger age and may give the appearance of being much better than youngsters of a similar age who have not started early. This does not mean that a better athlete has been developed but merely that the youngster has peaked earlier. Indeed, some educators believe that early starters burn out early. The strongest argument for starting children at an early age is that they have more free time available for practice. However, children also need time for their total development—social, academic, and physical—and youth sport practice often becomes the only important activity in the child's life.

6. Studies have shown that skeletally mature children tend to play skilled positions in youth sports (Hale 1956). This creates a situation in which the skilled become more skilled and the unskilled remain unskilled. The gap between skilled and unskilled becomes greater, and the unskilled student feels incompetent and drops out of the activity. Such tendencies must be guarded against.

DEVELOPING UNIT PLANS FOR SPORTS

A unit plan is a sequence of learning experiences planned around an activity that covers several weeks. Sport instruction lends itself to unit planning. Instructional direction can be based on the charts included at the beginning of the sport chapters. Selection of lead-up activities and target games is necessary, for more games and materials are presented in the sport chapters than can be used. A *target game* is defined as the game that serves as the ultimate achievement of the unit. Sideline Basketball (p. 491), for example, might be the target game for a unit on basketball at the 5th-grade level. The unit would be organized to develop the skills and techniques needed to participate successfully in the game.

Other emphases can give direction to a unit. A particular kind of skill competency or a set of skills can be the overall unit goal. Skills, however, should be tested in a competitive situation, which takes one back to the target game or lead-up activity.

A day-by-day schedule or lesson plan should be formulated for the first week, with subsequent schedules determined by the students' progress.

Skill techniques and drills should dominate the early phases of a sport unit. In other activities, fundamental skills for the activity should be achieved before more advanced activities are introduced. While the unit gives overall direction, progress is determined by the achievement of the students.

FORMAT OF THE UNIT PLAN

The unit plan has the following components.

General Purposes or Objectives of the Unit

A statement in broad terms of what the unit is attempting to accomplish should be formulated.

Specific or Target Goals

The specific objectives should be so constituted that when they have been met individually and collectively, the general purpose of the unit has been accomplished.

Cognitive Understandings. Knowledges and understandings to be acquired during the unit are stated in terms of the children's participation in the lessons.

use no more than 3 weeks per unit / game

Affective Domain. Social and ethical concepts planned as an outgrowth of the learning experiences are formulated, as well as habits and attitudes that need attention.

Psychomotor Goals. Skills, techniques, and strategies to be included as part of the learning experiences should be listed in proper progression as they appear in the unit.

Activity Experiences. Drills, forms of competition, formations, races, games, and other selected experiences that contribute to the acquisition of cognitive, affective, and psychomotor factors are also part of the plan.

Facilities and Equipment

The items necessary for instruction throughout the unit are listed.

Instructional Procedures

Instructional procedures are listed, with attention given to class management and organization. Safety measures are stated, and procedures for evaluating the achievements of specific goals are identified.

Educational Media

Bibliographical materials for student use are listed. These should include items needed at the lesson site and those in the school library. Materials—pamphlets, mimeographed sheets, and other papers—to be distributed to students are listed. Audiovisual aids needed for the unit, including projection equipment and media, bulletin board materials, and the like, are listed.

The Weekly Schedule

The schedule for the first week should be outlined in enough detail so that lesson plans can be made to conform with unit sequencing.

A SAMPLE BASKETBALL UNIT PLAN

The following basketball unit plan uses the format described and shows how such a plan can facilitate the teaching process.

Grade level: Fourth-grade boys and girls

Unit length: Three weeks

General Objective of the Unit

The students will develop a basic understanding of the game as well as developing competence in the techniques and skills used in basketball.

Specific Goals

Cognitive Understandings

The students will be able to recognize dribbling and traveling violations and comprehend the out-of-bounds rule.

Affective Domain

1. The students will develop an understanding of and sensitivity toward differences in individual ability among their peers.

2. The students will value basketball as a team game rather than as an individual sport.

3. The students will learn to value fair play when they compete in lead-up games.

Psychomotor Goals

The students will learn the two-handed chest pass, the one- and two-handed underhand passes, the one-handed set shot, the right- and left-handed lay-up shots, right- and left-handed stationary dribbling, right- and left-handed dribbling while moving.

Activity Experiences

The students will participate in the following skill drills: Shuttle Dribbling, Dribble and Pivot, lay-up shooting, and Set-Shot Formation. The students will play the following lead-up games: Review End Ball, Birdie in the Cage, Captain Ball.

Facilities and Equipment Needed

1. One junior basketball or 8½-in. playground ball per student

2. Six baskets adjusted to 8- and 9-ft levels

3. Eight hula hoops (for Captain Ball)

4. Eight cones (for drills)

5. Pinnies of different colors for opposing teams

Instructional Procedures

1. Concentrate on skill development. Choose drills that add variety and breadth.

2. Make sure that each child has a chance to practice all skills.

3. All skills should be performed with both sides of the body. (It is important that the children learn to dribble, pass, and shoot with either hand.)

4. Use as many balls as are available during drills to enhance skill development. (Other balls, such as soccer and playground balls, can be used successfully in the practice basketball skills.)

5. Lower baskets to 8 or 9 ft to help the children develop a proper shooting touch.

Educational Media

Textbooks

Cousy, R. 1972. *Basketball concepts and techniques.* Boston: Allyn and Bacon.

Dauer, V. P., and Pangrazi, R. P. 1986. *Dynamic physical education for elementary school children.* 8th ed. Minneapolis: Burgess Publishing.

Wooden, J. 1966. *Practical modern basketball.* New York: Ronald Press.

Films

Cinema Eight. *Sport films.* New York.

Eastman Kodak Company. *Basketball teaching films.* Rochester, N.Y.

Schedule (First Week)

Monday

Introductory Activity: Run and freeze on signal

Fitness Development Activity: Astronaut Drills

Lesson Focus

1. Introduction of two-handed chest pass
2. Introduction of stationary dribbling

Game or Drill: Shuttle Dribbling Drill

Tuesday

Introductory Activity: Run and pivot on signal

Fitness Development Activity: Astronaut Drills

Lesson Focus

1. Review of two-handed chest pass
2. Introduction of one- and two-handed underhand passes
3. Introduction of one-handed set shot

Game or Drill: Set-Shot Formation Drill

Wednesday

Introductory Activity: Run and change direction on signal

Fitness Development Activity: Astronaut Drills

Lesson Focus

1. Discussion of out-of-bounds rules
2. Review of stationary dribbling and one-handed set shot
3. Introduction of right- and left-handed dribbling while moving

Game or Drill: End Ball

Thursday

Introductory Activity: Run and jump on signal

Fitness Development Activity: Astronaut Drills

Lesson Focus

1. Review of dribbling while moving
2. Introduction of right-handed lay-up shot
3. Introduction of lay-up shooting drill

Game or Drill: Birdie in the Cage

Friday

Introductory Activity: Walk, trot, and run on signal

Fitness Development Activity: Astronaut Drills

Lesson Focus

1. Review of lay-up shot
2. Introduction of Dribble and Pivot Drill

Game or Drill: Birdie in the Cage (emphasize quick, short passes)

Second Week

Continue skill practice as determined by student progress. Introduce Captain Ball if indicated.

Third Week

Continue skill practice as needed. Play Captain Ball.

TOURNAMENTS

Depending on the teacher's preference, the level of the students, the time available, and the limitations of facilities and equipment, tournaments can be an enjoyable culmination of a sport unit. Various types of tournament drawings can be used with success.

ROUND ROBIN TOURNAMENT

The round robin drawing is a good choice when there is a fair amount of time. In round robin play, every team or individual plays every other team or individual once. Final standings are based on win-loss percentages. To determine the amount of time required for completion of the tournament, the following formula can be used:

$$\frac{TI(TI - 1)}{2}$$

where *TI* is the number of teams or individuals. For example, if there are five teams in a volleyball unit, $5(5 - 1)/2 = 10$ games to be scheduled.

To arrange a tournament for an odd number of teams, each team should be assigned a number (number the teams down the right column and up the left column). All numbers rotate, and the last number each time draws a bye. An example using seven teams follows.

Round 1	Round 2	Round 3	Round 4
7–Bye	6–Bye	5–Bye	4–Bye
6–1	5–7	4–6	3–5
5–2	4–1	3–7	2–6
4–3	3–2	2–1	1–7

Round 5	Round 6	Round 7
3–Bye	2–Bye	1–Bye
2–4	1–3	7–2
1–5	7–4	6–3
7–6	6–5	5–4

To arrange a tournament for an even number of teams, the plan is similar, except that the position of team number 1 remains stationary, and the other teams revolve around it until the combinations are completed. An example of an eight-team tournament follows.

Round 1	Round 2	Round 3	Round 4
1–2	1–8	1–7	1–6
8–3	7–2	6–8	5–7
7–4	6–3	5–2	4–8
6–5	5–4	4–3	3–2

Round 5	Round 6	Round 7
1–5	1–4	1–3
4–6	3–5	2–4
3–7	2–6	8–5
2–8	8–7	7–6

LADDER TOURNAMENT

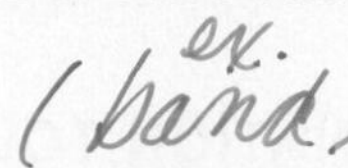

A ladder format can be used for an ongoing tournament that is administered either formally by the teacher or informally by students. Competition occurs by challenge and is minimally supervised. Arrangements vary, but usually a participant may challenge only opponents who are two steps above his present ranking. If the challenger wins, he changes places with the loser. The teacher can establish an initial ranking, or positions can be drawn from a hat. A shuffleboard tournament could be handled by a ladder ranking (Figure 26.2).

SHUFFLEBOARD TOURNAMENT

1. ______
2. ______
3. ______
4. ______
5. ______
6. ______
7. ______

FIGURE 26.2. Ladder ranking

PYRAMID TOURNAMENT

A pyramid tournament is similar to a ladder tournament, but has more challenge and variety because the choice of opponents is wider (Figure 26.3). In the pyramid tournament, a player may challenge any opponent one level above her present ranking. Another variation is that a player must challenge someone on her level and beat that person before challenging a player at a higher level.

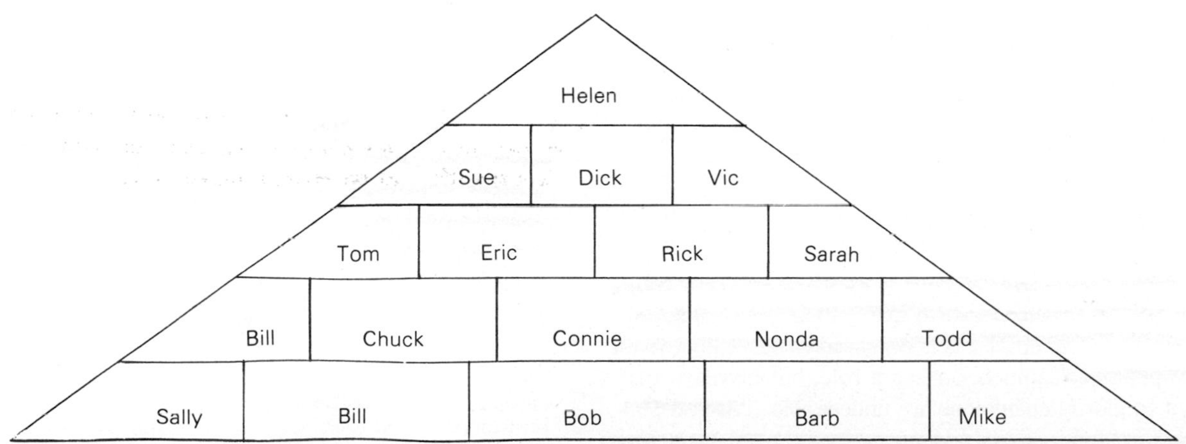

FIGURE 26.3. Pyramid tournament

ELIMINATION TOURNAMENT

An elimination tournament is not the best format for elementary school youngsters, because teams that lose early have to sit out and observe. In many cases, these are the teams that need more participation and success, rather than less. An example of a simple elimination tournament for six teams is illustrated in Figure 26.4.

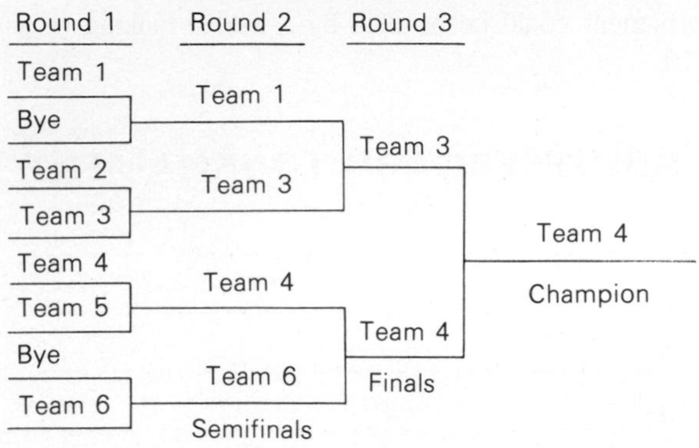

FIGURE 26.4. Simple elimination tournament for six teams

CLUBS AND SPECIAL INTEREST GROUPS

Clubs and special interest groups have not been exploited enough. Club work can provide extra opportunity for sport practice and can cater to special interests—archery, backpacking, swimming, gymnastics, rhythmics (dancing), baton twirling, cycling, tennis, skiing, skating, bowling, golf, and wrestling, among others. Competent leadership is vital and may have to be sought outside of the school family.

Club activities satisfy the urge for adventure, for something different and new. These activities also provide the highly skilled with an opportunity for effective participation.

Clubs can be organized within a school, but the most effective special interest groups usually are organized in larger systems. One of the district schools can be specified as the location of a weekly interest group meeting, supervised by qualified personnel. Parents must assume responsibility for getting interested children in the district to the school and back home.

PLAYDAYS

A playday is a festival setting in which children from one or several schools meet to take part in physical education activities. The emphasis is on social values, rather than on competition. Competition has a role, but playdays that attempt to glorify champions are undesirable. The real purpose of a playday is to have everyone be on a team and to have a team for everyone.

A playday may be held within a particular school, but the more usual situation is for a playday to be held between schools. It can occur during the school day, after school, or on a Saturday. The program may consist of sports activities, or it may include simple games, relays, and contests. Stunts, individual athletic events, and even rhythms are the bases of activities in some meets. The programs vary according to the size of the participating schools and the grade level of the children.

The children should have a large part in the planning. This experience gives them an opportunity to act as hosts or as guests in a social situation. The program may emphasize activities that have been previously practiced or rehearsed, or it can include new and unique events that broaden the scope of the physical education experience.

INTRAMURAL PROGRAMS

The intramural[1] program for the elementary school should grow out of and be an extension of the physical education program. The program should begin in 3rd or 4th grade. Its purpose is to provide a recreational and competitive program to serve all children, including the handicapped.

A few administrators believe misguidedly that an extramural competitive sports program meets the needs of the majority of students, and for some educators this becomes an excuse not to operate an intramural program. Unfortunately, heavy emphasis on interschool sports often monopolizes the available facilities and leaves little time for intramurals. The problem of extramural emphasis can be further compounded by some parents of skilled children who bask in the reflected glory of their prodigy's participation.

The first requirement for a functioning intramural program is a commitment by the school community, based on recognition of the program's potential value for children.

This commitment must have two premises: (1) a quality physical education program is the basis of a successful intramural program, and (2) the extramural program should grow out of intramural participation (Figure 26.5).

For an intramural program to be an extension of the physical education program, a close relationship between the two must exist. The physical education program concentrates on skill learning with minimal concern for the amount of playing time. In the intramural program, in contrast, playing time is the central focus.

An important element of a successful intramural program is qualified, interested, and enthusiastic direction. This should be an assigned duty with appropriate compensation

1. The term *intramural* literally means "within the walls" and describes a program conducted within the confines of the school and its grounds. The term *extramural* refers to a program outside of the school, normally a competitive interschool program, but in a broader context the term can include visits to local bowling alleys, swimming pools, and the like.

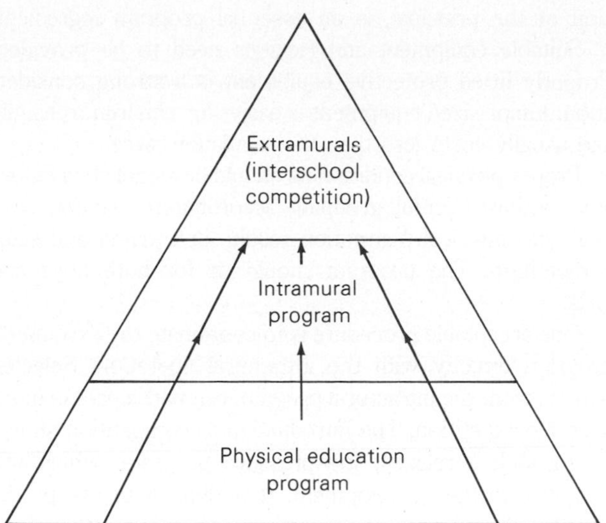

FIGURE 26.5. Interrelationship between the physical education program and other sports programs

for the service. To rely on volunteer direction provides a weak basis for a continuing program, but student volunteers can form a cadre of managers, referees, timers, scorers, and other aides. Positive reinforcement and recognition should be given to these officials. A school intramural council, composed chiefly of students and headed by the director of intramurals, can provide direction and act as a sounding board for student opinion and preferences.

SUGGESTED OPERATING PROCEDURES

The following are considerations in setting up an elementary intramural program.

1. All available times should be used. After-school hours are ideal, but the hour before school, the noon hour, and Saturdays merit consideration. Some evening participation is a possibility.

2. The program should be open to *all* interested students. Teams should be composed of enough children to ensure successful play but should not be so large that some members become spectators. Usually one or two (no more) beyond the required team number is a good standard. A minimum playing time for each team member should be set, with the goal being to have players share the playing time equally. Free substitution should be the rule. Rotating positions can help prevent domination by the more skilled participants.

3. Rules should be modified according to facilities, equipment, and level of skill. Elimination games or single elimination tournaments should be avoided and participation stressed.

4. Some method of team selection to equalize competition is needed. Teams and team leaders can be changed frequently. During competition, each team should be designated clearly by pinnies, armbands, or other means. Modest team shirts are acceptable, but elaborate and costly uniforms should be banned.

5. Boys and girls should receive equal opportunity to participate and should have equal access to quality equipment, programming, and facilities.

6. Safety awareness and procedures should be emphasized to participants.

7. A bulletin board with pertinent information is important. Rules of play governing each activity can be posted, and individual and team rosters listed. Tourney information and progress should be displayed. A place to pick up intramural information should be at or near the bulletin board.

8. Forfeits are the bane of any competitive system, and every effort should be made to avoid the nonappearance of opponents.

9. Although the emphasis is on enjoyment and participation, some system of awards or points can help stimulate involvement.

10. Publicity is a key to involvement. Good publicity has two phases. The first consists of announcements of upcoming events, with follow-up publicity as the second phase. Time and effort spent on publicity will be reflected in increased student participation.

11. Specialized equipment needs should be minimal. Most supplies and equipment should be drawn from the physical education materials.

12. Handicapped and atypical children should have the opportunity to participate as determined by individual capabilities.

13. Parental permission slips may be desirable for students who arrive early or stay late.

INTRAMURAL PROGRAMMING

A wide variety of programming possibilities exist, ranging from highly structured to informally organized activities, even to activities pursued simply for the pure enjoyment. A number of categories, with suggested activities, follow.

Team Sports

The team sports selected should be those in which prior skill training has been offered. Modification of rules is essential so a high degree of activity is possible. For example, in basketball, one might play three on three in half-court play. In soccer, the rules might call for 5- or 7-person teams, rather than for 11-person teams. In softball, play might feature Tee-Ball or Two-Pitch. Volleyball activities might stress Beach Ball Volleyball. Low-organization team games such as Alaska Baseball, dodgeball games, and the like are a good idea.

Track and Field

Track and field activities can be individual or team oriented. Entry in each event should be limited. Modified cross-country racing is excellent. The concept of a track and field day can be broadened to include nonstandard events such as the softball throw, the triple standing long jump, Frisbee throwing, the football target or distance throw, and the predicted time jog.

EXTRAMURAL COMPETITION

The extramural program should grow out of the intramural program. In launching and operating extramural sport competitions for elementary school children, the school system must make a number of commitments. The program should be under the control of the school, and the competition level should be appropriate to the maturity of boys and girls. Schedules should be limited, and the aim should be to provide friendly competition between nearby schools. In short, the program is not a miniature secondary school program. At the elementary level, there is little place for pep rallies, ornate uniforms, victory celebrations, elaborate recognition ceremonies, excessive publicity, playoffs, or bowl contests. Contests should take place after school or on Saturdays, so academic time is not sacrificed. Admission should be free. Publicity should focus on team achievement rather than on individual performances.

The safety and welfare of the children are paramount, and certain controls are vital. Parental permission should be required, and medical examination or screening should be required before participation. Insurance coverage is a consideration. Emergency care procedures and attention to counteracting the hazards of the sport are also of utmost importance. Qualified leadership, under the general supervision of the principal, is an essential program ingredient.

Suitable equipment and facilities need to be provided. Properly fitted protective equipment is a strong consideration. Junior-sized equipment is easier for children to handle and usually costs less than the regulation sizes.

Proper physical conditioning should be established before competition. Careful grouping according to weight, size, skill, and physical maturation results in equated and safer competition. The program should be for both boys and girls.

One acceptable procedure is to coordinate the extramural program directly with the intramural operation. Selected players from the intramural program can participate in interschool competition. The introduction to competition should be through a relaxed, low-pressure program, which will stimulate further development. It is difficult to escape the fact that the purpose of competing is to win, but the motto should be "Win with the good sportsmanship code, with your head and honor held high."

REFERENCES

Greene, D., and Lepper, M. R. 1975. Turning play into work: Effects of adult surveillance and extrinsic rewards on children's internal motivation. *Journal of Personality and Social Psychology* 31: 479–86.

Hale, C. 1956. Physiological maturity of Little League baseball players. *Research Quarterly* 27: 276–84.

Thomas, J. R., ed. 1977. *Youth sports guide for coaches and parents.* Washington, D.C.: Manufacturer's Life Insurance Company and the National Association for Sport and Physical Education.

CHAPTER 27

Basketball

Basketball is an activity enjoyed by many American boys and girls. The reinforcement offered when a basket is made renders it an attractive game, and this, when coupled with the impact that basketball has on the cardiorespiratory system of participants, makes it a strong contribution to the total curriculum.

Basketball instruction in the elementary school should focus on developing skills and competence so students will choose to participate later in life. Often, elementary basketball programs have sought to develop future high school stars with little concern for less talented youngsters. The emphasis should be on lead-up games that allow all students to experience success and enjoyment. A range of fundamental activities should be offered.

With the emphasis on instruction and skill development in the physical education setting, little time is available for regulation basketball during school hours. More skilled and interested students should be given additional opportunities through intramural programs, recreational leagues (e.g., the Youth Basketball Association), or an educationally sound interschool competitive league.

Ball-handling skills should be developed slowly and are an outgrowth of fundamental skills learned in the primary grades. Primary-grade children learn the elements of catching, bouncing, passing, and dribbling using many types of objects. As they progress in the intermediate grades, shooting, offensive and defensive play, and comprehension of rules are added to this base. Program suggestions begin at the 3rd-grade level.

Modifying the equipment used by elementary school children is important. Smaller balls and lower baskets help develop technically correct patterns, increase the success of the participants, and maintain motivation.

INSTRUCTIONAL EMPHASIS AND SEQUENCE

Table 27.1 shows the sequence of basketball activities for the 3rd through the 6th grade.

THIRD GRADE

Little emphasis is placed on regulation basketball in the 3rd grade. Concentration should be on the fundamental skills of passing, catching, shooting, and dribbling. Lead-up games such as Birdie in the Cage, Circle Guard and Pass, and Basketball Tag allow participants to learn their skills in a setting that offers enjoyment and success. Movement of players is somewhat limited, and this increases the opportunity for a positive experience.

FOURTH GRADE

Fourth grade is a good level for beginning instruction in regulation basketball. Emphasis is on fundamental skills, with modification and improvement of these skills for specialized use. The goal is to develop a range of skills, including passing, catching, dribbling, and shooting. The lay-up shot and the one-handed push shot receive instructional attention. Captain Ball adds elements of simple defense, jump balls, and accurate passing. Rules covering traveling and dribbling are taught.

FIFTH GRADE

At the 5th-grade level, several games are introduced. Shooting games, such as Twenty-one and Freeze Out, be-

TABLE 27.1. SUGGESTED BASKETBALL PROGRAM

	Third Grade	Fourth Grade	Fifth Grade	Sixth Grade
Skills				
Passing	Chest or push pass Baseball pass Bounce pass	Underhand pass: One-handed Two-handed One-handed push pass	All passes to moving targets	Two-handed overhead Long passes Three-player weave
Catching	Above the waist Below the waist		While moving	
Dribbling	Standing and moving	Down and back Right and left hands	Figure eight Pivoting	Practice with eyes closed
Shooting	One-handed push shot	Lay-up, right and left One-handed push shot	Free throws	Jump shot
Guarding and stopping			Feinting Pivoting	Parallel stop Stride stop
Knowledge	Dribbling	Violations: Dribbling Traveling Out-of-bounds	Held ball Personal fouls: Holding Hacking Charging Blocking Pushing	Conducting the game Officiating
Activities	Circle Guard and Pass Basketball Tag Birdie in the Cage	Captain Ball Around the Key	Captain Basketball Sideline Basketball Twenty-one Freeze Out	Flag Dribble One-Goal Basketball Five Passes Basketball Snatch Ball Three-on-Three Basketrama
Skill Tests		Dribble	Figure-eight dribble Wall pass test	Figure-eight dribble Baskets per minute Free throws

come favorites. Sideline Basketball and Captain Basketball offer meaningful competition. Continued practice on fundamental skills is necessary to ensure a good base of motor development. Drills to enhance skill performance are used, and rules for regulation basketball are presented.

SIXTH GRADE

Sixth grade is a time for refinement of skills. Shooting games are continued, and new games such as Basketball Snatch Ball and One-Goal Basketball, with its formations, lineup, and other details, are covered to prepare participants for regulation games. Officiating should be taught so youngsters learn to appreciate the importance and difficulty of refereeing. They should also be able to conduct some games through self-officiating.

BASKETBALL SKILLS

Skills needed in basketball at the elementary level can be divided into the following categories: passing, catching, dribbling, shooting, defending, stopping, and pivoting. Feinting should be taught as part of the passing, dribbling, and offensive maneuvers.

PASSING

Certain factors are common to all passes regardless of which pass is used. For firm control, the ball should be handled with the thumb and finger pads and not with the palms of the hands. The passer should step forward in the direction of the receiver. Passes should be made with a quick arm extension and a snap of the wrists, with thumbs and fingers providing momentum. After the pass is released, the palms should be facing the floor.

Passers should avoid telegraphing the direction of the pass. They should learn to use peripheral vision and keep their eyes moving from place to place to develop an awareness of their teammates' positions. At the same time, they should anticipate the spot toward which a teammate will be moving to receive the pass.

Chest (or Two-Handed) Push Pass

For the chest, or two-handed, push pass, one foot is ahead of the other, with the knees flexed slightly. The ball is held at chest level, with the fingers spread on each side of the ball (Figure 27.1). The elbows remain close to the body, and the ball is released by extending the arms and snapping the wrists as one foot moves toward the receiver (Figure 27.2).

FIGURE 27.1. Ready for a chest push pass

FIGURE 27.2. Chest push pass

Baseball (or One-Handed) Pass

For the baseball, or one-handed, pass, the passer imitates the action of a baseball catcher throwing the ball to second base. The body weight shifts from the back to the front foot. Sidearm motion should be avoided, because it puts an improper spin on the ball. Figure 27.3 shows a left-hander throwing the pass.

FIGURE 27.3. Baseball pass

One-Handed Push Pass

For a one-handed push pass, the passer holds the ball with both hands but supports the ball more with the left than with the right, which is a little back of the ball. The ball is pushed forward, with a quick wrist snap, by the right hand.

Bounce Passes

Any of the preceding passes can be adapted to a bounce pass. The object is to get the pass to the receiver on the first bounce, with the ball coming to the receiver's outstretched hands at about waist height. Some experimentation determines the distance. The ball should be bounced a little more than halfway between the two players to make it come efficiently to the receiver.

Underhand Pass

For a two-handed underhand pass, the ball should be held to one side in both hands, with the foot on the opposite side toward the receiver. The ball is "shoveled" toward the receiver and a step is made with the leading foot (Figure 27.4). The one-handed underhand pass is made like an underhand toss in baseball.

Two-Handed Overhead Pass

The two-handed overhead pass is effective against a shorter opponent. The passer is in a short stride position,

FIGURE 27.4. Underhand pass

with the ball held overhead (Figure 27.5). The momentum of the pass comes from a forceful wrist and finger snap. The pass should take a slightly downward path.

CATCHING

Receiving the ball is a most important fundamental skill. Many turnovers involve failure to handle a pass properly. The receiver should move toward the pass with the fingers spread and relaxed, reaching for the ball with elbows bent and wrists relaxed. The hands should give as the ball comes in.

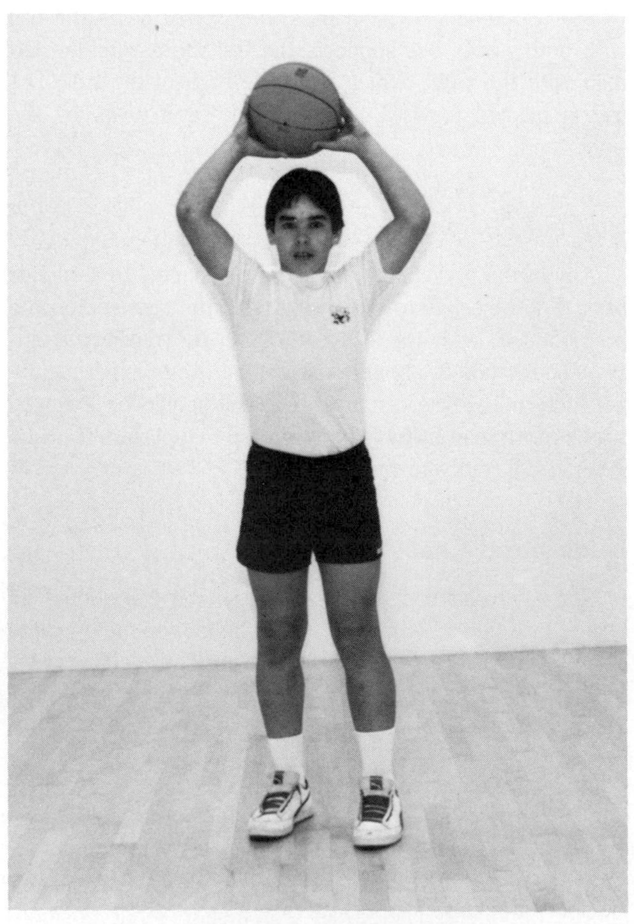

FIGURE 27.5. Two-handed overhead pass

DRIBBLING

Dribbling is used to advance the ball, break for a basket, or maneuver out of a difficult situation. The dribbler's knees and trunk should be slightly flexed (Figure 27.6), with hands and eyes forward. Peripheral vision is important. The dribbler should look beyond the ball and see it in the lower part of the visual area. The ball is propelled by the fingertips with the hand cupped and relaxed. There is little arm motion. Younger children tend to slap at the ball rather than push it. The dribbling hand should be alternated, and practice in changing hands is essential.

FIGURE 27.6. Dribbling

SHOOTING

Shooting is an intricate skill, and students need to develop consistent and proper technique rather than be satisfied when the ball happens to drop in the basket.

1. Good body position is important. Both the toes and the shoulders should face the basket. The weight should be evenly distributed on both feet. In preliminary phases, the ball should be held between shoulder and eye level.

2. A comfortable grip, with fingers well spread and the ball resting on the pads of the fingers, is essential. One should be able to see daylight between the palm of the hand and the ball. For one-handed shots, the shooting elbow is directly below the ball.

3. As soon as the decision is made to shoot, the eye is fixed on the target (the rim or the backboard) for the rest of the shot.

4. As the shot starts, the wrist is cocked.

5. The follow-through imparts a slight backspin to the ball. The arms are fully extended, the wrist is completely flexed, and the hand drops down toward the floor. The arc should be 45 degrees or a little higher.

One-Handed Push Shot

The one-handed push shot is usually a jump shot at short distances and a set shot at longer distances. The ball is held at shoulder-eye level with both hands; the body is erect, and the knees are flexed slightly in preparation for a jump. For a jump shot, the shooter executes a vertical jump, leaving the floor slightly (Figure 27.7). (In a set shot, the shooter rises on his toes.) The supporting (nonshooting) hand remains in contact with the ball until the top of the jump is reached. The shooting hand then takes over with fingertip control, and the ball rolls off the center three fingers. The hand and wrist follow through. Visual concentration on the target is maintained throughout. Proper technique should be emphasized rather than accuracy.

FIGURE 27.7. One-handed push shot

FIGURE 27.8. One-handed jump shot

Lay-up Shot

The lay-up is a short shot taken when going in toward the basket either after receiving a pass or at the end of a dribble. In a shot from the right side, the takeoff is with the left foot, and vice versa. The ball is carried with both hands early in the shot and then shifted to one hand for the final push. The ball, guided by the fingertips, should be laid against the backboard with a minimum of spin.

Free-Throw Shot

Free-throw shooting can be performed successfully with different types of shots. The one-handed foul shot is now the most popular. Complete concentration, relaxation, and a rhythmic, consistent delivery are needed. Some players find it helpful to bounce the ball several times before shooting. Others like to take a deep breath and exhale completely just before shooting. The mechanics of the shot do not differ materially from those of any shot at a comparable distance. Smoothness and consistency are most important.

Jump Shot

The jump shot has the same upper-body mechanics as the one-handed push shot already described. The primary difference is the height of the jump. The jump should be straight up, rather than at a forward or backward angle. The ball should be released at the height of the jump (Figure 27.8). Since the legs cannot be used to increase the force applied to the ball, the jump shot is difficult for those youngsters who lack strength. To develop proper shooting habits, the basket should therefore be at a lower level and a junior-sized basketball should be used.

DEFENDING

Defending involves a characteristic stance. The defender, with knees bent slightly and feet comfortably spread (Figure 27.9), faces the opponent at a distance of about 3 ft. The weight should be distributed evenly on both feet to allow for movement in any direction. Sideward movement is done with a sliding motion. The defender should wave one hand to distract the opponent and to block passes and shots. A defensive player needs to learn to move quickly and not be caught flat-footed!

STOPPING

To stop quickly, the weight of the body is dropped to lower the center of gravity and the feet are applied as brakes (Figure 27.10). In the parallel stop, the body turns sideward and both feet brake simultaneously. The stride stop comes from a forward movement and is done in a one-two count.

FIGURE 27.9. The defensive position

FIGURE 27.10. Stopping

On one count, one foot hits the ground with a braking action, and the other foot is planted firmly *ahead* on the second count. The knees are bent, and the center of gravity is lowered. From a stride stop, the player can move into a pivot by picking up the front foot and carrying it to the rear and, at the same time, fading to the rear.

PIVOTING

Pivoting is a maneuver that protects the ball by keeping the body between the ball and the defensive player. The ball is held firmly in both hands, with elbows out to protect it. One foot, the pivot foot, must always be in contact with the floor. Turning on that foot is permitted, but it must not be dragged away from the pivot spot. The lead foot may, however, step in any direction (Figure 27.11).

If a player has received the ball in a stationary position or during a jump in which both feet hit the ground simultaneously, either foot may become the pivot foot. If a player stops after a dribble on a one-two count, the pivot foot is the foot that made contact on the first count.

FIGURE 27.11. Pivoting

FEINTING

Feinting masks the intent of a maneuver or pass and is essential to basketball. Feinting is a deceptive motion in one direction when the intent is to move in another direction. It can be done with the eyes, the head, a foot, or the whole body. In passing, feinting means faking a pass in one manner or direction and then passing in another.

INSTRUCTIONAL PROCEDURES

1. Many basketball skills, particularly at the 3rd-grade level, do not require the use of basketballs. Other balls, such as volleyballs or rubber balls, can be used successfully.

2. Many skills can be practiced individually or in pairs with playground balls. This allows all children to develop at their own pace, regardless of skill level. Dribbling, passing, and catching skills receive more practice when many balls are used.

3. Baskets should be lowered to 7 ft, 8 ft, or 9 ft, depending on the size of the youngsters. If the facility is also used for community purposes, adjustable baskets—preferably power driven—are the key. Baskets of 5- or 6-ft height are good for children in wheelchairs. This height also allows for experimentation by younger children. These lower baskets can be mounted directly on a wall and set up and removed as needed. No backboard is necessary. When the baskets are mounted to one side, handicapped children can shoot baskets even though they may not be able to participate in other basketball activities.

4. The program should concentrate on skills and include many drills. Basketball offers endless possibilities, and using many drills gives variety and breadth to the instructional program. Each child should have an opportunity to practice all skills. This is not possible when a considerable portion of class time is devoted to playing regulation basketball on a full-length court.

BASIC BASKETBALL RULES

The game of basketball played at the elementary school level is similar to the official game played in the junior and senior high school, but it has modifications in keeping with the capacities of younger children. The following basic rules apply to the game for elementary school children.

TEAMS

A team is made up of five players, including two guards, one center, and two forwards.

TIMING

The game is divided into four quarters, each 6 minutes in length.

OFFICIALS

The game is under the control of a referee and an umpire, both of whom have an equal right to call violations and fouls. They work on opposite sides of the floor and are assisted by a timer and a scorer.

PUTTING THE BALL INTO PLAY

Each quarter is started with a jump ball at the center circle. Throughout the game, the jump ball is used when the ball is tied up between two players or when it is uncertain which team caused the ball to go out-of-bounds.

After each successful basket or free throw, the ball is put into play at the end of the court under the basket by the team against whom the score was made.

VIOLATIONS

The penalty for a violation is to award the ball to the opponents near the out-of-bounds point. The following are violations.

1. Traveling—taking more than one step with the ball without passing, dribbling, or shooting (sometimes called *walking* or *steps*).

2. Stepping out-of-bounds with the ball or causing the ball to go out-of-bounds.

3. Taking more than 10 seconds to cross the center line from the back to the front court. (Once in the forward court, the ball may not be returned to the back court by the team in control.)

4. Double dribbling, which is taking a second series of dribbles without another player's having handled the ball; palming (not clearly batting) the ball; or dribbling the ball with both hands at once.

5. Stepping on or over a restraining line during a jump ball or free throw.

6. Kicking the ball intentionally.

7. Remaining more than 3 seconds in the area under the offensive basket, which is bounded by the two sides of the free-throw lane, the free-throw line, and the end of the court.

PERSONAL FOULS

Personal fouls are holding, pushing, hacking (striking), tripping, charging, blocking, and unnecessary roughness. When a foul is called, the person who was fouled receives one free throw. If she was fouled in the act of shooting and the basket was missed, she receives two shots. If, despite the foul, the basket was made, the score counts and one free throw is awarded.

TECHNICAL FOULS

Technical fouls include the failure of substitutes to report to the proper officials, delay of game, and unsportsmanlike conduct.

DISQUALIFICATION

A player who has five personal fouls called against him is out of the game and must go to the sidelines. Disqualification also can result from extreme unsportsmanlike conduct or from a vicious personal foul.

SCORING

A basket from the field scores two points and a free throw one point. The team that is ahead at the end of the game is declared the winner. If the score is tied, an overtime period of 2 minutes is played. If the score is still tied after this period, the next team to score (one or two points) is declared the winner.

SUBSTITUTES

Substitutes must report to the official scorer and await a signal from the referee or umpire before entering the game. The scorer will sound the signal at a time when the ball is not in play so the official on the floor can signal for the player to enter the game.

OFFENSIVE TIME LIMIT

A time limit (30 seconds) may be established during which the offensive team must score or give up the ball.

BASKETBALL DRILLS

In working with drills, instructors should use the technique suggestions for the skill being practiced and apply movement principles (pp. 26–30). The drills presented here cover both single skills and combinations of skills.

PASSING DRILLS

In passing practice, good use should be made of the various movement formations (Chapter 6), including two-line, circle, circle-and-leader, line-and-leader, shuttle turn-back, and regular shuttle formations. A number of other drills should be considered.

Slide Circle Drill

In the slide circle drill, a circle of four to six players slides around a person in the center. The center person passes and receives to and from the sliding players. After the ball has gone around the circle twice, another player takes the center position.

Circle-Star Drill

With only five players, a circle-star drill is particularly effective. Players pass to every other player, and the path of the ball forms a star (Figure 27.12). The star drill works well as a relay. Any odd number of players will cause the ball to go to all participants, assuring that all receive equal practice.

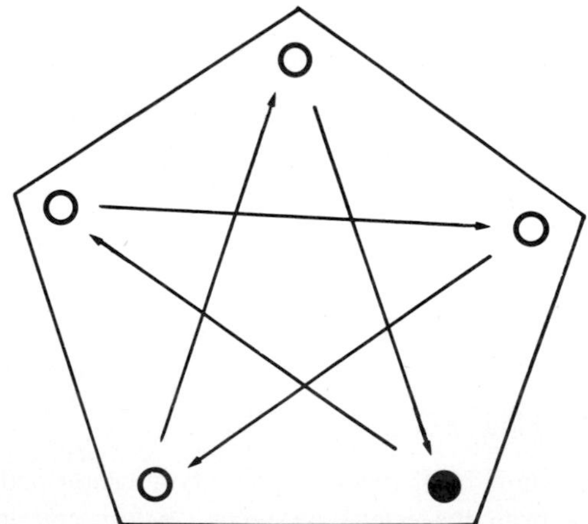

FIGURE 27.12. Circle-star drill formation

Triangle Drill

Four to eight players can participate in the triangle drill. The ball begins at the head of a line and is passed forward to a player away from the line. This player then passes to a teammate out at a corner, who then passes back to the head of the line (Figure 27.13). Each player passes and then moves to the spot to which he passed the ball, thus making a continual change of positions.

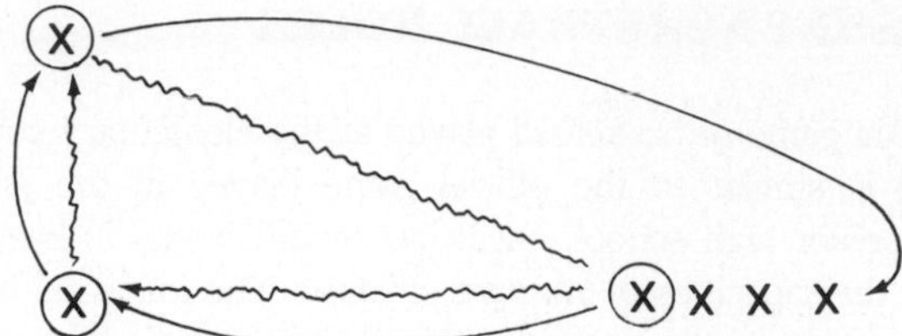

FIGURE 27.13. Triangle drill formation

Three-Player Weave

Another valuable drill is the three-player weave. This drill needs explanation and practice. The player in the center always starts the drill. She passes to another player coming across in front and then goes behind that player. Just as soon as she goes behind and around the player, she heads diagonally across the floor until she receives the ball again. The pass from the center player can start to either side.

DRIBBLING DRILLS

Dribbling can be practiced as a single skill or in combination with others.

File Dribbling

In file dribbling, players dribble forward around an obstacle (such as an Indian club, a cone, or a chair) and back to the line, where the next player repeats (Figure 27.14). A variation has each player dribbling down with one hand and back with the other.

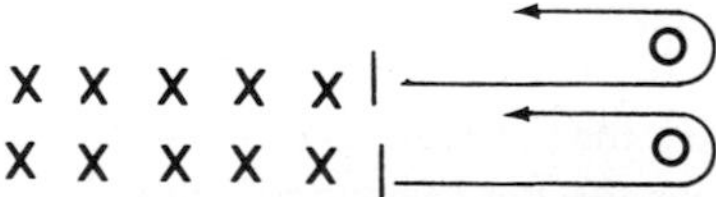

FIGURE 27.14. File dribbling

Shuttle Dribbling

Shuttle dribbling begins at the head of a file. The head player dribbles across to another file, and hands the ball off to the player at the head of the second file. He then takes a place at the end of that file (Figure 27.15). The player receiving the ball dribbles back to the first file. A number of shuttles can be arranged for dribbling crossways over a basketball court.

FIGURE 27.15. Shuttle dribbling

Obstacle, or Figure-Eight, Dribbling

For obstacle, or figure-eight, dribbling, three or more obstacles are positioned about 5 ft apart. The first player at the head of each file dribbles in and around each obstacle, changing hands so that the hand opposite the obstacle is the one always used (Figure 27.16).

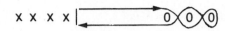

FIGURE 27.16. Obstacle, or figure-eight, dribbling

DRIBBLING AND PIVOTING DRILLS

In dribbling and pivoting drills, the emphasis is on stopping and pivoting.

File Drill

For the file drill, each player in turn dribbles forward to a designated line, stops, pivots, and faces the file, passes back to the next player, and runs to a place at the end of the line (Figure 27.17). The next player repeats the pattern.

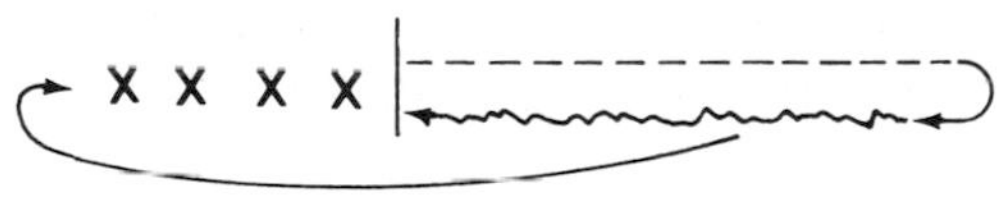

FIGURE 27.17. File drill

Dribble-and-Pivot Drill

For the dribble-and-pivot drill, players are scattered by pairs around the floor (Figure 27.18). One ball is required for each pair. On the first whistle, the front player of the pair dribbles in any direction and fashion on the court. On the second whistle, she stops and pivots back and forth. On the third whistle, she dribbles back and passes to a partner, who immediately dribbles forward, repeating the routine.

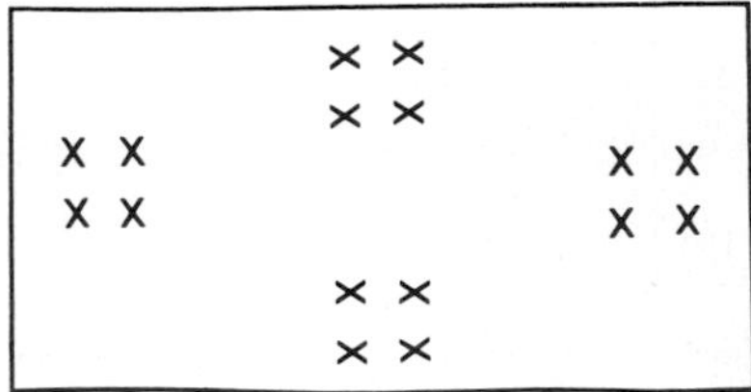

FIGURE 27.18. Dribble-and-pivot drill

SHOOTING DRILLS

Shooting drills may involve just shooting or a combination of shooting and other skills.

Simple Shooting Drill

In one simple shooting drill, players form files of no more than four people, and take turns shooting a long and a short shot or some other prescribed series of shots.

File-and-Leader Drill

For a file-and-leader drill, the first player in each file has a ball and is the shooter. He passes the ball to the leader, who returns the ball to the spot that the shooter has selected for the shot (Figure 27.19).

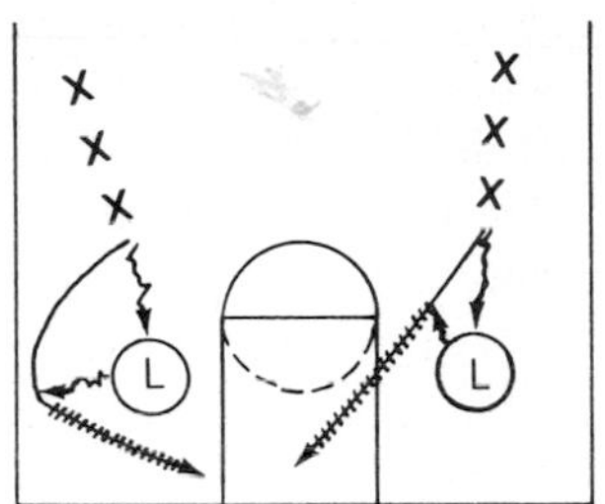

FIGURE 27.19. File-and-leader drill

Dribble-and-Shoot Drill

For the dribble-and-shoot drill, two files are established on one end of the floor. One file has a ball. The first player dribbles in and shoots a lay-up. A member of the other file recovers the ball and passes it to the next player (Figure 27.20). As each person in turn either shoots or retrieves, she goes to the rear of the other file. After some proficiency in the drill has been developed, two balls can be used, allowing for more shooting opportunities.

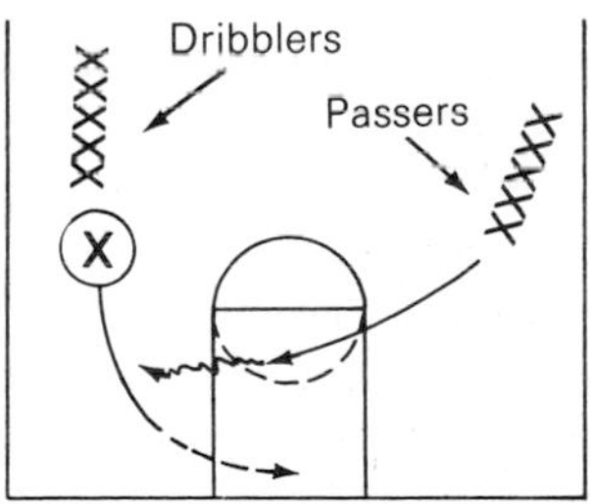

FIGURE 27.20. Dribble-and-shoot drill

Set-Shot Drill

In the set-shot drill, players are scattered around a basket in a semicircle, with a leader in charge (Figure 27.21). Players should be close enough to the basket so they can shoot accurately. The leader passes to each in turn to take a shot. The leader chases the ball after the shot. A bit of competition can be injected by allowing a *successful* shooter to take one step back for the next shot, or a player can shoot until she misses.

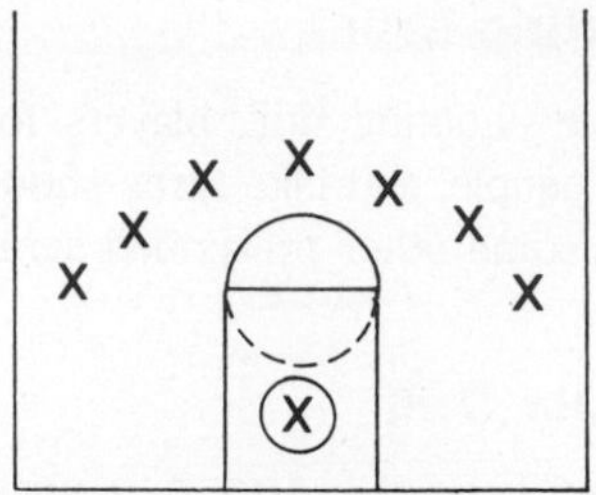
FIGURE 27.21. Set-shot drill formation

Lay-up Drill

The lay-up drill is a favorite. One line passes to the other line for lay-up shots (Figure 27.22). Shooters come in from the right side first (this is easier), then from the left, and finally from the center. Each player goes to the end of the other line.

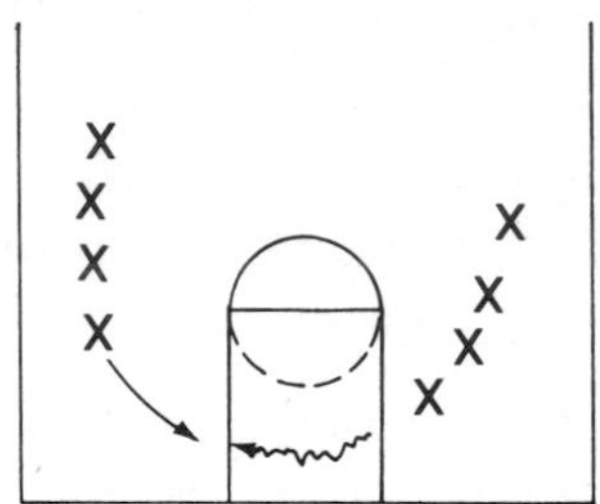
FIGURE 27.22. Lay-up drill

Jump-Shot Drill

The jump-shot drill is similar to the lay-up drill, except that the incoming shooter receives the ball, stops, and takes a jump shot. The line of shooters should move back so that there is room for forward movement to the shooting spot. As soon as the passer releases the ball to the shooter, he moves to the end of the shooter's line. The shooter goes to the passer's line after shooting (Figure 27.23).

One extension of this drill is to allow a second jump shot when the shooter makes the first. In this case, the incoming passer passes to the shooter taking a second shot as well as to the next shooter. Another extension, which creates a gamelike situation, is having both the shooter and the incoming passer follow up the shot when the basket has not been made. As soon as the follow-up shot is made or there are three misses by the followers, the passer passes the ball to the new shooter. The avenues by which the shooters approach should be varied, so children practice shooting from different spots.

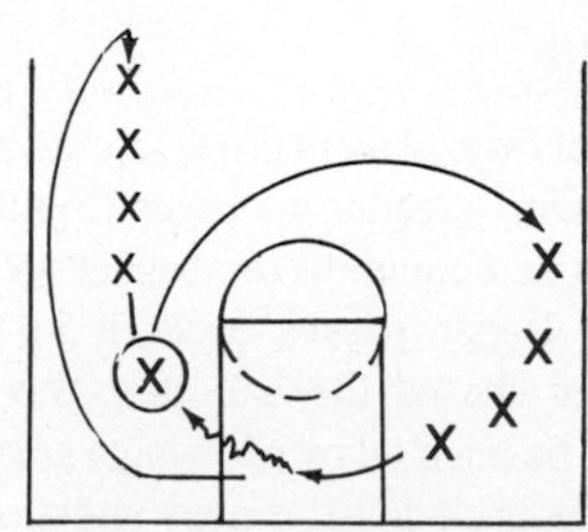
FIGURE 27.23. Jump-shot drill

OFFENSIVE AND DEFENSIVE DRILLS

Group Defensive Drill

For the group defensive drill, the entire class is scattered on a basketball floor, facing one of the sides (Figure 27.24). The instructor or the student leader stands on the side, near the center. The drill can be done in a number of ways.

1. The leader points in one direction (forward, backward, or to one side) and gives the command "Move." When the students have moved a short distance, she commands, "Stop." Players keep good defensive position throughout.

2. Commands can be changed so that movement is continuous. Commands are "Right," "Left," "Forward," "Backward," and "Stop." The leader must watch that movement is not so far in any one direction that it causes players to run into obstructions. Commands can be given in order, and pointing can accompany commands.

3. The leader is a dribbler with a ball. He moves forward, backward, or to either side, with the defensive players reacting accordingly.

It is important to stress good defensive position and movement. Movement from side to side should be a slide. Movement forward and backward is a two-step, with one foot always leading.

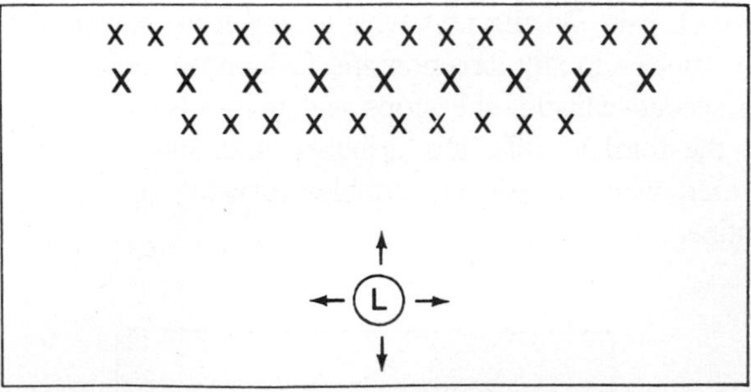

FIGURE 27.24. Group defensive drill

Offensive-Defensive Drill With a Post

The offensive-defensive drill with a post consists of an offensive player, a defensive player, and another player who acts as a passing post. The post player generally remains stationary and receives the ball from and passes to the offensive player. The player on offense tries to maneuver around or past the defensive player to secure a good shot (Figure 27.25). Plays can be confined to one side of an

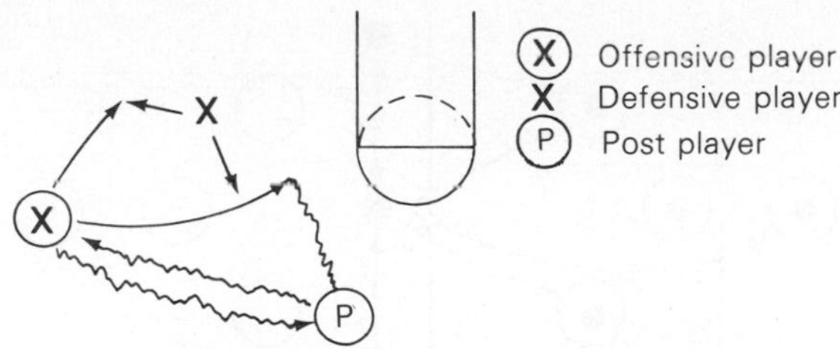

FIGURE 27.25. Offensive-defensive drill with post

offensive basket area, thus allowing two drills to go on at the same time on one end of the basketball floor. If there are side baskets, many drills can be operated at the same time. After a basket has been attempted, a rotation of players, including any waiting player, is made.

The defensive player's job is to cover well enough to prevent shots in front of her. Some matching of ability must occur or the drill is nonproductive.

BASKETBALL ACTIVITIES

THIRD GRADE

Circle Guard and Pass

Playing Area: Any smooth surface with circle markings

Players: Eight to ten per team

Supplies: A basketball or playground ball

Skills: Passing, catching, guarding

The offensive team moves into formation around a large (30 ft diameter) circle. One of the offensive players moves to the center. The defensive team is in position around a smaller (20-ft) circle inside the larger circle. On signal, the offensive team tries to pass the ball to the center player. They may pass the ball around the circle to each other before making an attempt to the center. The defensive team must bat the ball away but cannot catch it. After a stipulated time (1 minute), offensive and defensive teams trade positions. If score is kept, 2 points are awarded for each successful pass.

Variation: More than one ball can be used and different types of passes can be stipulated. The defensive team also can earn points for each time they touch the ball.

Basketball Tag

Playing Area: Gymnasium or playground area, 30 by 50 ft

Players: Eight to ten per team

Supplies: A basketball, pinnies

Skills: Catching, passing, dribbling, guarding

A player from each team is designated to be it and wears a pinny. The object of the game is to tag the other team's target player with the ball. The player who is it may move only by walking. Players can move the ball by dribbling and by passing the ball to teammates. The player who is it tries to avoid moving near the ball, while others try to pass, dribble, and move near the roving it. The team without the ball plays defense and tries to intercept the ball.

Variation: More than one ball can be used and more than one player per team can be identified as it.

Birdie in the Cage

Playing Area: Any smooth surface with circle marking

Players: 8 to 15 per team

Supplies: A soccer ball, basketball, or volleyball

Skills: Passing, catching, intercepting

Players are in circle formation with one child in the middle. The object of the game is for the center player to try to touch the ball. The ball is passed from player to player in the circle, and the center player attempts to touch the ball on one of these passes. The player who threw the ball that was touched takes the place in the center. In case of a bad pass resulting in the ball leaving the circle area, the player who caused the error can change to the center of the ring.

Teaching Suggestions: The ball should move rapidly. Passing to a neighboring player is not allowed. If touching the ball proves difficult, a second center may join the first. Play can be limited to a specific type of pass (bounce, two-handed, push).

Variation: As few as three children can play, with two children passing the ball back and forth between them while a third tries to touch it. An excellent version of this game calls for four players, with three forming a triangle and positioning themselves about 15 ft apart.

FOURTH GRADE

Captain Ball

Playing Area: Playground or gymnasium area, about 30 by 40 ft

Players: Seven on each team

Supplies: A basketball, pinnies, eight hoops

Skills: Passing, catching, guarding

Two games can be played crosswise on a basketball court. A center line is needed (Figure 27.26); otherwise, the normal out-of-bounds lines can be used. Hoops can provide the circles for the forwards and the captains. Captain Ball is a very popular game that is played with many variations. In this version, a team is composed of a captain, three forwards, and three guards. The guards throw the ball to their captain. The captain and the three forwards are each assigned to respective circles and must always

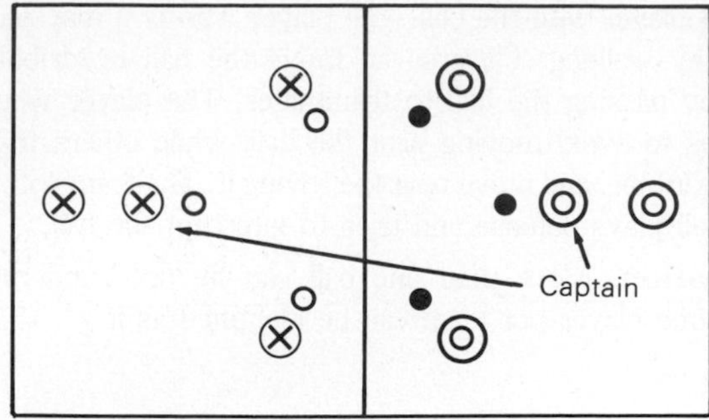

FIGURE 27.26. Formation for Captain Ball

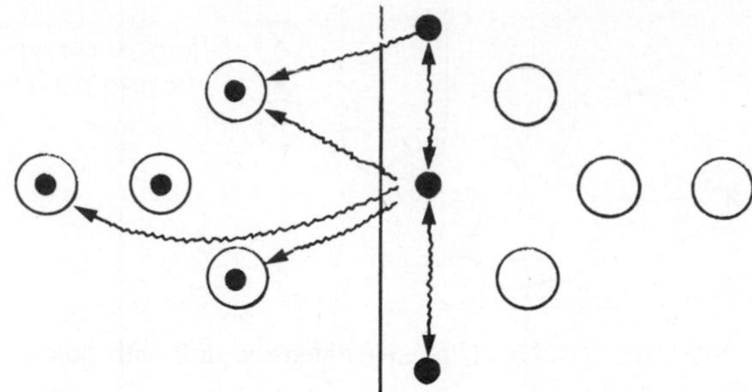

FIGURE 27.27. Most effective offensive formation in Captain Ball

keep one foot inside the circle. Guarding these four circle players are three guards.

The game is started by a jump at the center line by two guards from opposing teams. The guards can rove in their half of the court but must not enter the circles of the opposing players. The ball is put into play after each score in much the same manner as in regular basketball. The team scored on puts the ball into play by a guard throwing the ball in bounds from the side of the court.

As soon as a guard gets the ball, he throws it to one of the forwards, who must manuever to be open. The forward then tries to throw it to the other forwards or in, to the captain. Two points are scored when all three forwards handle the ball and then it is passed to the captain. One point is scored when the ball is passed to the captain but has not been handled by all three forwards.

Stepping over the center line is a foul. It is also a foul if a guard steps into a circle or makes personal contact with a circle player. The penalty for a foul is a free throw.

For a free throw, the ball is given to an unguarded forward, who has 5 seconds to get the ball successfully to the guarded captain. If the throw is successful, one point is scored. If it is not successful, the ball is in play. Successive fouls rotate free throws among the forwards.

As in basketball, when the ball goes out-of-bounds, it is awarded to the team that did not cause it to go out. If a forward or a captain catches a ball with *both* feet out of her circle, the ball is taken out-of-bounds by the opposing guard.

For violations such as traveling or kicking the ball, the ball is awarded to an opposing guard out-of-bounds. No score may be made from a ball that is thrown in directly from out-of-bounds.

Teaching Suggestions: Some instruction is necessary for children to absorb the basic strategy of the game. The most effective offensive formation seems to be one in which the guards are spaced along the center line (Figure 27.27). Only the offensive team is diagrammed. By passing the ball back and forth among the guards, the forwards have more opportunity to be open, since the passing makes the guards shift position.

The guards may dribble, but this should be held to a minimum and used for advancing the ball only when necessary. Otherwise, dribbling accomplishes little.

The forwards and the captain should learn to shift back and forth to become open for passes. Considerable latitude is available, since they need keep only one foot in the hoop. Short and accurate passing uses both high and bounce passes. Circle players may jump for the ball but must come down with one foot in the circle.

Variations

1. Four guards can be used, but scoring is then more difficult.

2. A five-circle formation can be used, forming a five spot like that on a die. Nine players are needed on each team—four forwards, four guards, and one captain.

3. A platform 6 to 8 in. high and 20 in. square can elevate the captain to make reception of the ball easier.

Around the Key

Playing Area: One end of a basketball floor

Players: Three to eight

Supplies: A basketball

Skill: Shooting

Spots are arranged for shooting as indicated in Figure 27.28. A player begins at the first spot and continues until a miss. When a miss occurs, the player can stop and wait for her next opportunity and begin from the point where the miss occurred, or she can "risk it" and try another shot immediately from the point where the first try was missed. If the shot is made, the player continues. If the shot is missed, the player must start over on the next turn. The winner is the player who completes the key first or who makes the most progress.

Variations

1. Each child shoots from each spot until a basket is made. A limit of three shots from any one spot should be set. The child finishing the round of eight spots with the lowest number of shots taken is the winner.

2. The order of the spots can be changed. A player can start on one side of the key and continue back along

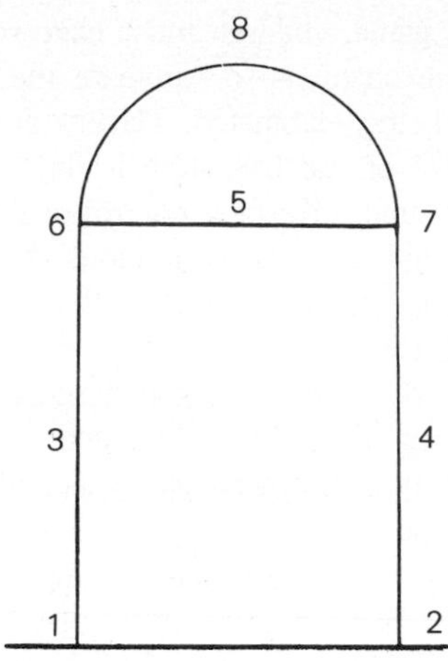

FIGURE 27.28. Shooting positions for Around the Key

the line, around the free-throw circle, and back down the other side of the key.

3. An easier version of the game permits two shots from each spot, thus increasing the chances for success.

FIFTH GRADE

Captain Basketball

Playing Area: A basketball court with center line

Players: Six or eight on each team

Supplies: A basketball, pinnies

Skills: All basketball skills except shooting

A captain's area is laid out by drawing a line between the two foul restraining lines 4 ft out from the end line. The captain must keep one foot in this area. Captain Basketball is closer to the game of basketball than Captain Ball. The circle restrictions of Captain Ball limit movements of the forwards. Captain Basketball brings in more natural passing and guarding situations, and the game is played in much the same way as basketball.

A team normally is composed of three forwards, one captain, and four guards. The captain must keep one foot in his area under the basket. The game is started with a jump ball, after which the players advance the ball as in basketball. No player may cross the center line, however. The guards must therefore bring the ball up to the center line and throw it to one of their forwards. The forwards maneuver and attempt to pass successfully to the captain. A throw by one of the forwards to the captain scores 2 points; a free throw scores 1 point.

Fouls are the same as in basketball. In addition, stepping over the center line or a guard stepping into the captain's area draws a foul.

In the case of a foul, the ball is given to a forward at the free-throw line. She is unguarded and has 5 seconds to pass successfully to her captain, who is guarded by one player. The ball is in play if the free throw is unsuccessful.

Teaching Suggestions: A folding tumbling mat can be used to designate the captain's area at each end of the court. Use of a mat tends to discourage intrusion by guards into the captain's area.

While players are required to remain in their own half of the court, they should be taught to move freely within that area. Short, quick passes should be stressed, because long passes are not effective. This is also good practice for proper guarding techniques.

Sideline Basketball

Playing Area: Basketball court

Players: Entire class

Supplies: A basketball, pinnies

Skills: All basketball skills

The class is divided into two teams, each lined up along one side of the court, facing the other. The game is played by three or four active players from each team. The remainder of the players who stand on the sideline can catch and pass the ball to the active players. Sideline players may not shoot, nor may they enter the playing floor. They must keep one foot completely out-of-bounds at all times.

The active players play regular basketball, except that they may pass and receive the ball from sideline players. The game starts with the active players occupying their own half of the court. The ball is taken out-of-bounds under its own basket by the team that was scored upon. Play continues until one team scores or until a period of time (2 or 3 minutes) elapses. The active players then take places on the left side of their line and three new active players come out from the right. All other players move down three places in the line.

No official out-of-bounds on the sides is called. The players on that side of the floor simply recover the ball and put it into play by a pass to an active player without delay. Out-of-bounds on the ends is the same as in regular basketball. If one of the sideline players enters the court and touches the ball, it is a violation, and the ball is awarded out-of-bounds on the other side to a sideline player of the other team. Free throws are awarded when a player is fouled. Sideline players may not pass to each other but must pass back to an active player. Sideline players should be well spaced along the side.

Twenty-One

Playing Area: One end of a basketball court

Players: Three to eight in each game

Supplies: A basketball

Skills: Shooting

Players are in file formation by teams. Each child is permitted a long shot (from a specified distance) and a follow-up shot. The long shot, if made, counts 2 points and the short shot counts 1 point. The follow-up shot must be made from the spot where the ball was recovered from the first shot. The normal one-two-step rhythm is permitted on the short shot from the place where the ball was recovered.

The first player scoring a total of 21 points is the winner. If the ball misses the backboard and basket altogether on the first shot, the second shot must be taken from the corner.

Variations

1. A simpler game allows dribbling before the second shot.

2. Players can continue to shoot as long as every shot is made. This means that, if he makes *both* the long and the short shot, a player goes back to the original position for a third shot. All shots made count, and the shooter continues until a miss.

3. The game works well as a team competition, with each player contributing to the team score.

4. Various combinations and types of shots may be used.

Freeze Out

Playing Area: One end of the basketball court

Players: Four to eight

Supplies: A basketball

Skill: Shooting under pressure

There are many types of freeze-out shooting games. This version is an interesting shooting game that culminates quickly and allows players back in the game quite soon.

Each player can have three misses before she is out. After the first miss, the player gets an *O;* after the second, a *U;* and after the third, a *T*. This spells *OUT* and puts the player out. The last player remaining is the winner.

The players start in file formation. The first player shoots a basket from any spot desired. If the basket is missed, there is no penalty and the next player shoots. If the basket is made, the following player must make a basket from the same spot or it is scored as a miss. Players keep track of their own misses. Players should remember that, if the player ahead of them makes a basket, they must do likewise or have a miss scored against them. If the player ahead of them misses, they may shoot from any spot they choose without penalty.

SIXTH GRADE

Flag Dribble

Playing Area: One end of a basketball floor or a hard-surfaced area outside with boundaries

Players: 4 to 15

Supplies: A basketball and a flag for each player

Skill: Dribbling

To play this game, children must have reasonable skill in dribbling. The object is to eliminate the other players while avoiding being eliminated. Players are eliminated if they lose control of the ball, if their flag is pulled, or if they go out-of-bounds. Keeping control of the ball by dribbling is interpreted to mean continuous dribbling without missing a bounce. A double dribble (both hands) is regarded as a loss of control.

The game starts with players scattered around the area near the sidelines. Each has a ball and a flag tucked in the back of her belt. Extra players wait outside the area. On signal, each player begins to dribble in the area. While keeping control of the dribble and staying in bounds, they attempt to pull a flag from any other player's back. They can also knock aside any other player's ball to eliminate that player. As soon as the game is down to one player, that player is declared the winner. Sometimes two players lose control of their basketball at about the same time. In this case, both are eliminated. Sometimes, two players are left and the game results in a stalemate. In this case, both are declared winners and the game starts over.

Variations

1. If using flags is impractical, the game can be played without this feature. The objective then becomes to knock aside or deflect the other basketballs while retaining control of one's own ball.

2. Flag Dribble can be played by teams or squads. In this case, each squad or team should be clearly marked.

One-Goal Basketball

Playing Area: An area with one basketball goal

Players: Two or four on each team

Supplies: A basketball, pinnies (optional)

Skills: All basketball skills

If a gymnasium has four basketball goals, many children can be kept active with this game. If only two goals are available, a system of rotation can be worked out. The game is played by two teams according to the regular rules of basketball but with the following exceptions.

1. The game begins with a jump at the free-throw mark, with the centers facing the sidelines.

2. When a defensive player recovers the ball, either from the backboard or on an interception, the ball must be taken out beyond the foul-line circle before offensive play is started and an attempt at a goal is made.

3. After a basket is made, the ball is taken in the same fashion away from the basket to the center of the floor, where the other team starts offensive play.

4. Regular free-throw shooting can be observed after a foul, or some use can be made of the rule whereby the offended team takes the ball out-of-bounds.

5. If an offensive player is tied up in a jump ball, he loses the ball to the other team.

Fouls are something of a problem, because they are called on individuals by themselves. An official can be used, however.

Variations

1. A system of rotation can be instituted whereby the team that scores a basket holds the floor and the losing team retires in favor of a waiting team. For more experienced players, a score of three or more points can be required to eliminate the opponents.

2. *One-on-One.* This variation differs from One-Goal Basketball primarily in the number of players. Only two play. Otherwise, the rules are generally the same. The honor system should be stressed since officials usually are not present and players call fouls on themselves. There is more personal contact in this game than in One-Goal Basketball. The game has value because of its backyard recreational possibilities. It is popular because it has been featured on television broadcasts of professional basketball players.

Five Passes

Playing Area: Half of a basketball floor

Players: Four or five on each team

Supplies: A basketball and colored shirts, markers, or pinnies

Skills: Passing, guarding

Two teams play. The object of the game is to complete five consecutive passes, which scores a point. On one basketball floor, two games can proceed at the same time, one in each half.

The game is started with a jump ball at the free-throw line. The teams observe regular basketball rules in ball handling, traveling, and with regard to fouling. Five consecutive passes must be made by a team, which counts out loud as the passes are completed.

The ball must not be passed back to the person from whom it was received. No dribbling is allowed. If for any reason the ball is fumbled and recovered or improperly passed, a new count is started. After a successful score, the ball can be thrown up again in a center jump at the free-throw line. A foul draws a free throw, which can score a point. Teams should be well marked to avoid confusion.

Variations

1. After each successful point (five passes), the team is awarded a free throw, which can score an additional point.

2. After a team has scored a point, the ball can be given to the other team out-of-bounds to start play again.

3. Passes must be made so that all players handle the ball.

Basketball Snatch Ball

Playing Area: Basketball court

Players: 6 to 15 on each team

Supplies: Two basketballs, two hoops

Skills: Passing, dribbling, shooting

Each of two teams occupies one side of a basketball floor. The players on each team are numbered consecutively and must stand in the numbered order. The two balls are placed in two hoops, one on each side of the center line. When the teacher calls a number, the player from each team whose number was called runs to the ball, dribbles it to the basket on her right, and tries to make the basket. As soon as a successful basket is made, she dribbles back and places the ball on the spot where she picked it up. The first player to return the ball after making a basket scores a point for her team. The teacher should use some system to keep track of the numbers so all children have a turn. Numbers can be called in any order.

Teaching Suggestion: In returning the ball, emphasis should be placed on legal dribbling or passing. In the hurry to get back, illegal traveling sometimes occurs.

Variations

1. Players can run by pairs, with either a pair of players assigned the same number or the teacher calling two numbers. Three passes must be made before the shot is taken and before the ball is replaced inside the hoop.

2. Three players can run at a time, with the stipulation that the player who picks up the ball from the hoop must be the one who takes the first shot. All players must handle the ball on the way down and on the way back.

3. To make a more challenging spot for the return, use a deck tennis ring. This demands more critical control than placing the ball in a hoop. In either case, the ball must rest within the designated area to score.

4. A more demanding task calls for a single player to pass the ball to each of his teammates successively on the way down and on the way back. Teammates scatter themselves along the sideline after the number has been called.

Three-on-Three

Playing Area: Half of a basketball court

Players: Three to five teams of three players each

Supplies: A basketball

Skills: All basketball skills

An offensive team of three stands just forward of the center line, facing the basket. The center player has a basketball. Another team of three is on defense and awaits the offensive team in the area near the foul line. The remaining teams, waiting for their turn, stand beyond the end line.

Regular basketball rules are used. At a signal, the offensive team advances to score. A scrimmage is over when the offensive team scores or when the ball is recovered by the defense. In either case, the defensive team moves to the center of the floor and becomes the offensive unit. A waiting team comes out on the floor and gets ready for defense. The old offensive team goes to the rear of the line of waiting players. Each of the teams should keep its own score. Two games can be carried on at the same time, one in each half of the court.

Variations

1. If the offensive team scores, it remains on the floor, and the defensive team drops off in favor of the next team. If the defense recovers the ball, the offensive team rotates off the floor.

2. If a team has a foul (by one of the players), that team rotates off the floor in favor of the next team.

3. A team wins when it scores 3 points. The contest becomes a regular scrimmage in which the offensive team becomes the defensive team upon recovering the ball. When a team scores 3 points, the other team is rotated off the floor. Rules for One-Goal Basketball prevail.

4. The game can be played with four against four.

Basketrama

Playing Area: Area around one basket

Players: Usually two

Supplies: A basketball for each player

Skill: Shooting under pressure

On signal, two players, each with a basketball, begin to shoot individually as rapidly as possible, taking any kind of shots they wish, until one scores 10 baskets and becomes the winner. Each player must handle his own basketball and must not impede or interfere with the other's ball. Naturally, the balls do collide at times, but deliberate interference by knocking the other ball out of the way or kicking it means disqualification.

Balls should be marked, so there is no argument as to ownership. This can be done by using different types of basketballs or by marking with chalk or tape. Each player can count out loud each basket he makes, or another student can keep score for each contestant.

Variations

1. The game can be played with more than two players, but this can cause confusion and mix-ups of the respective basketballs.

2. The scoring method can be varied. A time limit can be set, and the player's score is the number of baskets that she makes during the set time. Another method is to time the player to see how many seconds it takes her to make 10 baskets.

BASKETBALL SKILL TESTS

Tests in basketball cover dribbling, passing, shooting, and making free throws. For each of the first four tests presented here, a stopwatch is needed.

STRAIGHT DRIBBLE

A marker is placed 15 yd down the floor from the starting point. The dribbler must dribble around the marker and back to the starting position, where she finishes by crossing the starting line. The marker must remain standing or disqualification results. The teacher should allow two or three trials and take the best time.

FIGURE-EIGHT DRIBBLE

Four obstacles (Indian clubs, bases, or cones) are placed 5 ft apart in a straight line beginning 5 ft from the starting line. The player must dribble in and out of the markers in the path of a figure eight, finishing at the point where he started. The teacher can allow two or three trials and take the best time.

WALL PASS TEST

A player stands 5 ft from a smooth wall. She is given 30 seconds to make as many catches as she can from throws or passes against the wall. The two-handed or chest pass is generally used. Balls must be caught on the fly to count. Another student should do the counting. Only one trial is allowed. A board or mat provides a definite restraining line.

BASKETS FOR 30 SECONDS

A player stands near the basket in any position he wishes. On signal, he shoots and continues shooting for a period of 30 seconds. His score is the number of baskets he makes during the time period. Another student should do the counting. Only one trial is allowed.

FREE THROWS

Score is kept of the number of free throws made out of ten attempts. The player should get three or four warm-up trials and announce when she is ready. Score should be kept by another student with pencil and paper. An X is marked for a basket made, and a O for a miss.

CHAPTER 28

Football

Football is truly the great American game. With television exposure to professional football keyed by the game of the week and culminating in the Super Bowl, public interest in this game has grown considerably. The names of professional football players have become household words.

The shape of the football makes throwing and catching more difficult than with a round ball. Specialized skills are needed, which means that the teacher must spend more time on football skills if children are to enjoy participating.

Touch and Flag Football are modifications of the game of American football. A ball carrier usually is considered down in Touch Football when touched by one hand. Some rules do call for a two-handed touch, however. In Flag Football, a player wears one or two flags, which the opponents must seize to down the ball carrier, hence the name Flag Football.

Flag Football has advantages over Touch Football in that there is more twisting and dodging, which makes the game more interesting and challenging. In addition, in Flag Football, argument over whether the ball carrier was downed is less likely.

INSTRUCTIONAL EMPHASIS AND SEQUENCE

Table 28.1 shows the sequence of activities for the 4th through 6th grade.

FOURTH GRADE

Passing, centering, and catching make up the 4th-grade program. Most of the instructional time should be spent on skills. The lead-up games of Five Passes and Football End Ball make use of the skills listed.

FIFTH GRADE

The 5th grade should review the skills learned at the 4th-grade level. The emphasis then shifts to passing skills, with moving receivers in football drills. Punting and kicking games are introduced.

SIXTH GRADE

More specialized skills, such as blocking, carrying the ball, exchanging the ball, and football agility skills provide lead-up work for the game of Flag Football.

FOOTBALL SKILLS

PASSING

Forward Pass

Skillful forward passing is needed in Flag Football and in the lead-up games; passing is a potent weapon. The ball should be gripped lightly behind the middle with the fingers on the lace. The thumbs and fingers should be relaxed (Figure 28.1).

In throwing, the opposing foot should point in the direction of the pass, with the body turned sideways. In preparation for the pass, the ball is raised up and held over the shoulders. The ball is delivered directly forward with an overhand movement of the arm and with the index finger

TABLE 28.1. SUGGESTED FOOTBALL PROGRAM

	Fourth Grade	Fifth Grade	Sixth Grade
Skills	Forward pass Centering Catching	Stance Pass receiving Punting	Blocking Carrying the ball Running and dodging Ball exchange Lateral pass
Knowledge			Football rules Plays and formations
Activities	Football End Ball Five Passes	Kick-Over Fourth Down	Football Box Ball Flag Football Pass Ball
Skill Tests	Passing for distance Centering	Kicking for distance Passing for distance	Passing for accuracy Passing for distance

pointing toward the line of flight. A left-hander is used in Figure 28.2.

Lateral Pass

Lateral passing is pitching the ball underhand to a teammate (Figure 28.3). The ball must be tossed sideward or backward to qualify as a lateral. It should be tossed with an easy motion, and no attempt should be made to make it spiral like a forward pass.

FIGURE 28.1. Preparing to pass

CATCHING

In catching, the receiver should keep his eyes on the ball and catch it in his hands with a slight give (Figure 28.4). As soon as the ball is caught, it should be tucked into the carrying position. The little fingers are together for most catches.

CARRYING THE BALL

The ball should be carried with the arm on the outside and the end of the ball tucked into the notch formed by the elbow and arm. The fingers add support for the carry (Figure 28.5).

FIGURE 28.2. Passing

FIGURE 28.3. Ready for a lateral pass

CENTERING

The centering player takes a position with his feet well spread and toes pointed straight ahead. His knees are bent, and he should be close enough to the ball to reach it with a slight stretch. The right hand takes about the same grip as is used in passing. The other hand is on the side near the back of the ball and merely acts as a guide (Figure 28.6). Center passing for the T-formation is with one hand, however. The other arm rests on the inside of the thigh.

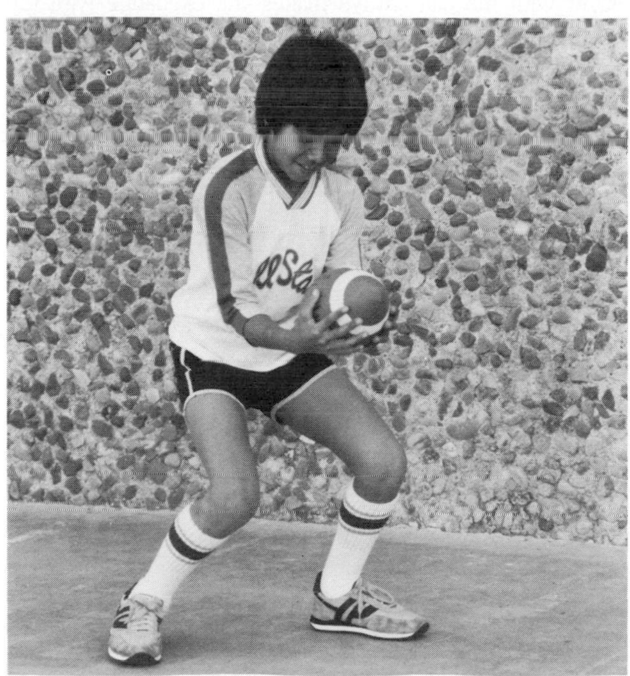

FIGURE 28.4. Catching a pass

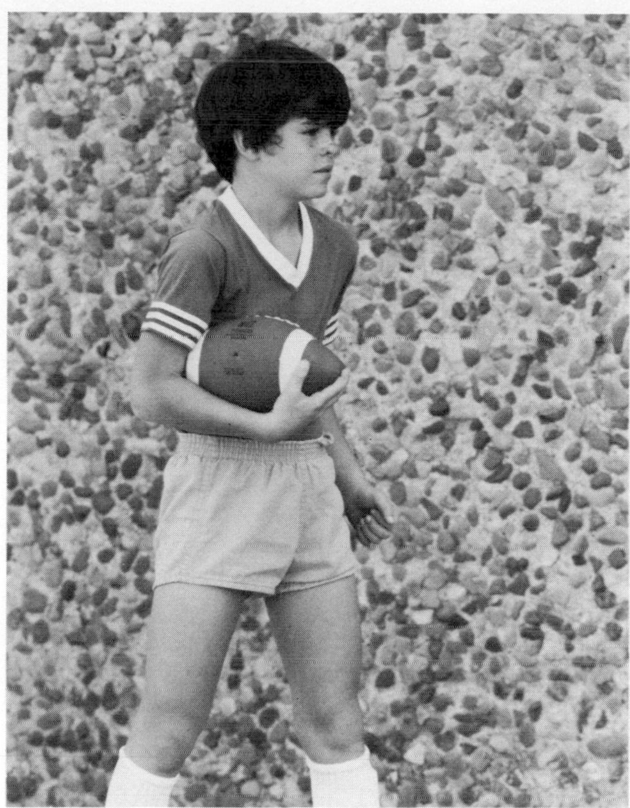

FIGURE 28.5. Carrying the ball securely

STANCE

The three-point stance is the offensive stance most generally used in Flag Football. The feet are about shoulder width apart and the toes point straight ahead, with the toe of one foot even with the heel of the other. The hand on the side of the foot that is back is used for support; the knuckles rest on the ground. The player should look

FIGURE 28.6. Centering (note the hand and finger positions)

FIGURE 28.7. Offensive three-point stance

straight ahead and always take the same stance (Figure 28.7).

Some players prefer the parallel stance, in which the feet, instead of being in the heel-and-toe position, are lined up evenly. In this case, either hand can be placed down for support. Some defensive players like to use a four-point stance, as shown. Both hands are in contact with the ground (Figure 28.8).

BLOCKING

In blocking for Flag Football, the blocker must maintain balance and not fall to the knees. The elbows are out and the hands are held near the chest. The block should be more of an obstruction than a takeout, and should be set with the shoulder against the opponent's shoulder or upper

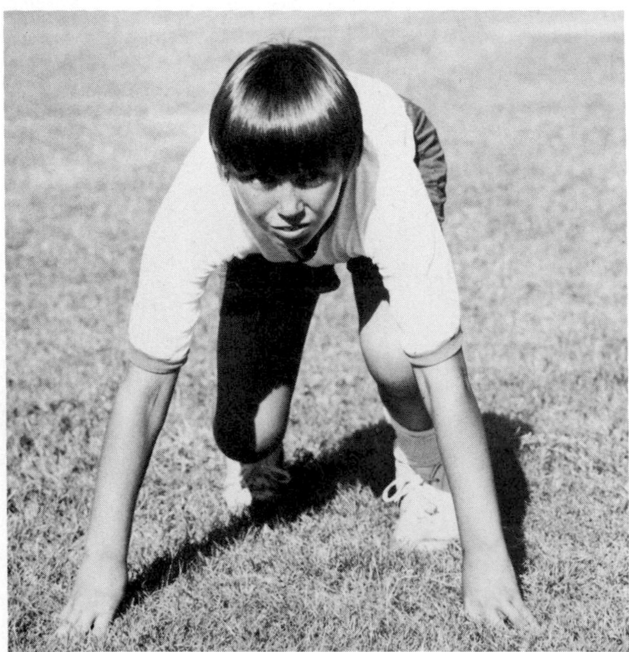

FIGURE 28.8. Defensive four-point stance

FIGURE 28.9. Blocking position

body (Figure 28.9). Making contact from the rear in any direction not only is a foul but could cause serious injury.

EXCHANGING THE BALL

Children enjoy working plays where the ball is exchanged from one player to another, as for a reverse. In a reverse, the object is to start the play in one direction and then give the ball to another player heading in the opposite direction. The ball can be handed backward or forward. The player with the ball always makes the exchange with the inside hand, the one near the receiving player. The ball is held with both hands until the receiver is about 6 ft away. The ball then is shifted to the hand on that side, with the elbow bent partially away from the body. The receiver comes toward the exchange player with the near arm bent and carried in front of the chest, the palm down. The other arm is carried about waist height, with the palm up (Figure 28.10). As the ball is handed off (not tossed) to him, the receiver clamps down on the ball to secure it. As quickly as possible, the receiver then changes to a normal carrying position.

A fake reverse, sometimes called a bootleg, is made when the ball carrier pretends to make the exchange but keeps the ball instead and hides it momentarily behind his leg.

PUNTING

The kicker stands with the kicking foot slightly forward. The fingers are extended in the direction of the center. The eyes should be on the ball from the time it is centered until it is kicked, and the kicker should actually see the foot kick the ball. After receiving the ball, the kicker takes

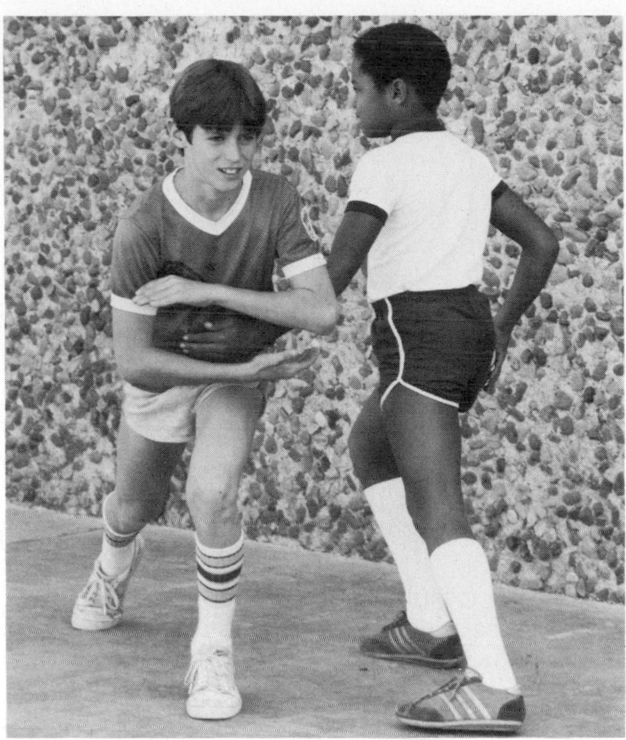

FIGURE 28.10. Exchanging the ball

a short step with the kicking foot and then a second step with the other foot. The kicking leg is swung forward and, at impact, the knee is straightened to provide maximum force. The toes are pointed, and the long axis of the ball makes contact on the top of the instep. The leg should follow through well after the kick (Figure 28.11). Emphasis should be placed on dropping the ball properly. Beginners have a tendency to throw it in the air, making the punt more difficult.

FIGURE 28.11. Punting

INSTRUCTIONAL PROCEDURES

1. All children need the opportunity to practice all skills, and a system of rotation should be set up to ensure this.

2. Drills should be performed with attention to proper form, and they should approximate game conditions. When going out for passes is being practiced, the proper stance should be employed.

3. Junior-sized footballs should be used. At least six to eight footballs should be available for football drills. The best teaching situation is to have one football for each pair of children.

4. Roughness and unfair play must be controlled by supervision and strict enforcement of the rules.

ORGANIZING FOR INSTRUCTION

The differences between sexes should be allowed for in football activities. The instruction may follow one of two patterns. Skills are taught together but the sexes are separated for other phases, or the skills and simple selected lead-up games may have coeducational participation.

Blocking and scrimmage play are not suitable for mixed participation. When boys are participating in Flag Football, Fourth Down, or Pass Ball, girls might do likewise in another area. Noncontact games such as Football Endball, Five Passes, or Football Box Ball may have mixed participation.

Passing and catching skills can be practiced informally. More room is needed for kicking skills. Ball exchange drills work well with three or four children. Informal work gives children a chance to experiment and explore without pressure.

For more effective instruction, groups can be organized by skill level. Combining two or more skills in one drill means that the practice should be more structured. Group size still should be kept small.

FOOTBALL DRILLS

Ball Carrying

Formation: Scattered

Players: Four to six

Supplies: A football, a flag for each player, cones to mark the zones.

The ball carrier stands on the goal line—ready to run. Three defensive players wait at 20-yd intervals, each one stationed on a zone line of a regular Flag Football field, facing the ball carrier (Figure 28.12). Each defender is assigned to the zone that she is facing and must down the ball carrier by pulling a flag while the carrier is still in the zone. The ball carrier runs and dodges, trying to get by each defender in turn without having her flag pulled. If the flag is pulled, the runner continues, and the last defender uses a two-handed touch to down the ball carrier. After the runner has completed the run, she goes to the end of the defender's line and rotates to a defending position.

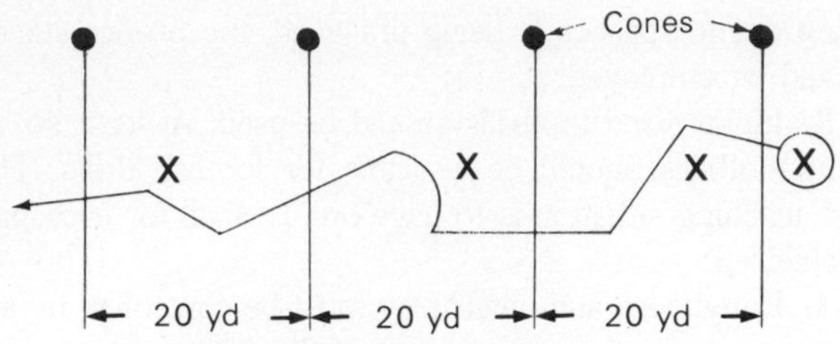

FIGURE 28.12. Ball carrying drill

Ball Exchange

Formation: Shuttle, with the halves about 15 yd apart

Players: Four to ten

Supplies: A football

The two halves of the shuttle face each other across the 15-yd distance. A player at the head of one of the files has a ball and carries it over to the other file, where he makes an exchange with the player at the front of that file (Figure 28.13). The ball is carried back and forth between the shuttle files. The receiving player should not start until the ball carrier is almost up to him. A player, after handing the ball to the front player of the other file, continues around and joins that file.

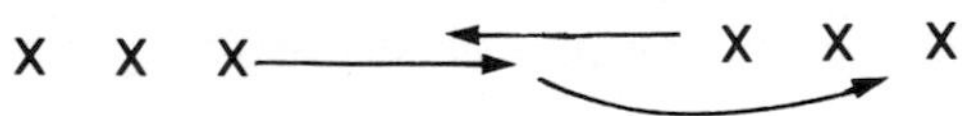

FIGURE 28.13. Ball exchange drill

Combination

Formation: Regular offensive formation with passer, center, end, and ball chaser

Players: Four to eight

Supplies: A football

Passing, centering, and receiving skills are combined in one drill. Each player, after her turn, rotates to the next spot. A minimum of four players is needed. The center player centers the ball to the passer; the passer passes the ball to the end; the end receives the pass; and the ball chaser retrieves the ball if missed by the end, or takes a pass from the end (if she caught the ball) and carries the ball to the center spot, which is her next assignment (Figure 28.14).

The rotation follows the path of the ball. This means that the rotation system moves from center to passer to end to ball chaser to center. Extra players should be stationed behind the passer for their turns.

One-on-One Defensive Drill

Formation: Center, passer, end, defender

Players: Eight to ten

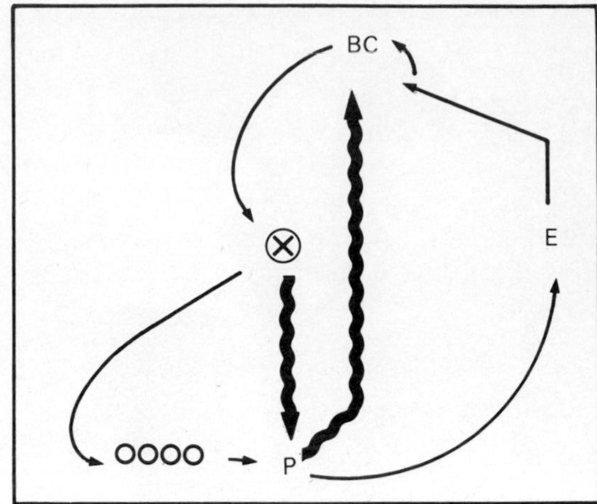

FIGURE 28.14. Combination drill

Supplies: A football

The one-on-one defensive drill is as old as football itself. A defensive player stands about 8 yd back, waiting for an approaching end. The passer tries to complete the pass to the end while the defender tries to break up the pass or intercept the ball. One defender should practice against all of the players and then rotate (Figure 28.15). The passer must be able to pass well, or this drill has little value.

Variation: The drill can be played with two ends and two defenders. The passer throws to the end who appears to be the most unguarded.

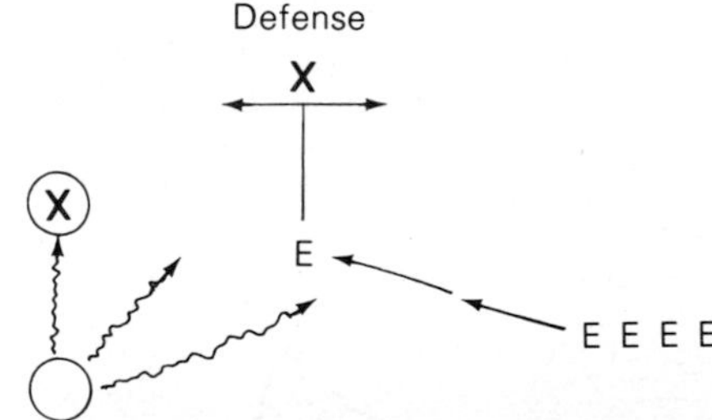

FIGURE 28.15. One-on-one defensive drill

Punt Return

Formation: Center, kicker, two lines of ends, and receivers

Players: 10 to 20

Supplies: A football, a flag for each player

The object of the drill is for the receiver to catch a punted ball and return it to the line of scrimmage while two ends attempt to pull a flag or make a tag. Two ends are ready to run downfield. The center snaps the ball to the kicker, who punts the ball downfield to the punt receiver. The ends cannot cross the line of scrimmage until the ball has been kicked. Each end makes two trips downfield as a "tackler" before rotating to the punt receiving position.

Teaching Suggestions: An effective punter is necessary for this drill. Only children with the degree of skill required to punt far enough downfield should be permitted to kick. It is also important for the ends to wait until the ball is kicked, or they will be downfield too soon for the receiver to have a fair chance of making a return run.

Stance

Formation: Squads in extended file formation

Players: Six to eight in each file

Supplies: None

The first person in each file performs and when finished with his chores, goes to the end of his file. On the command "Ready," the first person in each file assumes a football stance. The teacher can correct and make observations. On the command "Hip," the players charge forward for about 5 yd (Figure 28.16). The new player at the head of each line gets ready.

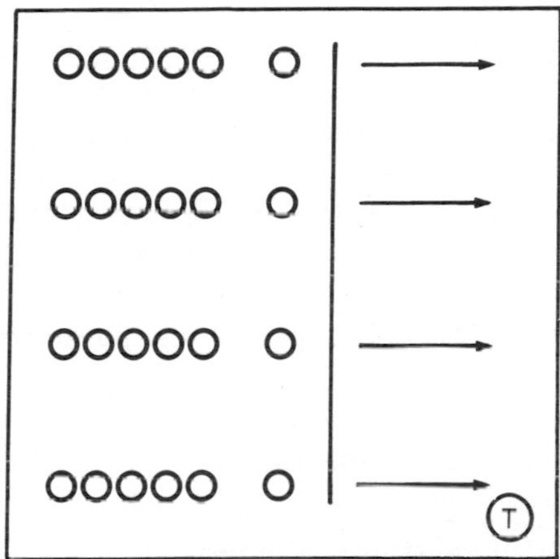

FIGURE 28.16. Stance drill

FOOTBALL ACTIVITIES

FOURTH GRADE

Football End Ball

Playing Area: A court 20 by 40 ft

Players: 9 to 12 on each team

Supplies: Footballs

Skills: Passing, catching

The court is divided in half by a center line. End zones are marked 3 ft wide, completely across the court at each end. Players on each team are divided into three groups—forwards, guards, and ends. The object is for a forward to throw successfully to one of the end-zone players. The players from each team are positioned as diagrammed in Figure 28.17. End-zone players take positions in one of the end zones. Their forwards and guards then occupy the half of the court farthest from this end zone. The forwards are near the center line, and the guards are back near the end zone of their half of the court.

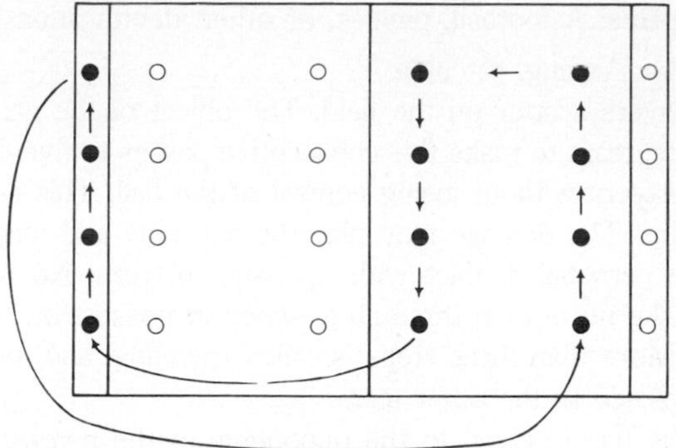

FIGURE 28.17. Player positions for Football End Ball

The ball is put into play with a center jump between the two tallest opposing forwards. When a team gets the ball, the forwards try to throw over the heads of the opposing team to an end-zone player. To score, the ball must be caught by an end-zone player with *both feet* inside the zone. No moving with the ball is permitted by any player. After each score, play is resumed by a jump ball at the center line.

A penalty results in loss of the ball to the other team. Penalties are assessed for the following.

1. Holding a ball for more than 5 seconds
2. Stepping over the end line or stepping over the center line into the opponent's territory
3. Pushing or holding another player

In case of an out-of-bounds ball, the ball belongs to the team that did not cause it to go out. The nearest player retrieves the ball at the sideline and returns it to a player of the proper team.

Teaching Suggestions: Fast, accurate passing is to be encouraged. Players in the end zones must practice jumping high to catch the ball while still landing with both feet inside the end-zone area. A system of rotation is desirable. Each time a score is made, players on that team can rotate one person. (See Figure 28.17.)

To outline the end zones, some instructors use folding mats (4 by 7 ft or 4 by 8 ft). Three or four mats forming each end zone make a definite area and eliminate the problem of defensive players (guards) stepping into the end zone.

Five Passes (Football)

Playing Area: Football field or other defined area

Players: Six to ten on each team

Supplies: A football, pinnies, or other identification

Skills: Passing, catching

Players scatter on the field. The object of the game is for one team to make five consecutive passes to five different players without losing control of the ball. This scores 1 point. The defense may play the ball only and may not make personal contact with opposing players. No player can take more than three steps when in possession of the ball. More than three steps is called traveling, and the ball is awarded to the other team.

The ball is given to the opponents at the nearest out-of-bounds line for traveling, minor contact fouls, after a point has been scored, and for causing the ball to go out-of-bounds. No penalty is assigned when the ball hits the ground. It remains in play, but the five-pass sequence is interrupted and must start again. Jump balls are called when the ball is tied up or when there is a pileup. The official should call out the pass sequence.

FIFTH GRADE

Kick-Over

Playing Area: Football field with a 10-yd end zone

Players: Six to ten on each team

Supplies: A football

Skills: Kicking, catching

Teams are scattered on opposite ends of the field. The object is to punt the ball over the other team's goal line. If the ball is caught in the end zone, no score results. A ball kicked into the end zone and not caught scores a goal. If the ball is kicked beyond the end zone on the fly, a score is made regardless of whether the ball is caught.

Play is started by one team with a punt from a point 20 to 30 ft in front of its own goal line. On a punt, if the ball is not caught, the team must kick from the spot of recovery. If the ball is caught, three long strides are allowed to advance the ball for a kick.

Teaching Suggestion: The player kicking next should move quickly to the area from which the ball is to be kicked. Players should be numbered and should kick in rotation. If the players do not kick in rotation, one or two aggressive players will dominate the game.

Variation: Scoring can be made only by a dropkick across the goal line.

Fourth Down

Playing Area: Half of a football field or equivalent space

Players: Six to eight on each team

Supplies: A football

Skills: Most football skills, except kicking and blocking

Every play is a fourth down, which means that the play must score or the team loses the ball. No kicking is permitted, but players may pass at any time from any spot and in any direction. There can be a series of passes on any play, either from behind or beyond the line of scrimmage.

The teams line up in an offensive football formation. To start the game, the ball is placed in the center of the field, and the team that wins the coin toss has the chance to put the ball into play. The ball is put into play by centering. The back receiving the ball runs or passes to any of his teammates. The one receiving the ball has the same privilege. No blocking is permitted. After each touchdown, the ball is brought to the center of the field, and the team against which the score was made puts the ball into play.

To down a runner or pass receiver, a two-handed touch above the waist is made. The back first receiving the ball from the center has immunity from tagging, provided that she does not try to run. All defensive players must stay 10 ft away unless she runs. The referee should wait for a reasonable length of time for the back to pass or run. If the ball is still held beyond that time, the referee should call out, "Ten seconds." The back must then throw or run within 10 seconds or be rushed by the defense.

The defensive players scatter to cover the receivers. They can use a one-on-one defense, with each player covering an offensive player, or a zone defense.

Since the team with the ball loses possession after each play, the following rules are used to determine where the ball should be placed when the other team takes possession.

1. If a ball carrier is tagged with two hands above the waist, the ball goes to the other team at that spot.

2. If an incomplete pass is made from *behind* the line of scrimmage, the ball is given to the other team at the spot where the ball was put into play.

3. Should an incomplete pass be made by a player *beyond* the line of scrimmage, the ball is brought to the spot from which it was thrown.

Teaching Suggestions: The team in possession should be encouraged to pass as soon as is practical, because children tire from running around to become free for a pass. The defensive team can score by intercepting a pass. Since passes can be made at any time, on interception the player should look down the field for a pass to a teammate.

Variation: The game can be called Third Down, with the offensive team having two chances to score.

SIXTH GRADE

Football Box Ball

Playing Area: Football field 50 yd long

Players: 8 to 16 on each team

Supplies: A football, team colors

Skills: Passing, catching

Five yards beyond each goal is a 6-by-6-ft square, which is the box. The teams should be marked so they can be distinguished. The game is similar to End Ball in that the teams try to make a successful pass to the captain in the box.

To begin the play, players are onside, which means that they are on opposite ends of the field. One team, losing the toss, kicks off from its own 10-yd line to the other team. The game then becomes a kind of keep-away, with either team trying to secure or retain possession of the ball until a successful pass can be made to the captain in the box. The captain must catch the ball on the fly and still keep both feet in the box. This scores a touchdown.

A player may run sideward or backward when in possession of the ball. Players may not run forward but are allowed momentum (two steps) if receiving or intercepting a ball. The penalty for illegal forward movement while in possession of the ball is loss of the ball to the opponents, who take it out-of-bounds.

The captain is allowed only three attempts to score or one goal. If either occurs, another player is rotated into the box. On any incomplete pass or failed attempt to get the ball to the captain, the team loses the ball. If a touchdown is made, the team brings the ball back to its 10-yd line and kicks off to the other team. If the touchdown attempt is not successful, the ball is given out-of-bounds on the end line to the other team.

Any out-of-bounds ball is put into play by the team that did not cause the ball to go out-of-bounds. No team can score from a throw-in from out-of-bounds.

In case of a tie ball, a jump ball is called at the spot. The players face off as in a jump ball in basketball.

Players must play the ball and not the individual. For unnecessary roughness, the player is sidelined until a pass is thrown to the other team's captain. The ball is awarded to the offended team out-of-bounds.

On the kickoff, all players must be onside, that is, behind the ball when it is kicked. If the kicking team is called offside, the ball is awarded to the other team out-of-bounds at the center line. After the kickoff, players may move to any part of the field. On the kickoff, the ball must travel 10 yd before it can be recovered by either team. A kickoff outside or over the end line is treated as any other out-of-bounds ball.

A ball hitting the ground remains in play as long as it is in bounds. Players may not bat or kick a free ball. The penalty is loss of the ball to the other team out-of-bounds. Falling on the ball also means loss of the ball to the other team.

Teaching Suggestion: A 4-by-7-ft or a 4-by-8-ft folding tumbling mat can be used to define the box where the captain must stand to catch the ball for a score.

Flag Football

Playing Area: Field 30 by 60 yd

Players: Six to nine on a team

Supplies: A football, two flags per player (about 3 in. wide and 24 in. long)

Skills: All football skills

The field is divided into three zones by lines marked off at 20-yd intervals. There also should be two end zones, from 5 to 10 yd in width, defining the area behind the goal in which passes may be caught. Flag Football is played with two flags on each player. The flag is a length of cloth that is hung from the side at the waist of each player. To down (stop) a player with the ball, one of the flags must be pulled.

Flag Football should rarely, if ever, be played with 11 players on a side. This results in a crowded field and leaves little room to maneuver. If 6 or 7 are on a team, 4 players are required to be on the line of scrimmage. For 8 or 9 players, 5 offensive players must be on the line.

The game consists of two halves. A total of 25 plays makes up each half. All plays count in the 25, except the try for the point after a touchdown and a kickoff out-of-bounds.

The game is started with a kickoff. The team winning the coin toss has the option of selecting the goal it wishes to defend or choosing to kick or receive. The loser of the toss takes the option not exercised by the first team. The kickoff is from the goal line, and all players on the kicking team must be onside. The kick must cross the first zone line or it does not count as a play. A kick that is kicked out-of-bounds (and is not touched by the receiving team) must be kicked over. A second consecutive kick out-of-bounds gives the ball to the receiving team in the center of the field. The kickoff may not be recovered by the kicking team unless caught and then fumbled by the receivers.

A team has four downs to move the ball into the next zone or they lose the ball. If the ball is legally advanced into the last zone, then the team has four downs to score. A ball on the line between zones is considered in the more forward zone.

Time-outs are permitted only for injuries or when called by the officials. Unlimited substitutions are permitted. Each must report to the official.

The team in possession of the ball usually huddles to make up the play. After any play, the team has 30 seconds to put the ball into play after the referee gives the signal.

Blocking is done with the arms close to the body. Blocking must be done from the front or side, and blockers must stay on their feet.

A player is down if one of her flags has been pulled. The ball carrier must make an attempt to avoid the defensive player and is not permitted to run over or through the defensive player. The tackler must play the flags and not the ball carrier. Good officiating is needed, because defensive players may attempt to hold or grasp the ball carrier until they are able to remove one of her flags.

All forward passes must be thrown from behind the line of scrimmage. All players on the field are eligible to receive and intercept passes.

All fumbles are dead at the spot of the fumble. The first player who touches the ball on the ground is ruled to have recovered the fumble. When the ball is centered to a back, she must gain definite possession of it before a fumble can be called. She is allowed to pick up a bad pass from the center when she does not have possession of the ball.

All punts must be announced. Neither team can cross the line of scrimmage until the ball is kicked. Kick receivers may run or use a lateral pass. They cannot make a forward pass after receiving a kick.

A pass caught in an end zone scores a touchdown. The player must have control of the ball in the end zone. A ball caught beyond the end zone is out-of-bounds and is considered an incomplete pass.

A touchdown scores 6 points, a completed pass or run after touchdown scores 1 point, and a safety scores 2 points. A point after touchdown is made from a distance of 3 ft from the goal line. One play (pass or run) is allowed for the extra point.

Any ball kicked over the goal line is ruled a touchback and is brought out to the 20-yd line to be put into play by the receiving team. A pass intercepted behind the goal line can be a touchback if the player does not run it out, even if she is tagged behind her own goal line.

A penalty of 5 yd is assessed for the following.

1. Being offside.
2. Delay of game (too long in huddle).
3. Failure of substitute to report.
4. Passing from a spot not behind line of scrimmage. (This also results in loss of down.)
5. Stiff-arming by the ball carrier, or not avoiding a defensive player.
6. Failure to announce intention to punt.
7. Shortening the flag in the belt, or playing without flags in proper position.
8. Faking the ball by the center, who must center the pass on the first motion.

The following infractions are assessed a 15-yd loss.

1. Holding, illegal tackling.
2. Illegal blocking.
3. Unsportsmanlike conduct. (This also can result in disqualification.)

Teaching Suggestions: Specifying 25 plays per half eliminates the need for timing and lessens arguments about a team's taking too much time in the huddle. Using the zone system makes the first-down yardage point definite and eliminates the need for a chain to mark off the 10 yd needed for a first down.

Pass Ball

Playing Area: Field 30 by 60 yd

Players: Six to nine on a team

Supplies: A football, flags (optional)

Skills: All football skills, especially passing and catching

Pass Ball is a more open game than Flag Football. The game is similar to Flag Football with these differences.

1. The ball may be passed at any time. It can be thrown at any time beyond the line of scrimmage, immediately after an interception, during a kickoff, or during a received kick.
2. Four downs are given to score a touchdown.
3. A two-handed touch on the back is used instead of pulling a flag. Flags can be used, however.
4. If the ball is thrown from behind the line of scrimmage and results in an incomplete pass, the ball is down at the previous spot on the line of scrimmage. If the pass originates otherwise and is incomplete, the ball is placed at the spot from which this pass was thrown.
5. Since the ball can be passed at any time, no downfield blocking is permitted. A player may screen the ball carrier but cannot make a block. Screening is defined as running between the ball carrier and the defense.

FOOTBALL SKILL TESTS

Tests for football skills cover centering, passing, and kicking (punting).

CENTERING

Each player is given five trials to center at a target. The target should be stationed 6 yd behind the center. Some suggestions for targets follow.

1. An old tire can be suspended so the bottom of the tire is about 2 ft above the ground. For centering the ball through the tire, 2 points are scored. For hitting the tire but not going through it, 1 point is scored. The possible total is 10 points.
2. A baseball pitching target from the softball program can be used. Scoring is the same as with the tire target.
3. A 2-by-3-ft piece of plywood is held by a player at the target line in front of his body, with the upper edge even with the shoulders. The target is held stationary and is not to be moved during the centering. For hitting the target, 1 point is scored. The possible total is 5 points.

PASSING FOR ACCURACY

To test accuracy in passing, each player is given five throws from a minimum distance of 15 yd at a tire suspended at about shoulder height. (To make the tire fairly stable, it can be suspended from goal posts or from volleyball standards.) As skill increases, increase the distance.

For throwing through the tire, 2 points are scored. For hitting the tire but not passing through, 1 point is scored. The possible total is 10 points.

PASSING FOR DISTANCE

Each player is allotted three passes to determine how far he can throw a football. The longest throw is measured to the nearest foot. Reserve the test for a relatively calm day, because the wind can be quite a factor (for or against the player) in this test.

The passes should be made on a field marked off in 5-yd intervals. Use markers made from tongue depressors to indicate the first pass distance. If a later throw is longer, the marker should be moved to that point. When individual markers are used, the members of a squad can complete the passing turns before measuring.

KICKING FOR DISTANCE

Punting, place-kicking, and drop-kicking can be measured for distance by using techniques similar to those described for passing for distance.

FLAG FOOTBALL FORMATIONS

A variety of offensive formations are shown in Figure 28.18, including the T-formation. The T-formation has limited strategical use in Flag Football, because the passer (i.e., the quarterback) is handicapped by being too close to the center. Emphasis should be on using a variety of formations and on spread formations, with flankers and ends positioned out beyond normal placement.

The following formations are based on a nine-player team, with four in the backfield and five on the line. The formations will vary if the number on each team is decreased. Presenting a variety of formations to the children

Balanced (tight ends):

E O X O E

Unbalanced right (tight ends):

E X O O E

Line over right (tight end):

X E O O E

Right end out (can be one or both):

E O X O (5 yards) E

Right end wide (can be one or both):

E O X O (15 yards) E

Right end wide, left end out (can be reversed):

E (5 yards) O X O (15 yards) E

Spread (3 to 5 yards between each line position):

E O X O E

FIGURE 28.18. Offensive line formations

```
Single wing:
          E O X O E
                     B
                B
               B
             B

Double wing:
          E O X O E
     B          B        B
            B

Punt:
          E O X O E
           B  B
                B
            B

Flanker right:
          E O X O E
                B
               B        B
             B

Wing right, flanker left:
          E O X O E
                        B
     B         B
            B

Wing right, flanker right:
          E O X O E
                    B        B
               B
            B

T-formation (regular):
          E O X O E
             B
          B  B  B

Wing T:
          E O X O E
             B          B
            B B

Spread:
          E O X O E
     B         B                B
              B

Shotgun:
          E O X O E
      B                 B
             B
               B
```

FIGURE 28.19. Offensive backfield formations

makes the game more interesting. Backfield formations can be right or left (Figure 28.19).

OFFENSIVE LINE FORMATIONS

Only the formation to the right is presented. The center is indicated by an X, backs by B, ends by E, and line positions by O.

OFFENSIVE BACKFIELD FORMATIONS

The formations diagrammed in Figure 28.19 can be combined with any of the offensive line formations. For purposes of clarity, however, the illustrations for all formations show a balanced line with tight ends.

PASS PATTERNS

The pass patterns illustrated in Figure 28.20 may be run by the individual pass catcher, whether she occupies a line position or is a back. They are particularly valuable in practice, when the pass receiver informs the passer of her pattern.

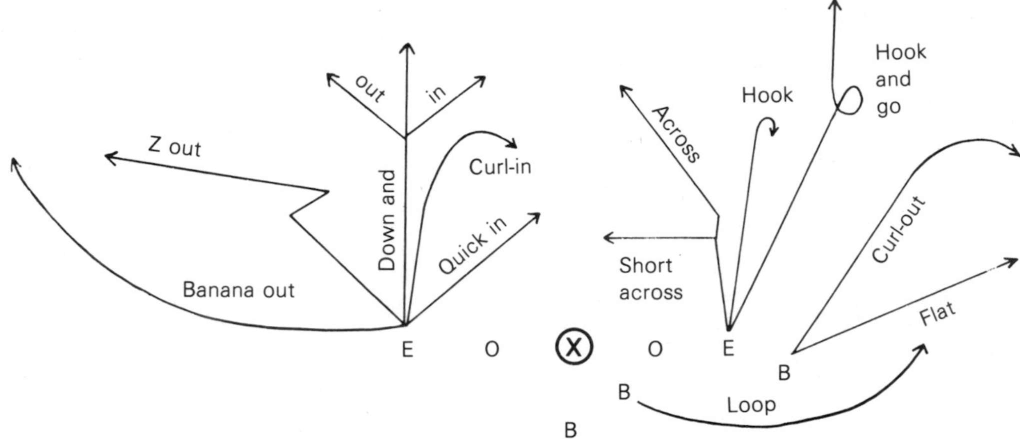

FIGURE 28.20. Pass patterns

CHAPTER 29

Hockey

Hockey is a fast-moving game that can be adapted for use in the elementary school. Hockey at the elementary level is a lead-up to ice hockey as well as to field hockey, which is popular among girls and women. With a plastic puck, hockey can be played indoors. Outdoors, a plastic whiffle ball is used (Figure 29.1). Play can be mixed, with boys and girls playing on an equal basis. Shin guards are not needed in elementary school hockey.

Success at hockey demands much running and team play. Children should develop good fundamental skills and learn position play, rather than the disorganized "everyone chase the puck" style of hockey often played in schools.

FIGURE 29.1. Hockey equipment

INSTRUCTIONAL EMPHASIS AND SEQUENCE

Table 29.1 lists the hockey activities sequence for the 4th through 6th grade. Emphasis is on fundamental skills needed to play the game of hockey.

FOURTH GRADE

In the 4th grade, little strategy is introduced. Drills are used to develop the fundamental skills. Learning to dribble loosely, fielding the ball, and making short passes should receive the most attention.

FIFTH GRADE

In the 5th grade, skill development continues, with more emphasis on ball control and passing accuracy. Lead-up games that use the skills involved in regulation hockey are played. The drills presented are designed to foster team play.

SIXTH GRADE

At the 6th-grade level, strategy for successful play is emphasized. The rules of regulation hockey are introduced, and the actual game is played. Skills should be reviewed and practiced through the use of selected drills and lead-up games.

TABLE 29.1. SUGGESTED HOCKEY PROGRAM

	Fourth Grade	Fifth Grade	Sixth Grade
Skills	Gripping and carrying the stick Front field Quick hit Goalkeeping	Controlled dribble Side field Tackle Dodging Face-off	Driving Jab shot
Knowledge	Simple rules	Ball handling and passing strategy	The game of hockey Team play and strategy
Activities	Circle Keep-Away Star Wars Hockey Modified Hockey	Goalkeeper Hockey Sideline Hockey	Regulation elementary hockey
Skill Tests		Passing for accuracy Dribbling for speed	Fielding Driving for distance

HOCKEY SKILLS

GRIPPING AND CARRYING THE STICK

The hockey stick should be held with both hands and carried as low to the ground as possible. The basic grip puts the left hand at the top of the stick and the right hand 8 to 12 in. below the left hand (Figure 29.2). The player should learn to carry the stick to the right of the body, with the blade close to the ground, while running. To ensure accuracy as well as safety, the stick must not be swung above waist height.

FIGURE 29.2. Gripping and carrying

DRIBBLING

Loose Dribble

The loose dribble is an elementary form of moving the ball under control. It demands less skill than controlled dribbling. In loose dribbling, the ball is pushed 10 to 15 ft in front of the player. The player then runs to the ball and gives it another push, repeating the sequence. This type of dribble is used in open-field play when there is little chance that an opponent will intercept the ball. The loose dribble also allows skilled players to run at maximum speed. The ball must be pushed with the flat side of the blade and kept in front of the body.

Controlled Dribble

The controlled dribble consists of a series of short taps in the direction in which the player chooses to move. The hands should be spread 10 to 14 in. apart to gain greater control of the stick. As the player becomes more skilled, the hands can be moved closer together. The stick is turned so the blade faces the ball. The grip should not be changed, but rather, the hands should be rotated until the back of the left hand and the palm of the right hand face the ball (Figure 29.3). The ball can then be tapped just far enough in front of the player to keep it away from the feet but not more than one full stride away from the stick. The emphasis should be on controlling the ball during heavy traffic so opposing players cannot easily intercept it.

FIELDING

The term *fielding* refers to stopping the ball and controlling it. Fielding the ball in hockey is as important as catching the ball in basketball. As a skill, it requires much practice.

FIGURE 29.3. Starting the dribble

Front Field

For the front field, the student must keep an eye on the ball, move to a point in line with its path, and extend the flat side of the blade forward to meet the ball (Figure 29.4). The faster the ball approaches, the more the player must learn to give with the stick to absorb the momentum of the ball. The player should field the ball in front of the body and not permit it to get too close.

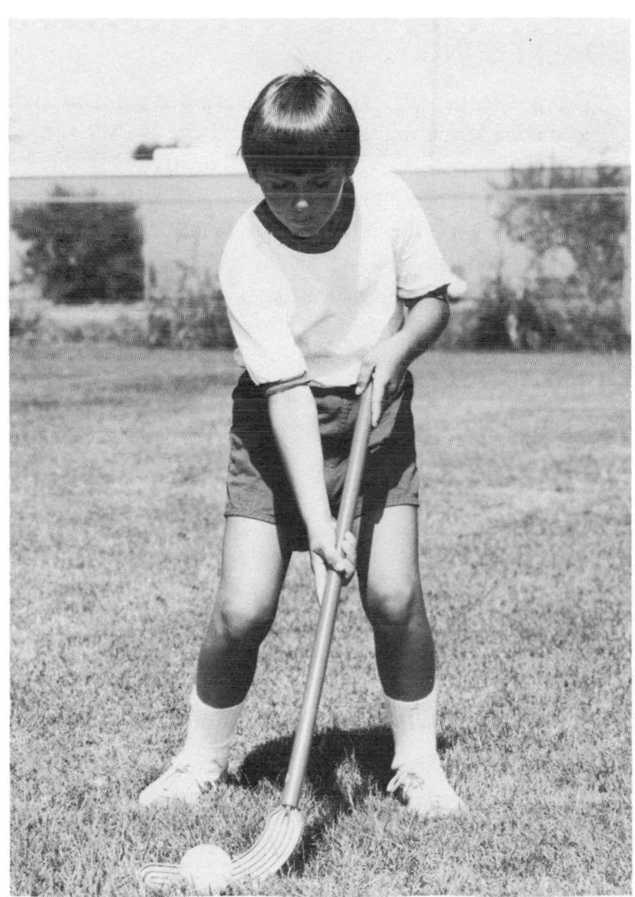

FIGURE 29.4. Front field position

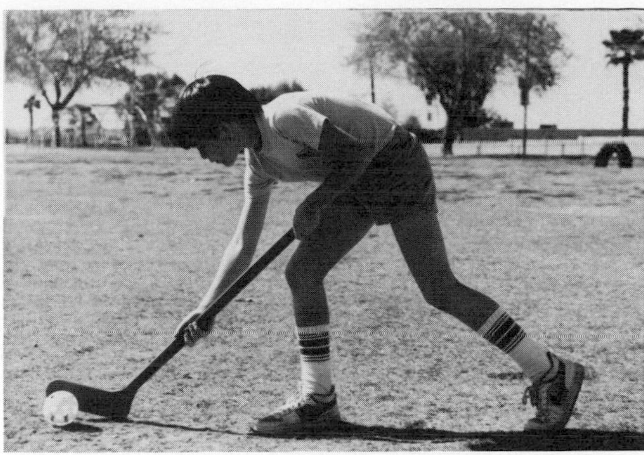

FIGURE 29.5. Side field position

Side Field

A ball approaching from the left or right side is more difficult to field than one approaching from the front. When the ball is approaching from the player's left, he must allow the ball to travel in front of his body before fielding it. If the ball is approaching from the right, it must be intercepted before it crosses in front of his body (Figure 29.5). The player's feet should be pointed in the direction in which he plans to move after controlling the ball. Regardless of the direction of the ball, the side of the blade must always be used to field it.

QUICK HIT

The quick hit is a short pass that usually occurs from the dribble. It should be taught before driving, because the quick hit requires accuracy rather than distance. The player spreads the feet with toes pointed slightly forward when striking. He approaches the ball with the stick held low and brings the stick straight back, in line with the intended direction of the hit. The hands should be the same distance apart as in the carrying position, and the stick should be lifted no higher than waist level. The player's right hand guides the stick down and through the ball. The head should be kept down with the eyes on the ball. A short follow-through occurs after contact.

TACKLING

The tackle is a means of taking the ball away from an opponent. The tackler moves toward the opponent with the stick held low. The tackle is timed so the blade of the stick is placed against the ball when the ball is off the

FIGURE 29.6. Tackling

opponent's stick (Figure 29.6). The tackler then quickly dribbles or passes in the direction of the goal. Throwing the stick or striking carelessly at the ball should be discouraged. Players need to remember that a successful tackle is not always possible.

DODGING

Dodging is a means of evading a tackler and maintaining control of the ball. The player dribbles the ball directly at the opponent. At the last instant, the ball is pushed to one side of the tackler, depending on the direction the player is planning to dodge. If the ball is pushed to the left, the player should move around the right side of the opponent to regain control of the ball, and vice versa. Selecting the proper instant to push the ball is the key to successful dodging. Dodging should not be attempted if a pass would be more effective.

DRIVING

Driving (Figure 29.7) is used to hit the ball moderate to long distances and to shoot at the goal. It differs from the quick hit in that the hands are brought together more toward the end of the stick. This gives the leverage necessary to apply greater force to the ball and results in more speed and greater distance. The swing and hit are similar to the quick hit. Stick control should be stressed so that wild swinging does not occur.

FIGURE 29.7. Driving

FACE-OFF

The face-off is used at the start of the game, after a goal, or when the ball is stopped from further play by opposing players. The face-off is taken by two players, each facing a sideline, with their right sides facing the goal that their team is defending. Each player hits the ground on her side of the ball and the opponent's stick over the ball, alternately, three times. After the third hit, the ball is played, and each player attempts to control the ball or to pass it to a teammate. The right hand can be moved down the stick to facilitate a quick, powerful movement. An alternate means of starting action is for a referee to drop the ball between the players' sticks.

JAB SHOT

The jab shot is used only when a tackle is not possible. It is a one-handed, poking shot that attempts to knock the ball away from an opponent.

GOALKEEPING

The goalkeeper may kick the ball, stop it with any part of the body, or allow it to rebound off the body or hand. He may not, however, hold the ball or throw it toward the other end of the playing area. The goalkeeper is positioned in front of the goal line and moves between the goal posts (Figure 29.8). When a ball is hit toward the goal, the goalkeeper should attempt to move in front of the ball and to keep his feet together. This allows the body

FIGURE 29.8. The goalie in position

to block the ball should the stick miss it. After the block, the ball is passed immediately to a teammate.

INSTRUCTIONAL PROCEDURES

1. For many children, hockey is a new experience. Few have played the game and many may never have seen a game. Showing a film of a hockey game as an introduction may be helpful.

2. Since few children have had the opportunity to develop skills elsewhere, it is necessary to teach the basic skills in a sequential manner and to allow ample time in practice sessions for development.

3. Hockey is a rough game when children are not taught the proper methods of stick handling. They need to be reminded often to use caution and good judgment when handling hockey sticks.

4. Ample equipment increases individual practice time and facilitates skill development. A stick and a ball or puck for each child are desirable.

5. If hockey is played on a gym floor, a plastic puck should be used. If played on a carpeted area or outdoors, a whiffle ball is used. An 8-ft folding mat set on end makes a satisfactory goal.

6. Hockey is a team game that is more enjoyable for all when the players pass to open teammates. Excessive control of the ball by an individual should be discouraged.

7. An individual who is restricted to limited activity can be designated as a goalkeeper. This is an opportunity for a handicapped child to participate and receive reinforcement from her peers. An asthmatic child, for example, might serve as a goalkeeper.

8. Fatigue may be a problem, for hockey is a running game that demands agility and endurance. Children should be in reasonably good physical condition to participate. Rotation and rest periods help prevent fatigue.

HOCKEY DRILLS

DRIBBLING DRILLS

1. Successful hockey play demands good footwork and proper stick handling. To develop these skills, all players can spread out on the field, carrying the stick in proper position, in a group mimetic drill. On command, players move forward, backward, and to either side. Quick reactions and good footwork are the focus.

2. Each player with a ball practices dribbling individually. Dribbling should be practiced first at controlled speeds and then at faster speeds as skill develops.

3. Players can practice in pairs, with their partners standing about 20 ft apart. One player dribbles the ball toward a partner, goes around the partner, and returns to the starting spot (Figure 29.9). The ball is then passed to the partner,

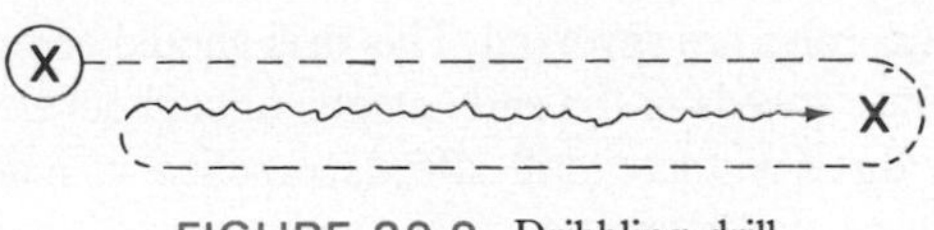

FIGURE 29.9. Dribbling drill

who moves in a similar manner. A shuttle type of formation can be used with three players.

PASSING AND FIELDING DRILLS

1. In pairs, about 20 ft apart, players pass the ball *quickly* back and forth. Emphasis should be on passing immediately after fielding the ball. The cue phrase might be "Field, pass."

2. One player passes the ball to his partner, who fields the ball, dribbles twice, and passes back to the other. Passes should be fielded from various angles and from the right and left side.

3. The shuttle turn-back formation can be used in which two files of four or five players face each other. The first person in the file passes to the first person in the other file, who in turn fields the ball and returns the pass. Each player, when finished, goes to the end of the file.

4. The downfield drill is useful for polishing passing and fielding skills while moving. Three files of players start at one end of the field. One player from each file proceeds downfield, passing to and fielding from the others until the other end of the field is reached. A goal shot can be made at this point. The players should remain close together for short passes until a high level of skill is reached.

5. Driving for distance and accuracy can be practiced with a partner.

DODGING AND TACKLING DRILLS

1. Players are spread out on the field, each with a ball. On command, they dribble left, right, forward, and backward. On the command "Dodge," the players dodge an imaginary tackler. Players should concentrate on ball control and dodging in all directions.

2. Three players form the drill configuration as diagrammed in Figure 29.10. Player number 1 has the ball in front, approaches the cone (which represents a defensive player), dodges around the cone, and passes to player number 2, who repeats the dodging maneuver in the opposite direction. Number 2 passes to number 3, and the drill continues in that manner.

3. Players work in pairs. One partner dribbles toward the other, who attempts to make a tackle. If the tackle is

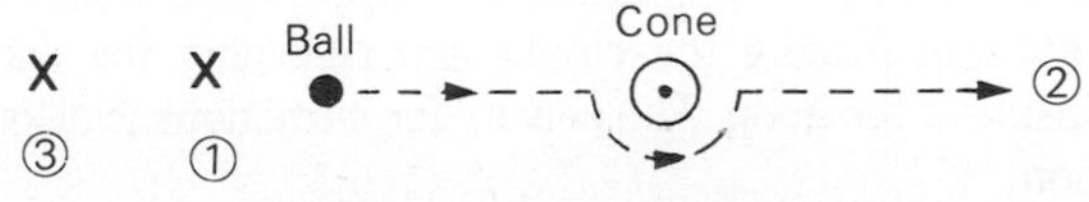

FIGURE 29.10. Shuttle-type drill

successful, roles are reversed. This drill should be practiced at moderate speeds in the early stages of skill development.

4. A three-on-three drill affords practice in many skill areas. Three players are on offense and three are on defense. The offense can concentrate on passing, dribbling, and dodging, while the defense concentrates on tackling. A point is given to the offense when they reach the opposite side of the field. The defensive team becomes the offensive team after a score.

HOCKEY ACTIVITIES

FOURTH GRADE

Circle Keep-Away

Playing Area: A 20- to 25-ft circle

Players: Eight to ten

Supplies: One stick per person, a ball or puck

Skills: Passing, fielding

Players are spaced evenly around the circle with one player in the center. The object of the game is to keep the player in the center from touching the puck. The puck is passed back and forth, with emphasis on accurate passing and fielding. If the player in the center touches the puck, the player who last passed the puck takes the place of the center player. A change of players also can be made after a passing or fielding error.

Star Wars Hockey

Playing Area: Playground, gymnasium

Players: Four teams of equal size

Supplies: One stick per player, four balls or pucks

Skill: Dribbling

Each team forms one side of a square formation. The game is similar to Star Wars (p. 438), with the following exceptions.

1. Four pucks are used instead of Indian clubs. When a number is called, each player with that number goes to a ball and dribbles it out of the square through the spot previously occupied, around the square counterclockwise, and back to the original spot. Circles 12 in. in diameter are drawn on the floor to provide a definite place to which the puck must be returned. If the game is played outdoors, hoops can mark the spot to which the balls must be returned.

2. No player is permitted to use anything other than the stick in making the circuit and returning the ball to the inside of the hoop. The penalty for infractions is disqualification.

Modified Hockey

Playing Area: Hockey field, gymnasium

Players: 7 to 11 on each team

Supplies: One stick per person, a ball or puck

Skills: Dribbling, passing, dodging, tackling, face-off

The teams may take any position on the field as long as they remain inside the boundaries. The object of the game is to hit the ball through the opponent's goal. No goalies are used. At the start of the game and after each score, play begins with a face-off. Each goal is worth one point.

Teaching Suggestion: The distance between goal lines is flexible but should be on the long side. If making goals is too easy or too difficult, the width of the goals can be adjusted accordingly.

FIFTH GRADE

Goalkeeper Hockey

Playing Area: A square about 40 by 40 ft

Players: Two teams of equal size

Supplies: One stick per player, a ball or puck

Skills: Passing, fielding, goalkeeping

Each team occupies two adjacent sides of the square (Figure 29.11). Team members are numbered consecutively from left to right. Two or three numbers are called by the instructor. These players enter the playing area and attempt to capture the ball, which is placed in the center of the square, and to pass it through the opposing team. A point is scored when the ball goes through the opponent's side. Sideline players should concentrate on goalkeeping skills. When a score is made, the active players return to their positions, and new players are called.

Teaching Suggestions: The teacher needs to keep track of the numbers called, so all players have an equal opportunity to play. Different combinations can be called.

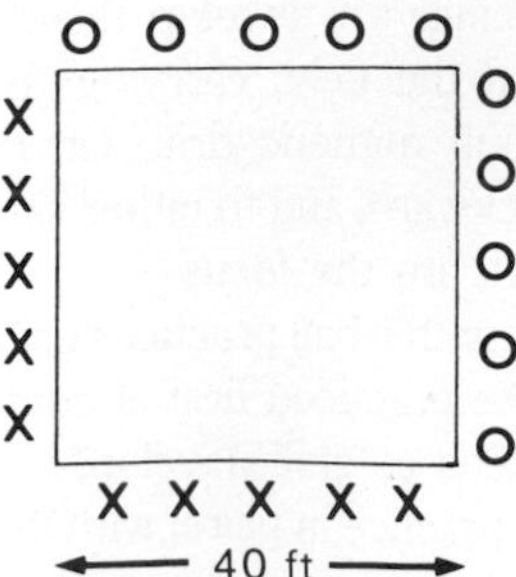

FIGURE 29.11. Team positions for Goalkeeper Hockey

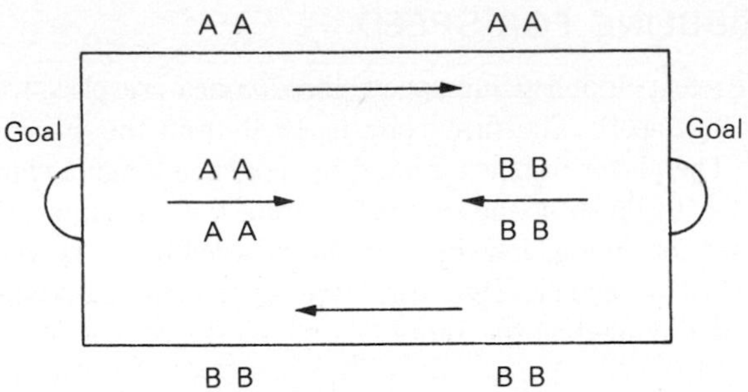

FIGURE 29.12. Team positions for Sideline Hockey

Sideline Hockey

Playing Area: Hockey field or gymnasium area, 60 by 100 ft

Players: 6 to 12 players on each team

Supplies: One hockey stick per player, a ball or puck, two 4-by-8-ft folding tumbling mats

Skills: Most hockey skills, except goaltending

Each team is divided into two groups. They are positioned as indicated in Figure 29.12, which shows eight players on each team. Half of each team is on the court; these are the active players. The others stand on the sidelines. No goalkeeper is used. A face-off at the center starts the game and puts the ball into play after each score. Each team on the field, aided by the sideline players, attempts to score a goal. The sideline players help keep the ball in bounds and can pass it onto the court to the active players. Sideline players may pass only to an active player and not to each other.

Any out-of-bounds play on a sideline belongs to the team guarding that sideline and is put into play with a pass. An out-of-bounds over the end line that does not score a goal is put into play by the team defending the goal. The group of players on the field change places with the sideline players on their team as soon as a goal is scored or after a specified time period.

Illegal touching, sideline violations, and other minor fouls result in loss of the ball to the opposition. Roughing fouls and illegal striking should result in banishment to the sideline for the remainder of the competitive period.

Teaching Suggestion: Some attention must be given to team play and passing strategies rather than all players simply charging the ball. Teams should use the sideline players by passing to them and receiving passes from them in return. Teams can be rotated, so the same two teams do not face each other continually.

SIXTH GRADE

Regulation Elementary Hockey

Playing Area: Hockey field or gymnasium area, approximately 40 to 50 ft by 75 to 90 ft

Players: Six on each team

Supplies: One stick per player, a ball or puck

Skills: All hockey skills

In a small gymnasium, the walls can serve as the boundaries. In a large gymnasium or on an outdoor field, the playing area should be delineated with traffic cones. The area should be divided in half, with a 12-ft restraining circle centered on the midline. This is where play begins at the start of the periods, after goals, or after foul shots. The official goal is 2 ft high by 6 ft wide, with a restraining area 4 ft by 8 ft around the goal to protect the goalie (Figure 29.13). Each team has a goalkeeper, who stops shots with her hands, feet, or stick; a center, who is the only player allowed to move full court and who leads offensive play (the center has her stick striped with black tape); two guards, who cannot go beyond the center line into the offensive area and who are responsible for keeping the puck out of their defensive half of the field; and two forwards, who work with the center on offensive play and who cannot go back over the center line into the defensive area.

A game consists of three periods of 8 minutes each, with a 3-minute rest between periods. Play is started with a face-off by the centers at midcourt. Other players cannot enter the restraining circle until the ball has been hit by the centers. The clock starts when the puck is put into play and runs continuously until a goal is scored or a foul is called. Substitutions can be made only when the clock is stopped. If the ball goes out-of-bounds, it is put back into play by the team that did not hit it last.

Whenever the ball passes through the goal on the ground, one point is scored. If, however, the ball crosses the goal line while in the air, it must strike against the mat or back wall to count for a score. Under no circumstances can a goal be scored on a foul. The puck can deflect off a player or equipment to score, but it cannot be kicked into the goal.

The goalkeeper may use her hands to clear the ball away from the goal, but she may not hold or throw it toward the other end of the playing area. She is charged with a foul for holding the puck or ball. The goalkeeper may be pulled from the goal area but cannot go beyond the center line. No other player may enter the restraining area without being charged with a foul.

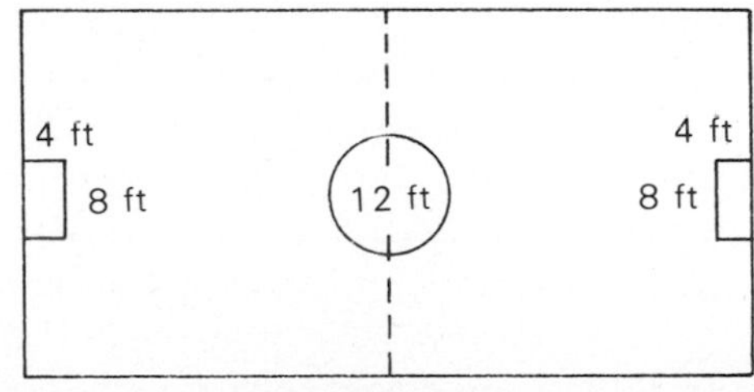

FIGURE 29.13. Regulation elementary hockey playing field

The following are fouls and are penalized by loss of the ball at the spot of the foul.

1. Illegally touching the ball with the hands
2. Swinging the stick above waist height (called *sticking*)
3. Guards or forwards moving across the center line
4. Player other than the goalie entering the restraining area
5. Goalie throwing the ball
6. Holding, stepping on, or lying on the ball

Defenders must be 5 yd back when the puck is put into play after a foul. If the spot where the foul occurred is closer than 5 yd to the goal, only the goalkeeper may defend. This ball is then put into play 5 yd directly out from the goal.

Personal fouls include any action or rough play that endangers other players. A player committing a personal foul must retire to the sidelines for 2 minutes. The following are personal fouls.

1. Hacking or striking with a stick
2. Tripping with either the foot or the stick
3. Pushing, blocking

HOCKEY SKILL TESTS

PASSING FOR ACCURACY

In passing for accuracy, the player has five attempts to pass the ball into a 3-by-3-ft target. The target can be drawn or taped on the wall, or a 3-ft square of cardboard can be used. The player must pass from a distance of 30 ft. He can approach the 30-ft restraining line in whatever fashion he chooses. Two points are awarded for each successful pass.

DRIBBLING FOR SPEED

To test dribbling for speed, three cones are placed in line 8 ft apart. The first cone is 16 ft from the starting line. The player dribbles around the cones in a figure-eight fashion to finish at the original starting line. A stopwatch is used for timing, and the score is recorded to the nearest tenth of a second. Two trials are given, and the faster trial is recorded as the score.

FIELDING

Three players are designated as passers and pass from different angles to a person being tested in fielding. The ball must be definitely stopped and controlled. The instructor can judge whether the pass was a good opportunity for the player to field. Six passes, two from each angle, are given, and one point is awarded for each successful field.

DRIVING FOR DISTANCE

Driving for distance should be tested outdoors only. A restraining line can be used as a starting point. Each player is given five trials, and the longest two attempts are recorded as the player's score. Distance is measured to the nearest foot. Players can be lined up in four or five squads behind restraining line can be used as a starting point. Each player is given five trials, and the longest two attempts are recorded as the player's score. Distance is measured to the nearest foot. Players can be lined up in four or five squads behind the restraining line. At any one time, one third of the class can measure distances and return the balls. After players have taken their five trials, they can exchange places with someone who is measuring or returning balls. The test should be done on grass, because solid ground permits the ball to roll unimpeded.

CHAPTER 30

Soccer

Soccer is a game of "educated" feet. If players are to improve their playing ability, organized practice that emphasizes handling the ball as often as possible and being in possession of the ball for as long as possible is essential for each child. Maneuvering the ball with the feet must become second nature, and this is accomplished by frequent opportunities on offense to kick, control, dribble, volley, and shoot and frequent opportunities on defense to mark, guard, tackle, and recover the ball.

Teachers should avoid the tendency to place children in soccer playing without the needed skills. Success in soccer depends on how well individual skills are coordinated in team play. Effective soccer stresses position play, in contrast to a group of children dashing around the ball like bees around a honey pot.

MODIFICATIONS OF SOCCER FOR ELEMENTARY SCHOOL CHILDREN

The 11-person game is not suitable for elementary children and should be played only as a matter of orientation. The predominant game should be Mini-Soccer, with 6 or 7 players on a side. Two games can be played crosswise on a regulation soccer field. With the exception of a penalty area and the out-of-bounds lines, the field does not have to be marked.

The official regulation soccer goal, 24 ft wide and 8 ft high, is too large for elementary play. The size should be such that teams have a reasonable chance of scoring as well as preventing a score. The suggested size is from 18 to 21 ft in width and 6 to 7 ft in height. The size can be further scaled down as determined by the character of the game. If a line of players make up the goal, the ball should be required to pass below either waist or shoulder height to count as a score.

INSTRUCTIONAL EMPHASIS AND SEQUENCE

Table 30.1 summarizes the program for the 4th through 6th grade.

FOURTH GRADE

The two basic skills in soccer are (1) controlling or stopping the ball with the foot so the ball is in a position to be kicked and (2) passing the ball with the foot to another player or to a target. Fourth-grade material should stress games and drills that facilitate practice and involvement of these fundamental skills. To maximize involvement, one ball for every two players should be available.

FIFTH GRADE

The two basic skills continue to be most important throughout the learning of the game and are developed further. To enhance control of the ball, dribbling skills are introduced and students are also taught to control the ball with other parts of the body, such as the thigh and chest. Passing should still be the major emphasis so that small-side games or Mini-Soccer, with two to five players per team, can be introduced. The basic goalkeeping skills of catching low and high balls can be taught.

TABLE 30.1. SUGGESTED SOCCER PROGRAM

	Fourth Grade	Fifth Grade	Sixth Grade
Skills	Inside of foot kick Instep kick Sole-of-the-foot control Foot trap Goalkeeping	Dribbling Outside foot kick Body control Passing Tackling	Kicking goals Kickoff (placekicking) Punting Volleying Heading
Knowledge	Simple rules	Ball control and passing	The game of soccer Team play and rules
Activities	Circle Kickball (review) Soccer Touch Ball Diagonal Soccer Dribblerama Bullseye Sideline Soccer	Pin Kickball Addition Soccer Over the Top Line Soccer Mini-Soccer	Mini-Soccer Six Spot Keepaway Regulation Soccer
Skill Tests	Sole-of-the-foot control Kicking for accuracy (from a stationary position)	Figure-eight dribbling Controlling (three types) Kicking for accuracy	Figure-eight dribbling Punting for distance Placekicking Penalty kicking Kicking for accuracy

SIXTH GRADE

Further development of the basic skills is recommended, along with the introduction of shooting, tackling, heading, jockeying, and the concept of two-touch soccer for the more advanced players. Fundamentals of team and positional play can be introduced, along with the important rules of the regular game. The 7-player game is a much better substitute for the 11-on-a-side game, as it increases player involvement.

A unit of study focusing on soccer as an international game is of value, because few American children realize how important this game is in other countries.

SOCCER SKILLS

Offensive skills that should be taught in the elementary grades are passing, kicking, controlling, dribbling, volleying (including heading), and shooting. Shooting is defined as taking a shot at the goal with the intent to score. Defensive skills include marking, guarding, jockeying, tackling, and recovering the ball.

PASSING

Balance and timing provide the key to accurate passing. The basic purposes of passing are to advance the ball to a teammate or to shoot on goal. Occasionally, a pass is used to send the ball downfield so a team has a chance to regroup, with their opponents having an equal chance to recover the ball.

The elements of accurate passing are as follows:

1. The nonkicking foot should be placed alongside the ball.

2. The head should be kept down, with the eyes focused on the ball during contact.

3. The arms should be spread for balance.

4. The kicking leg should follow through in the intended direction of the ball.

5. Kicking with the toe lacks control and accuracy, and is not used in soccer. The outside or inside of the foot makes contact with the ball.

6. All passing skills should be practiced with the left and right foot.

THE SHORT PASS

The short pass is used for accurate passing over distances of up to 15 yd. Because of the technique used, this pass is sometimes referred to as the *push pass.*

Using the Inside of the Foot

The nonkicking foot is placed well up, alongside the ball. As the kicking foot is drawn back, the toe is turned out. During the kick, the toe remains turned out so the inside of the foot is perpendicular to the line of flight. The sole is kept parallel to the ground. At contact, the knee of the kicking leg should be well forward, over the ball, and both knees should be slightly bent (Figure 30.1).

FIGURE 30.1. Preparing for an inside foot kick

Using the Outside of the Foot

The nonkicking foot is placed more to the side of the ball than for the inside foot kick, and the approach of the kicking leg is from directly behind the ball. The kicking foot is fully extended and contact with the ball is on the outside of the foot between laces and sole-line. This pass can be used effectively while running, without breaking stride, or for pushing the ball to the side.

THE LONG PASS

For longer passes, a run at the ball is usually required. The best approach is from behind the ball at a 45-degree angle—using a sweeping action with the kicking leg. Once again, the nonkicking foot is alongside the ball, with the kicking leg cocked in the backswing. Just before contact, the kicking foot is locked so the toe is down. Contact is made with the lower part of the shoe near the lower shoelaces. The passer gives the lower leg a good forward snap at the knee. A normal follow-through in the intended direction of the pass completes the action.

If the ball is contacted close to the ground, with the body leaning slightly backward, a lofted or chip pass will result. This pass is made over the opposition.

BALL CONTROL (TRAPPING)

Learning to receive a ball and how to place it in the ideal position for making a pass or shot is vital. In fact, one of the best measures of a skilled player is how quickly she can bring the ball under control by using either the feet, legs, or torso. An advanced player is able to achieve this in one smooth movement, with one touch on the ball. The second touch occurs when the pass is made.

FIGURE 30.2. Controlling with the inside of the foot

For efficient control, a large surface should be presented to the ball. On contact, the surface should be momentarily withdrawn to produce a spongelike or shock-absorbing action, which decelerates the ball and allows it to drop in an ideal position about a yard in front of the body. The pass or shot can then be made.

1. *Using the inside of the foot.* This is the most common method of control, and is used when the ball is either rolling along the ground or bouncing up to knee height. The full surface of the foot, from heel to toe, should be presented perpendicular to the ball (Figure 30.2).

2. *Using the sole of the foot.* This method of control is sometimes called "trapping the ball," and is occasionally used to stop the ball. With beginners, it is not as successful a method as the inside-of-the-foot control, because the ball can roll easily under the foot. The sole is also used to roll the ball from side to side in dribbling, and to adjust for a better passing position (Figure 30.3).

3. *Using other parts of the body.* The inside of the thigh and the chest also are used to deflect the ball downward when it is bouncing high. When deflecting the ball with the upper body, girls should cross their arms for protection.

DRIBBLING

Dribbling is moving the ball with a series of taps or pushes to cover ground and still retain control. It allows a player to change direction quickly and avoid opponents. The best contact point is the inside of the foot, but the outside of the foot will be used at faster running speeds.

FIGURE 30.3. Sole-of-the-foot control

The ball should be kept close to the player to maintain control.

HEADING

Heading is a special kind of volleying in which the direction of flight of the ball is changed through an impact with the head (Figure 30.4). In heading, the neck muscles can be used to aid in the blow. The eye must be kept on the ball until the moment of impact. The point of contact is the top of the forehead at the hairline. In preparation for contacting the ball with the head, the player should stand in stride position, with knees relaxed and trunk bent backward at the hips. At the moment of contact, the trunk moves forward abruptly, driving the forehead at the ball. Heading can be achieved in midair, and is especially useful in beating other players to the ball. This can be done by a running one-footed takeoff or a standing two-footed jump.

DEFENSIVE MANEUVERS

Tackling is a move by a player to take possession of the ball away from an opponent who is dribbling. The most

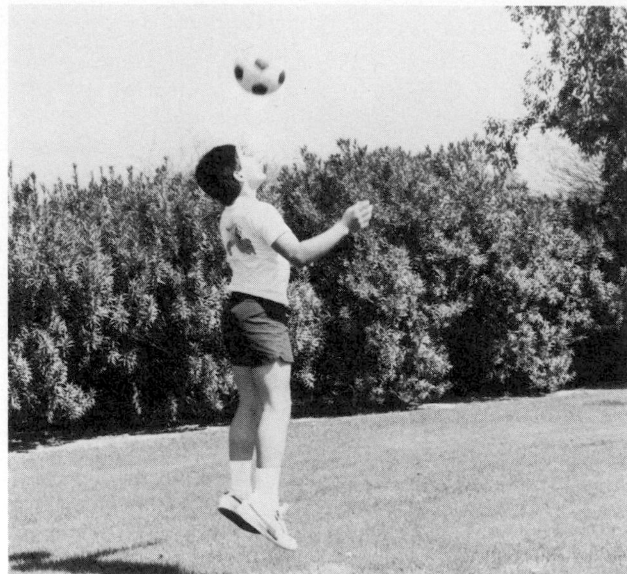

FIGURE 30.4. Heading

common tackle is the front block, which involves contacting the ball with the inside of the foot just as the opponent touches it. The tackler presents a firm instep to the ball, with his weight behind it. The stronger the contact with the ball, the greater the chance of controlling it. Body contact should be avoided, as this may constitute a foul. Other tackles may be made when running alongside the player with the ball.

How much tackling to teach in elementary school programs is a question of concern. In most cases, it is probably best to teach tackling skills that involve the defensive player's remaining on her feet. Methods like the hook slide and split slide are of little value in elementary school instructional programs.

Jockeying

Knowing when and when not to make a tackle is one of the most difficult skills to learn. A failed tackle may mean that an attacker breaks through with a free shot on goal. Often, defenders should jockey until defensive support arrives. This means backing off while staying close enough to pressure the advancing player. The defender should stay on his toes, watch the ball rather than the opponent's feet, and keep within 1 to 2 yd of the ball.

THROW-INS

The throw-in from out-of-bounds may be executed from a standing or running position. Both feet must remain on the ground, and be on or behind the line. The feet often are placed one behind the other, with the rear toe trailing along the ground. Delivery of the ball should be from behind the head, using both arms equally. Release should be from in front of the forehead with arms outstretched.

SHOOTING

Scoring is the purpose of the game, and shooting skills should be practiced both while stationary and on the run. As with passing, the inside, outside, and top of the foot can be used.

GOALKEEPING

Goalkeeping involves stopping shots by catching, stopping, or otherwise deflecting the ball. Goalkeepers should become adept at catching low rolling balls, diving on rolling balls, catching airborne balls at waist level and below (Figure 30.5), and catching airborne balls at waist height and above.

Youngsters should practice catching low rolling balls in much the same manner as a baseball outfielder does. The goalie gets down on one knee, with the body behind the ball to act as a backstop, and catches the ball with both hands, fingers pointing toward the ground.

If the goalie must dive for the ball, he should throw his body behind it and cradle it with his hands. A goalie should always try to get his body behind the ball.

When catching a ball below the waist, the thumbs should point outward and the arms reach for the ball, with body and arms giving and bringing the ball into the abdomen. For balls above waist level, the thumbs should be turned inward, arms reaching to meet the ball and giving to guide it to the midsection.

Drills for goalies should offer opportunities to catch the different shots described. All students should receive goaltending practice.

FIGURE 30.5. Goalie catching a ball below waist level

Punting

Used by the goalkeeper only, the punt can be stationary or can be done on the run. The ball is held in both hands at waist height in front of the body and directly over the kicking leg. For the stationary punt, the kicking foot is forward. A short step is taken with the kicking foot, followed by a full step on the other foot. With the knee bent and the toe extended, the kicking foot swings forward and upward. As contact is made with the ball at the instep, the knee straightens, and additional power is secured from the other leg through a coordinated rising on the toes or a hop (Figure 30.6).

The goalkeeper has an advantage if she can develop a strong placekick. Distance and accuracy are important in setting up the next attack. Over shorter distances, throwing both underhand and overhand are sometimes more accurate than kicking. A straight arm should be used for rolling or throwing the ball to players.

FIGURE 30.6. Punt

INSTRUCTIONAL PROCEDURES

1. Soccer skills must be developed if children are to participate successfully in the sport. Controlling the ball and passing should predominate in practices. Drills and activities should be organized to maximize the involvement of all children. One ball is needed for every two children.

2. Many combination drills featuring both offense and defense should be included. Enjoyment is the key to continued learning. Drills and lead-up activities can be used to make the skills challenging, but all activities should be appropriate to the developmental level of the children.

3. Small-group games (between two and five players) should be used frequently to ensure maximum activity. The number of team members can be increased as skill improves.

4. Lead-up games should encourage the use of the skills practiced in drills. For example, if long passing is the skill of the day, lead-up games requiring and rewarding long passing should be played. In the early stages of learning soccer, it may be best not to allow tackling.

5. Using cones or chalk, a grid system of 10-yd squares can be marked on a playing field. The grid can be useful when organizing drills, activities, and small-sized games.

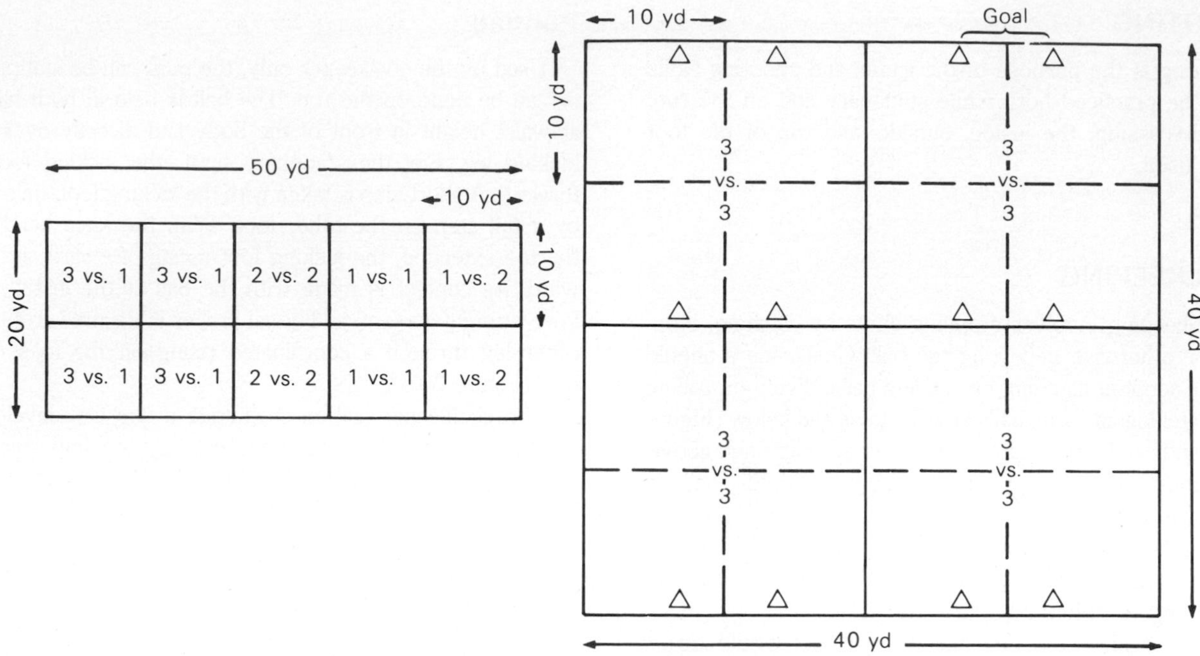

FIGURE 30.7. Examples of grid layouts and usage

The number of squares needed depends on the size of the class, but at least one square for every three students is recommended. Possible layouts are shown in Figure 30.7.

Squares can be used as confines for tackling, keeping possession, and passing diagonally or sideways. Drill and game areas can be defined easily, so a number of small-sized games can be played simultaneously.

6. Balls smaller than the regular soccer ball should be used. Molded rubber balls or partially deflated 8½-in. rubber playground balls can be used, provided that their quality is good enough to withstand the kicking. Another excellent ball for novices is the *dense* foam rubber training ball. It withstands heavy usage and does not hurt youngsters on impact. The key to soccer practice is to have plenty of balls available. Rubber balls mean more fun, because they can be kicked far, controlled easily, and even headed without discomfort. Junior-sized soccer balls are also excellent but are more expensive.

7. Soccer, with its attack and defense, can be a rough game. Rough play like pushing, shoving, kicking, and tripping must be controlled. Rules need to be strictly enforced. Attention to proper heading, volleying, and kicking techniques helps eliminate injuries that result from contacts with the ball. Players need to watch for kicked balls, which may strike them in the face or head unexpectedly. Glasses should be removed when possible, and shin guards are recommended in very competitive situations.

8. Soccer is a vigorous game, so the teacher should use methods of rotation to help rest players. Children can rotate in and out of the goalkeeper position (generally the least demanding position). Stretching should be emphasized before and after each session to minimize injuries.

9. Scoring can be modified in keeping with the children's capabilities. To score must be a challenge—neither too easy nor too difficult. To avoid arguments in situations in which the ball is to be kicked through a line of children, the height of the kick should be limited to shoulder level or below. This emphasizes an important soccer principle: control of the ball on the ground. Cones, jump standards, and similar devices can be used to mark goal outlines. Formal soccer goals are not necessary for the elementary school program.

SOCCER DRILLS

In soccer drills, two approaches should be recognized. The first is the practice of technique with no opposition from any defense. The second is the skill approach, which involves both offensive and defensive players and perhaps a target. In drills using the skill approach, the goal is to outmaneuver the opponent. Some drills begin with the technique approach and then move to the skill approach.

Individual practice can be carried on early, particularly with dribbling techniques, but most work should be with combinations of two or three students and small groups.

Communication becomes a problem when children are scattered over a playing area. One solution is a central demonstration location. On signal, children leave the soccer balls at their respective areas and come to the demonstration point for instructions.

The type of surface has a marked effect on the quality of soccer practice. Grass is the most desirable practice surface, but some schools have only hard-top surfaces. In this case, balls should be deflated slightly to approximate how they travel on grass. If space is to be restricted, the areas can be outlined by cones, beanbags, jugs, or boundary boards. Ten-yard lines on a football field make convenient grid lines to outline practice areas.

INDIVIDUAL WORK

Dribbling practice is well suited to individual work. Activity can begin by having youngsters dribble in various directions and encouraging them to make right and left turns. As a variation, children can react to signals: one whistle means turn left, two means turn right, and three means reverse direction. Ten cones or so can be scattered around the area. The children dribble around one cone clockwise and then around another cone counterclockwise.

Heading can be practiced by players tossing the ball to themselves and heading it. This is followed by a short period of dribbling and then repeated. The teacher can signal to remind youngsters to pick up the soccer ball and begin heading again.

A child can drop a ball and learn to smother it with a foot. Another gambit is to toss the ball in the air and let it bounce, followed by a kick to oneself with an instep kick so the ball can be caught. Yet another trick is to toss the ball high and use the instep kick to control the ball.

Rebounding to oneself continuously, although not actually used in the game of soccer, is an excellent way to learn ball control. (This is sometimes called foot juggling.) Begin by dropping the ball so it bounces at waist height, and then follow this pattern:

1. Rebound the ball with alternating feet, letting it bounce between contacts.

2. Play the ball twice with one foot, let it bounce, and then play it twice with the other foot.

3. Toss the ball so it can be handled with the thigh and then catch. Add successive rebounds with the thigh.

4. Play ball with the foot, thigh, head, thigh, foot, and catch.

Other combinations can be devised. The teacher needs to move slowly with these skills, for some children will find them difficult.

The foot pickup can be learned in two ways. The first is to put the ball between the feet, jump up, and hoist the ball so it can be caught. The second is the toe pickup. Put the toe on top of the ball. Pull the toe back and down, so the ball spins up the instep from which it can be hoisted to the hands.

Another bit of individual work is toe changing on top of the ball. Put the ball of the foot on top of the ball. On signal, change feet. This movement can also be done to music using the Bleking step (see p. 262–263). During the first part of the music, the rhythm is slow, slow, fast, fast, fast. During the second part of the music, players dribble in diverse directions. Repeat.

DRILLS FOR TWO PLAYERS

Many introductory drills can be practiced by paired players. Students are scattered in twos, with space needs determined by the type of drill. The pairs can sometimes be arranged in two lines so both students react to the same challenges.

One of the best ways to organize partner drills is to use grid lines, mentioned earlier, placed 10, 20, or 30 yd apart. The distance between the grids depends on the skill to be practiced. Partners position themselves opposite each other so two lines of players are formed, which gives the teacher a clear view of the class in action (Figure 30.8). This approach is recommended for introducing all new skills such as passing with both sides of the foot, ball control, and heading. Skill combinations can be used such as throw-ins by one partner, and control-and-pass by the other. Within the grids, partners can work on passing, dribbling in a confined space, keepaway, and one-on-one games.

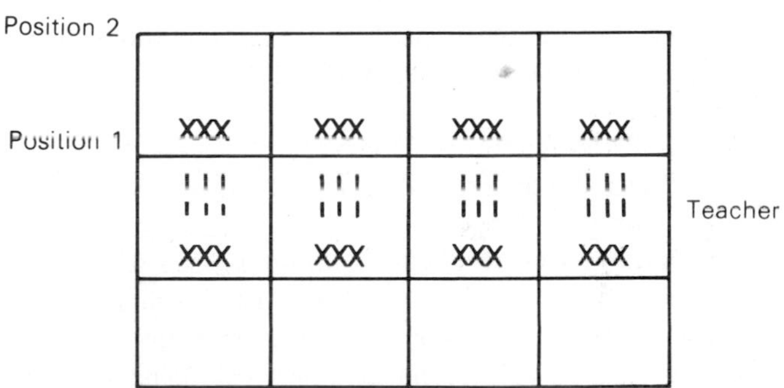

FIGURE 30.8. Class organized along grid lines

The following are examples of drills that can be used in partner formation.

1. *Dribbling, marking, and ball recovery.* Pairs are scattered, with one player in each pair having a soccer ball. That player dribbles in various directions, and the second player attempts to stay close to her (marking). As skill development occurs, the defensive player can attempt to recover the ball from the dribbler. If successful, roles are reversed.

2. *Dribbling.* One player of the pair has a ball and dribbles in different directions. On signal, she passes to her partner who repeats the dribbling, continuing until another signal is given.

3. *Dribbling, moving, and passing.* Two lines of paired children face each other across a 40- to 60-ft distance, as illustrated in the diagram (Figure 30.9). Each child in one

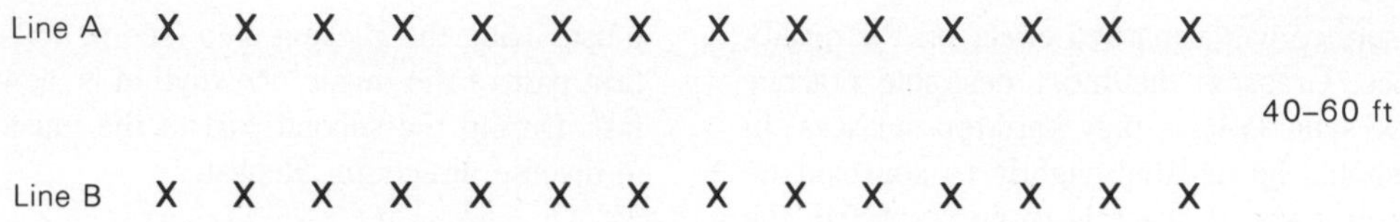

Line A X X X X X X X X X X X X X X

40–60 ft

Line B X X X X X X X X X X X X X X

FIGURE 30.9. Dribbling, moving, and passing

of the lines has a ball and works with a partner directly across from him. A player with a ball from Line A moves forward according to the challenges listed below. When he moves near his partner, he passes to him, and the partner (Line B) repeats the same maneuver back to Line A. Repeating the maneuver immediately results in both players returning to their starting place.

a. Dribble across to partner. Dribble using the outside of either foot.

b. Gallop across, handling the ball with the front foot only. On return, lead with the other foot.

c. Skip across, dribbling at the same time.

d. Slide across, handling the ball with the back foot. On return, lead with the other foot.

e. Hop across, using the lifted foot to handle the ball. Be sure to change feet halfway across.

f. Dribble the ball to a point halfway across. Stop the ball with the sole of the foot and leave it there. Continue to the other line. In the meantime, the partner from Line B moves forward to dribble the ball back to Line A.

g. Player A dribbles to the center and passes to player B. Player A now returns to Line A. Player B repeats and returns to Line B.

4. *Heading, volleying, and controlling.* Pairs of players are scattered. One player in each pair has a ball and acts as a feeder, tossing the ball for various receptive skills—heading, different volleys, and controlling balls in flight. Controlled tossing is essential to this drill.

DRILLS FOR THREE PLAYERS

With one ball for three players, many of the possibilities suggested for pair practice are still possible. An advantage of drills for three players is that fewer balls are needed.

1. *Passing and controlling.* The trio of players set up a triangle with players about 10 yd apart. Controlled passing and practice in ball control should occur.

2. *Heading, volleying, controlling.* One player acts as a feeder, tossing to the other two players who practice heading, volleying, and controlling air flight balls.

3. *Dribbling and passing.* A shuttle-type drill can be structured as shown in Figure 30.10. Players keep going back and forth continuously. Player no. 1 has the ball and dribbles to no. 2, who dribbles the ball back to no. 3 who, in turn, dribbles to no. 1. Players can dribble the entire distance or dribble a portion of the distance and then pass

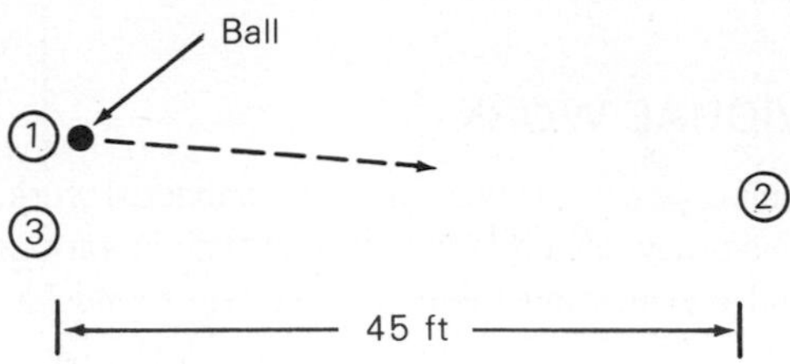

FIGURE 30.10. Shuttle-type dribbling drill

the ball to the end player. Obstacles can be set up to challenge players to dribble through or around each obstacle.

4. *Dribbling and stopping the ball.* Three dribblers are in line, each with a ball. The leader moves in various directions, followed by the other two players. On signal, each player controls her ball. The leader circles around to the back ball, and the other two move one ball forward. The dribbling continues for another stop. A third stop puts the players back in their original positions.

5. *Passing.* Players stand in three corners of a 10-yd square. After a player passes, he must move to the empty corner of the square, which is sometimes a diagonal movement (Figure 30.11).

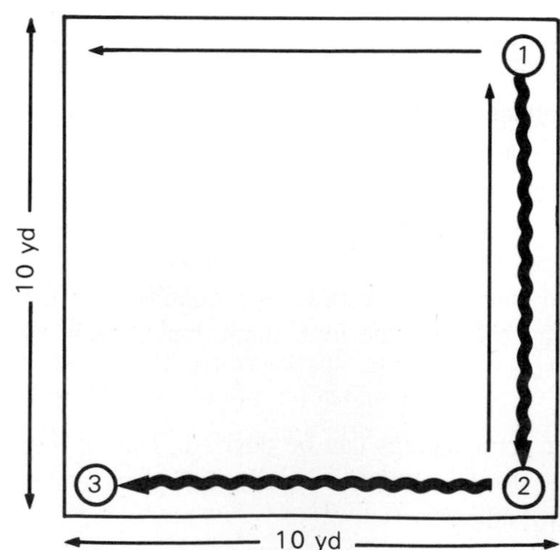

FIGURE 30.11. Passing drill

6. *Passing and defense.* One player is the feeder and rolls the ball to either player. As soon as he rolls the ball, he attempts to block or tackle the player receiving the ball to prevent a pass to the third player, who, if the pass is completed, attempts to pass back (Figure 30.12).

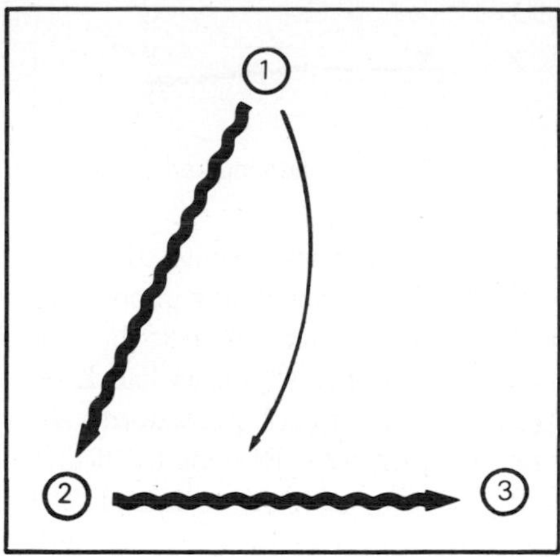

FIGURE 30.12. Passing and defense drill

DRILLS FOR FOUR OR MORE PLAYERS

Drills for four or more players should be organized so a rotation gives all players an equal opportunity to practice skills.

1. *Dribbling.* Four players are in line as diagrammed in Figure 30.13. Each player in front has a ball. Both front players dribble to the center where they exchange balls and continue dribbling to the other side. The next players perform similarly. A variation is to have the two players meet at the center, exchange balls, and dribble back to their starting point. Action should be continuous.

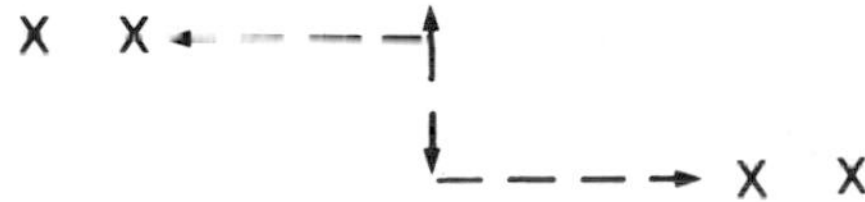

FIGURE 30.13. Dribble exchange drill

2. *Passing, guarding, and tackling.* Four players occupy the four corners of a square respectively (Figure 30.14). One player has a ball. Practice begins with one player rolling the ball to the player in the opposite corner, who, in turn, passes to either of the other two players. There should be two attempts each round so kicks are possible both ways. The next progression calls for the player who rolled the ball to move forward rapidly to block the pass to either side. Several tries should occur before another player takes over the rolling duties.

3. *Shooting, goalkeeping, and defense.* A shooting drill against defense can be run with four players and a 15-ft goal set off with cones or other markers (Figure 30.15). One player has the ball. He advances and attempts to maneuver around a second player so he can shoot past the goalkeeper guarding a goal. A fourth player acts as the retriever. Rotate positions.

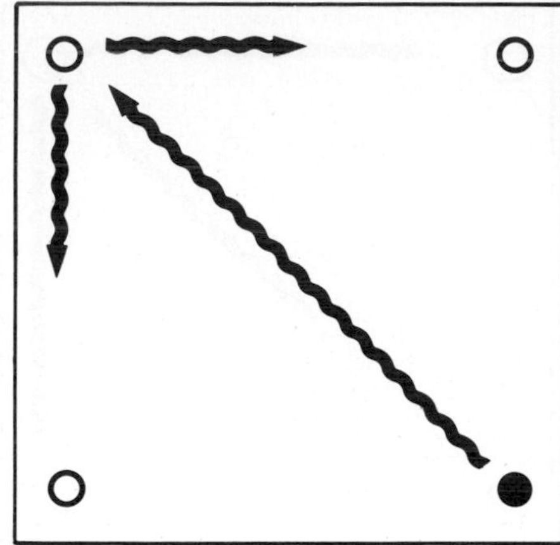

FIGURE 30.14. Passing, guarding, and tackling drill

FIGURE 30.15. Shooting, goalkeeping, and defense

4. *Dribbling.* Four or five players, each with a ball, form a line. A "coach" stands about 15 yd in front of the line. Each player, in turn, dribbles up to the coach, who indicates with a thumb in which direction the player should dribble past him. The coach should give the direction at the last possible moment.

5. *Passing, controlling, and defense.* Four players stand in the four corners of a square, 10 yd on a side. Two defensive players are inside the square. The corner players stay in place within the square and attempt to pass the ball among themselves, while the two defenders attempt to recover the ball (Figure 30.16). After a period of time, another two players take over as defenders.

6. *Shooting.* For two-way goal practice, two to six players are divided, half on each side of the goal. The width of the goal can vary, depending on the skill of the players. Two types of shooting should be practiced—(1) kicking a stationary ball from 10 to 20 yd out and (2) preceding a kick with a dribble. In the second type, a restraining line 12 to 15 yd out is needed. This line can be marked by cones as illustrated (Figure 30.17).

Use at least four balls for this two-way drill. After a period of kicking, the groups should change sides. Ball chasers are those players at the end of each line.

7. *Shooting and goalkeeping.* Scoring can also be practiced with a goalkeeper (Figure 30.18). Practice should be done with a stationary ball from 12 yd out (penalty distance) and with kicks preceded by a dribble. The goalie and the chaser should remain for one complete round and then rotate. Having a second ball to play with saves time, because

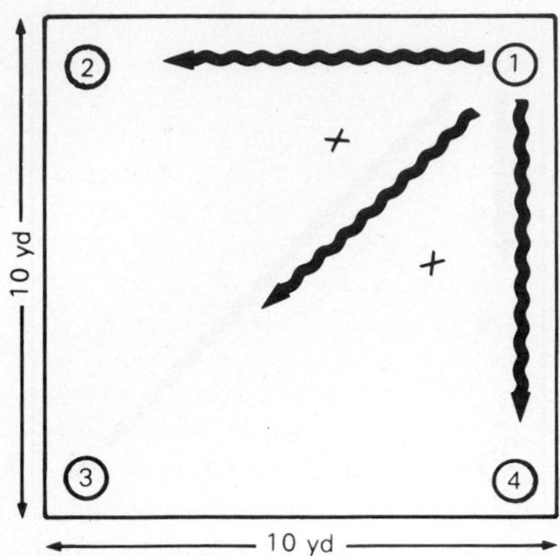

FIGURE 30.16. Passing, controlling, and defense[1]

1. The following symbols are used in soccer game formation diagrams:
X Defensive player
O Offensive player
→ Player moving without the ball
--→ Player dribbling
~~→ Pass, kick, or shot on goal

play can continue while the chaser is recovering the previous ball.

8. *Kicking and trapping.* This is an excellent squad drill. Approximately eight players form a circle 15 yd in diameter. Two balls are passed back and forth independently. Passes should be kept low, using primarily the side-of-the-foot kick. Using three balls can be tried also.

9. *Passing and shooting.* The drill can be done with four to six players. Two balls are needed. A passer is stationed about 15 yd from the goal, and a retriever is behind the goal. The shooters are in line, 20 yd from the goal and to the right. The first shooter passes to the passer, and then runs forward. The passer returns the ball to the shooter. The shooter tries to time his run forward so he

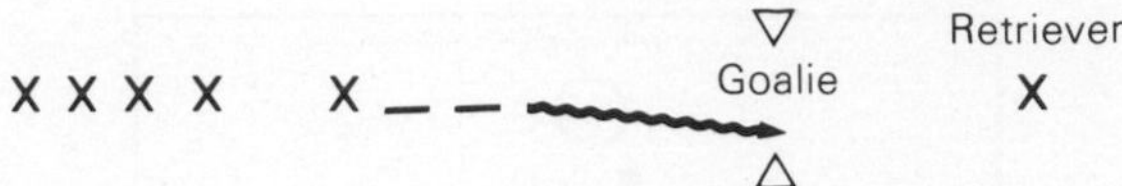

FIGURE 30.18. Shooting and goalkeeping

successfully shoots the pass through the goal. Both the passer and the retriever should stay in position for several rounds of shooting and then rotate to become shooters. The first pass can be from a stationary ball. Later, however, the kicker can be allowed to dribble forward a short distance before making the first pass. Reverse the field and practice from the left, shooting with the nondominant leg (Figure 30.19).

10. *Tackling and ball handling.* A defender is restricted to tackling in the area between two parallel lines, which are 1 yd apart. The field is 20 by 40 yd (Figure 30.20). Four to six players can practice this drill. Player no. 1 advances the ball by dribbling and attempts to maneuver past the defender. After he has evaded the defender, he passes to player no. 2 and takes his place at the other side of the field. Player no. 2 repeats the routine, passing the ball off to the next player in the line. If the ball goes out of control or is stopped by the defender, it is rolled to the player whose turn is next. Play is continuous, with the defender maintaining his position for several rounds.

BASIC SOCCER RULES FOR LEAD-UP GAMES

The ball may not be played deliberately with the hands or arms, but incidental or unintentional handling of the ball should be disregarded in the early stages. Eventually, a violation leads to a direct free kick in which the ball is placed on the ground with the opposition a specified distance away (10 yd on a full-sized field). A goal can be scored directly from this type of kick.

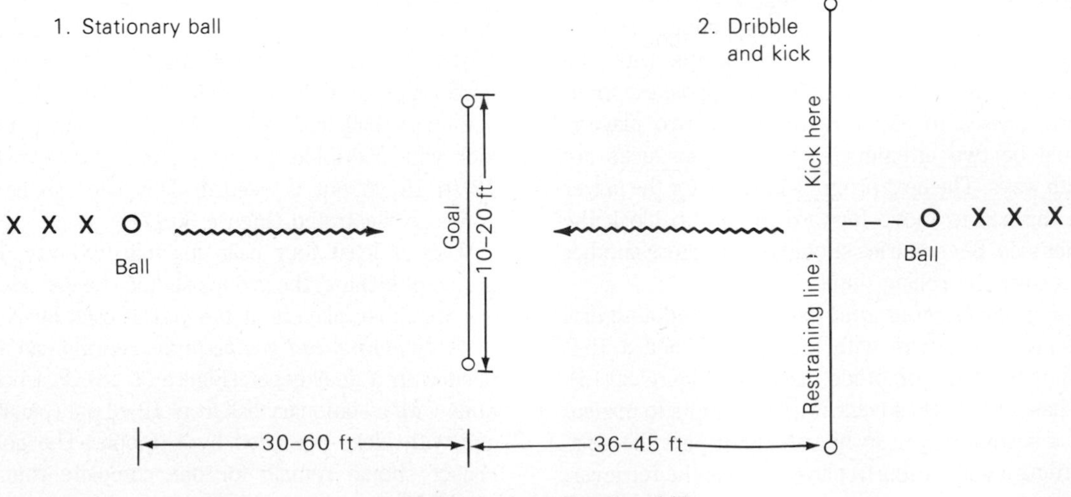

FIGURE 30.17. Shooting drill

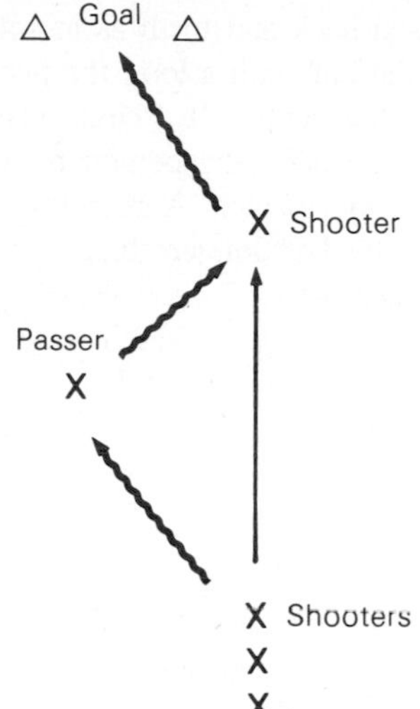

FIGURE 30.19. Passing and shooting

The goalkeeper is allowed to handle the ball *within his area* by catching, batting, or deflecting with the hands. If the goalie has caught the ball, he may not be charged by the opponents. While the goalie is holding the ball, official rules limit him to four steps. In elementary school play, the teacher should insist on the goalkeeper's getting rid of the ball immediately by throwing or kicking. This removes the temptation to rough up the goalie. In some lead-up games, a number of students may have the same ball-handling privileges as the goalie. The rules need to be clear, and ball handling should be done within a specified area.

All serious fouls, such as tripping, kicking a player, holding, or pushing, result in a direct free kick. If a defender commits one of these fouls or a handball in his own penalty area, a penalty kick is awarded. Only the goalkeeper may defend against this kick, which is shot from 12 yd out. All other players must be outside the penalty area until the ball is kicked. In lead-up games, consideration should be given to penalty fouls committed in a limited area near the goal by the defensive team. A kick can be awarded or an automatic goal can be scored for the attacking team.

The ball is out of play and the whistle blown when the ball crosses any of the boundaries, when a goal is scored, or when a foul is called. The team that last touched the ball or caused it to go out-of-bounds on the side of the field loses possession. The ball is put into play with an overhead throw-in using both hands (Figure 30.21).

If the attacking team causes the ball to go over the end line, the defending team is awarded a kick from any point chosen near the end line of that half of the field. If the defense last touched the ball going over the end line, then the attacking team is awarded a corner kick. The ball is taken to the corner on the side where the ball went over the end line, and a direct free kick is executed. A goal may be scored from this kick.

The game is normally started by a kickoff with both teams onside. In lead-up games, the ball can be dropped for a free ball. In some games, the teacher may find it advisable simply to award the ball for a free kick in the backcourt to the team not making the score.

Lead-up games can continue for a set length of time (by halves) or until a predetermined score is attained. In a regular soccer game, the play is timed.

When the ball is ensnarled among a number of players or when someone has fallen, a quick whistle is needed.

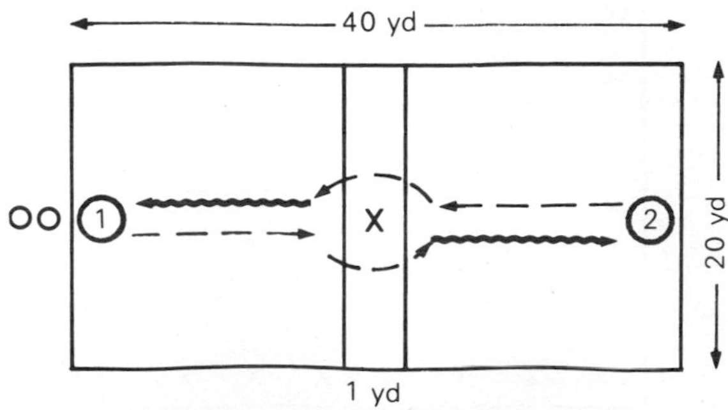

FIGURE 30.20. Tackling and ball handling drill

FIGURE 30.21. Throwing in, from out of bounds

The ball can be put into play by dropping it between players of the opposing teams.

While the offside rule is of little value in elementary school play, children should understand the rule and the reasons for it. Its purpose is to prevent the "cheap" goal (i.e., a player on offense waits near the goal to take a pass behind the defenders and to score easily against the goalkeeper). Although the concept of offsides involves a number of details, it essentially means that a player on offense who is ahead of the ball must have two defensive players between her and the goal when the ball is kicked forward. One of these players is, of course, the goalkeeper. The offside rule does not apply when the player receives the ball directly from an attempted goal kick, from an opponent, or on a throw-in, corner kick, or when the player is in her own half.

Players should not raise their feet high or show the soles or cleats when other players are in the vicinity. This constitutes dangerous play, and an indirect free kick is awarded.

SOCCER ACTIVITIES

THIRD GRADE

Circle Kickball

Playing Area: Playground, gymnasium

Players: 10 to 20

Supplies: Two soccer balls or 8-in. foam rubber balls

Skills: Kicking, controlling

Players are in circle formation. Using the side of the foot, players kick the balls back and forth inside of the circle. The object is to kick a ball out of the circle *beneath* the shoulder level of the circle players. A point is scored against each of the players where a ball leaves the circle between them. If, however, a lost ball is clearly the fault of a single player, then the point is scored against that player only. Any player who kicks a ball over the shoulders of the circle players has a point scored against him. Players with the fewest points scored against them win. Players must watch carefully since two balls are in action at one time. A player cannot be penalized if she leaves the circle to recover a ball and the second ball goes through her vacated spot.

FOURTH GRADE

Soccer Touch Ball

Playing Area: Playground, gymnasium

Players: Eight to ten

Supplies: A soccer ball

Skills: Kicking, controlling

Players are spaced around a circle 10 yd in diameter with two players in the center. The object of the game is to keep the players in the center from touching the ball. The ball is passed back and forth as in soccer. If a center player touches the ball with a foot, the person who kicked the ball goes to the center. If a circle player commits an error (i.e., misses a ball), the person responsible changes places with a center player. A rule that no player may contain or hold the ball longer than 3 seconds tends to keep the game moving.

Diagonal Soccer

Playing Area: A square about 60 by 60 ft

Players: 20 to 30

Supplies: A soccer ball, pinnies (optional)

Skills: Kicking, passing, dribbling, some controlling, defending, and blocking shots

Two corners are marked off with cones 5 ft from the corners on both the sides, outlining triangular dead areas. Each team lines up as illustrated in Figure 30.22 and protects two adjacent sides of the square. The dead area on the opposite corner marks the opposing team's goal lines. To begin competition, three players from each team move into the playing area in their own half of the space. These are the active players. During play, they may roam anywhere in the square. The other players act as line guards.

The object of the game is for active players to kick the ball through the opposing team's line (beneath shoulder height) to score. When a score is made, active players rotate to the sidelines, and new players take their place. Players on the sidelines may block the ball with their bodies but cannot use their hands. The team against whom the point was scored starts the ball for the next point. Only active players may score. Scoring is much the same as in Circle Kickball in that a point is awarded for the opponents when any of the following occur.

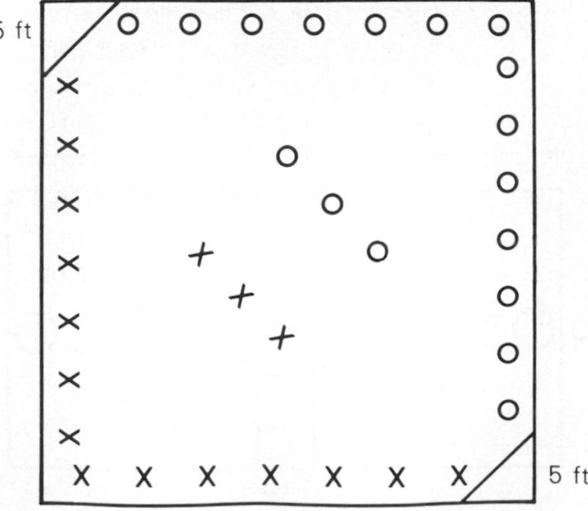

FIGURE 30.22. Formation for Diagonal Soccer

1. A team allows the ball to go through its line below the shoulders.

2. A team touches the ball illegally.

3. A team kicks the ball over the other team above shoulder height.

Variations

1. If the class is large, a bigger area and more active players can be used.

2. If scoring seems too easy, the line defenders can use their hands to stop the ball.

Dribblerama

Playing Area: Playground

Players: 10 to 20

Supplies: One soccer ball for each player

Skills: Dribbling and protecting the ball

The playing area is a large circle or square, clearly outlined. All players dribble within the area. The game is played on two levels.

Level 1: Each player dribbles throughout the area, controlling the ball so that it does not touch another ball. If a touch occurs, both players go outside the area and dribble counterclockwise around the area. Cut the remaining area in half again if necessary.

Level 2: While dribbling and controlling the ball, each player attempts to kick any other ball out of the area. When a ball is kicked out, the player owning that ball takes it outside and dribbles around the area. Play continues until only two or three players are left. These are declared the winners. Bring all players back into the game and repeat.

Bullseye

Playing Area: Playground

Players: Six to ten

Supplies: One soccer ball per player

Skills: Dribbling and protecting the ball

The playing area is a large outlined area—circle, square, or rectangle. One player holds a ball in her hands, which serves as the bullseye. The other players dribble within the area. The player with the bullseye attempts to throw her ball (basketball push shot) at any other ball. The ball that is hit now becomes the new bullseye. The old bullseye becomes one of the dribblers. A new bullseye cannot hit back immediately at the old bullseye. A dribbler should protect the ball with her body. If the group is large, have two bullseyes. No score is kept and no one is eliminated.

Sideline Soccer

Playing Area: Rectangle about 100 by 60 ft

Players: 10 to 12 on each team

Supplies: A soccer ball, four cones, pinnies (optional)

Skills: Most soccer skills, competitive play

The teams line up on the sidelines of the square. Three or four active players from each team are called from the end of the team line (Figure 30.23). These players remain active until a point is scored, and then they rotate to the other end of the line.

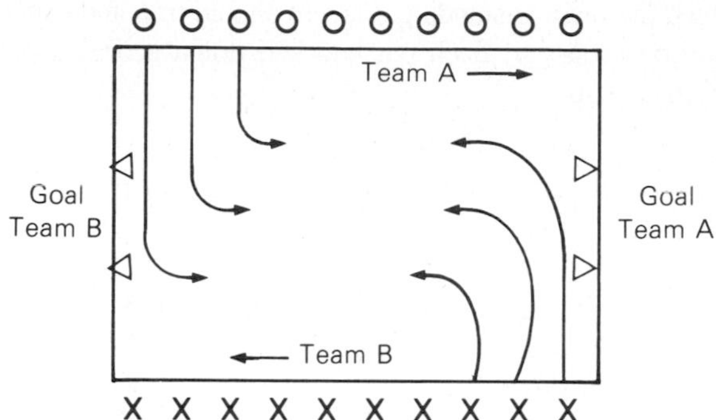

FIGURE 30.23. Formation for Sideline Soccer

The object is to kick the ball between cones that define the scoring area. The active players on each team compete against each other, aided by their teammates on the sidelines.

To start play, a referee drops the ball between two opposing players at the center of the field. To score, the ball must be kicked last by an active player and must go through the goal at or below shoulder height. A goal counts one point. Sideline players may pass to an active teammate, but a sideline kick cannot score a goal.

Regular rules generally prevail with special attention to the restrictions of no pushing, holding, tripping, or other rough play. Rough play is a foul and causes a point to be awarded to the other team. For an out-of-bounds ball, the team on the side of the field where the ball went out-of-bounds is awarded a free kick near that spot. No score can result from a free kick. Violation of the touch rule also results in a free kick.

Teaching Suggestions: A system of rotation in which active players move to the opposite end of the sideline and new players come forth is necessary. More active players can be added when the class is large, and the distance between goals can be increased. After some expertise is acquired, the cones should be moved in to narrow the goal area. If the ball goes over the end line but not through the goal area, the ball is put into play by a defender with a kick.

FIFTH GRADE

Pin Kickball

Playing Area: Playground, gymnasium

Players: Seven to ten on each team

Supplies: Six or more pins (cones, Indian clubs, or bowling pins), two soccer balls

Skills: Kicking, controlling

Two teams start about 20 yd apart, facing each other. At least six pins are placed between the two lines of players. One ball is given to each team at the start of the kicking (Figure 30.24). Kicks should be made from the line behind which the team is standing. Players should trap and concentrate on accuracy. Each pin knocked down scores a point for that team.

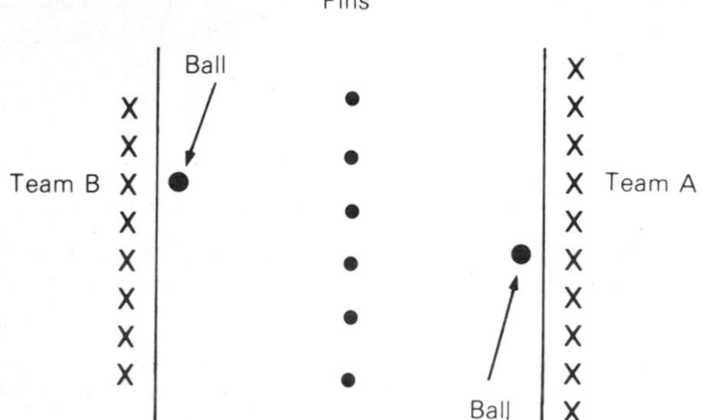

FIGURE 30.24. Formation for Pin Kickball

Teaching Suggestions: This is a flexible game; the number of pins, balls, and players can be varied easily. The type of kick can be specified, or it can be left up to the player to choose. Domination of the game by one or two players can be controlled somewhat by having those who have just scored go to either end of the line. More soccer balls can be added when the game seems slow. As accuracy improves, the distance between the teams can be increased. Players on each end of the lines are the ball chasers. After all of the pins have been knocked down, they are reset, and the game resumes.

Addition Soccer

Playing Area: Playground

Players: 10 to 15

Supplies: One soccer ball per player, except for the person who is designated as defender

Skills: Dribbling and ball control

One player is designated to defend against the other players. The remainder of the players dribble throughout the area, trying to keep the defender from touching any ball with his foot. The first ball that he touches makes the owner of that ball the ball collector at the ball control station.

The defender now tries to touch any other ball with his foot. When the ball is touched, that player rolls the ball to the ball control station and joins hands with the defender to become his partner. They operate as a twosome and must keep hands joined as they chase to touch other balls. When another ball is touched, that player takes the ball to the control station and waits until yet another ball is touched to provide her with a partner. The new twosome now become defenders, too, adding their efforts to that of the first twosome. Play continues until all balls are in the ball control station and all players have been caught.

If partners break joined hands in touching a ball, the tag is voided. The last one caught becomes the defender for the next match. The game is similar to Addition Tag (page 431).

Over the Top

Playing Area: Playground

Players: Two teams, five to seven on a team

Supplies: Each player on offense has a ball

Skills: Dribbling, ball control, guarding, and tackling

One team is on offense and one on defense, placed according to Figure 30.25.

Defensive players must stay in their respective area. On signal, all offensive players begin to dribble through the three areas. A player is eliminated if her ball is recovered by a defensive player or goes out-of-bounds. The offensive team scores 1 point for each ball that is dribbled across

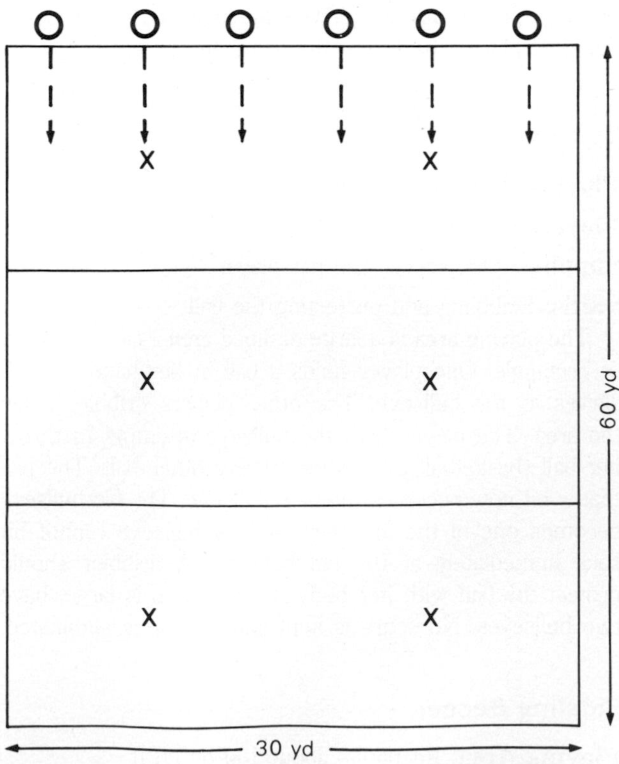

FIGURE 30.25. Over the Top

the far end line. Reverse roles and give the other team a chance to score.

Field markings need to be definite to keep the defensive players in their respective zones. Some teachers like to put neutral zones between the active zones.

Line Soccer

Playing Area: Soccer field

Players: Eight to ten players on each team

Supplies: A soccer ball, four cones, pinnies

Skills: Most soccer skills, competitive play

Two goal lines are drawn 80 to 120 ft apart. A restraining line is drawn 15 ft in front of and parallel to each goal line. Field width can vary from 50 to 80 ft. Each team stands on one goal line, which it defends. The referee stands in the center of the field and holds a ball (Figure 30.26). At the whistle, three players (more if the teams are large) run from the right side of each line to the center of the field and become active players. The referee drops the ball to the ground, and the players try to kick it through the other team defending the goal line. The players in the field may advance by kicking only.

A score is made when an active player kicks the ball through the opposing team and over the end line (provided the kick was made from outside the restraining line). Cones should be put on field corners to define the goal line. A system of player rotation should be set up.

Line players act as goalies and are permitted to catch the ball. Once caught, however, the ball must be laid down immediately and either rolled or kicked. It cannot be punted or drop-kicked.

One point is scored when the ball is kicked over the opponent's goal line below shoulder level. One point is also scored in case of a personal foul involving pushing, kicking, tripping, and the like.

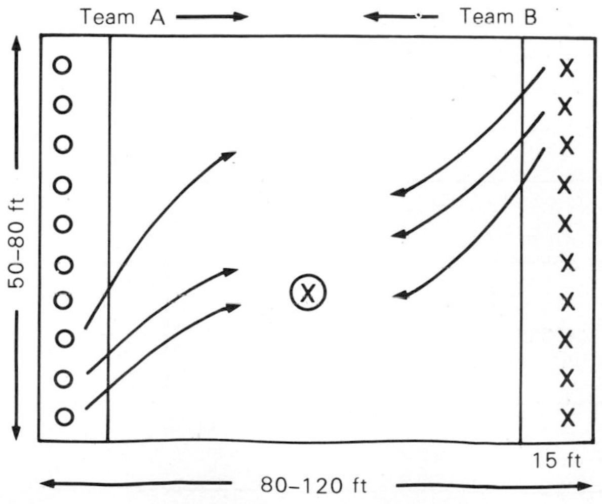

FIGURE 30.26. Line soccer

For illegal touching by the active players, a direct free kick from a point 12 yd in front of the penalized team's goal line is given. All active players on the defending team must stand to one side until the ball is kicked. Only goalies defend.

A time limit of 2 minutes is set for any group of active players. If no goal is scored during this time, play is halted and the players are changed.

An out-of-bounds ball is awarded to the opponents of the team last touching it. The regular soccer throw-in from out-of-bounds should be used. If the ball goes over the shoulders of the defenders at the end line, any end-line player may retrieve the ball and put it into play with a throw or kick.

Teaching Suggestion: Line Soccer should be played with the regular soccer rules when possible.

Variations

1. If there is enough space, the teams can count off by threes. They need not keep any particular order at the end lines but simply come out as active players when their number is called. By using numbers, the teacher can pit different groups against each other.

2. Instead of giving a score for a personal foul, a penalty kick can be awarded. The ball is kicked from 12 yd out, and only three defenders are permitted on the line.

Mini-Soccer

Playing Area: Any large area 100 by 150 ft, with goals

Players: Seven on each team

Supplies: A soccer ball, pinnies or colors to mark teams, four cones for the corners

Skills: All soccer skills

Each end of the field has a 21-ft wide goal marked by jumping standards. A 12-yd semicircle on each end outlines the penalty area. The center of the semicircle is at the center of the goal (Figure 30.27).

The game follows the general rules of soccer, with one goalie for each side. One new feature, the corner kick, needs

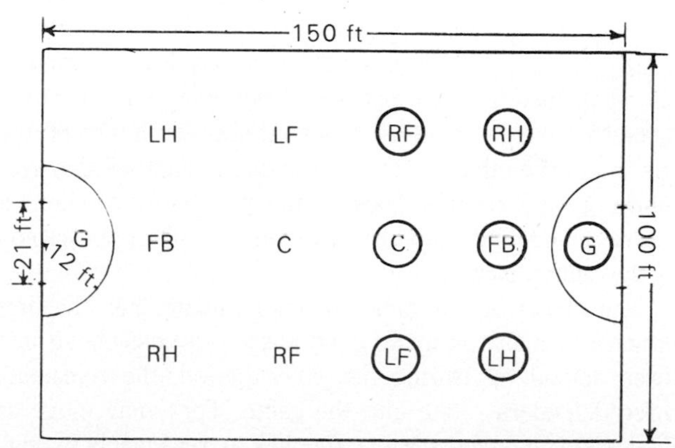

FIGURE 30.27. Formation for Mini-Soccer

to be introduced. This kick is used when the ball, last touched by the defense, goes over the end line but not through the goal. The ball is taken to the nearest corner for a direct free kick, and a goal can be scored from the kick. In a similar situation, if the attacking team last touched the ball, the goalkeeper kick is awarded. The goalie puts the ball down and placekicks it forward.

The players are designated as center forward, outside right, outside left, right halfback, left halfback, fullback, and goalie. Players should rotate positions. The forwards play in the front half of the field, and the guards in the back half. Neither position, however, is restricted to these areas entirely, and all may cross the center line without penalty.

A foul by the defense within its penalty area (semicircle) results in a penalty kick, taken from a point 12 yd distant, directly in front of the goal. Only the goalie is allowed to defend. The ball is in play, with others waiting outside the penalty area.

Teaching Suggestion: Position play should be emphasized. The lines of three should be encouraged to spread out and hold reasonable position.

Variation: The number of players can vary, with some games using as few as three on a side in a more restricted area. If teams have more than seven players, the seven-player game should be maintained but with frequent substitutions.

SIXTH GRADE

Mini-Soccer

Mini-Soccer, introduced in the 5th grade, should be an important part of the 6th-grade program as well.

Six Spot Keepaway

Playing Area: Playground, gymnasium

Players: Two teams, six on each side

Supplies: One soccer ball, stopwatch

Skills: Passing, ball control, guarding

There is a total of six offensive players. Five are arranged in a pentagon formation with one player in the center (Figure 30.28). The pentagon is about 20 yd across. For the offense, play is divided into two periods of one minute each. Three defenders from the other team attempt to interrupt the passing of the offensive team from one to another. A player may not pass the ball back to the person from whom it was received. The game begins with the ball in possession of the center player.

The object of the game is, for 1 minute (i.e., the first period), to make as many good passes as possible against three defenders. During the other period, the remaining three defenders rotate into the game. They may move as they wish. Offensive players should stay reasonably in position. Change offense and defense and repeat.

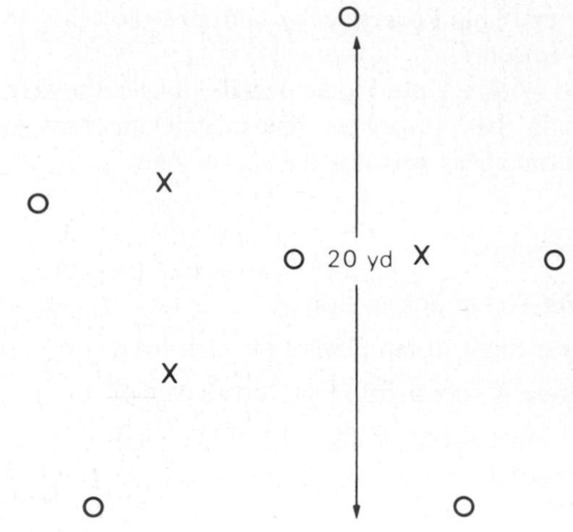

FIGURE 30.28. Six Spot Keepaway

Regulation Soccer

Playing Area: Soccer field (Figure 30.29)

Players: 11 on each team

Supplies: A soccer ball, pinnies

Skills: All soccer skills

A team usually consists of three forwards, three midfield players, four backline defenders, and one goalkeeper. Forwards are the main line of attack. They need to develop good control, dribbling, and shooting skills, and they must have a strong desire to score. They should be encouraged to shoot frequently. Midfield players tend to be the powerhouse of the team. They need good passing and tackling skills as well as a high level of cardiovascular fitness. Defenders should work well together and know when to tackle. They should play safely by clearing the ball away from their own penalty area, and not risk dribbling or passing toward their own goal unless it is absolutely safe to do so. Goalkeepers must be quick and agile, good decision makers, and must have ball-handling skills.

On the toss of the coin, the winning team gets their choice of kicking off or selecting which goal to defend. The loser exercises the option not selected by the winner.

On the kickoff, the ball must travel forward about 1

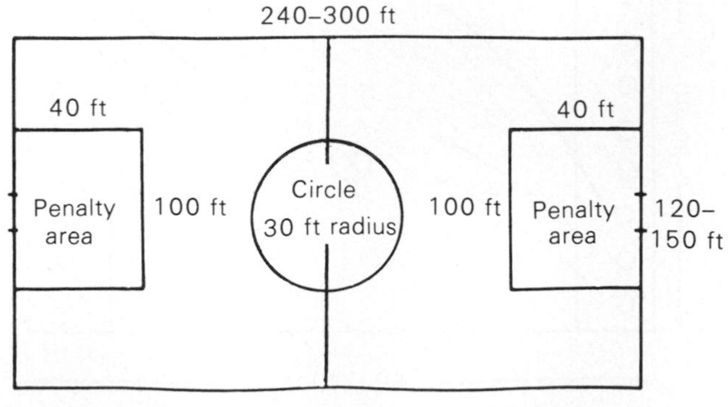

FIGURE 30.29. Regulation soccer field

yd, and the kicker cannot touch it again until another player has kicked it. The defensive team must be 10 yd away from the kicker. After each score, the team not winning the point gets to kick off. Both teams must be onside at the kickoff. The defensive team must stay onside and out of the center circle until the ball is kicked. Regular soccer rules call for scoring by counting the number of goals made.

Elementary school children usually play 6-minute quarters. There should be a rest period of 1 minute between quarters and 10 minutes between halves.

When the ball goes out-of-bounds on the sideline, it is put into play with a throw-in from the spot where it crossed the line. No goal may be scored, nor may the thrower play the ball a second time until it has been touched by another player. All opponents are to be 10 yd back at the time of the throw.

If the ball is caused to go out-of-bounds on the end line by the attacking team, a goal kick is awarded. The ball is placed in the goal area and kicked beyond the penalty area by a defending player who may not touch the ball twice in succession. If the ball is touched by a player before it goes out of the penalty area, it is not yet in play and should be kicked again.

If the defensive team causes the ball to go out-of-bounds over the end line, a corner kick is awarded. The ball is placed 1 yd from the corner of the field and kicked into the field of play by an attacking player. The 10-yd restriction also applies to defensive players.

If the ball is touched by two opponents at the same time and caused to go out-of-bounds, a drop ball is called. The referee drops the ball between two opposing players, who cannot kick it until it touches the ground. A drop ball also is called when the ball is trapped among downed players.

If a player is closer to the opponent's goal line than to the ball at a time when the ball is played in a forward direction, it is an offside infraction. Exceptions exist, and a player is not offside when she is in her half of the playing field, when two opponents are nearer their goal line than the attacking player at the moment when the ball is played, or when the ball is received directly from a corner kick, a throw-in, or a goal kick.

Personal fouls involving unnecessary roughness are penalized. Tripping, striking, charging, holding, pushing, and jumping an opponent intentionally are forbidden.

It is a foul for any player, except the goalkeeper, to handle the ball with the hands or arms. The goalkeeper is allowed only four steps and must then get rid of the ball. After the ball has left her possession, the goalkeeper may not pick it up again until another player has touched it. Players are not allowed to screen or obstruct opponents, unless they are in control of the ball.

Penalties are as follows.

1. A direct kick is awarded for all personal fouls and handballs. A goal can be scored from a direct free kick. Examples of infringements are pushing, tripping, kicking a player, and holding.

2. A penalty kick is awarded if direct free-kick infringements are committed by a defender in his own penalty area.

3. An indirect free kick is awarded for offsides, obstruction, dangerous play such as high kicking, a goalkeeper taking more than four steps or repossessing the ball before another player has touched it, and playing the ball twice after a dead-ball situation. The ball must be touched by a second player before a goal can be scored. The referee should signal if the kick is indirect by pointing one arm upward vertically.

Teaching Suggestions: Players should be encouraged to use the space on the field to the best advantage. When a team is in possession of the ball, players should attempt to find a position from which they can either pass behind the player with the ball to give support, or toward the goal to be in a better position to shoot. When a team is forced into defense, the defenders should get "goalside" of attackers (between the attackers and their own goal) to prevent them from gaining an advantage.

From an early stage, players should be taught to give information to each other during the game, especially when they have possession of the ball. Valuable help can be given by shouting instructions such as "man on," "you have time," "player behind," and also calling for the ball when in a good position to receive a pass.

SOCCER SKILL TESTS

The tests for soccer skills cover various kinds of kicks, dribbling, and controlling.

PASSING AGAINST A WALL

Players pass the ball from behind a line between 5 and 10 yd away from a wall. The student should be encouraged to control the ball before kicking. The score is the number of passes made from behind the line in 1 or 2 minutes. This is an excellent test of general ball control and short passing skill.

FIGURE-EIGHT DRIBBLING

For a figure-eight dribbling test, three obstacles or markers are arranged in a line, 4 yd apart, with the first marker positioned 4 yd from the starting line. The finish line is 4 yd wide. A stopwatch is used, and the timing is done to the nearest tenth of a second.

Each player gets three trials, with the fastest trial taken as the score. On each trial, the player dribbles over the figure-eight course and finishes by kicking or dribbling the ball over the 4-yd finish line, at which time the watch is stopped. The test is best done on a grass surface, but if a hard surface must be used, the ball should be deflated somewhat so it can be controlled.

CONTROLLING

For the controlling test, the formation is a file plus one. A thrower stands 15 to 20 ft in front of the file and rolls or bounces the ball to the player at the head of the file. Three trials each are given for the sole-of-the-foot control, the foot control, and body control. The ball must be definitely stopped and controlled. A score of 9 points, one for each successful control, is possible.

The thrower should adopt one type of throw for all controls and for all players. If the scorer judges that the roll was not a good opportunity, the trial is taken over. For the 4th grade, the only control taught is the sole-of-the-foot control. Five trials can be allowed.

PLACEKICKING AND PUNTING FOR DISTANCE AND ACCURACY

To test punting for distance, a football field or any other field marked in gridiron fashion at 5- or 10-yd intervals is needed. One soccer ball is required, but when three are used, considerable time is saved. A measuring tape (25 ft or 50 ft) plus individual markers complete the supply list.

Each player is given three kicks from behind a restraining line. One child marks the kick for distance, while one or two others act as ball chasers. After three kicks, the player's marker is left at the spot of the longest kick. This is determined by marking the point at which the ball *first touched* after the kick. Measurement is taken to the nearest foot.

Every student in the squad or small group should kick before the measurements are taken. The punt must be from a standing, not a running, start. If a child crosses the line during the kick, it counts as a trial and no measurement is taken.

Placekicking for distance is tested in the same way as punting for distance, with two exceptions. The ball is kicked from a stationary position. It must be laid on a flat surface and not elevated by dirt, grass, or other means. The child is given credit for the entire distance of the kick, including the roll. The kicking should be done on a grassy surface, because the ball will roll indefinitely on a smooth, hard surface. If the surface presents a problem, the test can be limited to the distance the ball has traveled in flight.

PENALTY KICKING AND SHORT PASSING ACCURACY

In the penalty-kicking test, the kicker faces a target area from a point 12 yd out where the ball has been placed. The target area is formed by a rope stretched tight 6 ft above the ground. Four ropes, at distances 5 ft apart, are dropped from the stretched rope. This outlines three target areas 6 ft high and 5 ft wide. The center target area scores 1 point and the side areas 2 points (Figure 30.30). (This reflects the principle that a penalty kick should be directed away from a goalkeeper toward either corner of the goal.) Each child is allotted five kicks at the target. A score of 10 points is possible.

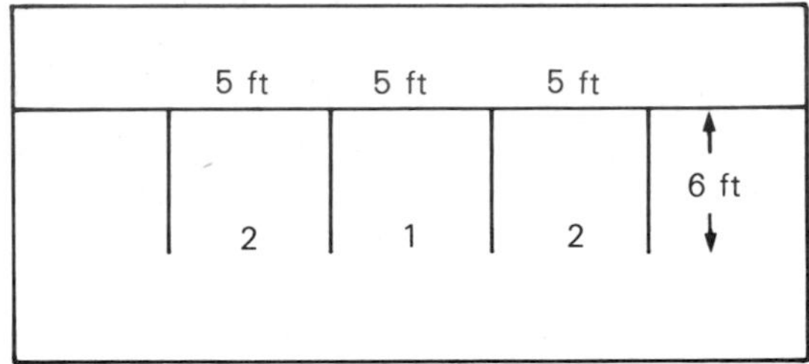

FIGURE 30.30. Penalty-kicking target area

The same target is used for kicking for accuracy, but the center area scores 2 points and the side areas 1 point each. A balk line is drawn about 20 ft from the target. The child is back another 20 ft for the start. The player dribbles the ball forward and must kick the ball as it is moving and before it crosses the balk line. Five trials are given and a score of 10 points is possible.

The test can be done with a stationary kick (placekick) by 4th-graders. The kicking distance depends on the capacities of the group.

CHAPTER 31

Softball

The main emphasis in softball should be on instruction and lead-up games. Children have adequate opportunity during recess, at the noon hour, and at other times to play the regulation game. In many physical education classes, too much softball participation is of the "choose sides and let 'em go" variety. Youngsters enjoy softball, and a good program should make use of this drive.

Because the experiences of individual children with softball vary so much, the allocation of skills and knowledges for a progressive program is difficult. The formal program should begin at the 3rd-grade level and progress through the 6th grade. By the time children are in the 5th grade, they should be playing softball modified for their level.

INSTRUCTIONAL EMPHASIS AND SEQUENCE

Table 31.1 summarizes the programs for the 3rd through 6th grade.

THIRD GRADE

The fundamental skills of batting, throwing, and catching are emphasized in the 3rd grade. Batting must receive attention, for softball is little fun unless children can hit. Proper form and technique in all three fundamental skills should be part of the instruction, with attention paid not only to the *how* but also to the *why.* A wide range in skill levels should be expected. Lead-up games for the 3rd grade are simple, but they provide an introduction to the basic rules of the game. At this level, there is little emphasis on the pitcher or the catcher.

FOURTH GRADE

In the 4th grade, specific skills for pitching, infield play, base running, and batting make up the instructional material. Proper pitching technique is important to the budding softball player.

FIFTH GRADE

The 5th-grade student should develop the background to play the game of regulation softball. Instructional material is aimed at this goal. The 4th-grade program is expanded through the addition of techniques useful in the regular game of softball. Tee Ball provides a good opportunity for developing all softball skills except pitching and catching. Home Run and the ever-popular Scrub (Work-up) provide a variety of experiences, while Batter Ball stresses hitting skills.

SIXTH GRADE

Experiences with batting, throwing, catching, and infield play are continued in the 6th grade. New pitching techniques, situation play, and double-play work are added. Slow-Pitch Softball provides lots of action. Babe Ruth Ball emphasizes selective hitting.

SOFTBALL SKILLS

Children can find many ways to execute softball skills effectively by trial and error and through instruction. Care must be taken not to attempt to mold every child into a prescribed form, but to work toward making the most of each child's movement patterns.

TABLE 31.1. SUGGESTED SOFTBALL PROGRAM

	Third Grade	Fourth Grade	Fifth Grade	Sixth Grade
Skills				
Throwing	Gripping the ball Overhand throw Underhand toss	Continued practice Around the bases	Throw-in from outfield Side-arm throw	Continued practice
Catching and fielding	Catching thrown balls Catching fly balls Grounders	Continued practice Fielding grounders in infield Sure stop for outfield	Catching flies from fungo batting Infield practice	Flies and infield practice
Batting	Simple skills Tee batting	Fungo hitting Continued practice Tee batting	Different positions at plate Tee batting	Bunting
Fielding positions		Infield practice How to catch	Infield positions Backing up other players	Double play
Base running	To first base	To first base and turning Circling the base	Getting a good start off base Tagging up on fly ball	Sacrifice
Pitching	Simple underhand	Application of pitching rule	Target pitching	Slow pitches
Coaching			Coaching at bases	
Knowledge, rules	Strike zone Foul and fair ball Safe and out	Foul tip Bunt rule When the batter is safe or out	Pitching rule: Position Illegal pitches Infield fly Keeping score Base running	Review all rules Situation quiz
Activities	Throw-It-and-Run Softball Two-Pitch Softball	Two-Pitch Softball (review) Hit and Run Kick Softball In a Pickle	Five Hundred Batter Ball Home Run Tee Ball Scrub (Work-up)	Slow-Pitch Softball Babe Ruth Ball Hurry Baseball Three-Team Softball
Skill Tests	None	Throwing for accuracy Throwing for distance	Pitching Throwing for distance Circling the bases	Tee batting Pitching Throwing for distance Circling the bases Fielding grounders

GRIPPING THE BALL

The standard softball grip calls for the thumb to be on one side, the index and middle fingers on top, and the other fingers supporting along the other side (Figure 31.1). Younger children with small hands may find it more comfortable to use a full-hand grip, in which the thumb and fingers are spaced rather evenly (Figure 31.2). Regardless of the grip used, the pads of the fingers should control the ball.

FIGURE 31.1. Gripping the ball, two-finger grip

THROWING (RIGHT-HANDED)

Overhand Throw

In preparation for throwing, the child secures a firm grip on the ball, raises the throwing arm to shoulder height,

FIGURE 31.2. Gripping the ball, full grip (the little finger supports on the side)

and brings the elbow back. For the overhand throw, the hand with the ball is then brought back over the head so it is well behind the shoulder at about shoulder height. The left side of the body is turned in the direction of the throw, and the left arm is raised in front of the body. The weight is on the back (right) foot, with the left foot advanced and the toe touching the ground. The arm comes forward with the elbow leading, and the ball is thrown with a downward snap of the wrist (Figure 31.3). The body weight is brought forward into the throw, shifting to the front foot. There should be good follow-through so the palm of the throwing hand faces the ground at completion of the throw. The eye should be on the target throughout, and the arm should be kept free and loose during the throw.

FIGURE 31.3. Throwing overhand

Sidearm Throw

The sidearm throw is much the same as the overhand throw, except that the entire motion is kept near a horizontal plane. The sidearm throw is used for shorter, quicker throws than the overhand and employs a quick, whiplike action. On a long throw, the sidearm throw curves more than the overhand, because a side-spinning action is usually imparted to the ball on release. There is generally some body lean toward the side of the throwing arm.

Underhand Throw

For the underhand throw, the throwing hand and arm are brought back, with palm facing forward, in a pendulum swing. The elbow is bent slightly. The weight is mostly on the back foot. The arm comes forward, almost in a bowling motion, and the ball is tossed. The weight shifts to the front foot during the toss. The flight of the ball should remain low and arrive at about waist height.

Pitching

Official rules call for the pitcher to have both feet in contact with the pitcher's rubber, but few elementary schools possess a rubber. Instead, the pitcher can stand with both feet about even, facing the batter, and holding the ball momentarily in front with both hands. The pitcher takes one hand from the ball, extends the right arm forward, and brings it back in a pendulum swing, positioning the ball well behind the body. A normal stride taken toward the batter with the left foot begins the throwing sequence for a right-handed pitcher. The arm is brought forward with an underhanded slingshot motion, and the weight is transferred to the leading foot. Only one step is permitted. The follow-through motion is important (Figure 31.4).

The windmill is an alternate pitching motion in which the arm describes a full arc overhead, moving behind the body and then forward toward the batter. The arm goes into full extension on the downward swing in the back, gathering momentum as the forward motion begins. The pitch is otherwise the same as the normal motion. The windmill is generally a difficult style for youngsters to master.

FIGURE 31.4. Pitching

READY POSITION FOR FIELDERS

Infielders should assume the ready position, a semicrouch, with legs spread shoulder width apart, knees bent slightly, and hands on or in front of the knees (Figure 31.5). As the ball is delivered, the weight is shifted to the

FIGURE 31.5. Ready position for the infielder

balls of the feet. The outfielder's position is a slightly more erect semicrouch.

FIELDING

Fly Balls

There are two ways to catch a fly ball. For a low ball, the fielder keeps the fingers together and forms a basket with the hands (Figure 31.6). For a higher ball, the thumbs

FIGURE 31.6. Catching a low fly ball

FIGURE 31.7. Catching a high fly ball

are together, and the ball is caught in front of the chin (Figure 31.7). The fielder should give with her hands, and care must be taken with a spinning ball to squeeze the hands sufficiently to stop the spinning. The eye is on the ball continually until it hits the glove or hands. The knees are flexed slightly when receiving and aid in giving when the ball is caught.

Grounders

To field a grounder, the fielder should move as quickly as possible into the path of the ball (Figure 31.8) and then move forward and play the ball on a good hop. The eyes must be kept on the ball, following it into the hands or glove. The feet are spread, the seat is kept down, and the hands are carried low and in front (Figure 31.9). The weight is on the balls of the feet or on the toes, and the knees are bent to lower the body. As the ball is caught, the fielder straightens up, takes a step in the direction of the throw, and makes the throw.

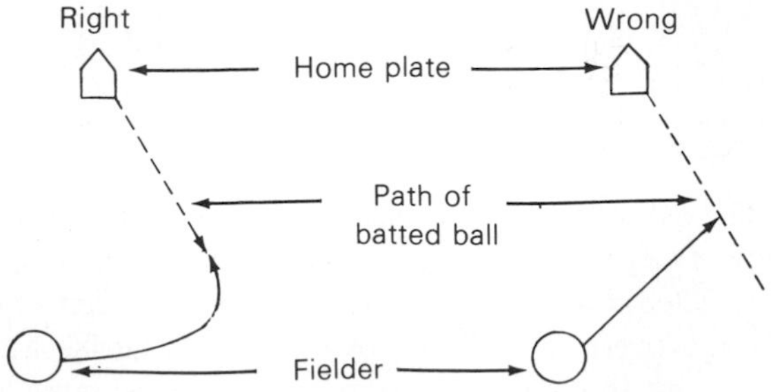

FIGURE 31.8. Fielding a grounder correctly

FIGURE 31.9. Fielding a grounder

Sure Stop for Outfield Balls

To keep the ball from going through the hands and thus allowing extra bases, the outfielder can use his body as a barrier. The fielder turns half right and lowers one knee to the ground at the point toward which the ball is traveling (Figure 31.10). The hands catch the rolling ball, but if it is missed, the body will generally stop the ball.

First-Base Positioning

When a ball is hit to the infield, the first-base player moves to the base until the foot is touching it. She then judges the path of the ball, stepping toward it with one foot and stretching forward. The other foot remains in contact with the base (Figure 31.11).

FIGURE 31.10. Sure stop

FIGURE 31.11. First-base player stretching for a catch

Catcher's Position

The catcher assumes a crouched position with the feet about shoulder width apart and the left foot slightly ahead of the right. He should use a glove and wear a mask. A body protector is desirable. The catcher is positioned just beyond the range of the swing of the bat (Figure 31.12).

BATTING (RIGHT-HANDED)

The batter stands with the left side of the body toward the pitcher. The feet are spread and the weight is on both feet. The body should be facing the plate. The bat is held with the trademark up, and the left hand grasps the bat lower than the right. The bat is held over the right shoulder, pointing both back and up. The elbows are away from the body (Figure 31.13).

The swing begins with a hip roll and a short step forward in the direction of the pitcher. The bat is then swung level with the ground at the height of the pitch. The eyes are kept on the ball until it is hit. After the hit, there must be good follow-through.

The batter should avoid the following: lifting the front foot high off the ground, stepping back with the rear foot, dropping the rear shoulder, chopping down on the ball,

FIGURE 31.12. Catcher's position

FIGURE 31.13. Batter's position

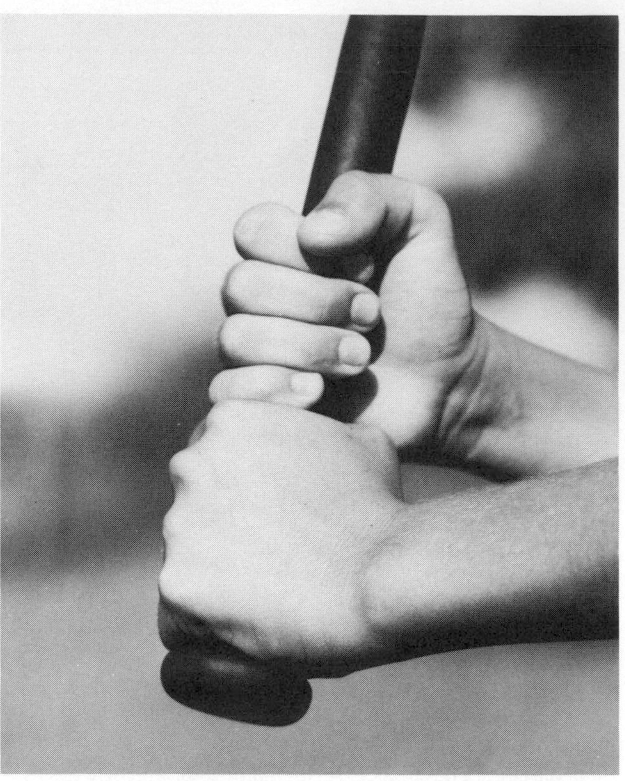
FIGURE 31.15. Long grip

FIGURE 31.14. Choke grip

golfing, dropping the elbows, or crouching or bending forward. Failure to keep the eyes on the ball is a serious error.

Youngsters should get experience with the choke grip (Figure 31.14), the long grip (Figure 31.15), and the middle grip (Figure 31.16). Beginning batters can start with the choke grip. In any case, the grip should be light, because this relaxes the forearm muscles.

BUNTING (RIGHT-HANDED)

To bunt, the batter turns to face the pitcher, the right foot alongside home plate. As the pitcher releases the ball, the upper hand is run about halfway up the bat. The bunter holds the bat loosely in front of the body and parallel to the ground to meet the ball (Figure 31.17). The ball can be directed down the first- or third-base line.

The surprise, or drag, bunt is done without squaring around to face the pitcher. The batter holds the bat in a choke grip. When the pitcher lets go of the ball, the batter runs the right hand up the bat. She directs the ball down either foul line, keeping it as close as possible to the line in fair territory.

BASE RUNNING

When the batter hits the ball, he should run hard and purposefully toward first base, no matter what kind of hit

FIGURE 31.16. Middle grip

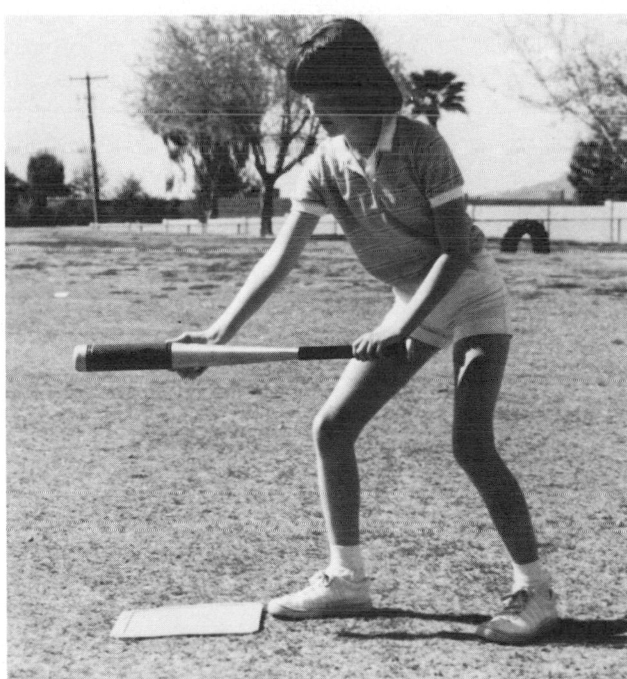

FIGURE 31.17. Regular bunt position

it is. The runner should run past the bag, tagging it in the process, and should step on the foul-line side of the base to avoid a collision with the first-base player.

Since a runner on base must hold the base position until the pitcher releases the ball, securing a fast start away from the base is essential. With either toe in contact with the base, the runner assumes a body lean, the weight on the ball of the leading foot and the eyes on the pitcher. After the pitch is made, the runner takes a few steps away from the base in the direction of the next base.

INSTRUCTIONAL PROCEDURES

1. Safety is of the utmost importance. The following precautions should be observed.
   a. Throwing the bat is a constant danger. The members of the batting team should stand on the side opposite the batter. For a right-handed batter, the batting team members should be on the first-base side and vice versa.
   b. The following techniques help keep the batter from throwing the bat.
      (1) Have the batter touch the bat to the ground before dropping it.
      (2) Call the batter out if the bat is thrown.
      (3) Have the batter carry the bat to first base.
      (4) Have the batter change ends with the bat before dropping it.
      (5) Have the batter place the bat in a 3-ft circle before running.
   c. Sliding can lead to both bodily injury and destruction of clothing. No sliding should be permitted. Runners should be called out when they slide into base.
   d. If a catcher stands close behind the plate while catching, she must wear a mask. A body protector is also recommended.
   e. Colliding while running for the ball can be held to a minimum if players call for the ball and do not trespass on another player's area.
   f. When changing fields at the beginning of an inning, the batting team stays on the first-base side of the infield. The fielding team goes to bat via the third-base side of the infield.
   g. Soft softballs should be used, particularly in the lower grades. Fleece balls are excellent for introductory throwing skills.
   h. All bats should be taped. Broken or cracked bats should not be used, even when taped.
2. Batting skills must be stressed. There is no more ego-shattering experience for a youngster than to stand at the plate and demonstrate an ineptness that draws scorn and ridicule from peers. Make sure that youngsters know the correct stance and proper mechanics of batting. Improved hitting will come with practice.

3. The spoiler of many softball games is the pitcher-batter duel. If this becomes prolonged, the other players become justifiably bored from standing around. Having a member of the batting team pitch is one way to eliminate the problem.
4. Players should rotate positions often. A good rule in physical education classes is that everyone, including the pitcher, should rotate to another position at the start of a new inning.
5. The distance between the bases greatly affects the game. The distance should be lessened or increased according to the game and the capacities of the children.
6. Umpires can be appointed, or the team at bat can umpire. A convenient rule to follow is that the person who made the last out of the previous inning will be the umpire for the next inning. All students should receive instruction in umpiring. To expect a child to umpire properly without proper instruction is poor teaching.
7. Good players should be encouraged to recognize and give approval and support to those who are less skillful. Because there will be many differences in ability, the opportunity is present for a lesson in tolerance. It is important not to let an error become a tragedy to a child.
8. Each player should run out a hit, no matter how hopeless it seems.
9. Each lead-up game should be analyzed for its purpose. The needed skills should be practiced before inclusion in the game.
10. Children must recognize that the perfection of softball skills comes only through good practice.
11. Respect for officials and acceptance of the umpire's judgment must be taught. The disreputable practice of baiting the umpire should not be a part of the child's softball experiences.
12. Care of equipment is the responsibility of all. The bat trademark should be kept up when the ball is contacted, and the bat should be used to bat softballs only. Hitting rocks and sticks with the bat injures it and lessens its effectiveness and life expectancy. The bat should be carried, not thrown, from one person to another.

ORGANIZING FOR INSTRUCTION

It is essential that students develop skills in softball and acquire knowledge about the various phases of the game. The amount of field space and the equipment available determine the instructional organization. To cover the many phases of the game, a multiple-activity or station pattern is best. The approach should use the following guidelines.

1. Children should have many opportunities to practice the different skills. Even with rotation, there should be as many small groups as possible. Throwing and fielding grounders can be practiced between two children, for example.

2. The basis of the rotational system can be the squad, with responsibility centered on the captain for the conduct of the practice at different stations.

3. The Little League problem cannot be ignored. These "stars" generally have higher skill levels than others in the class. Their skills can be used in various phases of instruction, provided sufficient direction for these efforts is given. Boys are more likely to have Little League experience than girls, but this is changing.

4. Activities and procedures to be stressed at each station should be carefully planned and communicated to all participants. Prior meetings with captains and other helpers are valuable. Appropriate softball rules should be covered.

5. Complete rotation of stations is not necessary at each class session. During a class session, teams may practice at one station for part of the time and then use the remainder of the time to participate in an appropriate lead-up game.

6. There must be directions for each station, and individuals also must assume responsibility for cooperating during the planned activities and for making the most of the skill development opportunities.

7. The use of the rotational station system does not rule out activities involving the class as a whole. Mimetic drills (i.e., drills without equipment) are valuable for establishing fundamental movement patterns for most skills. Students can practice such techniques as batting, pitching, throwing, and fielding without worrying about results. Correct technique should be emphasized. Discussions of rules and various demonstrations for the entire class are fruitful.

8. Station teaching provides an excellent opportunity for visiting high school students to provide assistance. In many school systems, high school students visit elementary schools on a regular basis for observation and educational experiences, some of which are admittedly sterile. Here is an opportunity to make good, meaningful use of these visitors.

9. The teacher's role in the rotational system is to circulate from one station to another to provide encouragement, correction, coaching, and motivation for learning.

10. A motivational factor can be introduced through comparisons of the rotational system with varsity or major league practices. This gives the activity an adult flavor.

11. Selection can be made from the list of lead-up games, particularly for activities that are suitable for squads or smaller groups.

BASIC SOFTBALL RULES

Most sporting goods establishments have copies of the official rules for softball. Although an official rule guide should be used by students when they are studying rules, a general idea of the basic rules of the game can be obtained from the following discussion.

PLAYING AREA

The official diamond has 60-ft baselines and a pitching distance of 46 ft. Play in the intermediate grades should be with baselines no longer than 45 ft and a pitching distance of 35 ft or less.

PLAYERS

The nine players on a softball team are the catcher, pitcher, first-, second-, and third-base players, shortstop, and left, center, and right fielders. The right fielder is the outfielder nearest first base.

BATTING ORDER

Players may bat in any order, although having them bat according to their positions in the field is at times convenient in class. Once the batting order has been established, it may not be changed, even if the player changes to another position in the field.

PITCHING

The pitcher must face the batter with both feet on the pitching rubber and with the ball held in front with both hands. The pitcher is allowed one step toward the batter and must deliver the ball while taking that step. The ball must be pitched underhanded. The pitcher cannot fake a pitch or make any motion toward the plate without delivering the ball. It is illegal to roll or bounce the ball to the batter. No quick return is allowed before the batter is ready. To be called a "strike," a pitch must be over the plate and between the knees and shoulders of the batter. A "ball" is a pitch that does not go through this area.

BATTING

The bat must be a softball bat. The batter cannot cross to the other side of the plate when the pitcher is ready to pitch. If a player bats out of turn, he is out. A bunt that goes foul on the third strike is an out. A pitched ball that touches or hits the batter entitles the batter to first base, provided he does not strike or bunt at the ball.

STRIKING OUT

A batter is out when she misses the ball on the third strike. This is called "striking out."

BATTER SAFE

The batter who reaches first base before the fielding team can field the ball and throw it to first is safe.

FAIR BALL

A fair ball is any batted ball that settles on fair territory between home and first base and home and third base. A ball that rolls over a base or through the field into fair territory is a fair ball. Fly balls (including line drives) that drop into fair territory beyond the infield are fair balls. Foul lines are in fair territory.

FOUL BALL

A foul ball is a batted ball that settles outside the foul lines between home and first or between home and third. A fly ball that drops into foul territory beyond the bases is a foul.

FLY BALL

Any fly ball (foul or fair), if caught, is an out. A foul fly, however, must rise over the head of the batter or it is ruled a foul tip. A foul tip caught on the third strike, then, puts the batter out.

BASE RUNNING

In base running, no leadoff is permitted. The runner must stay on base until the ball leaves the pitcher's hand on penalty of being called out. On an overthrow when the ball goes into foul territory and out of play, runners advance one base beyond the base to which they were headed at the time of the overthrow. On an overthrow at second base by the catcher with the ball rolling into center field, the runners may advance as far as they can. The runner may try to avoid being tagged on a baseline but is limited to a 3-ft distance on each side of a direct line from base to base. A runner hit by a batted ball while *off* the base is out. The batter, however, is entitled to first base. Base runners must touch all bases. If a runner fails to touch a base, it is an appeal play, which means that the fielding team must call the oversight to the attention of the umpire before he will rule on the play.

Runners may overrun first base without penalty. On all other bases, the runner must maintain contact with the base or be tagged out. To score, the runner must make contact with home plate.

SCORING

A run is scored when the base runner makes the circuit of the bases (i.e., first, second, third, and home) before the batting team has three outs. If the third out is a force out, no run is scored, even if the runner crossed home plate before the out was actually made.

The situation needing the most clarification occurs when a runner is on base with one out and the batter hits a fly ball that is caught, making the second out. The runner is forced to return to the base previously occupied before the ball reaches that base, or she, too, is out. If she makes the *third* out as a result of her failure to return to the base in time, no run is scored.

SOFTBALL DRILLS

Softball drills lend themselves to a station setup. For a regular class of 30 students, four squads with 7 or 8 students each is suggested. Activities at each station can emphasize a single skill or a combination of skills. Situational drills can also be incorporated. Children should realize that constant repetition is necessary to develop, maintain, and sharpen softball skills.

The multitude of softball skills to be practiced allows for many different combinations and organizations. The following are examples of combinations and organizations that can be used in station teaching.

1. Batting can be organized in many ways. One key to an effective program is to ensure that each child has many opportunities to hit the ball successfully. Sufficient area is needed.

a. Use a batting tee. For each station, two tees are needed, with a bat and at least two balls for each tee. Three to five children are assigned to each tee. There should be a batter, a catcher to handle incoming balls, and fielders. When only three children are in a unit, the catcher should be eliminated. Each batter is allowed a certain number of swings before rotating to the field. The catcher becomes the next batter, and a fielder moves up to catcher.

b. Organize informal hitting practice. A batter, a pitcher, and fielders are needed. Two batting groups should be organized at each station. A catcher is optional.

c. Practice hitting a foam rubber ball thrown underhanded. The larger ball is easier to hit.

d. Practice bunting with groups of three—a pitcher, batter, and fielder.

2. To practice throwing and catching, do the following drills.

a. Throw back and forth, practicing various throws.

b. Throw ground balls back and forth for fielding practice.

c. One player acts as a first-base player, throwing grounders to the other infielders and receiving the put-out throw.

d. Throw flies back and forth.

e. Hit flies, with two or three fielders catching.

f. Establish four bases and throw from base to base.

3. Proper pitching and catching form should be used for pitching practice.

a. Pitch to another player over a plate.

b. Call balls and strikes. One player is the pitcher, the second is the catcher, and the third is the umpire. A fourth player can be a stationary batter to provide a more realistic pitching target.

c. Pitch toward pitching targets, either a wooden target (see p. 548) or a similar area outlined on a wall.

4. For infield drill, children are placed in the normal infield positions—behind the plate, at first, second, and third base, and at shortstop. One child acts as the batter and gives directions. The play should begin with practice in throwing around the bases either way. After this, the batter can roll the ball to the different infielders, beginning at third base and continuing in turn around the infield, with each player throwing to first to retire an imaginary runner. Various play situations can be developed. If the batter is skillful enough, he can hit the ball to infielders instead of rolling it, thus making the drill more realistic. Using a second softball saves time when the ball is thrown or batted past an infielder, because players do not have to wait for the ball to be retrieved before proceeding with the next play. After the ball has been thrown to first base, other throws around the infield can take place. The drill can also be done with only a partial infield.

5. Various situations can be arranged for practicing base running.

a. Bunt and run to first. A pitcher, a batter, an infielder, and a first-base player are needed. The pitcher serves the ball up for a bunt, and the batter, after bunting, takes off for first base. A fielding play can be made on the runner.

b. Bunt and run to second base. The batter bunts the ball and runs to first base and then on to second, making a proper turn at first.

6. Play Pepper. (This is one of the older skill games in baseball.) A line of three or four players is about 10 yd in front of and facing a batter. The players toss the ball to the batter, who attempts to hit *controlled* grounders back to them (Figure 31.18). The batter stays at bat for a period of time and then rotates to the field.

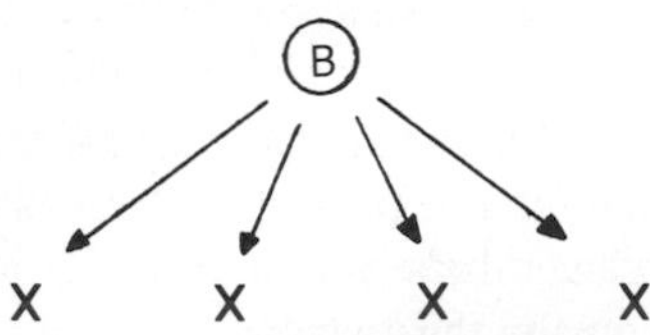

FIGURE 31.18. Play Pepper

7. Some of the game-type activities, such as Batter Ball, In a Pickle, Five Hundred, and Scrub, can be scheduled at stations.

Stations might be organized as follows. (Numbers and letters refer to the drills just listed. Page numbers refer to activities not yet discussed.)

Station 1—Batting (see 1a)
Station 2—Throwing, fielding grounders (see 2c)

Station 3—Base running—In a Pickle (see p. 544)
Station 4—Bunting and base running (see 5a)

Another example of station arrangement is the following.

Station 1—Batting and fielding—Pepper (see 6)
Station 2—Pitching and umpiring (see 3b)
Station 3—Infield practice (see 4)
Station 4—Batting (see 1b)

Stations might also be arranged as follows.

Station 1—Fungo hitting, fielding, throwing
Station 2—Bunting and fielding (see 1d)
Station 3—Pitching to targets (see 3c)
Station 4—Batting (see 1a and 1b)

SOFTBALL ACTIVITIES

THIRD GRADE

Throw-It-and-Run Softball

Playing Area: Softball diamond reduced in size

Players: 7 to 11 (usually 9) on each team

Supplies: A softball or similar ball

Skills: Throwing, catching, fielding, base running

Throw-It-and-Run Softball is played like regular softball with the following exception. With one team in the field at regular positions, the pitcher throws the ball to the batter, who, instead of batting the ball, catches it, and immediately throws it into the field. The ball is then treated as a batted ball, and regular softball rules prevail. No stealing is permitted, however, and runners must hold bases until the batter throws the ball. A foul ball is an out.

Variations

1. *Under-Leg Throw.* Instead of throwing directly, the batter can turn to the right, lift the left leg, and throw the ball under the leg into the playing field.

2. *Beat-Ball Throw.* The fielders, instead of playing regular softball rules, throw the ball directly home to the catcher. The batter, in the meantime, runs around the bases. A point is scored for each base that she touches before the catcher receives the ball. A ball caught on the fly would mean no score. Similarly, a foul ball would not score points but would count as a turn at bat.

Two-Pitch Softball

Playing Area: Softball diamond

Players: 7 to 11 on each team

Supplies: A softball, a bat

Skills: Most softball skills, except regular pitching

Two-Pitch Softball is played like regular softball with the following changes.

1. A member of the team at bat pitches. A system of rotation should be set up so every child takes a turn as pitcher.

2. The batter has only two pitches in which to hit the ball, and must hit a fair ball on one of these pitches or he is out. The batter can foul the first ball, but if he fouls the second, he is out. There is no need to call balls or strikes.

3. The pitcher does not field the ball. A member of the team in the field acts as the fielding pitcher.

4. If the batter hits the ball, regular softball rules are followed. No stealing is permitted, however.

Teaching Suggestions: Since the pitcher is responsible for pitching a ball that can be hit, the pitching distance can be shortened to give the batter ample opportunity to hit the ball. The instructor can act as the pitcher.

Variation: *Three Strikes*—In this game, the batter is allowed three pitches (strikes) to hit the ball. Otherwise, the game proceeds as in Two-Pitch Softball.

FOURTH GRADE

Two-Pitch Softball

Introduced in the 3rd-grade program, Two-Pitch Softball should be emphasized in the 4th grade as well.

Hit and Run

Playing Area: Softball field, gymnasium

Players: 6 to 15 players on each team

Supplies: A volleyball or soccer ball or playground ball, home plate, and base markers

Skills: Catching, throwing, running, dodging

One team is at bat, and the other is scattered in the field. Boundaries must be established, but the area does not have to be shaped like a baseball diamond. The batter stands at home plate with the ball. In front of the batter, 12 ft away, is a short line over which the ball must be hit to be in play. In the center of the field, about 40 ft away, is the base marker.

The batter bats the ball with the hands or fists so that it crosses the short line and lands inside the area. She then attempts to run down the field, around the base marker, and back to home plate without being hit by the ball (Figure 31.19). The members of the other team field the ball and throw it at the runner. The fielder may not run or walk with the ball but may throw to a teammate who is closer to the runner.

A run is scored each time a batter runs around the marker and back to home plate without getting hit by the

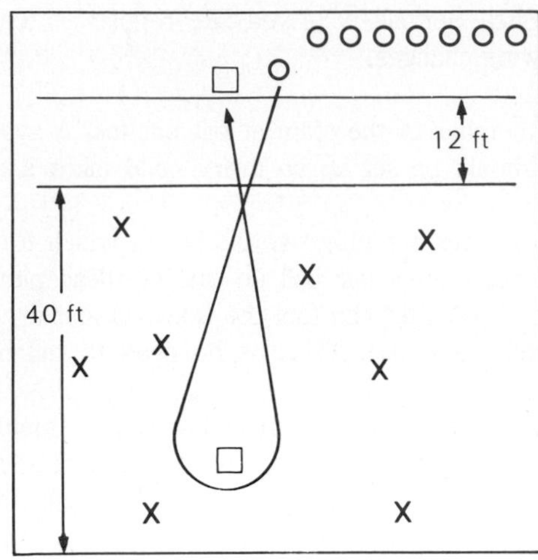

FIGURE 31.19. Hit and Run

ball. A run also is scored if a foul is called on the fielding team for walking or running with the ball.

The batter is out in any of the following circumstances.

1. A fly ball is caught.
2. He is hit below the shoulders with the ball.
3. The ball is not hit beyond the short line.
4. The team touches home plate with the ball before the runner returns. (This out is used *only* when the runner stops in the field and does not continue.)

The game can be played in innings of three outs each, or a change of team positions can be made after all members of one team have batted.

Teaching Suggestion: The distance the batter runs around the base marker may have to be shortened or lengthened, depending on the children's ability.

Variation: *Five Passes*—The batter is out when a fly ball is caught or when the ball is passed among five different players of the team in the field, with the last pass to a player at home plate beating the runner to the plate. The passes must not touch the ground.

Kick Softball

Playing Area: Regular softball field with a home base 3-ft square.

Players: 7 to 11 on each team

Supplies: A soccer ball or another ball to be kicked

Skills: Kicking a rolling ball, throwing, catching, running bases

The batter stands in the kicking area, a 3-ft-square home plate. The batter kicks the ball rolled on the ground by the pitcher. The ball should be rolled at moderate speed. An umpire calls balls and strikes. A "strike" is a ball that rolls over the 3-ft square. A "ball" rolls outside this area. Strikeouts and walks are called the same as in regular softball. The number of foul balls allowed should be limited. No base stealing is permitted. Otherwise, the game is played like softball.

Variations

1. The batter kicks a stationary ball. This saves time, since there is no pitching.

2. *Punch Ball.* The batter can hit a volleyball as in a volleyball serve or punch a ball pitched by the pitcher.

In a Pickle

Playing Area: Any flat surface with 60 sq ft of room

Players: Three or more

Supplies: A softball, two bases 45 to 55 ft apart

Skills: Throwing, catching, running down a base runner, and tagging

When a base runner gets caught between two bases and is in danger of being run down and tagged, she is "in a pickle." To begin, both fielders are on bases, one with a ball. The runner is positioned in the base path 10 to 15 ft away from the fielder with the ball. The two fielders throw the ball back and forth in an attempt to run down the runner between the bases and tag her. If the runner escapes and secures a base, she gets to try again. Otherwise, a system of rotation is established, including any sideline (waiting) players. No sliding is permitted.

FIFTH GRADE

Five Hundred

Playing Area: Field big enough for fungo hitting

Players: 3 to 12 (or more)

Supplies: A softball, a bat

Skills: Fungo batting, catching flies, fielding grounders

There are many versions of the old game of Five Hundred. A batter stands on one side of the field and bats the ball to a number of fielders, who are scattered. The fielders attempt to become the batter by reaching a score of 500. Fielders earn 200 points for catching a ball on the fly, 100 points for catching a ball on the first bounce, and 50 points for fielding a grounder cleanly. Whenever a change of batters is made, all fielders lose their points and must start over.

Variations

1. The fielder's points must total exactly 500.

2. Points are subtracted from the fielder's score if a ball is mishandled. If a fly ball is dropped, for example, 200 points are lost.

Batter Ball

Playing Area: Softball diamond

Players: 8 to 12 on each team

Supplies: A softball, a bat, a mask

Skills: Slow pitching, hitting, fielding, catching flies

Batter Ball involves batting and fielding but no base running. It is much like batting practice but adds the element of competition. A line is drawn directly from first to third base. This is the balk line over which a batted ball must travel to be fielded. Another line is drawn from a point on the foul line 3.5 ft behind third base to a point 5 ft behind second base and in line with home plate. Another line connects this point with a point on the other baseline 3.5 ft behind first base. The blue area in the diagram is the infield (Figure 31.20).

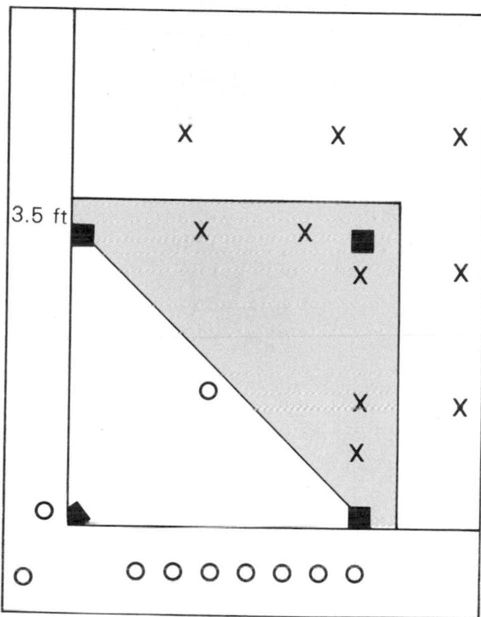

FIGURE 31.20. Field for Batter Ball

Each batter is given three pitches by a member of his own team to hit the ball into fair territory across the balk line. The pitcher may stop any ground ball before it crosses the balk line. The batter then gets another turn at bat.

Scoring is as follows.

1. A successful grounder scores one point. A grounder is successful when an infielder fails to handle it cleanly within the infield area. Only one player may field the ball. If the ball is fielded properly, the batter is out.

2. A line drive in the infield area is worth one point if not caught. It can be handled for an out on any bounce. Any line drive caught on the fly is also an out.

3. A fly ball in the infield area scores one point if not caught. For an out, the ball must be caught legally by the first person touching it.

4. A two-bagger scores two points. Any fly ball, line drive or not, that lands fairly in the outfield area without being caught scores two points. If it is caught, the batter is out.

5. A home run scores three points. Any fly ball driven over the head of the farthest outfielder in that area scores a home run.

Three outs can constitute an inning, or all batters can be allowed one turn at bat and then the team changes to the field. A new set of infielders should be in place for each inning. The old set goes to the outfield. Pitchers should be limited to one inning. They also take a turn at bat.

Teaching Suggestions: Many games of this type require special fields, either rectangular or narrowly angled. This game was selected because it uses the regular softball field with the added lines. The lines can be drawn with a stick or can be marked using regular marking methods.

The pitcher has to decide whether he should stop the ball. If the ball goes beyond the restraining line, it is in play even if he touched it.

Variations: Batter Ball can be modified for use as a station in rotational teaching, with the emphasis on individual batting and squad organization. One member of the squad would be at bat and would get a definite number of chances (e.g., five) to score. She keeps her own point total. The other squad members occupy the necessary game positions.

Home Run

Playing Area: Softball diamond (only first base is used)

Players: Four to ten

Supplies: A softball, a bat

Skills: Most softball skills, modified base running

The crucial players are a batter, a catcher, a pitcher, and one fielder. Any other players are fielders; some can take positions in the infield. The batter hits a regular pitch and on a fair ball must run to first base and back home before the ball can be returned to the catcher.

The batter is out whenever any of the following occurs:

1. A fly ball (fair or foul) is caught.

2. He strikes out.

3. On a fair ball, the ball beats the batter back to home plate.

Teaching Suggestions: To keep skillful players from staying too long at bat, a rule can be made that, after a certain number of home runs, the batter automatically must take a place in the field. A rotation (work-up) system should be established. The batter should go to right field, move to center, and then to left field. The rotation continues through third base, shortstop, second base, first base, pitcher, and catcher. The catcher is the next batter. Naturally, the number of positions depends on the number of players in the game. If there are enough players, an additional batter can be waiting to take a turn.

The game can be played with only three youngsters, eliminating the catcher. With only one fielder, the pitcher covers home plate. The first-base distance should be far enough away to be a challenge but close enough so that a well-hit ball scores a home run. The distance depends on the number playing and the capacities of the children.

Variations

1. This game can be played like softball—allowing batter to stop at first base if another batter is up.

2. A fly ball caught by a fielder puts that player directly to bat. The batter then takes a place at the end of the rotation, and the other players rotate up to the position of the fielder who caught the ball. This rule has one drawback. It may cause children to scramble and fight for fly balls, which is not desirable in softball. The ball belongs to the player in whose territory it falls.

3. *Triangle Ball.* First and third bases are brought in toward each other, thus narrowing the playing field. Second base is not used. The game gets its name from the triangle formed by home plate and the two bases. The batter must circle first and third bases and return home before the ball reaches home plate. This game can also be played with as few as three players, with the pitcher covering home plate.

Tee Ball

Playing Area: Softball field

Players: 7 to 11 on each team

Supplies: A softball, a bat, a batting tee

Skills: Most softball skills (except pitching and stealing bases), hitting a ball from a tee

This game is an excellent variation of softball and is played under softball rules with the following exceptions.

1. Instead of hitting a pitched ball, the batter hits the ball from a tee. The catcher places the ball on the tee. After the batter hits the ball, the play is the same as in regular softball. With no pitching, there is no stealing. A runner stays on the base until the ball is hit by the batter.

2. A fielder occupies the position normally held by the pitcher. The primary duty of this fielder is to field bunts and ground balls and to back up the infielders on throws.

Teams can play regular innings for three outs or change to the field after each player has had a turn at bat.

Teaching Suggestions: A tee can be purchased or made from a radiator hose. An improvised batting tee is shown in Figure 31.21 (for another type of tee, see p. 585). If the tee is not adjustable, three different sizes should be available.

The batter should take a position far enough behind the tee so that, in stepping forward to swing, she will hit the ball slightly in front of her.

Tee Ball has many advantages. There are no strikeouts, every child hits the ball, there is no dueling between pitcher and batter, and fielding opportunities abound.

FIGURE 31.21. An improvised batting tee

Scrub (Work-up)

Playing Area: Softball field

Players: 7 to 15

Supplies: A softball, a bat

Skills: Most softball skills

The predominant feature of Scrub is the rotation of the players. The game is played with regular softball rules, with each individual more or less playing for herself. There are at least two batters, generally three. A catcher, pitcher, and first-base player are essential. The remaining players assume the other positions. Whenever the batter is out, she goes to a position in right field. All other players move up one position, with the catcher becoming the batter. The first-base player becomes the pitcher, the pitcher moves to catcher, and all others move up one place.

Variation: If a fly ball is caught, the fielder and batter exchange positions.

SIXTH GRADE

Slow-Pitch Softball

Playing Area: Softball diamond

Players: Ten on each team

Supplies: A softball, a bat

Skills: Most softball skills

The major difference between regular softball and Slow-Pitch Softball is in the pitching, but there are other modifications to the game as well. With slower pitching, there is more hitting and thus more action on the bases and in the field. Outfielders are an important part of the game, because many long drives are hit. Rule changes from the game of official softball are as follows.

1. The pitch must be a slow pitch. Any other pitch is illegal and is called a ball. The pitch must be slow with an arc of 1 ft. It must not rise over 10 ft from the ground, however. Its legality depends on the umpire's call.

2. There are ten players instead of nine. The extra one, called the roving fielder, plays in the outfield and handles line drives hit just over the infielders.

3. The batter must take a full swing at the ball and is out if he chops at the ball or bunts.

4. If the batter is hit by a pitched ball, she is not entitled to first base. The pitch is merely called a ball. Otherwise, balls and strikes are called as in softball.

5. The runner must hold base until the pitch has reached or passed home plate. No stealing is permitted.

Teaching Suggestion: Shortening the pitching distance somewhat may be desirable. Much of the success of the game depends on the pitcher's ability to get the ball over the plate.

Babe Ruth Ball

Playing Area: Softball diamond

Players: Five

Supplies: A bat, a ball, four cones or other markers

Skills: Batting, pitching, fielding

The three outfield zones—left, center, and right field—are separated by four cones. It is helpful if foul lines have been drawn, but cones can define them (Figure 31.22). The batter calls the field to which he intends to hit. The pitcher throws controlled pitches so the batter can hit easily. The batter remains in position as long as he hits to the designated field. Field choices must be rotated. The batter gets only one swing to make a successful hit. He may allow a ball to go by, but if he swings, it counts as a try. There is no base running. Players rotate.

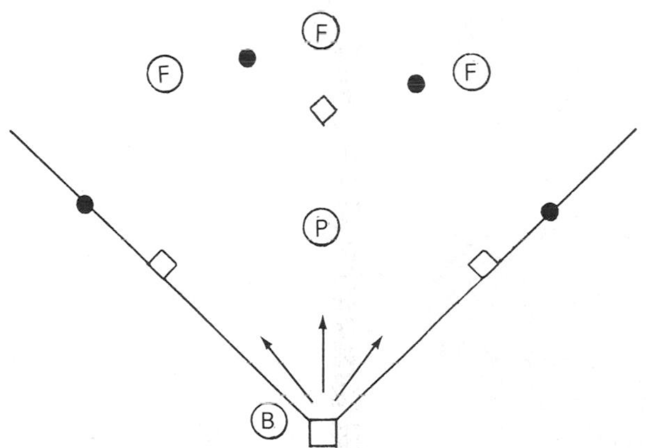

FIGURE 31.22. Babe Ruth Ball

Teaching Suggestions: Children play this game informally on sandlots with a variety of rules. Some possibilities to consider are these. What happens when a fly ball is caught? What limitations should be made on hitting easy grounders? Let the players decide about these points and others not covered by the stated rules.

Hurry Baseball (One-Pitch Softball)

Playing Area: Softball diamond

Players: 8 to 12 on each team

Supplies: A softball, a bat

Skills: Slow pitching, most softball skills except stealing bases and bunting

Hurry Baseball demands rapid changes from batting to fielding, and vice versa. The game is like regular softball, with the following exceptions.

1. The pitcher is from the team at bat and must not interfere with, or touch, a batted ball on penalty of the batter being called out.

2. The team coming to bat does not wait for the fielding team to get set. Since it has its own pitcher, the pitcher gets the ball to the batter just as quickly as the batter can grab a bat and get ready. The fielding team has to hustle to get out to their places.

3. Only one pitch is allowed to a batter. The batter must hit a fair ball or she is out. The pitch is made from about two thirds of the normal pitching distance.

4. No stealing is permitted.

5. No bunting is permitted. The batter must take a full swing.

The game provides much activity in the fast place changes that must be made after the third out. Teams in the field learn to put the next hitter as catcher, so she can bat immediately when the third out is made. Batters must bat in order. Scoring follows regular softball rules.

Three-Team Softball

Playing Area: Softball diamond

Players: 12 to 15

Supplies: A mask, a ball, a bat

Skills: All softball skills

Three-Team Softball works well with 12 players, a number considered too few to divide into two effective fielding teams. The players are instead divided into three teams. The rules of softball apply, with the following exceptions.

1. One team is at bat, one team covers the infield (including the catcher), and the third team provides the outfielders and the pitcher.

2. The team at bat must bat in a definite order. This means that, because of the small number of batters on each side, instances can occur when the person due to bat is on base. To take a turn at bat, the runner must be replaced by a player not on base.

3. After three outs, the teams rotate, with the outfield moving to the infield, the infield taking a turn at bat, and the batters going to the outfield.

4. An inning is over when all three teams have batted.

5. The pitcher should be limited to pitching one inning only. A player may repeat as pitcher only after all members of his team have had a chance to pitch.

SOFTBALL SKILL TESTS

THROWING FOR ACCURACY

To test accuracy in throwing, a target with three concentric circles of 54, 36, and 18 in. is drawn on a wall. Scoring is 1, 2, and 3 points, respectively, for the circles. Five trials are allowed, for a possible score of 15. Balls hitting a line score the higher number.

Instead of the suggested target, a tire can be hung. Scoring allows 2 points for a throw through the tire and 1 point for simply hitting the tire. A maximum of 10 points is possible with this system.

THROWING DISTANCE

In the test of throwing for distance, each child is allowed three throws, and the longest throw on the fly is recorded.

FIELDING GROUNDERS

A file of players is stationed behind a restraining line. A thrower is about 30 ft in front of this line. Each player in turn attempts to field five ground balls. The score is the number of balls fielded cleanly. It is recognized that inconsistencies will occur in the throw and bounce of the ground balls served up for fielding. If the opportunity was obviously not a fair one, the child should get another chance.

CIRCLING THE BASES

Runners are timed as they circle the bases. A diamond with four bases is needed, plus a stopwatch for timing. Two runners can run at one time by starting from opposite corners of the diamond. Two watches are needed with this system.

The batter can bunt a pitched ball and run around the bases. The timing starts with the bunt and finishes when the batter touches home plate.

PITCHING

Pitching is one of the easier skills to test in softball and is certainly one of the most popular with children. Two basic methods are used for testing. In the first, each child takes a certain number of pitches at a target. Scoring is on the basis of the number of strikes that can be thrown. In the second, each child pitches regularly, as if to a batter, with balls and strikes being counted. Batters are either struck out or walked. The test score is the number of batters the child is able to strike out from a given number at bat. This is expressed as a percentage.

In either method, a target is needed. It should be 19 in. wide and 42 in. high. It can be outlined temporarily on a wall with chalk or paint. The lower portion of the target should be about 18 in. above the ground or floor. If the target is constructed from plywood or wood, some means of support or of hanging the target will be needed.

The boundaries of the target should be counted as good. The pitching distance should be normal (35 ft), and regular pitching rules should be observed.

Old Woody is the name of a pitching target in the form of a stand that can be moved from school to school. The target size is shown in Figure 31.23. A sturdy frame holds the target and allows it to be used in almost any spot.

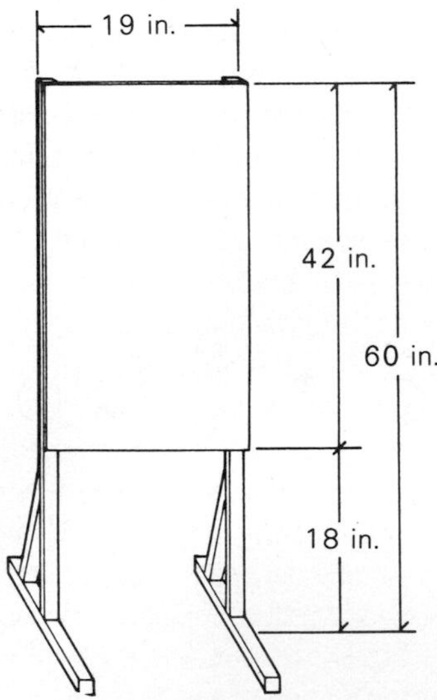

FIGURE 31.23. Old Woody pitching target

CHAPTER 32

Track, Field, and Cross-Country Running

Track, field, and cross-country activities carry much of their own motivation. Extensive television coverage and international and Olympic competitions have elevated track and field to a high status. These factors, coupled with the urge of boys and girls to run and jump and race against others, make track and field activities an exciting part of the program.

All children can benefit from track and field instruction. The opportunities to set personal goals are many. In the program, more attention should be given to progress toward a personal goal than to beating classmates; however, the desire to come out on top must not be lost. The instructional program should have as one of its aims the stimulation of all students to their best effort.

The elementary program in track and field should consist of short sprints (40 to 100 yd), running and standing long jumps, high jumps, hop-step-and-jumps, and relays. Jogging and distance running should be encouraged throughout the program. The primary emphasis should be on practice and personal accomplishment, but modified competition in cross-country running is quite acceptable. The idea that distance running is harmful to children is fast disappearing. Children should learn to establish a pace. Hurdling can be included when the equipment is available.

Children must understand the difference between walking, sprinting, running, striding (for pace), and jogging. Sprinting techniques are particularly important, with instruction centering on the correct form for starting, accelerating, and sprinting. Speed and quickness are important individual attributes that govern the degree of success in many play and sport activities. In many nations, teaching children how to sprint is considered as basic as teaching them to write.

Rules for the different events also should be covered. Since few elementary schools have a permanent track, laying out and lining the track (see p. 556) each year can be a valuable educational experience.

Some type of culminating meet is desirable to provide a goal for participants and a finishing touch to the unit of instruction. A discussion of meets is included at the end of this chapter.

INSTRUCTIONAL EMPHASIS AND SEQUENCE

A suggested program covering the 4th through the 6th grade is shown in Table 32.1.

FOURTH GRADE

The 4th-grade program should stress running short distances, learning different starting positions, and participating in the two types of long jump. Some running for distance is included and cross-country meets are introduced.

FIFTH GRADE

More serious efforts to achieve proper form begin in the 5th grade. The scissors style can be introduced in high jumping, and experimentation with other styles can be encouraged. Students should begin to use check marks with the running long jump. Running for distance should be started as well as relay work, including baton passing. Cross-country activities are continued through the 5th and 6th grades.

TABLE 32.1. SUGGESTED TRACK, FIELD, AND CROSS-COUNTRY RUNNING PROGRAM

	Fourth Grade	Fifth Grade	Sixth Grade
Skills			
Track and cross-country running	40- to 60- yard dashes Standing start Sprinter's start Jogging and cross-country running	50- to 80-yard dashes Sprinter's start Distance running Relays Jogging and cross-country running	60- to 100-yard dashes Sprinter's start Distance running Hurdling Relays Jogging and cross-country running Baton passing
Field	Standing long jump Running long jump	Standing long jump Running long jump High jump	Standing long jump Running long jump Hop-step-and-jump High jump

SIXTH GRADE

Hurdling, primarily for practice, is an addition to the program in the 6th grade. This activity should use modified hurdles. In the high jump, critical points of the Straddle Roll and the Western Roll should be explained. Developing pace in distance running without strong elements of competition is important. Relaxed, flowing running is the goal.

The hop-step-and-jump extends the range of jumping activities. Relays and baton passing are given attention. Sprinting instruction should emphasize the start, acceleration, and drive for the finish line. The Potato Shuttle Race adds a novel event to the program.

TRACK AND FIELD SKILLS

STARTING

Standing Start

The standing start should be practiced, for this type of start has a variety of uses in physical education activities. Many children find it more comfortable than the sprinter's start. As soon as is practical, however, children should accept the sprinter's start for track work.

In the standing start, the feet should be in a comfortable half-stride position. An extremely long stride is to be avoided. The body leans forward, so the center of gravity is forward. The weight is on the toes, and the knees are flexed slightly. The arms can be down or hanging slightly back (Figure 32.1).

Norwegian Start

The Norwegians use the standing start in a novel way. On the command "On your mark," the runner takes a position at the starting line with the left foot forward. On "Get set," the right hand is placed on the left knee and the left hand is carried back for a thrust (Figure 32.2). On "Go," the left hand comes forward, coupled with a drive by the right foot. The advantage claimed for this start is that it forces a body lean and makes use of the forward thrust of the arm coordinated with the step off on the opposite foot.

Sprinter's Start

There are several kinds of sprinter's starts, but teachers are advised to concentrate on a single one. The "On your mark" position places the toe of the front foot from 4 to 12 in. behind the starting line. The thumb and first finger are just behind the line, with other fingers adding support.

FIGURE 32.1. Standing start

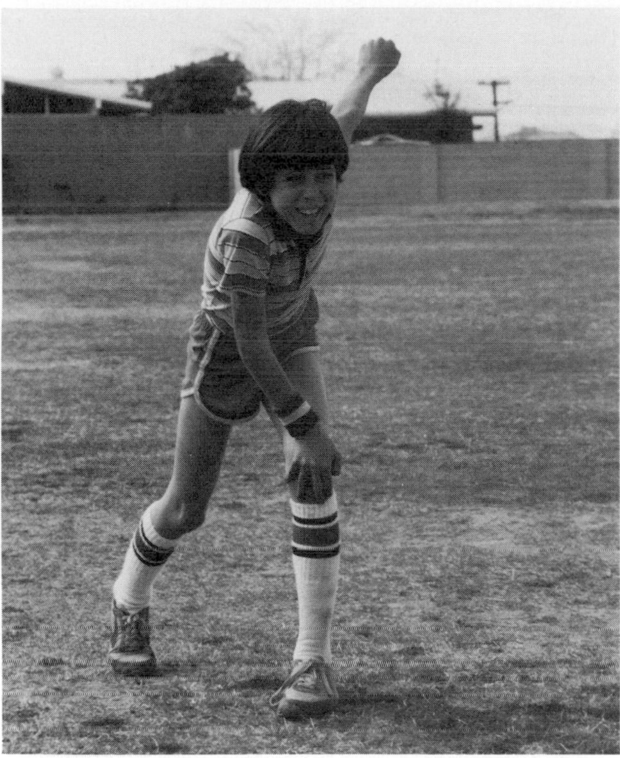

FIGURE 32.2. Norwegian start

The knee of the rear leg is placed just opposite the front foot or ankle (Figure 32.3).

For the "Get set" position, the seat is raised so it is slightly higher than the shoulders. The knee of the rear leg is raised off the ground, and the shoulders are moved forward over the hands. The weight is evenly distributed over the hands and feet (Figure 32.4).

FIGURE 32.3. Sprinter's start—"On your mark"

FIGURE 32.4. Sprinter's start—"Get set!"

On the "Go" signal, the runner pushes off sharply with both feet, with the front leg straightening as the back leg comes forward for a step. The body should rise gradually and not pop up suddenly.

The instructor should watch for a stumbling action on the first few steps. This results from too much weight resting on the hands in the "Get set" position.

RUNNING

Sprinting

In proper sprinting form, the body leans forward, with the arms swinging in opposition to the legs. The arms are bent at the elbows and swing from the shoulders in a forward and backward plane, not across the body (Figure 32.5). Forceful arm action aids sprinting. The knees are lifted sharply forward and upward and are brought down with a vigorous motion, followed by a forceful push from the toes. Sprinting is a driving and striding motion, as opposed to the inefficient pulling action displayed by some runners.

FIGURE 32.5. Proper sprinting form

Distance Running

In distance running, as compared with sprinting, the body is more erect and the motion of the arms is less pronounced. Pace is an important consideration. Runners should try to concentrate on the qualities of lightness, ease, relaxation, and looseness. Good striding action, a slight body lean, and good head position are also important. Runners should be encouraged to strike the ground with the heel first and then push off with the toes (Figure 32.6).

FIGURE 32.6. Proper running form

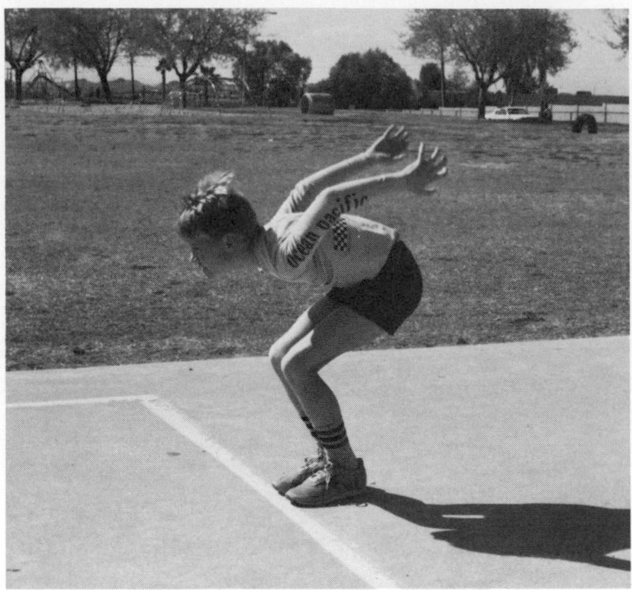

FIGURE 32.7. Standing long jump (note position of the hands and arms)

BATON PASSING

In baton passing, the runner exchanges the baton from her left hand to the right hand of the runner ahead. The runner should carry the baton like a candle when passing it to her teammate. The receiver reaches back with her right hand, fingers pointing down and thumb to the inside, and begins to move ahead when the advancing runner is 3 to 5 yd back. The receiver grasps the baton and immediately shifts it to her left hand while moving. The exchange to the next runner should be made on the move, with the front runner timing her start and increasing her speed to the pace of the runner coming in. If the baton is dropped, it must be picked up, or the team is disqualified.

An alternate way to receive the baton is to reach back with the hand facing up. The first method is considered more suitable for sprint relays.

JUMPING

In both the standing and running long jump, the measurement is made from the takeoff board or line to the nearest point on the ground touched by the jumper. It is therefore important for children not to fall or step backward after making the jump.

Standing Long Jump

In the standing long jump, the child toes the line with feet flat on the ground and fairly close together. The arms are brought forward in a preliminary swing and are then swung down and back (Figure 32.7). The jump is made with both feet as the arms are swung forcibly forward to assist in lifting the body upward and forward. In the air, the knees should be brought upward and forward, with the arms held forward to sustain balance.

Long Jump

For the running long jump, a short run is needed. The run should be timed so the toes of the jumping foot contact the board in a natural stride. The jumper takes off from one foot and strives for height. The landing is made on both feet after the knees have been brought forward. The landing should be in a forward direction, not sideward.

More efficient jumping is achieved when a checkpoint is used. The checkpoint can be established about halfway down the run. Competitors can help each other mark checkpoints. Each jumper should know how many steps back from the takeoff board the checkpoint is located. On the run for the jump, the student hits the mark with the appropriate foot (right or left) so as to reach the board with the correct foot in a normal stride for the jump.

The jumper should arrive at the checkpoint at full speed. The last four strides taken before the board should be relaxed in readiness for the takeoff. The last stride can be shortened somewhat (Figure 32.8).

A fair jump takes off behind the scratch line. A foul (scratch) jump is called if the jumper steps beyond the scratch line or runs into or through the pit. Each contestant is given a certain number of trials (jumps). A scratch jump counts as a trial. Measurement is from the scratch line to the nearest point of touch.

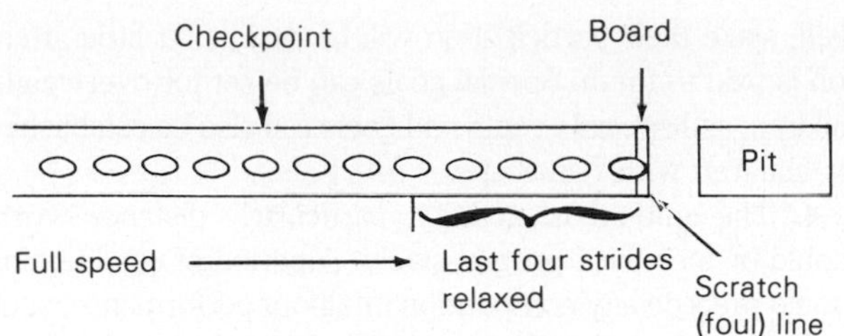

FIGURE 32.8. Long jump

Hop-Step-and-Jump

The hop-step-and-jump event is increasing in popularity, particularly because it is now included in Olympic competition. A takeoff board and a jumping pit are needed. The distance from the takeoff board to the pit should be one that even less skilled jumpers can make. The event begins with a run similar to that for the long jump. The takeoff is with one foot, and the jumper must land on the same foot to complete the hop. He then takes a step followed by a jump. The event finishes like the long jump, with a landing on both feet (Figure 32.9).

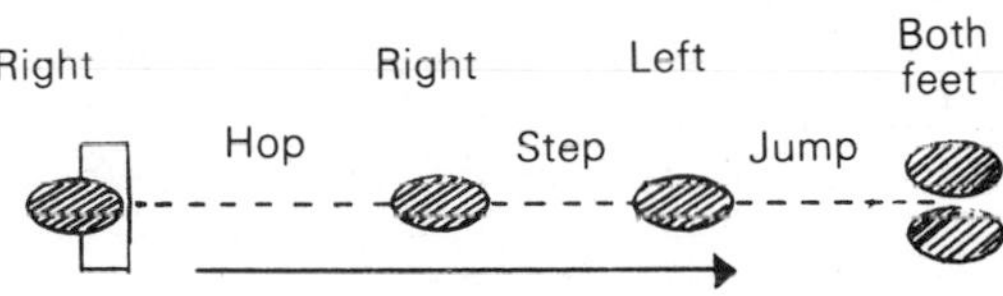

FIGURE 32.9. Hop-step-and-jump

The pattern can be changed to begin with the left foot. A checkpoint should be used, as for the long jump.

The jumper must not step over the takeoff board in the first hop, under penalty of fouling. Distance is measured from the front of the takeoff board to the closest place where the body touches. This is usually a mark made by one of the heels, but it could be a mark made by an arm or another part of the body if the jumper landed poorly and fell backward.

High Jump

High-jump techniques are developed by practice. The bar should be at a height that offers challenge but allows concentration on technique rather than on height. Too much emphasis on competition for height quickly eliminates the poorer jumpers who need the experience most. The practice of keeping the entire class together on a single high-jump facility is poor methodology. This arrangement determines who are the best jumpers in class but does little else.

Scissors Jump

For the Scissors Jump, the high-jump bar is approached from a slight angle. The takeoff is by the leg farthest from the bar. The near leg is lifted and goes over, followed quickly in a looping movement by the rear leg. A good upward kick with the front leg, together with an upward thrust of the arms, is needed. The knees should be straightened at the highest point of the jump. The landing is made on the lead foot followed by the rear foot.

Straddle Roll

For the Straddle Roll (Figure 32.10), the approach is made from the left side at an angle of no more than 45 degrees. There are four basic parts to the jump with respect to coaching. Each jumper should seek to develop his own style.

1. *Gather.* The last three steps must be fast and vigorous, with the body leaning back a bit. The takeoff is on the left foot.

2. *Kick.* The right leg is kicked vigorously as the jumping foot is planted.

3. *Arm movement.* An abrupt lift with both arms is made, with the left arm reaching over the bar and the right moving straight up. This puts the jumper in a straddle position as he goes over.

4. *Back leg clearance.* Clearance is accomplished by straightening the body, rolling the hips to the right (over the bar), or dropping the right shoulder.

Good pit protection is needed. A crash pad or a foam rubber pad cushions the fall well.

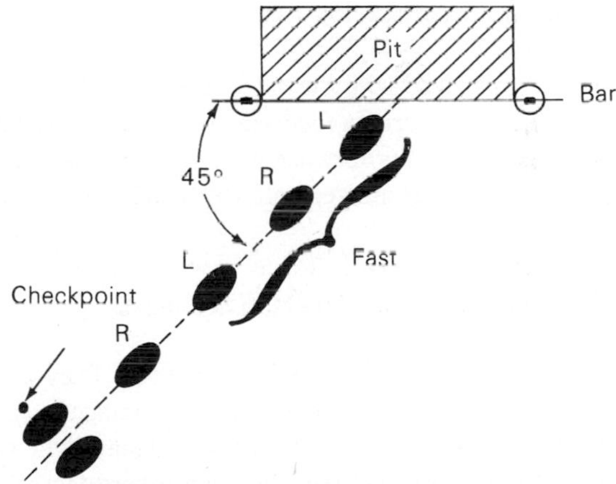

FIGURE 32.10. Straddle Roll

Western Roll

For the Western Roll, the approach, gather, and kick are the same as for the Straddle Roll, but instead of being facedown the jumper clears the bar by lying parallel to it on her side. The left arm is pointed down at the legs just at crossing and then is lowered. The head is turned toward the pit after clearance, and the landing is made on both hands and the left (takeoff) foot.

HURDLING

Hurdling is an interesting activity, but it poses equipment problems. Hurdles can be formed from electrical conduit pipe (see pp. 586–587 for a diagram). Wands supported on blocks or cones can also be used as hurdles. Hurdles should begin at about 12 in. in height and increase to 18 in. They should be placed about 25 ft apart. Using six hurdles, a 60-yd (180-ft) course can be established as diagrammed in Figure 32.11.

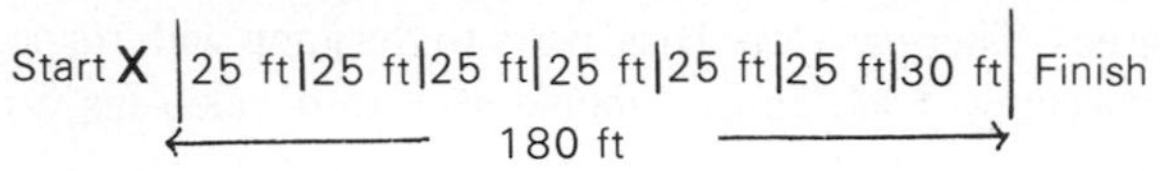

Start X | 25 ft | 25 ft | 25 ft | 25 ft | 25 ft | 25 ft | 30 ft | Finish
←—— 180 ft ——→

FIGURE 32.11. Hurdling course

A single or double course can be set up for practice. If there is competition, it should be on a personal best time basis. If regular hurdles are available, practice on lower temporary hurdles should precede work on regular hurdles. A hurdles course or practice area can be set up in a location other than on the track. In this way, the hurdles can be left in place for more concentrated use.

Several key points govern good hurdling technique. The runner should adjust his stepping pattern so the takeoff foot is planted 3 to 5 ft from the hurdle. The lead foot is extended straight forward over the hurdle, the rear (trailing) leg is bent, with the knee to the side. The lead foot reaches for the ground, quickly followed by the trailing leg. The hurdler should avoid floating over the hurdle. Body lean is necessary.

A hurdler may lead with the same foot over consecutive hurdles or he may alternate the leading foot. Some hurdlers like to thrust both arms forward instead of the single arm as described. A consistent step pattern should be developed.

INSTRUCTIONAL PROCEDURES

1. Spiked running shoes are not permitted. They create a safety problem and also give an unfair advantage to those children whose parents can afford them. Many light gym or running shoes are available. Running in bare feet is not recommended.

2. Form should be stressed at all times, but it should be appropriate to the individual. The child should realize that good results are due to good form and diligent practice. Each child should be encouraged to develop good technique within her own style. Observation of any event at a track meet bears out the fact that many individual styles are successful.

3. The program should offer something for all—boys and girls, the highly skilled and the less skilled, and those with physical problems. Children with weight problems need particular attention. They must be stimulated and encouraged, since their participation will be minimal if little attention is paid to them. Special goals can be set for overweight children, and special events and goals can also be established for children with handicaps.

4. The amount of activity, particularly distance work, should be increased progressively. A period of conditioning should precede any competition or all-out performance, such as the 1600-m run-walk test. If this procedure is followed, children will show few adverse effects.

5. Warm-up activity should precede track and field work and should include jogging as well as bending and stretching exercises.

6. Pits for the long jump and the high jump must be maintained properly. They should contain sand, sawdust mixtures, or loose dirt for long jumping. For high jumping, commercial impact landing pads are necessary though expensive. If they are not available, high jumping should be restricted to the scissors style with stacked tumbling mats used for the landing area.

7. The metal high-jump crossbar is economical in the long run, although it will bend. Sometimes bamboo poles can be procured from rug and carpet establishments. A satisfactory crossbar also can be made of nylon cord with a weight on each end to keep it taut while still allowing it to be displaced. In Europe, small leather bags with shot are used as weights to keep the ropes level. Magic ropes (rubberized stretch ropes) can be adapted for low-level jumping practice.

8. The use of a track starter signal is recommended. The clapboard track starter approximates the sound of the usual starter's gun and does not have the drawback of requiring expensive ammunition. (See Figure 34.38 for a diagram showing how to construct this starting device.)

9. The goal of the program should be to allow students to develop at their own rate. The instructional sessions should be strenuous enough to ensure some overload but not so strenuous that students become discouraged or physically ill. The instructor needs to be perceptive enough to determine whether students are working too hard or too little. Special attention must be given to those who appear disinterested, dejected, emotionally upset, or withdrawn.

ORGANIZING FOR INSTRUCTION

Track, field, and cross-country running differ from other areas of the elementary school program in that considerable preparation must be made before the classes begin.

1. A track or a cross-country course must be laid out when there are no permanent courses. This can be done with marking lime. Lanes for sprinting are of value but are not an absolute requirement.

2. A hurdling area should be similarly outlined in an appropriate location.

3. Separate pits should be placed for the running long

jump, the high jump, and the hop-step-and-jump. These should be spaced well apart to minimize interference.

4. High-jump equipment should be checked. Standards with pins, crossbars (or cord substitutes), and cushioned landing pads are needed.

5. Takeoff boards for the long jump and hop-step-and-jump should be in place. Jumping without the use of a takeoff board is not a satisfying experience. Pits should be filled with fresh building sand of a coarse variety.

6. Accessory materials should be gathered, including batons, starter clapboards, watches, hurdles, and yarn for the finish line.

7. The value of starting blocks is debatable. Doubtless, they add interest to the program, but their use and adjustment are sometimes difficult for the elementary student to master.

The organization of students is as important as the organization of equipment. Height and weight are factors affecting the degree of physical performance in track, field, and cross-country activities. More efficient instruction is possible when children are grouped by height and weight. They also can be arranged by sex. The following groups serve as a basis for instruction: (1) heavier and taller boys, (2) shorter and lighter boys, (3) heavier and taller girls, and (4) shorter and lighter girls. A simple way to form groups is to rank boys and girls separately according to the following formula, which yields a standard number.

$$\text{Score} = 10 \times \text{Age (to the nearest half-year)} + \text{Weight in pounds}$$

After the boys have been ranked, the upper 50% are assigned to group 1 and the remainder to group 2. A similar division is made with the girls. Some decisions regarding borderline cases must be made.

Some track and field skills can be practiced with a single-activity organization. Starting skills can be practiced with perhaps one fourth of the children at one time. Four groups can practice baton-passing skills at one time. Striding for distance can be practiced with each group running as a unit.

The predominant plan of organization should be one of multiple activity. Four stations can make use of the selected group organization, but more stations are desirable. If eight stations are used, two stations can be assigned to each group. Stations can be selected from the following skill areas: (1) starting and sprinting, (2) baton passing, (3) standing and running long jump, (4) hop-step-and-jump, (5) high jump, (6) hurdles, (7) striding for distance and pace judgment, and (8) the Potato Shuttle Race (see the following section).

It is generally not sound to have children practice at all stations in any one class session. The entire circuit can be completed during additional sessions. Putting written directions at each station is helpful. The directions can state what is to be accomplished as well as offering points of technique.

In later instruction, students can select the skills that they desire to practice. With guidance, the choice system could embrace the entire program, with children determining each session those areas on which they would like to concentrate. This choice approach can be related to individualized or contract instruction.

TRACK AND FIELD DRILLS AND ACTIVITIES

Potato Shuttle Race

The Potato Shuttle Race is an adaptation of an old American custom during frontier harvest celebrations. For each competitor, a number of potatoes were placed in a line at various distances. The winner was the one who brought in his potatoes first, one at a time. He won a sack of potatoes for the best effort.

The modern version of this race uses blocks instead of potatoes, and each runner runs the following course. A box is placed 15 ft in front of the starting line, with four blocks in individual circles, which are the same distance (15 ft) apart (Figure 32.12). The runner begins behind the starting line and brings the blocks, one at a time, back to the box. She can bring the blocks back in any order desired, but all blocks must be put inside the box. The box should be 12 by 12 in., with a depth of 3 to 6 in. Blocks must be placed or dropped, not thrown, into the box.

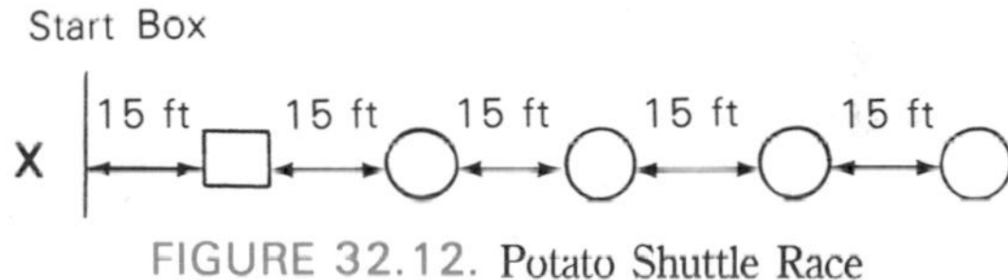

FIGURE 32.12. Potato Shuttle Race

The most practical way to organize competition in this race is to time each individual and then award places on the basis of elapsed time, for the race is physically challenging. The competitors must understand that each person is running individually and that they should strive for their best time, regardless of position or place of finish in the race.

Timers can act as judges to see that the blocks are not thrown into the box. A block that lands outside the box must be placed inside before the student goes after another. Blocks should be about 2 in. square, but this can vary.

The race can be run as a relay. The first runner brings all of the blocks in, one at a time, and then tags off the second member of the team, who returns the blocks, one at a time, to the respective spots. The third relay member brings the blocks in again, and the fourth puts them out again. For this race, it is necessary to have pie tins, floor tiles (9 by 9 in.), or some other items in addition to the box so that, when the blocks are put out by the second and fourth runners, it can be determined definitely that they rest in the proper spot. A block must be on its spot in the proper fashion before the runner delivers the next one.

Running for Pace

Children should have some experience in running for moderate distances to acquire an understanding of pace. The running should be loose and relaxed. Distances up to 1600 m may be part of the work. To check their time, each runner needs a partner. Someone with a stopwatch counts loudly the elapsed time second by second, and the partner notes the runner's time as he crosses the finish line.

Allowing children to estimate their pace and time can be motivating. On a circular track, at a set distance, let each runner stipulate a target time and see how close she can come to it.

Interval Training

Children should know the technique of interval training, which consists of running at a set speed for a specified distance and then walking back to the starting point. On the one-eighth-mile track, children can run for 110 yd and then walk to the starting point, repeating this procedure a number of times. They can also run the entire 220 yd, take a timed rest, and then repeat. Breathing should return to near normal before the next 220-yd interval is attempted.

RELAYS

Two types of relay are generally included in a program of track and field for children.

Circular Relays

Circular relays make use of the regular circular track. The baton exchange technique is important, and practice is needed.

On a 220-yd or 200-m track, relays can be organized in a number of ways, depending on how many runners are spaced for one lap. Four runners can do a lap, each running one quarter of the way; two can do a lap, each running one half of the distance; or each runner can complete a whole lap. In these races, each member of the relay team runs the same distance. Relays can also be organized so that members run different distances.

Shuttle Relays

Since children are running toward each other, one great difficulty in running shuttle relays is control of the exchange. In the excitement, the next runner may leave too early, and the tag or exchange is then made ahead of the restaining line. A high-jump standard can be used to prevent early exchanges. The next runner awaits the tag with the arm around the standard. A difficulty with this technique is providing a standard for each team.

SUGGESTED TRACK FACILITY

The presence of a track facility is a boon to any program. Few elementary schools have the funds or space for a quarter-mile track. A shorter track facility that can be installed permanently with curbs or temporarily with marking lime is suggested. Discarded fire hoses can be used to mark curbs and can be installed each spring with spikes.

The short facility is one-eighth mile (220 yd) in length and has a straightaway of 66 yd, which is ample for the 60-yd dash (Figure 32.13). It allows flexibility in relays, since relay legs of 55, 110, and 220 yd are possible. In keeping with international practice, a 200-m track may be preferable (Figure 32.14). Sixth-grade classes might practice number concepts by helping to lay out the track and by calculating distances from the dimensions.

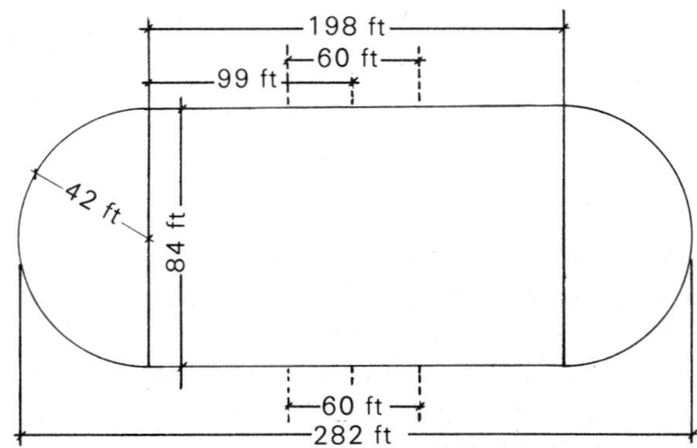

FIGURE 32.13. One-eighth-mile (220-yd) track

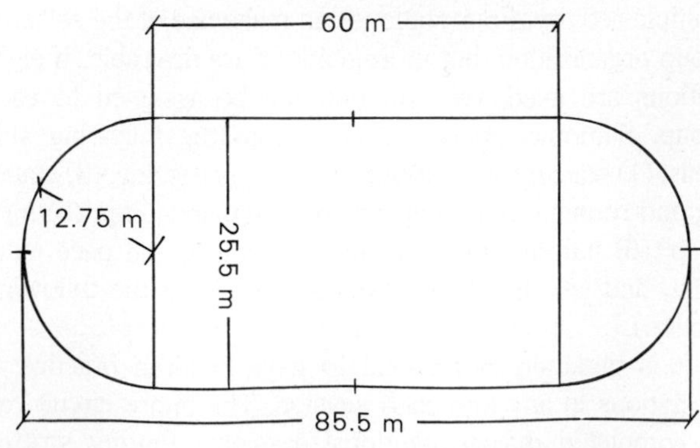

FIGURE 32.14. 200-m track

CONDUCTING TRACK AND FIELD DAYS

Track and field days can range in organization from competition within a single classroom to competition between selected classes, from an all-school playday meet to a meet between neighboring schools or an areawide or all-city meet. In informal meets within a class or between a few classes, all children should participate in one or more events. Each student can be limited to two individual events plus one relay event, with no substitutions permitted. An additional condition could be imposed that competitors for individual events enter only one track event and one field event.

For larger meets, two means of qualification are suggested.

1. Qualifying times and performance standards can be set at the start of the season. Any student meeting or bettering these times or performances is qualified to compete.

2. In an all-school meet, first- and second-place winners in each class competition qualify for entry. For a district or all-city meet, first- and second-place winners from each all-school meet become eligible.

Generally, competition is organized for each event by sex and grade. This does not preclude mixed teams competing against mixed teams in relays. Height and weight classifications can be used to equalize competition.

PLANNING THE MEET

The order of events should be determined by the type of competition. Relays are usually last on the program. If preliminary heats are necessary, these are run off first. Color-coded cards should be given to the heat qualifiers. This helps get them into the correct final race.

The local track coach can give advice about details of organizing the meet. Helpers can be secured from among school patrons, secondary students, teacher-training students, and service clubs. Adequate and properly instructed help is essential. A list of key officials and their duties follows.

1. *Meet director.* The meet director should be positioned at a convenient point near the finish line, with a table on which all official papers are kept.

2. *Announcer.* The announcer can be in charge of the public address system. Much of the success of the meet depends on her abilities.

3. *Clerk of the course.* The clerk of the course has charge of all entries and places the competitors in their proper starting slots.

4. *Starter.* The starter works closely with the clerk of the course.

5. *Head and finish judges.* There should be one finish judge for each awarded place, plus one extra. The first competitor "out of the money" is identified in case there is a disqualification. The head judge can cast the deciding vote if there is doubt about the first- and second-place winners.

6. *Timers.* Three timers should time first place, though fewer can be used. If another timer is available, he can time second place. Timers report their times to the head timer, who determines the correct winning time. Accurate timing is important if records are a factor.

7. *Messenger.* A messenger takes the entry card from the clerk of the course to the finish judge, who records the correct finish places and the winner's time after the race is completed. The messenger then takes the final record of the race to the meet director's table.

8. *Field judges and officials.* Each field event should be managed by a sufficient crew, headed by a designated individual. Each crew head should be given a clipboard with the rules of the event that she is judging fully explained.

9. *Marshalls.* Several marshalls should be appointed to keep general order. They are responsible for keeping noncompetitors from interfering with the events. Competitors can be kept under better control if each unit has an assigned place, either in the infield or in the stands. Only the assigned officials and competitors should be present at the scenes of competition.

In smaller meets, first, second, and third places are usually awarded, with scoring on a 5-, 3-, and 1-point basis, respectively. Relays, because of multiple participation, should count double in the place point score. For larger meets, more places can be awarded, and the individual point scores can be adjusted.

Ribbons can be awarded to winners but need not be elaborate. The name of the meet should be printed on the ribbon, with the individual event and the place designated. Blue ribbons are given for first place, red for second, and white for third. They are usually awarded after each event. Awarding ribbons at the conclusion of a large interschool meet is anticlimactic, since many spectators already will have left.

An opening ceremony, including a salute to the flag, is desirable for larger meets. Competitors from each unit can be introduced as a group, with announcements and instructions emphasized or clarified at this time. Holding the event on a school morning or afternoon gives status to the affair and allows all children to participate.

It is helpful if the competitors wear numbers. Safety pins, rather than straight pins, should be used to keep the numbers in place. Numbers can be made at the individual schools prior to the meet when well-defined instructions pertaining to the materials, colors, and sizes have been given.

ORGANIZING THE COMPETITION

The overriding goal of elementary school competition is to have many children take part and experience a measure of success. The determination of individual champions and of meet winners is lower in priority. Track and field competition can take many forms.

In informal competition, competitors are assigned to different races and compete only in those races. There are no heats as such, nor is there advancement to a final race. Races are chosen so that individuals on the same team usually do not run against each other. Points may or may not be given toward an overall meet score. The informal meet is more like a playday and can include nontrack events also, such as the softball throw, the football kick, and the Frisbee throw.

In individual competition, winners and place finishers are determined for all events, with no team scoring and no meet winner.

In team competition, individual winners are determined, and each contributes points toward a team score. The team with the highest score wins. Different team winners can be determined for different grade levels and for boys and girls.

Relay competition is a carnival in which a number of relays make up the program. Performances can be combined for several individuals if field events are to be included. Few, if any, uncombined scores are taken into consideration. A number of relays should be part of track and field days under any plan. Relays increase student participation. Mixed relays are a possibility.

CROSS-COUNTRY RUNNING

Many youngsters are motivated by running laps around a track. Others soon tire of these circular efforts, however, and can be motivated by cross-country running. Students can run marked or unmarked courses for enjoyment of the competition. Emphasis is on improving one's personal time rather than on winning. This enables all students to have personalized goals and an ongoing incentive for running.

Cross-country courses can be marked with a chalk line and cones so runners follow the course as outlined. Check points every 220 yd offer runners a convenient reference point so they can gauge accurately how far they have run. Three courses of different length and difficulty can be laid out. The beginning course can be 1 mi in length, the intermediate 1.25 mi, and the advanced 1.5 mi. Including sandy or hilly areas in the course increases the challenge. When students run cross country, they can select the course that challenges them appropriately.

It is important for students to learn the concept of pace when running long distances. One technique for teaching students how to pace themselves is to place cones at similar intervals and to challenge students to run from cone to cone at a specified rate. A student or the instructor can call out the time at each cone, and students can adjust their running to the desired pace. Another method is to break down long-distance runs into smaller segments and times, which enables youngsters to get a feel for how fast they must run the shorter distances to attain a certain cumulative time over the longer distance. Table 32.2 gives times for the 40- and 100-yard dashes.

CROSS-COUNTRY MEETS

Cross-country meets provide a culminating activity for youngsters involved in distance running. The attractiveness of cross-country competition lies in the fact that it is a team activity and all members of the team are crucial to its success. Teams may win or lose a meet based on the finish of their slowest member, thus making all youngsters feel important.

Youngsters should learn how to score a meet. Probably the easiest way to keep team scores is to assign seven (depending on class size) members to each team. Points are assigned to finishers based on their placement in the race. For example, the first-place runner receives 1 point,

TABLE 32.2. TIMES FOR 40- AND 100-YARD DASHES

To run a mile in:	Runner has to run 40-yd dash 44 times—each dash run in:	Runner has to run 100-yd dash 17.6 times—each dash run in:
3:48 minutes (world record time)	5.18 seconds	12.95 seconds
5:00 minutes	6.81 seconds	17.04 seconds
6:00 minutes	8.18 seconds	20.45 seconds
7:00 minutes	9.55 seconds	23.87 seconds
8:00 minutes	10.90 seconds	27.25 seconds
10:00 minutes	13.62 seconds	34.08 seconds

TABLE 32.3. **SUGGESTED DIVISIONS FOR CROSS-COUNTRY MEETS**

Division	Age	Sex	Distance (in miles)
1	8–9	M	1
2	8–9	F	1
3	10–11	M	1.25
4	10–11	F	1.25
5	12–13	M	1.5
6	12–13	F	1.5

the tenth-place runner 10 points, and so on. The points for all team members are totaled, and the team with the lowest score is declared the winner.

Teams can be equalized by having youngsters run the course ahead of the meet and their times recorded. Teams can then be organized by the teacher so that members are somewhat matched. As a guideline, Table 32.3 offers suggested competitive divisions and distances to be run. Divisions 5 and 6 are classed as open divisions, which any child in the elementary school may enter, even if below the age of 12. Ages are defined by birthdays, that is, a child is classified as being a certain age until the next birthday.

A primary concern is that the child gauge her running pace so she is able to finish the race. Improvement of previous times should be the focus of the activity, with placement at the finish of the race a secondary goal. The timekeeper can voice the time as each runner finishes to help children evaluate their performance.

A funnel, made of cones, at the finish line prevents tying times (Figure 32.15). As runners go through the funnel, the meet judges and helpers can hand each one a marker with the place of finish on it. This simplifies scoring at the end of the meet. Each team captain can total the scores and report the result.

Cross-country runners should learn to cool down on completion of a race. Youngsters have a tendency to fall down rather than to move. They should jog gently until they are somewhat rested. Since runners do not all finish at the same time, it is sometimes helpful to have some recreational activities set out near the track so the youngsters can stay involved in activity.

FIGURE 32.15. Funneling runners at the finish line

CHAPTER 33

Volleyball

Volleyball is an activity that should be started in the elementary grades, with instruction serving as a basis for later high school participation. An advantage of volleyball is that boys and girls can participate together coeducationally. Television exposure of volleyball played recreationally and in Olympic competition, plus increased interschool volleyball competition have put the sport in the public eye.

For volleyball to be played successfully on the elementary level, a skill foundation must be established. This requires sufficient practice of serving and passing skills, and development of hand-eye and body coordination for effective ball control. Attention to proper technique is essential. Informal practice should begin in the primary grades with activities that mimic volleyball skills—passing, serving, and rebounding of all types. Beginning in the 4th grade, more volleyball-type activities can be scheduled. Setting and spiking are questionable inclusions in the regular class lesson plans. Even at the 6th-grade level only a few children are able to employ these more advanced techniques successfully. Blocking can receive some attention as it occurs in normal play.

INSTRUCTIONAL EMPHASIS AND SEQUENCE

Indoor facilities are sometimes a problem with volleyball. In some gymnasiums, the lack of court space means playing with 12 to 15 children on a side in a single game. This arrangement usually results in little activity for the majority of participants. A few skilled players on each side dominate the game. The usual basketball court should be divided into two volleyball courts on which the children play crosswise. Nets should be lowered to 6 ft for the 4th grade and to 6.5 to 7.0 ft for the 5th and 6th grade. Attachments on the walls should reflect these varied net heights. Furthermore, the nets should be attached firmly so that both the upper and lower net cords are tight. A loosely hanging net does not allow for ball recovery from the net. Walls may not be suitable for rebounding activities.

The number of volleyballs also can be a problem. When children practice individually with a ball, the number of balls can be supplemented with beach balls and foam balls of comparable size. Few schools have 30 to 35 volleyballs available. When possible, all volleyballs should be properly inflated. In larger school systems, the problem of volleyball supply can be solved by having a rotating schedule of volleyball activities from school to school. Few practice activities require a net, so outdoor participation is possible. The wind and the sun can create problems at times.

The skills of the overhand serve, the setup, the spike, and blocking should be introduced only when a competitive situation exists, as in intramurals or an interschool program, in which the emphasis shifts to winning. Normally, in physical education classes, the program dwells on keeping the ball in play, thereby increasing activity, skill development, and enjoyment. As a matter of game orientation, however, students should know about the setup, the spike, and blocking techniques.

In the primary grades, children should have had ball-handling experiences related to volleyball skills. Rebounding and controlling balloons is an excellent related experience, particularly for younger children. Included in ball-handling experiences with beach balls or foam rubber training balls should be exploratory work in batting with the hands and other body parts. This preliminary experience in visual

TABLE 33.1. SUGGESTED VOLLEYBALL PROGRAM

	Fourth Grade	Fifth Grade	Sixth Grade
Skills	Underhand serve Simple returns	Overhand pass Forearm pass	Overhand serve Setup Spike Blocking
Knowledge	Simple rules Rotation	Basic game rules	Game strategy Additional rules
Activities	Beach Ball Volleyball Informal Volleyball Shower Service Ball	Keep It Up Cageball Volleyball Mini-Volleyball Regulation volleyball	Three-and-Over Volleyball Four-Square Volleyball Regulation volleyball
Skill Tests		Simplified serving Wall volleying	Serving for accuracy Wall volleying

tracking is advantageous for volleyball. Table 33.1 summarizes the volleyball program for the 4th through the 6th grade.

FOURTH GRADE

Fourth-grade experiences should be based on the use of the beach ball and should culminate in the game of Beach Ball Volleyball. A beach ball is larger and more easily handled than a volleyball and allows a level of success not possible with a smaller ball. Simple returns and underhand serves can be practiced with beach balls. Later in the instructional sequence, serving the volleyball should be introduced. The game of Informal Volleyball should be played with a volleyball. Shower Service Ball should be played with volleyballs.

FIFTH GRADE

Beach balls can be used in the early stages of instruction in the 5th grade, but a shift to volleyballs should be made as soon as is practical. Foam rubber training balls (8-in.) are excellent substitutes for volleyballs (Figure 33.1). They cannot hurt youngsters and they move more slowly, which affords more opportunity for successful play. Students in the 5th grade should begin to exhibit good basic technique in handling high and low passes. They should review the serve and polish this skill. Basic game rules should be used in modified volleyball games. The game of Keep It Up calls for controlled passing. Cageball Volleyball is an interesting variation of the regular game.

SIXTH GRADE

For 6th-grade students, the program should introduce the overhand serve, the setup, the spike, and blocking. The volleyball rules that affect these phases of the game should be covered. An introduction to elementary strategy should be part of the instruction. Four-Square Volleyball provides an interesting form of competitive volleyball. The game Three-and-Over Volleyball is a basic game for the program.

FIGURE 33.1. Beach ball and foam training ball

VOLLEYBALL SKILLS

SERVING

Underhand Serve

Directions are for a right-handed serve. The player stands facing the net with the left foot slightly forward and the weight on the right (rear) foot. The ball is held in the left hand with the left arm across and a little in front of the body. The ball is lined up with a straight forward swing of the right hand. The left-hand fingers are spread, and the ball rests on the pads of these fingers. On the serving motion, the server steps forward with the left foot, transferring the weight to the front foot, and at the same time brings the right arm back in a preparatory motion. The right hand now swings forward and contacts the ball just below center. The ball can be hit with an open hand or with the fist (facing forward or sideward). An effective follow-through with the arm ensures a smooth serve (Figure 33.2).

FIGURE 33.2. Underhand serve

Children should explore the best way to strike the ball, with the flat of the hand or the fist. Each player can select the method that is personally most effective.

Overhand Serve

For the right-handed serve, stand with the left foot in front and the left side of the body turned somewhat toward the net. The weight is on both feet. The server must master two difficult skills—how to toss the ball and how to contact the ball. The ball is held in the left hand directly in front of the face. The ball must be tossed straight up and should come down in front of the right shoulder. As the ball is tossed, the weight shifts to the back foot. The height of the toss is a matter of choice, but from 3 to 5 ft is suggested. As the ball drops, the striking arm comes forward, contacting the ball a foot or so above the shoulder. The weight is shifted to the forward foot, which can take a short step forward. The contact is made with the open palm or with the fist. An effective serve is one that has no spin—a floater.

PASSING (OR RETURNING)

Overhand Pass

The overhand pass, or return, must be mastered if there is to be interesting, competitive play. If the ball is served and not returned well or often, the game is dull. To execute an overhand pass, the player moves underneath the ball and controls it with the fingertips. Feet should be in an easy, comfortable position, with knees bent. The cup of the fingers is made so that the thumbs and forefingers are close together and the other fingers are spread. The hands are held forehead high, with elbows out and level with the floor. The player, when in receiving position, looks ready to shout upward through cupped hands (Figure 33.3).

The player contacts the ball at above eye level and propels it with the force of spread fingers, not with the palms. At the moment of contact, the legs are straightened and the hands and arms follow through. If the ball is a pass to a teammate, it should be high enough to allow for control. If the pass is a return to the other side, it can be projected forward with more force.

Forearm Pass (Underhand Pass)

The forearm pass takes the place of the old underhand pass, in which the ball was contacted with the palms of the hands. The body must be in good position to ensure a proper volley. The player must move rapidly to the spot where the ball is descending to prepare for the pass. Body position is important. The trunk leans forward and the back

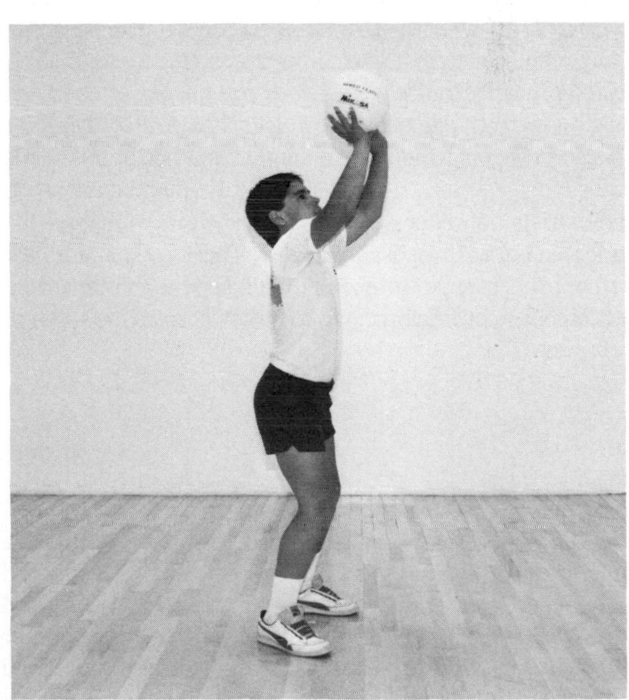

FIGURE 33.3. Completing an overhand pass

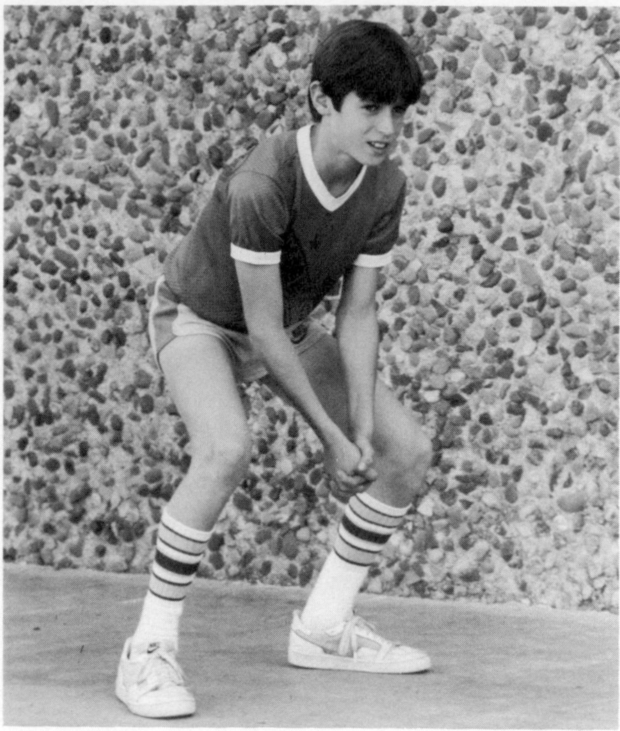

FIGURE 33.4. Forearm (underhand) pass position

is straight, with a 90-degree angle between the thighs and the body. The legs are bent, and the body is in a partially crouched position, with the feet shoulder width apart (Figure 33.4).

The hands are clasped together, so that the forearms are parallel. The clasp should be relaxed, with the type of handclasp a matter of choice. In one method, the thumbs are kept parallel and together, and the fingers of one hand make a partially cupped fist, with the fingers of the other hand overlapping the fist. In another method, both hands are cupped and turned out a little, so the thumbs are apart. The wrists, in either case, are turned downward, and the elbow joints are reasonably locked. The forearms are held at the proper angle to rebound the ball, with contact made with the fists or forearms between the knees as the receiver crouches.

Dig Pass

The dig pass is an emergency return when neither the overhand nor the forearm pass is possible. It is a stiffened rebound from one arm, contact being made with the cupped fist (Figure 33.5), the heel of the hand, or the inside or outside of the forearm. The dig pass should not be employed as a standard return.

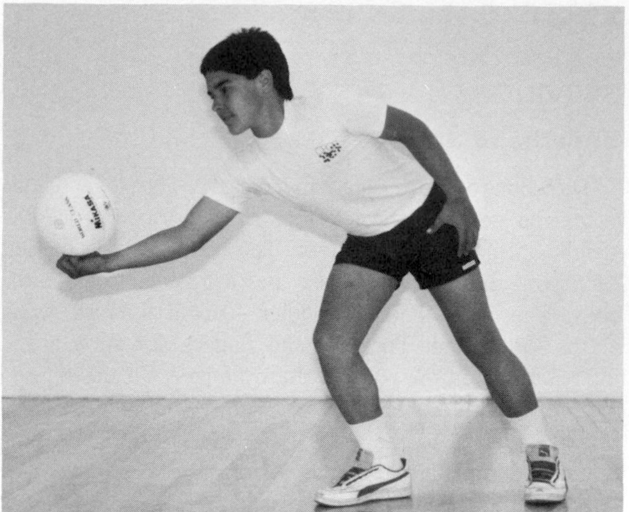

FIGURE 33.5. Dig pass

SETUP

The term *setup* applies to a pass that sets the ball for a possible spike. The object is to raise the ball with a soft, easy pass to a position 1 or 2 ft above the net and about 1 ft away from it. The setup is generally the second pass in a series of three. An overhand pass is used for the setup. It is important for the back line player, who has to tap to the setter, to make an accurate and easily handled pass.

SPIKE

The spike is the most effective play in volleyball, and when properly done, is extremely difficult to return. Its success depends a great deal on the ability of a teammate to setup properly. At the elementary school level, spiking should be done by jumping high in the air and striking the ball above the net, driving it into the opponent's court. Experienced players may back up for a short run, but the jump must be made straight up so the player does not touch the net, and the striking hand does not go over the net.

BLOCKING

Blocking involves one or more members of the defensive (receiving) team forming a screen of arms and hands near the net to block a spike. At the elementary school level, blocking is usually done by a single individual, and little attention is given to multiple blocking.

To block a ball, a player jumps high with arms outstretched overhead, palms facing the net, and fingers spread. The jump must be timed with that of the spiker, and the blocker must avoid touching the net. The ball is not struck but, rather, rebounds from the blocker's stiffened hands and arms. Students should know about blocking even if it is used infrequently in elementary play.

INSTRUCTIONAL PROCEDURES

1. Most volleyball-type games begin with a serve, so it becomes critical that this be successful. Regular volleyball rules call for one chance to serve the ball over the net without touching the net. Three modifications can achieve more successful serving. The first is to serve from the center of the playing area instead of the back line. A second is to allow another serve if the first is not good. A third is to allow an assist by a team member to get the ball over the net.

2. To save time, instruct players to roll the ball back to the server. Other players should let the ball roll to its destination without interception.

3. Effective instruction is possible only when the balls can be rebounded from the hands and arms without pain. A heavy or underinflated ball takes much of the enjoyment out of the game.

4. The predominant instructional pattern should be individual or partner work. For individual work, each child needs a ball.

5. An 8½-in. foam rubber training ball has much the same feel as a volleyball but does not cause pain. The foam balls should be used early in skill practice.

6. The use of the fist to hit balls on normal returns causes poor control and interrupts play. Except for dig passes, both hands should be used to return the ball. Teachers should rule hitting with the fist a loss of a point if the practice persists.

7. Rotation should be introduced early and used in lead-up games. Two rotation plans are illustrated (Figure 33.6).

Two lines

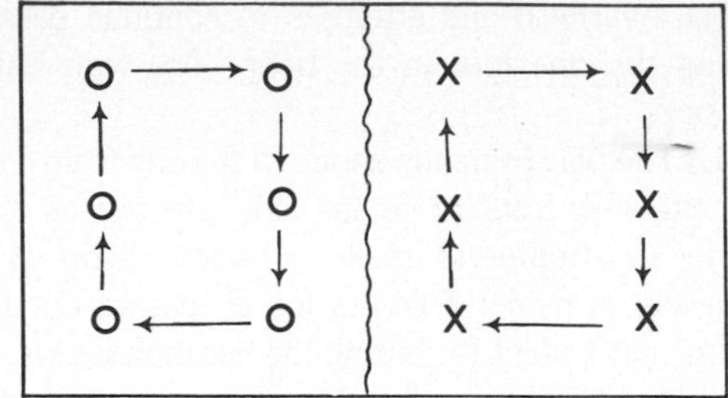

Three lines

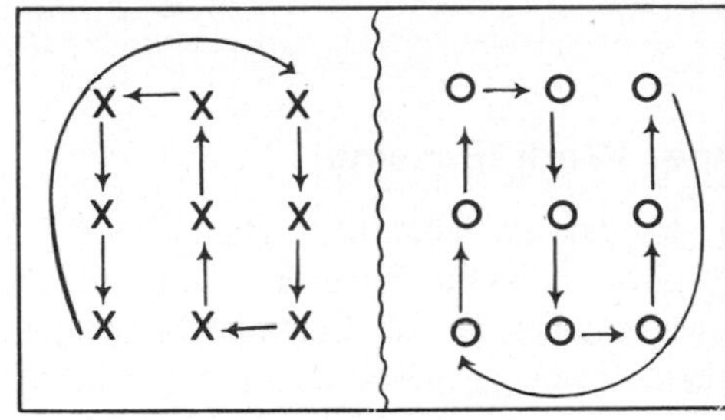

FIGURE 33.6. Rotation plans

ORGANIZING FOR INSTRUCTION

Practice sessions can be categorized as individual play, partner work, or group work. These tasks can be prefaced by "Can you . . ." or "Let's see if you can. . . ." A skill to learn early is a toss to oneself to initiate a practice routine. This occurs when the practice directions call for a pass from one individual to oneself or to another.

Individual Play

1. For wall rebounding, stand 6 ft away from a wall. Throw the ball against the wall and pass it to the wall. The player then catches and begins again. Allow two passes against the wall before a catch is made. A further extension is to pass the ball against the wall as many times as possible without making a mistake.

2. From a spot 6 ft from the wall, throw the ball against the wall and alternate an overhand pass with a forearm pass. The player then catches the ball.

3. In another wall-rebounding exercise, the player throws the ball to one side (right or left) and then moves to the side to pass the ball to the wall. Catch the rebound.

4. The player passes the ball directly overhead and catches it. Try making two passes before catching the ball. Later, alternate an overhand pass with a forearm pass and catch the ball. A further extension of the drill is to keep the ball going five or six times with one kind of pass or with alternate passes. This is a basic drill and should be mastered before proceeding to others.

5. The player passes the ball 10 ft high and 10 ft forward, moves rapidly under the ball, and catches it. Later, make additional passes without the catch.

6. The player passes the ball 15 ft overhead, makes a full turn, and passes the ball again. Vary with other stunts such as touching the floor, making a half turn, clapping the hands at two different spots, and others. Allow choice in selecting the stunt.

7. Two lines 3 ft apart are needed. The player stands in front of one line, makes a backward pass overhead, moves to the other line, and repeats the procedure.

8. The player passes 3 ft or so to one side, moves under the ball, and passes it back to the original spot. The next pass should be to the other side.

9. The player passes the ball directly overhead. On the return, she jumps as high as possible to make a second pass. Continue.

10. The player stands with one foot in a hoop. He passes the ball overhead and attempts to continue passing while keeping the one foot in the hoop. Try with both feet in the hoop.

11. The player stands about 15 ft away from a basketball goal, either in front or to the side. He passes toward the goal in an attempt to make a basket. Score 3 points if the basket is made, 2 points for no basket but for hitting the rim, and 1 point for hitting the backboard only. A further challenge would be for the player to make a pass to himself first and the second pass toward the goal.

Partner Work (Passing)

1. Players are about 10 ft apart. Player A tosses the ball (controlled toss) to Player B, who passes the ball back to A, who catches the ball. Continue for several exchanges and then change throwers. Another option is for Player B to make a pass straight overhead, catch the ball, and then toss to Player A. Yet another variation is to have one player toss the ball slightly to the side. Player B then makes a pass to Player A. Player A can make the toss in such a fashion that Player B must use a forearm return.

2. Two players are about 15 ft apart. Player A passes to herself first and then makes a second pass to Player B, who catches the ball and repeats. This can be followed with a return by Player B.

3. Players A and B try to keep the ball in the air continuously.

4. Players are about 15 ft apart. Player A remains stationary and passes in such a fashion that Player B must move from side-to-side. An option is to have Player B move forward and backward.

5. Players are about 10 ft apart. Both have hoops and attempt to keep one foot in the hoop while passing. Try keeping both feet in the hoop.

6. Two players pass back and forth—making contact with the ball while off the ground.

7. Players are about 15 ft apart. Player B is seated. Player A attempts to pass to Player B. A second method is for both players to stand. Player A passes to Player B and then sits down quickly. Player B attempts to pass the ball back to Player A, who catches in the seated position.

8. Player A passes to Player B and does a complete turnaround. Player B passes back to Player A and also does a full turn. Other stunts can be used.

9. Player A is stationed near a basketball goal, with Player B in the lane. Player A passes to Player B in the lane, who attempts a pass to the basket. Count 3 points for a basket, 2 points for a miss that hits the rim, and 1 point for hitting the backboard only. Any pass from Player A that lands outside the center lane is void, and another chance is given.

10. Partners stand on opposite sides of a volleyball net. The object is to keep the ball in the air. The drill can be done by as many as four or six players.

11. One player stands on a chair in front of the net and holds a ball in such a fashion that spikers can knock the ball out of her hands. The next progression is to toss the ball about 2 ft above the net for spiking practice.

12. If the net is stretched properly, recovery can be practiced. One player throws the ball against the net, and the active player recovers with a forearm pass.

Partner Work (Serving and Passing)

1. Partners are about 20 ft apart. Partner A serves to Partner B, who catches the ball and returns the serve to Partner A.

2. Partner A serves to Partner B, who makes a pass back to Partner A. Change responsibilities.

3. Play Service One-step. Partners begin about 10 ft apart. Partner A serves to Partner B, who returns the serve with Partner A catching. If there is no error and if neither receiver moved his feet to catch, both players take one step back. This is repeated each time no error or foot movement by the receiver occurs. If an error occurs or if appreciable foot movement is evident, the players revert to the original distance of 10 ft and start over.

4. A player stands at the top of the key on a basketball court. The object is to serve the ball into the basket. Scoring can be as in other basket-making drills—3 points for a basket, 2 points for hitting the rim, and 1 point for hitting the backboard but not the rim. Partner retrieves the ball.

Group Work

1. A leader stands in front of not more than four other players who are arranged in a semicircle. The leader conducts the same routine with each of the circle players. She tosses to each player in sequence around the circle, and they pass the ball back to her. After a round or two, another player comes forward to replace the leader.

2. For blocking, six players are positioned alongside the net, each with a ball. The players take turns on the other side of the net—practicing blocking skills. Each spiker tosses the ball to himself for spiking. A defensive player moves along the line to block consecutively a total of six spikes. The next step is to have two players move along the line to practice blocking by pairs.

3. Setup and spiking can be practiced according to the drill shown in Figure 33.7. A back player tosses the ball to the setup player, who passes the ball properly for a spike. The entire group or just the spikers can rotate.

4. Two groups of children stand on opposite sides of a net. Eight to ten balls must be available to make this a worthwhile experience. The children serve back of the baseline and recover balls coming from the other team. The action should be informal and continuous.

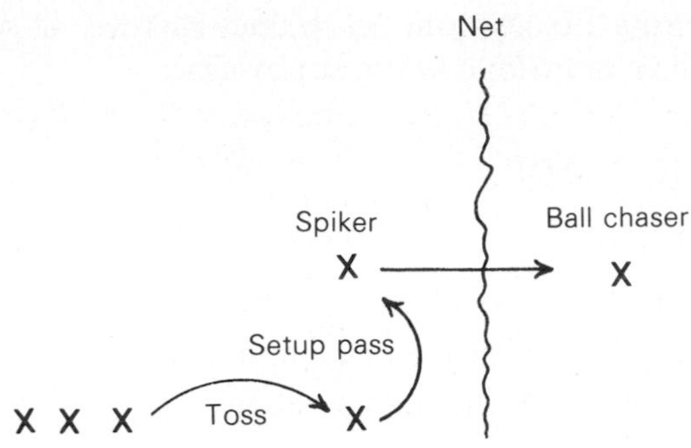

FIGURE 33.7. Setup and spiking drill

BASIC VOLLEYBALL RULES

Officially, six players make up a team, but any number from six to nine makes a suitable team in the elementary school program.

To begin, captains toss a coin for the order of choices. The winner can choose to serve or to select a court. The opposing captain takes the option that the winner of the toss did not select. At the completion of any game, teams change courts, and the losing side serves.

To be in the proper position to serve, a player must have both feet behind the right one third of the end line and must not step on the end line during the serve. The server covers the right back position.

Only the serving team scores. The server retains the serve, scoring consecutive points, until his side loses a point and is put out. Members of each team take turns serving, the sequence being determined by the plan of rotation.

Official rules allow the server only one serve to get the ball completely over the net and into the opponent's court. Even if the ball touches the net (a net ball) and goes into the correct court, the serve is lost.

The lines bounding the court are considered to be in bounds, that is, balls landing on the lines are counted as good. Any ball that touches or is touched by a player is considered to be in bounds, even if the player who touched the ball was clearly outside the boundaries at the time.

The ball must be returned over the net by the third volley, which means that the team has a maximum of three volleys to make a good return.

The major violations that cause the loss of the point or serve are these:

1. Touching the net during play.

2. Not clearly batting the ball—sometimes called palming or lofting the ball.

3. Reaching over the net during play.

4. Stepping *over* the center line. (Contact with the line is not a violation.)

A ball going into the net may be recovered and played, provided that no player touches the net.

The first team to reach a score of 15 points wins the game if the team is at least 2 points ahead. If not, play continues until one team secures a 2-point lead.

Only players in the front line may spike, but all players may block. No player may volley the ball twice in succession.

VOLLEYBALL ACTIVITIES

FOURTH GRADE

Beach Ball Volleyball

Playing Area: Volleyball court

Players: Six to nine on each team

Supplies: A beach ball, 12 to 16 in. in diameter (Figure 33.1)

Skills: Most passing skills, modified serving

The players of each team are in two lines on their respective sides of the net. Serving is done, as in volleyball, by the player on the right side of the back line. The distance is shortened, however, because serving a beach ball successfully from the normal volleyball serving distance is difficult. The player serves from the normal playing position *on the court* in the right back position. Scoring is as in regular volleyball. Play continues until the ball touches the floor.

A team loses a point to the other team when it fails to return the ball over the net by the third volley or when it returns the ball over the net but the ball hits the floor out-of-bounds without being touched by the opposing team. The server continues serving as long as she scores. Rotation is as in regulation volleyball.

Teaching Suggestions: The server must be positioned as close to the net as possible while still remaining in the right back position on the court. Successful serving is an important component of an enjoyable game.

Variations

1. In a simplified version of Beach Ball Volleyball, the ball is put into play by one player in the front line, who throws the ball in the air and then passes it over the net. Play continues until the ball touches the floor, but the ball may be volleyed any number of times before crossing the net. When either team has scored 5 points, the front and back lines of the respective teams change. When the score reaches 10 for the leading team, the lines change back. Game is 15.

2. Any player in the back line may catch the ball as it comes initially from the opposing team and may immediately make a little toss and pass the ball to a teammate. The player who catches the ball and bats it cannot send it across the net before a teammate has touched it.

Informal Volleyball

Playing Area: Volleyball court, 6-ft net

Players: Six to eight on a team

Supplies: A volleyball

Skills: Passing

This game is similar to volleyball, but there is no serving. Each play begins with a student on one side tossing to herself and passing the ball high over the net. Points are scored for every play, as there is no "side out." As soon as a point is scored, the nearest player takes the ball and immediately puts it in play. Otherwise, basic volleyball rules govern the game. Rotation occurs as soon as a team has scored 5 points, with the front and back lines changing place. Action is fast, and the game moves rapidly since every play scores a point for one team or the other.

Shower Service Ball

Playing Area: Volleyball court

Players: 6 to 12 on each team

Supplies: Four to six volleyballs

Skills: Serving, catching

A line parallel to the net is drawn through the middle of each court to define the serving area. Players are scattered in no particular formation (Figure 33.8). The game involves the skills of serving and catching. To start the game, two or three volleyballs are given to each team and are handled by players in the serving area.

Balls may be served at any time and in any order by a server who must be in the back half of the court. Any ball served across the net is to be caught by any player near the ball. The person catching or retrieving a ball moves quickly to the serving area and serves. A point is scored *for* a team whenever a served ball hits the floor in the other court or is dropped by a receiver. Two scorers are needed, one for each side.

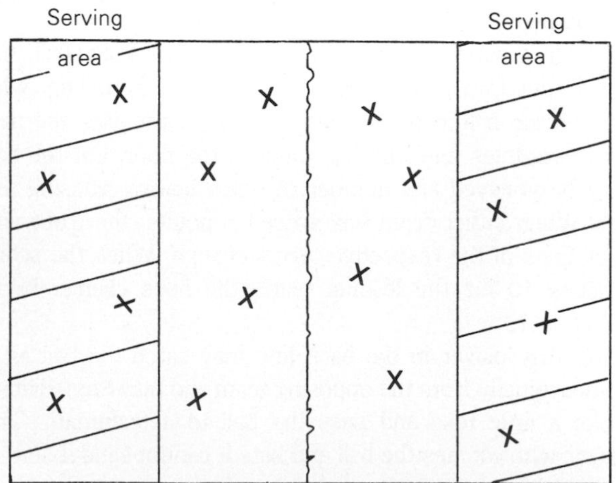

FIGURE 33.8. Formation for Shower Service Ball

Teaching Suggestion: As children improve, all serves should be made from behind the baseline.

FIFTH GRADE

Keep It Up

Playing Area: Playground, gymnasium

Players: Five to eight on each team

Supplies: A volleyball for each team

Skills: Overhand, forearm, and dig passes

Each team forms a small circle of not more than eight players. The object of the game is to see which team can make the greater number of volleys in a specified time or which team can keep the ball in the air for the greater number of consecutive volleys without error.

On the signal "Go," the game is started with a volley by one of the players. The following rules are in force.

1. Balls are volleyed back and forth with no specific order of turns, except that the ball cannot be returned to the player from whom it came.
2. A player may not volley a ball twice in succession.
3. Any ball touching the ground does not count and ends the count.

Teaching Suggestions: Players should be responsible for calling illegal returns on themselves and thus interrupting the consecutive volley count. The balls used should be of equal quality, so one team cannot claim a disadvantage. Groups should be taught to count the volleys out loud, so their progress is known.

Cageball Volleyball

Playing Area: Volleyball court

Players: Six to nine on each team

Supplies: A cageball

Skills: Most volleyball skills

Cageball Volleyball is a variation of regular volleyball. The ball used is a cageball, 18 to 24 in. in diameter. The following special rules govern this game.

1. The serve is made by a player in the back line in normal playing position by tossing the cageball in the air and batting it toward the net. Other players can assist the ball on its way over.
2. Any number of hits may be made in any combination or in any order by the players, but the ball must be clearly batted and *not* lofted or carried.
3. Scoring and rotation follow volleyball rules.

Teaching Suggestions: A 24-in. ball is the largest one that can be used for this game; a larger ball is difficult to handle legally by volleyball rules. The referee must be alert to violations involving momentarily resting or supporting the ball to keep it from hitting the floor.

Mini-Volleyball

Playing Area: Gymnasium, badminton court

Players: Three on each team

Supplies: A volleyball

Skills: Most volleyball skills

Mini-Volleyball is a modified activity designed to offer opportunities for successful volleyball experiences to children between the ages 9 and 12. The playing area is 15 ft wide and 40 ft long. The spiking line is 10 ft from the center line. Many gymnasiums are marked for badminton courts that are 20 by 44 ft with a spiking line 6.5 ft from the center. This is an acceptable substitute court.

The modified rules used in Mini-Volleyball are as follows.

1. A team consists of three players. Two substitutions may be made per game.

2. Players are positioned for the serve so that there are two front line players and one back line player. After the ball is served, the back line player may not spike the ball from the attack area or hit the ball into the attack area unless the ball is below the height of the net.

3. The height of the net is 6 ft, 10 in.

4. Players rotate positions when they receive the ball for serving. The right front line player becomes the back line player, and the left front line player becomes the right front line player.

5. A team wins a game when it scores 15 points and has a 2-point advantage over the opponent. A team wins the match when it wins two out of three games.

The back line player cannot spike and thus serves a useful function by allowing the front players to receive the serves while he moves to the net to setup for the spikers.

Teaching Suggestions: This game can be modified to suit the needs of participants. Sponge training balls work well in the learning stages of Mini-Volleyball.

Rotation Mini-Volleyball

Playing Area: Basketball or volleyball court

Players: Three on each team

Supplies: A volleyball

Skills: All volleyball skills

Three games, involving 18 active players, can be played at the same time crosswise, on a regular basketball court. The remaining children, organized in teams of 3, wait on the sideline with teams designated in a particular order. Whenever a team is guilty of a "side out," it vacates its place on the floor and the next team in line moves in. Each team keeps its own running score. If, during a single side in, 10 points are scored against a team, that team vacates its place. Teams in this arrangement move from one court to another and play different opponents. The one or two extra players left over from team selection by threes can be substitutes and should be rotated into play on a regular basis.

Regulation Volleyball

Playing Area: Volleyball court

Players: Six on each team

Supplies: A volleyball

Skills: All volleyball skills

Regulation volleyball should be played in the 5th grade, with one possible rule change: in early experiences, it is suggested that the server be allowed a second chance if she fails to get the first attempt over the net and into play. This should apply only to the initial serve. Some instructors like to shorten the serving distance during the introductory phases of the game. It is important for the serving to be done well enough to keep the game moving.

A referee should supervise the game. There are generally three calls.

1. "Side out." The serving team fails to serve the ball successfully to the other court, fails to make a good return of a volley, or makes a rule violation.

2. "Point." The receiving team fails to make a legal return or is guilty of a rule violation.

3. "Double foul." Fouls are made by both teams on the same play, in which case the point is replayed. No score or side out results.

Teaching Suggestion: There should be some emphasis on team play. Back court players should be encouraged to pass to front court players, rather than merely batting the ball back and forth across the net.

Variation: The receiver in the back court is allowed to catch the serve, toss it, and propel it to a teammate. The catch should be limited to the serve, and the pass must go to a teammate, not over the net. This counteracts the problem of children in the back court being unable to handle the serve to keep the ball in play if the served ball is spinning, curving, or approaching with such force that it is difficult to control.

SIXTH GRADE

Three-and-Over Volleyball

Playing Area: Volleyball court

Players: Six on each team

Supplies: A volleyball

Skills: All volleyball skills

The game Three and Over emphasizes the basic offensive strategy of volleyball. The game follows regular volleyball rules with the exception that the ball *must* be played three times before going over the net. The team loses the serve or the point if the ball is not played three times.

Rotation Volleyball

Playing Area: Volleyball court

Players: Variable

Supplies: A volleyball

Skills: All volleyball skills

If four teams are playing in two contests at the same time, a system of rotation can be set up during any one class period. Divide the available class time roughly into three parts, less the time allotted for logistics. Each team plays the other three teams on a timed basis. At the end of a predetermined time period, whichever team is ahead wins the game. A team may win, lose, or tie during any time period, with the score determined at the end of the respective time period. The best win-loss record wins the overall contest.

Four-Square Volleyball

Playing Area: Volleyball court

Players: Two to four on each team

Supplies: A volleyball

Skills: All volleyball skills

A second net is placed at right angles to the first net, dividing the playing area into four equal courts. The courts are numbered as in Figure 33.9. There are four teams playing, and an extra team can be waiting to rotate to the number 4 court. The object of the game is to force one of the teams to commit an error. Whenever a team makes an error, it moves down to the number 4 court or off the courts if a team is waiting. A team errs by not returning the ball to another court within the prescribed three volleys or by causing the ball to go out-of-bounds.

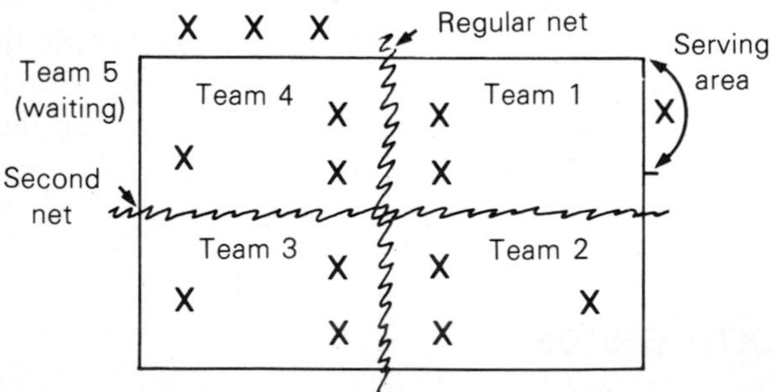

FIGURE 33.9. Four-square volleyball courts

The ball is always put in play with a serve by a player from the number 1 team, the serve being made from any point behind the end line of that team. Players must rotate for each serve. The serve is made into court number 3 or 4. Play proceeds as in regular volleyball, but the ball may be volleyed into any of the other three courts. No score is kept. The object of the game is for the number 1 team to retain its position.

Teaching Suggestion: The game seems to work best with five or more teams. With four teams, the team occupying court number 4 is not penalized for an error, because it is already in the lowest spot.

Regulation Volleyball

The playing of regulation volleyball should be continued, with increased attention to team play. The concept of offensive volleyball should be introduced, with some attention given to the skill of spiking. Similarly, blocking can receive some attention, but the emphasis on setting up and spiking should not be overriding. The continued practice of the fundamental skills of serving and volleying is an important part of the instruction. Close attention to the details of good technique makes the play more efficient.

Wheelchair Volleyball

Children in wheelchairs can participate successfully in some phases of volleyball. For example, a child confined to a wheelchair can compete against a nonhandicapped child on a one-on-one basis when courts are laid out as illustrated in Figure 33.10. The difference in size of the playing areas equalizes the mobility factor. The net should be about 6 ft in height. Serving by the normal child is done from behind the back line and by the handicapped child with the wheels on the back line. Rules should be adjusted as necessary.

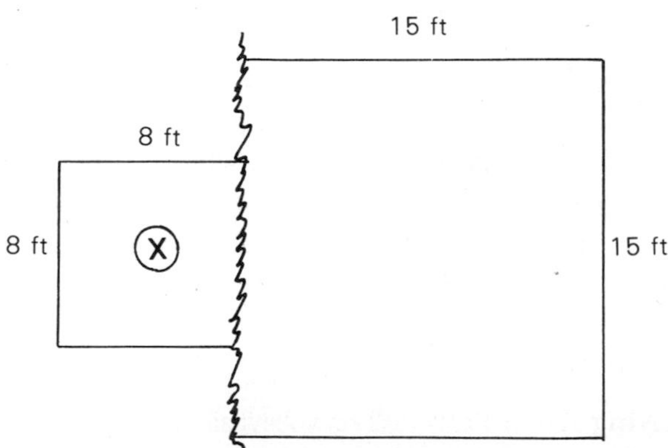

FIGURE 33.10. Court for Wheelchair Volleyball

VOLLEYBALL SKILL TESTS

Serving and volleying are the skills to be tested in volleyball. Serving is tested in two ways: (1) with a simple serve and (2) with an accuracy score.

SIMPLIFIED SERVING

In the simplified serving test, the child to be tested stands in normal serving position behind the end line on the right side and is given a specific number of trials in which to serve. The score is the number of times he serves successfully out of ten trials. The serve must clear the net without touching and land in the opponent's court. A ball touching a line is counted as good.

SERVING FOR ACCURACY

To test serving for accuracy, a line is drawn parallel to the net through the middle of one of the courts. Each half is further subdivided into three equal areas by lines drawn parallel to the sidelines. This makes a total of six areas, which correspond to the positions of the members of a volleyball team. The areas are numbered from 1 to 6 (Figure 33.11).

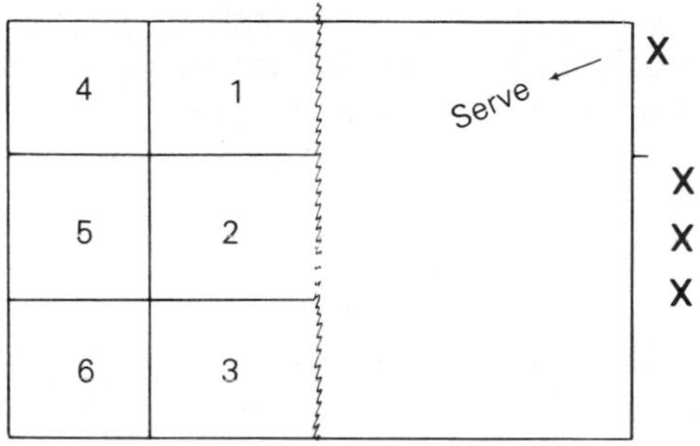

FIGURE 33.11. Layout of court for service testing

Each child is allowed one attempt to serve the ball into each of the six areas in turn. Two points are scored for serving into the designated court area. One point is scored for missing the designated area but landing in an adjacent area. No points are scored otherwise.

WALL VOLLEYING

For the wall volleying test, the player stands behind a restraining line 4 ft away from a wall. A line, representing the height of the net, is drawn on the wall parallel to the floor and 6.5 ft up. A player is allowed 30 seconds to make as many volleys as she can above the line while staying behind the restraining line. A counter is assigned to each testing station to count the successive volleys.

To start, the child makes a short toss to herself for the first volley. If time permits, more than one 30-second period can be allowed, with the best count being taken as the score. A mat can mark the restraining line. Stepping on top of the mat makes that volley illegal.

CHAPTER 34

Facilities, Equipment, and Supplies

The facilities for physical education can be classified in two categories—outdoor and indoor. Climatic conditions should determine which type of facility is more important for the school. Usually, outdoor space provides enough room for several classes to work simultaneously. Where weather conditions require frequent use of indoor space, a minimum of one indoor teaching station for every eight classrooms is needed. In addition, to meet the needs of the handicapped (as required by Public Law 94–142), another indoor play area, separate from but close to the regular indoor facility, is needed.

Physical education facilities should be planned in terms of maximum projected enrollment. Too often, planning is done in terms of the present situation. Later, when classrooms are added to the school, they are added without change in the physical education areas. What was previously an adequate arrangement now becomes a scheduling problem. Adding physical education facilities is difficult because of generally escalating costs and the relatively high cost of physical education facilities in comparison with the cost of adding regular classroom space.

OUTDOOR FACILITIES

The standards for outdoor play areas call for a minimum of 10 acres for the school, with an additional acre for each 100 pupils in the maximum projected enrollment. Parking areas, cycle racks, and entry roads are in addition to these standards. The outdoor areas should include field space for games, a track, hard-surfaced areas, apparatus areas, play courts, age-group-specific play areas, covered play space, and a jogging trail.

Fields should be leveled, drained, and turfed, because grass is the most usable field surface. An automatic sprinkler system is desirable, but the sprinkler heads must not protrude to become safety hazards. Automatic installations permit sprinkling during the evening and night, so the fields are not too soggy for play the next day.

A hardtop area should be marked for a variety of games, such as tetherball, volleyball, and basketball courts. Four-square courts, hopscotch layouts, and circles for games are examples of other markings that can be put on these surfaces. Simple movement pattern courses can also be marked.

Some administrators prefer a hard surface for the entire play area, because this eliminates the mud problem, the need for sprinkling, and in general lowers maintenance costs. Hard surfaces are usually used when play space is limited and when the number of students makes keeping a good turf surface difficult. On hard surfaces, however, more injuries are likely to occur than on grass.

An official track (440 yd or 400 m) may be installed when the interest in track and field is high. Space also should be provided for a smaller track (220 yd or 200 m), and it should be placed in an area where it will not interfere with other activities. For schools where a permanent installation is not practical, a temporary track can be laid out each spring (see p. 556).

Separate play spaces for different age-groups should be included in the planning. Such areas should contain apparatus designed for each age-group. The play area for primary-level children should be well away from areas where footballs and softballs are used.

Small, hard-surfaced play courts can be located strategically near the edges of the outdoor area, thus spreading out the play groups. These courts, approximately 40 by 60 ft, can be equipped for basketball or volleyball or for both. A covered shed can be divided for use by different age-groups. Climatic conditions would dictate the need for such facilities.

A jogging trail can stimulate interest in jogging. Small signs indicating the distances covered and markers outlining the trail are all that are needed. Stations with exercise tasks can be placed at intervals. For example, a station could have directions to accomplish a specified number of Pull-ups or to do a Flexed-Arm Hang for a specified number of seconds. Such a circuit is popularly called a *parcourse.*

An area set aside as a developmental playground is an important part of the total play space. The area should contain equipment and apparatus and should be landscaped to have small hills, valleys, and tunnels for children. A recommended approach is to divide the playground into various developmental areas, so children must use different body parts in different areas of the play space. For example, one area might contain a great deal of climbing equipment to reinforce arm-shoulder girdle development, and another area might challenge the leg and trunk region. Equipment and apparatus should be abstract in nature; creation and imagination are left to the children. Apparatus can be manipulated and changed to suit the needs and desires of the youngsters.

INDOOR FACILITIES

The gymnasium must be well planned for maximum use. The combination gymnasium-auditorium-cafeteria facility leaves much to be desired and creates more problems than it solves. Although it may be labeled a "multipurpose room," a better description is probably "multiuseless." The cafeteria poses a particular problem. The gymnasium must be vacated before the lunch hour so chairs and tables can be set up, and the facility is not available again for physical education activities until it has been cleaned, which usually involves mopping. This eliminates any noon-hour recreational use, thus leaving little play area for the children during inclement weather. In extreme cases, a lack of help postpones gymnasium use for the early part of the afternoon, until the custodian has completed cleaning chores. Special programs, movies, and other events necessitating chairs and the use of the area also complicate the situation.

The gymnasium should be located in a separate wing connected with the classrooms by a covered corridor. It should provide ready access to play areas. Isolating the gym from the rest of the school minimizes the noise problem and allows after-school and community groups to use the facilities without access to other parts of the school.

The indoor facility should be planned in such a way that athletic contests can be scheduled there at times, but the primary purpose of the gymnasium is *not* as an athletic facility. Consideration for spectators should not be a major planning concern. Only after basic physical education needs have been met should the needs of spectators be considered.

In the gymnasium, markings and boundaries should be put on the floor to outline convenient areas for the more common activities. The markings should be painted on the floor after the first or second sealer coat has been applied. A finish coat should then be applied on top of the line markings. Figure 34.1 is an example of how floor markings can maximize the usefulness of a facility.

Temporary lines needed occasionally during the year can be applied with pressure-sensitive tape. These tapes are, however, difficult to remove completely and are likely to take off the finish when removed. A hardwood, preferably maple, floor is recommended for the gymnasium. Other surfaces limit community use and create both safety and maintenance problems.

For safety reasons and for rebound practice, walls should have a smooth surface for a distance of 8 to 10 ft up from the floor. Walls and ceilings should have acoustical treatment. In original construction, a recess for each set of ropes on tracks is an excellent feature. Insulation should conform to modern health standards, and older buildings should be scrutinized for unacceptable insulation materials such as asbestos fibers and certain formaldehyde-based plastics.

The lighting should be of sufficient intensity and fixtures should be recessed to prevent damage. Lights should be arranged so they can be serviced from the floor. Exposed beams should be available for attaching apparatus, and all walls should have electrical outlets. A permanent overhead public address system is desirable, permitting permanent installation of a record player for easy and quick access. In original construction, the record player can be recessed.

Windows should be placed high on the long sides of the gymnasium. Protection from glare and direct sun should be provided.

If baskets and backboards need to be raised and lowered often, a motor-driven system eliminates laborious hand cranking. The system switch should be activated with a key.

Adequate storage space must be given careful thought. The storage space needed for the equipment and instructional supplies used in present-day physical education is considerable, and the area should be designed so the materials are readily available.

One problem frequently associated with a combination auditorium-gymnasium facility is the use of the physical education storeroom for storage of bulky auditorium equipment such as portable chairs on chair trucks, portable stages, and lighting fixtures and other paraphernalia for dramatic productions. Unless the storage facility is quite large, and most are not, an unworkable and cluttered facility is the result. The best solution is two separate storerooms for the dual-purpose facility, or at least one very large storeroom.

A separate storage area of cabinets is essential for outside groups that use the facility. These groups should not have

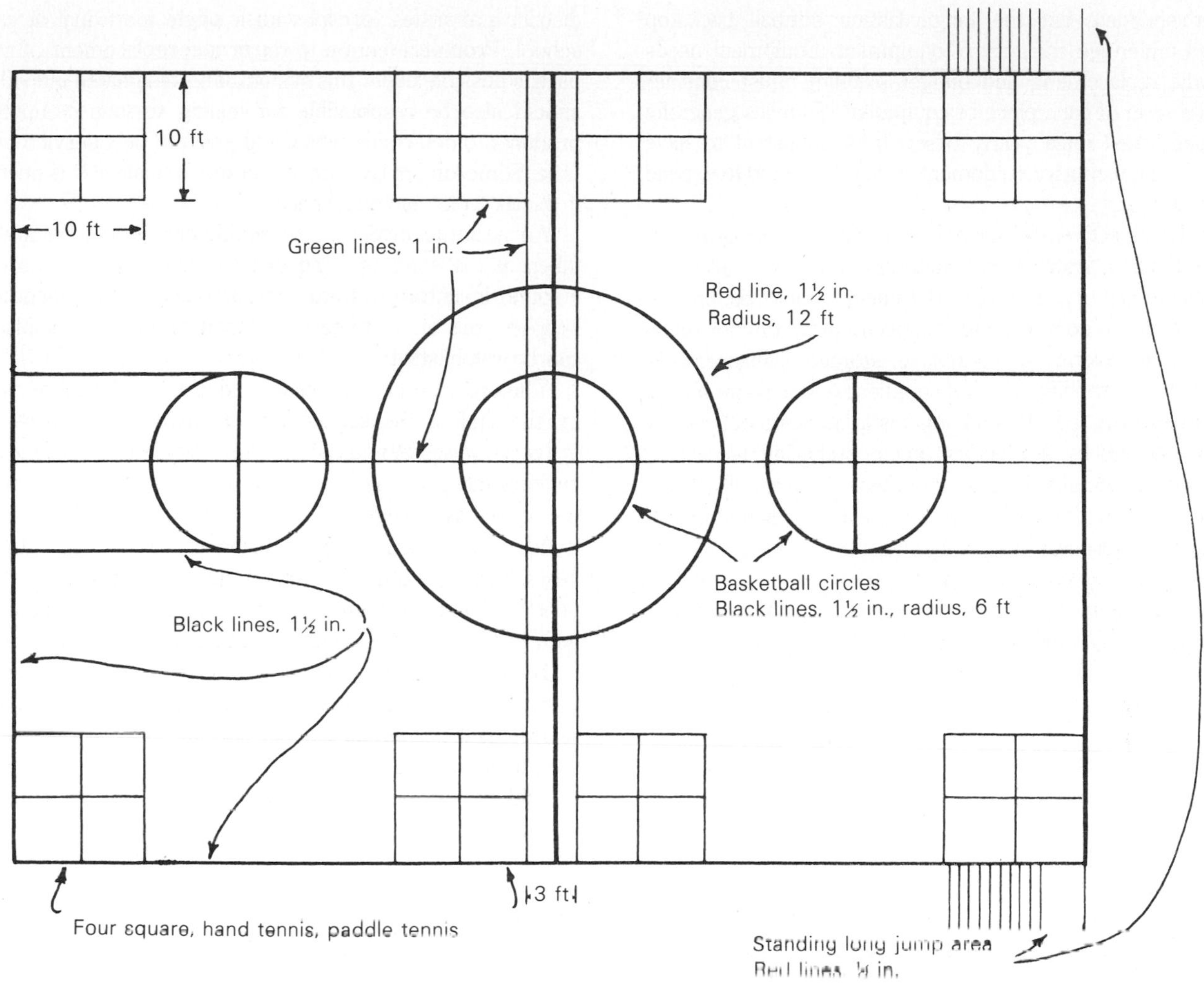

FIGURE 34.1. Floor markings to maximize gymnasium use

access to the regular physical education supply room. If they are permitted to use school equipment, the equipment should be checked out to the group and later checked in again.

Many storage areas in European schools have doors on tracks, similar to American overhead garage doors. This design has a number of advantages, the main one being that the overhead opening makes the handling of large apparatus much easier.

Most architects are unaware of the storage needs of a modern physical education program. Teachers can only hope that the architects designing new schools will be persuaded to allow for sufficient storage.

For the physical education specialist, an office-dressing room is desirable. The office should contain a toilet and a shower.

If contract or task approaches are important in the instructional process, an area to house instructional materials is also desirable. This should be a place where the children can go to search through materials and view loop films and videotapes as they complete their learning packets.

The children should also have a place to change to play clothing and gym shoes. Provision must be made for the storage of play clothing. The storage space for kindergarten through 4th grade can be arranged in the classroom, thus enabling the teacher to make sure that each child has the necessary items each day.

For grades 5 and 6, dressing rooms and shower facilities large enough to accommodate peak capacity should be available. Because it is advisable for children in grades 5 and 6 to change to play clothing and to shower after activity, different provisions for clothing storage should be made. A storage area away from the regular classroom removes the odor problem, which occurs when the play clothes (particularly gym shoes) of the older children are stored in the classroom.

EQUIPMENT AND SUPPLIES

Equipment refers to items of a more or less fixed nature. *Supplies* are those nondurable items that have a limited period of use. To illustrate the difference, a softball is listed under supplies, but the longer-lasting softball backstop comes under the category of equipment. Equipment needs periodic replacement, and budget planning must consider the life span of each piece of equipment. Supplies generally are purchased on a yearly basis. It is important to have adequate financing for equipment and supplies and to expend funds wisely.

If the objectives of the physical education program are to be fulfilled, instructional materials must be available in sufficient quantity. Enough equipment should be present so the children do not waste practice time waiting for turns.

Policies covering the purchase, storage, issuance, care, maintenance, and inventory of supplies are necessary if maximum return on the allotted budget is to be realized. Program features should be decided first and a purchasing plan should then be implemented based on these features. Having a minimal operational list of instructional supplies stabilizes the teaching process.

Equipment constructed by the school staff and homemade equipment should be considered. Quality must not, however, be sacrificed. Articles from home (e.g., empty plastic jugs, milk cartons, old tires, and the like) should be regarded as supplementary materials. Care must be taken that the administration does not look for the cheap, no-cost route to securing supplies and thus sacrifice valuable learning experiences when the program needs require an appreciable investment.

Some articles can be constructed adequately at the school or in the home, and these merit consideration for the sake of economy. Such items as yarn balls, hoops, lummi sticks, balance beams, bounding boards, and others can be made satisfactorily by school staff, parents, and in some instances by students. For other articles, the administration must be reminded that constructed equipment is usually a temporary solution only, undertaken in the early phases of a program when equipment costs are high and cannot all be met immediately.

PURCHASING POLICIES

The purchase of supplies and equipment involves careful study of need, price, quality, and material. The safety of the children who will use the equipment is of vital concern.

Quantity buying by pooling the needs of an entire school district generally results in better use of the tax dollar. However, cooperative purchasing may require compromises on equipment type and brand to satisfy different users in the system. If bids are requested, careful specifications are necessary. Bids should be asked for only on specified items, and "just as good" merchandise should not be accepted as a substitute.

One individual within a school should be made responsible for the physical education supplies and for keeping records of equipment, supplies, and purchasing. Needs will vary from school to school, and it is practical for school district authorities to deal with a single individual at each school. Prompt attention to repair and replacement of supplies is possible under this system. The designated individual should also be responsible for testing various competing products to determine which will give the best service over time. Some kind of labeling or marking of materials is needed if this is to be accomplished.

An accurate inventory of equipment should be undertaken at the start and end of each school year. Through a sound inventory system, the durability of equipment and supplies and an accounting of supplies lost or misplaced can be established.

The ordering of supplies and equipment should be done by the end of the school year or earlier, if possible. A delivery date in August should be specified, so orders can be checked and any necessary adjustments made before the school year begins.

Most equipment of good quality will last from 7 to 10 years, thus keeping replacement costs to a minimum. The policy of some purchasing agents of selecting low-cost items with little regard for quality is financially unsound.

Budgetary practices should include an allotment for the yearly purchase of instructional supplies as well as major replacement and procurement costs for large items, which are usually staggered over a number of years. Once sufficient equipment and supplies have been procured, the budget considerations are for replacement and repair only.

RECOMMENDED OUTDOOR EQUIPMENT

Two criteria are important in selecting outdoor equipment. First, each piece of equipment must contribute to the development of the child (Figure 34.2). For this reason, items that allow only "sit and ride" experiences (swings, teeters, merry-go-rounds) are not recommended. The value of slides is questionable, but some educators believe that the slide is a help in learning to overcome fear of height. The second criterion is that each piece of equipment be safe. Many of the circular supported pieces, such as the giant slide, have proved to be dangerous.

Climbing Structures

There are many brands and many fine varieties of climbing structures (Figure 34.3). Items such as jungle gyms and castle towers have value in attaining physical fitness.

Horizontal Ladders

Horizontal ladders are valuable pieces of playground equipment. They come in a variety of combinations and forms. Arched ladders are quite popular, and allow children to reach the rungs easily. Uniladders, consisting of a single beam with pegs on each side, offer good challenge to children. An equipment set consisting of two arched ladders

FIGURE 34.2. Creative playground equipment

crossing each other at right angles at the center offers the children numerous movement experiences.

Climbing Ropes

In some geographic areas where the weather is not too severe, schools are installing climbing ropes outside. These should not be over 12 or 14 ft in height and should be equipped with circular stops at the top.

Balance Beams

Balance beams made of 4-by-4-in. beams can be permanent installations. They can be arranged in various patterns

FIGURE 34.3. Climbing equipment on the playground

but should not be more than 12 to 18 in. above the floor surface.

Turning Bars

Turning bars made from 3-in. galvanized pipe offer exciting possibilities for children. The bars can be from 6 to 10 ft in length and 30 to 36 in. above the ground.

Horizontal Bar Combinations

A set of three horizontal bars of different heights is a valuable piece of apparatus.

Basketball Goals

Outdoor basketball goals may or may not be combined with a court. Youngsters play a lot of one-goal basketball, and a regulation court is not needed for this game. The goals should be in a surfaced area, however. Outdoor baskets for elementary school use should be 8 to 9 ft above the ground. The lowered height sometimes poses a problem, because children can jump up and grasp the front of the rim, which may damage or tear loose the basket. Strong construction that withstands such abuse is one solution. Some schools have reverted to the 10-ft-high basket, thus putting it out of reach of most children.

Volleyball Standards

Volleyball standards should have flexible height adjustments, including a low height of 30 in. for use in paddleball.

Softball Backstops

Softball backstops can be either fixed or portable.

Tetherball Courts

Tetherball courts should have fastening devices for the cord and ball so they can be removed from the post for safekeeping. The immediate playing area should be surfaced.

Track and Field Equipment

Jumping standards, bars, and pits should be available. These must be maintained properly.

Challenge Courses

Considerable choice exists in setting up outdoor Challenge Courses, which are a new development in the equipment market. Many interesting and challenging obstacles can be put together to create an effective course.

Other Playground Equipment

Many other items can be used as part of the outdoor playground plan. These include large concrete sewer pipes (24 in. or more in diameter) placed variously, posts in combination for stepping stones (Figure 34.4), forts made of railroad ties or building blocks, tractor tires placed in pyramid fashion, a giant tractor tire placed flat, a series of jumping posts for Leapfrog, steps and platforms from which to jump, and simulated locomotives and trains. Truck tires embedded halfway in the ground make an interesting playground addition.

Today, much emphasis is placed on the creative playground, and many creative and imaginative pieces of apparatus are available from commercial sources.

FIGURE 34.4. Playground equipment constructed from railroad ties and posts

RECOMMENDED INDOOR EQUIPMENT

Several principles should govern the choice of indoor equipment. First, a reasonable variety and amount of equipment should be available to keep children active. Included should be items to facilitate arm-shoulder girdle development (i.e., climbing ropes, climbing frames, ladders, and similar apparatus). A criterion for selection is that most, if not all, indoor equipment be of the type that the children themselves can carry, assemble, and disassemble. A regular trampoline, for example, would not meet this criterion.

Mats for Tumbling and Safety

Mats are basic to any physical education program. Enough mats must be available to provide a safe floor for climbing apparatus. At least eight should be present. The light, folding mats are preferable because they are easy to handle and store. They stack well and can be moved on carts. Mats should have fasteners so two or more can be joined (Figure 34.5). The covers should be plastic for easy cleaning. (The one objection to plastic covers is that they are not as soft as the type of mat cover used for wrestling.) Mats should be 4 ft wide and 7 or 8 ft long. Heavy hand-me-down mats from the high school program, some with canvas covers, may prove counterproductive, because they are difficult to handle and bulky to store.

Other mats that might be considered are thick, soft mats (somewhat similar to mattresses) and inclined mats. Soft mats are generally 4 in. or more thick and may entice the timid to try activities that they otherwise would avoid. Inclined mats are wedge shaped and provide downhill momentum for rolls. Both types of mat are excellent for the handicapped.

Individual Mats

Strong consideration should be given to obtaining a supply of 30 to 35 individual mats to be used mostly for the primary-level program. The mats, which can be 20 by 40 in. or 24 by 48 in. are useful for practicing many interesting movement experiences and introductory tumbling activities.

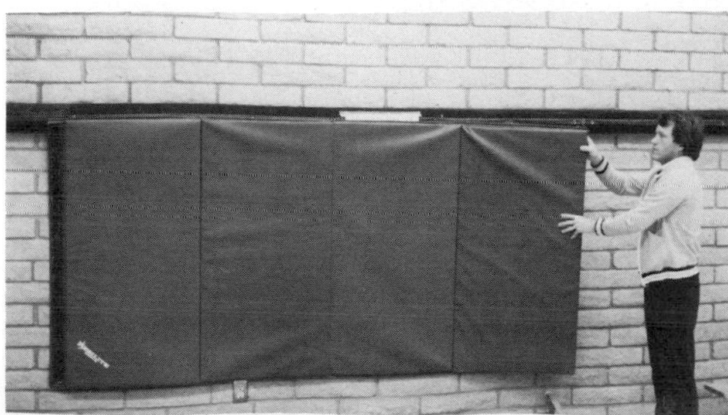

FIGURE 34.5. Tumbling mats stored on walls with Velcro fasteners

Expense is, however, a key factor. The initial outlay, including a carrying cart, is quite high, but the mats do last indefinitely with care and add much to the program.

Record Player

A good record player with a variable speed control is a necessity. Pause control is also helpful. There is enough demand to justify the physical education program's having its own record player. A tape recorder is also helpful.

Balance Beam Benches

Balance beam benches have double use. They can serve as regular benches for many types of bench activity, and when turned over, they can be used for balance beam activities. Wooden horses or their supports can serve as inclined benches. Six benches are a minimum for class activity.

Balance Beams

A wide beam (4 in.) is recommended for kindergarten and 1st grade. Otherwise, a 2-in. beam should be used. Balance beams with alternate surfaces (2 and 4 in.) can be constructed from common building materials.

Chinning Bar

The chinning bar is especially useful for physical fitness testing and in body support activities. The portable chinning bar installed in the gymnasium doorway is an acceptable substitute.

Climbing Ropes

Climbing ropes are essential to the program. At least eight should be present, but more than eight allows better group instruction. Climbing rope sets on tracks are most efficient to handle (Figure 34.6). With little effort or loss of time, the ropes are ready for activity. Ropes on tracks are available in a variety of materials, but good-quality manila hemp seems to be the most practical. Ropes should be either 1¼ or 1½ in. in diameter.

Good-quality climbing ropes made of synthetic fibers are appearing on the market. The best are olefin fiber ropes, which are nonallergenic and have nonslip qualities, thus forestalling the problem of slickness, a characteristic of plastic ropes and even of older cotton ropes. Climbing ropes on tracks and other large apparatus can be purchased from the Robert Widen Company, P. O. Drawer 2075, Prescott, AZ 86301.

Volleyball Standards

Volleyball standards should adjust to various heights for different grade levels and games.

FIGURE 34.6. Climbing ropes on tracks

Bounding Boards

Bounding boards are 2 by 6 ft and are made of ¾-in. marine plywood. Six boards should be constructed for the primary program.

Balance Boards

Four to six balance boards of different styles are a desirable extension of apparatus experiences.

Supply Cart

A cart to hold supplies is desirable. Other carts can be used for the record player and for regular and individual mats.

Jumping Boxes

Small boxes used for jumping and for allied locomotor movements extend the opportunities to work on basic movement skills. For kindergarten, boxes should be 8 and 16 in. high. For other children, boxes 12 and 24 in. high offer sufficient challenge (Figure 34.7). The shorter box can be 16 by 16 in. and the taller box 18 by 18 in. (The smaller box can then be stored inside the larger box.) The top of the box should have carpet padding and be covered with leather or durable plastic. Holes drilled through the sides provide fingerholds for ease of handling. Eight boxes, four of each size, are a minimum number for the average-size class.

Horizontal Ladder Sets

Horizontal ladders that fold against the wall make an excellent indoor equipment addition. The ladder may be combined with other pieces of apparatus in a folding set.

Climbing Frames

A type of frame that has been well received in this country and in Canada is the Centaur Frame, which can be ordered from the Robert Widen Company, P.O. Drawer 2075, Prescott, AZ 86301. This wall-mounted frame comes

FIGURE 34.7. First-graders using 16-in. jumping boxes

FIGURE 34.8. Wall-mounted climbing frame

from England and was originally called the Southhampton frame. Many variations and designs (Figure 34.8) are available.

Other Indoor Items

A portable chalkboard is desirable, as is a wall screen for viewing visual aids. A large bulletin board and a wall chalkboard should be located near the main entrance to the gym. The wall chalkboard permits quick announcements or notes.

An audiovisual cart or stand for projectors is helpful. It should contain sufficient electrical cord to reach wall outlets.

Rebound nets for throwing and kicking have excellent utility. They do, however, pose storage problems.

Substitute goals for basketball and related games can be designed. One suggested goal is 4 ft square with the rim 5 ft above the ground. Beginners and the handicapped can find success with this goal design. The frame can be made of 1-in. pipe or plastic (PVC) tubing.

A plank, supported horizontally on sawhorses, also adds to the equipment possibilities.

SUPPLIES FOR PHYSICAL EDUCATION

A basic list and an optional list of supplies should be established for each program. The basic list stipulates the instructional materials that should be available for teaching. In addition, extra basic-list items should be held in storage for replacement during the year. Optional supplies depend on personal preferences and available funds.

Basic Supply List

Ball inflator with gauge (1)
Balloons, rubber (1 for each child and extras in reserve)
Balls
  Beach balls, 12 to 16 in. (2 to 6)
  Cageballs, 24 in. (2 with an extra bladder in reserve)
  Playground balls, rubber, mostly 8½ in. (1 for each child)
  Small balls, sponge or tennis, in assorted colors (50)
  Sport balls (for primary) in a variety of sponge or plastic forms, such as footballs, soccer balls, volleyballs, and basketballs (8 of each type)
  Sport balls (junior size), football, basketball, soccer ball, volleyball (8 of each)
  Yarn or fleece balls (1 for each child)
Basketball nets (6 in reserve)
Batting tees for softball (4 to 6)
Beanbags, in assorted colors (2 for each child)
Cones, rubber, for boundary markers (24)
Eyeglass protectors (4 or more)
Gym scooters (4 for relays or 1 for every two children for games)
Hockey sets (2)
Hoops, 36 or 42 in. (1 for each child with extras in reserve)
Indian clubs (16 or more)
Individual mats (1 for each child)
Jump ropes, individual, in a variety of lengths (1 for each child)
Jump ropes, long (8)
Jump-the-shot ropes (3)
Lummi sticks (32 pairs)
Magic (stretch) ropes (8)
Measuring tape, 50 ft or longer (1)
Paddles, wooden (1 for each child)
Parachute, 24 or 28 ft (1)
Pinnies or other team markers (1 for every two children)
Records, a sufficient supply
Scoops, bottle (1 for each child)
Softball equipment—balls, gloves, masks, bases, bats, protector
Stopwatches, $\frac{1}{5}$ or $\frac{1}{10}$ second (3)
Tambourine (1)
Tetherball sets as needed
Tinikling pole sets, 10-ft poles (6)
Tom-tom or dance drum (1)
Tote bags for balls (12 or more)
Track and field equipment—batons (8), jump boards, hurdles, crossbars or ropes, starter, jump standards
Tug-of-war ropes, individual (1 for every two children)
Volleyball nets (2)
Wands (1 for each child)
Whistles (8)
Wire baskets for holding items (6 or more)

Optional Supply List

Bongo boards (8)
Broom handles (8)

Deck tennis rings (16)
Footsteps, tiles or rubber footprints (40)
Frisbees (16)
Fun balls, in a variety of forms (36)
Hockey sticks, 12-in. size for scooter or hand hockey (2 sets)
Lime for marking fields
Liner, dry, for marking fields
Microphone for record player (1)
Parachute, 10 or 12 ft (1)
Pitching targets (2)
Pogo sticks (8)
Repair kit for balls (1)
Shuffleboard equipment
Stilts, regular (6 pair)
Stilts, tin can (6 pair)
Table tennis equipment
Tape, colored, for temporary marking of gymnasium floor
Tires, auto
Tires, bicycle
Tool chest—saw, hammer, pliers, and so on
Tubes, auto, oversized and inflatable (6)
Tug-of-war rope, 60 ft or more (1)
Wooden blocks, 1 by 1 in. for relays (24)
Other miscellaneous items purchased commercially or made at home

STORAGE PLANS

When a class goes to the gymnasium for physical education, the teacher has a right to expect sufficient supplies to be available to conduct the class. A master list stipulating the kinds and quantities of supplies in storage should be established. A reasonable turnover is to be expected, and supply procedures should reflect this. Supplies in the storage facility should be available for physical education classes and for organized after-school activities. The supplies should not be used for games played during recess or for free play periods; each classroom should have its own supplies for such purposes.

A system should be established for the storage of equipment and supplies. "A place for everything and everything in its place" is the key to good housekeeping. Bins, shelves, and other assigned areas where supplies and equipment are to be kept should be labeled.

Both teachers and students must accept responsibility for maintaining order in the storage facility. Squad leaders or student aides can assume major responsibility. At the end of the week, the teacher in charge of the storage area can assign older children to help tidy the area, put any stray items back in place, and repair or replace articles as needed. A principal will be more favorably inclined toward purchase requests when obvious care is taken of instructional materials.

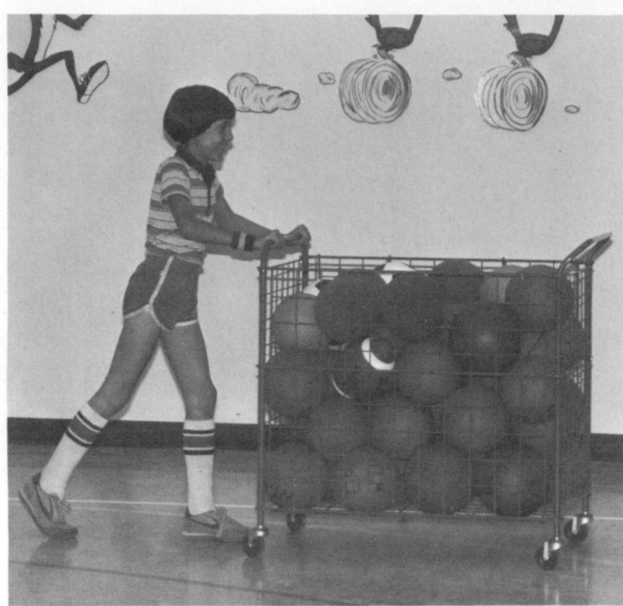
FIGURE 34.9. Portable ball cart

Some schools use small supply carts of the type pictured in Figure 34.9. The carts hold those articles used most frequently. They take up some additional space but do save time in accessing needed items. The carts can be built inexpensively to meet specific needs or commercially manufactured equipment carriers can be purchased. A cart that holds the record player and carts that store and move mats and balls are helpful.

An off-season storage area, where articles not in present use can be kept, should be established. Equipment not in current use should be kept in this separate area, perhaps under lock and key.

CARE, REPAIR, AND MARKING

A definite system should be developed for repairing supplies and equipment. A quick decision must be made about whether to repair an item locally or whether to send it out of the area for repair. If the repair process is lengthy and not cost-efficient, using the article until it can no longer be salvaged may be preferable to being deprived of its use. An area should be established for equipment needing repair, so all articles to be repaired are evident at a glance.

Balls must be inflated to proper pressures. This means using an accurate gauge and checking the pressures periodically. The inflation needle should be moistened before insertion in the valve. Children should kick only those balls made specifically for kicking (i.e., soccer balls, footballs, and playground balls).

Softball bats and wooden paddles should not be used to hit rocks, stones, or other hard materials. Neither should bats be knocked against fences, posts, or other objects that might cause damage. Broken bats should be discarded; they are unsafe, even when taped around the break. Children should learn to keep the trademark up when batting. Bats should be taped to prevent slippage.

Cuts, abrasions, and breaks in rubber balls should be repaired immediately. In some cases, repairs can be made with a vulcanized patch, such as one uses for repair of tire tubes. In other cases, a hard-setting rubber preparation is of value. In some instances, repair may be beyond the scope of the school, and the ball should be sent away for repair.

For off-season storage, balls should be deflated somewhat, leaving just enough air in them to retain the shape. Leather balls should be cleaned with an approved conditioner.

Mats are expensive, and proper care is needed if they are to last. A place where they can be stacked properly must be provided, or if the mats have handles, they should be hung from those. A mat truck is another storage solution, if there is space for storing the truck. The newer plastic or plastic-covered mats should be cleaned periodically with a damp, soapy cloth.

For small items, clean plastic ice-cream bucket containers make adequate storage receptacles. Most school cafeterias have these and other containers that can be used in the storage room to keep order. Small wire baskets also make good storage containers.

All equipment and supplies should be marked. This is particularly important for equipment issued to different classrooms. Marking can be done with indelible pencil, paint, or stencil ink. Few marking systems are permanent, however, and remarking at regular intervals is necessary. Sporting goods establishments have marking sets. An electric burning pencil works well but must be used with caution so as not to damage the equipment being marked.

Rubber playground balls come in different colors, and assignment to classrooms can be made on the basis of color. A code scheme with different-colored paints can be used also. It is possible to devise a color system by which the year of issue is designated. This offers opportunity for documentation of equipment usage and care.

CONSTRUCTING EQUIPMENT AND SUPPLIES

We have divided this section into two parts. In the first part, we offer recommendations for sources and materials needed to construct equipment and supplies, as well as recommending equipment usages. In the second part, we provide diagrams and specifications for building equipment in an economical manner. If the recommended equipment can be described adequately without an illustration, we have included the description in the first part.

RECOMMENDATIONS FOR CONSTRUCTING EQUIPMENT AND SUPPLIES

The supply of balls can be augmented with tennis balls or sponge balls. Discarded tennis balls from the high school tennis team are useful. Holes can be poked in the tennis balls if they are too lively for young children to handle. Sponge balls are inexpensive and with care last indefinitely.

A good supply of ropes for jumping is essential. We are partial to the newer plastic-link jump ropes, because these have good weight, come in attractive colors, can be shortened easily (by removing links), and can be purchased with color-coded handles. The handles provide good leverage for turning. Ropes, however, can be made from cord. Heavy sash cord or hard-weave polyethylene rope is suitable. The ends should be whipped, heated, or dipped in some type of hardening solution to prevent unraveling. The lengths can be color coded with dye or stain. Kindergarten through grade 2 use mostly 7-ft ropes, with a few 6- and 8-ft lengths. Grades 3 through 6 use mostly 8-ft ropes, with a few 7- and 9-ft lengths. Instructors will require 9- or 10-ft ropes.

Enough ropes should be available in the suggested lengths to provide each child with a rope of the correct length. The supply of ropes should include eight to ten long ropes (14 or 16 ft) for long-rope jumping activities. A jump-the-shot rope can be made by tying an old, completely deflated volleyball on one end of a rope.

Beanbags are made easily. Good-quality, bright-colored muslin is suitable as a covering. Some teachers have asked parents to save the lower legs of worn-out denim jeans; this material wears extremely well and is free. Some instructors prefer a beanbag with an outer liner that snaps in place to allow for washing. Another idea is to sew three sides of the beanbag permanently. The fourth side is used for filling and has an independent stitch. The beans can be removed through this side when the bag is washed. Beanbags should be about 4 by 4 in. and 6 by 6 in. and can be filled with dried beans or peas, wheat, rice, or even building sand.

For games requiring boundary markers, pieces of rubber matting can be used, or small sticks or boards, painted white, are excellent. A board 1 by 2 in. across and 3 or 4 ft in length makes a satisfactory marker.

Tetherballs should have a snap-on fastener for easy removal.

Old tires, even those from bicycles, can be used. Chapter 20 contains many ideas for tire use.

Schools near ski areas may be able to get discarded tow ropes. These make excellent tug-of-war ropes.

Indian clubs can be turned in the school shop, or suitable substitutes can be made. For example, pieces of 2-by-2-in. lumber cut short (6 to 10 in.) stand satisfactorily. Lumber companies usually have dowels 1 to 1½ in. in diameter.

Sections of these make a reasonable substitute for Indian clubs. Broken bats also can be made into good substitute clubs.

White shoe polish has numerous marking uses and can be removed from the floor with a little scrubbing.

Three-pound coffee cans can be used as targets. Empty half-gallon milk cartons also have a variety of uses.

Inner tubes can be cut in strips and used as resistance exercise equipment. The tube should be cut crossways in 1½-in. wide strips.

Old bowling pins can be obtained from most bowling alleys free of charge. Because the standard pins are too large for the children to handle easily, cutting 2 to 4 in. off the bottom is recommended. Parallel cuts through the body of the pin provide hockey pucks and shuffleboard disks. Another way to trim bowling pins is described on p. 586.

For kindergarten and 1st-grade children, improvised balls can be made from crumpled newspaper bound with cellophane tape. Papier-mâché balls are also useful. Light foam rubber cubes can be trimmed to make interesting objects for throwing and catching.

Bamboo for making tinikling poles can sometimes be procured from carpet stores, which use the poles to give support to the center of a carpet roll. Plastic tinikling sticks are available commercially.

Good savings on rubber traffic cones can be realized if these are purchased from a highway department supply source, where they are usually less expensive than cones purchased from physical education equipment supply firms. Plastic jugs, half filled with sand, can be used in place of traffic cones.

DIAGRAMS AND SPECIFICATIONS FOR CONSTRUCTING EQUIPMENT AND SUPPLIES

Safety standards should apply to all school-constructed equipment; the construction and the materials used should not create or introduce any safety hazards. The design must be educationally sound and utilitarian.

Balance Beam

The balance beam is used for many kinds of activity. Two types of stand for a two-by-four beam are shown in Figure 34.10. The beam can be placed with the wide or the narrow side up, depending on the skill of the performer. If the beam is longer than 8 ft, a third stand should be placed in the middle. Care must be taken to sand and apply multiple coats of finish to the beam to prevent splintering and cracking.

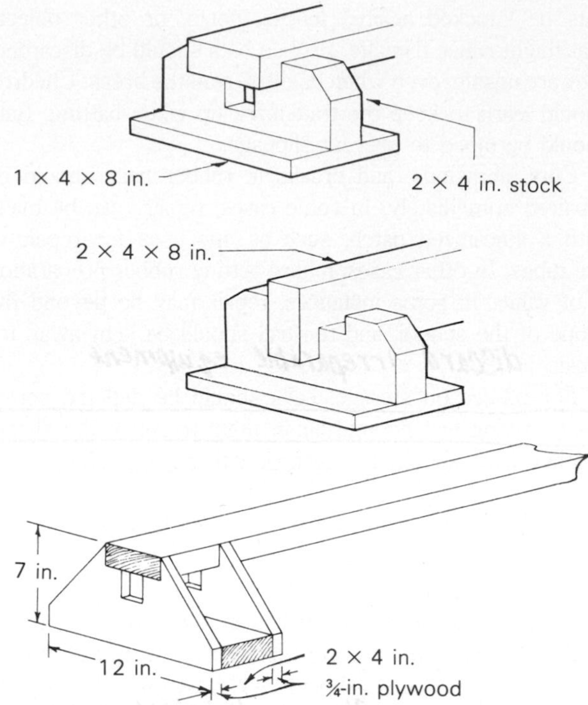

FIGURE 34.10. Balance beam with stand

Balance Beam Bench

The balance beam bench is a versatile piece of equipment. Its dimensions can be modified depending on the age of the users (Figure 34.11). It should be made of hardwood or hardwood plywood, and should be well finished. Hooks can be fastened to the underside of the bench to provide even more uses for this important piece of apparatus.

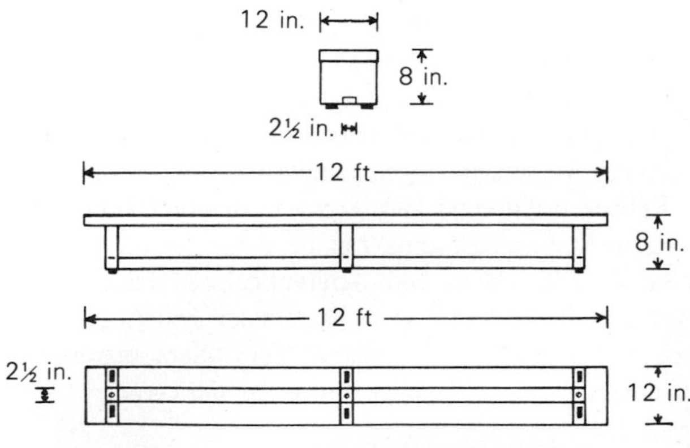

FIGURE 34.11. Balance beam bench

Balance Boards

Many different styles of balance board can be constructed, depending on the materials available and on individual needs (Figure 34.12). The board should have a piece of rubber matting glued to the top to prevent slipping, and should be placed on an individual mat or on a piece of heavy rubber matting. A square board is easier to balance than a round one, for its corners touch the floor and give more stability.

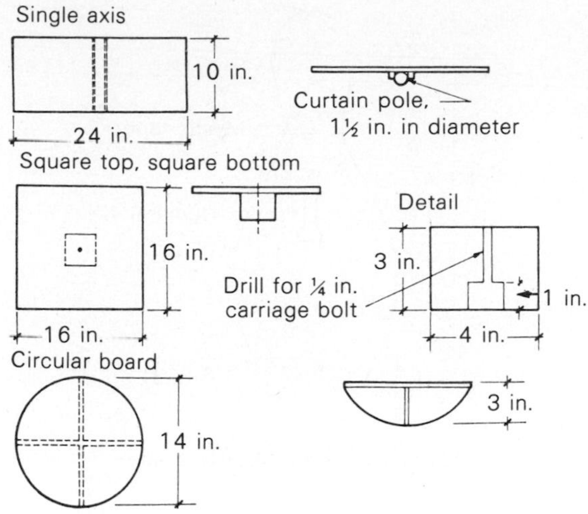

FIGURE 34.12. Styles of balance board

Batting Tee

Ideally, the batting tee should be adjustable to accommodate batters of various heights (Figure 34.13). Constructing an adjustable tee takes time, however, and the results are not always satisfactory. An alternative is to make several nonadjustable tees of different heights.

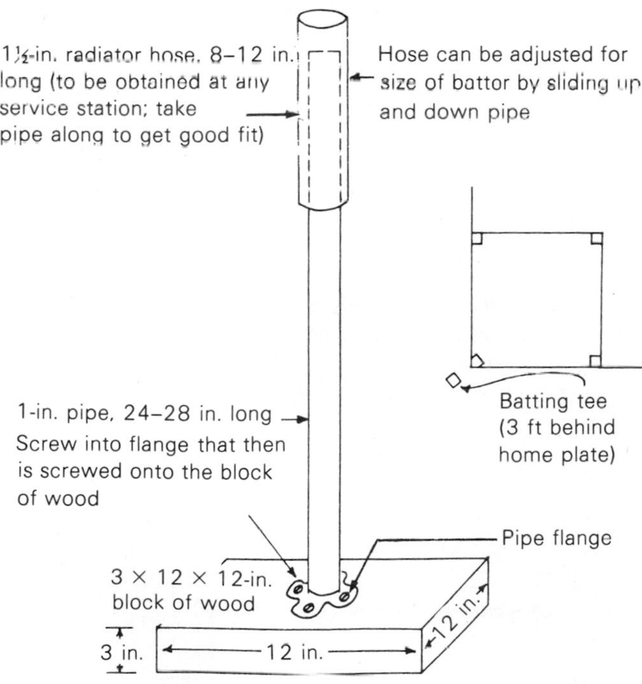

FIGURE 34.13. Batting tee construction

Materials

One piece of 1-in. pipe, 24 to 28 in. long

One piece of radiator hose, 8 to 12 in. long, with an inside diameter of 1½ in.

One block of wood, 3 by 12 by 12 in.

One pipe flange for 1-in. pipe, to be mounted on the block

Screws and hose cement

Directions: Mount the flange on the block and screw the pipe into the flange. Place the radiator hose on the pipe. Paint as desired. To secure a good fit for the radiator hose, take the pipe to the supply source. If the hose is to remain fixed, then secure it with hose cement.

An alternate method is to drill a hole in the block and to mount the pipe directly in the hole with mastic or good-quality glue. Note that 1-in. pipe has an outside diameter of approximately 1½ in., allowing the hose to fit properly over it.

Blocks and Cones

Blocks with grooves on the top and on one of the sides are excellent for forming hurdles with wands. A four-by-four, cut in lengths of 6, 12, and 18 in., yields a variety of hurdle sizes. Cones can be notched and used in place of the blocks (Figure 34.14).

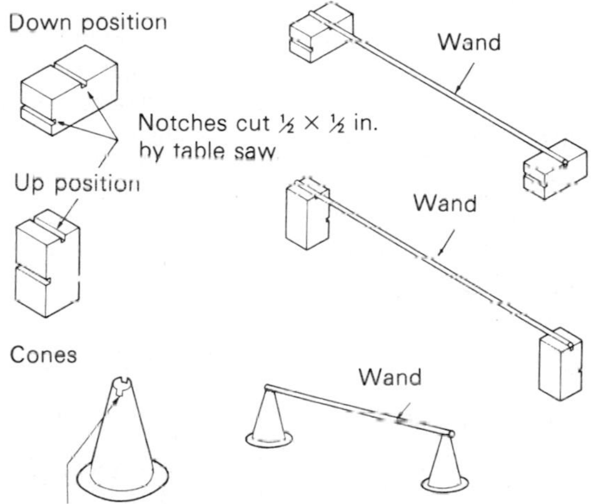

FIGURE 34.14. Notching blocks and cones to make hurdles

Bongo Boards

Bongo boards are excellent for helping students learn the concept of static balance. Roller sizes can be increased to make the challenges more difficult.

Materials

One piece of ¾-in. plywood, 8 by 36 in.

One piece of 1-by-2-in. lumber, 3 ft long

One roller, 2 to 5 in. in diameter

Directions: On the bottom of the plywood board, glue and screw down the 1-by-2-in. piece of lumber. This pro-

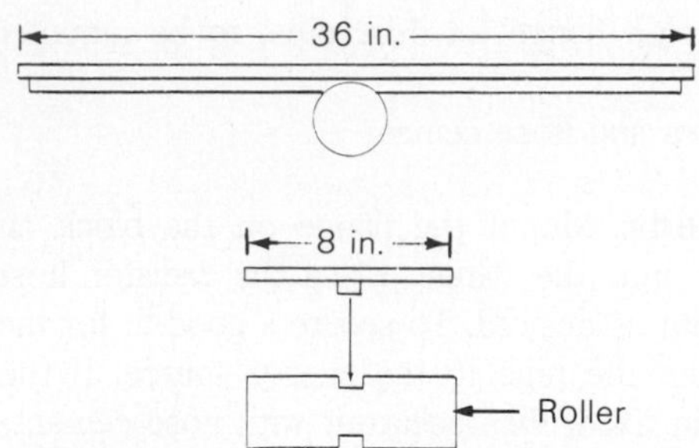

FIGURE 34.15. Bongo board construction

vides a guide to prevent the roller from moving out from under the board. The roller should be cut in such a way that the guide fits inside the slot on the roller with a clearance of not more than ⅛ in. (Figure 34.15).

Bounding Boards

Bounding boards should be made from good-quality, ¾-in. marine plywood, which is strong and holds up under repeated bounding. If the board exhibits a tendency to break, a stop can be put under the middle. A 2-by-4-in. padded board attached across the width of the bounding board usually works adequately.

Finishing the boards is not necessary. Different lengths of board give various amounts of bounce and can be adapted to the size of the student. Heavier students should not bound on boards made for younger children.

Materials

One piece of ¾-in. marine plywood, 2 by 6 ft

Two 4-by-4-in. boards, 2 ft long, trimmed as shown in Figure 34.16

Six carriage bolts, ⅜ by 4 in.

Two pieces of carpet, about 8 by 24 in.

Glue

Directions: Glue and bolt the two boards to the edges of the plywood, as shown in Figure 34.16. Glue the pieces of carpet to the boards for padding.

Bowling Pins

Bowling alleys give away old tenpins, which can be used for many purposes. Some suggested uses are as field and gymnasium markers, for bowling games, and for relays. The bottom 2 in. of the pin should be cut off, and the base sanded smooth (Figure 34.17). Pins can be numbered and decorated with decals, colored tape, or paint.

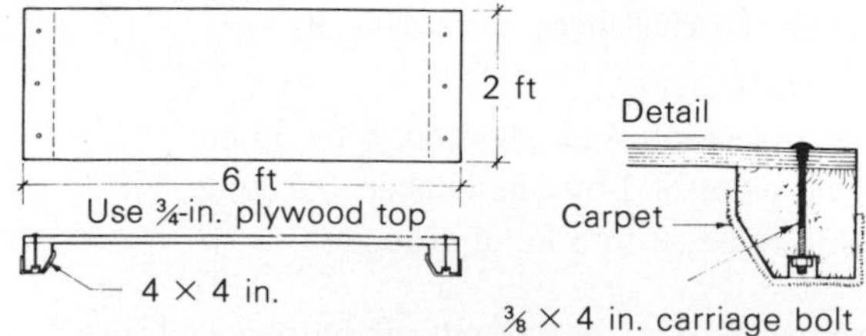

FIGURE 34.16. Bounding board construction

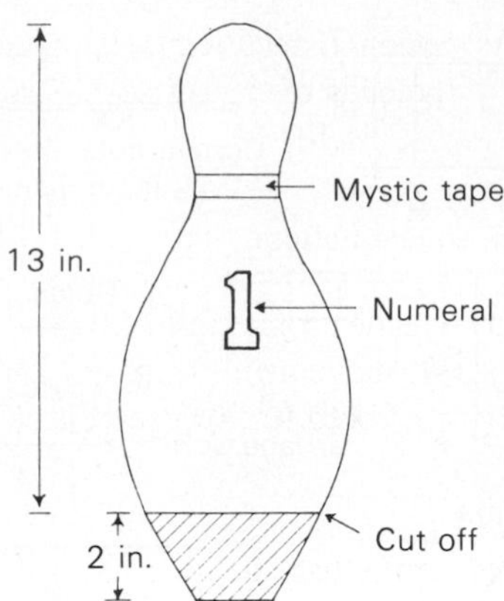

FIGURE 34.17. Bowling pin

Conduit Hurdles

Conduit hurdles are lightweight and easy to store. Because they are not weighted and fall over easily, children have little fear of hitting them. The elastic bands can be moved up and down to create different heights and different challenges. Conduit can be purchased at most electrical supply houses.

Materials

One piece of ½-in. electrical conduit pipe, 10 ft long

One piece of 1-in. stretch elastic tape

Wood doweling, ½ in. in diameter

Directions: Bend the piece of conduit to the following dimensions: uprights should be 30 in. high, the base should be 30 in. wide, and the sides of the base should be 15 in. long. A special tool for bending the conduit usually can be purchased from the supply house where the conduit was bought. Sew loops on each end of the elastic tape, so the tape will slide over the ends of the hurdles with a

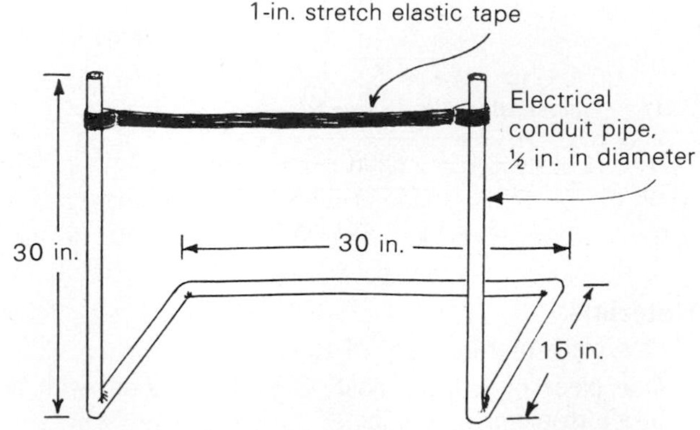

FIGURE 34.18. Conduit hurdle construction

slight amount of tension. If necessary, short pieces of doweling can be put in the ends of the conduit to raise the height of the hurdle (Figure 34.18).

Footsies

Footsies can be made economically by the children. They provide an excellent movement challenge. The activity requires coordination of both feet to keep the footsie rotating properly.

Materials

Plastic bleach bottle, half-gallon size
One piece of ⅛-in. clothesline-type rope
Old tennis ball
Large fishing swivel, preferably with ball bearings

Directions: Cut a circular strip about 2 in. wide out of the bottom of a bleach bottle. Cut two holes in the strip about 1 in. apart. Thread a 3-ft piece of clothesline through the holes, and tie a knot on the outside of the strip. Cut the clothesline in half and tie the swivel to each end of the cut cord. The swivel prevents the rope from becoming twisted.

Puncture the tennis ball with an ice pick, making two holes directly across from each other. Thread the line through the holes with a piece of wire or a large crochet hook. Tie a large knot near the outer hole so the line cannot slip back through (Figure 34.19).

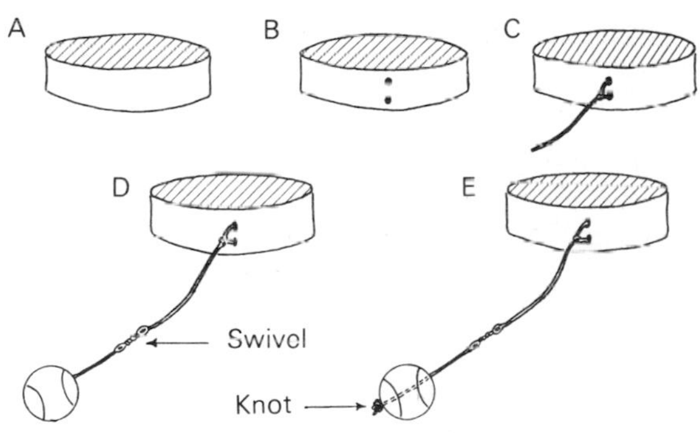

FIGURE 34.19. Footsie construction

Gym Scooters

Scooters are easily constructed from readily available materials and can be made in many sizes and shapes. The casters should be checked to make sure that they do not mark the floor. Scooters have many activity applications, as previously described, and can also be used to move heavy equipment.

Materials

One piece of 2-in. yellow pine board, 12 by 12 in.
Four ball-bearing casters with 2-in. wheels of hard rubber
Protective rubber stripping, 4 ft in length, and cement
Screws and paint

Directions: Actual dimensions of the board are around 1⅝ by 11⅝ in. Two pieces of ¾-in. plywood glued together can be substituted. Cut and round the corners, smoothing them with a power sander. Sand all edges by hand, and apply two coats of paint. Fasten the four casters approximately 1½ in. diagonally in from the corners. A rubber strip fixed around the edges with staples and cement (Figure 34.20) will cushion the impact of the scooter on other objects.

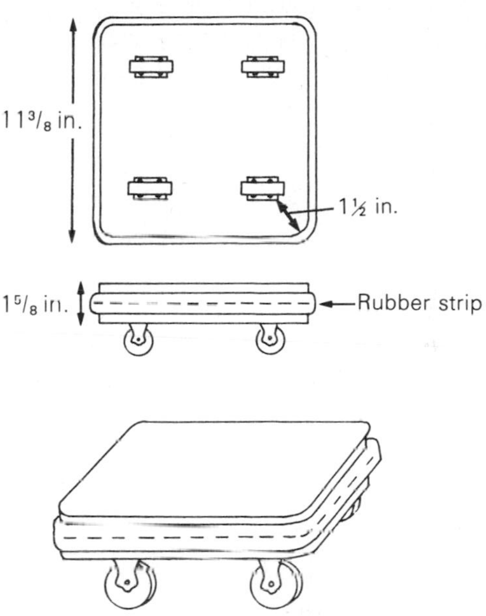

FIGURE 34.20. Gym scooter construction

Hoops

Hoops can be constructed from ½-in. plastic water pipe, which unfortunately is available in drab colors only. The cost savings of using the pipe are, however, great. Hoops can be constructed in different sizes. A short piece of doweling, fixed with a power stapler or tacks, can be used to join the ends together (Figure 34.21). An alternate joining method is to use special pipe connectors. Weather-stripping cement helps make a more permanent joint.

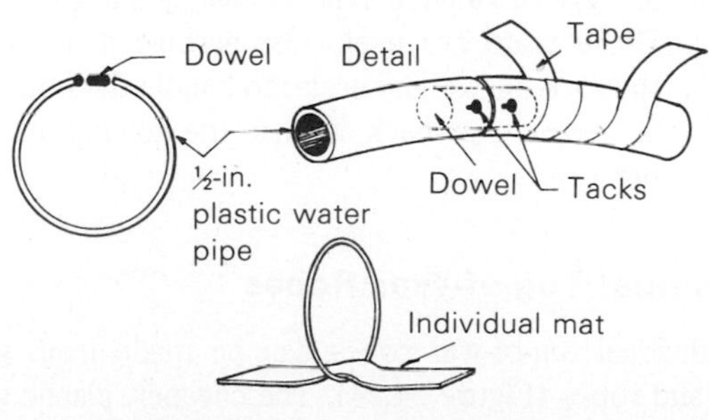

FIGURE 34.21. Hoop construction

Hurdle and High-Jump Rope

The weighted hurdle and high-jump rope is ideal for beginning hurdlers and high jumpers who may fear hitting the bar. The rope can be hung over the pins of the high-jump standards; the weights keep the rope fairly taut.

Materials

One piece of ⅜-in. rope, 10 ft long
Two rubber crutch tips (no. 19)
Tacks (no. 14) and penny shingle nails
Lead (this can be purchased at plumbing outlets)

Directions: Drive a carpet tack through the rope approximately ¾ in. from each end. Drive three nails into the bottom of each of the two rubber crutch tips. Place the rope ends inside the crutch tips and fill the tips with hot lead (Figure 34.22).

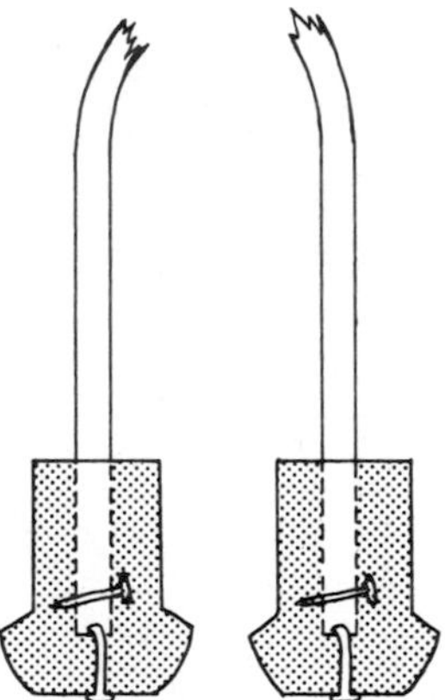

FIGURE 34.22. Weighted hurdle and high-jump rope construction

Individual Mats

Individual mats can be made from indoor-outdoor carpeting that has a rubber backing. This prevents the mat from sliding on the floor and offers some cushion. The mats also can be washed easily when they become soiled. Mats of different colors are preferable, because they can be used for games, for color tag, and for easy division of the class according to mat color. Carpet stores often have small pieces and remnants that they will sell cheaply or give away.

Another type of individual mat is designed to fold (Figure 34.23). These mats are useful for aerobic dance classes because they are lighter and easier to handle than the carpet mats. The major drawback is that the folding mats are more expensive.

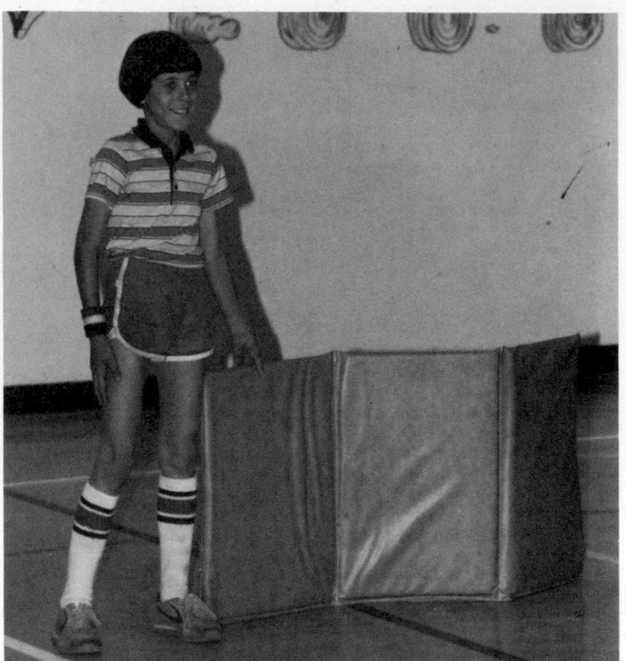

FIGURE 34.23. Folding individual mat

Individual Tug-of-War Ropes

Individual tug-of-war ropes can be made from garden hose and ropes (Figure 34.24). The cheaper, plastic garden hose (⅝ in. in diameter) works much better than the more expensive rubber hose. The plastic hose does not crease as easily and gives the hands more protection. The white, soft, braided nylon rope (¼ in. in diameter) offers adequate strength and is much easier to handle than other types of rope. A bowline knot should be used, because it does not slip and tighten around the hands. The ends of the nylon rope should be melted over a flame to prevent them from unraveling.

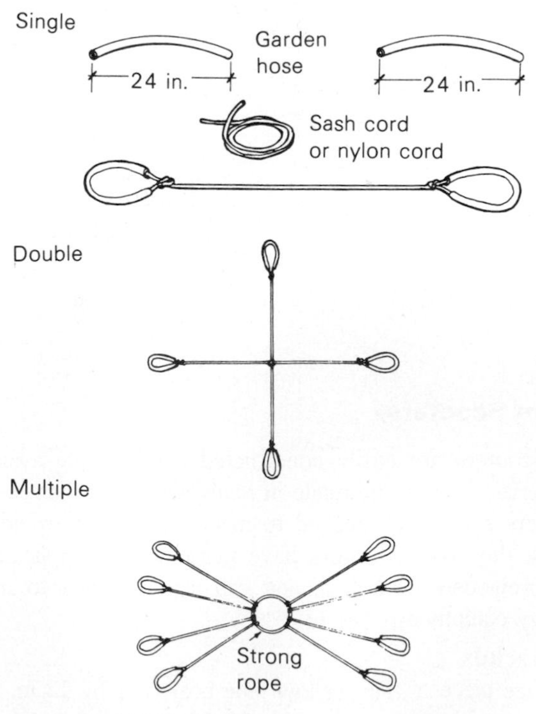

FIGURE 34.24. Tug-of-war ropes

Jumping Boxes

Jumping boxes are used to develop a wide variety of body management skills. The dimensions can be varied to satisfy individual needs, but if the boxes are made to fit inside each other, storage is less of a problem. The boxes also can be used to transport equipment and supplies when they are not being used for their primary purpose.

Materials

¾-in. marine plywood
Wood screws, paint, and glue
Carpet pad remnants
Naugahyde or similar material to cover box top
Upholstery tacks

Directions: Cut the four sides to similar dimensions and then sand them together to make sure they are exactly the same size. Use a countersink and drill the screw holes, apply glue at the joints, and screw the sides together. When the box is assembled, sand all edges to remove any sharpness. Paint the boxes, preferably with a latex-base paint, because it does not chip as easily as oil-base enamel. If handholds are desired, drill holes and then cut them out with a saber saw (Figure 34.25). Cut a carpet pad remnant to match the size of the top of the box, and cover with a piece of Naugahyde. The Naugahyde should overlap about 4 in. on each side of the box so it can be folded under a double thickness and then tacked down.

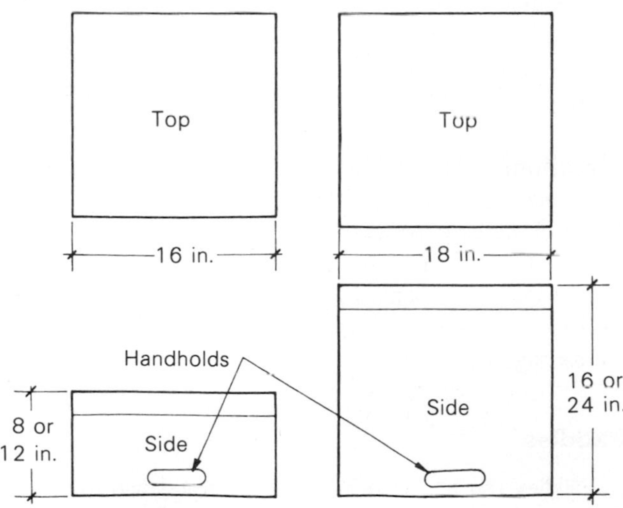

FIGURE 34.25. Jumping box construction

Jumping Standards

Jumping standards are useful for hurdling, jumping, and over-and-under activities. Many shapes and sizes are possible (Figure 34.26).

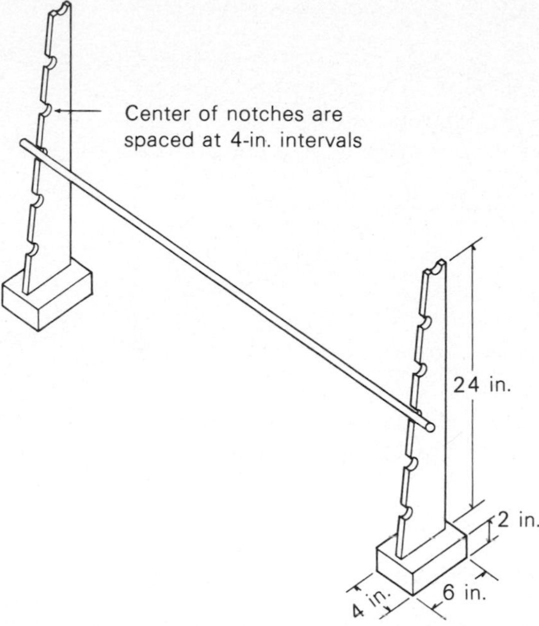

FIGURE 34.26. Jumping standard construction

Materials

Two pieces of ¾-in. plywood 25 in. long, cut as shown
Two blocks of wood, 2 by 4 by 6 in.
Glue and paint
Broomstick, 48 in. long

Directions: The wood blocks should be mortised lengthwise, about 1 in. deep. After the uprights have been cut to form, set them with glue into the blocks—making sure the uprights are plumb. Paint as desired. Small circles of various colors can be placed at each of the corresponding notches of the uprights for quick positioning of the crosspiece.

Ladder

A ladder laid on the floor or on a mat provides a floor apparatus for varied movement experiences and has value in remedial programs and programs for exceptional children. Sizes may vary (Figure 34.27).

Materials

Two straight-grained 2-by-4-in. timbers, 9½ ft long
Ten 1¼-in. or 1½-in. dowels, 20 in. long
Glue
Paint or varnish

Directions: Round the ends and sand the edges of the timbers. Center holes for the ladder rungs 12 in. apart, beginning 3 in. from one end. Cut the holes for the rungs $\frac{1}{16}$ in. smaller than the diameter of the rungs. Put glue in all of the holes on one timber, and drive in all of the rungs. Next, glue the other timber in place. Varnish or paint the ladder.

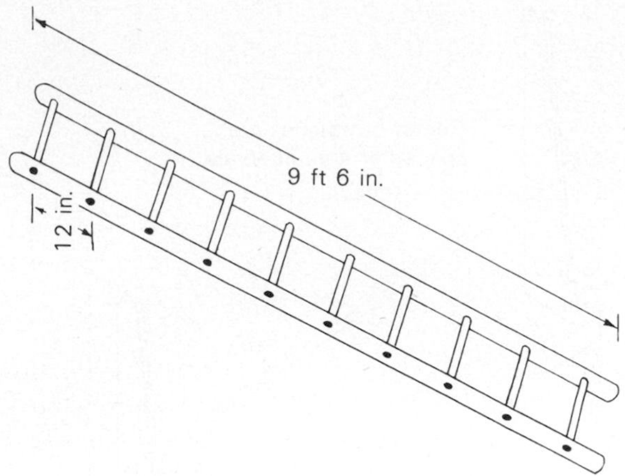

FIGURE 34.27. Ladder construction

Lummi Sticks

Lummi sticks are excellent tools for developing rhythmic skills. The sticks can also be used as relay batons.

Materials

1-in. doweling, in 12-in. lengths
Paint and varnish

Directions: Notches and different colors are optional, but these decorations do make the sticks more attractive. If desired, use a table saw to cut notches ⅛ in. wide and ⅛ in. deep. Round off the ends and sand the entire stick. Paint and varnish the stick as shown in Figure 34.28.

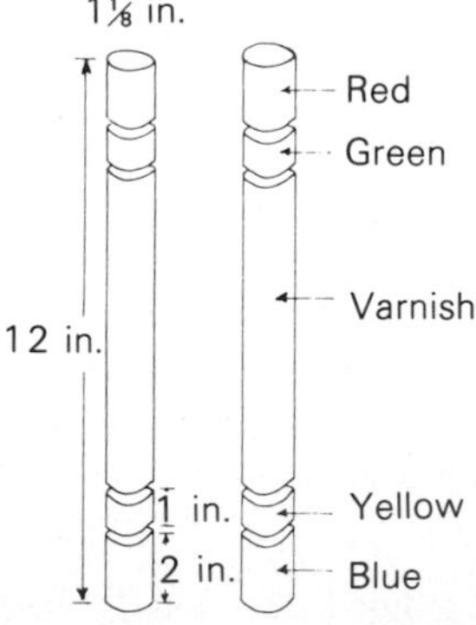

FIGURE 34.28. Lummi stick construction and decoration

Magic Ropes

Magic or stretch ropes can be made by stringing together 25 to 30 large rubber bands. Common clothing elastic also can be used to make the ropes (Figure 34.29). Some teachers have had success with shock cord, which usually can be purchased at a boating marina or hardware store.

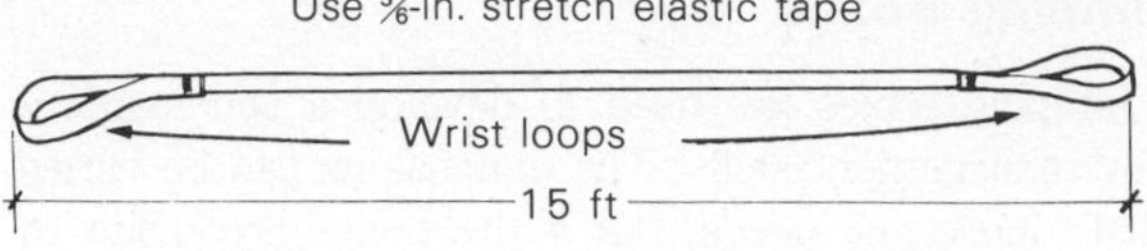

FIGURE 34.29. Magic rope construction

Outdoor Bases

There are many satisfactory methods for constructing bases. They can be made from heavy canvas by folding the canvas over three or four times and stitching it together. Heavy rubber matting can be cut to size. More permanent bases can be made from outdoor plywood and painted (Figure 34.30).

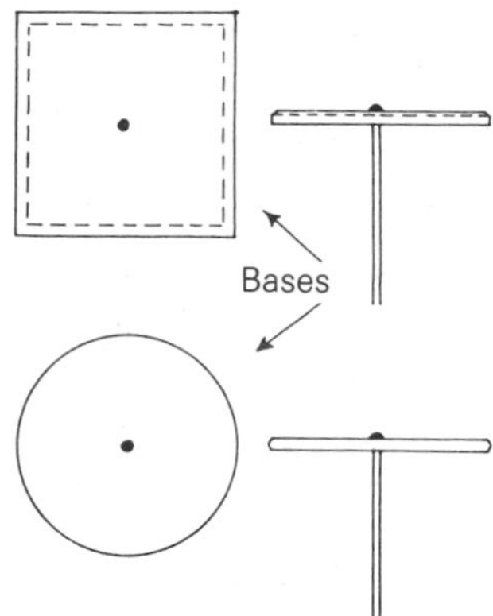

FIGURE 34.30. Outdoor base construction

Materials:

Exterior ¾-in. plywood
One ½-in. carriage bolt, 14 in. long
Paint

Directions: Cut the plywood into 12-by-12-in. squares. Bevel and sand the top edges. Drill a ½-in. hole in the center of the base and then paint the base. When the paint has dried, place the carriage bolt in the center hole and drive it into the ground. More holes can be used to make the base more secure. Large spikes can be substituted for the carriage bolt.

Paddles

Paddles can be made in many sizes and with different thicknesses of plywood (Figure 34.31). Usually, ¼-in. plywood is recommended for kindergarten through grade 2, and ⅜-in. plywood for grades 3 through 6. Paddles can be painted or varnished, and the handles taped to give a better grip. Holes can be drilled in the paddle area to make it lighter and to decrease air resistance. Good-quality plywood, perhaps marine plywood, is essential.

For hitting a foam rubber ball or a newspaper ball, nylon-stocking paddles can substitute quite effectively for wooden

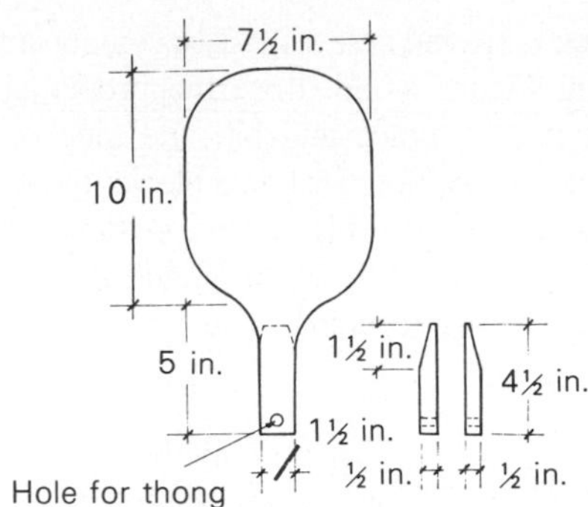

FIGURE 34.31. Paddle construction

paddles. Because of their light weight, they do not cause injuries. They are therefore excellent for primary-age children. A badminton bird can be used with the paddle for various activities, such as hitting over a net, and for many individual stunts.

Materials

Old nylon stocking
Wire coat hanger
Masking tape or athletic tape
String or wire

Directions: Bend the hanger into a diamond shape. Bend the hook into a loop, which becomes the handle of the paddle (Figure 34.32). Pull the stocking over the hanger, beginning at the corner farthest from the handle, until the toe of the nylon is as tight as possible against the corner point of the hanger. Hold the nylon at the neck of the hanger and stretch it as tight as possible. Tie the nylon securely with a piece of heavy string or light wire. Wrap the rest of the nylon around the handle to make a smooth, contoured surface. Complete the paddle by wrapping tape around the entire handle to prevent loosening.

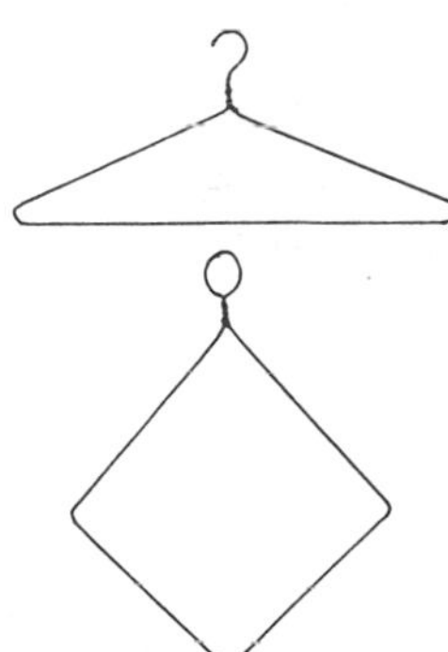
FIGURE 34.32. Frame for nylon-stocking paddle

Paddle Tennis Net Supports

The advantage of paddle tennis net supports is that they stand by themselves on the floor and still provide proper net tension. The stands come apart easily and quickly and can be stored in a small space. For lengths up to 8 ft or so, a single center board, with holes on each end, can be used, thus eliminating the need for bolting two pieces together (Figure 34.33).

Materials

Two broomsticks or ¾-in. dowels, 2 ft long
Two 1-by-4-in. boards, 2 ft long
One or more additional 1-by-4-in. boards
Glue

Directions: For the upright supports, drill a hole 11/16 in. in diameter in the center of each one-by-four. Drive the dowel into the hole, fixing it with glue. The dowels can be notched at intervals for different net heights.

The length of the crosspiece depends on how much court width is to be covered. If a single crosspiece is to be used, holes should be bored in each end. The holes should be big enough (⅞ in.) so the dowel slides through easily. If the crosspiece is in two halves, then ¼-in. bolts are needed to bolt the halves together, as indicated in the diagram.

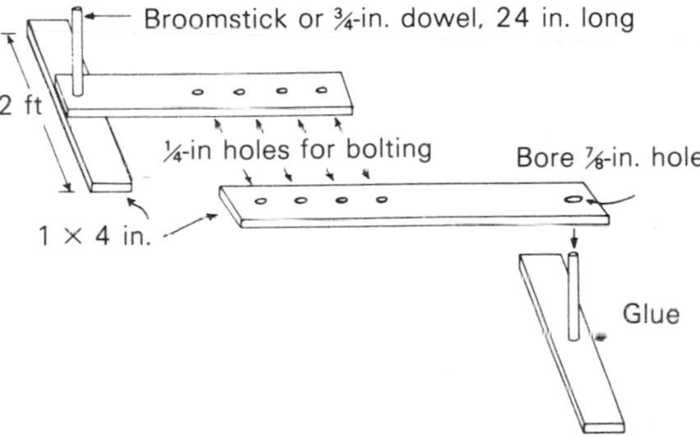

FIGURE 34.33. Paddle tennis net support construction

Plastic Markers and Scoops

One-gallon plastic jugs filled halfway with sand and recapped make fine boundary markers. The markers can be painted different colors to signify goals, boundaries, and division lines. The jugs also can be numbered and used to designate different teaching stations. Plastic bottles can be cut down to make scoops (Figure 34.34), which have many activity possibilities.

Rings, Deck Tennis (Quoits)

Deck tennis is a popular recreational net game that requires only a ring as basic equipment. The rings can be made easily by the students and are useful for playing catch and for target throwing. They can be fashioned from heavy rope by braiding the ends together, but the construction method illustrated in Figure 34.35 is easier. Weather-stripping cement helps strengthen the joints.

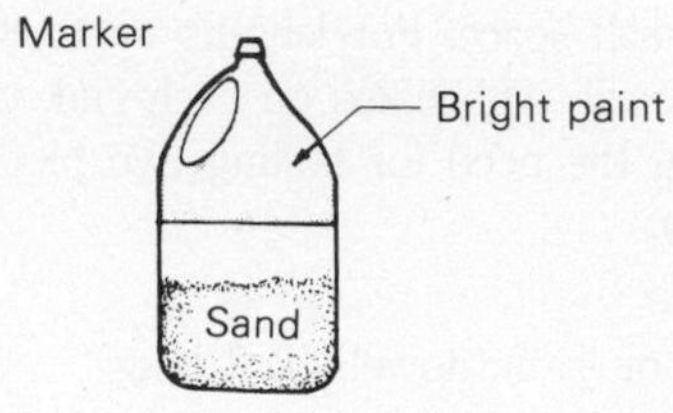

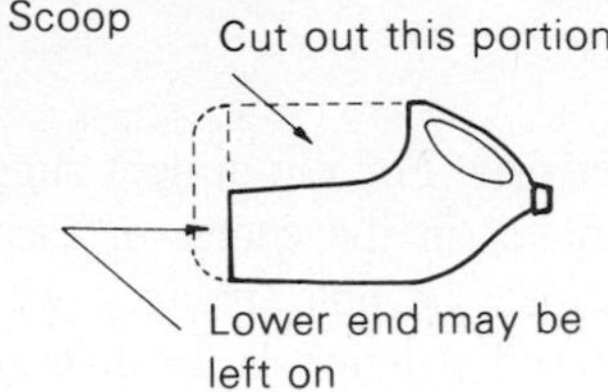

FIGURE 34.34. Plastic marker and scoop

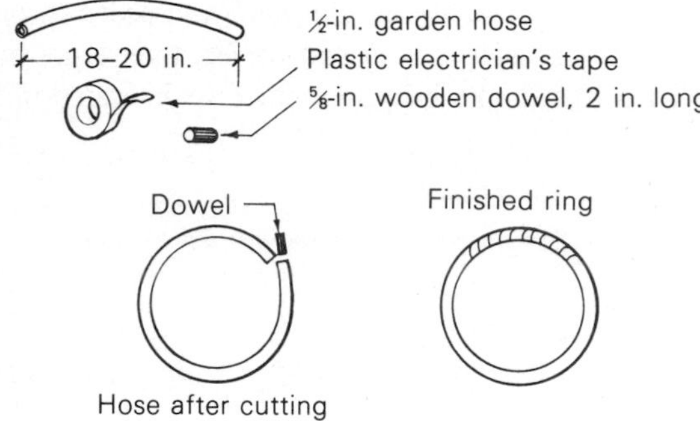

FIGURE 34.35. Ring construction

Ring Toss Target

Many ring toss targets can be made from 1-by-4-in. lumber and old broom or mop handles. They can be made to hang on the wall or to lie flat on the ground. The quoits, constructed from garden hose, are excellent for throwing at the targets. The target pegs can be painted different colors to signify different point values.

Materials

Two 1-by-4-in. boards, 18 to 20 in. long
Five pegs, 6 in. long (old broom handles)
Screws and paint

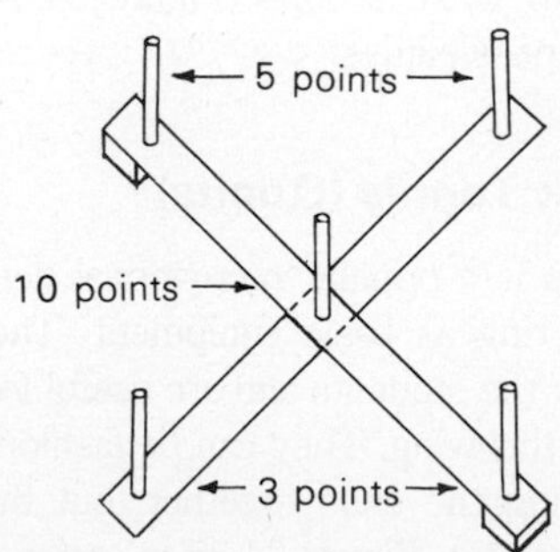

FIGURE 34.36. Ring toss target construction

Directions: Glue and screw the 1-by-4-in. boards together, as shown in Figure 34.36. Bore the proper size holes in the boards with a brace and bit, and glue or screw the pegs into the holes. Note that two blocks must be screwed on the ends of the board placed on top so the target stands level. Paint the base and the sticks, and if desired, number the sticks according to point value.

Tire Stands

Tire stands keep tires in an upright position (Figure 34.37). The upright tires can be used for movement problems, over-and-through relays, for vaulting activities, and as targets. Tires are much cleaner and more attractive when they are painted both inside and out.

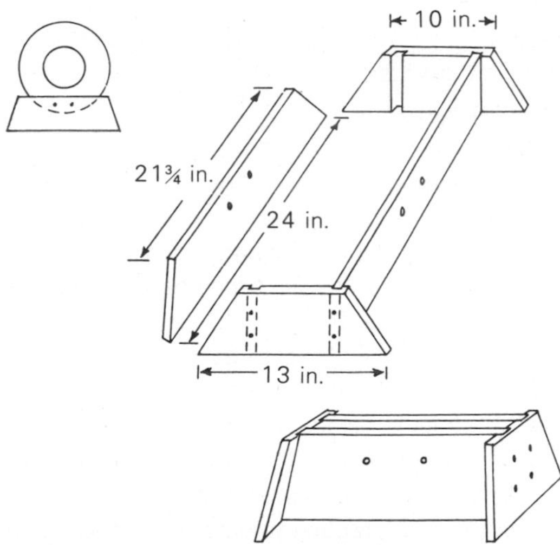

FIGURE 34.37. Tire stand construction

Materials

Two 1-by-6-in. boards, 24 in. long, for side pieces
Two 1-by-6-in. boards, 13 in. long, for end pieces
Four ⅜-in. carriage bolts, 2 in. long
Glue, screws, and paint
One used tire

Directions: Cut the ends of the side boards at a 70-degree angle. Dado each end piece with two grooves ¾ in. wide and ¼ in. deep. The distance between the grooves is determined by the width of the tire. Round off the corners and sand the edges. Glue and screw the stand together. Install the tire in the frame by drilling two ⅜-in. holes in each side of the frame and in the tire. Secure the tire inside the frame with the bolts. Paint both the tire and the frame a bright color. Note that the frame dimensions will vary according to the size of the tire, making it necessary to adjust the frame dimensions to the tire.

Track Starter

The track starter is an ingenious device that simulates a gun report. If many starters are made, the children can start their own races.

Materials

Two 2-by-4-in. boards, 11 in. long

Two small strap hinges

Two small cabinet handles

Directions: Cut the boards to size, and sand off any rough edges. Place the two blocks together, and apply the two hinges with screws. Add the two handles on the outside of the boards. Open the boards and then slam them together quickly to obtain a loud bang (Figure 34.38).

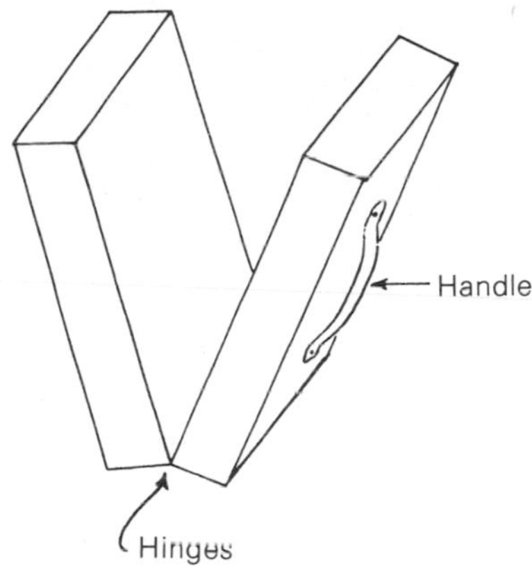

FIGURE 34.38. Track starter

Wands

Handles from old brooms or mops make excellent wands (Figure 34.39). The handles may have different diameters, but this is not an important factor. The ends can be sanded and the wands painted different colors. If noise is a concern, rubber crutch tips can be placed on the wand ends.

⅝-in. or ¾-in. doweling

Lengths: grades K–1 = 30 in., 2–3 = 36 in., 4–6 = 42 in. or 1 m

FIGURE 34.39. Wand dimensions

Yarn Balls

Yarn balls can be used to enhance throwing and catching skills and for many games. They have an advantage over balls in that they do not hurt when they hit a child, and they can be used in the classroom or in other areas of limited space. Yarn balls can be made by the older children or by the PTA. Two construction methods are offered here; both work well. When possible, wool or cotton yarns should be used, because the balls will then shrink and become tight when soaked in hot water or steamed. Nylon and other synthetic yarns are impervious to water and so do not shrink and bond.

Materials for Method One

One skein of yarn per ball

One piece of box cardboard, 5 in. wide and about 10 in. long

Strong, light cord for binding

Directions for Method One: Wrap the yarn 20 to 25 times around the 5-in.-wide dimension of the cardboard. Slide the yarn off the cardboard, and bind it in the middle with the cord to form a tied loop of yarn. Continue this procedure until all of the yarn is used up and tied in looped bunches. Next, take two of the tied loops and tie them together at the center, using several turns of the cord. This forms a bundle of two tied loops, as illustrated in Figure 34.40. Continue tying the bundles together until all are used. Now cut the loops, and trim the formed ball. The cutting should be done carefully, so the yarn lengths are reasonably even, or considerable trimming will be needed.

FIGURE 34.40. Yarn ball, method one

Materials for Method Two

Two skeins of yarn per ball

Two cardboard doughnuts, 5 or 6 in. in diameter

Strong, light cord for tying

Directions for Method Two: Make a slit in the doughnuts so the yarn can be wrapped around the cardboard.

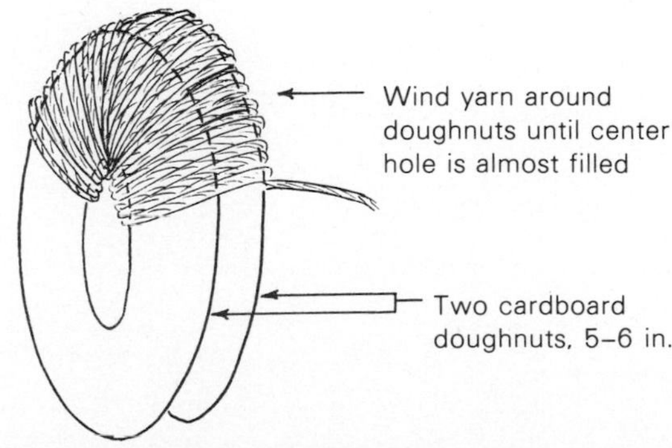

FIGURE 34.41. Yarn ball, method two

Holding strands from both skeins, wrap the yarn around the doughnut until the center hole is almost completely filled with yarn (Figure 34.41). Lay the doughnut of wrapped yarn on a flat surface, insert a scissors between the two doughnuts, and cut around the entire outer edge. Carefully insert a double strand of the light cord between the two doughnuts and catch all of the individual yarn strands around the middle with the cord. Tie the cord as tightly as possible with a double knot. Remove the doughnuts, and trim the ball if necessary.

Index

Student Survey

Victor P. Dauer and **Robert P. Pangrazi**
Dynamic Physical Education for Elementary School Children, Eighth Edition

Students, send us your ideas!

The authors and the publisher want to know how well this book served you and what can be done to improve it for those who will use it in the future. By completing and returning this questionnaire, you can help us to develop better textbooks. We value your opinion and want to hear your comments. Thank you.

Your name (optional) ______________________ School ______________________

Your mailing address ____

City ______________________ State ______________ ZIP ______________

Instructor's name (optional) ______________________ Course title ______________________

1. How does this book compare with other texts you have used? (Check one)
   □ Superior □ Better than most □ Comparable □ Not as good as most

2. Circle those chapters you especially liked:
   Chapters: 1 2 3 4 5 6 7 8 9 10 11 12 13 14 15 16 17 18
   19 20 21 22 23 24 25 26 27 28 29 30 31 32 33 34

   Comments:

3. Circle those chapters you think could be improved:
   Chapters: 1 2 3 4 5 6 7 8 9 10 11 12 13 14 15 16 17 18
   19 20 21 22 23 24 25 26 27 28 29 30 31 32 33 34

   Comments:

4. Please give us your impressions of the text. (Check your rating below)

	Excellent	Good	Average	Poor
Readability of text material	( )	( )	( )	( )
Logical organization	( )	( )	( )	( )
General layout and design	( )	( )	( )	( )
Up-to-date treatment of subject	( )	( )	( )	( )
Match with instructor's course organization	( )	( )	( )	( )
Illustrations that clarify the text	( )	( )	( )	( )
Selection of topics in the text	( )	( )	( )	( )
Explanation of difficult concepts	( )	( )	( )	( )

5. List any chapters that your instructor did not assign. ______________________

____

6. What additional topics did your instructor discuss that were not covered in the text? ______________________

____

(Over, please)

7. Did you buy this book new or used? ☐ New ☐ Used

   Do you plan to keep the book or sell it? ☐ Keep it ☐ Sell it

   Do you think your instructor should continue to assign this book? ☐ Yes ☐ No

8. After taking the course, are you interested in taking more courses in this field? ☐ Yes ☐ No

   Is your major physical education? ☐ Yes ☐ No

9. Did you purchase the Pangrazi-Dauer *Lesson Plans* to accompany the text? ☐ Yes ☐ No

   If not, and you want more information, please read the boxed information below.

10. GENERAL COMMENTS:

May we quote you in our advertising? ☐ Yes ☐ No

To mail, remove this page and mail to:

Marketing Department • Burgess Publishing Company • 7110 Ohms Lane • Edina, MN 55435

THANK YOU!

LESSON PLANS
for *Dynamic Physical Education for Elementary School Children*

By Robert P. Pangrazi and Victor P. Dauer
Fourth Edition 1986. 342 pages, paperbound.

Lesson Plans for Dynamic Physical Education for Elementary School Children provides an entire year's physical education program in weekly units. Each unit lists the supplies and equipment needed, specific activities, learning objectives, teaching hints, and references by page number to the eighth edition of *Dynamic Physical Education for Elementary School Children.* The pages in *Lesson Plans* are perforated for easy removal and are three-hole punched.

The purchase price of *Lesson Plans* is $10.50 net. Orders accompanied by payment (check or money order payable to Burgess Publishing) will be sent postage and handling free. Please allow two weeks for delivery.

☐ Yes, I wish to place an order for *Lesson Plans.* My payment of $10.50 net payable to Burgess Publishing is enclosed. Please send to:

NAME ______________________

MAILING ADDRESS ______________________

____

CITY ________ STATE ________ ZIP ______